W9-DIH-108

THE ENCYCLOPEDIA
OF
JUDAISM

THE ENCYCLOPEDIA

OF

JUDAISM

VOLUME I

A – I

Edited by

JACOB NEUSNER

ALAN J. AVERY-PECK

WILLIAM SCOTT GREEN

PUBLISHED IN COLLABORATION WITH THE
MUSEUM OF JEWISH HERITAGE
NEW YORK

CONTINUUM • NEW YORK

1999

The Continuum Publishing Company
370 Lexington Avenue
New York, NY 10017

Distribution in the United States and Canada by The Continuum Publishing
Company, 370 Lexington Avenue, New York, NY 10017-6503, USA

Distribution in the rest of the world by Brill, Plantijnstraat 2, P.O.Box 9000,
2300 PA, Leiden, The Netherlands

This book is printed on acid-free paper.

Printed in The Netherlands

Library of Congress Cataloging-in-Publication Data

The encyclopedia of Judaism / editors, Jacob Neusner, Alan J. Avery
-Peck, William Scott Green.
    p.   cm.
  Includes bibliographical references and index.
  Contents: v. 1. A–I.
  ISBN 0–8264–1178–9 (set : alk. paper)
    1. Judaism—Encyclopedias.   I. Neusner, Jacob, 1932–
II. Avery Peck, Alan J. (Alan Jeffery), 1953–   III. Green, William
Scott.
  BM50.E63   1999
  296'.03—dc21   99–34729
                                                    CIP

Volume 1   ISBN 0-8264-1175-4

TABLE OF CONTENTS

PREFACE

THE ENCYCLOPEDIA OF JUDAISM provides a full and reliable account of the religion, Judaism, beginning in ancient Israelite times and extending to our own day. About Judaism, the religion, its diverse history, literature, beliefs past and present, observances, practices and world-view, and place in the context of society and culture, this is what we know. In context and proportion, here is how we think we know it. All principal topics required for the systematic description of any religion—[1] the world view, [2] way of life, [3] theory of the social entity constituted by the faithful—are addressed here. In all cases information is set forth in historical and systemic context. Therefore facts take on meaning and produce consequences.

These systematic entries are essays written both to be read for enlightenment and also to be used for ready-reference to on-the-spot facts. The table of contents identifies the topical program, and two elaborate indices make the volumes immediately useful for finding quick definitions of facts, persons, places, things, events, practices, and the like. The work speaks to anyone interested in religion, in understanding what religion—viewed through the example of Judaism—is, and in comprehending the difference religion makes in general. It is written for people of all ages and backgrounds and not only for specialists in the subject or practitioners of Judaism or any other religion. No special pleading for or against religion in general or for Judaism or any particular viewpoint therein finds a place in the pages of this work. Nor is there room here for partisanship within Judaism. The religion, Judaism, is represented by the entire range of Judaic systems of belief and behavior put forth over time and in our own times.

For our highly qualified editorial board of specialists, we have sought as broad and representative a variety of viewpoints within the faith and about the faith as we could assemble. The editorial consultants advised us on the entire range of topics to be covered, not only their own, and each wrote the principal entry in his or her area of specialization. The program of THE ENCYCLOPEDIA OF JUDAISM therefore responds to the viewpoints of a great many scholars of Judaism, not only of the editors. Objectivity and academic authority characterize the presentation throughout. Numerous editors from universities and other centers of learning and enterprises of culture, originating in every place where Judaism is practiced and studied today—North America, South Africa, Great Britain, Eastern, Central, and Western Europe, the State of Israel, and elsewhere—helped plan the program and executed it. In identifying our co-workers, we imposed no conditions concerning religious belief or practice. We therefore claim to offer a consensus of responsible and objective learning on each topic and to cover nearly all subjects required systematically to describe, analyze, and interpret the religion, Judaism.

Judaism deserves such full-scale treatment because of its place among the great religions of human civilization. It is practiced throughout the world, both in the State of Israel, where it is the majority-religion, and throughout Europe, South Africa, Australia, New Zealand, the Western hemisphere, North and Latin America, and elsewhere. It is an indispensable example of a religion for all who study religion, exemplifying as it does the power of religion to speak to diverse settings of history and culture over nearly the whole of recorded history. Additionally, Judaism has exercised profound influence on, and engaged in dialogue with, the two other mono-theist religions, Christianity and Islam. Its relationships with those kindred religions prove complex and illuminating. But of still more interest: Judaism has retained the loyalty of its practitioners over nearly the entire course of recorded history and under duress as in times of ease. Even though, through most of the history of the Jews, abandoning the faith and people of holy Israel promised worldly advantages, Jews affirmed their religion and, at great personal sacrifice, adhered to its way of life and community. The power of the faith over long centuries to retain the commitment of those that kept the faith attracts attention. More important, still, in an era of chal-lenges of another sort, Judaism provides a fine case of a vital contemporary reli-gion, showing how an ancient, continuous tradition makes a compelling statement to the contemporary world. In concrete everyday terms, Judaism shapes the com-munity of the faithful, and it defines in various systems a distinctive way of life and world-view. So by reason of its antiquity, influence on other world religions, power to persuade the faithful of its truth, and contemporary vitality, Judaism demands sustained attention.

THE ENCYCLOPEDIA OF JUDAISM focuses in a comprehensive way upon Juda-ism the religion, presenting accounts of the history, literature, practices and beliefs, theology and philosophy, and contemporary practice of that faith. The history of Judaism is laid out both by periods and by regions, that is, Judaism in Christian Europe and in the Muslim Middle East and North Africa. The important holy books of Judaism, from ancient Israelite Scripture ("Tanakh," meaning, Torah, or Pen-tateuch, Nebi'im or Prophets, and Ketubim or Writings, called by Christianity "the Old Testament"), to the Dead Sea Scrolls, the writings of the sages of ancient times, including the Mishnah, Midrash, and Talmuds, writings of theology, philosophy and mysticism—all are introduced. The liturgy of the synagogue is spelled out, as well as synagogue architecture, art, and material culture. The practice of Judaism in important centers of the religion, the U.S.A., Britain, Russia, France, South Africa, the State of Israel, and elsewhere, is described. So too is the practice of Judaism in significant times and circumstances, e.g., in the time of the Holocaust, in the cir-cumstance of life in central and eastern Europe, in Muslim countries, in medieval Christendom.

Besides the normative Judaism defined by the ancient rabbis and called Classical or Rabbinic or—in the world today—Orthodox, other Judaisms are described, in-cluding the Essene Judaism of Qumran, Karaite Judaism, Reform, Conservative, and Reconstructionist Judaisms, and the like. Jewish mysticism and Kabbalah in par-ticular receive systematic treatment. Philosophy, numerous theological topics with-in the paramount, Rabbinic Judaism, ethics, law, and other normative components of the religion are explained in detail. The life cycle of Judaism is spelled out, as are the components of everyday piety, religious observance, and liturgy and worship. The material culture of Judaism, synagogue architecture, and other concrete matters are presented.

How Judaism relates to other religions and the views upon Judaism expressed by outsiders, ancient Greek and Latin historians and philosophers, Christian and Muslim theologians both in ancient times and in the world today, are covered. How Judaism makes its impact upon politics, the relationship of Judaism to natural science, psychology, and economics, all are expounded. Numerous special topics of religious thought and theological systemization of religious ideas, such as theological anthropology, sin, the soul, evil, suffering, tradition, death and afterlife, are set forth. Topics of acute contemporary interest, such as medical ethics, women and Judaism, Zionism and Judaism, are treated in a thorough and objective manner. In all, the table of contents shows a comprehensive and thorough treatment of a complex religion, revealing what we believe is required in the systematic and descriptive study of a religion.

The articles serve two purposes, reading and reference. In this way we have learned from the excellent idea of the Encyclopaedia Britannica, which presents a macropaedia, with long, readable articles, and a micropaedia, ready reference for basic facts of various topics. Our entries are meant to accomplish the same double purpose. First, they are written to be read, so that anyone in search of a systematic account of a topic will find here a cogent and comprehensive statement. The editors hope that readers will find many occasions to follow a topic from beginning to end, as the many contributors to these pages organize knowledge of their respective subjects.

Second, the articles are meant for ready reference in looking up facts, so that people in search of specific information will find it conveniently via the index at the end. Alongside names, places, and concepts, this index includes topical references, so that each individual topic covered in a protracted entry is made accessible. Through these references, readers may locate the individual paragraphs that form the counterpart to the brief entries of dictionaries and quick-reference encyclopedias. To take a simple example, a reader who wants to know about the Sabbath, the Festival of Sukkot, or Passover will be directed by the index to the relevant references in the long article, Calendar of Judaism. There concrete information is available on each of the holy times and seasons of Judaism. But that information is put in a context in which the Sabbath or the Festival of Sukkot or Passover forms part of a larger picture, the system of keeping time, of celebrating holy days and festivals, of an entire religion. The advantage of seeing details in their larger contexts is formidable.

The editors hope in this way both to inform by providing information and also to enlighten by placing facts into the setting in which they take on meaning, and forming out of them significant generalizations about the religion, Judaism. Above all, by seeing things whole and in context, readers may form a judgment concerning matters of proportion and significance, assigning to some matters appropriate weight, to others a lesser priority in the assessment of the whole.

In providing both ready-references and large-scale, comprehensive statements, THE ENCYCLOPEDIA OF JUDAISM differs from all other dictionaries and encyclopedias of

Judaism to date. These have tended to supply short entries, containing facts and defining words, but to neglect the larger framework in which facts take on meaning. But to describe the religion, Judaism, as we propose to do in these pages, facts out of context do not illuminate, and information without an effort at interpretation yields knowledge of only limited consequence. We cannot know a religion without mastering the facts that religion generates, but we also cannot understand a religion without some broader conception of its principal points of emphasis and contention. These impart to the whole that shape and structure that turn information into knowledge and produce insight for purposes of comparison and contrast.

While the knowledge we convey in these pages rests on a detached and objective foundation, one bias does dictate proportion and structure, defining our priorities throughout. This bias is to insist that Judaism is a living religion, not only a phenomenon out of the past. That is why many articles are devoted to the practice of Judaism in various parts of the world today, and many others to how Judaism is practiced in general, its piety, liturgy, calendar, and other practices. We wish Judaism to emerge in these pages as a set of vivid religious systems, all of them capable of sustaining and maintaining communities of "Israel," however defined, and every one of them rich in nourishment of individual and family life as well.

From the very beginning we signal our bias. Every contributor to THE ENCYCLOPEDIA OF JUDAISM, whether a practitioner of Judaism, some other religion, or no religion at all, whether of Jewish origin or otherwise, writes about Judaism with respect for a living religious community, its world view and way of life as these cohere, respectively, to form a self-evidently valid response to an urgent and paramount question. If we may use the word "passion" in speaking of learning, what the contributors bear in common is a passion for their subject, which they treat with respect and unfailing dignity. But the statements made in each of the more than one hundred entries are objective, factual, and non-partisan. No particular position within Judaism dominates, and every group and viewpoint is covered in a manner we believe to be fair and balanced. The list of contributors includes specialists from the major universities of the State of Israel, Europe, and the U.S.A. and Canada, as well as other parts of the world; scholars of Orthodox and Reform and Conservative and Reconstructionist origin; Jews and gentiles, women and men, a wide range of convictions and engagements. Judaism is set forth as both a religious tradition and also a living religion, practiced by large and cogent communities of the faithful today. The editors mean not only to inform and enlighten, but to advance understanding of Judaism in its own terms and in the framework of the study of religion generally. That is why, among the articles, approaches of social science and comparative religion are represented, as well as studies of Judaism in its own terms and setting.

To understand the plan of the ENCYCLOPEDIA overall, its inclusions and omissions, a particular complication in studying Judaism requires attention. Judaism, the religion, bears intimate relations with a particular nation-state, the State of Israel, on the one side, and a trans-national ethnic group, the Jewish people, on the other. We here take account of the confusion of the national, ethnic, and political with the religious that complicates the study of Judaism as a religion. Take the national first of all. The State of Israel recognizes Judaism and supports that religion. But Judaism the religion is trans-national and does not tie itself to any secular political entity, even with the State of Israel. Then there is the ethnic, often a matter of individual self-definition or identification, called "Jewish identity." The ethnic may or may not engage with the religious at all. In the ethnic framework the Jews, viewed individually as defining themselves in some way or another as Jewish, by reason of shared history, sentiment, and culture claim to constitute a group formed around shared history and memory. Finally, among Judaic religious communities are those that reject the nationality offered by the State of Israel and also dismiss the ethnic ties that to many Jews are binding. These categories—national, ethnic, political, religious—complicate the work of defining the task of THE ENCYCLOPEDIA OF JUDAISM.

Clearly, the border between the religion, Judaism, and the secular, ethnic group, the Jews, or between that religion and the State of Israel, cannot be drawn very rigidly or with much precision. But it is obvious that, because of its intimate tie to the Jews as individuals and the Jewish people, an ethnic group, Judaism also helps to define the secular culture of Jews wherever they live, whether or not they practice the religion, Judaism, no religion, or some other religion altogether. And the religion, Judaism, further contributes many of the critical mythic and symbolic elements of Zionism and shapes many aspects of the cultural life of the State of Israel. We have tried to take account of the interplay of the national, the ethnic, and the religious dimensions of Jewish existence, while focusing upon the religion in particular. Accordingly, while paying most attention to Judaism, the religion, THE ENCYCLOPEDIA OF JUDAISM presents the entire range of contexts in which that religion affects human life and culture. These include areas often deemed essentially secular, such as the impact of Judaism upon systems of politics and economics, psychology, and the supposedly secular life of contemporary Jews living in conditions of religious freedom. Given the rich and diverse religious heritage of Judaism, from ancient Israel to the modern State of Israel, such descriptions claim a central position within the analysis of Judaism, the religion.

* * *

The Editors take special pride that THE ENCYCLOPEDIA OF JUDAISM finds a place as one of the first major educational projects under the sponsorship of the new MUSEUM OF JEWISH HERITAGE, in New York City. The ENCYCLOPEDIA reached its final stages just as the Museum opened its doors. Through the Museum's collaboration with our work from the very beginning and through the participation of its director, Dr. David Altshuler, as chairman of the editorial board, the Museum helped both to create THE ENCYCLOPEDIA OF JUDAISM and also to define its educational program and scholarly mission. It is the link between THE ENCYCLOPEDIA OF JUDAISM and its editors and publishers, on the one side, and the educational mission of the organized Jewish community, on the other. Just as the MUSEUM OF JEWISH HERITAGE speaks to the entire public world of learning and culture, so we mean in these pages to do the same.

Special thanks are owed to Dr. Altshuler for opening to us the Museum of Jewish Heritage's extensive photo-archives. We benefited as well from the help of the Museum's staff, in particular, Louis Levine, Director of Collections and Exhibitions, and from the painstaking work of Shari Segel, Curator of Photography, who identified appropriate materials in the Museum's collection. Identification and acquisition of photos from other collections was the result of the hard work of our photo-researcher, Rhoda Seidenberg, who also prepared all of the captions and photo credits. We benefitted tremendously from her expertise and great dedication to this project.

For a companion to this Encyclopedia, providing easy access to facts and definitions, the editors call attention to their now-complete and in-print reference-work, *Dictionary of Judaism in the Biblical Period, from 450 B.C. to 600 A.D.* (N.Y., 1995: Macmillan Publishing Co.). That systematic work facilitates ready-reference to persons, places, events, and the like in the period in which Judaism took shape.

The editors found much pleasure in the professionalism of the scholarly executives of Brill, who sustained the project from the moment it was proposed to them. These are Elisabeth Erdman-Visser, now retired, the first, and Elisabeth Venekamp, the second, of Brill's editors assigned to THE ENCYCLOPEDIA OF JUDAISM. Both not only supported every proposal and initiative aimed at producing a still more ambitious work than originally contemplated. They also identified with the project and took as much pleasure in the results as have the editors, noting the excellent quality of the entries as they made their appearance and appreciating the ever-expanding range of coverage of the work. Among the European and international academic imprints in the field of Judaism, Brill has long taken the principal position as the leading publisher. Our uniformly positive experience with the firm explains why. The editors also enjoyed the counsel and acumen of Werner Mark Linz and Justus George Lawler and the staff of Continuum. We take special pride in the participation in this project of two such formidable publishers.

The editors express their thanks to their respective universities, which sustain their research and scholarly projects. The University of South Florida and Bard College, The College of the Holy Cross, and the University of Rochester make possible the work and careers of the three, respectively, including the rather considerable enterprise that reaches fruition here. Along with the collaboration of the MUSEUM OF THE JEWISH HERITAGE in the largest Jewish community in the world, this diverse mixture of academic sponsors—a huge, municipal and public university, a tiny private college, a Catholic college, and a major private research university—matches the mixture of personalities and viewpoints comprised by the entire editorial board.

To the Board of Consulting Editors, who advised on the planning of the project and produced the articles, is owed the credit for the successful completion of THE ENCYCLOPEDIA OF JUDAISM. Given the vast range encompassed by the history and contemporary practice of Judaism, the diversity that characterizes the Board of Consulting Editors proves entirely appropriate to the subject and the task of elucidating it. Many talents contributed to the project. That explains why the editors also owe their genuine gratitude to the dozens of contributors. Each a principal expert in his or her field, they not only did their work as assigned and on time but turned in their best work and produced first rate scholarship in literate and interesting articles. THE ENCYCLOPEDIA OF JUDAISM forms a felicitous indicator of where we now stand in the study of Judaism within the academic study of religion today. To the many contributors to these pages we pay tribute for the excellence that their entries evince and express our thanks for the learning, wit, intelligence, and responsibility that they brought to this collaborative project. It is hardly necessary to say we could not have done it without them!

THE EDITORS

JACOB NEUSNER
UNIVERSITY OF SOUTH FLORIDA, TAMPA, FLORIDA, AND BARD COLLEGE,
ANNANDALE-UPON-HUDSON, NEW YORK
ALAN J. AVERY-PECK
COLLEGE OF THE HOLY CROSS, WORCESTER, MASSACHUSETTS
WILLIAM SCOTT GREEN
UNIVERSITY OF ROCHESTER, ROCHESTER, NEW YORK

LIST OF ILLUSTRATIONS AND MAPS

Art and Material Culture

Figure 1: Bible, Majorca, 1325.

Figure 2: Passover plate, probably Valencia, fifteenth century, lusterware.

Figure 3: Hanukkah lamp, Germany, fourteenth century, bronze.

Figure 4: Set of nested beakers, Bohemia, before 1330-1335, silver.

Figure 5: Hanging lamp, Germany, fourteenth century, bronze.

Figure 6: Torah finials, Spain or Sicily, fifteenth century, silver, stones.

Figure 7: Torah shield, Florence, 1747.

Figure 8: Torah shield, Augsburg, ca. 1725, Zacharias Wagner, silver: gilt.

Figure 9: Torah shield, Germany, late eighteenth century, silver.

Figure 10: Torah shield, Izmir, nineteenth century, silver.

Figure 11: Torah crown and finials, Istanbul, 1845/1846-1879/1880, silver.

Figure 12: Torah crown, Johann Friedrich Wilhelm Borcke, Berlin, 1821-1839, silver: gilt.

Figure 13: Valance for Torah ark, Prague, 1718/1719, silk and metallic threads.

Figure 14: Torah curtain, Venice?, 1698/1699, linen embroidered with silk and metallic threads.

Figure 15: Torah binder, Germany, 1153, linen embroidered with silk threads.

Figure 16: Beaker for the Burial Society of Worms, Nürnberg, 1711/1712, Johann Conrad Weiss, silver.

Figure 17: Tiered Passover plate, Poland, eighteenth century, brass, wood, silk.

Figure 18: Spice container, Frankfurt, ca. 1550, silver.

Figure 19: Hanukkah lamp, Frankfurt, 1710, Johann Michael Schuler, silver.

Figure 20: Purim Megillah case, Galicia, eighteenth century, silver: gilt.

Judaism, Contemporary Expressions of; New Age Judaisms

Judaism, History of, Part I. Ancient Israel. To 586 B.C.E.

Judaism, History of, Part III. Late Antiquity

Judaism, History of, Part V. A. Modern Times in Europe

Liturgy of Judaism. History and Form

Music in Judaism

Women and Judaism

Zionism, Judaism and

MAPS

FIGURE AND MAP CREDITS

All artifacts listed below from the Collection of the Museum of Jewish Heritage were photographed by Peter Goldberg.
Figures 1-23 are from The Photo Archives of the Jewish Museum, New York.

Figure 1: The Jewish Museum.

Figure 2: Israel Museum, Jerusalem, 134/57.

Figure 3: Congregation Imanu-el of the City of New York.

Figure 4: Germanisches Nationalmuseum, Nuremberg.

Figure 5: The Jewish Museum, New York, JM 200-67.

Figure 6: Cathedral Treasury of Palma de Majorca.

Figure 7: Communita Israelitica. Florence.

Figures 8-9: The Jewish Museum, New York, F 70c. Photograph: John Parnell.

Figure 10: Israel Museum, Jerusalem, 148/2117.

Figure 11: Israel Museum, Jerusalem, 146/33; 147/213a,b.

Figure 12: Gift of Dr. Harry G. Friedman. The Jewish Museum, New York, F 1649. Photograph: Ambus Hiken.

Figure 13: The Jewish Museum, New York, S 1. Photograph: Frank J. Damstaedter.

Figure 14: The Jewish Museum, New York, F 3432. Photograph: Frank J. Damstaedter.

Figure 15: The Jewish Museum, New York, F 5036. Photograph: Frank J. Damstaedter.

Figure 16: The Jewish Museum, New York, JM 30-51. Photograph: Frank J. Damstaedter.

Figure 17: The Jewish Museum, New York, D 115. Photograph: Frank J. Damstaedter.

Figure 18: The Jewish Museum, New York, JM 23-52. Photograph: Frank J. Damstaedter.

Figure 19: Musée de Cluny, Paris, Inv. 12241.

Figure 20: The Jewish Museum, New York, JM 27-64, purchased by the Purim Ball Committee. Photograph: Graydon Wood.

Figure 21: Gift of Milton Rubin, The Jewish Museum, New York, JM 33-48.

Figure 22: Promised gift of Sylvia Zenia Wiener, The Jewish Museum, New York. Photograph: John Parnell.

Figure 23: Collection of Patricia and Alan Davidson, New York.

Figure 24: Collection of Ruth Cernea and Itic and Tili Svartz-Kara.

Figure 25: Gift of Rabbi W. Gunther and Elizabeth S. Plaut, Museum of Jewish Heritage, New York.

Figure 26: Gift of J. Nina Lieberman in memory of Rabbi Dr. David Samuel Margules, Museum of Jewish Heritage, New York.

Figure 27: Gift of Sal Kluger in memory of Charlotte and Bernhard Kluger, Museum of Jewish Heritage, New York.

Figure 28: Rabbi W. Gunther and Elizabeth S. Plaut, Museum of Jewish Heritage, New York.

Figure 29: Gift of Vera Freeman, Museum of Jewish Heritage, New York.

Figure 30: © Beryl Goldberg, Photographer.

Figure 31: Gift of Helen Elbaum, Museum of Jewish Heritage, New York.

Figure 32: Gift of Louis Heidelberger, Museum of Jewish Heritage, New York.

Figure 33: Collection of Anne Lisa Erlanger Rotenberg.

Figure 34: Collection Joseph A. and Dorothy Frank Bamberger.

Figure 35: Collection of Shoshana Dagan.

Figure 36: Gift of Natalie Kaplansky Gomberg, Museum of Jewish Heritage, New York.

Figure 37: Gift of Nathan Solomon, Museum of Jewish Heritage, New York.

Figure 38: Beth Hatefutsoth, The Nahum Goldmann Museum of the Jewish Diaspora, Tel Aviv.

Figure 39: Gift of Frank Barnett, Museum of Jewish Heritage, New York.

Figure 40: Gift of Dr. Leslie M. Hammel, Museum of Jewish Heritage, New York.

Figure 41: Gift of Elsie O. Sang in memory of Phillip Sang, Museum of Jewish Heritage, New York.

Figure 42: Anonymous donation, Museum of Jewish Heritage, New York.

Figure 43: Gift of Jean Schreider Friedland and Marion Schreider Seitzman, Museum of Jewish Heritage, New York.

Figure 44: Collection of Naomi Rothschild.

Figures 45-46: Israel Antiquities Authority.

Figure 47: Gift of Isaac, Doris, and Nina Moinester in memory of David and Ida Sidewitz, Museum of Jewish Heritage, New York.

Figure 48: Gift of Barbara Mathes, Museum of Jewish Heritage, New York.

Figure 49: Collection of Jacques Heller.

Figure 50: Gift of Stanley Stern, Museum of Jewish Heritage, New York.

Figure 51: Gift of Carol Biermann, Museum of Jewish Heritage, New York.

Figure 52: Gift of Dr. Ervin Varga, Museum of Jewish Heritage, New York.

Figure 53: Gift of Salamon and Jolan Katz, Museum of Jewish Heritage, New York.

Figure 54: Collection of Rabbi David Lipman.

Figure 55: Gift of Sigrid Jean Ansbacher Strauss, Museum of Jewish Heritage, New York.

Figure 56: Gift of Ludwig Ehrenreich, Zachary Ehrenreich and Margaret E. Heching, Museum of Jewish Heritage, New York.

Figure 57: Museum of Jewish Heritage, New York.

Figure 58: Gift of Menora Studios, Brooklyn, New York, Yaffa Eliach Collection donated by the Center for Holocaust Studies, Museum of Jewish Heritage, New York.

Figure 59: Collection of Edita Reich-Alexander.

Figure 60: Gift of Hana Rothchild, Yaffa Eliach Collection donated by the Center for Holocaust Studies, Museum of Jewish Heritage, New York.

Figure 61: Gift of Herbert von Peci, Museum of Jewish Heritage, New York.

Figure 62: Gift of Judah Nadich, Yaffa Eliach Collection donated by the Center for Holocaust Studies, Museum of Jewish Heritage, New York.

Figure 63: Memorial Scrolls Trust on permanent loan to the Museum of Jewish Heritage, New York.

Figure 64: © Bill Aron.

Figure 65: © The British Museum.

Figures 66-70: Israel Antiquities Authority.

Figure 71: Gift of Lew Sonn, Museum of Jewish Heritage, New York.

Figure 72: Beth Hatefutsoth, The Nahum Goldmann Museum of the Jewish Diaspora, Tel Aviv.

Figure 73: Gift of Irene White, Museum of Jewish Heritage, New York.

Figure 74: Gift of Herman and Norbert Strauss, Museum of Jewish Heritage, New York.

Figure 75: Gift of Hilda Newton, Museum of Jewish Heritage, New York.

Figure 76: Barbara Pfeffer Collection, Museum of Jewish Heritage, New York.

Figure 77: Gift of Carol Biermann, Museum of Jewish Heritage, New York.

Figure 78: Gift of Fredric and Rosalie Frost, Museum of Jewish Heritage, New York.

Figure 79: © Zion Ozeri.

Figure 80: Gift of Belle Davis, Museum of Jewish Heritage, New York.

Figure 81: Gift of Vivian Zilberman, Museum of Jewish Heritage, New York.

Figure 82: Gift of Rose Boyarsky, Museum of Jewish Heritage, New York.

Figure 83: Gift of Rhoda Gordon, Museum of Jewish Heritage, New York.

Figures 84-85: Gift of Ernestine Cline Rachlis, Museum of Jewish Heritage, New York.

Figure 86: Gift of Roberta Goldman, Museum of Jewish Heritage, New York.

Figures 87-88: Museum of Jewish Heritage, New York.

Figure 89: Collection of Michael M. Cernea.

Figure 90: Gift of Joseph A. and Dorothy Frank Bamberger.

Figure 91: Gift of Irene Zimmer, Museum of Jewish Heritage, New York.

Figure 92: Gift of Herbert Buxbaum, Yaffa Eliach Collection donated by the Center for Holocaust Studies, Museum of Jewish Heritage, New York.

Figure 93: Hilda Bixon and Edith Kupferman, Museum of Jewish Heritage, New York.

Figure 94: Barbara Pfeffer Collection, Museum of Jewish Heritage, New York.

Figure 95: Yad Izhak Ben-Zvi Archives, Jerusalem.

Figure 96: Richard T. Nowitz.

Figure 97: Amsterdam University Library.

Figure 98: Gift of Naomi Rothschild, Museum of Jewish Heritage, New York.

Figure 99: Gift of Helen Hershoff in honor of Henry, Mary, and Israel Hershoff, Museum of Jewish Heritage, New York.

Figure 100: Collection of Saul and Hope Bell.

Figure 101: Barbara Pfeffer Collection, Museum of Jewish Heritage, New York.

Figure 102: National Archives, Amsterdam.

Figure 103: Amsterdam City Archives.

Figure 104: Gift of Henry Morley, Museum of Jewish Heritage, New York.

Figure 105: Gift of Rose Sigal-Ibsen in memory of Albert Dov Sigal, Museum of Jewish Heritage, New York.

Figure 106: Gift of Edith Riemer, Museum of Jewish Heritage, New York.

Figure 107: Gift of Max Adolf, Museum of Jewish Heritage, New York.

Figure 108: Gift of Judith G. Thaler, Museum of Jewish Heritage, New York.

Figure 109: Gift of Stella Sardell Sanua, Museum of Jewish Heritage, New York.

Figure 110: Collection of Solomon Chasin.

Figure 111: Gift of Max Lucash, Museum of Jewish Heritage, New York.

Figure 112: Gift of Anita Beer, Museum of Jewish Heritage, New York.

Figure 113: Gift of Shlomo and Rivka Shulsinger, Museum of Jewish Heritage, New York.

Figure 114: By Permission of the British Library. Hebrew MS Add. 19776.

Figures 115-117: Reconstructionist Rabbinical College.

Figure 118: © Peter Goldberg.

Figure 119: Gift of Yehuda Tamir, Museum of Jewish Heritage, New York.

Figure 120: Gift of Mr. and Mrs. George Klein and Family, Museum of Jewish Heritage, New York.

Figure 121: Gift of Joseph A. Bamberger and Family, Museum of Jewish Heritage, New York.

Figure 122: © Bill Aron.

Figure 123: Anonymous donor, Museum of Jewish Heritage, New York.

Figure 124: Anonymous donor, Museum of Jewish Heritage, New York.

Figure 125: Gift of Cypora and Josef Glikson, Museum of Jewish Heritage, New York.

Figures 126-127: © Ryan Noik.

Figures 128-129: Barbara Pfeffer Collection, Museum of Jewish Heritage, New York.

Figure 130: © Leonard Freed/Magnum Photos.

Figure 131: © Archaeological Exploration of Sardis/Harvard University.

Figures 132-134: Yale University Art Gallery, Dura-Europus Archive.

Figure 135: Israel Antiquities Authority.

Figures 136-168: The Photo Archives of the Jewish Museum, New York.

Figure 169: Gift of Hilda Lourie and Arthur Lourie, Museum of Jewish Heritage, New York.

Figure 170: Gift of Fruma Dushnitzer, Yaffa Eliach Collection donated by the Center for Holocaust Studies, Museum of Jewish Heritage, New York.

Figure 171: Gift of Joseph Eden, Museum of Jewish Heritage, New York.

Figure 172: Barbara Pfeffer Collection, Museum of Jewish Heritage, New York.

Figure 173: © Peter Goldberg.

Figure 174: Gift of Ma'yan, The Jewish Women's Project of the Jewish Community Center on the Upper West Side, New York, Museum of Jewish Heritage, New York.

Figure 175: Gift of Rabbi Amy Levin, Museum of Jewish Heritage, New York.

Figure 176: Anonymous donation, Museum of Jewish Heritage, New York.

Figure 177: Anonymous donation, Museum of Jewish Heritage, New York.

Figure 178: Anonymous Donor, Museum of Jewish Heritage, New York.

Figure 179: Collection of Abraham Grussgott.

Figure 180: Gift of Gedalia Segal, Yaffa Eliach Collection donated by the Center for Holocaust Studies, Museum of Jewish Heritage, New York.

Maps 1, 3-7 are drawn after © Carta, Jerusalem.

Map 2 is drawn after © Oxford University Press.

A

ART AND MATERIAL CULTURE OF JUDAISM—
MEDIEVAL THROUGH MODERN TIMES:[1]
While works of Jewish ceremonial art fulfill
functions mandated by Judaism's obligatory
ritual practices, their forms and decoration
often are drawn from those of the surrounding cultures in which Jewish communities
have lived. As a result, although the function of a ceremonial object made in a particular cultural area will be identical to one
created within another culture, and while
they may share a common vocabulary of
symbols, their shape, techniques, and decorative motifs will differ. Therefore, a work
of Jewish art or material culture must always
be studied within two frames of reference:
its place within the practice of Judaism, and
its relationship to the art and material culture of its place of origin.

Medieval illuminated manuscripts: In
the realm of art, illuminated manuscripts link
the culture of ancient Israel with the later
culture of the diaspora. Several fragments of
manuscripts that were written in the ninth-
tenth centuries are decorated with both carpet pages of overall, repeated motifs and
with pages bearing the implements of the
wilderness Tabernacle and the Temple in
Jerusalem.[2] Some of these early illuminations
are formed through micrography, the use of
letters to shape forms, which became a distinctive feature of Hebrew manuscript illumination into the modern era, although the
technique is not exclusive to books written
in Hebrew.

The same decorative schemes are found
in later manuscripts created in Cairo and in
Spain.[3] Carpet pages are also a feature of illuminated Korans, and the corpus of Hebrew
and Arabic Bibles extant from medieval

Spain share a common repertoire of carpet
page compositions and motifs, as both were
produced within the iconoclastic culture of
Islam. In Hebrew Bibles, additional pages
bear images of the Tabernacle and Temple
instruments, continuing the iconography of
earlier Tiberian manuscripts (fig. 1). Inscriptions surrounding the Spanish compositions
elucidate their meaning: the Bible is the
mikdash me'at, the small sanctuary, that sustains Jewish belief until the reestablishment
of the holy Temple in the messianic age.

With the spread of Christian hegemony
over the Iberian Peninsula and the influence
of new artistic models in the early fourteenth
century, an innovative type of Hebrew manuscript appeared in Barcelona and its environs, the illuminated haggadah or service
book for the Passover seder. The decoration
of these Sephardic haggadot was influenced
by the Christian tradition of figurative manuscript decoration. It includes a prefatory
cycle of biblical pictures tracing the history
of the world from the creation through the
death of Moses, or some portion of that
history.[4] Illuminated haggadot also incorporate textual illustrations, such as the four
sons and the symbolic foods, and even genre
scenes depicting preparations for Passover,
for the seder, and the enactment of the seder
itself.

The genre scenes are important sources
for the history of a Jewish ceremonial art
that largely disappeared with the expulsion
from Spain in 1492 and from Portugal in
1497. For example, a deep dish (*brasero*)
inscribed with Hebrew names of three symbolic Passover foods is in the Israel Museum
(fig. 2). Its exact use is unknown, but one
illuminated fourteenth-century haggadah

shows the master of the house distributing matzah to his household from a similar dish.[5] Such information on the forms of ceremonial art is invaluable in the light of the losses suffered by the Jews of Iberia because of edicts forbidding them to leave Spain and Portugal with their gold and silver. Both synagogual and private ceremonial objects were melted down and used to compensate cities for the loss of tax revenues caused by the expulsion of Jewish citizens.

Genre illustrations of Judaica also appear in manuscripts created in Ashkenaz, whose Jews lived within a dominant Christian culture with a long tradition of using images as both an aid to devotion and for education. Scenes depicting Jewish ceremonial objects appear in prayer books, even those used in the synagogue, and haggadot.[6] Despite periodic persecutions, the Jews of Ashkenaz did not suffer the wholesale expulsions inflicted on the Sephardim, with the result that greater numbers of actual ceremonial objects remain from the French and German-speaking areas of medieval Europe.

The High Middle Ages (twelfth-fifteenth centuries): Hannukah lamps constitute the earliest group of ceremonial objects extant from the medieval period, with their characteristic row of eight lights all on the same level. A twelfth-century bench-type lamp, designed to sit on a surface, was excavated in Lyons.[7] Made of stone from a nearby quarry, its row of oil and wick containers are shaped as horseshoe arches, a motif drawn from the Islamic art of nearby Spain.

A change in usage occurred in the thirteenth century. Hanukkah lamps began to be hung on the wall. Three bronze examples from northern France or the Rhineland are known (fig. 3).[8] Above their oil and wick containers rises a backplate formed of an interlaced arcade similar to that on Norman buildings of the thirteenth century, and a gable housing animals in relief framed in roundels. A century later, a group of lamps with simplified gables and arcades appeared.[9] Their major motif is a Gothic rose window.

Recent excavations in the old Jewish quarter in Teruel, which was a center for the manufacture of pottery during the Middle Ages, have uncovered fragments of three fifteenth-century ceramic Hanukkah lamps.[10] They are bench type and glazed cream, purple, and green like other Teruel ceramics of the period. Painted eyes animate the oil containers, giving them a face-like appearance.

Other excavations along the Rhine and in the mining town of Kutna Hora, the Czech Republic, revealed additional domestic Judaica. One type is the *kiddush* cup. At Lingenfeld near Speyer, beakers were found along with a coin hoard dated 1348, their burial probably due to the persecution of Jews following the Black Death .[11] A set of nested beakers was found in an administrative building in Kutna Hora (fig. 4). Although originally made for a queen named Elizabeth, whose coats of arms appear on the bottoms of the beakers, these cups were later acquired by a Jew named Wolf, who added his Hebrew name to the shield bearing that animal.

The double cup, a very elaborate drinking vessel whose cover was formed to serve as a second cup, was popular as a wedding present from the thirteenth through the sixteenth centuries. The symbolism of two combining into one made these vessels highly appropriate as marriage gifts. One example dated to the fourteenth century was found with the Lingenfeld coin hoard. An even more elaborate example of jasper was commissioned by a Jew named Zvi, then acquired at some point by the archbishop of Erbach, who substituted his own coats of arms for that of the prior Jewish owner.[12] The miniatures of fifteenth-century Ashkenazic haggadot attest to the presence of both nested *kiddush* cups and the more elaborate double cups in wealthy Jewish homes, those also capable of commissioning illuminated manuscripts.[13]

Seder scenes in both Ashkenazic and Sephardic haggadot commonly show a star-shaped hanging lamp above the festive table.[14] The form was in general use in medieval Europe, but was eventually superseded by other forms of lighting. Among Jews, however, the lamp became a traditional type so that, by the sixteenth century, it became known among German goldsmiths as a *Judenstern*. The star-shaped hanging lamp was utilized by central- and east-European

Jews for Sabbaths and holy days into the twentieth century. One medieval survivor of Jewish ownership was found in Deutz (fig. 5). Made of bronze, its faceted form indicates a date in the first half of the fourteenth century. An engraved six-pointed star on the base together with its discovery in an area inhabited by Jews suggest Jewish ownership.

Excavations of medieval sites have also yielded distinctive Jewish marriage rings, whose bezels are formed in the shape of small buildings. The earliest was found at Weissenfels, near Halle, in a hoard dated to the first half of the fourteenth century.[15] Another example found with a fourteenth-century coin hoard comes from Colmar, and a third was in the Munich Schatzkammer before 1598.

Another medieval object, the aquamanile in the form of a lion, was used by Jews both in the home and in the synagogue. An example in the Walters Art Gallery, Baltimore, is engraved with the Hebrew blessing said after washing the hands and was probably used in the home.[16] Two others were published in 1928 as the property of German synagogues; their whereabouts are today unknown. One may be identical with a damaged example, now in a private collection, that bears a Hebrew inscription indicating its dedication to a synagogue by a woman whose father was a *kohen*, a member of the priestly class. It may have been used for washing the hands of *kohanim* prior to their blessing the congregation.

According to Rabbinic responsa and to documents such as the lists of objects belonging to various synagogues found in the Ben Ezra geniza in Cairo, the Torah finial was an independent object as early as the twelfth century.[17] It is most often called a *rimmon* (pomegranate), implying that its shape was round or fruit-like. This is the form found in medieval miniatures and in the earliest extant Sephardic finials, dated 1601/2 and discovered in Pest, in an area occupied by the Ottomans.[18] The only medieval pair to survive, however, is formed as a tower, a symbol of the heavenly Jerusalem used by both Christians and Jews since the

early Byzantine period (fig. 6). The finials were made in Sicily during the fifteenth century, when that island was under Spanish rule, and are close in form to the verges, the ceremonial stave ends, used by the church.[19] This may account for their survival to this day in the Cathedral Treasury of Palma de Majorca. These Sicilian Torah finials are decorated with horseshoe arches and filigree, as well as with semiprecious and glass stones. Hebrew inscriptions appear on all four sides of the towers.

Although the Sicilian finials and earlier Torah finials dated as far back as the twelfth century were created independent of the Torah scroll, other finials were fashioned from the Torah's wooden staves themselves. They can be seen in manuscript illustrations where the rod of the stave terminates in a bulbous form and in one extant pair of stave decorations dated to the late fifteenth century.[20] The stave finials were created for Nathanael Trabuto, who worked as a punctuator and scribe of Hebrew manuscripts and may have adorned a Torah scroll that he copied. They are carved with Gothic motifs: multiple lancet windows, a frieze of leaves that appear on metalwork of the late fifteenth century, and the name of their owner.

Unfortunately, none of the Torah crowns mentioned in Rabbinic responsa and seen in miniatures such as the one in the Spanish Sarajevo Haggadah of the second quarter of the fourteenth century survive.[21] These Sephardic crowns were sometimes used individually, but were often placed together with a pair of finials on the staves of the Torah scrolls, a usage that has been followed throughout the Sephardic diaspora and in eastern communities until the present day.

A detailed description of a medieval crown was found in a French archive, in a contract dated March 24, 1439, written between an Avignon silversmith, Robin Asard, and the Jewish community of Arles.[22] The contract indicates what materials were to be used and the working conditions and restrictions mandated by the community, who also specified the forms to be incorporated into their Torah ornament. Robin Asard was required to make a hexagonal crown whose corners were marked by pillars, each adorned with the head of a lion from whose mouth three chains emerged bearing bells. The sides of the crown were to be articulated as masonry and topped by crenellations to give the appearance of a fortress. This literary description recalls the polygonal polycandelons donated to important German churches beginning in the twelfth century.[23] Latin inscriptions on these large lamps indicate that their patrons saw them as representations of the heavenly Jerusalem, a meaning appropriate to a Torah crown as well. The Arles contract also describes the renovation of an older crown belonging to the congregation that likewise was to be furnished with towers, interesting testimony to a desire to modernize an older work by investing it with symbols matching those on the new crown.

Only one other type of ceremonial object associated with the Torah survives from the Middle Ages. It is represented by a single silver pointer, a rod with a terminal in the form of a hand, made in Ferrara, Italy, in 1488, for use by the reader in following the text.[24] The Talmudic prohibition against touching the sacred Torah scroll with the naked hand or finger (B. Meg. 32a) gave rise to the practice of covering the hand with a piece of silk or the corner of a prayer shawl. Documents from Prague indicate that in 1581 the Jews of that city commissioned pointers from Christian silversmiths attached to the court of Rudolf II, who were considered to be better-trained than their Jewish counterparts, but none survive.[25] Although the new instrument appeared in the late fifteenth century, both means of following the text, the silver pointer and a textile wrapped around the hand, survived into the late sixteenth century.[26]

When not in use, the Torah scroll was placed in an ark, which, as in the period of the early synagogues, could be part of the building fabric or an independent wooden structure. Until *Kristallnacht*, the synagogue in Worms, dated to 1174/75, was the oldest in Europe, and its ark was an aedicula. A similar ark, dated ca. 1265, still exists in the Altneuschul, Prague, now the oldest surviving European synagogue.[27] The gable of the ark contains a stone relief of the Tree of Life, a motif repeated over the entrance door to the men's prayer hall.

Both Ashkenazic and Sephardic manuscript illuminations depict wooden arks as independent pieces of furniture. A surviving example stems from Modena and is today in the Musée de Cluny, Paris. Although its inscription indicates a date of 1472, in the midst of the Renaissance, the Modena ark is decorated with Gothic motifs, notably a series of lancet openings. The old-fashioned style of this ark may indicate it was based on a preexisting work that the congregation wished to replace. Just a few years later, ca. 1500, the Jews of Urbino commissioned an ark in Renaissance style, whose basic scheme appears to derive from the *studioli* of their duke in his palaces at Gubbio and Urbino.[28] The temporal coexistence of different styles remains characteristic of Jewish ceremonial art into the modern age.

The sixteenth-nineteenth centuries— Torah ornaments: The development of Jewish ceremonial art in the post-medieval period was governed by many of the same conditions that affected the production of European decorative arts in general. Of major significance was the increased availability of silver in Europe as the result of the discoveries of the Americas, which led to the creation of greater numbers of silver vessels and tableware. The ownership and display of works in silver came to express the power and wealth of their possessor. Not only individuals but corporate entities such as city governments and guilds commissioned quantities of silver plate that were placed on view at ceremonial occasions. Jewish participation in this trend can be seen in the commissioning of large numbers of silver ritual objects whose forms were known in the Middle Ages, finials, crowns, and pointers, and in the creation of an important new ornament for the Torah scroll: the Torah shield, a plaque indicating the biblical book and chapter to which the scroll was rolled.

In 1530, a Jewish convert to Catholicism, Antonius Margaritha, wrote that he saw silver plaques hanging by means of chains over the mantles of the Torah scroll.[29] Other mid-sixteenth-century evidence for Torah shields are entries in the register of the Frankfurt goldsmiths' guild. They list a "Jewish plaque," "a Moses plaque engraved with the Ten Commandments," and two "silver covers for Jewish Torah scrolls."[30] One shield made in Frankfurt in 1587 survives, as does another made in Trieste in 1599.[31]

The Frankfurt shield is an oblong topped by a crown and, in the middle, has a holder for small plaques that were engraved with the names of special readings used to indicate the place to which the scroll was rolled. The Trieste shield is oriented vertically and lacks accommodations for interchangeable plaques. Instead, it is engraved "the third scroll." It became traditional for Italian synagogues to own three such plaques, engraved "first," "second," and "third." Rather than heralding specific readings, these indicated the order in which the scrolls were to be used on a given Sabbath or holy day (fig. 7). From their earliest appearance through the beginning of the twentieth century, Torah shields were useful appurtenances that marked the scroll turned to the reading of the day. They were also decorative. Only in the twentieth century did they lose their practical purpose and become exclusively ornamental.

The few shields that survive from the seventeenth century are oblong like the early example from Frankfurt and preserve the large proportions of the interchangeable plaques relative to the size of the shield as a whole.[32] Two examples were made by silversmiths from Emden, and the remainder stem from Strasbourg.

A new period begins in the later seventeenth century, a great age of experimentation with the form of the Torah shield, when some of the most impressive examples of the genre were created. During the last decades of the century, silversmiths in several German centers added framing columns to the repertoire of motifs on the shields, thereby establishing a vertical orientation that soon became commonplace. The columns were frequently topped by confronted lions that "guarded" the motif at center, usually a

crown symbolic of the Torah. Within this basic scheme many individual variations occurred, such as the 1717-1718 shield of Zacharias Wagner of Augsburg, whose columns are multiplied to form a garden pavilion (fig. 8) and the Bohemian and Moravian shields, whose crowns copy the imperial Austrian regalia. In the works of two Prague goldsmiths of the second quarter of the nineteenth century, the guardian lions are often playful, as in the works of Carl Skremenec, or they disappear in favor of dragons on the shields of Thomas Hoppfl.[33] This unusual iconography was probably inspired by the fourteenth-century statue of Saint Michael Vanquishing the Dragon, a landmark sculpture that stood in front of Prague's St. Vitus Cathedral.

Although the framing columns, guardian animals, and even crowns could be interpreted as Jewish symbols and often are labeled as such, these motifs in fact come from the general repertory of seventeenth- and eighteenth-century decorative silver. Other shields made in the same period display specifically Jewish iconography, including biblical subjects such as Abraham and the three angels or the Offering of Isaac,[34] while others bear scenes showing the celebration of Jewish holy days or the furnishings of the Temple. This last iconographic theme was also popular on Torah curtains, mantles, and valances of the period.[35] The most commonly found biblical theme is the pairing of Moses holding the Tablets of the Law and Aaron holding a censer. This iconographic scheme appeared first on the title pages of Latin books during the 1520s and later on the title pages of Hebrew books printed in the late seventeenth century. Since the Torah shield announced the specific contents of the scroll on which it hung, the shield functioned like a title page and came to assume the iconography of printed examples.

Figures of Moses and Aaron are most commonly found on shields produced in Breslau and other German cities (fig. 9). In the early nineteenth century, Moses Sofer, rabbi in Pressburg and a proponent of strict orthodoxy, discussed the propriety of shields with figures of the Lawgiver and the High Priest.[36] He ruled that they were permissible, since the iconography of Moses and Aaron was widely known and their figures would not be mistaken for idols. Nevertheless, a diminution of the human forms by cutting off the tips of their noses or the tops of their ears was preferable.

As was the case with Moses and Aaron, various compositional schemes were particularly popular in specific regions. Following the fire in the Frankfurt Judengasse of 1711, a series of simple shields of cast rectangles to which were attached molded appliqué symbols were quickly made to replace the synagogue silver lost in the conflagration.[37] In Augsburg and Nuremberg, a composition focused on a vertical arrangement of the Temple menorah, the reading plaques, and the Tablets of the Law, all flanked by columns supporting lions, was popular into the early nineteenth century, while in eastern Europe, shields devoid of pictorial decoration were dedicated in honor of newborn children.[38] Later, many east-European shields were embellished with filigree as was other Judaica from the region. Immigrants from Russia and Poland continued to produce filigree shields in the United States, often stamped with false Russian marks to assure other immigrants of their quality.

Prior to the mid-nineteenth century, Torah shields, although a characteristic form of Ashkenazic Judaica, were unknown in Sephardic and eastern lands. The few that were made were ornamental and were often formed from an existing object (fig. 10). They do not fulfill the common function of Ashkenazic shields of indicating the lection.

On the other hand, Torah finials were used in Sephardic and eastern communities throughout the Middle Ages and afterward, as attested by Rabbinic responsa and other documentary evidence. As we have seen, the earliest pair, found in Budapest and dated 1601, is of spherical form. Fruit-shaped finials continue to be used in eastern, Italian and other Sephardic communities until the present day, sometimes in combination with crowns on the top of a scroll or on the top of

tikim housing scrolls, or placed at the corners of the reader's desk.[39]

Tower-formed finials found in the synagogues of eastern communities in the nineteenth and twentieth centuries suggest European influence, as in the Italianate finials used in North Africa until the recent emigration of the community (fig. 11). Ashkenazic communities, on the other hand, favored the tower-form finial from the beginning, although this shape underwent many changes and varied from naturalistic towers with apertures and articulated masonry, some actually copying local landmarks, to others whose tower form disappeared beneath an overlay of baroque ornament.[40] The Torah crown was usually employed as an alternative to finials in Ashkenazic lands, sometimes reserved for holy days as opposed to routine Sabbaths. Its form varied from region to region, reflecting the regalia of local rulers of the cities in which it was made (fig. 12).

A variety of literary and visual evidence, together with a few extant works, suggest that the Torah curtain and mantle as articulated compositions including both iconographic and decorative elements first developed in the mid-sixteenth century. The curtains depicted in medieval miniatures were made of un-embellished textiles, but a responsum of Joseph Caro, 1488-1575, discusses the permissibility of hanging curtains with woven designs.[41] In his answer, Caro wrote that the custom of placing a figured and embroidered Torah curtain before the ark had spread throughout the diaspora.

The earliest extant curtains are a carpet with Mamluk borders and motifs whose framing architecture was modeled on the title page of a Hebrew text printed in Padua, and an embroidered silk curtain made by Solomon Perlsticker of Prague in 1592, whose columned frame likewise echoes a printed example.[42] A major inspiration for the creation of articulated curtain compositions may have been the adoption of decorated title pages by the printers of Hebrew texts who, in turn, often modeled their works on Latin title pages.

On the Perlsticker curtain, the inscription, rows of squared letters of equal height, is placed in a block frame at the top of the textile, a compositional element that remained constant on Central European curtains and mantles into the nineteenth century. The remainder of the curtain or mantle consisted of a beautiful woven or embroidered textile, as on the earliest mantle, that commissioned by Mordecai Meisel in 1592.[43] Sometimes, an independent, elaborately decorated valance hung atop the curtains. Its scallops were richly embroidered with the implements of the Temple, while two stumpwork eagles, representing the cherubim, and the inscription filled the horizontal field (fig. 13).

The iconography of the Prague valances was taken up in Bavaria during the 1720s by the embroiderer Elkone of Naumberg, who signed the elaborate curtain and valance sets that were his specialty.[44] His compositions were a model for the works of Jakob Koppel Gans, active in the 1770s, who integrated the design of the valance with that of the curtain, and who treated inscriptions in a freer manner than did his counterparts in Prague. The basic iconography found on their curtains became standard in the nineteenth and twentieth centuries in both western and eastern Europe, although often reduced to framing columns, confronted lions, and the menorah or Tablets of the Law.

Most Italian Torah curtains consist of beautiful fabrics without any additional decoration. A number of works are exceptional, however, and are formed of elaborately embroidered or needlework compositions with sophisticated iconographic programs (fig. 14). Executed by women, whose achievement was sometimes engraved on their tombstones, these curtains echo the complexity of meaning found in altarpieces of baroque churches. Italian Jewish women also embroidered binders for the Torah, as well as mantles.

Women in the Ottoman Empire similarly played a role in furnishing textiles for the synagogue, both new pieces and ones made from previously used works. Ceremonial bedcovers, tablecovers, and dresses embroidered with gold thread were donated to the synagogue and used to form Torah curtains, reader's desk covers, and the like.[45] At the same time, the carpet curtain first known in Padua, where it was probably knotted by an itinerant Egyptian rug maker, was the forerunner of a series of Ottoman Torah curtains modeled on prayer rugs, whose iconographic elements (framing columns and lamps) were transposed into Ottoman forms.[46] They continued to be made into the twentieth century.

Besides differing in style and materials, the Ottoman curtains and those made elsewhere in the Mideast contrast with Ashkenazic examples in their avoidance of animal imagery. While lions and other guardian figures were acceptable in Ashkenaz, they were avoided by the Jews of countries whose dominant religious art was severely iconoclastic. Some European Jewish communities went so far as to allow human forms on Torah shields, as we have seen, and on curtains and mantles. These exceptional textiles were made in Alsace and Germany in the eighteenth and nineteenth centuries.[47]

A similar distinction exists between the Torah binders used by Sephardim and those used by Ashkenazim to hold the parchment rolls of the scroll together. Until *Kristalnacht*, textile binders dating to the sixteenth century were part of the holdings of the Synagogue in Worms. The inscription dominated these long rectangle binders. Embroidered with the name of a young boy, his date of birth, and wishes that he grow to knowledge of the Torah, the wedding canopy, and to good deeds, the binders became the demographic record of Jewish communities. The main inscription, designed by a male scribe, was often decorated with motifs appropriate to the boy's name, his zodiac sign, his father's name, and the blessings that follow (fig. 15).

Sephardic binders served the same generic purpose but represented different social concerns. They were made by women to commemorate a major life cycle event, such as marriage and the birth of a child.[48] Their inscriptions do not dominate the compositions but are equivalent or subsidiary to decorative elements, such as floral or abstract ornaments. Often, a beautiful fabric is used as a binder without the addition of any embroidery. Sephardi women also made and dedicated elaborate reader's desk covers, the cloths on which the Torah scroll is laid for reading. Although some Torah textiles in Ashkenazic communities were given to the synagogue by women, either together with their husbands or as widows, their role in provisioning the synagogue was less consistent than in countries like Italy, whose Roman rite prayer book acknowledges their role in the passage, "[bless] every daughter of Israel who makes a mantle or cover for the Torah."

Other Judaica was commissioned by communal associations affiliated with one or more synagogues. These included societies to furnish dowries for poor brides, to pay for circumcision feasts for indigent families, to maintain the lamps in the synagogue, and to provide for the general needs of the poor. Prominent above all these associations was the Burial Society, which cared for the ill and dying, provided a proper internment, and looked after survivors. By the seventeenth century, societies began to acquire regalia of the type owned by Christian guilds, whose social services they emulated. Large inscribed drinking vessels of silver or enameled glass were commissioned and used at the society's annual banquet to mark the induction of new members (fig. 16). Some Burial Societies even owned sets of dishes and silver tableware for use at the banquet, as well as flags that were carried in the processions so popular in the eighteenth century. Inscribed sets of silver combs and nail cleaners were used for the members' central task, preparing the dead for burial, silver frames, for the prayers recited during the rites, and alms boxes, for the collection of charity at the cemetery. The manuscript record books of all types of societies bore miniatures depicting members carrying out their duties.[49]

The sixteenth-nineteenth centuries— Domestic Judaica: Because Judaism is a home-centered religion as well as one focused on the synagogue, many significant ceremonial objects were created for domestic use. There are, first of all, those known from the Middle Ages, like the *Judenstern*,

whose kindling marked the onset of the Sabbath. The star-shaped lamp remained traditional for Sabbaths and holy days in Germany and eastern Europe, although many used candlesticks and candelabra after wax candles came into widespread use.

The silver *kiddush* cup is another medieval type that continued to be made in the modern era in a variety of styles and forms: beakers, footed vessels, cups with covers. As long as the cup for *kiddush* was clean, had an unbroken rim, and encompassed the minimum volume specified in Jewish law, its form was left to individual choice. Sometime in the seventeenth century, the elaborate double cup known from the Middle Ages was supplanted by a simpler type, the barrel shape that separates into two.[50] Like its medieval predecessor, it was used for marriage ceremonies and at circumcisions, both of which require the use of two cups.

The *mohel* (circumcisor) worked as an individual but was considered a community functionary. His basic implement was a knife with a rounded tip, whose handle was often of silver or semiprecious stones, sometimes engraved with an appropriate biblical quotation. Supplementary implements included the double cups mentioned above, plus bowls and flasks for various unguents. Custom-made sets were provided with specially fitted containers and were passed down from one generation to another.[51]

A third type of object known from the Middle Ages that continued to be used in later centuries is the seder plate. Numerous European examples in pewter that survive from the seventeenth century onward are decorated with inscriptions, usually the order of the seder service and the owner's initials, and with symbols and scenes drawn from the haggadah, but lack containers for the symbolic foods.[52] In the eighteenth century a new tiered type appeared in which three trays for the matzot are capped by a tray bearing food containers and the Cup of Elijah. The earliest example has a Danzig (Gdansk) provenance but was probably brought there from Poland (fig. 17). Brass grill work similar to that on Hanukkah lamps surrounds the wooden trays for matzot; the footed cups for food are of wood. Early in the nineteenth century, the artisans of Vienna translated the tiered seder plate into silver, sometimes interpreting the food holders as workers with wheelbarrows and baskets.

The earliest example of another Judaica object, used both in the home and synagogue and mentioned in a medieval source, dates to the mid-sixteenth century. Ephraim of Regensburg, who lived in the twelfth century, reportedly owned a glass container for spices that he used during the ceremony of *havdalah*, performed at the close of Sabbaths to separate the holy day from the workday week. Because of the olfactory function of a spice container, it was termed either *Rauchfass* (censer) or *Hedes* (myrtle) in the list of works created by Frankfurt goldsmiths in the sixteenth century. The form of these spice boxes was generally a tower, which had been used for church censers since the early Byzantine period and, as we have noted, symbolized the heavenly Jerusalem (fig. 18).

That this iconography was acceptable to Jewish patrons is indicated by the one extant example from the mid-sixteenth century, now in The Jewish Museum, New York, and by a drawing found in the records of a court case in Frankfurt of the same period.[53] Joseph Goldschmidt sued a goldsmith because the spice box he had produced was not like that of Goldschmidt's father, recorded in the sketch. By the time of the court case, the tower form had become traditional among Ashkenazim, and it remains the most popular form to this day, despite the appearance of other shapes.[54] Sephardim have adhered to a more ancient manner of fulfilling the need to smell spices during *havdalah*. Those living in lands with warmer climates continue to use freshly picked branches of myrtle or other aromatic trees and do not use spice containers at all.

The Hanukkah lamp is the final type known from the Middle Ages, which continues to be made to our own day. Both medieval forms, the bench type and the hanging lamp, were popular in succeeding centuries, although the motifs used as decoration on later examples are more varied. The decorative motifs of most of the surviving medieval lamps are architectural, perhaps because the lamps were always placed by the door, opposite the *mezuzah*, when lit. On later lamps with backplates, the style of the architecture or alternative motif changes with the country of origin and date of the lamp.[55]

The earliest post-medieval Hanukkah lamps with backplates stem from Renaissance Italy. Some echo architectural shapes, while other Italian backplates are filled with figures from classical mythology, such as nereids, combined with motifs drawn from the decorative repertoire of Renaissance bronzes that have no iconographic relationship to Hanukkah. An exception is the late-sixteenth-early-seventeenth century lamp from the workshop of Joseph de Levis (1552-1611/14), a Jewish bronze caster of Verona, which is the single known attempt to create a Hanukkah lamp with a Jewish theme.[56] The scene of Judith beheading Holofernes appears in relief on the backplate, while figures of reclining Hasmoneans appear in repose below a three-dimensional figure of Mattathias. That most of the Italian Hanukkah lamps dated to the sixteenth century and later are of bronze must be due to the prestige of bronze sculpture in the Renaissance.

An innovative development of the late seventeenth century in Germany was the creation of a menorah-form Hanukkah lamp of a size suitable for use in the home. The large menorot found in ancient synagogues are represented in a few late medieval Hebrew manuscripts, but the actual examples that survive were made for Carolingian and Romanesque churches to signify that the church was successor to the synagogue. In the late seventeenth century, a silversmith of Altona fashioned a small silver version with bare, tube-like arms, stems, and supports.[57] A few decades later, the type was taken up in Frankfurt by a group of silversmiths who produced seven examples that adhere more closely to the biblical description of the menorah as a branched lampstand with knops and flowers (fig. 19). Small molded figures of Judith with the head of Holofernes stand atop the center shafts. She was associated with the

Hasmonean family in antiquity and in Renaissance Italy became a symbol of virtue and civic pride.

The Hanukkah lamps of eastern Europe are generally made of brass and feature openwork, sometimes inhabited by paired deer, lions, and birds. Their bench form provided a place for the Hanukkah lights on the "seat" level, while the "arms" supported two candleholders. One could be used as the servitor, while both together functioned as candleholders for the Sabbath of Hanukkah. An outstanding, large example from the Mintz Collection in The Jewish Museum, New York, incorporates pairs of each of the animals found singly on other lamps, plus a rampant bear and gorilla, muzzled like circus animals.[58]

The second minor holiday of the Jewish year, Purim, is celebrated by listening to the story of Esther recited from a handwritten scroll, by giving gifts of foods to friends in accord with the custom of the Jews of ancient Persia, and by donating alms to the poor. Three forms of ceremonial art were created around these practices. The first is the illuminated *megillah* or scroll, whose ornamentation could be decorative, composed of scenes from the Purim story, or a combination of both.[59] These scrolls, as well as undecorated ones, were placed in an ornamented cylindrical case (fig. 20). In central and eastern Europe, the decoration often took the form of bands, executed in relief, of scenes that told the Esther story. Purely ornamental cases are known from the same regions and are common in Arabic countries. The third art object associated with Purim is a special plate for sending *mishloah manot*, gifts of foods to friends. In some areas known for ceramic workshops, like Alsace, the plates are painted ceramics, while pewter was common in Central Europe. Alms containers bearing inscriptions specifying their use on Purim are also known; the oldest dates to the thirteenth century and comes from Spain.[60]

The twentieth century: In general, the Judaica produced in the second half of the nineteenth century was derivative of earlier types. The sterility of invention that characterized this period was bolstered by the "Historismus" movement in Germany, which called for repeating decorative arts themes of the past. Only in the last decade of the century did a new aesthetic emerge, based on forms drawn from nature. Called Art Nouveau in France and Jugendstil in German, the new style emphasized sinuous outlines and foliate forms and broke with the artificial ornament that had been the rule since the baroque. One of its German practitioners was Friedrich Adler (1878-1942), a designer of interiors, decorative arts, and fabrics, who was the first to create Judaica in a modern style. In 1908, he designed a silver spice container with clean lines, whose perforated cover rises in the center to form a handle. Three years later, he created a bulbous Torah crown for the Hamburg Temple based on nineteenth-century shapes, whose surface, however, is an expression of Judgendstil artistic principles.[61] Plain areas of polished silver alternate with perforated panels composed of sinuous leafy forms. The companion Torah shield was completely covered with ornament. In 1912 and 1913, Adler created multiples of Judaica for domestic use: a seder set, *kiddush* goblets, etrog and spice containers, and candlesticks. His seder plate has a new broad and low outline, enclosing solid areas of silver contrasting with perforated ornament based on nature.[62] In 1914, he formed an association with a firm in Regensburg to produce a line of pewter and brass Judaica. The culmination of these efforts was Adler's design for the interior of a synagogue, exhibited in 1914 at the Werkbund Exhibition in Cologne, which was cited for its unity of forms and decoration.[63]

By the second decade of the twentieth century, German architects and designers were espousing a new, modernist aesthetic in which form followed function and works emphasized the beauty of materials rather than ornamentation. Among the chief proponents of the new trend were Mies van der Rohe and his colleagues at the Bauhaus school in Weimar. One of their students was a Hungarian Jew, Gyula Pap (1899-1983), who created a brass synagogue menorah in

1922, whose appeal lies in the beauty of its curved brass forms and their finely calibrated proportional relationships.[64]

Judaica following the new aesthetic was also created in workshops that followed the artistic principles established in the Bauhaus, but without any formal affiliation with the Weimar school. The textile workshop of Rudolf Koch in Offenbach used traditional techniques following the pattern of early Weimar production. Koch worked primarily as a designer of typefaces and books, and the commission given him by the collector and patron of Judaica, Siegfried Guggenheim, in 1924 was for a series of hangings incorporating Jewish texts (fig. 21). The Hebrew alphabet used in some of the hangings was designed by Koch's Jewish pupil, Bernard Wolpe, who created a stylized alphabet that mimicked the simplified letters of Koch's Latin typefaces.[65] For both men, lettering was the prime means of decoration, a principle that would be adopted by a great many younger artists creating Judaica in the second half of the twentieth century.

The revolutionary Hebrew alphabets and modernist forms created for books and wall hangings in the 1920s also influenced the shape of inscriptions and symbols embroidered on Torah curtains, as on a series created in Berlin during the 1920s whose symbolic forms are as dense and compact as Adler's seder plate and whose lettering is stylized in the manner of the Koch-Wolpe hangings.[66]

Ludwig Wolpert (1900-81) was another pioneer influenced by the Bauhaus who applied its stylistic principles to Judaica in metal. One of his surviving pre-war works is a silver pointer whose shape is an abstract curve devoid of ornament.[67] It is a sharp renunciation of the type used to follow the text in the eighteenth and nineteenth centuries, which consisted of a baluster-like handle and stem terminating in a hand with extended finger.[68] Another work that represents a rethinking of an older type of Judaica is Wolpert's three-tiered seder set of 1930 (fig. 22). The original, lost in the war, was recreated in the 1960s. It has the same broad and low proportions of Adler's set, but unlike the earlier example relies solely on the beauty of the materials, the forms of the parts, and the decorative use of script to convey a modernist aesthetic.

Following several years of teaching at the Bezalel School in Jerusalem, Wolpert came to New York's Jewish Museum in 1956 to head its Tobe Pascher Workshop. With a larger clientele, many of them new suburban synagogues of the postwar era, Wolpert was able to produce a wide variety of Judaica for both the home and the synagogue. He also began to mass produce his designs, with the result that his Judaica influenced the taste of generations of patrons and, through classes held in the workshop, his aesthetic principles were transmitted to silversmiths working in the field.

Wolpert's most outstanding pupil at the Bezalel School had been Moshe Zabari (b. 1935), a Jerusalemite of Yemenite ancestry, who followed his teacher to New York in 1961, becoming artist-in-residence at the Jewish Museum workshop. His art, formed under the International Style espoused by the teachers at Bezalel, was recast under the influence of new trends in American art, such as the kinetic sculpture of the 1950s. From this combination of sources came Zabari's Torah Crown of 1968, whose curved tubes of silver and dangling pearls vibrate with the movement of the scroll.[69] In the 1970s, he explored the structural and decorative uses of Hebrew script and, in other works, the forms of Art Nouveau, which had served as a major influence on early works of the Bezalel School. Zabari's works of the 1980s reflect the principles of post-modernism, a movement that allowed the artist to incorporate a richer repertoire of symbols into his Judaica for home and synagogue (fig. 23).

In the 1980s, Zelig Segal (b. 1933), Zabari's former schoolmate at Bezalel, joined him in New York. Today, both have returned to Israel, a move that symbolizes the internationalism characteristic of contemporary Judaica. Both Israeli and diaspora artists train with the same masters and compete at the same competitions and fairs, with the result that their works draw on similar vocabularies of form and decoration. Whereas the Judaica of earlier centuries was closely tied to the visual culture of individual countries, and even to that of particular cities, the international character of modernism is now characteristic of Judaica.

Bibliography

Altshuler, David, ed., *The Precious Legacy: Judaic Treasures from the Czechoslovak State Collections* (New York, 1983).

Grafman, Rafi, *Crowning Glory: Silver Torah Ornaments in the Collection of the Jewish Museum*, ed. Vivian B. Mann (New York and Boston, 1996).

Grossman, Grace Cohen, *Jewish Art* (New York, 1995).

Hachlili, Rachel, *Ancient Jewish Art and Archaeology in the Land of Israel* (Leiden, New York, Copenhagen, Cologne, 1988).

Kleeblatt, Norman, and Vivian B. Mann, *Treasures of The Jewish Museum* (New York, 1985).

Notes

[1] On this topic, see also SYNAGOGUES, ANCIENT TIMES, and SYNAGOGUES, MEDIEVAL AND MODERN.

[2] Bezalel Narkiss, *Hebrew Illuminated Manuscripts* (Jerusalem, 1969), pl. 1.

[3] Vivian B. Mann, Thomas F. Glick, and Jerrilyn Dodds, eds., *Convivencia: Jews, Muslims and Christians in Medieval Spain* (New York, 1992), figs. 46-47.

[4] Narkiss, op. cit., pl. 8.

[5] Bezalel Narkiss, *Hebrew Illuminated Manuscripts in the British Isles* (Jerusalem and London, 1982), fig. 186.

[6] Mendel Metzger and Thérèse Metzger, *Jewish Life in the Middle Ages* (Fribourg, 1982), figs. 90, 93, 98, 145, 152.

[7] Bezalel Narkiss, "Un Objet de culte: La lampe de Hanuka," in Bernhard Blumenkranz, ed., *Art et archéologie des Juifs en France médiévale* (Toulouse, 1980), pp. 200-201.

[8] See also, Susan L. Braunstein, "Hanukkah Lamp," in *Sigmund Freud's Jewish Heritage*, (Binghamton and London, 1991), n.p.

[9] Mann, Glick, Dodds, op. cit., fig. 13.

[10] Mann, Glick, Dodds, ibid., cat. no. 79, fig. 65.

[11] Vivian B. Mann, "'New' Examples of Jewish Ceremonial Art from Medieval Ashkenaz," in *Artibus et Historiae* 17 (1988), fig. 9.

[12] On these items, see ibid., figs. 10-14.

[13] Ibid., fig. 15 and note 55.

[14] Metzger and Metzger, *Jewish Life*, figs. 133, 152.

[15] Mann, op. cit., fig. 2.

[16] Ibid., fig. 6.

[17] Maimonides, *Teshuvot ha-Rambam*, vol. II, ed. Jehoshua Blau (Jerusalem, 1960), no. 165; Shlomo David Goitein, "The Synagogue Building and Its Furnishings according to the Records of the Cairo Genizah," in *Eretz-Israel* 7 (Hebrew: 1964), p. 91.

[18] Alexander Scheiber, *Jewish Inscriptions in Hungary* (Budapest and Leiden, 1983), no. 153.

[19] Mann, "Torah Ornaments before 1600," figs. 8-9 and n. 54.

[20] Metzger and Metzger, *Jewish Life*, fig. 94; Vivian B. Mann, *Gardens and Ghettos* (Berkeley, Los Angeles, and Oxford, 1989), no. 115.

[21] Metzger and Metzger, *Jewish Life*, fig. 90.

[22] See [George Stenne], *Collection de M. Strauss* (Poissy, 1878), pp. VIII-X.

[23] For discussions of monumental church polycandelons, see Peter Lasko, *Ars Sacra 800-1200* (Harmondsworth, 1972), pp. 178-79, 216, pls. 187, 246-247; Percy Ernst Schramm and Florentine Mütterich, *Denkmäle der Deutschen Könige und Kaiser* (Munich, 1962), no. 177.

[24] Umberto Nahon, *Holy Arks and Ritual Appurtenances from Italy in Israel* (Hebrew: Tel-Aviv, 1970), p. 153.

[25] Otto Muneles, ed., *Prague Ghetto in the Renaissance Period* (Prague, 1965), p. 119.

[26] Antonius Margaritha, *Der Gantz Jüdisch Glaub* (Leipzig, 1705), p. 268.

[27] David Altshuler, ed., *The Precious Legacy: Judaic Treasures from the Czechoslovak State Collections* (New York, 1983), fig. 53.

[28] Vivian B. Mann, "The Recovery of a Known Work," in *Jewish Art* 12-13 (1986-87), pp. 269-278.

[29] Margaritha, op. cit., pp. 267-268.

[30] Wolfgang Scheffler, *Goldschmiedes Hessens* (Berlin and New York, 1976), pp. 92, 96, 106.

[31] Mann, "Torah Ornaments before 1600," fig. 12; Hava Lazar, "Du nouveau dans l'art sacre Juif," in *L'Oeïl* 288/289 (1979), pp. 62-63.

[32] William Gross, Rafi Grafman, and Annette Weber, *Zeugnisse einer zerstörten Vergangenheit. Jüdisches Kulturgerät aus Emden 1639-1806* (Emden, 1992), figs. 6, 7, 9.

[33] On all these shields, see Altshuler, *The Precious Legacy*, figs. 122-123, 125.

[34] Iris Fishof, pp. 50-51.

[35] Norman Kleeblatt and Vivian B. Mann, *Treasures of The Jewish Museum* (New York, 1985), pp. 106-09; Altshuler, *The Precious Legacy*, fig. 113.

[36] Moses Sofer, *She'elot u-Teshuvot* (Hebrew: Jerusalem, 1970), part 6, no. 6.

[37] Vivian B. Mann, "The Golden Age of Jewish Ceremonial Art in Frankfort," in *Leo Baeck Institute Yearbook* 231, 1986, pp. 392-395.

[38] Grafman, op. cit., nos. 2-32, 50-60, 136-143.

[39] On these items, see Grafman, op. cit., nos. 406, 414-17, 426-29; Mann, *Gardens and Ghettos*, fig. 115; Fishof, op. cit., pp. 42-43, 46-47.

[40] Mann, ibid., figs. 107, 112.

[41] Metzger and Metzger, *Jewish Life*, figs. 97-98; Joseph Caro, *Avkat Rokhel* (Jerusalem, 1960), no. 66.

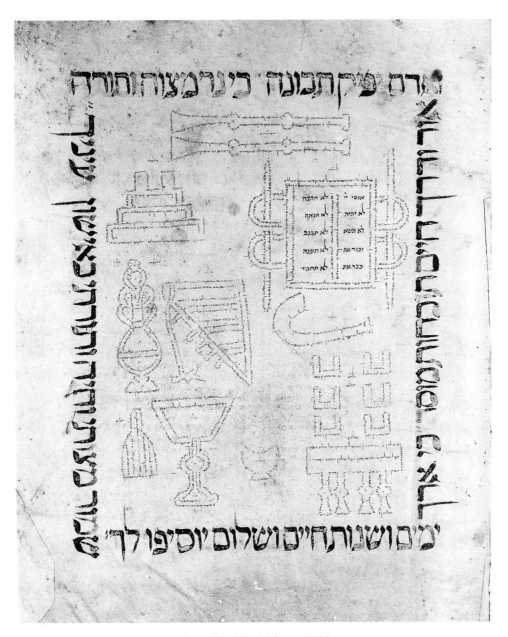

Figure 1. Bible, Majorca, 1325.

Figure 2. Passover Plate, probably Valencia, fifteenth century, lusterware.

Figure 3. Hanukkah Lamp, Germany, fourteenth century, bronze.

Figure 4. Set of nested beakers, Bohemia, before 1330-1335, silver.

Figure 5. Hanging lamp, Germany, fourteenth century, bronze.

Figure 6. Torah finials, Spain or Sicily, fifteenth century, silver, stones.

Figure 7. Torah shield, Florence, 1747.

Figure 8. Torah shield, Augsburg, ca. 1725, Zacharias Wagner, silver: gilt.

Figure 9. Torah shield, Germany, late eighteenth century, silver.

Figure 10. Torah shield, Izmir, nineteenth century, silver.

Figure 11. Torah crown and finials, Istanbul, 1845/1846-1879/1880, silver.

Figure 12. Torah crown, Johann Friedrich Wilhelm Borcke, Berlin, 1821-1839, silver: gilt.

Figure 13. Valance for Torah ark, Prague, 1718/1719, silk and metallic threads.

Figure 14. Torah curtain, Venice?, 1698/1699, linen embroidered with silk and metallic threads.

Figure 15. Torah binder, Germany, 1153, linen embroidered with silk threads.

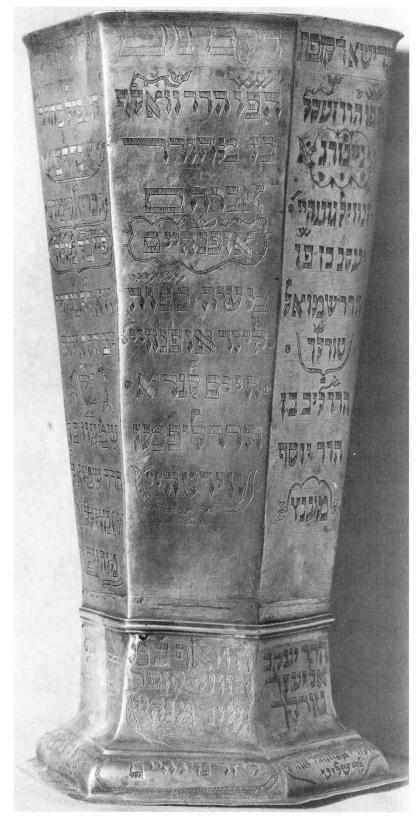

Figure 16. Beaker for the Burial Society of Worms, Nürnberg, 1711/1712, Johann Conrad Weiss, silver.

[42] Mann, *Gardens and Ghettos*, figs. 25, 31; Muneles, op. cit., figs. 42, 56-57.

[43] Muneles, ibid., fig. 27.

[44] Franz Landsberger, "Old-Time Torah Curtains," in *Beauty in Holiness* (n.p., 1970), pp. 147-156.

[45] Esther Juhasz, ed., *Sephardic Jews in the Ottoman Empire* (Jerusalem, 1990), figs. 5-7, 19-22, 24-25, pl. 9.

[46] Ibid., pls. 17-20.

[47] E.g., Barbara Kirschenblatt-Gimblett, *Fabric of Jewish Life* (New York, 1977), no. 137.

[48] Mann, *Gardens and Ghettos*, nos. 124-125, 128.

[49] On these materials, see Altshuler, *The Precious Legacy*, no. 85, 150-155, 163-167, and Ilona Benoschofsky and Alexander Scheiber, eds., *The Jewish Museum of Budapest* (Budapest, 1989), nos. 214, 217-219.

[50] On kiddush cups, see Benoschofsky and Scheiber, ibid., nos. 1-17, and Grace Cohen Grossman, *Jewish Art* (New York, 1995), p. 133.

[51] On these objects, see Altshuler, *The Precious Legacy*, no. 192, and Kleeblatt and Mann, op. cit., pp. 156-157.

[52] Benoschofsky and Scheiber, nos. 136-142.

[53] Kleeblatt and Mann, pp. 34-35.

[54] Grossman, op. cit., pp. 182-183.

[55] Ibid., pp. 184, 226-235.

[56] Mann, *Gardens and Ghettos*, fig. 38.

[57] Stephen Kayser and Guido Schoenberger, *Jewish Ceremonial Art* (Philadelphia, 1959), no. 141.

[58] Kleeblatt and Mann, p. 127.

[59] Mann, *Gardens and Ghettos*, figs. 29, 91.

[60] On objects associated with Purim, see Grossman, op. cit., p. 240; Benoschofsky and Scheiber, no. 116-17; Mann, Glick, and Dodds, op. cit., no. 104.

[61] Birgitte Leonhardt, Dieter Zühlsdorf, and Norbert Götz, eds., *Friedrich Adler: zwischen Jugenstil und Art Déco* (Stuttgart, 1994), nos. J1, J3.

[62] Grossman, op. cit., p. 254.

[63] Leonhardt, et al., op. cit., pp. 104-107.

[64] Grossman, op. cit., p. 272.

[65] For the Guggenheim commissions, see Kleeblatt and Mann, pp. 176-177.

[66] Kirshenblatt-Gimblett, op. cit., no. 66.

[67] E.g., Grafman, 1996, no. 637.

[68] Ibid., nos. 520-524.

[69] Kleeblatt and Mann, op. cit., p. 194.

VIVIAN B. MANN

B

THE BIBLICAL FOUNDATIONS OF JUDAISM: The Pentateuch, the five books of Moses, as a single narrative, constitute the primary canon of every ancient Judaism known to us. They contain an account of the creation of a polity, Israel. Having set out the adventures of humans from a single creature (Adam) in a restricted environment (a garden) to a set of nations distributed throughout the world, the narrative depicts the creation of one particular family (Abraham's). First it depicts the ancestor on his way from the core (Mesopotamia) to the periphery (Canaan) of the inhabited world in accordance with the divine program of settlement (see Gen. 1:28: "fill the earth") and subsequent to the scattering of humans from the city of Babel. The racial[1] basis of Israel is firmly established.

In the book of Exodus the nation exists as a "family of Jacob" but without any further identity except in relation to another culture and society: it is a nation of slaves. But it then receives what is viewed as constitutive of a fully-fledged nation: a leader, a law, and a land. Such a definition of nationhood belongs perhaps less to the world of the ancient Near East than to the Hellenized Levant. The notion that a nation needs an ancestor, lawgiver, constitution, and its own territory is arguably the product of a fusion of Oriental and Greek ideas and is reflected not only in the Judean literature but in the great national histories written (in Greek!) by Manetho, Berossus, and Philo of Byblos.

The problem of dating this narrative does not matter so much as its function. Central to the notion of national identity is a constitution. In a monarchy, that role may be taken by the king—indeed, the very idea of "nation" tends to be replaced by "subjects of the king." But in an imperial context, national identity required other symbols, such as a distinctive cult or law. For from the Persian empire onwards, the Jewish "nation" had, in fact, been encouraged to live according to its own laws and to focus upon its own Temple. It was very probably at that time rather than earlier that the literature of the Mosaic canon originated. The bringer of that defining constitution is the ancient figure of Moses, who, if not acknowledged as the founder of the Temple itself (if Hecataeus is incorrect), was the founder of the cult, in the form of the institution of ark, tent, and priesthood as well as of the laws by which Israel was to be distinguished from other nations.

The Mosaic Torah, then, is an account of the foundations of a *nation*, Israel, living in a land (which is narratively only anticipated) and organized in a certain way. It is, however, neither an historically accurate account nor created from a single conception. As a composite narrative, it reflects a number of discrete programs, each defining the newly-established Mosaic polity in a different way and, indeed, each set at different points in the narrative. It is a reasonable (if unprovable) conclusion that once the framework of Israel's origins were outlined, then, during the literary evolution of the Mosaic canon, into that narrative were inserted at slightly different points several different "Mosaic constitutions." From the combination of these (idealized) constitutions the Judaic systems of the late Second Temple period onwards have been created.

In this canonical narrative, the nation is born in the transition from slavery to conquest, from leaderless to led, from landless to landed, and from formless to rigidly structured. There are three places in this transition at which the nation is formed, and these provide the narrative points at which three different approaches to the constitution of Israel are found: Sinai, the wilderness trek, and the plains of Moab. These places, and these moments, correspond approximately to the scrolls of Leviticus, Numbers, and Deuteronomy. The Sinai narrative of Exodus itself, centering on the so-called "Book of the Covenant" (or *Mishpatim*), does not afford a systematic description: no "constitution of Israel" can really be derived from it. But each of the last three books of the Mosaic canon projects a distinct, and different, definition of the nature of Israel, its society, and its world, and, together and separately, they have defined what "Israel" means.

The following analysis leaves aside the question of the composition of these books but does not assume they are unitary. In the ancient world scrolls did not as a rule survive copying unedited, and, in these particular instances, there are many signs of a literary history. But the evolution of these scrolls has not, I suggest, obscured the underlying program.

The three constitutions will be treated not in *narrative* order, but with Deuteronomy first and Leviticus last. The reason is partly that this plausibly reflects the order in which each program came to maturity (though the priority is both unprovable and irrelevant); and partly rhetorical: Leviticus, with its holiness agenda, has provided Rabbinic Judaism with its dominant classification, despite, or perhaps because of, the disappearance of the functions of priesthood. By contrast, the programs of Deuteronomy and Numbers apply more readily to a political entity possessed of land and tight social organization, though the Deuteronomic invention of the category "covenant" has been highly influential.

The constitution of Israel in Deuteronomy: Thanks to the influence of Deuteronomy on the books of Joshua-Kings, the dominant biblical narrative of the founding of Israel as a polity[2] comprises the following elements: a law book, a law-reading, and a covenant ceremony, including blessings and curses. The relationship between the people and the deity is construed as a formally legal one, in which rescue from slavery is a "down payment" and land is promised in return for obedience to the terms of the covenant (i.e., the laws).

For the last two millennia, the equation of Judaism with obedience to divine laws is so prominent that it may escape attention that this construct is a Deuteronomic invention. The framers of this Deuteronomic theory built, in all probability, upon an existing narrative in which Moses received laws at Sinai, and they may have expanded upon (as well as glossing: the term "covenant" appears here and there in Exodus) an already existing collection of laws. But in Deuteronomy, the laws have been put into a new context: a *legal religion* according to which obligations on either side cease if the conditions are broken. The entire concept is then framed literarily in the form of a testamentary address by Moses immediately before the Israelites cross to possess the land in fulfillment of the deity's part of the contract.

The patron-client relationship that underlies nearly all ancient Near Eastern (one might even say, Mediterranean) social exchange is here applied to a nation and its god, and the (usually) implied conditions of such relationships are constituted by the divinely-originating law code (a stereotype of ancient Near Eastern monarchies). The conditions of the Deuteronomic covenant boil down to a rigid maintenance of both cultic and racial identity, implying a community surrounded by peoples who are cultically and racially very similar (especially problematic when, as the Deuteronomistic History explains, Israelites behaved just like Canaanites in matters of religion). Had this not been the case, such differentiation would not have been so violently endorsed, even to the point of genocide (which, it goes without saying, is a rhetorical feature and not a program for action).

The covenant-making scene recurs elsewhere. It is repeated in Josh. 24, Neh. 8-10, and, outside the Scriptures, at Qumran in the Damascus Document and 1QS, where Israel is being reconstituted in a sect. Israel is a nation constituted by allegiance to a particular deity who has already chosen it. The term "covenant" has also become so fundamental that it find its way into other parts of the Mosaic canon, where covenants abound: with Abraham, with Noah, with Phineas. These covenants, however, are with individuals rather than nations, and they have more the character of a one-sided (divine) *appointment*, without any freedom on the part of the human to accept or reject, but without any obligations on the part of humans either; in other words, the term has become embedded so firmly that it is even used of relationships that are not properly covenantal at all! The fact that the word *berit* is used so widely and loosely illustrates the influence of Deuteronomy's central concept.

From the point of view of a historian of Judaism, it is important to recognize that Deuteronomy does not offer a *description* of "Israelite" religion at any stage of history and certainly not even a realistic fiction for the monarchic period. A direct legal bond between a whole people and a god is a *theory*, and one that more probably reflects early Second Temple society, which, as far as we can tell, was hierocratic and in which a small immigrant society was establishing itself around a temple and in the midst of an indigenous population of similar racial stock and, indeed, with some similar religious practices. The account of Neh. 8-10 pretends that an existing "book of the law" was brought from the Temple by Ezra and read out; that the history of the people was rehearsed, and a solemn covenant signed. But again, we are dealing with idealized narratives, not history. Ezra and Nehemiah are quite distinct characters who meet only in the few central chapters of Nehemiah, where the first-person narrative is interrupted; it is impossible to reconcile their functions or their historical relationship, and Ezra is unknown to Ben Sira, while the book of Nehemiah presupposes a schism with the Samaritans. The interesting aspect of Ezra and Nehemiah is the effort to fuse them and establish, out of two independent and partly conflicting narratives, a common legend about the (re)foundation of Judaism by means of a covenant renewal, in which the Deuteronomic pattern is replicated. The revived Israel, rescued this time not from Egypt but from Babylonia, is reconstituted as a covenant people, to whom (as Deuteronomy itself prescribed) the law was read out.

In the Damascus Document (CD), whose date of composition may not be too far removed from that of the Ezra story,[3] a very similar narrative about the (re)foundation of Judaism is implied. The exilic punishment on Israel led to the restoration of a remnant, to whom the true divine will about Sabbaths, feasts, and laws was given. While the rest of Israel went astray, this chosen remnant remained to await the divine judgment on Israel and on the gentiles, anticipating salvation and vindication for themselves.[4] The revelation of the law and the foundation of this "true Israel" is credited to a figure known as the "Interpreter of the Law" (*doresh ha-*

Torah). The differences in scope, in literary form, and in some details from both Ezra and Nehemiah are mostly attributable to the literary genre in which the story is embedded and to the fact that CD's "Judaism" is yet again different from that implicitly advanced in either Ezra or Nehemiah.

The similarities among the three accounts are even more striking and significant; they presuppose the same story of Israel's "pre-exilic" past (though the historical narrations of that period have quite different emphases)[5] and the exile as punishment for that past. All three accounts, significantly, speak of a covenant with the members of the elect group that is based on a lawgiving, and all three allude to a process of interpretation of that law and deal with issues of holiness and separation from "outsiders" (and indeed from other potential Judeans, such as Samaritans, "people of the land," or "builders of the wall").

In these respects the accounts all reflect a certain common perspective on Judaism, namely a Deuteronomic one. Israel is founded by a lawgiver who has the people make a covenant in which their exclusivity is legally enjoined. The Deuteronomic Israel is a *people*, defined by race and law. Their land, accordingly, is not theirs by birth or by nature but by *gift*. The land in the Deuteronomic constitution is the deity's part of the covenant, and its possession is therefore conditional (see Neh. 9:36-37 for a most eloquent expression of this).

The constitution of Israel in Numbers: If, as we may imagine, Deuteronomy was written by a lawyer, Numbers was authored by a soldier. More precisely, there is a distinctive concept around which the disparate materials that now make up the book have been structured. The book opens directly with a census of those "able to go to war" (1:3), and from that point onwards a military portrait of the nation is offered. Such a portrait suits well the narrative context chosen for it, in which the nation is, like a campaigning army, on the march towards a destination to be conquered, living off the terrain and constantly on the alert for attack. Thus, ch. 2 describes the disposition of the camp and the order of marching. The following chapters deal with priestly and cultic matters, but the section ends (in ch. 10) with instructions for the priests to blow the trumpets in time of war as well as on cultic occasions—linking the two kinds of activity. There follows a description of the Israelite army marching from Sinai, following their divine leader's cloud. The closing words of this opening section also link the central cultic object, the ark, *and its deity,* to warfare: whenever it was moved, Moses was to say, "Arise, Yahweh, let your enemies be scattered and your foes flee before you," and on its stopping, "Return, Yahweh of the massed armies of Israel" (Num. 10:35-36).

The organization of Israel, then, according to Numbers, is military. The nation is divided into families and tribes, but these are all reconfigured as military units, and they provide specified numbers of young men to fight. The spatial arrangement of Israel is also important, for it assumes the form of a military camp; on each of the four sides is a group of three tribes. The camp as a whole apparently represents the land, since as far as geography allows, the tribes occupy positions corresponding to their regions of settlement, with Reuben, Gad, and Simeon on the south; Dan, Asher, and Naphtali on the north; Benjamin, Ephraim, and Manasseh on the west; and Judah, Issachar, and Zebulon (somewhat unsatisfactorily grouped) on the east. At the center of the camp/land is the Temple/tent of meeting, with the three levitical families camped on the north, south, and west and the priests guarding the entrance on the east. Towards the close of Numbers (ch. 34), attention moves to the imminent occupation of the land and its divisions, and the disposition for the tribal allotments is given, followed by allotments for the Levites, as the geography of the camp is converted in anticipation into the geography of the land.

The attitude of Numbers towards discipline also reflects a military disposition. The "rebellion" (*mrd, mrh*) of the people, who wish to go no further, is a constant theme (see chaps. 14, 17, and 20), and the issue of Moses' leadership stands very obviously as a motif of the entire book, climaxing in a challenge by Miriam (ch. 12) and by Korah, Dathan, and Abiram (ch. 16). Such disobedience to the appointed leader is, naturally, harshly punished. The military discipline recalls the book of Joshua, in which Achan's breach of the ban (Josh. 7) is punished with even more severity. Both Numbers and Joshua in fact describe the events of a successful military campaign ending with the distribution of land, reminding one of the Greek institution of cleruchies, whereby troops were awarded allotments of land to sustain them, or, possibly, the more generally followed custom of allotting agricultural and residential land to military colonies. Both Numbers and Joshua clearly wish above all to demonstrate the necessity of firm leadership and the rewards of obedience, and both go out of their way to demonstrate the perils of insubordination. The theme of both books is obedience not so much to the covenant as to the military leader.

It is worth recalling at this point the previously mentioned observation by Hecataeus that Moses had instituted a military education and led the people to many conquests against neighboring tribes, after which he apportioned the land equally, but reserving larger portions for the priests. These data look like a precis of Numbers. But whence the idea of this military constitution? Was it devised merely for the narrative of the wilderness itinerary, or does it have a historical basis? The military aspects of scriptural Israel and the historical Judah of the Second Temple period have not been as greatly emphasized in scholarly research as has the theological notion of Yahweh as the "divine warrior," which is, nevertheless, one part of the phenomenon. For the name *Yhwh Tzeba'ot* probably means "Yahweh of armies," and this title should be given due weight, for whether the armies in question are heavenly or human, it seems probable that this deity is a warrior god or has a very strong military component to his cult.

Indeed, there is a good deal of evidence, if not conclusive, of the military reputation of Israelites and Judeans.[6] The military colony at Elephantine, probably set up by the Assyrians, was composed of Judeans, who continued to serve under the Persians. If we are to believe the claims of Josephus (*Apion* I.192ff.), Alexander, Ptolemy I, and Ptolemy Philadelphus likewise recruited Jewish mercenaries. There were Jewish garrisons in Egypt, Libya, and Cyrenaica. The city of Leontopolis, founded by Onias IV, included a military colony, while in Asia Minor, Antiochus III settled two thousands Judean soldiers from Babylonia. As is well known, Caesar's concessions to the Judeans also stemmed from military assistance rendered him by forces led by Antipater.

Thus, even if not a major occupation of Judeans, military service as mercenaries seems to have been something of a tradition, and, accordingly, it can be concluded that the success of the Judeans in the Maccabean wars and the subsequent expansion of the Judean kingdom was built on considerable native military experience. Hengel's suggestion that such military colonies may have been a major factor in the spreading of the Jewish diaspora should be seriously considered, though whether such an explanation throws into doubt the strength of Sabbath observance among certain Jews is at least an interesting question. Perhaps, as Hengel also suggests, Hecataeus' comment about Jewish military education stems not from any data derived from Numbers or Joshua but from the many Judean military colonies in Egypt and, perhaps, elsewhere.

In all events, there is certainly adequate evidence to suggest that among the Judeans of the Persian period (perhaps earlier as well), a strong military ethos was present, and such an ethos is a plausible context for the insertion into the Mosaic "constitution" of an Israel organized like a mobile military colony; indeed, it may have been directly inspired by such a Judean colony: if not, its likely author was in any case someone who had enjoyed a military career.

Be this as it may, Number's definition of Israel was revived in the Qumran *War Scroll*, in which the powerful and direct influence of Num. 1-10 is evident (especially in cols. 2-19) and in which a surprising degree of knowledge of military hardware, maneuvers, and regulations seems to be evident behind the ridiculously choreographed performance of the army itself. No less than the legal definition of Deuteronomy, the military ideal elaborated in the book of Numbers, then, exerted an enduring influence on the character of Judaism towards the end of the Second Temple period. This may go some way to explaining the motivation, and the considerable initial success, with which, in the first century C.E., the Jewish war with Rome was conducted.

The constitution of Israel in Leviticus: Like Numbers, Leviticus describes the dwelling place of its ideal Israel as a "camp," but here, not a military camp. The camp is the site of an ideological cosmos on which the contours of purity and pollution are drawn. The emphasis is primarily on the social relations pertaining between the members of Israel and their god, but not, unlike in the case of Deuteronomy, in terms of the administration of justice. The vision is not that of the legal but the priestly scribe.

As Mary Douglas has argued, Leviticus' underlying organizing principle is "order," achieved through a series of taxonomies. Animals are divided into clean and unclean and also into their proper spheres: land, sea, air. In Douglas' view, taboo ("unclean") animals are those seen not to fit any normative classification. While this explanation does not fit all of Leviticus' details, as we shall see, the underlying perception is sound.[7]

Even if no anthropological explanation can entirely fit the data of Leviticus, the notion that its authors demand an ordered world, in which things clean, holy, and proper are kept separate from those that are not, seems the best analysis of the system. Such a reading is supported to some extent by the account of creation in Gen. 1, where order is made out of chaos through the creation of contrasting categories (light vs. darkness, dry vs. wet), by the placing of the appropriate creatures in their proper domain, and by the marking of divisions of time. Such a classification in Leviticus extends beyond animals to types of sacrifices, bodily emissions, and human sexual relations. It continues, indeed, beyond Israel ("the camp") to the unclean word beyond, and it constitutes Israel, like

the sanctuary itself, as a center of holiness relative to the unclean environment in which the people live.

The function of the land in this scheme is different from either Deuteronomy or Numbers. The land is not to be enjoyed, Canaanite-free, as a covenant gift; nor is it to be captured by a disciplined army. It is to be maintained as an ordered cosmos, kept holy through the separation of clean and unclean, of distinct classifications of living things, of Sabbath from non-Sabbath, and of tithed produce from untithed. The camp of Leviticus embraces the ark, the tent, the area of the priests, of Israelites, then of the world beyond: concentric spheres of holiness to be mapped onto the land. This is not the "camp" of Numbers, nor its Israel.

Central to the well-being of Leviticus' Israel is the sacrificial system and the priesthood, because Israel's holiness is directed to, and sustained by, the holiness of its god; and the sacrificial system regulates Israel's contact with its deity, while the priesthood ensures that this contact is maintained in an orderly way, for the contours of holiness must not be ruptured. Hence, the first five chapters of Leviticus deal with the various kinds of sacrifices, and the next two with the ordination of the priests (with chap. 10 as a warning against illegitimate priestly behavior). Then various other issues are covered: animals, childbirth, skin diseases, and bodily discharges, culminating in the ceremony by which all Israel can achieve atonement (chap. 16). The so-called "Holiness Code" (chaps. 17-26), in which it is possible to detect slight differences in ideology, rehearses the uncleanness of blood, sexual relations, sacrificial laws, and, finally, the holiness of times and seasons.

The system represented by Leviticus is concerned above all with regulating the transition of humans between various states. The sanctuary and its trappings and the priesthood must be holy; but the remainder of Israel may, and will, contract uncleanness from time to time: sexual emissions, blood, and corpses, for example, will impart uncleanness (for all of these, significantly, have to do with life: its creation, preservation, and withdrawal). But such uncleanness must be removed with reasonable promptness, because it has the capacity to affect the holiness of the sanctuary and thus to threaten the continuation of the divine presence within it. The second part of Leviticus, however, appears to extend the realm of holiness over the entirety of Israel, thus reducing the distinction between priesthood and laity and raising the responsibility of each Israelite to maintain a holiness that is not limited to the cult.

But the literary history of Leviticus is not our concern here,[8] nor the dating of its composition or completion. The origin of its classifications system and its relations to an actual cult are matters much discussed, with both pre-exilic and post-exilic dates being defended. Whatever its origin, its definition of Israel as a society dedicated to holiness came to be extremely influential in a community in which the presence of the Temple and a large priestly population probably dominated the life of the city of Jerusalem, from which, in Persian times, no part of the province of Judah was more than a day's walk.

Indeed, the issue of priestly holiness played an important role in the development of the Jewish "schools," that is, the religious parties such as the Pharisees and the communities of the Dead Sea Scrolls. Perhaps following the trend observable in Lev. 17-26, both groups seem to have been concerned to extend more widely the regulations regarding priestly holiness. The associations known as *haburot*—fellowships—devoted themselves in particular to strict observance of tithing and dietary rules and extended Levitical purity beyond the priestly sphere.

As for the Qumran scrolls, difference of interpretation of the rules of purity between the writers of 4QMMT and their addressees (those then in power in the Temple) may have led to the separation of the former from "the way of the people," perhaps represented in their founding of the kinds of "camp" communities encountered in the *Damascus Document*, in which accusations are made that the Temple is being defiled by breaches in the laws of sexual relations (uncle-niece marriage, intercourse during the period of

"uncleanness;" see CD 4-5). This clearly reflects Leviticus' principle that impurity defiles the Temple whether or not such defilement takes place in or near it. For the "city of the sanctuary," according to the Damascus Document, obliges its inhabitants to a special degree of purity, and sexual intercourse is entirely forbidden within its walls.

It is also clear from Jacob Neusner and his students' analyses of the development of the Mishnah that the issue of purity (including tithing) formed the earliest stage of that document's growth. The Mishnah as a whole legislates for a holy people in a pure land, and, while by the middle of the second century C.E. the land itself was not accessible to most members of Israel and the priesthood had disappeared, the ideal of such an Israel remains at the heart of Rabbinic Judaism.

The heritage of the Mosaic constitution(s): The biblical foundations of Judaism may be said to reside in the three definitions contained in the Mosaic canon. Even though their differing perspectives could not be entirely harmonized, their fusion into a single narrative, contained in a single canonical *Torah*, yielded a single vision. From the Deuteronomic constitution, the word *Torah* was perhaps the most important bequest, for it is Deuteronomy that describes itself as a book of *Torah*. This word then spread to cover the Mosaic canon and other sacred writings as well. But the notion of covenant remained fundamental to the characterization of the religion of Israel, though it extended beyond the episode at Sinai to embrace a wider (and perhaps largely diaspora) Judaism that traced the origins of its identity to Abraham and *his* covenant (and even to the Noahide covenant with non-Jews). The *legal* basis of the bond between humanity and Israel and its god remained, and thus Rabbinic Judaism is a religion of law, because that is the mode of human response to the divine will. Yet because of the vision of Leviticus, the law is transformed into a mechanism of holiness: this gives Torah its purpose and extends the goal beyond obedience towards the ideal of human perfection and beyond doing the will of God to becoming holy like God.

The influence of the unique vision of Numbers on the encompassing system of Mosaic Judaism has been less evident than that of either Deuteronomy or Leviticus. But it remains the one ancient constitution for an Israel without land, an Israel surrounded by enemies and caught between a past that seems temptingly luxurious (as the "rebels" claim) and a future that is precarious, for the destined land is full of giants. The specter of destruction in an alien environment that implicitly justifies the militarism of Numbers is raised both by Esther and Daniel, where the Jews rely respectively on the benignity of a foreign king to allow them to kill their enemies and on the hope of a final heavenly vindication of the righteous.

Bibliography

Davies, Philip R., *In Search of Ancient Israel* (Sheffield, 1982).
Mullen, E.T., Jr., *Ethnic Myths and Pentateuchal Foundations* (Atlanta, 1997).
Nodet, Etienne, *A Search for the Origins of Judaism* (Sheffield, 1997).

Notes

[1] The term is strictly correct, because "ethnic" is not a synonym and refers to a system of social identification that is at least partly elective. Used without any pejorative overtones, "racial" here means simply an identity predicated purely upon biological descent.

[2] For the initial suggestion, see S. Dean McBride, "Polity of the Covenant People," in *Interpretation* 41 (1987), pp. 229-244.

[3] CD and "Damascus Document" strictly speaking refer to the medieval manuscripts of a text known to have originated in the same way as many of the Qumran texts. Unfortunately, from the Qumran fragments, it is impossible to reconstruct with certainty any supposedly original form, despite assertions to the contrary. Much of the Qumran material simply does not overlap. For a survey of the Qumran material and its readings, see M. Broshi, ed., *The Damascus Document Reconsidered* (Jerusalem, 1992).

[4] For fuller discussion, see Philip R. Davies, *The Damascus Covenant* (Sheffield, 1982), pp. 56-104.

[5] Neh. 9; CD 2.14-3.12.

[6] For details, see Hengel, op. cit., vol. 1, pp. 15ff., and vol. 2, pp. 11-12.

[7] *Purity and Danger. An Analysis of the Concepts of Pollution and Taboo* (London, 1966). An alternative characterization of Leviticus' system suggests that at stake is not normative classifications but what animals eat, with herbivores deemed clean and carnivorous animals unclean. This explanation coheres well with Gen. 1, in which God designates vegetation alone as food for humans and beasts.

[8] See Jacob Milgrom, *Leviticus 1-16* (New York, 1991), pp. 42-51.

PHILIP R. DAVIES

BRITAIN, PRACTICE OF JUDAISM IN: Historically British Jews tried to represent themselves as a purely religious minority. While they differed from other British citizens in regard to their private religious beliefs, they wished to be seen as resembling others in their public conduct, social attitudes and, above all, national allegiance and loyalty. Thus, British Jewish leaders, at least until World War II, promoted the image of Jews as "Englishmen of the Mosaic persuasion."[1] They sought to avoid differentiation on the grounds of culture, language, or ethnicity, and they discouraged the development of separate Jewish schooling, the use of Yiddish and, in particular, communal support for Zionism.

The aim of this policy was to protect the achievements and social position of the established Jewish community by emphasizing its Anglicized character and limiting its distinctiveness to the private religious domain. But while the British government appeared to accept the notion of the Jews as a purely religious minority, it is not clear that Jews themselves were persuaded by the argument. Certainly by the second half of the twentieth century, the unidimensional image of the Jew had begun to crumble. Historical events—the Holocaust, the establishment of the state of Israel, and the development of a multiculturalism in Britain—opened the way not only to greater religious differentiation between Jew and Jew but also to the evolution of Jewish identities based on feelings, beliefs, and social ties that were not intrinsically religious. Support for Zionism, the desire to fight antisemitism, attachment to Jewish culture, feelings of ethnic consciousness—these and other themes became alternative currencies for the expression of Jewish identity and for the development of new Jewish sub-cultures. By the turn of the century, survey data show that very few British Jews see their Jewishness *solely* in religious terms, while many see it as essentially secular and ethnic.

Sources of data on British Jewry: The many different and overlapping manifestations of Jewish identity make it difficult to provide a simple overview of Jewish practice and belief in the U.K. The problem is exacerbated by the paucity of data sources: there is no communal database providing information on the synagogal affiliation of British Jews, and even the enumeration of Jewish population is complicated by the absence of a question on religion in the decennial census.

Social scientific descriptions of British Jewry therefore rely on sample surveys and other ad hoc studies carried out by academic or community-based research groups. Four principle sources of data on the practice of Judaism and the demography of British Jews exist. The first and most comprehensive is the "JPR survey," a sample survey of more than two thousand British Jews conducted by the Institute for Jewish Policy Research in 1995. This survey maps the religious behavior, beliefs, and attitudes of a broad sample of self-identifying Jews selected mainly, but not entirely, by probability sampling from the British electoral register. Two smaller sample surveys, one of Jewish women and another of members of the largest synagogal body in Britain, the United Synagogue, also provide useful information on the beliefs and practices of the more affiliated sections of the community.[2] Finally, the Community Research Unit (CRU) of the Board of Deputies of British Jews produces regular, high quality, demographic and statistical reports, covering trends in synagogue membership, births, deaths and marriages. These sources will be referred to respectively as the JPR survey, the Women's survey, the US survey, and CRU reports.[3]

Jewish population—Size and location: In the absence of census data on British Jews, two other approaches to the estimation of population size have been considered: projection from synagogue membership statistics and estimation from national random sample surveys. The former method is subject to unacceptable distortions,[4] and the latter is impractical given the small size and patchy geographical distribution of British Jews.

Instead, an indirect method of estimation has been developed based on quinquennial mortality statistics, i.e., the number of burials and cremations performed under Jewish religious auspices in a given five year period. Using age- and sex-specific mortality rates, it is possible to calculate the size of the living population, which yields an estimate of approximately 300,000 Jews.[5] This figure *excludes* people who are Jewish according to Halakhah but whose links with the community are so weak that neither they nor their surviving family requests a Jewish burial; equally, it *includes* some individuals who would not be classified as Jewish by Orthodox authorities, but who meet the criteria for burial or cremation under the auspices of a Progressive synagogue. The figure of 300,000 may therefore be regarded as a rough estimate of the size of the "effective Jewish community," based on the minimal criteria of desire for and eligibility for a Jewish burial or cremation. Jews thus constitute approximately 0.5% of the British population.

The geographical distribution of British Jews is monitored by the CRU and has been described in a number of reports, which show that British Jewry is highly urbanized. About two-thirds of the population (200,000) is found in greater London and its immediate surroundings, with particular concentrations in three areas: North-West London and Hertfordshire, Stamford Hill in North London, and Redbridge and S.W. Essex. A further 10% of British Jews (30,000) lives in greater Manchester, and there are major concentrations in Leeds (10,000 = 3%) and Glasgow (6000 = 2%). The remaining 20% of the affiliated Jewish community is spread over seventy or more locations, including retirement towns on the south coast and larger towns throughout the U.K. These communities generally number less than two thousand Jews each and are subject to significant demographic erosion. Thus, for practical purposes, the ethos and development of the

British Jewish community is driven by organizations based in London and Manchester.

The religious/secular divide: It is easier to map the Jewish population geographically than to disentangle the secular and religious sub-populations. While the JPR survey provides a great deal of data on the beliefs and practices of British Jews, these data do not support the notion of a clear cut distinction between secular and religious lifestyles. The problem hinges on providing a clear operational definition of a secular Jew:

One approach is to ask respondents to classify themselves as secular or not, without providing formal criteria. All three communal surveys adopted this technique, asking respondents to characterize their pattern of religious observance by choosing a description from the following list:

Non-practicing, i.e., secular Jew
Just Jewish
Progressive (e.g., Liberal or Reform)
Traditional (not strictly Orthodox)
Strictly Orthodox (e.g., would not turn on a light on the Sabbath)

Using this self-classification scale, about a quarter of British Jews (26% in the JPR sample) describe themselves as "non-practicing, i.e., secular." However, it turns out that some of these "secular" respondents do in fact observe a number of common Jewish rituals (fasting on Yom Kippur, lighting Sabbath candles, refraining from work on Rosh Hashanah), and about 16% of them belong to a synagogue; indeed about 8% belong to an *Orthodox* synagogue. If criteria are introduced to exclude synagogue members or those who engage in ritual practice, then the proportion of British Jews who qualify as secular is correspondingly reduced:

Criteria for being "secular"	Percentage who qualify
Self-classification (as "non-practicing i.e., secular")	26%
Self-classification *and* avoidance of key mitzvot	19%
Self-classification *and* avoidance *and* no synagogue membership	16%

Now, if the criteria are made even less stringent—to include, for example, someone who regards "participation in Jewish religious life" as "not at all important" to his or her personal sense of Jewishness—then the proportion rises to 45%. If the definition is extended to include those who reject the divine origin or inspiration of the Torah, then 56% qualify as secular. And if rejection of, or uncertainty about, God's role in the creation is used as a criterion, then almost 70% must be classified as secular.

Prominent secular Jews in Great Britain have adopted the more extensive definition. Thus, Felix Posen[6] comments on the "glaring facts" that "well over 50% of the Jews . . . are secular—people for whom the concept of God and the keeping of *mitzvot* are no longer an option." But the evidence shows that the boundary between the secular and the religious is not that clear cut. And it is the disjunction between the very aspects of Judaism that Posen puts together, belief and practice, that makes the boundary fuzzy. If a secular Jew is to be defined behaviorally as someone who avoids all religious rituals, then the vast majority of British Jews would qualify as religious; but if the criterion is to be based on lack of belief or rejection of the key elements of Jewish religious dogma, then the majority would be classified as secular.

For practical purposes, in the description that follows, the self-report criterion has been used to delineate the secular respondents. In doing this, it is recognized that some of "secular Jews" participate in a few basic religious practices; and equally, that some who are classified as "religious" are in fact non-believing Jews whose involvement in Jewish practice leads them to avoid the label "secular."

Typology of secular Jews: Secular Jews fall into two broad categories, those who are relatively detached from anything Jewish but recognize their Jewish origins ("remote" secular Jews) and those who have a personally meaningful Jewish identity expressed in one or more non-religious ways ("active" secular Jews).

The JPR survey shows that the majority of secular Jews (57%) falls in the remote category, defined as those who accept their Jewish origin but "do not think of (themselves) as being Jewish any longer" or "do not think about it very often." Predictably, remote Jews have low levels of involvement in Jewish life; more than 90% are not affiliated to any kind of Jewish organization, and 92% have no desire to increase their involvement in Jewish activities. If asked to characterize the basis of their Jewish identity, remote Jews are most likely to cite psychological factors ("feeling Jewish inside," "loyalty to my Jewish heritage"), but only a small minority (10%) regards these as important factors. The majority of Jews in this category see themselves as "more British than Jewish" (70%); of those who are married, 76% are married to non-Jews.

In contrast, active secular Jews (43% of the total) are more keenly aware of their Jewishness. They are defined as those who feel "quite strongly Jewish" or are "extremely conscious" of it. This is expressed through feelings of attachment to the Jewish heritage, to fellow Jews, and to aspects of their own personality perceived to be intrinsically Jewish (56% regard these factors as being "very important"); a further 35% cite Israel, Jewish culture, or Jewish home life as being important. Predictably, active secular Jews feel either more Jewish than British or at least equally so (74%), and a somewhat smaller proportion is married to non-Jews (63% of those who are married). Active secular Jews are more likely to be involved in events of

There are a number of Jewish organizations in Britain whose membership is predominantly secular (e.g., The Jewish Socialist Group), but attempts to establish cultural or educational bodies whose mission is to develop Jewishly knowledgeable, culturally or ethnically committed *secular* Jews have failed. Hence, there is no obvious organizational base in Britain for people who see "secular Judaism" not as a contradiction in terms but as a critical element in the battle for Jewish survival.

How to measure a religious lifestyle?
Any attempt to classify and describe religious practice is at once confounded by the tendency of British Jews, unlike their American counterparts, to retain membership in their parents' (and by extension their grandparents') synagogal body. Whether for reasons of family loyalty, nostalgia, convenience, or distaste for Reform and Liberal services, the great majority of affiliated British Jews belong to an Orthodox synagogue.[7] Since only a small proportion of the members of these synagogues are themselves fully observant, it follows that synagogue affiliation *per se* is a very poor indicator of Jewish lifestyle. Based on the profile of synagogue membership in the U.K.,[8] the distribution of religious practice should resemble that shown in column A below. However, the distribution of *self-reported* religious practice among synagogue members (JPR data) tells a very different story (column B):

It is apparent that synagogue membership

A		B	
Profile of synagogue affiliation		Self-reported religiosity of synagogue members	
Orthodox	71%	Orthodox (Sabbath observant)	14%
Masorti (Conservative)	2%	Traditional (not strictly Orthodox)	44%
Progressive (Liberal/Reform)	27%	Progressive (Liberal/Reform)	21%
		Just Jewish	15%
		Non-practicing secular	6%

Jewish interest; 34% would like to increase their involvement. If an index of "communal involvement" is constructed and applied to *all* secular Jews, the distribution is clearly bimodal, indicating that the remote and active sub-groups are quite distinct from one another.

patterns vastly exaggerate the proportion of practicing Orthodox Jews and correspondingly under-estimate the substantial number of traditionally oriented, non-Orthodox Jews (sometimes referred to as the "nominal" Orthodox). However, it is not simply the case that Orthodox synagogues contain both

Orthodox and Traditional members, while Progressive synagogues contain both Progressive and secular members. The relationship is more complex than that (see Table 1), involving a significant spread of religious practice in each of the categories of synagogue membership. This underlines the weak relationship between synagogue affiliation and self-reported religious observance and justifies the separate analysis of each.

Ritual observance among non-secular British Jews: In this section we focus on the ritual observance of members of the four self-defined religious sub-groups and disregard divisions based on synagogue affiliation. The four groups (Strictly Orthodox, Traditional, Progressive, Just Jewish) comprise approximately 74% of British Jewry, the remaining 26% being those who describe themselves as secular.

Each of the sample surveys (the JPR, US, and Women's surveys) provides data on the observance of a range of common Jewish rituals and practices. The surveys are consistent in showing very marked differentiation among the four sub-groups in regard to the particular rituals observed and the proportion of adherents who observe them. Table 2 shows the typical pattern.

These findings illustrate the general decline in ritual observance as one moves across the religious spectrum. They also show the relative persistence of three core practices—attending a Seder, fasting on Yom Kippur, and refraining from work on Roah Hashanah—kept by the majority of respondents in all groups. Following American trends, it is clear that the more convenient annual rituals tend to survive, while the more demanding, daily or weekly obligations are prone to disappear. For most respondents, practical convenience seems to override Halakhah, suggesting that the practices that do survive are more likely to be expressions of ethnic belonging than religious conviction.

The strictly Orthodox: The one group in which the Halakhah remains supreme is the Strictly Orthodox, comprising some 13% of religiously active Jews, who are consistent and meticulous in their observance of a wide range of religious practices. These include the more intensive practices associated with the Sabbath and kashrut, which clearly impede social integration with the non-Jewish world and which have been shown to reflect devotional rather than ethnic dimensions of Jewish identity.[10]

The qualification "strictly" is used here to avoid any confusion with "nominal" Orthodoxy (i.e., the practices of non-observant members of Orthodox synagogues), but it is not meant to exclude the observant members of central Orthodox movements who, together with the genuinely stricter right-wing Orthodox groups, make up the "Strictly Orthodox" classification. Naturally, variations in religious practice occur within and between these various groups, but the measurement scales used in the British research are not sensitive enough to pick these up. While the survey data describe the Orthodox group as a whole, some information about the cen-

Table 1: The religious lifestyle of members of the main types of synagogue (JPR data; N = 1376; row percentages shown)

Religious Lifestyle

Synagogue type	Secular	Just Jewish	Progressive	Traditional Orthodox	Strictly	Total
Orthodox	4	16	2	58	20	100
Masorti	5	18	14	63	0	100
Reform	9	11	75	5	0	100
Liberal	13	18	60	9	0	100

Note: Percentages for Masorti are unreliable due to the very small sample size (N = 22)

Table 2: **Percentage observance of key rituals in the four self-rated religious groups**[9]
(JPR data, N = 1607)

	Strictly Orthodox	Traditional	Progressive	Just Jewish
% of total sample are "religious" Jews	(13%)	(42%)	(20%)	(25%)
Attends a Seder every/most years	**100**	96	87	62
Refrains from work on Jewish New Year	**100**	96	85	57
Fasts on Yom Kippur	**100**	94	81	56
Prefers to stay home on Friday night	**100**	88	65	39
Lights candles every Friday evening	**100**	69	36	17
Buys Kosher meat (excludes vegetarians)	**100**	79	17	19
Does not mix milk and meat	**100**	68		8
Attends synagogue each Shabbat (men)	**100**	35	19	1
Refrain from traveling on Sabbath	**100**	17	1	2

tral and right-wing sub-groups is included below in the discussion of synagogue membership statistics.

Research on Strictly Orthodox communities has been confined mainly to the assessment of their individual religious behavior, but observation of Jewish life in the U.K. reveals a significant increase in the vibrancy and public expression of Orthodox lifestyles over the past two decades. This is evidenced, for example, by the custom among modern Orthodox Jews of wearing a kippah in public, the expansion of full-time Orthodox Jewish schooling, the growth in the number of non-Orthodox Jews who turn to Orthodox practice, the wide range of opportunities for and styles of Torah learning, and, more prosaically, the dramatic growth in the numbers of kosher restaurants and snack bars in areas of Orthodox concentration.

Traditional Jews: The profile of observance among the strictly Orthodox is loosely mimicked by the 42% who classify themselves as Traditional, but with the crucial difference that Traditional Jews neglect the strict requirements of Sabbath observance, are less likely to observe the more demand-ing aspects of kashrut, and tend to neglect the requirements of ritual purity.[11] Traditional Jews are not, however, entirely consistent; while the majority eat kosher meat at home, they are more-or-less equally divided on the practice of eating only kosher meat outside of the home (48% do, 52% do not; US survey), and they exhibit wide variation in the frequency of synagogue attendance and in the level of observance of the pilgrimage and minor festivals. In effect, Traditional Jews fall on a continuum of ritual observance from a basic minimum at one pole (fasting on Yom Kippur, eating kosher meat at home, marking Rosh Hashanah, Passover, and the Sabbath in some way) through quite extensive ritual observance at the other, covering most but not all of the practices relating to the holidays, prayer, kashrut, and Shabbat.

What unites Traditional Jews across this continuum is an emotional attachment to Orthodoxy, a feeling that it represents authentic Judaism, a Judaism to which they aspire in theory, though not entirely in practice. This attachment should not, however, be confused with deep spiritual or religious commitment.

Progressive Jews: The attachment to some kind of normative model of Judaism distinguishes Traditional Jews from the remaining 20%, who classify themselves as Progressive. Progressive Jews also observe a set of core practices, but they do not see these practices, even in theory, as halakhic imperatives or requirements of authentic Judaism, so much as voluntary expressions of religious or ethnic identity. In effect, this means that Progressive Jews observe a smaller set of key rituals related mainly to social and family aspects of Jewish life, with very low levels of observance of kashrut and rejection of the precise ritual requirements of Sabbath observance. Further, the pattern of ritual observance of individual Progressive Jews is less consistent than for members of other groups. Thus a Progressive Jew who, for example, lights Sabbath candles, may neglect a more common practice such as refraining from work on Rosh Hashanah or fasting on Yom Kippur. Such reversals occur in all religious groups, but are more frequent among Progressive Jews, reflecting their more flexible approach to the concept of Mitzvah.[12]

Anecdotal evidence suggests that Progressive Jews are becoming more traditional and religiously observant, and there are observable changes, such as the establishment of a Reform ritual bath (*mikveh*) in North West London and the creation of Reform *havurot* (prayer groups). However, as noted by Marmur, such changes do not reflect a reversal of attitude to the Halakhah, so much as an increased desire for more traditional, but essentially voluntary, expressions of Jewish identity.

Just Jewish: The final 25% of the "religiously active" sub-group of British Jews comprise those who classify themselves as Just Jewish. These people are effectively on the boundary between religious and secular; they engage in very few ritual practices (Yom Kippur, Seder, and Rosh Hashanah), with about 60% observing each particular ritual and 81% observing at least one of the set (JPR survey). The distinction between this group and Progressive Jews seems to relate to the place of religious observance in their global sense of Jewish identity; Progressive

Jews (and Traditional Jews even more so) view participation in Jewish religious life as relatively important to their sense of Jewishness (73% say it is "very" or "quite important"), whereas Just Jewish respondents generally regard it as "not at all important" (71%). In this respect, Just Jewish respondents resemble Secular Jews.

There seems to be no qualitative distinction between the Just Jewish and Secular groups, although the former are somewhat more observant than the latter; 81% of Just Jewish respondents against 32% of the Secular keep at least one of the key practices (JPR data). It would seem then that the somewhat higher levels of observance have an effect on the choice of descriptor, even though both groups express non-religious attitudes. Thus, as far as religious practice is concerned, Just Jewish and Secular respondents may be regarded as falling on a single continuum, reflecting the non-religious expression of Jewish identity, and extending from weak (= Just Jewish) to zero (= Secular) levels of ritual observance.

Belief systems and ritual observance: The previous sections provide a behavioral description of the practices of each British religious sub-group but say relatively little about the belief systems that serve those practices. Religious beliefs are of interest not only as a means of understanding the psychological reality of religious practice but also as a tool for interpreting the prevailing trends in religious practice. The core data for examining the religious beliefs of British Jews also come from the JPR survey. Table 3 lists four statements reflecting fundamental aspects of Jewish religious faith and records the proportion of respondents in each group who agree (or strongly agree) with each proposition.

Two features of these data are of interest: first, the overall levels of belief are low in absolute terms; apart from the Strictly Orthodox, only about a third of the religiously active are found to accept each of these basic articles of faith, and separate analysis shows that only about 10% accept all four of them. Second, levels of belief do not decline steadily across the four religious groups

Table 3: Percentage agreement with belief statements in four religious sub-groups (N = 2147)

	Strictly Orthodox	Traditional	Progressive	Just Jewish
Praying to God can help over-come personal problems	90	49	44	36
Rejects: Universe came about by chance	94	36	27	21
Belief in God is central to being a good Jew	82	35	28	22
Jews have a special relationship with God	96	58	43	32

(as was the case with ritual observance), but, rather, there is a big step between the Strictly Orthodox and Traditional groups, with a relatively shallow decline thereafter. Very similar profiles of religious belief were obtained in the samples collected for the US and Women's survey.[13]

These findings suggest that, outside of the Strictly Orthodox grouping, the small variations in religious faith are insufficient to explain the large variations in ritual observance. In that case, another hypothesis suggests itself, that among the non-Orthodox, variations in observance have more to do with individual differences in ethnic affiliation (defined as a feeling of closeness to other Jews and association with the Jewish heritage) than with the strength of a person's religious conviction. Certainly, if the strength of ethnic identity is measured for each of the religious groups, the profile that emerges matches the trend in religious observance far better than the profile for religious belief. For example, the question "How important to your sense of Jewish identity is a feeling of closeness to other Jews?" elicits the response "very important" from 80% of the Strictly Orthodox, 57% of Traditional Jews, 37% of Progressive Jews, and 25% of the Just Jewish category. This steady decline across the four groups mimics the trend in ritual observance illustrated in Table 2.

A more rigorous test of this hypothesis can be achieved by constructing an index to measure each respondent's level of practice (P), level of belief (B), and strength of ethnic identity (E). If this is done, the cor-

relation (strength of relationship) between practice and belief on the one hand can be compared with the correlation between practice and strength of ethnic identity on the other. For the JPR sample the results are:

Correlation between P and B
(with E held constant) $r = +0.1$
Correlation between P and E
(with B held constant) $r = +0.8$

These findings provide strong support for the idea that when non-Orthodox Jews perform a religious ceremony—when they celebrate the Seder or light Sabbath candles—they are primarily expressing their ethnic identity and only rarely are driven by a feeling that these practices derive from the transcendent authority of God.

It should not be concluded from this that Strictly Orthodox Jews are an exception and that they are wholly motivated by religious faith. As Table 3 indicates, a small proportion reject key articles of faith, including (not shown above) some 17% who subscribe to the notion of the Torah as "the inspired word of God, but not everything should be taken literally" rather than to the view that "the Torah is the actual word of God." It seems likely, therefore, that, in some cases, strict observance of the Halakhah may be driven mainly by non-religious influences, such as habit or emotional attachment.

The religious characteristics of British Jews: The research reported in the previous sections yields a four dimensional structure for classifying religious life in the U.K. The dimensions are religious faith or belief, religious practice, ethnic identity, and religious attachment. The first three dimensions already have been defined operationally; the fourth refers to a person's emotional attachment or positive attitude to Jewish religious life, independent of his or her level of religious faith or belief. The four religious subgroups can then be represented in terms of their positions on each of these dimensions.

The Strictly Orthodox, whether modern or right-wing Orthodox, are unique in British Jewry in having high levels of religious faith that in most cases can be assumed to underpin their strict observance of the Halakhah. In this respect, they resemble adherents of non-Jewish religious groups who demonstrate a strong association between belief and practice. The Orthodox are also strongly identified on ethnic measures and have an emotional attachment to religious life, but in most cases these factors reinforce the role of religious conviction rather than substituting for it.

The remaining three groups (Traditional, Progressive, and Just Jewish) have roughly equivalent, rather weak levels of religious belief, so that they cannot be differentiated on this basis. Further, they differ only by degree on the scale of religious practice, although there is wide variation extending from the highest levels of observance of Traditional Jews (elements of Sabbath, kashrut, prayer, and observance of the holidays) through the intermediate level of Progressive Jews (mainly annual family practices, some recognition of the Sabbath) to the minimal practices of the Just Jewish category (one or two annual practices such as Seder, Rosh Hashanah). In the same way, the three groups differ only as a matter of degree on the scale of ethnic identity; and again the variation is very marked. The strong association between variations in ethnic identity and variations in level of ritual observance leads to the suggestion that ethnic identity is the main determinant of religious practice in these groups.

This analysis leaves Traditional, Progressive, and Just Jewish respondents occupying adjacent regions of a hybrid "practice/ identity" continuum but not clearly differentiated in qualitative terms. However, the three groups can be distinguished by reference to the fourth dimension, religious attachment. On this dimension, Traditional Jews are characterized by their emotional attachment to Orthodox "style" Judaism, which they see as authentic and to which they aspire (in a theoretical rather than practical sense). Progressive Jews do not attribute halakhic authenticity to Orthodox practices, and they have of course sought to "modernize" many synagogue practices, but they do tend to view religious life as an important part of their Jewish identity. In contrast, Just Jewish respondents do not see themselves as being psychologically engaged in Jewish religious life at all; they observe one or two annual practices solely as a matter of habit or ethnic affiliation. They are therefore very similar to Secular Jews, except that they are marginally more observant.

In summary, non-Orthodox Jews differ only marginally from one another with regard to their religious faith but differ significantly in terms of religious practice and in terms of the ethnic affiliation that fuels their practice. However, the qualitative distinctions between the three groups emerge only in the attitudinal and affective domains, having to do with the preferred style of religious practice and the psychological significance of religious life to their sense of Jewish identity.

Synagogue movements and their membership: Although it has been argued that synagogue membership statistics do not accurately represent the religious topography of British Jewry, some basic details are necessary to an understanding of communal trends and to an appreciation of the religious context of Jewish life. Particularly so, since there are only a handful of general Jewish "community centers" in Britain, and synagogues are therefore the prime focus of religious, educational, and cultural Jewish life.

There are approximately 370 synagogues, shtiebls (prayer rooms), and *minyanim* (small prayer groups) in the U.K., extending from the Liberal end of the religious spectrum (ideologically equivalent to American Reform) to the ultra-Orthodox *Haredi* groups. They provide a home—spiritual, social, ethnic, or sometimes just formal—to approximately two-thirds of Britain's self-identifying Jews (JPR survey); for some they provide little more than a route to a Jewish burial.

The breakdown of synagogue membership (Table 4) replicates the information given but provides greater detail. The 7.1% membership of right-wing Orthodox synagogues includes Hassidic and other congregations, all of whose members can be assumed to observe Jewish law strictly. They make up part of the 13% who classify themselves as "strictly Orthodox" in the various sample surveys. The remaining 6% is drawn from the membership of central Orthodox synagogues, emphasizing again that the vast majority of that membership is not strictly Orthodox. This generates the bizarre situation that central Orthodox synagogues can claim through their membership statistics to represent the majority (64%) of synagogue-affiliated British Jews, while, religiously speaking, they represent only a very small minority (i.e., 6%). Meanwhile, the Masorti movement, which dates back only to 1964 and which represents only a minute proportion of British synagogue members, is probably closer ideologically to the traditional majority than any other movement. The membership statistics of the Reform and Liberal synagogues are relatively well matched to the real numbers of Progressive Jews, although Table 1 shows that these synagogues also contain some members whose natural religious stance falls to the right or left of the institutional position.

Trends in religious practice and synagogue affiliation: The picture so far has been static. But British Jewry is probably undergoing more rapid change in its religious and institutional composition than at any stage in its history. Here we describe and contextualize these trends, integrating where possible data on synagogues with information about the religious lifestyle of their members. The starting point for this analysis is the most religiously ambivalent and potentially unstable group, the traditional Jews.

As noted, traditional Jews (the "nominal" or "non-observant" Orthodox) constitute the majority religious grouping in the U.K. Virtually all traditional Jews (94% of them) are members of Orthodox synagogues: they make up about 67%[14] of the membership of central Orthodox synagogues such as the United Synagogue (US survey), 44%[15] of the membership of all synagogues (JPR survey), and 31% of the entire Jewish population (JPR survey). Until comparatively recently, Traditional Jews were regarded as the Jewish establishment, and even if that is no longer quite the case, they are by no means the spent force that some judge their counterparts in America to be.[16]

Traditional Jews are interesting because of the significant mismatch between their non-Orthodox lifestyle and the ideology of their synagogues. In America, a similar disparity led to almost wholesale migration from the Orthodox synagogues of the first generation to the more fitting, Conservative synagogues of the second.[17] This has not yet happened on any scale in the U.K., but it is fair to say there is significant maneuvering and communal debate around the issue. It is clear where

Table 4: Congregations and Household Membership by Synagogal Grouping in 1996 (CRU Report: Schmool and Cohen, 1997)

	Congregations	% Households
Right-wing Orthodox (Union of Orthodox Hebrew Congregations)	84	7.1%
Central Orthodox (United Synagogue, Federation of Synagogues, Sephardi, etc.)	206	64.1%
Masorti (Conservative)	6	1.5%
Reform	41	18.8%
Liberal	28	8.5%

the interests of the competing religious institutions lie. The central Orthodox rabbinate views the continued allegiance of the non-observant majority as a financial necessity and spiritual challenge. Commenting on the latter, the British Chief Rabbi, Dr. Jonathan Sacks says:[18]

> Sadly, there are those who see it as a *weakness* of the United Synagogue that it includes among its members those who do not yet keep every one of the 613 commandments, and that . . . ninety per cent of its membership are only "traditional" or non-observant. I use the word "sadly" advisedly, because those who take this view have no understanding of what Torah and the sages meant by "the congregation of Israel." . . . . The time has come for the United Synagogue to stop being apologetic for what is in fact its greatest strength and its most authentic Torah value: that it embraces all Jews from the most to the least observant and that it forges from this range of commitments a deep sense of community.

The exhortation of the Chief Rabbi to create a more welcoming, inclusive, creative, and spiritually dynamic Orthodox community has struck a chord with both lay and religious leaders. The need to retain the allegiance of traditional Jews, and the threat of their defection to the religious left, has somehow enhanced their status. It has encouraged the development of more diverse educational and cultural programs within Orthodox synagogues, including the now ubiquitous "explanatory service," educational Sabbaths, and institutionalized "welcoming" duties. There is also evidence of religious concessions being made to less observant members, for example, the adoption of a more relaxed attitude to carrying and the bringing of pushchairs to synagogues on the Sabbath, outside of an Eruv. Some of this resembles the historical tolerance of the United Synagogue of the early 1900s, which seemed to welcome not only the nominal Orthodox but also nominal Orthodoxy. Commenting on this period in its history, Geoffrey Alderman talks of the United Synagogue as "nothing less than an organized hypocrisy . . . the bulk of whose members professed an orthodoxy they delighted in not practicing," but he goes on to say that it "undoubtedly played a major part in helping to retain within the formal framework of orthodoxy many who might otherwise have drifted away."[19] The question to which we now turn is whether the United Synagogue in particular, and mainstream Orthodoxy in general, is likely to manage a repeat performance.

Part of the answer to this question will be determined by the attitudes of traditional Jews themselves. Their continuing allegiance is explained in part by their emotional and nostalgic attachment to Orthodox practice, a strong desire to perpetuate what they see as authentic Judaism, and a feeling that they can do so vicariously by remaining formally within the Orthodox fold. In this context, it is not surprising that even among those who have considered leaving, the tension between personal practice and the religious ethos of the synagogue is not a prime factor. Indeed, where religious style is concerned, traditional Jews give as one of their reasons for remaining in an Orthodox synagogue a distaste for what is perceived to be the "church-like" atmosphere of a Reform or Liberal service.[20]

However, in a changing religious marketplace, that unflattering image of Progressive synagogues must be set against the evidence that Reform synagogues are becoming more traditional. In addition, there is the possible appeal of the Masorti (Conservative) movement, which is now promoting itself more actively and which offers a logical home for traditional Jews who have difficulty with the notion of a Torah dictated by God, who want an Orthodox-style service, and who favor a more effectual role for women. Further, the intrinsic appeal of Masorti and other left-leaning movements may have been enhanced by a series of disputes between the Chief Rabbi and other Orthodox and non-Orthodox rabbis that created the impression, whether justified or not, of an intolerant Orthodoxy unable to put inclusivism into practice.[21] Further, there is the impact of the Lubavitch rabbis who now occupy the pulpits of a number of central Orthodox synagogues, filling the void left by the inadequate supply of "mainstream" rabbis historically trained by Jews' College, and creating both a more exotic and more right-wing religious ethos.

It is not yet clear what the operational effects of these conflicting pressures will be. The statistical evidence on synagogue membership shows an unambiguous contraction in the central Orthodox share of the market—down from 70% in 1990 to 64% in 1996—while right-wing Orthodoxy has grown from 5.7% to 7.1%, and the left-of-center from 24% to 29%.[22] This religious polarization, which in statistical terms is quite reliable, might be thought to represent the migration of traditional Jews to the left and strictly Orthodox Jews to the right, in effect, the beginnings of the demise of middle-of-the-road Judaism. But this would be a misreading of the data, since the trends are caused largely by demographic factors: the right-wing community has a high birth rate and is growing larger; the Central Orthodox group is aging and contracting. It is possible that, over and above these natural demographic trends, there has been some voluntary switching of synagogues—some traditional Jews may have moved to the left—but there is certainly no evidence of a significant disengagement from central Orthodoxy at this stage.

Of course, that is not to say that traditional Judaism (or indeed any other form of Judaism) may not decline to the point of extinction in the longer term, due to the combined effects of demography and assimilation. That will depend on the capacity of traditional Judaism to transmit itself to future generations and to resist the pressures of assimilation. But that is not a question about the synagogue preferences of the currently affiliated community.

On the question of transmission, however, the data are clear: rates of outmarriage increase systematically as one moves across the religious spectrum from children raised in Strictly Orthodox homes through Traditional and Progressive to the Just Jewish. Only the Strictly Orthodox have achieved a balance between fertility and assimilation that exceeds the replacement level. Similarly, on the question of retention within a given synagogue movement, the offspring of members of right-wing synagogues are the most

likely to remain within their parent's grouping, followed by the offspring of Orthodox synagogue members, then Reform, and finally the Liberal (JPR data). Those who move from their parent's synagogal grouping move predominantly to the left. A proportion do not join a synagogue at all, this also following a linear trend across the religious groupings.

The implications of this for the religious community, if the trends remain unchecked, are that all but the strictly Orthodox community will disappear. Between now and then, there will be further polarization of the religious community, arising not from the greater assimilation rate of the traditional group (it is currently lower), but from the inter-generational shift to the left; i.e., the offspring of traditional Jews will replace, temporarily, the Progressive Jews who are assimilating at a greater rate. These are temporary dynamics that might be changed by the development-strategies of individual movements, but the overall trend is clearly towards the erosion of all but the strictly Orthodox.

The recognition of this stark fact has galvanized the minds of communal leaders and thinkers and created a Jewish continuity industry of considerable energy but disputed potential. The question for the coming millennium is whether modes of transmission can be developed that can transform ethnic identity into religious passion as surely as history has operated in the reverse direction.

Bibliography

Kalms, Stanley, ed., *A Time for Change: The United Synagogue Review* (London, 1992).

Miller, Stephen, "Religious Practice and Jewish Identity in a Sample of London Jews," in Webber, Jonathan, ed., *Jewish Identities in the New Europe* (Oxford, 1994), pp. 193-204.

Schmool, Marlena, and Stephen Miller, *Women in the Jewish Community* (London, 1994).

Schmool, Marlena, and Frances Cohen, *British Synagogue Membership in 1996* (London, 1997).

Notes

[1] Chaim Bermant, *The Jews* (London, 1977), p. 4. See too Geoffrey Alderman, "British Jewry: Religious Community or Ethnic Minority," in Jonathan Webber, ed., *Jewish Identities in the New Europe* (Oxford, 1994), pp. 189-192.

[2] Marlena Schmool and Stephen Miller, *Women in the Jewish Community* (London, 1994); Stanley Kalms, ed., *A Time for Change: The United Synagogue Review* (London, 1992).

[3] Where no other source is given, statistics are from the JPR survey. Some statistics are derived from the original data set and appear for the first time in this article.

[4] Schmool and Cohen, op. cit.

[5] Steven Haberman and Marlena Schmool, "Estimate of British Jewish Population, 1984-88," in *Journal of Royal Statistical Society, Series A*, 1995, 158, part 3, pp. 547-562.

[6] Felix Posen, "Judaism is Jewish Civilisation: Routes of Secular Return," in *Judaism Today*, no. 5 (Autumn, 1996).

[7] See Judy Citron in Kalms, op. cit.

[8] Schmool and Cohen, op. cit.

[9] Note that the base for the percentages given here is religious (i.e., non-secular) Jews, whether synagogue members or not.

[10] Stephen Miller, "The Structure and Determinants of Jewish Identity in the UK," in *Proceedings of the International Workshop on Jewish Identity* (Bar Ilan University, March 1997).

[11] Schmool and Miller, op. cit., p. 18.

[12] Stephen Miller, "Religious Practice and Jewish Identity in a Sample of London Jews," in Webber, op. cit., pp. 196-197.

[13] See, e.g., Miller, ibid., p. 198.

[14] The remaining 33% are not all strictly Orthodox. In fact only 10% of central Orthodox members are strictly Orthodox, 67% Traditional, and 23% Progressive, Just Jewish, or Secular. Note that the breakdown shown in Table 1 applies to all Orthodox synagogues.

[15] The 42% figure shown in Table 2 gives the percentage of all non-secular Jews who are Traditional, whether synagogue members or not. The 44% figure is based on synagogue members only.

[16] Norman Lamm, "The Jewish Jew and Western Culture," in Webber, op. cit., pp. 101-106.

[17] Calvin Goldscheider, *Jewish Continuity and Change: Emerging Patterns in America* (Bloomington, 1986), pp. 151-169.

[18] Jonathan Sacks, *A Time for Renewal: A Rabbinic Response to the Kalms Report* (London, 1992), pp. 6-7.

[19] Geoffrey Alderman, "The Disunited Synagogue," in *Judaism Today* 4 (1996), p. 36.

[20] Miller and Schmool, op. cit., p. 254; Citron, op. cit., p. 202.

[21] Alderman, op. cit.

[22] Figures are from Schmool and Cohen, op. cit.

STEPHEN MILLER

C

CALENDAR OF JUDAISM: Unlike the solar calendar that guides Christian worship and the lunar calendar that governs Muslim religious observances, the Jewish year (from which both Christian and Muslim religious calendars stem) harmonizes solar and lunar rhythms. In this system, the lunar calendar has a certain primacy. In ancient times, special watch was kept in Jerusalem for the first appearance of the new moon, for this marked *Rosh Hodesh*, the beginning of a new month. This was honored everywhere as an important day of rest and special liturgical assembly. During the Second Temple period, complex relays of messengers and signals brought to diaspora communities rapid notification of the new moons and festival commencements in the land of Israel (for all festivals continued to be regulated by the relation of the heavens and the seasons in the Land of Israel). The practice of adding an extra day to each festival developed in the diaspora to ensure that observances would in any case be correctly timed. In the post-Biblical period, Rosh Hodesh was gradually demoted to minor liturgical status, and the prohibition on work was removed.[1]

Despite the lunar foundation, the annual solar cycle was acknowledged. While Jewish months generally alternate between twenty-nine and thirty days, to keep harmony with the moon's phases, if only these lunar cycles governed the calendar, the months would move out of their congruence with the solar cycle, the actual seasons, and agricultural life. So the Great Sanhedrin in antiquity had the task of determining which years would have an added month, Adar II, following the month of Adar that usually ends the year. Through the addition of Adar II seven times over a period of nineteen years, the lunar and solar cycles were ingeniously synchronized. Finally, repression by the newly

Christian Roman Empire led the fourth century C.E. patriarchate in Palestine to disseminate a fixed calendar incorporating the nineteen year adjustments, so that local communities no longer depended on the Great Sanhedrin for establishing their religious calendar.

The names of the months have varied. In the Biblical period, they were known by their numbered sequence: the first month (of the year), the seventh month, etc. Canaanite names were also applied (e.g., Passover falls in "Aviv," Exod. 13:4, 23:15, Deut. 16:1, etc.). Following the Babylonian Exile, Babylonian names were adopted, and they still govern usage. From the first month on, they are Nisan, Iyyar, Sivan, Tamuz, Av, Elul, Tishre, Marheshvan, Kislev, Tevet, Shevat, Adar (and Adar Sheni, "Second Adar" or "Adar II," in leap years).

Passover, in Nisan, which generally falls in April-May, begins the cycle of the Jewish festivals, so, in Scripture, Nisan is "the first month" (Exod. 12:2). Nevertheless, presently the Jewish year is reckoned from Rosh Hashanah, "the Head of the Year," the first day of what Scripture calls the seventh month, Tishre, which falls in September-October. Tellingly, "Head" here can have the meaning of "goal/purpose" or of "beginning." As the seventh month, Tishre is the sabbath of the months of the year, the time especially dedicated to God and creation. Jubilee years began in Tishre. Rosh Hashanah and the holy period it inaugurates are indeed the goal and purpose of the yearly festival cycle. The Talmudic sages thus debated whether to date the creation of the universe from Nisan or from Tishre. For reasons that have a great deal to do with the deeper meanings of the Tishre holy days, it was agreed that Rosh Hashanah celebrates the beginning of time and, as we shall see, also prefigures the end of days. So the Jewish year incorporates two beginnings, a heavenly year and an earthly one, placed six months apart. The former marks the beginning of God's cosmic rule with Rosh Hashanah in Tishre; the other the beginning of humanity's response with Passover in Nisan. Nisan is also the new year for human kings and is the reference point for measuring the length of their reigns.[2]

In antiquity, Jewish writers generally dated events from epochal historical changes, as did the general non-Jewish population. Thus Second Commonwealth datings, for instance, were usually from the start of the Seleucid empire. The present practice of dating the Jewish religious year from creation arose in the Middle Ages. The Tosafists of the twelfth century indicate that this practice was already customary then in France and Germany. Applying this dating to our own time, the secular year 2,000 will bridge 5760 and 5761 in the Jewish calendar.

A phenomenological-structural approach—Comparing the autumn and spring festivals: Although there are many accounts of the Jewish festivals, few have attempted to explain the festival cycle as a single patterned and logical whole. Instead, discussions of the festivals generally treat each in isolation from the others, viewing them in a "just-so" fashion, as survivals from pre-Mosaic nature-festivals and the happenstance accumulation of later customs. The High Holidays of Rosh Hashanah and Yom Kippur are usually analyzed by themselves; Sukkot (Tabernacles), though it immediately follows Yom Kippur, is separately grouped with Passover and Shavuot (Pentecost) as "pilgrimage festivals;" and the "lesser feasts and fasts" are dealt with in no particular order and often almost as after-thoughts. But studies of ritual calendars in almost all religions disclose that the annual festival calendar as a whole, and the details of each festival, normally are coordinated in a systematic and coherent way. Each festival, its timing and meaning determined by the specific religion and world view, plays a particular role in the annual experience of worshippers, even if they cannot articulate this explicitly. Customs are rarely mere "survivals," but, rather, exemplify tacit meanings still actively structuring the observances. Most significant, the "survival" theory cannot explain why some customs survive and others do not.

Considering the Jewish festivals as a coherent totality reveals a great deal. We begin at the most general and obvious level, with the holidays that remain important even for non-observant and secularized Jews in the modern period: the High Holidays (more traditionally called the "Days of Awe," the ten days bracketed by Rosh Hashanah and Yom Kippur) and Passover. These holidays divide the year, falling about six months apart. Each is known as a "New Year," and they complement each other with peculiar exactitude, as is clear when we compare their specific traits (see Table 1).[3]

The contrasts are systematic and far-reaching. They extend from small details of ritual practice to overall mood and meaning. In regard to meaning, the High Holidays have a universal and timeless significance as "the birthday of the world," and they pertain to all living things: at this season God reviews the deeds of all creatures and determines their fate in the coming year. In a lesser enactment of the ultimate Day of Judgment at the end of time, every soul stands before God. Pass-

over, by contrast, is a historical and particularistic festival celebrating "the birthday of the Jewish people" as such, the Exodus from Egypt. Here, the Jewish people alone stand before God. During the High Holidays, everyone wears the simplest clothes to stress their humility before God: one wears no leather on Yom Kippur, and no jewelry. But on Passover every Jew is freed from slavery and is the equal of aristocrats, able to recline on pillows at home in elegant clothes like the Graeco-Roman nobility used to do. The details of observance further underline this complementarity. High Holiday worshippers spend most of the *daylight* hours in the *synagogue*, in *public* and *formal* prayer. Its climactic day, Yom Kippur, *concludes* the ten-day period and is devoted to *fasting* and intense prayer, which ends precisely when night falls. Passover, on the other hand, although an eight-day festival, has its climactic observance at the *beginning*, which *starts*

THE HIGH HOLY DAYS AND PASSOVER COMPARED

THE HIGH HOLY DAYS	PASSOVER
Formal mode of observance	Informal mode of observance
Synagogue-centered and Biblical (Hebrew language; Torah text)	Home-centered and Rabbinic (Aramaic & vernacular Haggadah)
Services held throughout day	Night-time celebration most central
High Priest and Temple imagery (Rabbi/cantor conducts service)	Clan, family and rabbis imaged (Family elder conducts service)
Solemn atmosphere	Playful and joyous atmosphere
Ascetic renunciation, repentance	Feasting and wine-drinking
Adult-oriented	Child-oriented
Self-examination, personal renewal (Introvert penitent emphasis)	Communal and family solidarity (Extrovert emphasis)
Humility in clothes, e.g., no jewels, no leather (all Israel equally humble, poor)	Nobility in clothes and usages, e.g., reclining at table, best clothes (all Israel equally aristocratic)
Focus on eternity (the Last Judgment, beyond death) ("the birthday of the world") (Israel, each Jew a sacrificial offering)	Historical focus (the first formation of Israel) (the birthday of the Jewish people) (Israel as people to rejoice in life)
All humanity and all living things (universal vision unifying world) (service is on behalf of all beings)	The people Israel the subject (group struggle produces Israel) (service is on behalf of Israel)
Transcendental call from God	The human community's response

Table 1

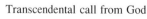

when *night* falls, at a bounteous *feast* at *home*. The night-time emphasis is so strong that the Torah directs that the feast may last throughout the night, for the sacrificial lamb must be completely eaten before dawn, and certain Talmudic rabbis are praised in the Haggadah that is read during the home service for so extending their discussion of deeper meanings of the Exodus that they talked right through until the time for morning prayers. The tradition emphasizes that the longer it takes to get through the service, and the more insights, laughter and enjoyment, the more praiseworthy the act. Such variety, spontaneity, and intimate informality certainly contrast strongly with the formal public High Holiday rituals.

Both festivals elaborate a symbolism of substitutionary sacrifices—offered in place of Jewish children—that establishes the Jewish community and vocation. But the Passover symbolisms invert the High Holidays' pattern. In Rosh Hashanah morning services, the Torah portions deal with the birth of Isaac and his almost-sacrifice by Abraham (the *Akedah*); these events provided the model and rationale for the later Temple sacrificial services and for Israel's covenantal destiny. Here the father initiates a sacrifice that his son trustingly and lovingly participates in, even allowing himself to be bound on the altar. Although Isaac queries his father about what is happening, he rests content in the assurance that God will provide the answer. And in the end a ram was provided and accepted as a substitute for Isaac/Israel. Later generations understood this to promote the ideal of Israel as a Suffering Servant who exhibits heroic faithfulness to the covenant of the ancestors, accepting even to the point of martyrdom the trials history inflicts, relying on the merciful promise of God that Israel will ultimately survive and be vindicated. But in Passover, where triumphant liberation, rather than acceptance of defeat, is expressed, the children, the builders of the future, must take the initiative, even to the point of asking their father about the meaning of the ritual. The father then responds lovingly and at length, with song and chant, retelling the story of the Exodus, including

the account of the sacrifice of the Egyptians' first-born sons and the substitution of first-born lambs for the Hebrews' sons. That the children initiate the symbolic sacrifice with love and with rejoicing in their lot ensures the perpetuation of the Jewish people. The two festivals together thereby anticipate the prophetic promise that in the End of Days, "the hearts of fathers will turn to their children, and the hearts of children unto their fathers" (Mal. 4:6). A foretaste of that millennial communion of past and future is given in the High Holidays and Passover festivals, for on this communion has always depended the persistence of the Jewish people through the generations of exile.

One more link between the two festival periods of autumn and spring must be mentioned. Passover does not exist as an isolated festival, but, from its second day, announces the coming of Shavuot. The "Counting of the Omer" day by day, for forty-nine days, heightens the sense that the Exodus of Passover is merely a prologue and preparation for Shavuot (also called *Atzeret*, day of special "Assembly") on the fiftieth day, the day of the Israelites' arrival at Mt. Sinai and the receiving of Torah. The spring festival of Passover thus starts a fifty-one-day countdown (fifty-two days in the diaspora, where a second day of Shavuot is added), which ends in a joyful celebration of Torah, with the synagogue decked with green branches, for the Torah is "the Tree of Life."[4]

We find a very similar structure in the autumn, too, in which there is a long countdown within a framework of 51/52 days, ending with an *Atzeret*-day of Torah celebration and rejoicing with the synagogue filled with greenery. This period begins with the month of Elul and comes to a climax in the High Holidays that begin the month of Tishre; it continues through Sukkot, Shemini Atzeret, and Simhat Torah. The first of Elul, one month before Rosh Hashanah, marks the beginning of the season of repentance with the blowing of the shofar in the synagogue (anticipating the central role of the shofar in the High Holidays). A full month of introspection and self-purification follows, leading up to Rosh Hashanah, which in turn begins a yet more intense ten day period of preparation, culminating in the yearning prayers of Yom Kippur and the triumphal conclusion at its end, as night falls. But even Yom Kippur does not conclude the cycle. In a sense the eight days of Sukkot are the extension of Yom Kippur and its positive resolution: on Sukkot, God provides the blessings of life and plenty and Jews dwell trustingly in booths open to the sky. The Sukkot liturgy stresses this continuity with High Holidays by echoing some of the key phrases of the Days of Awe. In the Middle Ages, the seventh day of Sukkot even came to be called *Yom Kippur Hakatan*, "the lesser Yom Kippur," for it was considered a final opportunity to seek true repentance and divine forgiveness. The entire holiday is pervaded by an exuberant sense of God's mercy and an assurance that God has responded to the penitent with gifts of life. These gifts are above all symbolized for farmers in the rains. The final climax of the autumn cycle, the last day of Sukkot or added to it, comes fifty-one days after the first of Elul. It is called *Atzeret*, or rather *Shemini Atzeret*, "Eighth day of Assembly" (that is, the eighth day concluding Tabernacles), or *Simhat Torah*, "Rejoicing in the Torah" (which in the diaspora is celebrated on the next day, fifty-two days after the first of Elul), a time of dancing in the synagogue, which is filled with rustling tree branches. So we find again in the autumn the 51/52-day pattern that we noted in the spring, involving a count-down period of spiritual preparation and a conclusion in a special *Atzeret*-day of celebration of the Torah, when the synagogue is filled with greenery.

But Sukkot and Shavuot also contrast in the same way that the High Holidays and Passover do. Just as Passover in early spring stresses historical and particularistic meanings, the Exodus from Egypt of a "mixed multitude," so does Shavuot in late spring point to the historical arrival of that multitude at Mt. Sinai, where they finally understood their vocation, accepted the Torah and became the Jewish people. By contrast, the autumn High Holidays stress universalistic and cosmic meanings, as is confirmed by the Sukkot prayers for mercy and rain for all the earth. Simhat Torah, which concludes Tabernacles, celebrates the Torah as the underlying source and pattern for the entire universe, and the Torah portion read on Simhat Torah tells of the Creation of the universe and Adam and Eve's story in Eden. Commentators who emphasize the historical associations of Passover and Shavuot generally ignore any historical symbolisms in the High Holidays and Sukkot. So the complementary contrasts between universal and particular themes, timelessness and history, humanity and Israel, are repeated in the contrasts between Sukkot and Shavuot.

The meaning of the summer fast days: If there is any wider pattern of meaning in the Jewish year, however, it must include the summer and winter holy days. So we must turn to the observances that occur between Shavuot and the first of Elul and see if there is any coherent structure of meaning linking the spring and autumn cycles of 51/52 days. The major observances during the summer are the fasts of the Seventeenth of Tamuz and the Ninth of Av. The former falls exactly forty days after Shavuot. It traditionally is explained as commemorating and atoning for the sin of the Golden Calf (and all similar sins of the Jewish people down through history). The Torah does indeed tell us that the sin of the Golden Calf occurred precisely forty days after the arrival at Mt. Sinai and Moses' ascent of the mountain. On the fortieth day, the seventeenth of Tamuz, Moses descended the mountain with the tablets of the Torah and found the people worshipping God through the image of the calf. He broke the tablets, purged the people of their false leaders, and disposed of the calf. Two days later, he re-ascended Mt. Sinai for a further forty days. Some Torah passages suggest that this second period of prayer and communion of Moses with God was necessary to renew the bond of blessings between God and Israel, while other passages suggest that Moses only needed a new set of tablets. In any case, forty-two days after the seventeenth of Tamuz brings us precisely to the thirtieth of Av. This was the day on which Moses descended for a second time from Mt. Sinai;

on the morning of the next day, the first of Elul, shofar blasts called the people together and marked the beginning of their full reconciliation with God. Shofar blasts forever after are associated with the first of Elul and sound on that day in the synagogues: rally and return to God! We now understand why the season of exemplary penitence begins at this time. So it is clear that the spring cycle is tightly linked with the autumn cycle after all. The events of the Mosaic generation, beginning with the Exodus and including the revelation at Mt. Sinai, overarch both cycles. This explains why Shavuot, which celebrates the revelation at Mt. Sinai, is so brief and underemphasized: in fact it only commemorates the first days of this revelation. The later festivals, including the High Holidays and Sukkot, elaborate deeper and later events at Sinai, all precisely as related in the Torah.

For example, the Ninth of Av, a fast day not specifically commanded in the Torah, is nevertheless implied by the Torah's account: it falls exactly at the mid-point between the events of the Golden Calf and Moses' second descent, twenty-one days after the seventeenth of Tamuz and twenty-one days before the first of Elul. It represents therefore the absolute nadir of Israel's estrangement from God. According to tradition, the three weeks following the Golden Calf incident is the time *Bein Hamatzarim*, "Between the Fences" (Lam. 1:3: "All her pursuers caught her between the fences"—or "in the midst of [her] distress"). This remains in Jewish lore the time when over the past 3,000 years the worst persecutions and pogroms have befallen the Jews. Ascetic and mourning practices are adopted, for Jews are most vulnerable then. Not only has Israel's idolatrous misconception of the way to God broken the bridge to him, but her own true guides, the greatest sages and saints, are absent from her midst and are interceding with God in obscurity.[5] So it is the hardest time to reach God or to know how to proceed: Israel is then most friendless, ill led, divided, and vulnerable to attack.

The High Holidays as a sealing of the Torah's covenant: But the next three weeks after the ninth of Av are a period of increasing mercy, climaxing in Moses' second return from the mountain-top with the news of God's merciful renewal of the covenant. Possibly, according to some Torah passages, and certainly according to the standard Rabbinic interpretation of the Torah narrative, this second period of forty days was spent by Moses interceding with God on behalf of the sinful People of Israel. When Moses came down on the first of Elul, he announced that God would accept their repentance, so from that time they could begin to purify their hearts, removing the roots of their sinful ways and preparing themselves for a whole and integral communion with God. This explains why Israel's preparation for the High Holidays begins on the first of Elul. The Torah is interpreted to teach that, on the first of Elul, after informing Israel of God's covenantal love, Moses again ascended the mountain and stayed away a further (and final) forty days, returning at last with a second set of tablets of the Torah. If we add forty days to the first of Elul, we come to Yom Kippur, the holiest day in the Jewish calendar. That day is now revealed as commemorating the perfected acceptance of the (second) tablets of the Torah, when God's presence was truly in the people's midst. A great sense of rejoicing and awed reconciliation filled the Israelites, and they set eagerly to work building the tabernacle in accordance with God's own instructions (Exod. 35ff.). The beginnings of this are commemorated in the festival of Sukkot.

Despite some doubt about when Moses descended with the second tablets, it appears that, from pre-exilic times, the number of days between the fasts and festivals has exactly followed the Torah's account. The neat repetition of sets of forty days, and the 51/52-day cycles of spring and autumn, and especially the symbolic contents, the rituals, moods, and meanings of the festivals themselves, have too closely followed the events of Moses' own generation to be coincidental. Contrary to what an entire generation of Biblical scholars has insisted, it is difficult if not impossible to explain these complex, deeply interwoven, and, above all, interdependent patterns as merely a Judaic after-thought to randomly appropriated earlier pagan rites (with Shavuot, for example, being a pure nature and harvest festival and only gaining a Sinaitic connection late in the Second Temple period!). It appears instead that a Judaic pattern determined the overall festival cycle and its details from the earliest period: particular elements might be borrowed, and certainly many customs were added from time to time, but these endured only if they spoke to later generations in other lands and enhanced the original meaning. The festival cycle did not have its roots in pagan Canaanite cult.

In any case, we must conclude that the spring and autumn cycles are presently directly linked together through the summer fasts as a single drama centering on the revelation at Mt. Sinai, with the specific timing and themes of these festivals determined by the Torah's account of the first year following the Exodus from Egypt. In this account the revelation at Mt. Sinai is understood as the culmination of universal history, the pivot of time. It is above all commemorated by the autumn festivals. The seemingly merely universalistic and non-historical cycle of holy days in the autumn, and the clearly historical spring cycle, actually express one historical sequence. This story starts from particularity, in the Exodus of Passover, but it expands to universality at Mt. Sinai, to include the world and all humanity in the High Holidays and Sukkot. In this, Israel's vocation is fulfilled. The entire yearly cycle is part of a single drama that merges particularity and universality, history and eternity.

The centrality of the Torah in this understanding of the High Holidays illuminates the many references in the autumn festivals to the "Book of Life." Throughout the period of Elul and the Days of Awe, people greet each other with the saying, "May you be inscribed for a good life." The imagery of a Book of Life (sometimes imaged as several books of different fates) into which God writes the destiny of every person is a major theme tying together the weeks from Elul to Yom Kippur (see, e.g., B. R.H. 16b). God is

still composing this book during this period. The inscription determined for each person is inchoate and can still be modified, but it gets clearer and is fixed by the end. "All are judged on Rosh Hashanah, and the verdict is sealed on Yom Kippur" (T. R.H. 1:12). This Book of Life into which the lives of all worthy creatures are inscribed and sealed, and which is finished by God and presented on Yom Kippur, is typologically similar to the Torah and the tablets themselves, which were finally brought down and presented to Israel on the first Yom Kippur (in fact, being inscribed in—or blotted out—of the Torah, depending on one's sins, is explicitly mentioned in Exod. 32:32-33). In effect, through penitence, those living today become worthy to be included in the covenant of life sealed at Sinai. The Days of Awe are the time for the reconversion of the people of Israel to God, as they break through the barriers of time and stand again at Mt. Sinai. And Sukkot celebrates the universal vision of the harmonies of the universe that flow from this breakthrough, in which Israel is a kingdom of priests serving all humanity. In the Temple period, during Sukkot, seventy bullocks were offered up on behalf of the seventy peoples of the earth, and Zech. 14:16-19 tells us that in the messianic era all the nations will come up to Jerusalem to observe Sukkot: it will be their one obligatory festival!

The meaning of the winter feasts: The vision of the Garden of Eden, which is reviewed in the Torah reading on Simhat Torah, also includes the account of Adam and Eve's expulsion from Eden into a difficult world of striving and imperfections. The long cold, wet period of winter that begins after the joyous Sukkot celebrations is a time of suffering and struggle. The only biblically mandated fast day during this season, the Tenth of Tevet, sets its theme: it commemorates the commencement of the final siege of Jerusalem in 589 B.C.E. by the Babylonian army, the event leading to diasporic exile. (But coming before that, and mourning the deeper cause of the Tenth of Tevet, is the Fast of Gedaliah, immediately after Rosh Hashanah, which acknowledges that Israel's wintry exile was brought on by her own fanatics, her schisms and sins.) Henceforth Israel must wander in a dark wilderness. Quite simply, the three major observances that mark winter's middle and end are meditations on how to sustain Israel and the light of Torah in a world that fights against them. Hanukkah, Purim, and Passover itself all concern intensifying degrees of challenge.

Hanukkah centers on an attempt by hostile Hellenistic despots to outlaw Judaism; Purim goes further with an account of a plot by government ministers to murder all Jews; but Passover in this context presents the most chilling and insidious spiritual possibility of all (one being faced anew in our own post-Holocaust era), that the Jewish people will be so seduced by, or enslaved to non-Jewish cultures that they will simply cease to exist as a people at all, half-voluntarily, half-involuntarily. But each of the winter festivals insists that no matter how dark the forces oppressing the Jewish people and their religion, they do now have the Torah-Tabernacle in their midst, and a light will continue to endure within them from the Sinai revelation (the ritual symbolism of light within and darkness without marks all these winter festivals and is especially evident in Hanukkah and the night-time feast of Passover). This translates into the promise that God will always succor his people, inspiring them to resist as a whole people and bestowing miraculous signs (Hanukkah), by invisibly shaping the natural "secular" forces of history, and even acting through assimilated Jews (Purim), or by direct intervention when all else fails (Passover). The ultimately triumphant God-is-with-us meanings of winter are the complement to the pained and confused search for God by sinning Israel during the summer fasts. Just as the summer fasts of the Seventeenth of Tamuz and the Ninth of Av contrast the dark confusion within the hearts even of the pious to the burning arid summer without, so do the feasts of the cold wet winter months contrast the light within with the surrounding threatening dark forces.

There are other complementarities and contrasts of ritual themes and practices between the winter and summer festivals too systematic to be merely coincidental. They complete each other's meaning, and both focus above all on the chief threats to the maintenance of the Torah covenant established in the spring and autumn festivals. One category of threat arises from within, the unfaithful or erring heart; the other category arises from without, in the hatred of humanity at large for God and for those who follow God's way. Both treat of Israel's relationship to humanity and with itself during the long period of history before the end of days. God may eternally summon (the autumn festivals) and Israel may joyfully respond (the spring festivals), but the two must be tied together through painful historical events testifying again and again to flawed responses by Israel (summer fasts) and by humanity at large (winter feasts). Both summer and winter tell us of the purgations of history.

The festivals as time past, present, and future: All this reminds us that the festivals do not merely commemorate the primal Mosaic history of the Exodus and Sinai. In their traditional interpretation they also contain constant references to the later history of Israel, for the events of the first year of Judaism were so paradigmatic, so archetypal, that they echo still down through time, and their meaning continues to unfold. The tendency of each generation to depict and anchor yet more passing events in the relevant parts of the calendar came in fact to overwhelm the underlying Sinaitic history and to displace it from the awareness of the faithful. Eternity triumphed over time, creating a baroque superstructure of custom and exegesis. So, despite the consistent reference to the Mosaic events in Rabbinic interpretations of particular festivals, from the Talmudic era through the Middle Ages to the present day this structure has generally been lost to view or is seen as secondary and accidental when it is the basic key to all else.

But we do not exhaust the meaning of the festivals to their practitioners when we add post-Mosaic, even post-Biblical, historical and present references to the Mosaic signi-fications of the rituals (this seems to have begun around the time of the Babylonian Exile, when the fall of the First Temple was linked to the Seventeenth of Tamuz and the Ninth of Av). It is true that in this way the festivals are made to embrace in their inten-tions and spiritual exegesis the full range of later and contemporary Jewish history and to give that history shape and meaning within a sanctified universe. There are in addition, however, a multitude of future-oriented mes-sianic and millennial symbolisms. We need only think of Passover's references to the cup of Elijah, the proclamation at the end of that feast, "Next Year in Jerusalem!" and the "Had Gadya" song that foretells the over-coming of death itself. Similarly, we recall the High Holidays' references to the great Shofar blast that will herald the End of Days, the motif of the Day of Judgment's uniting the living and the dead, and the subsequent Sukkot references to millennial joy and har-mony (e.g., as symbolized in the Lulav and Etrog, especially in the myrtle branches; cf., Isa. 55:12-13).

It thus is possible to see the annual festi-vals as moving in a three-fold spiral of tem-poral reference. The first spiral recalls the Mosaic generation's experience of the first year after the Exodus, centering on the rev-elation at Mt. Sinai, which lays the founda-tion for all the rest. The second spiral sweeps through later Jewish history, with references to the glories of the two Temples (evoked in the course, for example, of the High Holi-days and of Passover), but also to the dis-asters that arose from Israel's own sins (bringing about, for example, the destruc-tion of those Temples, remembered on the summer-time fasts) and the miracles of salva-tion worked by God, which saved exilic Israel from annihilation at the hands of enemies (recalled in the winter festivals). The third spiral pictures the events of the future and of final things, with the meanings of each festival contributing in logical sequence to the ultimate events: the coming of Elijah (suggested in Passover's cup of Elijah), which spurs a period of unification culminating in a renewal of Jewish faith (Shavuot), a time

of apocalyptic woes and confusion (Seven-teenth of Tamuz and the Ninth of Av; al-though Zech. 8:19 assures us that in those days the fast will be transformed into "glad-ness and cheerful feasts"), the final day of judgment (High Holidays), and the millennial blessings that follow (when all the nations shall come up to Jerusalem to celebrate Tab-ernacles, Zech. 14:16-19). Hanukkah and Purim have no end of days references at all and so do not relate to this third and ultimate spiral.

As we can see, there is a normative Juda-ism. Based on their acceptance of revelation, a hundred generations of Jews have enacted the same basic structure of festivals (e.g., the Ethiopian Jewish calendar also includes the Torah-mandated festivals). These obser-vances have articulated a clear vision of Israel's identity and purpose. The festival calendar is too coherent and too interwoven with complementary features to have devel-oped its holy days in happenstance fashion; each festival in its timing and meaning is determined by the Torah's account and ac-tually implies the others. Once they appeared, they appeared as a whole. In his outstanding study, *The Jewish Way: Living the Holidays* (New York, 1988), Irving Greenberg argues that the Exodus is the fundamental motif of the festivals. Our study suggests rather that the revelation at Mt. Sinai is at their heart.

The practices of the festivals—Passover: At Passover, the descendants of Jacob to-gether with all others seeking liberation from slavery (a "mixed multitude:" Exod. 12:38, Num. 11:4) went forth out of Egypt, accom-panied by mighty signs and wonders and protected by God. So began the redeemed family or people of Israel. Hence the month in which this happened became the first month in the Jewish year (Exod. 12:2: start-ing the new year in the spring and ground-ing it in a historical event of liberation was a radical innovation in the ancient world). Family observances are the core of the festi-val. Just as the slaves had too little time to prepare properly cooked food for their flight, so for the entire seven or eight days of the festival everyone must eat bread baked too briefly for the yeast to rise, flat *matzah*. No leavened bread may be eaten or other grains associated by custom with leaven (wheat, spelt, rye, barley, oats, and, for Ashkenazi Jews, rice, millet, corn, and legumes). Leaven must be cast out of the home, to make the home participate in the Exodus and its symbolic purgation of slave-like tendencies, the "leaven" in the heart (as midrashic commentaries stress).

Every year at this time there is a thorough spring-cleaning, and the night just before Passover, traditionalist Jews make a special search of the home and property to remove all leavened things; it is collected together and burnt or otherwise disposed of ("sold," for example, to a cooperative non-Jew). Special dishes and utensils are gotten out for Passover, or the usual ones are "kashered," cleansed in a specially intensive way. The dinner itself on the first night of Passover (the first two nights in the diaspora) is filled with symbolic references to the events of the Exodus, in part to arouse the children's curiosity. A special plate on the dinner table contains

objects representing the paschal sacrifice, the bitterness of slavery, etc. These are pointed out and explained in the course of the traditional Passover *Seder* or "Order," which includes a narration of the Exodus followed by the meal, the Grace after Meals, and various songs. The Exodus account is read out from the *Haggadah* or "Narration," an originally Aramaic text almost completely fixed by the end of the Second Temple period; a copy of this *Haggadah*, usually with a vernacular translation, may be put next to each plate. Cushions are provided so that guests may recline like free persons or nobility of antiquity, at least symbolically. There is an extra cup of wine "for Elijah" (the messianic messenger) in addition to those set out for every guest (figs. 36, 106).

The youngest child (in traditional circles, the youngest male) starts the formal narration by chanting the "Four Questions:" why is this night so different from all other nights, with its matzah, reclining on cushions, etc.? The father or other person leading the *seder* then

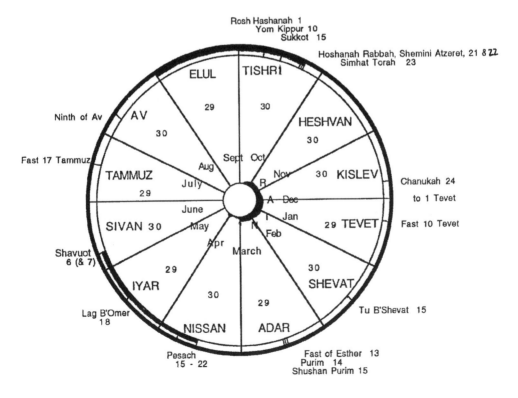

THE ANNUAL CYCLE OF FESTIVALS

responds with the narration of the Haggadah itself. The longer this narration takes and the more interpolations, questions, and comments on the Exodus narrative, the more meritorious the service, according to the liturgy itself. The symbolic and transhistorical nature of the narrative is explicitly emphasized, for as the Haggadah puts it, "Every person in every generation must regard himself as having been personally freed from Egypt" (cf., Deut. 6:20-25).

Spontaneity, informality, and a happy atmosphere are encouraged. Adult celebrants drink four cups of wine (children drink grape juice). There are diversions for the children: the door is opened and Elijah, the forerunner of the messiah, invisibly visits the home to see if all are ready for redemption. Among Ashkenazic Jews the children either spirit away and hide the *Afikomen*, the matzah portion that must be eaten for dessert before the service can conclude, or an adult hides it and they must find it. In any case, for its return the children get a gift of sweets. Among Sephardic Jews, at the start of the service a child knocks on the door with the Afikomen tied to his shoulder, and a dialogue ensues in which the child says he is on his way to Jerusalem, but he agrees to linger for the feast and asks the Four Questions. At the end of the evening there are also boisterous children's songs teaching the main categories of religious faith (*"Ehad mi yodea?"*) or with the deeper religious message that ultimately even death shall be overthrown (*"Had Gadya"*).

The communal historical focus of the festival is very clear: it is the story of the creation and protection of the Jewish people. The salvific miracles that aided the Exodus (the Ten Plagues, the parting of the Red Sea) are emphasized to underline God's direct intervention and grace. Amazingly, but not accidentally, in the Ashkenazi rite there is only one minor reference to Moses. In the Sephardic, there is none. All praise is to God.

The synagogue service the following morning contains the standard festival liturgy and Torah readings from Exod. 12:21-51 and Num. 28:16-25, which command observance of the Passover. After nightfall, during the evening prayer, the first "Counting of the Omer" is recited, a short declaration of how many days remain until Shavuot. In the diaspora the meal this evening repeats the seder of the first night, and the Torah reading on the second morning is Lev. 22:26-23:44, which describes the festivals, including the laws of the Omer. As is usual with festival periods, one may work on the intermediate days of the festival, but they retain a holy character. The Torah is read every day (the passages mostly relate to the commanding of the festival). The seventh day (and the diaspora eighth day) has a greater holiness; work is not allowed, and the synagogue service mirrors those of the first days of Passover. On this day, it is said, the People of Israel crossed the Red Sea, and the Torah portion describing this (Exod. 13:17-15:26) is read (on the eighth day, Deut. 15:19-16:17). *Yizkor*, a memorial service for the dead, is also recited.

The counting of the Omer and Lag B'Omer: In the late spring, less than two months after Passover, falls *Atzeret*, "special assembly," more commonly termed *Shavuot*, the festival of "Weeks" or "Pentecost" (Deut. 16:10-12). The very term underlines its connection with Passover, for it falls "a week of weeks," i.e., seven weeks, plus one day, after Passover. "The counting of the Omer" is in effect a countdown to Shavuot. In ancient times, a measure of newly harvested wheat, referred to as an "omer," was brought to the Temple every day for forty-nine days (Lev. 23:9-16), and the counting is still a part of the evening prayers. It is a period of progressive purgation. Despite the ban on leaven, people eat meat on Passover; but Shavuot is a dairy and vegetarian festival. Through Omer-period abstinences (no new clothes or haircuts, no marriages or setting off on journeys, etc.; the renunciatory emphasis was quite strong in antiquity) Israel rises from one to the other. In fact the first daily gathering of the Omer was of the manna from heaven that sustained the Israelites as they journeyed to Mt. Sinai (Exod. 16:16); as the Torah says (Exod. 16:3-4), it was hard to wean the former slaves from the "flesh-pots of Egypt" and to teach them to prefer the "bread from heaven."

Within these weeks, *Lag B'Omer*, the thirty-third day of the Omer period, is a day of sanctioned release from the prohibitions and so is especially favored for marriages. Hair may be cut, and there is dancing and exuberance (following the geonic custom, the modern Conservative movement allows marriage celebrations any time from Lag B'Omer onwards). Medieval mystics from Sefat in northern Israel began the custom of making joyful pilgrimage to the graves of saints on Lag B'Omer. Because this period is the time of the betrothal of Israel to God, with the Torah itself the wedding covenant, it was already in ancient times the practice to read the Song of Songs during the Sabbath of the Passover festival, and under medieval Kabbalistic influence Sephardic Jews recite the Song of Songs on all the Sabbaths between Passover and Pentecost.

Shavuot: *Shavuot* ("Weeks," "Pentecost") comes on the fiftieth day after the start of the Omer count (Lev. 23:16-21). It marks transcendent completion: just as the week itself is made up of six full work-days, a complete sum in hexagesimal systems, plus one day for transcendence, so fifty is seven times seven, plus one. Moses ascended Mt. Sinai then and returned with the first revelation of the Ten Commandments and some other commandments; Israel accepted the covenantal bond even before learning of all the commandments, saying "We will do them and will listen" (Exod. 24:7). So Shavuot, in addition to being a *Yom Habikkurim* (first-fruits offering, Num. 28:26) or *Hag Hakatzir* (wheat harvest festival: Exod. 23:16, cf., 34:22) represents the moment when essential aspects of the Torah were first revealed at Mt. Sinai. The "first-fruits harvest" is of Torah and of the bounty (crops, etc.) springing from Torah observance.

After the evening service beginning Shavuot, the especially pious stay up all night studying key passages of Torah, so as to be worthy of receiving Torah the next day. The actual liturgy of Shavuot, however, is not much different from other festival days. The Torah readings are from Exod. 19-20, telling of the giving of the Torah, and Num. 28:26-31, commanding the festival. Ezek. 1:1-28 and 3:12, relating the ecstatic vision of God, is the Haftorah. The Book of Ruth, which tells of Ruth's conversion, is also read (on the second day in the diaspora), appropriate on a day commemorating the conversion-like experience of Israel and the "mixed multitude" at Mt. Sinai. King David, from whose line will come the messiah, was a descendant of Ruth, so there may also be a messianic significance in the choice of this work, i.e., that all the world will turn to Judaism eventually. Milk and vegetarian dishes are traditional for Shavuot. The tree branches and plants that bedeck the synagogue at this time are also said to acknowledge that Shavuot is the day the world is judged regarding the fruits of the trees (M. R.H. 1:2). This theme of repentance recalls Sukkot, as does the joyful emphasis on fruits and trees. Interestingly, the Torah does not state explicitly that Shavuot is the "Time of the Gift of our Torah," the Talmudic phrase; as with most other festivals it merely stipulates the working details needed by the priests, namely the precise kinds and numbers of sacrifices that were required.

The summer observances—The Seventeenth of Tamuz: On the seventeenth of Tamuz, the fortieth day after he ascended Sinai, Moses came down with the two tablets of the Torah. Reaching the assembled People of Israel, he saw the Golden Calf and threw down the tablets, splitting them, and spent two days purging the evil from Israel (Exod. 32-33). Then he went up Mt. Sinai again, where he stayed another forty days.

The fast of the Seventeenth of Tamuz recalls the sin of the Golden Calf (cf., M. Ta. 4:6). Following the Babylonian Exile, however, it came to be seen as a fundamental modality of Jewish history, for on or around this day the fortifications around Jerusalem were breached in 586 B.C.E. and again in 70 C.E., preceding the falls of the First and Second Temples (cf., Jer. 39:2 and M. Ta. 4:6). Other catastrophes of the late Second Temple period were associated with this date, and the fast from dawn to dusk recalls and mourns all of them. Pregnant women, nursing mothers, and the sick are exempt from this and all fasts. Working and bathing are permitted, as they are on the other lesser fasts. There are a few relatively minor changes to the regular prayers to underline the penitential significance of the day. Consoling passages from the Torah are read twice, in the morning and in the afternoon services: Exod. 32:11-14, 34:1-10 tells of God's mercy following the incident of the Golden Calf; the Haftorah is Isa. 55:6-56:8, which speaks generally of God's forgiveness to the penitent and of Israel's ultimate redemption.

The Seventeenth of Tamuz is followed by "the Three Weeks," also called the time "between the fences," *Bein Hamatzarim.* This is a period of mourning for the three weeks that elapsed between the breaching of Jerusalem's walls and the fall and burning of both the first and the second Temples, traditionally dated to the Ninth of Av. Weddings are not held then, there is no listening to music, nor dancing, nor pleasure trips; new garments are not worn, new fruits eaten, nor any enterprise started. Restrictions intensify with the coming of the month of Av: the pious neither eat meat nor drink wine (except on Sabbaths) and do not cut their hair. Throughout this period and on the Ninth of Av, no ornaments are worn (in obedience to Exod. 33.4-6, which dictate the proper demeanor of contrition for the sin of the Golden Calf). The three Sabbaths of this period have special Haftarot (Jer. 1:1-2.3; Jer. 2:4-28, 3:4, 4:1-2; Is. 1:1-27), telling of Israel's sins, her punishment, and her restoration to blessings.

The Ninth of Av: The Ninth of Av climaxes this period of mourning. It is the second most important fast in the Jewish year, after only Yom Kippur. As on Yom Kippur, its fast lasts 24-hours, from evening to evening, and work, conjugal relations, and bathing are prohibited. It mourns events that fell around this day, such as the fall of both Temples and of Betar (the last hold-out at the time of the Bar Kokhba messianic uprising), the plowing up of Jerusalem (M. Ta. 4:6), the edict expelling the Jews from England (in

1290), the expulsion of the Jews from Spain in 1492, and even the breaking out of World War I (some say World War II and the Holocaust as well). In the morning service, as a sign of desolation, traditionalists do not wear leather in the synagogue and do not put on a prayer shawl (*Tallit*) or phylacteries (*Tephillin*). In the evening service beginning the fast, following the Amidah and the Kaddish, congregants sit on the ground or on overturned or low stools for the reading of the Book of Lamentations. This is followed by laments, *Kinnot,* describing the sorrows of the centuries. The Kinnot are also recited in mourning postures (e.g., head in hands) after the Torah reading the next morning. The Torah reading is from Deut. 4:25-40, warning of the exile and torment awaiting Israel if it takes up idolatrous ways, and Jer. 8:13-9:23, reinforcing these warnings, is the Haftorah. There is also a repetition of the Torah reading in the afternoon service.

The seven Sabbaths that follow the Ninth of Av are designated Sabbaths of consolation, in which the Haftarot, mostly from Deutero-Isaiah (chapters 40ff.), are progressively more comforting ones; the first lines of each of the Haftarot when read in sequence construct a dialogue between Israel and God in which God responds finally with great love to Israel's desolation and yearning. These seven weeks conclude with the High Holidays. They thus echo on a higher level the seven weeks between Passover and Shavuot and suggest that the whole month of Tishre constitutes a deeper form of the Shavuot experience.

On the Thirtieth of Av, Moses finally returned from seclusion (Exod. 34). The next day is the first of Elul, the beginning of the autumn's 51/52-day cycle.

The month of Elul: During the month of Elul the ram's horn is blown in the synagogue each morning, to urge the pious to deepen their prayers, to examine their deeds, to seek forgiveness from all those they have wronged in the course of the year, and to affirm their affection for those they hold dear. This is a time nowadays to send greeting cards, cakes, etc., to friends and relatives, expressing the hope that they be "inscribed [in the Book of Life] for a good year." It is customary during morning services in Elul to recite *selichot*, penitential prayers, and sometimes also in special midnight services on Saturday nights; Torah-study sessions often accompany the special night-time services. The morning *selichot* on the day before Rosh Hashanah are especially extensive. People may visit the graves of dear ones, and contributions to charities on this day are especially encouraged.

Rosh Hashanah: The High Holidays, Awesome Days, or Days of Awe, *Yamim Noraim*, the ten days begun by Rosh Hashanah and ending with Yom Kippur, are the most important Jewish holy days. Even many laxly observant Jews attend synagogue for the Rosh Hashanah and Yom Kippur services, crowding synagogues to bursting. People wish each other "a good and sweet year," and at Rosh Hashanah meals it is customary to dip bread in honey (rather than salt) and to invoke the hope for a good and sweet year. It is believed that "On Rosh Hashanah all the inhabitants of the world pass before God [in judgment] like a flock of sheep" (M. R.H. 1:2). All are judged on Rosh Hashanah, and the verdict is sealed on Yom Kippur. The worthy are written into the Book of Life, the unworthy blotted out (cf., Exod. 32:32-33) or entered into a Book of Death (sometimes a third book for undecided cases is mentioned). Severe decrees can be averted through repentance, prayer, and deeds of charitable lovingkindness, as the prayers during the Days of Awe repeat like a refrain. During these days worshippers face God in eternity, for he rules past, present, and future. Rosh Hashanah, the first day of the seventh month, was the first Sabbath day of creation, the rabbis taught (B. R.H. 11a). The blowing of the shofar recalls the horn-blasts at Sinai when the Torah was revealed.

The service is dense with historical references. And, as a Day of Judgment, *Yom Hadin*, and Day of Blowing the Shofar, *Yom Hateruyah*, Rosh Hashanah also prefigures the end of days, the Last Judgment, when all souls shall appear before God. The prayers are particularly awesome. The Amidah liturgies on Rosh Hashanah have added to

them lofty prayers given entirely over to the praise of God (these prayers center on *Malchuyot*, celebrating God as creator and king of the universe, *Zichronot*, recalling God's mighty judgments in history, and *Shofarot*, Shofar verses, which celebrate God as future messianic redeemer). The shofar is blown at regular intervals throughout these lengthy prayers, as if awakening the soul to and symbolizing in its sounds all of the implications of Malchuyot, Zichronot, and Shofarot. In the afternoon of Rosh Hashanah, or on the second day if the first day falls on a Sabbath, it is a custom, called *Tashlikh*, "Casting," from the Middle Ages to go to the banks of a river, lake, or ocean, and recite appropriate verses while emptying pockets and symbolically "casting all their sins into the depths of the sea" (Mic. 7:19). The experience of nature at this time adds greater depth to the services and relates them to the cosmos.

Even in the land of Israel, Rosh Hashanah is celebrated for two days, with the second day spent mostly in the synagogue in a repetition of the first day. Work is then permitted during the days that follow up to Yom Kippur. But on these days, regular synagogue services are longer than usual, with penitential prayers recited every morning before regular morning prayers.

It was once customary to fast on each of the ten days until the evening, but in any case the day following Rosh Hashanah is the Fast of Gedaliah, mourning the death of the Governor of Judah whose assassination by a fanatical Jew set in motion the final destruction of the First Commonwealth (2 Kgs. 25:25). This fast therefore presages the coming winter fasts and feasts. However, during the hours just before the evening start of Yom Kippur, the Talmud rules (B. Yom. 81b), one should eat well, in preparation for the twenty-four hour fast and the strenuous praying.

The Sabbath that falls during the intermediate days between Rosh Hashanah and Yom Kippur is called *Shabbat Shuvah*, the Sabbath of Repentance, and the Haftorah (Hos. 14:2-10) begins with the exhortation, *Shuvah Yisrael*, "Return, O Israel." The day before Yom Kippur a medieval custom (*Kapparot*, still followed by ultra-Orthodox) had each person wave about a chicken that was subsequently slaughtered and donated to the poor.

Yom Kippur: *Yom Kippur*, "Day of Atonement-sacrifice," is a total fast (although ill persons and children are exempt). Leather shoes and belts, signs of luxury, are not worn by traditionalists, at least in the synagogue itself, recalling the Temple practice that people left their shoes at the gates (cf., Moses at the Burning Bush, Exod. 3:5) and even more pointedly recalling the prohibitions on ornaments when atoning for the sin of the Golden Calf (Exod. 33:4-6). The prohibitions on work are as strict as those for the weekly Sabbath, and somber abstention and self-examination are emphasized. The first service of Yom Kippur, in the evening, is called *Kol Nidrei*, "All vows," after its opening declaration, which mournfully allows the absolution of vows made to God that one cannot fulfill; by Talmudic law vows made to other people are not annulled. It focuses on the mercifulness of God in contrast to the mere humanity of the congregation. The liturgy that follows is basically that of the evening service for festivals and is fairly brief, but it includes the confession of sins at the end of the Amidah, at which one should beat one's breast (in obedience to a midrashic interpretation of "And the living will lay it to his heart;" Eccles. 7:2). This is the only evening service in the year on which men wear their prayer shawls, otherwise worn only for morning and afternoon prayers.

On Yom Kippur itself the prayers go on throughout the day, adding to the standard daily services numerous prayers, confessional passages, and entire commemorative segments, many dating from the Middle Ages. The Torah readings are of Lev. 16 and Num. 29:7-11, both of which describe the sacrificial offerings of Yom Kippur; the Haftorah is Isa. 57:14-58:14, which emphasizes that fasting and repentance are of no value if they do not produce justice and mercy in actual society. After the Torah reading the Additional service (Musaf) includes a lengthy description (drawn from the Mishnah) of the ceremonies and prayers in the Temple on Yom Kippur, focusing on the confession recited by the High Priest in the Holy of Holies. The person who leads the service at this point imitates the prostrations of the High Priest before the ark; in some synagogues, the entire congregation does the same. Another special addition to the Musaf is a recitation of the martyrdom of Ten Sages of the Talmudic era, for whose sake God will assuredly redeem later generations. *Yizkor*, a memorial service for the dead, is recited. The late afternoon supplications lead up to an intense climax and end at the coming of darkness (*Neilah*). These prayers suggest that with the waning of the light the gates of heaven are slowly closing; these are the last moments when penitential prayers will be heard. As darkness comes, and just as the gates shut, the service concludes with affirmations of God's all-encompassing mercy, unity (the Shema), and glory.

The formality, ascetic exaltation, mournful but also somehow joyful character of the High Holiday observances stand out; all Israel contemplates the heavy burden of their sins and wrong-turnings and repents of them, relying on God's lovingkindness and covenantal pledge. From the perspective of eternity one can see the preciousness, frailty, and transitoriness of our lives. Although the prayers are in the plural and thus relate to the common human condition, they speak to the individual soul. Outside of time, one stands before God sustained by God alone.

Sukkot: "Booths" or "Tabernacles", which falls four days after Yom Kippur, is very much a part of the Days of Awe. Building of the sukkah-tabernacle, it is taught, should begin right after Yom Kippur, and some indeed make the first preparations in the night hours following the end of Yom Kippur. Also called the Festival of Ingathering or even simply "The Festival," Sukkot is a seven day festival beginning on the fifteenth of Tishre. *Shemini Atzeret*, formally a separate holy day, comes at the end and constitutes a biblically ordained additional eighth day. The first two days are full holidays, on which work of most kinds is prohibited, and the five days that follow retain some aspects of the festival. Sukkot is traditionally so strongly associated with joyful celebration (cf., Deut. 16:14-16) that it is often simply called *Zeman simhatenu*, "the season of our rejoicing." The most characteristic trait of the festival is the erecting of temporary booths, open to the sky and usually hung with greenery and fruits. As the Torah states explicitly, this is to remind every generation of the booths in which the Israelites lived after the Exodus (Lev. 23:43). Green boughs are laid across the open rafters, and fruits are often hung from them. The walls too may covered with representations of prosperity and abundance of life.

For the Biblical farmers, this festival was a time for rejoicing in the harvest as a gift from God and anticipating God's mercies in the coming year. As elaborated in the Second Temple period and by the Talmudic rabbis (developing Lev. 23:40), blessings are pronounced in the course of festival prayers in the synagogue over a bundle of three plant branches (the *lulav*) and a large lemon-like fragrant fruit (the *etrog*, citron): the two are held together, waved and shaken in the air, with prayers to assure that their benign influence spreads life and vigor to all the four quarters of the compass (B. Suk. 37b). The four species (citron, palm branch, myrtle, and willow) are associated with flowing waters and the coming of life-giving rains. They symbolize all vegetable life (some Talmudic era sages also saw in the lulav bundle a representation of the organic unity of all sectors of the Jewish people or of the human body: Pesikta Rabbati 51.2; Lev. Rab. 30:14, etc.). The synagogue is decked in green branches, and there are prayers for rain to come as a blessing to the earth and its inhabitants everywhere. Indeed, in the land of Israel Sukkot comes just before the season of the rains. These prayers are said to benefit the entire world, and the universal thrust of this festival is shown in the fact that on it, when the Temple still stood, sacrifices for the seventy nations of humanity were offered up. Rain is associated in the liturgy and in the Torah with the blessings of life bestowed by God. Torah itself is likened to rain.

The Book of Ecclesiastes, with its emphasis on the universal rhythms of nature, is read on the Sabbath of the intermediate days, or on Shemini Atzeret if it falls on a Sabbath. The Sabbath Torah reading is Exod. 33:12-34:36, ordaining the festival, and the Haftorah is Ezek. 31:18-39:16, because of a tradition that the victory at Armageddon, marking the beginning of the messianic age, will take place on Sukkot. The lulav and etrog are waved and chants praising God are sung when the Torah is taken out. Those holding lulav and etrog follow the reader who carries the Torah around the Bimah, in a procession. The rustlings of the branches, the chants, and the procession create a joyful atmosphere (fig. 29).

On Hoshana Rabba, the seventh day of Sukkot, there are seven processions around the synagogue, with people waving bunches of willow branches mingling with those carrying all the synagogue's Torah scrolls. The name *Hoshana Rabba* developed in the Middle Ages and refers both to the willow branches themselves and to the long drawn-out chants made during these processions, pleading for God's mercies. By the later Middle Ages, Hoshana Rabba was regarded as a lesser Yom Kippur.

Shemini Atzeret-Simhat Torah: On *Shemini Atzeret* ("Eighth Day of Special Assembly") in the diaspora there is no procession, since this day is considered in a formal sense to be its own festival, separate from Tabernacles, but on *Simhat Torah* ("Rejoicing in the Torah;" in the diaspora, Simhat Torah is a separate day following Shemini Atzeret), the Torah scrolls are again taken out and people dance around the synagogue with them. Sometimes the processions spill into the streets (fig. 30). In Israel the celebrations of Shemini Atzeret and Simhat Torah are combined. On Shemini Atzeret the Torah reading is the same as on the eighth day of Passover, Deut. 14:22-16:17, describing the sabbatical year of liberation and renewal, and the festivals; the Maftir is Num. 29:35-30:1. The Haftorah (1 Kgs. 8:54-66) relates King Solomon's blessing upon the people at the conclusion of his consecration of the Temple, at the time of Sukkot-Tabernacles. The prayer for rain is inserted in the Musaf, corresponding to the prayer for dew that is said on the first day of Passover; the prayer is recited in a plaintive melody, since this day is still a kind of day of judgment. Shemini Atzeret is said to mark the beginning of the rainy season in Israel. The sense of new beginnings is enhanced still further by the practice on Simhat Torah of calling up honored members of the congregation to read the last sections of the Pentateuch (concluding the annual cycle of readings) and the first section of the Pentateuch (to start the annual cycle anew). These people are hailed as the "bridegrooms" of the Torah. They are often honored at parties afterward. The reading of the first chapter of Genesis makes the sense of cosmic renewal and regeneration all the stronger: this is the time of Eden and the fusion of heaven and earth.

In the Bible, the Jubilee, or fiftieth, year, a period of cosmic restoration and renewal in which the entire land returns to God, began on Yom Kippur and had its immediate actualization in Tabernacles.

The winter period—the Fast of the Tenth of Tevet: As if in immediate response to the autumn period's supplications and celebrations, sometimes during Sukkot itself the rains commence and in Israel the temperature rapidly drops. The winter is a surprisingly chilly, dark period of frequent heavy rains. But the fields soon turn green, and flowers appear. The festival calendar reflects this contrast of outer darkness but inner light and life by focusing its special winter observances on post-Exilic history, during which Israel bears the Torah through the dark wilderness of the world. The only biblically ordained fast-day of this season, the fast-day of the tenth of Tevet, recalls the day in 589 B.C.E. on which the army of Nebuchadnezzar, emperor of Babylonia, surrounded Jerusalem, commencing the siege that ended three years later with Jerusalem's fall and the Babylonian Exile (cf., 2 Kgs. 25:1). The fast thus mourns the beginning of diasporic existence, the "wanderings in the wilderness." The chief festivals of this period are the "minor feasts" of Hanukkah and Purim, instituted in the Second Temple era.

These celebrate miraculous redemptions in the face of persecution and give a sustaining confidence in God's presence despite Exile and other torments of history.

Hanukkah: *Hanukkah* ("Dedication") is an eight day festival starting on the twenty-fifth of Kislev (usually around mid-December). It is a "minor" festival (i.e., it is not biblically instituted, although some Rabbinic authorities link it to the building of the Tabernacle; Yalkut Melachim 184), but because it is the first joyous celebration to occur during the long winter months and is oriented towards children, it has always been fondly regarded. It commemorates the restoration of Temple worship by the Hasmoneans, who rebelled against the Seleucid empire that had prohibited practice of Judaism. The rededication of the Temple was the most triumphant, seemingly miraculous, moment in the Hasmonean creation of a Jewish commonwealth in Judea, around 166 B.C.E. The cleansing and partial reconstruction of the Temple took eight days, which gave rise to the Talmudic story that a day's supply of pure oil miraculously burned for eight days, supplying the Temple's eternal light until additional proper oil could be made. Hanukkah is not much noted in the prayer service; there is an insertion into the Amidah during Hanukkah of a brief grateful reference to the "miracles and wonders" God bestowed upon his people. This is also included in the Grace after Meals during those days. The Torah portion, parts of which are read each day of Hanukkah, is Num. 7, which tells of the gifts the princes of Israel brought at the dedication of the Tabernacle in the wilderness. Hallel is also recited in the daily service, and each night special blessings accompany the candle or lamp lighting. An additional light is lit each night, until by the last night eight lights are burning (plus the central *shamas* light, used to ignite the others).

The real celebration of Hanukkah is in the home. The candle-lighting ritual, for example, seems to have spread from the home into the synagogue. The Hanukkah lights are placed near to windows, so that their illumination shines in the darkness (figs. 31, 32). Although not obligatory, special festive meals are customary among the pious, with discourse on Torah themes and miraculous deliverances. Songs generally follow the lamp-lighting at home, especially the song *Maoz tzur*, "Rock of Ages," emphasizing trust in God's salvations, and other songs equating light and Torah. Sweets and coins (often including chocolates in the form of coins but bearing on their face Torah symbols) and in recent generations gifts of toys are distributed to children. Distinctive games are played by the children, most notably those centering on the *dreidel*, a spinning top each face of which contains a Hebrew letter or word relating to the miraculous salvations of God.

Ten days after Hanukkah occurs the Fast of the Tenth of Tevet, already mentioned. And mid-way through the next month of Shevat there is *Tu B'Shevat* ("Fifteenth of Shevat"), the "New Year for trees" (a reference to fruit-tithing practices when the Temple still stood), which has no special synagogue observance. It is customary at this time to eat a fruit not yet enjoyed that year, hopefully a fruit from the land of Israel, so that one can recite the blessing *Shehecheyanu*, thanking God for allowing one to reach this season. Many people like to walk in the forest at this time.

Purim: *Purim* ("Lots," as in "casting lots") is the other significant celebration of the winter months. It really involves two days: the Fast of Esther on the thirteenth of Adar and Purim itself on the fourteenth; in a few communities in Israel a third day, *Shushan Purim*, is celebrated on the fifteenth, in which the Purim reading of the *Megillah* (the Book of Esther in handwritten parchment scroll form) is repeated. It is interesting that on the Sabbath before Purim (*Shabbat Zachor*, "Sabbath of Remembrance") two Torah scrolls are taken from the Ark; from one the congregation reads the regular weekly portion, and from the other is read the passage including the line, "Remember what Amalek did to you" (Deut. 25:17-19). The Haftorah is from 1 Sam. 15:1-34, explaining that kingship was grudgingly allowed to the Jewish people, as a defensive measure against Amalekites. So the point is made clearly that Purim involves the relationship between Israel and the Amalekites of history, the rabid antisemites.

Purim specifically commemorates a great deliverance of the Jewish people in the Persian empire during the Second Commonwealth, but beyond the account in the Book of Esther, we know nothing about the actual precipitating events, not even their century (probably the fourth B.C.E.). Nevertheless, Purim and the synagogue reading of the Megillah had attained general inclusion in the festival calendar by late in the Second Commonwealth, and the Fast of Esther remains the only non-biblical fast to be universally observed among pious Jews. The Fast of Esther, like all other fasts except for the Ninth of Av and Yom Kippur, is a relatively short daylight hours fast. It is customary to give generously to charity on this day, and indeed throughout the Purim period, for uniting the community in love and winning God's favor is a chief way to counter one's enemies ("the Amalekites"). Gifts, including gifts of food (*mishloach manot*, "sending portions"), are also sent to friends and relatives on Purim, and they are especially given to children, who are Israel's future. On Purim itself, the Megillah is read twice in the synagogue, in the evening service just before the Alenu, and in the following morning service after the Torah reading, usually to raucous noise-making each time the name of Haman, the imperial advisor who wished to have all Jews killed, is mentioned. Often special noisemakers called *graggers* or *clackers* are used, a custom from the Middle Ages.

Children are given sweets, and there are festive meals, which include meat and wine. Some however stress vegetarian meals, claiming that Esther kept such a diet to avoid eating non-kosher food. The main meal is supposed to be on Purim starting very early, right after the afternoon (Minchah) service, and it should extend well into the night. This is the only festival of the year in which one is actually encouraged by Talmudic rulings to get drunk, or at least tipsy enough so that one cannot distinguish between Haman and Mordecai (the Jewish advisor to the emperor who together with Esther thwarted Haman). In many respects Purim is about release, informality, and the ambiguous blurring of boundaries. Authority and priggishness are lampooned. Late medieval celebrations, influenced by carnival celebrations among non-Jews, even included Purim comedies in which men dressed as women and women dressed as men, something otherwise strictly forbidden. One still sometimes sees this, and even in the modern period children often dress up as adults on this day, act out comic and mocking plays (usually based on the Purim story), and parade about in the streets (figs. 33-35).

Modern additions to the festival calendar: The soul-shattering and -exalting events of the twentieth century, the Holocaust and the establishment of the State of Israel, have added two new days to the festival calendar, although there is still some controversy about their observance. In particular the time and contents of Holocaust Remembrance Day, *Yom Hashoah*, have been debated. Some ultra-Orthodox, maintaining that the Holocaust was merely another of the terrible tribulations of history Jews have suffered in some part for their own sins, wish to merge its observance with the Ninth of Av. Others want to assign it to the winter months, and perhaps stress the Suffering Servant theme: not for Israel's sins but because of the world's hostility to the People of God did Israel suffer. But the official Israeli observance is on the twenty-seventh of Nisan, following Passover. In the diaspora, April 19 is often chosen. The datings refer to the April 19, 1943, start or 27 Nisan "ending" of the Warsaw Ghetto Uprising, whose spirit of undaunting resistance to unjust persecution underlies the State of Israel today. Memorial speeches and the closing of entertainment centers are the chief observances. Liturgical forms are still fluid.

Yom Haatzmaut, Israel's "Independence Day," falls on the fifth of Iyyar, the month after Nisan, on the day in 1948 that Israel declared its formal establishment. The previous day in Israel is *Yom Hazikaron*, the Day of Remembrance of all those who fell in the fight to create and then to defend the state. Candles are lit in the synagogue, and yizkor is recited along with other mourning prayers. In the afternoon, sirens sound throughout the state, and all movement halts for a few minutes of mourning. Yom Haatzma'ut follows, and the mood changes to one of celebration. Hallel may be recited in the synagogue, and there are festive meals.

Bibliography

Goodman, Philip, *The Sukkot and Simhat Torah Anthology* (Philadelphia, 1973).

Greenberg, Irving, *The Jewish Way: Living the Holidays* (New York, 1988).

Knobel, Peter, *Gates of the Seasons* (New York, 1983).

Kitov, Eliyahu, *The Book of Our Heritage* (New York, 1978).

Zuesse, Evan, "The Jewish Year," in *Australian Journal of Jewish Studies*, 7, no. 1, 1993, and 8, nos. 1-2, 1994.

Notes

[1] Since the Talmudic period, aside from the recitation of Hallel and special Musaf prayers, there remains little that is different about the service, but from the 1970s Rosh Hodesh observances have again been developed by some women's groups to provide celebration of women's spirituality.

[2] Of lesser note is Tu B'Shevat which marks the new year for trees and the first of Elul when cattle are tithed (M. R.H. 1:1).

[3] For a detailed account of the practices of each of the festivals, see below.

[4] Strangely enough, the actual festival is very brief and simple considering that the revelation of Torah is central to Judaism; why this is we shall discuss below.

[5] The legend that there are thirty-six intercessors with God evidently has Mosaic roots, for during this period, according to the Torah, Moses was up on the mountain interceding with God for Israel; cf., Exod. 32-34; also note Num. 14:11-20.

EVAN ZUESSE

CHARITY IN JUDAISM: The charitable donation of money, goods, or services to the needy is understood in both secular and religious cultures to be a free tribute, given out of the liberality of one person to help in the support of another. People accordingly associate charity with generosity and comprehend it primarily to be an act of free will, in which one individual makes a personal decision to help another who is in need. Judaism, especially in modern times, comparably, recognizes the personal choices involved in decisions regarding when to give, how much to give, and to whom to give. Referring to charity by the Hebrew word *Tzedakah* ("righteousness") as well as by the term *Gemilut Hasadim* ("the bestowing of kindness"), Judaism acknowledges the free will aspect of charity and the extent to which it represents a special act of human kindness. At the same time, at its foundation, Judaism views supporting the needy to be a duty imposed upon each person under the terms of the covenant with God. Unlike secular notions that see in charity only an act of individual free will, under Jewish law, individuals are obligated to provide for the needy. By legislating a system of social welfare run by the community, Jewish law dictates standards of support and assures that individuals and communities will provide for the basic needs of all members of society.

Charity in the Hebrew Bible: Judaism's view of charity as an obligation emerges from the idea first expressed in the Hebrew Bible that God created the world and therefore has a claim upon all that it produces. This claim is expressed, for instance, in the understanding that the first produce of each season's crop (Exod. 23:19) as well as specific portions of all that is harvested belong to God.[1] God's claim upon the produce is satisfied, in part, when specific portions are given in support of the poor, widows, orphans, strangers, and others who have a special dependence upon God for sustenance. Scripture thus assigns to the poor that which grows in the corner of a field ("*peah*;" Lev. 19:9, 23:22), gleanings ("*leqet*;" Lev. 19:9, 23:22), forgotten sheaves ("*shikhah*;" Deut. 24:19), a tithe in each third year ("*maaser ani*;" Deut. 14:28-29), separated grapes ("*peret*;" Lev. 19:10), defective clusters ("*olelot*;" Lev. 19:10, Deut. 24:21), and all of the produce of the Sabbatical year (Exod. 23:11). Through these tithes and other agricultural offerings, the poor are maintained directly out of that which, in the first place, is understood to belong to God.

The earliest forms of support for the poor in Israelite religion thus do not comprise what commonly would refer to as "charity" at all. In Scripture, rather, support for the needy takes the form of obligatory transfers of food to the poor. Through these payments the farmer satisfies his debt to God for God's participation in the production of the crop, through the provision, for instance, of the land, sun, and rain. Alongside this aspect of support for the poor, Scripture further details the obligation that people of means provide those who are in need with loans, which normally are to be repaid. The extent to which such loans are understood to be charitable, however, is reflected in the rule for how people are expected to behave when the Sabbatical year, in which all loans of money are canceled, is approaching (Deut. 15:7-11):

> If there is among you a poor man, one of your brethren, in any of your towns within your land which the Lord your God gives you, you shall not harden your heart or shut your hand against your poor brother, but you shall open your hand to him, and lend him sufficient for his need, whatever it may be. Take heed lest there be a base thought in your heart, and you say, "The seventh year, the year of release is near," and your eye be hostile to your poor brother, and you give him nothing, and he cry to the Lord against you, and it be sin in you. You shall give to him freely, and your heart shall not be grudging when you give to him; because for this the Lord your God will bless you in all your work and in all that you undertake. For the poor will never cease out of the land; therefore I command you, you shall open wide your hand to your brother, to the needy and to the poor, in the land.

The passage makes a number of important points. The first is to make explicit the Israelite understanding that the existence of needy people is not a deviation from the order of the world as God created it but is, rather, part of the created order. People cannot therefore blame the poor themselves for their predicament or propose that society has no responsibility for them. Rather, God ordered the world in such a way that there always will be people in need, and God also mandated that, to meet that need, people of means must provide support.

The second point is that this support is not defined as what we usually think of as charity, that is, as a free gift for which repayment is not anticipated. Rather, the passage suggests that support for the poor normally is in the form of a loan that in due course will be repaid. The passage, however, adds the important point that such loans must be made even though the coming Sabbatical Year will cancel them. Thus, while monetary support for the poor normally is repaid, even when it will not be, such support must be given. Even though, in the Israelite conception, supporting the needy may look like a business transaction—a loan to be repaid—it is not. Supporting the poor is, rather, an act of compliance with the covenant that has little to do with free will and everything to do with the fulfillment of one's obligations to God.

Third, the passage introduces a conception that becomes extremely important in the development of the Jewish theory of charity, that free and ungrudging support of the poor brings in return special blessings from God. Even though aiding the poor is a religious requirement and, especially in Talmudic times, is formalized in a system of communal welfare supported by taxation, those who are profligate and whole-hearted in their giving earn special merit in the eyes of God.

Charity in the Rabbinic literature: The rabbis develop the several aspects of support of the poor introduced in Scripture: they spend considerable time developing a sophisticated system of procedures through which Scripture's agricultural offerings are to be distributed to and used by the poor, and they supplement this system of tithes and loans by developing rules for a community chest and other charitable organizations. The rabbis additionally explore the reasons for the existence of poverty and discuss the nature of the obligation to alleviate the problems presented by the existence of needy people. Finally, they detail the way in which giving charity affects God's relationship with the Israelite people, and they describe the rewards that God grants to individuals who are particularly generous.

The fundamental question of whether or not people should in fact care for the poor receives attention. If, as Deut. 15:10-11 states, God intentionally created a class of needy people, one might question whether or not it is in any event the prerogative of others to support, and so change the cir-

cumstance of, these individuals. Perhaps doing so is comparable to lessening a punishment imposed by God. This issue is explored in a Talmudic story about a dispute between Aqiba and a gentile philosopher (B. B.B. 10a):

A. The wicked Turnus Rufus asked R. Aqiba, "If your God loves the poor, how come he does not provide for them?"

B. He said to him, "It is so that through them we ourselves may be saved from the judgment of Gehenna."

C. [Turnus Rufus] said to him, "To the contrary! That is precisely what makes you liable to the sentence of Gehenna. I shall provide you with a parable. To what is the matter to be likened? To the case of a mortal king who was angry with his servant and put him in prison and gave orders not to feed him or give him drink. But somebody came along and gave him food and drink. When the king heard, would he not be angry with him? And you people are called servants: 'For to me the children of Israel are servants' (Lev. 25:55)."

D. Said to him R. Aqiba, "I shall provide you with a parable [proving the contrary]. To what is the matter to be compared? To the case of a mortal king who grew angry with his son and threw him into prison and gave orders not to feed him or give him drink. But somebody came along and gave him food and drink. When the king heard, will he not send a gift to him? And we are called sons: 'Sons are you to the Lord your God' (Deut. 14:1)."

E. [Turnus Rufus] said to him, "Well, you are called sons, and you are called servants. When you do the will of the Omnipresent, you are called sons, but when you do not do the will of the Omnipresent, you are called servants. And now [in giving charity] you are not doing the will of the Omnipresent!"

F. [Aqiba] said to him, "Lo, Scripture says [Is. 58:7, referring to the 'fast' that God desires], 'Is it not to deal your bread to the hungry and to bring the poor who are cast out to your house?' When should you 'bring the poor who are cast out to your house'? Now! And it says, 'Is [what I want] not to deal your bread to the hungry?'"

Aqiba makes a number of important points regarding the nature and purpose of charity and the status of the Israelites before God. The central point is that the people of Israel are like "sons" of God, not servants. This means that whatever God does to the people is done out of love and that God, accordingly, would prefer that all his people were well cared for. Thus, even though God has created a world in which there is poverty, he actually desires that no one be in need. From this emerges the passage's second point, that giving charity is both a social and religious obligation, a means of maintaining the community while fulfilling God's desires. The final issue introduces the conception we already encountered at Deut. 15:7-11, concerning why, if God indeed means for the poor to be supported, he does not himself provide that support. The answer to this appears at B: The opportunity to care for the poor provides a chance to improve one's merit before God. In providing for the poor, Israelites act on behalf of God, distributing God's share of the earth's produce to those God designated for its benefit. Foregoing one's own wealth to act as God's agent brings a reward, the merit that saves one from Gehenna.

Support for the poor in the Mishnah and Tosefta: The idea that one who gives charity acts on behalf of God is expressed clearly in the Mishnah, which elaborates the law for the payment to the poor of the agricultural tithes listed in Scripture. At the heart of the Mishnah's conception is that, in leaving gifts for the poor, one does not act primarily out of generosity of spirit. Rather the Mishnah's authorities comprehend the payment of gifts to the poor as a transfer of produce directly from God to the needy. These gifts are foods over which the individual farmer has no claim of ownership in the first place, so that their designation for the poor is not a matter of a free will gift at all. It is, rather, a procedure through which the farmer allows the needy to take that which is understood to be theirs in the first place.

Mishnah Peah makes this clear when it details the rules for distribution to the poor of produce that grows in the corner of the field and is left unharvested, gleanings, and forgotten sheaves. The rabbis' central principle is that the farmer may play no active role in setting aside the specific portions of produce for the poor. Rather, the produce for the poor is identified as that which gets left behind accidentally, when the farmer leaves some grain unharvested, drops a few stalks in the field, or forgets to collect some of the sheaves. Since, in Rabbinic Judaism, that which happens unintentionally is associated with the will of God, the Mishnah's view of the payment of poor offerings suggests a recognition of the poors' direct claim upon God for support. God owns the land and hence has a right to all that grows on it. Those portions of food that the farmer "accidentally" leaves behind are understood to have been designated directly by God for the needy.

Alongside agricultural gifts, in the increasingly urban society of the period of the Mishnah, other methods of providing for the community's poor were developed, such that, by the third century C.E., the poor were supported through a number of community institutions. Among these was a community chest that provided indigent townspeople and travelers with provisions and clothing appropriate to their particular circumstance and in relation to the amount of time they had been or would be in the community (T. Pe. 4:8-15). All needy people were entitled to sufficient food for a week. Local residents and those who had been in the area for a month additionally received clothing as required, and, after six months in the community, a homeless person was entitled to shelter as well. Alongside the community chest, a soup kitchen provided food on a day-to-day basis.

As in the case of the agricultural gifts, the community chest and soup kitchen were not funded as charities through free will offerings. Rather, in line with the ideology that holds charity to be a religious responsibility, funds to maintain the institutions of public welfare derived from a tax levied on all residents who had been in the community for a year. Indeed, in light of this communal approach to supporting the poor, the Mishnah holds that householders are not obligated to offer provisions or money to beggars who go door-to-door. Judaism in this way views the support of the poor not primarily as an individual decision, in which one acts out of generosity when confronted with a particular case of need. Rather, support of the poor is a corporate responsibility of the community, which is charged under the law with looking after the welfare of all permanent and temporary residents.

Charity in the Talmud: In Talmudic times, the development of a cash economy, the inaccessibility of farm lands to most poor people, and the fact that most Jews lived outside of the land of Israel, in areas in which the biblical system of agricultural offerings did not apply, led to the growth of community chests and others methods of support for the poor. As a result, Talmudic Judaism developed new and intricate procedures for maintaining the needy, and the rabbis expected all members of the community actively to assure that the poor were fed and clothed. Alongside this development of specific procedures for collecting and distributing welfare, the theological significance of individual support of the poor was elaborated. What emerged was a focus on the merit earned through supporting the poor, a sense of value encapsulated in the Rabbinic notion that the giving of charity, along with repentance for sins, is a person's greatest advocate before God (B. Shab. 32a).

This concept of the merit earned through the giving of charity is expressed in a series of passages at B. B.B. 10a. Many of these examples depend upon the rabbis' association of the Hebrew term translated "righteousness" with giving charity in particular:

36.A. It has been taught on Tannaite authority:

B. Said R. Eleazar b. R. Yose, "Every act of charity and mercy that Israelites do in this world brings about peace and great reconciliation between Israel and their father in heaven: 'Thus says the Lord, do not enter into the house of mourning, nor go to lament, nor bemoan them, for I have taken away my peace from this people . . . even loving kindness and tender mercies' (Jer. 16:4)—loving kindness refers to acts of mercy, and 'tender mercies' to charity."

37.A. It has been taught on Tannaite authority:

B. R. Judah says, "Great is charity, for it draws redemption nearer: 'Thus says the Lord, keep judgment and do righteousness [charity], for my salvation is near to come and my righteousness to be revealed' (Is. 56:1)."

C. He would say, "Ten strong things have been created in the world. Rock is strong, iron shatters it. Iron is strong, fire melts it. Fire is strong, water quenches it. Water is strong, clouds carry it. Clouds are strong, wind scatters them. Wind is strong, the body can withstand it. The body is strong, fear crushes it. Fear is strong, wine overcomes it. Wine is strong, sleep removes it. Death is strongest of all, but charity saves from death: 'Righteousness delivers from death' (Prov. 10:2)."

38.A. Expounded R. Dosetai b. R. Yannai, "Come and note that the trait of the Holy One, blessed be he, is not like the trait of a mortal. If someone brings a splendid gift to the king, it may or may not be accepted from him, and should it be accepted from him, he may or may not see the king. But the Holy One, blessed be he, is not that way. Someone gives a penny to a poor person, and he has the merit of receiving the face of the Presence of God: 'And I shall behold your face in righteousness, I shall be satisfied when I awake with your likeness' (Ps. 17:15)."

39.A. R. Eleazar would give a penny to a poor man and then go and recite the [statutory] prayer, in line with the verse, "And I shall behold your face in righteousness" (Ps. 17:15).

Charity reconciles Israel with God, bringing redemption. In this regard it can be said that charity actually saves from death. It is an act of "righteousness" that allows one to "see God's face," that is, to have such contact with God that one's prayers are particularly efficacious and that one receives from God special rewards.

The saving power of charity was understood not simply in a metaphorical or eschatological sense, as one of the human acts that advance the coming of the messianic age. Rather, as the following passage makes clear, the merit of giving to those in need was understood to accrue to the individual's own personal store of blessings from God (B. B.B. 11a):

47.A. It has been taught on Tannaite authority:
   B. They said concerning Benjamin the righteous that he was in charge of the charity fund. One time a woman came before him during years of famine. She said to him, "My lord, take care of me."
   C. He said to her, "By the Temple service! There is nothing in the charity fund."
   D. She said to him, "My lord, if you don't take care of me, lo, there is a woman [that is, me] and her seven sons who are going to die."
   E. He went and took care of her out of his own property.
   F. After some days he fell ill and was tending toward death. The ministering angels said before the Holy One, blessed be he, "Lord of the world, you have said, 'Whoever preserves a single Israelite life is as though he had preserved a whole world,' and Benjamin the righteous kept alive a woman and her seven sons, so should he die after so few years?"
   G. Forth with they tore up the decree concerning him.
   H. A Tannaite statement: they added twenty-two years to his life.

Along with defining the power of the merit that derives from giving charity, the passage reflects the broader communal attitude towards support for the poor in the Talmudic period. The expectation was that the poor would be supported out of the community chest, with funds collected through the system of taxation. Only the inability of this fund to support a particular needy person leads Benjamin to give charity out of his own resources. This was a supererogatory act of righteousness, for which he was found to be particularly meritorious and deserving of reward.

Many passages concern the appropriate manner of giving. The point, expressed many times at B. B.B. 11a, is that one must not give charity for self-aggrandizing purposes. It should, rather, be an act of giving of one's own substance solely for the benefit of others. This leads to the conclusion that the most

meritorious act of charity is anonymous, as B. Ket. 67b illustrates:

10.A. There was a poor man in Mar Uqba's neighborhood, into whose door-socket he anonymously would toss four *zuz* a day. Once the man thought, "I'll go and see who is doing me this goodness."
   B. On that day Mar Uqba was late at the school house, and his wife was coming home with him; when the man saw them moving the door, he went out after them.
   C. They ran away from him and jumped into a furnace from which the fire had just been swept out.
   D. Mar Uqba's feet started to burn.
   E. His wife said to him, "Raise your feet and put them on mine."
   F. He was upset [that she merited divine protection from the hot oven while he did not]. [To explain] she said to him, "I'm usually home, so what I give is direct" [that is, a gift in kind; Mar Uqba by contrast gave money, which brings only indirect help].
   G. So why did they go to so much trouble anyhow?
   H. It is in line with what Mar Zutra bar Tubiah said Rab said, and some say, said R. Huna bar Bizna said R. Simeon the Pious, and some say, said R. Yohanan in the name of R. Simeon b. Yohai, "It would be better for someone to throw himself into a heated furnace than embarrass someone else in public.
   I. "How do we know this? From the case of Tamar: 'when she was brought forth, she sent to her father-in-law' (Gen. 38:24)."

The passage makes two separate points. First, Mar Uqba felt it better to risk his own life by jumping into a hot oven than to compromise the humility with which he had been daily giving charity. The thanks he would receive when recognized as the donor would have lessened the degree of selflessness that the giving of charity was meant to entail. Second, the highest level of merit is earned by giving food or other goods that directly meet the poors' needs. Mar Uqba's wife earned greater merit than did he, since she gave food she had prepared, while he gave only money. As a result, her feet, but not his, were protected from the oven's hot floor.

Despite the tremendous rewards earned by giving charity, the benefits of giving were to be balanced by the need to maintain one's own estate and not to become dependent upon others (B. Ket. 67b; see also B. Ket. 50a):

> 12.A. When Mar Uqba was dying, he said, "Bring me my account books for charity." He found written, "Seven thousand gold *dinars* of Sianaq." He said, "The provisions are scanty and the way is long." He went and donated half of his entire estate to the poor.
>
> B. But how could he act in such a way? And did not R. Ilai say, "In Usha they ordained: he who distributes his wealth to the poor should not give away more than a fifth of his estate"?
>
> C. That is the case when one is alive, lest he lose his money [and himself become dependent on charity], but after death, there is no objection to one's doing so with his estate.

Rabbinic Judaism thus differs from the attitude of certain Essene writings found at Qumran and from that expressed by the early Christian community, which advocated divestment of all of one's earthly possessions as a way of entering the spiritual realm. Compare, for instance, the statement at Mat. 19:21: "Jesus said to him, 'If you would be perfect, go, sell what you possess and give to the poor, and you will have treasure in heaven; and come, follow me.'" The rabbis, by contrast, balanced the need to support the poor—viewed, as we have seen, largely as a communal and not an individual obligation— with responsibility to one's self and family— viewed as one's primary duty, the proper fulfillment of which itself was deemed worthy in the eyes of God.

Despite the concern that people not give away that which they needed themselves, the seriousness of the obligation to give charity was such that, while Rabbinic authorities were careful not to give to those who were not in need, they preferred that this would happen on occasion than that they would fail to give to someone who was truly needy (B. Ket. 67b):

> 13.A. R. Abba would bind up money in his scarf, sling it over his back, and make himself available to the poor [who would take the money quietly]. But he kept a sharp eye out for frauds.
>
> 14.A. There was a poor man near R. Hanina, to whom he would regularly send four *zuz* every Friday. One day he sent the money through his wife, who came home and said to him, "He doesn't need you."
>
> B. He said to her, "What did you see?"
>
> C. She said, "I heard that people said to him, 'On what do you want to eat, on silver cloth or gold cloth?'"
>
> D. He said, "That's in line with what R. Eleazar said, 'We have to be grateful to frauds, for if it weren't for them, we would sin every day: "And he cry unto the Lord against you and it be sin unto you" (Deut. 15:9).'"
>
> 15.A. R. Hiyya bar Rab of Difti set forth as a Tannaite statement: "R. Joshua b. Qorhah says, 'Whoever hides his eyes from the needs of philanthropy is as though he worships idols. Here it is written, "Beware that there not be a base thought in your heart and your eye will be evil against your poor brother" (Deut. 14:9), and with regard to idolatry, "Certain base fellows are gone out" (Deut. 13:14). Just as there the ultimate sin is idolatry, so here, idolatry is involved.'"

The three units together make the central point. One should be careful not to give to those who are not needy. But making such a gift is preferable to possibly failing to support someone who really is in need. For one is obligated to fulfill what is required by Deut. 15:9, that one give to *whoever* cries out for support. The reason is made clear in the final unit. The appearance of the word "base" in the context of support for the poor and in a description of those who worship idols proves that failure to give charity is itself comparable to idol worship.[2]

Charity in the medieval period: The theology of charity as it develops in Judaism in the medieval period is summarized clearly by the thirteenth century Sefer Hasidim:[3]

> As God gives riches to the wealthy and does not give to the poor, he gives to the one sufficient to sustain a hundred—The poor come and cry to God: you gave to this one sufficient to sustain a thousand and yet he is unwilling to give me charity. [Accordingly] God punishes the rich man as though he had

robbed many poor; he is told, "I gave you riches so that you could give according to the ability of your riches to the poor, ant you did not give. [Thus] I shall punish you as though you had robbed them, and you had repudiated My pledge, for I gave you riches that you might divide them among the poor and you appropriated them for yourself."

The rich are charged with distributing their wealth as demanded by the (divine) rules of social justice and equality. While the medieval Jewish community developed sophisticated systems of social welfare, in this theory, the ultimate responsibility of caring for the poor and needy devolved first and foremost upon the individual: people of means were commanded to use their resources to support those in need. Failure to do so not only disgraced one in the social and communal sphere. It further comprised a failure to adhere to God's demands and therefore was a serious sin, a violation of the covenant punishable exactly like other violations of God's law.

Similar in perspective to the statement of the Sefer Hasidim, Maimonides' *Mishneh Torah* (Book 7, Chapter 10) presents one of the most complete and well known medieval formulations of the specific rules for giving and receiving charity. Maimonides' larger point regarding the nature of charity is in line with the Rabbinic perspective with which we already are familiar. Charity is not simply a tax imposed upon the wealthy. It is, rather, a religious obligation, the fulfillment of which depends not primarily upon the physical distribution of the alms but, more importantly, upon the mental attitude of the individual who offers the donation. To give charity in the proper way is an aspect of righteousness before God, bringing to the donor manifold rewards. The complete text of Maimonides' statement is as follows:[4]

1. We are obligated to be more scrupulous in fulfilling the commandment of charity than any other positive commandment, because charity is the sign of the righteous man, the seed of Abraham our Father, as it is said, "For I know him, that he will command his children . . . to do righteousness" (Gen. 18:19). The throne of Israel is established and the religion of truth is upheld only through charity, as it is said, "In righteousness shall you be established" (Is. 54:14). Israel is redeemed only through charity, as it is written, "Zion shall be redeemed with judgment and they that return of her with righteousness" (ibid. 1:27).

2. No man has ever become impoverished by giving charity and no evil or damage has ever resulted from charity, as it is said, "and the work of righteousness is peace" (Is. 32:17).

   Whosoever displays mercy to others will be granted mercy himself, as it is said, "And He will grant you mercy, and have compassion upon you, and multiply you" (Deut. 13:18).

   If someone is cruel and does not show mercy, there are sufficient grounds to suspect his lineage, since cruelty is found only among the other nations, as it is said, "They are cruel and will not show mercy" (Jer. 50:42).

   All Jews and those attached to them are like brothers, as it is said, "You are sons to the Lord your God" (Deut. 14:1), and if a brother will not show mercy to his brother, then who will have mercy on him? And to whom can the poor of Israel look for help—to those other nations who hate and persecute them? They can look for help only to their brethren.

3. Whosoever refuses to give charity is called Belial, the same term which is applied to idol-worshipers. With regard to idol-worshipers it is said, "Certain base fellows [literally, children of Belial] have gone out" (Deut. 13:14), and with regard to those who refuse to give charity it is said, "Beware that there be not a base [Belial] thought in your heart" (ibid. 15:9); and he is called a wicked man, as it is said, "The tender mercies of the wicked are cruel" (Prov. 12:10); and he is called a sinner, as it is said, "And he cries to the Lord against you, and it be sin in you" (Deut. 15:9).

   The Holy One, blessed be He, is close to the cries of the poor, as it is said, "You hear the cries of the poor" (paraphrase of Job 34:28). Therefore, one should heed their cries, for a covenant has been made with them, as it is said, "And when he will cry to Me I shall listen because I am merciful" (Exod. 22:26).

4. Whosoever gives charity to a poor man ill-manneredly and with downcast looks has lost all the merit of his action even though he should give him a thousand gold pieces. He should give with good

grace and with joy and should sympathize with him in his plight, as it is said, "Did I not weep for him that was in trouble? Was not my soul grieved for the poor?" (Job 30:25). He should speak to him words of consolation and sympathy, as it is said, "And I gladdened the heart of the widow" (ibid. 29:13).

5. If a poor man requests money from you and you have nothing to give him, speak to him consolingly. It is forbidden to upbraid a poor person or to shout at him because his heart is broken and contrite, as it is said, "A broken and contrite heart, O God, You will not despise" (Ps. 51:19), and it is written, "To revive the spirit of the humble, and to revive the heart of the contrite" (Is. 57:10). Woe to him who shames a poor man. Rather one should be as a father to the poor man, in both compassion and speech, as it is said, "I am a father to the poor" (Job 29:15).

6. He who persuades and constrains others to give shall have a reward greater than that of the giver himself, as it is said, "And the work of righteousness shall be peace" (Is. 32:17). Concerning such that solicit charity (for others) and their like, it is said, "And they that turn the many to righteousness [shall shine] as the stars" (Dan. 12:3).

7. There are eight degrees of charity, one higher than the other. The highest degree, exceeded by none, is that of the person who assists a poor Jew by providing him with a gift or a loan or by accepting him into a business partnership or by helping him find employment—in a word, by putting him where he can dispense with other people's aid. With reference to such aid, it is said, "You shall strengthen him, be he a stranger or a settler, he shall live with you" (Lev. 25:35), which means strengthen him in such manner that his falling into want is prevented.

8. A step below this stands the one who gives alms to the needy in such manner that the giver knows not to whom he gives and the recipient knows not from whom it is that he takes. Such exemplifies performing the meritorious act for its own sake. An illustration would be the Hall of Secrecy in the ancient sanctuary where the righteous would place their gift clandestinely and where poor people of high lineage would come and secretly help themselves to succor.

The rank next to this is of him who drops money in the charity box. One should not drop money in the charity box

unless one is sure that the person in charge is trustworthy, wise, and competent to handle the funds properly, as was Rabbi Hananya ben Teradyon.

9. One step lower is that in which the giver knows to whom he gives but the poor person knows not from whom he receives. Examples of this were the great sages who would go forth and throw coins covertly into poor people's doorways. This method becomes fitting and exalted, should it happen that those in charge of the charity fund do not conduct its affairs properly.

10. A step lower is that in which the poor person knows from whom he is taking but the giver knows not to whom he is giving. Examples of this were the great sages who would tie their coins in their scarves which they would fling over their shoulders so that the poor might help themselves without suffering shame.

11. The next degree lower is that of him who, with his own hand bestows a gift before the poor person asks.

12. The next degree lower is that of him who gives only after the poor person asks.

13. The next degree lower is that of him who gives less than is fitting but gives with a gracious mien.

14. The next degree lower is that of him who gives morosely.

15. There have been great sages who, before praying, would give a coin to the needy, because it is said, "I will behold your face in righteousness" (Ps. 17:15).

16. A species of charity is the maintenance of one's minor sons and daughters who have passed the age at which the father is obligated to support them, provided the purpose of such maintenance be that of educating the sons in sacred lore and of keeping the daughter in the right path, removed from shame. Similarly to be classed as charity is the maintenance of one's father and mother.

In giving charity, precedence should be accorded to one's own relatives.

He who lets poor people and orphans partake of food and drink at his table shall call upon the Lord and find, to his delight, that the Lord will answer, as it is said, "Then shall you call and the Lord will answer" (Is. 58:9).

17. The sages have enjoined that one's domestics should consist not of bondmen but of poor folk and orphans. Better to employ the latter and let the descendants of Abraham, Isaac, and

Jacob benefit from one's possessions than to have that advantage go to the seed of Ham. Day by day, one who adds to the number of his bondmen augments the world's sin and iniquity. But hour by hour, one who takes the poor as members of his household increases virtue and merit.

18. A man should always exert himself and should sooner endure hardship than throw himself, as a dependent, upon the community. The sages admonished, "Make your Sabbath a weekday sooner than become dependent." Even one who is learned and honored should, if impoverished, work at various trades, yes, despicable trades, in order to avoid dependency. Better to strip the hides of beasts that have sickened and died than to tell people, "I am a great sage, my class is that of a priest, support me." Thus spoke the sages.

Outstanding scholars worked as hewers of wood, as carriers of beams, as drawers of garden water, as iron workers, as blacksmiths, rather than ask anything of the community and rather than accept any proffered gratuity.

19. He who, having no need of alms, obtains alms by deception will, ere he die of old age, fall into a dependency that is real. Such a person comes under the characterization: "Cursed is the man that trusts in man" (Jer. 17:5).

One, however, who does stand in need, and who, like an aged or sick or afflicted person, cannot live without help but who, in his pride, declines to accept help is a shedder of blood, guilty of attempts on his own life. Out of his misery, he gets naught but trespasses and sins.

But one, impoverished otherwise, who endures privation and exerts himself and lives a life of hardships rather than burden the community will, ere he die of old age, possess the means out of which he will succor others. Concerning such a person, it is written "Blessed is the man that trusts in the Lord" (Jer. 17:7).

At the heart of Maimonides' depiction of charity is the understanding, taken directly from Scripture, that the poor are especially beloved by God, upon whom they have a claim for support. In sustaining such individuals, people of means thus carry out the will of God, in whose place they stand. The result is that they themselves become deserving of divine reward.

Equally important is that, as a religious obligation, charity must be given with an openness of spirit and clear desire to carry out God's work. Maimonides' eight degrees of the giving of charity depend upon this notion, familiar already from B. Ket. 67b, cited above. At the highest level of giving is the offering to the poor of the means to support themselves, so that they might no longer depend upon others at all. Below this, however, the greatest acts of giving are those in which neither the donor nor the recipient has any knowledge of the other. This mode of giving is laudable because it is totally selfless, since no thanks or feeling of indebtedness of the poor person to the rich are possible. In this circumstance, the giving of charity—like the fulfillment of other religious commandments—is truly an act done for its own sake alone. Isadore Twersky (p. 134) describes this point as follows:

> Maimonides' original classification of the "eight degrees of benevolence" is one of the gems of rabbinic literature, illustrating the need for sensitivity, tact, and graciousness in the act of charity. The formal, objective act of giving charity is deficient and defective if it is not characterized by kindness and sympathy. A benevolent act is easily vitiated by rudeness or impatience—hence the need, for example, to supplement hospitality with escorting one's guests. This is the meaning of the dictum that "the reward of charity depends entirely upon the measure of the kindness in it" (Sukkah 49b).

Developing this theme of the importance of kindness in the giving of charity, Jacob Neusner describes the underlying motivation behind Maimonides schema as follows:[5]

> What the law requires, therefore, is consideration for the humanity of the poor person, who remains no different from us who give. The poor are not less than us or different from us. They have not only needs, but also feelings. They want not only bread, but also respect.
>
> When we give to the poor, we must do so in such a way that the equality of the giver and receiver is acknowledged. This is not an act of grace or an expression of affection. It

is an act of respect, an expression of duty. The use of the word tzedakah in the sense of doing what is right and required is deliberate and definitive. We give not because we feel like it, but because it is our obligation. We do so in a way that will not make us feel superior, and in a way that will not make the poor person feel inferior.

For this reason we begin with the notion that the best way to do tzedakah is to find work for the poor, to relieve the poor of the necessity of begging. Failing that, the next best thing is to ensure that we do not discover who is receiving our charity, in order that we not develop a sense of self-importance, thinking ourselves "Lady Bountifuls." It is less suitable if the donor knows but the recipient does not know the source of the funds. Still, the recipient enjoys dignity. Finally, the poor person may know the source of the money; the wealthy one not know the recipient.

The overall purpose of these laws, in Maimonides' own words, is "instilling pity for the weak and the wretched, giving strength in various ways to the poor, and inciting us . . . not to afflict the hearts of the individuals who are in a weak position" (cited by Twersky, ibid.).

The institutions of charity in medieval Judaism: The specific societal structure for supporting the poor may be briefly outlined. Medieval Jewish communities generally supported a community chest (*kuppah*), which became the major means of collecting and distributing funds, as well as a system for giving gifts in kind, e.g., through a soup kitchen (*tambui*). Supported by a tax, the community chest was the universal norm in Jewish communities, but it was joined as well by the benevolent activity of privately organized charitable societies. Such societies were found all over Europe and contributed to the feeding, clothing, and sheltering of the poor, to the educating of orphans and the children of the poor, to providing dowries so that poor women could be married, to visiting and caring for the sick and aged, for ransoming captives, and for providing for burials. Communities would often support a number of different benevolent societies, each dedicated to a distinct area of charity (for recent examples, see figs. 37-42).

Alongside this structure of community in-stitutions, care of one's own needy relatives continued to be seen as a weighty individual obligation, the fulfillment of which was particularly meritorious:[6]

Anyone who was known to be related came within the terms of the injunction, "Hide not thyself from shine own flesh" (Is. 58:7). This text, as interpreted by the Talmud, constituted a proverbial expression denoting a person's obligation to come to the assistance of his less fortunate relatives.

Aid to one's relatives implied, first of all, supporting them in the event of economic setbacks and actual poverty. Ancient religious law obliged the benefactor to give his relatives preference over the poor in general. According to the view prevalent in the period we are studying [the late middle ages], a person was expected to help his needy relatives more substantially than he would an ordinary charity case. Particular emphasis was placed on the duty of helping to marry off the daughters of one's poor relatives, particularly if the girl's father was dead. To bring up and eventually marry off the orphan of a poor relative was regarded as an especially meritorious deed, and one which charitable persons took pride in performing.

The obligation to support one's relatives was regarded as an accepted norm in society, although the degree of such support naturally varied from person to person. In this readiness to aid one's relatives, the object of preserving the family honor constituted, at the most, a secondary motive. For even the richest families were not in a position to maintain a uniform socio-economic standard among all their members. The fundamental condition necessary for the purpose was lacking: namely, property of permanent value, such as land. Business methods and conditions led to fluctuations in the social hierarchy. Well-to-do families kept their poor relations in mind; they could perhaps save them from destitution, but they could not sustain their socio-economic position.

The obligation of inter-family assistance constituted a norm which evolved out of the actual functions discharged by ties of kinship under the prevailing social conditions. The chief economic activity of this society was intimately bound up, as we have seen, with its continued unity despite the geographical dispersion of its members. The possibility of constant communication with people living in other countries, with whom there existed a kinship of language and culture, gave an economic advantage to the Jews, who were scattered over many lands.

But even in the competition of the members of this society between one another, the connections of secondary groups, whose members were related and loyal to each other, constituted an advantage over individuals without any outside ties. This advantage was not confined to the economic sphere alone. To the extent that common political interests existed, whether these involved intercession with outside authorities or with the internal organizations, primary ties were regarded as an asset. Connections with persons outside the immediate locality were helpful in every field of activity which was not completely parochial in character. The roving talmudic student, the rabbi who was called to serve another *kehilla*, and even a person who had made a match with someone in a distant city, needed assistance or, at least, information. The family was the only institution or agency to which the individual could turn for assistance in making contact with persons outside his locality.

The obligation to support the poor arose in part out of strong feelings of family honor but, more importantly, out of the unique social and economic circumstance of the Jews. Scattered across many lands and lacking the economic resources or civil protections to assure consistent personal safety and financial security, Jews were particularly susceptible to problems of dislocation and poverty. Mutual acceptance of the obligation to support the community's needy and, in particular, the poor of one's own family brought to all Jews an otherwise unattainable level of security and safety—political, economic, and social. The family, through its attention to the needs of its kin, attempted as best it could to assure the success of all relatives. On this same model, Jews as individuals and as a society provided assistance to all Jews in need, working to assure that all members of the community could achieve at least a minimum level of subsistence.

While in the medieval period charity took many forms, in general, people were understood to be required to support the needy with a minimum of a tenth of their income, comparable to the biblically mandated tithe of produce. Following the Talmudic mandate, people were discouraged from giving more than a fifth, so as not to risk impoverishing themselves.

Conclusion: Judaism obligates people of means to sustain the needy. Accordingly, communities of Jews from biblical to contemporary times have developed sophisticated systems of collecting and dispersing funds. In this way they assure, on the one hand, that the burden of supporting the poor is fairly assessed upon all members of the community. On the other, they guarantee that those in need will be sustained in an appropriate and dignified manner.

Even as it sees charity as an aspect of the communal system of taxation, however, Judaism is clear on the importance of personal giving of charity, and thus it defines charitable giving as an act of righteousness that brings manifold heavenly rewards. The point is explicit at B. Shab. 151b:

A. It has been taught on Tannaite authority:
B. Rabban Gamaliel beRibbi said, "'And he shall give you mercy and have compassion on you and multiply you' (Deut. 13:17)—whoever has mercy on other people will be shown mercy from Heaven, and whoever does not show mercy to other people will not be shown mercy from Heaven."

The relationship between individual Jews and the poor of their community is parallel to the relationship between the Jews and God. The greater the extent to which a person shows mercy to others, the greater the mercy that God will show that person.

Understood in this way, acts of charity are in the same category as acts of righteousness, and it is for this reason, of course, that "charity" is referred to by the Hebrew term "*tzedakah*." Charity and other acts of selfless giving for the benefit of others are deemed more desirous to God than even the sacrifices of the Jerusalem Temple (B. Suk. 49b):

A. A Tannaite authority of the house of R. Anan taught, "What is the sense of Scripture's statement, 'The roundings of your thighs' (Song 7:2)?
B. "Why are the teachings of Torah compared to the thigh?
C. "It is to teach you that, just as the thigh is kept hidden, so teachings of Torah are to be kept hidden."
D. That is in line with what R. Eleazar said, "What is the sense of the verse of Scripture, 'It has been told you, O man, what

is good, and what the Lord requires of you: only to do justly, to love mercy, and to walk humbly with your God' (Mic. 6:8)?

E. "'To do justly' refers to justice.

F. "'To love mercy' refers to doing deeds of loving kindness.

G. "'And to walk humbly with your God' refers to taking out a corpse for burial and bringing the bride in to the marriage-canopy.

H. "And is it not a matter of argument a fortiori:

I. "Now if, as to matters that are ordinarily done in public, the Torah has said, 'To walk humbly,' matters that are normally done in private, all the more so [must they be done humbly and in secret, that is, the giving of charity is done secretly]."

J. Said R. Eleazar, "Greater is the one who carries out an act of charity more than one who offers all the sacrifices.

K. "For it is said, 'To do charity and justice is more desired by the Lord than sacrifice' (Prov. 21:3)."

L. And R. Eleazar said, "An act of loving kindness is greater than an act of charity.

M. "For it is said, 'Sow to yourselves according to your charity, but reap according to your loving kindness' (Hos. 10:12).

N. "If a man sows seed, it is a matter of doubt whether he will eat a crop or not. But if a man harvests the crop, he most certainly will eat it."

O. And R. Eleazar said, "An act of charity is rewarded only in accord with the loving kindness that is connected with it.

P. "For it is said, 'Sow to yourselves according to your charity, but reap according to your loving kindness' (Hos. 10:12)."

Acts of charity are to be done humbly and in private, not for personal aggrandizement but selflessly, for the betterment of the world in which the individual lives. It is perhaps this fact of charity, that it has an economic purpose and will be especially appreciated by the recipient, that leads certain rabbis to deem it secondary to other acts of righteousness. Such other acts involve the person's self and not just his wealth. They can benefit those who are unable to offer thanks (e.g., the dead) and may be done for those who do not in a concrete way "require" the act (e.g., the rich). This point is made in the continuation of the passage at B. Suk. 49b:

A. Our rabbis have taught on Tannaite authority:

B. In three aspects are acts of loving kindness greater than an act of charity.

C. An act of charity is done only with money, but an act of loving kindness someone carries out either with his own person or with his money.

D. An act of charity is done only for the poor, while an act of loving kindness may be done either for the poor or for the rich.

E. An act of charity is done only for the living. An act of loving kindness may be done either for the living or for the dead.

Given the rabbis' overall focus upon the importance—and religious necessity—of supporting the poor, the point here is hardly that people should not take extremely seriously their obligation to give charity. Rather, we see here the extent to which the giving of charity is not viewed as an act in which a person should take particular pride, as though he or she has behaved in a totally selfless way or done that which is not, in all events, expected. The giving of charity, rather, is only one type of act of loving kindness. Insofar as it uses the wealth given to the individual by God in the first place, and insofar as the one who gives charity experiences the recipient's gratitude, that person should not feel overly smug about his or her deed. The giving of charity, rather, can be valued only in accordance with the level of human kindness and true concern for the poor with which that act is performed.[7]

Notes

[1] God's additional claim upon the first-born both of people and animals (Exod. 13:15, Num. 18:5, etc.) is explained contextually as flowing from the fact that, when God killed the first born of Egypt, he saved—and thereby took possession of—the first born of Israel. The larger point is the same however: God has a claim upon all that exists through God's generosity. These things God directs for use in purposes he chooses, whether the support of the cult, as in the case of the first born of people and animals, or in the support of the needy, as explained in the following.

[2] The Mishnah, for its part, holds that those who, to collect charity, pretend to be lame, dumb, or handicapped will not die of old age before they actually develop such an infirmity (M. Pe. 8:9).

[3] Ed. Wistinezki, par. 1345, p. 331; cited in Haim Ben-Sasson, "Charity," in *Encyclopedia Judaica*, vol. 5, col. 345.

[4] Cited from Isadore Twersky, *A Maimonides Reader* (New York, 1972), pp. 135-139. As in the Rabbinic texts, note throughout the association of the terms "charity" and "righteousness," which represent the same word in Hebrew.

[5] Jacob Neusner, *Tzedakah: Can Jewish Philanthropy Buy Jewish Survival* (Atlanta, 1990), p. 13.

[6] Jacob Katz, *Tradition and Crisis: Jewish Society at the End of the Middle Ages* (New York, 1958), pp. 150-151.

[7] On charity in Judaism in North America in modern times, see NORTH AMERICA, PRACTICE OF JUDAISM IN.

ALAN J. AVERY-PECK

CHRISTIANITY ON JUDAISM IN ANCIENT AND MEDIEVAL TIMES: At its inception a movement within Judaism,[1] the dramatic process by which Christianity came to be defined systemically as distinct from Judaism may be traced within the principal sources of the New Testament. That process was part and parcel of a redefinition of Israel, a redefinition that lead to a debate with Israel after the flesh during the period between the second and the fourth centuries. From the fourth century, with the emergence of Christianity as the principal religion of the Roman Empire, Judaism came to be treated as apostasy, an unacceptable deviation from the prophetic faith. By the Middle Ages, the sense of alienation from Judaism had grown within Christianity and resulted in the perception of Judaism as a threat that subverted the truth of Christ and human reason itself.

The redefinition of Israel in primitive Christianity—"Q": Recent discussion of the source known as "Q" has brought about a remarkable consensus that at least some of the sayings within it were circulated a few years after the crucifixion, around the year 35 C.E. A recent study assigns to the earliest version of "Q" a charge to Jesus' disciples (Luke 10:3-6, 9-11, 16), a strategy to cope with resistance to their message (Luke 6:27-35), examples of how to speak of the kingdom (Luke 6:20b-21; 11:2-4, 14-20; 13:18-21), curses to lay on those who reject those sent in the name of the kingdom (Luke 11:39-48, 52), and a section relating John the Baptist and Jesus as principal emissaries of the kingdom (Luke 7:24b-26, 28a, 33-34).[2]

Q is best seen as evolving in two distinct stages. In the first, Jesus' teaching was arranged by his disciples in a form which they could readily use. A "mishnah" in this period was an authoritative statement, usually in oral transmission, of a rabbi's rulings and principles. In the form of a mishnah, Jesus' teaching would commend itself to the attention of those who were familiar with the emerging Rabbinic ethos. They thus took up a ministry in Jesus' name that was addressed to Israel at large after the resurrection. The mishnaic form of Q was preserved orally in Aramaic and explained how the twelve were to discharge their mission. It included just the materials that have already been specified, instructions to Jesus' disciples, a strategy of love to overcome resistance, paradigms to illustrate the kingdom, threats directed towards enemies, and a reference to John the Baptist that would serve as a transition to baptism in the name of Jesus. It seems likely, in addition, that Q also preserved at least one saying in reference to eucharist (Luke 22:15).[3] As specified, that is probably the original, mishnaic order of Q. It is the order that accords with Q's purpose within the mission to Israel.

At the final stage, Q's order was changed to become quasi-biographical, in accordance with the order of the teaching in the circle of Peter. At that stage, for example, material concerning John the Baptist was moved to the beginning, and the story of Jesus' temptations (Luke 4:1-13) was added, in order to make the transition to an unequivocal focus upon Jesus rather than John. The final redaction of Q probably took place a decade after the mishnaic stage of Q was composed, probably in Syria, an environment in which both Aramaic and Greek were spoken.[4] Although in Q "Israel" remains the target of the disciples' mission, crisis in the face of a significant rejection of that mission is an evident feature of the source. Such statements as John the Baptist's claim that God could raise up children for Abraham from stones in order to replace those of Israel who refused to repent (Luke 3:8) suggest a palpable—albeit pre-conceptual—distance from Israel as usually defined.

The circle of Peter: Peter shared with Jesus the hope of a climactic disclosure of divine power, signaled in the willingness of nations to worship on Mount Zion. That hope is certainly attested within sources extant by the first century. Chief among them, from the point of view of its influence upon the New Testament, is the book of Zechariah. Zechariah provided the point of departure for Jesus' inclusive program of purity and forgiveness as the occasions of the kingdom. Jesus is said to have mentioned the prophet by name (see Mat. 23:34-36; Luke 11:49-51).

Peter perpetuated that vision by means of his fidelity both to breaking bread at home with the disciples and in worship within the Temple (see Acts 2:42-47). The common ownership of possessions in Jerusalem, which is emphasized in the description of Petrine practice (in addition to Acts 2:44-45, see 4:32-5:11), also has its roots in the Zecharian vision. Commonality of goods in the vicinity of the Temple implied that no buying or selling would be at issue (see Zechariah 14:20-21); it was an extension of just the principle that Jesus had died defending. At the same time, Acts portrays Peter's activity much further afield; he is active in Samaria (8:14-25), Lydda (9:32-35), Joppa (9:36-43), and Caesarea (10:1-48; 12:19). Paul refers, as if as a matter of course, to Peter's presence personally in Antioch (see Gal. 2:11-14), and by the time of the pseudepigraphic 1 Peter (written around 90 C.E.), he is pictured as writing from Rome with Silvanus (see 1 Peter 5:12-13) to churches in the north of Asia Minor (1:1, 2). If, then, Jerusalem was a center for Peter in the way it was not for Jesus, it was certainly not a limit of his operations. Rather, the Temple appears to have featured as the hub of a much wider network of contacts that linked Jews from abroad and even gentiles (see Acts 10:1-48; 11:1-18, 15:1-11 with Gal. 2:1-14) in common recognition of a new, eschatological fellowship defined by the teaching of Jesus.

The key to the connection between Peter's residence in Jerusalem and his activity in Syria and beyond is provided by the vision he relates as the warrant for his visit to the house of Cornelius, the Roman centurion (Acts 10:1-48). Peter is praying on a roof top in Joppa around noon. His vision occurs while he is hungry and concerns a linen lowering from heaven, filled with four-footed animals, reptiles, and birds. A voice says, "Arise, Peter, slaughter and eat," and he refuses (in words reminiscent of Ezek. 4:14). But a voice again says, "What God has cleansed, you will not defile" (see Acts 10:9-16).

Peter defends his baptisms in the house of Cornelius on the basis of his vision in the course of a dispute with those who argued that circumcision was a requirement of adherence to the movement (Acts 11:1-18). He also cites his activity among non-Jews at a later point, in the context of what has come to be called the Apostolic Council (Acts 15:7-11). Throughout, the position of Peter appears to have been consistent: God may make, and has made, eschatological exceptions to the usual practice of purity. Those exceptions include the acceptance of uncircumcised men in baptism, and fellowship with them.

Peter's emphasis upon the importance of spirit determined his attitude toward the Scriptures of Israel. In the Transfiguration (see Mark 9:2-8 and parallels), for example, Jesus stands side by side with Moses and Elijah; the son of God and the prophetic covenant together mediate God's own spirit. But social policy is left undefined under Peter's approach. According to Acts 15, Peter concluded on the basis of God's gift of the spirit to gentiles that they could not be required to be circumcised (Acts 15:6-11). On the other hand, Paul shows in Gal. 2 that Peter was not willing to reject Mosaic requirements as a general principle and that he could change his mind when confronted with differing interpretations and practices. But his apparent ambivalence reflects a commitment to the twin loyalties of a single son and a single law, together mediating the same spirit.

Despite the consistency of Peter's position with Jesus', it could not serve as a practical guide in framing a social identity for the followers of Jesus after the resurrection. The policy of taking Israel as you found it was wise in the case of Jesus, owing to the cultural and geographical limitation of his ministry. But as soon as his movement extended beyond the land—and more especially beyond the culture—of what was commonly agreed to be Israel, that policy could be portrayed as intellectually bankrupt and morally inconsistent. Was a group of non-Jewish believers who accepted baptism an example of Israel or not?

The circle of James: Hegesippus—as cited by Eusebius (see *History* II.23.1-18)—characterizes James, Jesus' brother, as the person who exercised immediate control of the church in Jerusalem. Although Peter had initially gathered a group of Jesus' followers in Jerusalem, his interests and activities further afield left the way open for James to become the natural head of the community there. That change, and political changes in Jerusalem itself, made the Temple the effective center of the local community of Jesus' followers. James practiced a careful and idiosyncratic purity in the interests of worship in the Temple. He abstained from wine and animal flesh, did not cut his hair or beard, and forsook oil and bathing. According to Hegesippus, those special practices gave him access even to the sanctuary. Josephus reports he was killed in the Temple, circa 62, at the instigation of the high priest Ananus, during the interregnum of the Roman governors Festus and Albinus (*Antiquities* 20.9.1, 197-203). Hegesippus gives a more circumstantial, less politically informed, account of the martyrdom.

In addition to the sort of close association with the Temple that could and did result in conflict with the authorities there, the circle of James is expressly claimed in Acts to have exerted authority as far away as Antioch, by means of emissaries who spoke Greek (Acts 15:13-35). The particulars of the dispute will be discussed in the next section. What is of immediate import is that James alone determines the outcome of apostolic policy. James in Acts agrees that gentiles who turn to God are not to be encumbered with needless regulations (15:19), and yet he insists they be instructed by letter to abstain "from the pollutions of idols, and from fornication, and from what is strangled, and from blood" (v. 20).

The grounds given for the Jacobean policy are that the law of Moses is commonly acknowledged (Acts 15:21); the implication is that to disregard such elemental considerations of purity as James specifies would be to dishonor Moses. Judas Barsabbas and Silas are then dispatched with Paul and Barnabas to deliver the letter in Antioch along with their personal testimony (vv. 22-29) and are said particularly to continue their instruction as prophets (v. 32, 33). They refer to the regulations of purity as necessities (v. 28), and no amount of Lukan gloss can conceal that what they insist upon is a serious challenge of Paul's position (cf., 1 Cor. 8).

James' devotion to the Temple is also reflected in Acts 21. When Paul arrives in Jerusalem, James and the presbyters with him express concern at the rumor that Paul is telling Jews who live among the gentiles not to circumcise. Their advice is for Paul to demonstrate his piety by purifying himself, paying the expenses of four men under a vow, and entering the Temple with them (Acts 21:17-26). The result is a disastrous misunderstanding. Paul is accused of introducing "Greeks" into the Temple, a riot ensues, and Paul himself is arrested (21:27-36). James is not mentioned again in Acts, but Hegesippus' description shows his devotion to the Temple did not wane.

Typically, the circle of James applied the Scriptures directly to the situation of Jesus' followers, on the understanding of their regulative authority. James cited the reference of Amos to the restoration of the house of David (in Amos 9:11-12). As James develops the meaning of Amos in Acts 15:16-21, the gentiles are to recognize the triumph of David and that implies that they are to remain gentiles. They are not a part of Israel, although they are to keep basic rules of purity in order to honor the law of Israel.

James' focus was on Jesus' role as the ultimate arbiter within the Davidic line, and there was never any question in his mind but that the Temple was the natural place to worship God and acknowledge Jesus. Embracing the Temple as central meant for James, as it meant for everyone associated with worship there, maintaining the purity that it was understood God required in his house and keeping it better than many of those associated with the priesthood. According to James, Jesus' purity involved excluding from the interior courts of the Temple gentiles, even those who, out of loyalty to the Mosaic law, acknowledged some rudiments of purity. There, only Israel was to be involved in sacrifice, and followers of Jesus were to accept particular responsibility for such sacrifice (so Acts 21:17-36). The line of demarcation between Israel and non-Israel was no invention within the circle of James but a natural result of seeing Jesus as the triumphant scion of the house of David.

Peter's imprisonment by Herod Agrippa can be dated rather precisely to the year 44 C.E.[5] By that time, James had emerged as a prominent authority, the natural leader of the group in Jerusalem. Earlier, in reference to his visit to Jerusalem in 35 C.E., Paul refers to meeting Peter and James, but he alludes to receiving instruction only from Peter (see Gal. 1:18-19). During the intervening period, c. 40 C.E., the circle of James promulgated its own instructional gospel, comparable to Peter's and building upon it. That was the basis of James' authority, which the apostolic council reflected in Acts 15 confirmed. That council is usually dated in the year 49 C.E. When Judas Barsabbas and Silas were sent by the council to deliver its judgment (which was originally James' opinion) in Antioch, it authorized James' version of the gospel to be delivered in Greek. When Acts 15:32-33 refers to Judas and Silas as prolonging their visit in Antioch after they had read the letter from the council, we are given a glimpse into to process by which materials originally framed in Aramaic were rendered into Greek. At the same time, we are shown how James' classic understanding of Israel was considered authoritative, even for the largely non-Jewish congregation in Antioch. Here, in the place where Jesus' followers were first called "Christians" (so Acts 11:26),[6] it is accepted

after a considerable controversy that, although gentiles may not be required to circumcise, neither may they be considered one with Israel. James' Israel consisted of those who recognized Jesus, the scion of the Davidic line, as the guardian of true, non-commercial purity in the Temple.

Paul: Sometime around 53 C.E., Paul wrote a letter to a group of churches in the northern part of Asia Minor (present-day Turkey). He communicated to communities he himself had founded, where Christians were embroiled in a deep and destructive controversy. As Paul sees the matter (Gal. 2), in churches he founded, he had established the practice of common fellowship at meals, including eucharistic meals. Such fellowship of course included Jews who became Christians, signaling their acceptance of Jesus' teaching by being baptized. But it also—and increasingly—saw the participation of non-Jews who had been baptized, but not circumcised. Paul won the agreement of Christian leaders in Jerusalem that circumcision should not be required of non-Jewish members.

The remarkable and early agreement that Jews and non-Jews could be included in the movement established a radical principle of inclusion. But it also brought about one of the greatest controversies within the early Church. Paul's version of events in Galatians (seconded by Acts 15) is the best available. At Antioch, Jews and non-Jews who had been baptized joined in meals of fellowship together. According to Paul, Peter fell in with the practice. Peter—whom Paul also calls "Cephas," the Aramaic word for "rock"— was a founding apostle of the church in Jerusalem, whose nickname came from Jesus himself.

Paul's policy of including gentiles with Jews in meals, as well as in baptism, needed the support of authorities such as Peter, in order to prevail against the natural conservatism of those for whom such inclusion seemed a betrayal of the purity of Israel. When representatives of James, the brother of Jesus and the pre-eminent figure in the church in Jerusalem, arrived, that natural conservatism re-asserted itself. Peter "separated himself," along with the rest of the

Jews, and even Barnabas (Gal. 2:12, 13). Jews and gentiles again maintained distinct fellowship at meals, and Paul accuses the leadership of his own movement of hypocrisy (Gal. 2:13).

The radical quality of Paul's position needs to be appreciated before his characteristic interpretation of Scripture may be understood. He was isolated from every other Christian Jew (by his own account in Gal. 2:11-13, James, Peter, Barnabas, and "the rest of the Jews"). His isolation required that he develop an alternative view of authority in order to justify his own practice. Within Galatians, Paul quickly articulates the distinctive approach to Scripture as authoritative that characterizes his writings as a whole.

In Scripture, Paul finds what he needs in the example of Abraham. He says that when believers hear with faith, they are "just as Abraham, who believed in God, and it was reckoned to him as righteousness" (Gal. 3:6). The characterization of Abraham is taken from Gen. 15:5-6, when Abraham is promised that his descendants shall be as the stars of the heavens: his trust in what he is told makes him the father of faith, and in the course of the sacrifice that he subsequently offers, God seals his promise as the solemn covenant to give the land that would be called Israel (Gen. 15:7-21).

Paul understands the role of Abraham as the patriarch of Judaism, but he argues that Abraham's faith, not his obedience to the law, made him righteous in the sight of God (Gal. 3:7): "Know, therefore, that those who are of faith are sons of Abraham." Paul was capable of remarkable elaborations of that theme, in Galatians and elsewhere, but the essential simplicity of the thought must not be overlooked. Abraham, for Paul, embodied a principle of believing that was best fulfilled by means of faith in and through Jesus Christ. Descent from Abraham, therefore, was a matter of belief, not a matter of genealogy.

The circle of Barnabas: In Galatians, Barnabas is blamed by Paul for being taken up in the "hypocrisy" of Peter and the "rest of the Jews," because Peter had separated from

the company of gentiles he had formally eaten with (Gal. 2:11-13). Peter's position, as we have seen, was a function of his conviction that God's spirit in baptism overcame the impurity of non-Jews, without abrogating God's choice of Israel. Barnabas can be expected to have been more rigorous than Peter in regard to questions of purity and impurity. As a Levite from Cyprus (Acts 4:36), he had an awareness of what it meant to live with priestly concerns in a Hellenistic environment. His devotion to the Petrine understanding of pure worship is marked by his willingness to sell off his property in order to join the group in Jerusalem (Acts 4:37).

Barnabas, then, was associated with Peter before he was associated with Paul, so that Paul's attempt (as reflected in Galatians) to claim Barnabas' loyalty in opposition to Peter had little chance of success. After all, it was Barnabas' introduction that brought Paul into contact with the apostles in Jerusalem, despite Paul's well deserved reputation as an enemy of the movement (Acts 9:27-30). Whatever disagreements might have stood between James and Barnabas, Barnabas enjoyed the implicit trust of the church in Jerusalem. When followers of Jesus from Cyprus and Cyrene preached to non-Jews in Antioch and enjoyed success, Barnabas was commissioned to investigate (see Acts 11:19-26). It was during the course of a sojourn that lasted over a year that Barnabas introduced Paul to Antioch.

Adherents of the movement came to be known as "Christians" (meaning partisans of Christ) in Antioch (Acts 11:26), and they embraced that term of intended ridicule. The use of the term by outsiders high-lights the marginal status of non-Jews who accepted baptism. Without conversion to Judaism, they were not Jews in the usual understanding; having rejected the gods of Hellenism by being baptized, they were also no longer representative of the Graeco-Roman syncretism which was then fashionable. By calling disciples Christiani, a term analogous to Caesariani and Augustiniani, outsiders compared the movement more to a political faction than to a religion. It would be as if, in English, we called a disciple a "Christite," on the model of Thatcherite, Reaganite, Clintonite, etc.

Acts describes Barnabas in the context of his visit in Antioch as "a good man, full of holy spirit and faith" (Acts 11:24). The reference to the spirit attests his connection with the Petrine understanding of discipleship that he had fully accepted. Unlike Peter, however, Joseph—called Barnabas—was a Levite (Acts 4:36). Given that fact, and the confidence invested in Barnabas by the church in Jerusalem when an issue of purity arose (Acts 11:22), it is natural to infer that Barnabas was discrete in his social contacts with non-Jewish believers. Even Paul does not say of Barnabas, as he does of Peter, that he ate commonly with non-Jews and then separated when emissaries from James arrived (see Gal. 2:11-13). Barnabas' policy was probably consistent and accepted non-Jews in baptism, although they continued to be treated as non-Jews after baptism.

Barnabas represents a committed attempt to convert Peter's dual loyalty to the spirit in baptism and to circumcision and purity within Israel into a coherent social policy. Paul calls the attempt hypocritical because he did not agree with it; in fact it was a brilliant effort to combine inclusiveness with integrity. Acts attempts to minimize the difference between Barnabas and Paul, turning it into a limited matter of who should accompany them in a visit of churches at which they had previously preached (see Acts 15:36-41). In fact, their dispute after the council devolved upon what had always divided them: Barnabas' commitment to separate fellowship in order to preserve the purity of Israel. The person Barnabas wanted to come with them, John—called Mark—had been associated with the circle of Peter and was well received in Jerusalem (see Acts 12:12-17, 25; 13:5, 15). Paul no doubt feared that John would further extend the influence of James. Barnabas stood by the policy that fellowship among non-Jewish Christians was authorized and endorsed, but that the fellowship of Israel was also to be maintained.

The social policy of the community as envisaged by Barnabas is instanced in the two signs of feeding, of the five thousand and the four thousand. Both stories reflect a eucharistic fellowship with Jesus, one for Israel and one for non-Jews. That crucial meaning is the key to what has long perplexed commentators, the significance of the numerological symbols embedded in each story, which function in contrast to one another.

In the first story (Mat. 14:13-21; Mark 6:32-44; Luke 9:10b-17), the eucharistic associations are plain: Jesus blesses and breaks the bread prior to distribution (Mat. 14:19; Mark 6:41; Luke 9:16). That emphasis so consumes the story, the fish—characteristic among Christian eucharistic symbols—are of subsidiary significance by the end of the passage (compare Mark 6:43 with Mat. 14:20 and Luke 9:17). Whatever the pericope represented originally, it becomes a eucharistic narrative in the Barnaban presentation. Jesus gathers people in orderly way (see Mat. 14:18; Mark 6:39, 40; Luke 9:14, 15), by "symposia" as Mark literally has it (6:39); without that order, they might be described as sheep without a shepherd (Mark 6:34).

The authority of the twelve is a marked concern within the story. In Mat. 14:12b-13, Mark 6:30-31, and Luke 9:10a, their return after their commission occasions the feeding, and their function is definite: Jesus gives them the bread to give it to others (Mat. 14:19; Mark 6:41; Luke 9:16). The divine support for what they do is manifest in the assertion that twelve baskets of fragments were gathered after the five thousand ate. The lesson is evident: the twelve, the counterparts of the twelve tribes of Israel, will always have enough to feed the church, understood to realize the identity of Israel in the wilderness.

The story of the feeding of the four thousand (Mat. 15:32-39; Mark 8:1-10) follows so exactly that of the five thousand that its omission by Luke may seem understandable, simply as a redundant doublet. But there are distinctive elements in the second feeding story, elements that are clearly designed to articulate the significance of the story for those outside of Israel as usually understood. The four thousand are a multiple of the four points of the compass, the story follows that of the Canaanite or Syrophoenician woman

(Mat. 15:21-28; Mark 7:24-30) and concerns a throng from a number of different areas and backgrounds (see Mat. 15:21, 29; Mark 7:24, 31). The issue of non-Jewish contact with Jesus is therefore marked here in a way it is not in the case of the feeding of the five thousand. Likewise, the number seven, the number of bushels of fragments here collected, corresponds to the deacons of the Hellenists in the church of Jerusalem (cf., Acts 6:1-6) and is related to the traditional number of the seventy nations within Judaism. Even the liturgical practice of the non-Jewish constituency of Christianity is reflected here. The reference to Jesus as giving thanks (*eukharistesas*) over the bread in Mat. 15:36 is significant. Mark 8:6 better corresponds to the Hellenistic version of the Petrine eucharist in Luke 22:17, 19 and 1 Corinthians 11:24 than does "he blessed" (*eulogesen*) in Mat. 14:19; Mark 6:39, which better corresponds to the earlier Petrine formula in Mat. 26:26; Mark 14:22.

The Lukan omission of such stories, in fact of the whole of what corresponds to Mark 6:45-8:26 (conventionally designated as "the great omission" of Mark by Luke), seems natural once their meaning is appreciated: they concern the sense of Jesus in an environment characterized by a mixture of Jews and gentiles. Luke takes up that theme in Acts and regards its reversion into the ministry of Jesus as an anachronism.

After the second feeding, Jesus rebukes his disciples for a failure to understand when he warns them about the leaven of the Pharisees and Sadducees and asks whether they truly grasp the relationship between the number twelve and the five thousand and the number seven and the four thousand (Mat. 16:5-12; Mark 8:14-21). In the mind of the Hellenistic catechesis, the meaning is clear, and its implications for eucharistic discipline are evident. Celebration of eucharist in its truest sense is neither to be limited to Jews, as the Jacobean program would have it, nor forced upon communities in a way which would require Jews to accept reduced standards of purify, as the Pauline program would have it. There is for the Hellenistic catechesis of which the Synoptic transformation is a monument an on-going apostolate for Jews and gentiles, prepared to feed as many of the Church that gather.

Hebrews and the Revelation: Where the obvious question in what went before Hebrews (Paul included) was the nature of Israel, the natural question that emerges from Hebrews is the nature(s) of Christ. We can see an indication of that change immediately by placing the "Israel" of Hebrews in the context of the concern to define Israel within the movement of Jesus from its earliest phase.

Jesus had insisted upon a policy of treating all of Israel as Israel, pure enough by means of its customary practice to accept and enter the kingdom of God. For Peter, that made Jesus a new Moses: just as there is an implicit analogy between the followers of Jesus and the Israel that followed Moses out of Egypt, the prophetic covenant of Moses and the divine sonship of Jesus stand side by side, linked by their common source in the spirit of God. James' point of departure was David, rather than Moses. Here, the belief of gentiles achieves, not the redefinition of Israel, but the restoration of the house of David, which is committed to preserve Israel in its purity. But Paul began with Abraham, who in his theology embodied a principle of believing that was best fulfilled by means of faith in and through Jesus Christ. The Synoptic Gospels, in their variety, posit an analogy between Jesus and the figures of the Hebrew Bible. Christ becomes the standard by which Israel's Scripture is experienced, but not superseded; a separation between Jews and non-Jews remains. John's nuance is sophisticated, but plain: Jesus is the true Israel, attested by the angels of God (see John 1:51), by whom all who believe might become children of God (see John 1:12-13).

All such options are brushed aside in Hebrews. The author understands Israel, literally, as a thing of the past, the husk of the first, now antiquated covenant. He says the word "Israel" just three times. Twice in chapter 8, he refers to Israel but simply as part of his quotation of Jer. 31:31-34, where to his mind a completely new covenant is promised

(Heb. 8:8, 10). The point of that citation, as elaborated by the author, is that the new covenant makes the former covenant obsolete (8:13). Accordingly, when the author speaks of Israel in his own voice, it is simply to refer to "the sons of Israel" in the past, at the time of the exodus from Egypt (11:22). (The mention is in reference to Joseph's command for the disposal of his own bones, a fitting context for the attitude toward "Israel" in Hebrews!) Melchizedek is a positive, theological category. Israel is no longer and remains only as a cautionary tale from history.

The ability of the author of Hebrews to relegate Israel to history is related to the insistence, from the outset of the epistle, that the son's authority is greater than that of the Scripture. Once, God spoke in many and various ways through the prophets; now, at the end of days, he speaks to us by a son (Heb. 1:1, 2). The comparative judgment is reinforced when the author observes that, if the word delivered by angels (that is, the Torah) carried with it retribution for transgression, how much more should we attend to what we have heard concerning the son (Heb. 2:1-4). The implication of both statements is clear: Scripture is only authoritative to the extent that it attests the salvation mediated by the son (1:14; 2:3-4). The typology framed later in the epistle between Jesus and the Temple derives directly from the conviction of the prior authority of the son of God in relation to Scripture.

The dual revaluation, of Israel and Israel's Scripture, is what permits Hebrews to trace its theology of Christ's replacement of every major institution, every principal term of reference, within the Judaisms of its time. Before Hebrews, there were Christian Judaisms in which Christ was in various ways conceived of as the key to the promises to Israel. Hebrews' theology proceeds from those earlier theologies, and it remains a Christian Judaism in the sense that all of its vocabulary of salvation is drawn from the same Scriptures that were axiomatic within the earlier circles.

But the Christian Judaism of Hebrews is also and self-consciously the system of an autonomous Christianity, because all that is Judaic is held to have been provisional until the coming of the son, after which point it is no longer meaningful. There is a single center within the theology of Hebrews. It is not Christ with Moses, Christ with Temple, Christ with David, Christ with Abraham, Christ with Scripture, Christ with Israel. In the end, the center is not really even Christ with Melchizedek, because Melchizedek disappears in the glory of his heavenly archetype. Christ is the beginning, middle, and end of theology in Hebrews, just as he is the same yesterday, today, and forever (Heb. 13:8). Everything else is provisional—and expendable—within the consuming fire which is God (12:29).

The Revelation of John: The Revelation was written at the close of the period during which the New Testament as a whole was composed. John of Patmos particularly developed themes that are sounded in the Gospel according to John, although his theological vocabulary is by no means limited to what he learned from that source. The identity of the writer is unknown, except that he wrote around the year 100 C.E. for churches in the vicinity of Ephesus (where John's Gospel was also composed).

The key to an understanding of the Revelation (written some five years after Hebrews) is that it is what it says it is, an apocalypse (from the term *apokalupsis* in Greek), a disclosure of the heavenly court. In aid of the deliberately visionary medium of the work, the tone of intellectual argument (as, for example, in the letters of Paul) is avoided. Everything unfolds as a matter of what is seen and heard rather than as a result of speculation.

The lamb of God, an image sounded in the fourth Gospel, is especially developed in the Revelation of John. When John the Baptist identifies Jesus as "the lamb of God which takes away the sin of the world" (John 1:29, cf. v. 36), an association with Passover is evident. It has been objected that the image of the lamb in itself is not necessarily paschal, and that the removal of sin might more readily be associated with the daily offering (the *tamid*) than with the paschal lamb. When the image is taken in isolation, that observation is apposite. But paschal imagery permeates the fourth Gospel with eucharistic meaning. The moment of Jesus' death in John corresponds to the time at which paschal lambs were normally slain: that Jesus was crucified during the afternoon of the day of preparation, just prior to Passover, is emphasized (19:14, 31). Moreover, John 19:36 cites a regulation concerning the paschal lamb, that no bone shall be broken (Exod. 12:46), in respect of Jesus' body on the cross. The sponge of vinegar raised on hyssop (specified only in John 19:29) may recollect the hyssop used to apply the paschal blood in Exod. 12:22. The Johannine theology is specific: Jesus here is identified as the paschal lamb in 1:29, 36, just as he is identified as the true manna in 6:30-58.

Jesus' discourse in John 6:30-58, in which he identifies himself as the true bread of life that must be eaten for eternal life, arouses opposition within his Jewish audience (see 6:41, 52) and even among the disciples (see 6:61). The eucharistic theology involved is obviously highly developed. The Revelation takes up the paschal imagery of the Gospel within its own version of the Johannine portrayal of eucharist as that which provokes controversy within Judaism. The document itself is written in a Semitized Greek, with self-consciously bad grammar: some errors of case and tense, for example, are below a rudimentary level, a flaunting of the grammar even an elementary student would be aware of. Such attempts at archaism can scarcely convince, when Jewish congregations are dismissed as instances of a "synagogue of Satan" (2:9; 3:9).

Separation from Judaism is also flagged in the Revelation by a theological development: Jesus as the divine lamb is now explicitly an object of worship. The lamb of John 1:29, 36 has become a surreal "lamb standing as slain" (Rev. 5:6). The attribution to the lamb of divine status is obvious both in its placement, in the midst of the throne and the living creatures, among the elders, and in its possession of seven eyes, "which are the spirits of God sent out into all the earth." The term used for "lamb" (*arnion*) connotes the helplessness of a lamb, so that the fact of

its slaughter is emphasized, yet the focus of the Revelation is the power that proceeds from the lamb as a consequence of its slaughter. The lamb is worthy of heavenly and human worship (5:8, 13; 7:9-10) precisely as slain (5:12). That is the source of its authority to open the seals (5:1-5, 7; 6:1f.) and exercise judgment with God (6:15-16; cf., 14:9, 10; 17:12-14).

The essential focus of the Synoptic catechesis regarding eucharist, the solidarity of believers in the witness of a faithful martyr, is assumed in the Revelation. Indeed, that solidarity is combined with the imagery of Jesus as a sacrifice for sin in the portrayal of Christian martyrs as those who have whitened their robes in the blood of the lamb (7:14). They enjoy the presence of the lamb in their midst, now portrayed as shepherding them (7:17). It is telling that the image appears after reference to the sealing of the 144,000 of Israel (7:4-8) and to the worshipping throng "from every country, tribe, people and tongue" (7:9-12). The union of Jewish and non-Jewish followers of Jesus within the heroic sacrifice, implicit within the Synoptics, is unmistakable within the Revelation. The notion of whitening in blood is no paradox once it is understood that the underlying issue is the purification Christ as sacrifice effects.

Rev. 7 represents, in visionary form, the consensus of the New Testament regarding the global identity of the Church. The scope of the vision is marked by the number of the four angels, assigned to the four corners of the earth (7:1). Another angel arises to "seal" the servants of God, to mark them as slaves might be identified. Those marked first are 144,000 from Israel, 12,000 from each of the twelve tribes (7:2-8). Here, the image in the Gospels of twelve baskets gathered at the feeding of the five thousand has reached its apocalyptic climax. Israel in the numerical structure of the biblical promise is guaranteed its place in the judgment to come.

The number seven, the number of the baskets associated with the feeding of the four thousand, is also central within the Revelation, especially at this point in the book. The lamb is about to open the seventh and final seal in the presence of seven angels, to whom seven trumpets are given (8:1-2). As in the case of the feeding of the four thousand and the number of the deacons of the Hellenists in Jerusalem, the number seven derives from the book of Zechariah, where "the seven eyes of the Lord" are said to "range through the whole earth" (4:10). Seven is the number of the limitless reach of the divine kingdom. So here, in the Revelation (as it happens, chapter 7) the perfected number of Israel is joined by "a great multitude which no one could number, from every nation—all tribes and peoples and tongues—standing before the throne and before the lamb, clothed in white robes with palm branches in their hands" (7:9).

The debate with Israel after the Flesh: Christianity and Gnosticism challenged the sensibilities of the Greco-Roman religious philosophies of the second century. Both of them had discovered the idiom of philosophy in order to develop and convey their claims, crafting a distinctive view of the divine "Word" (logos) that conveys the truth of God to humanity. For most Christians, that Logos was Jesus Christ, understood as the human teacher who at last fully incarnated what philosophers and prophets had been searching for and had partially seen. Gnostics were inclined to see that "Word" as a fully divine, ahistoric revelation of the truth.

Justin Martyr was the theologian who articulated that doctrine most clearly from the perspective of Christianity, on the basis of the Gospel according to John. In 151 C.E., he addressed his Apology to the Emperor himself, Antonius Pius. Such was his confidence that the "true philosophy" represented by Christ, attested in the Hebrew Scriptures, would triumph over the other options available at the time. Justin himself had been trained within some of those traditions, and by his Samaritan birth he could claim to represent something of the wisdom of the east. Somewhere between 162 and 168, however, Justin was martyred in Rome, a victim of the increasing hostility to Christianity under the reign of Marcus Aurelius.[7]

Justin argued that the light of reason in people is put there by God and is to be equated with the Word of God incarnate in Jesus. His belief in the salvation of people as they actually are is attested by his attachment to millenarianism, the conviction that Christ would return to reign with his saints for a thousand years. That conviction, derived from Revelation 20, was fervently maintained by catholic Christians during the second century, in opposition to the abstract view of salvation that Gnostics preferred.

In strictly religious terms, Christianity did not compete well within the second century. Greco-Roman preferences were for ancient faiths, and the movement centered on Jesus was incontrovertibly recent. Moreover, it could and often did appear to be subversive of the authority of the Emperor. After all, Christians did not accept the Imperial title of *divi filius* ("Son of God"), applying it instead to their criminal rabbi. Moreover, this "Son of God" was a rabbi who was not even a rabbi, for the recognized authorities of Judaism did not accept Christians among their numbers. For such reasons, by the time Justin wrote, the persecution of Christianity had been an established policy of state for nearly a century.

The Christianity Justin defended, however, was as much a philosophy as it was a religion. His claim was that the light of reason in humanity, which had already been indirectly available, actually became fully manifest in the case of Jesus Christ. Jesus, therefore, was the perfect sage, and Socrates as much as Isaiah was his prophet. In that sense, Christianity was as old as humanity; only its open manifestation was recent.

In order to make his case, Justin used arguments previously employed by Philo of Alexandria, but on behalf of Judaism. Philo also identified the logos, the prophetic word articulated in Scripture, as the reason by which God created the world and animates humanity. (Unlike Justin, of course, Philo draws no conclusions about Jesus, his contemporary.) Philo even makes out the historical case that Moses was an influence on Plato, so that the extent to which Greek philosophy illuminates God's wisdom is quite derivative. Justin is even bolder in his Platonism, in that his argument does not rely on such an historical argument, but on the contention that in Jesus the primordial archetype of humanity and of the world itself, the logos, became accessible and knowable in a way it was not before.

One can easily imagine a debate between Philo and Justin. Had it occurred, it would have been the only encounter between Judaism and Christianity on the philosophical terrain they both claimed and were comfortable on. Philo's case, argued in his brilliant continuous commentary on the Pentateuch in Greek, identified the creative logos behind our world and in our minds as the Torah that God revealed perfectly to Moses. Justin, in a less voluminous way, more the essayist than the scholar, insisted that our knowledge of the logos implies that it is eternally human and that its human instance is Jesus.

The comparison between Philo and Justin shows how Judaism in the first century and Christianity in the second both relied upon the revival of Platonism, which provided each with a means of demonstrating that their respective religions were philosophically the most appropriate. The Platonic picture of perfect intellectual models was their common axiom, invoked in Philo's rounded, elegant Greek, and in Justin's controversial, rhetorical Greek. Had they met and disputed, Judaism and Christianity would have been represented for the only time in their history as approximate equals and on a level playing field.

But that meeting never happened. What divided them was not only one hundred years but watershed events. The Temple in Jerusalem had been burned under Titus in 70 C.E. and taken apart by Hadrian's order in 135. Judaism was still tolerated in a way Christianity was not, but it was a movement now under suspicion, and it needed to reconstitute itself in the wake of the failed revolts against Rome that resulted in the double destruction of the Temple. The rabbis who re-invented Judaism during the second century did so, not on the basis of Platonism, but on grounds of a new intellectual contention. They held that the categories of purity established in their oral teaching as well as in Scripture were the very structures according to which God con-

ducted the world. The Mishnah, the principal work of the rabbis, is less a book of law (which it is commonly mistaken for) than a science of the purity that God's humanity—Israel—is to observe.

So complete was the Rabbinic commitment to systematic purity at the expense of Platonism that Philo's own work was not preserved within Judaism but only became known as a result of the work of Christian copyists. And the same philosophical idiom that the rabbis turned from as a matter of survival, apologetic argument, was what Justin turned to, also as a matter of survival.

Justin sets his *Dialogue with Trypho, A Jew* in the period after the revolt under Simeon called Bar Kokhba (*Dialogue*, chapter 1) of 132-135 C.E. Thematically, Justin disputes Trypho's conception of the permanent obligation of the law (chapters 1-47) and sees the purpose of scriptures in their witness to Christ's divinity (chapters 48-108), which justifies the acceptance of non-Jews within the Church (chapters 109-136). Trypho, that is, is portrayed as arguing that the systemic meaning of the Scriptures is the law, while Justin argues that their systemic meaning is Christ.

Justin describes his own development from Platonism to Christianity as a result of a conversation with an old man. The sage convinced him that the highest good Platonism can attain, the human soul, should not be confused with God himself, since the soul depends upon God for life (chapter 6). Knowledge of God depends rather upon the revelation of God's spirit (chapter 7):

> Long ago, he replied, there lived men more ancient than all the so-called philosophers, men righteous and beloved of God, who spoke by the divine spirit and foretold things to come, that even now are taking place. These men were called prophets. They alone both saw the truth and proclaimed it to men, without awe or fear of anyone, moved by no desire for glory, but speaking only those things which they saw and heard when filled with the holy spirit. Their writings are still with us, and whoever will may read them and, if he believes them, gain much knowledge of the beginning and end of things, and all else a philosopher ought to know. For they did not employ logic to prove their state-

ments, seeing they were witnesses to the truth. . . . They glorified the creator of all things, as God and Father, and proclaimed the Christ sent by him as his Son. . . . But pray that, before all else, the gates of light may be opened to you. For not everyone can see or understand these things, but only he to whom God and his Christ have granted wisdom.

Here is a self-conscious Christianity, which distinguishes itself from Judaism and proclaims itself the true and only adequate philosophy. Justin's account of the truth of the logos depends upon two sources of revelation, resonant with one another: the prophetic Scriptures that attest the Spirit and the wise reader who has been inspired by the Spirit.

Justin is quite clear, then, that his concern is not with the immediate reference of Scripture, what we would call its historical meaning. That has also come to be known (rather confusingly) as its literal meaning. The description "immediate reference" is more accurate: the meaning of Scripture within the conditions in which it was produced. In his *Dialogue*, Justin portrays Trypho as being limited to the immediate reference of Scripture, enslaved by its specification of laws.

Justin is committed to a typological reading of Scripture, the Christian norm during the second century. The prophets were understood to represent "types" of Christ, impressions on their minds of the heavenly reality, God's own son. Isaac, for example, was taken to be a type of Jesus; while Isaac was *nearly* offered on Mt. Moriah in Gen. 22, Jesus was *actually* offered on Golgotha. That typology, which Paul had initiated in the first century (see Rom. 8:32), became a typical motif during the second century. Trypho, by contrast, is portrayed as becoming lost in the immediate minutiae of the prophetic text. So prevalent was this understanding of Judaism, by the end of the century, Christians such as Clement of Alexandria (see his *Pedagogue* 1.6.34) called any limitation to the immediate reference of Scripture (its "literal meaning") the "Jewish sense."

Anyone who is familiar with the development of Judaism from the second century onward will see the irony of this understanding of Judaic interpretation. The second cen-

tury was just the period when Scripture was being interpreted in terms of its eternal meaning, when any limitation to its immediate reference came to be overridden by an appeal to the significance of the eternal Torah. Gen. 22 is a case in point: from the second century, it came to be asserted that Isaac was slain on Moriah, that he accepted his fate as a fully grown adult, and that God raised him from the dead. In other words, Isaac was a type in Judaism as well, but of a different truth: an emblem of a martyr's obedience to the Torah rather than of a prophet's vision of Christ.[8]

So what is presented by Justin as a meeting of minds is in fact a missing of minds. Both Justin and Trypho in fact make the immediate reference of Scripture ancillary to its systemic significance. But because Christianity is now committed to the logos as its systemic center, and Judaism is now committed to the Torah as its systemic center, the two cannot understand one another. Any objection from one side to the other seems silly: it misses the systemic point.

Judaism as apostasy: In 388 C.E., a mob of Christians—at the instigation of their bishop—looted and burned the synagogue in Callinicum, a town on the Euphrates. The Emperor Theodosius demanded the punishment of those responsible and also directed that the property of the synagogue be restored and the structure rebuilt at the expense of the bishop. That evidently just sentence was vehemently resisted by Ambrose, bishop of Milan and one of the most important counselors to the Emperor.

Ambrose's intensity, as expressed in a letter (usually numbered 40 in collections), may seem surprising and irrational (40.8):

> This, Master, is my request: that your turn your vengeance upon me, and if you consider this act a crime, that you impute it to me. . . . I proclaim that I set the synagogue on fire, or at least ordered others to do so, that there might not be left a building in which Christ is denied.

When Theodosius simply ignored Ambrose, the latter preached directly to him in the cathedral in Milan (see the letter numbered 41).

Theodosius relented and in effect condoned what had happened at Callinicum.

Around this time, Ambrose composed his extensive sermon on the patriarch Joseph. Here his theology of Judaism is plain, and the formative influence of his theology on his political counsel becomes obvious. On his reading, the story of Joseph concerns Jewish recalcitrance. Jacob's rebuke of his son for the dream in which his family bowed to the ground before him reflects "the hardness of the people of Israel" (*Joseph* 3.8). But such relatively straightforward connections do not suffice for Ambrose. His reading of minor images is even more striking. Referring to the pit into which Joseph was thrown (Gen. 37:23-24), he comments (3.16): "As for the pit's being dry, what wonder if the pit of the Jews does not have water? For they abandoned the fountain of living water and made for themselves broken pits."

Ambrose here alludes to Jer. 2:13, where God complains that "they have forsaken me, the fountain of living water, and dug out for themselves cracked cisterns that can hold no water," but through a particular lens. In John 4:7-15, Jesus promises living water to those who ask him, and the Samaritan woman to whom he speaks compares his gift to the well of Jacob. To some extent, Ambrose argues as he does because his approach to Scripture, influenced by the neo-Platonism already evident in Justin, enables him to see in the biblical text types that are worked out in his own experience.

Within that experience, the issue of the rule of the Empire has been amalgamated with the issue of the identity of the Church. Part of Ambrose's argument, as he puts it to Theodosius, is that the usurper Theodosius had recently defeated (Maximus) had ordered that a synagogue in Rome should be rebuilt (letter 40.23). Whatever the particulars involved, he holds that this is bad policy, and for a simple reason: "The maintenance of civil law is secondary to religious interests" (letter 40.11). The position of the Emperor is like that of the Israelites (letter 41.26):

> You, like the Israelites, have entered the promised land: do not say, "By my own strength and righteousness I have obtained

these things," but "The Lord God gave them to me, Christ in his mercy conferred them on me." Cherish, therefore, the body of Christ, which is the Church; pour water on his feet, and kiss them, not merely forgiving those who have been taken in sin, but also by your pardon restoring them to peace and rest; anoint his feet, that the whole house wherein Christ reposes may be filled with the odor of your ointment, and that all those sit at table with him may be delighted with its fragrance. In plain words, honor the least of Christ's disciples and pardon their faults, that the angels may rejoice, that the apostles may exult, that the prophets may be glad.

The claims of typology, in which Israel becomes the Empire, have here overwhelmed any sense that "Israel" in itself may have a positive meaning left over. The people who are more usually called "the Jews" by this stage simply typify the rejection of Christ, and for Ambrose they are just "unbelievers." If Theodosius were to permit their synagogue to be rebuilt, they could inscribe on the front, "Temple of Impiety erected out of the spoils of the Christians" (letter 40.10). By Ambrose's day, Judaism represents that which resists Christ; actual dialogue is not even a theoretical possibility.

Judaism as a subversive threat: By the Middle Ages, distinguished Jewish teachers found themselves under inquisition because their interpretation was not sufficiently literal, at least as concerns the coming of the messiah. In 1263, Moses ben Nahman (also called Nahmanides) was convened in Barcelona before King Philip of Aragon and made to answer arguments put to him by a Jewish convert to Christianity. One charge he was made to respond to concerned his not taking his own Talmud seriously:[9]

> That man resumed, and said, In the Talmud it is said that Rabbi Joshua ben Levi asked Elijah, When will the messiah come? To which he replied, Ask the messiah himself. He said, Where is he? Elijah said, At the gate of Rome among the sick people. He went there and found him and asked him some questions. So, he has come, and is in Rome: that is, he is Jesus, who rules in Rome.
>
> I said, Is it not obvious from this that he has not come? For Rabbi Joshua asked Elijah, When will he come? Also, it is stated that Rabbi Joshua asked the messiah himself,

When will the master come? If so, he has not come yet, although according to the literal sense of these traditions, he has been born; but personally I do not believe that.

Then our lord the King spoke, If he was born on the day of the destruction of the Temple, which was over 1,000 years ago, and he still has not come, how can he ever come? For it is not in the nature of a human being to live 1,000 years.

I said to him, The agreement was that I would not dispute directly with you, and that you would not join in the discussion. Still, among the ancients, there were Adam and Methuselah, who lived for nearly 1,000 years; and Elijah and Enoch lived even longer, in that they are still alive with God.

The king asked, So where is the messiah today?

I said, That is not relevant to the debate, and I will not answer you. But if you send one of your runners, maybe you will find him at the gates of Toledo. (I said that ironically.)

Then they adjourned. . . .

King Philip and his associates were therefore saved from making further fools of themselves. Nahmanides' whole point, which his disputants have difficulty grasping, is that a discussion with Elijah (from B. San. 98a) is not to be pressed in its immediate reference. That is why his reference to Elijah as immortal, along with Enoch, is telling: he reminds the listener (to no avail) that conversations with such figures are outside the conditions of time. Then Philip compounds the literalism by raising the issue of the messiah's birth at the time of the destruction of the Temple. That discussion reverts to a much earlier argument about a different text (Lam. Rabbah 2.57). Philip is cast in the role of the dullest student in the seminar, who cannot follow what is going on. Instead of admitting he is lost, he invents questions that only show the thread of the argument escapes him.

Nahmanides' fun at the king's expense did not go unnoticed. The official record of the same disputation, composed in Latin, puts a very different cast on matters (Maccoby, pp. 149-150):

> . . . when he could not explain the textual authorities mentioned, he said publicly that he did not believe in the authorities which were cited against him, though they were in ancient, authoritative books of the Jews, because, he said, they were sermons, in which

their teachers, for the sake of exhorting the people, often lied. For this reason, he dismissed both the teachers and the scriptures of the Jews. . . .

The insistence on a single, consistent meaning in theological argument, in other words, was not just an artifact of Philip's difficulty in following the argument. Any inconsistency is taken here to be an indication of bad faith, and the official record concludes that Nahmanides had engaged in an attempt "to escape the disputation by lies." We are very far indeed from any appeal to typology or inspiration.

Between Justin Martyr and King Philip there lies not only a millennium but a different understanding of how Scripture may be understood to have meaning. By the time of the disputation at Barcelona, the powerful influence of Aristotle upon theology had been exerted. The world of Platonic types and ideals had been largely abandoned. Instead, the claim became increasingly fashionable that the immediate reference and the spiritual meaning of Scripture were one and the same. In the case of Nahmanides, he simply should have read his own texts, and he would have known the issue of the messiah was acute. That he failed to do so was proof of either ignorance or bad faith, perhaps some combination of the two.

The role of appeal to immediate reference grew as the Middle Ages progressed. It went hand in hand with the growth of the influence of Thomas Aquinas. He had baptized Aristotle by claiming that empirical knowledge and revealed knowledge complemented one another. The corollary of that picture of knowledge for interpretation was that the immediate reference of a text would lead one on to the spiritual sense. Any argument to the contrary was subversive of reason and knowledge together, which immediately implied that Judaism in itself was to be taken and countered as a threat to rational order.

Conclusion: Even as the movement of Jesus continued to address Israel after the resurrection, it is plain from the source called "Q" that the problem of the rejection of message of Jesus' followers was severe. The circle of Peter responded to that situation, and to the willingness of non-Jews to be baptized, with the association of Jesus with Moses and Elijah as sources of the spirit of God for those who believe. James' focus was the Temple and the maintenance of purity there, with the result that non-Jewish followers of Jesus were placed in a more ancillary position. Where the Pauline approach to the issue of non-Jewish discipleship was radical inclusion within a new definition of Israel, Barnabas (represented by the Synoptic Gospels) represented moderation—a separate apostolate for Jews and gentiles. Although that practice may have been dominant for much of the first century, by the close of the period of the New Testament, "Israel" (as Hebrews and the Revelation show us) had taken a subsidiary place in the definition of the people of God.

Justin Martyr's contention during the second century that Jesus, as the word of God, is the systemic center of all Scripture—whether the Scriptures of Israel or the apostolic memoirs—is therefore a direct, philosophical development of the position reached within the New Testament at the end of the first century. By the fourth century, Ambrose shows how that claim is translated into recommendations of public policy: the rejection of Christ, especially Israel's, is recalcitrance to the point of apostasy. The encounter between Nahmanides and his inquisitors in 1263 makes any such recalcitrance into a threat against rationality itself.

Bibliography

Chilton, Bruce, *A Feast of Meanings. Eucharistic Theologies from Jesus through Johannine Circles* (Leiden, 1994).
——, *Targumic Approaches to the Gospels. Essays in the Mutual Definition of Judaism and Christianity* (Lanham and London, 1986).
Maccoby, Hyam, *Judaism on Trial. Jewish-Christian Disputations in the Middle Ages* (Washington, 1993).
Neusner, Jacob and Chilton Bruce D., *The Body of Faith. Israel and the Church: Christianity and Judaism— The Formative Categories* (Valley Forge, 1996).

Notes

[1] See on this JESUS AND JUDAISM.
[2] See Leif E. Vaage, *Galilean Upstarts. Jesus' First Followers According to Q* (Valley Forge, 1994).
[3] Bruce Chilton, *A Feast of Meanings. Eucharistic Theologies from Jesus through Johannine Circles* (Leiden, 1994), pp. 72-74, 94-96.
[4] See Siegfried Schulz, *Q. Die Spruchquelle der Evangelisten* (Zürich, 1972).
[5] See C.K. Barrett, *The Acts of the Apostles: The International Critical Commentary* (Edinburgh, 1994), p. 592.
[6] Ibid., pp. 556-557.
[7] See Henry Chadwick, *The Early Church* (London, 1993), pp. 29, 74-79.
[8] See Bruce Chilton, *Targumic Approaches to the Gospels. Essays in the Mutual Definition of Judaism and Christianity* (Lanham and London, 1986).
[9] The account is Nahmanides' own. See Hyam Maccoby, *Judaism on Trial. Jewish-Christian Disputations in the Middle Ages* (Washington, 1993), pp. 113-114.

CHRISTIANITY ON JUDAISM IN MODERN TIMES: From the late sixteenth through the seventeenth century, Christendom, splintered by the Protestant Reformation, continued to develop its centuries old hate-love conception of Judaism. On the one hand, Judaism was a fossil that inexplicably refused to act like a fossil. Since it had long ago been replaced in God's economy by Christianity and the Church, it had to be eradicated, preferably by the conversion of its adherents to Christianity. On the other hand, the Christian "Old Testament" was Judaism's Bible, and the Bible was the rock upon which the Reformation stood.

Both Catholics and Protestants had been invested with Renaissance curiosity for things ancient, including "dead" languages such as Hebrew. Thus by the end of the sixteenth century, at the same time the printing press made these texts available far and wide, the number of Christian scholars capable of reading Scripture as well as Rabbinic commentaries in the original tongue had grown. Even as texts from the Church Fathers, with their diatribes against the Jews, became widely available, so was a broad spectrum of Jewish thought. A whole new encounter with Judaism was under way, resulting in the flowering of what came to be called Christian Hebraism.

The Protestant Reformation: Though the discontent with abuses, particularly the sale of indulgences, had been simmering for numbers of years earlier, the Protestant

Reformation is generally considered to have begun publicly in Wittenberg (Germany) on October 31, 1517, when Martin Luther nailed his "95 Theses" to the door of the Castle Church. The impact of this ecclesiastical dispute on Christian attitudes towards Jews and Judaism differed according to the theological positions of major reformers, particularly Martin Luther (1483-1546) and John Calvin (1509-1564).

Though early in his career Luther had proclaimed that Jesus was a Jew and had been certain that Jews would flock to his Christian reform movement, in his old age his vitriol against Jews knew no bounds, including admonitions to burn synagogues and drive Jews from their homes. This ambiguity in Luther's position was reflected in his monumental translation of the Bible into German, a translation that did for the German language what the King James version did for English. While making the Old Testament available to the masses, Luther's translation intentionally served his theological agenda, ensuring that Christ was found in almost every Old Testament word. For Luther, and the Lutherans who followed him, the Old Testament was misunderstood unless read through the lens of the New Testament. An implication for Lutheran reformers of this theological conviction was that Rabbinic interpretations of the Hebrew Bible were collections of lies. An important task was to ferret out and refute those lies, found in every facet of Rabbinic literature, including most especially the Talmud. Nothing of positive value for Christians was to be found in any Jewish literature later than the Bible. This conviction was to have fateful consequences for Jews and Judaism throughout the centuries to come.

John Calvin's perception of Jews and Judaism was considerably more complex than Luther's, often exhibiting contradictory judgments. For instance, he denied the allegation that the covenant of God with Israel had been taken over by the Church (supersessionism). But at the same time his understanding of the "Old Testament covenant" contained anti-Jewish convictions, including that it had been revealed to Israel in a veiled form and was "fulfilled" only in the coming of Christ.

Calvin also took a less dogmatic stance towards Scripture. Since the training of a learned clergy was an imperative for him, the academy he established in Geneva required the mastery of Hebrew as well as Greek and Latin. But he tended to ignore inconsistencies in the Bible, finding no need for elaborate exegesis or allegory, and he thought that Old Testament authors such as Moses, although they knew the relevant facts about, for example, creation, chose to speak in language common people could understand. In this sense, Calvin was more of a humanist, a fact that, along with his ambivalent approach to the covenant, could partially explain the development in the seventeenth century in the Netherlands of a genuine encounter of Calvinist scholars/clergy with rabbis and Jewish students of Rabbinics and Scripture, something that Calvin himself apparently never did.

Protestant assignment of religious authority solely to Scripture encouraged the application to the Old Testament of humanist scholarly tools even as it endorsed consultation of Jewish critical scholarship. Well into the eighteenth century the Old Testament was assumed to be the property of Christians—with Jews therefore usurpers of it. But Jews nevertheless were recognized as the custodians of centuries of learned commentary and tradition. A few Jewish thinkers even became guides of sorts for Protestants. Conservative reformist groups considered Maimonides (1135-1204) to be a defender of religion; Spinoza (1632-1677), who went so far as to suggest that the Old Testament books were composed in different centuries, was feared by some as a heretic but privately lauded in radical Protestant circles.

The Roman Catholic reaction to the Protestant Reformation—the Counter-Reformation—produced not only the lavish and ornate decoration of baroque churches (a highly visible rejection of the Reformers' iconoclasm) but also brought charges that Protestants were "Judaizers." In Spain and elsewhere, based on what were purported to be passages from the Talmud and other

Rabbinic writings, Catholic theologians continued to write learned treatises charging Judaism with the most amazing perversions.

The Council of Trent, which met intermittently between 1545 and 1563, came close to banning the printing of the Talmud and, had not Jews agreed to a "voluntary" censorship of their own, would have done so under the leadership of Pope Paul IV (1555-1559), who earlier had burned the Talmud in Rome. Later sixteenth-century popes, such as Pius V (1566-1572) and Gregory XIII (1572-1585), issued various bulls against the Jews, forbade Talmud reading, and supported the establishment of ghettoes. Nevertheless, the dawning of the seventeenth century saw an explosion of attention to Judaism as Christians, both Protestants and Catholics, searched Jewish sources in order to further their own theological agendas, including controversies with one another.

Christian attention to Rabbinics: In the seventeenth century, under the related impulses of humanism and the Reformation, the view that the Bible is a seamless whole inspired by God equally in all its parts began to break down. Distinctions were recognized among the three parts of the Hebrew Bible: the Torah, the Prophets, and the Writings. The Torah (Genesis, Exodus, Leviticus, Numbers, Deuteronomy) was held to be more sacred, because in it God had spoken directly to Moses. But the prophets and psalms were of most value to Christians, for there the direct announcement of the coming of Christ was thought to be found. As the European world turned away from belief in the miraculous, it seemed more reasonable, particularly for Protestants, to countenance prophesy than to trust in miracles.

The stubborn refusal of Jews to acknowledge Jesus as the messiah could be attributed in part to the fact that regular synagogue readings included the entire Torah but not all the prophets. Thus, even as Christians, through ever broader and deeper study of the Bible and of Rabbinic material, were gleaning valuable wisdom to support various Christian doctrines, it was thought that Jews simply refused to know the truth of their own Scriptures.

All Hebrew or Aramaic writings were lumped under the category "Rabbinic," and vast amounts of them were translated, often loosely, into Latin. This was primarily for the use of scholars, who frequently took great liberties in interpretation. But translations were made into the vernacular as well, though not in as great a quantity, as interest in Judaism spread into disciplines other than theology and to audiences that were curious about this "strange" people, the Jews, who lived among them.

Christian Hebraists were indebted particularly to the work of Johann Buxtorf the Elder (1564-1629) and his son, Johann Buxtorf the Younger (1599-1664) of Basel, Switzerland. Between them the Buxtorfs translated and published a vast amount of Judaica, including an extremely influential *Lexicon* and Buxtorf the Elder's monumental explication of the synagogue, *Synagoga Judaica* (1603). Intended as a popular guide, the latter work served, with scholarly apparatus, to perpetuate common Christian stereotypes of Judaism as a confused religion with a completely random collection of rituals that had no sense of God's holiness.

In his later years, Buxtorf the Younger moved away from his father's fixation on Judaism's "empty" rituals towards a growing reliance on the rational in religion. He justified his translations of Maimonides' *Guide for the Perplexed* and Judah Halevi's *Kuzari* by declaring that nothing is so totally evil that some good could not be found in it. In other words, the younger Buxtorf led the way towards an understanding of scholarship for scholarship's sake that was to result in an even wider study of the Hebrew language and the development of huge collections of Judaica in private and university libraries. Thus, by the end of the seventeenth century a considerable amount of information about Judaism was available to literate people, even to those without facility in Latin or Hebrew.

Though without doubt some of the attention to Rabbinics and Hebrew studies was purely scholarly, the principal use to which it was put served specifically Christian purposes, primarily the mission to convert Jews to Christianity. Since Judaism was considered an internally inconsistent religion that misunderstood its own Scripture, refutation of its untenable beliefs could best be done by citing the rabbis against themselves. That few Christians were inclined, or able, to grasp anything more than caricatures of Rabbinic Judaism did not deter them from their duty to destroy it on its own ground.

The more Christian clergy and academics knew, or thought they knew, about Rabbinic writings, the more they became concerned about the anti-Christianity they discerned there. The search was on for hidden names in the Talmud and later Jewish material that might conceal hostility towards the Church or even blasphemy. Printing was now widespread and not only the Bible but commentaries and theological works, both Christian and Jewish, were available to all who could read. Censorship followed, and the Catholic Index of Published Books canvassed Jewish material, frequently provided by converted Jews, for works worthy of being banned.

Seventeenth-century Christians, like their predecessors, understood the vexing problem of the survival of Judaism in two ways. On the one hand, the prophets of the Hebrew Bible had foretold the coming of the messiah, at which time, Israel would be renewed. Jesus, the messiah, had come, but the Jews had refused to recognize him as such and had, in fact, orchestrated his crucifixion. As a consequence, the suffering of the Jews had been magnified a thousand times, and they were condemned to wander homeless over the earth. Judaism was a dead religion that lived on only as a fossil.

On the other hand, since the holy books of Judaism contained testimony to the coming of Christ, a prophesy that had been fulfilled, the very existence of Jews and Judaism was witness to the truth of the crucifixion: these people had killed Christ, even though he was of their flesh and blood. They and their religion persisted in order to exhibit that testimony to generations to come. Judaism and living Jews thus were a theological necessity for Christians and the Church, Protestant and Catholic alike.

The Enlightenment: The intellectual and social movement known as the Enlightenment, which began in the seventeenth and peaked in the eighteenth century, initiated fundamental changes in Christian attitudes towards Judaism. The spirit of the Enlightenment in general was egalitarian, tolerant, and, above all, rational. But in this "age of reason" frontal attacks on the Church and Christianity were hallmarks of an increasingly secular society, and attacks on Christianity meant, at the same time, attacks on Judaism. Nevertheless, the situation was far from unambiguous. It was consistent in the Enlightenment for "rational" thinkers to sympathize with the plight of Jews, who were the victims *par excellence* of Christian religious and cultural intolerance. But there was a world of difference between and among Jews, Judaism, and Judaism's influence on Christianity and society.

For the first time, Christians began to recognize that the Hebrew Bible was a *Jewish* book, not (solely) an extended introduction to the New Testament. As a consequence, attempts were made entirely to separate Christianity from Judaism and thus to deny the theological dependence upon Judaism that had earlier prevailed. The Old Testament now became *literature*, and its tales of mighty battles and mythical beasts were compared with those of Homer, while the God who would order the destruction of hordes of Israel's enemies was decried as a barbarian.

English Deists and French philosophes: Deists such as Lord Herbert of Cherbury, Matthew Tindal, and Thomas Chubb taught that "natural religion" was intrinsic to human society, and, although the moral precepts of the Bible were valid, the practices of all religions were deeply flawed with impurities. This was particularly so in the case of Judaism, which Christianity had believed was the original locus of monotheism. The Deists held, however, that natural religion was monotheistic, while all polytheisms were mere superstitions. This meant that the Egyptians, Chinese, and other early peoples were monotheists before the Jews. Judaism was nothing special, as even the most anti-Judaic of the Christian Hebraists had always assumed. Once Christianity was relieved of its pagan and Jewish ritual, not to mention its convoluted and irrelevant theology, it could be shown to be identical with primordial natural religion.

As the implications of awareness that the books of the prophets were independently Jewish, not Christian, began to sink in, the Deists even called into question the seventeenth-century reliance on the Hebrew prophets for proof of Christianity. If the prophesies actually reflected events that happened, or were to happen, long before the advent of Christ, then—so the argument went—they could hardly be fulfilled in Jesus Christ. The Old Testament, therefore, became irrelevant for Christianity, and a direct corollary was the irrelevancy of Judaism itself.

Becoming irrelevant, however, did not exempt Jews and Judaism from disapprobation by the Deists. Enlightenment thinkers judged institutions and peoples by the degree to which they could be considered civilized, a cardinal characteristic of which was the presence (or lack) of a system of laws. In that regard, Judaism was without question civilized. But the laws of Judaism rested on a barbaric foundation: the bloodthirsty tribal God of the Old Testament and his bandit chieftain, David, plus the human-scarificers, Abraham and Jephthah. Judaism accordingly could not stand as a "civilized" religion, much less as a progenitor of Christianity.

By the middle of the eighteenth century the English Deists had proved to their own satisfaction that Christianity was all but fatally corrupted by Judaism. Everything that was fanatical (a particularly despised characteristic), priestly, or devoted to "mammon" had come from Judaism. In the eyes of the Deists, Judaism retained no valid reason for existence, not even the perverse reason that it was testimony to the unspeakable crime of deicide.

Though some of the English Deists, among them Thomas Morgan—a philosopher who took it upon himself to save Christianity by exposing its pernicious corruption by Juda-

ism—considered themselves to be Christian, the violent attacks on Christianity, using Judaism as the whipping boy, by French philosophes such as Voltaire (1694-1778) and Paul d'Holbach (1723-1789) by any normal criterion denied them the Christian label. Be that as it may, and though the churches as institutions and Christianity as a religion managed to survive the onslaughts of the philosophes, they had a determinative influence on decades of Christian understandings of Jews and Judaism.

Voltaire's agenda was the intellectual destruction of Christianity, which for him was a malign superstition. His assault on Judaism, therefore, was instrumental to his attack on Christianity. Like the English Deists, Voltaire thought of the Hebrews, the predecessors of the Jews, as barbarians without civilization. The Jews and Judaism of his own day were no different. How could they be when their origins were so polluted?

Jean Jacques Rousseau (1712-1788), on the other hand, claimed Moses as one of the great law-givers of the ancient world, but such a one as he could only come around once and, after him, the Jews had followed an ever descending slope. But what a man was Moses! Rousseau, like few other major Enlightenment figures, understood something of Judaism, but, for him, Jews would nevertheless always be outsiders; they could not become Christians.

Enlightenment churchmen: Though the Deists and philosophes set the principal intellectual tone of the eighteenth century— a tone that led eventually to the political emancipation of Jews throughout Europe but without changing the centuries-long evaluation of Judaism as a corrupt and corrupting religion—they were not without their challengers within the Catholic and Protestant churches.

In 1722 an older contemporary of Voltaire, Benedictine Abbot Augustin Calmet (1672-1757) published his *Dictionnaire historique, critique, chronologique, géographique, et littéral de la Bible*. A responsible work that reflected the Enlightenment spirit, it concentrated on precision in dating and geography and on concise literalism in description. As such, it treated Judaism fairly and spoke favorably of Jewish intellectual giants such as Maimonides, though it evidenced far less familiarity with Hebraic sources than had the Christian Hebraists of the century preceding. Calmet's Dictionary and his other, more popular, writings were derided by Voltaire but became a foundation upon which other Catholics could build as they became conscious of the danger to Christianity posed by the philosophes.

Abbé Antoine Guénée took it upon himself in 1769 to refute Voltaire's calumnies on the ancient Israelites by the novel device of publishing what were purported to be letters to the reigning philosophe from German and Polish Jews, in which Voltaire's readings of Old Testament passages were set beside the originals. The result was to reveal the manifold mistakes and contradictions Voltaire had made and, through obvious irony, to provide evidence of the superiority of Moses' laws and, indeed, of Moses himself. Guénée's work went into several editions and was occasionally reprinted even in the twentieth century for use by those who continued to refute Voltaire.

Another abbé, Nicholas Bergier, was responsible for a three-volume revision of the theology section of Diderot's *Encyclopédia* in which, among other things, he attempted to rehabilitate Old Testament figures who had been maligned by Voltaire and Holbach. Israelite religion, far from being barbaric as depicted by the philosophes, was pure and holy. And the purported intolerance of Jews toward gentiles was nothing of the kind. Instead, it was intolerance of idolatry and the "abominations" flowing therefrom.

In Germany during the eighteenth century only the pietists showed evidence of the tolerance towards Judaism present in England or France. Lutherans had not forgotten Luther's invective against the Jews, nor had they learned anything different. In Leipzig, even such an Enlightenment figure as Leibniz was not immune to the anti-Judaic virus, and the Grand Complete Universal Lexicon (*Grosses Vollständiges Universal Lexicon*)

published there in 1735 contained some of the most extreme vitriol against Judaism seen in over a century.

There were, however, a few exceptions. Johann David Michaelis (1717-1791), a noted advocate of the historical-critical approach to the Old Testament, viewed the Mosaic code as genuinely human. Compared with the true abominations of Canaanite religion, the horrors of which Michaelis painted vividly, the laws of Moses were superb examples of eighteenth-century jurisprudence. He saw the punishments meted out to the Hebrews who violated the laws of God to be wholly just and the destruction of cities condemned by God to be comparable to a holocaust sacrifice.

However, Michaelis would have nothing to do with the rabbis or the literature of Rabbinic Judaism, including not only the Talmud but also the greats of Jewish philosophy such as Maimonides and Rashi. Though he glorified the Mosaic code as valid in its own right, unlike many of his predecessors who had esteemed the Old Testament law as valid until superseded by the "law" of the New Testament, for him it had become totally corrupted by Rabbinism.

Idealization of ancient Judaism was carried even further by Johann Gottfried von Herder (1744-1803). A Lutheran pastor and progenitor of German romanticism whose advocacy of intuition over rationality greatly influenced Goethe, Herder found his philosophical inspiration in Kant. Not surprisingly, therefore, like Michaelis, he found little to admire in the Judaism he saw around him and was suspicious of Jews' efforts to integrate into German society.

The universal moral principal Emmanuel Kant (1724-1804) called the "categorical imperative" applied to all rational beings and was independent of any personal or national motive or desire. It thus retained no place for the Rabbinic rulings that were relevant only to Jews and, as far as Kant was concerned, actually were detrimental to the rational functioning of society. Of course if the laws of Moses were stripped of their particularistic accretions, the remaining core would come close to his own moral law. But that would mean the destruction of Judaism, the religion, a solution Kant thought would best serve Jews by transforming them into Deists, indistinguishable from Christian Deists like himself.

As the eighteenth century drew to a close with the French Revolution, Count Stanislas de Clermont-Tonnerre summed up the Enlightenment judgment on Jews and Judaism when he announced in the French National Assembly of 1789 that "Everything should be denied to the Jews as a nation; everything should be granted to them as individuals. Every Jew must individually become a citizen; if they do not want this, they must inform us and we shall then be compelled to expel them. The existence of a nation within a nation is unacceptable to our country."

Enlightenment continues—The nineteenth century: The intense attention to Judaism by Christian intellectuals in the seventeenth century—which, in the eighteenth century, gave way either to idealistic romanticizing of ancient Israel or to forcing the religion into a Deistic mold—came almost to a halt in the early nineteenth century. The Enlightenment and the rapidly expanding political emancipation of Jews throughout Europe focused Christian attention on Jews as individuals who, free to practice their own religion, were encouraged to assume their proper place in society as citizens.

The Enlightenment's solidification reversed Judaism's importance for Christianity. Throughout the preceding centuries Judaism had played a necessary role in the Church's theological self-understanding. Not only had the Church taken the Hebrew Scriptures for its own, but the continuing presence of Judaism provided the foil against which Christianity could establish its own validity. Under the Enlightenment's emphasis on the individual, however, an increasingly secularized world began to view religion as a private affair. Judaism, the religion of the Jews, was of no more social significance than was privatized Christianity. Christendom, well on its way to collapse, no longer felt compelled itself to judge either the truth or falsity of Judaism. And conversion of the Jews no longer was necessary for the working out of the Church's—or the world's—eschatological destiny.

Biblical scholars and Higher Criticism: Instead of the theological interest in Judaism that had characterized the sixteenth and seventeenth centuries, Christian academics in the nineteenth century—like Jewish scholars of the *Wissenschaft des Judentum* school of the same period—asked historical and philosophical questions. For instance, Georg W.F. Hegel (1770-1831), whose dialectical theory shaped virtually all subsequent philosophy throughout the century, delivered a famous series of lectures on the philosophy of history at the University of Berlin in which, though without prejudice to Jews, he relegated Judaism to the byways of history.

Biblical scholars now treated their material as they would secular texts, with the result that the so-called Higher Criticism revealed the complex nature of the Old and New Testaments, including their multiple sources and myriad authors. The work of German scholars such as F.C. Baur, Johann G. Eichhorn and, later, Hermann Gunkel and Julius Wellhausen and their colleagues and students turned biblical criticism on its head. They intended to discover historical truth and in order to do so an even better knowledge of biblical and cognate languages was required, as well as deeper insight into the religions supported by texts originally in those languages. Scripture was no longer treated as sacrosanct, but the knowledge of biblical religion was immeasurably increased and the historical, not simply theological, relation between Christianity and Judaism began to be evident.

The conclusions drawn by these scholars about Judaism as a religion were anything but complimentary, however. The schema developed by Wellhausen was generally accepted: Judaism began with the simple piety of Moses' time, developed into the sublimity of the prophets' monotheism, degenerated into mere legalism after the return from Babylonian exile ("late Judaism"), and finished with the dead religion of Rabbinism.

"Late Judaism" was the result of Rabbinic concentration on rites in the Jerusalem Temple and failure to recognize that the essence of Judaism was to be found in the nomadic conditions of Moses' time. Rather than a nation, Jews were a religious community destined to remain nomadic.

Theologians and racial theory: When applied to the New Testament, Higher Criticism lead to the attempt to ferret out the origins of Christianity and specifically to a look at the Judaism of Jesus' time. A favorite distinction was between the religion *of* Jesus and religion *about* Jesus, with a decided preference for the former, which—when coupled with newly-found interest in comparative philology and theories of race—resulted in another variant of the hoary estimation of Judaism as a degenerate religion.

David Strauss (1808-1874), whose *Life of Jesus* caused a theological uproar that lasted well into the twentieth century, was concerned to free Christianity from dependence on Jesus' miracles. He thus called into question the historicity of the Gospels, particularly the Gospel of John, and in the process demonstrated that the religion of the Jesus of history was grounded in Judaism. The Christ of faith, on the other hand, represented the transformation of the historical Jesus into a powerful myth that represented a higher truth than mere history could provide. As for Judaism itself, Strauss saw in myths about Christ the evidence that inadequate Second Temple Judaism, the religion of the Pharisees, Sadducees, and Essenes, had been transcended and lifted to a far higher spiritual plane. Contemporary Rabbinic Judaism was all but totally ignored. The old theory of Christian supersession of Judaism was taken for granted.

By the middle of the century, under the influence of Joseph Arthur de Gobineau (1816-1882) and others, the originally purely linguistic designations "Semitic" and "Aryan" had been converted into racial categories with assigned characteristics; "racial" antisemitism became popular as a political slogan through Europe. Most overt antisemitism was not specifically religious in nature, though Judaism was never far from the surface. Par-

ticularly was this so in eastern Europe and Russia, where the "blood libel," the charge that Judaism required the ritual murder of Christians as part of religious festivals, was actively spread by Russian Orthodox Christians, resulting in bloody pogroms.

Like other nineteenth-century Christian academics who dealt with Judaism, Joseph Ernest Renan (1823-1892) was primarily interested in Jesus and Christianity; Judaism merely came with the territory. Nevertheless his extremely popular *Life of Jesus* and his more intellectually significant works, *History of the Origins of Christianity* and *History of the People of Israel*, painted a picture of biblical Israel as a group of pastoral nomads that was to have a lasting effect on Christian perceptions of Jews and Judaism. Whereas Gobineau had seen the Semitic races (principally Jews and Arabs) as inferior to the Aryan races (principally Europeans), Renan viewed them simply as different, with unique qualities, each adding to the creative mix of humanity.

By including ancient Israel (and by extension modern Jews) in the general Semitic linguistic, racial, and religious category, however, Renan diluted the "uniqueness" that Judaism supposedly had for Christianity. In his history of Israel, for instance, he counted the kings of Israel as no better or worse than those of the peoples they conquered, the miracles of Moses as corruptions, and credited only the eighth- and ninth-century prophets with value. The value of these prophets was so great, however, that they represented the moral force that continued in Jesus Christ and, consequently, in Judaized Christianity and from there into the modern scientific world. From Renan's time until the present, the Hebrew prophets have remained the part of Israel's Scripture that Christians, particularly Protestant Christians, have considered to be most legitimate.

But the nineteenth-century work that was most to influence the understanding of Judaism among Christian theologians and seminarians was *A History of the Jewish People in the Time of Jesus* by Emil Schürer (1844-1910). Published in various editions from 1886 to 1890, Schürer's *History* became a standard source for everything Jewish, including archeology, geography, political and religious institutions, chronology, cults, and sects. His purpose, of course, was to delineate the context of the rise of Christianity, but in doing so he produced a mass of accurate and valuable information about what was still called "late Judaism."

Schürer's stance towards Judaism itself, though, did not deviate from the long-standing Christian perception that Judaism and "legalism" were identical. In the Jewish view, God kept a record book in which adherence to or violation of the law was meticulously recorded. Judaism's function, consequently, was to ensure the keeping of external regulations, to the total neglect of inward motive and conviction.[1]

Missions to Jews: Since discrimination against Jews in education, business, and the professions remained the norm rather than the exception, the temptation for Jews to convert to Christianity, which, after all, was presented as only slightly different from Judaism, was great. And the churches and, particularly, Protestant mission organizations took full advantage of the new opportunities. The concept of a covenant people or nation was submerged in the Enlightenment's progressive individualism: Jews were individuals who should be converted one by one. Earlier curiosity about Jewish beliefs and rituals abated and, though some missionaries to Jews became knowledgeable about Judaism, most Christian theologians paid scant attention to the details of the religion of the Jews who lived among them.

Beginning in the eighteenth century, the reaction by Christian pietists to the rationalism of the Enlightenment had resulted in the religious revivals known in England as the "Evangelical Awaking" and in the United States as the "Great Awakening." The nineteenth century saw the expansion of the vast colonial empires of the British, French, and Dutch and, with it, the pietist Protestant Missionary Movement that, by the end of the century, was characterized by John R. Mott's slogan, "The Evangelisation of the World in this Generation." The oldest missionary movement in the world, that directed towards Jews, was caught up by the fervor for Christian mission but attracted little attention outside the relatively small circle of evangelical Christians who took as their mandate St. Paul's testimony that "I am not ashamed of the gospel: it is the power of God for everyone who has faith, *to the Jew first* and also to the Greek" (Rom. 1:16).

In Germany the first institute for the study of Judaism designed to train missionaries to the Jews was established at Halle in 1728 and produced, *inter alia*, a Yiddish translation of the New Testament. It was disbanded in 1791, but almost a century later (1886) Franz Delitzsch (1813-1890) established the Institutum Judaicum at Leipzig. Upon his death "Delitschianum" was added to the institute's name; it remains in existence in Münster.

Delitzsch combined a genuine knowledge of Judaism, both ancient and modern, with a desire that Jews be brought into the Christian fold. Toward that end he produced a number of biblical commentaries and a Hebrew translation of the New Testament. At the same time he argued publicly against Christians who demonized the Talmud and other Jewish writings. When August Rohling, a professor of Catholic theology at the University of Prague, author of a collection of distorted and forged quotations from the Talmud, went on trial for slander, Delitzsch was instrumental in exposing the fallacy of his work, arguing forcefully for the religious validity of the Talmud.

Academic institutions like the Delitschianum supported, and were supported by, missionary agencies such as the "London Society for Promoting Christianity Amongst the Jews," founded in 1809. Missionaries came to know more about Judaism as it was actually practiced during the nineteenth and early twentieth centuries than any of their Christian contemporaries and, in the process, developed a genuine appreciation for Judaism as a religion. The missionaries believed that, because Judaism was a "good religion," it was more difficult to change Jews, as opposed to "pagans," into Christians. Utterly opposed to antisemitism, seen as a barrier to evangelization, they were among the most stalwart defenders of Judaism when it was denigrated or attacked by other Christians. They did not hesitate, however, to act on their conviction that Judaism was woefully inadequate when compared to Christianity, for, though it had the "law and the prophets," it did not have Christ.

By adhering to Judaism when they had every opportunity to know better, Jews showed that they needed salvation above all others. The evangelical motive of the missionaries was "pure," which is to say that they offered Christianity as the only viable alternative to Judaism out of genuine concern for the welfare of *Jews*, not in order to enhance Christianity, which by definition was not in need of enhancement. These were Christian individuals addressing individual Jews, and they were unconcerned that *Judaism* would be destroyed if their efforts were successful.

Genocide and ecumenicism—The twentieth century: Christianity's attitude towards Judaism shifted radically after the Shoah, the destruction of European Jewry by the Nazis in 1933-1945. But the events of the preceding three decades—large-scale Jewish migration as the result of pogroms in Eastern Europe and Russia, the upheavals caused by the Great War, the rise of political Zionism—had done little to alter prevailing Christian perceptions of Judaism. If anything, Judaism was perceived to be even more degenerate, a judgment that Jews themselves were believed to accept since, no longer having the ghetto to "protect" them, they were, so it was thought, abandoning the faith in droves. As for Zionism, it was viewed by many Christians as a naturalistic form of Judaism, Christianity's real rival for the Jewish soul.

Theological ambiguity: Reaction against the optimistic liberal theology of the nineteenth century took the form of "neo-Reformation" or "neo-orthodox" theology, of which Karl Barth (1886-1968) is representative, both of the theological trend itself and of its stance concerning Judaism. Arguably, no twentieth-century theologian, Protestant or Catholic, has influenced the century's theology more than Barth. But Barth's theology

vis-à-vis Judaism was not different from that of the missionaries to Jews, in that he resisted antisemitism—hatred and persecution of *Jews*—while characterizing *Judaism* in most ambiguous ways. He could, on the one hand, insist that Judaism embodied the revelation of God while, in almost the same breath, declaring that apart from Christ, Judaism is "nothing." He could say that no one could be chosen without being either "a Jew or heart and soul on the side of the Jews," and yet maintain that Judaism opposed and denied its own election by rejecting God's grace in Jesus Christ. Be this as it may, Barth's thought prefigured some of the themes that would emerge following the Shoah, such as the long-delayed recognition that the covenant between God and Israel remains valid even after the advent of Jesus Christ.

Ambiguity concerning Judaism continued into the Nazi period, when the overriding theological issue in fact became the integrity of the Church itself. Among Lutheran and Reformed Protestants, we find, on one side, the "German Christians," who supported Nazi ideology, and the "Confessing Church," which fought against Nazi take-over of the church (the "Church Struggle"), on the other. Though the underlying issue was the Nazis' intention to eradicate biblical religion, both Jewish and Christian, neither group of Protestants directly addressed earlier assessments of Judaism, the religion. The basic position remained the same. In the words of a paper written by Confessing Church pastors, "The place of the Old Testament people of the covenant was taken not by another nation, but by the Christian Church, called out of and living among all nations." In other words, supersession of Judaism by Christianity.

Catholic perceptions of Judaism remained substantially as they had been since the Middle Ages: Christianity had taken the place of Judaism in the economy of God. But, as with the Protestants, the spirit of Enlightenment tolerance had led to the recognition of the humanity of Jews. Many Catholics therefore resisted Nazi antisemitism and Catholic, as well as Protestant, missionaries to Jews engaged in oft-times heroic efforts to rescue Jews from their Nazi fate. Pope Pius XI, in a famous 1939 speech, declared that "Spiritually we are Semites," but his successor, Pius XII, was widely criticized for failing to condemn Nazi "race" policy for fear of losing the support of German Catholics.

The deadly antisemitism of the Nazis, though not directly perpetrated by Christianity, could scarcely be imagined apart from the age-long Christian theological denigration of Judaism and thus of Jews.

Christianity's historic reversal: With the closure of the death camps across Europe in 1945, Protestants and Catholics alike woke up to the horrendous consequences implicit (when not explicit) in their theological denigration of Judaism. A new recognition emerged, not only of the guilt of Christians, or even churches, for involvement in the genocide of Europe's Jews, but of the necessity to reevaluate the relationship between Christianity and Judaism. This process continues as the twentieth century draws to a close.

At its founding assembly in 1948, the World Council of Churches issued a statement designed primarily to encourage the evangelization of Jews, including a phrase that was to be copied by many subsequent Protestant statements: "Antisemitism is sin against God and man." Legislative bodies of Protestant churches in Europe and North America followed in the next years with similar statements that condemned antisemitism, though for the most part they remained within a missionary context, indicating that the fundamental perception of Judaism remained substantially unchanged. Nevertheless, to label antisemitism a sin was a significant theological judgment that spoke of Christian rejection of hatred and prejudice against *Jews* but said nothing necessarily about *Judaism*.

An attempt to enlarge the scope of the Council's perception of Christianity's relation to Judaism (still within the missionary framework) was unsuccessfully made at the second assembly in 1954. Only in 1961, at its third assembly, was the ecumenical body able to say, "In Christian teaching, the historic events which led to the crucifixion should not be so presented as to impose upon the Jewish people of today responsibilities which must fall on all humanity, not on one race or community." For the first time in Christian history, a representative body of the world-wide Church denied the charge of deicide, the charge that "the Jews" killed God and are still today responsible for that act.

The breakthrough that ushered in a surge of Christian reevaluation of Judaism came with the promulgation by the Second Vatican Council in 1965 of a statement entitled "Declaration on the Relationship of the Church to Non-Christian Religions" (better known by its opening Latin words, "Nostra Aetate"). Section 4 acknowledged that "True, the Jewish authorities and those who followed their lead pressed for the death of Christ; still what happened in His passion cannot be charged against all Jews, without distinction, then alive, nor against the Jews of today." A significant advance over the World Council of Churches' 1961 statement in that it exonerated Jews of Jesus' day as well as modern Jews from responsibility for the death of Christ, this rejection of the deicide charge by the Roman Catholic Church legitimated Christian scholars and churches' addressing in refreshingly new ways the questions of Christianity's relation to Judaism.

Beginning in the earliest days of gentile Christianity and Rabbinic Judaism, "dialogue" between Jews and Christians had been a one-sided affair, in which Christians attempted to prove the superiority of their religion over that of their opponents. But in the wake of Vatican II, dialogue more and more became a discussion between equals. The 1979 "Guidelines on Dialogue" of the World Council of Churches stated the principle upon which Jewish-Christian dialogue now would be conducted: "One of the functions of dialogue is to allow participants to describe and witness to their faith in their own terms. . . . Listening carefully to the neighbors' self-understanding enables Christians better to obey the commandment not to bear false witness against their neighbors. . . ."

For the first time in their history, Christians thus began to acknowledge Judaism as a valid religion in its own right that could provide positive contributions to Christian identity. Once it became unnecessary to castigate Judaism it was possible for Christians to take with theological seriousness the obvious historical fact that Jesus was a Jew who practiced one of the forms of Judaism that were the precursors of both gentile Christianity and Rabbinic Judaism.

Other theological issues that had been buried in supersessionist Christianity also began to surface, among them the role of God's covenant with Israel, the place of Torah (usually understood by Christians as "law"), and even the validity of the Hebrew Scriptures ("Old Testament") apart from the orthodox Christian conviction that their function was to predict the coming of Christ. Each of these issues continued to be debated in the churches, but the debate itself would have been impossible in earlier epochs, when nothing in Judaism was seen as having intrinsic value.

Among the many positive statements of official church theology regarding Judaism that appeared in the second half of the twentieth century, that of the Synod of the Evangelical Church of the Rhineland in 1980 stands out. In addition to confessing the guilt of "German Christendom for the Holocaust," the statement announced belief in "the permanent election of the Jewish people as the people of God and realize(d) that through Jesus Christ the church is taken into the covenant of God with his people." This theme—that Israel's covenant with God remains valid—was repeated by Protestant church assemblies throughout Europe and North America. The theological and ecclesiastical implications cry out for explication, but that remains a task for church theologians of the twenty-first century.

In 1982, the Executive Committee of the World Council of Churches issued a position paper entitled "Ecumenical Considerations on Jewish-Christian Dialogue" that attempted to summarize the thought of the Protestant and Orthodox ecumenical movement to that date. Among its many salient points was a note concerning the Talmud, the appreciative tone of which was in startling contrast with the position of earlier periods: "Judaism, with its rich history of spiritual life, produced the Talmud as the normative guide for Jewish life in thankful response to the grace of God's covenant with the people of Israel. . . . For Judaism the Talmud is central and authoritative. Judaism is more than the Scriptures of Israel."

The Vatican issued two papers as guidance for the implementation of Nostra Aetate, "Guidelines and Suggestions for Implementing the Conciliar Declaration" (1975) and "Notes on the Correct Way to Present the Jews and Judaism in Preaching and Catechesis in the Roman Catholic Church (1985). Promoted through the Church's bureaucratic structures, these documents led to the rewriting of curriculum materials to eliminate prejudice again Jews and Judaism and to the encouraging of local, national, and international dialogue-meetings between Jews and Christians.

In sum, the post-Shoah Christian reevaluation of the Jewish people produced a climate of acceptance of Jews unprecedented in Christian history. The degree to which a similar change took place relative to Judaism the religion, however, is debatable. The perceived Christian imperative to seek converts from Judaism remains solidly in place, particularly among more conservative Protestant churches. Even among mainline churches, including Roman Catholicism, the missionary impulse, albeit muted from time to time, is a constant in preaching and teaching. Though God's covenant with Israel is no longer disavowed and the churches deny taking Israel's place in the divine economy, the superiority of Christianity over Judaism (and all other religions) remains a given. The logical contradiction has never been acknowledged, so that much theological work remains to be done.

Bibliography

Brockway, Allan, et al., eds., *The Theology of the Churches and the Jewish People: Statements by the World Council of Churches and Its Member Churches* (Geneva, 1988).
Manuel, Frank E., *The Broken Staff: Judaism*

through Christian Eyes (Cambridge, 1992).

Wigoder, Geoffrey, *Jewish-Christian Relations Since the Second World War* (Manchester, 1988).

Williamson, Clark M., *A Guest in the House of Israel: Post-Holocaust Church Theology* (Louisville, 1993).

Notes

[1] The third volume of Schürer's *History*, where his discussion of "legalism" principally appeared, was revised and republished in 1987 by Geza Vermes, Fergus Millar, and Martin Goodman.

ALLAN R. BROCKWAY

CIRCUMCISION: *Milah* ("circumcision"), or, more properly, *brit milah* ("the covenant of circumcision"), consists of the removal of the foreskin from the penis of a baby boy, with the purpose of initiating him into the "covenant of Abraham." The term borrowed from the Rabbinic reading of Gen. 17, where Abraham and all his male heirs in perpetuity are told to practice circumcision as a sign of the covenant that God establishes with the people of Israel. As the physical and ritual rite of initiation into the covenant, circumcision is thus performed also on male converts to Judaism, regardless of their age. Already circumcised male converts undergo a shortened form of the ritual entitled *hatafat dam*, literally "a drop of blood." In this ritual, a single drop of blood is drawn from the penis as a representation of circumcision, which is performed not merely as a surgical procedure but as a religious act that brings about entry into the Jewish covenant.

In keeping with the Abraham narrative, circumcision normally occurs on the eighth day of an infant's life, counting the first day of birth (no matter what time of day birth occurs) as day one. The dictate to circumcise on the eighth day is considered so important that circumcision occurs on that day even if it is a Sabbath or holy day, even on Yom Kippur, when all "work" normally is prohibited. The rite occurs in the daytime hours, not at night, and it usually is performed in the child's home. Here guests gather, technically, to witness the covenant's being passed to another generation, and to celebrate the event by sharing a meal thereafter known as a *se'udat mitzvah*, "a feast entailed by a com-

mandment." Despite the weightiness of the obligation to circumcise on the eighth day, circumcision may be delayed—indefinitely, if need be—for reasons of health (e.g., hemophilia) as established by medical experts. In some contemporary liberal Jewish circles, circumcision is considered optional, not mandatory, for converts.

Jewish law requires three surgical steps: (1) *milah* (lit., "circumcision" proper), that is, the removal of the outer foreskin that covers the tip (the *glans*) of the penis; (2) *periyah*, whereby an underlying mucous membrane that lies below the foreskin is peeled back and stripped away; and (3) *metsitsah*, the stanching of the blood so that the wound is fully cauterized. Today, through the use of a surgical clamp (see below), *milah* and *periyah* usually occur simultaneously.

The man (in liberal circles nowadays, a woman may serve as well) who performs the operation is known as a *mohel* (fem.: *mohelet*, pl.: *mohalim*). *Mohalim* are professionally trained in the religious ritual and surgical practice, so as to perform the ceremony rapidly and hygienically, often using modern equipment such as a surgical clamp that streamlines and facilitates the procedure according to the canons of modern medicine but in keeping with the spirit and law that marks Jewish tradition. *Mohalim* consider their job a means of serving God and are expected to exemplify Jewish wisdom and character in all they do. Nowadays, the *mohel* is commonly assisted in the ritual part of the operation by a rabbi who recites the requisite liturgy, names the child, and invokes blessing upon the boy and his family.

Circumcision in the Bible: Male circumcision is well attested in the various strands of Hebrew Scripture. Israel's narrative is organized so that it virtually begins when Abraham circumcises Isaac (Gen. 21:4) after circumcising himself and Ishmael and all the other male members of his retinue (Gen. 17:23-27). Thereupon, the Bible presents circumcision as a custom that is taken for granted as normative for all Israelite men. Jacob's sons, for instance, tell Chamor and Shechem that Israelite women cannot have uncircumcised husbands, since an uncircumcised condition for males is "a disgrace among us" (Gen. 34:13-16). When the people of Israel leave Egypt, God instructs Moses to prepare a Passover offering, of which only the circumcised may eat (Exod. 12:44, 48). Zipporah circumcises Moses' son when his uncircumcised condition threatens him with danger (Exod. 4:24-26), and Joshua assures that all Israelite males are circumcised before the people enter the Promised Land (Josh. 5:2-8). With Lev. 12:2-3, circumcision enters Israel's legal regulations for all time: "When a woman at childbirth bears a male . . . on the eighth day, the flesh of his foreskin shall be circumcised."

But the biblical editor's carefully orchestrated presentation of circumcision as a covenantal custom stretching back endlessly and without change from Abraham on is not without lacunae. Deuteronomy presents Moses' final charge to Israel as if the covenant and circumcision have nothing to do with each other. It knows a covenant involving the gift of the Land, which the Israelites will enjoy if they follow all of God's Torah, but as for circumcision, it records only the metaphoric vision that "God will circumcise your heart" (30:6), a usage picked up a century later by Jeremiah (Jer. 9:25).

If we survey the biblical narrative according to the probable date at which its several interwoven strands were composed rather than the canonical chronology imposed by the final editors, it becomes clear that even though Israelite men were indeed circumcised from a very ancient time, it was only in the post-exilic period that circumcision was associated with covenanthood. Prior to that, circumcision was associated not with covenant at all, but with the belief that circumcised males would prove more fertile. For instance, the foreskin that is stripped away is called the *orlah*, as is the first fruit of a tree that is removed while still unripened (Lev. 19:23). The male member thus is likened to a tree trunk, with its unripe growth requiring removal if the male child, like a young sapling, is to be able to bear fruit in abundance later in life.

Deuteronomy and the pre-exilic prophets do believe in the existence and importance of the covenant, but they see it as the condition by virtue of which Israel has been deeded God's chosen Land, not in any way linked to circumcision. The covenanted people must choose life over death, blessing over curse, says Moses in his final peroration (Deut. 30). Nowhere does he stipulate that they must choose also to be circumcised. The early account of the Abrahamic covenant given in Gen. 15, and datable to the Davidic-Solomonic monarchy, thus emphasizes landedness, not circumcision, an appropriate agenda for an era demanding justification for the establishment of an independent Israelite kingdom for the first time.

After the exile, however, and under theocratic hegemony, circumcision was reinterpreted theologically to be the sign of the covenant. Gen. 15 was thus recast in Gen. 17 to picture circumcision of Israelite men as the normative condition on which the covenant depends, and Leviticus—newly composed as the middle and ideologically central chapter in Israel's narrative—portrayed circumcision as a foundational cultic responsibility. By contrast, Jeremiah's pre-exilic metaphor of a circumcised heart was ignored until Christian exegetes used it to support the arguments of those within the early church who denied the necessity of circumcision (see, e.g., Rom. 4:10-12).

Circumcision becomes a sign of the covenant, therefore, only in the final strata of the Torah. Assuming a fifth century B.C.E. date for the Torah's redaction, we are left with some six or seven hundred years until the first canonical Rabbinic document, the Mishnah, comes into being. For most of that time, circumcision was practiced as a covenantal rite, not merely (or perhaps no longer at all) as a precaution against infertility, but there was still no accompanying liturgical ritual. Only at the end of that period, probably in the Tannaitic era (c. 70-200 C.E.), was a ritual script to accompany the physical operation elaborated.

The Rabbinic ritual in context: The ritual in question took shape through the Tannaitic era and into the early Amoraic era as well (c. second-fourth cents.), and comprised five liturgical parts, all of which are present today:

1. The circumciser (the *mohel*) recites an opening blessing, "Blessed art Thou, Lord our God, King of the universe, who has sanctified us by your commandments and commanded us concerning circumcision."

2. The father, on whom Jewish legal responsibility to circumcise his son technically devolves, says, "Blessed art Thou, Lord our God, King of the Universe, who has sanctified us by your commandments and commanded us to admit him [the child] to the covenant of Abraham our father."

3. Those in attendance originally responded, "As you have brought him into the covenant, so may you admit him to the study of Torah and marriage." By the second or third century, this response was altered in two ways. First, to "study of Torah and marriage," the phrase, ". . . and to good deeds" was added. A midrashic fragment (Ec. Rab. 3:3) suggests that the addition was a response to a folk belief that good deeds, a prophylactic against early death, should be sought at the moment of circumcision when demonic forces threaten to cut short a child's life. In addition, the inclusion of "good deeds" probably played a polemical role in the Jewish-Christian debate on the efficacy of works over faith.

Second, it was recognized that good deeds (unlike Torah study and marriage) constituted something to which the father could not reasonably be expected to admit his son. Instead of charging the father to continue raising his child in proper covenantal fashion by admitting him to Torah, marriage (and now, good deeds as well), the bystanders began voicing the pious wish, "Just as he [the child] has entered the covenant of circumcision, so may he enter Torah, marriage and good deeds"—that is, the burden of responsibility was rhetorically displaced from the father onto the child himself, in a rephrasing of the response that is found to this day.

4. The *Mohel* adds:

> Blessed art Thou, Lord our God, King of the universe, who sanctified the beloved one [Abraham] in the womb. He [God] set a

statute in his [Abraham's] flesh, and he [Abraham] stamped his descendants with the sign of the holy covenant. Therefore, as a reward for this, O living God, our Portion and our Rock, command [i.e., the imperative; or, in other texts, the perfect, or past, tense, "commanded"] that the beloved of our flesh shall be delivered from the pit. Blessed art Thou, Lord, who makes a covenant.

Our current version of this blessing differs somewhat, containing redundant material added through the ages; the designation of the subject—given here in brackets—follows, in part, medieval exegesis, on which, however, opinion differed, some authorities believing that the prayer included reference to all three patriarchs, Abraham, Isaac, and Jacob (cf. Tosafot to B. Shab. 137b, s.v. *yedid*).

The struggle with early Christianity is evident throughout this blessing, which polemicizes in favor of the salvific character of circumcision, in contrast to the Pauline epistles, and even uses identical language to Paul (Rom. 4:11)—terminology defining circumcision as a seal or signet ring demonstrating ownership. For Paul, the seal of circumcision was just an outward sign of Abraham's prior faith, so that ever after, it was faith that mattered, while circumcision was allowed to lapse. For the rabbis, circumcision remained the eternal sign of the covenant. Church fathers continued to interpret circumcision as the visible outward sign of a similarly outward covenant of the flesh, which had been superseded by an inner covenant of the spirit. Circumcision remained an outward sign, they charged, but only of that very Jewish contumacy that lost the Jews their covenanted Land of Israel (Tertullian, *An Answer to the Jews*). The rabbis responded by reaffirming the eternal validity of the covenant, the absolute necessity of circumcision, and Israel's everlasting ownership of the Land. They therefore inserted reference to the obligation of circumcision in the second blessing of the Grace after Meals (*Birkat Ha'aretz*), which thanks God for the gift of the Land.

5. There is reason to believe that the early ritual contained at least some sort of prayer to name the baby. John the Baptist was

named at his circumcision (Luke 1:59-63). The absence of any prayer ritual in that account may indicate only its author's lack of concern with whatever blessings people normally said; or it may be that the liturgy in question postdates Luke's account and must be dated only in the second century, after Luke but before the Mishnah's codification. In either case, however, we know at least that names were bestowed at the circumcision, even if we do not know what prayers were said at the naming. In any event, we do have a naming prayer in today's rite. Its traditional version reads in part:

> Our God and God of our fathers, sustain this child to his father and to his mother, and let his name in Israel be (so-and-so, son of so-and-so, his father). Let the father rejoice in what has come forth from his loins, and let the mother be happy with the fruit of her womb, as it is written: "Let your father and mother rejoice, and let her that bore you be happy" (Prov. 23:25); and it is said, "I passed by you and saw you wallowing in your blood, and I said to you: 'In your blood, live;' I said to you: 'In your blood, live'" (Ezek. 16:6).

This particular prayer is unattested in the Tannaitic record. But neither the Mishnah nor the Tosefta contains comprehensive records of Tannaitic ritual, and at least one medieval authority (Eliezer ben Joel Halevi, c. 1140-c. 1225) says he saw this prayer in his edition of the Palestinian Talmud. Moreover, a parallel prayer can be found in *Seder Rav Amram* (ninth cent.), petitioning also for the health of mother and child. Its composition in Palestinian Aramaic suggests that it was an early alternative to the version that eventually became customary. We may conclude, therefore, that the early ritual too ended with naming the child and praying for his health and that of his mother.

Of greatest interest here is Ezek. 16:6, which is cited prominently in today's prayer but which occurs also in second-century sources, within the context again of anti-Christian polemic: "I passed by you and saw you wallowing in your blood, and I said to you: 'In your blood, live;' I said to you: 'In your blood, live.'" Its significance in the con-

text of the debate on the efficacy of works over faith is evident from the following second century midrash (*Mekhilta Bo*, Chap. 5.):

> Rabbi Matia ben Cheresh used by say, "Behold, it says, 'I passed by you and looked at you and saw it was a time of love' (Ezek. 16:8). This means the time had arrived for God's vow to Abraham to be fulfilled, namely, that He would save his children. But as yet they had no commandments to perform, by virtue of which they might merit redemption.... As it says, "Your breasts were fashioned and your hair had grown, but you were naked" (Ezek. 16:8), meaning that they were naked of all commandments. God therefore assigned them two commandments: the sacrifice of the paschal lamb, and circumcision, which they were to perform so as to merit being saved, as it says: "I passed by you and saw you wallowing in your blood, and I said, 'By your blood live.... By your blood live'" (Ezek. 16:6).... *One cannot obtain reward except by deeds.*

As the Ezekiel exegesis demonstrates, the central symbol of the circumcision ritual was its blood. Regularly, therefore, we find reference not only to the salvific nature of the rite in general, but more specifically, to the saving merit of circumcision blood. Nowadays, a blessing accompanies the symbolic placing of wine on the lips of the baby boy just after the circumcision wound has been cauterized. It is virtually certain that in early Rabbinic Jewish tradition, as in Christian, wine symbolized blood: Y. Pes. 10:3, for instance, defines wine-made *charoset*—a paste of honey and nuts eaten at Passover to symbolize the mortar used by the Israelite slaves—as "a remembrance of the blood [of the paschal lamb]." In the circumcision ceremony, the blessing over the wine was probably added at a later time, when the original symbolic value of the wine as blood had been forgotten. Originally, no blessing was recited here, since the wine was never meant to be consumed as such, certainly not by the adult participants; it was instead regarded as an oral transfusion of wine (= blood) for the child. In a nutshell: blood escapes the system; wine as blood enters it.

At any rate, the symbolic value of circumcision as an act of salvation is evident throughout our second century sources. It is the sign of the covenant that saves. The blood drawn in the act is equivalent to the blood of the paschal lamb that Israelites smeared on their doorposts to warn off the angel of death on the night the first-born Egyptians were slaughtered (Exod. 12:22-23). It is the paradigmatic salvific example of a good work, practiced in every generation from Abraham onward. As such, it has commanded the universal allegiance of Jews throughout history.

Medieval additions: Medieval European Jews added to the symbolic prism through which circumcision's merit was perceived. An earlier midrash (Pirkei deRabbi Eliezer, chap. 29) had designated Elijah as an appropriate visitor to the circumcision, and assigned him a "seat of glory" (*moshav kavod*) there. Following the Crusades and paralleling Christian expectations of an imminent second coming of Christ, this theoretical notion crystallized in actual ritual practice, as Jews began invoking Elijah's presence in happy anticipation of messianic deliverance. In thirteenth-century Italy (*Shibbolei Haleket, Hilkhot Milah*, Section 8), the child was expressly welcomed with words indicating that he might be the messiah himself, born of the house of David. He was seated on the special seat defined by the midrash, but eventually renamed *kisei eliyahu*, "Elijah's chair."

Although the messianic symbolism has by now been forgotten, the practice of welcoming the child and calling on Elijah has been retained. The child is normally brought into the room accompanied by the recitation of biblical verses on the theme of deliverance; he is greeted at the outset with the messianic invitation from Ps. 118:26, "Blessed be he who comes" (cf., Matt. 21:9, Mark 11:9, Luke 19:38), and then placed on the chair of Elijah, who is summoned to be present at the event.

Originally, mothers had carried their sons to their circumcision, holding them during the operation. John's mother is therefore portrayed as being present in the Lukan account, and mothers drink wine and are prayed for in the ninth century *Seder Rav Amram* text. By the thirteenth century, however, Rabbi Samson bar Tzaddok of Germany complains on behalf of his teacher, Meir of Rothenberg (known as Maharam), that mothers should be removed from the ceremony because it is unseemly for women to mix with men, especially in the synagogue (where the ceremony occurred in his day), and all the more so during morning worship (when the rite was usually scheduled). A spiritual descendant of the strict pietism that dominated post-Crusade Germany, Maharam became the most influential leader of his generation, so that within a century, his opinion prevailed: women were henceforth excluded from the rite, and a newly developed ritual role of *sandek* (related etymologically to the Christian term for Godfather) evolved in the mother's place. Now the *sandek*, not the mother, held the boy for the operation.

In time, two other roles became somewhat common: the *kvatter* and the *kvatterin*, a man and a woman honored with the task of presenting the child to the *mohel*, who then gives him to the *sandek* for the procedure. The role of *sandek*, however, remained particularly valued as time went on. This is because kabbalistic theory likened the ritual more and more to a sacrifice, especially the near-sacrifice of Isaac on Mt. Moriah. In keeping with this metaphor, the current traditional rite therefore prays:

> Creator of the universe, may it be your will that this child be considered and accepted positively by You, just as if I had brought him before your throne of glory. In your great mercy, send by means of your sacred messengers [angels] a holy a pure soul to this circumcised child. . . . May his heart be open to your holy Torah like the opening of the doorway to the Temple hall.

The fourteenth century German master Jacob Moellin (known as Maharil), the leading exponent of German Jewish thought after Maharam even held that acting as a *sandek* "is greater than the commandment performed by the *mohel*, since his knees are likened to an alter as if he were offering incense to heaven" (*Sefer Maharil, Hilkhot Milah*). The sixteenth century Polish savant, Moses Isserles, codified the whole development by deciding that "the *sandek* takes precedence over the *mohel* in being called to the Torah, since a *sandek* is likened to someone who offers incense at the altar" (*Shulchan Arukh, Yoreh Deah*, 265:11).

By the sixteenth century, the ceremony had been expanded to include considerable celebration during the night prior to the actual circumcision. Medieval exegetical tradition traced the evening's festivity to a Talmudic party known in the Mishnah as *Shavua Haben* and identified in the Gemara as *Yeshua Haben*. The etiology is false, since the Mishnaic and Talmudic events are more likely aspects of birth festivities celebrating the birth of a boy or girl and having nothing to do with circumcision *per se*, except the coincidental fact that since the celebration consumed an entire week after the baby's delivery, its final night fell by chance on the eve prior to circumcision, if the baby was a boy. Nonetheless, the heightened messianic expectation reinforced by Kabbalistic doctrine in particular established an evening celebration prior to the circumcision. It was known by various names in the vernacular, for instance, *Wachnacht* (in Germany), a term that still expresses the messianic night of watching (akin to Passover eve or the Jewish roots of the Easter vigil) as well as folkloristic motifs of protecting the boy from harm that night. The practice continues in some circles, although it has been moved to the Friday night prior to the event, and renamed *Shalom Zakhar*, or, more commonly, the Yiddish, *Shol'm Zoch'r*.

Various artistic embellishments testify to the growth of circumcision as a folkloristic highlight in the late Middle Ages, chief among them the wimple, or swaddling cloth, which goes back to sixteenth century Germany. Composed of linen (or silk for those who could afford it), it was used to wrap the infant and then cut length-wise into strips, sewn end to end to constitute a banner, and inscribed with the boy's name and birth date, as well as the wish, "As he entered the covenant, so may he enter Torah, marriage, and good deeds." The wimple would be used to wrap the Torah scroll when, years later, the boy became a *bar mitzvah* and when, later

still, he was called to the Torah to be granted the honor of reciting blessings over the Sabbath Torah lection on the Sabbath prior to his marriage.

The ritual art associated with circumcision includes also circumcision knives, double-cup sets (one cup to hold the wine, and another to catch the circumcision blood), and elaborate chairs of Elijah, often a bench with two seats, one on which the boy is briefly placed during the introduction to the ritual, and the other on which the *sandek* sits while holding him for the operation.

Modern issues: During the nineteenth century, some emancipated Jews began having second thoughts about the circumcision rite. European boys were not universally circumcised, so that Jewish practice stood out as unusual, possibly even primitive, given the mores of the period. Particularly embarrassing for Jews intent on demonstrating that they were worthy of being granted citizenship and civil rights was the fact that the sanitary bureau of Frankfort had been investigating some cases of infant fatality that were said to be traceable to the operation. When a lay society announced its intention of jettisoning the age-old rite on the grounds that it no longer represented the essence of their Mosaic faith, they encountered universal condemnation by German rabbis, even the liberals, some of whom personally opposed circumcision themselves, but who were loath to say so publicly. The rite therefore continued despite reservations that many had about its propriety (figs. 43, 44).

Again in our time, the issue has been addressed, this time on different but related grounds. Nineteenth-century opposition was rooted in evolutionism, the assumption that a mature Judaism could safely pare away the dysfunctional ritual of its youth. Today's objections come in part from feminist circles where this very masculine rite is seen as reinforcing outmoded notions of a covenant solely with men. Objections emerge also from the perception that the rite may entail sexual mutilation. Supporters of the rite champion its age-old centrality in Jewish consciousness, mentioning especially the fact that in times of persecution, Jews have willingly died rather than give up the sign of the covenant. They deny the charge of mutilation, noting that the operation may even be in the child's best interest for other than religious reasons (medical opinion goes back and forth on that score). Liberal Jews have thus tended to retain the rite, but to do so in a way that mutes its objective features. A small local anesthetic does away with any pain that the child might encounter, and a revised ritual script emphasizes the theological status of covenanthood into which boys and girls are now equally inducted. The blessing structure of the rite is thus recited for both sexes, and the actual operation attendant upon it and relevant only to boys is relegated to the background. In the foreground is the liturgical (and egalitarian) liturgical script that emphasizes the continuity of covenanthood from generation to generation, but not the actual act of circumcision which is taken as a secondary manifestation, for boys only. The primary item becomes the covenant itself that is duly celebrated for every child now, male or female.

For many, therefore, circumcision now is hardly the central act of faith that it once was. Almost no one is aware any more of the salvific symbolism it once contained: the blood that saves, the parallelism between circumcision blood and blood of the paschal lamb, the very real hopes once invested in the child as potential messiah, or the cultic symbolism of sacrifice that dominated centuries of Rabbinic thought. But the rite still maintains its hold on the popular imagination, at least in most circles. Since baby boys in North America are systematically circumcised anyway, Jews who advocate Jewish circumcision as a religious responsibility are at least sheltered from the need to justify their own practice in the light of a contrary cultural trend, such as Germany presented a century and a half ago.

Bibliography

Barth, Lewis M., *Berit Milah in the Reform Context* (New York, 1990).

Boyarin, Daniel, "'This We Know to Be the Carnal Israel': Circumcision and the Erotic Life of God and Israel," *Critical Inquiry* 18 (1992), pp. 474-505.

Hoffman, Lawrence A., *Covenant of Blood: Circumcision and Gender in Rabbinic Judaism*, (Chicago, 1996).

Horowitz, Elliott, "The Eve of Circumcision: A Chapter in the History of Jewish Nightlife," *Journal of Social History* 23 (1989), pp. 45-69.

LAWRENCE A. HOFFMAN

CONSERVATIVE JUDAISM: With roots in the German Judaic response to the development of Reform, then Orthodox Judaism, on the one side, and the immigrant response to the conditions of American life in the twentieth century, on the other, Conservative Judaism seeks a centrist position on the issues of tradition and change. The Historical School, a group of a nineteenth century German scholars, and Conservative Judaism, a twentieth century Judaism in America, took the middle position, each in its own context. They form a single Judaism, because they share a single viewpoint. The Historical School began among German Jewish theologians who advocated change but found Reform extreme. They parted company with Reform on some specific issues of practice and doctrine, observance of the dietary laws and belief in the coming of the Messiah for example. But they also found Orthodoxy immobile. Conservative Judaism in America in the twentieth century carried forward this same centrist position and turned a viewpoint of intellectuals into a Judaism: a way of life, world view, addressed to an Israel. The Historical School shaped the world view, and Conservative Judaism later on brought that view into full realization as a way of life characteristic of a large group of Jews, nearly half of all American Jews by the middle of the twentieth century.

The Historical School in Germany and Conservative Judaism in America affirmed a far broader part of the received way of life than Reform, yet rejected a much larger part of the world view of the system of the dual Torah than did Orthodoxy. Calling itself "the Historical School,"[1] the Judaism at hand concurred with the Reformers in their basic philosophical position, but with the Orthodox in their concrete way of life. The Reformers had held that change was permissible and claimed that historical scholarship would show what change was acceptable and what was not. The proponents of the Historical School differed in matters of detail. The emphasis on historical research in settling theological debates explains the name of the group. Arguing that its positions represent matters of historical fact rather than theological conviction, Conservative Judaism maintained, that "positive historical scholarship" will prove capable, on the basis of historical facts, of purifying and clarifying the faith, joined to far stricter observance of the law than the Reformers required. Toward the end of the nineteenth century rabbis of this same centrist persuasion organized the Jewish Theological Seminary of America, in 1886-1887, and from that rabbinical school the Conservative Movement developed. The order of the formation of the several Judaisms of the nineteenth century therefore is, first, Reform, then Orthodoxy, finally, Conservatism—the two extremes, then the middle. Reform defined the tasks of the next two Judaisms to come into being. Orthodoxy framed the clearer of the two positions in reaction to Reform, but, in intellectual terms, the Historical School in Germany met the issues of Reform in a more direct way.

The centrist position between Reform and Orthodoxy: The centrist viewpoint had one name, the Historical school, in Germany, another, Conservative Judaism, in America. But the Historical School in Germany did not constitute a Judaism—a doctrine and way of life realized in a social group that deemed itself "Israel." The Historical School added up to a handful of scholars writing books, and a book is not a Judaism. In America, by contrast, Conservative Judaism did reach full realization in a way of life characteristic of large numbers of Jews, a world view that, for those Jews, explained who they were and what they must do, a clearly articulated account of who is Israel—a Judaism. The circumstance of its success helps in identifying the urgent question that it answered. In his *Conservative Judaism*, Marshall Sklare argued that Conservative Judaism served to express the particular viewpoint of the children of the immigrants to America from Eastern Europe who came at the end of

the nineteenth century. Those children laid emphasis on the folk aspect—the way of life—while rejecting the world-view—the supernaturalism—of the received system of the dual Torah. Sklare further identified Conservative Judaism with the area of second settlement, that is to say, the neighborhoods to which the Jewish immigrants or their children moved once they had settled down in this country. Still, the middle position's fundamental definition of the urgent issues and how they were to be worked out in both nineteenth century Germany and twentieth century America proved remarkably uniform, beginning to the present.

The stress of the Historical School in Europe and Conservative Judaism in America lay on two matters, first, scholarship, with historical research assigned the task of discovering those facts of which the faith would be composed, second, observance of the rules of the received Judaism. A professedly free approach to the study of the Torah, specifically through what was called "critical scholarship" would yield an accurate account of the essentials of the faith. But, second, the scholars and lay people alike would keep and practice nearly the whole of the tradition just as the Orthodox did. The ambivalence of Conservative Judaism, speaking in part for intellectuals deeply loyal to the received way of life, but profoundly dubious of the inherited world view, came to full expression in the odd slogan: "Eat kosher and think *traif*." (*Traif* means, not kosher.) That statement meant people should keep the rules of the holy way of life but ignore the convictions that made sense of them. Orthopraxy is the word that refers to correct action and unfettered belief, as against Orthodoxy, right doctrine. Some would then classify Conservative Judaism in America as an orthoprax Judaism defined through works, not doctrine.

The middle position then derived in equal measures from the two extremes. The way of life was congruent in most aspects with that of the Orthodox, the thought-world, with that of the Reform. The two held together in the doctrine of Israel which covered everyone. Conservative Judaism saw the Jews as a people, not merely a religious community, and celebrated the ethnic as much as the more narrowly religious side to the Jews' common life. Orthodoxy took a separatist and segregationist position, leaving the organized Jewish community in Germany as that community fell into the hands of Reform Jews. Reform Judaism, for its part, rejected the position that the Jews constitute a people, not merely a religious community. Conservative Judaism emphasized the importance of the unity of the community as a whole and took a stand in favor of Zionism as soon as that movement got under way.

What separated Conservative Judaism from Reform was the matter of observance. Fundamental loyalty to the received way of life distinguished the Historical School in Germany and Conservative Judaism in America from Reform Judaism in both countries. When considering the continued validity of a traditional religious practice, the Reform asked why, the Conservatives, why not. The Orthodox, of course, would ask no questions to begin with. The fundamental principle, that the world-view of the Judaism under construction would rest upon (mere) historical facts, came from Reform Judaism. Orthodoxy could never have concurred. The contrast to the powerful faith despite the world, exhibited by the founder of modern orthodoxy, Samson Raphael Hirsch's stress on the utter facticity of the Torah, presents in a clear light the positivism of the Conservatives, who, indeed, adopted the name "the *positive* Historical School."

History as an instrument of reform: The emphasis on research as the route to historical fact, and on historical fact as the foundation for both change and, also, the definition of what was truly authentic in the tradition further tells us that the Historical School was made up of intellectuals. In America, too, a pattern developed in which essentially non-observant congregations of Jews called upon rabbis whom they expected to be observant of the rules of the religion. As a result many of the intellectual problems that occupied public debate concerned rabbis more than lay people, since the rabbis bore responsibility—so the community maintained—for not only teaching the faith but,

on their own, embodying it. An observer described this Judaism as "Orthodox rabbis serving Conservative synagogues made up of Reform Jews." But in a more traditional liturgy, in an emphasis upon observance of the dietary taboos and the Sabbath and festivals—which did, and still does, characterize homes of Conservative more than of Reform Jews—Conservative Judaism in its way of life as much as in its world-view did establish an essentially mediating position between Orthodoxy and Reform. The conception that Conservative Judaism is a Judaism for Conservative rabbis thus in no way accords with the truth. That Judaism for a long time enjoyed the loyalty of fully half of the Jews in America and today retains the center and the influential position of Judaism in America. The viewpoint of the center predominates even in the more traditional circles of Reform and the more modernist sectors of Orthodoxy.

The point at which a school achieved the status of a Judaism is not difficult to locate. The school—the Historical School in Germany, a handful of moderate rabbis in America—defined itself as a movement in Judaism (in my terms, a Judaism) in response to a particular event. It was the adoption, by the Reform rabbis, of the Pittsburgh Platform of 1885. At that point a number of European rabbis now settled in America determined to break from Reform and establish what they hoped would be simply "traditional" Judaism in America. When, in 1886, they founded the Jewish Theological Seminary of America, Conservative Judaism as a religious movement began. The actual event was simple. The final break between the more traditional and the more radical rabbis among the non-Orthodox camp occurred with the formation of a group that sponsored this new rabbinical school for "the knowledge and practice of historical Judaism."[2]

Reform Judaism defines its competition: The power of Reform Judaism to create and define its opposition—Orthodoxy in Germany, Conservative Judaism in America—tells us how accurately Reform had outlined the urgent questions of the age. Just as Reform had created Orthodoxy, it created

Conservative Judaism. Reform, after all, had treated as compelling the issue of citizenship ("Emancipation") and raised the heart of the matter, how could Jews aspire to return to the Holy Land and form a nation and at the same time take up citizenship in the lands of their birth and loyalty? Jews lived a way of life different from that of their neighbors, with whom they wished to associate. A Judaism had to explain that difference. The answers of all three Judaisms accepted the premises framed, to begin with, by Reform. Orthodoxy maintained one could accept citizenship and accommodate political change but also adhere loyally to the Torah. To Orthodoxy, certain changes, necessary in context, represented trivial and unimportant matters. Conservative Judaism in its German formulation took up a mid-position, specifying as essential fewer aspects of the received way of life than did Orthodoxy but more than Reform. In this way therefore Reform Judaism defined the agenda for all of the Judaisms of the nineteenth century, and its own success lies in its imposing of its fundamental perspective on its competition.

If we want to understand Conservative Judaism, we have to follow its mode of sorting out the legitimate changes from the unacceptable ones, for that method marked the middle off from the extremes on either side. The way in which the Historical School coped with political change, in particular the secularization of politics and the challenge to reframe the political teleology—and associated way of life and world view—of Judaism—through historical study. The search for precedent need hardly surprise us, since the Reformers took the same route. The fundamental premise of the Conservatives' emphasis on history rested on the conviction that history demonstrated the truth or falsity of theological propositions.

We should look in vain in all of the prior writings of Judaic systems for precedent for that fact, self-evident to the nineteenth and twentieth century system-builders. The appeal to historical facts was meant to lay upon firm, factual foundations whatever change was to take place. In finding precedent for change, the Conservatives sought reassurance that some change—if not a great deal of change—would not endanger the enduring faith they wished to preserve. But there was a second factor. The laws and lessons of history would then settle questions of public policy near at hand. Both in Germany in the middle of the century and in America at the end the emphasis throughout lay on "knowledge and practice of historical Judaism as ordained in the law of Moses expounded by the prophets and sages in Israel in Biblical and Talmudic writings," as the articles of Incorporation of the Jewish Theological Seminary of America Association stated in 1887. Calling themselves "traditionalists" rather than "Orthodox," the Conservative adherents accepted for most Judaic subjects the principles of modern critical scholarship. Conservative Judaism therefore exhibited traits that linked it to Reform but also to Orthodoxy, a movement very much in the middle. Precisely how the historical school related to the other systems of its day—the mid- and later-nineteenth century—requires attention to that scholarship that, apologists insisted, marked the Historical School off from Orthodoxy.

The principal argument in validation of the approach of the Historical School and Conservative Judaism derived from these same facts of history. Change now would restore the way things had been at that golden age that set the norm and defined the standard. So by changing, Jews would regain that true Judaism that, in the passage of time, had been lost. Reform added up to more than mere change to accommodate the new age, as the Reforms claimed. This kind of reform would conserve, recover, restore. That is what accounts for the basic claim that the centrists would discover how things had always been. By finding out how things had been done, what had been found essential as faith, in that original and generative time, scholarship would dictate the character of the Judaic system. It would say what it was and therefore what it should again become, and, it followed, Conservative Judaism then would be "simply Judaism," to which all Jews could adhere. Reform identified its Judaism as the linear and incremental next step in the unfolding of the Torah. The Historical School and Conservative Judaism later on regarded its Judaism as the reversion to the authentic Judaism that in time had been lost. Change was legitimate, as the Reform said, but only that kind of change that restored things to the condition of the original and correct Judaism.

The Conservative apologetic: That position formed a powerful apologetic, because it addressed the Orthodox view that Orthodoxy constituted the linear and incremental outgrowth of "the Torah" or "the tradition," hence, the sole legitimate Judaism. It also addressed the Reform view that change was all right. Conservative Judaism established a firm criterion for what change was all right: the kind that was, really, no change at all. For the premise of the Conservative position was that things should become the way they had always been. And scholarship would tell how things had always been and dictate those changes that would restore the correct way of life, the true world view, for the Israel composed of pretty much all the Jews—the center. Historical research therefore provided a powerful apologetic against both sides. That is why the weapon of history in the nineteenth century was ultimate in the struggle among the Judaisms of the age. The claim to replicate how things always had been and should remain thus defined as the ultimate weapon historical research, of a sort. That was, specifically, a critical scholarship that did not accept at face value as history the stories of holy books, but asked whether and how they were true, and in what detail they were not true. That characteristically critical approach to historical study would then serve as the instrument for the definition of Conservative Judaism, the Judaism that would conserve the true faith, but also omit those elements, accretions of later times, that marred that true faith.

The issue of the Oral Torah: At issue in historical research, out of which the correct way of life and world view would be defined, was the study of the Talmudic literature, that is, the Oral Torah. The Hebrew Scriptures enjoyed immunity. Both the Reformers and the Historical School theologians stipulated that the written Torah was God given. The Conservatives and Reformers concurred that God gave the written Torah, but man made the oral Torah. So the two parties of change, Reformers and Historical School alike, chose the field of battle, declaring the Hebrew Scriptures to be sacred and outside the war. They insisted that what was to be reformed was the shape of Judaism imparted by the Talmud, specifically, and preserved in their own day by the rabbis whose qualification consisted in learning in the Talmud and approval by those knowledgeable therein. That agreement on the arena for critical scholarship is hardly an accident. The Reform and Historical School theologians revered Scripture. Wanting to justify parting company from Orthodox and the received tradition of the Oral Torah, they focused on the Talmud because the Talmud formed the sole and complete statement of the one whole Torah of Moses our rabbi, to which Orthodoxy and, of course, the traditionalists of the East, appealed. Hence in bringing critical and skeptical questions to the Talmud, but not to the Hebrew Scriptures, the Conservatives and Reformers addressed scholarship where they wished, and preserved as revealed truth what they in any event affirmed as God's will. That is why the intellectual program of the Historical School in Germany and Conservative Judaism in America consisted of turning the Talmud, studied historically, into a weapon turned against two sides: against the excessive credulity of the Orthodox, but also against the specific proposals and conceptions of the Reformers.

The role of scholarship being critical, Conservative Judaism looked to history to show which changes could be made in the light of biblical and rabbinic precedent, "for they viewed the entire history of Judaism as such a succession of changes," Arthur Hertzberg explains.[3] The continuity in history derives from the on-going people. The basic policy from the beginning, however, dictated considerable reluctance at making changes in the received forms and teachings of the Judaism of the dual Torah. The basic commitments to the Hebrew language in worship, the dietary laws, and the keeping of the Sabbath and festivals, distinguished the

Historical School in Europe and Conservative Judaism in America from Reform Judaism. The willingness to accept change and to affirm the political emancipation of the Jews as a positive step marked the group as different from the Orthodox. So far as Orthodoxy claimed to oppose all changes of all kinds, Conservative Judaism did take a position in the middle of the three

The Positive-Historical School in the nineteenth century: If history, or rather, History, the chosen discipline for Judaic theological argument in the nineteenth century, gave its name to the Judaism at hand, the particular area of history that defined discourse by no means surfaced as a matter of accident. People made a very deliberate choice in the matter. What they studied, that is, subjected to critical processes of analysis, proof and disproof, was no more indicative than what they refrained from reading in that same detached and critical manner. They did not study Scripture in the critical way. They did study the documents of the Oral Torah in accord with the canons of contemporary academic scholarship. Why the difference? The principal theological issues under debate derived from the Judaism of the dual Torah. No one argued about whether or not Moses gave the Ten Commandments. But people did have to work out for themselves a relationship to the Judaism of the dual Torah—and, by definition, that meant, to the documents of the Oral Torah. So the historical question applied, in particular to that matter, and, of course, as to the oral part of the dual Torah people raised questions of origins, meaning, authority: where did it come from, is it part of the revelation of Sinai?

The Orthodox answers left no ambiguity. The entirety of the Torah came from God, not from mortal humanity; the entire Torah retains authority, such as it had from the very beginning; and, of course, the Talmud and the other rabbinic writings represented by it form part of the revelation of Sinai. The Reformers' answers took an opposite and equally coherent position. The oral Torah forms part of the accidents of history; it comes from human authors; it is not part of the Torah of Sinai. Addressing these issues, then, would occupy scholars who thought that they could produce "positive, historical" knowledge, which would secure reliable facts in answer to the questions of faith. When history forms the arena for scholarship, in the Judaic context at hand, the history of the oral component of the dual Torah will attract attention and debate. That rule derives from the debates between Reform and Orthodox theologians. Both concurred on the divine origin of the written component of the dual Torah, but the former denied what the latter affirmed, which is the divine origin of the oral part of that same Torah.

The Historical School's principal contribution to the debate derived from two historians, Zechariah Frankel and Heinrich Graetz. They founded the study of the rabbinic literature as a historical source. Since the theological motive for the work is now clear to us, we can understand that the beginnings of the study of the Talmud as history lie in nineteenth-century Germany. With Reform well defined and Orthodoxy coming to an articulate view of itself, the Historical School made its appearance third in line. This was in the 1850s. The definition of the modern debate about the Talmud, in mostly historical terms, was supplied in that single decade from 1851 to 1859. Four books were published in less than ten years that defined the way the work would be done for the next one hundred years, and three of the four—Krochmal, Graetz, and Frankel—were identified (in Krochmal's case, posthumously) with the Historical School. These four were Leopold Zunz's posthumous publication of Nahman Krochmal's *Moreh nebukhe hazzeman* ("guide to the perplexed of our times," a title meant to call to mind Maimonides' *Guide to the Perplexed*), 1851; Heinrich Graetz's fourth volume of his *History of the Jews from the Earliest Times to the Present*, which is devoted to the talmudic period, 1853; Geiger's *Urschrift und Uebersetzungen der Bibel*, 1857; and Zechariah Frankel's *Darkhé hammishnah* ("ways of the Mishnah"), 1859. These four volumes, Zunz and Geiger marking the Reform contribution, Graetz and Frankel the positive-historical school's contribution, placed the Talmud into the very center of the debates on the reform of Judaism and address the critical issues of the debate: the divine mandate of Rabbinic Judaism.[4] For three generations there would be no historical work on the Talmud deriving from Orthodoxy. And what came later on represented no constructive program at all.

The Talmudic period defines the arena of the struggle over reform because the Reform theologians made it so and because Conservative ones affirmed that same decision, for essentially the same reason. They had proposed that by exposing the historical origins of the Talmud and of the Rabbinic form of Judaism, they might "undermine the divine mandate of rabbinic Judaism."[5] As Ismar Schorsch points out, Geiger's work indicates the highwater mark of the attack on Rabbinic Judaism through historical study. Krochmal, Graetz, and Frankel presented a sympathetic and favorable assessment. That is the point at which, in historical work, they would take their leave of Reform Judaism and lay the foundations for the Historical School of Conservative Judaism. In so doing, however, they adopted the fundamental supposition of the Reformers: the Talmud can and should be studied historically. They conceded that there is a history to the period in which the Talmud comes forth. The Talmud itself is a work of men in history.

The method of Graetz and of Frankel was essentially biographical. The two provided spiritual heroes, a kind of academic hagiography, imparting color and life to the names of the talmudic canon. One third of Frankel's book is devoted to biographies of personalities mentioned in the Talmud. He collects the laws given in the name of a particular man and states that he appears in such and such tractates, and the like. His card file is neatly divided but yields no more than what is filed in it.[6] Joel Gereboff comments on Frankel as follows:

> For Frankel Rabbi was the organizer and the law-giver. He compiled the Mishnah in its final form, employing a systematic approach. The Mishnah was a work of art; everything was "necessary" and in its place. All these claims are merely asserted. Frankel

gives citations from Mishnaic and Amoraic sources, never demonstrating how the citations prove his contentions. Frankel applied his theory of positive-historical Judaism, which depicted Jewish life as a process combining the lasting values from the past with human intelligence in order to face the present and the future, to the formation of the Mishnah. The Mishnah was the product of human intelligence and divine inspiration. Using their intelligence, later generations took what they had received from the past and added to it. Nothing was ever removed. Frankel's work has little lasting value. He was, however, the first to analyze the Mishnah critically and historically; and this was his importance.

What is important is not what he proves but what he implicitly concedes, which is that the Mishnah and the rest of the rabbinic literature are the work of men. Graetz likewise stresses the matter of great men. As Schorsch characterizes his work:

> Graetz tried valiantly to portray the disembodied rabbis of the Mishnah and Talmud as vibrant men, each with his own style and philosophy and personal frailties, who collectively resisted the disintegrating forces of their age. . . . In the wake of national disaster, creative leadership forged new religious institutions to preserve and invigorate the bonds of unity. . . . He defended talmudic literature as a great national achievement of untold importance to the subsequent survival of the Jews.[7]

Now why, in the doing of history, the biographies of great men should be deemed the principal work is clear: the historians of the day in general wrote biographies. History was collective biography. Their conception of what made things happen is tied to the theory of the great man in history, the great man as the maker of history. The associated theory was of history as the story of politics, thus of what great men did. The beginnings of the approach to the Talmud as history meant biography. But the historians of the day in general did not lay the foundations for religious movements, nor did they ordinarily engage in vigorous debate on theological questions. Graetz and Frankel, by contrast, strongly opposed Reform and criticized not only the results of Reform scholarship but the policies of Reform Judaism.

If we place the historical scholarship of Graetz and Frankel into the context of the age, we realize that their program fit more comfortably into a theological than a critical-historical classification, however much they invoked the status of critical-historical and positive-historical knowledge for their results. And that fact places a quite different construction on the Historical School. Measured by the standards of its day, it proved far less critical, far less historical, and far more credulous and believing, than its adherents admitted. For a broad range of critical questions escaped the attention of the Historical School. These questions had to do with the reliability of sources. Specifically, in both classical and biblical studies, long before the mid-nineteenth century a thorough-going skepticism had replaced the gullibility of earlier centuries. Alongside the historicistic frame of mind shaped in the aftermath of the Romantic movement, there was an enduring critical spirit, formed in the Enlightenment and not to be eradicated later on. This critical spirit approached the historical allegations of ancient texts with a measure of skepticism. So for biblical studies, in particular, the history of ancient Israel no longer followed the paths of the biblical narrative, from Abraham onward.

In the work of writing lives of Jesus, the contradictions among the several gospels, the duplications of materials, the changes from one gospel to the next between one saying and story and another version of the same saying and story, the difficulty in establishing a biographical framework for the life of Jesus—all of these and similar, devastating problems had attracted attention. The result was a close analysis of the character of the sources as literature, for example, the recognition—before the nineteenth century—that the Pentateuch consists of at least three main strands: JE, D, and P. It was well known that behind the synoptic Gospels is a source (called Q, for source, in German, *Quelle*) containing materials assigned to Jesus, upon which the three evangelists drew but reshaped for their respective purposes. The conception that merely because an ancient story-teller says someone said or did something does not mean he really said or did it goes back before the Enlightenment. After all, the beginnings of modern biblical studies surely reach into the mind of Spinoza. He was not the only truly critical intellect in the field before Voltaire. But as a powerful, socially rooted frame of mind, historical-critical and literary critical work on the ancient Scriptures is the attainment of the late eighteenth and nineteenth centuries. And for the founders of talmudic history, Graetz, Frankel, and Krochmal, what had happened in biblical and other ancient historical studies was either not known or not found to be useful. And it was not used. The issues on which they worked derived from a religious and not an academic or narrowly-scholarly debate.

And yet the model of German Protestant theological scholarship in biblical studies made slight impact. For a considerable critical program had already taken shape, so that scholarship on religion observed the critical norms worked out in other historical subjects. No German biographer of Jesus by the 1850s, for example, could have represented his life and thought by a mere paraphrase and harmony of the Gospels, in the way in which Graetz and Frankel and their successors down to the mid-twentieth century would paraphrase and string together talmudic tales about rabbis, and call the result "history" and biography. Nor was it commonplace, by the end of the nineteenth century, completely to ignore the redactional and literary traits of documents entirely, let alone their historical and social provenance. Whatever was attributed to a rabbi, in any document, of any place or time, was forthwith believed to provide evidence of what that rabbi really said and did in the time in which he lived. So the claim of the positive Historical School to produce that same positivist data that historians in general claimed to present certainly fails. The reason that fact matters is simple. The theologians of the Historical School claimed to present "mere" facts, but the bulk of the facts they did produce derived from a reading of sources in as believing, not to say credulous, a spirit as the Orthodox brought to Scripture. By the standards of their own day, the scholars at hand proved not at all critical. What matters, then, is the theological program, not the scholarly outcome.

We therefore must wonder quite how much change the Historical School admitted. It was less than people alleged. For while calling themselves "positive-Historical," none of the scholars at hand could claim to contribute to history in the way in which, in general, critical historical work was carried on in their time. Yet the change, in the context of the received and available Judaisms, nonetheless was formidable. For the Conservatives took a delicately balanced position between Orthodox and Reform theologians. Admitting [1] that the Talmud and related writings came from mortals—an enormous reform—the historian-theologians then [2] took at face value—exactly as did the Orthodox—all of the tales and treated the document with a faith that, in the setting of biblical studies, would have earned the title, uncritical or even fundamentalist. In this regard Orthodoxy cannot have objected to the results of historical study, only to its premises. Since the work of talmudic history was methodologically obsolete by the critical standards of its own age, we must correct the notion that the scholarship at hand pursued an essentially secular and "objective" program and cannot be deemed the foundation of a Judaism.

Quite to the contrary, the scholarship in historical sciences aimed at theological results. The world-view that would emerge in Conservative Judaism, with its stress on scholarship, simply insisted on the facticity of matters of faith—no less than did Hirsch, but with less reason. So the middle position emerged in a simple way. On the one side, the historian-theologians of the Historical School chose to face the Orthodox with the claim that the Talmud was historical. On the other they chose to turn their backs on the critical scholarship of their own day with that very same claim that the Talmud *was* historical. That formed a powerful weapon against Reform, and it was the weapon of the Reformers' own choice (as Geiger indicated in so many words). So as with the Reformers and the Orthodox, so for the Conserva-

tives the place and authority of the Oral Torah, embodied in the Talmud, formed the arena for debate. Facing the one side, the Historical School treated the Talmud as a document of history, therefore a precedent for paying attention to context and circumstance, so to admit to the possibility of change. But facing the other side, the Historical School treated the Talmud as a uniformly reliable and inerrant source for historical information. The Talmud was the target of opportunity. The traditionalists trivialized the weapon, maintaining that history was essentially beside the point of the Talmud: They used an argument such as this: The historians can tell us what clothes Rab wore, and what he ate for breakfast. The Talmudists can report what he said. But, it goes without saying, polemical arguments such as these, no less than the ones of the Reformers, were important only to the people who made them up.

Two purposes—biography and theology—define the character of nearly all of the historical work done in talmudic literature for the century from the decade of foundation onward. Graetz set the style for such history as was attempted; Frankel for biography. At the end let me quote Schorsch's definitive judgment of Graetz, which forms an epitaph to the whole enterprise of talmudic history from the 1850s onward:

> Above all, Graetz remained committed to the rejuvenation of his people. His faith in God's guiding presence throughout Jewish history, as witnessed by two earlier instances of national recovery, assured him of the future. His own work, he hoped, would contribute to the revival of Jewish consciousness. He succeeded beyond measure. As a young man, Graetz had once failed to acquire a rabbinic pulpit because he was unable to complete the delivery of his sermon. There is more than a touch of irony in the remarkable fact that the reception accorded to Graetz's history by Jews around the world made him the greatest Jewish preacher of the nineteenth century.[8]

That none of this reveals a narrowly historical task scarcely requires proof. In fact we deal with a theological program, one which resorts to facts to make its points, and which imagines that history settles questions. The reliance on precedent, of course, will not have surprised proponents of the dual Torah. But the entire program, with its treating as this-worldly and matters of history what the received system of Judaism understood to form an entirely supernatural realm, surprised and deeply offended those proponents.

Orthopraxy as Conservatism: Alexander Marx and Louis Ginzberg: We therefore come to the question of who joined Historical Judaism in Europe and Conservative Judaism in America. Of particular interest are the system-builders, the intellectuals: the historians, Talmudists, and other scholars. They are the ones, after all, who defined the ideas and expressed the values and the attitudes that made all of the Judaisms before us systems, whole and complete, each with its world-view, way of life, theory of an Israel—and powerful appeal to an Israel too. Since nearly all of the first generations of Conservative Jews in America and adherents of the Historical School in Europe had made their way out of that received system of the dual Torah, the motivation for the deeply conservative approach to the received system requires attention. For that basis assuredly cannot emerge from matters of doctrine. Indeed, once scholar-theologians maintained that the oral part of the Torah derived from mortals, not God, disagreements with Reformers on matters of change can have made little difference. For by admitting to the human origin and authority of the documents of the Oral Torah, the historian-theologians had accomplished the break with Orthodox, as well as with the received system. Then differences with Reform were of degree, not kind. But these differences sustained a Judaism for a very long time, a Judaism that would compose its world-view, its way of life, its audience of Israel, in terms that marked off that system from the other two successor-Judaisms we have already considered. Where and how did the differences emerge? To answer the question, we turn to two Europeans turned Americans, who typify the first mature generation of Conservative Judaism.

Professors at the Jewish Theological Seminary of America for the first half of the twentieth century, important authorities in their fields of learning, Louis Ginzberg and Alexander Marx form the counterpart to Abraham Geiger and Samson Raphael Hirsch. Together they typify the principal points of emphasis of Conservative Judaism in its formative age. They will serve as our interlocutors in pursuing the questions of this study. For what we want to find out—to remind ourselves—is not the sociology, or even the theology, of the successor-Judaisms of the nineteenth century. We want to know where and how people made the passage from self-evidence to self-awareness, how we may identify what changed and specify what continued within the received way of life and world view. The answers to these questions tell us how people identified and answered urgent questions and so constructed a social world in which to live out their lives.

In the case of the Historical School of Germany in the nineteenth century and Conservative Judaism in the U.S.A., the answer is clear. Keeping the way of life of the received tradition, to which the Conservatives felt deep personal loyalty because of upbringing and association, would define the way of life of Conservative Judaism. Ignoring the intellectual substance of the received system and striking out in new directions would define the method of thought, the worldview. We have already met their cynical apophthegm, "Eat kosher and think *traif* (that is, not kosher)," meaning keep the practical rules of the established way of life, but pursue your scholarly interests wherever they may lead you. Conservative Judaism thus began—and for many years persisted—as a blatant orthopraxy—think what you like but conform to the law. What we learn is that the inherited way of life exercised profound power over the heart of the Conservative Jew of the early generation. The received viewpoint persuaded no one. So keep what could not be let go, and relinquish what no longer possessed value. To justify both sides, historical scholarship would find reassuring precedents, teaching that change is not Reform after all. But no precedent could provide verification for orthopraxy, the most novel, the most interesting reform among the Judaisms of continuation.

We turn to two substantial figures, who show us how Conservative Judaism actually worked in the lives of first rate intellects. The first was Alexander Marx (1878-1953), who in his *Essays in Jewish Biography* introduces people he knows and loves. His book presents a classic statement of the philosophy of the founders of Conservative Judaism. As such Marx teaches us where Conservative Judaism came from—which, in his person, was out of the Westernized Orthodoxy of nineteenth century Germany. Marx carried forward the legacy of his father-in-law, David Hoffmann, and Hoffmann's father in law, Rabbi Hildesheimer—the two intellectual giants, after Hirsch, of Orthodoxy in Germany. So Marx explains the choices of those whom he provides with biographies: "The works of Rashi have attracted me since my early youth." "My interest in Saadia was aroused by the greatness and originality of his work and the unusual story of his life." As to the eight modern scholars, he either knew them personally or was deeply influenced by them in his scholarly career. So he says, "I had a personal reason for selecting these men. In one way or another each of them either affected my own scholarly career or was bound to me by ties of close friendship." Hoffmann, for example, was his father in law, and Solomon Schechter, the true founder of the Jewish Theological Seminary of America just after the turn of the twentieth century, his friend.

But there is more to it than that. The notion that orthopraxy without a world view characterized Conservative Judaism is wrong. The mode of scholarship in the study of the Talmudic corpus, while different from that of Orthodoxy as well as of the system of the dual Torah called "traditional," in fact remained entirely within the programmatic and topical interests of the Orthodox and the traditionalists alike. In the case of Marx this fact emerges clearly. His book is a party-document—a work of theology masquerading as descriptive history. Orthopraxy contained its own world-view, remarkably like that of Orthodoxy—except where it differed. There are deep convictions in his book, beliefs about right and wrong, not only about

matters of fact. That is why Marx proves more interesting than, in his day, people might have predicted. So he wrote an intellectual autobiography, expressed through the biographies of others—a powerful and subtle medium. A reticent but solid scholar in these pages reflects on himself through what he says about others, reveals his ideals through what he praises in others. Here is an authentic judgment on the nineteenth and twentieth century and its principal intellectual framers: Marx's masters, friends, and heroes

Marx himself was born in Eberfeld, in what was later East Germany. In his youth he served as a horseman in a Prussian artillery regiment. That hardly constituted a routine vocation for a rabbinical student, any more than did Hirsch's attendance at university. Only later did he go to the rabbinical seminary in Berlin. There, in that center of Orthodoxy, he married David Hoffmann's daughter. Hoffmann was the son-in-law of the founder of that same seminary. So there is a continuity within the intellectual leadership of Western Orthodoxy: Hildesheimer, Hoffmann, then, via the Jewish Theological Seminary of America, Marx. But then there is the break: who carried on the tradition in Conservative Judaism? While Hoffmann was an intellectual founder of Germany's westernized Orthodoxy, Marx in 1903 accepted Solomon Schechter's call to America. Schechter was the founding president of the Jewish Theological Seminary of America. He brought major scholars from Europe, and Marx was one of them.

Perhaps Marx hoped that the Jewish Theological Seminary of America would reproduce the intellectual world of German Orthodoxy: intellectually vital and religiously loyal to tradition. In any case Marx became professor of history and librarian at the Jewish Theological Seminary of America. Indeed, in his day, JTSA surely found a comfortable niche on the Western shores of Orthodoxy. To be Conservative in Judaism then meant to make minor changes in the law but to make much of them, at the same time making major innovations in the intellectual life of Judaism and minimizing them. Marx fit that pattern—but so did many of those about whom he writes. What were the consequences for learning? A kind of intellectual counterpart to orthopraxy yielded facts without much interpretation. In the case of Marx, the scholarship was erudite but not terribly original or productive. He formed a personal embodiment of a Judaism that made much of facts—observances—but did little with them.

In that regard he carried on the intellectually somewhat arid tradition of Frankel and Graetz, collecting information and making up sermons about it, but engaging in slight analysis or sustained inquiry of a sophisticated character. He published in the areas of history and bibliography. His most popular work was his *History of the Jewish People* (written with Max L. Margolis) published in 1927. This one-volume history must rank as among the most boring of its uninspired genre, but it does provide an accurate catalogue of important facts. So Marx's intellectual strength lay in his massive erudition, not in his powers of imagination and interpretation. To him, history was a sequence of facts of self-evident importance and obvious significance. That, of course, constituted a theological not merely an academic conviction. For the theological data of the Historical School derived from historical facts, which, then, bore self-evident consequence.

But that view did not derive from Marx; it was a commonplace then and even today that the facts of history bear self-evident theological meaning. Because things once happened, today people find themselves compelled to do or not to do, to believe or to disbelieve. That is the view of theology to which Marx, as his entire generation of German and American scholars of Judaism, subscribed. Scholarship for Marx and his fellows was comprised of brief, topical, *ad hoc*, and unconnected papers—hence, ideas too. Graetz's history, made up of tales, and Frankel's biographies, thumbnail sketches based on paraphrases of talmudic stories, fall into the same classification. Given the stress on the self-evident meaning of facts, one can understand why, in simply establishing a fact, Marx and his generation saw a message and

derived a meaning. So brief, ad hoc articles bore their self-evident importance too. But even though two of the three books are made up of short essays, they contain important statements of broad significance and general interest. The modern figures of interest to Marx find a place at the center of the movement for the intellectual modernization of Judaism. All of them stood within the Western camp, but also took a traditionalist position in that camp.

Ginzberg: And that brings us to Louis Ginzberg (1873-1953), a still more typical and influential figure.[9] He typifies the entire group of theologian-historians, in that he grew up within the heartland of the Jewish world of Eastern Europe, but left for the West. In that important respect he stands for the experience of departure and of alienation from roots that characterized the generality of earlier Reformers, the earliest generations of Conservative theologians, and the Orthodox of the age as well. Later on some of these figures would lay down the rule that, to be a scholar in Judaism, one had to grow up in a yeshiva—a school of advanced Talmudic learning—and leave! That counsel raised alienation to a norm. Obviously, it bore no relationship whatsoever to the received system of the dual Torah. None of the representative figures in the early generations found urgent the replication of the way of life and world view in which he grew up. The policy of orthopraxy then formed a mode of mediating between upbringing and adult commitment—that is, of coping with change.

Ginzberg himself traced his descent to the Vilna Gaon, Elijah, a formidable and legendary figure in the life of the communities of the dual Torah. But while born and brought up in Lithuania, heartland of the intellectual giants of the received system, Ginzberg left. He went to Berlin and Strasbourg, where he studied with Semitists, historians, and philosophers—practitioners of disciplines unknown in the study of the dual Torah. Ginzberg's next move, from the central European universities, brought him to the U.S.A., where, in 1899, he found employment at Hebrew Union College. But the appointment he had received was canceled when Ginzberg's position on biblical criticism became known. Specifically, Ginzberg affirmed the validity of critical approaches to the Hebrew Scriptures, and that fact made him unacceptable at the Reform seminary. Critical scholarship flourished within carefully circumscribed borders; within the frontier lay the oral Torah, outside—and beyond permissible criticism—the written. That distinction, central to Reform and Conservative positive-historical scholarship, placed Ginzberg outside of the camp for Reform seminaries. Instead, in 1900 he found employment at the Jewish Encyclopedia, and, in 1903, he accepted an appointment in Talmud at the Jewish Theological Seminary of America, yet another of the founding faculty collected by Solomon Schechter. Why Schechter found Ginzberg's views on biblical scholarship acceptable is not known, but, of course, Ginzberg taught Talmud, not Scriptures. A fixture at the Jewish Theological Seminary for fifty years, Ginzberg is called by Arthur Hertzberg, a leading second generation Conservative rabbi,[10] simply, "a principal architect of the Conservative movement."

His scholarly work covered the classical documents of the oral Torah, with special interest in subjects not commonly emphasized in the centers of learning which he had left. So the subject changed, and changed radically. But the mode of learning remained constant. Ginzberg's work emphasized massive erudition, a great deal of collecting and arranging, together with episodic and ad hoc solutions to difficult problems of exegesis. But the work remained primarily textual and exegetical, and, when Ginzberg ventured into historical questions, the received mode of talmudic discourse—deductive reasoning, ad hoc arguments—predominated. So, for example, he propounded the theory—famous in its day—that differences on issues of the law represented class differences. In "The Significance of the Halakhah for Jewish History" (1929), the repeated enunciation of the thesis followed by exemplifications of how the thesis might explain differences of opinion took the place of rigorous analysis and cool testing of the thesis. So Ginzberg maintained that the liberals expressed the class interests of the lower classes, the conservatives of the upper classes. He then found in details of the law as two parties debated it ample exemplifications of this same theory. Just as in the yeshiva-world Ginzberg had left, enthusiastic argument took the place of sustained analysis and the critical exercise of testing, so in the world Ginzberg chose to build, the same mode of thought persisted, changed in context, unchanged in character.

The claim to critical scholarship forms, for Conservative Judaism, the counterpart to Orthodoxy's appeal to the Torah as God's will. Much is made in the theologies of Conservative Judaism of historical fact, precedent, discovering the correct guidelines for historical change. But the essential mode of argument accords with the received patterns of thought of the Yeshiva-world from which Ginzberg took his leave. For Talmudists such as Ginzberg, who acquired a university training, including an interest in history, and who also continued to study Talmudic materials, never fully overcame the intellectual habits ingrained from their beginnings in *yeshivot*.

Characteristic of Talmudic scholarship is the search, first, for underlying principles to make sense of discrete, apparently unrelated cases, second, for distinctions to overcome contradictions between apparently contradictory texts, and third, for *hiddushim*, or new interpretations of a particular text. That exegetical approach to historical problems which stresses deductive thought, while perhaps appropriate for legal studies, produces egregious results for history, for it too often overlooks the problem of evidence: How do we know what we assert? What are the bases in actual data to justify *hiddushim* in small matters, or, in large ones, the postulation of comprehensive principles (*shitot*) of historical importance? Ginzberg's famous theory that disputes reflect economic and social conflict is not supported by reference to archaeological or even extra-Talmudic literary evidence. Having postulated that economic issues were everywhere present, Ginzberg proceeded to use this postulate to "explain" a whole series of cases. The "explanations" are supposed to demonstrate the validity of the postulate, but in fact merely repeat and illustrate it. None of these theses in their exposition and demonstration bears much in common with then-contemporary humanistic learning. For humanistic history, even then, derives its propositions from inductive, not deductive, proof. In Ginzberg's case what is lacking in each particular case is the demonstration that the data could not equally well—or even better—be explained by some other postulate or postulates. At best we are left with "this could have been the reason" but with no concrete evidence that this was the reason. Masses of material perhaps originally irrelevant are built into pseudo-historical structures which rest on nothing more solid than "we might suppose that." The deductive approach to the study of law ill serves the historian.

We have dwelt at some length on Ginzberg's practice of historical scholarship so that we have a clear picture of the approach he worked out. Its problems aside, none of this, of course, in any way could find a point of compatibility with Orthodoxy. And that explains the orthopraxy of formative Conservative Judaism, captured in the saying, "eat kosher and think *traif*." That is, keep the practice laws of Judaism but ignore the dogmatic theological principles of the received system (or claim there are none). While such inconsistency of belief and practice may strike some as difficult to sustain, in fact for those who hold this world-view, imputing to religious practice enormous value, while ignoring the received mythic basis for the practice in favor of some other, provides ample explanation for the way of life at hand. The story is reported by Ginzberg's son that, when he visited Hebrew Union College, "they inquired of young Ginzberg whether he was observant and he replied affirmatively; they next asked whether he 'believed' and the reply was in the negative."[11] Both answers, in the context of the Reform seminary he was visiting, were the wrong ones.

Ginzberg very explicitly stressed that Judaism "teaches a way of life and not a theol-

ogy."[12] At the same time he conceded that theological systems do "expound the value and meaning of religion in propositional form," but doctrines follow practices: "Theological doctrines are like the bones of the body, the outcome of the life-process itself and also the means by which it gives firmness, stability, and definiteness of outline to the animal organism." So Ginzberg rejected "the dogma of a dogma-less Judaism." Religious experience, in context meaning observance of the way of life, comes first and generates all theological reflection. The role of history: "Fact, says a great thinker, is the ground of all that is divine in religion and religion can only be presented in history— in truth it must become a continuous and living history." This extreme statement of the positive-historical school will not have surprised Frankel and Graetz. It does provide a guide to the character of Conservative Judaism in the context of the changes of the nineteenth and twentieth century. The appeal to fact in place of faith, the stress on practice to the subordination of belief—these form responses to the difficult situation of sensitive intellectuals brought up in one world but living in another. Ginzberg's judgment placed experience prior to thought: "Religious phenomena are essentially reactions of the mind upon the experienced world, and their specific character is not due to the material environment but to the human consciousness."[13] Ginzberg's capacity for a lucid statement of his own theological views belied his insistence that theology followed upon, and modestly responded to, what he called "religious experience," but what, in fact, was simply the pattern of religious actions that he learned in his childhood to revere.

So orthopraxy eased the transition from one world to another. The next generation found no need to make such a move; it took as normal, not to say normative, the stress on deed to the near-exclusion of intellect that, for Ginzberg and the Positive Historical School, as much as for Orthodoxy, explained why and how to keep in balance a world-view now utterly beyond belief and a way of life very much in evidence. His address in 1917 to the United Synagogue of America, of which he served as president, provides a statement of his system of Judaism:

> Looking at Judaism from an historical point of view, we become convinced that there is no one aspect deep enough to exhaust the content of such a complex phenomenon as Judaism, no one term or proposition which will serve to define it. Judaism is national and universal, individual and social, legal and mystic, dogmatic and practical at once, yet it has a unity and individuality just as a mathematical curve has its own laws and expression. By insisting upon historical Judaism we express further our conviction that for us Judaism is no theory of the study or school, no matter of private opinion or deduction, but a fact . . . If we look upon Jewish History in its integrity as a simple and uniform power, though marked in portions by temporary casual parenthetical interruptions, we find that it was the Torah which stood forth throughout the history of Israel as the guiding star of his civilization."[14]

While some may find this statement gibberish, affirming as it does everything and its opposite, we nonetheless discern a serious effort at a statement of deeply held convictions. The key to much else lies in the capital H assigned to the word History, the view that History possesses "integrity as a simple and uniform power." Here history—fact—proves theological propositions.

That position cannot surprise us, when we remember that the facts of the way of life impressed Ginzberg far more than the faith that, in the context of the dual Torah, made sense of those facts and formed out of that way of life a Judaism. In fact Ginzberg did not possess the intellectual tools for the expression of what he had in mind, which is why he found adequate resort to a rather inchoate rhetoric. Assuming that he intended no mere political platform, broad enough to accommodate everyone whom he hoped would stand on it, we reach a single conclusion. Conservative Judaism, in its formative century from Frankel to Ginzberg, stood for the received way of life, modified in only minor detail, along with the complete indifference to the received world view. To take the place of the missing explanation—theology—"Jewish History" would have to

make do. That history, of course, supplied a set of theological propositions; but these demanded not faith, merely assent to what were deemed ineluctable truths of history: mere facts. At what price the positivism of the founding generation? The intellectual paralysis that would follow. But to what benefit? The possibility of defining a position in the middle, between the Reform, with its forthright rejection of the received way of life, and the Orthodox, with the equally forthright rejection of the new mode of thought.

Continuity or new beginning: The question, continuity or new beginning, finds a facile answer. In its formative century Conservative Judaism carried forward the received way of life, hence, a Judaism professedly continuous with its past. But in its forthright insistence that no world-view one could delimit and define accompanied that way of life, Conservative Judaism imposed a still more radical break than did Reform Judaism between itself and the received tradition. Above all, Conservative Judaism denied the central fact of its system: its novelty. The change effected by Frankel, Graetz, and Ginzberg involved not a scarcely-articulated change of attitude, but a fully spelled out change of doctrine. For the one thing that Hirsch, all the more so his critics in the traditionalist-world, could not concede proves central to Ginzberg's case: "Judaism" is everything and its opposite, so long as Jewish History defines the matter. Is this an incremental development or new beginning? The answer is self-evident.

Conservative Judaism formed a deeply original response to a difficult human circumstance. In its formative century it solved the problem of alienation: people who had grown up in one place, under one set of circumstances, now lived somewhere else, in a different world. They cherished the past, but they themselves had initiated the changes they now confronted. In the doctrine of orthopraxy they held on to the part of the past they found profoundly affecting, and they made space for the part of their present circumstance they did not, and could not, reject. A Judaism that joined strict observance to free thinking kept opposed weights in equilibrium—to be sure, in an unsteady balance. By definition such a delicate juxtaposition could not hold. Papered over by a thick layer of words, the abyss between the way of life, resting on supernatural premises of the facticity of the Torah (as Hirsch rightly understood), and the world view, calling into question at every point the intellectual foundations of that way of life, remained. But how did the successor generation propose to bridge the gap, so to compose a structure resting on secure foundations?

We look for the answer to a representative Conservative theologian of the second generation, beyond Ginzberg. The claim of Reform Judaism to constitute an increment of Judaism, we recall, rested on the position that the only constant in "Judaism" is change. The counterpart for Conservative Judaism comes to expression in the writings of Robert Gordis, since, for their day, they set the standard and defined the position of the center of the religion. Specifically, we seek Gordis' picture of the Judaism that came before and how he proposes to relate Conservative Judaism to that prior system. We find a forthright account of "the basic characteristics of Jewish tradition" as follows:

> The principle of development in all areas of culture and society is a fundamental element of the modern outlook. It is all the more noteworthy that the Talmud . . . clearly recognized the vast extent to which rabbinic Judaism had grown beyond the Bible, as well as the organic character of this process of growth . . . For the Talmud, tradition is not static—nor does this dynamic quality contravene either its *divine origin* or its *organic continuity* [all italics his]. . . . Our concern here is with the historical fact, intuitively grasped by the Talmud, that *tradition grows*.[15]

Gordis appeals to historical precedent But the precedent derives from a Talmudic story—which by itself is scarcely historical at all. The story, as Gordis reads it, recognizes that tradition is not static. Let us read the story in Gordis's words and ask whether that is, in fact, its point:

> Moses found God adding decorative crowns to the letters of the Torah. When he asked the reason for this, the lawgiver was told: "In a future generation, a man named Akiba son of Joseph is destined to arise, who will derive multitudes of laws from each of these marks." Deeply interested, Moses asked to be permitted to see him in action, and he was admitted to the rear of the schoolhouse where Akiba was lecturing. To Moses' deep distress, however, he found that he could not understand what the scholars were saying and his spirit grew faint within him. As the session drew to a close, Akiba concluded: "This ordinance which we are discussing is a law derived from Moses on Sinai." When Moses heard this, his spirit revived![16]

While Gordis's view, that the story "clearly recognized the vast extent to which rabbinic Judaism had grown beyond the Bible, as well as the organic character of this process of growth," certainly may be found in the tale, his interpretation hardly impressed the Orthodox and traditionalists who read the same story. More important, if we did not know that "the principle of development . . . is fundamental," we should not have necessarily read the story in that context at all. For the emphasis of the story, not adduced as a proof-text for the Conservative position, lies on the origin at Sinai of everything later on. And that point sustains the principal polemic at hand: the divine origin of the oral Torah, inclusive, even, of the most minor details adduced by the living sage. We know, of course, the issue urgent to the story-tellers of both the Talmud of the Land of Israel and that of Babylonia, namely, the place of the sages' teachings in the Torah. And that polemic, fully exposed here, took the position that everything sages said derived from Sinai—which is precisely the opposite of the meaning imputed to the story by Gordis. That is not to suggest Gordis has "misinterpreted" the story, only that he has interpreted it in a framework of his own, not in the system which, to begin with, created the tale. That forms evidence of creativity and innovation, an imaginative and powerful mind proposing to make use of a received tradition for fresh purpose: not incremental but a new birth.

This small excursus on talmudic exegesis serves only to underline the fresh and creative character of Conservative Judaism. For without the slightest concern for anachronism, the Conservative theologians found in the tradition ample proof for precisely what they proposed to do, which was, in Gordis's accurate picture, to preserve in a single system the beliefs in both the divine origin and the "organic continuity" of the Torah: that middle-ground position, between Orthodoxy and Reform, that Conservative Judaism so vastly occupied. For Gordis's generation the argument directed itself against both Orthodoxy and Reform. In the confrontation with Orthodoxy Gordis points to new values, institutions, and laws "created as a result of new experiences and new felt needs." But to Reform Gordis points out "instances of accretion and of reinterpretation, which . . . constitute the major modes of development in Jewish tradition." That is to say, change comes about historically, gradually, over time, and change does not take place by the decree of rabbinical convocations. The emphasis of the positive Historical School upon the probative value of historical events, we now recognize, serves the polemic against Reform as much as against Orthodoxy. To the latter, history proves change, to the former, history dictates modes of appropriate change.

Gordis thus argues that change deserves ratification after the fact, not deliberation before hand: "Advancing religious and ethical ideals were inner processes, often imperceptible except after the passage of centuries." Gordis, to his credit, explicitly claims in behalf of Conservative Judaism origin in an incremental and continuous, linear his-tory of Judaism. He does so in an appeal to analogy:

> If tradition means development and change . . . how can we speak of the continuity or the spirit of Jewish tradition? An analogy may help supply the answer. Biologists have discovered that in any living organism, cells are constantly dying and being replaced by . . . ones . . . If that be true, why is a person the same individual after the passage of . . . years? The answer is twofold. In the first instance, the process of change is gradual . . . In the second instance, the growth follows the laws of his being. At no point do the changes violate the basic personality pattern. The organic character and

unit of the personality reside in this continuity of the individual and in the development of the physical and spiritual traits inherent in him, which persist in spite of the modifications introduced by time. This recognition of the organic character of growth highlights the importance of maintaining the method by which Jewish tradition . . . continued to develop. This the researches of Jewish scholars from the days of Zacharias Frankel and Isaac Hirsch Weiss to those of Chaim Tchernowitz and Louis Ginzberg have revealed. . . .[17]

The incremental theory follows the modes of thought of Reform, with their stress on the continuity of process, that alone. Gordis sees the ongoing process of change as permanent. The substance of the issues, however, accords with the stress of Orthodoxy on the persistence of a fundamental character to Judaism. The method of Reform then produces the result of Orthodoxy, at least so far as practice of the way of life would go forward.

Like Orthodoxy, Conservative Judaism defined itself as "Judaism, pure and simple." But it did claim to mark the natural next step in the slow evolution of "the tradition," an evolution within the lines and rules set forth by "the tradition" itself. Appeals to facts proved by scholars underlines the self-evidence claimed in behalf of the system in its fully articulated form. The incapacity to discern one's own anachronistic reading of the past in line with contemporary concerns further sustains the claim that, at hand, we deal with a system of self-evidence. And yet, when we realize the enormous abyss between Louis Ginzberg and his ancestor, the gap that separated Alexander Marx from his wife's family, not to mention the striking difference between the viewpoint of the Talmud's storyteller and the reading of the story by Gordis, the fact becomes clear. What truths Conservative theologians hold to be self-evident they have uncovered through a process of articulated inquiry. The answers may strike them as self-evident. But they themselves invented the questions. And they knew it. The appeal to an incremental and linear history, a history bonded by a sustained method and enduring principles that govern change, comes long after the fact of change. Assuredly,

Conservative Judaism forms a fresh system, a new creation, quite properly seeking continuity with a past that has to begin with been abandoned. For processes of change discerned after the fact and in the light of change already made or contemplated are processes not discovered but defined, then imputed by a process of deduction to historical sources that, read in other ways, scarcely sustain the claim at hand. The powerful scholarship of Conservative Judaism appealed to a reconstructed past, an invented history: a perfect faith in a new and innovative system, a Judaism discovered by its own inventors.

Notes

[1] Arthur Hertzberg, "Conservative Judaism," in *Encyclopaedia Judaica*, vol. 5, col. 901-906.
[2] Ibid., col. 902.
[3] Ibid., col. 901.
[4] Ismar Schorsch, *Heinrich Graetz. The Structure of Jewish History and Other Essays* (New York, 1975), p. 48.
[5] Ibid.
[6] Joel Gereboff, "The Pioneer: Zecharias Frankel," in J. Neusner, ed., *The Modern Study of the Mishnah* (Leiden, 1973), pp. 59-75.
[7] Schorsch, op. cit., p. 48.
[8] Ibid., pp. 61-62.
[9] Arthur Hertzberg, "Louis Ginzberg," in *Encyclopaedia Judaica*, vol. 7, col. 584-586.
[10] Ibid., col. 584.
[11] Eli Ginzberg, *Keeper of the Law. Louis Ginzberg* (Philadelphia, 1966), p. 82.
[12] Ibid., p. 145.
[13] Ibid., p. 148.
[14] Ibid., pp. 159-160.
[15] Robert Gordis, *Understanding Conservative Judaism* (New York, 1978), pp. 26-27.
[16] Ibid., p. 26.
[17] Ibid., pp. 39-40.

JACOB NEUSNER

CONVERSION IN JUDAISM: The possibility and desirability of non-Jews' converting to Judaism has always been a complex issue. This is because, encompassing an ethnic as well as religious component, the very nature of Jewish identity has been hard to conceptualize. From the first century C.E. forward, on the one hand, all children of Jewish mothers have been deemed Jews, whether or not they undergo any ritual of entry into the community, accept any theological doctrine, or perform any of the religious and cultural practices Jews view as commanded by God.

In this respect, Judaism functions as any racial identity: one is Italian, French, or Jewish as a happenstance of birth. But, on the other hand, from the Hellenistic period onward, Jews have recognized and respected the possibility of non-Jews' conversion to Judaism, accomplished on the basis of their accepting fundamental Jewish doctrines and religious practices.

The ambivalent meaning of being a Jew yields a number of difficult questions regarding converts and conversion. For instance, a good deal of the Jewish discussion of conversion concerns whether or not converts to Judaism are in all regards equal to native-born Jews. At base, this question mirrors the debate over whether or not born-Jews, members of the holy nation chosen by God, are *essentially* different from non-Jews, so that even someone who converts cannot be deemed in all respects to have become a Jew. A second issue, which emerges from such discussions, concerns the advisability of encouraging, or even accepting, converts into the Jewish community. On the one hand, numerous statements throughout Jewish history advocate acceptance of converts, some even arguing that the Jews were sent into exile for the explicit purpose of bringing converts into the community. But, on the other hand, from the Babylonian Talmud forward, certain traditions attribute Israel's troubles—exile, loss of the Temple cult, persecution—to the presence of converts within the community.

Alongside these theoretical issues, Jewish attitudes towards conversion have been shaped and reshaped by the status Jews and Judaism have had within various historical contexts. For much of the past fifteen hundred years, Jews had a marginal position in Christian Europe. Beginning in the fourth century, Byzantine/Christian law outlawed conversion, in some cases making it a capital offense. Even apart from such laws, conversion to Judaism was hardly an attractive option, given the Jews' generally low economic and social status and the fact that, in the Middle Ages, Jews were viewed as the paradigmatic threat to human existence, the devil's representatives on earth. In contrast, the openness of American society and the high rate of intermarriage among contemporary American Jews make conversion a viable and attractive option. Thus we see the extent to which, historically, the place of conversion in Judaism has depended as much upon the social, political, economic, and legal realities of Jewish existence as upon theoretical discussions of the nature of Jewishness or membership in the Jewish community.

The psychology of conversion: The word conversion derives from the Latin *convertere*, which refers to a "spiritual reorientation."[1] The terms for conversion in Greek, Hebrew, and Latin all refer to "motion" or "change." As Thomas Finn writes:[2]

> They denote a "turning towards, from, away, return. . . ." The Hebrew root is *shub*; the Greek, *[s]trephein*; the Latin, *[con]vertere*. All three point directly to a physical or material move or change, yet indirectly to a change of spirit or mind, specifically to a change of conviction and way of life.

Contemporary scholars have argued that conversion and commitment are discrete acts that may occur at different times, so that one may convert to a new religion before one has fully committed to the group's doctrines and beliefs.[3] But conversion does necessitate that one *eventually* accept a new system of thoughts and ideas, so that conversion is essentially a process of self-transformation, entailing "the displacement of one universe of discourse by another."[4] As Alan Segal has written, "the central aspect of conversion is a decision to reconstruct reality."[5]

People always convert for a reason, generally understood to be the inability of an existing system of beliefs to explain one's current circumstance. Thus Griel postulates that people continue to adhere to a fixed set of solutions to everyday problems and to work with a specific "stock of knowledge" for so long as the solutions and knowledge function effectively in the situations in which the individuals find themselves. But if their "stock of knowledge" ceases to be useful, they "learn something new," "work out the answer," or "realize that what [they] thought was true has been wrong all along." Additionally, because people's beliefs emerge as

a function of their reference group, the search for new sets of knowledge may occur not only when old paradigms fail to work but also simply in times of rapid social change or when one's social setting becomes increasingly heterogeneous. In all of these instances, one's previous perspective is often discredited, so that new avenues and solutions are explored. For this reason, a significant other's use or adoption of a new set of knowledge will often lead the individual to follow.[6]

Of course, conversion is not only an intellectual event but also a sociological transformation, in which "effective bonds" must be created with individuals in the new community. For this reason, "significant others" play a particularly important role in shaping one's frame of reference and in causing one to change communities. Segal draws an analogy between the "socialization of children" and the "way in which conversion works in developing commitment," stating that "conversion resembles a new and conscious choice to socialize to a particular group—resocialization." Gaventa similarly points to the importance of the converts' establishing "a relationship of interdependence with other believers" and of their moving into "a community of mutual responsibility and commitment."[7]

Conversion in the early books of the Hebrew Bible: The ethnic and tribal identity of the biblical Israelites precluded outsiders' easily joining the group. Israelites described themselves as *benai yisrael*, the children of Israel/Jacob, that is, as stemming from a common ancestor. From the point of view of the Bible's authors, the covenant with God was a compact between a particular deity, Yahweh, and a specific descent group, Abraham, Isaac, Jacob, and Jacob's children. Notably Jacob became the principle progenitor of this people, because he alone of the patriarchs could claim that all of his offspring accepted Yahweh as their deity. Abraham had fathered Ishmael as well as Isaac, and Isaac had sired both Esau and Jacob.

The importance of kinship in Israelite identity is stressed by Genesis' emphasis on the fact that, even before they married, the patriarchs and matriarchs shared a lineage. By contrast, Ishmael's and Esau's "foreign" wives symbolize their exclusion from the main line of Israelite descent.[8] These are among the factors that explain why the concept of conversion does not appear in the earlier books of the Hebrew Bible, where *ger*, the term that later means "convert," refers only to a non-citizen who resides among the Israelites. It does not indicate that the individual has accepted Yahweh as his or her sole deity.[9] These early books hold that non-Israelites may perform Israelite rituals *without* converting. For instance, a non-native-born male could enjoy the Passover sacrifice so long as he were circumcised, and Moses married the daughter of a priest of Midian, who saved her husband's life by circumcising their sons (Exod. 2:16-22, 4:24-26). But these texts do not speak of conversion.

Conversion in the later biblical books: It is not clear exactly when the practice of conversion entered Judaism. Neither Ezra nor Nehemiah seems to have considered the possibility of the "foreign wives" converting to Judaism.[10] Is. 56:6-8, for its part, mentions "the foreigners who attach themselves to YHWH, to minister to him . . . to be his servants, all who keep the Sabbath and hold fast to the covenant." The prophet tells them that God will bring them to the Temple and accept their prayers and sacrifices. The author of Is. 66:20-22 similarly asserts that God will make priests and Levites from among the gentiles. But as Cohen states,[11] the anonymous prophet does not provide us with any information about these people or the process by which they became followers of Yahweh. That is, Isaiah does not outline a formal process of conversion, and at least the latter reference speaks of an eschatological future. In this messianic period, non-Israelites may become Yahweh's servants, observe the Sabbath, and worship at the Temple. But they still are not called *benai yisrael*.

Conversion in the Hellenistic period: Cohen maintains that the first clear evidence for conversion to Judaism—"belief in the true God accompanied by circumcision and a change of identity"[12]—appears at Jud. 14:10:

"When Achior saw all that the God of Israel had done, he believed in God completely. So he was circumcised and was admitted to the community of Israel, as are his descendants to the present day."[13] While the book may derive only from the second century B.C.E., it contains some elements that reflect the Persian period, so that Nickelsburg suggests that it is "a tale which originated in the Persian period [that] has been rewritten in Hasmonean times."[14]

Even if Judith originated in the Persian period, only in Maccabean times do we encounter several concrete examples of conversion to Judaism. John Hyrcanus forcibly circumcised the Idumeans who fought alongside native-born Jews in the war against Rome of 67-73 C.E. (Josephus, *Antiquities* 13:257, 319, 397). Horace (65-8 B.C.E.) compares "a big band of poets" to the Jews who "will compel you to make one of our throng."[15] Stern comments that "[t]he comparison implies strong Jewish missionary activity in Rome." Valerius Maximus attributes the expulsion of the Jews from Rome in 139 B.C.E. to the fact that they "attempted to transmit their sacred rites to the Romans."[16]

Josephus (*Antiquities* 13:257, 319, 397) reports that rulers of Adiabene converted to Judaism. A traveling Jewish merchant, Charax Spasini, taught Izates's harem how to worship God "after the manner of Jewish tradition," while another Jew had taught Judaism to Helena, Izates's mother. After learning about his mother's commitment to Judaism, Izates decided to convert. However, when he maintained that a true convert must be circumcised, Helena attempted to dissuade her son, fearing that his subjects would violently reject their king's allegiance to "rites that were strange and foreign to them." While Ananias agreed with Helena and advised the king not to be circumcised, another Jew, Eleazar, "who came from Galilee and who had a reputation for being extremely strict when it came to the ancestral laws," urged Izates to undergo the rite. Josephus reports that after the king was circumcised, God prevented his subjects from rebelling against him.[17]

These events in conjunction with Mat.

23:15 ("Woe to you, scribes and Pharisees, hypocrites! For you traverse sea and land to make a single proselyte") have led some scholars to argue that, beginning in the Hellenistic period, Jews undertook a concerted policy of proselytizing.[18] Others have written extensive refutations of this position, and, overall, while there is evidence that, at least as early as the Hellenistic period, people converted to Judaism, no evidence shows that the Jews actively sought converts then or in the Rabbinic period. Importantly, the appearance of conversion in Hellenistic Jewish texts may reflect a larger cultural expression in the complex Hellenistic world at large, for there are good examples of conversion to the Greco-Roman mystery religions and to the philosophical schools of antiquity, including Apuleius' *Metamorphoses*—"the biography of a Pagan convert," Lucius. Finn similarly maintains that Iamblichus' description of the philosophical life fits well within a discussion of converts and conversion.[19]

The fact that conversion increases during periods of social instability may further explain its appearance in Judaism during the Hellenistic period. Hellenism clearly represented a challenge to the religion of biblical Israel, the thought of classical Greece, and the cultures of Asia, for Alexander's joining of Europe and Asia produced new forms of religion, philosophy, theology, art, poetry, drama, science, and language. It brought the Jews into immediate contact with new universes of thought, and it introduced Judaism and its god to a variety of new peoples and cultures. The political turmoil that followed Alexander's death turned the land of Israel and Jerusalem into unwilling prizes in the struggles between the Ptolomies and the Selucids, as well as homes for many non-Jewish soldiers, slaves, merchants, and hangers-on. In this setting Judaism was increasingly recognized as a Hellenistic religion, merely one of the local, national forms of Hellenistic culture. Some non-Jews, of course, did not fully understand the religion or its failure to have a representation of its deity in its Temple. But they did comprehend its ethical system, its sacrificial rituals, its concern with ritual purity, and its concept of

an ancient divine law given to an extraordinary political ruler. While Romans thought the Jews lazy for wasting time on the Sabbath and unfriendly for refusing to eat with them, they appreciated Judaism's antiquity. Thus Julius Caesar recognized Judaism as a legitimate religion and gave the Jews certain liberties, so that they might live in the Roman Empire and still practice their ancient customs in peace.[20] In this setting, to many Romans, especially women among the upper class, Judaism was a viable, stable, and venerable religious option, and the stage for conversion was set.

Conversion in the Rabbinic period: As we turn to the Rabbinic period, it is important to remember that Rabbinic documents do not present the testimony of converts but only view conversion from the rabbis' points of view. Thus we find here no first hand evidence about the converts or why they chose to enter the Jewish community. Second, this is the literature of a religious elite, and it therefore does not reveal how common people dealt with converts or the idea of conversion. Third, since the Talmudic literature is largely theoretical and utopian, it does not necessarily inform us of what actually was practiced or of history as it actually occurred. The rabbis, for instance, claim that virtually every enemy of the Jews eventually converted to Judaism, including the Roman emperors Nero and Antoninus. How much else they tell us was simply part of their imagination? Fourth, the rabbis exploit the topic of conversion to present their larger legal theories and concerns rather than honestly to inform about this topic. So it is unclear how much we really learn from the Rabbinic literature about conversion at all.

As we might accordingly expect, a careful study of the diverse Rabbinic compilations reveals contradictory statements about converts and conversion.[21] We find that, even within the limited purview of the rabbis, different communities performed different rituals, and diverse sages held conflicting opinions of how one could convert to Judaism, how a convert fits into the Jewish community, and how the Jewish community should view conversion and converts. This diversity of views may be an accurate reflection of the multiplicity of groupings within the Jewish communities of late antiquity, for, as Segal writes, "different Jews . . . reached different opinions about proselytism and behaved accordingly."[22] Thus, as McKnight[23] writes, "conversion is a local factor. One does not . . . convert to Judaism so much as one converts to a local display of Judaism."

Although present-day Judaism has a carefully delineated conversion ritual and process Jews trace back to Rabbinic documents, those texts themselves do not exhibit the consistency often attributed to them. Some scholars hold that acceptance of the Torah, circumcision, for males, immersion, and sacrifice were required for conversion from Second Temple times and on.[24] But the Rabbinic documents themselves do not support this claim. Indeed, in Sifre Numbers, from the middle of the third century C.E., Judah the Patriarch first mentions these rituals. And even at this late point in history, an examination of the full Rabbinic corpus reveals considerable inconsistency concerning the nature, meaning, and importance of the sacrifice. Several explanations appear for why converts must bring offerings and undergo ritual immersion. Other passages concern the necessity of circumcision for male converts. Finally, some held that a male convert did not need ritual immersion, because his being circumcised effected his conversion. It appears that, throughout the Rabbinic period, the conversion ritual was inchoate, with the variety of opinions reflecting a lack of agreement concerning the nature of the process by which a non-Jew became a Jew. Furthermore, only in the Babylonian Talmud do we hear of detailed education and examination of the convert, which, in this text's view, take place at conversion itself, not before.

The rabbis disagreed about the importance of a convert's motives. Ideally, non-Jews entered the Jewish community "for the sake of heaven." Some sages would not permit gentiles to convert in order to marry Jews. Rav, however, encourages such conversions, because he believes that the converts will eventually become true followers of Yahweh. Others held that if people converted for im-

proper reasons, they should undergo a second conversion ritual for the correct reasons. A few maintained that children would not understand their conversion, so that they should undergo the ritual again when they were adults. Some even permitted gentiles who converted as children to renounce their conversion when they became adults.

Once individuals converted to Judaism, they seem to have been required to fulfill the same obligations as the native-born Jews. Rabbinic sources frequently repeat the biblical injunction that there should be one law for the native-born and the *ger*, which now refers to the convert. From the Tosefta onward, one reads that a convert must follow the entire Torah; however, at least a passage in the Palestinian Talmud, at Y. Shab. 6:1, suggests that it could take some time for converts completely to reject their former way of life. In addition, some passages imply that because converts had not been raised in the Jewish tradition, they could not be trusted to follow all of the laws and rituals connected with the Sabbath and Passover. Despite these limitations, the Rabbinic documents make it clear that while gentiles are not required to follow the Jewish agricultural laws and purity laws immediately, upon their conversion, they are required to observe all Jewish practices and mitzvot.

Even while consistently arguing that converts are to be treated like native-born Jews, Rabbinic documents note that they are different. Converts could not recite the avowal that stated that God had given the land of Israel to the ancestors of the Jews, and converts, unlike native-born Jews, do not have inherent rights to portions of the land of Israel, because their ancestors were not among the original tribes. Another essential difference between converts and Jews concerned family relationships. According to most rabbis, it was virtually impossible for born-Jews to die without leaving heirs, while converts, who had severed their ties with their gentile families, most likely would not have legitimate heirs or relatives who could attend to the estate or inherit the property. In fact, for the rabbis, converts represent a unique legal category of people who die without any heirs.

It is inconceivable to the rabbis that native-born Israelites could be in this category.

Also unlike native-born Israelites, converts could marry Israelites of impaired lineage, but, according to many authorities, could not, because of their genealogy, marry priests (excluded by the Torah only from marrying women with presumed or known previous sexual experience). Similarly, because converts were not native-born members of the Israelite community, we find numerous discussions of the applicability to them of the laws of Levirate marriage. Other restrictions also applied to converts. According to some, they could not serve in the Sanhedrin; the Mishnah holds that they cannot be judges, while the Babylonian Talmud permits them to judge only civil cases. Nor, according to some, may they own Israelite slaves.

Despite these many ways in which converts differed from born-Jews, Rabbinic texts assume that gentiles would seek to convert and, in many statements, deemed them an integral part of the people Israel from its inception. This is especially clear in the notion that the soul of converts, or their "guiding star," was present at the revelation on Mt. Sinai, suggesting that some rabbis believed that converts had always been and would always be a legitimate element within the Israelite community. The Mishnah deems converts a recognized segment of the Israelite community that accompanied Ezra back to the land of Israel from Babylonia, and a passage in the Palestinian Talmud states that God "traverses the earth, and whenever he finds a righteous person he attaches him to Israel." Similarly, Simeon b. Yohai suggests that converts are more precious to God than native-born Israelites, "for those whom the king loves are greater than those who love the king." We are also told that God revealed himself in the desert and not within a specific country, so that any who wished to convert could do so. So that gentiles would realize that they could convert at any time during their lives, Abraham was not circumcised until the age of ninety-nine.

The Babylonian Talmud maintains that noted rabbis were the descendants of converts, many of whom even were Israel's ene-mies. Meir was related to Nero, whom the Talmud says converted to Judaism, and Shemaia and Abtalion were descended from Sennacherib. Haman's descendants learned Torah in Benei Berak, and Sisera's descendants taught children in Jerusalem. These imagined genealogies negate the hostility of many of Israel's foes, and they blur the lines between converts and rabbis. Ruth the Moabite was David's ancestress, and Rahab, the harlot of Jericho, married Joshua son of Nun. Their descendants included Israelite priests and prophets.

Despite such ideas, the Rabbinic documents remain ambivalent, containing a number of negative comments about converts. Eliezer referred to converts' inherent "bad streak," and he claimed that the "enemy" in Exod. 23:4 is a convert. Sifre Numbers states that converts occupied the actual fringes of the Israelite camp during their travels from Egypt to the land of Israel. The "rabble" who accompanied the Israelites out of Egypt were converts, and they caused the Israelites to sin. Helbo compared converts to sores on Israel's body, and Isaac stated that "evil upon evil comes to those who receive converts." An anonymous sage claimed that converts were among those who were delaying the messiah's arrival.

Thus, even as the entire range of Rabbinic texts assumes that gentiles will convert to Judaism and find a place within the Jewish community, the Rabbinic collections consistently present the converts as marginal beings, situated in the liminal space between the Jewish and non-Jewish communities. They had severed their ties with the gentile community but in some sense remained on the outer edges of that community. While they were no longer gentiles, their gentile background was important in certain contexts. Similarly, while they were not fully equated with native-born Israelites, they shared many traits in common, so as to be both "alien and familiar at the same time."[25]

The Rabbinic period was a time of great change in the Near East and Asia Minor. The rise of Christianity, the struggles between Rome and the Sassanian governments, the rise and fall of peoples as Rome moved north, and the gradual destruction of the Palestinian Jewish community testify to social and cultural instability. Peter Brown begins his classic study of late antiquity by stating, "This book is a study of social and cultural change."[26] For the reasons indicated above, it is not surprising that late antiquity would witness a great number of conversions. But, while we know that this was the case for Christianity, to which a multitude converted, we have no idea how many became Jews. We know that, to some extent, the rabbis dealt with converts and conversion. But we do not have the impression that large numbers converted to Judaism or that conversion was a pressing issue for the rabbis or Jews. At the least, it is clear that no single Rabbinic view of conversion, the conversion process, or the nature of converts existed.

Conversion in the fourth and fifth centuries: There were few Christians in ancient Babylonia, but, in Asia Minor, the growing power of Christianity made it difficult for non-Jews to convert to Judaism. This was especially the case by the fourth century, under Byzantine-Christian law. Already before the year 300 C.E., the jurist Paul decreed that a Roman citizen who allows himself to be circumcised should be exiled, with the state confiscating his property and the doctor who performed the circumcision being executed. In 329, Constantine again imposed these punishments on anyone who approached "their nefarious sect" and "join[s] himself to their conventicles." In 339, Constantine II decreed that if a Jew purchases a non-Jewish slave and circumcises him, "not only shall he suffer the lost of the slave, but he shall be punished, indeed, by capital punishment." Furthermore, Jews who encouraged female weavers to join their religion were subject to capital punishment. In 353/354, Constantine II decreed that the state would confiscate any property belonging to a Christian who became a Jew. Again in 409, Honorius and Theodosius II legislated against conversion to Judaism.[27]

In addition, many of the Church Fathers composed virulent condemnations of the Jews and Judaism, meant to keep Christians from associating with Jews and being attracted to

Judaism or Jewish practices.[28] For example, Cyril of Alexandria wrote:[29]

> The Jews are the most deranged of all men. They have carried impiety to its limit, and their mania exceeds even that of the Greeks. They read Scriptures and do not understand what they read. Although they had heavenly light from above, they preferred to walk in darkness. They are like people who had neither their mind nor their thinking faculty. Accordingly, they were seized by darkness and live as in the night. They were deprived completely of the divine light. . . .

And Cyprian wrote:

> I have comprised in my undertaking two books of equally moderate length; one wherein I have endeavored to show that the Jews, according to what had before been foretold, had departed from God, and had lost God's favor, which had been given them in past time . . .; while the Christians had succeeded to their place. . . .

These condemnations of Jews and Judaism—rather mild by later standards—serve as a transition from Asia Minor and Europe of late antiquity to the Middle Ages.

The practice of conversion in the Middle Ages: It is impossible to generalize about the Jews in medieval Europe, as the situation varied from century to century and from country to country. However, after the First Crusade, a negative picture of the Jew appeared frequently in medieval Christian Europe, especially among the common people. After 1144, the charge that Jews killed innocent Christians, especially children, was found throughout Europe, appearing even in the twentieth century.[30] The Fourth Latern Council in 1215 sought to end any possibility that Christians might be put in a subordinate position to Jews and decreed special clothing for Jews in order to prevent any "accidental" commingling of Jews and Christians. Beginning in 1239, the papacy had the Talmud burned, and, in this same century, Christian rulers began a policy of expelling Jews from their realms. More or less sporadic persecutions of Jews occurred at various times during the Middle Ages, and the anti-Jewish polemic continued to flourish in many places.[31]

Despite these restrictions, persecutions,

and polemics, for brief periods of time, canon lawyers protected some Jewish rights. They supported the binding nature of the Jewish laws of marriage, divorce, and parental rights, and some even permitted Jews to serve in public office, provided that they performed duties Christians could not easily render. In light of this complex picture of the position of the Jew in medieval Europe, many assume that Jews neither sought nor accepted converts, and this line of reasoning has been supported by reference to the almost uniformly low economic and social position of the medieval Jews. In most locations and during most centuries, one gained few advantages through conversion. And yet, as we shall now see, direct evidence shows that, during this period, hundreds, perhaps thousands, of people anyway converted to Judaism.

During the medieval period, a convert had to be formally accepted by a Jewish court of three sages, a procedure that non-Jewish authorities often openly opposed. As a result, the Talmud's ambiguity concerning the advisability of accepting converts is echoed in writings of several medieval sages. Even so, "the desirability of *gerey sedeq*, 'righteous proselytes' (i.e., those who became Jews through conviction), was taken for granted." Clearly, Christians who converted to Judaism did so on "an exclusively religious level," for there were no practical or material advantages in becoming a Jew. Thus, in the thirteenth century, Rabbi Moses of Coucy urged the Jews to treat gentiles fairly, because God indeed had sent the Jews into exile specifically to gain converts. Only if Jews dealt honestly and fairly with non-Jews could their mission to the gentiles be fulfilled. For some, such as Rabbi Moses, the conversion of the gentiles was the first step in the redemption of the world.[32]

Latin sources provide information about the earliest medieval European convert to Judaism, Bodo, or Puota, a deacon in Louis the Pious' court. This nobleman, described as a "scion of a German tribe," converted to Judaism around 838. He subsequently engaged in debates with Christians and, according to one source, convinced the Muslim

rulers in Spain to force Spanish Christians to convert to Judaism or Islam.[33] Similarly, in an epistle probably from the ninth century, Father Nestor writes that he was "one who loved the Lord 'with all his heart and all his soul,' who despised the religion of the uncircumcised and their errors, and sought shelter under the wings of the Shechina, the Holy Presence." After examining several religions, Father Nestor had become convinced that Christianity lacked value; he wrote the epistle to present the theological reasons he abandoned Christianity for Judaism. Another individual, Wecelin, served Duke Conrad of Carinthia early in the eleventh century. A literate cleric from a prominent family, after his conversion to Judaism, he was forced to flee his homeland. At the end of life, he actively opposed Christianity.[34]

Fragments from the Cairo Genizah likewise speak of clerics who became Jews.[35] One reports that after he was circumcised, he sought to convince others to follow his example. He was thrown into jail but was aided in escaping by one of his guards, to whom the Lord had spoken in a dream. The Genizah also provides extensive information about a certain Andreas, Archbishop of Bari from 1062-1066, and about a female convert whose family was from Normandy. After her conversion, she fled to Narbonne, where she married David, of the Todros family. Upon hearing that her family was pursuing her, she and her husband fled to Monieux. Her husband was murdered, and two of her children were kidnapped during a pogrom six years later, about the time of the First Crusade.

In addition to information about the converts mentioned above and several others, the Genizah fragments provide the memoirs of Johannes son of Dreux, who, upon his conversion in 1102, took the name Obadiah. An expert in the Hebrew language and calligraphy, he also knew Arabic and Latin, and he is described as an expert in Christian literature. He was the younger of twins born to Maria, the wife of Dreux in Oppido. As a young teen, he dreamed he was a priest in the basilica in Oppido. We learn nothing about the next twenty years of his life, so that we do not know why he eventually became a Jew. By the time of the First Crusade, however, he had begun to study Judaism. In several fragments of his writings, he chronicles the events of the First Crusade, at one point citing Joel 3:4 in Latin, written in Hebrew characters. He seems to have converted in 1102, six years after the beginning of the Crusades, and shortly thereafter he moved to Syria. In Aleppo he received a letter of reference from Barukh b. Isaac, the head of the Talmudic academy. After an undetermined period of time, Obadiah left for Baghdad, where the Jewish community supported him. He resided in the synagogue's living quarters and was eventually invited "to be with the orphan youths in order to learn the Torah of Moses and the words of the prophets in the writing of the Lord and the language of the Hebrews."[36] Fortunately Obadiah saw himself as a chronicler, carefully recording events leading to the First Crusade, the teachings of certain false messiahs he heard about in Baghdad, and the siege of Aleppo by Roger of Antioch, around 1118.

It is important to note, as Golb does, that, for every proselyte "actually described or mentioned in the extant records of the Cairo Geniza"[37] there were hundreds more who received no such mention. Thus it seems likely that the phenomenon of conversion to Judaism in this period was much larger than scholars normally concede.

Other documents found in the Cairo Genizah shed additional light on this topic, especially on the eighth century conversion to Judaism of the Khazars, a people living in southern Russia.[38] From the sixth century on, apparently as part of the Hun Empire, they occupied most of the region between the Black and Caspian Seas, at one point controlling the Ukraine, including Kiev. In the eighth century, Khakan Bulan and his court led a mass conversion to Judaism. Most of our evidence about those events comes from a series of letters between the tenth century Spanish Jewish statesman Hasdai ibn Shaprut and Khakan Joseph, then the Khazar king. These letters describe Bulan's inviting to his palace sages from Islam, Christianity, and Judaism. After hearing the case for each religion, he selected Judaism. This account forms the basis for Judah Halevi's *Khuzari*.

According to the Genizah documents, Jews seeking refuge from Byzantine persecution had settled among the Khazars and intermarried with them. Among the Khazars, a deceased king was succeeded by his bravest general. At one point, a prominent general selected to be Khakan revealed after he took the throne that he was Jewish. Now the disputation among the religions took place, and Judaism was made the official religion of the people.

Medieval Jewish philosophers on conversion: Like the Talmudic sources, medieval Jewish writers present a variety of views concerning converts and conversion. The thinking of Maimonides and Judah Halevi gives us a glimpse at the extent of the differing views.

Maimonides implies that even born-Jews were converts at Sinai, when they underwent the three-fold ritual of circumcision, immersion, and sacrifice that now is required of all converts. He holds that Jews should do everything possible to attract converts and that, once someone expresses an interest in Judaism, Jews must do all they can to make that person a Jew. Reflecting the Talmudic point that the sages should not overburden converts with the details of the punishments they may receive for not following the law, Maimonides writes:[39]

> We neither belabor the point nor enter into details; lest this trouble him and cause him to turn from a good way to a bad way. For at the beginning one only attracts a person with soft and pleasing words, and so it says [in Hosea 11:4], *I will draw them with cords of a man* and only afterwards *with bonds of love.*

Elsewhere Maimonides even suggests that while we must instruct the convert in the principles of faith, the Talmud mandates that Jews not to go into a lengthy discussion of the commandments.

Maimonides holds in general that it is permissible to teach the Torah to Christians, who otherwise misinterpret it. By learning the correct meaning, they will be attracted to Judaism. Thus Maimonides seems to have held not only "a positive attitude toward proselytes but a positive attitude toward proselytization."[40]

Maimonides' attitude on this topic stems from his overall view of human beings, who, he argues, are all essentially the same. Since no one is born with a fully developed soul, Jews and non-Jews are alike, able to acquire a soul through intellectual activity. What differentiates Jews from non-Jews are not inborn traits but what they do with their intellects. The absence of an essential difference between Jews and gentiles makes it relatively easy for non-Jews to become Jews. All they have to do is learn the principles of Judaism and live their lives accordingly.

Judah Halevi held very different ideas about people and about converts. Believing that Jews are essentially distinct from other human beings, he held that converts could never become the same as born Jews. Thus he wrote:[41]

> Any Gentile who joins us sincerely shares our good fortune, but he is not equal to us. If the Torah were binding on us because God created us, the white and the black man would be equal since He created them all. But the Torah (is binding) because He led us out of Egypt and remained attached to us. For we are the pick of mankind.

Elsewhere Halevi wrote, "Those who become Jews do not take equal rank with born Israelites, who are especially privileged to attain to prophecy, whilst the former can only achieve something by learning from them, and can only become pious and learned, but never prophets."[42] Thus while Halevi wrote the *Kuzari* to explain that Judaism is open to non-Jews, his theory of Judaism did not allow him to equate native-born Jews and converts.

The Jewish mystical tradition similarly had a problem with converts, for the Zohar and the tradition out of which it came believed that Jews and gentiles are *essentially* different. They do not have the same types of souls or similar essential beings. The Zohar teaches that individual souls are pre-existent with the divine: "Since the day when it occurred to God to create the world and even before it was really created, all the souls of the righteous were hidden in the divine idea, even in its peculiar form."[43] The souls of the people Israel thus were pre-ordained and pre-counted before the creation of the world, and they are different from those of non-Jews, which were not carved from God's very being.

The Jews' uniqueness is symbolized by the complex of meanings of the phrase *knesset yisrael*, referring to the earthly Israel, the spiritual Israel, and the Shekhinah, the creative aspect of God and the lowest of the ten divine emanations (*sefirot*). Because God interacts with humankind and the created world through the Shekhinah and *knesset yisrael*, the community of Israel is a liminal entity, alone among the peoples of the earth straddling the boundary between the divine and mundane. Within this understanding, conversion was possible, but only on the basis of the Zohar's doctrine that an entirely new soul descends upon converts. Even this soul, however, was understood to be of lesser spirituality than the soul of a born Jew.[44]

The spread of Judaism in medieval times: During the medieval period and even earlier, Judaism spread throughout Asia, India, China, and Africa. Some have argued that Jews settled in Cochin, India, as early as the sixth or seventh century. While some claim that Jews were in China before the time of Ezra, Chinese Jews themselves argue that their ancestors reached the Orient during the first three centuries of the common era. A seventeenth century Jesuit in China—supported by a contemporary inscription—complains that Jews there actively sought converts.[45]

The Abyssinian annals record the conversion of the Queen of Sheba, and some claim that all of Abyssinia was Jewish before it became Christian in the early part of the fourth century. The Falashas are the best known of the Ethiopian converts. Seligson[46] writes that:

> The skin pigmentation of many modern North African Jews and the religious practices of many African non-Jews indicate that much intermarriage and interchange of

religious ideas and practices took place in this vast area and that a far-flung missionary work was carried on for a long period of time. There is an abundance of legends and popular folktales all over the hinterlands of Egypt and North Africa to indicate the influence of Judaism on native peoples.

The situation in Europe is similar, with conversion invariably being at least an issue. In 1539, an eighty year old Catholic woman, Catherine Zaleshovska, was tried by a court of priests and convicted of blasphemy for holding Jewish beliefs. After she was burned at the stake, rumors abounded that throughout Poland Christians were converting to Judaism. Sigismun I sent two commissioners to Lithuania to investigate, but they returned with no evidence supporting the rumors. Still, the priestly hierarchy told the king that Lithuanian Jews and their new converts were about to flee to Turkey. The king investigated the rumors, found them baseless, and, in 1540, promised the Lithuanian Jews that he would not bother them again unless he found unquestionable evidence that they were seeking converts.[47]

In Hungary, large numbers of conversions are known to have occurred. After Suleiman the Magnificent conquered Hungary, a significant number of Christians converted to Judaism, because the Sultan mistreated Christians while favoring Jews. In the sixteenth and seventeenth centuries, the tolerant religious environment of Transylvania encouraged Jews to seek converts, and they were quite successful. Simon Pechi, Chancellor of Transylvania, not only converted to Judaism but was said to have persuaded twenty thousand peasants to convert with him. When Prince George Rackoczi II ascended the throne, Pechi was thrown into prison. Eventually he escaped to Constantinople, where he joined Donna Gracia Mendesia's printing firm and spent his life translating Hebrew religious works into Hungarian.[48]

During the sixteenth and seventh centuries, Sefardic Jews witnessed several examples of Catholics being burned alive for having converted to Judaism. Diogo da Assumpcao, a Franciscan monk, believed he was descended from Jews. In 1603, the Inquisition burned

him at the stake in Lisbon. The ancestors of Francisco Maldonado da Silva, a prominent surgeon living in Peru, were Marranos, and he became convinced of the truth of Judaism. When he tried to convert his sisters, one of them denounced him to the Inquisition. He was burned at the stake in 1639. Don Lope deVera, a Spanish nobleman, had no Jewish blood but became convinced of the truth of Judaism after studying Hebrew at the University of Salamanca. His brother turned him over to the Inquisition in 1639, and, in 1644, he was executed in Valladolid, Spain.

Throughout Europe, we find examples of Jewish converts during these centuries. In 1607, Conrad Victor, a professor of classical languages at the University of Marburg, migrated to Salonica in order to convert to Judaism. Born a Catholic, Nicholas Antione became a Protestant minister. Early in his ministry he sought to convert to Judaism but was rebuffed by the rabbis of Metz, Venice, and Padua. He remained a minister but secretly professed Judaism. Eventually, he was arrested for heresy and tried in Geneva. He was founded guilty, strangled to death, and his body was burned at the stake on April 20, 1632.

As suggested by this final example, we do find at this time strong voices within the Jewish community discouraging conversion. Isaiah Horowitz's *Sheney Luhoth Ha-Berith* ("Two Tables of the Covenant"), completed in 1623, treats the term *ger* in its biblical sense of stranger, not in its post-biblical meaning of convert. One of the strongest voices against accepting converts was the great Polish Halakhic scholar, Solomon Luria, who died in 1574. He argued that as long as Jews lived in exile, "in a country not our own, like slaves beneath the hands of their owners," they should not accept converts. As for any Jew who sought converts, "let his blood be on his own head, whether he himself engages in proselytization, or whether he merely knows of such. . . ." Luria's arguments result partly from his historical circumstance and partially from his view, similar to that of the Zohar, that Jews and non-Jews are different types of human beings with different souls.[49]

The Middle Ages thus produced a full spectrum of ideas concerning conversion and a least some number of Christians who actually became Jews. These include prominent individuals, who we no doubt know about because of their ability to record their actions. But how many other, common people made the transition we will never know. Nor do we know how common Jews related to such converts. In all, the Jewish sources are varied, complex, and wide-ranging, revealing little, hiding much.

Conversion in the modern period: The Enlightenment changed everything for the Jews, with Jews entering European society for the first time in centuries and some non-Jewish thinkers even believing that Jews, like all other human beings, could make important contributions to culture and society. Indeed, if the Jews would just discard the irrationalities of the Talmud and Rabbinic law, they could be fully integrated into European society. In this philosophical setting, the negative images of the Jew that prevailed in the Middle Ages were de-emphasized, and it was theoretically possible for Jews and Christians to live, work, socialize, and study together.

During the eighteenth century, some Jewish intellectuals began to de-emphasize the differences between Judaism and Christianity, and others sought to disengage Christian ethics and civility from Christian theology. Thus the concept of a common reason and ethics promised to bridge the gap between Judaism and Christianity, even as the theological claims of both religions were rejected as irrational and inappropriate foundations upon which to build a life. Solomon Maimon, accordingly, expressed his willingness to convert to Christianity so long as he did not have to accept its theology, and David Friedländer, a foremost disciple of Moses Mendelssohn, proposed that Jews would join Wilhelm Abraham Teller's Protestant Church, if they could maintain their skepticism about Christian dogma and confess only to the religion of nature.[50]

In this setting, numbers of Jews converted to Christianity, justifying their action on the basis of the shared ethics of the two religions and the practical benefits they gained by becoming Christian. Yet, while some Christians agreed that the two religions shared a common ethical systems, they tended less frequently and dramatically to blur the lines between the two faith communities. If, as some Jews argued, Judaism and Christianity really were the same, then converting to Christianity was the only reasonable action, as Johann Lavatar declared in 1769 in his famous challenge to Moses Mendelssohn.[51] In reality, then, the situation in modern Europe was not so different from that of medieval Europe. In theory, the Enlightenment had brought an end to the negative image of the Jews. But the rise of Romanticism that soon followed again precluded a radical integration of the Jews into European society or the possibility of Judaism's becoming attractive to significant numbers of Christians. Notably, Jews in Europe were not anxious to be seen as encouraging non-Jews to convert. Instead, the struggle to prevent Jews from becoming Christians occupied enough of their time.

The situation in nineteenth century America was somewhat different. Founded on the principles of the Enlightenment, American culture had never encompassed the negative image of Jews and Judaism familiar from medieval society. Nor had Christian anti-Judaism ever permeated American thought as it had European imaginations and mythologies. As a result, a number of leaders of the American Jewish community saw a realistic possibility of Christians' becoming Jews. Thus, in 1869, thirteen leaders of liberal Judaism in America met in Philadelphia. David Einhorn, who was in charge, proposed that the son of a Jewish mother would be considered Jewish whether or not he was circumcised, a position that the Frankfort Society of Friends of Reform had taken in 1842.[52] Isaac Meyer Wise went further, proposing that male converts to Judaism did not have to undergo circumcision. Einhorn opposed this, stating, "The acceptance of proselytes, through which Judaism acquires many impure elements, must be made more difficult and it is precisely circumcision which can form a barrier against the influx of such elements." Wise stated: "Let us open the gates so that 'On that day the Lord shall be one' will become a reality." Wise's view was debated but tabled. By 1893, however, the Central Conference of America Rabbis, the rabbinical organization of American Reform Judaism, resolved that converts could be accepted, "without any initiatory rite, ceremony or observance whatever." Only knowledge and commitment were required for conversion.[53]

Conversion to Judaism in America steadily rose from the 1950s. A study in 1953 estimated that two thousand non-Jews had converted to Judaism, and, by the late sixties, probably seven thousand were converting to Judaism yearly. Women composed the majority of the converts, and about 90% converted because they were marrying a Jew. Already in 1947, the Central Conference of American Rabbis had stated that sincere candidates for conversion should be welcomed, even if they were converting because of marriage. By the 1950s, the Central Conference began an active effort to bring converts—as well as unaffiliated Jews—into Judaism, while the Union of American Hebrew Congregations, the association of Reform temples, launched a program to make conversion available to non-practicing Christians. The focus was on knowledge of Judaism, and many temples in larger communities offered courses on Jewish beliefs, practices, and community institutions. Often the prospective convert and his or her intended spouse attended such a course together. By 1964, at least 10% of families affiliated with Reform congregations included converts.[54] While, throughout the fifties and the sixties, Reform rabbis did not require converts to undergo circumcision or ritual immersion, in the 1970s, as part of its return to ritual and the attempt to build bridges with the more traditional American Jewish movements, Reform began to encourage converts to participate in these ritual acts.

In 1978, Rabbi Alexander Schindler, president of the Union of American Hebrew Congregations, outlined a procedure for welcoming converts and proposed the creation of an outreach program for "unchurched" Americans seeking a spiritual home. Schindler's proposal, made in a speech before the Union's board of directors, responded to the high rate of marriage between Jews and non-Jews and to the declining number of Jews in America. He emphasized the need to encourage non-Jewish spouses to convert to Judaism and argued that Judaism should actively promote itself as a viable option for non-affiliated Americans searching for a religious community and way of life. Schindler's call initiated much debate within the Reform movement and the American Jewish community at large, especially as it pointed to an important new factor in Jewish opinion on conversion. With the high rate of intermarriage, the issue of conversion had taken on a new importance, especially as the conversion of a non-Jewish spouse is an important factor in whether or not the children of an intermarriage are raised as Jews.

Twenty years later, there remains less than unanimous endorsement of Schindler's ideas. For the most part, Reform and Conservative Jewish organizations have continued to lead initiatives to support conversion and the full acceptance of converts. At the same time, the range of opinions found throughout Jewish history continues to appear, both in the liberal wings of contemporary Judaism and in American Orthodoxy. Rabbi Emanuel Rackman—echoed by Rabbi Marc D. Angel—views conversion as a means of averting the "astronomical losses" that may result from intermarriage. On the other hand, some orthodox rabbis continue to boast that they have never performed a conversion ceremony.[55]

Conclusion: Within Judaism, conversion is an ambiguous and complex phenomenon. The inherent ethnicity of the Jewish community means that, under all circumstances, converts are more or less liminal beings. At the same time, the general openness of the Jewish community and its belief that God created all of humankind to do God's will means that Jews in general have and will always welcome converts into their midst. From at least the first century C.E., Judaism has recognized the convert as a viable part of the Jewish community, a segment that some held stood before God alongside the native-born population at the foot of Sinai. Thus, in all historical periods, conversion to Judaism has been an important phenomenon: in antiquity, in medieval and pre-modern Europe, and increasingly in contemporary America, where, both for reasons of marriage and as the result of personal spiritual quests, many gentiles seek to become Jews.

Bibliography

Finn, Thomas A., *From Death to Rebirth: Ritual and Conversion in Antiquity* (New York and Mahwah, 1997).

Golb, Norman, *Jewish Proselytism—A Phenomenon in the Religious History of the Early Medieval Period* (Cincinnati, 1987).

McKnight, Scot, *A Light among the Gentiles: Jewish Missionary Activity in the Second Temple Period* (Minneapolis, 1991).

Porton, Gary G., *The Stranger within Your Gates: Converts and Conversion in Rabbinic Literature* (Chicago and London, 1994).

Notes

[1] Shaye J.D. Cohen, "Conversion to Judaism in Historical Perspective: From Biblical Israel to Postbiblical Judaism," in *Conservative Judaism*, 1983, 36, no. 4 (Summer), p. 31.

[2] Thomas A. Finn, *From Death to Rebirth: Ritual and Conversion in Antiquity* (New York, 1997), pp. 19-20.

[3] Rosabeth Kanter, *Commitment and Community* (Cambridge, 1972). Alan F. Segal, *Paul the Convert: The Apostolate and Apostasy of Paul the Pharisee* (New Haven and London, 1990), p. 76, puts matters this way: "conversion most often precedes commitment, so that the phenomenon of commitment includes more aspects than merely conversion. Conversion merely begins a process of commitment to the group."

[4] David A. Snow and Richard Machalek, "The Sociology of Conversion," in *Annual Review of Sociology* 10 (1984), p. 170. See also C.L. Staples and Armand L. Mauss, "Conversion or Commitment? A Reassessment of the Snow and Machalek Approach to the Study of Conversion," in *Journal for the Scientific Study of Religion* 26 (1987), p. 146.

[5] Segal, op. cit., p. 75.

[6] On the preceding, see Arthur L. Griel, "Previous Dispositions and Conversion to Perspectives of Social and Religious Movements," in *Sociological Analysis*, 38, 2 (1977), pp. 118-121, and Max Heirich, "Change of Heart: A Test of Some Widely Held Theories About Religious Conversion," in *American Journal of Sociology*, 83, 3 (November, 1977), pp. 674-675.

[7] On this see Griel, ibid., Segal, op. cit., p. 74, and Beverly R. Gaventa, *From Darkness to Light: Aspects of Conversion in the New Religions* (Beverly Hills and London, 1986), pp. 45-46.

[8] Naomi Steinberg, *Kinship and Marriage in Genesis: A Household Economics Perspective* (Minneapolis, 1993).

[9] Morton Smith, *Palestinian Parties and Politics that Shaped the Old Testament* (New York and London, 1971), pp. 178-182; Cohen, ibid., pp. 33-34.

[10] Smith, ibid., p. 180; Cohen, ibid., p. 35.

[11] Ibid., p. 35.

[12] Ibid., p. 35. See also Finn, op. cit., p. 93, who maintains that Judith, "takes conversion for granted."

[13] Carey A. Moore, *Judith: A New Translation with Introduction and Commentary. The Anchor Bible* (Garden City, 1985), p. 231. On the following, see p. 67 and Finn, op. cit., p. 93.

[14] George W.E. Nickelsburg, *Jewish Literature between the Bible and the Mishnah: A Historical and Literary Introduction* (Philadelphia, 1981), pp. 108-109.

[15] Menaham Stern, *Greek and Latin Authors on Jews and Judaism: Edited with Introductions, Translations, and Commentary. Volume One: From Herodotus to Plutarch* (Jerusalem, 1974), p. 323.

[16] Ibid., pp. 323 and 357-358.

[17] See Lawrence H. Schiffman, "The Conversion of the Royal House of Adiabene in Josephus and Rabbinic Sources," in Louis H. Feldman and Gohei Hata, eds., *Josephus, Judaism, and Christianity* (Detroit, 1987), pp. 293-314; Jacob Neusner, *A History of the Jews of Babylonia: I. The Parthian Period* (Leiden, 1969), pp. 61-67; Finn, op. cit., p. 96; Cohen, op. cit., p. 36.

[18] See Scot McKnight, *A Light Among the Gentiles: Jewish Missionary Activity in the Second Temple Period* (Minneapolis, 1991), pp. 1-4; see also Martin Goodman, *Mission and Conversion: Proselytizing in the Religious History of the Roman Empire* (Oxford, 1994), pp. 7-9.

[19] Finn, op. cit., pp. 68-84.

[20] Among numerous important works on this topic, see Louis H. Feldman, *Jew and Gentile in the Ancient World: Attitudes and Interactions from Alexander to Justinian* (Princeton, 1993), and Smith, op. cit., pp. 57-192.

[21] See Gary G. Porton, *The Stranger Within Your Gates: Converts and Conversion in Rabbinic Literature* (Chicago and London, 1994).

[22] Segal, op. cit., p. 79.

[23] McKnight, op. cit., p. 7.

[24] See Lawrence H. Schiffman, *Who Was a Jew? Rabbinic and Halakhic Perspectives on the Jewish-Christian Schism* (Hoboken, 1985), p. 19. Porton, op. cit., p. 133, lists others who argue for the antiquity and consistency of the requirement that converts participate in these rituals.

[25] Porton, op. cit., p. 215.

[26] Peter Brown, *The World of Late Antiquity:*

From Marcus Aurelius to Muhammad (London, 1971), p. 7.

[27] Amnon Linder, *The Jews in Roman Imperial Legislation* (Detroit, 1987), pp. 117-120, 124-132, 144-154, and 256-262. For discussions of this legislation, see Michael Avi-Yonah, *The Jews of Palestine: A Political History from the Bar Kokhba War to the Arab Conquest* (New York, 1976), pp. 147-148, 162-163, and 214-215. See also Mark R. Cohen, *Under Crescent and Cross: The Jews in the Middle Ages* (Princeton, 1994), pp. 32-36.

[28] Rosemary Ruether, *Faith and Fratricide: The Theological Roots of Anti-Semitism* (New York, 1974); Marcel Simon, *Verus Israel: A Study of the Relations Between Christians and Jews in the Roman Empire (135-425)* (Oxford, 1986), pp. 202-233, 306-338.

[29] Robert L. Wilken, *Judaism and the Early Christian Mind: A Study of Cyril of Alexandria's Exegesis and Theology* (New Haven and London, 1971), p. 1. The following quote is on p. 17.

[30] See Joshua Trachtenberg, *The Devil and the Jews* (New York, 1966), and Alan Dundes, *The Blood Libel Legend: A Casebook in Anti-Semitic Folklore* (Madison, 1991).

[31] Cohen, *Under Crescent*, pp. 42, 38-39, 140-194. On the following, see pp. 77-136.

[32] Jacob Katz, *Exclusiveness and Tolerance: Studies in Jewish-Gentile Relations in Medieval and Modern Times* (New York, 1973), pp. 77-79, 104-105.

[33] Norman Golb, *Jewish Proselytism—A Phenomenon in the Religious History of the Early Medieval Period. The Tenth Annual Rabbi Louis Feinberg Memorial Lecture* (Cincinnati, 1987), pp. 2-3; David J. Seligson, "In the Post-Talmudic Period," in David Max Eichhorn, ed., *Conversion to Judaism: A History and Analysis* (New York, 1965), pp. 69-73.

[34] Golb, op. cit., pp. 3-8; Seligson, op. cit., pp. 73-74.

[35] Based on manuscripts from the Cairo Genizah, Golb, op. cit., demonstrates the pervasiveness of conversion to Judaism during the early medieval period. On the following, see pp. 9-31.

[36] Ibid., p. 27.

[37] Ibid., p. 33.

[38] Seligson, op. cit., pp. 74-76; Golb, op. cit., pp. 38-39.

[39] Menachem Kellner, *Maimonides on Judaism and the Jewish People* (Albany, 1991), pp. 52-53.

[40] Ibid., p. 55.

[41] Isaak Heinemann, "Jehuda HaLevi: The Kuzari," in *Three Jewish Philosophers* (New York, 1965), p. 35.

[42] Hartwig Hirschfeld, *The Kuzari* (New York, 1971), p. 79; Katz, op. cit., pp. 146-147; Julius Guttmann, *Philosophies of Judaism: A History of Jewish Philosophy from Biblical Times to Franz Rosenzweig* (New York, 1973), pp. 143-144.

[43] Gershom Scholem, *Major Trends in Jewish Mysticism* (New York, 1973), p. 242.

[44] Katz, op. cit., pp. 146-147.

[45] Seligson, op. cit., pp. 88-90.

[46] Ibid., p. 91.

[47] David Max Eichhorn, "From Expulsion to Liberation (1492-1789)," in Eichhorn, op. cit., pp. 98-99.

[48] Ibid., pp. 99-101. On the following, see pp. 112-115.

[49] Katz, op. cit., pp. 144-148.

[50] Jacob Katz, *Out of the Ghetto: The Social Background of Jewish Emancipation 1770-1870* (New York), pp. 104-123.

[51] Alexander Altmann, *Moses Mendelssohn: A Biographical Study* (Philadelphia, 1973), pp. 194-264.

[52] David Philipson, *The Reform Movement in Judaism* (London, 1907), p. 163. On the differences between America and Europe with regard to the Jews, see Ben Halpern, "America Is Different," in Marshall Sklare, ed., *The Jew in American Society* (New York, 1974), pp. 67-92.

[53] Michael Meyer, *Response to Modernity: A History of the Reform Movement in Judaism* (New York and Oxford, 1988), pp. 257, 280.

[54] Ibid., pp. 380-381.

[55] See Charles E. Silberman, *A Certain People: American Jews and Their Lives Today* (New York, 1985), p. 319, and Michael Goldberg, *Why Should Jews Survive? Looking Past the Holocaust Toward a Jewish Future* (New York and Oxford, 1995), p. 112.

GARY G. PORTON

COSMOLOGY, JUDAIC THEORIES OF: "Theories of the cosmos" present general pictures of what the universe (meaning, everything that exists) looks like. Such theories form a critical part of every primary text of Jewish theology, from the Hebrew Scriptures through the historical development of Jewish philosophy and mysticism well into the twentieth century. This is because Jewish communal and individual religious life have always been conceived in terms of obligations or duties incumbent upon Jews in consequence of the people of Israel's relationship with the creator deity of the universe, who is their redeemer. These duties form a coherent whole that can be expressed as a moral system, and, in turn, generalized as two seemingly distinct imperatives, which Jewish tradition calls "duties of the mind" and "duties of the limbs." These imperatives are, "Believe what is true!" and "Do what is right!"

Doing what is right constitutes the sub-system of Jewish law (Halakhah); believing what is true constitutes the sub-system of Jewish belief (Aggadah). While in some ways these sub-systems are parallel, at base Judaism conceives them in different terms: Jewish law is more specifically determined and subject to strong communal enforcement in a formal or informal Jewish polity. Jewish belief is more general, and its specification tends to be left more to the individual. Hence, while Rabbinic and other leaderships of Jewish communities have tended to be rigorous about overseeing communal behavior, such rigor has not occurred in rewarding beliefs the community judges to be true and punishing convictions it judges false. Note, however, that contrary to what is often thought, this is not because (at least before the twentieth century) religious authorities considered belief less important to religious life than practice. On the contrary, the two have always been viewed as interrelated, so that true belief is seen to teach and promote right behavior and right behavior to encourage true belief. Rather, the emphasis has always had to do with what the community in fact is able to enforce.

For a similar reason, right practice is primarily a matter of correct behavior and only secondarily a matter of correct intention. To be sure, to intend to do what is right is better than not to, but doing what is right without intention is better than doing what is wrong with the best of intentions, and since external action is readily observable while internal intention is not, the community can create an objective structure to judge and instruct divinely obligated morality. The situation is just the reverse in questions of proper faith. True belief is primarily a matter of correct conception and only secondarily a matter of correct expression. To say what is true is better than not to, but for individuals to say what is true when they either do not understand at all what they are saying or even understand their words to be something false does not in any sense constitute true belief, and since internal conception is not obvious from words externally uttered, the community can not readily create an objective structure to judge divinely obligated true belief. Hence, in its attempt to fulfill the collective's duty to profess truth, the community is forced to rely on tools to instruct and encourage true faith rather than tools to obligate and enforce true utterance.

The primary means of this instruction has always been the publication by different rabbis of books that present reasons for believing what is true. Since the foundations of these arguments always rest on an understanding of the character of the universe as a whole, we can see clearly how, within Judaism, cosmologies become so central. For, as we noted above, Judaism asserts that the same God who reveals to the people its moral obligations is the creator of the universe and the redeemer of the Jewish people. In other words, Judaism affirms the existence of a God who creates the universe as a whole, reveals morality to the people Israel, and, through this creating and revealing, also redeems the people, in particular, and the universe, in general. This complex statement presupposes an adequate conception of what it means for both God and the Jewish people to exist in relationship to each other by way of the relationship of both to something called "the universe." Such a conception is a cosmology.

All Jewish conceptions of cosmology have their origin in images drawn in the Hebrew Scripture, which presents two dominant pictures, the account of creation in Gen. 1:1-2:3, referred to as *Ma'ase Bereshit*, and the account of the chariot in Ezek. 1:1-28, called *Ma'ase Ha-Merkavah*. While, in general, all Judaic theories of the cosmos are interpretations of these two biblical texts, at different periods in history each text has had more influence than the other. The first collections of speculation of these texts are found in the compilations of Rabbinic midrash attributed to the early rabbis. Here the focus is primarily on the account of creation, although the influence of the account of the chariot is also apparent. Beyond midrash, the sources for Jewish theories of the universe are independent manuscripts and biblical commentaries attributed either to Jewish philosophers or to Jewish mystics. In the ages when the primary form of Jewish speculation about the nature of the universe was philosophic, the account of creation dominated, but in ages in which the primary form of Jewish speculation on this subject was mystic, the account of the chariot dominated. Still almost all Rabbinic readers, at least until modern times, believed that the pictures drawn in both biblical texts are the same, or, at least, coherent and consistent with each other.

In the following, we begin by summarizing what both biblical texts say. Then we turn to see how these texts were interpreted in Rabbinic speculation through the subsequent centuries, including in Rabbinic midrash, in the classic Jewish philosophy that begins around the tenth century in the Eastern Muslim Empire, and in those written Jewish texts generally associated with Jewish mysticism, called "Kabbalah" (lit., "tradition").

Genesis' account of creation:[1] The Hebrew Bible opens with a general picture of the origin and nature of the universe. This functions as a cosmological framework for understanding the central narrative that follows, which presents an epic history of the rise and fall of the first Jewish theocratic nation state. The framework includes the origins of the universe (Gen. 1:1-2:3), humanity (Gen. 2:4-3:24: the story of the Garden of Eden), diverse human families (Gen. 4:1-5:32: the story of Cain and Abel and its aftermath), and diverse human nations (Gen. 6:1-11:32: the stories of the flood and the tower of Babel and their aftermaths). Our focus is exclusively on the cosmological part of the framework, concerning the origin of the universe.

The creation story is divided into seven distinct units, identified in the biblical text as "days." Creation itself is an intentional act by which God transforms a pre-existent space into diverse regions (days 1-3), which in turn act as God's agent to produce the forms of living entities (days 4-6). Each of the first three days marks the separation of a distinct region of space out of a pre-existent region— light out of dark (called respectively "day" and "night") on day one, a separation of earth and water (called "sky") on day two, and the separation of a portion of the surface of the earth from the water (called respectively "dry land" and "seas") on day three. Also on day three God generates the vegetation that covers the entire surface of the earth. This vegetation is in or transitional between the already generated space and the living occupants of that space that will be generated in the next three days. It functions as the basis of the food chain intended to nurture the unlimited number of yet-ungenerated material life forms commanded to occupy the space of the universe.

On the next three days, God orders the appropriate spaces to generate a single general form for the subsequent generation, through an endless serial chain of acts of procreation, of spatial occupants. On day four, the light of day, created on day one, creates multiple objects made from light (the sun, moon, and other celestial objects). On day five, the pre-existent water creates the form of a swarming sea life (fish and other entities, such as sea serpents, that live in water), while the sky, created on day two, generates from its material the form of life that can fly above the surface of the dry land (birds). Next, on day six, the pre-existent earth generates the form of living earthly entities (wild and domestic animals) that roam the dry land formed on day three. In addition, God joins the earth in creating a final creature, the human. This being (*ha-adam*) is a single form that contains within it the potential to be differentiated into two genders (called "male" and "female"). This potential does not become actual until the following story of the Garden of Eden.

Note that this cosmology presupposes that initially God is not alone. Prior to God's act of creation, on what we (but not the text) can call "day zero," there are undifferentiated regions of space. The initial universe is a sphere with a central earth core, surrounded by a ring of water, above which hovers something that the text calls "God's wind" (*ruah elohim*). The earth, water, and (possibly also) divine wind are the stuff from which God creates. God creates by speaking. In general, the verbs used to express God's activity describe the action of an absolutely powerful ruler who need simply states that something be done for it to be accomplished. God is a ruler of such power that, in his case, to "say" something and to "make" something are the same. The only things that God makes as such are the light and the spread (*raqiy'a*, most often translated "firmament"), which he creates alone on the first and second days respectively, and the human, which he creates in partnership with the earth on day six. In every other case, what God "says" constitutes a commandment to his already generated creatures to do the actual work.

On day one, God says that there should be light, which there is, and which God perceives. The light is then set to contain the region of dark encompassing the material world into a distinct region. God names the light and its region "day," and the dark and its separate region "night." Note that the terms "day" and "night" designate regions of space and not time. Nothing in the text suggests that any of these distinct acts collectively called "creation" take place in time.

On the second day, God inserts a ring of distinct material into the ring of water that divides the water into two separate, discrete rings of the same material, called "upper and lower waters." He makes this divider by saying that it should exist and naming it "sky." Then, on day three, he tells the waters below the sky to collect together in such a way that some of the surface of the globe of the earth emerges at the surface of the sky ring. God names the earth surface facing the sky "dry land" and the water space and material bordered by the earth and the sky "seas." With these two acts of naming, God completes his differentiation of the space of the universe. Then, still on day three, he initiates his creation of the living occupants of this space.

The picture that dominates God's generation of living occupants of his created space is political. One political feature we already have noted. God acts by speaking, meaning, in God's case, as an absolute ruler, for him to say something is sufficient for it to happen. The other crucial features in this story of God as a ruler are that he commands laws for his subjects to obey, and he assigns agents over each of his regions to govern the subjects and territories on his behalf. On day three he tells the earth to make plants and fruity trees sprout on its surface, the earth produces the vegetation that makes fruit, and God perceives that what he commanded happens. On day four, God separates day and night and says that there should be celestial objects to govern them by enlightening the earth and functioning as signs for the seasons, days, and years. Again, God perceives that what he said in fact happens. Next, on day five, God tells the water to generate a swarm that swarms in the seas and a flier that flies in the sky. He perceives that they do what he said they should do, and then he blesses the sea-swarm. He then tells the flier to increase on the earth and the sea-swarm to be fruitful, increase, and fill the water. Finally, on day six, he tells the earth to produce a "fresh life" (*nefesh hayah*) and to join him in making the human. The human is then made the governor of all these creatures below the domain of the celestial objects. God then blesses the human and commands him/her to be fruitful, increase, and to fill, conquer, and subdue the earth. In addition, he authorizes all of his life forms to eat the plants. Then, once again, he perceives that everything that he has said has come to be.

The last stage of the story is the creation of the seventh day, about which we are explicitly told practically nothing other than that God finished making his task. The story ends with God's blessing and sanctifying the seventh day.

Ezekiel's account of the Chariot:[2] At the initiation of his prophecy, in chapters one and ten, Ezekiel creates a visual image. I treat these two chapters as alternative descriptions of the same experience, which I begin by setting in context. Ezekiel ben Buzi, a priest of Zadok, is sitting by the river Chebar, which in all likelihood is another name for the Euphrates, on the fourth day of the month of Tammuz, in the fourth year of his, and his people's, exile from the holy city of Jerusalem, which dates the vision around 592 B.C.E. At this specific time and place, Ezekiel is hit by a strong, stormy wind (*ruah*) from the north. He finds himself sitting in the middle of a great cloud, surrounded by electrical fire, and within this fire he sees a vision, which he, like many other priest-prophets before him, identifies as a word (*davar*), also called a "hand," from the Lord. In general, his vision is not unlike those of others. God calls him and tells him what he must say to his people. But unique in this case is that the aural description is preceded by a relatively lengthy (for the Hebrew Scriptures) visual description.

At the bottom of Ezekiel's picture is a set of wheels, which, while spatially separate from the creature, were the mechanical means by which it moved. But the wheels were not the cause of the motion. Rather, they were moved, constantly back and forth, by the wind. Above, but spatially separate from, the wheels is a compound living thing (*hayot*) with four sides. On each side can be seen a face, attached to a body with human hands that are covered by a set of wings, attached to straight legs that end in the feet of a calf. Additionally, from each body there spreads out a second pair of wings, which in conjunction produce the appearance of an interconnected, organic, single entity. All of the feet, like the four bodies, are uniform in appearance and color; they sparkle and have the color of burnished brass. All that is different about the creatures is their faces. According to Ezekiel chapter one, the four faces in order were of a human (*adam*), a lion, an ox, and an eagle; according to chapter ten, they were in order the faces of a cherub, a human, a lion, and an eagle.

The living creature and its wheels, set firmly upon the earth, belong to a spatial domain distinct from the envisioned space above the life form. What separates the two domains is a spread (*raqiy'a*). Above the spread is a seat or throne, above which is a human, which Ezekiel calls "the glory of the Lord." This is generally described as "the appearance of the divine," but it is not. First, everything described above the spread is only something "like an appearance" and not an actual appearance. Second, within this kind of appearance the throne isn't really a

throne; it is "the likeness" of a throne. Third, the appearance of the human above the throne is only a likeness of something like the appearance of a human. This two-steps-removed-from-an-actual-appearance-of-the-human is ablaze in fire. Thus, what Ezekiel sees is a fire in what is sort of like a human shape, which is also like a rainbow in a cloud, and, at the same time, is like the glory of the Lord.

The first half of the last sentence of Ezekiel's vision in Ezek. 1:28 describes the association of the image of the human with the image of God's glory. The second half of the sentence reads, "I looked, fell on my face, and I heard a voice/sound (*qol*) speaking." What it speaks is the word/hand of God. In other words, where the visual image ends, with the identity of the human and divine glory, the aural begins. Presumably, the aural is to be understood as a higher form of knowledge; to hear what God says to the human transcends seeing whom God and the world are.

So end the two primary cosmological pictures of the universe found in the Hebrew Scriptures. What follows is how these verbal images were interpreted in subsequent ages of Jewish civilization. These interpretations, here considered in historical sequence, constitute the different cosmologies of Rabbinic Judaism.

Midrash Genesis Rabbah:[3] The single most important collection of early Rabbinic discussions of the meaning of the Genesis creation text is Genesis Rabbah. Whenever it was written, the interpretations presented in this collection are the oldest Rabbinic sources for cosmology. The account has a number of distinctive characteristics in relationship to and in contrast with the range of literal meanings of the biblical text itself. First, it sees creation as a single event, in which the list of days is to be understood as specifying a logical rather than a temporal order. Second, its authors were well aware of a dispute as to whether or not the pre-existent material out of which God creates the world is itself created, and the midrash's overall tendency is to reconcile both views rather than to choose between them. The rabbis make this move by positing other universes from which the materials of the creation of this world are drawn. Third, the rabbis introduce angels who, while they are present in other places in the Pentateuch, play no role in the biblical account of creation.

Once angels are introduced, the rabbis question whether they pre-exist or are created. As with the pre-existent materials explicitly mentioned, they affirm that they both pre-exist and are created. Consequently, fourth, the rabbis affirm that our world is not the only one. Here the term "world" does not merely specify a domain of spatial-temporal continuity. Different worlds have different natures. One such world is the Garden of Eden. There, for example, the sun and moon have the same size, and trees are as edible as their fruit. Furthermore, there exist species in the Garden of Eden that have never existed in This-World of ours, and humans are by nature vegetarians. The rabbis also discuss other worlds that co-exist with ours in time as well as at least one more world, the World-To-Come, that will exist when our world comes to an end. Actually, not everything that Scripture says was created was created for our world. Notably, the original light created to limit the dark on day one is set aside from This-World for the World-To-Come.

Medieval Jewish philosophy and science—Ibn Daud's *Exalted Faith*:[4] Ibn Daud wrote his *Exalted Faith* at the time that Aristotelian philosophical science was just beginning to gain dominance over the more Stoic-oriented, atomistic philosophy of Kalam. Stoicism, which began around 300 B.C.E. with Zeno of Citium in Cyprus, grew in influence until, in less than a century, it dominated the world of Roman intelligentsia. Among its more famous exponents were Chrysippus, Panaetius of Rhodes, Cicero, Seneca, Epictetus of Phrygia, and even the emperor Marcus Aurelius. At its ontological core was a view that reduced every thing and event in the universe to small, indivisible, qualitatively indistinguishable materials (i.e.,

atoms) that interact with force. This dominant, popular, general philosophy was taken over more or less uncritically by the earliest apologists for Islam, who presupposed and made use of it in promoting the new faith of Islam. The form of rhetoric used by these thinkers was called "Kalam" (speech), which Jewish thinkers, influenced by Islamic culture, subsequently associated with the Hebrew term "dibbur."

By the eighth century C.E., both terms came to refer to speech using logic as well as rhetoric, and those who used it became known as "reasoners" (*mutakallimun* in Arabic; *ha-medabbrim* in Hebrew), or, simply, "those who love wisdom", i.e., "philosophers." By the tenth century, in polemics with Karaites, Muslims, and Christians, these Jewish philosophic theologians developed precise formulations of the beliefs of Rabbinic Judaism. Those formulations presupposed a Megarian scientific over-view of the universe. This school of Greek philosophy had developed in Mégara, located in eastern central Greece on the Saronic Gulf, from the late fifth century B.C.E. through the third century B.C.E. Its founders, Euclid of Mégara and Eubulides, made major contributions to the then beginning scientific study of argumentation, that is, logic. Their work assumed that logic entails ontology (the theory of what is), and the ontology it entailed was the source for the subsequent materialist atomism of the Stoics.

On this view, the universe consists of discrete material entities occupying discrete spaces in discrete time, where events occur either by chance or will. That science had been superseded by an over-view of the universe that held that everything occupied a distinct hierarchic place relative to everything else and in which change was understood primarily in terms of a natural intentional or unintentional movement by which the subject of the change sought to become better. Individual members of species were uniquely more or less like ideal prototypes that defined their species, and each member, when unhindered by external forces, sought to become more like the prototype, and, therefore, better than it was. Similarly, species were uniquely more or less like an ultimate ideal first cause of the universe that alone was not subject to change because it and it alone was perfectly what it could wish to be.

Ibn Daud sought in his *Exalted Faith* to show how the most basic beliefs affirmed by Rabbinic Judaism could be demonstrated rationally within the conceptual framework of the new Aristotelian science. But the audience for his work knew little of this science. Hence, the first part of the *Exalted Faith* is a primer for educated Jews in Aristotelianism as Ibn Daud understood it. In a word, "Aristotelianism" refers to that philosophy developed through the so-called middle ages by Muslims, Jews, and Christians whose source was the writings of Aristotle (384-322 B.C.E.). Its content is not identical with the philosophy of Aristotle but grew out of independent observations and arguments deeply influenced, but not entirely determined, by what Aristotle wrote, as those writings were translated from Greek into the vernacular and interpreted by commentators influenced by the translated works of Plato (about 427-347 B.C.E.), Aristotle's teacher. The major voices in this tradition of interpretation included Aristotle's own students, notably Theophrastus and subsequently Alexander of Aphrodisias (third century C.E.), Themistius (about 317-388 C.E.), and John Philoponus (about 490-580 C.E.).

Ibn Daud's primer on Aristotelian philosophy more or less determined the overview of the universe through which Rabbinic philosophers interpreted Jewish faith until at least the sixteenth century. Book I of the *Exalted Faith* consists of eight chapters, the last four of which—on the first mover, the soul, angels, and the heavens—constitute a general view of the universe. The resulting scientific cosmology provides the presuppositions for Ibn Daud's demonstration of the nature of divine action in his Basic Principle 4 in Book II. That principle is the conceptual key to his demonstration of the final principle of the book, Principle 6, that attempts to explain divine providence within the framework of an Aristotelian science.

Ibn Daud's general view of the universe can be summarized as follows: The first principle and final cause of everything that exists is what the new science identifies as the Absolute One and what the Jewish, revealed tradition of the Mosaic Torah recognizes as the God of Israel. From this single source emanate or overflow two distinct orders of entities, one spiritual and the other material. The spiritual order consists of a series of spherical shaped spaces, simply called "spheres," that are alive, which means that they are intimately associated with forces, called "intellects" or "souls," that initiate in their spaces motion. Ibn Daud lists ten such spheres, some of which (but not all) contain material bodies. The first, the Absolute One, lies itself beyond the cosmos. In its domain resides "The Essence of the Throne," which, in turn, is the domain of the second intellect or mover. Each succeeding sphere and its associated intellect or mover is located within the preceding sphere, the former being subject to the motion of the latter. The second intellect governs the sphere of the universe in general and is called "The All-Encompassing Sphere," "the First Sphere," and "The Right Sphere." This sphere is divisible into a northern and southern inclined sphere. It also initiates what is called "the motion of the Same," and it produces the forms of the material elements. Within the first sphere resides the second intellect that governs the third sphere, called "the Eccentric Sphere," "the Ecliptic," or "the Zodiac." It initiates the contrary "motion of diversity," and it produces the common matter that, in conjunction with the elementary forms, produces the four elements from which all material entities are composed.

Beyond these three intellects and two spheres are the different spherical heavens whose intelligible movers themselves are subject to natural motion. The fourth intellect governs the third sphere in which resides the planet Saturn and the fifth intellect. The fifth governs the fourth sphere of Jupiter, the sixth governs Mars, the seventh governs Mercury, the eighth governs Venus, and the ninth governs our sun. Finally, the tenth intellect, called "the Active Intellect," governs the sphere of our moon, within which resides the globe of the moon and the globe of the earth. Rabbinic tradition identifies this intellect with the Shekhina (the divine presence), through whose agency some human beings receive prophecy.

This spiritual chain of emanation governs and directs the mechanical causal chain by which material objects are generated within spiritual space by other material objects. Through different combinations of the four elements—fire (viz., the celestial substance), air (viz., gas), water (viz., liquid), and earth (viz., solid)—minerals, vegetation, life in the sea and on the earth, humans, and celestial beings are generated in hierarchical order. The lower the species the more dominant is the element earth, and the higher the species the more dominate is the element fire.

Notably absent from Ibn Daud's application of the new science is a doctrine of creation. Presumably it is missing because Ibn Daud did not believe it could be explained in terms of the new science, mainly because in this Aristotelian universe species have no temporal beginning or end. However, Gersonides, coming at the time of the maximum development of Aristotelianism, some four hundred years later, was able to reconcile the by then dogma of creation with Aristotelianism. He showed through his commentary on Genesis that the creation spoken of there is not itself a temporal event. Rather, the movement of the constant flow of procreated individual members of species, as well as the movement of species themselves, are to be understood as asymptotic functions, i.e., movements towards a motivating, infinitely remote end. As such, while the motions themselves occur in time, neither their origin nor their end are within time. Rather, both the origin and the end of the motion are eternally and infinitely remote from the temporal motions they move respectively as a first and final cause. The end is identified in Jewish tradition as the end of days or the World-To-Come, and the origin is the creation of Genesis.

Kabbalah—The Zohar:[5] An early source for Kabbalistic cosmology is the Sefer Yetzirah ("the book of creation"), which was compiled from materials as early as the third century C.E. but did not reach its final form until the ninth century, when it was combined with a commentary by Saadiah. There we learn of thirty two distinct paths to wisdom about God, the nature of the universe, and human happiness, constituted through some kind of interaction between the ten spheres and the twenty two letters of the Hebrew alphabet. The spheres are identified as divine attributes that are imagined anthropomorphically with special reference to the fingers, the tongue, and the foreskin. These attributes are also identified with divine potencies for action, ten depths (beginning, end, goodness, evil, height, depth, east, west, north, and south), and the elements of being (holy spirit [voice, speech, spirit], spirit from spirit, the elements water and fire, and the cosmic dimensions height, depth, east, west, north, and south). The Hebrew letters are identified as the very material of reality situated in three places—the space of the universe (olam), the time of the year (shanah), and the microcosm of life (nefesh). The permutations of these different sets of factors—spheres and letters—have parallels in the cosmology of the equally authoritative Shiur Qomah.

By the twelfth century in Provence, notably in the Sefer Ha-Bahir ("the bright book"), the spherical divine powers, now called "sayings," become visualized as a tree whose limbs function symbolically in much the same way that the human fingers functioned in earlier Kabbalistic texts. These limbs are seen to be minimally symbols for the essence of the divine reality. Against this background, the Zohar presents the ten spheres, associated with divine names, in two pictures. One is a geometric web and the other is a human form. The spheres are crown (keter) associated with the divine I am (ehyeh), wisdom (hokhmah) associated with yah, understanding (binah) associated with the Lord (yhwh) vocalized as God (elohim), mercy (hesed) with el, judgment (din) or power (gevurah) associated with elohim, beauty (tiferet) with yhwh, eternity (nezah) with the Lord of Hosts (yhwh zevaot), majesty (hod) with elohim zevaot, foundation-element (yesod) with the living el (el hai) or el shaddai, and the sphere of kingdom (malchut) or divine presence (*shekhina*) associated with the divine name of my Lord (*adonai*). In its human form, the crown, wisdom, and understanding constitute the head of the primordial human created in God's image, while the two arms are represented by mercy and judgment, the two legs by eternity and majesty, and the male and female genitalia are represented respectively by the foundation-element and the kingdom.

How these representations of God in Kabbalistic cosmologies are to be understood is not altogether clear. Superficially these pictures of the cosmos differ radically from the pictures drawn in Jewish philosophy. But this judgment is only superficial. The critical difference between them is not their intent, which in both cases is to provide a model for understanding the universe, humanity, and divinity, and to depict how the three are related. Rather, the difference, to the extent there is one, is epistemological, found in the respective judgments by the two sets of cosmologists on the extent that human imagination can be used to augment the way that human reason makes reality comprehensible. The more that Jewish cosmologists relied on scientific reasoning to express their images, they were philosophers; the more that they relied an aesthetic imagination to express their conceptions, they were mystics.

The difference between the two ultimately has to do with a preference for one of two dominant forms of mathematical reasoning, one algebraic and the other geometric. Thanks to René Descartes (1596-1650), we know that algebra and geometry are alternate expressions of the same logic, i.e., the same formalized way of thinking out systematically the solutions to a problem, for it was Descartes who first demonstrated through the use of what are called "Cartesian coordinates" that any geometric figure can be expressed as an algebraic operation, and any algebraic expression can be represented as a geometric form. Prior to Descartes' work in mathematics in the seventeenth century, geometry and algebra were seen to be distinct logical disciplines. Which one was utilized in constructing solutions to problems depended on the nature of the problem.

Generally, operations that can be expressed in finite, definite terms lend themselves to questions about linear equations most readily solvable algebraically, and operations that must be expressed in infinite, indefinite terms lend themselves to questions about non-linear equations most readily solvable geometrically. Historically in western thought, at least outside of the domain of those skilled in pure mathematics, the terms "rational" and "logical" have tended to be applied almost exclusively to the former kinds of questions, expressions, and solutions, while the latter kinds, because their expressions are indefinite or "fuzzy," and their solution techniques involve imaginative use of pictorial constructions, have tended to be called "irrational" or "emotional." In fact, most issues in topics as abstract as cosmology involve both kinds of thinking, but the history of western thought in general has tended to alternate in a wave-like movement between the two, which translates in terms of the history of Jewish thought as a movement to mysticism from philosophy and to philosophy from mysticism, i.e., from reliance on imaginative concrete paradigmatic pictures (mystical reasoning) to reliance on so-called rational abstract symbolic expressions (philosophical reasoning), and back. This tendency is no less apparent in contemporary Jewish thought than in classical and medieval Jewish philosophy and Kabbalah.

Applications of tradition to modern Jewish cosmologies: Jewish philosophy is no less continuous than Jewish mysticism throughout Jewish history. In fact, the lines that separate them are somewhat arbitrary, at least flexible, since Jewish philosophy tends to flow into Jewish mysticism and visa versa. Still, there is a difference in emphasis that gives some justification for the separation. While none of the earliest works of Judaism—the Hebrew Scriptures and the collections of Rabbinic midrash—are either philosophical or mystical in primary intent, clearly both contain philosophical and mystical content, and both played a role as authoritative texts in the subsequent development of Jewish philosophy and mysticism. If a distinction can be drawn between these two modes of thought, it may be made on the basis of the kind of cosmologies both tended to advance.

In general, three kinds of views of the universe emerge. At times the view of the universe is atomistic, in which what happens is believed to occur solely by chance and/or necessity, without purpose. This view dominates in the modern Newtonian period and is most clearly expressed by Spinoza (the Netherlands, 1634-1677). But it is equally the case in the pre-tenth century Muslim world, in which the dominant model for cosmology exploited by the Mutakallimun was a composition of ancient Greek Megarianism with Roman Stoicism. Jewish philosophy and mysticism exist in both periods, but neither thrives in this intellectual atmosphere. At other times the view of the universe is a process view, in which what happens occurs primarily through directionality towards some kind of end or limit. This view dominates in the medieval Aristotelian period and is the setting in which medieval Jewish philosophy prospers. Conversely, at other times the view of the universe is a static conception of ideal entities related to each other through principles of imitation. This view dominates in periods in which the dominant philosophical model is Neoplatonic and is the setting in which medieval and early modern Jewish mysticism thrives. However, these two directions combine in the tradition of twentieth century European neo-Kantian, Marburgian philosophy initiated by Hermann Cohen (Germany, 1842-1918), where the actual universe is seen in terms of a procession towards infinitely remote and fixed ideals (called "asymptotes" in mathematics) that constitute reality. This view is most clearly expressed in the creationist philosophical theology of Franz Rosenzweig (Germany, 1886-1929).

Note that the above general characterizations of kinds of Jewish cosmology are simply that, general characterizations that, as such, make lines of separation far stricter than they are in fact in the texts considered. Creationists use emanationists' themes, and emanationists include elements of the creationist view of the universe. The differences here have to do with emphasis only, and the drawing of these lines in any specific case is not self-evident to any not-so-predisposed reader of these texts. But these differences are not trivial.

Modern science, dominated by the atomist conception of a cosmos ruled exclusively by mechanical notions of chance and/or probabilistic chance, has tended to see the world, because it lacks any inherent purpose, as amoral. Although it is possible for a scientist to approach his or her work as a moral enterprise and as a theist, this way of conceptualizing the universe tends to favor belief that there is no deity (since a deity has no place within the cosmology) and there are no real moral duties (since ethics seem tied to notions of purpose, and this cosmology has no place for purpose). In contrast, the mystic's emanationist view of the universe definitely affirms the existence of some kind of deity, but generally this entity is seen to be something whose reality lies within the individual thinker. Although it is possible for a mystic to approach his enterprise with moral sensitivity to other human beings, this way of conceptualizing the universe tends to dull, even negate, moral consciousness. In general, we human beings learn moral responsibility when confronted by other human beings whose needs are not our own.

Moral sense is a response to that concrete need, but for people whose primary religious road is to turn ever inward to find the God within, especially when that God is identified with the mystic's true self that is seen to be the only reality, it is not surprising that these emanationists tend not to be aware of the needs of others beyond themselves, for how can others place real moral obligations on us when ultimately in truth there are no others except the deity within who is the sole reality. Hence, the multiple forms of creationist cosmology, from Aristotle's universe of material motions to Cohen's world of asymptotic functions, tend to be most supportive as a foundational philosophy for sensitizing thinkers to both the divine and the moral. Here the world is seen in terms of functions that originate in distinct human individuals and move towards radically other distinct human individuals, forming a chorus of voices directed at an ultimate, utterly radical divine individual. In such a theistic directed cosmology, as is most apparent in the philosophical and theological writings of Rosenzweig's disciple Emmanuel Levinas (1906-1996), ethics play as primary a role as they did in the creation model of the author of Genesis and the chariot vision of the prophet Ezekiel.

Notes

[1] This account primarily summarizes my *The First Seven Days: A Philosophical Commentary on the Creation of Genesis* (Atlanta, 1992).

[2] The account presented below summarizes my "Three Comparative Maps of the Human," in *Zygon: Journal of Religion and Science*, vol. 31, no. 4 (December, 1996), pp. 695-710.

[3] The account presented below primarily summarizes my *Judaism and the Doctrine of Creation.* (Cambridge, 1994), pp. 113-135.

[4] The account presented reviews my *The Exalted Faith of Abraham Ibn Daud* (Cranbury, 1986), pp. 108-126.

[5] The following depends upon Lawrence Fine, "Kabbalistic Texts," in Barry W. Holtz, ed., *Back to the Sources: Reading the Classic Jewish Texts* (New York, 1984), pp. 305-359, and Elliot R. Wolfson, "Jewish Mysticism: A Philosophical Overview" and Hava Tirosh-Rothschild, "Jewish Philosophy on the Eve of Modernity," in Daniel H. Frank and Oliver Leaman, eds., *History of Jewish Philosophy* (New York and London, 1997), pp. 450-573.

NORBERT SAMUELSON

COVENANT: The term covenant signifies a formal agreement between two parties, in which "one or both make promises under oath to perform or refrain from certain actions stipulated in advance."[1] In the religion Judaism, the term covenant refers in particular to the agreement God made with the people of Israel at Sinai. This agreement calls for the Jews to follow God's law, embodied in Torah. In return God promises to make of the Israelites a great nation dwelling in peace in the Promised Land. Described at Exod. 19-20 and elaborated in the legal materials of the books of Exodus, Leviticus, Numbers, and Deuteronomy, this covenant is understood also to encompass the later expansions and interpretations of Scripture found with-

in the Talmudic literature and subsequent codes of Jewish law. In light of this association with the system of Rabbinic law and learning, for Jews from the Rabbinic period and on, the term covenant has been tantamount to the concept of Torah.[2] Covenant, this is to say, refers in Judaism to the entire body of revelation that defines the agreement between God and Israel, that states the obligations Israel has accepted upon itself, and that details what the nation can expect from God in return.

From biblical times and on, groups both within and outside of Judaism have claimed to be the successor community to the covenant God made with Abraham. These groups see themselves as the "true" Israel, standing in a distinct and special relationship with the God of the Hebrew Scriptures. The community at Qumran, for instance, saw its law as the embodiment of the terms of the Sinai covenant and declared its members to be the truly chosen among Israel. The early gentile Christian community, for its part, also viewed its relationship with God as the product of a new covenant that superseded the earlier one between God and the Jews. Christians thus saw themselves as the true children of Abraham, replacements of the Jews, who claimed membership in the covenant as a matter of birth (see, e.g., Rom. 4). For these communities and others, the concept of covenant defined a unique relationship with God, facilitated self-definition, and legitimated a distinctive theology and way of life.

In these ways, covenant has served as the central metaphor for a range of forms of Judaism and associated religions that have emerged from biblical times to the present. The comprehension that a group stands in a distinctive, covenanted relationship with God defines the group as uniquely under divine protection, assures special access to ultimate salvation, and legitimates the group's beliefs and practices as solely correct. Most important, the faith that one participates in a unique relationship with God, defined by a bilateral covenant, elevates the believer above all other people: uniquely right, uniquely blessed, uniquely saved.

Covenant in the Hebrew Bible: The Hebrew term for covenant, *brit*, is of uncertain etymology but apparently is associated with the concept of "binding." Alongside this term, the Hebrew Scripture uses the term *edut*, referring to the solemn charge that comprises the contents of the covenant, and *alah*, meaning oath and frequently used in conjunction with the term *brit*. These terms refer to agreements between individuals (e.g., 1 Sam. 18:3), between nations of either equal or unequal strength (e.g., Josh. 9), between sovereigns and their people (2 Kgs. 11:4, 11:17), between husbands and wives (Ezek. 16:8), and even, figuratively, between humans and animals (Hos. 2:20).

As in the Hebrew Scriptures, in the ancient Near East in general the concept of covenant was used to describe many types of relationships. But its use to define the relationship between a deity and a people is unique to Israelite religion.[3] This usage apparently emerged as a result of the Israelites' distinctive conception that their deity demanded exclusive loyalty and that the people could have no attachment nor show any devotion to any other god. The idea of a covenant accurately defined an exclusive relationship such as this, which could be understood in terms comparable to those familiar, for instance, in treaties between a people and a human king, to whom a nation similarly would pledge sole fealty.

The biblical concept of covenant has its specific origins in the Syro-Hittite age of the ancient near east, a period for which treaties represent our major source of historical knowledge.[4] These treaties are characterized by a fixed structure and set of elements that are found as well in the Hebrew Bible's depiction of the covenant between Yahweh and the people of Israel. This structure includes:

1) the identification of the covenant giver, generally indicating the name of the great king who is entering into the covenantal relationship with an inferior party. The implication is that "the relationship of the vassal to the overlord had to be an exclusive one: the vassal could not engage in treaty or other relationships with other independent monarchs without being guilt of treason."[5] Such an identification of the covenant giver is found at Exod. 20:2, which reads simply: "I am the Lord your God. . . ."

2) a historical prologue, recounting the monarch's past deeds that benefited the vassal, deeds that comprise the foundation of the vassal's obligation to that monarch. Thus, at the heart of the Hittite treaty form, represented as well in the Israelite notion of covenant, stands the idea of reciprocity: because the monarch/deity has done this for you, you are to be subject to that monarch's/deity's demands, outlined in the terms of this treaty. The continuation of Exod. 20:2 presents exactly such a historical prologue, stated briefly: ". . . who brought you out of the land of Egypt, out of the house of bondage."

3) the stipulations, which indicate the specific terms of the covenant that the deity/ monarch expects of the vassal in return for past protection and to assure future harmonious relationships. Thus Exod. 20:2 continues with the commandment, "You shall have no other gods before me" followed by the remainder of the book of Exodus's statement of covenantal law.

4) deposit and periodic reading of the covenant. In the ancient Hittite texts, as in the Hebrew Bible, the covenant was treated as a sacred object, often deposited in the temple of the local deity and publicly announced. Its terms thus could be followed as public policy and law. The Israelite parallel is found in the building of the ark of the covenant, so central in Israelite cultic life (Exod. 25:10ff.) and in the description of the tablets' formal deposit in a sanctuary, Josh. 24:26. Moses also reads the law to the people (Exod. 24:7), a feature of the covenant that recurs in the period of Ezra (Ezra 8:1-9:37). Ritual reading of the law may be implied at Exod. 23:17 and Deut. 27:11-26 as well.

5) witnesses, in particular:

> deities or deified elements of the natural world . . . [often a list] so lengthy that it justifies the conclusion that it was intended to be exhaustive: all gods relevant to *both* parties were called upon as witnesses, so that

there was no god left that the vassal could appeal to for protection if he wanted to violate his solemn oath.[6]

Witnesses also included heaven and earth. Like the provisions for deposit (4) and blessings and curses, which follow (6), the idea of witnesses is not found in the Sinai narrative of Exod. 20. But the notion of heaven and earth as witnesses to God's covenant with Israel is explicit at Deut. 32, Is. 1:2, and Mic. 6:1-2.

6) blessing and curses, detailing the punishments or rewards that will result from obedience or disobedience to the terms of the covenant. Absent from the earlier text of Exodus, the blessings and curses of the Sinaitic covenant are elaborated in exceptional detail at Deut. 28.

7) a ratification ceremony, through which the treaty is formally adopted and made binding on both parties. Methods of ratifying treaties varied greatly in the ancient world. In Exodus, two ratification elements are present, the people's verbal agreement to the covenant (Exod. 19:8 and 24:3: "All that the Lord has spoken we will do") and the sacrificial ritual during which, in association with Moses's public reading of the covenant law, the blood of a sacrifice is tossed upon the people and the altar (Exod. 24:4-8), thereby binding the people to the deity with whom the covenant has been made. A different covenant ratification ceremony appears at Exod. 24:9-14, where, once the people have declared their acceptance of the covenant, Moses and the seventy elders climb Sinai and experience the presence of God, with whom they share a meal (Exod. 24:11). Josh. 24 describes a covenant renewal ceremony at Shechem that also contains many of the elements commonly found in suzerain treaties such as are described here.

The array of formal features found in the Sinaitic covenant suggests the extent to which it is presented as a carefully developed contract that will assure the people's acquiescence to a detailed system of social and religious laws. This assurance derives at least in part from the fact that the Sinai covenant is conditional, depicting God's continuing protection of Israel and the fulfillment of the promise to make of the people a great and mighty nation as dependent upon the people's own behavior *vis a vis* God. Notably, this well developed concept of the covenant relationship, so central in all subsequent Jewish thinking about Israel's relationship with God, depicts but one stage in the evolving Israelite perception of the covenant. This relationship begins with what Scripture depicts as God's original *unconditional* promise to make of Abraham a great nation. A complete statement of the content and purpose of the covenant with Abraham is at Gen. 17 (see also Gen. 12:1-7, Gen. 15, Gen. 22):

> When Abram was ninety-nine years old the Lord appeared to Abram, and said to him, "I am God Almighty; walk before me, and be blameless. And I will make my covenant between me and you, and will multiply you exceedingly." Then Abram fell on his face; and God said to him, "Behold, my covenant is with you, and you shall be the father of a multitude of nations. No longer shall your name be Abram, but your name shall be Abraham; for I have made you the father of a multitude of nations. I will make you exceedingly fruitful; and I will make nations of you, and kings shall come forth from you. And I will establish my covenant between me and you and your descendants after you throughout their generations for an everlasting covenant, to be God to you and to your descendants after you. And I will give to you, and to your descendants after you, the land of your sojournings, all the land of Canaan, for an everlasting possession; and I will be their God." And God said to Abraham, "As for you, you shall keep my covenant, you and your descendants after you throughout their generations. This is my covenant, which you shall keep, between me and you and your descendants after you: Every male among you shall be circumcised. You shall be circumcised in the flesh of your foreskins, and it shall be a sign of the covenant between me and you. He that is eight days old among you shall be circumcised; every male throughout your generations, whether born in your house, or bought with your money from any foreigner who is not of your offspring, both he that is born in your house and he that is bought with your money, shall be circumcised. So shall my covenant be in your flesh an everlasting covenant. Any uncircumcised

male who is not circumcised in the flesh of his foreskin shall be cut off from his people; he has broken my covenant." And God said to Abraham, "As for Sarai your wife, you shall not call her name Sarai, but Sarah shall be her name. I will bless her, and moreover I will give you a son by her; I will bless her, and she shall be a mother of nations; kings of peoples shall come from her." Then Abraham fell on his face and laughed, and said to himself, "Shall a child be born to a man who is a hundred years old? Shall Sarah, who is ninety years old, bear a child?" And Abraham said to God, "O that Ishmael might live in thy sight!" God said, "No, but Sarah your wife shall bear you a son, and you shall call his name Isaac. I will establish my covenant with him as an everlasting covenant for his descendants after him. As for Ishmael, I have heard you; behold, I will bless him and make him fruitful and multiply him exceedingly; he shall be the father of twelve princes, and I will make him a great nation. But I will establish my covenant with Isaac, whom Sarah shall bear to you at this season next year."

The foundational elements of covenantal theology are introduced here. God's selection of Abraham for a special relationship means that Abraham is to follow God's righteous ways and, in return, will be made the father of a great nation and of many kings. The covenant with God is hereditary; its obligations and its rewards will apply as well to Abraham's descendants through a designated son. While Ishmael, like his father, will be the father of princes, the covenant itself will follow only through the line of Isaac, who, along with his sons, will enjoy the special benefits of this relationship with God, in particular, possession of the land of Canaan. Finally, just as this covenant has rewards, so it entails obligations, both moral and ritual. Here in particular, as a sign of the covenant, God demands that all of the males of the line of Abraham undergo circumcision. From this point on, circumcision, referred to in later Judaism as *Brit Milah*, the covenant of circumcision, becomes the central symbol of the male Israelite's membership in the community subject to God's covenant.[7]

Genesis depicts God's covenant with Abraham as a permanent pact, the conditions of which are immediately to be fulfilled by both parties. Abraham does what God demands of him, and God too is prepared immediately to fulfill his obligations: Abraham and Sarah will parent the child through whom the terms of the covenant can be fulfilled. This concept of a realized covenant appears as well in the biblical descriptions of the Davidic monarchy, which hold that, in accord with God's covenant with David, a Davidic king *always* will rule on the throne of Israel. The striking difference between these notions of covenant and what is portrayed in the conditional covenant at Sinai, to the details of which we now turn, is explained through reference to the actuality of Israelite history, in particular, the Babylonian exile and destruction of the first Temple in 586 B.C.E. In the Sinai narrative, which reached final form in the period of the exile, the reality of the loss of Israelite power and control over the promised land was explained not as evidence of God's failure to keep the covenantal promises but as proof of the covenant's continuing validity: the people's exile from and loss of sovereignty over the Holy Land was the punishment earned for the people's failure to observe the terms of covenantal law.

In later Judaic history, the persistence of exile and the delay in God's fulfilling of the covenantal promises led to other significant developments as well. In particular, post-biblical Jewish theology added an eschatological aspect to thinking about the covenant, seeing God's promises as destined to be fulfilled only at some undisclosed future time, with the coming of a messiah, the resurrection of the dead, and the direct rule of God on earth.[8] But we should be clear that in the earlier statements of covenantal thinking throughout the Pentateuch, the realization of the covenant's promises, like Abraham's fulfilling of the covenant's demands, is a this-worldly matter. Within time as we know it, Abraham's descendants will become a great and mighty nation and possess Canaan. The end of time, a coming messiah, resurrection of the dead have no place in this picture.

The covenant at Sinai: The culmination of the Hebrew Scripture's delineation of the covenant between God and the people occurs at Exod. 19-20. Following the miraculous redemption of the nation of Israel from Egyptian bondage, God brings the people to Sinai, where, speaking directly to Moses, he conveys to them the terms of the covenant. At the heart of the agreement is the people's exclusively loyalty to Yahweh, to whom they shall be a "kingdom of priests and a holy nation." God deserves the people's sole fealty because of the acts he has performed for them, in particular, their release from Egyptian bondage:

> On the third new moon after the people of Israel had gone forth out of the land of Egypt, on that day they came into the wilderness of Sinai. And when they set out from Rephidim and came into the wilderness of Sinai, they encamped in the wilderness; and there Israel encamped before the mountain. And Moses went up to God, and the Lord called to him out of the mountain, saying, "Thus you shall say to the house of Jacob, and tell the people of Israel: You have seen what I did to the Egyptians, and how I bore you on eagles' wings and brought you to myself. Now therefore, if you will obey my voice and keep my covenant, you shall be my own possession among all peoples; for all the earth is mine, and you shall be to me a kingdom of priests and a holy nation. These are the words which you shall speak to the children of Israel." So Moses came and called the elders of the people, and set before them all these words which the Lord had commanded him. And all the people answered together and said, "All that the Lord has spoken we will do." And Moses reported the words of the people to the Lord. And the Lord said to Moses, "Lo, I am coming to you in a thick cloud, that the people may hear when I speak with you, and may also believe you for ever." Then Moses told the words of the people to the Lord. And the Lord said to Moses, "Go to the people and consecrate them today and tomorrow, and let them wash their garments, and be ready by the third day; for on the third day the Lord will come down upon Mount Sinai in the sight of all the people. And you shall set bounds for the people round about, saying, 'Take heed that you do not go up into the mountain or touch the border of it; whoever touches the mountain shall be put to death; no hand shall touch him, but he shall be stoned or shot; whether beast or man, he shall not live.' When the trumpet sounds a long blast, they shall come up to the mountain." So Moses went down from the mountain to the people, and consecrated the people; and they washed their garments. And he said to the people, "Be ready by the third day; do not go near a woman." On the morning of the third day there were thunders and lightnings, and a thick cloud upon the mountain, and a very loud trumpet blast, so that all the people who were in the camp trembled. Then Moses brought the people out of the camp to meet God; and they took their stand at the foot of the mountain. And Mount Sinai was wrapped in smoke, because the Lord descended upon it in fire; and the smoke of it went up like the smoke of a kiln, and the whole mountain quaked greatly. And as the sound of the trumpet grew louder and louder, Moses spoke, and God answered him in thunder. And the Lord came down upon Mount Sinai, to the top of the mountain; and the Lord called Moses to the top of the mountain, and Moses went up.

The passage continues with the ten commandments, understood to be the foundational principles of the covenant. These commandments are followed by a large compendium of detailed social, economic, and ritual laws that the people also must follow as the requirements of the covenant. The results of adherence to or violation of the requirements of the covenant are delineated later in the Pentateuch, at Deut. 30:15-20:

> See, I have set before you this day life and good, death and evil. If you obey the commandments of the Lord your God which I command you this day, by loving the Lord your God, by walking in his ways, and by keeping his commandments and his statutes and his ordinances, then you shall live and multiply, and the Lord your God will bless you in the land which you are entering to take possession of it. But if your heart turns away, and you will not hear, but are drawn away to worship other gods and serve them, I declare to you this day, that you shall perish; you shall not live long in the land which you are going over the Jordan to enter and possess. I call heaven and earth to witness against you this day, that I have set before you life and death, blessing and curse; therefore choose life, that you and your descendants may live, loving the Lord your God, obeying his voice, and cleaving to him; for that means life to you and length of days, that you may dwell in the land which the Lord swore to your fathers, to Abraham, to Isaac, and to Jacob, to give them.

Figure 17. Tiered Passover plate, Poland, eighteenth century, brass, wood, silk.

Figure 18. Spice container, Frankfurt, ca. 1550, silver.

Figure 19. Hanukkah lamp, Frankfurt, 1710, Johann Michael Schuler, silver.

Figure 20. Purim Megillah case, Galicia, eighteenth century, silver: gilt.

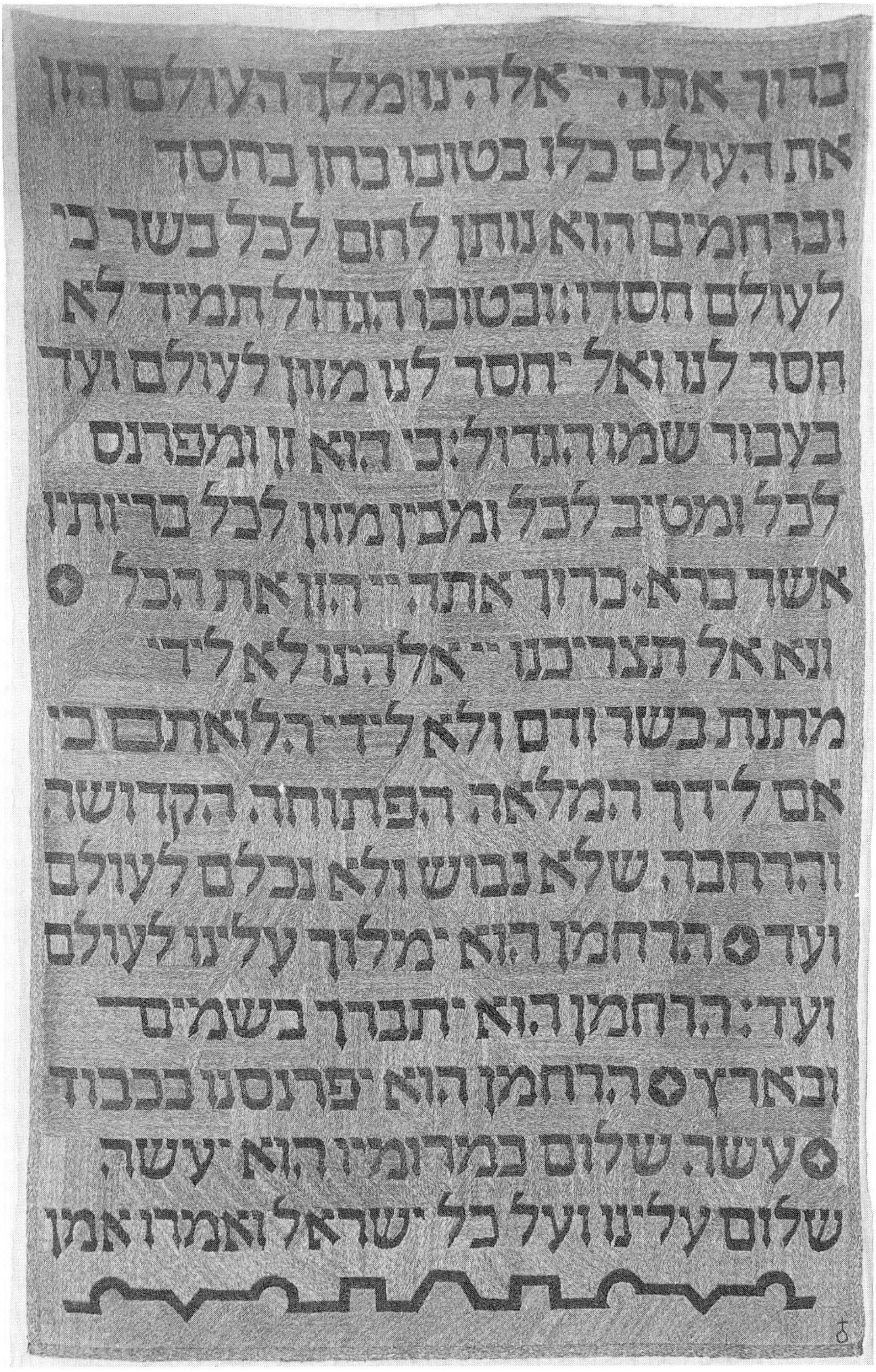

ברוך אתה יי אלהינו מלך העולם הזן
את העולם כלו בטובו בחן בחסד
וברחמים הוא נותן לחם לכל בשר כי
לעולם חסדו ובטובו הגדול תמיד לא
חסר לנו ואל יחסר לנו מזון לעולם ועד
בעבור שמו הגדול כי הוא זן ומפרנס
לכל ומטיב לכל ומכין מזון לכל בריותיו
אשר ברא ⬦ ברוך אתה יי הזן את הכל ⬦
ונא אל תצריכנו יי אלהינו לא לידי
מתנת בשר ודם ולא לידי הלואתם כי
אם לידך המלאה הפתוחה הקדושה
והרחבה, שלא נבוש ולא נכלם לעולם
ועד ⬦ הרחמן הוא ימלוך עלינו לעולם
ועד ⬦ הרחמן הוא יתברך בשמים
ובארץ ⬦ הרחמן הוא יפרנסנו בכבוד
⬦ עשה שלום במרומיו הוא יעשה
שלום עלינו ועל כל ישראל ואמרו אמן

Figure 21. Wall hanging: grace after meals, 1925, Berthold Wolpe, workshop of Ruolf Koch, linen.

Figure 22. Ludwig Wolpert, Passover set, Frankfurt, 1930, silver, ebony, glass.

Figure 23. Moshe Zabari, spice container, 1982, silver, stones.

Figure 24. This embroidered challah cover was used by Puri and Zisla Marcovitch, Iasi region, Romania.

Figure 25. A silver challah knife with the inscription, "In honor of the holy Sabbath," used by Jonas and Selma Plaut and their sons, W. Gunther and Walter, prior to World War II in Berlin, Germany.

Figure 26. Silver filigree spice box used by Rabbi and Mrs. David Samuel Margules for havda-lah, the ceremony marking the transition from the Sabbath to the weekday, Tachov, Czechoslovakia, c. 1920s.

Figure 27. Jewish New Year greeting card for the United States market, made in Germany, c.1880-1910.

Figure 28. Lithograph published in 1871 in New York depicts an 1870 Yom Kippur service of Jewish soldiers of the German Army. An inscription reads, "Have we not all the same Father? Have we not all been created by the same God?"

Figure 29. Silver etrog box used by a Hungarian Jewish family, undated.

Figure 30. Members of Congregation Ansche Chesed dance with the Torah to celebrate Simhat Torah, New York City, c. 1982. Photograph by Beryl Goldberg.

Figure 31. Girls from the Bais Yaacov school celebrating Hanukkah, Bardejov, Czechoslovakia, 1935.

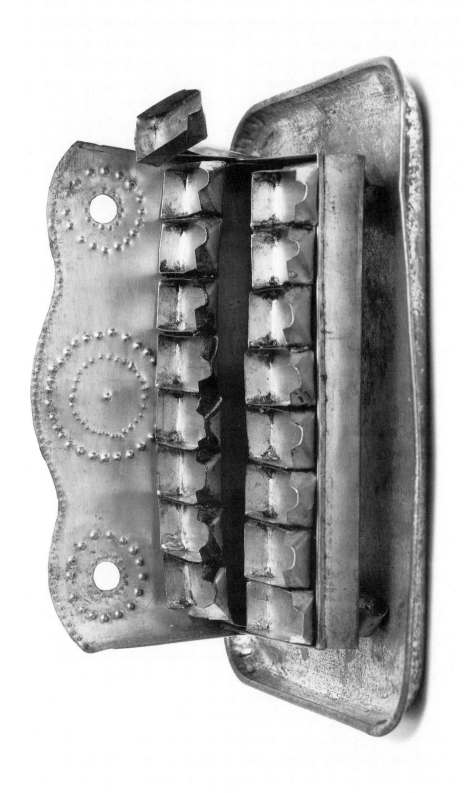

Figure 32. Hanukkah lamp, Flehingen, Germany, 1914-1918. The Heidelberger family lit this oil-burning lamp during World War I, when candles were unavailable. Two rows of eight cups let two families use it at the same time.

This passage follows a long listing of the blessings that come with adherence to the terms of the covenant and the curses that result from violations. In this phrasing of matters, the passage illustrates the special power with which the author of Deuteronomy considers the topic of covenant: the law is not simply a set of rituals and idiosyncratic national practices. It is, rather, a source of pride and blessings to the Israelites, the foundation on which they will build the lives God has promised them as a great and mighty nation.

At the same time that the idea of a unique covenant with God assured Israel of its destiny as a great nation, these materials placed in sharp focus theological and social issues increasingly significant in ancient Israel's cultural, religious, and monarchical life. The people's new life in Canaan will place before them significant temptations. At stake in the people's ability or inability to withstand these temptations is their relationship with God and, ultimately, their very success as a distinctive national entity. In the face of this challenge, God pleads for continued loyalty and love as the conditions for life in the Promised Land. While this issue becomes a particular focus of Moses's farewell address at the end of the book of Deuteronomy, its main point emerges here: failure to abide by the law established by the covenant, in particular the sin of worshipping foreign gods, means the cessation of God's support of the people. The result is removal from the land and denial of the fullness of life enjoyed by those under God's protection. The covenant truly is a matter of great moment. Through their actions, the people choose blessing or curse, life or death.

The covenant in the prophetic literature: To make immediate and real the significance of the people's covenantal responsibilities, especially in the prophetic literature the concept of the people's exclusive relationship with God is portrayed metaphorically. The covenant is viewed as the union between a husband and wife, on the one hand, or as a relationship between a king and his people, on the other. At Ezek. 16:8-14, for instance, the maiden Israel is understood to have been adopted through marriage into God's covenant. Thus she became queen and enjoyed extravagant raiment and bountiful foods:

> When I passed by you again and looked upon you, behold, you were at the age for love; and I spread my skirt over you, and covered your nakedness: yea, I plighted my troth to you and entered into a covenant with you, says the Lord God, and you became mine. Then I bathed you with water and washed off your blood from you, and anointed you with oil. I clothed you also with embroidered cloth and shod you with leather, I swathed you in fine linen and covered you with silk. And I decked you with ornaments, and put bracelets on your arms, and a chain on your neck. And I put a ring on your nose, and earrings in your ears, and a beautiful crown upon your head. Thus you were decked with gold and silver; and your raiment was of fine linen, and silk, and embroidered cloth; you ate fine flour and honey and oil. You grew exceedingly beautiful, and came to regal estate. And your renown went forth among the nations because of your beauty, for it was perfect through the splendor which I had bestowed upon you, says the Lord God.

Within the terms of the covenant, God equally may be viewed as a king, to whom Israel is a vassal (Ps. 47:6-9):

> Sing praises to God, sing praises! Sing praises to our king, sing praises! For God is the king of all the earth; sing praises with a psalm! God reigns over the nations; God sits on his holy throne. The princes of the peoples gather as the people of the God of Abraham. For the shields of the earth belong to God; he is highly exalted!

The strength of these metaphors is their ability to depict more than the majesty of the covenant relationship in times in which the people of Israel perform their obligations. Rather, these metaphors equally describe the anguish and pain caused by Israel's abandonment of its responsibilities. Just like a human king, for instance, God expresses outrage at his people's lack of loyalty, their failure to abide by the terms of his rule (Jer. 8:19):

> Hark, the cry of the daughter of my people from the length and breadth of the land: "Is the Lord not in Zion? Is her King not in her?"

"Why have they provoked me to anger with their graven images, and with their foreign idols?"

Jeremiah similarly invokes the image of Israel as wife to portray the deep hurt caused by the nation's failure to follow its obligations under the covenant (Jer. 2:2-5, 3:1-2):

> Go and proclaim in the hearing of Jerusalem, Thus says the Lord, I remember the devotion of your youth, your love as a bride, how you followed me in the wilderness, in a land not sown. Israel was holy to the Lord, the first fruits of his harvest. All who ate of it became guilty; evil came upon them, says the Lord. Hear the word of the Lord, O house of Jacob, and all the families of the house of Israel. Thus says the Lord: "What wrong did your fathers find in me that they went far from me, and went after worthlessness, and became worthless?
>
> If a man divorces his wife and she goes from him and becomes another man's wife, will he return to her? Would not that land be greatly polluted? You have played the harlot with many lovers; and would you return to me? says the Lord. Lift up your eyes to the bare heights, and see! Where have you not been lain with? By the waysides you have sat awaiting lovers like an Arab in the wilderness. You have polluted the land with your vile harlotry.

Within these metaphors, the result of the people's abrogation of their covenant responsibilities is deeply felt. Whether imagined as an unfaithful wife or as a vassal nation that swears fealty to a foreign king, the people of Israel's failure to abide by the covenant leads to God's intense anger and withdrawing of his divine protection from the people. Within Scripture, the concept of covenant thus not only assures the people of Israel of God's protection and eventual salvation but also explains the fate of a nation that has not been faithful to God and to the demands of God's law.

The covenant in Rabbinic Judaism: In the first centuries C.E., an emerging group of Jewish leaders called rabbis struggled to make sense of a set of circumstances that challenged the inherited notion of covenant. Despite the multifaceted life of the Jewish people in the land of Israel and in the exilic communities during the centuries preceding the destruction of the Second Temple,[9] the theological and cultic center of Jewish life had remained Jerusalem and the Temple of God that stood there. Sovereignty over the land of Israel and the continued operation of the priestly cult had from biblical times and on provided all Jews with a concrete symbol of their relationship to God and of the anticipated fulfillment of God's covenantal promises. The destruction of the Temple and the failed Bar Kokhba revolt accordingly meant for all Jews the end of the covenant relationship as it previously had been experienced.

In 70 C.E., as in 586 B.C.E., the cult ceased operation. But this time, the failure of the Bar Kokhba revolt of 132-135 C.E. and, still later, the ascent of Christianity to world domination meant that any expectation of the quick rebuilding of the Temple or the return of Israelite sovereignty was unrealistic. Accordingly, in the period of the Mishnah and the later Rabbinic literatures, both the political and theological contexts in which Judaism existed had been dramatically altered. Jews lived under foreign dominion, leaving open the question of the viability of God's promise that the people would be sovereign in their own land. The Temple, the visible sign of God's presence and power, was gone; the cult, through which the people of Israel had acknowledged God's lordship and appealed to his mercies, had ceased. The loss of all that had signified God's concern for the Israelite people left open the question of whether or not God continued to rule over and care about the chosen people, whether or not the covenant remained intact at all.

In response, the rabbis developed a system of belief and practice that, even when not overtly addressing the character of the Israelites' covenant with God, carefully rethought the meaning and purpose of that covenant. On the one hand, the rabbis exhibited a deep conservatism, claiming that, just as Scripture promised and just as seemed to be the case while the Temple stood, God still rules over and moves in response to the actions of the Israelite people. The covenantal relationship, the rabbis thus argued, continued unchanged, and the promises first made to Abraham would, at some undisclosed point in the future, be fulfilled. Yet to support this claim that nothing had changed, the rabbis developed a new Jewish theology and a revised understanding of how the people were to interpret the Bible's covenantal promises and to fulfill the terms of covenantal law.

The rabbis' central message was that the events of the first centuries signified neither the end of the covenantal relationship with God nor the termination of life lived within the sacred circle once established by the presence, in the nation's midst, of the holy Temple and its cult. Just as when the Temple stood, the Jewish people would raise families, would carry out their day-to-day vocations, and would worship God through prayer and by following divine law. What changed is that, by creating a system of law and practice that remade the home in the model of the Temple, the rabbis shifted the sacred circle from its station around the Temple, firmly centering it instead around the life and home of each individual Israelite. In place of the sacrifices once offered by priests in the Temple, common Israelites would now truly become a nation of priests, eating their common food, conducting their personal and communal lives, and worshipping God according to a strict code of holiness.

By significantly expanding the legislation understood to comprise covenantal law, the rabbis created a system under which all of the people's actions were to be carried out on the basis of a detailed model believed to derive from God. This emergent system of law allowed the rabbis and people to understand that the sacred circle remained intact. The impact of the destruction of the Temple was ameliorated as common Israelites increasingly could see themselves living as a nation of priests, with their own villages taking on the aspect of the Temple. In the midst of political and social chaos, the rabbis thus reestablished a world whose order and sense were informed by the nature of God's original creation and by the terms of the covenant enacted between God and the Israelite people.

In this way, the rabbis developed into a complete system ideas introduced, while the Temple still stood, by the group known as Pharisees. The rabbis of the Mishnah shared with the Pharisees the central idea that the holiness represented in the Temple could and should be imposed upon the homes and daily activities of all Israelites. Ordinary Israelites, in this view, should eat their food and lead their lives as though they were priests offering sacrifices at the Temple altar. They would accomplish this by following the same laws for ritual purity and food cleanness that, according to Scripture, apply only in the Temple cult. All Israelites then would become truly like priests. While the historical connection between the Pharisees and the later rabbis is not entirely clear, the rabbis did eventually claim the Pharisees as their immediate forebears.[10] The ideology that removed matters of cult and sanctification from the sole control of the priests became the hallmark of Rabbinic Judaism. The rabbis thus provided a new theory of the character of Jewish existence, a fresh concept of the meaning of history, and a revised perception of the source of the power to assure salvation, seen now to reside in the people's adherence to the details of Torah.

Through these developments, the rabbis assured that under widely ranging political and social conditions, each member of the Jewish community would know that the covenant formalized at Sinai still was in affect. This reassurance was a product of the most basic Rabbinic claim: wherever they are, the people of Israel can fulfill their requirements as God's chosen nation, and, as a result, can play a direct and immediate role in prompting God to fulfill the promise of salvation. This is because, in the rabbis' perspective, through observance of the details of covenant law, each Jew participates in the shaping of the world in the image in which God originally created and sanctified it. In place of the lost cult and its priesthood, the common Jew's own actions are primary in the creation of a perfected world and in the bringing of salvation, that is, in helping to fulfill the covenant's promises.

This notion, that through observance of

the law Israelites help bring about the perfection of the universe, means that, within the Rabbinic literature, the concept of covenant as a theoretical construct is less a topic of discussion than is the specific content of the law through which the covenant is upheld. This fact has led many Christian scholars and theologians to criticize Rabbinic Judaism. Following the essence of the perspective first articulated by Paul, that the law, to which no person can perfectly adhere, cannot be the foundation of justification before God, these individuals have argued that the Rabbinic perspective, which focuses upon the merit earned through fulfillment of God's demands, is untrue to the biblical idea of covenant, which they say is primarily about God's mercy. This purported distinction between the biblical and post-biblical views was phrased by H.A.A. Kennedy as follows:[11]

> it must not be forgotten that [in the Hebrew Scriptures] the conception of the revealed legal system presupposed the existence of the Covenant. It is given to the community as standing within the Covenant. And that relationship in turn presupposed what we can only call faith in the mercy and goodness of God. So that all that is done by the worshipping people in the later ritual is not for the purpose of reaching fellowship with God: its aim is to maintain the fellowship unbroken. . . . But for this period [of post-biblical Judaism], the crowning proof of Israel's election is its possession of the Law. Obedience to the Law, therefore, is the chief token of its acknowledgment of the Divine grace. But as this obedience came to involve the observance of minute regulations, the notion of merit [which had to be earned] was bound to insinuate itself, and so the rigid contract-conception overshadowed that of the Covenant, which rested on the mercy of God.

In this reading, post-biblical, and in particular Rabbinic, Judaism essentially denied what is viewed as the original essence of the idea of covenant, that, as an act of mercy and without regard to the nation's "works," God chose freely to protect and save the Israelite people. With its emphasis upon the law, by contrast, later Judaism twisted the earlier conception, totally denying the role of God's grace as the essential element in salvation.

E.P. Sanders responds to this reading of post-biblical Judaism by arguing that, at its foundation, stood a conception of what he calls covenantal nomism, that is, the idea that the obligations between the people of Israel and God were viewed as reciprocal. This meant that, since God consistently fulfilled his duties under the covenant, so the people of Israel needed carefully to fulfill their responsibilities, even though they understood that this alone, absent God's mercy, could not lead to redemption. Sanders (pp. 421-422) phrases matters as follows:

> I would venture to say that this is the *fundamental nature of the covenant conception which largely accounts for the relative scarcity of appearances of the term "covenant" in Rabbinic literature.* The covenant was presupposed, and the Rabbinic discussions were largely directed toward the question of how to fulfil the covenantal obligations. The very arguments and the way in which the questions are worded show the conviction that the covenant was in force—that God was being true to his covenantal promises. The question was precisely how Jews should be true to their covenantal obligation. Similar observations could be made about most of the rest of the literature. The covenant is directly mentioned in the Dead Sea Scrolls relatively frequently because the very existence of the sect was based on the sectarians' conviction that they had the true covenant (or the true interpretation of it) and because of the need to define special requirements for being admitted to and staying in the covenant. Generally, however, the word does not much appear in the literature of the period, even though covenantal ideas are absolutely common. Further, obedience is universally held to be the behaviour appropriate to being in the covenant, not the means of earning God's grace. . . .

> There are two different formulations concerning mercy and justice. One is that of Rabbinic literature: God's mercy is greater than his justice. In the other literature, the usual formulation is that God punishes the wicked *for their deeds*, while bestowing *mercy on the righteous*. The theme of mercy to the righteous is worked out especially elaborately in the Dead Sea Scrolls and the Psalms of Solomon, and it appears also in Ben Sirach, Jubilees and I Enoch. The themes of mercy and retribution or justice are not actually in competition, but serve different functions.

Statements to the effect that God pays each man his just due serve to assert the justness of God and to assure both sinners and the righteous that what they do matters. God is not capricious. He will neither punish for obedience nor reward transgression. The theme of mercy—whether put in terms of God's mercy in electing Israel, God's mercy in accepting repentant sinners (repentance does not earn a reward, but is responded to by God in mercy), or God's "rewarding" the righteous because of his mercy—serves to assure that election and ultimately salvation cannot be earned, but depend upon God's grace.

Judaism, in particular Rabbinic Judaism, thus is about both law and mercy, and the religion that emerges from this interplay of human and divine responsibility to the terms of the covenant is characterized by the following structure (Sanders, p. 422):

> (1) God has chosen Israel and (2) given the law. The law implies both (3) God's promise to maintain the election and (4) the requirement to obey. (5) God rewards obedience and punishes transgression. (6) The law provides for means of atonement, and atonement results in (7) maintenance or re-establishment of the covenantal relationship. (8) All those who are maintained in the covenant by obedience, atonement and God's mercy belong to the group which will be saved. An important interpretation of the first and last points is that election and ultimately salvation are considered to be by God's mercy rather than human achievement.

In this reading, supported by the texts of Rabbinic Judaism cited below, the important points are the first and the last. While central to the process of salvation, the law is but one element in bringing about personal and national redemption. At the heart of the covenant relationship, that is, is not simply the obligation of the people to observe the law. Rather, that relationship is maintained as well through acts of repentance, through which people may be reconciled with God, and on the foundation of God's mercy, which assures that God desires the people to succeed in their efforts at righteousness, that God is accepting of their sincere acts of atonement. This means that the post-biblical and especially the Rabbinic conception of law carries with it a deep sense of God's mercy and of

the centrality of God's grace in the maintenance of the covenant relationship.

Talmudic sources on covenant: We see that the earliest rabbis responded to the devastating events of the first centuries C.E. by providing a new sense of what the people must do to maintain their obligations under the covenant. At the same time, they answered the question of what could now be expected of God by rethinking God's own obligations under that covenant. At the heart of this rethinking was the belief that the people's own actions in following the covenant's law play a direct role in perfecting the world. Further, the rabbis proposed that suffering such as Jews in the first centuries experienced did not necessarily result from the people's failure to follow God's law. The rabbis, rather, understand the covenantal relationship to be extremely complex, so that individual and national suffering, even exile, need not be read as direct indicators either of the nation's having abandoned the covenant or of God's having stopped loving and caring for the nation. Suffering, instead, was to be seen as part of the process of redemption itself.

In the aftermath of the Babylonian exile in 586 B.C.E., Jews expressed certainty that their suffering was the result of their sins against God, in particular their idolatrous behavior and failure to follow the terms of the covenant (see, e.g., Amos 5:25-27). While the same idea—that the destruction of the Second Temple and loss of the land of Israel in the first centuries was a punishment for sin—finds expression in the Rabbinic literature and in the liturgy that is formalized in this period, this inherited ideology takes its place alongside a quite different view of matters. While conceding that the people behaved improperly, T. Men. 13:22, for instance, holds that the Second Temple was not destroyed because of idolatry or violations of specific laws of the covenant at all:

> A. Said R. Yohanan b. Torta, "On what account was Shiloh[12] destroyed? Because of the disgraceful disposition of the Holy Things which were there.
> B. "As to Jerusalem's first building, on what

account was it destroyed? Because of idolatry and licentiousness and bloodshed that were in it.

C. "But [as to] the latter [building], we know that they devoted themselves to Torah and were meticulous about tithes.

D. "On what account did they go into exile? Because they love money and hate one another.

E. "This teaches you that hatred of one for another is evil before the Omnipresent, and Scripture deems it equivalent to idolatry, licentiousness, and bloodshed."

Being scrupulous towards covenantal law, C, is not enough to assure God's blessing. Rather, the nation is expected to perfect itself in all ways, so as to live according to the highest moral values and standards of righteousness, beyond what is directly expressed in the terms of the covenant. Since the passage distinguishes these matters, D, from "devotion to Torah," C, it makes clear that simple observance of Israel's obligations under the covenant offers no assurance of God's protection and support. The people, rather, must do more. By creating a morally and socially perfect society, D, they initiate the process of redemption, themselves creating the sort of world that God had originally intended and promised to create.

While diverging from the inherited notion that observance of the letter of the law is sufficient to assure God's protection, T. Men. 13:22 still expresses the overall concept of divine providence developed within the Bible's theory of the covenant: in essence the passage holds that exile has resulted from the people's failings before God, that is, from sin, even if the sin is not depicted as a violation of a specific law of the covenant. Other passages appear not to grant even this. They hold, rather, that no fixed relationship at all exists between sin and suffering. Exile is not primarily the result of Israel's failure to follow the covenant at all. God in this view chastens the people of Israel not as punishment for past sins but in order to assure their future adherence to the covenant, with its promise of *eventual* redemption. The implication of this reading is that, contrary to what the events of the first centuries might have seemed to mean, the nation's sorrows

did necessarily result from the people's abandoning of the covenant. They could not be explained using the inherited biblical model of divine retribution for sin. The people's suffering, rather, was a product of God's love, and it vouchsafed a future redemption (B. Ber. 5a):

A. R. Jacob bar Idi and R. Aha bar Hanina differed. One of them said, "What are sufferings brought on by God's love? They are any form of suffering that does not involve one's having to give up studying Torah.

B. "For it is said, 'Happy is the man whom you chasten, O Lord, and yet teach out of your Torah' (Ps. 94:12)."

C. The other said, "What are sufferings brought on by God's love? They are any form of suffering that does not involve having to give up praying.

D. "For it is said, 'Blessed be God, who has not turned away my prayer nor his mercy from me' (Ps. 66:20)."

E. Said to them R. Abba, son of R. Hiyya bar Abba, "This is what R. Hiyya bar Abba said R. Yohanan said, 'Both constitute forms of suffering brought on by God's love.

F. "'For it is said, "For him whom the Lord loves he corrects" (Prov. 3:12).

G. "'What is the sense of the Scripture's statement, "And you teach him out of your Torah"? Do not read it as "You teach him," but "You teach us."

H. "'This matter you teach us out of your law, namely, the argument [concerning the meaning of the suffering brought on by God's love] *a fortiori* rests on the traits of the tooth and the eye:

I. "'Now if, on account of an injury done to the slave's tooth or eye, which are only one of a person's limbs, a slave goes forth to freedom, sufferings that drain away the whole of a person's body, how much the more so [should a person find true freedom on their account]!'"

J. This furthermore accords with what R. Simeon b. Laqish said.

K. For R. Simeon b. Laqish said, "A 'covenant' is stated in respect to salt, and a covenant is mentioned with respect to suffering.

L. "With respect to a covenant with salt: 'Neither shall you allow the salt of the covenant of your God to be lacking' (Lev. 2:13).

M. "With respect to a covenant with suffering: 'These are the words of the covenant' (Deut. 28:69) [followed by discourse on Israel's suffering].

N. "Just as the covenant noted with salt indicates that salt sweetens meat, so the covenant noted with suffering indicates that suffering wipes away all of a person's sins."

Within Scripture, the nation's collapse before its enemies and its suffering under the burden of exile are explicit signs that the people have failed in their covenantal obligations and that God, as a result, has punished them. The Rabbinic materials offer a new and quite different perspective. Now suffering is seen as an integral element of the covenantal relationship, as a tool God uses to purify the people and to make possible their eventual redemption. The rabbis thus depict the covenantal relationship not only as still intact but, despite the appearance of matters in the first centuries, as being certain to yield salvation for the people of Israel and the fulfillment of the promises made by God in the Hebrew Scriptures.

Ideas such as these assured the people that loss of the Temple and Holy Land and the suffering of the nation in exile did not signify the end of the covenantal relationship with God. Gen. Rabbah XLIV.5 makes this point explicit, stating that, from the time of Abraham and on, no nation, no matter what its particular merit, could replace the Israelites as the holders of the covenant with God:

A. "After these things" (Gen. 15:1): [This suggests that] there were some second thoughts [about the covenant].

B. Who had second thoughts? Abraham did. He said before the Holy One, blessed be he, "Lord of the ages, you made a covenant with Noah that you would not wipe out his children. I went and acquired a treasure of religious deeds and good deeds greater than his, so the covenant made with me has set aside the covenant made with him. Now is it possible that someone else will come along and accumulate religious deeds and good deeds greater than mine and so set aside the covenant that was made with me on account of the covenant to be made with him."

C. Said the Holy One, blessed be he, "Out of Noah I did not raise up shields for the righteous, but from you I shall raise up shields for the righteous. And not only so, but when your children will fall into sin and evil deeds, I shall see a single righteous man among them who can say to the attribute of justice, 'Enough.' Him I shall take and make into the atonement for them all."

God's covenant with Abraham superseded the covenant that, following the flood, God had made with Noah and, through Noah, with all people (Gen. 9:1-17). Under the covenant with Abraham, by contrast, the people of Israel alone received special blessings and promises from God. But if God once chose to make a new covenant that superseded an old one, could he not do so again? This passage offers an assurance that, no matter how the events of history might presently make things look, God's agreement with Abraham cannot be superseded: the covenant with Israel is eternal. Such rhetoric appears to be a direct response to the Christians' claim to have replaced the people of Israel—shown by their degraded stature to have been rejected by God—as the bearers of a "new" covenant. Stating that God has promised never to forsake his special relationship with Israel, this passage explains that, even if the people of Israel sin, the merit of Abraham, or the righteous deeds of someone like Abraham, appease God's anger. So God's covenant with and protection of Israel is permanent. In the eyes of God, no other nation, even if it is characterized by righteous behavior, can take the place of the people of Israel.

Most striking in their conception of the covenant is the rabbis' ability to imagine that Israel rightly may accuse God of delay in fulfilling his covenantal responsibilities. This is a quite different approach from that of Scripture, where Israel's sin clearly leads to God's punishing of the nation. While in Scripture God thus waits for Israel properly to observe the terms of the covenant and to become worthy of redemption, the passage before us depicts the people of Israel's impatience: the nation, faithful to God and true to the covenant, steadfastly awaits redemption. This is despite God's disquieting delay in fulfilling his responsibility under the covenant (Pesikta deRav Kahana XIX:IV):

1.A. R. Abba bar Kahana in the name of R. Yohanan: "The matter may be compared to the case of a king who betrothed a noble lady and wrote for her in the marriage settlement a sizable pledge: 'So and so many marriage canopies I shall prepare for you, such and so ornaments I shall provide for you, so and so many treasurers I shall give you.'

B. "He then left her and went overseas, and she waited there for many years. Her friends were making fun of her, saying, 'How long are you going to sit? Get yourself a husband while you are still young, while you are still vigorous.'

C. "And she would go into her house and take the document of her marriage-settlement and read it and find comfort. After some time the king came home from overseas. He said to her, 'My daughter, I am amazed at how you have had faith in me all these years.'

D. "She said to him, 'My lord, king, were it not for the substantial marriage settlement that you wrote out for me, my friends would have made you lose me.'

E. "So too, since in this world, the nations of the world ridicule Israel, saying to them, 'How long are you going to be put to death for the sake of your God and give your lives for him and be put to death for him? How much pain does he bring on you, how much humiliation he brings on you, how much pain he brings on you. Come to us and we shall appoint you commanders and governors and generals.'

F. "Then the Israelites enter their meeting places and study halls and take the scroll of the Torah and read in it: 'And I shall walk in your midst, and I shall make you prosper, and I shall make you numerous, and I shall carry out my covenant with you' (Lev. 26:9).

G. "When the end will come, the Holy One, blessed be He, will say to Israel, 'I am amazed at how you have had faith in me all these years.'

H. "And Israel will say before the Holy One, blessed be He, 'Lord of the ages, were it not for the scroll of the Torah which you wrote out for us, the nations of the world would have succeeded in destroying us for you.

I. "That is in line with this verse of Scripture: 'I recall to mind therefore I have hope' (Lam. 3:21).

J. "And so too David says, 'Unless your Torah had been my delight, I should then have perished in my affliction' (Ps. 119:92)."

It is hard to imagine a more powerful response to the history of the Jewish people from the destruction of the Second Temple and on. Rather than Scripture's image of God's waiting for the return to faith of the sinful people of Israel, the rabbis depict the people's need for strength and patience as they await God's salvation, working all the while themselves to perfect the world. In light of what has happened to them on the stage of earthly history as an apparent result of God's inaction, they have legitimate reason to give up hope. Instead, their possession of, study of, practice of the covenant—embodied in the Torah—provides them with the needed strength and assures them that salvation eventually will come. While they wait, the covenant, creating of them a nation of priests and righteous people, sustains them and assures that in some undisclosed future time, the promises made originally with Abraham will be kept.[13]

The idea of covenant in modern Judaism: The rabbis of classical Judaism conceived of the covenant as the defining element of their civilization and religion, that which bound the people of Israel to each other and to God and separated them from all other nations. And yet, as we have seen, the rabbis did not often speak directly of the covenant or of its nature, preferring instead to speak of Torah and *halakhah*, that is, of the laws through which the people were to carry out their obligations under the covenant. This approach was appropriate in light of the rabbis' understanding that observance of the law both recognized God's past protection of the nation and encouraged God finally to fulfill the messianic promises that stood at the heart of covenant. At the same time, movement away from direct discussions of the concept of covenant perhaps responded to the ascendance of Christianity, with its claim to comprise a *new* covenant that had superseded the one made originally with the Jews. By not speaking directly of the concept of covenant, the rabbis may have intended to reduce any sense of interaction with Christianity and its claims.[14] By speaking of Torah and not covenant, classical Judaism retained its own independent way of thinking about the relationship between God in heaven and people on earth.

While factors such as these led the authorities of classical Judaism to speak of Torah and not covenant, it is clear that the concept of covenant, in much the form it had emerged in the biblical literature, underlies their conception of the relationship between God and Israel. This overall perspective changed radically only with the emergence of enlightenment thinking and in the face of the nineteenth and twentieth century movement of Jews into the mainstreams of western culture. Now the very concept of covenant—which spoke of a unique relationship between Israel and God—became problematical. In the face of the modern idea of the equal legitimacy of all religions and in light of the increasing reception of Jews into western society, Jews more and more wished to be viewed as citizens of the world rather than as members of a parochial national and cultural group. No longer did they wish to be identified as members of the *nation* of Israel, distinguished by its exclusive covenant. They wished, rather, to be recognized as adherents of Judaism, a religion like all others, and as citizens only of the countries in which they lived.

Within this intellectual and social setting, the concept of covenant was overly confining. It suggested that Jews still believed themselves to be different from and, as bearers of a special relationship to God, better than all other people. Thus the very idea of covenant, as much as the laws it encompassed, stood in the way of the Jews' desired cultural and social homogenization. Scripture held that the covenant would make of the Jews "a kingdom of priests and a holy people" (Exod. 19:6). The question was how this could be, and what the meaning of covenant would be, when Jews largely "jettisoned those patterns of life which tended to make them different from their fellow citizens."[15] Leonard Kravitz phrases the problem as follows:

Within the philosophical and theological categories in which this new religious thinking was framed, the idea of a personal God who could command and choose and thus make a covenant with a particular people was problematical. As for the medieval philosophers, so for the early Reform thinkers, God was more idea than commanding presence, more the absolute than He who in love had given the Torah to His people Israel. For such thinkers, the idea of covenant would remain a very abstract concept, if it existed at all.

Thus, even as early Reform thinkers continued to insist on the existence of a special mission of the Jews, for instance, to bring pure ethical monotheism to the world, they left unclear the manner in which this mission could be accomplished. Living as undifferentiated citizens, similar to all other members of the nations in which they were found, in what regard did the Jews form the sort of collective through which they could carry out their covenantal mission? What, indeed, could be the meaning or significance of the concept of covenant if the Jews were not to be viewed as having a *unique* relationship to God but only, perhaps, a *special* one, just as all peoples were now understood, each in their own way, to be special to God?

In the early modern period, the concept of covenant thus was controversial and not comfortably spoken of either by Jewish thinkers or within the Jewish public at large. For covenant signified a parochial separateness at a time when Jews wished to think in universal terms, conceiving of themselves as no different from any other religious group. Only in recent times, in particular since the Nazi Holocaust, have Jewish attitudes towards the idea of covenant begun again to change. This change has come in the face of the general rejection of the possibility, or desirability, of total Jewish assimilation and, in the United States in particular, in response to the widespread discarding of the concept of America as melting pot. The new desire for pluralism rather than homogenization, that is, has left considerable room for, even demanded, the assertion of one's own ethnicity. As a result Jews are considerably less embarrassed by the concept of covenant, and Jewish thinkers have begun to explore covenant as a context for reaffirming ties to tradition.[16] This process unfolds, of course, even as Jews continue to develop positive and appropriate relationships to the non-Jewish world.

Explorations of the meaning of covenant lead in diverse directions. But they all grapple with the same central problem of how to formulate a contemporary conception of covenant that is true to the traditional ideal and yet appropriate to the unique circumstance of modern Jews. Note that the very notion of the existence of a covenantal relationship between God and Israel asserts that God has characteristics—appeared to Moses to reveal the law, acts in history to reward obedience or punish sin, is bound by promises recorded in Scripture—that many moderns refuse to attribute to God. Equally, the covenant's concept of a unique, and not just special, relationship between God and the people of Israel is troubling as Jews continue to fight for an end to religious intolerance. Jews equally struggle with the notion, intrinsic to the traditional concept of covenant, of obligatory ritual practices. And, finally, in an age in which religion increasingly is viewed as a matter of personal belief and individual formulation, many Jews are troubled by the covenantal idea's inescapable communal dimension.[17]

Yet, the centrality to Judaism of the idea of covenant, which in all periods of Jewish history has stood at the foundation of the essence of being a Jew, means that, despite these difficulties, Jews continue to view their membership in the people of Israel through the prism of the covenantal idea. Through the idea of covenant Jews continue to express their sense that they are the products not just of a collective history but of an advancing civilization. Through the concept of covenant they persist in declaring their sense of obligation, in the present, to creating a better world. And through the idea of covenant they still express their hope for the future, the hope that the progress humans make towards that better world ultimately will flower as the advent of the messianic age.[18] However the idea of covenant has changed from its earliest formulations within the narratives of the Pentateuch, it remains at the heart of what it means to be a Jew today.

Notes

[1] George Mendenhall and Gary Herion, "Covenant," in *Anchor Bible Dictionary*, vol. 1, p. 1179.

[2] B. Shab. 33a is explicit in this matter, stating that, in Scripture, the term covenant refers to Torah.

[3] Moshe Weinfeld, "Covenant," in *Encyclopaedia Judaica*, vol. 5, col. 1021.

[4] The following discussion of the ancient treaty form depends upon Mendenhall and Herion, op. cit., pp. 1180-1183.

[5] Op. cit., p. 1180.

[6] Op. cit., p. 1181.

[7] See CIRCUMCISION.

[8] See MESSIAH IN JUDAISM.

[9] Note for instance the philosophical and theological deliberations recorded in the wisdom literature, the messianic fervor of the apocryphal writings, the intellectual and philosophical readings of the nature of Judaism found in Philo, and Josephus' representation of Jewish participation in Hellenistic civilization. These examples all testify to vibrant and varied forms of Jewish religion, religious practice, and culture.

[10] See Jacob Neusner, *From Politics to Piety: The Emergence of Pharisaic Judaism* (New York, 1973), *passim*. For a discussion based upon the evidence of the Mishnaic Division of Agriculture, see Alan J. Avery-Peck, *Mishnah's Division of Agriculture. A History and Theology of Seder Zeraim* (Chico, 1985), pp. 359-362.

[11] "The Significance and Range of the Covenant-Conception in the New Testament," in *The Expositor*, 10, 1915, pp. 389 and 392, cited by E.P. Sanders, *Paul and Palestinian Judaism* (Minneapolis, 1977), pp. 419-420. Pp. 33-58 of Sanders' study document the pervasive view within New Testament scholarship that, in its focus upon the law, post-biblical Judaism represents an ossification of biblical religion.

[12] Prior to Solomon's building of the Temple in Jerusalem, Shiloh was the major center of Israelite worship of Yahweh, located in Canaan, north of Bethel. Scripture, unlike the Rabbinic literature, depicts Shiloh as having been abandoned (Jer. 7:12-14, 26:6-9), not destroyed.

[13] On the idea of covenant in contemporary, and, in particular, post-Holocaust Judaism, see JUDAISM, PHILOSOPHY AND THEOLOGY OF, IN MODERN TIMES IN THE USA, and HOLOCAUST, JUDAIC THEOLOGY AND THE.

[14] Elliot Dorff, "The Meaning of Covenant: A Contemporary Understanding," in Helga Croner and Leon Kleinicki, eds., *Issues in the Jewish-Christian Dialogue. Jewish Perspectives on Covenant Mission and Witness* (New York, 1979), p. 38.

[15] For the quote and on the preceding, see

Leonard Kravitz, "The Covenant in Jewish Tradition," in Croner and Kleinicki, op. cit., pp. 31-32.

[16] See Dorff, op. cit., pp. 38-39.

[17] This description of the issues in the formulation of a contemporary conception of covenant draws upon Dorff's description of the covenant as an "organizing concept for modern Jewish life," op. cit., pp. 50-57.

[18] Here I paraphrase Dorff, p. 58.

ALAN J. AVERY-PECK

CREEDS: Formal statements of fundamental belief, or articles of faith, do not exist in Judaism in the same way in which they exist in Christianity and Islam. While, especially beginning in the medieval period, Jewish philosophers made many attempts to reduce the content of Judaism to a short statement of dogma, such creeds lacked the backing of a supreme ecclesiastical body, which does not exist in Judaism. Thus, while certain of these statements have been incorporated into the Jewish liturgy and function for many as encapsulations of Jewish belief, the popularity and importance of specific creedal statements always have been a function of the fame and credentials of their authors. No attempts have been made, or can be made, to impose acceptance of any creed as an obligation incumbent upon all Jews or even as a precondition of conversion into the Jewish community. Judaism, as a result, has yielded no articles of faith comparable to the three great creeds of the Catholic Church—the Apostles' Creed, the Nicene Creed, and the Athanasian Creed—or to the Muslim *Kalimat As-Shahadat*, the first of the five pillars of Islam, which it is a duty for every believer to recite at least once in his or her life-time. By contrast, despite the interest of medieval Jewish philosophers in systematizing Jewish belief, Judaism offers no defining doctrines or obligatory articles of faith.

The absence of a central body that could validate and mandate a creedal statement is but one reason that Judaism has not produced any universally required creeds. An additional factor is that, since biblical times and to the present, membership in the Israelite community has been almost exclusively a function of birth and not the result of a confession of faith or the acceptance of a dogma at all. Since antiquity, anyone born to a Jewish mother has automatically been considered a Jew (and this, without regard for the religion of the father). For a person born into Judaism, practice of the religion's rituals and laws and the self-perception of being a Jew generally have been understood to be definitive. Indeed, even a born Jew who never practiced Judaism, or one who consciously rejects that faith, remains a Jew according to Jewish law. In hardly any circumstance can the status conferred by birth be erased. This means that, according to the dominant view, even an apostate may return to full participation in the community without making an explicit confession of faith or formally indicating acceptance of any set dogmas understood within the Jewish community to define the religion.[1] In Judaism, therefore, creeds have never had a role in answering the very important question of who is a Jew. Unlike in Christianity, for instance, in Judaism this question has been answered solely through evaluation of the individual's lineage.

Alongside the centrality of lineage in defining who is a Jew, the absence in Judaism of significant missionary trends has reduced the need for the development of creeds. Through history, Jews have not actively sought converts and so have not required a clear definition of the faith that could be used in setting standards for the admission of proselytes. Similarly, the absence of significant heresies that might tear apart the religion has meant that little pressure existed for the development of a creed. People's standings as Jews, rather, has been defined by their birth and behaviors, by how they live rather than what they believe. Such an attitude is not conducive to the production of concise statements of the essence of the religion or of the principles Jews are deemed obligated to accept in order to be considered members of the community, subject to God's saving power. Again, in this regard, Judaism differs from Christianity, in which precise, fixed creeds began to appear in the third and fourth centuries as ways of determining exactly who had the right, based upon the character of their faith alone, to claim membership in the emerging Christian community.[2]

The disinterest among Jews in formulating creeds, evidenced through antiquity and into the Talmudic period, changed primarily beginning in the tenth century, when formal statements of fundamental beliefs began to appear. Such statements of dogma were prepared by Jewish philosophers in response to internal pressure from the Karaite movement, which rejected the Rabbinic concept of the Oral Torah, and in reaction to corresponding theological discussions then occurring within Islam, in which intense efforts were underway to define precisely the content of Muslim belief. These developments within medieval Jewish theological writings distinguish this period from the eras of the Hebrew Bible and the Talmudic literature, in which the focus was as much or more upon correct forms of behavior than upon correct belief. At the same time, insofar as the biblical and Talmudic literatures describe the fundamental theological doctrines of Judaism and delineate the elaborate details of Jewish practice, they provided the basis for medieval, as well as modern, articles of the Jewish faith. This being the case, while neither the Hebrew Scriptures nor Talmudic literature contains encompassing statements of dogma *per se*, these documents form an appropriate starting point for our discussion of creeds in Judaism.

Creeds in the Hebrew Scriptures: The historical credos at Deut. 26:5-9 and 6:20-25 and the declamatory affirmations of membership in the Israelite people at Deut. 6:4-5 and 1 Kgs. 18:39 provide the earliest short summaries of the nature Israelite identity. The historical credos reflect the extent to which Israelite religion was not founded upon a system of philosophical or theological beliefs about the attributes of God. Rather, as these statements make clear, membership in the Israelite people was defined as a response to God's actions in history on behalf of the nation. Later medieval creedal statements define God and delineate central beliefs about God's future eschatological actions. The biblical credos, by contrast, focus on history, on the fact that what God has done for the people justifies God's demands that the people respond in certain ways. At issue is not what God *is* but what God *has done*, as Deut. 6:20-25 makes clear:

> When your son asks you in time to come, "What is the meaning of the testimonies and the statutes and the ordinances which the Lord our God has commanded you?" then you shall say to your son, "We were Pharaoh's slaves in Egypt; and the Lord brought us out of Egypt with a mighty hand; and the Lord showed signs and wonders, great and grievous, against Egypt and against Pharaoh and all his household, before our eyes; and he brought us out from there, that he might bring us in and give us the land which he swore to give to our fathers. And the Lord commanded us to do all these statutes, to fear the Lord our God, for our good always, that he might preserve us alive, as at this day. And it will be righteousness for us, if we are careful to do all this commandment before the Lord our God, as he has commanded us."

Children are to be taught the great deeds that God did on behalf of the Israelite people. This is the foundation of and justification for the demand that the people accept and observe the law. At issue is not the philosophical nature of God or the reason that God has come to act in one way and not another. Rather, history makes clear that following the will of God leads to the preservation of the nation. The same point is made at Deut. 26:5-9, which describes the confession pilgrims to Jerusalem are to make when they present the first fruits of their crop at the altar of God's Temple:

> And you shall make response before the Lord your God, "A wandering Aramean was my father; and he went down into Egypt and sojourned there, few in number; and there he became a nation, great, mighty, and populous. And the Egyptians treated us harshly, and afflicted us, and laid upon us hard bondage. Then we cried to the Lord the God of our fathers, and the Lord heard our voice, and saw our affliction, our toil, and our oppression; and the Lord brought us out of Egypt with a mighty hand and an outstretched arm, with great terror, with signs and wonders; and he brought us into this place and gave us this land, a land flowing with milk and honey."

The pilgrim recalls the mighty acts of God that were manifested in the Exodus from

Egypt and the conquest of Canaan. He thus declares his personal recognition of what is at the heart of Israelite identity: since God acted on behalf of the people, bringing the nation out of Egyptian bondage and into a land that would be their own, God is owed the people's obedience and singular faithfulness. On this foundation, the individual affirms acceptance of the terms of the covenant.

Such biblical formulations of the foundation of the Israelite way of life are the antecedents of later attempts in Christianity as well as in Judaism to formulate creeds that detail the fundamental facts about God. At the heart of the later creeds is the notion that sincere belief in the truth of their statements about God—even without any corresponding actions on the part of the believer—assures God's protection and, hence, the individual believer's salvation. The historical credos we have just reviewed, by contrast, entail no such thinking. They only present the justification for the Israelite code of ritual and communal law. Deut. 26:5-9, like Deut. 6:20-25, that is, adduces God's past behavior on behalf of the people as the reason that the people are now and forever obligated to accept and follow God's commandments. The practice of the law, in turn, identifies the individual as a member of the Israelite community and assures God's future protection. These goals are not understood to be accomplished by acceptance of the creed without the actions that the Bible comprehends that acceptance to bring in its wake.

The historical credos of the Hebrew Bible thus differ from later articles of faith. Unlike the later creeds, they view the actualization of the individual's relationship with God not to be a simple result of the acceptance of the credo. Rather, in the view of the Hebrew Bible, a correct relationship with God is a consequence only of the individual's carrying out of the actions described in the covenant. What is central in the historical credos thus is behavior and not belief at all.

Elsewhere in the Bible, declamatory affirmations of the divinity of God comparably serve as a foundation of faith. Here again, however, the declaration does not claim to comprise the totality of that faith, only to explain what is required of the Israelite. Deut. 6:4-5 presents perhaps the earliest such formulation:

> Hear, O Israel: The Lord our God is one Lord; and you shall love the Lord your God with all your heart, and with all your soul, and with all your might.

These verses rephrase as a positive affirmation the first commandment of the Decalogue ("You shall have no other gods besides me," Deut. 5:7). Since there is only one God, the people of Israel is to have only one loyalty. But, again, what follows immediately upon this statement is the obligation that the people abide by the covenantal law set down by God, carrying out the actions that signify love of God. It is not enough to "believe" or to have faith in the claim that God is one. The fact that God is one, rather, obligates the individual to follow the terms of the covenant established by God with the Israelite people.

1 Kgs. 18:39 presents another context in which the Israelites succinctly declare what they see as central in the nature of the deity and their relationship to him. The passage describes Elijah's challenging of the prophets of Baal to prove that Baal, like Yahweh, can act powerfully on behalf of those who turn to him. Baal's followers get no response when they demand that Baal reveal himself. By contrast, fire from heaven consumes the offerings laid out by Elijah, proving the presence and power of the Israelite God. The gathered Israelites respond as follows:

> And when all the people saw it, they fell on their faces; and they said, "The Lord, he is God; the Lord, he is God."

Like the previously cited historical credos, this passage presents the people's response to God's self-revelation in history, expressed here an affirmation of the divinity of Yahweh. These passages are in the category of creeds insofar as they describe the foundation for allegiance to God and the reason the people must accept the terms of the covenant, with its complex system of social, ethical, and ritual laws. But these statements are not dogmas in the sense that such articles of faith have existed in other, later religions. For

Scripture neither states nor implies that failure to accept the claims of these brief credos yields dismissal from the nation or loss of protection by God. Rather, as we have said, membership in the Israelite nation is established by birth or adherence to the covenant's strict system of regulations. Simple acceptance of a set of philosophical or theological tenets is not contemplated by Scripture as an important element in what demarcates the Israelite community and assures God's continued adherence to his responsibilities under the covenant.

Philo's scriptural truths: The first careful attempt to delineate the foundational beliefs expressed by the Hebrew Bible occurs in the work of Philo, the Alexandrean Jewish philosopher of the first century C.E. Philo's underlying conception was that Scripture expressed the absolute truths that stand at the foundation of all philosophical thinking. These are basic realities of God and the world with which, to be legitimate, philosophical reasoning must concur.[3] Throughout Philo's writings, eight such truths are listed, together comprising the fundamental beliefs that Philo understood Moses's account of the creation of the world to teach. The first five central truths are enumerated at *Opificio Mundi* 61, 170-172: "(1) the existence of God; (2) the unity of God; (3) the creation of the world; (4) the unity of the world; (5) divine providence." *Moses* II, 3, 14, speaks of two additional beliefs: (6) that the laws of Moses are the word of God not the invention of humans, and (7) the hope that these laws will remain for all future ages. Finally, at *Special Laws* I, 60, 327-363, in his enumeration five sorts of people who deny ideas that are fundamental to Scripture and so must be said to have no religion, Philo adds one additional principle to those already listed: (8) the existence of incorporeal ideas.

Striking in this listing of Scripture's fundamental presuppositions is that six of Philo's eight foundational beliefs—the existence and unity of God, the creation and unity of the world, divine providence, and the existence of incorporeal ideas—are central principles taught in Greek philosophy. The elaboration of these ideas throughout Philo's work suggests the ways in which he disagrees with some of the specifics of these conceptions as they are expressed in the variety of Greek philosophical schools. At the same time, as in his work as a whole, in enumerating these Scriptural principles, one of Philo's central goals was to legitimate Judaism by illustrating the extent to which its beliefs about God and the world concur with those of the philosophical world in which he lived.

The point is that even in his explicit enumeration of principles that he holds constitute the presuppositions of Judaism, Philo does not claim to be delineating the sum total of Jewish belief or to be listing articles of faith, acceptance of which assures salvation. We have here, rather, in Wolfson's words, a "preamble of faith," viewed primarily by Philo as constituting the principles to which "philosophy must accommodate itself" (p. 164). For Philo, as for the Hebrew Bible, and, as we shall now see, for the rabbis as well, certain central principles exist at the heart of Judaism. But their enumeration does not delineate the sum total of Judaism nor define what all Jews must consciously accept as a condition of salvation. Interestingly, for Philo, such encompassing principles do, in fact, exist. They are comprised of the two remaining fundamental beliefs that he lists but that have no parallel in Greek philosophical thinking: that the law in all its details is the word of God, transmitted directly by the deity to Moses, and that this law is eternal and immutable. While Philo argues that each element of the law represents a philosophical truth, he still concurs with the approach to Judaism that is central in Scripture and the later Rabbinic literature: Judaism is defined not primarily by a creed or by what one believes but, rather, by the ritual actions and observance of the law that define the Jewish way of life. There is no doubting that, despite his philosophical explanation of the law and his listing of Scripture's underlying principles, what for Philo defines the proper Jew is what he does and not what he believes.

Creeds in the Rabbinic literature: In addressing the Rabbinic literature, it is important to distinguish between creeds, or statements of religious dogma, and the formulation of distinct aspects of faith. We have already seen that statements of dogma do not appear in Judaism, where identity as a Jew depends upon birth and in which righteousness before God is a result not of what one believes but of one's strict adherence to law.

At the same time, as we have seen in Philo, by late antiquity, Jews found great benefit in articulating specific elements of Jewish belief, understood to be fundamental to the religion as a whole. In Philo, statements of the fundamental beliefs of Judaism showed that the Jewish religion was a legitimate expression of contemporary philosophical thinking. Similarly, in the Rabbinic literature, elaborations of the principles of Judaism helped to delimit the Jewish community and to identify legitimate vs. heretical theologies. This function of the delineation of fundamental beliefs is clear, for instance, at M. San 10:1, which lists what a Jew must believe in order to gain a place in the messianic world to come:

A. All Israelites have a share in the world to come,
B. as it is said, "Your people also shall be all righteous, they shall inherit the land forever; the branch of my planting, the work of my hands, that I may be glorified" (Is. 60:21).
C. And these are the ones who have no portion in the world to come:
D. (1) He who says the resurrection of the dead is a teaching that does not derive from the Torah, (2) and Torah does not come from Heaven, and (3) an Epicurean.
E. R. Aqiba says, "Also: He who reads in heretical books,
F. "and he who whispers over a wound and says, 'I will put none of the diseases upon you which I have put on the Egyptians, for I am the Lord who heals you' (Exod. 15:26)."
G. Abba Saul says, "Also: he who pronounces the divine Name as it is spelled out."

To be assured divine salvation, one must accept the central tenets of Rabbinic Judaism, in particular the principles of the coming resurrection of the dead and the divine origin of the Torah. Note that the term "Torah" appears here without the definite article and so should be distinguished from the Penta-

teuch, that is *the* Torah. Reference is to what the rabbis perceive to be the complete revelation of God to Moses, encompassed in the oral codes of Rabbinic Judaism as well as in the written Scriptures.

The claim that this list defines as heretical those who reject Rabbinic teachings in particular is strengthened by the inclusion of an "Epicurean." In Rabbinic literature, this term applies in general to Jews and gentiles opposed to Rabbinic teaching and thus means "skeptic" or "heretic." Its phonetic similarity to the name of the Greek thinker Epicurus is serendipitous, since Epicurean teaching rejected the existence of divine providence or divine intervention in the world. The title Epicurean thus appropriately designated one who rejected Rabbinic teachings so as, from the perspective of the Rabbinic movement, to be seen as a heretic. But the larger point should be clear: from the Rabbinic perspective, one who rejects the validity of the oral Torah and so practices none of its laws fails to live a pious life and so is excluded from God's redemption. But, at the same time, acceptance of the doctrine of the Oral Torah absent the practice of its laws is only marginally better. As in Scripture's presentation of matters, what appears to count is not so much belief as the ritual and other legal practices that are based on that belief.

This is not to say that the Talmudic rabbis could not, or never did, conceive of the essential human obligation to God as being faith. Indeed, as we shall see in the following passage, just as Pauline Christianity is marked by Paul's concept that God deemed Abraham righteous as a result of Abraham's faith, absent any "works" at all, so certain rabbis declared that Abraham, and later the children of Israel, were rewarded by God simply for their faith. At the same time, as other passages make clear, the preponderance of Rabbinic thinking rejects this view, holding that the essential element in attaining proper stature before God is fulfillment of the commandments that define the covenantal relationship. Thus, as we shall see, the rabbis are certain that Abraham fulfilled the covenant even before the Torah had been revealed at Sinai, and they make clear that his reward of becoming wealthy and a "king" resulted from his willingness to act as God demanded, even to the point of sacrificing his son.

The notion that faith alone may assure proper standing before God appears in Mekhilta deRabbi Ishmael, Bashallah 7:

25.A. Great is faith before the one who spoke and brought the world into being [that is, God].
B. For as a reward for the act of faith that the Israelites made in the Lord, the Holy Spirit rested upon them and they sang the song, as it is said, "and they believed in the Lord and in his servant Moses. Then Moses and the people of Israel sang this song [to the Lord, saying, 'I will sing to the Lord, for he has triumphed gloriously; the horse and his rider he has thrown into the sea]'" (Exod. 15:1).
26.A. R. Nehemiah says, "How do you know that whoever takes upon himself the obligation to carry out a single religious duty in faith is worth that the Holy Spirit should rest upon him?
B. "For so we find in the case of our ancestors that as a reward for the act of faith that they made, they achieved merit, so that the Holy Spirit rested on them, as it is said, 'and they believed in the Lord and in his servant Moses. Then Moses and the people of Israel sang this song [to the Lord, saying, "I will sing to the Lord, for he has triumphed gloriously; the horse and his rider he has thrown into the sea]."'"
27.A. So you find that Abraham our father inherited this world and the world to come only as a reward for the faith that he believed, as it is said, "And he believed in the Lord; [and he reckoned it to him as righteousness]" (Gen. 15:6).
B. So you find that the Israelites were redeemed from Egypt only as a reward for the faith that they believed, as it is said, "And the people believed" (Exod. 4:31).
C. "The Lord preserves the faithful" (Ps. 31:25). He calls to mind the faith of the fathers.
D. "And Aaron and Hur held up his hands" (Exod. 17:12).

These passages argue that divine reward may result from faith alone. All three units are explicit that, as a result of their faith and apart from the observance of any commandments, the people of Israel were rewarded with redemption from Egypt. Unit 27.A, for its part, makes the same point regarding Abraham: his reward in this world as well as the assurance of salvation in the coming world depended not upon any deed but only upon his faith, as Gen. 15:6 seems to propose. While unit 26.A refers to an individual's fulfilling of a commandment, its point is in line with the larger context: what matters is not the nature of the one commandment the person performs but that its performance is associated with perfect faith. This faith is rewarded with possession of the Holy Spirit.

This text from the Mekhilta de Rabbi Ishmael is notable in that it portrays a notion of faith most commonly associated with Pauline thinking. For Paul asserts that Abraham earned merit before God through faith alone and that, on that model, faith continues to be the essence of righteousness. This is what, in Paul's view, God demands, not observance of the law. Paul expresses this view clearly at Rom. 4:1-5:

What then shall we say about Abraham, our forefather according to the flesh? For if Abraham was justified by works, he has something to boast about, but not before God. For what does the scripture say? "Abraham believed God, and it was reckoned to him as righteousness." Now to one who works, his wages are not reckoned as a gift but as his due. And to one who does not work but trusts him who justifies the ungodly, his faith is reckoned as righteousness.

Similar to the Rabbinic attitude, in the passage just cited, for Paul, Abraham is the model of what God demands and rewards: perfect faith brings perfect justification before God. Yet Paul develops this view of righteousness in a manner that completely distinguishes it from the approach of the rabbis. For beyond asserting the role of faith in determining righteousness—a claim with which the rabbis, as we have seen, can concur—Paul rejects the idea that the law has any role in determining merit before God at all. In Paul's view, rather, righteousness cannot be earned through works, in the manner of a salary. Justification before God is given, instead, only as a free gift, in response to faith. Equally important for Paul is the premise that no person successfully can follow the entirety of the law without error. This means that, in the end, the law constitutes nothing more than a stumbling block. It assures that people will fail correctly to fulfill God's will. For Paul, therefore, unlike the rabbis, the law can have no role in achieving righteousness before God; faith alone accomplishes this.

We thus see that even the rabbis' assertion of the importance of faith provides only a limited parallel to Paul's—and later Christianity's—conception of Abraham as the model of the man of faith. For even as the rabbis accept the power of faith, unlike Paul, they simultaneously focus upon the importance of "works." And hence we find their most common perspective, that correct standing before God is first and foremost a result of one's following the commandments. This idea is expressed in general terms as well as for the particular case of Abraham in the second half of M. Qid. 4:14, which initially concerns trades that one appropriately should teach his son:

M. R. Nehorai says, "I should lay aside every trade in the world and teach my son only Torah."

N. "For a man eats its fruits in this world, and the principal remains for the world to come.

O. "But other trades are not that way.

P. "When a man gets sick or old or has pains and cannot do his job, lo, he dies of starvation.

Q. "But with Torah it is not that way.

R. "But it keeps him from all evil when he is young, and it gives him a future and a hope when he is old.

S. "Concerning his youth, what does it say? 'They who wait upon the Lord shall renew their strength' (Is. 40:31). And concerning his old age what does it say? 'They shall bring forth fruit in old age' (Ps. 92:14).

T. "And so it says with regard to the patriarch Abraham, may he rest in peace, 'And Abraham was old and well along in years, and the Lord blessed Abraham in all things' (Gen. 24:1).

U. "We find that the patriarch Abraham kept the entire Torah even before it was revealed, since it says, 'Since Abraham obeyed my voice and kept my charge, my commandments, my statutes, and my laws' (Gen. 26:5)."

In a way that nothing else can, studying and observing Torah assures divine reward. Indeed, contrary to what is suggested in the previously cited Rabbinic passage and unlike what Paul asserts, here we find the more common Rabbinic concept that merit before God results primarily from observing commandments. Thus, in the view of this passage, even Abraham's divine reward came not as a result of faith but because Abraham observed the entire Torah, even though it had not yet been given.

This idea that Abraham was rewarded not for faith or for any arbitrary reason is expressed again at Gen. Rab. 55:1, which associates Abraham's merit before God not with faith but with his specific actions:

1.A. "And it came to pass after these things God tested Abraham" (Gen. 22:1):

B. "You have given a banner to those that fear you, that it may be displayed because of the truth, selah" (Ps. 60:6).

C. [Since the word for "banner" shares the consonants of the word for "test," we interpret:] test after test, one attainment of greatness after another, so as to test them in the world and so as to endow them with greatness in the world, like the ensign of a ship.

D. And all this why? ". . . because of the truth, selah" (Ps. 60:6).

E. [Since the word for "truth" and the word for "validate" share the same consonants, we interpret:] it is so that the attribute of justice may be validated in the world.

F. For if someone should say, "He gives riches to whomever he wishes, and he impoverishes whomever he wishes, and whomever he wishes he makes king [all this without justice], and so too as to Abraham, when [God] wanted, he made him rich, and when he wanted, he made him king [and all this without justice], you may reply to him, saying, "Can you do what Abraham did?"

G. "Abraham was a hundred years old when Isaac, his son, was born to him" (Gen. 21:5). And after all that anguish [that led to the birth of Isaac and the conflict between Sarah and Hagar, Isaac and Ishmael], it was stated to him, "Take your son" (Gen. 22:2).

H. And he did not demur.

I. Accordingly: "You have given a banner to those that fear you, that it may be displayed because of the truth, selah" (Ps. 60:6).

J. "And it came to pass after these things God tested [i.e., displayed] Abraham" (Gen. 22:1).

Ps. 60:6 is used because it highlights the key word of the base verse, Gen. 22:1, "try" or "test." The result is to demonstrate that what God did in favoring Abraham rested on justice, not capriciousness: Abraham was rewarded for what he was willing to do, to sacrifice the son who he so loved. The point is clear and underlies the overall Rabbinic theory of what brings merit from God, what is regarded as righteousness. This is actions, the individual's willingness and ability not simply to express faith in God but to carry out all that God demands.

Still, the rabbis are cognizant of the existence in Judaism of some fundamental concepts, which on occasion they demarcate, as in the previously cited passage at M. San. 10:1. Another of these central ideas is the notion that at the heart of Judaism is the belief in the existence of two Torahs, one oral and one written. B. Shab. 30b, for instance, holds that all proselytes must accept the validity of the Oral, as well as the Written, Torah:[4]

A. Our rabbis have taught on Tannaite authority:

B. There was the incident of a certain gentile who came before Shammai. He said to him, "How many Torahs do you have?"

C. He said to him, "Two, one in writing, one memorized."

D. He said to him, "As to the one in writing, I believe you. As to the memorized one, I do not believe you. Convert me on condition that you will teach me only the Torah that is in writing."

E. [Shammai] rebuked him and threw him out.

F. He came before Hillel. He said to him, "Convert me." [ARN: "My lord, how many Torahs were given?" He said to him, "Two, one in writing, one memorized." He said to him, "As to the one in

writing, I believe you. As to the memorized one, I do not believe you."]

G. On the first day [Hillel] said to him, "Alef, bet, gimel, dalet." The next day he reversed the order on him.

H. He said to him, "Well, yesterday, didn't you say it differently?"

I. He said to him, "Didn't you depend on me then? Then depend on me when it comes to the fact of the memorized Torah too." [ARN for G-I: He said to him, "My son, sit." He wrote for him, Alef, bet. [Hillel] said to him, "What is this?" He said to him, "An alef." [Hillel] said to him, "This is not an alef but a bet." [Hillel] said to him, "What is this?" He said to him, "Bet." [Hillel] said to him, "This is not a bet but a gimel." [Hillel] said to him, "How do you know that this is an alef and this a bet and this a gimel? But that is what our ancestors have handed over to us—the tradition that this is an alef, this a bet, this a gimel. Just as you have accepted this teaching in good faith, so accept the other [regarding the Oral Torah] in good faith]."

Hillel and Shammai concur that it is imperative for the proselyte to accept as a matter of faith the divine origin of the Oral Torah. The difference between them, expressed in the following passage as well, is the result of their distinctive personalities, not a theological disagreement: Shammai has no patience for the prospective convert. Hillel, by contrast, takes the time to encourage the gentile's emerging acceptance of Jewish beliefs. Hillel argues that all things, at one level or another, are dependent upon faith, even learning the alphabet. Similarly, the convert should be willing to accept the fundamental premise that the Oral Torah, like the written one, derives from God.

While Hillel and Shammai concur that acceptance of the doctrine of the Oral Torah is essential to a legitimate Jewish ideology, they hardly propose that this is all that is required. Rather, such an article of faith functions as no more than a starting point, on the basis of which the individual must go on to learn the full extent of the theology and practice of Judaism. Fundamental doctrines of Judaism thus exist, and, as we shall see in the following, they may even be understood as encapsulating the overall meaning of the religion. Even so, these beliefs serve as no more than starting places for a complete life as a Jew. Simple acceptance of their truth brings no special merit before God. This is made clear in the continuation of the preceding passage, at B. Shab. 30b:

> A. There was another case of a gentile who came before Shammai. He said to him, "Convert me on the stipulation that you teach me the entire Torah while I am standing on one foot."
> B. He drove him off with the building cubit that he had in his hand.
> C. He came before Hillel: "Convert me."
> D. He said to him, "What is hateful to you, to your fellow do not do. That is the entirety of the Torah; everything else is elaboration. So go, study."

Again the difference between Hillel and Shammai results from their respective personalities, not from different perceptions of what one must believe or do to be a Jew. Hillel, no different from Shammai, asserts that Judaism demands observance of all of the commandments. But he, unlike Shammai, is patient with the perspective convert and able to articulate a moral message that he understands to lie at the heart of the commandments: do not do to your neighbor that which is hateful to you. But even for Hillel, acceptance of this moral imperative is only a beginning, to be followed by study and, we must assume, acceptance of the rules of Jewish behavior and practice of the entire range of Jewish laws and rituals. This is what Hillel demands of the convert when he adjures him to "go, study."

While Hillel is made the hero of the preceding narrative, Shammai's perspective makes clear the extent to which, within the Rabbinic perception of matters, it is possible to live as a Jew, or even to become a convert to Judaism, without knowing or acknowledging the truth of a maxim such as Hillel says encapsulates all of Torah. This is because, within the Rabbinic system, knowing and accepting some truth believed to stand behind all of the laws in no event is sufficient. What matters, rather, is the actual observance of the Torah's laws. This means that even one who accepts as true all of Judaism's articles of faith cannot be considered to be living properly as a Jew unless he or she also has knowledge of and practices the individual laws of Torah.

The long passage at B. Mak. 23b-24a illustrates the extent to which, for the Talmudic rabbis, the reduction of Judaism to a creed was an intellectual exercise rather than a reflection of a practical interest in determining the few single ideas the acceptance of which defines the good Jew. In the passage before us, the Talmudic rabbis search through Scripture for lists of moral principles to which all people largely can agree. The point is not that the six hundred and thirteen commandments can be replaced by the acceptance of one or two such principles, only that, through such principles, one can understand the purpose and intent of the commandments:

> A. R. Simelai expounded, "Six hundred and thirteen commandments were given to Moses, three hundred and sixty-five negative ones, corresponding to the number of the days of the solar year, and two hundred forty-eight positive commandments, corresponding to the parts of man's body."
> B. Said R. Hamnuna, "What verse of Scripture indicates that fact? 'Moses commanded us Torah, an inheritance of the congregation of Jacob' (Deut. 33:4). The numerical value assigned to the letters of the word Torah is [24A] six hundred and eleven, [to which you must add the two additional commandments], 'I am' and 'you shall have no other gods,' [which] have come to us [directly] from the mouth of the Almighty."
> C. [Simelai continues:] "David came and reduced them to eleven: 'A Psalm of David: Lord, who shall sojourn in thy tabernacle, and who shall dwell in thy holy mountain? (1) He who walks uprightly and (2) works righteousness and (3) speaks truth in his heart and (4) has no slander on his tongue and (5) does no evil to his fellow and (6) does not take up a reproach against his neighbor, (7) in whose eyes a vile person is despised but (8) honors those who fear the Lord. (9) He swears to his own hurt and changes not. (10) He does not lend on interest. (11) He does not take a bribe against the innocent' (Ps. 15)."
> D. "He who walks uprightly:" this is Abraham: "Walk before me and be wholehearted" (Gen. 17:1).
> E. "and works righteousness:" this is Abba Hilqiahu.

F. "speaks truth in his heart:" for instance R. Safra.

G. "has no slander on his tongue:" this is our father, Jacob: "My father might feel me and I shall seem to him as a deceiver" (Gen. 27:12).

H. "does no evil to his fellow:" he does not go into competition with his fellow craftsman.

I. "does not take up a reproach against his neighbor:" this is someone who befriends his relatives.

J. "in whose eyes a vile person is despised:" this is Hezekiah, king of Judah, who dragged his father's bones on a rope bed.

K. "honors those who fear the Lord:" this is Jehoshaphat, king of Judah, who, whenever he would see a disciple of a sage, would rise from his throne and embrace and kiss him and call him, "My father, my father, my lord, my lord, my master, my master."

L. "He swears to his own hurt and changes not:" this is R. Yohanan.

M. For said R. Yohanan, "I shall continue fasting until I get home."

N. "He does not lend on interest:" not even interest from a gentile.

O. "He does not take a bribe against the innocent:" such as R. Ishmael b. R. Yose. . . .[5]

U. [Simelai continues:] "Isaiah came and reduced them to six: '(1) He who walks righteously and (2) speaks uprightly, (3) he who despises the gain of oppressions, (4) shakes his hand from holding bribes, (5) stops his ear from hearing of blood (6) and shuts his eyes from looking upon evil, he shall dwell on high' (Is. 33:25-26)."

V. "He who walks righteously:" this is our father, Abraham: "For I have known him so that he may command his children and his household after him" (Gen. 18:19).

W. "speaks uprightly:" this is one who does not belittle his fellow in public.

X. "he who despises the gain of oppressions:" for example, R. Ishmael b. Elisha.

Y. "shakes his hand from holding bribes:" for example, R. Ishmael b. R. Yose.

Z. "stops his ear from hearing of blood:" who will not listen to demeaning talk about a disciple of rabbis and remain silent.

AA. For instance, R. Eleazar b. R. Simeon.

BB. "and shuts his eyes from looking upon evil:" that is in line with what R. Hiyya bar Abba said.

CC. For said R. Hiyya bar Abba, "This is someone who does not stare at women as they are standing and washing clothes.

DD. Concerning such a man it is written, "he shall dwell on high" (Is. 33:5).

EE. [Simelai continues:] "Micah came and reduced them to three: 'It has been told you, man, what is good and what the Lord demands from you, (1) only to do justly and (2) to love mercy, and (3) to walk humbly before God' (Mic. 6:8)."

FF. "only to do justly:" this refers to justice.

GG. "to love mercy:" this refers to doing acts of loving kindness.

HH. "to walk humbly before God:" this refers to accompanying a corpse to the grave and welcoming the bride.

II. And does this not yield a conclusion *a fortiori*: if matters that are not ordinarily done in private are referred to by the Torah as "walking humbly before God," all the more so matters that ordinarily are done in private.

JJ. [Simelai continues:] "Isaiah again came and reduced them to two : 'Thus says the Lord, (1) Keep justice and (2) do righteousness' (Is. 56:1).

KK. "Amos came and reduced them to a single one, as it is said, 'For thus says the Lord to the house of Israel. Seek Me and live.'"

LL. Objected R. Nahman bar Isaac, "Maybe the sense is, 'seek me' through the whole of the Torah [so that this is not really a single encompassing commandment at all]?"

MM. Rather, [Simelai continues:] "Habakkuk further came and based them on one, as it is said, 'But the righteous shall live by his faith' (Hab. 2:4)."

The individuals—Abraham, Eleazar b. Simeon—whose lives illustrate some of the progressively shorter encapsulations of the commandments point to what Judaism in fact demands. This is not simply to accept an article of faith. Rather, it is to act in a way that is commensurate with that dogmatic statement. At base, this is to say, the Talmud presents here not articles of faith so much as moral principles that Jews are intended not only to accept but also to act upon in everyday life. Judaism, for instance, stands for being humble before God. But this principle is presented here not as a theological statement about the nature of God and humankind but, rather, as the foundation for a number of specific commandments: one must accompany a corpse to the grave, one must welcome a bride. Thus, even when we get to the end of the list, to the single idea that the rabbis argue encapsulates the entire Torah—"The righteous shall live by his faith"—we are not being told the single thing that one must *believe* in order to be a proper member of the Jewish community. The point, rather, is to represent in a few words what one is *doing* when one observes the totality of the law of Judaism. To live by this faith, in the sense of a system of life and practice, is to be righteous before God. That status of righteousness, according to Judaism, cannot be achieved simply through the acceptance of a creed but only through practice of the laws that the creed explains.

Creeds in the medieval period: By the tenth century, in response to internal pressure from the Karaite movement, which denied the authority of the Oral Torah, Jewish thinkers began in earnest systematically to formulate statements on Jewish belief. The goal of comprehensively expressing the content of Jewish belief so as to define who should or should not be deemed a good Jew paralleled similar efforts underway in the Islamic philosophical schools of that period. The Jewish thinkers referred to the articles of faith that resulted as "obligations of the heart" (*hovot halevavot*), "primary principles" (*hathalot*), "cornerstones" (*pinot*), and, most frequently, as "foundational beliefs" (*iqqarim*). The best known of these creeds were developed by Maimonides, Crescas, and Abravanel.

Maimonides: Although not the earliest formulation of a creed of Judaism, the thirteen principles of Maimonides (1135-1204) is among the best known and most important of all Jewish articles of faith. Presented in the context of his commentary to Mishnah Sanhedrin Chapter 10, Maimonides' principles define the "Epicurean" who, according to the Mishnah, has no share in the world to come. In the thirteen principles, Maimonides thus delineates the beliefs he holds to be nec-

essary and sufficient to assure an individual's salvation.

According to Maimonides, Judaism's fundamental principles are (1) that God exists and (2) is uniquely unitary; (3) God is not corporeal and cannot be accurately described in anthropomorphic terms; (4) God is eternal and (5) alone is to be worshipped; (6) God designated prophets, (7) the greatest of whom was Moses, who (8) received the entire Torah; (9) the Torah cannot be abrogated or in any way altered; (10) God knows people's deeds and (11) rewards or punishes them as appropriate; (12) the messiah will come, and (13) the dead will be resurrected.

Maimonides' thirteen principles became central in Judaism when, by about 1300, they were formulated as a hymn ("Yigdal"), which appears in almost all forms of the Jewish daily liturgy. By the mid-sixteenth century, these principles circulated in a clearly creedal formulation, introduced with the statement, "I believe with perfect faith that. . . ."

Crescas: Among the major critics of Maimonides' formulation, Chasdai Crescas (d. 1412) had the most enduring impact on the later development of Jewish creeds.[6] Crescas defined the formulation of a creed as a philosophical task, involving the logical ordering of beliefs so that basic axioms could yield secondary conceptions. Crescas additionally introduced the notion of intentionality, defining a heretic not by what he believes but by the perceived source of his belief. A heretic holds beliefs—whether right or wrong—that he understands to be independent of the teachings of the Torah. According to Crescas, but contrary to Maimonides, one who perceives his beliefs to derive from the Torah cannot be called a heretic, even if those beliefs are in fact false.

At the foundation of Crescas' creed are the notions of God's (1) existence, (2) unity, and (3) incorporeality. Six pillars stand on these root principles: (1) God's knowledge of people's deeds, (2) divine providence, (3) God's omnipotence, (4) the appointment of prophets, (5) free will, and (6) the role of the Torah in assuring eternal happiness. These pillars lead to eight additional beliefs that Crescas sees as characteristic of Judaism but not fundamental. These include (1) God's creation of the world, (2) human immortality, (3) divine retribution, (4) resurrection, (5) the immutability of the Torah, (6) that Moses was the greatest prophet, (7) the divine origin of priestly instruction, and (8) the coming of the messiah.

Abravanel: Isaac Abravanel (1437-1508) devoted an entire treatise to the formulations of Jewish belief developed by Maimonides, Crescas, and Joseph Albo (ca. 1380-ca. 1440). While raising numerous objections to Maimonides' thirteen principles, Abravanel ultimately allied himself with Maimonides, defining heresy, for instance, on the basis of the content of one's faith, without regard for the perceived source of the specific beliefs. At the same time, Abravanel broadly rejected the claim that any narrow selection of beliefs can accurately encompass the content of Judaism. He held, rather, that, since the Torah was divinely revealed, everything it contains must be accepted; no hierarchy of belief is possible. The rejection of any Jewish belief is heresy and denies the individual a place in the world to come.

Abravanel's unique attitude may result from his having composed it just two years after the expulsion of the Jews from Spain. The declaration that Jews must accept all aspects of Jewish belief possibly was intended to prevent any lessening of Jewish commitment in this trying circumstance. In Abravanel's view, Jews must accept the entirety of Judaism's beliefs, since all of the tenets of Judaism have equally salvific value.

The modern period: The modern period in the formulation of Jewish creeds was heralded by Moses Mendelssohn (1729-1786), who argued that Judaism, unlike Christianity, contains no dogmas. Judaism's truths, rather, are identical with the eternal truths discoverable through reason, independent of revelation. These truths are (1) that God, who created and rules all things, is one; (2) that God knows all and metes out rewards and punishment through natural and supernatural means; and (3) that God made his will known through Scripture. In Mendelssohn's view, these truths, which represent the content of all natural religions, are to be distinguished from Judaism's ritual laws, the only part of Judaism that depends upon revelation rather than reason.

The intellectual and social forces that stood behind Mendelssohn's formulation were harbingers to a new approach to Judaism that, between 1782 and 1884, led to the publication of some one hundred and sixty textbooks that systematically presented the Jewish religion. Among these were thirty-five catechisms, intended specifically to prepare students for the newly introduced Jewish ceremony of confirmation.[7] Previously, children had learned the fundamentals of Jewish belief through study of Rabbinic texts and, especially, through Rashi's commentary on the Pentateuch. Now, facing the increasing number of secular subjects that took up students' time and experiencing an intensifying disdain for traditional Talmudic study, more and more Jews found the traditional and time-consuming method of Torah-study to be unacceptable. At the same time, and perhaps most important, these enlightened Jews wished to understand Judaism as a modern "religion," intelligible on the same terms on which they increasingly accepted Christianity as a legitimate system of religion and ethics. Stripped of any special claim to legitimacy, Judaism, like all other faiths, was to be understood through reference to its "universal foundations and moral contents, without too much concern for its many observances" (Petuchowski, p. 53). Judaism thus was to be viewed as but one manifestation of, or supplement to, what was understood as a universal religious truth. In 1808, Herz Homberg phrased matters as follows (cited in Petuchowski, pp. 53-53):

> Any man, of any nation in the world, attains to spiritual bliss if, while still alive, he fills his soul with wisdom, and conducts himself in all of his actions according to the ways of righteousness and wisdom, which are acceptable to God and man. That is why the Talmudists said: "The righteous of the nations of the world have a share in the World-to-Come."

While Homberg goes on, as did Mendelssohn, to argue that Jews have the special and unique obligation to observe the entire law of the Torah, his fundamental perspective is clear. Judaism, like all religions, is legitimated by the fact that it stands for righteousness and wisdom. Judaism thus is no different from and has no advantage over any religion that leads to the attainment of happiness and bliss, acquired through the promotion of righteousness and wisdom. Judaism thus is and can be defined as a "confession," exactly similar to the other religions whose acceptance Jews in this period craved.

In line with this approach, the textbooks and creeds of this period are primarily concerned not with Jewish ritual observances but with ethical duties and creedal affirmations. The ethical duties generally are introduced through the ten commandments, which frequently are described as representing the sum total of what God directly revealed to Israel. These creeds thus mark the emergence of the new approach to Judaism later to be formalized in the Reform movement. If the Ten Commandments, *but not the rest of Torah*, were given by God, then a wide range of practices and rituals that previously defined the Jewish way of life may now be rejected as unrelated to the authentic core contents and meaning of the faith. The creedal affirmations, for their part, generally depend upon Maimonides' Thirteen Principles, the truth of which was understood to accord with and be discernible through reason (Petuchowski, pp. 55-56).

The Pittsburgh Platform: The most complete and profound modern statement of the content and meaning of Judaism was produced beginning in 1869 by a committee of Reform rabbis that including the well known David Einhorn and was chaired by Samuel Hirsch. The resulting platform was ratified by the Central Conference of American Rabbis in Pittsburgh in 1885, at a meeting called by Kaufmann Kohler, son-in-law of the by-then deceased Einhorn. Through the Pittsburgh Platform, the American Reform rabbinate responded to the issues that divided Jews concerning Jewish belief and obligatory ritual practice. They worked to produce an authoritative statement that would express the position of the Reform movement on the overall nature and content of Judaism.[8]

Striking is that Reform rabbis in this period felt such an urgent need to specify the content and purpose of Judaism and that they conceived of a process of debate and discussion as an appropriate means to achieve this formulation. While, as we have seen, in their period, catechisms increasingly were being written, theirs was the most ambitious attempt yet to produce a final and authoritative characterization of a totally modern Judaism. We must keep in mind that prior to the modern period, conceptions of the content and meaning of Judaism had not even, for the most part, emerged as mandates from rabbis, and they certainly were not the products of democratic debate. Rather, the worldview of Judaism generally had been defined by what the people actually did, by the rituals they performed and by the lives they lived within their closed communities. This Jewish world-view hardly had been reducible to a formal statement of creed at all. It was, rather, located only in the consensus of Jews about how things are to be done, how life is to be lived. In the contrast between the new Reform approach and the way Judaism previously had been defined, we see the extent to which the Reform movement represented a truly new kind of Judaism, a Judaism specifically addressed to the issues that faced Jews in the nineteenth and then twentieth centuries.

In Pittsburgh, American Reform rabbis issued a concise statement that was to represent to the American public as a whole, as much as to Reform Jews, the essential purpose and content of Judaism. The complete text of the Pittsburgh Platform is as follows:[9]

> First—We recognize in every religion an attempt to grasp the Infinite One, and in every mode, source or book of revelation held sacred in any religious system the consciousness of the indwelling of God in man. We hold that Judaism presents the highest conception of the God-idea as taught in our holy Scriptures and developed and spiritualized by the Jewish teachers in accordance with the moral and philosophical progress of their respective ages. We maintain that Judaism preserved and defended amid continual struggles and trials and under enforced iso-

lation this God-idea as the central religious truth for the human race.

Second—We recognize in the Bible the record of the consecration of the Jewish people to its mission as the priest of the One God, and value it as the most potent instrument of religious and moral instruction. We hold that the modern discoveries of scientific researches in the domains of nature and history are not antagonistic to the doctrines of Judaism, the Bible reflecting the primitive ideas of its own age and at times clothing its conception of divine providence and justice dealing with man in miraculous narratives.

Third—We recognize in the Mosaic legislation a system of training the Jewish people for its mission during its national life in Palestine, and today we accept as binding only its moral laws and maintain only such ceremonials as elevate and sanctify our lives, but reject all such as are not adapted to the views and habits of modern civilization.

Fourth—We hold that all such Mosaic and Rabbinical laws as regulate diet, priestly purity and dress originated in ages and under the influence of ideas altogether foreign to our present mental and spiritual state. They fail to impress the modern Jew with a spirit of priestly holiness; their observance in our day is apt rather to obstruct than to further modern spiritual elevation.

Fifth—We recognize in the modern era of universal culture of heart and intellect the approach of the realization of Israel's great Messianic hope for the establishment of the Kingdom of truth, justice and peace among all men. We consider ourselves no longer a nation but a religious community, and therefore expect neither a return to Palestine, nor a sacrificial worship under the administration of the sons of Aaron, nor the restoration of any of the laws concerning the Jewish state.

Sixth—We recognize in Judaism a progressive religion, ever striving to be in accord with the postulates of reason. We are convinced of the utmost necessity of preserving the historical identity with our great past. Christianity and Islam being daughter religions of Judaism, we appreciate their mission to aid in the spreading of monotheistic and moral truth. We acknowledge that the spirit of broad humanity of our age is our ally in the fulfilment of our mission, and therefore we extend the hand of fellowship to all who co-operate with us in the establishment of the reign of truth and righteousness among men.

Seventh—We reassert the doctrine of Judaism, that the soul of man is immortal, grounding this belief on the divine nature of the human spirit, which forever finds bliss in righteousness and misery in wickedness. We reject as ideas not rooted in Judaism the belief both in bodily resurrection and in Gehenna and Eden (hell and paradise), as abodes for everlasting punishment or reward.

Eighth—In full accordance with the spirit of Mosaic legislation which strives to regulate the relation between rich and poor, we deem it our duty to participate in the great task of modern times, to solve on the basis of justice and righteousness the problems presented by the contrasts and evils of the present organization of society.

The Pittsburgh Platform conceives Judaism as but one religion among many, an evolutionary and progressive faith that contains an essential core of moral-laws and concepts of God. The platform sees Scripture and later Rabbinic texts as human writings that record conceptions of the divine in the primitive terms appropriate to people of prior ages. This means that Judaism, in its essence, should not be viewed as contradicting the essential truths of science and philosophy, even if these truths necessitate the rejection of inherited laws and traditional attitudes and beliefs. Indeed, at the heart of this Reform statement is an absolute trust in science and modern philosophical thinking, a certainty that, through these human activities, people will move the world towards a perfect state, themselves bringing about the messianic age.

Rather than a nation or political entity obligated to maintain an inherited culture and system of behaviors, Jews comprise a religious confession. They are united by their dedication to promoting social justice and their devotion to the other causes that will lead humankind to perfect morality and equality. Thus one of its most striking elements is the Pittsburgh Platform's rejection of all ritual that does not have a specific and discernible function in elevating the human spirit towards the fulfillment of the goals seen here to define Judaism. Judaism, and religion in general, is no longer to be viewed as a comforting context for tradition and ethnicity, as a mode of creating and sustaining social alliances and distinctive communities. It is, rather, primarily an agent for social progress and the achievement of broad moral and economic goals, goals that all people and all religions share.

The world-view expressed here thus emphasizes the as-yet unrealized but soon-to-come perfect age, an age that it is the mission of the Jews to help bring about. Only in light of this special mission do the Jews continue to form a group at all. Unlike in all past understandings of Judaism, that is, their separateness is now seen to result only from their membership in a distinctive confession. But they are not any longer to be conceived of as a nation or political entity, and, indeed, the way of life defined here admits no cultural or religious traits that would distinguish Jews from others. This is because morality is universal, applicable in the same way to everyone. And so just as Judaism is but one among many "true" religions, so Jews are just like everyone else, demarcated only by the faith into which they are born.

Emet ve-Emunah: The modern Conservative movement's first attempt at a statement of beliefs and principles was published in 1988, under the heading *Emet ve-Emunah: Statement of Principles of Conservative Judaism*. In this document, the leaders of the movement, who had long been criticized for their inability to produce a positive statement of the movement's principles, finally attempted to delineate a Conservative approach on a wide range of issues. The result, however, is not a statement of creed such as the Pittsburgh Platform or the modern catechisms that preceded it. Rather, in *Emet ve-Emunah*, the traditional notion of Judaism as a religion defined primarily by what one does rather than by what one believes means that, particular attention is devoted to the current status of Jewish law. Jack Wertheimer describes this Conservative attitude as it emerges in *Emet ve-Emunah* and a number of new Conservative prayer books and other documents:[10]

> Although the new publications do not speak with one voice or suggest anything resembling unanimity, several trends are evident. First and foremost, Conservative Judaism reiterated its desire to occupy the center of the religious spectrum: the statement of prin-

ciples speaks of "the indispensability of Halakhah" and "the norms taught by the Jewish traditions." By emphasizing a normative approach to Jewish religious behavior, the Conservative movement rejected the Reform and Reconstructionist positions. Simultaneously, the statement distances itself from Orthodoxy by taking note of "development in Halakhah," and though cautioning that "the burden of proof is on the one who wants to alter" Jewish laws, it affirms the right of Conservative religious authorities to interpret and adjust Jewish law as understood by the halakhic process of Conservative Judaism.

Important here is that, at the center of the Conservative definition of Judaism remains the concept of Halakhah, that Jews are defined not so much by what they believe as by what they do.[11] The central issue in defining Judaism thus remains, as Wertheimer's description makes clear, the development of a theory of how Halakhah is to be applied in modern times. Conservative Judaism is demarcated as "seeking a centrist path between extreme positions" (Wertheimer, p. 151). It understands Judaism not as a system of core beliefs that can be delineated in a code, but as a "disciplinary way of life that is dynamic and evolving."[12]

Conclusion: Jewish thinkers have continually attempted to identify elements of Judaism that uniquely define its system of religious beliefs. Indeed, by 1937, Reform rabbis, now meeting in Columbus, Ohio, had reframed the system of the Pittsburgh Platform so as to express a world-view quite different from that of the half-century before.[13] In this way, theologians within Reform Judaism in particular have worked from decade to decade to respond to the distinctive needs of their day, offering clear guidance regarding the essential beliefs that derive from the writings of Judaism. By defining what Jews must believe, these reformers have still countered traditionalists, who continue to focus upon the rituals that Jews must practice rather than the beliefs they must hold.[14]

For the nineteenth and twentieth century Jew, as for the Jew of the enlightenment, the importance of such systematic statements of

Jewish belief cannot be underestimated. This is because, as Jacob Katz noted in reference to the nineteenth century, in an extended period marked by a steady decline of the traditional Jewish way of life, "when all other ties of the individual to the Jewish community disintegrated, these systems taught and promoted the consciousness of the peculiar value and meaning of the Jewish identity."[15]

Religions that have emerged over long periods of time naturally encompass a diversity of views and attitudes towards the essentials of the faith as well as towards the laws and practices through which that faith is expressed. For the reasons we have seen, this has been particularly true in the case of Judaism, which, despite the attempts of the period of the enlightenment, has not come to be defined through tenets of faith the acceptance of which demarcates the true believer from the heretic. Jews through history, rather, have been generally tolerant of a wide range of formulations of Jewish theology at the same time that, until modern times, Jewish elites have been unaccepting of variety and diversity in the area of practice. Contrary to the case for Christianity and Islam, Jews thus have largely been allowed to think what they will, while correct interpretation of canonical documents and practice of the Torah's law have determined proper standing in the community and before God.

Notes

[1] On this, see HERESY, APOSTACY.

[2] See John H. Leith, "Creeds, Early Christian," in *Anchor Bible Dictionary*, vol. I, p. 1204.

[3] On this, see Harry Wolfson, *Philo, Foundations of Religious Philosophy* (Cambridge, 1947),

vol. 1, pp. 164-199. The enumeration of Philo's truths cited in the following is on p. 164.

[4] The passage appears in an expanded version at *The Fathers According to Rabbi Nathan* XV:V.1. The expansions are included here in brackets, marked ARN.

[5] The following lines, P-T, which are omitted here, concern the meaning of the final verse of Ps. 15, not cited above at C and not relevant to the current discussion.

[6] For a complete account of Crescas' critique of Maimonides and an analysis of his own formulation, see JUDAISM, PHILOSOPHY AND THEOLOGY OF, IN MEDIEVAL TIMES.

[7] On the following, see Jakob Petuchowski, "Manuals and Catechisms of the Jewish Religion in the Early Period of Emancipation," in Alexander Altmann, ed., *Studies in Nineteenth-Century Jewish Intellectual History* (Cambridge, 1964), p. 47.

[8] For an additional discussion of the Pittsburgh Paltform, see REFORM JUDAISM.

[9] "Declaration of Principles Adopted by a Group of Reform Rabbis at Pittsburgh, 1885," in *The Yearbook of the Central Conference of American Rabbis* XLV (1935), pp. 198-200.

[10] *A People Divided: Judaism in Contemporary America* (New York, 1993), p. 151.

[11] The second and third elements that Wertheimer notes as emerging here are the open embrace of religious pluralism and support for gender equality.

[12] Ismar Schorsch, cited by Wertheimer, p. 152.

[13] This platform, however, was widely ignored and rejected for its positive attitude towards Zionism and its call for increased ritual practice, in particular its statement of the centrality of Hebrew and of the importance of Sabbath and festival observance.

[14] Note in this regard the position of Samson Raphael Hirsch (1808-1888), the first spokesman for a modern orthodoxy, who proposed that "the catechism of the Jew is his calendar."

[15] Jacob Katz, "Jewry and Judaism in the Nineteenth Century," in *Journal of World History* 4:894 (1958), cited in Petuchowski, p. 58.

ALAN J. AVERY-PECK

D

THE DEAD SEA WRITINGS: Medieval sources report about book scrolls found near the Dead Sea. It seems probable that the extant Geniza fragments of the *Zadokite Documents* and of the Hebrew *Ben Sira* represent remains of copies made from scrolls similar to them. These were found by Beduins in 1947 in caves near Khirbet Qumran, and it is there that, during subsequent archaeological campaigns, the so-called Dead Sea Scrolls were located. These consist primarily of leather pieces of various sizes, sewn together to form scrolls of sometimes considerable length. The longest of the more or less well preserved texts, the Temple Scroll (11Q19), is extant in manuscripts as long as 8.75 meters, and one of the so-called "Pentateuch paraphrases" (3Q364 + 365) was originally probably more than 20 meters long. Others are of a miniature size, for instance the scrolls containing texts from Canticles (4Q106-108).

The scrolls are written in columns of a more or less equal number of lines. Some of them are on papyrus, and these are in a bad state of preservation. But due to the excellent quality of the black, and in few instances red, ink that was used, the script in all events remains relatively easy to read. Of all the materials, only those from Cave 1 (of 11), in which the scrolls had been wrapped in linen clothes and stored in clay jars, are more or less whole and intact. Over time, most of the jars were smashed by falling stones, and thus even these scrolls were exposed to physical damage, including nibbling by mice. Some of the jars too appear to have been broken or taken away by Bedouins, who frequently entered the caves. Unaware of the material's worth, they may have removed and destroyed a considerable amount.

What can be said is that the careful process of storage of the scrolls in Cave 1 indicates a well planned activity of production and archiving over a long period. By contrast, about 700 scrolls of various sizes and lengths seem to have been placed in haste in the other caves, particularly Cave 4. This probably occurred after the beginning of the Jewish war against the Romans in 66 C.E.

The physical nature of the material has been carefully investigated, and according to improved methods of radio-carbon dating, the scrolls could not have been produced earlier than 250 B.C.E. or later than 68 C.E. This dating of the material corresponds perfectly to the paleographic evidence. The largest number of scrolls were written in the first century B.C.E., in the Hasmonean and early Herodian periods; a smaller number was produced during the second century B.C.E.; and a few texts are of an even earlier date. Another small portion was written or copied during the first century C.E. until 68 C.E., the late Herodian period.

Except for some early published scrolls that are still designated by abbreviations indicating the cave number and scroll contents (1QH, 1QM, 1QS, 1QGenAp, 1QIs^{a-b}, 1QpHab), it is now common practice to cite the individual scrolls or texts by their running numbers according to the cave in which they were found (1Q1-75; 2Q1-33; 3Q1-15; 4Q1-475; 5Q1-25; 6Q1-31; 7Q1-19; 8Q5; 9Q1; 10Q1; 11Q1-25). In some instances, the assignment of fragments remains difficult, time consuming, and uncertain, since, rather than assigning to every fragment a number of its own, the early editors simply numbered the photographs of whole groups of fragments. This was done even though the fragments in these photographs had been placed together by mere chance.

Manuscript, copy, text: For a long time it was deemed possible to establish the importance or authority of a text by evaluating its size and scribal characteristics. The form of the script and the particular use of the tetragrammaton and other names of God seemed to indicate the relative significance of the scroll within the corpus as a whole. This assumption has not been corroborated by the evidence of later publications. Thus the relationship between scribal character and manuscript form, on the one side, and authoritative or practical significance, on the other, is still unclear and needs further investigation.

The extant manuscripts are in most cases not original writings produced by their authors ("autographs") but copies of existing texts. Indeed, in some cases, we have numerous such copies, or fragments of copies, with more or less identical contents. While in most cases, we would expect a dating of the underlying text earlier than that of the copy, the situation is actually complex. This is because several manuscripts are composites, combining materials extant as literary units or as components of other writings that existed prior the redaction of the respective scrolls. Such pre-formulated fluctuent elements and compounds provoke significant questions concerning the dating and status or authority of the contents of a scroll.

In general it may be assumed that the

manuscripts served a practical purpose for the group that created them, such that a correspondence is likely between importance and number of extant exemplars. Application of this principle however is confounded by the differing contents even of exemplars of one and the same underlying text. Additionally, we must ask a number of pertinent questions: What of the materials was collected for purely archival objectives? What was written for programmatic purposes? What in fact comprised the regulations that, according to some statements in the scrolls, were to be observed until the end of a certain "period of iniquity" and the beginning of the new era under the "anointed ones of Aaron and Israel and a (new Torah) prophet" (1QS IX, 10-11; CD XIX-XX)? In addition, a sociological point of view should be considered: The Zadokite priests who produced and transmitted such manuscripts represented an intellectual elite, and their literary activities probably transcended the actual demands of any Jewish group of that time. Consequently, we should not deduce from the Qumran evidence a similar intellectual level and linguistic capacity (particularly in Hebrew) for the majority of these Zadokite priests' contemporaries.

Pre-Qumranic, non-Qumranic and Qumranic literary production: As just suggested, a crucial issue beyond the dating of entire scrolls and texts is the dating of the literary components incorporated in these documents' complex compositions. This dating depends upon literary analyses that routinely yields equivocal results and normally allows no more than a putative, relative chronological sequence of components; only in rare cases is a firm chronology possible. Even so, reconstruction of the history of literary activity at Qumran depends upon such analyses and datings, resulting to date in a great diversity of views.

Prior to the publication of the fragments from 4Q and 11Q, almost all descriptions of the scrolls and reconstructions of the history of the supposed community behind them were based on the dating of the scrolls from 1Q in their ultimate redactional shape. This

dating, correlated with the dates known from our main historical sources, Flavius Josephus and the *Books of the Maccabees*, placed the founding of the Qumran settlement in about 130 B.C.E. Today it is clear that the situation was by far more complicated and that the settlement at Qumran did not occur until about 100 B.C.E. Accordingly, a considerable number of texts regarded initially as testimonies of the Qumran community itself appear now to be pre-Qumranic, whether in whole or in part. All the same, the early published texts continue to provide for many scholars the decisive criteria for defining the "sectarian" character of the supposed Qumran *yahad*-community. A re-examination of the literary evidence and its chronological implications is, therefore, indispensable.

Of pre-Qumranic origin (third to early second centuries B.C.E.) we find (omitting biblical manuscripts):

(1) A fragment of a text called "Apocryphon Joseph[b]" or "Psalms of Joshua" (4Q372 frg. 1), written about 200 B.C.E.

(2) Texts written during the second century before ca. 130 B.C.E.: 4Q201, 4Q202, and 4Q213-214 (Test. Levi); 4Q216a (Jub.); 4Q365 ("Reworked Pentateuch"); 4Q378 (Psalms of Joshua); 4Q504 (*Dibrey ha-Me'orot*).

(3) Some of the manuscripts written during the early Hasmonean period (130-ca. 63 B.C.E.), consisting at least in part of pre-Qumranic components: 4Q123 ("Parabiblical Joshua"); 4Q124 (?); 4Q125 (?); 4Q156 (Targum on Lev.); 4Q298 (4QCryptic); 4Q318; 4Q409 (Liturgy); 4Q448 and 4Q502-4Q503 (liturgical texts); 4Q512 (ritual/legal text); 4Q529 ("Words of Michael"); 4Q534 (4QNoah); 4Q540-4Q541 (Test. Levi); 4Q542 (Test. Kahat); 5Q13 (historical/legal); 5Q14 (maledictions); 6Q8 (Book of Giants); 7Q2 (Epistle of Jer.); 11Q05 (Psalms).

Almost certainly pre-Qumranic as well are the large literary components (sources) of the Temple Scroll, and probably also its final redaction. As the Temple Scroll contains laws that in part correspond to regulations in the Zadokite documents, 4QMMT, and related legal texts from 4Q ("Ordinances"), these manuscripts together represent a remarkable pre-Qumranic heritage that cannot be regarded as "sectarian." The same is true for most liturgical texts that probably derive from official Temple liturgies in use before the reign of Antiochus IV.

The literary and historical analysis of the texts is still in its initial phases. Unfortunately, certain religious concepts of special importance within Christian thinking—particularly eschatology, messiah, and messianism—still determine the direction of the research, while the legal heritage and its application, the very core of the tradition and the controversies of that time, have long remained of only secondary interest. A re-evaluation of the Qumran literature should, therefore, begin with the analysis of the traditions that, according to the sources themselves, actually shaped the life and interests of the people behind the texts: Torah and related legal topics, including specific cultic and ritual regulations.

Script and language: A small number of manuscripts, all but one of these containing biblical books, was copied in the ancient Hebrew script: 1Q03 (Lev.), 2Q05 (Lev.), 6Q01 (Gen.), 6Q02 (Lev.), 11Q01 (Lev.), 4Q11 (Gen./Exod.), 4Q12 (Gen.), 4Q22 (Exod.), 4Q45 and 4Q46 (Deut.), 4Q101 (Job), 4Q123 (a Joshua text?), 4Q124 (= ?), 4Q125 (= ?). In some scrolls only the tetragrammaton appears in such characters: 1Q15, 3Q03, 4Q26, 4Q160, 4Q161, 4Q171, 4Q183, 11Q05. Sometimes the word 'el, God, appears this way as well: 1Q14, 1Q27, 1Q35, 3Q14, 4Q179, 4Q183, 4Q258, 4Q406, 6Q15, 6Q18. In cryptic texts single words or letter sometimes appear in ancient Hebrew and also in Greek (e.g., 4Q186). At present it remains impossible to determine the motives for the use of the ancient Hebrew script for some of the biblical texts. Maybe, as is supposed by some scholars, these manuscripts are of non-Qumranic origin.

About one hundred texts are written in Aramaic: 1Q20/1QGenAp, 1Q21 (Test. Levi), 1Q23 (Book of Giant), 1Q24, 1Q32 (New Jerusalem), 1Q63-1Q68, 2Q24 (New Jerusalem), 2Q26 (Book of Giants), 3Q12, 3Q13, 3Q14, 4Q156 (Lev.), 4Q157 (Job),

4Q196-199 (Tobit), 4Q201-207 and 4Q210-212 (1 Enoch), 4Q213-214 (Test. Levi), 4Q242 ("Prayer of Nabonid"), 4Q243-246 ("Pseudo-Daniel"), 4Q309-310, 4Q318 (calendrical text), 4Q342 and 4Q344-348 (contracts), 4Q355 and 4Q359 (administrative texts), 4Q488-490 (apocalyptic texts?), 4Q529 ("Words of Michael"), 4Q530-533 (Book of Giants), 4Q534 (Noah-text), 4Q535-536, 4Q537 ("Visions of Jacob"), 4Q538-539 (texts about the patriarchs), 4Q540-541 (Test. Levi), 4Q542 (Test. Qahat), 543-548 ("Visions of Amram"), 4Q549 (about Hur/Miriam), 4Q550 ("Proto-Esther"), 4Q551 (Daniel/Susannah), 4Q552-553 ("Four kingdoms"), 4Q554 ("New Jerusalem"), 4Q555-558 (visions), 4Q559 (chronology), 4Q560 (Proverbs), 4Q561 (horoscope), 4Q562-575. 5Q15 (New Jerusalem), 5Q24, 6Q08 and (?) 6Q14 (Book of Giants), 6Q19, 6Q23 (Speech of Michael), 6Q31, 11Q10 (Job), 11Q18 ("New Jerusalem"). Aramaic was the language of every day life and of affairs. Within Jewish usage, certain narrative and scientific traditions of a more international character, however, seem also to have been transmitted in that language.

Texts in Greek are relatively rare, most of them translations of biblical texts (4Q76-4Q82, 4Q119-4Q122; 4Q126-127) and, strikingly, all the (very badly preserved) papyrus fragments from Cave 7 (7Q01-7Q19). Some of the latter (particularly 7Q5) have been—unconvincingly—identified with New Testament passages.

Classification criteria—the impact of traditional concepts of the Jewish and Christian canon: Of far reaching consequence to research in the scrolls was the initial, intensive engagement primarily of Christian biblical scholars. Their interest and approach included presuppositions that matched their own religious conceptions more than they represented the reality of Judaism in the last three centuries B.C.E. The most significant presupposition imputed to the period of the scrolls a scriptural canon corresponding to the Christian "Bible" or, at least, the Rabbinic "Holy Scriptures." In line with this perspective, scholars categorized the texts as biblical or non-biblical and further defined those in the latter category according to their purported relationships to biblical sources. Thus we have paraphrases, interpretations, rewritten or reworked biblical texts, para-biblical texts, and apocryphal or pseudepigraphic writings. Notably, the Qumran texts themselves provide no basis for such a theory of classification and evaluation.

The fragmentary condition of most texts also has meant that definitions of individual pieces based on content and form cannot be maintained once numbers of fragments are identified and assembled. In light of the preponderance of fragmentary texts, it thus remains preferable to be cautious. Further, some of the better preserved manuscripts are collections of texts made up of formally diverse components from different ages. These contain various genres and lack a convincing compositional device that creates of the parts a unitary scroll. Thus the majority of the sources are unlike the Temple Scroll, which may be defined as a carefully redacted "Torah Book."

It is impossible to classify all of the material exclusively according to biblical criteria, a state of affairs demonstrated by F. García Martínez in his Spanish, English, and Italian translations. Instead, he allotted the texts to a number of groups: "Rules," "Halakhic texts," "Literature with eschatological contents," "Exegetical literature," "Para Biblical literature," "Poetic texts," "Liturgical texts," "Astronomical texts, calendars etc." Notwithstanding certain advantages, even this scheme yields inevitable contradictions. The Temple Scroll, for example, which presents itself as a book of Torah, appears under the rubric "Exegetical literature" but has nothing in common with the Pesharim, neither content, genre, nor purpose. The "Wisdom" texts, which offer important theological statements, appear as "Poetic texts," a label that also fits most of the "Liturgical texts." In light of such insoluble difficulties, the German translation of 1996 simply presented the texts according to their running numbers for cave and text.

The most convincing and informative manner of presenting the texts depends primarily upon their description, indicating contents and purposes. The composite character of many scrolls means that separate consideration must be given to each of their major components.

The relationship of the finds to biblical texts: Among the remains of ca. eight hundred manuscripts, a quarter are identified as belonging to biblical texts. This judgment applies to 137 of the 575 items from Cave 4; to 17 of 33 from Cave 2; to seventeen of seventy-six items from Cave 1; to ten of twenty-five items from Cave 11; to seven of twenty-five items from Cave 5; to seven of thirty-one from Cave 6; to three of fifteen from Cave 3; to two of five items from Cave 8; and to one of nineteen items from Cave 7 (excepting the texts in Greek). This is significant, since the Qumran scrolls are about a thousand years older than any other known biblical manuscripts. Contrary to widespread assumptions, the biblical texts from Qumran are not distinguished by specific scribal characteristics. Additionally, not all of the biblical books are well attested: Chronicles, Ezra/Nehemiah, and Esther are probably not extant at all, and some apparently biblical fragments may contain only citations or parallel passages.

In any case, the concept "biblical" or "canonical" is anachronistic when applied to the scrolls. Based on the number of manuscript exemplars and the intensity of their employment in citations, only a few biblical texts appear to have any special significance within the corpus. Except the Psalter, which, as a selection of "Psalms of David," had the reputation of prophetic poetry, most books now referred to as belonging to the hagiographa—the third part of the Jewish Scripture—played an inferior role compared even with non-biblical books, such as Jubilees, Enoch, the Zadokite documents, and others. The following list of extant exemplars of biblical books, showing the approximate number of citations or clear applications, demonstrates the rather low significance of a number of books.

Book	Exemplars	Citations
Genesis	17	40
Exodus	17 (15)	38
Numbers	7	29
Leviticus	12	76
Deuteronomy	29	110
Isaiah	20	112 (exc. pIs)
Jeremiah	5	17
Ezekiel	6	20
Daniel	7	
XII Prophets	8	
Amos	(1)	4
Habakkuk	4	4 (except 1QpHab)
Hosea		17
Joel		2
Malachi		4
Micah		13
Nahum		8 (except 4QpNah)
Zechariah		7
Zephaniah		2
Psalter	36 (38)	60 (exc. pPs)
Joshua	2	1
Judges	3	
Samuel	4	7
Kings	3	4
Chronicles	(1??)	
Job	6	3
Proverbs	2	3
Canticles	4	
Ecclesiastes	3	
Ruth	4	
Lamentations	4	4
Book of Jubilees	16	
Zadokite documents	12	
1QS	11 (13?)	
1QH	9	
Book of Giants	8	
Enoch books	7	
Shirot ʿolat ha-shabbat	8	
1QM	7	
4QMMT	6	
New Jerusalem	6	
Tobit	5	
11QTemple Scroll	3	
Sirach	1	2
Book HHGHW (= ?)		4

Of particular importance, evidently, were the books of the Pentateuch, with Deuteronomy in first place. This high status is due to the legal materials that, while not representing the whole of the (written) "Torah," form part of a concept of Torah that includes much more than the "canonical" materials. The significance of Genesis is different, since it includes narrative traditions employed to express certain legal and theological issues. It also appears from this evidence that the boundaries of the canon were deemed immaterial, with an impressive amount of non-canonical materials being used for the same purposes as the canonical books.

The books of the Prophets form the second important group of texts, and among them the book of Isaiah was of an obviously exceptional importance. A prominent position may be ascribed as well to the Psalter and, beyond it, probably to all liturgical compositions related to David (cf., 11Q05 XXVII,2-11: 4050 pieces!). Psalms of David had the reputation of prophetic poetry and were therefore also subject to Pesher-interpretation. Essentially, every text subject to such interpretation was deemed a prophetic revelation, whether part of a biblical prophetic book or not.

Remnants of Aramaic translations have been found for two biblical texts, one for Leviticus (second century B.C.E.) and two exemplars of Job (first century C.E.). Their relationship to the later Rabbinic Targums and their purpose remains unclear.

Items related to Biblical texts—The Pesher: A Pesher-interpretation is an easily identified literary genre in which biblical wording forms the basis of an alleged interpretative statement. Yet, as we shall see below, the Pesher provides no actual explanation of the text. Its hermeneutic procedure accordingly differs fundamentally from that of an authoritative juridical reading, designated in this literature by the term le-horot ("to direct a Torah command to somebody;" "to enact a Torah regulation") or lidrosh ("to proclaim a Torah regulation as valid for;" "to proclaim a Torah regulation as applicable . . .").

The paraphrase: While the so-called "paraphrases," that is, the "re-worked" or "rewritten" pentateuchal texts, such as 4Q364-367, originally were works of considerable length, they are all poorly preserved. Their relationship to their underlying pentateuchal sources and their purpose needs further investigation. Until now it has been assumed that the biblical text formed the foundation for the composition of the non-biblical content of the paraphrase.

Treatments of prophetic books: A wide range of writings is associated with the name of Ezekiel, from variant textual traditions of the biblical book to elaborate, independent compositions. Ezekiel was probably regarded primarily as a priestly prophet, concerned with knowledge about heavenly things. The Jeremiah traditions in 4Q385b may have formed part of a literature concerning the fate of the first Temple and the exile, with a purpose close to that of the liturgical Lamentations and Consolations. Striking also is the volume of texts and materials related to the prophet Daniel. These particularly involve eschatological interpretations of historical and actual events.

Extant non-biblical texts and their Qumranic context—1 Enoch: Known in its Ethiopic version as one book, 1 Enoch consists of large literary components that, at the time of the Qumran texts, still existed as independent books. They formed part of a rich pre-Qumranic tradition in Aramaic linked to the name Enoch, known as the initiator of cosmological and calendrical sciences. As in the case of materials related to pentateuchal narratives, these texts served, therefore, primarily as vehicles for cosmological and doctrinal issues. In 4Q201-202 and 204-212, fragments from all the parts of 1 Enoch are preserved, except for the "Book of Similitudes" (1 Enoch 37-71), and, possibly by mere chance, also for 1 Enoch 83-84. One of the Enoch books was the "Book of Giants" (1Q23-24; 4Q203, 530-533; 6Q14), which according to its contents corresponds to the "Book of Watchers" (1 Enoch 1-36). The fall of the angels, to which Gen. 6:1-4 contains only a faint reminiscence, seems to have been a widespread motif, for a variant of

this "Book of Giants" is known from the Manichean tradition. The story had its roots in old Mesopotamian traditions and was probably transmitted in priestly circles. In ancient times it served as an explanation of the origins of technical and cultural achievements. Its later adaptations, however, display a profound critical attitude toward certain effects of civilization, an attitude characteristic of a widespread trend during the second half of the first millennium B.C.E. In light of the Qumran evidence, all past datings of the Enoch literature must be revised: the individual Enoch books existed already in the early second century B.C.E., and some of them are of considerably older date.

Jubilees: According to the number of exemplars (1Q17-18; 2Q19-20; 4Q176b; 4Q216-224; 11Q12), the Book of Jubilees was one of the most authoritative works in the Qumranic tradition. Its narrative basis is more or less identical with that of the Biblical Genesis and of related works found among the Qumran texts, and consequently it is far more deeply embedded in specific Jewish traditions than Enoch. Additionally, unlike the Enoch literature, with its international, Aramaic background, Jubilees is written in Hebrew. Still, Jubilees corresponds in many ways to the Enochic traditions, and the choice of Hebrew, for instance, may be due to its specific aim, to demonstrate that certain disputed Torah regulations form part of a tradition that predates the revelation at Sinai. In the view of Jubilees, these regulations' were authoritative already in the days of the patriarchs and even in pre-diluvial times; essentially they are part of a cosmic and social pattern that coincides with the order of creation.

Unlike the Enoch books, the dating of Jubilees to about 160 B.C.E. has remained relatively undisputed. Still, this dating should be reconsidered on the basis of the book's relationship to the "Astronomical Book" of Enoch (1 Enoch 72-80). The latter concerns calendrical problems proper, and Jubilees provides the chronographic application deduced from the common calendrical basis. The evidence points to the third century as the concluding phase of a chronographic system calculated on the basis of the twenty four priestly courses (integrated in the calendar, cf., 4Q292; 4Q320-330). Importantly, Jubilees' depiction of the division of time in general and of the history from Adam to the entrance into the Land of Israel are presupposed by that system, which during the early second century B.C.E. already caused profound controversies in Jerusalem, apparently because of its practical consequences. Contrary to scholarly opinion, Jubilees may, therefore, have its origins in the early third century B.C.E. Both the Enoch literature and Jubilees witness a massive Qumranic tradition concerning cultic and calendrical topics (4Q292-293; 4Q320-330). This tradition resulted in a sophisticated system for the division of time and in a reconstruction of history since creation, concluding with a calculation of the eschatological periods.

Testaments of the Twelve Patriarchs: Some Qumran texts resemble parts of the Testaments of the Twelve Patriarchs, presenting variant forms of the manifold Levi-traditions that conveyed the self-definition of the priestly clan (1Q21?; 4Q213-214: 540-541). Also, fragments of a kind of "Testament of Judah" (4Q484) and a "Testament of Naftali" (4Q215) are preserved.

Tobit: The Book of Tobit, known from the Septuagint canon, is represented by fragments of four exemplars in Aramaic (4Q196-199) and one in Hebrew (4Q200). Its narrative content and form correspond to a widespread type of court tales (cf., the Story of Ahiqar; Dan. 1-6), which Jewish authors adapted for historiographic and apologetic purposes.

Sirach: Fragments of the Hebrew text of Sirach (known from a medieval copy in the Cairo Genizah) have been found in Qumran (2Q18) as well as on Masada. Sir. 51 appears also in 11Q5, a psalm scroll that includes five poetic compositions hitherto preserved only in Syriac translations.

Classification according to literary genres: Most of the extant, well preserved Qumran scrolls are composites. They contain various genres and so lack the distinctive literary traits that allow for their definition within a single literary category. This is the case except for the Pesher-commentaries and certain liturgical texts, which are uniform in genre and content.

Another exception is the Temple Scroll, which we already have referred to as a carefully composed book of Torah. Also the War Scroll from Cave 1 (1QM) appears to be a thoughtfully constructed, unitary composition, but like 1QS and the Zadokite documents, 1QM is only one among a number of more or less identical M-collections. The same is true for diverse psalm scrolls, which exhibit differing contents and, compared with the biblical Psalter, many deviations in sequence (figs. 45-46).

Scrolls that contain poetic collections, such as 1QH and related texts from 4Q and 11Q, consist of units that can be classified easily according to their poetic genres. Unfortunately, we still know very little about the liturgical organization of the group(s) behind these texts, particularly considering developments over time. Accordingly, classification of the individual pieces usually follows the criteria developed in biblical scholarship for hymns, songs of praise or thanks, poems of lament, etc. The same is true for parts of the liturgical material, especially for the benedictions. The forms of the prayers, however, vary considerably according to the associated liturgical events and according to the group for which they were intended: priests, Levites, laymen.

The well preserved 1QH (*Hodayot*) and the fragments of identical and related collections from 4Q (4Q427-433, 440, 498-499) contain only a restricted number of genres. In its preserved 28 columns, 1QH contains three or four collections of pieces that in most cases begin, "I praise/thank you, oh Lord" and, in some cases, "Blessed are you." The first pattern belongs to the genre of "individual songs of praise," which describe negative situations or circumstances and express thanks for a change to the better due to God's grace. Columns II-XI of the *editio princeps* (originally numbered: X-XIX) contain seventeen such songs of praise, which many scholars regard as written by the Teacher of Righteousness himself and believe to express his personal experiences. There is, however, not sufficient evidence for such a biographical and psychological interpretation. Significant in col. XX (XII), 11 is the phrase "and I as *maskil*." It indicates for the *Hodayot* a similar function as for other pieces introduced "For the *maskil*," suggesting a concrete mode of instruction. The title *maskil* appears also in connection with legal and didactic texts. Rather than referring to individual and personal religious experiences, the use of "I" in this case thus expresses the collective convictions of the same priestly elite that determined the content of Torah.

Some poetical pieces of liturgical character are incorporated in the War Scroll (1QM + 4Q491-496). 1QM X,8 for example, contains a poem that employs the repeating phrase *Mi kamokah* ("Who is like you?") that, in biblical and later synagogal compositions, introduces a thematic genre concerning the similar incomparibilities of God and his people, Israel. The following columns of 1QM contain various poems connected with the issue of the "holy war," evidently part of a vast heritage attested as well in other contexts in this period and, in particular, actualized in the Maccabean wars. Some of these poems follow a benediction pattern; others are of hymnic and didactic character. Finally col. XVIII,?-XIX,8a presents an impressive song of victory and triumph.

The fragments of 4Q179 and 4Q501 present remnants similar to passages in the biblical Lamentations. They were perhaps connected with commemoration rituals for the destroyed first Temple. Their counterparts seem to have been the *Tanhumim* ("consolations") of 4Q176a, so called according to a certain part in the synagogal liturgy reserved for individual supplicatory prayers. The Qumran *Tanhumim* were, however, part of a collection of liturgical pieces of varying genres. Not concerned with the individual, their main interest was the fate of the people and land of Israel and its sanctuary. The first extant pieces explicitly called *Tanhumim*, indeed, are simply an anthology of citations primarily from Second and Third Isaiah. Only in this respect is there a certain thematic parallel to the later synagogal liturgy, namely

to the "pericopes of consolation" in the prophetic lectionary cycle (*Haftarot*).

The benediction as the basic form of prayer appears in the Qumran texts in a variety of forms associated with the priestly liturgy. This is contrary to the comparatively simple features of the lay-oriented Pharisaic-Rabbinic tradition. The Qumran benedictions are by far less uniform than the Rabbinic ones, which, until the third or fourth centuries C.E., underwent a continuous process of standardization. The standard Rabbinic benediction reads: "Blessed are you, Lord, our God, king of the world, who. . . ." The possibilities for comparisons with Qumran benedictions are, for chronological and sociological reasons, restricted.

In poetical contexts, thanksgiving poems are introduced in the form of benedictions, beginning "*Baruk*. . . ." Thus we find in 1QH V,20, X,14; XI,27 (?); XI,32, XVI,8 a: "Blessed are you, Lord, who . . ."; or "Blessed are you, the God of mercy and of grace in your/because . . ." (1QH XI,29); "Blessed are you, Lord, for/because . . ." (1QH XI,32; 1QH XIII,20; 1QH XVIII,14); "Blessed are you, my God, who . . ." (1QS XI,15-22; 1QH frg. 4,15); "Blessed is God, who . . ." (1QH XXVI,5); "Blessed is the God of Israel, who . . ." (1QM XIV,3-8/ 4Q491 frg. 8-10,2-6); "Blessed is your Name, oh God of grace" (1QM XIV,8/4Q491 frg. 8-10,6-10); "Blessed is your name, God of the godlike ones . . ." (1QM XVIII,6). In 1Q20 GenAp XX,12-16, a supplicatory prayer begins in a prose context, "Blessed are you, Highest God, Lord of all eternities . . ."; and in 11Q5 XIX,7, "Blessed is the Lord, who . . ." is the beginning of a stanza in the "Plea of Deliverance." In the angelic liturgy "Songs of the Sabbath Sacrifice," a piece in 4Q403 frg. 1,28 is introduced, "Blessed is [the] L[o]rd, kin[g of] all, high above all benediction and. . . ." Such rich literary employment of benediction patterns presumably reflects a correspondingly dominant role of such patterns in daily life.

Other patterns begin with a self-invitation to praise as in 4Q434 frg. 1 i 1-2: "Bless, my soul, my Lord, because of . . . and blessed is his name, for he has. . . ." In the "Grace after meals," 4Q434a, of which the beginning is lost, the wording of lines 9-10 corresponds to the beginning of 4Q434: "Bless, my soul . . .," followed by reasons for praise; cf. 4Q511 frg. 63 ii + 64,2: "I will bless your name and on the fixed times of my testimonies I will tell your wonders. . . ."

Of a third type are pieces with persons as subject of the benediction. They begin with the optative form "*yebarek*. . . ." ("May bless . . .") or (passive) "May be blessed . . .," as in 4Q448 frg. 1 ii: "May your name be blessed. In 4Q537 frg. A + E,1-2 an angel speaks to Jacob: "May God bless you. . . ."

The daily prayers for the individual days of a month in 4Q503 all apparently began in the form of benedictions: "Blessed is the God of Israel, who . . ." (III,2.6; IV,6.8). Also the major part of the festival liturgies probably consisted of benedictions; but most of them are, unfortunately, in an extremely fragmentary state: 1Q34 3,7; 4Q507 frg. 2; 3 ("Blessed is the Lord, who . . ."); frg. 4,4; frg. 10, ii,6-7; frg. 18,3; frg. 23 ii,3.

Similar formulas may be found in collection of prayers that cannot be defined according their purpose. In 4Q510-511 ("Song of the Wise"), which originally contained about 21 columns, a variety of formulas is employed; in 4Q511 frg. 16,4: "Blessed are you, God of godlike ones;" in 4Q511 frg. 52-59,4: "Blessed are you, [my] God, king of glory, because . . .;" in 4Q511 frg. 63 iv (as a final clause!): "All your works bless regularly, and blessed is your name for ever in eternities. Amen, Amen!;" and in 11Q14,2-3: "Blessed is [-] and blessed is the name [of his] holin[ess]. . . ."

Benedictions appear in some rare cases in connection with ritual acts. 4Q502 has been defined a marriage ritual, but in fact it contained various genres, among others, some for Tabernacles and benedictions for different groups. 4Q502 frg. 19,6-7, for instance, regards men: "Blessed is the [Go]d of Israel, who . . .;" cf., the same formula in 4Q502 frg. 24,2-6 (for ?); cf., 4Q502 frg. 31; 96; 101; 125. Benedictions accompanying ritual purification acts are quoted in 4Q414 frg. 2 ii,6;

4Q512 iv frg. 33,6-7; vii frg. 30,6; frg. 42,3; frg. 54,3; cf. frg. 69,3; frg. 72,6-7 ("Blessed are you [. . .]," in complete form probably as in frg. 64,6: "Blessed are You, God of [Is]rael, who. . . ."

1Q28b (1QSb) is a collection of benedictions for high officials: High priest, priests, ruler. It is preserved in parts with an introduction such as, "Words of benediction for the *maskil* to bless . . ." (I,1; III,22); or in V,20 (for the ruler): For the *maskil* to bless. . . ." The beginning of I,3. III,25 reads: "May the Lord bless you from the abode of his Holiness . . .," but the benediction for the ruler in V,23 begins only with "May raise you. . . ."

A liturgical formula containing benedictions (of the optative pattern) opposite maledictions is enclosed in 1QS col. I-III,12; a literary application of this twofold pattern appears in 1QM XIII,1-5, employing, however, the *Baruk*-pattern: "Blessed is the God of Israel in all . . . and blessed are . . .," corresponding to, "Cursed be . . . etc.;" 4Q379 (Psalms of Joshua) frg. 22 ii.5f. is similar.

4QMMT (4Q394-399) is a composite, one component of which is constructed as a literary epistle in the form of a letter to a ruler. Its main part consists of a list of differences in Torah interpretation and practice that distinguished the group behind the text and the ruling majority. The stereotypical formulations of the rival positions misled some scholars to see here a parallel to the "antitheses" in the Gospels. This antithetic arrangement is probably due to didactic considerations, for the existence of at least six exemplars points to a practical purpose. The end of the epistle is formulated as admonitions (blessings and maledictions) directed at the ruler in the traditions of the law of the king, in a generalized form as blessings and maledictions also found in covenantal contexts such as in Deut. 27-29 or Lev. 26. It is not quite clear whether this epistle originated as a mere literary device or was sent as a real letter to an actual ruler (Alexander Yannai?).

Classification according to contents and purposes—Torah traditions, laws and orders: In Qumran research, the term "Torah" is usually regarded as signifying the Pentateuch or the laws contained in it. But in fact, in the Qumran texts, as in later Rabbinic Judaism, the concept of Torah encompasses far more than the pentateuchal laws. Rather, at Qumran, as for the rabbis, all absolutely binding legal traditions are Torah. The entire Torah as an ideal whole represents God's will, and the competent authorities need "from time to time" to enact regulations controlling actual practice. At Qumran, as in the outside community, the priestly authorities held this responsibility. At Qumran, accordingly, Torah regulations are referred to as "revealed," and such rules encompass as well "hidden" laws, parts of the ideal whole Torah that have not yet been detected and enacted or are no longer practiced. It is impossible to define with certainty the boundaries between Torah laws and regulations on the level of communal discipline, since, perhaps to maintain complete disciplinary control, the priestly authorities were not interested in marking this difference.

Some Qumran texts entirely concern legal issues, and many composite scrolls as well contain legal or disciplinary materials. Due to the concept of Torah that held that even that which is "revealed" still had to be enacted "from time to time," it is difficult to determine the extent to which and in what periods specific regulations found in the scrolls guided actual practice.

A striking example of a Torah document in the described sense is the Temple Scroll, extant in remnants of three copies: 11Q19, which consists of two parts of different age—11Q10A (= col. II-V) from the early first century C.E. and 11Q19B from the late first century B.C.E.—and 11Q20, from the early first century B.C.E. For this extensive composition the redactors combined components of different genres and contents. The redactional result was a precisely organized book of laws with a historical frame, not unlike Deuteronomy, set in the Sinai (cf., Exod. 34) just prior to the entrance into the promised Land (cf., Deut. 7). The basic device is a priestly point of view treating the subjects according to a scheme of graduated concentric realms, proceeding from the Holy of Holies in the Sanctuary to the peripheral realms of holiness and ritual purity. Regulations concerning the Temple are thus treated first, while laws of common interest are discussed in the last parts. The large components, originally probably independent sources, are clearly discernible and of different age and character:

(1) The "Temple source," a detailed and architecturally sophisticated plan for a first sanctuary in the Land for all of the twelve tribes of Israel.
(2) Incorporated in col. 13,9-30,?, a list of sacrifices according to the events within the solar oriented festival cycle.
(3) A ritual prescription related to the sanctuary and the city of the sanctuary (col. 48-51,10).
(4) A collection of general laws that contains the major part of the materials extant also in Deut. 16-22, and within this compound an elaborated "Law of the King" (col. 56,12-60,?).

Almost all of the laws (including those with parallels in Deuteronomy) are formulated as ordinances of God, speaking in the first person to Moses. The Temple Scroll is composed as a book of Torah, indeed, but scarcely as a "new" Torah, destined to replace the Pentateuch or Deuteronomy, or as an "eschatological Torah." What of this collection actually served as the law of the time, enacted by competent authorities, is difficult to determine.

4QMMT (4Q394-399) contains in the first preserved part a calendrical text followed by a list of legal regulations and practices disputed by the authors and their adversaries. The list is framed as an epistle but represents essentially one of the most important legal texts among the scrolls. Some of the controversial regulations have parallels in the Temple Scroll (11Q19-20), and it seems likely that both writings represent a rather early Zadokite legal tradition, extant already towards 200 B.C.E. Parts of this survived also in the later Sadducean group.

1QS and CD: 1QS and CD (the Zadokite documents) are collections of various texts. The first part of 1QS (col. I,1-III,12) is a liturgical composition destined for a yearly covenant festival (identical with Pentecost) and connected with the admission of new members and the re-arrangement of the ranking order within the community. A doctrinal section follows, defining in concise schematic prose some basic beliefs. A third part (col. V,1-IX,2) contains laws and regulations and is commonly regarded as the Manual of Discipline of the Qumran community. After col. IX,2 a number of appendices appear, the first of didactic and then, in col. X,1-XI, of poetic-liturgical character. A comparison with the S-exemplars in 4Q (4Q255-264) leads to the conclusion that 1QS reflects different strata of disciplinary regulations and didactic self-definitions of the *yahad*-community. The same is true for the legal parts in the Zadokite documents compared with the related D-texts from 4Q (4Q266-273). The D-laws concern cities or "camps." The legal parts in CD col. IX-XII differ in extent and date from the 4Q fragments. The paleographic evidence regarding certain manuscripts suggests for at least parts of the S and D traditions an older age than that of the installation at Qumran. Consequently, they cannot be regarded as specifically characteristic of the community that lived there only from the end of the second century B.C.E. Although the comparatively great number of exemplars attests a prominent significance of both collections, there is no way to establish the exact historical place and function of their rules. The same has to be admitted regarding other legal collections.

Teharot[a-f] is the name of six manuscripts (4Q274-279.281-283) of a legal collection that corresponds to regulations in the S and CD texts and the Temple Scroll. Many of the extant fragments concern older ritual issues that are here related to the conditions of the *yahad*. A similar case are the so-called Ordinances, 4Q159 and 4Q513-514. Both collections appear to have been of considerable size and of great importance. Close to them in content and character are also the remnants of 4Q284 (concerning ritual purity), 4Q284a, and 4Q375.

The use of early history: Jubilees, 1 Enoch, and the Testaments of the XII Patriarchs present contemporary rules and disputed regulations as though they were aspects of old traditions from prior to even the revelation of the Torah on Sinai. Other texts from Qumran similarly describe prediluvial and patriarchal history. Fragments of such texts, some of them primarily of a narrative nature, are related to the figures of Noah (1Q19; 4Q246; 4Q534), Abraham (1Q20/GenAp), Jacob (4Q537), and Joseph (4Q371-373). Also the so-called "Pentateuch paraphrases" or "reworked Pentateuch" texts (4Q364-368; 4Q422-422a; 4Q464) share with similar writings containing Genesis or pentateuchal materials (4Q249; 4Q253-255) the tendency to demonstrate that certain Zadokite traditions are very old or even part of the original cosmic order.

Numerous texts are associated with the name of Moses (1Q22; 2Q21; 4Q374; 4Q385a; 4Q387a/4Q388a; 4Q389 and 4Q390). Others are connected with Joshua (4Q123; 4Q378-379; 5Q9), Samuel (4Q160; 6Q9), and David (2Q22; 4Q373; 11Q05 XXVII,2-11; XXVIII,3-13); texts concerning Levi, Qahat, and Amram transmit priestly issues in particular.

Liturgical and ritual texts: The fragmentary condition of the texts prevents in many cases a definition of their literary genre and liturgical purpose. Apart from the benedictions (see above), this applies, for instance, to the remains of five non-canonical psalms in 4Q380-381 or the fragments in 1Q30-31; 1Q36-40; 3Q6; 6Q18; 4Q291; 4Q294-297; 4Q392-393; 4Q441-4Q477; 4Q500.

An extensive collection of poetic-liturgical pieces appears in 4Q510-4Q511 (4QShir[a-b]), the "Songs of the Sage." Fragments from eleven of originally ca. 21 columns are extant, and these apparently contain a variety of genres. At least some of these pieces were intended for priestly use, for a passage in 4Q511 frg. 10 resembles the solemn "Songs of the Sabbath Sacrifice" (cf., passages in 4Q286 and 287). Striking is the stress on regular praise of God, which should accord with the demands of cosmic powers (4Q511 frg. 1) and occur at appropriate times, determined by eternal rules (4Q511 frg. 2 i; frg. 63 ii + 64), that is, in accordance with a certain calendar, reflected also in 1QH XII

(XX),4-11; 1QS X,1-8 (and the parallel texts in 4Q258 and 4Q260).

4Q502 has been defined as a marriage ritual. But this papyrus scroll (of which 344 small fragments remain) in fact contains a variety of prayers, including some for Tabernacles. At least part of the scroll contains prayers related to topics such as family welfare. It mentions men, young ones, women, maidens, children, apparently all members of the priestly elite, the Sons of Zadok. Other pieces are introduced by the formula characteristic for laic prayers: "Blessed is the God of Israel."

A considerable number of explicitly liturgical Qumran texts unfortunately are preserved in a very fragmentary state. The fragments of 4Q448 contain in all probability prayers for "King Jonathan," apparently Alexander Yannai (103-76 B.C.E.). From the fragmentary remains, it is difficult to determine on what occasion prayers in a vast collection called "Dibre ha-me'orot^{a-c}" (4Q504, a copy from about 150 B.C.E., 4Q505; 4Q506) were recited. Different is the case of 4Q503, which includes prayers for every day of the month according to the following pattern: "On the . . . of the month at evening/at sunrise they shall bless and recite: Blessed is. . . ." Also the festival prayers of the collections 1Q34, 4Q507-508 (frg. 2 for the Day of Atonement), and 4Q509 (frg. 131 ii for the first fruit day) seem to have consisted essentially of benedictions.

Exemplars of one of the most phantasmal texts among the Qumran finds, the "Songs of the Sabbath Sacrifice" (4Q400-407, 11Q17; Ms Masada), are comparatively numerous. This collection contains meticulously constructed liturgical pieces for the thirteen Sabbaths of a quarter of the year (*tequfah*). It does not present, in fact, the texts of the songs themselves, but only descriptions of their liturgical performance in the heavenly realms. The descriptions are of an extremely monotonous and solemn style, full of technical cult terms and stereotypical formulations. As a whole the compositions represent priestly traditions of the highest liturgical level, fundamentally of pre-Qumranic origin and part of the cultic heritage of the Temple of Jerusalem before Antiochus IV. Presenting the angelic priests as heavenly counterparts of the earthly ones, these texts provide important insights into priestly self-consciousness in general.

1QS I-III,12 constitutes a liturgical formulary intended for the annual covenantal ceremony of Pentecost, connected with the admission of new members and the regular re-arranging of the ranking order. 1Q28b (1QSb) consists of benedictions for the introduction of priests and high officials. Liturgical pieces accompanying ritual purification acts are attested in fragments of 4Q414 frg. 2 ii,6, and 4Q512. 1Q29 has been called 4QTongues of Fire. The remnants presuppose a kind of mysterious oracle ceremony, obviously designed for a specific priestly practice.

Sapiential and theological texts: Many fragments, particularly from 4Q, display the characteristics of wisdom traditions: 1Q26 + 4Q423; 1Q27; 4Q180-181; 4Q184-185; 4Q299-308; 4Q408; 4Q426; 4Q474-476; 4Q486-487; 4Q525. The range of literary features is, however, wide. The basic traditions seem to have consisted of wisdom texts proper. These are proverbs or series of proverbs, in part collected or composed according to thematic points of view and similar to some components of Ben Sira, of which fragments have been found at Qumran and on Masada. Whole passages are concerned with practical questions of daily life and with social relations. In many cases we find, however, a tendency to stress the significance of essentially impenetrable aspects of the existent world, which only the wise are able to grasp. This "mystery of being" transcends the imminent order presupposed in the old wisdom texts and implies cosmogonical and cosmological connotations of a peculiar character. The wise man is no longer the normal transmitter of wisdom but, in his place, the *maskil*, a functionary of the organizational collective behind the texts, obviously consisting primarily of priests. The impression is of a continuous theologizing of standard wisdom materials, resulting in the formation of passages with a doctrinal character.

During the last stage of this evolution, doctrinal texts emerged in a formalized rhythmic prose style with many stereotypical formulations, in parts very like poetic pieces. The most famous text of this kind is 1QS III,13-IV,26, an impressive compendium of doctrinal issues. But the wisdom tradition was not the only foundation of this literature. The cultic-liturgical realm in particular provided additional formal and conceptual elements for the crystallization of this kind of doctrinal tractate.

Establishing harmony within the realms of spirits and men and safeguarding the latter against evil forces represented by Belial was one of the most important purposes of liturgical practices. Exorcistic conjurations accordingly aimed at deterring and frightening demons (see, e.g., parts of 11Q11, 4Q286 frg. 7, and 4Q560). In such contexts, dualistic and deterministic traits appear, apparently in their proper social context, while the doctrinal statements in passages such as 1QS III,13-IV,26 and 4Q176; 4Q177 X, 4Q180-181; 4Q215 frg. 1 ii; 4Q369 seem to reflect a more theological application. The liturgical texts thus are of a doctrinal as well as a historical character, a fact that presupposes that a metaphysical explanation for the profound controversies within post-exilic Judaism was transformed from a mythical explanation of the confrontation between Israel and its enemies as one between God and his enemies to an antagonism within Judaism itself.

Individual horoscopes concerning the participation of the individual in the realms of light and darkness, as in 4Q186, as well as physiognomic texts, such as 4Q561, formed part of the community's world view and were apparently also significant for the ranking of individual's within the group. These texts also illustrate some of the peculiar phrases used in 1QS III,13-IV,26, which presume that membership in the lot of light or darkness was predestined.

The literary evidence points finally to an evolution of the dualistic and deterministic concepts originally rooted in a priestly view of the world and humankind. This transformation took place within an increasingly exclusive group, whose members came to consider themselves to be not only the leading elite of Israel but also to constitute the only true community of Israel. In this evolution, heightened attention was paid to specific eschatological issues. Viewed in the context of a radicalized dualistic world view, these ideas led to a profound demonization of the cosmos, history, and nature of humanity.

Eschatological texts and traditions: The apocalyptic character of certain texts has been of great concern from the inception of Qumran research. It is difficult to determine the date to which these texts set the decisive turning point between normal history and the eschaton. CD I,6's calculation of 390 years after Nebuchadnezzar's capture of Judah in 587/6 B.C.E has been understood by many scholars to be a more or less symbolic statement. In light of the publication of 4Q390 frg. 1, however, where an interval of seven jubilee periods is mentioned, this date has to be re-examined. A comparison of CD I-II with 4Q390 and with the apocalypses in 1 Enoch 85-90 and 93 + 91,1-12 as well as with Dan. 9-12 and certain other calendrical texts proves that a chronographic calculation existed.

This calculation was based on the division of time into "year-weeks" (that is, six years concluding with a Sabbatical year), Jubilees ($7 \times 7 = 49$ years), and periods of $6 \times 49 = 296$ years, $7 \times 49 = 343$ years, and $10 \times 49 = 490$ years. The periodization in intervals of 490 years was the most important instrument of world chronography in this tradition, which calculated past and present on the basis of cycles prefigured in the organization of the 24 priestly courses at the sanctuary and which had the Sabbatical cycle as its backbone. The significance of the vast mass of calendrical texts and particularly the existence of an extensive list covering a whole period, as in 4Q319, is, therefore, not restricted to discussions about the application of a yearly calendar oriented around the course of the sun or moon. It extends so far as to the calculation of all time and history. Such calculations are reflected in the Pesher-interpretation of historical or present events and scriptural passages allegedly related to the actual period of 490 years (586-97 B.C.E) and, in particular, to the previous two Jubilees (198/7-97 B.C.E.).

The word *pesher* is derived from a verb meaning "to untie knots/to solve riddles/to interpret dreams," and it designates a kind of actualizing and eschatologically motivated interpretation of prophetic texts, in the form of single interpretations as well as running commentaries. The Pesher-commentary forms a distinctive and characteristic part of the scrolls concerned with biblical passages or contents. It accordingly is represented in an impressive number of texts, indicating an important function during a certain phase of the development of the group: 1QpHab; 1Q14 and 4Q168 (pMicah); 1Q15 and 4Q170 (pZepheniah); 1Q16, 4Q171 and 4Q173 (pPsalms); 3Q4, 4Q161-165 and 4Q515 (pIsaiah); 4Q166-167 (pHosea); 4Q169 (pNahum); 4Q172 (= ?); 5Q5 (pMal?).

While the actualizing interpretation of single passages is found elsewhere in ancient Judaism, the Pesher's running commentary appears to be characteristic in particular of the group headed by the Teacher of Righteousness. He claimed to understand the words of the prophets according to their real meaning, thanks to the spirit given to him by God (1QpHab II,8-10). This approach presumed that even the biblical prophet himself did not conceive the true meaning of the revelation (cf. 1QpHab VII,1-2). Invariably, this true meaning concerns events of the latter days. Past, present, and future events are arbitrarily connected. These form the real subject of an interpretive process that presents them as signs or elements of an eschatological drama, in which the Teacher of Righteousness, of course, plays a decisive initial part. So even as the Pesher quotes more or less continuous passages or sometimes single words of the Bible, it appends previously conceived interpretative statements, which often lack any foundation in the scriptural source at all. Thus the Pesher is not really an explanation of the text but a method of using scriptural elements as vehicles for expressing distinct views. In this genre, biblical statements are introduced, "Its Pesher is/concerns . . ." or by, "The Pesher of the word/subject is/concerns . . .," eventually followed by a reasoning clause. A single word or part of a cited passage may be addition-

ally interpreted, beginning with the phrase, "And if it is said . . . its Pesher is that. . . ."

4Q174 ("Florilegium") and 4Q177 are parts of one composite text treating in the extant fragments specific eschatological themes. It begins with a Pesher interpretation of 2 Sam 10-14 regarding three temples. The following section applies 2 Sam 7:14 to the Davidic ruler who is said to take over his office together with a new *doresh ha-Torah* (Torah-Enactor, cf., CD VII,18-19). The following pieces seem to have contained eschatological interpretations of actual events connected with polemics against other groups. Here events of the past are utilized in a typological manner for polemical purposes.

4Q175 ("Testimonia") is a piece from a rather early (100-75 B.C.E.) copy. Its name has been given to the text by the editors because of its certain resemblance to collections of messianic-Christological proof texts of the early Church. The first part combines a series of passages also extant in the Hebrew Bible but of remarkably differing text traditions: Deut. 5:28-29; 18:18-19; Num. 24:15-17; Deut. 33:8-11. This piece probably served as an introduction to a more elaborate eschatological treatise interpreting actual events, in the extant fragment particularly concerned with Hasmonean building activities at Jericho.

Eschatological interpretations of historical or actual events are also attested in Aramaic fragments like 4Q246, misleadingly labeled a "Son of God text," or defined as an apocalypse. The fragments of 4Q552-553 (called "Four kingdoms") belong to a similar text containing eschatological visions or revelations. The so-called "pseudo-Daniel" texts, 4Q243-245, share the same purpose and concern. Apparently a broad tradition of materials existed related to Daniel, one of the most important prophets in the eyes of the people behind the Qumran scrolls (the biblical book itself being extant in seven exemplars).

The famous Melchizedek text, 11Q13, is in its extant parts also of primarily eschatological concern. Here Melchizedek, in the Jewish tradition the prototype of the High

Priest of Jerusalem, executes a kind of eschatological judgment in terms of a ritual purification. The preceding passages consist of Pesher-interpretations of a series of biblical passages, which allowed a combination of calendrical-chronographic Jubilee-speculations with the motif of a final judgment. The date of the appearance of the Anointed Prince, seven "weeks" after a time indicated in Dan. 9:25, points to the chronographic calculations mentioned above.

The War Scroll, relatively well preserved as 1QM (+ 1Q33) with variants in 4Q491-496, also has a specific eschatological concern. The scroll consists of components with a specific pre-history of their own, combined together to form a phantasmal plan of the final war(s) between Israel and its enemies and, concurrently, between the forces of good and evil, in sum, between the sons of light and the sons of darkness. Striking is the combination of realistic practical traits—the information about weaponry, war banners, tactical provisions and measures—on the one hand, and phantasmal traits, on the other. Significant also is the priestly claim to lead the course of the operations by signals. As a whole the work appears to be a liturgical formulary based on a deterministic concept of the course of events. 1QM contains two versions (I and XV-XIX, and II and X-XIV) with two distinct concepts of war. The fragments from 4Q indicate a rich but rather fluctuating war tradition with ritual and liturgical elements combined or enclosed. Most of the material was apparently already formulated in a highly stereotypical prose style or consisted of poetic-liturgical pieces. Texts of at least partially similar contents are 4Q259, 4Q285, and 4Q471.

1Q28a (= 1QSa, originally part of 1Qs) is formally a kind of community rule with ritual regulations concerning functions during certain public and cultic events. It is, however, a rule destined for the whole of Israel at the end of days, and so describes a peculiar constitution including a high priest and a laic ruler, in sum, persons for whom the text 1Q28b (= 1QSb) specifies particular benedictions.

The New Jerusalem text (in Aramaic!) is extant in fragmentary form: 1Q32, 2Q24, 4Q454-455, 5Q15, and 11Q18. Its basic concept resembles Hellenistic town planning but applied to a device for the eschatological Jerusalem as "City of the Sanctuary." Its utopian measurements exceed even those of Ezek. 40-48, the oldest example for this kind of utopian-architectural tradition. Like Ezek. 40-48, the work included legal regulations concerning cultic issues. The relatively great number of copies points to a particular interest or purpose. Perhaps its function was critical, to present a final, ideal device in contrast to existing institutions and circumstances, while the Temple Scroll (in Hebrew!) presented a utopian device destined for realization after the entrance into the Land of Israel. Both texts exhibit certain common features, last but not least regarding the scheme of Israel as a people of twelve tribes and the application of their names to the twelve gates of the enclosing walls of the Temple courts and the city, a motif that also appears outside the scrolls.

Bibliography

Burrows, M., *The Dead Sea Scrolls of St. Mark's Monastery*, vol. 1: *The Isaiah Manuscript and the Habakkuk Commentary* (New Haven, 1950); vol. 2, fasc. 2: *Plates and Transcription of the Manual of Discipline*, ed. by Millar Burrows (New Haven, 1951).

Cross, Frank M., *The Ancient Library of Qumran and Modern Biblical Studies* (Sheffield, 1995).

Discoveries in the Judean Desert, Oxford. Vol. I: Barthélemy, D. and J.T. Milik, *Qumran Cave 1*, (1964); vol. III: Baillet, M., J.T. Milik and R. de Vaux, *Les "Petites grottes" de Qumran*, vol. I-II (1962); vol. IV: Sanders, J.A., *The Psalm Scroll of Qumran Cave XI (11QPsa)* (1965); vol. V: Allegro, J.M., *Qumran Cave IV.1 (4Q 158-4Q 186)* (1968); vol. VI: de Vaux, R. and J.T. Milik, *Qumran grotte IV.2 (4Q 128-4Q 157)* (1977); vol. VII: Baillet, M., *Qumran grotte IV.3 (4Q 482-4Q 520)* (1982); vol. IX: Skehan, P.W., E. Ulrich, and J.E. Sanderson, *Qumran Cave 4 IV. Palaeo Hebrew and Greek Biblical Manuscripts* (1992); vol. X: Qimron, E. and J. Strugnell, *Qumran Cave 4. V. Miqsat Ma'ase ha-Torah* (1994); vol. XII: Ulrich, E. and F.M. Cross, *Qumran Cave 4 VII. Genesis – Numbers* (1995); vol. XIII: Tov, E., *Qumran Cave 4 VIII. Parabiblical Texts, Part 1* (1995); vol. XIV: Ulrich, E., *Qumran Cave 4 IX. Deuteronomy, Joshua, Judges, Kings* (1995); vol. XVIII: Baumgarten, J.M. and J.T. Milik, *Qumran Cave 4 XIII. The Damascus Document (4Q266-273)* (1996); vol. XIX:

Tov, E., *Qumran Cave 4 XIV: Parabiblical Texts, Part 2* (1995).

Eisenman, R.H., and J.M. Robinson, *A Facsimile Edition of the Dead Sea Scrolls* (Washington, 1991).

Fitzmyer, Joseph A., *The Dead Sea Scrolls. Major Publications and Tools for Study* (Atlanta, 1992).

García, Martínez Florentino and Julio Trebolle Barrera, *The People of the Dead Sea Scrolls* (Leiden, 1995).

Maier, Johann, *Die Qumran—Essener: Die Texte vom Toten Meer*, 3 vol. (Munich, 1995-1996).

Stegemann, Hartmut, *The Library of Qumran* (Kampen, 1994).

Sukenik, E.L., *The Dead Sea Scrolls of the Hebrew University* (Jerusalem, 1955).

VanderKam, James C., *The Dead Sea Scrolls Today* (Grand Rapids, 1994).

Wacholder, Ben Zion and Martin G. Abegg, eds., *A Preliminary Edition of the Unpublished Dead Sea Scrolls. The Hebrew and Aramaic Texts from Cave Four* (Washington, 1991-1995).

JOHANN MAIER

THE DEAD SEA WRITINGS, THE JUDAISM(S) OF: Attempts to define the Judaism practiced at Qumran have on the whole been in vain, the result of a substantial lack of proper methodology. When the Dead Sea Scrolls were first studied, it was assumed that all the non-biblical ones were homogeneous in their content and constituted a single sectarian library. In this approach, their authors' doctrines, treated as uniform, could be discovered by reading across the manuscripts. Once identified, these doctrines could be contrasted with the beliefs of the monolithic "non-sectarian" Judaism understood to be practiced everywhere but at Qumran.

In light of our present awareness of the diversity of the contents of the scrolls and our knowledge of the variety of Judaisms practiced in this period, this uncomplicated approach is no longer the least bit plausible. Therefore, at the outset of any attempt to define the Judaism practiced at Qumran, it must be borne in mind that the enterprise may prove impossible, it not being entirely clear that the scrolls represent a "Judaism" at all. For a kind of "Judaism" is not simply *any* collection of doctrines or practices, but a complete religious system. While the question of what makes a collection of religious beliefs and practices a mode of "Judaism" is difficult definitively to answer, it is clear that the collection must at least encompass certain ideas, including a concept of "Israel" and a definition of the location of that Israel in time and space and in relation to its deity.

A fundamentally important distinction must also be made between literary and historical approaches, that is, between an approach that evaluates the religion depicted in a range of texts and one that examines only the documented beliefs and practices of an actual community at a given point in time. Following the former method, in theory it would be possible to conduct a purely literary exercise so as to construct a "Judaism of the Qumran *texts*," without reference to their various origins and actual life-settings. This approach assumes that everything stated in all the texts, viewed collectively, is to be assembled into a statement of Judaism, regardless of whether this statement represents any Judaism that ever existed. In principle, a purely literary method such as this can ignore the question of historical authors, preservers, and readers of the library. But why scholars should want to read any such archive as a single, coherent statement is not evident. In fact, those who undertake this exercise claim they are describing what they call the "Qumran community," a supposedly historical entity that in truly circular fashion is defined as a group practicing the artificially constructed "Judaism" of the archive.

Even such a method would find it necessary to distinguish three discrete categories of manuscripts among the scrolls. While scholars have defined in Qumran literature in different ways, they have tended to agree on three central categories: 1) "scriptural" texts, which the later talmudic rabbis classified as "defiling the hands," 2) "pseudepigraphal" texts, known outside of Qumran, but not scriptural, and 3) "sectarian" texts, altogether unknown outside of Qumran. Many scholars have regarded the first group as representing the scriptural foundation that the Qumran sectarians shared with other Judaisms and the last group as what was distinctive to them. The middle group then ranges between these two extremes. Accounts of the "Judaism of the Qumran scrolls" are accordingly distilled from the "sectarian" texts, with the pseudepigraphal manuscripts possibly pointing to a penumbra.

One underlying problem with this approach is its assumption that previously unknown scrolls or the ideas they contain are by definition "sectarian." But in the last decade, this idea has been recognized as problematic, and the question of the conditions under which a text may be considered "sectually explicit" (as Carol Newsom phrases it) is now fairly well recognized. It hardly needs to be said that a description of a "Judaism represented by hitherto unknown texts from Qumran caves" is a fairly useless exercise, though this has, in effect, been attempted.

A *historical* analysis, in which a select set of Qumran texts could be assigned to a specific group and thus interpreted as a historical Judaism, is similarly confronted by a host of uncertainties. Is there evidence of only one historical group behind these texts, and, if not, how are the various groups, their texts, and their Judaisms related (if at all)? Unfortunately these difficulties did not present themselves when the major manuscripts were recovered from Qumran Cave 1 in 1947 and published in the early 1950s. As a result, these all were fairly rapidly interpreted ("biblical" scrolls apart) as products of a single group, and the locale and identity of that group were, after some initial dissent, agreed upon by the scholars responsible for their editing.[1] These were, by general consent, Essene writings, and "the Essenes" lived at the nearby settlement of Qumran (perhaps once named the "City of Salt;" cf., Josh. 15:62). For some time since, and until quite recently, the consensus therefore has held that the Qumran scrolls represent an "Essene library." This theory, at times elevated almost to fact, has the advantage of imposing an internal cohesion among the "non-biblical" texts and, as seems to have been important, identifying and naming the authors.

The reasons for this theory are understandable and should be reviewed. First, the Cave 1 scrolls, taken together, plausibly depict various aspects a single Jewish community:

(a) an account of the beliefs and rules, teachings and organization of a religious community, the *yahad* (the Community Rule, 1QS).
(b) some of its hymns, including those apparently of an individual who had been persecuted and had founded the community, called the *moreh hatzedeq* [= "teacher of righteousness," "rightful teacher"] (the Hodayoth, 1QH).
(c) interpretations of biblical prophecy claimed to be fulfilled in scenes from the life and times of the persecuted founding "teacher" (the Habakkuk Pesher, 1QpHab).
(d) a description of the eschatological war between the forces of light and darkness (the War Scroll, 1QM).

Specific ideological links among these manuscripts could also be observed—in particular a distinctive dualistic doctrine of "light and darkness" or "truth and falsehood" found in both the Community Rule and the War Scroll and a correspondence between events alluded to in the Habakkuk Pesher's account of the life of the "teacher" and the experiences mentioned by the writer of the Hodayoth (e.g., that this person was persecuted, exiled, and formed a group of loyal followers). Many scholars thus supposed that the "teacher" himself wrote these hymns, or at least some of them. It was also suggested more than once that he even wrote the Community Rule.[2]

The "Qumran community" accordingly was defined as the group described in the Community Rule (calling itself the *yahad*), and it seemed natural to conclude that this community had placed the scrolls in the caves and thus had lived nearby. A crucial link was the report of the Roman traveler Pliny (Natural History 5:71-73), who in the first century C.E. described a colony of Essenes by the Dead Sea, not far from Ein Gedi. This society of celibate males was indeed fortunate, said Pliny (who may well have been relying on second-hand testimony), having neither money nor women and only palm trees for company. This ancient report brought the cave-hunters to the nearby ruin now widely identified as the site of that community's habitation. The Essenes are also mentioned in several places by two other first-century writers, Philo and Josephus, and certain features of their description correspond with details of the Community Rule. Josephus described them, among other things, as being agriculturists, as taking frequent baths, and as requiring a lengthy process of admission.[3]

At the beginning of Qumran scholarship, then, the scrolls, Qumran, and Essenes were firmly locked together. That initial configuration still has several influential proponents.[4] However, many of the key elements have since begun to disintegrate. Among the most important are the following:

1. As the number of previously unknown texts increased, the difficulty of harmonizing them exceeded the inventiveness of all but a few commentators. In particular, the Temple Scroll (11QT) and the Halakhic Letter (4QMMT) drove clefts through the consensus: there was disagreement, for example, about whether 11QT was a product of the *yahad*[5] and whether the legal positions adopted in 4QMMT were Essene or Sadducee.[6]

2. With the publication of virtually the entire corpus of texts, it was realized that the 800 or so original manuscripts that survive (mostly in small fragments) were written by a large number of different scribes and very few by the same scribe. This makes it doubtful that the scrolls were largely, if indeed at all, written at Qumran. They may instead represent the products or possessions of numerous individuals and should not automatically be read as representing the beliefs of a "Qumran community."

3. The connection between the site of Qumran and the cave scrolls has been questioned: the archaeological data were interpreted in the light of the scrolls from Cave 1 rather than independently, and clear evidence of a "monastery" (as the site was often dubbed) was never available.[7] Additionally, more sites to which Pliny might have referred have since been discovered in the vicinity of Ein Gedi, and Khirbet Qumran itself has been suggested, among other things, as a fort, trading post, villa, and factory.

A host of other objections has also been raised to the once prevalent theory: the Qum-ran cemeteries include tombs containing female skeletons; the presence of monumental pillar bases at the site suggests something more luxurious than a "monastic" lifestyle; no manuscripts fragments, either of parchment or papyrus, have been found on the site;[8] the manner of deposit of the scrolls differs from cave to cave; the distribution of the caves is curious, some being virtually part of the site of Khirbet Qumran, others a few miles away.

These points are not exhaustive. Nor perhaps are they conclusive, even cumulatively. But the disintegration of the once firm connection of scrolls, ruins, and Essenes has reached the point at which it can be seriously questioned whether the scrolls have any proven connection with the ruins or indeed with any particular groups at all. The most skeptical position is that of N. Golb,[9] who regards the scrolls as comprising several deposits brought to the area from Jerusalem on the eve of its siege by the Romans. Even if his view is not to be accepted entirely, the argument at least exposes the fragility of an agenda that once allowed one to speak easily of a "Qumran community" and to spell out its doctrines and practices.

The question now is not "what was Qumran Judaism?" but *whether* there was one. The answer cannot be found by seeking to establish who lived at Qumran or by attempting to identify them with an otherwise known group. These are worthwhile pursuits in themselves, but they address historical questions that perhaps cannot be answered definitively and in any case do not contribute directly to the task of defining a Judaic system. "Qumran" must be taken in the first instance to denote merely *the place of discovery* of the texts and nothing else.

Does this mean, after all, that the Judaism of Qumran must be reconstructed using a literary method? The answer is that literary analysis indeed must indeed be the first step, specifically in the form of an investigation of the ideology of discrete texts and not of hypothesized authors or groups. But this method, which Jacob Neusner has so successfully used for the Rabbinic materials, needs to be modified in some respects for the Qumran literature. It is possible in some cases to set out the system of a particular text (e.g., the Community Rule, the Damascus Document, the War Scroll), and that system will belong to the framer of the text. But these discrete exercises do not yield a "Judaism of the Qumran texts" and even less so an ancient Judaism existing beyond the literature. For while the systems of the various texts interrelate, they do not all relate in the same way, nor do they form a single system that can be synchronically described. Setting aside first the large number of texts that have no place in the system at all,[10] several of those that remain bear traces of a redactional history. This impels us towards a diachronic analysis and a description of evolving systems. In some cases at any rate, the presence of historical and social processes appears necessary to explain both the format of individual texts and their collective presence in a single archive or set of related archives.[11]

In practice, then, how should one proceed? The similarity of vocabulary, ideology, and genre between a number of texts makes it clear that these are related. Such overlaps, as we shall presently observe, include a calendrical reckoning based on solar years rather than lunar months, the application of a range of dualistic accounts of the world and human nature with often quite specific technical vocabulary (children of light/darkness; Belial; lot), a tendency towards regarding sexual relations as purely for procreation, technical terms such as "city of the sanctuary," "camps," *yahad*, and so on. These varied overlaps suggest at first glance a family relationship (or, better, a set of relationships) among many of the texts.

But to express the relationship systemically or even historically requires a method that does not adopt its own conclusions as its presuppositions, so as to argue in a circle. This means that concrete historical connections must be proven. To do this, paleography has frequently been used as a means of dating. But, since the variables are too many, it is entirely unreliable. Indeed, while the multiple copies and the evidence of redaction in several major scrolls allow us, in a few cases, to set a establish the point by

which particular redactions (represented by specific manuscripts) must have existed, we are dealing with a process of literary (and ideological) formation spanning perhaps several centuries.

This means that the only method, as far as I can see, by which secure results can be obtained is to commence with an analysis of a *single* document and then to compare its major systemic features to other specific redactions of concrete texts. In this approach, the danger to be avoided is declaring the initial document a definitive or "normative" statement of "Qumran Judaism." Such an error is often made, as, for instance, where the *Community Rule* is taken as an official account of the "Qumran Community," and the "Qumranicity" of other texts is then gauged by their convergence with it. A similar procedure, equally invalid, is to identify "documents employing terminology connected to the Qumran community,"[12] where "Qumran community" is a hypothesis substantiated by an amalgam of texts and not a datum. Moreover, the texts in which such terms appear may well differ in *other* respects, and, indeed, may display important systemic divergences. In either case the mistake is to identify a single "Judaism" and then to decide whether or not particular texts fit it.

Indeed, that there is a monolithic "Qumran Judaism" is in principle dubious, and even a superficial acquaintance with the range of texts shows such a presupposition to be false. At most it is possible to posit what might be a family of Judaisms in which many basic features and, more importantly, configurations, recur. In theory, it is not important with which member of a family one begins, as resemblances can be traced in many directions. In practice, however, the choices for a "base text" are rather few. The conditions it must fulfill are that it is capable of expressing a *system*, that it should share a large number of features and configurations with a number of other texts, and that it should, if possible, identify itself with a community or organization, because social structure is a highly important index of ideological structure, and the identification of social entities facilitates a broader and potentially *historical* comparison of Qumran texts.

The Judaism of the Damascus sect: The best point of departure for an exploration of the Judaism of Qumran is not the Community Rule, even though, since it was among the first scrolls to be published, it has played the dominant role in Qumran scholarship. For, despite its given name, that manuscript[13] does not constitute an actual community rule and is very obviously an amalgam of genres, with little discernible structure or plot and no historical statements (whether reliable or not). Both on internal grounds and on the basis of a comparison with the Cave 4 fragments, it may be seen as either a scribal assemblage of material or as a text that has evolved by a redactional process that can more or less be reconstructed.[14]

A much better foundation for the Judaism of Qumran is the Damascus Document. Unfortunately, the best preserved manuscripts come from the geniza of a medieval synagogue, and while these manuscripts overlap, they do so only partly, and their common text is not identical. The fragments from Caves 4, 5, and 6 nevertheless confirm that the contents are important in the Qumran archive and also that the texts of the Cairo manuscripts are reasonably reliable. But these represent two recensions, while the Qumran fragments belong to yet more recensions. Attempts to "correct" the Cairo manuscripts on the basis of a reconstructed original "Damascus Document" must be rejected, for the notion of a definitive edition is no more secure than in the case of the Community Rule. The chief value of the Qumran fragments is to assure us that the Cairo texts do not represent a Karaite rather than a Qumranic edition.

The Damascus Document is divided into two sections, customarily known as *Admonition* and *Laws* (1-9 [= ms. A] + 19-20; 10-16 [ms. B] respectively). The two sections belong together, as the Cave 4 fragments confirm. Unlike the Cairo manuscripts, the Qumran fragments do not in themselves allow us to reconstruct a single recension, because they divide more or less between *Admonition* and *Laws*. But the *Admonition*

(to a lesser extent the *Laws*) does exhibit a rhetorical structure and includes a number of statements about the origin of the group or groups to which it testifies, while the *Laws* contain a fairly extensive collection of community rules.

Only a cursory account can be given here of the main contours of the Judaism of the Damascus Document.[15] For the purposes of brevity as well as clarity the following considers three basic topics: Israel, Torah, and Temple. But from these three, what I shall call "the Judaism of D" can be reconstructed.

Israel: The authorship of the Damascus Document represents the community for which it speaks as "Israel" in the sense of the true remnant of Israel, hence, an Israel within an Israel (1:4-5; 3:13; 4:4-5, etc.). On the basis of this self-definition, along with the fact that this Israel segregated itself socially, I regard it as a sect, a definition supported by the group's speaking of the historical "Israel" that has gone astray in the past and continues to be in error (1:4; 3:14; 4:16; 5:21; 6:1, etc.). The review of Israel's history (2:16-18) shows that it came to grief through disobedience, the result of which was punishment at the time of the exile under Nebuchadnezzar (1:6). Israel's remnant was then reconstituted under a new covenant, a new law, and a new lawgiver (3:12-16; 6:2-11). This picture of the origins of the "New Covenant" community therefore parallels other accounts (e.g., Daniel, Enoch) that speak of a new start after the Babylonian exile, effectively writing off the earlier period as disastrous.[16] The claim that D's Israel is the true successor of scriptural Israel is underlined by an extensive use of quotations and allusions to the books of Moses and the prophets, to an extent that one may at places describe the Damascus Document's text as a tissue or mosaic.[17]

This true Israel, then, is situated within an historical "Israel" that itself lies within a non-Jewish world. Indeed, while the Damascus Document regulates dealings with non-Jews without any overt polemic, it carefully regulates contact with the Israel that is in reality non-Israel, a group it sees as still in serious error and as bound for imminent divine destruction. This group is to be strenuously avoided (although converts are welcome and perhaps even canvassed), since the fate of the "covenant of the former ones (*rishonim*)" will be repeated. Or, rather, it will be *completed*, for the present is part of an "age of wrath," extending from the time of the Babylonian exile onwards. During that long period, while the true Israel has been preserved, historical Israel has been led astray by Belial and its leaders. Members of the historical Israel accordingly can be designated "children of perdition" (*benei hashahat*, 13:14).

The relationship between historical Israel and the Israel of the New Covenant is also expressed in dualistic and predestinarian terms. At 2:2-13, God is said to have chosen some and rejected others "from eternity" and to foreknow their existence; in each generation a chosen remnant has been left. This passage, however, is unique, and it does not introduce the names of heavenly powers, while elsewhere the role of Belial is confined to leading astray the historical Israel (4:12-13) and trying to lure away members of the New Covenant (12:2, where "spirits of Belial" are mentioned). Nowhere is there an angelic counterpart to Belial: he is opposed only to God. It is important to note, therefore, that a cosmic or psychological dualism does not play a systemic role in the Judaism of D: there are merely those elected and those rejected (true and false Israel) and the activity of Belial among both.

The Israel of the Damascus Document is divided into "Israel" and "Aaron" (1:7; 6:2; 19:10-11), though four additional categories (14:3-4)—priests, Levites, Israelites, and alien residents (*gerim*)—are also specified. While *gerim* could of course indicate non-Jews, it seems more likely that the term has already acquired its later sense of "proselyte," probably in this case by an analogy: the *ger* in Ezekiel is a non-Israelite permitted to be reckoned among the tribes; from the perspective of the "true Israel" of the Damascus Document, other Jews being admitted to live within this sect (presumably with the intention of membership) would be accorded this status. Thus, historical Israel is placed not quite on the level of non-Jews (even the

slaves of members of the "Damascus" sect have to belong to the "covenant of Abraham"), but are regarded as analogous to foreigners permitted to share the land of Israel (for the moment) with the possibility of joining the true Israel.

Following the scheme of Numbers, the true Israel of the Damascus Document is also organized into "camps" and ordered into units of thousands, hundreds, fifties, and tens (13:1-2). This structure may reflect a view of New Covenant Israel as recapitulating the origins of historical Israel, with the wilderness period (immediately after its receiving of the old covenant) as a time to prepare for entry into the land. A period before settlement and sanctuary, however, may have been regarded as appropriate for a group that had withdrawn from many aspects of participation in the Temple cult (see below). That the D sect thought itself to be geographically as well as typologically living "in the wilderness" is very probable.

Torah: The Israel of the Damascus Document is constituted by scrupulous obedience to the Torah revealed to it when it was instituted as the remnant. Adherence to their own will and not to the divine Torah had led the old Israel to destruction in the first place, and, accordingly, the new covenant of the Damascus sect is conveyed by a revelation of Torah. Interestingly, this new Torah was almost certainly created by exegetical development of the scriptural Torah of Moses rather than by a new text. It is not impossible that the Temple Scroll or even the book of Jubilees (referred to in 16:3-4) were understood as texts of this Torah. A "book of the *hagu*" is also mentioned in 13:2. But more probably the Torah was represented by a number of texts, including the laws contained in cols. 9-16. These collections of laws (they are evidently a collection of separate lists, with some headings preserved, e.g., at 10:10, 14; 12:19; 13:7) are of particular interest, because they constitute the earliest examples we have of a set of rules governing communal life and derived from the books of Moses. They cover matters of holiness, discipline, Sabbath observance (a separate section, 10:14-11:18), and commerce, and their headings suggest separate sets of rules for those living in "cities" and in "camps." The members of the New Covenant swear to "return to the Torah of Moses," the details of which must be learned by every member before being examined by the *mebaqqer* (15:10-11).

The laws governing the life of this group, then, are regarded as Mosaic Torah, and a distinction is made between the written text that the New Covenanters share with historical Israel (i.e., the Pentateuch) and its fuller explication in terms of community regulations (*perush*; 6:14). The distinction between the commonly available Torah and that possessed by the sect is also expressed by the terms *nigleh* ("revealed") and *nistar* ("hidden") respectively.[18]

While there are interesting similarities in much of this with Rabbinic ideology, especially the notion that the results of human exegesis constitute revealed knowledge, there are also differences. The Damascus Document lacks the distinction central to the Judaism of the Dual Torah between "written" and "oral" law, not considering the law as "dual" at all; the sectarians do not deal with holiness and tithing as fundamental and original concerns; the Damascus Document legislates for a real but sectarian community (rather than the utopian vision of the earliest rabbis), and, in the Damascus Document, the Torah is not discussed by learned authorities, such as rabbis, but is presented as if divinely commanded verbatim. Indeed, many of its formulations mimic ones used in Scripture to present apodictic law. Whether the term "halakhah" is appropriate to the Torah of the Damascus Document depends on how narrowly one wishes to define the word. While the noun is not used, the verb *hlk*—to follow the path (of the law)—is employed in the relevant sense.

According to 3:13, the key elements of the special revelation of God to the founder of the group (the "Interpreter of the Law," *doresh ha-torah*, 6:7) are "his holy Sabbaths and his glorious set times" followed by the more general "righteous testimonies and true ways." The calendar is undoubtedly a major concern of this Judaism, and it is something

to which historical Israel is "blind." But the calendar itself (on which *Jubilees* is cited as an authority) is not spelled out. The major difference that the Damascus Document addresses repeatedly, namely, between the "true" and the "historical" Israel, concerns sexual relations (4:19-5:11), specifically intercourse during the menstrual period, divorce/polygamy, and marriage between uncle and niece. In all cases what is evidently a scriptural law (accepted as authoritative by either side) is invoked and then interpreted by the authors of the Damascus Document according to their own rules: no more than one wife is permitted in a lifetime, marriage is prohibited between aunts and nephews as between uncles and nieces ("what is written as applying to males applies also to females"), and (implicitly) a longer period of female uncleanness due to menstruation.

These rules are consistent with a view that regards sexual relations as purely for procreation. The Judaism of D, then, is much concerned with regulating sexual activity, which, outside of the legitimate bounds of marriage (as strictly defined), is denounced as "lust" (*zenut*). Sexual intercourse is regarded as intrinsically unclean and so may not take place in the "city of the sanctuary" (12:1-2). Hence, while the group's members may marry and raise children (7:6-8), the implication is that some do not. The hint of a celibate lifestyle among this group is the product, it seems, of a concern for holiness.[19] It follows that if a D settlement existed in Jerusalem, its members were celibate.

Another important feature of the Torah of D is that its validity is associated with a specific period of time, running from the exile and subsequent revelation of true law to the appearance of an eschatological teacher: ". . . to walk in them [i.e., the laws] during the whole period of wickedness . . . until there shall arise one who teaches righteousness at the end of days" (6:10-11; see also 15:6-7: ". . . likewise is the commandment [*mishpat*] during the whole period of wickedness . . ."). The "period of wickedness" is also referred to as the "period of wrath" (1:4; cf., 21; 2:21; 15:7), because the divine anger and the activity of Belial (which are related) both characterize it. The clear implication remains that the validity of this law will be affected by the arrival of this "teacher," who is also a messiah (12:23: ". . . walk in these [laws] during the period of wickedness until there shall arise the [messiah] of Aaron and Israel"). There is additionally some evidence of a calculation of this "period of wickedness/wrath" and thus of the appearance of the messiah-teacher (4:8-9: "completion of the period according to the number of these years"). Probably the 390 years of 1:5 also reflect such a calculation.[20]

Temple: Several laws in the Damascus Document reveal the extent of participation in the Temple cult by members of this community (6:17-18; 9:14; 11:18-19; 12:1-2; 16:13). From these it emerges that:

1. Offerings were made at the altar or could be sent, and several different kinds of offering are mentioned, including *'olot, minhot,* incense, wood, and sin-offerings. The performance of the daily *tamid*-offering is assumed.
2. If 12.1f. applies to visitors to Jerusalem, participation in the major festivals may be included.
3. Vows extend participation in the Temple cult to private and even voluntary acts.
4. The use of Prov. 15:8 in 11:18f. suggests the idea that offerings on the altar can be adequately replaced by righteousness and prayer. But here it is cited to defend the *sanctity* of the altar, which runs counter to both the spirit and the letter of the biblical text.

The key to the place of the Jerusalem Temple in the Judaism of the Damascus Document is in 6:11-14, which precedes a number of injunctions treating matters involving external and internal relations and echoes laws or criticisms found elsewhere in the document. The passage reads:

> And all who have entered the covenant are not to enter the sanctuary "to light my altar in vain" unless they follow the observances of the law prescribed for the period of wickedness.

If this translation is correct (the passage reads awkwardly and may have been emended), we are faced with a link between participation in the Temple cult and the "law for the period of wickedness." The Temple lies at the center of the "wickedness," for there is an allusion (20:22-23) to a "period when Israel sinned and made the sanctuary unclean." From 5:6-7, too, it could be deduced that all transgressions of the laws of purity defile the Temple. Historical Israel inevitably and habitually defiled the Temple. But that did not mean that those who possessed the (true) law should totally abandon it. Israel (specifically, its priests) might "light the altar in vain," but it could still be lit in some way by those who observed the law exactly. Thus, the Damascus Document partly (*not* totally) replaces the function of the Temple by its own institutions (7:14-19):

> As it says [or: as he said]: "And I will exile the booth of your king and the *kiyyun* of your images from my tent to Damascus." The books of the law are the booth of the king, as it says: "And I will raise the falling booth of David." The king is the assembly, and the *kiyyun* of the images are the books of the prophets whose words Israel despised. And the star is the interpreter of the law who comes (came/will come) to Damascus, as it is written: "A star shall come forth. . . ."

This exegetical text speaks of the exiling of the books of the Law and Prophets. The "tent" of God, from which the Law (which includes Prophets) has been exiled, is obviously the divine sanctuary, the Temple. However, while "booth of the king" is taken to mean "the books of the law," "king" is interpreted as "assembly" (*qhl*). In 11:22 (cf., 12:16 and 14:18), the "assembly" is set in a "house of worship;" perhaps, therefore, *qhl* is not to be understood in this text simply as a designation for the community—a sense it does not bear elsewhere in the Damascus Document—but as the worshipping congregation, the community as a liturgical unit. Hence, the sect's own place(s) of worship is/are the sites to which the law has been "exiled" from the previous place of worship, the Temple. The Temple is no longer the site of law, though it remains the site of whatever cultic observance is still permissible.

The Temple cannot, of course, validly be used by those outside the sect. Their Temple worship can only defile it because of their disobedience to Torah, whereas the sanctuary could (and *should*) be used by those who possessed and observed the law. It may be appropriate to speak of the Temple's being partly supplanted. But the central importance of sanctuary to the Damascus Document's Judaism is not in doubt; its holiness extends, as we have seen, to the entire city.

The "Damascus" sect: Although in defining a Judaism it is not necessary to consider how far and by whom it was realized, it can be maintained that the "Damascus" community was a sect. It drew ideological boundaries between itself and the rest of "Israel;" it realized those boundaries socially and even geographically in a segregated lifestyle; and it claimed exclusively to be the true "Israel." It lived in distinct groups in cities and in villages ("camps") with the "city of the sanctuary" at its ideological center. Its communities had an authority structure that combined lay and priestly functionaries (*mebaqqer* and priest; cf., 13:4-6), and a strict hierarchy apparently existed, though this may have applied more stringently to unmarried settlements: the basic social unit of married groups was the household, including slaves (members of the covenant of Abraham, not of the "new covenant;" 12:11).

This sect may in fact be the first attested case of a Judaism that attempted to apply scriptural law (as it understood this law) to a communal lifestyle, and it is significant that such an experiment was only possible in a sectarian mode, in which everyday relations with other Judaisms were impossible. The relevance of such a development for the history of Judaism is immense. In some important ways it foreshadows the revolution of the Judaism of the Dual Torah by the rabbis. In acknowledging this, we must not allow ourselves to assume some normative continuity between the exclusive "Damascus" and inclusive Rabbinic Judaism. Still, comparison and contrast are possible and potentially fruitful.

The Judaism of the *Yahad(s)*: The social-historical question of the structure of the "Damascus" sect is important because, together with redaction-critical analysis of the Damascus Document, it can illuminate the process by which another Judaism (that of

the Community Rule; hereafter, S[erek]) developed from it. That it did develop is an important insight, and derived only from a redaction-critical analysis of the Damascus Document. There is no other secure way to decide the historical-typological relationship between the two (and indeed, many scholars reverse the sequence, though without any evidence at all). The Cairo manuscript A (containing the *Admonition*) is itself the product of a revision of the Community Rule, because the expected messianic "teacher" appears as a *past* figure in 1:12, while even his death is referred to in 20:14-15. At the end of the *Admonition*, his voice, along with the sectarian law, constitutes supreme authority (20:27-28), again corresponding to his expected function in 6:11. It is significant, however, that the Community Rule has revised and not replaced the Damascus Document. Indeed, the Judaism of S is a *transformation* of the Judaism of D, or, in its own terms, its proper fulfillment, its final maturity. Simply put, the Community Rule represents the Judaism of D in which an interim (valid for the "period of wrath") devotion to the Mosaic law (correctly interpreted) shares authority with a charismatic leader believed to be a/the messiah forecast in S-redacted passages in the Damascus Document. The parallel between the Judaism of Christianity and other Judaisms is attractive: it should not be overemphasized, nor ignored, because the function of the common stock of Scriptures in emerging Christianity, which added its own scriptures, provides a helpful analogy to the continued use of D texts by the community of S, or *yahad*.

The role of the "teacher" in the Judaism of S is clear, not from the Community Rule (or the Cave 4 Community Rule fragments) but from the Damascus Document, while it is also reflected in the *pesharim*, which present him, from a later perspective, as the founder of the group and allude to the D group only by its leader (the "Liar"), who is accused of having rejected the "teacher" (the New Testament parallels again impress).

S's Judaism is thus best explained in terms of its transformation of D's Judaism and not independently of it. In its definition of

"Israel," its strong dualism is most notable; the Community Rule defines its members as "children of light," (1QS 1:8; 3:24) or "children of truth," (4:5), with (apparently) the remainder of the human race (whether Jew or non-Jew) as children of darkness or falsehood. This dualism, explicated in cols. 3-4, nevertheless combines not only several sets of terminology (light/dark, truth/false, righteousness/wickedness) but also offers simultaneously a cosmic and a psychological version of its dualism, in which the two "spirits" appear now as subordinate deities to the "God of knowledge" and as internalized dispositions similar to the Rabbinic good and evil inclinations (*yetzer*; the term does occur elsewhere in 1QS).

Israel: Thus, the *category* "Israel," maintained and intensified in D, has much less of a role in this Judaism: historical Israel is not the focus of opposition, nor is there an opposition of Israel and nations. The perspective is universalized both cosmically and psychologically. On an ethical level, the same transformation is evident in the final chapter of Daniel, where the nationalistic perspective of chaps. 2 and 7 is replaced by a dichotomy between righteousness and wickedness (notably, 1QS and Daniel took their existing shape in approximately the same period). The predestination that plays on the fringes of the Damascus Document here occupies a central place. The interim "period of wrath" of the Damascus Document, between revelation of true law and revelation of true teaching, is now an interim period of "dominion of Belial" (1QS 1:23-24) between the creation of two spirits at the very beginning of time and the final destruction of Belial and his heavenly and earthly followers.[21]

Temple: The hostile attitude of the Damascus Document towards the defiled Temple cult, which was a product of high reverence for the sanctuary, is replaced in the Community Rule by an apparent rejection of its efficacy: a group of men constituting a "council of the community" are described in terms that present them as a human sanctuary (8:5-9):

> . . . the community council shall be built on truth, like an eternal plantation, a holy house for Israel and the foundation of the

Holy of Holies for Aaron . . . to atone for the world . . . the tested rampart, the prized cornerstone . . . the most holy dwelling for Aaron . . . a house of perfection and truth.

Similarly, the Temple cult will be superseded (9:4-6):

> . . . in order to atone for guilt of rebellion and for sin of unfaithfulness so as to win [divine] favor for the land without the flesh of burnt offerings and the fat of sacrifices . . . rightly-offered prayer shall be the fragrance of righteousness and perfection of way a delightful freewill offering . . . the men of the *yahad* shall set apart a house of holiness for Aaron. . . .

In an even more radical manner, the function of water as a cleansing agent is downplayed: "it is by the holy spirit of the *yahad* in [God's] truth that [a man] can be cleansed from all his iniquities" (3:7-8). Also, circumcision is deemphasized, for "he shall rather circumcise in the *yahad* the foreskin of his *yetzer* . . .'" (5:5). The conclusion to be drawn is not that these common institutions of all Judaisms were abandoned, but that their efficacy was confined to the *yahad*. Every Jewish symbol is thus strictly disciplined into a single ideological and social construction: the *yahad*. A much tighter grid is here evident than with the D groups, who do not even give a name to their communities, regarding themselves rather as members of the new, true covenant between Israel and God.

It has long been taken for granted that the *yahad* was a celibate group, and this would be consistent with the general movement beyond D's Judaism. Conceived of more explicitly as a sanctuary itself (rather than, as in D, a place where the true law lives and right worship must be practiced), the *yahad* operated under the regime of priestly purity, in which women would have of necessity been excluded. But this orientation was not entirely unprecedented, for the attitude of D towards sex as intrinsically unholy and the evidence that some of its settlements consisted of celibate males mean that the custom was inherited, even though in the process it may have been reinterpreted (much as Paul's Christianity inherited bathing as a rite of entrance into Judaism but transformed its imagery into rebirth after Christ). Continuity of customs does not guarantee continuity of ideology. The possibility that women were in some way associated with the *yahad* nevertheless continues to be entertained, largely from the existence of female skeletons (with those of children) in a cemetery on the outskirts of Qumran, and from the mention of marriage in the Damascus Document and in 1QSa. Such opinions arise from a failure to distinguish among Qumran Judaisms and result in a composite portrait of a society and a Judaism that never existed.[22]

Torah: As for Torah, the importance of the "Torah of Moses" is retained and with it the importance of correct observation of set times, which implies, no doubt, the 364-day calendar (1:14-15). But in S's covenant, less importance is attached to obedience to the covenant Torah and more to possession of "knowledge." In D, "Torah" connotes a single body of revealed law as the basis for communal living. In S's Judaism, although the will of God and the law of Moses are invoked, the language is overwhelmingly of esoteric "knowledge" (1:1 1-2, etc.), "insight" (2:3, etc.), "counsel" (3:6, etc.), and "truth" (1:5, 11, etc.). The large number of wisdom texts now recovered from Cave 4 appear to strengthen the impression that the owners of these texts succumbed to a "wisdom" world view (which might explain their attachment to dualism). But the wisdom of the Community Rule resembles a form of gnosticism— a term that needs to be used with caution, but which may be justified. The Judaism of S, to be sure, does not separate the God of creation from the God of salvation, but it does appear to regard esoteric *knowledge* as a *sine qua non* of salvation. This is a decisive movement beyond the Damascus Document's notion of a specially revealed Torah. This esoteric body of knowledge is imparted to each member by an enlightened teacher (*maskil*; not a *mebaqqer*, as in D)—the term itself has roots in wisdom terminology (and also in Dan. 12).

Evidence that the *yahad* was a more rigorously regimented society is apparent in the emphasis on the allotted status of each member (2:20-23), repetition of the word "authority" (of Zadokites and others) as well, and the practice of sharing goods in common (not found in the Damascus Document). This is commensurate with a small group founded on the teachings of a charismatic leader and especially one threatened by a larger parent movement that was still regarded as hostile, having, in the view of the members of the *yahad*, "rejected" the Teacher.

It is therefore possible and proper to conclude that while the Judaisms of D and S are not identical, they exhibit an organic relationship. This can be expressed historically, in that the *yahad* of S appears to have been formed as a splinter group from the D sect. But it can also be expressed through the *transformation* of key ideological components while nevertheless preserving the same infrastructure: holiness as obedience to divine law rather than through Temple cult; sexual relations as a purity issue; a dualistic universe in which an historic Israel stands outside and Belial rules.

An essential difference is that while the Judaism of D is self-sustaining and replicates an Israel, the Judaism of S only partly does so, defining itself very much in terms of opposition to what it is not (i.e., the continuing "Damascus" sect). Founded by a charismatic and messianic figure, it is a Judaism transformed for the eschaton (perhaps like early forms of Christian Judaism). Over the course of time, such systems must inevitably change as the expected outcomes do not materialize (the phenomenon known as "cognitive dissonance").

There is no space here to explore the traces of such development within the Community Rule material or in other Qumran texts. Only some likely contours can be indicated, and much work needs to be done in this area. It is possible that the Judaism of D also developed, but, unlike that of S, its own dynamic did not require any transformation until or unless its awaited messiah arrived.

Where do we go from here? Other Qumran Judaisms? What we can identify clearly as "D" and "S" materials do not constitute the entirety, or even the bulk, of the

Qumran literature, leaving us to ask whether either of these Judaisms is reflected also in other texts. The Rule of the Congregation (1QSa) affords a particularly interesting case. It appears to describe a restored Israel, and the majority of scholars[23] regard this as an eschatological "congregation." But, from the perspective of the authors, the term "last days" (1:1) could apply to their own time or a future one. Equally, the closing words— "according to this ruling they shall proceed at every meal where ten men are gathered together"—could designate a continuing practice in the present or the future.

Stegemann has proposed that this text is in fact the earliest rule of the *yahad* (predating the rules of both the Damascus Document and the Community Rule, which he regards as applying to the same communities), while Hempel has argued that in its original form this was a non-eschatological rule of the D group (which she identifies as the "parent Essene movement"), though it has, like the Damascus Document itself, been revised from the perspective of the *yahad*.[24] It may well be that this text began within the D group and was taken over by the *yahad*; in which case the question remains whether it comprised an eschatological "rule" already within the D group or was given such an orientation only when taken over.

The case of "M" (*Milhamah*, war) material illustrates a further range of difficulties, for "M" does not stand here for a system, a Judaism, or a particular social organization, but merely for a topic.[25] Indeed, the War Rule (1QM) is a specific recension of materials found in other recensions in Cave 4, and it contains a combination of fragments of two or more ideological systems. The dualistic framework in which cols. 15-19 are cast must be compared with that of the Community Rule, where "children of light" and "children of darkness" (in 1QM the terminology is more consistent) constitute the opposing forces, though on the side of "darkness" stand the "Kittim" also. By contrast, cols. 2-9 (and most of col. 14) exhibit a nationalistic ideology in which Israel and the nations oppose each other. The various elements have probably been fused (with a limited success) in col. 1, where a dualistic battle precedes world-wide conquest.

1QM also includes fragments of a description of an Israel similar to that of 1QSa (but also derived from Numbers, which could be a common source) in 7:1-7, while in col. 2 the restored Temple service is depicted and both priestly and lay leadership are defined. Here again we are dealing with source-materials from an uncertain origin. We can say that 1QM is composed from a number of sources and influenced by the dualism of S; that is really all. But the relationship between it and any particular group to whom we might assign a Judaism is by no means clear.

We may well be dealing with a scribal recension (as we almost certainly are) that represents an individual effort at harmonizing varied texts into a coherent account of a final victory of light, Israel, and God, and the defeat of darkness, Rome, and non-Jewish nations. The texts used in such an exercise would have been drawn from the fabric of Qumran Judaisms and possibly represent just one author's vision, one that amalgamates strictly contradictory premises. The horrible suspicion that such a possibility raises is that in the Qumran archive we do not always (if at all) directly confront the ideological products of Jewish societies but archival texts that represent copied, edited, or even amalgamated versions of older texts. The possibility that the Community Rule itself is such a case cannot be ignored, and for that reason we cannot proceed simply to draw a system on the basis of a particular text; indeed, we can in some cases reverse the process and use our reconstruction of the system as a tool to indicate possible levels in the texts that point to a literary history.

The temptation must be resisted, then, of forcing as many texts as possible into the mold or molds just created (or discovered) for "D" and "S" Judaisms. It is clear that not all Qumran texts represent a single Judaism, but also that several texts do not imply, or do not allow us to infer, a systematic Judaism; some texts may even be eclectic in this respect. The reason for the composition (or preservation) of texts in the Qumran archive may in each separate case have much, little, or nothing to do with the articulation of a specific Judaism.

It is also necessary to resist the temptation to incorporate common denominators of Qumran texts into the reconstruction of a "Qumran Judaism"—for example the existence of a calendar following a 364-day year of twelve thirty-day months (plus four intercalated days). Several earlier studies have assumed the use (or even invention) of this calendar to be a definitive mark of the "Qumran community." But the prevalence of this calendar in the Qumran archive does not prove that all such texts represent a single "Qumran Judaism." A calendar alone does not make a Judaism, and it has not yet been demonstrated that 1 Enoch and Jubilees, where the same (or a similar) calendar is embraced, also articulate a similar Judaism. The same is true of the Song of the Sabbath Sacrifice collection. The heavenly liturgy to which this attests is *consistent* with a feature of S's Judaism, in which a human community constitutes itself as a "holy of holies." But the tradition of a heavenly temple cult to which humans may have access is itself widely attested outside this form of Judaism. The essential point is that we may well expect in Qumran to find texts *consistent* with a certain Judaism, but this does not mean that these texts actually express that Judaism. The number of texts amenable to fruitful comparison is, in fact, very small.

This being said, it remains possible (and desirable) to investigate the extent to which certain texts may reflect the Judaism of D, S, or, perhaps, some other as yet unknown Qumran Judaism. So, to end on a positive note, let us briefly consider two texts that are frequently claimed as being central to "Qumran Judaism," the Halakhic Letter (4QMMT) and the Temple Scroll (11QT).

The Halakhic Letter: Although this text[26] cannot deliver sufficient evidence of a system, several current commentators have taken the view that it exposes the origins of "Qumran Judaism" in a dispute between Temple authorities and a dissident group over issues of cultic (specifically purity) law. The fragments plausibly convey the impression of differing traditions, expressed with

some force but without downright hostility. 4QMMT may imply that some formal separation has already taken place, however (C7: "we have separated ourselves from the multitude of the people"). Some support for a formal separation may also be found in the description of Jerusalem as the "camp of holiness" and "head of the camps of Israel" (cf., B29-30, 60-62). Settlements called "camps" are distinctive of the organization of the D sect, which, as has been seen, also venerated the holiness of Jerusalem and the Temple. Further, a concern for what the writers regard as illicit sexual union is expressed more than once (B48, B75, B82), consistent with a major source of opposition between the writers of the Damascus Document and their opponents. It is therefore entirely reasonable to deem 4QMMT consistent with the Judaism of D, *though not of S*. Nevertheless, if, as seems to be the case, the writers had not yet constituted themselves as a sectarian Israel, understanding themselves to be a true Israel within Israel, it is uncertain whether they had yet sufficiently articulated a system we should identify as a distinct "Judaism."

The Temple Scroll: This text has also been taken from time to time as a central text of "Qumran Judaism," though, as mentioned earlier, its publication sparked a dispute concerning whether it was "sectarian," predicated on its similarities to the Community Rule. It can probably be concluded that these two texts have *no* marked affinities.

Some affinity with the Judaism of D, on the other hand, seems likely.[27] For instance, in both 11QT (45:11) and the Damascus Document (12:1) the phrase "city of the sanctuary" occurs, and, according to both texts, no sexual activity is permitted there. But the range of material available for comparison is not extensive, given the different subject matter of the two texts. The issue of precise legal correspondences between 11QT, the Damascus Document, and 4QMMT has been taken up by Schiffman,[28] though not definitively, because like so many Qumran scholars, he is concerned with aspects of Jewish systems and aspects of Qumran documents rather than with systems themselves.

Conclusion: How to identify and describe the Judaism(s) of the Dead Sea Scrolls is a question that has so far not been very rigorously addressed. The challenge is above all a methodological one, reflecting the difficulty of sorting out the distinct strands within a corpus of texts the origins and community functions of which remain unknown. But if, despite the many difficulties presented by the nature of the evidence, we wish to identify and articulate the Judaic system(s) represented by the Qumran scrolls, the approach now outlined seems the most promising, even if the results attained here are only a beginning.

Bibliography

Beall, T.S., *Josephus' Description of the Essenes Illustrated by the Dead Sea Scrolls* (Cambridge, 1988).

Davies, Philip R., *1QM, The War Scroll from Qumran* (Rome, 1977).

——, *The Damascus Covenant: An Interpretation of the "Damascus Document"* (Sheffield, 1982).

——, *Sects and Scrolls: Essays on Qumran and Related Topics* (Atlanta, 1996).

Golb, N., *Who Wrote the Dead Sea Scrolls? The Search for the Secret of Qumran* (New York, 1994).

VanderKam, J., *The Dead Sea Scrolls Today* (Grand Rapids and London, 1994).

Notes

[1] M. Burrows, ed., *The Dead Sea Scrolls of St. Mark's Monastery* (New Haven, 1955); E. Sukenik, *The Dead Sea Scrolls of the Hebrew University* (Jerusalem, 1955); Frank M. Cross, Jr., *The Ancient Library of Qumran and Modern Biblical Studies* (London and Garden City, 1961); J.T. Milik, *Ten Years of Discovery in the Wilderness of Judaea* (London, 1959); John M. Allegro, *The Dead Sea Scrolls: A Reappraisal* (London, 1956); Roland de Vaux, *Archaeology and the Dead Sea Scrolls* (Oxford, 1973).

[2] See, e.g., Milik, op. cit., p. 74, and J. Carmignac, "Les elements historiques des 'Hymnes' de Qumrân," in *Revue de Qumrân* 2 (1960), pp. 205-22; cf., James Charlesworth, *The Dead Sea Scrolls 1: Rule of the Community and Related Documents* (Tübingen and Louisville, 1994), p. 3.

[3] See T.S. Beall, *Josephus' Description of the Essenes Illustrated by the Dead Sea Scrolls* (Cambridge, 1988); Geza Vermes and Martin D. Goodman, *The Essenes According to Classical Sources* (Sheffield, 1989); R. Bergmeier, *Die Essener-Berichte des Flavius Josephus* (Kampen, 1993).

[4] E.g., J. VanderKam, *The Dead Sea Scrolls Today* (Grand Rapids and London, 1994).

[5] See Baruch A. Levine, "The Temple Scroll:

Aspects of Its Historical Provenance and Literary Character," in *Bulletin of the American Schools of Oriental Research* 232 (1978), pp. 5-23; Yigael Yadin, "Is the Temple Scroll a Sectarian Document?," in G.M. Tucker and D.A. Knight, eds., *Humanizing America's Iconic Book* (Chico, 1980), pp. 153-169; Lawrence Schiffman, "The Temple Scroll in Literary and Philological Perspective," in William S. Green, ed., *Approaches to Ancient Judaism 2* (Chico, 1980), pp. 143-158.

[6] Philip R. Davies, *Sects and Scrolls: Essays on Qumran and Related Topics* (Atlanta, 1996), pp. 127-138.

[7] Philip R. Davies, "How Not to Do Archaeology: The Story of Qumran," in *Biblical Archaeologist* 51 (1988), pp. 203-207; Philip R. Davies, "Khirbet Qumran Revisited," in M.D. Coogan, J.C. Exum, and L.E. Stager, eds., *Scripture and Other Artifacts. Essays on the Bible and Archaeology in Honor of Philip J. King* (Westminster, 1994), pp. 126-142.

[8] An inscribed ostracon possibly containing the word *yahad* was recovered from Khirbet Qumran by James Strange and others in 1996; see F.M. Cross Jr. and E. Eshel, "Ostraca from Khirbet Qumran," in *Israel Exploration Journal* 47 (1997), pp. 17-28.

[9] Norman Golb, *Who Wrote the Dead Sea Scrolls? The Search for the Secret of Qumran* (New York, 1994).

[10] Systemically inert texts would include some that are now called "biblical" manuscripts, because even if a set of Scriptures did function systemically within a particular Judaism, we cannot either prove that or demonstrate the system from these texts. There may also be a category of non-systemic texts (e.g., possibly the Copper Scroll) that do not, and did not, belong within the system. But to dismiss any texts as outside a system is always a provisional judgment; the most improbable texts possess the potential for being read within a system, and it is better to treat such texts as inert.

[11] The distribution of texts among the caves is neither random nor wholly rational. It is possible to suggest that more than one archive is represented here (for example, only Cave 7 contained texts in Greek). But so many texts exist in copies in several caves that one would have to posit similar collections. In practice a systemic analysis can ignore this question.

[12] As attempted in D. Dimant, "The Qumran Manuscripts: Contents and Significance," in D. Dimant and Lawrence Schiffman, eds., *Time to Prepare the Way in the Wilderness* (Leiden, 1995), pp. 23-57 (cf., pp. 27-29; 37-44).

[13] Strictly speaking it is only part of a manuscript, which contains material regarded as separate and dubbed 1QSa and 1QSb. Whether we should really speak of three texts rather than one is an interesting point; but for the sake of simplicity, let us adhere to the convention.

[14] J. Murphy-O'Connor, "La génèse littéraire de la Règle de la Communauté," in *Revue biblique*

76 (1969), pp. 528-549; J. Pouilly, *La Règle de la communauté de Qumrân: son évolution littéraire* (Paris, 1976).

[15] For a full treatment, see Davies, *Sects and Scrolls*, and Philip R. Davies, *The Damascus Covenant: An Interpretation of the "Damascus Document"* (Sheffield, 1982).

[16] A similar development is traceable in the stories of Ezra and Nehemiah, which also tell (when combined, as they originally were) of a new Israel (the *benei haggolah*) founded by an individual (Ezra or Nehemiah) who makes a covenant and has the law read out and explained.

[17] This has been explored in detail by Jonathan G. Campbell, *The Use of Scripture in the Damascus Document 1-8, 19-20* (Berlin, 1995).

[18] See Lawrence Schiffman, *The Halakhah at Qumran* (Leiden, 1975).

[19] A possible scriptural basis for the association of celibacy and holiness is explored in Philip R. Davies, "Who Can Join the 'Damascus Covenant'?," in *Journal of Jewish Studies* 46 (1995), pp. 134-142.

[20] A figure of 490 years from exile to eschaton would accord with Daniel, Enoch, and the Melchizedek midrash (11QMelch). But CD 1 has been revised in accordance with S (see below), and its data do not necessarily pertain to the Judaism of D.

[21] In 9:9-11, a messianic hope remains: a prophet and the two messiahs—of Aaron and Israel—are awaited; the members must still be ruled by the "former ordinances" (i.e., those of D). Such texts warn against our assuming 1QS to be homogenous. It is clearly a repository of several stages in the transition from D to S Judaism in the *yahad*; whether these stages can be reconstructed in detail remains dubious.

[22] See Joseph Baumgarten, "The Qumran-Essene Restraints on Marriage," in Lawrence H. Schiffman, ed., *Archaeology and History in the Dead Sea Scrolls: The New York University Conference in Memory of Yigael Yadin* (Sheffield, 1990), pp. 13-24, specifically p. 20: "... celibacy at Qumran was never made into a universal norm. It was confined to those who emulated a 'perfection of holiness' requiring uninterrupted purity, and even for them perhaps only in the later stages of their lives. This would account for the fact that the *Messianic Rule*, in describing the practices of Israel at large, assumes that marriage would continue to be the 'order of the land'" (quoting from CD 7:6).

[23] Including Lawrence Schiffman, *The Eschatological Community of the Dead Sea Scrolls: A Study of the Rule of the Congregation* (Atlanta, 1989).

[24] H. Stegemann, *Die Essener, Qumran, Johannes der Täufer und Jesus* (Freiburg, 1994); C. Hempel, "The Earthly Essene Nucleus of 1QSa," in *Dead Sea Discoveries* 3 [1996], pp. 253-269.

[25] Again the search for a definitive edition of this "document" is fruitless. Instead, it is necessary to focus on an actual text. The conclusions assumed here are those argued in Philip R. Davies, *1QM, The War Scroll from Qumran* (Rome, 1977).

[26] If it is a single text; see John Strugnell in E. Qimron and J. Strugnell, eds., *Qumran Cave 4, V.-Miqsat Ma'aseh Ha-Torah* (Oxford, 1994), pp. 203-206.

[27] See P.R. Davies, "The Temple Scroll and the Damascus Document," in G.J. Brooke, *Temple Scroll Studies* (Sheffield, 1989), pp. 201-210.

[28] Lawrence H. Schiffman, "The Temple Scroll and the Systems of Jewish Law of the Second Temple Period," in Brooke, op. cit., pp. 239-255.

PHILIP R. DAVIES

DEATH AND AFTERLIFE, JUDAIC DOCTRINES OF: Judaic doctrines on the afterlife form one of the three dimensions of Jewish eschatology. These doctrines deal with the ultimate destiny of the individual Jew (and, for some authorities, with that of the righteous non-Jew as well). The other two dimensions deal with the ultimate destiny of the Jewish people (the national dimension) and that of all peoples and of the cosmos as a whole (the universal dimension).

Two independent doctrines of the afterlife for the individual emerged in Judaism, probably during the last two centuries B.C.E.: the doctrine of the resurrection of bodies and that of the immortality of souls. In time (probably the first century C.E.), these two doctrines became conflated so as to yield the theory that, at the end of days, God will resurrect dead bodies, rejoin them with their souls, which never died, and the individual human being, reconstituted as he or she existed on earth, will come before God in judgment.

Various formulations of this conflated doctrine persisted until the dawn of the Jewish Enlightenment toward the close of the eighteenth century, when liberal thinkers began to perceive spiritual immortality to be more in tune with the temper of the age, and when the idea of bodily resurrection was rejected as primitive. In the last half of our century, this process has begun to be reversed, and the doctrine of bodily resurrection is being given serious reconsideration.

The etiology of death: What the Bible has to say about the origins of death depends largely on our interpretation of the story of

Adam and Eve in the Garden of Eden, specifically of four texts: Gen. 2:16-17, 3:4-5, 3:17-19, and 3:22.

Of the four possible interpretations of these texts, the most obvious one, enshrined in official Christian teaching as the doctrine of "original sin" (though it appears in modified form in some Rabbinic teachings as well, e.g., Sifre Deut. 323), suggests that Adam was sentenced to death as punishment for his having eaten the fruit of the tree of knowledge of good and bad and that death was subsequently transmitted to all of Adam's descendants. Gen. 3:17-19 seems to support this reading, as long as the last phrase "for dust you are and to dust you shall return" is understood to be part of the punishment.

But that text could also be read to support the notion that death was part of God's plan for human beings from the outset of creation. The last phrase should then be read not as part of the punishment (which now ends with the notion that Adam must earn bread from the sweat of his brow), but simply as a re-statement of what was known by all. On this reading, Adam was being told *when* he would die, not *that* he would die, for human beings were created to die. The problem with this reading is that nowhere in the text are we told explicitly that death was part of God's plan from the outset. Also, contrary to what is stipulated in Gen. 2:17, Adam did not die "as soon as" he ate of the fruit.

On the other hand, the problem with the first reading is that it ties the origins of death to a generic sin, not directly to the sin of eating the fruit of the tree of knowledge of good and bad. But Gen. 2:16-17 and 3:2-4 seem to suggest that there is such a direct connection. This has led some authorities, notably James Barr,[1] to suggest that death should not be understood as punishment for sin but rather as a trade-off for the dawning of human awareness, for the power of rational and moral discrimination, symbolized here by the eating specifically of the fruit of the tree of knowledge of good and bad.

A fourth possible reading of the narrative, supported also by passages such as Jer. 9:19-20, 1 Sam. 22:5-6, and Hos. 13:14, views death as a relic of an ancient pagan deity, *Mwt* (cognate for Heb. *mavet*, "death"), referred to in the Ugaritic myth preserved on the Ras Shamra tablets from the second millennium B.C.E. Death, here, is a viewed as a power that remains independent of God's will, part of the pre-existent chaos that God did not succeed in eliminating through creation.

Of these four theories, the last is the least explicitly documented in our texts. That death was part of God's creation from the outset is also not explicitly documented. The first, that death is punishment for sin, is the most obvious and the most popular, probably because of its incorporation into the Christian myth. But the problems noted above lead this author to prefer Barr's reading of the Genesis narratives; this reading alone views death as the result of humans' gaining some form of knowledge.

Death in the Bible: Despite the later emergence of Jewish doctrines of the afterlife, in the Bible itself, death is understood to be final. All biblical personalities, except for Enoch (Gen. 5:21-24) and Elijah (2 Kgs. 2:11) die, in most instances we are told of their deaths, and there is no hint that any of them enjoy an afterlife.

In contrast to the two enigmatic references to Enoch and Elijah, there are ample references to the fact that death is the ultimate destiny for all human beings, that God has no contact with or power over the dead, and that the dead do not have any relationship with God (see, *inter alia*, Ps. 6:6, 30:9-10, 39:13-14, 49:6-13, 115:16-18, 146:2-4). If there is a conceivable setting for the introduction of a doctrine of the afterlife, it would be in Job, since Job, although righteous, is harmed by God in the present life. But Job 10:20-22 and 14:1-10 affirm the opposite. Whatever blessings or punishments obedience or disobedience confer, they are limited to one's lifetime on earth (cf., Exod. 20:12, Deut. 5:16, 11:13-17, and 28:1-68).

Even more, death in the bible is understood to be the arch-source of ritual impurity. Contact with the dead, even entering under the same roof with a corpse, confers impurity (Num. 19). Necromancy is sharply prohibited (Lev. 19:31, 20:6, 6:27, Deut.

18:11), and Ps. 106:28 associates sacrificing to the dead with the pagan cult of Baal Peor.

Ezekiel's vision of the dry bones that come to life (chap. 37) is clearly a metaphor for Israel's national "resurrection" from exile (37:11). One can legitimately speculate about the very use of such a metaphor in the sixth century B.C.E., centuries before a doctrine of bodily resurrection emerged explicitly in a few biblical texts. That use suggests the possible awareness of such a doctrine much earlier than we might anticipate. But even in Ezekiel, the doctrine is not explicitly articulated in non-metaphorical terms.

Upon death, people go to *Sheol*. This term and its synonyms, *Abbadon, Bor*, and *Shahat*, appear throughout the Bible. It designates the nether world, the bowels of the earth, the limit, (together with the "heavens") of human awareness (Job 11:7-8). *Sheol* is typically portrayed in terrifying terms. It is a monster that devours all people and is never sated (Is. 5:14, Prov. 27:20). It is a place of maggots and decay (Job 17:13-16). There is no awareness among the inhabitants of *Sheol* (Job 14:21-22), nor do they have a relationship with God (Ps. 88:4-5, 11-13).

Despite the oft-repeated claim that no one returns from *Sheol* (Job 7:9-10, 10:20-21), the Bible preserves one narrative that tells of such a return. 1 Sam. 28 relates how Saul, desperate for God's reassurance before entering into the battle with the Philistines, has the woman from En-dor bring Samuel up from *Sheol*. In the enigmatic encounter that follows, the woman sees Samuel though Saul does not, and Saul hears Samuel's voice though she does not. The ensuing conversation is singularly unhelpful to Saul, for Samuel reiterates that God has deserted him and that he will die in battle. The *sui generis* nature of this narrative clearly establishes the biblical insistence that once in *Sheol*, people just remain there forever. The story is more a reflection on the deteriorating condition of Saul's mental health than on life after death.

A number of biblical texts seem to imply that God does have the power to rescue people from *Sheol*. However the correct interpretation of texts such as Ps. 30:2-4, 1 Sam.

2:6-7, and Jonah 2:6-7 is that God has the power both to let people die and to cure them, i.e. to bring people *to the brink of Sheol* and to redeem them from its clutches. The parallelism in Ps. 30:4 clearly demands such a reading. These passages celebrate God's power to prevent people from dying in the first place, not to resurrect them from the dead. Again the biblical phrase "'*ani memit umehaye*," "I kill and I make alive" (Deut. 32:39) does not mean that God brings death and *resurrects*, but rather that God decrees death or *continued life* to the living. The later Talmudic liturgy will reinterpret that phrase to mean that God kills and resurrects, but that is not its biblical sense.

Despite the fact that existence in *Sheol* means total oblivion, in one sense there is a form of continued existence there. Jacob claims that when he goes to *Sheol*, he will never know his son Benjamin again (Gen. 42:38). Samuel too clearly existed in some sense while in *Sheol*. This suggests that Jacob, Benjamin, and Samuel were "there" in some mysterious sense. This may simply reflect the psychological awareness that our dead are still "present" with us. Also, Abraham and Moses are two notable characters whose death is described in far more gentle terms (Gen. 25:8, Deut. 5-7), without references to the terrors of *Sheol*. This suggests that the term was used to signify a death that follows a particularly painful life experience.

Finally, if one were to speculate on the reasons for the biblical emphasis on the finality of death, two possibilities arise. The first is to distance biblical religion from pagan religions that worshipped the dead. The second rests on the biblical insistence that only God is immortal. Human beings die, and that is the difference between them and the deity.

Biblical sources on the afterlife: Only three biblical texts explicitly affirm that at least some humans will enjoy life after death: Dan. 12:1-3, 12:12, Is. 25:18, and 26:9.

Daniel 12 is the climax of a unit (chaps. 10-12) that includes a vision (10) and an oracle (11-12). The opening verse of the passage dates what follows "in the third year of King Cyrus of Persia" (ca. 540 B.C.E.), but the ensuing oracle, which describes the course of Israelite history between Alexander the Great and Antiochus IV, could only have been written by someone who was living through the events of the reign of Antiochus IV, specifically the persecutions that led to the Maccabean revolt and the eventual rededication of the Temple in 164 B.C.E.

The author's depiction of the events of the day is remarkably accurate until it reaches the site of Antiochus IV's death (11:45). In fact, Antiochus died in late 164 B.C.E., not "between the sea and the beautiful holy mountain (i.e. Jerusalem)," but in Persia. We must conclude that this text was written prior to Antiochus' death, probably immediately prior. That the author did not know the details of Antiochus' death nor of the ultimate success of the Maccabean revolt (referred to obliquely in 11:32-35) leads us to date this passage in 165 B.C.E.

The historical setting of this passage provides the existential justification for Dan. 12:2: "Many of those that sleep in the dust of the earth will awake, some to eternal life, others to reproaches, to everlasting abhorrence;" and for 12:12: "But you, go on to the end; you shall rest, and arise to your destiny at the end of days."

The author of this text clearly is writing for those Jews who have resisted the persecutions of Antiochus IV and are dying as martyrs. He is probably also one of them. The impulse behind the introduction of the theme of the afterlife is retribution. His theological issue is theodicy. Why be faithful to God and Torah if it leads to martyrdom and if there is no reward after death? And why do the evildoers prosper if God does not exact retribution after their death? Nothing in the Torah answers these questions satisfactorily. The predominant theodicy in the Torah itself teaches that suffering is punishment for sin, but here, where is the sin? Neither does God's concluding addresses to Job leave the martyr with much to which to cling. Now a revised eschatology emerges to answer the need for theodicy.

This author is not concerned with all the previous dead nor with those who are not actively engaged in the events of the day. He

is only concerned with two groups, the pious Jews who cling to Torah and God, and the Jewish evildoers who are persecuting them. These are the "some" and the "others" who will be raised from their graves, one group for eternal blessing and the other for eternal abhorrence. The author's use of the term "awaken" (Heb., *yakitzu*) indicates that he is explicitly repudiating other texts (e.g., Job 14:12) that teach that the dead will never "awaken."[2]

The other two texts come from a unit of Is. 24-27 commonly called the Isaiah Apocalypse: "He will destroy death forever, my Lord will wipe the tears away from all faces . . ." (25:8); and "Oh let your dead revive! Let corpses arise! Awake and shout for joy, you who dwell in the dust . . ." (26:19).

In contrast to Daniel, the dating of the Isaiah Apocalypse has not been established, but it is probably somewhat prior to Daniel. The setting is again eschatological, portraying God's ultimate judgment on the earth as a whole, the host of heaven and the nations of the world, particularly the oppressors of Israel. The linguistic parallels between Isaiah and Daniel are clear. But Daniel goes beyond Isaiah in two ways. For Isaiah, the resurrection of the pious is itself the vindication of God's justice; for Daniel, it is the step prior to the ultimate reward and punishment that will follow. Second, Isaiah promises only the resurrection of the pious; Daniel envisions a resurrection of both the pious and the evildoers. These internal differences could point to an earlier date for the Isaiah passages.

On the other hand, the first of these passages could be viewed as going beyond Daniel in suggesting not only bodily resurrection but also the very death of death itself, a notion that emerges only much later in Jewish texts. But it is also possible that the author prophesies not the end of death itself but rather the end of mass killings (as suggested in the footnote to the 1985 Jewish Publication Society *Tanakh* translation of the passage). Or, as the parallelism in the verse suggests, this may be a metaphorical allusion to the end of the national reproach that God's people has suffered. Since the dating of the Isaiah passage is uncertain, it may then be roughly contemporary with Ezekiel's vision of the dry bones, in which resurrection is also a metaphor for national revival. This would suggest a significantly earlier emergence of the doctrine of resurrection than Daniel itself posits.

The author of Dan. 12 also draws upon two other themes in Isaiah. His use of the term *deraon* ("abomination") recalls Is. 66:24, the only other appearance of the term in Scripture. In this passage, however, the punishment meted out to the evildoers is that their corpses will remain unburied, not that they too will be resurrected as in Daniel. Also, Dan. 12:3, "And the knowledgeable will be radiant like the bright expanse of sky, and those who lead the many to righteousness will be like stars forever," clearly echoes Isaiah's "Servant Songs," specifically 52:13 and 53:11. The author of Daniel uses the characterization "those who lead the many to righteousness" as an apt description of the leaders of his pietist group; they are Isaiah's servant. That they will be like stars is commonly interpreted to mean that they will become angels.[3]

As to the provenance of the notion of resurrection, two possibilities suggest themselves. If this is a case of cultural borrowing, the likely source is Zoroastrianism, where resurrection is also tied to eschatological judgment. Alternatively, this marks an evolution within the body of Jewish religious teaching itself. Indeed, the Talmudic rabbis struggle to find a textual basis for the doctrine in the Torah, but there clearly is none apart from Daniel and Isaiah. However, the notion that God will eventually emerge as more powerful even than death is surely implicit in the biblical image of God as all-powerful. The message of the bulk of the Bible is that God's power is not yet totally manifest. Given the proper existential setting, it becomes explicit. Antiochus IV's persecutions may well have provided that setting.

One other internal biblical development may have also led to the emergence of the idea of resurrection. By and large, biblical historiography is concerned with the fate of the Israelite community as a whole, not with that of individuals. There are significant exceptions to that rule, notably some Psalms and Job, but these are rare. But note the explicit repudiation of Exod. 34:7, that God visits the iniquity of the parents upon children and children's children, in Deut. 24:16, Jer. 31:29-30, and Ezek. 18:2-4. In these other texts, God is portrayed as relating to each individual in terms of his or her own destiny. This sets the stage for the further claim that God's power to shape that destiny extends beyond the grave.

A number of references to resurrection also appear in the Apocrypha and Pseudepigrapha, texts dating roughly from the three centuries that follow Daniel. The most notable of these is 2 Macc. 7, the story of the woman and her seven sons who die as martyrs in the Antiochene persecutions. Each son is allotted a brief speech before dying, and four of these refer to the promise of resurrection. Interspersed with the sons' speeches are two by the mother, who seems (in vv. 22-23) to resort to an *a fortiori* argument for resurrection: if God has the power to create a human being (apparently *ex nihilo*) in the womb, then God surely has the power to restore the dead body to life.

Other references in this literature are En. 91:10 and 92:2, 4 Ezra 7:32, Syb. Ora. 4:180, and Test. Ben. 10:6-8. In the last of these, resurrection is universalized, anticipating its later development in Talmudic literature.

A similar universalization of the doctrine is found in a text in the Messiah Apocalypse (ca. 100-80 B.C.E.), one of the Dead Sea Scrolls, which celebrates God's power to reverse the natural course of affairs. Thus, just as God "frees the captive, makes the blind to see . . .," God also ". . . will heal the sick, revive the dead. . . ." The author's source is clearly Ps. 146:5-9. Both texts anticipate a similar recitation of God's power in the later liturgical *Amidah* to which we will return below. Here, however, in contrast to Daniel and Isaiah, the impulse behind resurrection is no longer God's justice but rather God's power.

The immortality of the soul: A second doctrine of the afterlife enters Judaism not in the Bible itself but in the intertestamental period, i.e., the first century B.C.E.-first century C.E. This doctrine teaches that every human being is a composite of two entities, a material body and a non-material soul; that the soul pre-exists the body and departs from the body at death; that, though the body disintegrates in the grave, the soul, by its very nature, is indestructible; and that it continues to exist for eternity.

Not even a hint of this dualistic view of the human being appears in the Bible. The three terms that were eventually used to characterize the soul, *nefesh, neshamah*, and *ruah*, in the Bible itself mean "neck" or "throat," or, by extension, that which passes through the neck or throat, i.e., breath, or, by further extension, that which confers life, hence, "a living being," not an independent, spiritual entity. (See, *inter alia*, Ex. 1:5, Ps. 150:6, and Job 34:14-15). In the Bible, a human being is a single entity, a clod of earth that, according to Gen. 2:7, is vivified by *nishmat hayyim*, the "breath of life." What vivifies the clod of earth is not a spiritual entity but rather a spark or breath. The only possible biblical anticipation of the later doctrine that the human person is a composite of body and spirit is Eccl. 12:7, ". . . the dust returns to the ground as it was, and the lifebreath [*ruah*] returns to God who bestowed it," clearly a reference to the creation of the human person as described in Gen. 2:7. This passage may mark a way-station in the eventual emergence of a full-fledged doctrine of spiritual immortality in the Talmudic tradition. Or, it may simply restate the common biblical view that, at death, the spark of life simply dissipates (Ps. 146:4).

In contrast to the uncertainty about the provenance of the doctrine of resurrection, that of the doctrine of the immortality of souls is in Greek philosophy, most notably, Plato's *Phaedo*. Here, Socrates is portrayed as welcoming death because the very act of philosophy that he has been pursuing his entire life demands the soul's liberation from its bodily prison in order to contemplate the platonic Forms or Ideas, the ultimately true reality and the source of authentic knowledge. Philosophy, then, is intrinsically redemptive. The human soul that has been struggling to reach the world of Forms dur-

ing the lifetime of the philosopher now achieves that condition for eternity. This is the ultimate blessing; this is its immortality.

No explicit reference to this platonic doctrine occurs in the Bible. It is explicit, however, in the Wisdom of Solomon, the work of a Hellenized, Alexandrine Jew, dating probably from the middle of the first century C.E. Wis. 2:22-3:8 portrays the destiny of the righteous person: "The souls of the just are in God's hand. . . . In the eyes of the foolish they seem to be dead . . . But they are at peace. . . . Their hope is full of immortality."

Wisdom reflects a blending of platonic and biblical themes. From Plato, the author takes a body-soul dualism, a mild disparagement of the body (9:15), the notion that the soul represents the source of human value (2:24), and that the soul is the source of immortality. From the Bible, the author takes the notion that righteous living, not philosophy, leads to immortality. No echo occurs here that the soul is by nature immortal. Nor is it suggested that death is to be welcomed; it is not the ultimate blessing. Finally, the grand eschatological scenario in which God exercises judgment on the wicked and the righteous echoes both Daniel and the Isaiah Apocalypse.

These two doctrines of the afterlife seem to have entered into Jewish consciousness quite independently. Daniel knows nothing of immortal souls, and Wisdom knows nothing of resurrected bodies. In fact, the two doctrines can be viewed as contradictory: the first attributes immortality to bodies alone, the second to souls alone. Yet in the later tradition, the two doctrines merge and in this form remain a centerpiece of Judaism until the dawn of modernity.

There is one major theological difference between the two doctrines. Bodily resurrection demands an active, some would say miraculous, intervention on the part of God, for the body clearly disintegrates in the grave. In contrast, souls are immortal because that is the way souls are; as spiritual substances, they are properly indestructible. Apart from creating it in the first place, God does not have to "do" anything to guarantee a soul's immortality. This distinction will play an important role in the post-Enlightenment discussion of these two doctrines.

From the Bible to the rabbis: By some time in the early Talmudic period, the doctrine of an afterlife for the individual has become quasi-canonical. This is established by two texts. M. San. 10:1, first, stipulates that only three sorts of Israelites do not have a share in the age to come: "the one who says that the resurrection of the dead is a teaching that does not derive from the Torah; [the one who says that] the Torah is not from heaven; and the Epicurean." Some (probably earlier) versions of this text read the first category to be simply one who denies the resurrection of the dead. The Talmudic phrase for the eschaton, *'olam haba*, is typically translated as either "world to come" or "age to come," with *'olam* having either a spatial or temporal reference. This author prefers the temporal designation; the eschaton can sometimes signify a new "world," but it always signifies a new "age."

The second text is the *Gevurot* (God's "mighty acts" from Heb. *gibbor*, "mighty") benediction of the Eighteen Benedictions, the second of the introductory three benedictions that are used in every single version of the *Amidah*, that, to this day, is recited at least thrice daily by the worshipping Jew. The benediction celebrates God's mighty acts. In its current form, it reads:

> You are eternally mighty, O Lord.
> You revive the dead; great is your power to save.
> (You make the wind to blow and the rain to fall.)
> You sustain the living with compassion; you revive the dead with abundant mercy.
> You support the falling, heal the ailing, free the captive; and maintain the faith with those who sleep in the dust.
> Whose power can compare with yours, who is comparable to you O king who brings death and restores life and causes salvation to sprout?
> You are faithful to restore life to the dead
> Praised are you, Lord, who restores life to the dead.

These two texts mark the canonization of the doctrine of the afterlife, because the Mishnah (ca. 200 C.E.) is the first authoritative summation of the body of Jewish law after the

Bible; the inclusion of these three theological claims in what is otherwise a legal code is striking. The liturgy, for its part, is the primary device used to introduce authoritative Jewish belief into the daily consciousness of the Jew; thus, in time, when the doctrine of resurrection came to be questioned by modern Jews, one of the typical responses was to change the wording of this text.

Dating the *Amidah* passage is a complex issue, but a version of this text, if not the one we have before us today, probably dates from the first half of the first century B.C.E. The very fact that this doctrine is mentioned six times in this short passage probably reflects an age when it was still hotly disputed, which again suggests an early first century B.C.E. date.

The key Hebrew phrases in these two texts, *tehiyat hametim* ("the resurrection of the dead") and *mehaye hametim* (God "resurrects," "revives," or "gives life to the dead"), are taken from Is. 26:19, and the reference to "those who sleep in the dust" is from Dan. 12:2. The text is a reworking of Ps. 146, but now God's power to reverse the normal state of affairs includes God's power to bring the dead to life. But the more difficult question concerns just what this concise formula meant to its author(s). It could refer to bodily resurrection alone, or it could mean the broader scenario that incorporates a notion of the rejoining of the resurrected body with the immortal soul. It clearly does convey this latter meaning in some later (post-Mishnaic) Talmudic texts, but it may also be implied here.

Resolving that question involves tracing the evolution of the doctrines of the afterlife from the Bible and the intertestamental literature to the Talmud. One of the links in the chain is the references to the doctrines in the Apocrypha and Pseudepigrapha. Another lies in the ideology of the Pharisees.

We have three primary sources on the beliefs of the Pharisees: Josephus, the Gospels, and Talmudic literature. The problem with all of these sources is that they are dated at the earliest roughly two centuries after the Pharisees are believed to have emerged on the scene of history, i.e., the second half of the second century B.C.E. They may then tell us something about the beliefs of the later (i.e., first century C.E.) Pharisees, but we have no grounds for assuming that they are trustworthy accounts of what the Pharisees closer to Daniel's time believed. Also, each of these sources is a polemical document, not dispassionate history.

Both in his *Antiquities of the Jews* and in his *Wars of the Jews*, Josephus' listing of the beliefs of the Pharisees includes a reference to their belief in the afterlife and indicates that this is one of the beliefs that distinguished them from the Sadducees and the Essenes. The latter school believed in a full-fledged, platonic doctrine of the immortality of the soul. The former denied any form of immortality.

In contrast, in Ant. 18:1:3, Josephus claims that the Pharisees believe that ". . . souls have a deathless vigor . . ." and that the virtuous ". . . shall have the power to revive and live again. . . ." In War 2:18:14, they are described as believing that ". . . all souls are incorruptible; but that the souls of good men are only removed into other bodies, but that the souls of bad men are subject to punishment."

Josephus' characterization of Pharisaic belief seems to emphasize the doctrine of spiritual immortality, though *Antiquities* can be read to include bodily resurrection. Accordingly, in this context, the Pharisees, at least those with whom Josephus was familiar, had already incorporated the conflated version of the two doctrines.

However tempting it may be to read this Pharisaic belief back into the second century B.C.E. and thereby to connect Pharisaic thinking with the group of pietists that produced Daniel, such a reconstruction lacks explicit documentation.

As to the Gospels, Mark 12:18-27, Mat. 22:23-33, and Acts 23:6-7 link Jesus and Paul to the Pharisees and to their belief in resurrection. But again, this is a late first century reading of Pharisaic ideology.

Finally, as to the evidence from Talmudic sources, the rabbis clearly see themselves as the descendants of the Pharisees. They also affirm the composite doctrine of bodily res-

urrection and spiritual immortality as we shall see below. However the relationship of what came to be called the "Judaism of the rabbis" and the early Pharisees cannot be clearly defined.

In summary, then, the Pharisees are probably one significant link in the transmission of the doctrine from the Bible to the Talmud, but the exact nature of their contribution is in dispute. What is clear, however, is that probably some time in the first century C.E. and certainly by the time of the Mishnah, the doctrine of afterlife had become canonical. The six-fold repetition of the phrase in the *Amidah* can be accounted for by postulating a setting in which the issue was in dispute; this also favors an early first-century date, for after the 70 C.E. destruction of the Second Temple, there were no more Sadducees or Essenes. It is also probable that the doctrine included belief in both bodily resurrection and spiritual immortality.

One liturgical text that captures the conflated doctrine is a portion of the liturgy recited upon awakening from sleep. It is recorded in B. Ber. 60b and reads in part:

> My Lord, the soul that you have given me is pure. You created it . . . you fashioned it, you breathed it into me . . . and you will eventually take it from me and return it to me in the time to come. . . . Praised are you Lord who restores souls to dead bodies.

The use of the terms "soul" and "me" here, together with the notions that the soul pre-existed the body, exits from the body at death, and is later restored to the body, suggest a more dualistic view of the human person than anything recorded in the Bible itself.

But an even clearer picture of the conflated doctrine is in the analogy attributed to the late second century C.E. rabbi Judah the Prince (B. San. 91a-91b). The body and soul are likened respectively to a blind man (the body) and a lame man (the soul) who conspire to steal fruit from an orchard by the device of having the lame man sit on the shoulders of the blind man. When the owner comes to punish them, each seeks to exculpate himself by arguing that he is incapable of committing the crime. But the king places the blind man back on the shoulders of the lame man and judges them together as one person. So will the body and the soul of the individual be reunited and come before God in judgment at the end of days.

By the time of the Talmud, the hope for an afterlife has become thoroughly universalized; it applies to all Jews who had every lived and, according to some Talmudic teachings, to righteous gentiles as well (T. San. 13:2). It is also clear that the impetus for the doctrine is no longer God's justice as in Daniel and Isaiah, but God's power. If God is truly God, then God's power must extend even beyond the grave.

Though the doctrine of an afterlife for the individual is hardly explicit in the Bible, the Talmud abounds with attempts to see it there, one more fanciful than the other (B. San. 90b-92a). The rabbis were not overly concerned with what may be called the "mechanics" of resurrection. Some of the models suggested include the metaphors of seeds that break through the ground, awakening from sleep, the effects of the dew, the fashioning of a pot from clay, or of bricks from the earth (B. Ket. 111b, Tan. Toledot 19, Gen. Rab. 13:6, B. San. 91a).

Notably, though it may seem to be a short step from affirming resurrection to affirming the eschatological disappearance of death itself, there are very few texts from this period that say this explicitly. The clearest reference is Aquila's translation of the last word in Ps. 48:15, *almut* ("forever") as the Greek, *athanasia* ("deathlessness"). He reads that verse to mean that God will lead us to "a world in which there is no death" (Lev. Rab. 11:9). It is also explicit in the last verse of the folk ditty, *Had Gadya*, which concludes the Passover Haggadah, dating from the sixteenth century C.E. Here, after the Angel of Death slaughters the slaughterer, "then comes the Holy One Blessed be He and slaughters the Angel of Death."

Maimonides and the medieval philosophers: What we have called the conflated doctrine of the afterlife that emerged in the age of the Talmud retained its hold until the dawn of modernity. Even so, Jewish thinking in the Middle Ages showed a decided preference for the doctrine of spiritual immortality. Bodily resurrection was never explicitly rejected, as it would be in the Enlightenment. It simply could not be, given its canonical status. But it was frequently relegated to a secondary status or, in some instances, was designated an interim stage in the eschatological scenario.

Maimonides (1135-1204) furnishes the paramount example of that latter strategy. In three distinct statements at various stages of his career, he dealt with the issue of the afterlife: in his *Commentary to the Mishnah*, specifically in the extended introduction to M. San. 10:1 (commonly called "Introduction to *Helek*," the title of that chapter of the tractate, taken from the opening words of the Mishnah, "All Israel has a portion [Heb., *helek*] in the Age to Come"); in ch. 8 of the Laws of Repentance in his code, the *Mishneh Torah*; and, finally, in a separate monograph, the *Essay on Resurrection*. There is no discussion of this entire topic in the author's *Guide of the Perplexed*, probably because he does not consider it to be a philosophical issue.

In the *Essay*, Maimonides expresses considerable frustration at the misunderstanding that his previous statements had generated. He had been accused of denying resurrection or of dismissing it as a metaphor. He vehemently denies both charges, insisting that his writings are clear and explicit and should be carefully read. In fact, however, the chapter in the *Mishneh Torah* makes absolutely no mention of resurrection, and his discussion of resurrection in *Helek* is brief and obscure, both in its own right and in comparison with his discussion of spiritual immortality, with which he deals rhapsodically and at great length.

The proof-text to which Maimonides refers again and again in support of his views is at B. Ber. 17a: "In the age to come there is no eating, drinking, washing, anointing, or sexual intercourse; but the righteous sit with their crowns on their heads enjoying the radiance of the Divine Presence." Maimonides reads this text to mean that in the age to come, there will be no need for bodies, since bodies exist only to perform various functions; if there are no bodily functions in the age to come, there will be no need for bodies. He then interprets the text allegorically: the "crown" represents the knowledge of the truly essential nature of God; that the crown is "on the head" indicates the soul's firm possession of this ultimate idea; "to delight in the radiance of the Divine Presence" means that the souls enjoy "the blissful delight in attaining this knowledge which is like that experienced by the angels who know [God's] existence first hand." This discussion is repeated almost verbatim in the *Mishneh Torah*.

This is the "ultimate good," the "final end," the "incomparable good, for how could that which is eternal and endless be compared with anything transient and terminable?"

In contrast to this extended treatment of spiritual immortality, resurrection is discussed in one paragraph. Resurrection is "one of the cardinal principles established by Moses," and "one who does not believe it has no real religion, certainly not Judaism." The paragraph concludes with this enigmatic sentence: "All men must die and their bodies decompose." At the end of the Introduction, Maimonides lists his Thirteen Principles of Faith, the minimal creedal commitments required of every Jew. Each of the thirteen principles is explicated, but the thirteenth reads simply: "The thirteenth fundamental principle is the resurrection of the dead which we have already explained."[4]

Only in his last statement, the *Essay on Resurrection*, does Maimonides spell out clearly and explicitly what he believes on this issue. His view posits a theory of a double dying: we die once, we are then resurrected sometime around the coming of the Messiah (which, for Maimonides, is a period independent of and prior to "the age to come"); we then die a second time, and, after that, in the age to come, the souls of the righteous achieve the ultimate reward reserved for souls alone, as he described in *Helek*. Resurrection and spiritual immortality are both true, but they emerge sequentially.

Why has he treated these two topics at such different lengths? Because resurrection is a miracle; it simply has to be accepted as

such. Spiritual immortality, in contrast, is a "hidden" matter that has to be explicated. Why is the Torah silent on resurrection? Because it deals with the natural, familiar course of affairs; by nature, the dead do not come back to life. When the biblical texts deny resurrection, they simply affirm that it is impossible by nature. But God's miraculous power can transform the natural order.

Finally, Maimonides resorts to an evolutionary view of biblical religion. Were God to have revealed the miracle of resurrection in the early stages of Israelite history, the people would have rejected the entire Torah. When, however, the basic principles of Judaism had become firm and valid, resurrection could be introduced into the picture.

The tension between bodily resurrection and spiritual immortality is one instance of the broader tension that permeates Maimonides' thought as a whole between the claims of revelation (as embodied in Torah) and of reason (as embodied in the Greek philosophy). On this issue at least, the latter wins out. Maimonides could not conceive of anything material subsisting eternally. Yet he could not deny the revealed tradition he had inherited. His uneasy compromise, then, is to accept both views but to view them as two distinct acts in the eschatological drama.

On this matter, the *Essay* does not repudiate Maimonides' earlier views, but it does spell out, for the first time clearly and explicitly, what he probably believed all along but had never stated. His caution may have reflected his vulnerability to the views of certain fundamentalists, both Jewish and Muslim.[5] But this final formulation would have done little to mollify his critics. Maimonides may also have been concerned that those who believe in the eternal existence of bodies may be led to believe in God's corporeality as well, which, he believed, constituted the ultimate philosophical heresy and which he attacked throughout his career. His position also marks Maimonides as the primary Jewish exponent of a dualistic view of the human person.

We have almost contemporaneous evidence of the controversial nature of Maimonides' position in the comment of Abraham ben David of Posquieres (d. 1198), printed as a sidebar in the Hebrew edition of the *Mishneh Torah* (Laws of Repentance 8:2): "This man's words are in my eyes near to those who assert that there is no resurrection of the body but only of souls. But by my life, this was not the opinion of our sages. . . ." He proceeds to quote various Talmudic statements that teach that it is the body that will be resurrected, and he concludes: "All of which is conclusive proof that the dead will arise with their bodies and remain alive. . . ."

The tension between bodily resurrection and spiritual immortality is a familiar theme in the writings of the other major medieval Jewish philosophers who preceded and followed Maimonides.

Saadiah ben Joseph (882-942), in his *Book of Beliefs and Opinions*, quotes Dan. 12:2, Is. 26:19, and Ezek. 37 as providing the biblical proof-texts for bodily resurrection, which he then proceeds to defend on philosophical grounds by arguing that if God could create the world out of nothing, God should then be able to bring dead matter back to life (echoing the mother's speech in 2 Macc.). Matter is never destroyed but simply preserved in other forms. Saadiah argues further that there will be two resurrections: that of the righteous Israelites at the time of the Messiah (so that all righteous Israelites will participate in the messianic redemption of Israel) and of other righteous persons in the Age to Come. The resurrected body, merged with its souls, will then come before God in judgment.

The medieval thinker who most approximates Maimonides' own view is Abraham ibn Ezra (1092-1167). In his commentary to Dan. 12:2, he accepts the notion of a double dying, with the second resurrection remaining totally spiritual.

Maimonides' arch-opponent among the medievals, Moses ben Nahman, known as Nahmanides (mid-thirteen century), insisted that both body and soul would live eternally. Since bodies are needed in this world, they will be present in the future world as well, though our future bodily existence will be spiritually refined and will not experience physical needs. Nahmanides quotes Is. 25:8

as denying Maimonides' view of a double dying.

This critique of Maimonides is echoed by Hasdai Crescas (1340-1444), who also insists that both body and soul will enjoy eternal life as a reconstitution of the kind of life that was lived on earth. Finally, as the period draws to a close, Maimonides' views are reasserted by Joseph Albo (1380-1444) in his *Book of Principles.*[6]

The overriding concern throughout this material is the tension between the claims of Torah and those of philosophy. Maimonides remains the single most creative voice among the medievals on this issue as in so many others. By the close of the fifteenth century, the broad agenda of medieval Jewish philosophy as a whole has become moot, only to be revived again with the dawn of modernity at the close of the eighteenth century.

The mystical journey of the soul: Medieval Jewish mystics share with their philosophical colleagues a primary concern for the ultimate destiny of the soul. Bodily resurrection is never rejected, but it is never accorded the same degree of interest that the mystics exhibited with the story of the human soul, its history prior to its incarnation in the body, its vicissitudes during its bodily existence, and, pre-eminently, its journeys between the death of the individual and the grand resurrection to come. On this last issue, the primary contribution of Jewish mysticism (popularly called *Kabbalah*, the "received tradition") is the notion of the transmigration of souls, or, to use the more popular term, reincarnation.

Though this doctrine is not found in either the Bible or the Talmud, though it was opposed by philosophers such as Saadiah and Albo and ignored by others such as Maimonides, it became omnipresent in medieval mystical literature, and it persists in the popular imagination to this day.

The doctrine of reincarnation teaches that after death, some souls that have departed the bodies in which they were housed return to inhabit other bodies—how many depends on the stage of the development of the doctrine over time—until the resurrection. Jews probably inherited the doctrine from Oriental religions and medieval neo-platonism. It emerges for the first time in one of the earliest mystical texts, *Sefer haBahir* ("The Book of Illumination"), which appeared in the twelfth century in Southern France.

The impulse behind the emergence of the doctrine is retribution; it is, at root, a theodicy: the righteous must suffer because of the sins committed in an earlier incarnation. The doctrine thus becomes an expression of both God's judgment and God's mercy: judgment, because sin must be punished; and mercy, because God gives the soul innumerable opportunities to perfect itself prior to the final judgment. At the outset, the sins that reincarnation purges are limited to sexual offenses. It serves also as a justification for the practice of levirate marriage, the biblical command that the brother of a man who dies without progeny must marry the widow (Deut. 25:5-10). But by the time of the classic statement of Jewish mysticism, the Zohar (late thirteen century), its scope expands to deal with all human sin; it becomes a universal law of retribution.

Since one soul may become identified with many bodies, the resurrection of any one body affects the destiny of the many other bodies that housed this soul. This expanded, universalized form of the doctrine becomes central in the teachings of the sixteenth century school of Safed mystics under the leadership of Isaac Luria.

For Luria, the process of redemption is understood as a *tikkun* ("repair") of the "broken vessels," two key terms in the Lurianic myth. These vessels, designed to contain the emanated light of creation and order the created world, were broken in the act of creation. This brokenness serves as the symbol for the "brokenness" of all things in this age of history. All things, not only Israel, are in "exile," a metaphysical symbol or metaphor for the imperfections that characterize the world or history as we know it. Even God is in exile; God as *Shekhina* (the indwelling presence of God) is split away from God as *Ein Sof* (literally, "Infinity"). The idea of reincarnation as an opportunity for retribution for sin is pushed into the background, and now every soul has limitless opportunities to

achieve its individual *tikkun* through fulfilling more and more of God's commands until it reaches its state of perfection. Thus every individual *tikkun* affects the cosmic process of restoration, which leads ultimately to the redemption of Israel, the world as a whole, and even of God as well.

The master of Jewish mysticism, Gershom Scholem, captures the ultimate effect of Luria's teachings: "Lurianic Kabbalah placed the Jew in an ineluctable entanglement of transmigrations. . . . (A)ll things are in exile . . . all things must wander and transmigrate in order to prepare, through a combined effort, for redemption."[7]

For the mystics, Jewish eschatology was essentially an eschatology of the soul. Though severely derided by the scholars of the Enlightenment as primitive and embarrassing, Jewish mysticism as a whole and particularly its Lurianic version had an extraordinary impact on post-expulsion Jewish communities. Lurianic metaphors continue to appear in popular Jewish thinking to this day, and the doctrine of reincarnation has achieved wide popularity in what is commonly called "New Age" thinking and for a new generation of Jewish spiritual seekers.

In the Enlightenment: If medieval Jewish philosophy and mysticism exhibits a decided preference for the doctrine of the immortality of the soul over that of bodily resurrection, the Jewish Enlightenment accentuates that process even further. Belief in bodily resurrection is judged to be primitive, unsophisticated, even, astonishingly, not grounded in classical Jewish sources. Eventually, it is dismissed. In contrast, spiritual immortality is praised as more intellectually respectable, more elevating, more in tune with the enlightened temper of the age. Maimonides' teachings are omnipresent in the literature of this period.

A forecast of what was to come can be seen in *Phaedon or On the Immortality of the Soul* (1767) by the prototypical enlightened Jew, Moses Mendelssohn. As its name implies, this is an eighteenth century reworking of Plato's *Phaedo*, providing a series of rational arguments for the immortality of the soul. Though not primarily addressed to the author's Jewish contemporaries, it accurately captures the concerns of the age: what is important is the ultimate destiny of the soul, and the truth of that doctrine is demonstrated through rational argumentation.

The further evolution of this emphasis can be viewed through the writings of the leaders of the nascent Reform movement in nineteenth century Germany, primarily in their reformulations of classical Jewish liturgy. Reform was the first modern Jewish religious movement to face the challenges of the Enlightenment, and all future such movements, in one way or another, played off the teachings of what came to be called "Classical" (i.e. early nineteenth—mid-twentieth century) Reform. Since it was always the liturgy that brought central Jewish teachings into the consciousness of the Jew, and since it was the liturgical embodiment of doctrines of the afterlife in the Talmudic period that helped to canonize those teachings, the Reform rabbinate had to deal with the tensions between their own thinking and the traditional liturgy.

One way of tracing the progressive disenchantment from the doctrine of bodily resurrection is to study the changes that were progressively introduced into the closing words of the *Gevurot* benediction of the *Amidah*, referred to above. The earliest Reformers were loath to tamper with the traditional liturgy,[8] but at a conference of Reform rabbis in Brunswick in 1844, Abraham Geiger, the acknowledged ideological father of Classical Reform, suggests that his movement must deal with some liturgical doctrines that were foreign to the new age. One of these was the hope for an afterlife, which, he proposed, should now stress not the resurrection of the body but rather the immortality of the soul. In the 1854 prayer book Geiger edited for his congregation in Breslau, he kept the original Hebrew of the benediction, but translated its concluding passage, . . . *der Leben spendet hier und dort* (freely translated: "who bestows life in this world and the other").

The champion of the radical wing of Classical Reform was David Einhorn (1809-

1879). Einhorn was singularly responsible for transplanting Reform ideology from Germany to America. In his 1856 prayer book, *Olat Tamid: Book of Prayers for Jewish Congregations*, published for his congregation in Baltimore, Einhorn replaced the traditional Hebrew closing formula with a new version that praises God, "Who has planted immortal life within us." That formula was later used in the 1895 *Union Prayer Book*, which became standard in all American Reform congregations until 1975, when it was replaced by *The New Union Prayer Book*, more commonly known as *Gates of Prayer*. This latter prayer book, in turn, typically substitutes for the closing words of the benediction, the formula *mehaye hakol* (variously translated: "Source of life," or "Creator of life.")

These liturgical changes were echoed in the various platforms issued by American Reform rabbis as a way of giving their movement a measure of ideological coherence. An 1869 conference of Reform rabbis, held in Philadelphia, affirmed that "(t)he belief in the bodily resurrection has no religious foundation, and the doctrine of immortality refers to the after-existence of souls alone." This Philadelphia statement served as the basis for an even more influential statement of the principles of Reform, the Pittsburgh Platform, adopted in 1885. The sixth paragraph of that statement asserts that ". . . the soul of man is immortal." It continues, "(w)e reject as ideas not rooted in Judaism the belief . . . in bodily resurrection. . . ." Finally, the 1937 Columbus Platform states, "Judaism affirms that man is created in the image of God. His spirit is immortal."

Still a third expression of the shift in thinking among Reform rabbis can be seen in theological treatises such as Kaufman Kohler's *Jewish Theology: Systematically and Historically Considered* (republished, New York: Ktav Publishing House, 1968). Einhorn's son-in-law, Kohler (1843-1969) succeeded him as the champion of the radical wing of American Reform. He was responsible for convening the Pittsburgh Conference and for drafting its platform. Kohler's book devotes three full chapters to a historical overview of Jewish thinking on the afterlife and concludes that "... he who recognizes the unchangeable will of an all-wise, all-ruling God in the immutable laws of nature must find it impossible to praise God ... as the 'reviver of the dead,' but will avail himself instead of the expression ..., 'He who has implanted within us immortal life'" (pp. 296-297). For Kohler, God's power reveals itself not in the miraculous but rather in the "immutable laws of nature," which decree that all material things must die, that death is final, and that only the spiritual can live eternally.

Apart from American Reform, the other modern Jewish religious movement that dismissed bodily resurrection outright was Mordecai Kaplan's Reconstructionism. Kaplan (1881-1983) was arguably American Judaism's most innovative thinker. A thoroughgoing religious and theological naturalist, he propounded the view that Judaism was the "civilization" of the Jewish people. The Jewish people can then reformulate its beliefs and practices to make it possible for new generations of Jews to identify with their civilization.

In 1945, Kaplan published his *Sabbath Prayer Book*, which carried his ideological commitments into the liturgy. His Introduction to the prayer book lists the "Modification of Traditional Doctrines" reflected in his work, and one of these is the doctrine of resurrection (pp. xvii-xviii). Kaplan rejects resurrection, accepts spiritual immortality, but refuses to impose it on the traditional liturgical text of the *Amidah*. In place of the traditional formula, he uses a phrase from the High Holiday liturgy that praises God "... Who in love rememberest Thy creatures unto life." This was but one of the many changes in the traditional liturgy that led to Kaplan's excommunication by a group of Orthodox rabbis. A more recent Reconstructionist prayer book, *Kol Haneshamah* (1994), replaces Kaplan's phrase with a version of the Reform formula, "Who gives and restores life." A literal translation of the Hebrew *mehaye kol hai*, by contrast, would read simply "who gives life to all living things."

The Conservative Movement in contemporary American Judaism was born in 1886. As its name implies, it was a conservative reaction to what it viewed as the excesses of American Reform and its Pittsburgh Platform. In contrast to Reform, this Movement generally avoided ideological self-definition, largely because it perceived itself to be a broad coalition of the more traditionalist elements in American Judaism.

The various prayer books published by the Conservative movement generally (but not always) avoid tampering with the traditional Hebrew liturgy. The movement's preferred strategy for dealing with troublesome doctrines embodied in the liturgy is to retain the Hebrew text but to shade the translation to reflect a more acceptable reading of the doctrine. As an instance of this practice, the 1945 *Sabbath and Festival Prayer Book*, omnipresent in Conservative congregations in the middle decades of this century, translates the concluding words of the *Gevurot* benediction, "who calls the dead to life everlasting." In the Foreword to this prayer book, Robert Gordis, the Conservative rabbi and scholar who chaired the committee that edited the prayer book, justifies this translation by noting that this rendering of the traditional Hebrew "... is linguistically sound and rich in meaning for those who cherish the faith in human immortality, as much as for those who maintain the belief in resurrection" (pp. viii-ix).

Gordis' personal predilection for spiritual immortality over bodily resurrection is recorded in his *A Faith for Moderns* (revised and augmented edition, New York: Bloch Publishing Co., 1971): "The facet in man's nature which is deathless, the vital spark, the breath of life, we call the soul" (pp. 251-252).

A more recent prayer book for use in Conservative congregations, *Siddur Sim Shalom* (1985), is more aggressive in its liturgical changes, yet it retains the tradition Hebrew formula for the *Gevurot* benediction, which it translates "give life to the dead," or, more freely, "Master of life and death."

Finally, all prayer books for use in contemporary American Orthodox congregations, primarily the various editions compiled by Philip Birnbaum (New York: Hebrew Publishing Co.) and those under the Art Scroll imprint (New York: Mesorah Publications, Ltd.), retain the traditional Hebrew text of the liturgy and translate it literally as either ". . . who revives the dead" or ". . . who resuscitates the dead."

By the middle of the twentieth century then, the entire liberal wing of the American Jewish religious community had abandoned the doctrine of resurrection, either explicitly by modifying the Hebrew liturgy, implicitly by shading its translation in favor of spiritual immortality, or by adopting a deliberately ambiguous reading of the Hebrew.

The return to resurrection: The concluding decades of the twentieth century have witnessed a cautious but significant reappraisal of the doctrine of bodily resurrection. Some of the factors leading to this reappraisal may include a renewed interest in the language of theological discourse, specifically the sense that all of theology must be understood as mythical and symbolic; the emergence of what has come to be called "post modernism," a distancing, by scholars in diverse fields, from the critical, scientific, or rationalist temper of what, in contrast, has come to be called the "modern" temper; the Holocaust experience of mass dying and its implications for a contemporary understanding of survival and the afterlife; and a new focus on issues of Jewish spirituality and on the need to create new liturgies and rituals that evoke the modern human experience. This final factor has led to a generalized rebellion against the more institutional and conventional expressions of the Jewish experience that had reigned since the Enlightenment.

One of the more influential statements of this new impulse is in Will Herberg's *Judaism and Modern Man.* Herberg (1901-1977) was a former Marxist who returned to Judaism under the influence of the writings of Martin Buber, Franz Rosenzweig, and the Christian theologian Reinhold Niebuhr. His chapter on eschatology, "History: Meaning and Fulfillment," is built on the assumption that Marxism is a secular version of biblical thinking on the end of days.

Herberg's review of the major themes of Jewish eschatology culminates in a discussion of the doctrine of bodily resurrection, which, he insists, is properly "outrageous" but indispensable and should not be confused with the doctrine of spiritual immortality. Herberg affirms what he calls the "symbol" of bodily resurrection, because it claims that ". . . man's ultimate destiny is not his by virtue of his own nature—by possession of an 'immortal soul'. . .—but comes to him solely by the grace and mercy of God . . .;" because it affirms that what is to be fulfilled is not a disembodied soul, but ". . . the whole man— body, soul and spirit—joined in an indissoluble unity;" and because it affirms that God's promise of salvation marks (pp. 229-230):

> . . . the corporate redemption of men in the full reality of their historical existence. The whole point of the doctrine . . . is that the life we live now . . . the life of empirical existence in society, has some measure of permanent worth in the eyes of God, and will not vanish in the transmutation of things at the last day.

Herberg's disdain for the doctrine of spiritual immortality is rooted in his generalized disdain for what he calls the "otherworldly" and "antihistorical" outlook of Greek and Eastern dualism. In contrast, Herberg argues that Judaism affirms the value of history and of society and the actual world of human events, and he views the doctrine of bodily resurrection as a symbolic affirmation of this world-view.

Herberg's arguments are echoed by two theologians who share his existentialist orientation: Arthur A. Cohen, in his essay, "Resurrection of the Dead;" and Hershel Matt, in a monograph, "An Outline of Jewish Eschatology."[9] Cohen, like Herberg, claims that the doctrine of resurrection is paradoxical yet endures because if God is truly God, then God can work paradoxes. Resurrection, then, is the ultimate manifestation of God's power. Cohen also affirms the doctrine of bodily resurrection because it alone respects the concrete individuality of every human being: "God bestows upon the dead a unity analogous to that which he has won for himself—a unity of illuminated consciousness and perfected flesh."[10]

Matt's major contribution to the inquiry is his extended footnote[11] on theological language as mythical: "A 'mythical'. . . statement seeks to point to a truth . . . which is beyond the power of science to demonstrate, beyond the power of experience fully to confirm, beyond the power of logic to prove, beyond the power of rational discourse to convey." The truths affirmed by the doctrine of resurrection include: that God's purposes for humans are not ultimately defeated by death, that our ultimate fulfillment is beyond death and history, and that we must accept full responsibility for the life we have led. All eschatological language is inherently mythical, Matt claims, and that is precisely the source of its power.

Still another theological reaffirmation of the doctrine is in a monograph, "Resurrection," by Morton Wyschogrod in *Pro Ecclesia* 1:1 (Fall, 1992), pp. 104-112. Wyschogrod echoes his colleagues in claiming that ". . . because God is a redeeming God, it follows that death cannot be the last word. . . . Either death wins or God saves." Redemption marks God's ability to transform "whatever bad things happen to people," but the conquest of death is ". . . the one triumph of the negative over which we have not as yet seen any triumph" (p. 109). Wyschogrod makes the further claim that the major difference between Jewish and Christian eschatology lies in the fact that Christians can claim to have witnessed God's triumph over death (in the resurrection of Jesus of Nazareth), whereas Jews cannot.

This reconsideration of bodily resurrection is also taking place within the ranks of the Reform and Conservative movements. In an extended inquiry into the current state of Reform ideology in *Reform Judaism Today* (New York, 1983), the movement's reigning theologian, Eugene B. Borowitz, distances himself from the prevailing notion that what survives death is the human soul: "Our present difficulty is that the notion of such a spiritual substance as a soul is no longer intellectually tenable for most modern thinkers. . . ." He continues that ". . . we cannot believe that having shared so intimately in God's reality in life, we do not continue to share it beyond the grave," and he trusts that ". . . having reached such heights in our personhood, our individuality, we trust that our survival will likewise be personal and individual" (vol. 2, pp. 45-49).

One year later, Borowitz goes significantly beyond this cautious statement. He confesses that while he has no knowledge of what awaits him after death, he is ". . . inclined to think that my hope is better spoken of as resurrection than immortality for I do not know my self as a soul without a body but only as a psychosomatic self."[12]

The Conservative movement, for its part, issued its first statement of principles in a pamphlet entitled *Emet Ve-Emunah* (1988). Its statement on "Eschatology: Our Vision of the Future" includes an affirmation of both of the two classical Jewish doctrines on the afterlife and adds that these doctrines can be understood both literally or figuratively. A figurative understanding of bodily resurrection could be viewed as teaching that Judaism values ". . . our bodily existence in our concrete historical and social setting." Spiritual immortality, for its part, affirms that ". . . our identities and our ability to touch people and society does not end with the physical death of our bodies" (pp. 28-29).

Emet Ve-Emunah was never affirmed by any significant body within the Conservative movement apart from the committee of academicians, rabbis, and lay people who drafted it. The extent to which it reflects the thinking of the movement as a whole can then be legitimately questioned. The same applies to Borowitz's statement in regard to current thinking within Reform.

Indeed, this reaffirmation of bodily resurrection on the part of contemporary liberal thinkers is far from unanimous. The Conservative rabbi/theologian Louis Jacobs, in his *A Jewish Theology* (New York, 1973), affirms that ". . . we should be frank enough to admit that all the speculations regarding life here on earth after the resurrection simply do not 'ring a bell' for us whereas the more spiritual interpretation of a Maimonides does" (p. 319).

Finally, we should note two recent book-length inquiries into Jewish notions of the afterlife by Simcha Paull Raphael and this author, Neil Gillman. Both volumes review the history of the doctrines and both conclude with more personal statements of the authors' beliefs. Raphael's personal statement draws on the Jewish mystical tradition, hasidism, contemporary thanatology, Buddhism and Hinduism, and on the teachings of the transpersonal school of psychology.[13]

My own study views all eschatological discourse as mythical and claims that belief in resurrection is neither a biological statement nor primarily a prediction of events that will take place in some indefinite future. It is rather an integral portion of the classical Jewish religious myth, which is designed to help the individual Jew make sense of his or her existence in the here and now. For the rest, I draw on the writings of the authors mentioned above, primarily Herberg, Borowitz, and Wyschogrod, and the French Catholic philosopher, Gabriel Marcel. I thus affirm the indispensability of the doctrine of bodily resurrection understood precisely as a mythical statement, because it asserts the integrity of the body to the sense of self.[14]

Conclusion: It is too early to predict whether or not this recent reappraisal of bodily resurrection will have a lasting impact on post-millennial Judaism. One indicator will be the outcome of the ongoing discussion of liturgical change in Reform prayer books. A decision on the part of Reform rabbis and lay people to reintroduce the traditional Hebrew closure of the *Gevurot* benediction in forthcoming Reform prayer books would be a notable expression of the power of the traditional doctrines. Finally, it is not unlikely that the coming millennium will generate a renewed interest in eschatology in general and in the afterlife in particular.

Bibliography

Bailey, Lloyd R., Sr., *Biblical Perspectives on Death* (Philadelphia, 1979).

Barr, James, *The Garden of Eden and the Hope of Immortality* (Minneapolis, 1992).

Gillman, Neil, *The Death of Death: Resurrection and Immortality in Jewish Thought* (Woodstock, 1997).

Nickelsburg, George W.E., *Resurrection, Immortality and Eternal Life in Intertestamental Judaism* (Cambridge, 1972).

Raphael, Simcha Paull, *Jewish Views of the Afterlife* (Northvale, 1994).

Notes

[1] *The Garden of Eden and the Hope of Immortality* (Minneapolis, 1992), pp. 62-65.

[2] My interpretation of the Daniel passages follows that of George W.E. Nickelsburg, *Resurrection, Immortality and Eternal Life in Intertestamental Judaism* (Cambridge, 1972), pp. 11-28, and James J. Collins, *Daniel: A Commentary on the Book of Daniel* (Minneapolis, 1993), pp. 394-398.

[3] Collins, ibid., p. 393.

[4] For the complete text of this Introduction, see I. Twersky, ed., *A Maimonides Reader* (New York, 1972), pp. 401-423. For the complete text of the *Essay on Resurrection* and a discussion of its contents, see Abraham Halkin and David Hartman, *Crisis and Leadership: Epistles of Maimonides* (Philadelphia, 1985), pp. 209-292.

[5] This is proposed by Joshua Finkel, "Maimonides' Treatise on Resurrection: A Comparative Study," in *PAAJR* 9 (1939), ch. 4.

[6] A useful compendium of the views of medieval philosophers on this issue is in J. David Bleich, *With Perfect Faith: The Foundations of Jewish Belief* (New York, 1983), pp. 619-687.

[7] Gershom Scholem, *On the Mystical Shape of the Godhead: Basic Concepts in the Kabbalah* (New York, 1991), p. 241.

[8] Jakob J. Petuchowski, *Prayerbook Reform in Europe: The Liturgy of European Liberal and Reform Judaism* (New York, 1968), p. 215.

[9] Arthur A. Cohen and Paul Mendes-Flohr, eds., *Contemporary Jewish Religious Thought* (New York, 1987), pp. 807-813; in *Judaism* 17:2, Spring, 1968, pp. 186-196.

[10] Cohen, ibid., pp. 811-812.

[11] Op. cit., p. 191.

[12] Eugene B. Borowitz, *Liberal Judaism* (New York, 1984), p. 222.

[13] Simcha Paull Raphael, *Jewish Views of the Afterlife* (Northvale, 1994), pp. 357-402.

[14] Neil Gillman, *The Death of Death: Resurrection and Immortality in Jewish Thought* (Woodstock, 1997), pp. 243-274.

NEIL GILLMAN

E

EASTERN EUROPE, PRACTICE OF JUDA-ISM IN: Eastern Europe—Poland and Lithuania in particular—was, for many centuries, the domain of the largest and most important Jewish settlement in the world, a community that fashioned a distinctive and particularly intense form of traditional Jewish learning and religious practice. Jews first settled in Poland and the Grand Duchy of Lithuania in the twelfth century. From the second half of the fifteenth century until the Second World War, the Jewish population of Eastern Europe rose steadily and produced many of the most important and influential Jewish religious and educational institutions. On the eve of the Nazis' invasion in 1939, more than 3.4 million Jews lived in Poland, and another four million lived in Lithuania and Russia (including Ukraine and Belarus), the vast majority of whom were exterminated in the Holocaust.

Origins—Khazars and Karaites: There is some uncertainty regarding the religious and racial origins of the first Jews to settle in Poland and the Grand Duchy of Lithuania. Included among the earliest adherents of some form of the Jewish faith to reside in the region (as early as the first half of the twelfth century) were not only "Ashkenazic" Jews of Western European origin but Khazars and Karaites as well. The Khazars were a conglomerate of nomadic Turkic tribes from central Asia. Around the year 740 C.E., a Khazar king, Bulan, converted to Judaism, together with some elite members of Khazar society. Over the course of the next three centuries, many of the Khazar tribes migrated northwest into Russia.

The Karaites were a Jewish religious sect originating in North Africa that broke with normative Judaism in the eighth century, rejecting the rabbinical interpretations of the Bible contained in the Talmud and codes of Jewish law. Some Karaites migrated from the orient to Russia during the eleventh and twelfth centuries and from there apparently moved westward into Poland. The destiny of the Khazars in Eastern Europe, the extent of their representation in the subsequent Polish-Jewish population, and their influence on its religious practices are to this day debated by historians. The views on this matter range from the great nineteenth-century historian Heinrich Graetz's insistence that the Khazar conversion to Judaism had almost no effect on subsequent Jewish practice in Eastern Europe to Arthur Koestler's controversial book, *The Thirteenth Tribe*, which argues that a majority of Ashkenazic Jewry is descended from the Khazars. The latter claim notwithstanding, it is clear to scholars today that, over the course of the fourteenth and fifteenth centuries, most of the Khazars were assimilated into Poland's dominant Jewish community, which was overwhelmingly of Ashkenazic (Franco-Germanic) origin. The consensus among contemporary Jewish historians regarding the Khazars then generally follows Salo Baron's view that, while the conversion of the Khazar king and some members of his nobility was a significant event in medieval Khazar history, it had at the very most a marginal impact on the subsequent religious and ethnic identity of the Jewish population of Eastern Europe.

As for the Karaites, they gradually separated themselves entirely from the Ashkenazic Jews and maintained their own communities, traditions, and religious institutions. During the Nazi occupation of Eastern Europe, the Karaites successfully saved themselves from persecution by asserting that they were not Jews at all. A tiny Karaite community, with a synagogue and cultural center, remains today in the village of Trokai, near Vilnius, Lithuania.

Ashkenazic Judaism: The beginnings of a significant Ashkenazic Jewish community in Eastern Europe can be traced primarily to several major waves of immigration from Western and Central Europe. In the late thirteenth and fourteenth centuries, Jews, mostly fleeing intense anti-Jewish persecutions and a series of expulsions, migrated eastward from Germany and Bohemia into Poland and the Grand Duchy of Lithuania. There was a sharp rise in massive Jewish migrations to Eastern Europe over the course of the fifteenth century, largely in response to another wave of expulsions of Jews from more than a dozen cities and towns in Bohemia.

These Jews brought with them the distinctive form of Ashkenazic, or Franco-German, Judaism. Both culturally and spiritually, East European Jews remained Ashkenazic in nature until their extermination during the Holocaust. The liturgy and particular religious traditions of the Jews of Poland, Lithuania, and, later, Russia and Ukraine, followed those of the medieval Franco-German Jewish communities from which the majority of Polish Jewry had originated. Moreover, until the sixteenth century, most of the leading rabbis of Poland were émigrés from the west who had trained in the Ashkenazic rabbinical academies of Germany and Bohemia.

Unlike the Sephardic Jews (i.e., those of Spanish origin) who flourished in Spain, North Africa, and the Ottoman Empire, and who were profoundly influenced by the surrounding Islamic society and culture, Ashkenazic Jewish religion and culture were deeply insular, based almost entirely on the study of Rabbinic texts and adherence to the norms of Talmudic law. There was precious little interest in, or knowledge of, any aspects of the surrounding European culture. Among the main characteristics of the religion was its devotion to and reliance upon the Talmud, its commentaries, and the Rabbinic legal codes based on them as virtually the sole sources for religious practice, theology, and spirituality. Unlike the Sephardic Jews of Spanish and Portuguese origin who, in the more religiously tolerant and culturally open Iberian Muslim society, developed varied and sophisticated philosophical and mystical interpretations of Judaism as well as belletristic traditions, Ashkenazic Jews—largely because of their intellectual and cultural isolation from a hostile Christian society—focused almost solely on the extant Rabbinic literature in shaping their religious beliefs and practice.

Despite their profound alienation from the gentile culture and societies of Eastern Europe, Jews initially found far greater security in Poland and Lithuania than they had enjoyed in the Western European lands, thanks in large measure to a succession of *privilegia*, or charters, issued to them by the Polish and Lithuanian monarchs. The motive for the promulgation of these charters, which guaranteed the Jews basic rights and privileges, was clearly economic; they were intended to attract Jewish traders to Poland and Lithuania in order to bolster these young countries' infirm monetary resources and were not motivated by any spirit of religious tolerance or pluralism. The first of the "Jewish charters" was granted in 1264 by Prince Boleslav the Pious of Great Poland and Kalisz. This charter—known as the statute of Kalisz—was confirmed by Kazimir the Great in 1364 for the Jews of Poland and in 1367 for the Jews of Cracow, Sandomierz, and Lwow. In only slightly altered form, these charters were again confirmed by King Ladislas Jagiellow in 1387.

The basic content of the Jewish charters was to guarantee the Jews the rights of residence, physical protection from assault, the freedom to worship in their own traditions, and almost complete autonomy for their municipal governments and religious courts and other institutions. By the mid-sixteenth century, the Jews of Poland had developed an autonomy unprecedented in Jewish history. Jewish communities were well-organized, highly structured, and almost totally self-governing. Each major Jewish community, or *Kehillah*, had its own city council as well as both lay and religious court systems. The Kehillah governed virtually all aspects of Jewish civic life, such as taxation, the regulation of settlement and demographics, the adjudication of legal disputes, the maintenance of law and order, and the management of relations with the monarch and other gentile authorities. The kehillah also exercised much authority over the smaller Jewish communities in the surrounding villages. Regional, inter-kehillah synods, the largest and most important of which was known as the "Vaad Arba Aratzoth" (Council of Four

Lands), met regularly in the larger cities, such as Cracow and Lublin, to govern relations and settle any religious or civil disputes between the various Jewish communities.

From the very beginning, the leading rabbis of Eastern Europe were intimately connected with the powerful kehillah leadership. Not only did the kehillah appoint rabbis for the Jewish communities in cities and towns across Eastern Europe; it was very common for the sons and daughters of the rabbinate to marry into the wealthiest and most powerful families in the Jewish community. While the rabbinate and the kehillah leaders had differing responsibilities and authority, the intricate connections between the two often rendered them indistinguishable.

This extensive communal autonomy and Rabbinic influence, unprecedented in the history of the Jewish diaspora, secured Jewish life for centuries. But such autonomy also had the long term effect of radically separating Jews both socially and culturally from the larger society. As a consequence of this separation, Jewish learning and religious practice in Eastern Europe remained for centuries ingrown and almost entirely immune to outside intellectual and spiritual influences. Perhaps the most overt sign of this was the East European Jews' almost exclusive use of the Yiddish vernacular in daily life—a cognate of German written in Hebrew characters and incorporating a very large number of Hebrew and Talmudic-Aramaic terms. Even during the period of European enlightenment, when the Jewish intelligentsia strove to acclimatize the Jews to the larger European society and culture, the Jewish masses of Poland, Russia, Ukraine, and Lithuania largely remained culturally, linguistically, and religiously secluded.

While the royal privileges, particularly when compared to the dreadful conditions of Jewish life in Germany and Bohemia, rendered Poland an attractive place for Jews to settle, there was, from the beginning, significant anti-Jewish hostility in Polish society, particularly on the part of the Church. Anti-Jewish persecution was particularly fierce during the fifteenth century, largely due to the efforts of Cardinal Zbigniew Olesnicki, whose intense anti-Jewish agitations resulted in the Nieszawa statute of 1454, repealing all of the charters and privileges that had previously been granted the Jews. But despite these setbacks, by the first decade of the sixteenth century, most of the Jewish privileges in Poland had been re-instated by the king. There was, indeed, a constant tension generated by conflicting attitudes towards the Jews between the Church and the Polish monarchy. The Church preached that the Jews ought to be condemned to a life of perpetual poverty, subjugation, and serfdom, as a punishment for the crime of "deicide" (that is, the murder of Christ, for which medieval Christianity held the Jews responsible), while the Polish monarchs generally favored protecting the Jews and granting them basic freedoms.

Though originating in opposing attitudes to the Jews, the Church's antisemitism and the monarchs' protection of the Jewish community's autonomy converged in their impact on the nature of Eastern European Judaism. Communal separation and religious antagonisms combined to intensify the profoundly particularist quality of East European Judaism. Alienated from the larger society, deeply distrustful of gentiles, autonomous in their self-government, and excluded from general European learning and culture, East European Jews remained for centuries virtually untouched by outside, non-Rabbinic influences. Only the Talmud, its Rabbinic commentaries, and the codes of Jewish law were studied in the Jewish elementary schools and rabbinical seminaries. While this produced a population that was uniquely steeped in Rabbinic literature and culture, and a Rabbinic elite with unprecedented Talmudic erudition, with regards to any and all forms of non-Rabbinic knowledge, the masses of East European Jews were functionally illiterate until the twentieth century. The daily lives of the Jewish masses—particularly those living in the shtetls (small towns) and villages were almost completely governed by the norms and customs of Jewish law.

The Golden Age: The sixteenth century is usually described as the golden age of Polish Jewry. During this period, the community began to produce great educational and cultural institutions of its own. Perhaps the most important development was the creation of important Polish yeshivas (rabbinical schools), which eventually became famous for a distinctively complex and casuistic method of Talmudic study known as "pilpul." By the mid-seventeenth century, Poland had become the international center of rabbinical scholarship, and—in a dramatic reversal of earlier trends—Jewish communities in other countries, such as France and Germany, became dependent on the Polish yeshivas to provide them with religious leaders.

The founder of the first great rabbinical school in Poland was Jacob Polak of Lublin. Polak was born and educated in Bavaria and served as Chief Rabbi of Prague before moving to Poland. In 1492, he established Poland's first advanced talmudic academy in Cracow. His most distinguished student, Shalom Shakhna, established Poland's second great yeshiva in Lublin. For almost three centuries, Lublin and Cracow remained the most important centers of rabbinical scholarship in the world. Lublin was widely known as the "Jerusalem of Poland," and on the eve of the Second World War was the home of the most eminent yeshiva in Poland, "Hakhmei Lublin," founded by Meyer Shapiro in 1931.

One of the most distinguished disciples of Shalom Shakhna was Moses Isserles (1520-1572), who became known as the "Maimonides of Poland." Isserles, who became Chief Rabbi of Cracow after studying in the Lublin Yeshiva, was a distinguished Jewish theologian and a leading authority on Jewish law. His most important and influential work was a series of glosses to the Shulkhan Arukh Code of Jewish Law, which remain the authoritative basis for Jewish religious observance for orthodox Ashkenazic Jews to this day. Among the major Rabbinic authorities of this period were Solomon Luria, author of the Talmudic legal compendium *Yam Shel Shelomo*, and Mordechai Jaffe, author of the ten volume encyclopedia of Judaism, *Asara Levushim*.

Along with the precipitous growth of Poland's Jewish population, Jewish religious life and talmudic scholarship continued to deepen and flourish in the seventeenth century. In this period, significant numbers of Jews moved eastward however, following Poland's colonization of the Ukraine and the unprecedented economic opportunities this expansion afforded.

Persecution and religious decline: Many of the Jews who settled in eastern Poland and the Ukraine served as leaseholders, tax farmers, shopkeepers, and tavern managers for the Polish landowners, thus finding themselves in the uncomfortable role of economic middlemen between the Polish nobility and Ukrainian peasantry. Combined with their total religious, linguistic, and cultural alienation from the peasants, this engendered tremendous resentment of the Jews on the part of the Ukrainian masses. That anti-Jewish hostility exploded during the Cossack rebellions against the Poles of 1648-1649, led by the Ukrainian nationalist, Bogdan Chmielnitski. Along with the Polish Catholic clergy and nobility as well as members of the Uniate church, Jews were among the principal targets of the marauding Cossack warriors, who managed to devastate entire Jewish communities on both sides of the Dniepr River. Aside from the tens of thousands of Jews who were killed, many thousands were forced to accept Christianity. The ferocity and scope of the destruction inflicted on the Jewish population was unprecedented in Jewish history and left the Jewish communities across the region severely traumatized. Several Jewish authors of the period wrote chilling chronicles depicting the horrors of the Ukrainian revolt, the most extensive and accurate of which is *Abyss of Despair*, by Nathan Nata Hanover. Hanover documented in particular the eradication of the great Jewish religious and educational institutions, which had flourished during the sixteenth century "golden age" of Polish Jewry. He also provides the most vivid, if nostalgic, description of the rich Jewish religious life and institutions that flourished before the massacres.

Despite these tragic setbacks, the Jewish community continued to grow demographically, and Jewish religious life began once again to thrive during the eighteenth century. The population increase during this period was particularly dramatic. According to the census of 1764 (the year of the abolition of the Council of Four Lands), there were almost 600,000 Jews in Poland, more than sixty percent of whom were living in the eastern regions of the country and the Ukraine.

Superstition and messianism: Despite the dramatic demographic resilience of East European Jewry, the educational and religious institutions that had shaped Jewish life during the golden age never fully recovered from the trauma of the Ukrainian pogroms. With the numbers of yeshivas greatly diminished and the terrible memories of the pogroms still vivid, two very different forms of Judaism that deeply divided the Jewish community began to emerge: an effete, scholarly religious culture based exclusively on Talmudic erudition but restricted to an aristocracy of rabbis and the very wealthy members of the kehillah elite and an ignorant, intellectually unsophisticated and heavily superstitious faith of the hoi polloi, whose Judaism became increasingly dominated by a variety of primitive folk-beliefs and superstitions. The popularity of moralistic books of popular mysticism replete with superstitious belief in demons, magical amulets, the powers of curses, and a deep distrust of gentiles, such as *Yesod Yosef* and *Kav ha-Yashar*, both of which were translated into Yiddish for mass readership, reflects this phenomenon.

The intensification of antisemitic persecution and successive waves of Ukrainian pogroms in the seventeenth and eighteenth centuries not only deepened the isolation and religious primitiveness of Eastern European Jews. It also led to a rise in messianic expectations and a susceptibility to false messianism. The infamous messianic pretender, Shabbetai Zevi (1626-1676), gained a mass following in Poland and Ukraine. And Poland produced the most notorious messianic figure in Jewish history, Jacob Frank (1726-1791), who transformed the messianic doctrine into a bizarre antinomian faith, whose central teaching was that the ritualistic violation of the tenets of Jewish law would hasten the redemption. In 1759, after wreaking havoc in many Polish Jewish communities and participating in the public burning of the Talmud, Frank converted to Christianity. Sabbatean and Frankist believers subsequently concealed their faith in East European Jewish society because of fear of excommunication but persisted secretly in their beliefs and practices well into the nineteenth century.

Hasidism: In the context of such deepening superstition and perverse messianism, the populist-mystical Hasidic movement originated in the heavily Jewish populated southeastern regions of Podolia and Volhynia. Founded by a school of charismatic kabbalists and faith healers, Hasidism spread rapidly throughout Eastern Europe during the last decades of the eighteenth century, gaining hundreds of thousands of adherents and thereby transforming the spiritual life of Polish Jewry.

Although the mystical spirituality associated with hasidism developed in Eastern Europe during the late eighteenth and early nineteenth centuries, the actual founding of the movement is commonly identified with the personality of Israel b. Eliezer (1700-1760) of Mezibozh (a small town in Volhynia, in southeast Poland) and his circle of close disciples. Israel was a charismatic mystic popularly known as the *Besht*, an acronym for the Hebrew honorific, Baal Shem Tov (master of the divine name), a title he earned thanks to his reputed powers as a kabbalistic faith-healer. The Besht was part of a small coterie of religious pneumatics in Podolia and Volhynia, who, though never renouncing Jewish law, favored religious spontaneity and the ecstatic practice of the kabbalah over the more conventional Rabbinic disciplines of intense Torah study and traditional halakhic observance.

As the Besht's reputation as a charismatic mystical teacher and faith-healer spread across Poland and the Ukraine, he attracted an impressive cadre of disciples, many of whom had previously held distinguished rabbinical positions but were apparently attracted to the spiritual passion and personal magnetism of the Besht. According to the hasidic hagiography of the Besht, *Shivhay ha-Besht* (In Praise of the Baal Shem Tov), many of these rabbis were weary of the dry and perfunctory regnant Rabbinic culture and found the religious ecstasy promoted by the Besht to be a refreshing alternative to the arid and emotionless practice of conventional Talmudic Judaism.

The two most eminent of these Rabbinic disciples of the Besht were Jacob Joseph of Pollnoe (d. 1782) and Dov Ber of Mezeritch (d. 1772), both of whom were distinguished rabbinical figures before being attracted to his mystical teachings. Jacob Joseph was hasidism's first major literary figure. His biblical commentary, *Toledoth Yaakov Yosef*, which was the first hasidic work ever published (1780), created a storm of controversy in Eastern European rabbinical circles. This book is of singular theological importance because it contains dozens of teachings received first-hand from the Besht, who did not himself record his ideas. *Toledoth Yaakov Yosef* is also of tremendous historical significance since it includes a sustained critique of the rabbis of Jacob Joseph's generation, whom the author refers to using the shocking term "*Shaydin Yehudain*," or Jewish demons. Jacob Joseph's major complaint against the rabbis was their scholarly elitism and distance from the Jewish masses. He complained that they were far more interested in the fine points of Talmudic discourse and the minutiae of Jewish law than in the actual lives and daily spiritual struggles of the Jewish masses. In his writings, we find the first formulation of an alternative model of religious leadership, that of the hasidic *zaddik* (righteous man), or *rebbe*. Whereas the religious and communal authority of the Eastern European rabbis had always derived from their scholarship—specifically their mastery of the Talmud and the codes of Jewish law— the hasidic rebbes were primarily charismatic

leaders whose authority derived from their personal holiness and reputed spiritual powers. And, unlike the establishment rabbis who remained isolated and divorced from the Jewish masses in their Talmudic ivory towers, the hasidic rebbes dedicated their spiritual energies to helping the many simple Jews who did not enjoy the advantages of advanced Talmudic training.

At the very heart of hasidic life in Eastern Europe was the intimate relationship that developed early on in hasidic history between the masses and the *zaddikim*, or rebbes. The influence of the hasidic rebbes and their total command over the lives of their followers was, in fact, unprecedented in Jewish history. Unlike the traditional non-hasidic rabbis, the rebbes' domain of authority was not limited to matters of Jewish law and religious ritual. The rebbe was the final arbiter of every imaginable personal problem and predicament facing his flock.

While Jacob Joseph formulated an elaborate theology to advance the religious authority and vital social role of the rebbe, it was the other major disciple of the Besht, Dov Ber of Mezeritch (best known as the *Maggid*, or preacher, of Mezeritch), who put this theory into practice by preparing the members of his own circle themselves to serve as rebbes. The Maggid of Mezeritch was a highly charismatic cleric who created the model of a hasidic "court," from which the zaddik ruled the lives of his hasidim, or adherents, in truly regal fashion. This model of hasidic leadership has continued virtually unchanged since then and—successfully transplanted from Eastern Europe to hasidic communities in America and Israel—can be observed to this day. The Maggid not only trained a significant number of disciples in the ways of hasidic spiritual leadership; he strategically dispensed them throughout Eastern Europe to establish courts of their own. Among the most important of Dov Ber's disciples were Levi Isaac of Berditchev, Nahum of Tchernobil, Elimelekh of Lyzansk, Hayyim Haykel of Amdur, Aaron of Karlin, Shneur Zalman of Ladi, and Menahem Mendel of Vitebsk.

Beyond directing a revolution of sorts against the established Rabbinic order, Dov Ber inculcated in his disciples a deeply monistic mystical faith in divine immanence, the thorough omnipresence of God in the created world. Classical hasidism's conviction that "God is all" and that "there is no place uninhabited by his presence" constituted a rejection of the dualism that characterized earlier schools of Jewish mysticism as well as the conventional Rabbinic belief in, and legal reverence for, distinct realms of the pure and impure. This hasidic faith in the pervasive presence of God remains hasidism's central doctrine and still guides many aspects of hasidic life today.

Charged with the mystical enthusiasm of their mentor, Dov Ber's disciples in turn established hasidic courts of their own in Ukraine, Poland, Russia, Lithuania, Belarus, and Palestine. Thanks to their spiritual enthusiasm and inherently popular and optimistic religious message, hasidism spread and quickly became a major spiritual force in virtually every Ashkenazic Jewish community in the world—even in Lithuania, where hasidism was most vociferously opposed by the Rabbinic leadership. One of the most important and charismatic leaders in the history of hasidism was the mystic Jacob Isaac of Lublin, best known as the "Seer" of Lublin, whose many disciples ultimately became the spiritual leaders of more than one million Polish Jews before the Holocaust. One of the more subtle, but highly repercussive, effects of the hasidic revolt against the Rabbinic establishment was the decentralization of religious authority in Eastern Europe. Although the courts of hasidic rebbes were based in towns after whom each sect became known, their authority far transcended these locales. One could be a follower of Levi Isaac of Berditchev, for example, and live hundreds of miles from his Ukrainian town. Since the authority of each rebbe derived from his personal charisma rather than his formal appointment as a Chief Rabbi by the elected community elders, hasidim would flock from dozens of places across Eastern Europe to visit and receive the teachings, advice, and blessings of their chosen rebbes. At the same time, the allegiance of hasidic Jews to local rabbinical authorities declined precipitously.

By the third generation of the movement, then, hasidism had spread very rapidly as a revolutionary, populist alternative to traditional Rabbinic Judaism. Despite the reality that over the course of the nineteenth century Hasidism became, and remained, the most reactionary religious movement in Judaism, one must keep in mind that it itself began as a rebellion against the ossification of the Jewish faith by the Rabbinic oligarchy and kehillah authorities. The chief goal of that revolution was to restore spontaneity and spiritual enthusiasm to the alienated Jewish masses, and its net effect was the disengagement of those masses from the established Jewish community.

Aside from its break with the traditional Rabbinic leadership of the day, Hasidism's most important and revolutionary religious message centered around the concept of "*devekuth*," or mystical communion with God. Whereas, in Jewish spiritual life, any mystical activity had hitherto always been the exclusive provenance of a highly restricted, elite cadre of kabbalistic initiates, hasidism promulgated a popularized form of religious ecstasy, intended to be easily accessible to each and every Jew. Toward that end, the hasidic leaders broke ranks with the institutional religious life, establishing independent prayer houses where a kabbalistic variation of established liturgy was introduced and in which the prayers were performed with great mystical enthusiasm, marked feverish swaying, song, and dance. On account of its essential optimism and populism, the hasidic movement attracted many followers particularly among the least educated and most disenfranchised sectors of East European Jewish society, further exacerbating the rift between the wealthy learned elite and the untutored masses.

The hasidim also instituted a variety of new rituals and standards for religious observance. The most notable and socially repercussive of such ritual changes was the introduction of a stricter method of *shekhita*, the kosher method for the slaughter of animals. The creation of autonomous synagogues and the enactment of distinct dietary standards effectively disengaged the hasidic community from the rest of Ashkenazic Jewish society.

In the course of the nineteenth century, hasidism spread very rapidly throughout Poland and Galicia and from there made significant inroads into Hungary, Romania, and Czechoslovakia. Although never formally repudiating the religious and social radicalism of the movement's founders, over the course of the century, hasidism tended to grow increasingly conservative, largely in response to the spread of the Jewish enlightenment to Eastern Europe. While the radical mystical ideals of the Besht and the Maggid were officially preserved in the rhetoric and theoretical writings of the later hasidic masters, for all practical purposes, they became the most religiously conservative and politically reactionary of Jewish leaders in Europe. This conservatism was first reflected in the violent opposition of the hasidic rebbes to the changes in Jewish religious practice advocated by the enlightenment and reform movement and, later, in their hostility to the emergence of modern Jewish political ideologies, Zionism and the varieties of Jewish socialism in particular.

The very nature of hasidic leadership also eventually contributed to the internal degeneration and spiritual ossification of the movement. The early hasidic leaders were religious charismatics who rebelled against an ensconced Rabbinic elite that had become too powerful and alienated from the life and daily spiritual needs of the average Jew. However, by the middle of the nineteenth century, hasidic leadership had become almost exclusively dynastic, with rebbes bequeathing the mantel of leadership to their sons, regardless of their competence or qualifications for the challenges of religious leadership. The inherited nature of hasidic leadership, combined with the absolute authority granted by hasidim to the rebbe, led to much abuse and, in many sects, precisely the kind of exploitation of rabbinical po-

wer against which hasidism had originally revolted.

By the end of the nineteenth century, the hasidim accounted for almost half of the world's orthodox Jews. There were hundreds of hasidic societies, large and small, to be found throughout Eastern Europe. Among the largest and most important hasidic sects at the turn of the century were: Ger, Aleksander, and Rizhin in Congress Poland; Habad (or Lubavitch) in White Russia (today, Belarus); Bobov, Belz, and Vishnitz in Galicia; and, Munkacz, Sighet, and Satmar in Hungary and Carpathian Ruthenia (today, northern Romania). Though suffering some attrition as a result of the modernization of Jewish life in Europe and the seductions of the enlightenment, these important groups—along with many other minor hasidic sects—flourished until the eve of the Second World War.

The hasidic world was absolutely devastated by the Holocaust. While some of the most prominent rebbes managed to escape to Palestine, the overwhelming majority of their followers was completely wiped out by the Nazis. In fact, hasidim account for more than thirty percent of Hitler's Jewish victims. The hasidic rebbes' rejection of Zionism and their resistance to the emigration of their followers to America only made matters worse. For, on the eve of the war—aside from a few thousand hasidim in Jerusalem and New York City—hasidic life was restricted almost exclusively to Eastern Europe.

The Mitnagdim: Despite the rapid spread of the hasidic movement across Eastern Europe, Lithuania remained a bastion of traditional Rabbinic culture and was largely unreceptive to hasidism. This was largely due to the profound antagonism displayed towards hasidism by the greatest Talmudist of the time, Elijah ben Solomon of Vilna (1720-1797), commonly referred to as the Vilner Gaon ("the genius of Vilna"). He was the single most important figure in the formation of a distinctive Lithuanian form of Judaism. Although the Vilner Gaon was, for most of his life, a reclusive scholar who refused to accept any official post, in his last years he channeled all of his energies to lead the Rabbinic resistance to the spread of the hasidic movement. The Vilner Gaon directed an energetic campaign across Lithuania and Belorussia to block the hasidic rabbis from attaining any religious influence or communal authority. He even went so far as to declare meat slaughtered by hasidic rabbis as unkosher and to ban "intermarriage" between hasidic Jews and members of his own community.

The basis for the Vilner Gaon's hostility towards hasidism was ostensibly the movement's emphasis on religious ecstasy and mysticism at the expense of the Torah scholarship that had hitherto been the supreme value in Jewish religious life. As an antidote to hasidism's anti-intellectual spirituality, the Lithuanian disciples of the Vilner Gaon further elevated the role of Talmudic scholarship to the very epicenter of religious life.

One of the Vilner Gaon's most distinguished students, Hayyim ben Isaac (1749-1821), established a talmudical academy for advanced rabbinical students in the small town of Volozhin, near Vilnius, in 1802. Although numerous yeshivas had existed in Eastern Europe since at least the sixteenth century, the academy at Volozhin set new standards for scholarship and raised the prestige of yeshiva students to unprecedented levels. Through its graduates, the yeshiva in Volozhin generated similar elite rabbinical academies in such Lithuanian and Belorussian cities as Paneviecz, Kaminiecz-Litovsk, Slobodka, Telsiai, Kletsk, Mir, and Slutsk. The most important academic innovation of this network of Lithuanian yeshivas was the rejection of the old convoluted method of Rabbinic casuistry, *pilpul*, in favor of a more rational, conceptual approach to the Talmudic text.

Though this impressive network of Lithuanian Talmudical academies, which comprised a kind of "Ivy League" in the world of Jewish academia, was decimated by the Nazis, many were re-established after the war in the United States and Israel and still bear the names of their Lithuanian towns of origin. To this day, the orthodox Jewish world is divided between hasidim, whose leaders are charismatic mystical rabbis mostly of Polish and Hungarian origin and their descendants, and the *mitnagdim*, led by the deans of the Lithuanian yeshivas and their disciples.

One particularly important offshoot of the Lithuanian yeshivas was the emergence of the "Musar" movement, a religious revivalist faction of Lithuanian orthodox Judaism founded by Israel Lipkin of Salant (1810-1883), which emphasized rigorous moral introspection and ethical perfection along with Talmudic scholarship. By fashioning an intense Jewish spirituality rooted in study and ethical excellence, the Musar movement also served to obstruct the spread of hasidism as well as the Jewish enlightenment to Lithuania.

Largely as a result of the influence of the Vilner Gaon and his followers—the mitnagdim—Lithuania became famous as the home of one of the world's most learned and intellectually vibrant Jewish communities. The intensity of Jewish learning and the high level of Rabbinic scholarship in Lithuania were legendary. According to one tale, when Napoleon entered the Jewish quarter of the Lithuanian capital, Vilnius, he was so impressed by the plethora of Jewish religious and cultural institutions, that he declared: "This is the Jerusalem of Lithuania." Whatever the actual origins of that appellation, thanks to the unparalleled tradition of eminent Jewish scholarship that had developed there, Vilnius was widely known as the "Jerusalem" of Eastern Europe until the Nazis' liquidation of the Jewish ghetto there in 1943.

Aside from hasidism's derogation of Torah scholarship in favor of more mystical and spontaneous forms of Jewish spirituality, the mitnagdim maintained a more traditional, dualistic understanding of the Jewish faith. They rejected hasidism's popularization of the notion of divine immanence and its celebration of the earthly existence and its physical pleasures as the theater for spiritual experience, maintaining instead a more ascetic approach to religious life.

The social and theological divisions between hasidim and mitnagdim effectively divided East European traditional Judaism into two very distinct religious camps, through the modern period. Due to the enduring legacy of the Vilner Gaon, the vast majority of traditional Lithuanian Jews defined themselves as mitnagdim and remained the sober, dualistic, and ascetic opponents of hasidism's mystical enthusiasm right up to the eve of the Holocaust. The center of their spiritual universe was the yeshiva, which played a role equivalent to that of the rebbe's court in hasidic life.

In discussing Lithuanian Jewry, it is important to keep in mind that this historic community is neither defined by nor limited to those Jews who actually resided in the territory that finally came to be defined as Lithuania after the country achieved independence in 1918. In Jewish history and culture, Lithuanian Jews were distinguished from their Polish, Russian, and Ukrainian brethren by certain well-defined religious, linguistic, and social characteristics that transcended politics and national borders. These distinctive features, which defined Jews as "Litvaks" (Yiddish for Lithuanian Jews, as opposed to "Litviner," the Yiddish term for Lithuanian gentiles), included a particular Yiddish dialect, a rational, anti-mystical and anti-hasidic approach to Jewish religion and an intense intellectualism, reflected in the traditions of the great Lithuanian yeshivas. These religious and cultural distinctions were shared with the Jews of Lithuania by virtually all of the Jews of Belarus, or White Russia, which had a pre-war Jewish population of more than 400,000, as well as the culturally Lithuanian regions under Russian, and later Polish, rule, such as Vilnius, Bialystok, Novogrudek, and Pinsk, whose combined Jewish populations totaled about 550,000. Therefore, although no more than 175,000 Jews actually resided in the independent Lithuanian Republic in 1938, there were actually more than 1,000,000 "Litvaks" living in Eastern Europe on the eve of the Second World War. All but a few thousands were liquidated in the Holocaust.

Religious responses to modernity: The influence of the Vilner Gaon's intellectualism not only fostered a unique religious culture in Lithuania. It is also credited by many scholars with creating an environment conducive to the spread of rationalism and the ideals of the Jewish enlightenment. Indeed, while the Vilner Gaon himself was a rigid traditionalist who strongly opposed the infiltration of secularism into Poland and Lithuania from Western Europe, many of his disciples were attracted to the enlightenment and helped facilitate its spread in Lithuania and White Russia. Unlike Western Europe and Galicia however, where the Enlightenment often led to the radical reform of Jewish law and rituals, national self-denial and assimilation, in Lithuania—and later in Russia—it took on a particularly intense Jewish character. This was especially manifest in the eventual rise in Lithuania of the two most important movements of secular Judaism: Zionism and Yiddish culture.

The most significant distinction between Eastern and Western European Jewries' respective religious responses to modernity is the fact that it was only in Germany and the Austro-Hungarian empire that the liberalization of the Jewish religion—as manifest in the emergence of reform Judaism—developed over the course of the nineteenth century. The religious denominationalism that characterized modern Jewish life in Germany (and later in America) never took root in Poland or Russia. In Eastern Europe, largely because of the blatantly antisemitic nature of the Czars' attempts to control and "modernize" Jewish life, no accomodationist reforms of Jewish ritual and practice emulating the majority religion ever developed. Instead of transforming Judaism itself, the Jewish enlighteners—maskilim—of Eastern Europe developed distinctly secular alternatives to Jewish religious practice. A variety of secular Jewish cultural and political movements, expressing themselves in either Yiddish or Hebrew, flourished throughout Eastern Europe from the mid-nineteenth century. This tendency culminated in the establishment, in 1897, of the two largest secular Jewish political movements, Zionism and the Jewish Labor Movement, known as the Bund. Both the Zionists, who fostered the creation of a secular, modern Hebrew culture and literature, and the Bundists, who promoted secular Yiddish culture, were equally opposed by the hasidim and the mitnagdim, who came closer together as a consequence of their shared opposition to all forms of modern, secular Judaism.

The type of organized, self-conscious orthodox Judaism that developed in Germany and Hungary—which was largely a reactionary response to the reformation of religious practice in Central and Western Europe—therefore also never emerged in the east. In general, the East European rabbis and the masses of their followers opposed the politicization of Jewish life and rejected newfangled social organizations and political parties that were established by the more secular Jews. They preferred to be governed solely by the norms and mores of Talmudic Judaism, as interpreted by the rabbis.

Despite the traditional Jewish leaders' disdain for the conventions of modern political life and its institutions, by the beginning of the twentieth century they found it virtually impossible to remain immune to the forces of modernization. In 1912, the first orthodox Jewish political party—Agudath Israel—was formed, largely in opposition to the emergence of a religious Zionist movement, known as Mizrachi. After World War One, Agudath Israel functioned in Poland as a political party, elected delegates to the Seim (Polish Parliament), and strenuously opposed the platforms of the secular Jewish parties, such as the Bund and various Zionist movements. Agudah eventually became a major force in Jewish political life in interwar Poland. The leadership of Agudah spanned the traditional ideological spectrum, further uniting hasidim and mitnagdim in their battle against modernity. So, for example, two of the party's towering figures were Abraham Mordechai Alter (1866-1948), the hasidic rebbe of Ger (the single largest hasidic sect in Poland) and Hayyim Ozer Grodzinski (1863-1940), the mitnagdic Chief Rabbi of Vilna. In addition to its political work, the Agudah established a network of schools and published newspapers in the larger Jewish communities.

Still, despite the political and social changes that invaded even the most traditional segments of East European Jewry, Judaism, as practiced by the Jewish masses of Eastern Europe during the previous centuries, remained essentially unchanged, particularly in villages and small shtetls, in which the norms of halakhah and the authoritative rulings of the local rabbis continued to dominate all aspects of Jewish behavior and to define Jewish life. While in a few of the largest cities of Eastern Europe, a form of aestheticized, enlightened Judaism developed, practiced in majestic "choral synagogues" and presided over by official, Czarist-government-sanctioned rabbis, its impact on the great majority of East European Jews remained minimal until the eve of the Holocaust.

The most significant contribution of this modernized, but still halakhic, East European enlightenment Judaism was the development of the elaborate liturgical art of East European cantorial music, which borrowed heavily from the European classical and operatic traditions. Still, the popularity of this liturgical form was actually greater among the Russian Jewish émigrés to America than among the Jews who remained in Eastern Europe.

The traditional life of the shtetl: The traditional Jewish life of the shtetl has been captured in vivid, but highly nostalgic and romanticized, terms in literature, theater, music, and film. Perhaps the most popular rendition of the life of the shtetl is the depiction found in the award-winning Broadway musical (and later the film) "Fiddler on the Roof." While—like all artistic recreations of a lost world—there are many problems and inaccuracies with these depictions, the central, salient feature of shtetl life that is described is incontrovertible: the extent to which Jewish law and custom permeated every aspect of Jewish behavior. The Judaism of the shtetl was thoroughly mimetic; it completely governed, indeed saturated, the lives and conduct of the shtetl Jews. Probably the most vivid and accurate of the nostalgic descriptions of the spiritual life of the shtetl is Abraham Joshua Heschel's famous essay *The Earth is The Lord's*. This lost world has also been vividly described through the letters and documentary and oral history that survived its destruction in several anthologies, edited by Heschel, Dawidowicz, and Herzog.

Despite its insularity and endurance, however, the Judaism of the shtetl—whether hasidic or mitnagdic—began rapidly to disintegrate during the latter part of the nineteenth century. Aside from the inroads being made by secular Russian Jewish culture, the two external events that most threatened the old forms of traditional Ashkenazic Judaism were the rapid urbanization of Jewish life and the massive emigration to America that had been spawned by waves of increasingly brutal, government-sanctioned pogroms, beginning in 1881 and continuing to the 1920s. Since the small shtetls were most vulnerable to the pogroms, the depletion of their population was most pronounced. During the interwar period, the shtetls were rapidly disappearing and with them the thoroughly traditional Jewish life that had made them the last, unique representations of traditional East European Jewish religious life.

Bibliography

Dawidowicz, Lucy S., *The Golden Tradition: Jewish Life and Thought in Eastern Europe* (New York, 1967).
Etkes, Immanuel, *Rabbi Israel Salanter and the Musar Movement* (Philadelphia, 1995).
Herzog, Elizabeth, and Mark Zborowski, *Life Is with People* (New York, 1995).
Nadler, Allan, *The Faith of the Mithnagdim* (Baltimore, 1997).
Rabinowicz, Harry M., *Hasidism: The Movement and Its Masters* (Northvale, 1988).
Schochet, Elijah J., *The Gaon of Vilna and the Hasidic Movement* (Northvale, 1994).
Weinryb, Bernard Dov, *The Jews of Poland* (Philadelphia, 1973).

ALLAN NADLER

ECONOMICS, JUDAISM AND: In the opening passage of an essay on the relationship between economics and religion, Jacob Katz writes,[1] "Economics in its widest sense, i.e., efforts to satisfy human material needs, and religion as an expression of the spiritual, the metaphysical meaning of human life, require, prima facie, two separate arenas, and it is not inevitable that any contact between them evolve." Katz, for his part, rejects such a simplistic notion of the discontinuity between economics and religion for all but some very unique circumstances, for instance, prior to the expulsion from the Garden of Eden or in the wilderness following the Exodus from Egypt, when God's daily provision of manna saved the Israelites from the toil and trouble of working for their living.

Yet economists must reject the notion that even in such distinctive cases economics and religion are truly separate. The Garden of Eden was given to Adam "to till it and to keep it" (Gen. 2:15), interpreted by the medieval commentator Ibn Ezra as meaning that Adam was obligated "to water it and guard it from the wild beasts." And in exchange for the manna in the desert, the Israelites were expected to perform scores of acts with economic significance, from specific business and familial obligations to the offerings of sacrifices at the Sanctuary.

There are several possible ways of analyzing the relationship between religion and economics. The two most important are:

1. The harmonic view, which sees the two as centered in distinct but in some ways complementary poles of human activity, representing the two major foci of human life, the spiritual and the material. Religion and economics thus are both expected to contribute to the total welfare of the individual and the society, and one may even assume a kind of causal complementarity between them, whereby material contributions promote objectives of the religious institutions, and religious spirit and zeal enhance aspects of productivity.

2. The oppositional view, which argues that religion and economics are contradictory forces. By the nineteenth century, classical as well as Marxist schools of economic thinking both regarded religion as irreconcilable with, and therefore detrimental to, rational thinking (classical/neoclassical school) or to the promotion of proletarian self-consciousness (Marxism). Consequently religion undermines the objective function of the economic endeavor to maximize the material welfare of society. By contrast, many religious institutions, which strive to elevate society above what they call purely materialistic objectives, consider the ideology of "market oriented rationalism" a menace to the human spirit and social justice.

Religion is a complex and multifarious phenomenon, with different religions accentuating different idiosyncrasies of human behavior and social norms. Even for the case of Judaism alone, one must bear in mind the variety of dimensions that illuminate different yet vital angles of the Jews' world-view. Judaism is a set of philosophical postulates that constitute a comprehensive theological system of faith. It encompasses a body of prescribed behavioral and social norms, reflecting a value system, principles for interpersonal relationships, and a clear-cut pattern of rites and rituals. Finally, it comprises a network of institutions manned by officials and functionaries, clergy and laymen, who work to maintain and shape the Jews' behaviors, attitudes, and perspectives.

Since all of these dimensions have a direct or indirect relevance to economics, Judaism represents an economically analyzable phenomenon, in which religious behavior appears as one of many individual or group activities that confer utility—in this case, mainly of a spiritual nature—upon the rationally behaving religious individual. Importantly, since Judaism focuses upon human behavior more than upon the claims of theology and faith, it should be regarded more as a code of conduct than as a statement of belief. Therefore, within Judaism we are bound to encounter many more connections with economic realities than the routine performance of religious rituals would present. This is the case even though Judaism provides no broad economic guidelines detailing how people should treat economic life, and no ancient or medieval Jewish sage produced any encompassing work that can be considered an economic treatise.

Judaism and the economics of religion: The economics of religion has only recently drawn the interest of scholars. Until the 1960s religion was viewed as merely of historical importance and hence as the domain only of economic historians. Besides, due to the rapid process of worldwide secularization, economists considered religion's future significance to be minimal.

The last quarter of the twentieth century has witnessed some religious revival, seen not only in so-called fundamentalist movements but also among intellectuals in Europe and the United States. In the United States, contributions to religious organization are consistently about 50% of all charitable donations, reaching, in the late 1980s, $60 billion. Empirical studies conducted in recent years discovered no negative correlation between religiosity and education, suggesting that earlier hypotheses about religion's being the asylum of the ignorant should be rejected. Furthermore, those same studies discovered that religion is not an "inferior good," that is, that levels of religiosity have no tendency to decline with rising income. Here we find that another common belief, that "God is the comfort and salvation of the poor," tends to fall.

Statistics seem, therefore, to disprove the view that in modern times only the *victims* of modernization, the unlearned and the poor, cling to religion.[2] Economists, instead, have embarked upon attempts to model religious behavior with the accepted tools and assumptions of mainstream economic analysis. Their underlying hypothesis is that "widespread and/or persistent human behavior can be explained by a generalized calculus of utility maximizing behavior."[3] This hypothesis proposes that families maximize utility not only from the goods and services they buy but also from what they produce with the skills, time, and human capital at their disposal. According to this theory people or households chose to allocate their scarce resources in such a manner that their utility is maximized.

The extension required to encompass religion in such a routine economic paradigm is the inclusion of spiritual satisfaction into the utility function of the individual and the addition of religious activities to the "commodities" that compete for the individual's scarce resources. We thus can re-phrase the basic statement and suggest that people allocate their scarce resources (time and money) between religious and other commodities to maximize their spiritual and material utility. For an observant Jew the concept of sacrificing commodities, time, and money for the acquisition of religious "goods" is an everyday reality. Time for prayers, extra money for kosher food, forsaken income for the observance of the Sabbath are just three examples. Donations to causes with ritual or social objectives are also sacrifices with religious significance.

Within this theoretical framework, the religious behavior of the individual or family is quite analogous to behavior in economic matters. In general, people who face monetary constraints tend to reduce the acquisition of high price commodities. Similarly few observant Jews wake up nightly for midnight prayers (*Tiqqun Hatzot*) or insist on consuming only the high priced milk certified as *halav yisrael*. Religious behavior also encounters income constraints, so that individuals who are very short of time will probably seek to express devotion by monetary contributions rather than by time consuming ritual activities, and vice versa.

It bears noting that this is perhaps one explanation for the fact that in most countries in which Orthodox, Conservative, and Reform Jewish communities function alongside each other, the membership of the Conservative and Reform communities tends to be economically better to do, on average, than the members of the Orthodox communities. The daily rites and demands of Orthodox Judaism are much more time consuming and are much less substitutable by money than those of the Conservative or Reform communities. For these very reasons elderly people tend to yield much more of their time, and also of their money, for the acquisition of religious goods and have, probably, higher expectations for "afterlife consumption" than the young, who are at the peak of their economic vigor.

The organizational framework within which religious life takes place may also be examined through various models. One such model is the Institution—Consumer relationship, which holds that the church and its officials produce and sell religious goods, while the laity consumes them. Another, more democratic pattern, closer to the concept of the Jewish community in the west, can be presented within the Club Theory, which views the community as a club-like institution in which families and individuals combine the roles of production and consumption in order jointly to perform functions of worship, charity, and social activity. The club hires officials (rabbis, cantors) and finances its operations through membership dues. Since the present western religious communities are voluntary bodies, and the commodity they produce and consume is of a spiritual nature, they enjoy positive economies of scale; that is to say, the more members come and join their activities, the greater the utility for all members.

Economists analyze religious phenomenon using variants of neo-classical rational actor perspectives. That is, they treat religion under value-neutral assumptions and attribute, for analytical purposes, motives to the religious action that are comparable to the motives under which all other actions are interpreted. Yet religions are not value-neutral. They profess ideologies and have clear criteria for good and evil. This leads to the problem of conducting value-neutral inquiries on a phenomenon that is, by its very substance, value-loaded. Nevertheless, this approach is of great benefit in examining the impact of religious behavior on a person's daily functioning, as well as in comprehending the effect of religion on interactions with other persons, believers or not, in the social, economic, and demographic arenas of society.

Religiosity, because of its normative expectations, affects the daily behavior of its adherents, influencing the relative importance given to the spiritual vis-á-vis the mundane. Therefore, religiosity influences occupational preferences, income aspirations, and consumption and savings patterns. It also affects sociological and demographic attributes that have crucial economic implications: fertility, single parenthood, educational ambitions, intensity of criminal activities, and the like. In personal and business interactions, religion may also reduce what economists call "transaction cost." People of faith who internalize the values and the ideologies of their religion and believe in the trustworthiness of their neighbors and business partners often act without resorting to expensive and time-consuming external material enticements.

Under such circumstances human interaction becomes more efficient, and business is conducted with low transaction cost.[4] Thus, for instance, in the diamond industry, which has been predominantly in Jewish hands, contracts are sanctioned by mutually binding handshakes, saving complex and expensive paperwork.

On the other hand, allegiance to the economic interest of other members of the congregation may *reduce* cost efficiency by granting a measure of monopolistic power to club members who are suppliers of goods and services. In Judaism this is the economic manifestation of the principle *kol yisrael arevim ze baze* ("all Israel are sureties one for another;" B. Sheb. 39a), which was the ancient way of expressing the idea of mutual assurance. In a close knit community, members may prefer to utilize each others' economic services, even at the expense of higher cost, in order to reduce each other's level of economic uncertainty.

The modern welfare state took upon itself to provide social safety nets to all citizens, so that many particularistic economic guarantee plans through "clubs" became redundant and were utilized only by very coherent communities. However, the present tendency of welfare states to replace the model of the social safety net by a "swim or sink" competitive rationality may revive community oriented mutual assurance models.

While mainstream economists understood that their positive economic analysis had nothing to contribute to the issue of religious preferences, religious groups may argue that their reticence was tantamount to a sanctioning of the social order that emerged from the unbridled capitalism of the 1980s. They hold that religious values are relevant within the modern world, since, the claims of economists to the contrary, the social and distributional wrongs that emanate from unrestrained competition in the marketplace are themselves not value neutral. So long as welfare states responded to issues of social policy with a normative philosophy of social justice the distinctive messages advocated by religious institutions seemed irrelevant. By the end of the century, spokesmen of major religions, including Judaism, have taken more active stances in matters of social policy with direct economic implications.

Aspects of Jewish law—Theory of wealth: Jewish religious tradition relates extensively to economic concerns. Scripture is replete with references to economic issues, including strife over wells and water in the drought stricken Negev during the patriarchal period, the detailed reporting about the prudent inventory and macro-economic measures of Joseph, the Egyptian viceroy, and instructions regarding the remuneration of workers. The Talmud devotes two out of its six divisions (Agriculture and Damages) to matters that are basically economic. Medieval and post-medieval legal thinkers (Maimonides, Ben Asher, Caro, and others) dealt extensively with the application to their own times of inherited economic principles. Finally, in the course of close to a thousand years, the vast responsa literature dealt with a myriad of economic issues raised by people who desired to know how to harmonize their business interests with the expectations of Jewish law.

Despite an extensive treatment of these matters, ancient as well as later Rabbinic sources evidence an ambivalence towards economic subjects. The first and probably the best known example is Judaism's attitude towards work. Is work an unavoidable necessity and a curse, or is it a blessing? The famous expression at Gen. 3:19 states, "In the sweat of your face you shall eat bread." Here work is a curse, the punishment imposed on Adam for his transgression. Yet virtually the same statement recurs at Ps. 128:2, with the addition, "you shall be happy, and it shall be well with you," indicating that work was intended to be a blessing.

The same ambivalence is shown when the views of the great Talmudic sage Simeon bar Yohai are contrasted with those of others, among them the equally distinguished Ishmael. Simeon reportedly claimed that work, i.e., the cultivation of land, is an inferior occupation and should be subordinated to the sacred calling of life, service to God through the study of Torah. The economic cost to be paid for such a way of life is explicitly spelled out in M. Ab. 6:4: "This is the way that is becoming for the study of the Torah: a morsel of bread with salt you must eat, and water by measure you must drink; you must sleep upon the ground and live a life of trouble as you toil in the Torah."

In contrast to this feverishly austere Puritanism, Ishmael advocated a balanced division of time between work for the sustenance of worldly needs and study of Torah. Another outstanding sage, Eleazar b. Azariah, went so far as to suggest that a reciprocal dependence exists between the mundane and the spiritual, rejecting thereby the totalistic asceticism of Simeon bar Yohai. Eleazar is quoted at M. Ab. 3:21: "Where there is no flour there is no Torah; where there is no Torah there is no flour." The Talmud sums up the controversy pragmatically, recalling that those who tried to imitate Simeon bar Yohai failed, while those who followed the practice of Ishmael succeeded.

This summary of the attitude of traditional Judaism towards the acquisition of material wealth is clearly expressed by Maimonides, whose philosophy of moderation became a leitmotif in mainstream Jewish theology. Moderation, or in Maimonides' words "the middle road," meant dividing the day equally into three parts: household (meals and resting), work (material needs), and study (the spiritual). The complementarity between these activities is made clear by Maimonides' disproving totally of the idea of making Torah learning one's profession.

Following the guidelines of Ishmael and the ideas of Maimonides, mainstream Jewish theology has never made poverty an accepted path for devout piety and has rejected asceticism as a desirable expression of faithful religiosity. Nevertheless, Judaism also regards excessive preoccupation with the acquisition of riches as undesirable, since primacy is due the spiritual domain of life. Consequently, ostentation and wasteful consumption are not condoned, even when materially they can be afforded.

Obligations to the poor: The Judaic norms of behavior impose upon the wealthy members of the community obligations and responsibilities to support materially the op-

eration of communal institutions. In this respect Judaic values belie the assumptions of economists who consider all human actions to be motivated by the rational choices of purposive actors, and stand closer to social norm theories, which assume that behavior is determined by norms that constitute that portion of the social organization that tells people what to do and what not to do. Such norms are not mere constraints, as claimed by the rational choice economists, but are internalized by the devout members of the community, who modify their utilities by the norms, which "express what action is right and what action is wrong."[5]

In ancient times the well-off social class, usually independent farmers in a basically classless society, supported the clerical institutions through a wide assortment of offerings, including various tithes, which were the main public vehicles for the maintenance of the clergy. Alongside these liabilities to the clerical establishment, other social service and infrastructural obligations imposed on farmers were also called tithes and accorded religious significance. These included the poor tithe, a direct transfer payment paid twice in a cycle of seven years to the poor at the donor's discretion. The other major social imposition, characteristic of the agrarian economy, was the sharing of a part of the harvest with the landless poor by allowing them to gather the marginal crop: an edge on the field unreaped, the gleaning of the harvest, and forgotten sheaves.

All tithes were proportional to the volume of the crop and obligatory to the extent that the new harvest was not permitted for consumption until all the deductions were paid. Besides the liabilities to clerics and the poor, four times in a cycle of seven years a second tithe with a unique economic character was imposed. It was consumed by the donor and his family, with the single stipulation that the act of consumption had to take place in Jerusalem, with the explicit intention to strengthen the city's economy by enhancing consumers' demand for the city's goods and services. This second tithe aimed at improving the socio-economic infrastructure of the city and manifested the principle of direct responsibility of each family in the ancient Jewish peasant society for the prosperity of their principal public good, their spiritual center, without imposing a special "spiritual center tax."

Beyond the obligatory direct financial liabilities ordered by the Torah, other normative instructions existed of a more general, non quantitative nature, loaded with messages of social justice. They intended to support sectors of society that could not defend themselves in the open, competitive marketplace, including groups such as widows and orphans, slaves and day laborers, aliens, and the disoriented. These groups required active social intervention to avoid, or at least reduce, exploitation and abuse. Some injunctions were explicit and unequivocal, such as the instruction to behave with compassion to destitute debtors or to the day laborers who, living from hand to mouth, need their wage by the end of each day. Controlling behavior towards the widow and orphan, the poor, slaves and aliens, the blind, and simpletons, other commandments are more in the nature of moral exhortations, with or without promises of specific retributions.

Theories of the market: The ancient socio-economic codes laid down in the overwhelmingly rural environment of biblical times became the theological pillars of the vast legal system that, during the Mishnaic and Talmudic periods, crystallized into the Jewish behavioral code, the Halakhah. Generally speaking, the doctrines conveyed in this literature indicate an economic system based on freedom and competition, strongly respecting private ownership. Such deference towards property rights shows a profound understanding of human nature, a sense of market realities, a rational approach to the business interaction of the participants in the marketplace, and a grasp of the positive effect a well functioning market has on the welfare of society.

This attitude is well demonstrated by the Talmudic concept of market price. In a poignant contradiction to the notion of "Just Price," held by Christian theologians up to the time of Thomas Aquinas and beyond, the Talmud determines prices by the market at the approximated level of equilibrium between demand and supply (see, e.g., T. Dem. 4:13).

The main enemy of competition is the monopolistic accumulation of economic power. Its damaging effect on social welfare is today a commonplace. Scripture apparently predicted the hazards of land accumulation in an agrarian society and so introduced the Jubilee, which requires that every fifty years all land be returned to its original owner. When enforced this is an effective anti-monopolistic institution, a fact of which the later sages were very well aware. Thus Sefer Hahinnuch (Mitzvah 330) explains that God ". . . desired to convey to his people that everything is his and ultimately everything will return to whomever he wished to give it originally. . . . Then . . . people will keep well away from seizing the land of their fellow-man."

Jewish law utilizes highly institutional requirements to safeguard a congenial atmosphere for efficient business conduct. Besides the absolute divine sanction given to the fundamental rules of the social order—the prohibitions against killing, stealing, robbing, and perverting justice—numerous special injunctions enhance efficiency. Thus, while Judaism distinguishes among different causes of torts—the ox, pit, crop-destroying beast, and conflagration—the single principle that unites the four is plain. These things "customarily do damage, so that taking care of them is your [the owner's] responsibility." The owner of that which in fact causes damage "must pay compensation out of the choicest of his land" (M. B.Q. 1:1-2).

Another distinction in tort law reveals the tension between the draconian imposition of liabilities, which could be prohibitively costly for the one whose property caused the tort, and economic efficiency. The shadow of excessive liability may impede entrepreneurship. Therefore, when an ox (the major source of mobile energy in ancient economies) damaged, a distinction was made between an innocuous ox, which had no reputation for goring, pushing, biting, or the like, and a noxious ox, already notorious on these accounts. Since oxen were crucial to efficient farming, differences existed between the liability carried for an innocuous ox's actions, calculated at one half the damage and limited by the value of the ox, and those for a noxious ox, which incurred full damages.

Many more instances of realistic analytical treatment of circumstances with economic bearing occur, such as pricing in inflation or the practical exchange rates of diverse moneys with different liquidities. However, it would be misleading to claim that ancient and later economic models of Judaism are capitalistic in the way the term is interpreted at the threshold of the twenty-first century. Indeed, Judaism favors an economic system that is close to capitalism, even as it rejects some of the premises of capitalism's theoretical model. Most important, Judaism rejects the notion of "Perfect Knowledge," that is, the assumption that every participant in the marketplace has all relevant information about the price, quality, and availability of every commodity and service and makes buying or selling decisions in view of that information. This theory holds that nobody will buy anything at a price above the known one and that neither is anyone in a position to buy anything below that price. The same applies to sellers, who cannot sell above the market price and will not sell below it. Thus there is by definition one price for all. Likewise, in this theory, no monopolistic abuse can emerge when people behave rationally and their knowledge is perfect.

Judaism does not subscribe to these beliefs, for sages comprehended the economic reality as imperfect: knowledge is always incomplete and, without some central control, the market is inclined to fail. Therefore unbridled capitalism may lead to market distortions and social injustice. Although Judaism does not like price fixing, it does provide special rulings against fraud, which can result simply from imperfect knowledge. Thus Jewish law deems overcharging by one sixth the accepted market price or underpaying by a similar amount (about 17%) to be fraud. "Relief from overreaching is available both to the buyer and the seller" (M. B.M.

4:3). Such fraud is not punishable—the sages were aware of human nature—but the defrauded party was permitted to retract from the deal during a period of time sufficient to consult a relative or expert on the price paid or obtained.

Similarly, to prevent dishonesty in the use of weights and measures, Scripture did not rely on the effectiveness of the market. The Torah draws, rather surprisingly, an analogy between weights and court judgments. "You shall do no wrong in judgment, in measures of length or weight or quantity. You shall have just balances, just weights, a just ephah, and a just hin" (Lev. 19:35-36). Rashi, the great twelfth century commentator, explains: ". . . one who has to do with measuring is termed 'a judge' so that if he gives false measure he is like the judge who perverts justice," that is, undermines social stability. For their part, talmudic sages, aware of human nature, appointed market inspectors to check weights and to impose a profit margin that did not exceed one sixth, particularly on essential food.

Another manifestation of distrust in the unregulated market is the precept not to mislead the disoriented simpleton. The Torah's language is brief: "You shall not curse the deaf or put a stumbling block before the blind" (Lev. 19:14). The sages expand the term "blind" to include any person who is "blind about some matter," with the explicit purpose of improving society and communal life (Sefer Hahinnuch, Mitzva 232).

Probably the most profound evidence to attest the Jewish notion that market mechanisms alone are insufficient in matters of social policy is the case of income redistribution to help the poor. Judaism deems charity to be not merely an act of benevolence or philanthropy. It is, rather, an obligation, since, despite the expressed support of property rights, all riches belong to God, who gave them to the rich with the stipulation that they take responsibility for the sustenance of the poor. Charity, in Hebrew "Tzedakah," originates from the same root as "Tzedek," meaning justice. This provides the moral as well as legal justification for imposing on well-to-do members of the community taxes used to sustain the poor, sick, and disabled.

Judaism enforces charity, which means that it considers it a public good needed to rectify a socio-economic imbalance. Charity thus is like education, aimed to raise the level of human capital in the community. In this regard, it is also not unlike the maintenance of the synagogue and other religious services dedicated to the community's spiritual welfare, similarly seen as public goods. For this reason, Jewish concepts of charity do not conform to the modern welfare state's imposition of a "means test" upon those who apply for public help. The Judaic maxim is, "He who opens his palm (asking for alms)—open your (purse/heart) for him."

Because of trust in the impact of public shame, Jewish law has no concern that people might abuse such an open approach. To the contrary, recipients of charity are assumed to be sensitive to the loss of their dignity, and those responsible for the distribution of charity therefore must do their utmost to preserve it. Indeed, the nineteenth century rabbi Hatam Sofer considered shame to be the price paid by the poor for the assistance they receive.[6]

Monopolies: Rabbinical authorities' handling of economic matters may have deviated from the capitalistic postulates not only because of their rejection of assumptions concerning a perfect market and knowledge. For the rabbis also had fundamental disagreements with capitalism concerning the objective function of the market. Capitalist doctrines maintain that the best available state of affairs is obtained when conditions referred to as Pareto optimum are reached. These conditions safeguard maximum economic efficiency, and their essence is that every factor of production and every commodity receive their due reward. Under such conditions, material welfare reaches its optimum. The basic dictum of the system is, using the words of Joan Robinson, "the more the better."

This approach, however, overlooks questions of distribution and ignores the fate of the weak, who are unable successfully to fight for a position in the economy or who are victims of technological changes. Judaic thought often is willing to sacrifice efficiency for the sake of economic equality or even to preserve the livelihood of some inefficient yet powerless producers. Such is the spirit of the halakhic injunction against "landmark circumvention" (*hasagat g'vul*), in which the actions of one person or group infringe on other peoples' livelihood, for example, by competing in a manner than puts them out of business. In such cases, against capitalist economic wisdom, Rabbinic courts may pass verdicts to help the inefficient.

Still, as a rule, Talmudic law favors competition among producers and merchants. For instance, a series of statutes from Talmudic times through the sixteenth century assures the right of free entry of immigrants into the Jewish community. These immigrants acquired the right to open businesses and to use all public facilities on the sole condition that they shared with the rest of the community the financial cost of this right.

Free entry was an accepted custom throughout the Jewish diaspora. Only changing circumstances led to the emergence of a new attitude towards such liberal benefits to outsiders. When persecution shrank economic opportunities and made earning a livelihood difficult, the desire to preserve opportunities for existing residents overruled the customs and even the laws of free entry. Now communities introduced monopolistic practices and, in extreme cases, refused altogether to allow entry to immigrants. These monopolistic tendencies often developed into notions of entrenched rights of possession (*hezkat hayishuv*), with all the shortcomings of monopolies, such as opposition to change and innovation and rigid business practice.

Under similar conditions, the concept of rights of possession was widespread in the surrounding feudal economies of most of Christian Europe. Yet within the Jewish community, even as the eagerness to survive persecution proved stronger than previous custom and law, so a sense of solidarity with others in great danger from expulsion or pogroms proved even more powerful. Thus provisions of *hezkat hayishuv* often were suspended in order to save Jewish refugees of pogroms or persecution.

The impact of religious law: Rituals and the observance of religious precepts invariably involve material loss. For the economist these are constraints to be taken into consideration in the course of utility maximization. To the observant Jew, however, they are limitations that govern day-to-day life and behavior. Rabbinical authorities comprehended and worked to address conflicts that emerged between market considerations and the requirements of daily existence. Their general approach was to search for careful compromises through which they could circumvent problems without repealing the Halakhah itself. While numerous cases required attention, following the analysis of Jacob Katz,[7] we shall relate to three major issues: the price charged for money, the Sabbath, and kashrut.

The prohibition against usury: Modern economics considers interest the price paid for the utilization of capital, which, along with labor, is one of the two principal factors of production. Interest compensates the owner of capital either for losses realized in not investing it in an alternative enterprise or for the loss of pleasure attendant upon the failure to consume its value today.

This understanding of interest reflects today's capital intensive economy. But Scripture refers to interest in totally different circumstances: "And if your brother becomes poor, and cannot maintain himself with you, you shall maintain him; as a stranger and a sojourner he shall live with you. Take no interest from him or increase, but fear your God; that your brother may live beside you" (Lev. 25:35-36). Two of the main features of the reality in which loans were given are apparent here. First, a loan was used as relief for one who is poor. Second, the term translated "interest" (*neshekh*) in fact signifies "usury," a value loaded expression indicating exploitation.

Rashi contributes to the understanding of these circumstances by noting: "man's thoughts are greatly attracted by the idea of taking interest . . . on account of the fact that his money will otherwise remain unemployed." This accurately depicts the circumstance of an agrarian society with virtually no capital requirements, in which impoverished peasants, when in excessive distress, borrowed money *that otherwise would have stayed idle*. In such an economic setting, Scripture considered the charging of interest a very grave transgression.

Already during the period of the Mishnaic sages, conditions changed and the issue of loans and interest had to be reconsidered. In a rather complex marketplace with international trade and joint ventures involving active and inactive partners participating with different and changing shares of capital not all loans were granted to peasants in distress. An urgent need emerged to meet the capital requirements of such new types of enterprises.

Instead of repealing the prohibition of interest on loans, the rabbis allowed many financial transactions to be reshaped into business ventures (*iskah*) in which even the inactive creditors participated in risks and profits, as though they were part owners of the enterprise. In this circumstance, the capital they provided was not viewed strictly as a loan, and no violation of the prohibition against interest occurs. Another solution was to involve gentile intermediaries, to whom the prohibition against interest does not pertain.

The important point is that the more pressing the economic need became, the more receptive Rabbinic authorities were to halakhic adjustments. At the same time, the demand for consumption oriented loans to debtors increasingly was met by benevolent funds that granted small, interest free loans. Thousands of such usually small funds existed and exist, often associated with synagogues, schools, and charitable institutions.

The economics of kashrut: Thanks to the various devices of authorized circumvention, prohibitions on interest ceased to be a pressing limitation on orthodox businessmen. The issues of kashrut and Sabbath observance are different, since these obligations are not equally subject to circumvention. Nevertheless, in these matters too, as the conditions of Jewish life have changed, rabbis have sought viable compromises.

Kashrut involves an economic cost. Due to the special care taken in slaughtering, the prohibition on consuming various animals, parts of animals, and ingredients, and the need for separate utensils for dairy and meat products, kosher food is expensive. Additionally, the overall market for kosher food is limited, and, in light of technologies that increase economies of scale, production cost for such a small market is high.

In response to this issue, whenever and wherever possible, Rabbinic authorities made efforts to avoid excessive economic losses. They were and are cautious not to deem meat non-kosher as a result of a minor technical flaw. Toleration was even greater in the case of slaughtered poultry or a deficiency in Passover-kashrut if the victim of the possible loss was poor. Overall, the level of strictness in the application of the laws of kashrut depended on the magnitude of the potential loss. Slaughtered cattle found not to meet the requirements of kashrut, for instance, may be sold to producers of non-kosher meat. When prices for this meat were high, rabbis strictly enforced the criteria for kashrut; otherwise they were not so strict. Thus, within a permissible range of tolerance, rabbis used their judgment to minimize the economic costs of kashrut.

At the same time, the scrupulous preservation of the kashrut laws by the vast majority of Jews provided community authorities with a powerful financial vehicle. Virtually all communities in which ritual slaughtering facilities operated imposed on kosher meat an indirect tax, usually called the "gabelle." This tax signified an awareness of the very inelastic demand for kosher meat, that is, the knowledge that even as prices went up because of the tax, there were only relatively small declines in the quantity of meat demanded.

In order to prevent price competition between kosher slaughtering facilities of different communities, which would jeopardize a major source of tax and personal income in communities that operated economically inefficient slaughter houses, a ban was imposed on out-of-town kosher slaughtering. This ruling was widely accepted, and the utilization of the Rabbinic prerogative to withhold kashrut certificates solely for the preservation of the monopolistic privilege of the community was taken for granted. Defense of this financial resource of the community was considered more important to individual member's overall welfare than the availability of cheaper meat. Notably, similar Rabbinic authority was used to withdraw a license of kashrut when a cartel of fishmongers raised the price of fish above the level deemed fair. From this one can see that, even within the constraints of Halakhah, kashrut was an integral component in considerations about the material welfare of the community.

The economics of the Sabbath: The economic implications of Sabbath rest are of tremendous importance. The prohibition against doing constructive work is sweeping, set out in detail in the fourth commandment: "but the seventh day is a sabbath to the Lord your God; in it you shall not do any work, you, or your son, or your daughter, your manservant, or your maidservant, or your cattle, or the sojourner who is within your gates" (Exod. 20:10).

In periods of subsistence agriculture, the overall rest of all people and animals of the household was tenable. Centuries later, the problem became more complex, as the Sabbath restrictions led to the forfeit of many sources of livelihood and limited the economic activities Jews were able to pursue. The Jewish farmer's approach was that so long as he and his family did no physical work, there was no Sabbath desecration. However the requirement of Sabbath rest for gentile employees and animals was explicitly spelled out in Scripture. But other problems soon arose. For instance, when long maritime journeys in boats under non-Jewish control became a business necessity, was a Jew permitted to embark on a weekday for a journey that included the Sabbath?

In the northern and central parts of Europe, the strict preservation of ancient traditions regarding employees' Sabbath rest was impossible, for the short daylight and cold weather in the winter required lighting and heating of homes and synagogues on the Sabbath. Might the gentile employee be instructed to light candles and set fire in the oven? With the gradual sophistication of the economy and the increasing involvement of Jews in new business activities, closing on the Sabbath, as well as on Sunday, required for all, would have rendered businesses uncompetitive and non-viable. Could gentile employees operate Jewish businesses on the Sabbath? These are just some examples of the dilemmas facing Rabbinic courts in their efforts to solve the grave economic problems facing Jews in their struggle to survive in an in all events hostile social and economic environment.

Rabbinic responses, which also had to take into consideration the possibility that excessive strictness would lead to massive disobedience, varied. Some rabbis preferred not to be asked such questions, as it was preferable that, in the absence of an explicit Rabbinic pronouncement, the people transgressed inadvertently rather than deliberately. Most rabbis, however, searched actively for practical solutions, using the pretext that prohibitions that cause excessive damage to the congregation and that are rejected by the majority may be amended; only precepts with which the public can live may be imposed. Compromises sought in particular to relax the severity of the mandate of Sabbath rest for gentile employees and animals. This was accomplished by temporarily or permanently changing the gentile employee into a business partner, who was then charged with operating the business on the Sabbath. This is the foundation of the medieval institution of the "Shabbes goy."

The emergence of the concept of the Shabbes goy, extensively discussed by Jacob Katz,[8] sheds light on the historic debate on the long term expediency of passing permissive rulings in questions of Sabbath injunctions. Permissiveness contributed, no doubt, to improvements in the material welfare of Jews. Still, in the nineteenth and twentieth centuries, this approach's long term affects

raised heated controversy. Orthodox circles generally agree that the post-emancipation Jewish population in central and western Europe as well as in North America is an "Unruly Generation," widely disregarding the halakhic rules of behavior. The appropriate response to this state of affairs is, however, debated. The strict Rabbinic school advises uncompromising rulings in matters of the Sabbath, and, if the result is mass desertion from the orthodox way of life, so be it. Moderate thinking proposes the opposite, that "unruliness" should be met by understanding and by efforts to accommodate demands emanating from the requirements of modern times.

Modern times, defined by the Jews' achieving of full rights of citizenship, brought fundamental changes. The new, liberal atmosphere and increasing cosmopolitanism and secularism brought the Jews many economic and social opportunities. But the rules for survival in capitalist and industrial economies are quite different from those of the old days and the old countries. In the hearts of millions of Jews, the combined effect of the spiritual and the material created a new equilibrium between ritual precepts and participation in the joys and struggles of modern life. The result was that ". . . most immigrants deserted the traditional way of life, driven by their desire to find a livelihood for their family in their new environment."[9] As a result, in our day, for a large portion of the Jewish people, much of the discussion of the economic impact of the Sabbath and kashrut is mainly of theoretical interest.

The public sector: The Judaic value system is community oriented. Consequently, it must address issues concerning the public sector, comprising the tools and institutions that foster allegiance to the social and cultural norms of Judaism. This requires financing, which lies within the responsibilities of the lay leadership. For the Mishnah, the king symbolized the lay leadership, and it was understood that he had the right to confiscate private property in order to construct roads, passages, etc. (M. San. 2:4). Later, committees of lay leaders functioned under different names in different times and places. Descending from the national level to the town and its infrastructural and social service needs, the legal definition of the body of tax paying citizens was of basic importance. M. B.B. 1:5 writes:

> One [who dwells in a town] is compelled [to contribute towards the cost of building] a wall for the town [and towards the cost of] double doors and a bolt. . . . How long must one be in a town to be deemed a citizen, [required to pay taxes]? Twelve months. If one bought a dwelling house therein, he is immediately considered as a citizen of the town.

The period of residency after which one participates in the municipal social burden ranges from thirty days, for charity, to nine months, for contributing to the cost of burying the poor. The obligation to help support the poor is almost immediate, while physical defense of the town is required only after the immigrant has shown a direct, long term interest in dwelling there.

Taxation models presented in the Talmud and responsa are astonishingly comprehensive. B. B.B. 7b examines various principles for financing a city wall. If the wall's principle objective is to save life, it is fair to divide the cost equally among all households. But if the wall is meant primarily to protect wealth, the amount of tax imposed on the wealthy should be greater, in line with their greater risk. A third consideration in the distribution of the tax burden is the distance of the citizen's house from the wall. The closer it is, the more he pays, because the more he needs its protection. The principle is clear, as summarized by the medieval sage Rashbah: in a system of earmarked taxes, payment ought to accord with the utility of the service to each particular taxpayer.

This is an amazingly modern tax concept, which, though not particularly progressive, accords with the principles of Pareto optimum. It is, therefore, supplemented by a list of exceptional cases, including charity and social services, in which different principles apply. Thus, over the centuries, what was included in the tax base reflected the changing economic realities of Jewish communities. In periods and places in which farming and vineyards were considered high risk enterprises, they were exempted from taxation; when regarded as low risks, such exemptions were removed. The same applied to outstanding debts when money lending was widespread. When debt abrogation was not frequent, outstanding debt was a taxable asset. Yet, in times and places in which debt repudiation to Jews was common, outstanding debt to gentiles was no basis for tax. As long as gold was used as jewelry, it was not an economically active asset. When, however, it became a vehicle for hoarding wealth, it also was deemed a basis for taxation.

Again, the principle is clear. Only potential or actual income-generating wealth was considered as tax base. But, since systematic application of this principle could have violated some of the basic social and spiritual norms upon which the community's economy rested, ideologically and socially motivated exemptions from tax impositions were rather sweeping. Among the exempted sectors were 1) producers of merit goods (Torah scrolls, religious items, and learning), 2) rabbis and the clergy, 3) contributors to the land of Israel, 4) the poor. Notably, this method of general taxability, on the one hand, and exemptions motivated by merit considerations, on the other, is a widely accepted principle of the modern Value Added Tax.

The very same behavioral standards that served as guidelines for the public sector were expected to apply in business interactions. In a perfect market, under conditions of Pareto Optimum, no ethical considerations, per se, would be necessary, since perfect competition and perfect knowledge should suffice as safeguards against corrupt transactions. But, as we have seen, Jewish business ethics are not based upon a theory of a perfect market and do rely on value loaded principles.

The crucial underlying maxim is at Lev. 19:2: "You shall be holy; for I the Lord your God am holy." The obligations that emerge from this general notion are set out in the verses that follow: compassion to the poor

(9:10), honesty in business (9:11), decency to employees (9:13), integrity in dealings with the uninformed and the simpleton (9:14), emphasis on the impartiality of justice (9:15), sincerity in human relations (9:16-17), and the principle that epitomizes Judaic social ethics, "you shall love your neighbor as yourself" (9:18). Aqiba, among the greatest of the Mishnaic sages, maintained that this verse is a fundamental principle of the Torah.

To reinforce the validity of these exhortations, five verses in this brief passage conclude: "I am the Lord." This means that, in Judaism, the application of an ethical approach to business conduct is not based simply on a theory of reciprocity. Judaic business ethics therefore do not rely primarily on the judgment of the merchant, for instance, to maintain right scales for his own benefit. Neither does Judaism assume that the customers' vigilance will suffice. The free market theory puts the weight of alertness on the prudent customer: "let the buyer beware." Judaic ethics, by contrast, removes much of the buyer's burden, not for reasons of expediency but in line with the socio-religious claim that cheating in prices is ethically wrong. Business ethics thus are an integral part of the overall value system of the Judaic legacy.

The role of the Jew in the modern economy: The economic behavior of the Jews in their pursuit of a livelihood within a gentile majority was shaped by their own human capital and the internal constraints of their religious precepts, on the one hand, and the opportunities offered or refused by the outside world, on the other. Is there "any common repeatedly observed feature in the economic life of the Jews?" asked Simon Kuznets in his seminal work on this topic.[10] If the answer is indeed affirmative, should the similarities be attributed to factors specific to the Jews, their faith, culture, and historical heritage, or to their racial/genetic characteristics?

In the nineteenth and twentieth centuries, this question was asked by numerous historians and sociologists. Outstanding among them were Marx, Weber, and Sombart, who witnessed and studied the socio-economic and political movements that arose in the course of the first half of the nineteenth century: emancipation, industrial revolution, and modern capitalism. These movements had a dramatic impact on the fortunes of the Jews in Europe. Following their release from the ghettos, many Jews swiftly integrated into the rapidly growing economies, particularly in Western and Central Europe and in the United States, and occupied a visibly important role in many sectors. Social analysts, among them the three above mentioned scholars, searched for theories to explain the close correlation between the emergence of capitalism and the integration of the Jews into European economy, comprehended as "the role of the Jews in the development of capitalism."

A major essay of Karl Marx, "On the Jewish Question," written in 1843, in the early days of his career, was the only one he addressed solely to this topic. It was a vicious attack on Jews and Judaism, viewed as the perfect substantiation of capitalism and the capitalist ethos. The Jews were said to desire nothing more than to reap profit by manipulating the financial markets. The ultimate force behind this aspiration was the Jewish religion itself, from ancient times the supreme expression of rational, unscrupulous bourgeois spirit and thinking.

Admittedly, noted Marx, modern capitalism was not "created" by the Jews. However, due to the close spiritual kinship between them and capitalism, they internalized it and became some of the most important agents of social and economic modernization. Notably, Marx changed his position towards the Jews in his later writings, which were less saturated with rabidly anti-Jewish expressions. Now he reduced the Jews' role to that of hostile outsiders within authentic industrial capitalism. But posterity always quotes the early rather than the late Marx.

The great German sociologist Max Weber, in his analysis of the origins of capitalism (*The Protestant Ethic*, 1904, and *The Spirit of Capitalism*, 1905) as well as in his essay on the sociology of the Jewish religion, published post-mortem (*Das antike Judentum*,

1923), dealt extensively with the role of the Jews in the emergence of modern capitalism. Weber considered the Protestant ethic, principally in Calvinistic interpretation, through its ascetic discipline, modest consumption patterns, and rational as well as liberal attitude to industrial organization and work, to be the initiating spirit of modern capitalism. He saw capitalism, especially its industrial manifestation, as a positive phenomenon.

In his theory, constrained by the Jewish religion's precepts, the Jews in the diaspora were confined to a self-imposed isolation. This made them a "guest nation," fulfilling in various national economies only marginal functions, such as trade and finances. At the same time, through industrialization and technological change, modern capitalism stimulated genuine processes of structural transformation. As the direct corollary of their socio-economic status, Jews—the "pariahs" (a term coined by Weber) of the western economies—inevitably drifted to "pariah capitalism," that is, to activities at the fringes. Consequently, they cannot be regarded as a leading force in the evolution of western capitalism at all. Weber's empirical proof of his thesis was his statistical observation that the vast majority of the Jews, in his time at least, dwelled in the pre-capitalistic regions of the world, namely, in eastern Europe and the Muslim world.

The well known opponent of Weber on the issue of the Jews and capitalism was another German social economist, Werner Sombart. The long lasting controversy between them became a thought stimulating topic for many, particularly Jewish, social scientists. A common denominator for the two, and also for Marx, was contempt for trade and finance. Yet, in sharp contradiction to Weber, the very essence of Sombart's comprehension of capitalism was that it severed man's economic activity from toil for sustenance and converted it into a profit generating device (another idea learned from Marx).

Sombart conceived that the birth of capitalism was around the turn of the fifteenth century, when the Jews were expelled from Spain and Portugal and found refuge in the Netherlands and then in England. By Sombart's observations, wherever Jews settled in Europe the economy prospered, and when they were expelled, it declined. This proved that the Jews were the primary stimulators of modern capitalism. This empirical statement was invigorated by a theory supplied in Sombart's book, written as a reply to Weber, *Die Juden und das Wirtschaftsleben* (1911).

In Sombart's theory the main culprits in the commercialization and monetarization of European society were, apart from the unique economic conditions of the Jews prior to their full emancipation, the Jewish religion and the Jewish race. He argued that Judaism contains strong elements of self restraint and rationality. It contains no mystery, no indulgence, and no licentious creativity. Every interaction is based on contracts; even the relationship between the Jewish God and the Israelite people is founded on reciprocal contracts. Further, in his view, Judaism is an authentic reflection of the genetic characteristics of the Jews. They lean towards abstract and quantifiable notions and prefer logical reasoning over passionate affections. These features easily accommodate the universalistic character of capitalism and go perfectly well with the theoretical concept of the classical school of economics, the "homo economicus."

Contemporary research respects Marx and Weber as important scholars, while many criticize not only Sombart's theories but also the depth of his analysis and reliability of his sources. Nevertheless, recurrent quotations of his work, even today, attest to the considerable influence his writing has had on students of Jewish social and economic history. At the same time there is little doubt about his antisemitic inclinations and about the fact that Sombart lent his expertise and scholarly reputation to the service of the Nazi regime in Germany.

The Jews in contemporary economic theory: Recent studies of the economic behavior of Jews have had no need for such grand theories as were conceived by the nineteenth century scholars. The contributions of S. Kuznets and G. Becker to a theory of "Economics of Minorities" enable modern students to study the economic functioning of Jews as a permanent or temporary minority. They are to be identified as a minority because, to use Kuznets' categories:

1. They possess a common history that looks back to their original ancestry in the land of Israel.
2. They share the same religion, which is not shared with others.
3. They have a feeling of belonging to a specific group and care more about the fate of others in that group than about the fate of members of other groups.
4. They feel distinct from other groups in part because of recollections of past or present antisemitic discrimination.

Kuznets' model relates to small minorities that constitute less than one-tenth of the overall population and do not live together in a single territory over which they claim to have historical privileges. The model contends that the economic features of Jewish minorities in their countries of settlement (excluding Israel, where Jews are the majority) have the following characteristics:

1. The Jews' occupational composition differs from that of the population at large, with Jews concentrating in a narrower range of vocations. The closer the occupational composition of the minority to that of the general population, the faster the process of assimilation, leading ultimately to a loss of the minority's distinct identity.
2. Jews tend to gravitate to relatively new or rapidly expanding economic sectors because: 1) employment opportunities in these areas are better, as the acquisition of the needed skills takes longer for the majority, entrenched in old industries; and 2) such industries are more profitable than slow growing, stagnant ones.
3. Jews had an "economic heritage," the legacy of their countries of emigration and of their experiences prior to emancipation. This heritage constituted an historically accumulated human capital and played an important role in the initial process of occupation selection after emancipation or in their new countries.
4. As a result of past discrimination or apprehension about present discrimination, Jews tend to converge in industries already preferred by Jews. Since a Jewish presence in an industry is of expedience for new Jewish entrants, this pattern is likely to continue, unless the industry becomes stagnant. It may lead to a domination in certain niches of some industries. If these niches are visible, the situation may be exploited as an excuse for economic antisemitism.
5. For three reasons, in many countries the economic rise of the Jewish minority, expressed as an increase in per capita income, was larger than that of the general population: 1) Jews had a tendency to enter fast growing industries; 2) as immigrants, they received very low initial wages, so their progress was relatively rapid; 3) as a rule, urban minorities are more mobile and exploit new opportunities more easily than members of a ruling majority, firmly established in old positions.
6. The extent of economic inequality within Jewish communities tends to be smaller than among the general population.

Bearing in mind recent experience, one may add to these characteristics suggested by Kuznets that the pace and extent of the Jews' economic adjustment to their host countries has depended on the relative weight of the Jewish minority—the smaller it is, the easier its adjustment—and the "Jewish policy," that is, the general attitude of the host country and its government to minorities. Liberal governance eased economic integration. In this respect, Jews owe a debt to liberal capitalism with its main feature of competition, in which only performance counts and monopoly is viewed as discriminatory.

Examining these and other features, we may depict as follows the observable singularities of Jewish economic functioning in the twentieth century:

1. The absence of Jews from agriculture. Historically, the ownership of land was the most conspicuous target for economic discrimination. Beginning in the feudal period, Jews in most countries and in most ages had no right to owe land. When, in the nineteenth century, this limitation was removed, agriculture became a stagnant and later a declining industry. Jews had no "economic heritage" in agriculture, and they had no rational reason to enter it.

2. Jews have a demonstrated preference for urban life, and whenever permitted to choose their dwelling location, chose the city. This preference was paralleled in the late

nineteenth and twentieth centuries by much of the non-Jewish population, particularly in developed countries. The Jews, forerunners in many fields of modernization and also in early urbanization, sought economic, hygienic, and cultural improvements in the cities. Cities also provided advantageous conditions for maintaining community institutions at a sustainable cost. Finally, the big city was an ideal environment in which to find anonymity, a haven against antisemitic harassment.

3. Statistical calculations suggest amazingly high similarities between the occupational distributions of Jews in various European countries, pointing to the existence of a Jewish occupational pattern. Even so, it is difficult to generalize about Jewish occupations. For, contrary to the stereotype of Jews in banking and finance, after emancipation and the massive waves of Jewish migration, in much greater numbers they entered manufacturing, so that in many European countries, as well as in Canada, the ratio of Jewish industrial labor in the pre-World War II years was higher than that of non-Jewish, non-agricultural labor. The share of Jews in banking and finances decreased in part as a result of significant integration in the financial sector and the occupation of its more important positions by the privileged classes. In the era of finance capitalism, the traditional functions of Jews in pre-industrial finances—money lending and petty banking—became of marginal significance.

4. Regarding the manufacturing sectors preferred by Jewish entrepreneurs, two interdependent features should be mentioned. First, the great majority of Jews are in the production of final consumer goods, sold directly, in competitive markets, to non-institutional consumers. Such plants are moderately capital intensive, of relatively small size, and operated with intermediate technology. Second, relatively few Jewish entrepreneurs are found in steel, heavy engineering, and mining.

5. Similarly, Jews in commerce primarily operate retail businesses. They prefer to trade in consumer goods, such as clothing, footwear, food, and drink, much less in raw material and industrial inputs. The reason, as Kuznets argues, is that Jews seek projects with rapid capital turnover, which demand much ingenuity but small investment. They have a strong propensity for hard work, complemented with inventiveness. This substitutes for a lack of political leverage and connections, needed to do business in the public sector and in many of the basic industries.

6. Developments after World War II favored large scale and capital intensive enterprises and increased the economic share of the public sector, adversely affecting the economic equilibrium of the Jews. The viability of small private businesses declined, while the public sector became a dominant factor in production, commerce, and the labor market. Yet in most western countries the share of Jewish employees in the public sector remains lower than their percentage in the labor force. This is because, in the face of the declining profitability of small businesses, the Jews' stubborn preference for an independent status in the private, competitive market led many young Jews to enter the liberal professions as medical doctors, lawyers, engineers, and scientists.

Conclusion: From the point of view of economic position and status, active or passive belonging to the Jewish religion rendered the Jew a member of a minority within a national economy. In the past, being a Jew had a profound influence upon economic behavior and prospects. Although the liberal governmental policies pursued in the west have removed most formal limitations and allowed Jewish youths to choose careers of their liking, the legacy of the past continues to leave a meaningful imprint upon even their present occupational composition.

From quite an unexpected angle, higher standards of living and modern technology have affected the connection between Judaism and economic life. The reduction of the work week to five days removed a significant obstacle from Sabbath observance. No longer do synagogues sponsor early Sabbath morning worship services for those who need to hurry to work after Sabbath prayers. Longer annual holidays and flexible employment policies also have facilitated the observance of Jewish festivals that fall on weekdays. These changes have increased the pool of employment opportunities for observant Jews.

Additionally, recent technology has created possibilities for the reintroduction of cottage type industries, involving jobs such as programming, computerized accountancy, and the like. Offering tasks that can be done in the employees' homes and at their convenience, this has created new opportunities to productivize a potential labor force, including orthodox Jewish women with families, who heretofore kept away from the labor market. Modern technology also has enabled the production of kosher food at lower costs and in a vastly enlarged selection. Maintaining a kosher diet thus has become more affordable in terms both of economic and culinary cost.

Higher real income per capita and shorter working hours also have greatly expanded the options available for modern people to enrich their cultural and spiritual experience. More leisure time and higher real income have reduced the subjective cost of engagement in religious activities. For the modern person in the west, economic factors have become less of an obstacle in the pursuit of a way of life that accords with Judaic principles than at any time in the last two centuries.

Bibliography

Katz, Jacob, *The Shabbes Goy* (Philadelphia, 1989).

Kuznets, S., "Economic Structure and Life of the Jews," in Finkelstein, Louis, ed., *The Jews* (New York, 1960, 3rd ed.), vol. 2, pp. 1597-1665.

Tamari, Meir, *With All Your Possession: Jewish Ethics and Economic Life* (New York, 1987).

Notes

[1] Jacob Katz, "Thoughts on the Relationship between Religion and Economics," in M. Ben Sasson, ed., *Religion and Economy: Connections and Interactions. Collected Essays* (Jerusalem, 1995), p. 33.

[2] *Journal of Institutional and Theoretical Economics*, vol. 150, December, 1994, pp. 737-754, 769-775.

[3] G. Stigler and G. Becker, "De Gustibus Non Est Disputandum," in *American Economic Review*, 1977, vol. 67, p. 77.

[4] *Journal of Institutional and Theoretical Economics*, pp. 752-754.

[5] J.S. Coleman, "Norms as Social Capital," in G. Radinzky and P. Bernholz, eds., *Economic Imperialism* (N.Y., 1987), p. 135.

[6] Jacob Katz, *The Shabbes Goy* (Philadelphia, 1989), p. 249.

[7] Ibid.

[8] Ibid.

[9] Ibid., p. 44.

[10] S. Kuznets, "Economic Structure and Life of the Jews," in L. Finkelstein L., ed., *The Jews* (New York, 1960), vol. 2, p. 1579.

YEHUDA DON

EMOTIONS, DOCTRINE OF, IN JUDAISM: Rabbinic Judaism specifies the emotions and attitudes the faithful are to cultivate, favoring humility and the attitudes of conciliation and accommodation, not aggression. Israelite virtue was so formulated as to match Israel's political circumstance, which, from the first century, was one of defeat, alienation, and exile. Sages' Judaism for a defeated people prepared the nation for a long future. The vanquished people, the brokenhearted nation that had lost its city and its Temple, that had, moreover, produced another nation from its midst to take over its Scripture and much else, could not bear too much reality. That defeated people, in its intellectuals, as represented in the Rabbinic sources, found refuge in a mode of thought that trained vision to see things otherwise than as the eyes perceived them. Among the diverse ways by which the weak and subordinated accommodate to their circumstance, the one of iron-willed pretense in life is most likely to yield the mode of thought at hand: things never are what they seem. The uniform tradition on emotions persisted intact because the social realities of Israel's life proved permanent, until, in our own time, they changed. The upshot was that Rabbinic Judaism's Israel was instructed on how to tame its heart and govern its wild emotions, to accept with resignation, to endure with patience, above all, to value the attitudes and emotions that made acceptance and endurance plausible.

Humility, patience, endurance, and hope—The right feelings: The sages of Rabbinic Judaism taught not only what

Israel was supposed to do or not do, but also what Israel is supposed to feel. And that was how they accomplished their most difficult task, the transformation of the Jews to conform to the picture of "Israel" that the sages set forth and proposed to bring into being. From beginning to end, the documents of Rabbinic Judaism set forth a single, consistent, and coherent doctrine: the true Israelite was to exhibit the moral virtues of subservience, patience, endurance, and hope. These would translate into the emotional traits of humility and forbearance. And they would yield to social virtues of passivity and conciliation. The hero was one who overcame impulses, and the truly virtuous person was the one who reconciled others by giving way before their opinions.

All of these acts of self-abnegation and self-denial, accommodation rather than rebellion, required to begin with the right attitudes, sentiments, emotions, and impulses, and the single most dominant motif of the Rabbinic writings, start to finish, is its stress on the right attitude's leading to the right action, the correct intentionality's producing the besought decision, above all, accommodating in one's heart to what could not be changed by one's action. And that meant, the world as it was. Sages' prepared Israel for the long centuries of subordination and alienation by inculcating attitudes that best suited people who could govern little more than how they felt about things.

The notion that sages teach feelings is hardly puzzling. Since Israelites are commanded to love God, it follows that an emotion, love, becomes holy. If it is holy when the affection of love is directed to God, then, the same emotion, love, may become not only profane but sinful when it is directed to the wrong objects, self or power, for example. Accordingly, the definitive holy books of Judaism make plain the sages' conviction that feelings too come to the surface as matters of judgment. Emotions constitute constructions for which, they hold, we bear responsibility.

The repertoire of approved and disapproved feelings remains constant through the half-millennium of the unfolding of the canon of Judaism from the Mishnah through the Talmud of Babylonia. The emotions that are encouraged, such as humility, forbearance, accommodation, a spirit of conciliation, exactly correspond to the political and social requirements of the Jews' condition in that time. The reason that the same repertoire of emotions persisted with no material change through the unfolding of the writings of the sages of that formative age was the constancy of the Jews' political and social condition. In the view of the sages at hand, emotions fit together with the encompassing patterns of society and culture, theology and the religious life.

So the affective rules form an integral part of the way of life and world-view put forward to make sense of the existence of a social group. For sages it follows that how I am supposed to feel in ethos matches what I am expected to think. In this way, as an individual, I link my deepest personal emotions to the cosmic fate and transcendent faith of that social group of which I form a part. Emotions lay down judgments. They derive from rational cognition. The individual Israelite's innermost feelings, the microcosm, correspond to the public and historic condition of Israel, the macrocosm.

Private feelings, public policy: What Rabbinic Judaism teaches the private person to feel links her or his heart to what that same Judaism states about the condition of Israel in history and of God in the cosmos. All form one reality, in supernatural world and nature, in time and in eternity wholly consubstantial (so to speak). In the innermost chambers of deepest feelings, the Israelite therefore lives out the public history and destiny of the people, Israel. The genius of Rabbinic Judaism, the reason for its resilience and endurance, lies in its power to teach Jews to feel in private what they also must think in public about the condition of both self and nation. The world within, the world without, are so bonded, that one is never alone. The individual's life always is lived with the people.

The notion of the centrality of human feelings in the religious life of Israel presents no surprises. Scripture is explicit on both sides of the matter. The human being is commanded to love God. In the biblical biography of God, the tragic hero, God, will despair, love, hope, feel disappointment or exultation. The biblical record of God's feelings and God's will concerning the feelings of humanity—wanting human love, for example—leaves no room for doubt. Nor does the Judaism that emerges from late antiquity ignore or propose to obliterate the datum that "the merciful God wants the heart." The Judaism of the rabbis of late antiquity makes explicit that God always wants the heart. God commands that humanity love God with full heart, soul, mind, and might. That is the principal duty of humanity.

So without the Rabbinic canon and merely on the basis of knowledge that that canon begins in the written Torah of Scripture, the facts about the critical place of religious affections in Israel's religion would still prove clear and one-sided. Just as the sages framed matters of the Written Torah in a fresh and original way, all the time stating in their own language and categories the teachings of the Written Torah, so here too, we ask where, when, how, and for what purpose, did rabbinical authorships draw upon the legacy of the Written Torah, in concluding, as they did, "the Merciful God wants the heart."

Emotion as tradition: An epitome of the sages' treatment of emotions yields a simple result. From the first to the final document, a single doctrine and program dictated what people had to say on how Israel should tame its heart. So far as the unfolding components of the canon of Judaism portray matters, emotions therefore form part of an iron tradition. That is, a repertoire of rules and relationships handed on from the past, always intact and ever unimpaired, governed the issue. The labor of the generations meant to receive the repertoire and recipe for feeling proved one of only preserving and maintaining that tradition. As successive documents came to closure, we see each one adding its improvements, while leaving the structure basically the same. Like a cathedral that takes a thousand years to build but, through the construction and not only at the end, always looks uniform and antique, so the view of the affective life over centuries remained not only cogent but essentially uniform.

The sources, read sequentially, do not. So while the formative centuries of the history of Judaism overall mark a period of remarkable growth and change, with history consisting of sequences of developments in various substantial ideas and generative conceptions, here, in the matter of emotions, it does not. The single fact emerging from a canonical survey is that the sages' doctrine of affections remained a constant in an age of change. Early, middle, and late, a single doctrine and program dictated what people had to say on how Israel should tame its heart.

Emotions in the Mishnah: While the Mishnah casually refers to emotions, e.g., tears of joy, tears of sorrow, where feelings matter, it always is in a public and communal context. For one important example, where there is an occasion of rejoicing, one form of joy is not to be confused with some other, or one context of sorrow with another. Accordingly, marriages are not to be held on festivals (M. M.Q. 1:7). Likewise mourning is not to take place then (M. M.Q. 1:5, 3:7-9). Where emotions play a role, it is because of the affairs of the community at large, e.g., rejoicing on a festival, mourning on a fast day (M. Suk. 5:1-4). Emotions are to be kept in hand, as in the case of the relatives of the executed felon (M. San. 6:6). If one had to specify the single underlying principle affecting all forms of emotion, for the Mishnah it is that feelings must be kept under control, never fully expressed without reasoning about the appropriate context. Emotions must always lay down judgments.

We see in most of those cases in which emotions play a systemic, not merely a tangential, role, that the basic principle is the same. We can and must so frame our feelings as to accord with the appropriate rule. In only one case does emotion play a decisive role in settling an issue, and that has to do with whether or not a farmer was happy that water came upon his produce or grain. That case underlines the conclusion just now drawn. If people feel a given sentiment, it is a matter of judgment, therefore invokes the law's penalties. So in this system emotions are not treated as spontaneous but as significant aspects of a person's judgment. It would be difficult to find a more striking example of that view than at M. Makh. 4:5 and related passages, where the framers judge the farmer's feelings to constitute, on their own and without associated actions or even conceptions, final and decisive judgments on what has happened.

The reason that emotions form so critical a focus of concern in Rabbinic Judaism is that God and the human being share traits of attitude and emotion. They want the same thing, respond in the same way to the same events, share not only ownership of the Land but also a viewpoint on the value of its produce. This conception takes concrete form in the notion that man's and God's intentions are the same, so that if a farmer values produce, God, the farmer's partner in the holy land, values the produce too. So attitudes and emotions come to full exposure in the matter of intentionality.

For example, in the law of tithing, the produce becomes liable to tithing, such that a share of the crop of the Holy Land must be given to one of God's surrogates, when the farmer deems the crop to be desirable. Why is that so? When the farmer wants the crop, so too does God. When the householder takes the view that the crop is worthwhile, God responds to the attitude of the farmer by forming the same opinion. The theological anthropology that brings God and the householder into the same continuum prepares the way for understanding what makes the entire Mishnaic system work.

It is the matter of the intention and will of the human being as we move from theological to philosophical thought in the Mishnah's system. "Intention" stands for attitude, and, as we have already noted, there is no distinguishing attitude from emotion. For the discussion on intention works out several theories concerning not God and God's relationship to humanity but the nature of the human will. The human being is defined not only as sentient but also as a volitional being, who can will with effect, unlike beasts and, as a matter of fact, angels (who do not

figure in the Mishnah at all). On the one side, there is no consideration of will or attitude of animals, for these are null. On the other side, will and attitude of angels, where these are represented in later documents, are totally subservient to God's wishes. Only the human being, in the person of the farmer, possesses and also exercises the power of intentionality. And it is the power that intentionality possesses that forms the central consideration. Because a human being forms an intention, consequences follow, whether or not given material expression in gesture or even in speech. The Mishnah and the law flowing from it impute extraordinary power to the will and intentionality of the human being.

How does this bear practical consequences? The attitude of the farmer toward the crop, like that of the Temple priest toward the offering that he carries out, affects the status of the crop. It classifies an otherwise-unclassified substance. It changes the standing of an already-classified beast. It shifts the status of a pile of grain, without any physical action whatsoever, from one category to another. Not only so, but the attitude or will of a farmer can override the effects of the natural world, e.g., keeping in the status of what is dry and so insusceptible to cultic uncleanness a pile of grain that in fact has been rained upon and wet down. An immaterial reality, shaped and reformed by the householder's attitude and plan, overrides the material effect of a rainstorm.

The doctrine of emotions in Tractate Abot: Tractate Abot presents the single most comprehensive account of religious affections. The reason is that, in that document above all, how we feel defines a critical aspect of virtue. The issue proves central, not peripheral. The doctrine emerges fully exposed. A simple catalogue of permissible feelings comprises humility, generosity, self-abnegation, love, a spirit of conciliation of the other, and eagerness to please. A list of impermissible emotions is made up of envy, ambition, jealousy, arrogance, sticking to one's opinion, self-centeredness, a grudging spirit, vengefulness, and the like. People should aim at eliciting from others acceptance and good will and should avoid confrontation, rejection, and humiliation of the other. This they do through conciliation and giving up their own claims and rights. So both catalogues form a harmonious and uniform whole, aiming at the cultivation of the humble and malleable person, one who accepts everything and resents nothing. Here are some representative sentiments:

> 2:4.A. He would say, "Make his wishes into your own wishes, so that he will make your wishes into his wishes.
>   B. "Put aside your wishes on account of his wishes, so that he will put aside the wishes of other people in favor of your wishes."
> 3:10.A. He would say, "Anyone from whom people take pleasure—the Omnipresent takes pleasure.
>   B. "And anyone from whom people do not take pleasure, the Omnipresent does not take pleasure."
> 4:1.A. Ben Zoma says, "Who is a sage? He who learns from everybody,
>   B. "as it is said, From all my teachers I have gotten understanding (Ps. 119:99).
>   C. "Who is strong? He who overcomes his desire,
>   D. "as it is said, He who is slow to anger is better than the mighty, and he who rules his spirit than he who takes a city (Prov. 16:32).
>   E. "Who is rich? He who is happy in what he has,
>   F. "as it is said, When you eat the labor of your hands, happy will you be, and it will go well with you (Ps. 128:2) .
>   G. ("Happy will you be in this world, and it will go well with you in the world to come.")
>   H. "Who is honored? He who honors everybody,
>   I. "as it is said, 'For those who honor me I shall honor, and they who despise me will be treated as of no account' (I Sam. 2:30)."
> 4:18.A. R. Simeon b. Eleazar says, "Do not try to make amends with your fellow when he is angry,
>   B. "or comfort him when the corpse of his beloved is lying before him,
>   C. "or seek to find absolution for him at the moment at which he takes a vow,
>   D. "or attempt to see him when he is humiliated."

> 4:19.A. Samuel the Small says, "Rejoice not when your enemy falls, and let not your heart be glad when he is overthrown, lest the Lord see it and it displease him, and he turn away his wrath from him (Prov. 24:17)."

True, these virtues, in this tractate as in the system as a whole, derive from knowledge of what really counts, which is what God wants. But God favors those who please others. The virtues appreciated by human beings prove identical to the ones to which God responds as well. And what single virtue of the heart encompasses the rest? Restraint, the source of self-abnegation, humility, serves as the antidote for ambition, vengefulness, and, above all, for arrogance. It is restraint of our own interest that enables us to deal generously with others, humility about ourselves that generates a liberal spirit towards others.

So the emotions prescribed in tractate Abot turn out to provide variations of a single feeling, which is the sentiment of the disciplined heart, whatever affective form it may take. And where does the heart learn its lessons, if not in relationship to God? So: "Make his wishes yours, so that he will make your wishes his" (Abot 2:4). Applied to the relationships between human beings, this inner discipline of the emotional life will yield exactly those virtues of conciliation and self-abnegation, humility and generosity of spirit, that the framers of tractate Abot spell out in one example after another. Imputing to Heaven exactly those responses felt on earth, e.g., "Anyone from whom people take pleasure, God takes pleasure" (Abot 3:10), makes the point at the most general level.

Virtue in the Tosefta and the Yerushalmi: When the authors or compilers of the Tosefta finished their labor of amplification and complement to the Mishnah, they had succeeded in adding only a few fresh and important developments of established themes. Striking, first, is the stress upon the communal stake in an individual's emotional life. Still more striking is the Tosefta's authors' explicit effort to invoke an exact correspondence between public and private feelings. In both realms emotions are to be tamed, kept in hand and within accepted proportions. Public sanctions for inappropriate, or disproportionate, emotions depend themselves on emotions, for instance, shame. It need hardly be added that feeling shame for improper feelings once again underlines the social, judgmental character of those feelings. For shame is public, guilt private. People are responsible for how they feel, as much as for how, in word or deed, they express feeling. Hence an appropriate penalty derives from the same aspect of social life, that is, the affective life.

There is no more stunning tribute to the power of feeling than the allegation, surfacing in the Tosefta, that the Temple was destroyed because of vain hatred. That sort of hatred, self-serving and arrogant, stands against the feelings of love that characterize God's relationship to Israel. Accordingly, it was improper affections that destroyed the relationship embodied in the Temple cult of old. Given the critical importance accorded to the Temple cult, sages could not have made more vivid their view that how a private person feels shapes the public destiny of the entire nation. So the issues came to expression in a context in which the stakes are very high. But the basic position of the authors of the Mishnah, inclusive of their first apologists in Abot, seems entirely consistent. What Tosefta's authors accomplished is precisely what they claimed, which was to amplify, supplement, and complement established principles and positions.

A survey of this topic in the Yerushalmi confirms the one dominant result throughout. Emotions not taken up earlier now did not come under discussion. Principles introduced earlier enjoyed restatement and extensive exemplification. Some principles of proper feelings might even generate secondary developments of one kind or another. But nothing not present at the outset drew sustained attention later on. The system proved essentially complete in the earliest statement of its main points. Everything that followed for four hundred years served to reinforce and restate what to begin with had emerged loud

and clear. What then do the authors or compilers of the Yerushalmi contribute? Temper marks the ignorant person, restraint and serenity, the learned one. In general, we notice, where the Mishnah introduces into its system issues of the affective life, the Yerushalmi's authors and compilers will take up those issues. But they rarely create them on their own and never say much new about those they do treat. What we find is instruction to respect public opinion and cultivate social harmony.

What is most interesting in the Yerushalmi is the recognition that there are rules descriptive of feelings, as much as of other facts of life. These rules tells us how to dispose of cases in which feelings make a difference. The fact is, therefore, that the effects of emotions, as much as of opinions or deeds, come within the rule of law. It must follow, in the view of sages, the affective life once more proves an aspect of society. People are assumed to frame emotions, as much as opinions, in line with common and shared judgments. In no way do emotions form a special classification, one expressive of what is private, spontaneous, individual, and beyond the law and reason.

The Bavli's doctrine of emotions: The Bavli carried forward with little change the now traditional program of emotions, listing the same ones catalogued earlier and no new ones. The authors said about those feelings what had been said earlier. A leader must be someone acceptable to the community. God then accepts him too. People should be ready to give up quarrels and forgive. The correspondence of social and personal virtues reaches explicit statement. How so? The community must forbear, the individual must forgive. Communal tolerance for causeless hatred destroyed the Temple; individual vendettas yield miscarriages. In both cases people nurture feelings that express arrogance. Arrogance is what permits the individual to express emotions without discipline, and arrogance is what leads the community to undertake what it cannot accomplish.

A fresh emphasis portrayed in the Bavli favored mourning and disapproved of rejoicing. We can hardly maintain that that view came to expression only in the latest stages in the formation of the canon. The contrary is the case. The point remains consistent throughout. Excessive levity marks arrogance, deep mourning characterizes humility. So many things come down to one thing. The nurture of an attitude of mourning should mark both the individual and the community, both in mourning for the Temple, and also in mourning for the condition of nature, including the human condition, signified in the Temple's destruction.

A mark of humility is humble acceptance of suffering. This carried forward the commonplace view that suffering now produces joy later on. The ruin of the Temple, for example, served as a guarantee that just as the prophetic warnings came to realization, so too would prophetic promises of restoration and redemption. In the realm of feelings, the union of opposites came about through the same mode of thought. Hence God's love comes to fulfillment in human suffering, and the person who joyfully accepts humiliation or suffering will enjoy the appropriate divine response of love.

Another point at which the authors of the Bavli introduce a statement developing a familiar view derives from the interpretation of how to love one's neighbor. It is by imposing upon one's neighbor the norms of the community, rebuking the other for violating accepted practice. In this way the emotion of love takes on concrete social value in the norms of the community. Stories about sages cover the themes of humility, resignation, restraint, and perpetual good will. A boastful sage loses his wisdom. A humble one retains it. Since it is wisdom about which a sage boasts, the matching of opposites conforms to the familiar mode of thought.

The strikingly fresh medium for traditional doctrines in the Bavli takes the form of prayers composed by sages. Here the values of the system came to eloquent expression. Sages prayed that their souls may be as dust for everyone to tread upon. They asked for humility in spirit, congenial colleagues, good will, good impulses. They asked God to take cognizance of their humiliation, to spare them from disgrace. The familiar affective virtues and sins, self-abnegation as against arrogance, made their appearance in liturgical form as well. Another noteworthy type of material, also not new, in which the pages of the Bavli prove rich, portrayed the deaths of sages. One dominant motif is uncertainty in face of death, a sign of humility and self-abnegation.

The basic motif—theological as much as affective—encompassing all materials is simple. Israel is estranged from God, therefore should exhibit the traits of humility and uncertainty, acceptance and conciliation. When God recognizes in Israel's heart, as much as in the nation's deeds and deliberation, the proper feelings, God will respond by ending that estrangement that marks the present age. So the single word encompassing the entire affective doctrine of the canon of Judaism is alienation. No contemporary, surviving the Holocaust, can miss the psychological depth of the system, which joins the human condition to the fate of the nation and the world, and links the whole to the broken heart of God.

We therefore find ourselves where we started, in those sayings that state that if one wants something, he or she should aspire to its opposite. Things are never what they seem. To be rich, accept what you have. To be powerful, conciliate your enemy. To be endowed with public recognition in which to take pride, express humility. So too the doctrine of the emotional life expressed in law, scriptural interpretation, and tales of sages alike turns out to be uniform and simple. Emotions well up uncontrolled and spontaneous. Anger, vengeance, pride, arrogance— these people feel by nature. So feelings as much as affirmations and actions must become what by nature they are not.

So the life of the emotions, in conformity to the life of reflection and of concrete deed, will consist in the transformation of what things *seem* into what they *ought* to be. No contemporary psychologists or philosophers can fail to miss the point. Here we have an example of the view—whether validated by the facts of nature or not—that emotions constitute constructs, and feelings lay down judgments. So the heart belongs, together with the mind, to the human being's power to form reasoned viewpoints. Coming from sages, intellectuals to their core, such an opinion surely coheres with the context and circumstance of those who hold it.

Virtuous modes of thought: This theory of the emotional life, persistent through the unfolding of the canonical documents of Judaism, fits into a larger way of viewing the world. We may call this mode of thought an *as-if* way of seeing things. That is to say, it is *as if* a common object or symbol really represented an uncommon one. Nothing says what it means. Everything important speaks symbolically. All statements carry deeper meaning, which inheres in other statements altogether. So too each emotion bears a negative and a positive charge, as each matches and balances the other: humility, arrogance, love, hate. If natural to the heart is a negative emotion, then the individual has the power to sanctify that negative, sinful feeling and turn it into a positive, holy emotion. Ambition then must be tamed, so transformed into humility; hatred and vengeance must change into love and acceptance.

What we see is an application of a large-scale, encompassing exercise in analogical thinking—something is like something else, stands for, evokes, or symbolizes that which is quite outside itself. It may be the opposite of something else, in which case it conforms to the exact opposite of the rules that govern that something else. The reasoning is analogical or it is contrastive, and the fundamental logic is taxonomic. The taxonomy rests on those comparisons and contrasts we should call parabolic. In that case, what lies on the surface misleads. What lies beneath or beyond the surface—there is the true reality. People who see things this way constitute the opposite of ones who call a thing as it is. Self-evidently, they have become accustomed to perceiving more—or less—than is at hand. Perhaps that is a natural mode of thought for the Jews of this period (and not then alone), so long used to calling themselves God's first love, yet now seeing others with greater worldly reason claiming that same advantaged relationship.

Not in mind only, but still more, in the politics of the world, the people that remembered its origins along with the very creation of the world and founding of humanity, that recalled how it alone served, and serves, the one and only God, for hundreds of years had confronted a quite difference existence. The radical disjuncture between the way things were and the way Scripture said things were supposed to be, and in actuality would some day become, surely imposed an unbearable tension. It was one thing for the slave born to slavery to endure. It was another for the free man sold into slavery to accept that same condition.

The vanquished people, the brokenhearted nation that had in 586 B.C.E. and again in 70 C.E. lost its city and its Temple, that had, moreover, in the fourth century produced another nation from its midst to take over its Scripture and much else, could not bear too much reality. That defeated people, in its intellectuals, as represented in the sources we have surveyed, then found refuge in a mode of thought that trained vision to see other things otherwise than as the eyes perceived them.

Among the diverse ways by which the weak and subordinated accommodate to their circumstance, the one of iron-willed pretense in life is most likely to yield the mode of thought at hand: things never are, because they cannot be, what they seem. The uniform tradition on emotions persisted intact because the social realities of Israel's life proved permanent until our own time. The affective program of the canon, early, middle, and late, fits tightly in every detail with this doctrine of an ontological teleology in eschatological disguise. Israel is to tame its heart so that it will feel that same humility within that Israel's world-view and way of living demand in life at large. Submit, accept, conciliate, stay cool in emotion as much as in attitude, inside and outside—and the messiah will come.

Forbearance, aggression: The profound program of emotions, the sages' statement of how people should feel and why they should take charge of their emotions remained quite constant. No one can imagine that Jews in their hearts felt the way sages said they should. The repertoire of permissible and forbidden feelings hardly can have defined the broad range of actual emotions, whether private or social, of the community of Israel. In fact, we have no evidence about how people really felt. We see only a picture of what sages thought they should, and should not, feel. Writings that reveal stunning shifts in doctrine, teleology, and hermeneutical method form from beginning to end the one picture of the ideal Israelite. It is someone who accepts, forgives, conciliates, makes the soul "like dirt beneath other peoples' feet." These kinds of people receive little respect in the world we now know; they are called cowards. Self-assertion is admired, conciliatory attitudes despised. Ours is an age that admires the strong-minded individual, the uncompromising hero, the warrior whether on the battle-field or in the intellect. Courage takes the form of confrontation, which therefore takes precedence over accommodation in the order of public virtue.

Why sages counseled a different kind of courage we need hardly ask. Given the situation of Israel, vanquished on the battlefield, broken in the turning of history's wheel, we need hardly wonder why wise men advised conciliation and acceptance. Exalting humility made sense, there being little choice. Whether or not these virtues found advocates in other contexts for other reasons, in the circumstance of the vanquished nation, for the people of broken heart, the policy of forbearance proved instrumental, entirely appropriate to both the politics and social condition at hand. If Israel had produced a battlefield hero, the nation could not give him an army. If Jewry cultivated the strong-minded individual, it sentenced such a person to a useless life of ineffective protest. The nation required not strong-minded leadership but consensus.

The social virtues of conciliation moreover reinforced the bonds that joined the nation lacking frontiers, the people without a politics of its own. For all there was to hold Israel together to sustain its life as a society would have to come forth out of sources of inner strength. Bonding emerged mainly from within. So consensus, conciliation, self-abnegation and humility, the search for acceptance without the group—these in the literary culture at hand defined appropriate emotions because to begin with they dictated wise policy and shrewd politics.

Vanquished Israel therefore would nurture not merely policies of subordination and acceptance of diminished status among nations. Israel also would develop, in its own heart, the requisite emotional structure. The composition of individuals' hearts would then comprise the counterpart virtues. A policy of acceptance of the rule of others dictated affections of conciliation to the will of others. A defeated people meant to endure defeat would have to get along by going along. How to persuade each Jew to accept what all Jews had to do to endure? Persuade the heart, not only the mind. Then each one privately would feel what everyone publicly had in any case to think.

That accounts for the persistence of the sages' wise teachings on temper, their sagacious counsel on conciliating others and seeking the approval of the group. Society, in the canonical writings, set the style for the self's deepest sentiments. So the approved feelings retained approval for so long because emotions in the thought of the sages of the canon followed rules. They formed public, not personal and private, facts. Feelings laid down judgments. Affections therefore constituted not mindless effusions but deliberate constructions. Whether or not the facts then conformed to the sages' view (or now with the mind of psychology, philosophy, and anthropology) we do not know. But the sages' view did penetrate deeply into what had to be. And that is so, whether or not what had to be ever would correspond with what was.

The sages of the formative age of Judaism proposed for Israel the formation of exactly that type of personality that could and did endure the condition and circumstance of the exile. The doctrine of the messiah makes this point as well. In rejecting the heroic model of Bar Kokhba for the messiah-general's arrogance and affirming the very opposite, the sages who defined Judaism in the first seven centuries C.E. and whose heirs expanded and developed the system they had defined made the right choice. Living in other peoples' countries and not in their own land meant for Israel a long span of endurance, a test of patience to end only with the end of time. That required Israel to live in accord with the will of others. Under such circumstances the virtues of the independent citizen, sharing command of affairs of state, the gifts of innovation, initiative, independence of mind, proved beside the point. From the end of the second revolt against Rome in 135 to the creation of the State of Israel in 1948, Israel, the Jewish people, faced a different task.

The hero of Judaism: The human condition of Israel therefore defined a different heroism, one filled with patience and humiliation. To turn survival into endurance, pariah-status into an exercise in Godly living, the sages' affective program served full well. Israel's hero saw power in submission, wealth in the gift to be grateful, wisdom in the confession of ignorance. Like the cross, ultimate degradation was made to stand for ultimate power. Like Jesus on the cross, so Israel in exile served God through suffering. True, the cross would represent a scandal to the nations and foolishness to some Jews. But Israel's own version of the doctrine endured and defined the nation's singular and astonishing resilience. For Israel did endure and endures today.

If, then, as a matter of public policy, the nurture of the personality of the Israelite as a person of forbearance and self-abnegation proved right, within the community too, the rabbis were not wrong. The Jewish people rarely enjoyed instruments of civil coercion capable of preserving social order and coherence. Governments at best afforded Jews limited rights over their own affairs. When, at the start of the fifth century, the Christian Roman government ended the existence of the patriarchate of the Jews of the land of Israel, people can well have recognized the parlous condition of whatever Jewish authorities might ever run things. A government in charge of itself and its subjects, a territorial community able routinely to force individuals to pay taxes and otherwise conform where

necessary—these political facts of normality rarely marked the condition of Israel between 429 and 1948. What was left was another kind of power, civil obedience generated by force from within. The stress on pleasing others and conforming to the will of the group, so characteristic of sayings of sages, the emphasis that God likes people whom people like—these substitutes for the civil power of political coercion imparted to the community of Israel a different power of authority.

Both sources of power, the one in relationship to the public world beyond, the other in respect to the social world within, in the sages' rules gained force through the primal energy of emotion. Enough has been said to require little explication of that fact. A system that made humility a mark of strength and a mode of gaining God's approval, a social policy that imputed ultimate virtue to feelings of conciliation, restraint, and conformity to social norms had no need of the armies and police it did not have. The heart would serve as the best defense, inner affections as the police who are always there when needed. The remarkable inner discipline of Israel through its exacting condition in history from the beginnings of the sages' system to today began in those feelings that laid down judgments, that construction of affections, coherent with beliefs and behavior, that met the match of misery with grandeur of soul. So the vanquished nation every day would overcome the one-time victors. Israel's victory would come through the triumph of the broken heart, now mended with the remedy of moderated emotion. That union of private feeling and public policy imparted to the Judaic system of the dual Torah its power, its status of self-evidence, for the long centuries during which Israel's condition persisted in the definition imparted by the events of the third crisis in the formation of Judaism.

The Judaic doctrine of emotions: In the view of the sages of the dual Torah, attitudes or virtues of the heart, e.g., emotions, fit together with the encompassing patterns of society and culture, theology and the religious life. That accomplishment of Rabbinic

Judaism accounts for its power not only to respond to, but itself to define and shape, the condition of Israel, the Jewish people. What the dual Torah taught the private person to feel linked the individual's heart to what Judaism stated about the condition of Israel in history and of God in the cosmos. In successfully joining psychology and politics, inner attitudes and public policy, sages discovered the source of power that would sustain their system. The reason that Judaism enjoyed the standing of self-evident truth for so long as it did, in both Islam and Christendom, derives not from the cogency of its doctrines, but principally from the fusion of heart and mind, emotion and intellect, attitude and doctrine—and the joining of the whole in the fundamental and enduring politics of the nation, wherever it located itself.

In Christendom and Islam, Israel could survive—but only on the sufferance of others. But those others ordinarily accorded to Israel the right of survival. Judaism endured in Christendom because the later fourth century legislators distinguished Judaism from paganism. Judaism lasted in Islam because the Muslim law accorded to Judaism tolerated status. Israel therefore would nurture not merely policies of subordination and acceptance of diminished status among nations. Israel also would develop, in its own heart, the requisite emotional structure.

JACOB NEUSNER

ETHICS OF JUDAISM: The word ethics is used and understood in many different ways. This being the case, before describing Jewish ethics in particular, we begin by defining ethics in general. Questions of ethics are, broadly speaking, questions of value. The province of ethics within the commonwealth of evaluative issues is determined by the particular values it seeks to understand, define, and elucidate. These are generally accepted to be good and evil, right and wrong. Ethics, that is, deals with 1) the ends that truly fulfill human personality, 2) the character of moral agents, and 3) the nature of moral obligation.

Generally speaking, statements of or about ethics are divided into three groups: descriptive, normative, and meta-ethical. Descriptive ethics simply describes actual moral behavior (i.e., behavior that may appropriately be described as good or evil, right or wrong) and actual moral reasoning. It does not attempt to prescribe or to judge such behavior.[1] Normative ethics, by contrast, purports to evaluate moral behavior or to establish moral principles, to determine the norm or norms of moral behavior. Meta-ethics takes the judgments of normative ethics as its subject. It seeks not to make moral judgments but to analyze their nature. Judgments of meta-ethics describe and analyze words—such as "good" or "bad"—and judgments—such as "murder is wrong" or "one ought always seek to maximize the greatest good for the greatest number."

Traditionally, philosophers concerned with ethics sought to give general moral guidance. Such philosophers were not usually concerned with the details of moral behavior so much as with its basic principles and their justification. Since World War II, however, and until very recently, moral philosophers have increasingly given up the task of normative ethics in favor of pursuing the more purely philosophical questions of meta-ethics. The field of normative ethics was largely left to religious thinkers (often called "ethicists"), who had always been active in it.

The field of religious ethics is rather more difficult to define and describe than that of philosophical ethics. Broadly speaking, it may be construed as the study of the ethical teachings of the various religious traditions. In this sense it is purely descriptive. In the United States, however, in most academic contexts, "religious ethics" really means "Christian ethics," and it is most definitely normative (or sometimes meta-ethical) as opposed to descriptive. To characterize Christian ethics thus construed, we may say that it is primarily concerned with translating the general moral/religious teachings of the Christian faith into general principles of moral conduct and into specific moral injunctions. It is further characterized by the fact that almost all systems of Christian ethics seem to presuppose some single over-arching norm (often agape, or love). There is frequently disagreement over what the norm is or how to interpret it, but there is usually agreement that some such norm exists.

The situation in Christian ethics is conditioned by the fact that Christianity and its basic texts are fundamentally concerned with questions of faith. Thus, while no one could deny that the Christian religion is concerned with moral behavior, its specific teachings with respect to such behavior must be derived from the basic teachings of faith and are often a matter of dispute.

Jewish ethical teaching, on the other hand, is conditioned by the fact that Judaism as a religion emphasizes human behavior over general claims of theology and faith. It is, in the eyes of those who derogate its consistent concern with actions more than faith, a religion of pots and pans. Since Jewish tradition contains minutely detailed teachings regulating behavior, the problem facing the Jewish ethicist is not that of deriving moral obligations from general theological teachings. It is, rather, to justify his or her own undertaking in the face of the all-embracing Jewish law (halakhah), which seems to leave no room for supra-legal ethics as such. To characterize Jewish ethics provisionally, we may say that it attempts to show what Judaism, either in the guise of halakhah, or in some other form, teaches about moral issues.

The very concept "Jewish ethics" raises a number of problems, some of them inherent in the notion of any parochial ethic (be it Christian, Navajo, Marxist, or whatever) and some of them unique to Jewish ethics. With respect to the former, a fundamental assumption of contemporary ethical discourse since the time of Kant is that ethical principles must apply consistently and generally. Normative ethical statements on this view must be universal, applying across the board in every relevantly similar situation. This being the case, if Jewish ethics deserves the designation ethics (consistent, general, universal) at all, in what sense can it be (narrowly) *Jewish*, and if it is Jewish, in what sense can it be *ethics*? Even if we assume that this

problem is soluble—by rejecting or modifying Enlightenment conceptions of morality, for example—another raises its head. Can Jewish ethics satisfy another condition of Kantian moral discourse, that ethical actions be done for their own sakes and not in order to avoid punishment, earn reward, or for any other "heteronomous" reason? After all, if Jewish ethics is *commanded* by God, then those who feel themselves bound by those commands fulfill them in order to earn reward, avoid punishment, or, on a more sophisticated level, in order to express their love of God. In any event, they are not behaving in what Kant called "autonomous" fashion. Jewish thinkers have only recently begun to take account of these questions.[2] These issues, as noted above, are not unique to Jewish ethics but to any parochial ethic.

There are also questions of a programmatic nature unique to Jewish ethics. Some of these issues will be raised below after an historical description of the field of Jewish ethics. The rest of this entry, then, is divided into two parts, 1) describing that body of literature ordinarily denoted by the term "Jewish ethics," and 2) delineating some of the problems raised by the very notion of Jewish ethics.

The history of Jewish ethics—The Bible: We may conveniently divide the literature of what has been called Jewish ethics into four main periods: Biblical, Talmudic, Medieval, and Modern. Strictly speaking, the Bible and Talmud do not fall under our view here: they are the sources of Jewish ethics but do not in any systematic sense devote themselves to that subject. While permeated with moral concern, they contain almost no texts specifically given over to ethics. Certain recent scholars[3] have maintained that the Hebrew Bible is self-consciously aware of a distinct area of human activity parallel to what we call ethics. But, while the Bible is surely suffused with ethical concern, it does not see the laws mandating ethical behavior as being in any significant sense distinct from its laws governing civil, criminal, and ritual matters: they all *are given from one Shepherd* (Eccl. 12:11). Biblical Hebrew does not even have a word for "ethics" in our sense of the term. The Bible, then, teaches ethics, but not self-consciously. As such, it is a *source* of Jewish ethics while not seeing itself, so to speak, as an ethical text.

This said, the question remains, what are the ethical teachings of the Bible? The question presupposes that the Bible is, at least in moral and theological terms, a single unit. While that assumption may be rejected by historians of the Bible, it reflects the traditional Jewish approach to the text and will be adopted here. Perhaps the best-known of the ethical teachings of the Bible is the so-called Ten Commandments ("so-called" because there are many more than ten specific commandments in this passage), found in Exodus 20. Of the ten discrete statements in this text at least six have direct ethical import: 1) honor thy father and thy mother, 2) thou shalt not murder, 3) thou shalt not commit adultery, 4) thou shalt not steal, 5) thou shalt not bear false witness against thy neighbor, and 6) thou shalt not covet thy neighbor's possessions. The remaining four ("I am the Lord thy God . . .," that God alone may be worshipped, that God's name must not be taken in vain, and the observance of the Sabbath) relate to matters of theological and ritual importance.

The distinction between commandments that have ethical significance and those of theological and ritual importance reflects a division that later rabbis read out of (or into) the Bible. They distinguished obligations between one human and another from obligations between humans and God. Much of biblical legislation involves the first group, and herein may lie one of the basic contributions of Judaism to the Western religious tradition, that one worships God through decent, humane, and moral relations with one's fellows. (As the later rabbis were to put it at M. Ab. 1:2, the continued existence of the world depends upon three things: study of Torah, sacrifice and prayer, and acts of lovingkindness.) In other words, whatever morality might be, its basis is in God's will. Plato in the Euthyphro to the contrary, God is as relevant to morality as to religion itself.

The theological basis for God's demand

that we treat each other properly is apparently the biblical teaching that humans are created in the image of God (Gen. 1:27). It is obvious from this that one achieves the highest possible level of perfection or self-realization by becoming as similar to God as humanly possible. This is the basis for what may be the single most important ethical doctrine of the Hebrew Bible, that of *imitatio Dei*, the imitation of God. That humans are created in the image of God makes it possible for the Torah to command that Jews walk in God's ways, i.e., practice the imitation of God. It should come as no surprise that when Judaism, which emphasizes the practical over the metaphysical, introduces a doctrine that seems so clearly to beg for a metaphysical interpretation, it immediately insists on interpreting it in practical terms. The imitation of God is thus not treated in the Talmud as a metaphysical issue but as a practical, moral one. Jews are not commanded literally and actually to transcend their normal selves and to become in some sense *like* God; rather, they are commanded to act in clearly delineated God-like ways. Through the achievement of practical, moral perfection Jews imitate God and thus fulfill their destiny as individuals created in the image of God.

Ethics in the Rabbinic literature: As noted above, the Hebrew Bible is not self-consciously aware of morality as a distinct religious or intellectual category. This is also true of the corpus of Rabbinic writings that centers on the Mishnah and its ancillary texts. Here, too, we find no distinct text dealing with ethics in an explicit fashion and no apparent recognition of ethics as a department of thought that must be treated independently of other concerns. This is even true of the well-known Mishnaic tractate Abot, often called in English "Ethics of the Fathers," a compilation of maxims and homilies, many of which embody what we call ethical teachings. As the point of this treatise appears to be to describe the ideal human personality envisioned by the Mishnah, it is much more concerned with piety than with ethics.

Even more than the Bible, the vast corpus of Rabbinic writings is basically concerned with one issue: how human beings ought to live their lives so as to fulfill the commandment to make themselves holy by walking in God's ways. The Rabbinic response to this was the delineation of a body of detailed law designed to govern every aspect of behavior. That body of law, called Halakhah (homiletically if not etymologically derived from the Hebrew word for "the way" and thus taken as the specification of how one walks in God's ways), includes, but by no means is limited to, moral concerns.

Fully aware that no specification of legal obligations can cover every moral dilemma, to demand supererogatory behavior from the Jews, the rabbis of the Mishnah and Talmud point to a number of broad biblical commands. These include *Righteousness, righteousness, shalt thou pursue* (Deut. 17: 20), *Thou shalt do what is right and good in the sight of the Lord* (Deut. 6:18), and one of their own devising, the *obligation* to go beyond the letter of the law in the fulfillment of God's will. Such a demand may be justified on the grounds that one never fully satisfies the obligation to imitate God.

The centrality of the doctrine that human beings are created in the image of God (the basis, as noted above, for the commandment to imitate God) is emphasized in the well-known debate between two Mishnaic rabbis, Aqiba and Ben Azzai. Their debate (Sifra 7:4) centers on the question, "What is the great[est] maxim of the Torah?" Aqiba said, *Thou shalt love thy neighbor as thyself* (Lev. 19:18), while Ben Azzai insisted on, *This is the book of the generations of man, in the image of God created he him* (Gen. 5:1).[4] The important point for our purposes is that there is here no actual debate. Both Aqiba and Ben Azzai agree that the doctrine of humanity's having been created in the image of God is the central teaching of the Torah. Ben Azzai cites the doctrine itself, Aqiba, its clearest moral implication. Given the Jewish tradition's preference for practice over preaching, it is no surprise that in the popular Jewish mind at least, Aqiba is thought to have won the argument. This emphasis on the respect for others based on their having been created in the image of God also finds expression in what may be the best-known Rabbinic moral

teaching, Hillel's so-called "Golden Rule." When a non-Jew asked Hillel to teach him the entire Torah while the non-Jew stood on one foot, Hillel replied, "What you dislike do not do to others; that is the whole Torah. The rest is commentary. Go and learn" (B. Shab. 31a).

But, despite the importance of moral teachings in the Bible and Talmud, these texts know of no self-consciously worked-out moral system; they are not even aware of ethics as a distinct religious, intellectual, or human category. As sources for subsequent developments in Jewish ethics, they are, however, crucial. In an important sense, all Jewish ethics that takes halakhah seriously is Talmudic, not only because the Talmud is *the* source of halakhah, but because any attempt to determine a halakhic position on virtually any issue must begin with an analysis of the relevant Talmudic data. Still, while the study of Jewish ethics cannot ignore the Talmud, for the reasons explained above, we cannot speak of a Talmudic ethics as such.

Medieval Jewish ethics: The situation changes radically in the medieval period with the rise of a distinct Jewish ethical literature that seeks systematically to expound upon morals and human conduct. The literature of the period seems to fall rather naturally into four different and widely recognized categories: philosophic, Rabbinic, pietistic, and Kabbalistic. Joseph Dan points out[5] that medieval Jewish ethics appeared in many literary forms beyond what might be called the classical ethical literature of books and treatises on specific ethical issues. Among the many forms that ethical literature took, we find homiletical works, ethical wills and letters, moralistic storybooks and collections of ethical fables, poetry, and commentaries on the biblical book of Proverbs and on Tractate Abot. There were also concrete and specific manuals of behavior, the so-called *hanhagot*.

Jewish philosophy in the medieval period was deeply concerned with the question of the proper relationship between faith and reason. The literature of the Jewish philosophical ethics of the period reflects this concern in its emphasis on the problem of the proper relationship between religious and ethical perfection. The earliest of the Jewish philosophers to write on ethics, Saadia Gaon (Baghdad, 892-942) and Solomon ben Judah ibn Gabirol (Spain, 1021-1058), appear to have simply taken over systems of secular philosophic ethics whole, without making any serious attempt to root them in Judaism. Gabirol is the author of *On the Improvement of the Moral Qualities* (trans. I.M. Wise, New York, 1966) and *Choice of Pearls* (trans. A. Cohen, Ann Arbor, 1982). The situation was considerably changed by the appearance of *Duties of the Heart* by Bahya ben Joseph ibn Paquda, a Spanish thinker of the eleventh century (trans., M. Mansoor, London, 1973). Bahya sought not only to instruct the Jew in religious and moral behavior, but to develop an ethical system rooted in Judaism. In his book, Bahya distinguishes between the (halakhic) obligations of the body, which directly involve behavior, and inner obligations, the "duties of the heart" of his book's title. There are many halakhic works, he says, devoted to an elucidation of the outward duties of the Jew, but none devoted to his inward obligations, and it is this gap that he seeks to fill. Bahya's emphasis on inward disposition (*kavanah*) was perhaps the first expression of a motif that was to characterize and even dominate much of Jewish ethical literature and was to blossom much later in the Musar movement. This is the idea that proper moral behavior could best be attained through the religious perfection of the individual. This may possibly reflect the fact that the availability of halakhic guidelines for most moral problems made their analysis by ethicists superfluous. Whatever the reason, however, it is certainly the case that Jewish ethical texts tend to emphasize character development and personal virtues over social ethics. The latter are seen as depending upon the former.

Moses Maimonides and Jewish ethics: The greatest medieval Jewish philosophic ethicist was the most outstanding of the medieval Jewish philosophers, Moses Maimonides (1138-1204). Maimonides' general position was that faith and reason do not conflict, and this attitude is reflected in his ethics. He adopts the basic outline of Aris-

totle's golden mean, rooting it, however, in Judaism and modifying it to meet the exigencies of the tradition as he understood it.[6]

Maimonides is the author, among other things, of three major works: *Commentary on the Mishnah, Mishneh Torah*, and the *Guide of the Perplexed*. The first two of these contain material directly relevant to Jewish philosophical ethics, while the *Guide* can be read as a work of which the ultimate end is ethical. The introduction to Maimonides' commentary to Tractate Abot is a self-contained ethical treatise, called *Eight Chapters*.[7] In this text in particular he develops his ideas on the golden mean. The commentary to Abot itself is obviously also important here. Maimonides' code of Jewish law, the *Mishneh Torah*, contains a number of texts in which ethics plays an important role. In particular, two parts of the first section of the work, the *Book of Knowledge*, are important: "Laws of Ethics" and "Laws of Repentance."[8] Maimonides' discussion of messianism at the end of the *Mishneh Torah* contains material that played an important role in Jewish ethics in the modern period.

Throughout his writings, Maimonides presents a highly intellectualist version of Judaism, according to which individuals fulfill themselves as human beings only through intellectual perfection. Moral perfection is a necessary prerequisite for perfection of the intellect, but not an end in itself. At the very end of the *Guide of the Perplexed*, however, Maimonides teaches that the truly perfected individual will go beyond intellectual perfection and imitate God through the doing of "lovingkindness, justice, and righteousness" in the land. This turnabout has been interpreted in various ways,[9] but here Maimonides seems to be attributing a higher role to practical perfection than in his other writings.

Mention should be made here also of the philosophical commentary to the Pentateuch of Levi ben Gerson (Gersonides, 1288-1344). At the end of each Torah portion, Gersonides listed those *to'aliyot* or "advantages" to be derived from the portion. Many of these are explicitly mentioned as having an ethical character.

The tradition of medieval Jewish philosophy reached its apogee with the work of Maimonides; its descent thereafter was quick and precipitous. Certainly none of the philosophers who followed Maimonides, Gersonides included, had anything significant to add to his philosophic analysis of Jewish ethics. Indeed, given the general opposition to Jewish philosophy that followed the apostasy of so many Jews in Spain and Portugal in the fourteenth and fifteenth centuries (which was blamed, in part, on their devotion to philosophical pursuits), it is hardly surprising that there arose a trend in Jewish ethics directly opposed to philosophical ethics. Writers identified with this category of Jewish ethical literature sought to demonstrate that Rabbinic Judaism and its texts provided all that one required in order to generate a full-fledged ethical system. There was no need, they felt, to turn to the Greeks for ethical instruction. This literature contains little innovation and seeks rather to apply Rabbinic ethics directly to the conditions of the medieval world. The two most influential texts in this genre are Jonah ben Abraham Gerondi's *Gates of Repentance* (thirteenth century; trans., S. Silverstein, Jerusalem, 1967), and Isaac Aboab's *Candelabrum of Illumination* (fourteenth century).

Medieval Pietism and Jewish ethics: The third generally recognized category of medieval Jewish ethical literature is that associated with the Hasidei Ashkenaz, a pietistic movement in twelfth and thirteenth century Germany. The major work in this category is the *Book of the Pious*, an extensive compilation attributed to Judah ben Samuel he-Hasid of Regensburg (d. 1217). German pietistic literature is concerned largely with specific problems and actual situations. It is marked by deep piety and superstition and by an emphasis on the effort involved in a deed; the more difficult an action, the more praiseworthy it is judged. The *Book of the Pious* introduces the distinction between the law of the Torah and the much stricter law of Heaven. The pietist is marked by his adherence to the law of Heaven, which demands greater devotion and involves more difficulty than the law of the Torah, which applies to all. This attitude was greatly to in-

fluence the development of European Jewry, and its effects are still felt strongly today.

Two other works in the tradition of German pietism deserve mention. These are the anonymous *Ways of the Righteous* (trans., S.J. Cohen, New York, 1974) and Asher ben Jehiel's *Ways of Life* (trans., K.S. Orbach, Jerusalem, 1968). The *Ways of the Righteous* was probably composed in Germany in the fifteenth century. Extremely influential, it has been published over eighty times. Although its author was clearly influenced by Jewish philosophic ethics, there is no doubt that the book was written by one of the German pietists, as it is pervaded with the attitudes and values of that movement. Asher ben Jehiel (Asheri or Rosh), c. 1250-1327, was one of the leading halakhists of his generation. A refugee from Germany (where his father, his first teacher, was active in the pietist movement and was himself a student of Judah ben Samuel), Asher settled in Spain. His *Ways of Life*, often called *Ethical Manual of the Rosh* or *Testament of the Rosh*, consists of ethical sayings arranged for daily recitation.

Kabbalistic ethics: One of the major developments in the history of medieval Judaism was the rise of Kabbalah, Jewish mysticism. This had a clear impact on Jewish ethics, stimulating the development of a fairly well-defined class of kabbalistic-ethical texts. This literature is permeated with the kabbalistic idea that the actions of human beings have a profound impact on the very structure of the universe. There is a definite interdependence between the deeds of human beings and the mystical development of the world.

Of the many works in this category two of the most important are *Palm Tree of Deborah* (trans., L. Jacobs, London, 1960) by Moses ben Jacob Cordovero (1522-1570), and *Beginning of Wisdom* by Elijah ben Moses de Vidas (sixteenth century), a student of Cordovero's. Cordovero's work is a detailed guide to ethical behavior, relating moral perfection to mystical union with aspects of the deity. He seeks to unfold the mystical and ethical significance of God's thirteen attributes of mercy (enumerated in Exod. 34:6-7 and Mic. 7:18-20) and to explain how it is possible to imitate them, as the halakhah demands. De Vidas makes explicit use of kabbalistic texts and develops the idea that the cosmic struggle between good and evil is affected by the moral behavior of individual human beings.

What may be the most important work in the field of kabbalistic ethics, *The Path of the Upright* (trans., M. Kaplan, Philadelphia, 1964), is rarely considered to be in that category at all. This may simply reflect the fact that by the close of the Jewish middle ages (mid-eighteenth century), Kabbalah had so permeated all aspects of Jewish life that no one took special notice of a kabbalistic-ethical work. In addition to this, and more importantly, this work of Moses Hayyim Luzzatto made relatively little use of explicit kabbalistic texts, while still being overwhelmingly kabbalistic in tone. Luzzatto (1707-1746), an Italian mystic, playwright, and ethicist, leads the reader of his book along the path of the upright, which begins with the forsaking of sin and culminates in mystical contact with God. *The Path of the Upright* develops the Mishnaic concept of the world as a corridor leading to the world to come; human life must be devoted to preparation for the ultimate end. Luzzatto's book became enormously influential and popular; to this very day it is considered by many traditionalist Jews to be the Jewish ethical text *par excellence.*[10]

The Musar movement: Before turning to a discussion of contemporary developments in Jewish ethics, we must consider one important and still-influential outgrowth of medieval Jewish ethics, the Musar movement. At the end of the Jewish middle ages, Jewish life in Eastern Europe (specifically Poland and Russia) was characterized by a marked religious, cultural, and social decline. Eastern European Jewry suffered what can only be called a "failure of nerve" as a consequence of the Chmielnicki massacres of 1648, the collapse of effective government in Poland, which followed shortly thereafter in the face of the Ukrainian and Swedish wars, and the remarkable and pervasive despair and degradation of spirit engendered by the apos-

tasy of the false messiah, Shabbetai Zevi (1666). In the face of these calamities, Jewish education suffered terribly; Talmud study became cold, rigid, and formalistic; the democracy and sense of mutual responsibility that had formerly characterized the Jewish communal organizations degenerated, and there arose a huge mass of ignorant and only nominally observant Jews.

The best known reaction to this circumstance is the Hasidic movement, which sought to regenerate Jewish life and spirit. The Hasidic teachers, evangelical and charismatic religious leaders, tried to inject mysticism into everyday life and emphasized, as did the earlier pietists of medieval Germany, the importance of inwardness and intention as opposed to the formalistic obedience to law. The Musar (ethical reproof) movement may be seen as a non-Hasidic response to the same degradation of spirit that engendered Hasidism. Its followers sought to bridge the gap between Rabbinic training on the one hand and religious-ethical fervor on the other. The Musar movement was founded for the training of Jews in strict ethical/religious behavior. It emphasized character development (echoing one of the earliest and most consistent themes in medieval Jewish ethics) and concerned itself strongly with the psychological health of the individual. Followers of the Musar movement often organized themselves into small groups that met regularly to read ethical texts and to engage in mutual criticism and spiritual strengthening. By the early years of the present century, the *musar* ideal had been adopted by most of the great European rabbinical academies (yeshivot), almost all of which set aside a portion of each day for the study of ethical texts and many of which had individuals on their staffs specifically devoted to the ethical guidance of the students.

Modern Jewish ethics: The distinction between contemporary and medieval Jewish ethics reflects the great difference between pre-modern and contemporary Judaism. Up until the end of the eighteenth century, no country in Europe (and, outside of the United States, no country in the world at all) recognized its Jews as full-fledged citizens possessed of normal civil rights. The spread of Enlightenment ideals, however, led to the gradual emancipation of European Jewry. But the call of emancipation was often couched in terms such as, "To the Jew as Frenchman, everything; to the Jew as Jew, nothing!" Emancipation thus was predicated in almost every case upon assimilation. The Jews of Western Europe were faced with a situation unique in their experience and were confronted with a wholly new problem: how to remain Jewish while simultaneously participating in Western civilization. It was largely by way of response to this problem that the various religious movements of contemporary Judaism—Orthodoxy, Conservatism, Reform—developed and defined themselves.

Contemporary Judaism is distinguished from medieval Judaism, therefore, in that it is faced with an entirely new problematic and in that it presents a multiplicity of answers to that complex of problems. With respect to the subject at hand, we may say that contemporary Jewish ethics is distinguished from medieval Jewish ethics in that the problems it faces are largely those it shares with the surrounding culture (e.g., the problem of relating morality and religion and specific questions such as political obedience and medical ethics). In short, Jews and Judaism have become part of the modern world, and, to a significant degree, the modern world has become a factor that cannot be ignored by both Jews and Judaism. Contemporary Jewish ethics is further distinguished from its medieval counterpart in that it speaks with a divided voice. One must not ask today, "What is the Jewish position on such and such?" but, rather, "What is the Orthodox, Conservative, or Reform interpretation of the Jewish position on such and such?" Although many writers persist in presenting what they depict as *the* contemporary Jewish position on various subjects, it most often ought more correctly to be characterized as *a* Jewish position.

In order to understand fully the differences between Orthodox, Conservative, and Reform Judaism one ought to examine them in terms of their historical developments. For our purposes, however, it is sufficient to sketch out their basic theological differences. This can be done conveniently by examining their varying conceptions of revelation. Briefly put, Orthodoxy follows the traditional Rabbinic claim that the Torah represents the direct, conclusive revelation of God's will. Halakhah, which derives directly from that revelation, is the will of God. It is normative for all Jews in all places and at all times. Although Orthodoxy recognizes the fact of halakhic change, it insists that such change has come about and may come about only within the context of well-recognized halakhic mechanisms. The basic Orthodox contention with respect to the halakhah is that it is a divine, not a human system, and that as such it is not subject, in essence, to the sort of historical development that characterizes human institutions.

Reform Judaism, on the other hand, in both its classic and modern positions, entirely rejects the claim that the halakhah represents the revealed will of God. Revelation, it maintains, is progressive, akin to inspiration, and is ultimately concerned with ethics. This emphasis is summed up in the famous motto of early Reform, that Judaism is nothing more than ethical monotheism. While contemporary Reform thinkers have largely given up the classic Reform claim that Judaism took a quantum leap from the time of the prophets (in whose call for social morality early Reform thinkers saw God's revelation most clearly embodied) to the nineteenth century and the rise of Reform, it is still the case that Reform Judaism rejects the halakhah as a norm and still looks to the prophetic tradition for the "essence" of Judaism. Reform is further distinguished from most expressions of Orthodoxy by its insistence on seeing human autonomy as a central Jewish value.

The Conservative position is roughly midway between that of Orthodoxy and Reform. Conservative Judaism does not view revelation as God "talking" to the Jewish people, as it were, revealing to them exactly what it is they ought to do. Rather, Conservative Judaism maintains that the Jewish people have had what may be called "revelatory" experiences of God, to which they reacted by creating the Torah. Halakhah, then, is the way Jews have sought to preserve their experiences of God. Although taking its source in the Jews' experience of God, it is basically a human institution and undergoes change and historical development like all human institutions. It is normative in the conditional sense that one ought to obey the halakhah if one wants to preserve the insights and experiences of the Jewish people as a whole and of those Jews in particular who have confronted God directly in their own lives. Conservative Judaism thus sees the halakhah as the Jewish vocabulary for approaching God. But it does not see the halakhah as normative in the absolute sense that implies that obedience to it is explicitly demanded by God of every Jew.

These three different interpretations of revelation and halakhah give rise to different emphases within Jewish ethics. Generally speaking, Orthodox thinkers approach questions of ethics by seeking to determine the teachings of the halakhah on the issues at hand. That is not to say that they cannot recognize a super-halakhic realm of Jewish ethical teaching. But no Orthodox thinker will admit the possibility of there being a Jewish ethical teaching that might contradict halakhah. That possibility, by contrast, is explicitly stated by at least one important Conservative thinker, Seymour Siegel. "It is my thesis," he writes, "that according to our interpretation of Judaism, the ethical values of our tradition should have power to judge the particulars of Jewish law. If any law in our tradition does not fulfill our ethical values, then the law should be abolished or revised."[11] This position would most likely be rejected by Orthodox thinkers on the grounds that it sets human beings up as judges of God's law.

Generally speaking, at least until very recently, the Reform approach to ethics has been to identify Jewish ethics with prophetic teachings that, in turn, are interpreted in terms of contemporary liberalism. Of late, however, Reform thinkers have shown a new sensitivity to the teachings of the post-

Biblical Jewish tradition and generally seek to ground their ethical judgments in the Jewish tradition as a whole.

Summing up, we may say that the contemporary Jewish approach to ethical problems is distinguished from the medieval approach in at least two important ways. It is no longer informed by the basic unanimity of spirit that underlay medieval Jewish ethics in all its various styles and forms. Further, and as a result of the Jew's unprecedented level of integration into the surrounding world, Jewish ethics today faces an entirely new complex of problems. Although there are elements of continuity between medieval and modern Jewish ethics, the discontinuities are more important. This is one of the many ways in which the wrenching changes that accompanied the Jewish entry into the modern world are reflected.

Problematics of the term "Jewish ethics:" It is immediately evident, then, that no one definition of Jewish ethics is possible, since there are so many varieties of Judaism. But, even assuming that we know what the term "Jewish" means in the expression "Jewish ethics," fundamental problems still need clarification. While much of halakhah is given over to what we would today call religious or ritual law, it encompasses civil, criminal, and moral law as well. The moral component, however, is not distinguished in any way from the other components of halakhah and, at least from within the system, is seen as drawing its authority, as does the rest of the Torah, from God's command. Since halakhah contains an ethical component, we must ask whether "the Jewish tradition recognizes an ethic independent of Halakhah."[12] Can there be, that is, significantly *Jewish* ethical norms not included in halakhah?

This is a thorny problem. If Judaism recognizes the existence of two authentically Jewish yet independent realms, one of halakhah and one of ethics, how do they interrelate? Can halakhah be corrected on the basis of Jewish ethical considerations? This possibility is abhorrent to those Jews who maintain that halakhah is the unchanging expression of God's will on earth. Can ethics be corrected on the basis of halakhic considerations? This possibility would probably be unacceptable to those Jews who see halakhah as an expression of an early stage of God's dynamic and ongoing revelation. This issue may be rephrased as follows: if halakhah and Jewish ethics are both authentically Jewish, is one superior to the other? If not, what do we do when they conflict? If they never conflict, in what sense are they different?

And there are yet further problems: if a supra-halakhic Jewish ethic exists, what is its relationship to non-Jewish civil law (both in Israel and in the diaspora)? What is the obligation of the Jew with respect to imposing that ethic upon or offering it to non-Jews? Jews have always argued that halakhah applies to Jews only and have not generally sought the secular enforcement of halakhic norms. In other words, halakhah is parochial. Is supra-halakhic Jewish ethics parochial also? If it is, does that commit one to a form of relativism, to recognizing many different parochial moralities? Such a position seems inconsistent with a view of ethics rooted in revelation. But, on the contrary, if this Jewish ethic is universal, then we must indeed raise the question of "law and morality" and ask, to what extent must this "universal Jewish ethic" be imposed upon non-Jews? These questions are more than idle chatter in a period in which Jewish religious leaders (of all trends) regularly involve themselves, *as representatives of Judaism*, in ongoing public debates on issues like abortion and capital punishment.

More questions arise: if morality must be universally recognizable then not only must Jewish ethics apply to all human beings, but it must be available to them as well. If a supra-halakhic Jewish ethic exists, is it really universally available, and, if it is, what is specifically *Jewish* about it?

Until very recently discussions of Jewish ethics showed little in the way of the historical and philosophical self-consciousness that lie at the heart of the questions raised here. For many writers, wide-ranging erudition in halakhic sources and sophistication in the manipulation of Rabbinic texts were considered the appropriate and sufficient tools for a discussion of Jewish ethics. Rarely did they stop to ask themselves any methodological, historical, or philosophical questions.

This situation has changed dramatically in the last few years. Philosophical questions are being asked of the halakhic method of applying ancient texts and analyses to contemporary issues, and the philosophical presuppositions of classic texts are being laid bare. Louis Newman, for example, has been raising the question of what makes Jewish ethics Jewish and has raised important methodological questions about the possibility of applying considerations drawn from ancient discussions to problems raised by new medical technology in the fairly simple minded way in which it is often done in recent discussions of medical issues in halakhah and ethics.[13] In a series of studies, Avi Sagi and Daniel Statman have demonstrated that Jewish thinkers through the ages have (surprisingly) rejected the idea that divine command gives ethical imperatives their special force and have analyzed this historic datum for its contemporary implications.[14] Steven Schwarzschild, Marvin Fox, and David Novak have argued the place of natural law in Jewish ethics.[15]

At the end of the twentieth century, then, Jewish ethics seems poised to enter into a new phase. Thinkers steeped in ancient texts and traditions but also manipulating sophisticated new literary and philosophical tools are asking new questions and finding new answers.

Bibliography

Dorff, Elliot and Louis Newman, eds., *Contemporary Jewish Ethics and Morality: A Reader* (New York, 1995).
Kellner, Menachem, ed., *Contemporary Jewish Ethics* (New York, 1978).
Weiss, Raymond. *Maimonides' Ethics* (Chicago, 1991).

Notes

[1] I use the terms "ethics" and "morals" interchangeably here, even though there are some differences between them. The term "ethics" seems to have more of a practical, actional connotation than does "morals." Thus we say "medical ethics," for example, not "medical morals."
[2] See Menachem Kellner, "Reflections on the Impossibility of Jewish Ethics," in M. Hallamish,

ed., *Moshe Schwarcz Memorial Volume* (Ramat Gan, 1987), pp. 45-52; and D. Statman and A. Sagi, *Religion and Morality* (Amsterdam, 1995).

[3] See Israel Efros, *Ancient Jewish Philosophy* (Detroit, 1964), and Shubert Spero, *Morality, Halakhah, and the Jewish Tradition* (New York, 1983).

[4] On this text, see Chaim Reines, "The Self and Other in Rabbinic Ethics," in Menachem Kellner, ed., *Contemporary Jewish Ethics* (New York, 1978).

[5] "Ethical Literature," in *Encyclopedia Judaica* (Jerusalem, 1972), vol. 6, cols. 922-932.

[6] On how to understand Maimonides, see Marvin Fox, *Interpreting Maimonides* (Chicago, 1990), pp. 3-92; on Maimonides' ethics, pp. 93-228.

[7] See Eliezer Schweid, *Studies in Maimonides' "Eight Chapters"* (Cambridge, 1991).

[8] For these and others of Maimonides' ethical works, see R.L. Weiss and C. Butterworth, eds., *Ethical Writings of Maimonides* (New York, 1975).

[9] See Menachem Kellner, *Maimonides on Human Perfection* (Atlanta, 1991).

[10] On ethics in Kabbalah in general, see Joseph Dan, *Jewish Mysticism and Jewish Ethics* (Seattle, 1986).

[11] See Seymour Siegel, "Ethics and the Halakhah," in *Conservative Judaism* 25 (1971), pp. 33-40.

[12] This is the title of an article by Aharon Lichtenstein in Kellner, *Contemporary Jewish Ethics*.

[13] See his "Woodchoppers and Respirators: Interpretation in Jewish Ethics," in Elliot Dorff and Louis Newman, eds., *Contemporary Jewish Ethics and Morality: A Reader* (New York, 1995).

[14] For an English language study, see their "Divine Command Morality and Jewish Tradition," in *Journal of Religious Ethics* 23 [1995], pp. 39-67.

[15] See the latter's "Natural Law, *Halakhah*, and the Covenant," in *Contemporary Jewish Ethics and Morality: A Reader*.

MENACHEM KELLNER

EVIL AND SUFFERING, JUDAIC DOCTRINES OF: From the earliest canonical traditions of Israelite religion to contemporary Orthodox Judaism, suffering has been seen as punishment for the wickedness and sins of humanity. The persistence of this connection is evidence of its ability to explain the suffering of the people Israel and to provide comfort to sufferers. But, however powerful the explanation that associates suffering with sin, important questions always remain: Why is there evil in the first place? Why do humans pursue sin with such resourcefulness? Why do the innocent also suffer? These questions and others have repeatedly challenged the religious imagination of Israel to refine or find alternatives to the classical scheme.

The opening chapters of Genesis narrate a series of "falls" that, in combination, explain not only the human condition in general but human sin[1] and suffering in particular. Thus, in the well-known story of the temptation of Eve (Gen. 3), the first humans transgress God's prohibition of eating the fruit of the "tree of knowledge of good and evil" (Gen. 2:17). As a consequence, they are cursed with the pain of childbirth (Gen. 3:16), the sweat and toil of producing food, and death (Gen. 3:19). In the space of this brief chapter, the connection between transgression and punishment, manifested in human suffering, is firmly established. Crucially, so too is the root of human sin in temptation.

The punishment of an evil humanity by the waters of the flood (Gen. 6-7) shows that the cause-and-effect established in the Garden of Eden will oft be repeated. But, in this latter case, the source of human evil is more difficult to discern. According to Gen. 6:5, "the evil of humanity is great . . . for all the inclinations of the thoughts of his heart are evil all the day." Seemingly, there is a quality in the hearts of humans that inclines them to do evil. Why is this so? Though the text provides no clear answer to this question, the juxtaposition of Gen. 6:5's observation with the mythic narrative that precedes it suggests that, in the view of the biblical author, the cause of human evil may be divine beings.

According to the myth only hinted at in Gen. 6:2-4, at some time prior to the flood, "sons of gods" took human women for mates and produced from these couplings "the mighty men of old." There were on earth at the same time "*nephilim*" ("fallen ones"), who may be either the "sons of gods" themselves or their offspring. Whatever the precise meaning of this story, it is notable that the observation concerning human evil follows it immediately. It is difficult, therefore, to escape the conclusion that a transgression of the divine-human boundary by divine creatures was viewed as somehow at the root of human evil.

Abundant evidence throughout the Torah depicts evil and sin as the causes of suffering. This is especially so in God's promise of blessings and curses found in the penultimate chapter of Leviticus, and, even more, it is fundamental in the covenantal scheme that defines the central ideology of Deuteronomy. Thus, for example, we find at Deut. 28:15 + 25-26:

> If you (that is, Israel) fail to heed the voice of the Lord your God . . . then all of these curses will come upon you. . . . The Lord will allow you to be smitten before your enemies . . . and your corpse shall be food for the birds of the sky and the beast of the earth. . . .

The same explanation for military defeat is repeatedly offered in the Bible's royal history. This is most dramatically illustrated in the justification for the exiles of the kingdoms of Israel (2 Kings 17) and Judah (2 Kings 21).

Alternative biblical approaches: But the gravity of these latter catastrophes and the suffering that accompanied them challenged the plausibility of the inherited explanation. Even granting that suffering (such as exile) is punishment for sin, why does Israel not learn the lesson of repeated suffering and, if she does not, will suffering ever end? In response to this dilemma, both Jeremiah (31:30-3) and Ezekiel (36:26-7) propose that the heart of Israel—a heart of stone, in Ezekiel's imagery—must be replaced with a new heart, one inscribed with the Torah of the Lord. Sinful Israel thus was viewed as cursed with a sinful heart; sin was part of the people Israel's essence. This meant that the elimination of sin, and hence of suffering, demanded a fundamental reworking of human (or, at least, Israel's) nature.

In the course of Israel's travails, other understandings of the root of suffering also found their way into the canon. One of the most important of these (by virtue of its place in Christian interpretation) is Second Isaiah's image of a "suffering servant," a servant of the Lord who suffers on account of—and to atone for—the sins of others (Is. 52:13-53:12). In this explanation, suffering continues to be a consequence of sin, but not of the sin of those who themselves suffer.

The book of Job similarly offers an extended critique of traditional explanations of suffering, a critique made explicit in the statement that Job's accusers "do not speak rightly" (42:7). But, as the book of Job has come down to us, the "right" explanation of Job's suffering is the subject of competing redactional understandings. If the narrative introduction is to be granted priority, Job's suffering is a product of Satan's provocations of God (Job 1-2), and Job suffers even though he did not in any way sin. But if the voice of God speaking in response to Job is to be believed (Job 38), there is a reason for Job's suffering; it is simply that this reason is beyond human understanding. Job thus proposes that, in human terms, suffering and the God who brings it cannot be said to be just. But this is evidence of human, not divine, limitations.

Post-biblical Jewish literature: The ancient explanations of evil and suffering continued to play an important role in Jewish literature produced during the late second-Temple period (second century B.C.E.-first century C.E.). For example, the author of I Maccabees hints, through narrative juxtaposition, that the suffering of Israel at the hand of Antiochus is a consequence of their abandonment of traditional ways (1 Macc. 1:11-24, 52-4). In 2 Macc. 7:18, one of "the seven brothers" explains their torture at the hands of the Syrian Greeks as punishment for their sins against God.

But alternative explanations of sin and suffering flowered during this same period. The most striking of these, expressed in both 1 Enoch and Jubilees, grew out of the Torah myth spoken of above. In this latter-day version, the "nephilim" are fallen angels who rebel against God by leaving heaven, taking human women as mates, and spreading a variety of evil teachings and curses. From these encounters, humans learn temptation and the art of war, among other evils. In addition, according to Jubilees, following the flood, "demons" remained to lead the children of Noah (that is, humanity) astray. And, though Noah beseeched God to imprison the malevolent creatures forever, Mastema (that is, Satan) prevailed upon God to allow him to remain free and wreak havoc forever. Finally, the apparently suppressed myth has reasserted its power.

The most extreme Jewish expression of the mythical power of evil is offered in a sectarian scroll found near Qumran, known as the Code of Discipline. According to this scroll, God created two spirits—"the spirits of truth and of perversity." Those who follow the spirit of truth are "under the domination of the Prince of Lights," while those "who practice perversity are under the domination of the Angel of Darkness." This world is the battlefield on which the war between these two forces is fought, and all sin is a result of the (temporary) victories of the Angel of Darkness. This is the fate of the humankind "until the final age."

In literal terms, all of these various authors agree that sin leads to suffering. But ultimately, they claim, people are not at fault. They sin because of evil forces more powerful than them. Still, none of these authors, even the most extreme among them, denies Is. 45:7's claim that God "creates evil." Whether evil begins with rebellious angels, Satan, spirits of darkness, or a person's wicked heart, God created them all.

Following destruction: The deterioration of conditions under Herodian and Roman rule, leading to the destruction of the second Jerusalem Temple, combined to force Jews to seek alternative explanations of the suffering that surrounded them. When he explained the destruction as a product of fate, Josephus (*Jewish War* 6.250, 267-8) was probably reflecting a popular opinion among Hellenized Jews. But even more popular, if the literary record is to be believed, were various imaginations of the apocalypse, assumed by many to be at hand. Nascent Christianity, claiming that the messiah had actually arrived, testifies to this inclination. So too, in different ways, do the Apocalypses of Ezra and Baruch.

According to both of these books, the number of generations of humans was fixed at creation. When the last of these generations was born to life, history would come to an end and the final age would dawn. This dawning would be marked by unprecedented sufferings and catastrophes; much as a woman's labor is most painful immediately before birth, so too would the birth of the World-to-Come follow the most painful period in human history. There would be a final judgment. The wicked would suffer eternally, while the righteous would forever enjoy the rewards of the final era.

The classical Rabbinic canon: Writing a generation after the failure of the Bar Kokhba revolt (133-135 C.E.), the early Rabbinic authors could no longer imagine that the messiah would soon arrive. Instead, they turned their attentions to systematizing the law of God and Israel (in a document called the Mishnah), and they explained suffering—in thoroughly traditional terms—as punishment for sin. So, according to Simeon b. Eleazar, the pain humans experience while making a living is a consequence of our evil deeds (M. Qid. 4:14). In another illustrative teaching, women are said to die in childbirth for failure to observe three commandments specifically directed to them (M. Shab. 2:6). The Mishnah's general rule is this: "According to the measure with which a person measures, with it do we measure him" (M. Sot. 1:7). If a person sins, he or she will suffer punishment in kind.

Though rarely straying from this opinion, here and there, the early rabbis gave expression to important expansions or alternatives. According to one tradition, oft-quoted in subsequent Rabbinic compositions, suffering has superior power to atone for sin (second only to death; see T. Y.K. 4:8). Conceptually related, though rhetorically more powerful, is the claim that "sufferings cause God to pardon more even than sacrifices. . . . Because sacrifices are with one's property whereas sufferings are with one's body" (Sifre Deut. 32). Subsequent to the destruction of the Temple, it was surely difficult for Jews to imagine what would take the place of the sacrifices ordained in the Torah. If suffering could perform the task, one could hardly cavil. It is not surprising, therefore, that the midrash from which this teaching is quoted repeatedly comments, "precious are sufferings."

At the same time the rabbis were extolling suffering—and condemning any who would question the place of suffering in God's system of justice—they maintained a guarded silence concerning the origins of evil. On only a few occasions in their earliest teachings did they speak of the human inclination to do evil (*yetzer hara*), borrowing from the language of Gen. 6:5 to describe the cause of moral failure. From the traditions at hand, it is clear that they understood this inclination to lead to anger and transgression, seducing a person away from Torah and thus leading to his demise. But, at this early stage, the inclination for evil is not viewed as an independent force. Nor does Satan find more than an occasional place in the early Rabbinic tradition, where he serves more as a literary trope than a force to be reckoned with.

The condition just described will change in later Rabbinic literature, where the *yetzer hara* becomes a common reference, a force oft to be reckoned with. In the Babylonian Talmud, the evil inclination is described as speaking to a person, seeking to entice him to worship foreign gods. Not only does it incite a person to do evil in this world, but it also testifies against him in the World-to-Come. Stating matters with directness and clarity, Simeon b. Laqish declares, "Satan, the *yetzer hara*, and the Angel of Death are one and the same" (B. B.B. 16a).

Human suffering and the inclination to do evil are bound together in a massive apologia for God's justice, found in Gen. Rabbah 9. The midrash asks, at least by intimation, this question: Given the reality of human experience, how can we make sense of God's assessment that the created world is "very good" (Gen. 1:31)? In the course of defending this divine evaluation, the midrash argues for the goodness of death, suffering, hell (*gehinnom*), the evil inclination, and the oppressive earthly empire (Rome). Typical of the midrashic strategy is the justification of the evil impulse: if not for the *yetzer hara*, a man would not take a wife, build a house, have children, and engage in business. In other words, the *yetzer*, equated with ambition and sexual lust, has favorable con-

sequences. The force for evil, properly sublimated, yields good.

The only significant heterodox views concerning suffering in the classical Rabbinic canon are preserved in the Babylonian Talmud. At B. Shab. 55a-b, the Talmud concludes that suffering and death can come about without prior sin. The ancient link of sin and consequent suffering (as a result of punishment) is here definitively broken. In a related narrative (B. Hag. 4b-5a), the Talmud illustrates the reality of death by accident, death bearing no relationship to divine justice. And in the Talmud's most extended deliberation on human suffering (B. Ber. 5a-b), we find a repeated rejection of the classical apologia for suffering. Asked whether they find their sufferings "precious" (echoing the midrash quoted above), prominent sages reply: "neither them nor their reward."

The Middle Ages: Exponents of the medieval Jewish philosophical tradition represent a range of opinions regarding suffering and evil. Saadia, writing in the early tenth century, follows a traditional path. Beginning with the uncompromising insistence that humans have free will, he offers that suffering may be either punishment for the few sins a good person commits in this world (assuring his place in the future world) or a test from God, later to be compensated. Judah Halevi likewise writes (early twelfth c.) that a person's troubles serve to cleanse sins, and therefore he recommends a pious attitude of acceptance and joy.

In the *Mishneh Torah* (Laws of Repentance, ch. 5), Maimonides (twelfth c.) polemically insists that God has granted humans complete free will; he will allow no room for the opinion, evidently still popular, that God decrees the course a person will follow from his or her youth. Thus, evil caused by humans must be understood as the result of their freely chosen path. Those who fail properly to repent will, as the tradition suggests, die as a consequence of their sins. Obviously speaking from a philosophical perspective, Maimonides nevertheless employs the voice of Torah.

But in his *Guide for the Perplexed* (pt. 3, chapters 10-12), Maimonides forges a distinctive philosophical position. He begins with the assumption that God's created world is thoroughly good. Contrary to the claim of Isaiah, then, God cannot have created evil in any of its forms. If not, then how can the obvious evils of creation be explained? He answers that evil is privation, and privation, being not a thing but the absence of some thing or quality, is not created. By his enumeration, there are three species of evil: 1) evils that befall people because they possess a body that degenerates; 2) evils that people, because of their ignorance (that is, the absence of wisdom), cause one another; and 3) evils that people, because of their ignorance, cause themselves. God creates none of these evils or their associated sufferings. According to Maimonides' system, all are caused by natural forces, by essential human failings, or by human ignorance.

The opinions of medieval Jewish mysticism (Kabbalah) regarding evil and consequent suffering are varied and sometimes at odds. Early Kabbalistic texts record the belief that evil is a product of the unchecked growth of divine judgment. Judgment, untempered by mercy, is wicked. The domain of judgment gone awry is called the *sitra ara*, "the other side."

The great classic of the Kabbalah, the *Zohar*, gives credit to the view that evil originates in leftovers (*kelippot*) of earlier worlds that God destroyed. Alternatively, it suggests that evil was contained, *in potentia*, in the Tree of Knowledge (of Good and *Evil*), but was suppressed by the Tree of Life, to which the Tree of Knowledge was bound. When Adam "cut the shoots," separating one tree from the other, he activated the evil the tree had contained.

Perhaps the most enduring contribution of Kabbalah to the Jewish understandings of evil is that of Isaac Luria (sixteenth c.). According to the interpretation of Gershom Scholem, Luria's views, contained in his highly original cosmology, are a response to the great tragedy of the prior generation, the expulsion of the Jewish community from the Iberian peninsula. Struggling to understand why they had suffered so, Jews found unpar-alleled comfort in the interpretation that Luria promulgated.

According to Luria, in order to create the world, God—the *ein-sof* ("the limitless one")—had to contract into himself, leaving space for creation. In this space remained sparks of the divine light, preserved in special vessels. This light contained concentrated "shells" of stern divine judgment that, when the vessels were shattered (due to a flaw in the plan of creation), were scattered throughout creation. This, in the system of Lurianic Kabbalah, is the root of all evil. The system's popularity lay not only in its explanation of the suffering of Israel but also in its recipe for redemption: Redemption required that the vessels be repaired, and the tools of reparation were the *mitzvot* of the Torah performed even by common Jews.

The most extreme persecutions of these centuries provoked profoundly ambivalent responses, or so the evidence of contemporary liturgical compositions suggests. On the one hand, Jewish poets returned again and again to the notion that suffering is punishment for sin. In one of the most exemplary (and best known) of these poems, the "*Eileh ezkera*" (composed shortly after the first crusade in the late eleventh c.), the author justifies the Roman torture and execution of ten talmudic rabbis as punishment for the sin of Joseph's brothers who had "kidnapped" him and sold him into slavery. Of course, for the author and his readers, this is not history but theodicy; it explains their own suffering as well as that of their Rabbinic ancestors. It is appropriate, therefore, that in liturgical performance the reciter ends each stanza by declaring, "We have sinned . . . forgive us."

On the other hand, this and many similar compositions from the same broad period exhibit a considerable degree of horror and even anger, some complaining against the God who is "mute" or who "hides his face." This is a God who bids his children slaughter their own children on the altar, even as Abraham prepared to do to Isaac so long before. Still, the act of sacrifice—whether of Isaac or of their own sons and daughters—is justified as "sanctification of God's name."

It is an act both meritorious and cleansing.

Crucially, neither the availability of alternatives nor the experience of persecution caused Jews to abandon the ancient formula. Even Gluckel of Hameln, a woman of relative comfort and culture, returns to this piety on several occasions in her memoirs. Writing near the end of the seventeenth century, she clearly believes that sin is punished with suffering, which in turn atones the sin. God's judgment is just, she says, and to be accepted in modesty.

The turn of modernity: Jews entered modern culture in fits and starts. But enter they did, and with entrance came modern opinions, dominated by science and humanism. Thus, suffering now would more readily be seen as a consequence of natural law, the product of divine design, perhaps, but surely not of divine intervention. Without punishment, sin was a matter of pure theory, of little import to most but the clergy. The same could be said of the question of evil.

However, the anti-semitic upheavals of modernity—the Russian pogroms followed, less than a half a century later, by the Nazi Holocaust—made it impossible not to ask the question anew. Yiddish and Hebrew writers served as witnesses to the earlier of these crimes, employing the languages of traditional Judaism to critique and even betray that very tradition. H.N. Bialik, the great Hebrew poet, provides powerful examples. He mocks the cowering Jews who "crammed by scores in all the sanctuaries of their shame,/So sanctified my Name!" These pious cowards, crying out, "We have sinned!," do not even believe what they say—so Bialik writes. No God of might is listening; death "for the sanctification of the name" is therefore an obscenity.

If evil is a human quality and suffering the product of natural forces, human and natural, then only the active struggle for human dignity and freedom would suffice as a response. This view, already well-established in the rhetoric of early Zionism, would gain greater power following the Holocaust. For many Jews, the Holocaust meant that all hope in God, if imaginable at all in moder-

nity, was now lost. Secular power was the only power a Jew could have. For some, the turn to the exercise of human power would find theological underpinnings, the Holocaust and the founding of the State of Israel being interpreted according to prophetic paradigms. If God's will is revealed through history, then this history must mean that God will not protect Jews; responsibility for Jewish security must be taken into Jewish hands.

Eliezer Berkovits' *Faith After the Holocaust* remains illustrative of common approaches to the theological problems posed by the Holocaust. Like almost all Jews outside of extreme Orthodoxy, Berkovits categorically rejects the notion that the Holocaust was divine punishment. He calls it, instead, "injustice absolute." The God of the Holocaust is again the silent God, the God who hides His face. Jews are, following Isaiah, servants suffering by divine decree. But, Berkovits adds, "the world is sustained by the suffering of the guiltless." Moreover, there will be "a dimension beyond history in which all suffering finds its redemption through God." Strikingly, for those who insist on faith, tradition contains whatever explanations and promises might be needed.

For modern Jews unfamiliar with the theological tradition, a God whose might is demonstrated through silence, or one who hide's his face, is a cruel God, and thus unacceptable. As the popularity of Harold Kushner's *When Bad Things Happen to Good People* shows, the God these Jews (and non-Jews!) are prepared to consider is a God who is not all-powerful and is therefore not the source of their suffering. This God doesn't punish them. But he may help them, and he will surely provide them with comfort. The appropriate question to address to this God, writes Kushner, is not "Why are you doing this to me?" but "Can you help me?"

Bibliography
Berkovits, Eliezer, *Faith After the Holocaust*, (New York, 1973).
Kraemer, David, *Responses to Suffering in Classical Rabbinic Literature* (New York, 1995).

Roskies, David, *The Literature of Destruction* (Philadelphia, 1988).

Notes

[1] On this, see also SIN.

DAVID KRAEMER

EXEGESIS OF SCRIPTURE, MEDIEVAL RABBINIC: Understanding the Hebrew Scripture to be the authoritative teachings of God or, at least, the mediated message of God, Jews always have looked to the Bible as the ultimate source of knowledge of the divine will. To clarify and amplify this will, a tradition of analysis and commentary has emerged, stretching from the biblical period itself and continuing into the present day. Producing their works in diverse cultural, philosophical, and historical settings, including times of persecution and great anxiety, commentators on Scripture consistently have brought to their audiences a confidence in God's justice, have argued that all that happens is mandated by God, and have offered the nation a hope for the fulfillment of God's promises and for Israel's ultimate vindication.

These commentators additionally have addressed a number of technical issues that arise from the conception that Scripture has a divine origin. As the word of God, the Bible has been understood to contain neither redundancies nor contradictions. These are imperfections that the divine author could not have permitted. Biblical commentators accordingly have worked, for instance, to reconcile verses that appear to conflict with each other. One frequently cited example of this is the difference between Exod. 12:9, which states that the Passover lamb must not be cooked in water but only roasted on fire, and Deut. 16:7, which says it indeed must be cooked. The author of 2 Chron. 35:13 apparently preserves an ancient biblical commentary that reconciles the apparent discrepancy, using the verb associated with cooking in water in conjunction with the words "with fire." This yielded an amalgam of Exod. 12:9 and Deut. 16:7: "And they cooked the Passover lamb with fire as stipulated."

Especially in the medieval period, Scripture was searched from beginning to end by commentators who sought verses that would validate community practices and beliefs that had emerged over the generations. The model for their commentaries was the classic Rabbinic works of Talmud and Midrash, in which Rabbinic sages analyzed, abbreviated, sharpened, and reworked Scripture's words to meet the specific needs of their readerships. Some of these medieval commentaries came to be deemed so fundamental to properly understanding Scripture that they were assembled and arranged on the pages of Scripture themselves, in Rabbinic Bibles, called *Miqraot Gedolot* ("Expanded Scriptures"), which contain the major commentaries and Targumim alongside the biblical text. These commentaries do more than to transmit the sense of difficult passages in ways that both entertain and stimulate the mind. Rather, these commentaries quickly became the eyes through which Scripture consistently was read and understood, the full word of God of which the books of the Bible are but a laconic summary. Commentary, for the traditional student, thus becomes as divine and authoritative as the document for which it speaks.

We can see from the earliest extant translations and commentaries just how important these works were to Jews. Biblical commentary is present in all of the ancient sources that have survived: the Scriptures themselves, Jewish writings in Greek from the third century B.C.E. to the second century C.E. (primarily Septuagint, Pseudepigrapha, Apocrypha, Philo's and Josephus' works), and Jewish writings in Hebrew and Aramaic of that period (primarily the Dead Sea Scrolls, Targumim, and what is preserved in Rabbinic literature). These literary sources suggest the extent to which, in various communities, the meaning of Scripture was taught through commentaries. These commentaries identified the literary levels of Scripture, so as to ascertain what is to be taken as literal, as allegorical, or as mystical. They often endeavored to harmonize conflicting notions in Scripture. And in the way of all careful commentary from their day and on, they filled in omissions, elucidated strange wordings or awkward comparisons, and clarified difficult grammatical constructions.

In time the study of both legal (*halakhah*) and narrative (*aggadah*) passages became so refined that specific styles of commentary emerged making use of exegetical principles (*middot*) or alluding to earlier traditions in such ways as to be accessible only to scholars. At that point it became necessary formally to teach exegetical methods and to write super-commentaries. Commentary thus became a subject of study in its own right, and Scripture itself became subordinated to one or another exegetical approach. Three schools of commentary in particular continued the most ancient methods of biblical exegesis: The "midrash school" relied upon earlier Rabbinic commentary; the "*peshat* school" analyzed grammar and philology in order to identify Scripture's clear historical meaning and precise moral instruction; and the "philosophic/Kabbalistic school" elucidated Scripture by recourse to a reading strategy that revealed whole systems of "knowledge." Some commentators blended all three schools into their works.

The techniques of medieval commentary emerged in particular under Islamic rule of the ninth and tenth centuries, when the heads of the Rabbinic academies (Geonim) began to produce translations, dictionaries, and philosophic treaties that elucidated Scripture for the masses and that reacted against the threat of views opposed to mainstream Rabbinic belief, such as Karaism. A leader in these developments, Saadiah Gaon (882-942), the dynamic and fiery leader of the Sura academy, translated many (if not all) biblical books into Arabic. His commentaries revolved around grammatical, philosophical, and polemical points in order to demonstrate the necessity of Rabbinic oral tradition. While he generally focused upon literal meaning, he often utilized homiletic techniques when the literal would contravene the dictates of his reason or of accepted tradition. Saadiah's discussions organized Scriptural interpretation under the rubrics of hard and fast rules. While some of his rivals took exception to his methods, he exercised a vast influence upon future Geonim of Sura (e.g., Samuel ben Hophni.). Thus, as long as the cultural context of Arabic culture existed, with its emphasis upon grammar, rhetoric, philosophy, and science, Saadiah's commentaries and methods formed the foundation of Scriptural inquiry for the students of the Geonim in Kairouan, North Africa, and later in Spain.

During the eleventh century, under the hegemony of Islamic rule, the Spanish exegetes produced commentaries that, alongside elucidating grammar and word meanings, highlighted how historical information and literary motifs meshed aesthetically in biblical writing. Some Spanish rabbis wrote dictionaries and grammars, in which they illustrated their points through commentaries on specific biblical verses. Judah ben David Hayyuj (c. 950-1000) and Jonah ibn Janah (985-1040), who wrote *Sefer Ha-Rikma* and *Sefer Ha-Shorashim*, are foremost in this category. Moses ben Samuel Ha-Kohen ibn Gikatilla (eleventh c.) and Abraham ibn Ezra (1089-1164), by contrast, composed full commentaries utilizing grammatical principles. While these exposed the deep beauty and values of Scripture and occasionally were useful in countering the claims of Christians, Muslims, and Karaites, they did not incorporate the midrashic tradition of the classical sages of the Talmud. In this same period, allegorical interpretations spread, as did, surprisingly, critical approaches that identified the presence of late editorial hands that shaped certain chapters of early books of the Bible.

In France and Germany, under the rule of the Cross, other schools of commentary developed that brought the richness of the Rabbinic lore into the readings of biblical texts. These commentaries presented terse and direct summaries of large tracts of Talmud and midrash, simplified into bold proclamations of claims of definitive meaning. Their appeal was instantaneous. Soon more involved commentaries developed that no longer directly explained the text but that served, rather, as vehicles for new midrashic insight that went beyond the received corpus of the ancient rabbis. Midway between Spain and France, the two approaches merged in Provence for a brief period in the twelfth and thirteenth centuries. As the Cross pushed out the Crescent in Spain the method of commentary there became more and more like that of Northern Europe, except that the centrality of the philosophy/Kabbalah method became more pronounced than in the past. Thus the triumph of Spanish biblical commentary was the Zohar, a little known work in the fourteenth century, which several centuries later would have profound effects upon Jews.

With the expulsion of Spanish Jewries in 1492 and the re-establishments of their communities in the Ottoman Empire, North Africa, and Northern Europe, the methods of commentary remained stable into the Renaissance period. During and after the Enlightenment, from the middle of the eighteenth century until the middle of the twentieth century, a modern spirit entered the traditional methods of biblical commentary. The goal now was to mold the Jewish community according to the tastes of such modern groups as neo-orthodoxy or Hassidism or to combat the ideas of Protestant biblical criticism or the German Jewish Reform movements. In twentieth century America and Israel in particular, a number of important commentaries—both traditional and "scientific scholarly"—have been written, including ones by Reform and Conservative scholars.

Although in the following we discuss the innovations in biblical commentary introduced in different times and places, we must not be misled to imagine that the significance of any particular commentator results specifically from where or when he wrote. The truth of the matter, rather, is that the classical commentators Rashi and Ramban are read more widely, and have been from the time their works became available, than any contemporary commentators. Missing here as well are the hundreds and hundreds of commentaries that continue to be written that expand upon the ideas of classical commentators, asking questions and proposing solutions in order to develop some thesis that could have been in the back of the minds of the early commentators themselves. Continuing in the

traditional schools of exegesis, these works intend to strengthen religious practice even as they call for a renewed dedication to Jewish piety and Torah study in the face of what traditionalists perceive as the perversity of western values. To some extent, the textual and interpretive work of traditional scholars that began with the Italian Renaissance, in such works as Jedidiah Solomon ben Abraham Norzi's *Minhat Shai*, is ignored in modern times even by traditional scholars, who have turned their attention instead to the progressive Enlightenment that threatens orthodox religious values. Notwithstanding all of this, works such as Norzi's are preserved in current editions of Rabbinic Bibles and continue to play an important role in nurturing the continuing tradition of Rabbinic exegesis.

The major exegetes. Spain: The continuation of Saadiah's analysis of grammar, philology, and rhetoric appears in the commentaries of Isaac ben Judah ibn Geat (1038-1089), whose *Introductions* were methodical expositions of his approach of deriving ethical guidance from Scripture. Like Saadiah, Isaac was a first rate talmudist and paid careful attention to the traditions of the classical sages. His contemporary, Judah ben Samuel ibn Bilaam, wrote in terse Arabic fashion, glossing Scripture with his insights. Of all the Spanish commentators, however, the most influential throughout the ages has been Moses ben Nahman (1194-1274) of Aragon. He combined prodigious mastery of the classical Rabbinic sources with brilliant sensitivity to the nuance of Scriptural expressions, while, at the same time, alluding to the methods of early Spanish Kabbalah. He did not hesitate to take issue with Maimonides, Rashi, or ibn Ezra when he felt they missed the mark. The second most important Spanish exegete is certainly Abraham ben Meir ibn Ezra. He wrote long and short commentaries to many of the same books of the Pentateuch. For the most part his short commentaries have been popularized in editions of *Miqraot Gedolot*.

Abraham ibn Ezra (1089-1164): A Spanish Jew, Abraham ibn Ezra wandered throughout Christian Europe, writing his

Figure 33. Frankenheimer brothers in costume for Purim, Ichenhausen, Germany, c. 1906-1907.

Figure 34. Elsa, Siegmund, and Käte Buxbaum dressed in costumes for Purim, Würzburg, Germany.

Figure 35. Purim party in Jewish elementary school, Pleven, Bulgaria, March 27, 1920.

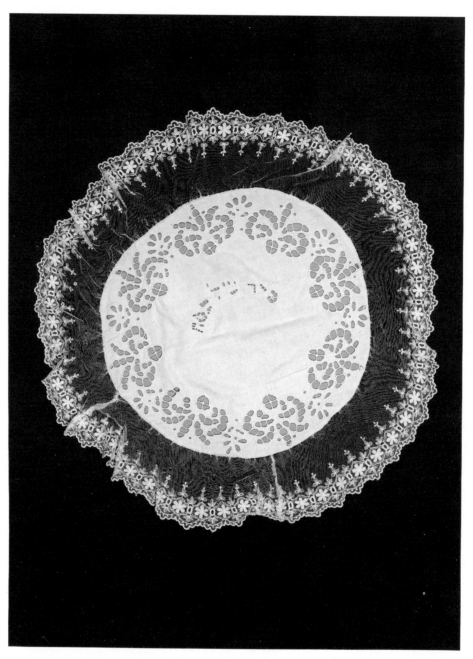

Figure 36. Matzah cover made by Frieda Ruda Kaplansky, Opatow, Poland, 1920s.

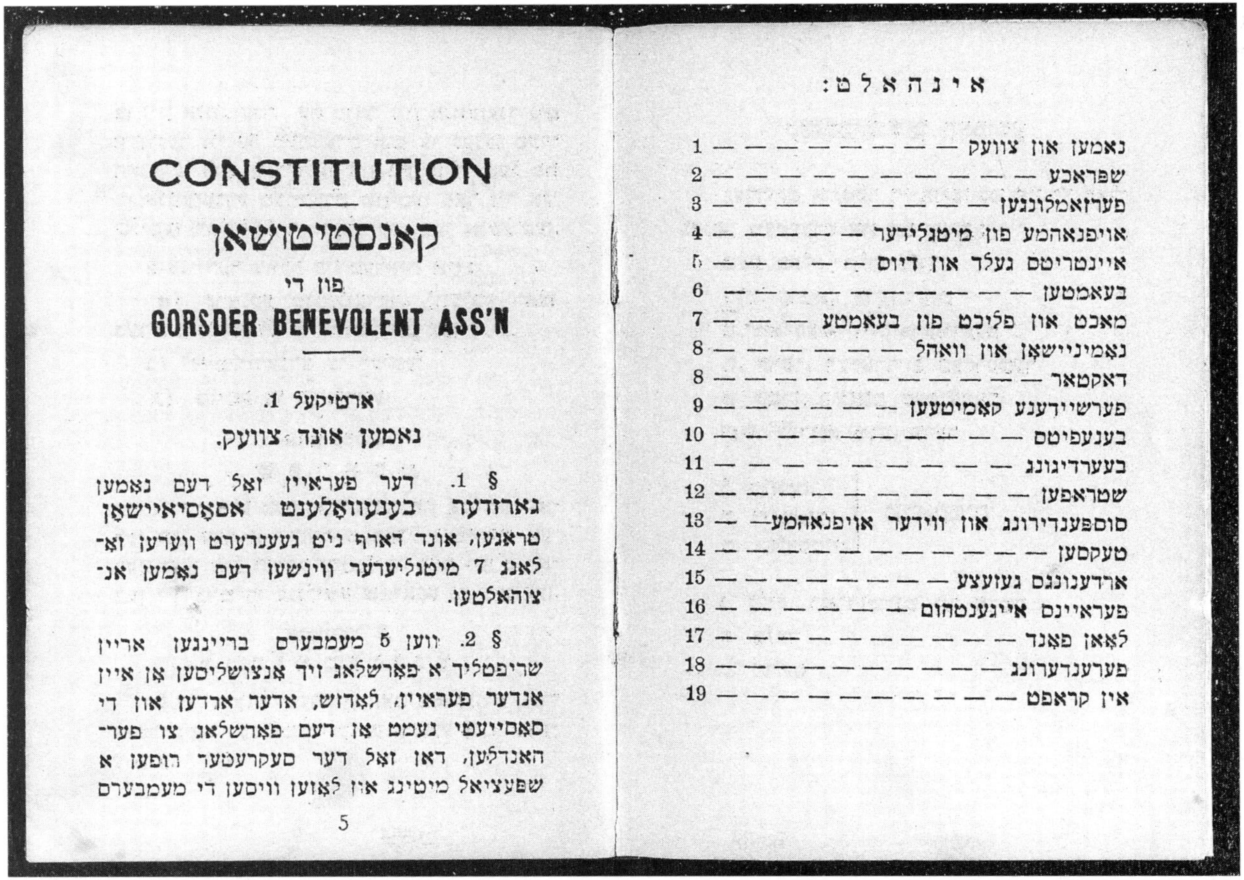

CONSTITUTION

פֿון די

GORSDER BENEVOLENT ASS'N

5

Figure 37. The Gorsder Benevolent Association was organized on June 3, 1903. This Constitution, the third revision of the Association's by-laws, was written in 1923.

Figure 38. Philanthropic Society for the Distribution of Food to Orphans, Salonika, Greece, 1925.

Figure 39. Gavel used by the Devenishker Verein of Greater New York, November 20, 1938. Immigrant organizations, known in Yiddish as landsmanshaftn, served as mutual aid societies and sent funds to the members' hometown.

Figure 40. Burial society (*chevra kadisha*) membership certificate of Tivadar and Malvin Hammel and their son Laszlo. The illustrated scenes and scriptural verse reflect the roles of the *chevra kadisha*. Budapest, Hungary, April 23, 1916.

Figure 41. Charity box made for a burial society in the Russian Empire, possibly Kiev, in 1864.

Figure 42. Poster for the first Jewish children's lottery in Lithuania. The advertisement announces a lottery at the Jewish bank of Vilna, April, 1918. Jewish communities often raised funds to support their own orphanages, old age homes, hospitals, and schools.

Figure 43. Edmund Schreider was dressed in this gown for his *brit milah* (circumcision ceremony) in Berlin, Germany, in 1896.

March 26, 1925 "Brithmealah" Daniel Herbert Bloom

Figure 44. The Bloom family during the circumcision of Daniel Herbert Bloom, New York City, March 26, 1925. The Blooms lived on Chrystie Street on the Lower East Side.

Figure 45. Dead Sea scroll fragment with excerpts from one of the oldest Psalm manuscripts, found in a Judean cave in 1956.

Figure 46. Closed Psalm scroll discovered in cave 11 at Qumran, Judean desert.

Deuxième Année. — Numéro 87

Cinq Centimes

JEUDI 13 JANVIER 1898

L'AURORE

Littéraire, Artistique, Sociale

Directeur
ERNEST VAUGHAN
ABONNEMENTS

Directeur
ERNEST VAUGHAN
143 — Rue Montmartre — 143

J'Accuse...!

LETTRE AU PRÉSIDENT DE LA RÉPUBLIQUE
Par ÉMILE ZOLA

LETTRE
A M. FÉLIX FAURE
Président de la République

Monsieur le Président,

Figure 47. Front page, L'Aurore, with Emile Zola's famous open letter, J'Accuse...! to the President of France, charging that the French government and army falsely accused Captain Alfred Dreyfus of treason, Paris, France, January 13, 1898.

commentaries wherever he went. These commentaries aimed to express the intent of the Scriptural authors by explaining grammatical and philological points, even when these yielded interpretations different from those of Talmudic rabbis. Ibn Ezra did not utilize word-plays or any other fanciful exegetical techniques to entertain or to validate postbiblical practices or beliefs. Rather, he rarely wavered from rational, sensible explanations. Additionally, his reliance on scientific ideas of his age informed his commentaries. For instance, he accepted astrology as a legitimate science and sometimes used it to explain biblical verses. This approach helped him explain why following God's commandments is humanly advantageous. At the same time, in line with his rational approach, ibn Ezra rejected Rabbinic reports of miracles not explicitly mentioned in Scripture but involving biblical characters. But he accepted the idea of God's mastery over nature, so as to accept as historical the miracles described in Scripture itself.

Unless absolutely necessary in his eyes, ibn Ezra never allegorized verses, recognizing instead the dangers of making Scripture appear to say anything and everything desired by the exegete. Still, in the case of the Songs of Songs, he appeals to allegorical motifs as had his predecessors. Upon occasion he writes a note to the prudent reader to keep silent about an interpretation that might suggest that prophets after Moses glossed Scripture. For example, he offers a pious interpretation of Gen. 12:6's statement that the Canaanite was "then" in the land, saying this means that the Canaanites arrived "prior" to Abraham. Alongside this interpretation, however, he adds a cryptic phrase suggesting that the verse actually reveals the work of a later hand. Its point is that, while the Canaanites were certainly in the land when Moses lived ("then"), they were not in the land when this glossator lived ("but not now"). At times he seems to propose that later prophets added editorial glosses to edify obscure references in earlier books. To say this outwardly might have been cause for complaint against his piety by the simple masses, and so he alludes to such

cases rather circumspectly. At the same time, he generally views prophecies that allude to the future, especially ones that utilize names and events unknown in the period of the prophet himself, as true predictions that even that prophet would not have understood very well.

Despite his propensity for critical thought, ibn Ezra shows great respect for Rabbinic legal tradition and often finds within Scripture's words a basis for Talmudic tradition. Still, what is stated as fact in Scripture, ibn Ezra accepts as fact, while what is stated by ancient rabbis he rejects if it does not match his own critical evaluation of Scripture. Moreover, he has no compunction about laying bare the faults of Scriptural heroes, and in doing this he differed from his predecessors and from Rabbinic tradition. He anticipates a modern understanding of the value of forms and their usages and often compares forms and usages from one passage in Scripture to another.

Editions of his works based on fine manuscripts have appeared over the last century. His comments are utilized by biblical commentators to this very day. Among the most popular of his works are those to the Pentateuch, the minor prophets, Isaiah, Jeremiah, Ezekiel, Psalms, Job, the five scrolls, and Daniel. Moses Kimhi's commentary to Job relies very heavily on ibn Ezra, and Kimhi's commentary to Proverbs was introduced into *Miqraot Gedolot* because it was mistaken for ibn Ezra's. In fact, it is unclear whether a commentary of ibn Ezra to Proverbs ever existed at all.

Moses ben Nahman (c. 1194-1274): A native of Gerona in the Spanish province of Catalonia, Nachmanides, or Ramban (his acronym), popularized the dialectic methods of French scholars, which he learned from Judah ben Yakar and combined with the approaches of classical Spanish talmudists. He was an outstanding legal scholar and Talmudic exegete whose method of Scriptural exegesis involved comparing prior interpretations of Rabbinic statements on the verse at hand. He utilized Targum, Talmud, Midrash, and even Apocrypha to search out the sense of the Bible in the light of Rabbinic teachings. Where called for, he differed from Rashi, ibn Ezra, and Maimonides as well as others. He had no difficulty criticizing biblical heroes when he felt they had acted wrongly.

Ramban steered an even course between presenting the text's plain meaning, which he almost always explains, reporting the more popular meanings the verse had acquired in Rabbinic midrash, and, rarely, mentioning its esoteric meanings (*derech emet*). While he never spells out precisely the esoteric teaching he derives from the verse, he indicates that the verse has some deeper meaning that an adept student might discover along certain specified lines. Throughout this interpretative process, he kept his eye on the most obvious context of the narrative he was explaining, while drawing out moral and ethical teachings and even hinting at future prophecies contained within the rather plain looking narratives. Often, such diverse meanings operate simultaneously.

Ramban also digressed into matters that he thought his audience should know but likely did not. In this, his great erudition still captivates readers. He often reconciles Rabbinic legal pronouncements with verses that seem at odds with them and defends traditional understandings of Scripture against those who would question the truth of Rabbinic commentary. His sense of rhetoric and grammar are typically Spanish in that his exegetical skills aim at combining diverse elements of a narrative to show how they work together to create a concrete, sequenced, unit of discourse. For him, Scriptural rules were not meant merely to accommodate primitive beliefs to a higher sense of monotheism but were in and of themselves means to enable the soul to perfect itself. His commentary to the book of Job, indebted in many ways to the work of Moses Kimhi of Narbonne, still bears his unique imprint in combining piety, mysticism, and rational philosophic inquiry.

In 1263 he was forced to debate the merits of Judaism against those of Christianity. Then, in 1267, to escape Pope Clement IV, who sought to punish him for speaking freely against Christianity during the course of the disputation, he made his way to the Land of Israel, where he completed his commentary to the Pentateuch.

Bahya ben Asher ben Hlava (thirteenth c.): Of great importance, Bahya's commentary to the Pentateuch simultaneously lists four interpretations of verses: the straightforward meaning, the midrashic interpretation, the rational exegesis, and the mystical explanation. These methods were widely used by Medieval Christian exegetes, and most scholars think they must have originated with some of the Church Fathers. The matter needs more investigation, since the authors Josephus and Philo as well as Rabbinic midrashic texts in general also identify various levels of meaning in textual analysis. The four-fold exegetical method also is prominent in the works of Joseph Gikatilla and Moses de Leon. Through Bahya's work one is able to discover the meaning of Nachmanides' terse hints concerning the Kabbalistic meanings of certain verses.

Jacob ben Asher (1270-1340): Although born in Germany, Jacob ben Asher adopted quickly to the ways of his new homeland of Spain. While his legal code reflects the practices of German Jewry, his Scriptural exegesis follows the methods of the Spanish school of Maimonides. His use of numerology (*gematria*) and his innovative interpretations of biblical texts were published separately, under the title "Baal Ha-Turim." Although not prominent in his major work, these methods reflect the entire school of exegesis of the Hassidei Ashkenaz, whose commentaries were highly influential in Germany throughout the Middle Ages.

Don Isaac Abravanel (1437-1508): Although a native of Portugal, he achieved prominence as a Spanish statesman. His commentaries to the Pentateuch, Prophets, and the Book of Daniel have been printed in many editions. He speculated upon why a biblical book appeared in one section of the bible rather than in another and addressed other historical problems, such as the authorship of specific books. He sought understanding wherever he could find it and did not hesitate to praise a Christian's comments on a certain problem. His style was to ask a series of questions at the beginning of a unit and to proceed to give clear answers that unraveled the problems. His commentary is filled with insights of politics and literary appreciation; he ignored Rabbinic tradition where he found it convenient to do so. For this he did not escape criticism.

France: Not much is known about the roots of French-German biblical commentary. We do know that the Biblical lexicons of Menahem ibn Saruk and Dunash ibn Labrat from Spain had reached there and that the scholarly community did not share the philosophic spirit of Geonic-Spanish commentary. There was a need to encode Jewish tradition within the minute details of Scriptural wording (*derash*) on the one hand and to lay bare the stark literal meanings of the Scriptural narratives (*peshat*) on the other hand.

While some few citations of the commentaries of Menahem ben Helbo were preserved in the biblical commentary of his nephew, Joseph Kara, the compellingly bold-stroked pen of Rashi dwarfed all others from the time of its first appearance until modern times. Rashi attempted to give the reader a sense of the dual *derash/peshat* approaches mentioned above. His commentary introduced a style of inquiry and a terse mode of discussion that set the standards for all future exegesis. Read by Jews and non-Jews, his mastery of Rabbinic materials and his brilliant manner of explaining difficult ideas very simply assured his commentary's becoming the standard against which all others would be judged.

The most surprising element in the history of Western European Jewish commentary is the emergence of a school of exegetes who separated the *derash* method represented in the Rabbinic tradition from the straightforward sense of the Bible revealed by the *peshat* method. This bifurcation is evident in the works of Rashbam, Joseph Kara, Joseph Bekhor Shor, and Eliezer of Beaugency, who considered Rabbinic exegesis often to be based on something other than the biblical text itself. The artistry of the French exegetes is best seen in Hezekiah ben Manoah's work, *Hizzekuni*. He combined the best of French exegetical approaches, often citing Rabbinic midrash, and wove the comments of his predecessors into perceptive and illuminating expositions of Scripture. While he reworks the oral tradition of the early rabbis, he does not ignore grammar, ethics, straightforward niceties, or even scientific observations. The medieval schools of exegesis in France and Germany are best represented by the following commentators:

Solomon ben Isaac (c. 1040-1105): Shelomo Yitzhaki, known as Rashi, was a native of Troyes, in the area of Champagne. He lived and worked there, but his schooling had been in Germany, with teachers in Mainz and Worms. He composed lucid commentaries on the Talmud and Scripture, which replaced those of his teachers and predecessors. He seemed to know precisely what points of the tradition students would stumble over and addressed those points with precision and authority. The separate statements addressing the traditional, Rabbinic understanding of the verse and his own contextual, straightforward readings were allowed to bear equal weight and to function simultaneously. Where there is a difficulty in knowing why the rabbis embellished Scripture, Rashi pointed out that without such embellishment there would be a difficulty in reading a word or two or understanding why Scripture had omitted certain important details in a key passage.

His grasp of material was such that he could feel free to differ with Targum or midrashic interpretations. Additionally, while he did not reject accepted legal decisions, he often showed how a text's primary meaning differed from the meaning assigned to it by the tradition, within which it validated a particular practice. That latter meaning was integral to the structure of Judaism but was secondary to the plain sense of Scripture. Rashi's extensive use of midrashic passages, which he often abridges, allows his commentary to serve as an entrance-way from study of Scripture to study of the Rabbinic literature. While he responds to many different kinds of problems that face the mature reader of the Bible, he does not hide his perplexity at some things, noting simply that he did not know their meaning.

Rashi's commentaries cover all of Scripture with the exception of Ezra, Nehemiah, Chronicles, and the last chapters of Job. The commentary that bear his name on these works are not from his pen. Students of Rashi added their own clarifications as they copied Rashi's commentary and today, despite the evidence of old manuscripts, it is difficult to pin-point all the additions. Among the super-commentaries to Rashi's commentary on the Torah are some produced in the Sephardic communities, for example, *Sefer Ha-Zikharon* of Abraham Boccarat. The best known super-commentaries are those of Elijah Mizrahi, the *Gur Aryeh* of Maharal of Prague, and the often printed *Siftei Hakhamim*, which was compiled from various sources. Another favorite is *Kli Yakar* by Solomon Ephraim Luntschitz.

Samuel ben Meir (c. 1080-1165): Rashbam was born in Northern France (Ramerupt), the grandson and student of Rashi, the brother of the illustrious Jacob Tam. Of his many books concerning Scripture, only his commentary to the Torah remains extant. His reputation as a commentator to Talmud, who supplemented Rashi's commentary to some major tractates, ensures his respect for all time. His Bible commentaries, lucid and penetrating, are meant to be read alongside Rashi's, revealing other facets of Scripture, not discussed by Rashi. These draw the student into an appreciation for an intelligent reading of Scripture created without reference to the plethora of important Rabbinic midrashic passages that inform the meaning of the text. Rashi had aimed to solve problems in the text and to show the connection between the Oral and Written Laws. Rashbam, by contrast, aimed to provide an appreciation of Scripture as a document in its own right. As a result he informs us that his commentary cannot be used to study the legal sense of laws in the Torah, which depend upon the Rabbinic reading, but only the ethical and human dimensions that the legal sense does not have.

Legal readings are informed by many techniques, and Rashbam had mastered the material thoroughly. Nevertheless, the lessons to be derived from such readings were prescriptive, and Rashbam broke new ground in showing that Scripture had more to say about law than the prescriptive aspects. The phrasing of the law often had a moral dimension, irrespective of the tradition's notion of the law's proper observance. It might even happen on rare occasion that the tradition reversed meanings in Scripture, for whatever practical reasons. Rashbam did not suggest that anyone should follow his readings in practice, but in theory they had much to teach about equity and fairness. These natural readings of Scripture were a luxury. So long as Rashbam was free from pressure to engage the meaning of the law, he could think about the holy text as a revelation in and of itself, beyond any other considerations.

Rashbam often opposed Rashi's interpretations (see E.Z. Melamed, *Bible Commentators* [in Hebrew, Jerusalem, 1978, vol. I, p. 458]) and also engaged in polemics against the Church Fathers. Nevertheless, he knew the Apocrypha from Christian sources, which he utilized when it was convenient for him to do so (see, e.g., his comment to Num. 12:1). His knowledge of Hebrew grammar and philology is prodigious, and he was able to make good use of Targumim to discuss such subjects and even to study the precise wordings of the textual tradition he had received. An able poet in his own right, he was the first to discuss certain facets of biblical poetry, for instance, that what is stated in the first hemistich of a line is embellished in the second. While his method of analysis drew the attention of the greatest minds of his generation who adopted his approach, overall his program was not followed extensively by subsequent exegetes in later generations. We do, however, have at least one super-commentary on the work of Rashbam.

Joseph Kara (eleventh-twelfth c.): This French scholar has been sadly neglected throughout the ages, and only his works on the Prophets and Job are extant. He formulated rules of narrative and literary techniques, for instance, that Scripture foreshadows events by introducing a subject briefly in one episode before elaborating upon it in great detail subsequently. He endeavored to portray Scripture as made up of cohesive units with a tight internal logic that merely had to be exposed by the commentator. He viewed traditional midrash as presenting secondary embellishments to the text rather than strict interpretations, and in many ways his essentialist approach is not much different from Rashbam's, whom he knew well. He had studied with his uncle, Menahem ben Helbo (11c), who himself wrote biblical commentaries.

Joseph ben Isaac (twelfth-thirteenth c.): Joseph ben Isaac, referred to as Rabbi Yosef Bekhor Shor of Orleans, was as prodigious and productive a talmudist and halakhist as was Rashbam. Like Joseph Kara he considered midrash to be secondary to the primary sense of Scripture, the larger literary structure of which he often explored. For instance, whereas modern scholars are inclined to see the legal exposition of Exod. 34 as divorced from the previous episodes concerning the golden calf, Rabbi Bekhor Shor demonstrates integral connections between the two sections. Unlike Rashi, especially in his exposition of legal passages, he did not rely on Talmudic and midrashic literature, following, rather, the style of Rashbam. He thus deviated from traditional exegeses in cases in which he felt the sense of Scripture was different from that upheld by the oral law, even though he obviously accepted that law as binding. In particular in cases with no practical implication for daily life, he upheld the literal meaning as opposed to that on which the binding, accepted rule was based.

He took pains to explain away anthropomorphic descriptions of God, and, similarly, he tended to rationalize miracles as much as possible, contrary to the midrashic approach. In engaging the literal meaning of texts he reacted bitterly against the figurative interpretations of Christian exegetes and even belittled Christians for the yearly Eucharist rite, in which they understand themselves to partake of the blood and the flesh of Jesus. (There is no reason to emend here the word "yearly." That was the current practice.) Polemics and apologetics were among his major concerns.

Of all the medieval Western European exegetes, the school of Rashi had the most lasting impact. Rashi had been content to speak of straightforward (*peshat*) and derivative (*derash*) meanings, without demeaning either approach. Rashbam and his colleagues, by contrast, had shown a marked preference for a purely straightforward method of exegesis. It remained for the continuators of Rashi's approach, the Baalei Ha-Tosafot of France and Germany, to produce commentaries, collected in many volumes, such as *Da'at Zekenim* and *Hadar Zekenim*, that justified the Rabbinic oral tradition and argued against any other approach, including Rashi's or even that of Targum Onqelos. These works were scholastic, cited others commentaries, and asked penetrating questions that were solved by very ingenious answers. The method now applied to the interpretation of Scripture was the same one used to study the Talmud.

Provence: Joseph Kimhi (c. 1105-1170) had come to Narbonne in Provence from Spain and established the methods of ibn Ezra there. His many commentaries (*Sefer Ha-Torah, Sefer Ha-Maqneh, Perush le-Sefer Mishlei, Perush le-Sefer-Iyov*) have survived, sometimes in partial form, but many have been lost. His work is philological and grammatical, paraphrasing units into the contemporary Hebrew, while often leaving the actual interpretation to the reader. He utilized his knowledge of Arabic to reveal meanings in biblical Hebrew, and his rationalist and occasionally neo-Platonist approach stands in stark contrast to the more romantic currents favored in Germany and France. Scattered throughout his grammatical works, such as *Sefer Hagalui*, one finds many explanations of biblical passages. His approach led him into disputations with Christian exegetes, and his polemics are recorded in his *Sefer Ha-Brit*. He was the teacher of Menahem ben Simeon of Posquières, who composed commentaries to the Books of Jeremiah and Ezekiel.

Moses Kimhi (c. 1120-1190): Taught by his father, Joseph Kimhi, Moses followed in his footsteps and achieved prominence as a first-rate grammarian. His biblical commentaries to Proverbs and Job have recently appeared in critical editions, and his work on

Ezra, Nehemiah, and Proverbs appears in Rabbinic Bibles under the title of Abraham ibn Ezra, whose methods Moses followed. His work is characterized by expositions of grammatical points, with ample examples given from other books of the Bible that illustrate the same matter. He also paraphrases verses to show how the units of Scripture hang together as literary units with substantial inner logic. He utilizes Targumim, reacts against earlier commentators who remain unnamed, borrows from Abraham ibn Ezra, and at times cites Rabbinic ideas. He taught his younger brother David, who was ten years old when their father died.

David Kimhi: Radak achieved more fame than his brother or his father. He combined their stark philological and grammatical approaches—which exposed the evident sense of verses—with passages from Rabbinic literature, so as to arrive at the essence of each biblical verse's meaning. He introduced both neo-platonic and Aristotelian notions into his commentaries. In the case of descriptions of the world's creation or the features of the heavenly realms, he utilized allegorical methods. Nevertheless, unlike his father and brother, with whom he disagreed in many ways, his work was meant to be popular and not just for scholars. On occasion he included discussions about proper behavior, ethics, and morals, while still clinging as best he could to what he saw as the straightforward meaning of the biblical text.

Among the examples in his grammar (*Mikhlol*) and his lexicon (*Shorashim*) can be found hundreds of interpretations of Scripture, and these are useful even for modern scholars. He traveled widely to look at various manuscripts of the Bible, so that he could free the text from copyists' errors. He wrote commentaries to the Pentateuch, and that to Genesis is still extant. While he may not have written any more than this one on the Pentateuch, some later references may suggest otherwise. Or, perhaps, there was a compilation, now lost, of his comments to the Pentateuch taken his other works. We have his commentaries to all the books of the Prophets, Psalms, Proverbs, and Chronicles. It does not seem that he commented on Job, and a

commentary to that book bearing his name is likely that of a student of Moses Kimhi. His influence was pronounced, and the King James Version of the Bible is largely based on his commentaries.

Joseph ben Abba Mari ibn Kaspi (1279-1340): Born in Spain, Joseph moved to Provence later in his life. He produced commentaries to almost the entire Scripture. He named his commentaries with the adjective "silver" (*kesef*), an illusion to the name Kaspi (*Tirat Kesef, Adnei Kesef, Asara Klei Kesef*, etc.). He combined a proto-modern approach to contradictory statements in the Bible, ascribing them to different contemporary accounts of the same incident. He was sensitive to the Masoretic cantillation notations, to grammar, to textual variants, and to ancient reality. It is of historical note that Kalonymos ben Kalonymos wrote him concerning the appearance of various names of God in one section of Genesis, different names in another section, and combined names in a third section. Kalonymos does not tell us what he made of this, except to intimate that on the surface it had no facile reason. Kaspi's philosophic approach to theological questions was in the framework of the Spanish schools, and of late scholars are recognizing his contributions.

Levi ben Gershom (1288-1344): He was well versed in the philosophic and *peshat* methods of his native Provence. His work covers almost the whole of Scripture, save for the Later Prophets, Lamentations, and some of the Hagiographa. He was a thorough rationalist and often reworked sentences that sounded miraculous, so that they seemed more natural. He did not minimize contradictions between various Scriptural books.

Italy. Isaiah ben Mali di Trani (first half of thirteenth c.): A well known Talmudist, his commentaries on the Prophets and Writings dealt with matters in a modern spirit, posing difficulties in chronology and noting implausible sequencing of narratives. He touched upon matters of theology and philosophy and showed a breadth of understanding detached from the stock answers that might have flowed from his Talmudic commentaries. A prolific writer, he followed the approach of Rashbam, and, like him, his methods were not widely appreciated.

Obadiah ben Jacob Sforno (c. 1470-1550): This halakhist and humanist was a true renaissance man, a philosopher, physician, and mathematician. His students were not only Jews but also famous Christians, like Johannes Reuchlin. A spirit of compassion and moral instruction fills his works. He weaves his knowledge of medicine and botany with his literary insights to create an intelligent, discriminating, and very illuminating commentary. He introduces his own insights to elaborate upon the works of his predecessors, in general following the thinking of Maimonides and deviating from his path only at rare times. He utilized passages from the Talmud more frequently than midrashic texts. His commentaries cover the Pentateuch, Song of Songs, Job, Psalms, Ecclesiastes, Habbakuk, Zechariah, and Jonah. His works remain popular to the present day, and his commentary to the Pentateuch is found in Rabbinic Bibles.

The later Sephardic tradition. Moses Alshekh (second half of sixteenth c.): His saintly character is evident throughout his commentaries to the Pentateuch, Prophets, Psalms, Proverbs, Song of Songs, Ruth, Lamentations, Ecclesiastes, Esther, and Job. A contemporary of the famed Kabbalist Isaac Luria, he wrote in the Land of Israel, reading ethical or philosophic insights into a verse by recourse to midrashic and talmudic texts and mystical allusion. The sheer beauty of his thought attracted much attention. It was added to some editions of Rabbinic Bibles and is widely read to this day.

Hayyim ben Moses Attar (1696-1743): A prominent Moroccan Kabbalist who founded an academy in the Land of Israel, he wrote an extensive commentary to the Pentateuch, called *Or Ha-Hayyim*. In this work he weaves together midrashic and Kabbalistic themes to develop profound speculations on the biblical text. The Western European Hassidic communities elevated his work to the status of Rashi's commentary, published it in their editions of Rabbinic Bibles, and read it weekly alongside the Biblical weekly portions.

The dawn of modernity: Included in current editions of the Rabbinic Bible under the titles *Metzudot David* and *Metzudot Zion*, David and Hillel Altschuler's comments to the Prophets and Writings (seventeenth c.) were copied from the best of earlier exegetes who had focused on the literal sense of verses. Their work stands at a transitional point in biblical commentary. Even as the emerging Hassidic commentaries brought a new midrashic thrust into the texts, the dawn of secularism gave rise to an new interest in philology and ancient history. The blossoming of modernity and its impact on religious life is fully portrayed in the currents of eighteenth, nineteenth, and twentieth centuries commentary.

Elijah ben Solomon, Gaon of Vilna (1720-1797): The Gaon was the towering figure of eighteenth century Jewry, there being no area of Rabbinic study that he did not master. He revitalized the study of Scripture in Poland, Germany and Lithuania. When he was dealing with the straightforward sense of Scripture he brought his powerful intellect to delve deeply into the precise sense of word usages, realia of history, geography, mathematics, and grammar; when dealing with esoteric matters he showed Kabbalistic connections in a brief but penetrating manner. His son annotated his *Aderet Eliyahu* on the Pentateuch.

Moses Mendelssohn (1729-1786): With the figure of Moses Mendelssohn we enter a new stage in Bible commentary. Mendelssohn was thoroughly dedicated to the Age of Reason and its ideals. Active in beginning the Berlin Enlightenment, he translated the Bible into German anew, even working into it the ideas of the medieval commentators and traditional *halakhah*. He organized a project of detailed, rational commentary called the *Beur*, which took several generations to complete. His commentary was meant to stimulate Jewry into an appreciation of the delights of rational, scientific thought on history, botany, textiles, etc., so as to unravel the ancient texts. He wanted to make it possible for Jews to learn proper German and good Hebrew, as opposed to their native Yiddish dialects that had been born in the ghettos. He revitalized the study of grammar as a tool to study Bible, accepted Rabbinic tradition, and followed midrash where the literal sense was too much at odds with the talmudic teaching about a verse, especially in legal matters. Mendelssohn paid close attention to the aesthetics of Biblical poetry and wrote brilliant introductions to many biblical books. Despite his modern and critical approach, his piety was unquestionable, including his belief that the text was divinely given to Moses. His collaborators were S. Dubno, N. Wessely, A. Jaroslaw, and N. Homberg, who based their comments on the works of the classical commentators but added gems of their own. The work in its entirety was called *Netivot Ha-Shalom*. The text was reprinted and expanded upon for a number of years and finally came to include the insights of Samuel David Luzatto and Elijah of Vilna.

As the Jewish Enlightenment in the early 1800s began to develop into a serious threat to religious traditions, and as the leaders of the Enlightenment began to utilize sections of Mendelssohn's translations and commentaries to teach German language and the goals of the Enlightenment to Jewish youth, the most prominent traditional scholars, including Hassidic masters, gathered to condemn the work and Mendelssohn himself. By the end of the century such scholars as Heinrich Graetz were writing German commentaries, suggesting emendations to the traditional text, and departing totally from the ancient traditional understandings. In Italy, Isaaco Samuel Reggio (1784-1855), a colleague of Samuel David Luzzatto, did in Italian on a smaller scale what Mendelssohn had done on larger scale, but his work already suggested emendations and departed from tradition more than Mendelssohn would have appreciated.

Samuel David Luzzatto (1800-1865): A sense of balance was introduced by this eminently pious Italian rabbi. In his piety he worked to demonstrate that the Pentateuch was not a composite work, as the emerging German Protestant scholars were claiming. Still, he was a rationalist in that he adopted the views of the emerging Protestant scholarly approach to the books of the Prophets

and the Writings and even emended texts on the basis of ancient versions. Known by the acronym Shadal, he labored to extract the plainest meaning possible and did not shirk from using comparative semitics and acknowledging the corrupt states of certain passages. In sum, what he derived as the proper sense would stand, no matter if it contradicted received tradition. He commented on the Pentateuch and Isaiah, each of which he saw as authored by a single hand. His work on Jeremiah, Ezekiel, Proverbs, and Job shows his dislike of Abraham ibn Ezra's disregard of Rabbinic tradition in his commentary to the Torah. In his lengthy essay on Ecclesiastes, he disregarded Kabbalistic approaches and ignored traditional Jewish philosophical expression in favor of common sense. Shadal was very much part of the Jewish Enlightenment in his Hebrew poems and innovative use of language. But in his theology and his yearning for the Holy Land, he was a disciple of Judah Halevi.

The climate for biblical scholarship, whetted by Shadal, continued into modern times. The works of Moses Isaac ben Samuel Tedeschi (1821-1898) are prolific and densely thought out; Arnold Bogumil Ehrlich (1848-1919) wrote commentaries aiming at philological precision in both Hebrew and Greek; Benno Jacob (1862-1945) totally rejected the biblical criticism of German Protestant scholarship and undertook a detailed philological and grammatical analysis of texts to show the unity of their meaning and message. Ehrlich's approach was utilized by N.H. Tur Sinai (Torczyner) in his *Peshuto shel Miqra* commentary to the Pentateuch and in his commentary to Job, both written in the middle of the twentieth century. His approach was also continued by the Italian scholar Umbretto Cassuto in his commentary to Exodus and parts of Genesis. Also writing in the middle of the twentieth century, Cassuto opposed the use of the documentary hypothesis, which explains textual difficulties by relegating different passages to distinct biblical authorships.

Jacob Zevi Meklenburg of Koenigsberg (1785-1865): His great work on the Torah, *Ha-Ketav ve-Ha-Qaballah*, delves into the meaning of each word in order to clarify its meaning and to show how much the oral tradition and accepted commentaries can be accommodated by these senses without straining the plain sense.

Naphtali Zevi Judah Berlin (1817-1893): This Lithuanian master talmudist and head of the great academy of Volozhin had an incisive mind and a mastery of Rabbinic works. His commentary to the Pentateuch, called *Ha'amek Davar*, attempts to show the consistency of Scripture's language and to demonstrate how the oral traditions illuminate the text and clarify difficult problems. In his footsteps it is fair to mention the later commentaries of Baruch Epstein's *Torah Temimah* and Meir Simha Cohen's *Meshech Hochmah*, which attempt to explain the connections between Midrash and Scripture.

Meir Leibush ben Yechiel Michel (1809-1879): Revealing wit and acumen, his commentaries are based on the large numbers of rules this Russian rabbi deduced for unraveling Scripture. In the main he wishes to show how Rabbinic interpretation is true to the meaning of the written Scripture, and he maintains the futility of the ideas of the Reform movement, which sought to discredit Rabbinic interpretations. Malbim (his name based on his acronym) also examined biblical poetry to illustrate that parallel stichs are not simply casual poetic redundancies but carry independent meaning and, when looked at closely, reveal deep theological and ethical teachings.

David Zevi Hoffmann (1843-19212): The products of a quick and critical mind, his German commentaries to Leviticus and Deuteronomy attempted to illustrate the insufficiencies of the documentary hypothesis and to portray the fundamental place of Rabbinic tradition in establishing the authorial meaning of Scripture.

Samson Raphael Hirsch (1808-1888): The prolific spiritual leader of the Jewish community of Frankfurt-on-Maine, he wrote commentaries to the Pentateuch. His goals and methods are similar to those of Malbim, but his method of writing is quite different. Malbim posed and then answered pointed questions. Hirsch by contrast sermonizes

eloquently, while never forgetting that the commentator's goal is to derive lessons from a close reading of the text. He speculates about the emotional and mental motivations of biblical characters, and at times he shows how social influences can determine behavior. The most recurrent technique he uses is creative etymology, which finds unsuspected meanings in words so as to open up new understanding of verses. Since he balances tradition with enlightened views of the value of the human spirit, Hirsch, like Malbim, has remained popular into the twenty-first century.

Judah Aryeh Leib Alter (1847-1905): A renowned talmudic scholar and author, the Sfas Emes (his pen name) was the chief rabbi of the Gur Hassidim in Poland. His biblical commentaries, unlike his talmudic commentaries, bring together ancient Rabbinic thought, Zohar, and creative Hassidic reformulations of law and lore with some contemporary point he wishes to address to his audience.

Modern criticism: The first third of the twentieth century saw the publication of the most thorough higher critical commentary on the Bible in Hebrew. Abraham Kahana organized a group of scholars to utilize the newest discoveries in ancient Semitic languages and the findings of scholars who accepted the premises of the documentary hypothesis. Yet this commentary did not have the popular appeal of either the "traditional" or the "enlightenment" methods. While there may or may not be further attempts at scientific commentaries in Hebrew, it is certain that the collecting and analyzing of the works of the classical commentators will continue into the future, and such works appear regularly. Also many of the Jewish biblical commentaries are continuing to be translated into English, among them: Attar's commentary on the Torah, 1995; the commentary of Abraham Ibn Ezra on the Pentateuch, 1986; Samuel ben Meir's commentary on Genesis and Exodus 1989-; Meir Leibush ben Yechiel Michel's commentary on the Torah, 1978; Sforno's *Beur al Ha-Torah*, 1987-1989; Ramban's commentary on the Torah, 1971-76; *Perush Rashi al Ha-Torah*, 1994; and Hirsch's

Pentateuch, 1958-1962. Of more significance to scholars are the new Hebrew editions of classical commentators, which are based on manuscript evidence and show how corrupt the current printed editions are.

The problem of levels of meaning in medieval interpretation: The study of biblical hermeneutics is a very new field, such that many central questions remain unanswered. One of these questions concerns whether or not there is a continuous tradition of exegetical methodology, so that, for instance, commentators in the eleventh century inherited approaches used by exegetes in the first century or earlier. This is an important issue in particular regarding the origins of the notion that the biblical text can be interpreted on several levels. For while some have argued that medieval Jewish exegetes referred to three or four levels of meaning because this approach was in use in the Christian schools of their time, it should also be clear that a precedent for this approach exists in the Jewish sources themselves.

The recognition of a tension between the literal meaning and the significant meaning is reflected as early as the first century by Josephus, who begins his *Antiquities of the Jews* (1:24) by noting that Scripture has three modes of writing: 1) the enigmatic veiled allusion that hides esoteric meanings; 2) the metaphoric expression that is meant to be interpreted; and 3) the simple, straightforward meaning. For Josephus, these various levels of meaning did not apply simultaneously to the same words. In the same period, however, Philo (*On the Confusion of Tongues* 183-190) understands words that have allegorical lessons still to bear their straightforward sense. Similarly the opening paragraph of the Rabbinic text Genesis Rabbah (1:1) reflects a threefold exegesis scheme, including the pedagogic, the hidden, and the veiled meaning. In later manuscripts and the printed editions, a fourth, Alexandrian allegorical meaning has been added as well. The Zohar (Midrash Ha-Neelam 83a, end) also holds that all four levels are simultaneously active in all places in Scripture.

The centrality in early Judaism of the question of how Scripture is to be interpreted is reflected in the fact that Talmudic rabbis already saw a certain tension between the literal and the belabored senses. The rabbis, or at least many of them, were unwilling to see a divine document as having been written wastefully. God, in this view, did nothing gratuitously, did not waste a jot or tittle. Everything, including the spellings of words and their numerical values, thus had meaning and needed to be interpreted. In line with this, B. Men. 29b pictures Moses himself as astounded when God shows him a vision of Aqiba interpreting what Moses saw as mere ornamental decorations of certain letters in Scripture. Finding meaning even in these decorations, Aqiba derives teachings from every aspect of the text, a procedure of which God clearly approves.

In presenting a model of this exegetical approach, the influence of the rabbis on medieval commentators was profound. For instance, Rashi explains M. Sot. 9:15's report that after the death of Aqiba the honor of the Torah was impoverished by stating that this is because Aqiba's methods of reading meaning into every jot and tittle was not practiced after he died as thoroughly as when he had encouraged it in his lifetime. Of similar importance was B. Meg. 18a's statement that Scripture itself elevates one who teases meanings out of every hair line in it. Scripture thus was not to be interpreted simply as the product of literary artistry. It comprises, rather, a highly complex structure of meanings to be thoroughly analyzed and processed.

At the same time, Scripture had always been recognized as a work of historical and narrative writing, such that even the Talmuds proclaim that the study of Scripture as a historical document is meritorious (even as the study of its minutiae to derive legal, philosophic, and mystical meaning was of the highest order). The outcome of this dual attitude towards scripture—viewed as artistic narrative, on the one side, and complex structure of meanings, on the other—was the emergence of the medieval notion that Scripture can and must be interpreted on a number of levels.

To appreciate this approach, let us look

at Gen. 33:16-20: "And Esau returned on that day on his way to Seir . . . And Jacob traveled to Sukkot . . . And Jacob came to Shechem . . . And he bought a portion of the field . . . And he erected there an altar; and he named it/him, Mighty, the God of Israel."

B. Meg. 18a tells us that one sage, Eliezer, rejected the ostensible meaning that Jacob named "it," that is, the altar, "Mighty, the God of Israel." He holds instead that the verse should be read "and Jacob (was) named it," that is, "and the God of Israel named Jacob, 'Mighty.'" While the Talmud presents no explicit explaination of why Eliezer chose this interpretation, Rashi is aware that Talmudic method requires that one show a problem in the obvious meaning of a verse before straining its sense to produce a creative meaning. Rashi thus understands the Talmud to have rejected the straightforward sense of the text only in order to present a sermonic meaning. But it is not uncommon for Rashi and others to present exactly such meanings that Talmudic sages rejected as the obvious and accepted sense. Thus Rashi comments:

> And he erected there an altar; and he named it, "Mighty, the God of Israel"—The altar was not called "the God of Israel;" rather in celebration of the fact that God was with him and had saved him [from Esau] he named the altar in celebration of that miracle. In this way praise of God would be conveyed in calling it this name. Specifically, He who is Mighty—being the Holy One blessed be He—is the God of me for my name is Israel. And likewise we find concerning Moses "he called its (his altar's) name "The Lord is my miracle-worker" (Exod. 17:15). The altar was not called "Lord;" rather in celebration of the miracle, he named the altar to convey the praise of God; The Lord, He is my miracle-worker. But the rabbis creatively interpreted it to mean that God called Jacob "Mighty." Now the words of the Torah are like what ensues when the hammer is smashed on a rock in that they become fragmented (Jer. 23:29) into many meanings (B. Shab. 88b). My intention is to settle the straightforward sense of Scripture.

There is no question that Rashi understands the meaning of the text to be that the altar was named "Mighty, God of Israel," that is, "Mighty is the God of Israel." What Rashi must address is why Jacob names his altar at all. Rashi did not find the Talmud's query— "How could Jacob have called his altar 'Mighty'"—to be anything more than a way of introducing a creative, midrashic reading of the text. But this reading was not to be understood as invaliding the explicit, surface meaning of the narrative.

Rashi's reading is not all together out of line with Targum Onqelos' paraphrase in other places, a point not lost on the Ba'alei Ha-Tosafot, who reject Rashi's waving aside of the seriousness of Eliezer's query in the Talmud. Thus the Tosafists (B. Meg. 18a) explained the Talmud's warning about accepting Gen. 33:20 at face value:

> Perhaps you might imagine that Jacob called his altar "Mighty!" Now although we can object and claim that we find this in line with places where it is written in Scripture that Moses called his altar's name "The Lord is my miracle-worker (Exod. 17:15)," or where Gideon called his altar's name, "God is the peace-worker" (Judg. 6:24), and the Aramaic paraphrase translates that "he offered sacrifices and prayed there," that is not a valid objection. We can say in these cases that they were celebrating the miracle or the peace that occurred to them in those narratives by naming the altars as such. But in the case of Jacob, we cannot find any event that warrants Jacob's naming his altar "Mighty." Had Jacob in fact called it "Mighty," Scripture would certainly have indicated it more clearly.

The Ba'alei Ha-Tosafot object to Rashi's claim, finding his parallels unconvincing. In those other settings, the name of the altar reflects the theme of the narrative, while in the Jacob story, there is no theme in which the concept "Mighty" plays a role. The Talmud's query therefore is taken as definitive and defended at the expense of Rashi's comparative and sensitive reading. The Talmud is giving the only acceptable sense; Rashi is wrong.

One does not sense that the Tosafists simply wanted to defend the Talmud's methods while in reality they might be prepared to grant Rashi's point. As one reads the volumes of biblical exegesis produced in the French academies, one will not find support for such a position. The attempt to read Scripture as a closed document with only one meaning was gaining currency, and even the immense statures of Rashi and the Spanish commentators were not able to stem the strong tide that swept through Provence in the twelfth century. By contrast, the method of reading Scripture as revealing diverse meanings is best seen in the words of Ramban who, after quoting Rashi's comment says:

> All this is the language of Rashi and the Master is correct as far as the straightforward meaning of the verse goes. . . . But Onqelos translated it, "And he worshipped upon it to the Mighty, God of Israel". . . . But the Kabbalistic meaning is like the interpretation of the rabbis in tractate Megillah: From whence do we know that the Holy One, blessed be He, called Jacob "Mighty?" As it is said, "and he named him 'Mighty'—the God of Israel (did)." "Mighty." And there is in this matter a profound mystery which was mentioned elsewhere in Genesis Rabbah in different words: Jacob said to him, "You are the Lord of the upper realms and I am the lord of the lower realms." And the rabbis thereby alluded to their constant dictum that

"the image of Jacob was engraved on the Throne of Glory" and the sense is that the Shekhina is focused upon the Land of Israel. The Kabbalist will follow the thread.

Here we see the range of simultaneous meanings: Jacob names the altar, he prays upon it, the personage of Jacob is given metaphysical meaning in the Kabbalistic, sefirotic system. These are not competing senses, as the Baalei Ha-Tosafot would see them, but complimentary ones.

Bibliography

Greenberg, M., *Parshanut Hamikra Ha-Yehudit: Pirke Mavo* (Jerusalem, 1983; reprinted from *Encyclopedia Biblica*, Jerusalem, 1982: vol. 8, 641-737).
Plaut, W. Gunther, *The Torah: A Modern Commentary* (New York, 1981).
Segal, M.H., *Parshanut Hamikra* (Jerusalem, 1971).
Soloveitchik, M., and Rubashov, S., *Toledot Bikkoret Ha-Mikra* (Berlin, 1925).

HERBERT W. BASSER

F

FAMILY IN FORMATIVE JUDAISM: In the view of Rabbinic Judaism, husbands and wives owe one another loyalty to the common task and reliability in the carrying out of their reciprocal obligations, which are sexual, social, and economic. Their relationship finds its definition, therefore its rules and obligations, in the tasks the social order assigns to marriage: child-bearing and child-raising, on the one side, and the maintenance of the political economy of the holy people, Israel, on the other. The purpose of marriage is to produce the next generation and to support it. Marriage thus finds its definition in the larger social contract that the Torah means to set forth for Israel.

In this perspective, affection and love may emerge out of mutual trust and shared achievements—children raised, the household maintained—and, for one example, sages counsel husbands to afford sexual sat-

isfaction to their wives, saying that if the wife reaches orgasm first, male children—which men are assumed to want—will result. But romantic attitudes do not enjoy a high priority in the Rabbinic view of marriage and family. The governing language is theological, with the key-word being "holiness." The family is formed when a man betroths a woman and consummates the betrothal, and the word for "betroth" is "sanctify." The relationship of that woman to that man is one of sanctification; she is uniquely his, having consented to consecrate herself to him. God, of course, has a heavy stake in what is set apart as sanctified, whether an offering in the Temple, or a wife in the household. When, as we shall see, the marital relationship breaks down, the same considerations enter in, now through a process of deconsecration of the originally-sanctified marital bond. There too, Heaven supervises.

In the polygamous society taken for granted in the classical Judaic sources, to be sure, the husband owes the wife not a counterpart relationship of sexual sanctification but reliable support, both material and conjugal, as we shall see. The wife can have sexual relations only with her husband. But since he may have several wives, the husband does not enter into a counterpart status of sanctification to her. Still, when it comes to adultery, sages condemn the husband's as much as the wife's. This view is expressed in the context of sages' discussion of the ordeal of bitter water (Num. 5:11-31) imposed upon a wife accused of adultery. The pertinent verse of Scripture is, "And the man shall be free from iniquity, and the woman shall bear her iniquity" (Num. 5:31). The passage is interpreted in this way (B. Sot. 5:1 I:1D/28A):

> The sense of the foregoing verse of Scripture is that when the man is free of transgression, the water puts his wife to the test, and if the man is not free of transgression, the water does not put his wife to the test.

The ordeal imposed on the wife is null if, to begin with, the husband is not free of transgression. It goes without saying that sages also condemn sexual relations for money.

But we should err if we saw the family in classical Judaism through contemporary spectacles. People conventionally think of the nuclear (or extended) family as the primary social unit, distinct from society and autonomous of the political economy that sustains the social order. But in the Torah as set forth by the ancient sages husbands and wives and their children do not form the primary social unit, the building block of society. The household does, and it is not quite the same thing as the family. In the household, the family—husbands and wives and children, the husband's extended family and dependents—finds its defining context. By "the household" in the setting of classical Judaism is meant a coherent social unit, built upon ties of consanguinity and/or dependency, which is also a unit of production, ordinarily meaning agricultural production.

Only when we grasp what is at stake in the family, which is the household, shall we understand the rules governing what the husband owes the wife and the wife to the husband. To ask about husbands, wives, and children in Judaism, we must find the context in which their mutual obligations take shape, and that means, how husbands, wives, and children work together to support the household.

All relationships within the household, even those deemed the most significant, between parents and among parents and children, are governed by the needs of the larger social unit, the household itself. That is what defines the smallest whole building block of the social order of Israel, so far as classical Judaism sees matters. The aim of the Torah as sages expound it is to provide for a stable, nurturing relationship between husband and wife. Both parties to the marriage are given a heavy stake in the stability and comfort of the household, and that is why neither party is likely to risk for little reason the material and social benefits of the marriage. Indeed, in a society that made scant provision for the isolated individual, housing being organized by households for example, everyone in the household had good reason to carry out his or her public duties. Households locate themselves in villages or towns, and, within them, in courtyards that themselves debouch onto alleyways, then opening into large public places. So to imagine the family in its social context as Judaism in its classical sources portrays the family, we have to conceive of a world in which mothers, fathers, and children, grandparents, aunts and uncles and cousins, servants (paid a wage in cash or in kind) and slaves (people who sell their work and make their master's will their own) not only share a common residence but also work together in a mostly-subsistence farm, part of a barter-economy.

It follows that the singularity of the household lies not in its physical let alone genealogical traits but in its definition of the "family" as a distinct unit of economic production. What made a household into a household was its economic definition of the "family" as a complete unit of production, and the householder—ordinarily male—was the one who controlled that unit of production; that fact made all the difference, and not that all of the household's members were related (that was not the fact at all), nor that all of them lived in a single building distinct from other single buildings, which certainly was not the case. What made the household into a social unit was the economic fact that all its constituents related to one another in some genealogical pattern and also worked within the same economic unit, in a setting distinct from other equivalently autonomous economic units. In the idiom of the Mishnah, the first document of formative Judaism, they *ate* at the same table, and eating should be understood as an abstraction, not merely as a reference to the fact that people sat down and broke bread together.

The Written Torah (that is, "the Hebrew Scriptures," "the Old Testament") does not prepare us for such a picture of society and its building blocks. Ancient Israelite thinkers in Scripture, e.g., the priestly authorship of Leviticus, the prophetic schools that produced Isaiah's and Amos's conceptions, discerned within, and as, "Israel" classes identified by their sacerdotal and genealogical traits and functions; or a mixed multitude of poor and rich. We look in vain in the imagination of the Deuteronomist writers in their several layers for a conception of an "Israel" composed of neatly arranged farms run by landowners, of families made up of households, an Israel with each such household arrayed in its hierarchy, from householder on top, to slave on bottom. But that is how the Oral Torah sees things. Critical to the system of the Mishnah that forms the foundation of classical Judaism is its principal social entity, the village, comprising households; and the progressive model, from the household to village to "all Israel," comprehensively describes whatever of "Israel" the authorship at hand has chosen to describe. The family then is subsumed within the community, its framework defined by the expectation of self-sufficiency, and its governance aimed at justice. Judaism in its classical sources thus focuses upon the society organized in relationship to the control of the means of production—the farm, for the household is always the agricultural unit. That is the context in which we address the situation of the family and the relationships within the family, in particular father and mother to children, and children to parents, husbands to wives and vice versa.

If we cannot define the family apart from its position at the heart of the household, we also should not confuse the household with class-status, e.g., thinking of the householder as identical with the wealthy. The opposite is suggested on every page of the Mishnah and the Talmuds, in which householders vie with craftsmen for ownership of the leavings of the loom and the chips left behind by the adz. The household, rather, forms an economic and a social classification, defined by function, specifically, its economic function. A poor household was a household, and (in theory, the Mishnah's authorship knows none such in practice) a rich landholding that did not function as a center for a social and economic unit, e.g., an industrial—not a subsistence, family—farm, was not a household. Within the household, all local, as distinct from cultic, economic, therefore social, activities and functions were held together. For the unit of production comprised also the unit of social organization, and, of greater import still, formed the building block of all larger social, now also political, units, with special reference to the village.

In the conception at hand, which sees Israel as made up of households and villages, the economic unit also framed the social one, and the two together composed, in conglomerates, the political one, hence a political economy initiated within an economic definition formed out of the elements of production. The law of the Mishnah makes a single cogent statement that the organizing unit of society and politics finds its definition in the irreducible unit of economic production. The Mishnah conceives no other economic unit of production than the household, though it recognizes that such existed; its authorship perceived no other social unit of organization than the household and the conglomeration of households, though that limited vision omitted all reference to substantial parts of the population perceived to be present, e.g., craftsmen, the unemployed, the landless, and the like. The social foundation of the economy of the Mishnah therefore rested on the household, which in turn formed the foundation of the village, imagined to comprise the community of households, in the charge of small farmers who were free and who owned their land.

How then shall we briefly define the family? The head of the house, or householder, is taken for granted also to be the father of the family around which the household takes shape. In that context we may define the family as the persons that stand to inherit the property of one another or benefit therefrom. Within the villages, any Israelite male was assumed to possess the potential to become a householder, that is, in context, the master of a domain, a landholder. So in that context, the householder also is the father. What about the mother—can the householder be the mother, not the father? I cannot point to a passage in which it is assumed that a woman is head of a household. But in the law of the Torah, women can own land and engage in the economic activities of a household, so the system theoretically could accommodate a woman-householder. In practice, however, a woman is always taken to relate to a man: to her father, then her husband, when he is alive, and, when he is deceased, to her male sons or step-sons by her deceased husband. These support her as a widow. It is further taken for granted that when a woman is divorced or widowed, she will remarry within a brief spell, so that the alimony provided in the marriage-settlement is meant to tide her over until she does so. Or she reverts to her "father's house," which means that she rejoins the household of her father, alive, if dead, of her brothers.

With these theoretical remarks in hand, let us turn to the practical statements of the law of the Torah set forth in the Mishnah. These define what the wife owes the husband and the husband the wife. The law focuses, for the wife, on the labor that she owes, and, for the husband, on the restraint he must exercise, the respect for the wife's auton-omy he must display. Stated simply: the wife or wives (we deal, in ancient times, with a polygamous society) represent participants in the household, and the wife owes the husband the fruit of her labor. The husband reciprocates by honoring the wife's desires and attitudes and refraining from trying to control and isolate her. The wife's domestic duties encompass these (M. Ket. 5:5):

A. These are the kinds of labor which a woman performs for her husband:
B. she (1) grinds flour, (2) bakes bread, (3) does laundry, (4) prepares meals, (5) gives suck to her child, (6) makes the bed, (7) works in wool.
C. [If] she brought with her a single slave girl, she does not (1) grind, (2) bake bread, or (3) do laundry.
D. [If she brought] two, she does not (4) prepare meals and does not (5) feed her child.
E. [If she brought] three, she does not (6) make the bed for him and does not (7) work in wool.
F. If she brought four, she sits on a throne.
G. R. Eliezer says, "Even if she brought him a hundred slave girls, he forces her to work in wool,
H. "for idleness leads to unchastity."
I. Rabban Simeon b. Gamaliel says, "Also: He who prohibits his wife by a vow from performing any labor puts her away and pays off her marriage contract. For idleness leads to boredom."

The wife is expected to conduct herself in a modest and pious manner, and if she does not do so, the husband may divorce her without paying the alimony that is required in the marriage-agreement—a huge incentive for the wife to keep the law (M. Ket. 7:6):

A. And those women go forth without the payment of the marriage contract at all:
B. She who transgresses against the law of Moses and Jewish law.
C. And what is the law of Moses [which she has transgressed]? [If] (1) she feeds him food which has not been tithed, or (2) has sexual relations with him while she is menstruating, or [if] (3) she does not cut off her dough-offering, or [if] (4) she vows and does not carry out her vow.
D. And what is the Jewish law? If (1) she goes out with her hair flowing loose, or (2) she spins in the marketplace, or (3) she talks with just anybody.

E. Abba Saul says, "Also: if she curses his parents in his presence."

F. R. Tarfon says, "Also: if she is a loud-mouth."

G. What is a loudmouth? When she talks in her own house, her neighbors can hear her voice.

The husband, for his part, owes his wives not only the required domestic support for which Scripture provides—food, clothing, conjugal relations—but also an allowance that she may spend as she sees fit (M. Ket. 5:9):

A. He gives her in addition a silver *ma'ah* [a sixth of a *denar*] for her needs [per week].

B. And she eats with him on the Sabbath night [when sexual relations are owing].

C. And if he does not give her a silver *ma'ah* for her needs, the fruit of her labor belongs to her.

D. And how much work does she do for him?

E. The weight of five *selas* of warp must she spin for him in Judea (which is ten selas weight in Galilee), or the weight of ten *selas* of woof in Judah (which are twenty *selas* in Galilee).

F. And if she was nursing a child, they take off [the required weight of wool which she must spin as] the fruit of her labor, and they provide more food for her.

G. Under what circumstances?

H. In the case of the most poverty-stricken man in Israel.

I. But in the case of a weightier person, all follows the extent of his capacity [to support his wife].

We see in the requirements of husband to wife and wife to husband heavy emphasis upon shared personal and material obligations. The wife brings to the marriage her dowry, which stands for her share in the father's estate; this reverts to her (hence to her father) in the event of divorce or the husband's demise. So the marriage represents the formation of a partnership based on quite practical considerations. Matters of emotion enter in—but mainly as the husband's responsibility.

What does the husband owe the wife? As to sexual relations, however many wives a husband has, each woman's rights are to be carefully respected; marital rape is forbidden, and a woman who invites sexual relations is highly praised and will produce remarkable children (B. Erub. 10:10:8 II.9/100b):

A. Said R. Ammi bar Abba said R. Assi, "It is forbidden for someone to rape his wife or force his wife to carry out the religious duty [of sexual relations]: 'And he that hastes with his feet sins' (Prov. 19:2)."

B. And said R. Joshua b. Levi, "Whoever rapes his wife will have unworthy children."

C. Said R. Samuel bar Nahmani said R. Jonathan, "Any man whose wife calls him to sexual relations will have children of the like of which the generation of our lord, Moses, didn't have, as it is said, 'Take you men wise, understanding, and known among your tribes and I will make them rulers over you' (Deut. 1:13); and 'So I took the chiefs of your tribes, wise men and known' (Deut. 1:15)—without reference to 'understanding.' And with reference to Leah, it is written, 'And Leah went out to meet him and said, you must come to me, for I have surely hired you' (Gen. 30:16), and it is written, 'Issachar is a large-boned ass' (Gen. 49:14), and elsewhere, 'And of the children of Issachar, who were men that had understanding of the times' (1 Chr. 12:33). This was Leah's reward, proving that it is meritorious for a woman to demand sexual relations."

That the perspective is the husband's presents no surprise, the entire system being framed by men. Correct behavior with women requires modesty and deference (B. Ber. 9:1 XVII.6, 8/61b):

A. He who counts out coins into a woman's hand from his own in order to have a chance to stare at her, even if such a one has in hand Torah and good deeds like Moses, our master, will not be quit of the judgment of Gehenna. For it is said, "Hand to hand, he shall not escape from evil" (Prov. 11:21). He shall not escape from the judgment of Gehenna.

So much for matters of sexual modesty and restraint. But the husband owes the wife much more than that. The husband may not abuse the wife, may not try to keep her away from the normal social relations that she should enjoy as an independent personality, and must accord to her all of the rights and dignities of a free woman (M. Ket. 7:1):

A. He who prohibits his wife by vow from deriving benefit from him

B. for a period of thirty days, appoints an agent to provide for her.

C. [If the effects of the vow are not nullified] for a longer period, he puts her away and pays off her marriage contract.

D. R. Judah says, "In the case of a [non-priestly] Israelite, for [a vow lasting] one month he may continue in the marriage, but for two [or more], he must put her away and pay off her marriage contract.

E. "But in the case of a [member of the] priestly [caste], for two months he may continue in the marriage, and after three he must put her away and pay off her marriage contract."

Since, in the marital negotiations, the husband receives property that, in the event of divorce, he must restore to the wife's father's household, divorce is not undertaken lightly. It involves not only a year of alimony, but also loss of considerable capital or real estate. Hence the husband has a strong incentive not to impose a vow upon the wife that denies her the right to gain benefit from him, e.g., eat at his table, share his bed, and the like.

The same considerations strongly discourage the husband from brow-beating or otherwise trying to manipulate or control the wife. If he imposes on her a vow not to eat even one sort of fruit or vegetable, he must divorce her, giving her her freedom and losing the capital she has brought into his household (M. Ket. 7:2):

A. He who prohibits his wife by vow from tasting any single kind of produce whatsoever must put her away and pay off her marriage contract.

B. R. Judah says, "In the case of an Israelite, [if the vow is] for one day he may persist in the marriage, but [if it is] for two he must put her away and pay off her marriage contract.

C. "And in the case of a priest, [if it is] for two days he may persist in the marriage, but [if it is] for three he must put her away and pay off her marriage contract."

The law shows remarkably little patience for the intrusive husband, who would transform his wife into his slave, lacking freedom of will. The same protection encompasses the wife's right to adorn herself as a beautiful woman (M. Ket. 7:3):

A. He who prohibits his wife by a vow from adorning herself with any single sort of jewelry must put her away and pay off her marriage contract.

B. R. Yose says, "In the case of poor girls, [if] he has not assigned a time limit [he must divorce them].

C. "But in the case of rich girls, [he may persist in the marriage if he set a time limit] of thirty days."

The husband must permit the wife to maintain a circle of friends and relationships beyond the limits of the household. The husband may not interfere in the wife's relationships with her father and family; he may not stop her from seeing her relatives (M. Ket. 7:4):

A. He who prohibits his wife by a vow from going home to her father's house—

B. when he [father] is with her in [the same] town,

C. [if it is] for a month, he may persist in the marriage.

D. [If it is] for two, he must put her away and pay off her marriage contract.

E. And when he is in another town, [if the vow is in effect] for one festival season he may persist in the marriage. [But if the vow remains in force] for three, he must put her away and pay off her marriage contract.

The wife thus has the absolute right to visit her father's household pretty much when her duties permit. Nor may the husband interfere with the wife's normal social intercourse. Here too, if he tries to keep her caged at home and to cut off her ties to other people, particularly the society of women, he loses heavily (M. Ket. 7:5):

A. He who prohibits his wife by a vow from going to a house of mourning or to a house of celebration must put her away and pay off her marriage contract,

B. because he locks the door before her.

C. But if he claimed that he took such a vow because of some other thing, he is permitted to impose such a vow.

Finally, intimate details of the marriage must be kept private; the woman has a right to her dignity:

D. [If he took a vow] saying to her, (1) "On condition that you say to So-and-so what you said to me," or (2) "what I said to you," or (3) "that you draw water and pour it out onto the ash heap,"
E. he must put her away and pay off her marriage contract.

In these and other ways, the husband is given a weighty incentive to treat the wife with enormous respect. And, as we have seen, if the woman behaves improperly, not keeping the Torah of Moses, committing adultery, for example, she too loses the assets she has brought to the marriage and the household. The provisions of her marriage-settlement are null; the husband keeps the dowry; and she loses everything.

How, then, is the mother-wife-daughter positioned within the household? Along with slaves and minors, women form a classification of Israelites deemed not fully capable of independent will, intentionality, entire responsibility, and action and therefore subject not only to God's will but also to the will of another, the husband or father in the case of the woman, the master in the case of the slave, and the parent in the case of the child. In a number of specific contexts, moreover, a man and woman are differentiated in the functions that they perform or to which they are obligated. A man imposes a Nazirite vow on his son, but a woman does not impose a Nazirite vow upon her son (M. Naz. 4:6). A man brings the hair offering for the Nazirite vow of his father, but a woman does not bring a hair offering for the Nazirite vow of her father. The man sells his daughter, but the woman does not sell her daughter, in line with Exod. 21:6. The man arranges for a betrothal of his daughter, but the woman does not arrange for the betrothal of her daughter (M. Qid. 2:1). A man who incurs the death penalty is stoned naked, but a woman is not stoned naked. A man is hanged after being put to death, but a woman is not hanged (M. San. 6:3-4). A man, but not a woman, is sold to make restitution for having stolen something (Exod. 22:2). The matter is further amplified at M. Qid. 1:7:

A. For every commandment concerning the son to which the father is subject—men are liable, and women are exempt.

B. And for every commandment concerning the father to which the son is subject, men and women are equally liable.
C. For every positive commandment dependent upon the time [of day or year], men are liable, and women are exempt.
D. And for every positive commandment not dependent upon the time, men and women are equally liable.
E. For every negative commandment, whether dependent upon the time or not dependent upon the time, men and women are equally liable,
F. except for not marring the corners of the beard, not rounding the corners of the head (Lev. 19:27), and not becoming unclean because of the dead (Lev. 21:1).

This matter is clarified at T. Qid. 1:10-11:

A. What is a positive commandment dependent upon the time [for which men are liable but women exempt (M. Qid. 1:7C)]?
B. For example, building the Sukkah, taking the *lulab*, putting on phylacteries.
C. What is a positive commandment not dependent upon the time (M. Qid. 1:7D)?
D. For example, restoring lost property to its rightful owner, sending forth the bird, building a parapet, and putting on *sisit* (show-fringes).
E. R. Simeon declares women exempt from the requirement of wearing *sisit*, because it is a positive commandment dependent upon time.
A. What is a commandment pertaining to the son concerning the father [to which men and women are equally liable (M. Qid. 1:7B)]?
B. Giving him food to eat and something to drink and clothing him and covering him and taking him out and bringing him in and washing his face, his hands, and his feet.
C. All the same are men and women. But the husband has sufficient means to do these things for the child, and the wife does not have sufficient means to do them,
D. for others have power over her.

In a moment, we shall see how the Talmud takes up the issue of what the father owes to the son.

It is taken for granted that women are subject to men, daughters to fathers, then wives to husbands; widows are assumed to return to their fathers' households. Marriage is the natural condition of man and woman (B. Yeb. 6:6 II.19-21):

A. Said R. Hanilai, "Any man who has no wife lives without joy, blessing, goodness: Joy: 'and you shall rejoice, you and your house' (Deut. 14:26). Blessing: 'to cause a blessing to rest on your house' (Ezek. 44:30). Goodness: 'it is not good that man should be alone' (Gen. 2:18)."

B. In the West they say: without Torah and without a wall of refuge. Without Torah: "Is it that I have no help in me and that sound wisdom is driven entirely out of me" (Job 6:13). Without a wall of refuge: "A woman shall form a wall about a man" (Jer. 31:22).

C. Raba bar Ulla said, "Without peace: 'and you shall know that your tent is in peace, and you shall visit your habitation and shall miss nothing' (Job 5:24)."

D. He who loves his wife as he loves himself, he who honors her more than he honors himself, he who raises up his sons and daughters in the right path, and he who marries them off close to the time of their puberty—of such a one, Scripture says, "And you shall know that your tabernacle shall be in peace and you shall visit your habitation and you shall not sin" (Job 5:24).

So much for the household as the setting for the relationship of husbands and wives. But what about the larger society of holy Israel, the world in which the Torah affords access to, and knowledge of, God through God's own self-manifestation?

Now, we realize, the supreme religious activity focuses upon Torah-study, ordinarily as a disciple to a master. But by definition a woman cannot become a disciple to a master; she is the wife of her husband, and no other social role is open to her. Then how do wives and mothers participate in the merit of Torah-study? It is rarely through active participation in the processes of learning and debate. Women come to listen to the study of the Torah and bring their children as an act of merit as well (Abot d'R. Nathan XVIII:II.1):

A. When R. Joshua got old, his disciples came to visit him. He said to them, "My sons, what was the new point that you had today in school?"

B. They said to him, "We are your disciples, and your water [alone] do we drink."

C. He said to them, "God forbid! It is impossible that there is a generation of sages that is orphaned [and without suitable guidance]. Whose week was it to teach?"

D. They said to him, "It was the week of R. Eleazar b. Azariah."

E. He said to them, "And what was the topic of the narrative today?"

F. They said to him, "It was the passage that begins, 'Assemble the people, the men and the women and the children' (Deut. 31:12)."

G. He said to them, "And what did he expound in that connection?"

H. They said to him, "This is how he interpreted it. 'The men come to learn, the women to listen, but why do the children come? It is to provide the occasion for the gaining of a reward for those who bring them.'"

I. He said to them, "You had a good pearl in your hands, and you wanted to make me lose it! If you had come only to let me hear this one thing, it would have been enough for me."

In the end, what is the husband's primary obligation to his wives? Apart from the three requirements that Scripture sets forth—food, clothing, conjugal relations—he must bring peace to his household; in the situation of polygamy, that represents a considerable assignment.

What do parents owe their children? A religion that constructs its system through normative rules and makes its statements by formulating laws has no difficulty answering questions of obligation. An explicit reply to the question at hand is set forth in a simple sentence. The father owes the son a number of specific duties. He must bring him into the covenant of Abraham through circumcision. He must redeem him, if the son is a firstborn and the father is not of the priestly caste, by handing over to a priest five silver coins (Exod. 13:11-16); he must teach him Torah; he must get him a wife; and he must teach him a trade. In these ways the father provides for the son's religious, personal, and economic future (T. Qid. 1:11F-H):

B. The father is responsible with respect to his son to circumcise him, to redeem him, to teach him Torah, to marry him off to a woman, and to teach him a trade.

C. And there are those who say, also to teach him to swim.

D. R. Judah says, "Anyone who does not teach his son a trade is as though he trains him to be a gangster."

But both parents also owe their children an honorable example of how to conduct themselves. And they owe the children a heritage of virtue and not of sin, because Scripture is explicit that God visits the iniquity of the fathers upon the children but shows steadfast love for a thousand generations of those who love him and keep his commandments (Exod. 20:5-6). Sages clarify the former matter: God punishes the sons who continue the sins of the father, but not those who repent of the fathers' sins (Mekhilta d'R. Ishmael LII:I):

> 8.A. "visiting the iniquity of the fathers upon the children:"
>   B. That is when there is no break in the chain, but not when there is a break in the chain.
>   C. How so?
>   D. In the case of a wicked person, son of a wicked person, son of a wicked person.
>   F. When Moses heard this matter, "Moses made haste and bowed his head toward the earth and worshipped" (Exod. 34:8).
>   G. He said, "God forbid, there cannot be among all the Israelites a wicked person, son of a wicked person, son of a wicked person."
> 9.A. Might one suppose that, just as the measure of punishment covers four generations, so the measure of goodness covers the same span of four generations?
>   B. Scripture says, "to thousands."
>   C. If "to thousands," might I understand that the minimum plural of "thousands" is two?
>   D. Scripture says, "to a thousand generations" (Deut. 7:9), that is to say, to generations beyond all discovery and all counting.

The question of fairness is implicit: if the father has sinned, what has the son done to merit punishment? The question finds its answer in a revision of the facts of the matter: only if the son continues the father's tradition will be punished as the father was.

Scripture assigns yet another obligation to the parents, defining what they owe to the community in the up-bringing of their children. Parents must raise honorable children and, if needed, take action to protect the community from them. This is explained by sages' conception that humanity will live beyond the grave, being raised from the dead at the last judgment. Then those who have sinned and atoned for their sin in this life will enter eternal life, as much as those who did not sin at all. If a sinner or criminal is put to death, that atones for the sin or crime; then the sinner or criminal dies innocent, and so will enjoy life eternal. Thus sages explain Scripture's rule that "a stubborn and rebellious son, who will not obey the voice of his father or the voice of his mother" is referred to the "elders of the city." The parents tell the government, "This, our son, is stubborn and rebellious, he will not obey our voices, he is a glutton and a drunkard," and, found guilty, this son is put to death (Deut. 21:18-21). Sages explain: "A rebellious and incorrigible son is tried on account of [what he may] end up to be. Let him die while yet innocent, and let him not die when he is guilty" (M. San. 8:5).

Sages provide so many alibis and exceptions that, they conclude, no one has ever been tried, convicted, and put to death as a "rebellious and incorrigible son." Still, this is a matter of theory worth attention in its own right. For the point sages wish to make is that parents owe their children the certainty that the child remains eligible to stand in judgment and to gain the resurrection out of the grave that is the promise of God to holy Israel. Parents thus bear responsibility for their children now and in the world to come. Having joined God in the creation of life—for three partners have a stake in every person, the mother, the father, and God—parents owe children the capacity to earn a living, the model of the life of honor and dignity, and a chance at the ultimate promise of the Torah, eternal life and triumph over death.

What do children owe their parents? The Ten Commandments deem honor of father and mother one of the principles of God's dominion; paying honor to parents represents a primary act of acceptance of God's rule (Exod. 20:12). Then sages take as their task to spell out what honor of parents means. They want concrete actions of respect, support, and obligation: supporting parents with food, drink, and clothing:

A. "Honor your father and your mother [that your days may be long in the land which the Lord your God gives you (Exod. 20:12)]:"
B. Might I infer that this is with words?
C. Scripture says, "Honor the Lord with your substance" (Prov. 3:9).
D. That means, with food, drink, and fresh garments.

That honoring parents is tantamount to honoring God is made explicit. The reason is not difficult to fathom. It is stated explicitly at B. Qid. 1:7 II.2/30B-31A:

A. *Our rabbis have taught on Tannaite authority:*
B. Three form a partnership in the creation of a human being, the Holy One, blessed be He, one's father, and one's mother. When someone honors father and mother, said the Holy One, blessed be He, "I credit it to them as though I had lived among them and they honored me."

The same view is spelled out: honoring parents is like honoring God, cursing parents is like cursing God (Sifra Qedoshim CXCV: II.2):

B. It is said, "Honor your father and your mother" (Exod. 20:12), and it is further said, "Honor the Lord with your wealth" (Prov. 3:9).
C. Scripture thereby establishes an analogy between the honor of father and mother and the honor of the Omnipresent.
D. It is said, "He who curses his father or his mother will certainly die" (Prov. 20: 20), and it is said, "Any person who curses his God will bear his sin" (Lev. 24:15).
E. Scripture thereby establishes an analogy between cursing father and mother and cursing the Omnipresent.
F. But it is not possible to refer to smiting Heaven [in the way in which one is warned not to hit one's parents].
G. And that is entirely reasonable, for all three of them are partners [in a human being].

Why should the parents be given the same honor as God? When we recall that the act of procreation recapitulates God's act of creation, making life, we realize, possessed of the power of creation, parents are like God. Since the parents compare with God, the honor owing to God extends to them.

So much for the matter in principle. What, in real life, is involved in honoring parents? Sages set forth cases to make their point that there is no limit within what is permissible in the Torah. They appealed to the example of a righteous gentile, who gave up great wealth in order not to disturb his father's sleep ((B. Qid. 1:7 II.2/30B-31A):

II.10C. Said R. Judah said Samuel, "They asked R. Eliezer, to what extent is one obligated to honor one's father and one's mother? He said to them, 'Go and observe how a certain gentile has treated his father in Ashkelon, and Dama b. Netinah is his name."
D. On one occasion they wanted to buy from him precious stones for the ephod, in the amount of six hundred thousand (*R. Kahana repeated as the Tannaite version*, eight hundred thousand) but the keys were lying under his father's pillow, and he would not disturb him. Another year the Holy One, blessed be He, gave him his reward, for a red cow was born to him in his corral, and sages of Israel came to him. He said to them, "I know full well that if I should demand of you all the money in the world, you will give it to me. But now I ask of you only that sum of money that I lost in honor of my father."
E. And said R. Hanina, "Now if someone who is not subject to commandments acts in such a way, then if someone who is subject to the commandment acts in such a way, all the more so! For said R. Hanina, 'Greater is he who is commanded and acts on that account than he who is not commanded and acts on that account.'"

Not only so, but honor of parents is relative to the case; there are no fixed rules:

II.13A. A Tannaite statement of Abimi b. R. Abbahu: There is he who feeds his father pheasant but this drives the son from the world, and there is he who binds his father up to the grinding wheel, and this brings the son into the world to come.

The first son fed his father pheasant, but when the father asked how he could afford it said, "It's none of your business, chew and eat." By contrast, a son who was grinding when his father was summoned for the corvée, said to him, "You grind for me and I'll go in your place."

Sages themselves set the example. They were treated with great deference, being holy men, but that did not stop them from accepting the most demeaning tasks for the parents:

> II.16A. R. Tarfon's mother—whenever she wanted to get into bed, he would bend down and let her climb up on his back, and when she wanted to get out, she would step down on him. He went and praised himself in the schoolhouse. They said to him, "So? You still haven't got to half the honor that is owing! Has she thrown down a money bag in your presence into the sea, without your answering back to her?"

Sages' theory that honoring parents was honoring God found realization in a specific sage's attitude:

> II.17A. R. Joseph—when he heard the sound of his mother's steps, he said, "Let me arise before the Presence of God, who approaches."

The emphasis upon the theological basis for honoring parents reminds us, once more, that Judaism in its classical statement sets forth not random teachings and wise sayings but a system in which each component fits together with all others. That is because the details of the system work in small ways to realize the system's larger message. Truisms about honoring parents turn out to recapitulate the main point, that God forms the center of Israel's existence, Israel's task is to know and love God by forming a holy society worthy of God's rule, so that, at the end of days, Israel—meaning, all who accept God's self-manifestation in the Torah—will stand in judgment and enter into eternal life. We have come a long way from the requirements of the Israelite household—but only to discover what is at stake in that household, with its union of this-worldly and transcendental tasks and obligations.

What happens when the family breaks down? If the relationship of the wife to the husband is sanctified, at her assent, through betrothal and consummation of the marriage, how and at whose initiative is that bond of sanctification dissolved—secularized? When the family breaks down, the husband has the power to dissolve the marriage. Then the wife returns to her father's house, with designated portions of her dowry, and supported by alimony for a year. That is the material result of the breakdown of the marriage; the household is left unaffected, except in the specific, material ways involving alimony and the dowry. But how is the original act of sanctification nullified? Our special interest focuses upon the way by which the status, or relationship, of sanctification is removed and how the woman reenters the status of the unattached woman. Here the foci of sages' interest prove consequential. For man's part in the matter, everything depends upon a document, which properly done on earth is ratified in Heaven as an act consequential in the sight of God. The media of sanctification involve the willing exchange of money, a writ, or sexual relations with betrothal the intent. The consummation of the union depends, further, on the provision of the marriage-contract, which protects the woman in the event of divorce or the husband's death by providing for alimony. In these transactions, the woman's former status is removed by the provision of a document that nullifies the token of betrothal and the relationship that represents and that brings about the enforcement of the marriage-contract and its provisions. So the document at the end—for which Scripture makes provision—completes the document at the outset, of which Scripture knows nothing, but for which the logic of the transaction, matching beginning to end, surely calls.

To understand how we deconsecrate what has been sanctified we have to consider the analogous situation, the sanctification of an animal for the altar of the Temple in Jerusalem, at which point the animal may not be used for any other purpose. When a farmer consecrates an animal for a particular cultic purpose, e.g., as a sin-offering, the transaction involves a very specific process. He must identify the particular sin that is to be expiated by the particular animal (or in the case of what is unclear, designate an animal in a way that takes account of his uncertainty as to the sin he has committed). He must then make certain that the officiating priest makes the offering "in the proper name," meaning, it must fall into the category of offering that is required and no other; the act of tossing the blood must be performed with the correct, appropriate, particular intentionality. Once the intentionality of the farmer has been realized in the tossing of the blood, what is left of the blood is no longer sacred. It may be used as fertilizer. So the key to the status of sanctification is the intentionality of the farmer, and the moment at which that intentionality has reached fruition, the status of the sacred falls away from what is no longer required to carry out that intention.

What happens if the person's intentionality in sanctifying the beast is not realized? If he does not utilize the animal he has designated, or consecrated, to the altar for his particular sin, he must undertake the appropriate process of disposing of the still-consecrated beast in a manner appropriate to its status and, more to the point, to the purpose that, by his act of will, he has planned to use the beast. When it comes to the transformation of the woman's status, from secular and available to any appropriate Israelite to sacred to a single, specified individual male, the process of sanctification is equally particular, and the result equivalently decisive.

Then what brings about the deconsecration of the woman takes on heavy significance, since Heaven, as much as man and woman, takes a keen interest in the process. The counterpart to the process of the disposition of the beast sanctified to the altar for a given purpose differs at one fundamental point. The man's act of will in consecrating the beast cannot be nullified by a corresponding act of will to deconsecrate it. Scripture is very clear on that point, forbidding even an act of substitution of one beast for another (Lev. 27: 11). If the man should decide he wishes to offer beast B rather than beast A, beast B is consecrated, but beast A retains its prior status. That is because an additional participant in the transaction has had his say and can-

not now be dismissed, and that, of course, is Heaven. Once consecrated, the beast leaves the status of consecration only with Heaven's assent, meaning, by following the procedures that the law deems appropriate.

Heaven has a different relationship to the marriage, and other parties enter in. When the husband determines that he wishes to deconsecrate the wife, he has the power to do so only in such a manner that the wife is fully informed and takes an active role in the transaction, receiving the writ of divorce—initiated solely on the husband's volition to be sure—on terms that she has the power to dictate. The law states eloquently that she must play a fully conscious role in the transaction when it says she may not be asleep when the writ is handed over to her, and she may not be misinformed as to its character. Thus she must know that the document is a writ of divorce; she must be awake; if she sets conditions for the reception of the document, these must be met. In these fundamental ways, she accedes to the process of deconsecration, to the secularization of her status within the Israelite household.

Does Heaven take an equivalent role to its engagement in the disposition of the sanctified beast and if so, where and how does that engagement take effect? The answer is that Heaven, not only the husband and wife, concerns itself with the change in the woman's status as holy. Where, in the repertoire of the law, does that concern express itself? It is in the valid preparation of the document itself. That document—properly written, properly witnessed, properly handed over—serves to deconsecrated the woman, as surely as the rites of disposition of the consecrated animal not used for its correct purpose deal with the change in status of that beast. The document is the medium of effecting, or of annulling, the status of consecration. What gives the document effect?

The answer is in two parts. First the witnesses who certify the document are the key-element in the process; the document is validated by valid witnesses, and lacking valid witnesses, even though it is correctly written and delivered, it has no effect at all. The witnesses attest not only to the facts of what is incised in the writing but also to the specificity of the writing: this man, this woman, this document. Then what is to be said about the witnesses to the preparation of the document, for whom do they stand? Given Heaven's stake in the transaction and the witnesses' status as non-participants, we may offer only one answer: the witnesses validate the document and give it effect because they stand as Heaven's surrogates. Israelite males not related to the parties, the witnesses accord cognizance on earth in behalf of Heaven to that change in intentionality and status that the document attests. They confirm what is at stake in the entire transaction: Heaven has been informed of the change of intention on the part of the husband, releasing the wife from her status of sanctification to him. So the change in intentionality must be attested on earth in behalf of Heaven. And that which is certified by the witnesses is not only the validity of the writing of the document but the explicit transaction that has brought about the writing: the husband has instructed the scribe to write the writ of divorce, that particular writ of divorce, for his wife, for the named wife and no other woman (even of the same name). When he has done that, pronouncing his intent to nullify the relationship of sanctification that he proffered and the woman accepted, then all else follows.

But Heaven wants something else as well. Not only must the intention be articulated explicitly in the transaction at hand and no other, but the document itself must give evidence of counterpart specificity. The law specifies irregularities of two classes, first, those that do not invalidate the transaction, second, those that so completely invalidate the transaction that the original status of sanctification retains effect, despite what the husband has said, despite what the wife has correctly received by way of documentary confirmation of the change of intentionality and therefore status, his and hers, respectively. That represents a most weighty result, with long-term consequences. What conditions do not nullify the transaction? Confusing the writ of divorce of two couples bearing the same names presents a situation

that can be sorted out. If the two writs of divorce are written side by side, so that the signatures have to be assigned to the respective writs, that is a problem that can be solved. The document may be spread over two sheets: If one left over part of the text and wrote it on the second page, and the witnesses are below, it is valid.

On the other hand, we have two explicit situations that produce the catastrophe of a totally invalid exchange, such that the woman remains sanctified to the husband who has indicated the intention of divorcing her. That is to say, in two circumstances the husband's intentionality does not register with Heaven (M. Git. 8:5, 8:8):

> If he wrote the writ of divorce dating it according to an era which is not applicable, for example, according to the era of the Medes, according to the era of the Greeks, according to the building of the Temple, according to the destruction of the Temple, [if] he was in the east and wrote, "In the west," in the west and wrote, "In the east," she goes forth from this one [whom she married on the strength of the divorce from the former husband] and from that one [the first husband]. And she requires a writ of divorce from this one and from that one.

> If the scribe wrote a writ of divorce for the man and a quittance [a receipt, given to the husband for the marriage contract payment] for the woman, and he erred and gave the writ of divorce to the woman and the quittance to the man, and they then exchanged them for one another, and if, after a while, lo, the writ of divorce turns up in the hand of the man, and the quittance in the hand of the woman—she goes forth from this one and from that one.

The two rules produce this question: who has the power to nullify even the effect of the intentionality of the husband? It is the scribe. If he errs in dating the document, or if he errs and writes down the wrong location of the participant, then, whatever the husband's intentionality and whatever the wife's impression of what has taken place, the writ is null, and the result is as specified, chaotic. So too if the scribe made a mistake in transmitting the documents that are to be exchanged, the transaction is null.

Then the question presses: why has the

scribe so critical a role in the transaction that he can utterly upset the intentionality of the one and the consequent conclusion drawn by the other party, husband and wife, respectively? The reason is clear: the law attributes to the scribe a role in the transaction as critical, in its way, as the role of the husband in commissioning the document and the wife in receiving it. And what is it that the scribe can do to ruin the transaction? First, he can commit the unpardonable sin of not delivering the document to the correct party at the husband's instructions. That is, the husband has told him to deliver the writ of divorce to the wife, but he has given her the quittance instead. The woman has never validly received the writ. The scribe must realize and not thwart the husband's intentionality.

But what about the other matter, misdating the document, mis-identifying the parties? Here the writ no longer pertains to those mentioned in it. The scribe has placed the parties in a different period from that in which they live, dating them, by reason of the document, in some other time; or he has placed them in a different locale from the one where they are situated. He has set forth a document for some others than the ones before him, and he has given to those before him a spurious time and place. So the law raises yet again its requirement on the acute localization of the piece of writing: this woman, here and now, her and her alone, this man, here and now, him and him alone. That is to say, the law has underscored the conception, the conviction really, that the moment and act of sanctification are unique, specific, not to be duplicated or replicated in any way or manner. When God oversees this holy relationship, he does not wish it to be confused with any other. That is why, when God is informed of the change of intentionality that has brought about the consecration of the woman to the man, he must be given exact information.

The law rests on profound reflection about the character of intentionality and its effects. What it ascertains encompasses not only the intentionality and will of the husband, not only the conscious, explicit cognizance of the wife, but the facts of the case. Specifically,

the law insists that the husband's act of will carries effect only when confirmed by valid action. Intention on its own is null. The full realization of the intention, involving valid provision for all required actions, alone carries effect. Not only so, but a third party, the scribe, intervenes in the realization of the husband's will. That means, facts beyond the husband's control and the wife's power to secure a right to supervise and review matters take over—with truly dreadful and permanent results.

So the wife, having acted on the writ invalidated by the scribe's, not her or her husband's actions or intentionality, emerges as the victim of circumstances quite in contradiction to anybody's will. The upshot is, by the rule of the law, she may not then claim that her intention—in this case, the acquiescence in a successive relationship of consecration—has been thwarted by the actions or errors of a third party and so ought to be honored in the breach. The law rejects that claim. She acted in accord with the rules of intentionality and in good faith—and it makes no difference. And the first husband, with all good will, cannot confirm that he intended to divorce the woman, and her actions fully accord with his initiatory intentionality. The law dismisses that allegation as well. Neither bears material consequence in the validation of what is, by reason of the facts of the case, an invalid transaction.

But the scribe possesses no intentionality in the transaction (other than the will we assume motivates his practice of his profession, that is, professionalism). The role accorded to the scribe, not to the contracting parties, underscores the position of the law. It is that intentionality not confirmed by correct deeds does not suffice. The scribe's errors stand athwart the realization of the intentionality of the husband and the participation (where possible) of the wife; but the scribe obviously did not intend to make mistakes. So what stands in judgment of intentionality and its effect are the facts of the case: the objective actions taken by third parties. In a legal system that has made a heavy investment in the priority of intentionality and the power of will, the statement made by the law of divorce sounds a much-needed note of warning. Good will and proper intentionality do not govern when facts intervene.

What one means to do contradicted by what one has done willy-nilly changes no facts but makes no difference at all. That is because Heaven still insists upon something more than the correct will. It does, in the end, scrutinize actions, and these alone serve not only to confirm, but also to carry out, the will of the principals in any transaction. And, if we refer to the generative myth of the Torah, where to begin with the power of humans to form and exercise intentionality is set forth, we find the reason why. The man and the woman in Eden enter the excuses that they gave way to the will of another, so their actions should be set aside. But God punishes all the parties to the act of rebellion, the snake, the woman, and the man. Then the lesson at the origin of all things—the power of humanity's will to stand against Heaven's will—finds its complement in its companion: what matters in the end is the deed, not only the intention.

That fact is underscored by another. Death too severs the marital bond. But on the occasion of death no document is involved, no scribe, no act of preparation, delivery, and attestation. The man's will to be confirmed by a deed plays no role whatever. God's will supersedes. Heaven intervenes, without the man's or the woman's consent. So what man accomplishes through a statement of intentionality confirmed by a documentary action, the writ of divorce, Heaven effects through the husband's death. Then the wife gains the right to enter a new consecrated relationship. That fact affords perspective on the deconsecration of the union that man accomplishes. Specifically, the document serves to attest in a tangible manner to the man's intentionality, the correct conditions of receipt of the document to the woman's conscious knowledge of what has happened. Neither person can claim not to know that the relationship has been severed, and Heaven confirms the act of intentionality embodied in the document.

That is not what happens when the husband dies. Here, since Heaven's will is done without man's consent or woman's articulated awareness, the law sees no need for documentary confirmation, in palpable form, of the desacralization of the marital bond. The widow automatically is free to marry some other man. No one ever articulates that fact, which is everywhere taken for granted. But it does represent a choice, the alternative—keeping the widow "sacred" to the deceased until her own death—never presents itself in either law or narrative as an option worthy of consideration. No writ of severance is involved; God's decisive action suffices.

Unconventional families, supernatural families: Were we to ignore the larger theological context that guides the sages' thinking about any particular topic, we should miss the radical revision of the definition of family—the element of the household related by blood—that until this point we have accepted. For the Torah revealed by God to Moses and handed on by tradition to the sages of the Mishnah, Midrash, and Talmuds, radically revises all this-worldly relationships and patterns. The Torah sees the natural world from a supernatural perspective, through God's spectacles, so to speak. Accordingly, when it comes to relationships of children to parents—and by extension, all other relationships—the Torah recasts matters in a radical manner.

For the Torah creates a supernatural family that takes priority over the this-worldly family. That is stated in so many words when the law specifies that the obligations a disciple owes his master transcend those he owes to his father (M. B.M. 2:11):

A. [If he has to choose between seeking] what he has lost and what his father has lost, his own takes precedence.
B. What he has lost and what his master has lost, his own takes precedence.
C. What his father has lost and what his master has lost, that of his master takes precedence.
D. For his father brought him into this world.
E. But his master, who taught him wisdom, will bring him into the life of the world to come.

F. But if his father is a sage, that of his father takes precedence.

G. [If] his father and his master were carrying heavy burdens, he removes that of his master, and afterward removes that of his father.

H. [If] his father and his master were taken captive,

I. he ransoms his master, and afterward he ransoms his father.

J. But if his father is a sage, he ransoms his father, and afterward he ransoms his master.

Matters are carried a step further. Holy Israel in its classical law is organized into castes, the highest being the priests, then the Levites, then the Israelites, and so on down. But a disciple of a sage, one in the lowest caste, takes priority over a high priest who has not mastered the Torah. So the family only exemplifies the Torah's deepest ordering of the social relationships of holy Israel, whether in the home or in the public piazza or in the Temple itself (M. Hor. 3:6-8):

3:6A. Whatever is offered more regularly than its fellow takes precedence over its fellow, and whatever is more holy than its fellow takes precedence over its fellow.

B. [If] a bullock of an anointed priest and a bullock of the congregation [M. Hor. 1:5] are standing [awaiting sacrifice]—

C. the bullock of the anointed [high priest] takes precedence over the bullock of the congregation in all rites pertaining to it.

3:7A. The man takes precedence over the woman in the matter of the saving of life and in the matter of returning lost property.

B. But a woman takes precedence over a man in the matter of [providing] clothing and redemption from captivity.

C. When both of them are standing in danger of defilement, the man takes precedence over the woman.

3:8A. A priest takes precedence over a Levite, a Levite over an Israelite, an Israelite over a *mamzer* [the child of parents forbidden by the law of the Torah to marry, e.g., a brother and a sister, or a married woman and someone other than her husband], a *mamzer* over a *Netin* [the descendant of a family of Temple servants],

a *Netin* over a proselyte, a proselyte over a freed slave.

B. Under what circumstances?

C. When all of them are equivalent.

D. But if the *mamzer* was a disciple of a sage and a high priest was an *am haares* [a person unlettered in the Torah learned through discipleship], the *mamzer* who is a disciple of a sage takes precedence over a high priest who is an *am haares*.

There can be no clearer way of setting forth the entire message of the system of classical Judaism than this passage, which treats even the holiest officials of the Temple itself as subordinate, in the social order, to Torah-learning. That is why, as a matter of course, family relationships also are subordinated to those relationships with God that Torah-study entails and sometimes even realizes.

JACOB NEUSNER

FRANCE, PRACTICE OF JUDAISM IN, FROM NAPOLEON TO DE GAULLE: Although Jews had been effectively banished from France from 1394 until 1790, the great purge of Jews in the Iberian peninsula following the *Reconquista* sent Portuguese and Spanish marranos fleeing to French coastal towns like Bordeaux or Bayonne, where they maintained their secret identity for generations.[1] The emancipation of the Jews, begun in the Revolution and completed in Napoleon's reign, likewise drew Jews, primarily from the numerous "German" domains to the east. After the loss of Alsace and Lorraine in the Franco-Prussian War, numerous "Alsatian" Jews, mostly representing more conservative religious traditions, moved either to the French side of the new border or to the capital directly. In political and demographic terms, by the mid-nineteenth century, French Jews were rather few in number (80,000) and Parisian (65%). Parisian Jews were highly acculturated to metropolitan styles of French culture. Outside the metropole, the main provincial Jewish communities were divided into either that of Alsace-Lorraine (Ashkenazic) or Bordeaux and Bayonne (Sephardic).[2] Beginning in the 1880s, however, this native French Jewish community would be challenged by the immigration into France of the

Jewish victims of persecutions in czarist Russia. They came in unprecedented numbers, and by 1914, virtually outnumbered the Paris population of French-born Jews.[3] Their arrival—and the antisemitic reaction to them—eventually changed the character of French Jewish identity and spirituality.

In so long a history, certain key moments in the collective life of the Judaism of the Jews of France need to be marked, especially as they concern the nature of Judaism in France. These are first, the impact of Napoleonic religious policies on French Jewry; second, the development of Jewish learning under the aegis of the Société des Études Juives and the *Revue des études juives*; third, the rise of antisemitism, especially "scholarly antisemitism;" fourth, the impact of the Eastern European Jews; fifth, the rise of Jewish collective self-assertion in the forms of cultural and political movements of the late nineteenth and early twentieth centuries.

Napoleon: Although the process of Jewish emancipation can be said to have already begun in 1789 under the Revolution, it was Napoleon's call of 1806 to convene the Parisian Sanhedrin that effectively realized the institutionalization of Revolutionary legislation. The Sanhedrin, a hand-picked group of one hundred and twelve Jewish "Notables," was convened to secure agreement to Napoleon's terms for Jewish incorporation into the French nation-state—in effect all those issues that would conform Jewish law and practice to French citizenship and would prevent any tendencies towards Judaism's becoming the basis for a state within a state. In the words of the Sanhedrin, "Israel no longer forms a nation."[4] Correspondingly, in renouncing its own national and political aspirations, the Sanhedrin accepted France as its "primary sociopolitical loyalty," and laid the conceptual foundations for the French Jewish identity in modern times.[5]

However benign the emperor's religious policies may appear, emancipation thus had its costs, as it did for Catholics and Protestants as well. Politically, while emancipation meant the establishment of a system of Jewish self-regulation, it brought the constant oversight of the community by the state through access to the Jews' official convocations. Economically, while emancipation meant that Judaism received state support in the form of annual salaries paid to rabbis, it also meant their supervision as members of the French civil service. In 1808, while Napoleon gave to Jews, with one hand, recognition as one of the official religions of France, he took away with the other, establishing state control over the Jewish community through the mechanism of the consistory system. Under this system, Jews were obliged to promote loyalty to the nation and render military service. In short, while Napoleon underwrote religion, he also quite deliberately subordinated it to the political realm.

In theological terms, emancipation also meant that Jewish self-understanding changed from one in which Jews claimed a distinct ancient national identity to one in which they were exclusively French nationals. No less a figure than the great French Jewish scholar James Darmesteter marked the precise date of this transformation, the declaration of emancipation by the French National Assembly: "From the 28th of September, 1791, there is no longer a history of Jews in France. There is only a history of French Judaism, as there is a history of French Calvinism or Lutheranism, and nothing more."[6] The surrender of Jewish national political identity meant that the domains of religion and politics would henceforth be distinct spheres. Once again, the Sanhedrin's statement of 1807 is clear:

> We therefore declare that the divine Law . . . contains within itself dispositions which are political and dispositions which are religious: that the religious dispositions are, by their nature, absolute and independent of circumstances and of age; that this does not hold true of the political dispositions which are taken for the government of the people of Israel in Palestine when it possessed its own kings, pontiffs and magistrates. . . .[7]

"Becoming a religion" in this new sense meant that French Jews came to be identified with a movable venue of worship like the synagogue, a system of explicit beliefs and (to a much lesser extent) practices, rooted in the *individual* conscience and concerning sacred things alone.

From Wissenschaft des Judentums to "La Science du Judaïsme:" Although French Jews gave up their independent political status as Jews, they gained a great deal in terms of access to the gentile world. Among the venues in which French Jews thrived, the most important from the viewpoint of the nature and development of Judaism was Jewish entry into higher education and the greatly respected world of scholarship. French Jews had their own version of the famous "Wissenschaft des Judentums" movement of the German-speaking world, which did so much to give intellectual legitimacy to Reform.

As articulated by the German Jewish scholar Immanuel Wolf in 1822, the "Wissenschaft des Judentums" was what its name indicated—a "science" of Judaism. As such, it

> treats the object of its study in and for itself, for its own sake, and not for any special purpose or definite intention. It begins without any preconceived opinion and is not concerned with the final result. Its aim is neither to put its object in a favorable nor in an unfavorable light in relation to prevailing views, but to show it as it is. Science is self-sufficient and is in itself an essential need of the human spirit.[8]

From the Jewish viewpoint, the situation in both France and Germany was on the whole bad for the critical study of Judaism. Where Judaism was studied, gentiles dominated the field. More typically, in the late eighteenth and early nineteenth centuries, when scientifically minded Jews wished to follow the lead of the new critical studies of the Jewish and Christian Bibles, they were rebuffed by state institutions. When Abraham Geiger proposed to establish Jewish studies in German universities, he was denied.[9] Likewise, when he sought to establish a Jewish faculty of theology at one of the universities, alongside Catholic and Protestant theology, he was denied government approval. Thus in 1819, Leopold Zunz founded an independent and

private organization for the scientific study of Judaism, the *Verein für Cultur und Wissenschaft der Juden.*[10] Geiger and Zunz launched the official journal of the movement, the *Monatschrift für Geschichte und Wissenschaft des Judentums*, expressly aimed to publish original work on all aspects of the history of Jewish life the world over. Under their leadership, in the first third of the nineteenth century, the Wissenschaft des Judentums movement took form.

Within a short time of the establishment of the "Wissenschaft des Judentums," the German movement was carried to France. In the 1830s, French Jews sought actively to lure these German Jewish scholars with the benefits of emancipation. Prominent among those who responded were two younger members of the *Monatschrift*'s original circle, Joseph Derenbourg and Solomon Munk. Arriving in Paris in the 1840s, Munk assumed a research post in Hebrew manuscripts as curator of oriental manuscripts at the Bibliothèque Nationale and as professor of Hebrew, Chaldaic, and Syriac at the Collège de France.[11] At about the same time, the French-born but German resident Joseph Derenbourg (1811-1895) joined Munk from Germany. In 1877, he became professor of Hebrew languages in the philological section of the École Pratique des Hautes Études. His son, Hartwig, followed his father's lead and became professor of Arabic and Islam. As the conservative French rabbinate kept these scholars and their heirs at arm's length, they, like other Jewish scholars, found their intellectual homes in the great secular institutions of the French state. At the École Pratique des Hautes Études, for instance, an entire generation of scholars from Jewish families, such as Durkheim, the various (unrelated) bearers of the Lévi surname—Emmanuel, Isidore, Israël—Marcel Mauss, the Reinach brothers, Hartwig Derenbourg, and others, established secular academic careers.

The École Pratique des Hautes Études, Fifth Section (philology), was unlike other institutions devoted to the study of religion elsewhere. And it fit beautifully the ambitions of scholars who preferred not always to be identified by their religious backgrounds to work out a career encompassing the study of religion. The Fifth Section was not aligned with any religious denomination and professed to treat the religions of the world with the same scientific procedures of investigation already established in the more general and better established historical disciplines. In this conception of science, the scholarship of the Fifth Section emphasized historical and philological erudition at the expense of theological or philosophical polemics or speculation.

The scientific study of Judaism in France remained however confined to the university, as the world of parochial Jewish learning still resisted the new history and philology, continuing to develop its own institutions of higher learning. Thus, in 1856, the slightly more worldly Séminaire Israëlite was established in Paris, still primarily organized to train young men for the rabbinate.[12] At best, the seminarians were permitted leave their schools for a scant two hours a week, and then only to visit Hartwig Derenbourg's class in Hebrew at the École Pratique. French Jewish learning thus still primarily meant provincial and conservative Talmudic training.

Only at the end of the nineteenth century did the "Science du Judaïsme" have any impact on the seminary education of the traditionally conservative French Jewish community, and then only because of the insistence of Jewish scholars at the university. Courses in Jewish and French history and literature were added to the curriculum that had prevailed in Metz.[13] Modern intellectuals like Paul Janet also lectured at the Séminaire. But despite these efforts to modernize education, the prevailing unscholarly and conservative "re-orthodoxing" trends of French Judaism at century's end prevented student rabbis from becoming unduly influenced by the new secular scholarship championed by the Wissenschaft des Judentums.[14]

The conservatives, however, gradually saw a way to exploit the Wissenschaft's historical positivism for their own purposes. The new scholarship offered both liberals and conservatives a set of ground rules for debate about religious change, providing a repertoire of precedents for ruling on current Jewish practice and the principle that all "legitimate reforms must be rooted in a respect for history." Exemplifying this dominant mood of progressive "conservative innovation, based on historical awareness," Chief Rabbi Isidor wrote in 1885 that "he had been trying to imitate the Adam of the midrashic legend, who had two faces, one turned toward the past, and the other turned toward the future."[15] Thus in an odd way, the Science du Judaïsme allowed both wings of French Jewry some measure of mutual accommodation. Typical of this ability to reconcile piety with scholarship were Sylvain and Israël Lévi,[16] critical scholars of the first order who tended to be more conservative about both religious belief and practice than the extreme liberal partisans of neo-Judaism, such as James Darmesteter, Louis-Germain Lévy, or Salomon Reinach.

Perhaps the man who did most to set the pace for these *avant garde* French Jewish scholars was Solomon Munk, whose influence can be seen in the work of Israël and Sylvain Lévi. For Munk, Judaism stood alongside other religious traditions like Islam and Christianity as an equal—and equally powerful—object of scientific study, not as a separate autonomous entity. Were Munk alive today, he would place the study of Judaism within the comparative study of societies, religious studies, history of philosophy, or comparative cultural history, and not within the more autonomous discipline of Jewish studies. Unlike his German Jewish mentors, Munk was a comparativist and an original proponent of interdisciplinary work who sought to orient the study of Judaism towards archeology, history of antiquity, and philology.[17] Munk showed, for example, how Jewish thinkers played important parts in making up the intellectual world of supposedly Christian medieval philosophy. The desire to show how Judaism and Christianity nurtured each other may likewise have guided some of the work of Israël Lévi.

The Société des Études Juives and the *Revue des études juives*: Much of Munk's spirit informed an institution that finally came to represent the ideals of the scientific study of Judaism in France, the Société des études juives. All the major Jewish figures of the late nineteenth and early twentieth centuries, referred to above, were members, as was renegade Catholic Ernest Renan. In 1879, Zadoc-Kahn founded the Société as the French parallel to the original German *Verein*. It was from this base in the Société, in the same year, that Zadoc-Kahn launched the *Revue des études juives*, a perfect mirror of the *Monatschrift für Geschichte und Wissenschaft des Judentums*, which recognized it as such.[18] In the inaugural number, the editors affirmed their "preoccupation with scientific truth"—even if this risked inducing a certain "aridity" into the pages of the *Revue*. Underlining their differences from the orthodox, they stated: "We are not in the business of making religious propaganda, nor are we even aiming at edification."[19] From its foundation, the Société des études juives took charge of "all aspects of the Jewish past excluding dogmatic or purely denominational matters," as its founder, Zadoc-Kahn declared.[20] Still, for Zadoc-Kahn, dedication to the ideals of a scientific study of Judaism did not entail indifference to specifically French Jewish values. First and foremost, he wanted to aid in building up the integrity of the Jewish community. He and others felt that both the Société and *Revue* should and could spur the evolution of Judaism, but must do so positively and "scientifically." But, from the beginning, the editors made clear that they had "patriotic" interests as well,[21] to create a specifically "*French* library of Jewish science and literature." Thus they wanted to "relieve France of its inferior position" in the study of the Jewish past.

The *Revue* thus put into practice values that Munk's scholarship asserted. Supporting Munk's opposition to Jewish studies as an autonomous endeavor, the editors extended their appeal to the study of the Jewish past of France naturally enough to Jews but also to "the public in general." Further "we neither ask those who write for the *Revue* who they are nor where they come from—only that they be serious and sincere." Recalling Munk's Jewish universalism and his interests in seeing how Judaism played a role in

the formation of modern European civilization, the *Revue* set out on the same path. The inaugural editorial wished, for example, to illuminate the nature of French Judaism of the middle ages because, said the editors, it showed a native "Jewish universalism" and thus bore the "imprint of the French spirit."[22]

The *Revue* also bore witness to Munk's belief in the importance of comparative studies in its openness to the new disciplines of folklore and ethnography and the general tendency to locate Judaism within the larger world of religious history. Louis-Germain Lévy, for example, authored an early piece on totemism.[23] Salomon Reinach wrote articles on the accusation of Jewish ritual murder, the Inquisition, the origin of prayers for the dead, and racism.[24] Lévi himself also published a comparative study of the sacrifice of Isaac and the death of Jesus.[25] In 1913, Israël Lévi took Sir James Frazer's *Golden Bough* to task for its insinuations about Jewish blood libel.

Not only to support the desire for religious reform was the new critical history practiced. Increasingly in the nineteenth century, positivist history also helped Jews defend their traditions against what one might call scholarly antisemitism, which first grew in the late 1800s. The strategy of the scholarly antisemites was to cast Jews born in France as indifferent to their own traditions and the writing of their own history. As Romain Rolland said flatly, "the past does not exist for the Jews."[26] Sylvain Lévi, then president of the Société des études juives, understood that such libels presented a "most pressing problem" to the well-being of the Jewish community. In 1904, he therefore addressed the general assembly of the Société des études juives and argued that Jews should take their place in the world, but without "renouncing their past or traditions." Giving eloquent voice to this ambition to write Jewish history—but within the context of human history—Lévi went on:

> When we rummage through libraries, decipher obscure scribbling, wrest bits of manuscript or fragments of inscriptions from the bowels of the earth, we mean to do work that is both fulfilling and positive and to draw

form these dead documents the secrets of our life. . . . Noble families of old kept in their archives the remembrances of the great deeds which had made them famous. And in so doing, they justified their social rank and fortune. Today, the whole of humanity wants to ennoble itself. Humanity wants its own archives. And it is from the historians that it expects them—[and expects them to be] faithful and sincere. In solidarity with the whole world, can we—without misuse or narrowness—reclaim the Jewish past?[27]

Lévi in effect answered the charges of Rolland clearly and positively in the style made possible by the Société des études juives. Yes, Jews—especially those like himself—can write such a history of themselves, because the "Jew is an historical being."[28]

But French Jews had to face more than skepticism concerning whether they were both capable and interested in writing their own histories. They had to confront the fact that in France prior to the rise of a "Science du Judaïsme," the study of the history and prehistory of Judaism was almost exclusively a gentile occupation and often profoundly antisemitic. The efforts of Munk on the whole played in the shadows, while the careers of gentile Semiticists sparkled in full view of the literate public. We have only to recall the celebrated career of Ernest Renan, who, before Darmesteter's Jewish publications of a generation later, was virtually the leading spokesman for Jewish religion and the Hebrew Bible in France. Thus, when we speak of Jewish learning in France, we should distinguish scholarship done *about* Judaism *by* Jews from that done by gentiles, as well as scholarship done by Jews on non-Jewish subjects. This distinction generates three possible categories of scholars:

1. *Jews Who Studied Judaism:*
   Specialists: Solomon Munk, Joseph Derenbourg, Isidore Lévi, Israël Lévi, Salomon Reinach, Theodore Reinach, Emmanuel Lévi.
   Secondary figures: Sylvain Lévi, Marcel Mauss, Joseph Reinach.
   Learned Journal: Revue des études juives.
   Learned Society: Société des études juives
2. *Jews Who Studied Non-Jewish Religions:*
   Specialists: James Darmesteter, Hartwig Derenbourg, Emile Durkheim, Robert Hertz, Sylvain Lévi, Louis-Germain Lévi, Lucien Lévy-Bruhl, Marcel Mauss, Salomon Reinach.
   Learned Journals: L'Année sociologique, Revue d'histoire des religions, L'Anthropologie.
   Learned Society: Société Française de Philosophie
3. *Gentiles Who Studied Judaism:*
   Specialists (Roman Catholics): Alfred Loisy, Ernest Renan.
   Learned Journals: L'Année sociologique, Revue d'histoire des religions, L'Anthropologie.
   Learned Society: Société Française de Philosophie

In their dominance of the study of Judaism, gentiles commanded access to Jewish Scripture and, in effect, exerted gentile power to determine what was important and worth studying in the Jewish heritage. In 1892, Darmesteter remarked that in France the Bible is "more celebrated than known." Continuing, he noted that German "Protestant theologians" have led the way in these studies and have done so "exclusively," resulting in studies in "the thralldom of theological and scholastic hierology."[29] Darmesteter here echoed the views of one of the founders of the Wissenschaft des Judentums, Edouard Gans, and thus recapitulated for French Jews the very reasons the Wissenschaft des Judentums was founded in the first place. Gans believed that Jews should be scandalized both by the dominance of Christian scholars over Jewish studies and the partisan Christian uses to which it was put:

> Any credible results [in the field of Jewish scholarship] are mainly due to the efforts of Christian scholars. But while the rabbis lacked the necessary freedom in their studies, the Christian approach to Judaism lacked independence: much too often it was turned into a discipline secondary, and merely ancillary, to Christian theology.[30]

Beyond feeling somewhat overshadowed by well-ensconced Christian students of the Jewish Bible, many Jews were sensitive to the antisemitic character of some Christian work—a conviction that goes back at least to 1818 with Leopold Zunz. This father of modern Jewish studies was quite clear about his feelings towards the treatment of the religion of Israel at the hands of some Christian theologians: "Nothing more distorted, more damaging, more dishonest has ever anywhere been written than that which has been written on the religion of Israel. The art of inciting malice has here reached its pinnacle."[31]

"Neo-Judaism" and Jewish modernism: Supported by the enlightened institutional ethos of the Société des Études Juives, a generation of creative Jewish thinkers, often called neo-Jews or Jewish modernists, came into prominence in the late nineteenth and early twentieth centuries. First among them, the real father of Jewish modernism, was Darmesteter, whose conception of Judaism as "prophetic Judaism,"[32] reminiscent of Moses Mendelssohn, dominated the thought of generations of liberal Jewish intellectuals from the 1880s through the years of the First World War.[33] Son of a poor bookbinder of Lorraine, James Darmesteter was reared in an orthodox Jewish home, where he received a classical Jewish education in texts and Jewish cultural lore. In 1852, the family migrated to Paris, where James' father believed his children would be better positioned for careers in the professions. Thanks to his education in Hebrew and Talmud, James was well prepared to work in the field of Oriental philology, where he eventually made for himself a great career. In short order, he developed into the greatest Avestan and Zoroastrian scholar of his generation.

Darmesteter was closely linked with the main figures in the broader field of the study of religion, especially his teacher, Ernest Renan. Indeed, Darmesteter was known affectionately in the liberal Jewish press as "un Renan Juif,"[34] and, after Renan's death, some even called him the most distinguished scholar in France. But Darmesteter was more than a philologist. A poet, folklorist, devotee of English literature, and man of broad personal cultivation, he is best remembered as an orientalist. He composed and published several articles and books of verse in English, the most remarkable of which celebrated the higher meaning of Jesus. While in Persia and India, he collected Afghanistani popular songs, partly for his own amusement, partly because he felt they showed traces of the Zend-Avestan language. Based on these songs, he also published an important essay on Afghan life. Late in life, he served as chief editor of the illustrious literary and political magazine, *La Revue de Paris*.

Darmesteter circulated in a world populated by like-minded liberal Jews and gentiles, including historians of religion, like Salomon Reinach, and liberal Protestants, such as Albert and Jean Réville.[35] Like Renan, Darmesteter feared that with the clerical party discredited in the cultural wars attending the foundation of the Third Republic, the French populace would dismiss religion totally.[36] Yet, while religions, especially Judaism, must change, Darmesteter felt that religion itself was important for the health of the nation. Traditional Judaism contained the seeds of a true universal religion and could be mined for this universal content, his "prophetic faith." In this approach, he traded on the reputation of the prophets as ethical reformers and iconoclasts opposed to the priestly, materialistic, and ritualistic tendencies of ancient Hebrew religion. A rationalist such as Darmesteter saw this prophetic faith as well fitted to the best of the modern spirit. It favored the irreverent and critical spirit of science; it opposed "superstition" and "magic." The prophets thus were the religious modernists of their time, opposed to the priesthood's ritualizing tendencies, which led people far from the inner ethical core of real religion, and against magic, the preoccupation of "charlatans and fools."[37] Thus reflecting implicitly the critical, libertarian, and iconoclastic heritage of the Revolution, Darmesteter held up the reforming religion of the ancient prophets as an ideal of what "modern" Judaism, and, like it, the modern religion of France, might be.[38] Republican France in a way fulfilled the promise of the prophets of Israel. This identification permitted Darmesteter to see the eternal message of the Jewish prophets symbolized in the republican political language of his own time.

Although a good deal less poetic than the gifted Darmesteter, Louis-Germain Lévy agreed with him that traditional

Judaism needed to undergo an inner reinterpretation. It

> only needs to cast off the practices, institutions and customs which have their *raison d'être* in other times and places, but which today are fossilized to the point of being encumbrances. Once relieved of all this dead weight, Judaism will present the necessary characteristics of religion in general and modern religion in particular. It will be a religion fitted out with all the positive and historical essentials, and at the same time be a rational and secular religion.[39]

Lévy simultaneously gave Jewish modernist approaches to religion a nationalist and Jewish spin. For, interpreted symbolically, Judaism qualified as "the religion" of France, thus replacing the *religions concrets* and laying a unifying moral floor under French national feeling. Although a "religion," Judaism, as Lévi read it, is not a "faith," for it is not fixed by doctrines, as the official Napoleonic conventions insisted that "religions" must be. Further, while the rites and doctrines of these so-called "religions" offend reason, Lévy's neo-Judaism does not. It is, rather, "perfectly compatible with the affirmations of modern thought" and science.[40] Thus Lévy rejected any idea of religion as "*passé*" or of Judaism as empty and ritualistic. The new Judaism, rather, was a version of the universal religion, a natural religion, religion-as-such: "in the last analysis," he says, "Judaism is not *a* religion among many others, but *the* religion . . .," capable of providing dynamogenic energy and idealistic direction to life.

By most standards of reputation, the key Jewish modernist of the *fin-de-siècle* was Salomon Reinach (1858-1932), born into a family of wealthy commercial investors and governmental professionals.[41] Salomon's two brothers, Joseph and Theodore, were famous in their own right. The elder, Joseph (1856-1921), was the author of a seven volume history of the Dreyfus Affair (1901-1908), *Histoire sommaire de l'affaire Dreyfus*. Because of his abilities as a journalist and political analyst, in 1881 he was appointed *Chef-du-Cabinet*, and, for several terms, he also served in the Chamber of Deputies, where he was an outspoken critic of the condemnation of Dreyfus (fig. 47). In 1886,

he was awarded the Legion d'Honneur. Salomon's younger brother, Theodore (1860-1928), was hardly less distinguished. Mixing scholarly and political roles as easily as Joseph, he was a classics scholar at the École Pratique des Hautes Études, Fifth Section, and wrote his *Histoire des Israélites* (1884) to present his version of the liberal position on the nature of Judaism. He opposed Zionism, arguing the standard line that since the Revolution, French Jews were not a nation but a religious community. For a time, he edited the *Revue des études grecques*, and later he won election to the Academie Française. Like Joseph, he was active in national politics, serving in the Chamber of Deputies from 1906-1914.

Salomon Reinach, the epitome of French "gentry Jewry," was a quintessential, if complex, iconoclastic Jewish modernist. A remarkable virtuoso intellectual, unlike his two more conventional brothers, he became perhaps France's greatest popularizer of the history of religions since Renan. An enormous literary success in anti-clerical France, his exposé of world religions, *Orpheus* (1909), was in its sixth edition by the end of its first year of publication. By the time Durkheim published the *Elementary Forms of the Religious Life* in 1912, *Orpheus* had passed into the sixteenth of its eventual thirty-eight editions and had already been translated into five languages. Salomon circulated easily in the social world of arts and letters and fell naturally into the company of the fashionable artists and intellectuals of the day. Like others of the *avant garde* milieu, Reinach's views on morality were progressive, and, in his opposition to social taboos, somewhat libertine. He even made his way along the edges of the *avant garde* world of the arts. Reinach and Max Jacob, for example, shared the favors of the *demi-mondaine*, Liane de Pougy.[42] A Dreyfusard, Reinach championed many left-wing causes of the day, and he was a talented journalist and self-interested chronicler of religious history.

Reinach was absorbed in the then new cross-cultural comparativist anthropological writings of British scholars like Robertson Smith and Sir James Frazer. In fact, at the time, he was recognized as the French *porte-parole* of these two great representatives of the *école anglaise*. Reinach was primarily concerned to apply the new ethnography to the in-house modernist task of reforming Judaism. Taking his cues from Frazer and Robertson Smith, he felt that Jewish dietary laws and other practices were nothing more than primitive "taboos" or "scruples" in hiding.[43] Reinach's goal was to eliminate these and all other taboos that had survived so long into the modern day and, in doing so, to liberate Judaism from the dead hand of the past. As a pious neo-Jew, Reinach believed such a strategy of exposing the primitive beneath the contemporary showed Judaism in its best light. Religions had all evolved and changed; Judaism was no exception. Ethnography indeed showed how much *better* Judaism had become over the years by gradually eliminating its barbaric elements. But why not encourage further evolution today? The new ethnography thus suggested the way in which religions of his day should reconsider their identities.

Despite his iconoclastic Voltairean reputation, Reinach was a sincere, if undeviatingly liberal, Jew, typical of his class and Parisian origins. Thus, using the standard modernist image of reform and regeneration, he says: "The old tree of Judah will let fall its dead leaves and in doing so, its powerful roots will not grow the less—a witness to its inexhaustible vitality."[44] His neo-Jewish reformist zeal turned the work of the British comparativists toward his critique of the conservative religiosity of his own community first, then, by extension, to the dominant Catholic religiosity of his country. Reinach accordingly was active in the leadership of Jewish affairs and proudly identified himself as Jewish. He was part of the pre-war Jewish renaissance and, in 1913, was joint founder, along with Israël Lévi, Darius Milhaud, and others, of the Amis du Judaisme.[45] On the other side, he was not an ethnic patriot. Jewish advancement meant progress along the critical, Enlightenment, and universalist axis. Like Solomon Munk and the other leaders of the French version of the Wissenschaft des Judentums, he held that

Judaism was an integral episode in the "moral and social history of humanity" rather than an objective end point of history. In a word, he cared more about what made Jews like other people and how Judaism contributed to the march of humanity than what set Jews apart.[46]

Reinach thus consistently opposed anything that would exaggerate Jewish exclusiveness. Typical was his distaste for North African and Eastern European Jews, whom he characterized as literally "unwashed masses," making a special point of attacking the new Jewish immigrants' lack of hygiene, even as these pious folk went to scrupulous lengths to insure ritual cleanliness.[47] Of the Hasidim, he said, "they constitute communities hostile to the modern spirit; their noisy and disorderly form of worship has all the appearances of a religious frenzy."[48] By the time of Reinach's maturity, the presence of these new Jews, with their foreign customs and habits, was seen as disturbing the hard-won modern and "French" identity of Franco-Jewry. But even as these models of Jewish particularity and ethnicity becoming more prominent, he opposed Zionism and denied the existence of a Jewish "race."[49] He was, in short, a model iconoclastic modernizer of Judaism: if the "tree" of Judaism was half-dead, as Reinach asserted, he assigned himself the task of reviving it through a severe pruning.

New Jews, new Judaism: At the height of some of the Reinach's greatest triumphs in the world of his day, social and political events began to challenge the historical course of the French Judaism he represented. One force was the arrival of the enthusiastic and unembarrassedly religious Jews of the East Europe, just mentioned;[50] the other was the rise of antisemitism, linked with dislike of these "outsiders" and fueled by renewed French nationalism in advance of World War I.

The arrival of East European Jews actually sparked two reactions: one was the rise of gentile antisemitism against the new immigrants; the other was the opposition of liberal, modernist French born Jews of Paris to the ritualistic, particularist, and collectively identified Eastern Europeans. Salomon Reinach's dislike for the newly arrived East European Jews, for example, fit right in with the feelings of other bourgeois French born Jews.[51] Always sensitive to the image of the Jew as outsider, native-born French Jews felt that the new immigrants threatened to overwhelm their small and largely Parisian population. In fact, by 1914, the Eastern European Jews virtually equaled in numbers the Paris population of French born Jews,[52] threatening to make Jews in general look alien once again.[53] By simple force of numbers and enthusiasm, these new arrivals in some degree succeeded in transforming the liberal Judaism of Reinach's peers.

The main theological upshot of the arrival of the new Jews from Eastern Europe was to challenge the highly individualized, spiritualized ("disembodied") form of Judaism that had developed as a result of the Napoleonic emancipation. While French Jews embraced the norms of official France, significant numbers were becoming more aware of the unavoidability of their own (at least perceived) differences and less agreeable to the official French doctrine of the liberal individualist values of the secular state.[54] These political trends were well prepared by the logic guiding Jewish thinking: had not the God of all creation spoken to the patriarchs and prophets and to Israel as a people and nation with a message meant for all humanity?

The new French Jews thus led the entire Jewish community to embrace a greater sense of Jewish social embodiment, what French Jewish scholars today call Judaism's need for the "acquisition of a proper physiognomy" in the wake of emancipation.[55] *Archives israélites'* editor, Hyppolite Prague, for example, claimed in 1900 that French Jews had just as much a right to concrete group identity as their Christian fellow citizens. For Prague, Judaism was "our laws and practices,"[56] which meant that Judaism was distinct and not "hyperspiritual" like Christianity.[57] It links matter and soul and achieves thereby "the perfect harmony of the human and divine in us."[58] For Prague, at least, such concerns for group identity and social em-

bodiment had practical religious and political roots. In an editorial five years later, he reported that both Catholics and Protestants were working to build up their communities in reaction to the law of Separation. Should not Jews put similar efforts into supporting their community?[59] Thus, by the end of the nineteenth century, Judaism was being regarded by significant representatives of the Jewish community in Paris along lines approaching the vision of the new Jews from Eastern Europe, as a fully social and concrete religion.

Zionism and "Les Amis du Judaism:" This notion of a re-socialized and politicized Judaism took at least three forms. First and most radical was the attempt to socialize Judaism through political or Herzlian Zionism. Second was the equally particularistic, but apolitical, attempt to embody Judaism culturally in the so-called "Jewish Renaissance" of "Les Amis du Judaism." Finally, alongside and often opposed both to political Zionism and the "Les Amis du Judaism," was an earlier movement among French born Jews that culminated in so-called "Franco-Judaism,"[60] perhaps still the most powerful Jewish societist trend, although often overshadowed by Zionism. Franco-Jews felt that Judaism should culminate in a religion of French nationalism, indeed that "Jewishness" gained its highest form of social and corporeal existence in "Frenchness." Let us consider the Zionist polemic against Judaism as a disembodied "religion" first.

Although until some years after the turn of the century Zionism represented a small minority position among French Jews, it would eventually become a solution for some to the problem of becoming a religion. Zionism rejected the idea of the individualized "religion" codified by Napoleon as well as the rather intellectual and ethical neo-Judaism of the modernists. The contradictions of modernity led the Zionists to reconsider the ideal of Judaism as a "people," in effect to reject the assumptions of the political *modus vivendi* worked out with the French state, by which the Jews of France became French Jews. If Judaism could not be socially embodied in France, it might reclaim its political and ethnic identity in a future state of Israel.

But, since the strength of *French* nationalist loyalties among French Jews was considerable, the leading Jewish intellectuals came to the Zionist solution with the greatest reluctance. Thus, however successful Zionist attempts to re-embody Judaism were to prove later in the century, they failed to rule the loyalties of the Jewish community in the *fin-de-siècle* and even later. Even when Zionism became a considerable force in the late nineteenth and early twentieth centuries, it was the newly arrived Eastern European and North African Jews who led the movement.[61]

Early in our century, Jewish liberals such as Salomon Reinach characterized the nascent Zionist national movement as superstitious, just "a new religion founded on the idea of a native land."[62] To the extent Reinach voiced feelings shared by the largely French born Jewish population, we can understand why: the Dreyfus Affair notwithstanding, Zionism was not yet compelling in France, and thus Franco-Jewish loyalties to the republic remained unshaken. As a result, James Darmesteter, the genie of Franco-Jewish theory, was deeply stirred by nationalist feeling from at least 1870. Taking leave of his spiritualist tendencies, he gradually came round to the view that Judaism required a more particular and concrete social embodiment than some sort of abstract "humanity." Without such concrete social embodiment, Judaism would only result in "deracinating Christianity and deracinating itself."[63] Therefore, Judaism must be incarnated in France herself. Paris would replace Jerusalem, and Jewishness would "dissolve" in "the catholic union of the future," which would be the "moral equivalent of the ancient Hebrew faith."[64]

On the other hand, some Jewish intellectuals preferred a cultural rather than political way of realizing a distinctive Jewish societal identity. As a path of Jewish cultural revival, they felt that Jews should find a third way between indifference to their Jewish identity and Zionist religious politics. Judaism was to be celebrated as a source of moral and intellectual wisdom of universal import. This entailed that Jews should not only cultivate their own rich cultural heritage for themselves but also foster the study of Judaism according to universal scientific principles of detachment, such as those promoted by the "*science du Judaïsme*."[65] Their movement, in many ways reminiscent of the Polish "Bund," took the positive form of French Jewish cultural assertion, the so-called "Jewish Renaissance" of 1906-18.[66] In line with this, early in the century, the previously mentioned "Les Amis du Judaisme" led the way to a virtual boom of self-conscious Jewish cultural activity. Prominent members of the group were major figures of French culture, such as Léon Blum and the composer Darius Milhaud, Sylvain Lévi, and Israël Lévi. Salomon Reinach, one of the group's founders wanted French Jews to assert their uniqueness and in so doing to enrich all forms of cultural activity in behalf of a renascent Judaism.[67]

Nationalist revival and Jewish patriotism: The revival of national feeling in France (1905-1914) greatly affected the traditional religions, including Judaism, somewhat opposing the trends of Jewish particularism just discussed. While, at first, some prominent Jews resisted the more extreme forms of French nationalist rhetoric, French Jews overall felt pressure to locate and celebrate their French "roots," to identify themselves with the nation, since Jews were routinely accused of a lack of patriotism or being too "cosmopolitan" or *deracinée*.[68] In light of the recent influx of East European Jews, the expanded French Jewish community was an especially easy target for antisemites who saw here a foreign "body." Irony of ironies, Jews were derided as "German," since many of them hailed from Alsace and had not learned to speak French until the middle nineteenth century.[69] In response to this attempt to cast Jews as strangers, the *Revue des études juives* featured regular article-length historical accounts of France's many long-lived Jewish communities, some even dating to Roman times. French Jews emphatically asserted that they belonged in France as much as members of any religious community, since they had been a living part of French history from its beginnings.

Accordingly, whether because of external pressures to conform or a natural attraction for republican values, French Jews happily adapted themselves to the conditions of the approaching war. As good citizens, they claimed to be "electrified" by the "cause."[70] Merging their own history with the present course of French history, in 1916, the *Archives israëlites* called the victory in the Battle of the Marne as much a providential act as was the deliverance of the Israelites in the book of Esther.[71] A 1915 editorial, "Le Soldat Juif," said that by taking an active role in the army, French Jews would defend France in the way their ancestors defended Jerusalem. Was not the "spirit of the Maccabees" evident enough in elite fighting units such as the Zouaves, where Jews numbered some 60% of the total?[72]

French patriotism among Jews was indeed extraordinary. This need to defend Jewish honor before their fellow citizens in a time of systematic antisemitism was felt right down to the grass roots of Jewish consciousness. A nameless descendant of recent Russian Jewish immigrants to France, identified only as "Litwack," penned this final letter before meeting death in a fatal assault:[73]

> So that the whole world might see that the Jews know how to die for liberty . . . we will demonstrate to France that the Jews know how to die for a country that makes no difference between its children. I am happy to die for a noble republican France, which is worthy of every sacrifice, because she will not forsake my wife, my child. . . . In an hour, we will march, and we will die for France, for Jews, for the emancipation of all Jews.

So potent was the force of French patriotism that Jews routinely preferred loyalty to France, even when this meant abandoning fellow Jews to the ravages of persecution and loss of life. Renewed pogroms by their Russian allies, for example, created an especially painful situation for French Jews, many of whom of course had themselves only recently fled Russia to escape the antisemitic campaigns of the 1880s. Normally, French Jews would have been vocal about these egregious Russian antisemitic policies. But with the Franco-Russian alliance a linchpin of national foreign policy, French Jews felt constrained to keep silent in the face of renewed Russian pogroms.[74]

Since the Holocaust and the recent trials of the state of Israel, such indifference to Jewish collective interests is as inconceivable for French Jews as is the once naive faith in the loyalty of France to its Jewish minority. Memories of the moral bankruptcy of the Vichy collaboration still stalk the nation, and questions about what seems an opportunistic French foreign policy in the Muslim world revive uneasiness among French Jews. Yet the moral territory inhabited by French Jews following World War II is like nothing before and is the common ground upon which all French Jews stand. Without minimizing these factors, in France today the entire range of Jewish self-conception is well represented. In the wake of the Israeli Six Day War, newer Jews, refugees from France's former North African colonies, still dominate major quarters of Paris, such as Belleville, and remind native-born Jews of the perils of minority status not only in their own country but in the world at large as well. Yet, for all that, a patriotic Franco-Judaism still claims the majority of French Jewish feelings, even as it thrives alongside its more skeptical brethren—Zionist or otherwise—sometimes within the same person.

Bibliography

Albert, Phyllis C., *The Modernization of French Jewry: Consistory and Community in the Nineteenth Century* (Hanover, 1977).

Hyman, Paula, *From Dreyfus to Vichy* (New York, 1979).

Marrus, Michael R., *The Politics of Assimilation: A Study of the French Jewish Community at the Time of the Dreyfus Affair* (Oxford, 1971).

Wilson, Stephen, *Ideology and Experience: Antisemitism in France at the Time of the Dreyfus Affair* (Rutherford, 1982).

Notes

[1] Arthur Herztberg, *The French Enlightenment and the Jews* (New York, 1968), p. 9.

[2] See the excellent work done by Michael R. Marrus, *The Politics of Assimilation: A Study of the French Jewish Community at the Time of the Dreyfus Affair* (Oxford, 1971); Phyllis C. Albert, *The Modernization of French Jewry: Consistory*

and *Community in the Nineteenth Century* (Hanover, 1977); Frances Malino and Phyllis Cohen Albert, eds., *Essays in Modern Jewish History* (Rutherford, 1982); Paula Hyman, *From Dreyfus to Vichy* (New York, 1979), pp. 23-28; Stephen Wilson, *Ideology and Experience: Antisemitism in France at the Time of the Dreyfus Affair* (Rutherford, 1982).

[3] Paula Hyman, "French Jewish Historiography since 1870," in Frances Malino and Bernard Wasserstrom, eds., *The Jews in Modern France* (Hanover, 1985), p. 335.

[4] The Parisian Sanhedrin, "Doctrinal Decisions," in Paul Mendes-Flohr and Jehuda Reiharz, eds., *The Jew in the Modern World* (Oxford, 1980), pp. 123-124.

[5] Hyman, *From Dreyfus to Vichy*, p. 5.

[6] James Darmesteter, "Essay on the History of Judaism," [1880] in Morris Jastrow, Jr., ed., *Selected Essays of James Darmesteter* (Boston, 1895), p. 270.

[7] Mendes-Flohr and Reiharz, op. cit., pp. 123-124.

[8] Immanuel Wolf, "On the Concept of a Science of Judaism," [1822] in Mendes-Flohr and Reinharz, op. cit, p. 194.

[9] Wissenschaft des Judentums," in *Encyclopedia Judaica* (New York, 1971), vol. 16, col. 576.

[10] Albert, op. cit., pp. 246, 251.

[11] Ibid., p. 250.

[12] There is evidence that government approval of the new *seminaire* was influenced by the belief that such an institution would be more "enlightened" than the old Talmudic school of Metz, even transferred to the secular setting of Paris. See Albert, op. cit., pp. 249, 252.

[13] Ibid., pp. 251-252, and Israël Lévi, *Rapport moral et financier sur le séminaire israélite et le Talmud-Thora, précédé d'une histoire des Juifs de France* (Paris, 1903), pp. 34-39.

[14] Albert, op. cit., p. 251.

[15] Phyllis Cohen Albert, "Nonorthodox Attitudes in Nineteenth Century French Judaism," in Malino and Albert, op. cit., pp. 128, 135.

[16] Maurice Level, "Sylvain Lévi," in *L'Univers Israëlite* 91/7 (8 November 1935), p. 97.

[17] Perrine Simon-Nahum, "Émergence et spécificité d'une 'science du Judaisme' française (1840-1890)," in Frank Alvarez-Pereyre and Jean Baumgartner, eds., *Les études juives en France* (Paris, 1990), p. 26.

[18] This fact was celebrated by the editors of the *Monatschrift* on the occasion of the inaugural publication of the *Revue*. See *Monatschrift für Geschichte und Wissenschaft des Judentums* 30 (1881), pp. 459-470. Throughout the years, the *Monatschrift* noted the publications of its French counterpart, especially the Derenbourgs.

[19] The Editors, "A Nos lecteurs," in *Revue des études juives* 1 (1880), pp. vii-viii.

[20] *Encyclopedia of Judaism*, vol. 14, p. 134.

[21] The Editors, op. cit., p. vi.

[22] Ibid., pp. v, vii.

[23] Louis-Germain Lévy, "Du totemism chez les Hébreux," in *Revue des études juives* 45 (1902), pp. 13-26.

[24] Salomon Reinach, "L'Origine des prières pour les morts," in *Cultes, mythes et religions*, vol. 1, 3rd ed. (Paris, 1922), pp. 316-331; "L'Inquisition et le Juifs," in ibid., vol. 2 (Paris, 1928), pp. 401-417; "La Prétendue race juive," in ibid., vol. 3 (Paris, 1928), pp. 457-471; "L'Accusation du meurtre rituel en 1892," in ibid., vol. 5 (Paris, 1923), pp. 451-474.

[25] Israël Lévi, "Le sacrifice d'Isaac et la mort de Jésus," in *Revue des études juives* 64 (1912), pp. 161-184. Sylvain Lévi published his comparative inquiries of Judaism and Hinduism there: "Problèmes indo-hébraïques," in ibid., 82 (1926), pp. 49-54.

[26] Hyman, *From Dreyfus to Vichy*, p. 22.

[27] Sylvain Lévi, "Allocution," to the General Assembly of the Société des études juives, 24 January 1904, in *Revue des études juives* 66 (1913), p. ii.

[28] Ibid.

[29] James Darmesteter, *Les Prophètes d'Israel* (Paris, 1892), p. 4; and "The Prophets of Israel," in *Selected Essays of James Darmesteter*, Morris Jastrow, Jr., ed. (Boston, 1895), p. 20.

[30] Edouard Gans, "A Society to Further Jewish Integration," (1822) in Mendes-Flohr and Reinharz, op. cit., p. 193. See also Salomon Reinach's tribute to Zadoc-Kahn, the founder of the Société des études juives and the *Revue des études juives* in his "Zadoc-Kahn," in *Cultes, mythes et religions*, vol. 5 (Paris, 1923), pp. 442-443.

[31] Leopold Zunz, "On Talmudic Literature," [1818] in Mendes-Flohr and Reinharz, op. cit., p. 198.

[32] Two pieces especially should be noted, James Darmesteter, *Les Prophètes d'Israel* and "The Religions of the Future," in his *Selected Essays*, pp. 1-15.

[33] *Selected Essays*, pp. v-xv.

[34] Darmesteter was the subject of Jean Muzlak-May's article, "Un Renan Juif: James Darmesteter (1849-1894)," in *Univers Israëlite* 90/10 (29 November 1935), pp. 151-152. This article began a series of seven that ran in *L'Univers Israëlite*.

[35] Salomon Reinach, "James Darmesteter," in *Cultes, mythes et religions*, vol. 5 (Paris, 1923), pp. 414-432.

[36] James Darmesteter, "La guerre et la paix intérieures (1871 à 1893)," in *Critique et politique* (Paris, 1895), p. 261.

[37] Darmesteter, *Les Prophètes d'Israel*, pp. vi, 12-14.

[38] See Jean Réville's review of Darmesteter's *Les prophètes d'Israel*, in *Revue d'histoire des religions* 25 (1892), pp. 253-256.

[39] Louis-Germain Lévy, *Une Religion rationnelle et laique: la religion du XXe siecle* (Dijon, 1904).

[40] Ibid.

[41] Salomon's father, Baron Jacques Reinach,

was an unhappy party to the scandal created around the Panama investment fraud of the late 1880s.

[42] See Salomon Reinach and Max Jacob, *Lettres à Liane de Pougy* (Paris, 1980). For his views on the relation of sex and marriage, see Salomon Reinach, "Une Mystique au XXe siècle, Antoinette Bourignon," [1894] in *Cultes, mythes et religions*, vol. 1, 3rd ed. (Paris, 1922), ch. 35.

[43] Salomon Reinach, "Réponse aux 'Archives Israëlites' sur le meme sujet," in *Cultes, mythes et religions*, vol. 2. Paris, 1923, p. 16.

[44] Salomon Reinach, "L'emancipation interieure du Judaisme," in *Cultes, mythes et religions*, vol. 2 (Paris, 1923), p. 436. Also see his confession of faith, "Pourquoi je suis juif," in *L'Univers israëlite* 13 April 1928, p. 135.

[45] Reinach's case confirms Phyllis C. Albert's thesis ("Ethnicity and Jewish Solidarity in the Nineteenth Century," in J. Reinharz and D. Swetschinski, eds., *Mystics, Philosophers and Politicians* (Durham, 1982)) of the degree of Jewish identification even of some of those most committed to the values of the Enlightenment and emancipation.

[46] Seymour De Ricci, "Salomon Reinach," in *Revue des études juives* 94 (1933), p. 6.

[47] Salomon Reinach, *Cultes, mythes et religions*, vol. 2 (Paris, 1923), pp. 426, 429. Similar expressions of Reinach's disgust for Tunisian Jews are in Michel Abitbol's account of his February 1884 report to the Alliance: "The Encounter between French Jewry and the Jews of North Africa: Analysis of a Discourse (1830-1914)," in Malino and Wasserstrom, op. cit., pp. 48f.

[48] Salomon Reinach, *Orpheus* (New York, 1930), p. 224.

[49] Salomon Reinach, "La pretendue race juive," (1903) in *Cultes, mythes et religions*, vol. 3. (Paris, 1923), pp. 470-471.

[50] Theodore Zeldin, *France 1848-1945: Anxiety and Hypocrisy* (Oxford, 1981), p. 274. Michel Abitbol, *Les Deux terres promises: Les Juifs de France et le sionisme* (Paris, 1989), p. 21.

[51] Michael R. Marrus, *The Politics of Assimilation: A Study of the French Jewish Community at the Time of the Dreyfus Affair* (Oxford, 1971), pp. 161-162.

[52] Paula Hyman, "French Jewish Historiography since 1870," in Malino and Wasserstrom, op. cit., p. 335.

[53] Hyman, *From Dreyfus to Vichy*, pp. 23-28.

[54] Vicki Caron, *Between France and Germany: The Jews of Alsace-Lorraine, 1871-1918* (Stanford, 1988), ch. 9, and Theodore Zeldin, *France 1848-1945: Anxiety and Hypocrisy* (Oxford, 1981), p. 274.

[55] Perrine Simon-Nahum, "Emergence et spécificité d'une 'science du Judaisme' française (1840-1890)," in Frank Alvarez-Pereyre and Jean Baumgartner, eds., *Les études juives en France* (Paris, 1990), p. 23.

[56] Henri Prague, editor's reply to an anonymous letter, *Archives israëlites* 61 (6 September 1900), p. 891.

[57] See, for instance, the spiritualist trends of liberal Protestantism, also a feature of Zeldin's conception of Cartesianism in Theodore Zeldin, *France 1848-1945: Intellect and Pride* (Oxford, 1981), pp. 224f. For an archetypal example of Liberal Protestant spiritualism, see Albert Réville, "Contemporaneous Materialism in Religion: the Sacred Heart," in *Theological Review* 44 (January 1874), pp. 138-156.

[58] Henri Prague, "La caractéristique du nouvel israelite," in *Archives israëlites* 66 (28 September 1905), p. 306.

[59] Ibid., p. 297.

[60] Caron, op. cit., pp. 8f.

[61] Ibid., pp. 192f.

[62] Salomon Reinach, "Pendant et après la guerre," [1922] in *Cultes, mythes et religions*, vol. 5 (Paris, 1923), p. 382.

[63] Darmesteter, *Les Prophètes d'Israel*, p. iii.

[64] Michael R. Marrus, *The Politics of Assimilation: A Study of the French Jewish Community at the Time of the Dreyfus Affair* (Oxford, 1971), pp. 100f, 108.

[65] Hyman, *From Dreyfus to Vichy*, pp. 45f.

[66] Aleksander Hertz, *The Jews in Polish Culture* (Evanston, 1988), p. 28.

[67] Hyman, op. cit., pp. 33, 42-46.

[68] Philippe Landau, "'La Patrie en danger': D'une guerre à l'autre," in Pierre Birnbaum, ed., *Histoire politique des juifs de France* (Paris, 1990), pp. 74-91, and Hyppolite Prague, "Politique juive et patriotisme antisemite," in *Archives israëlites* 27 (4 July 1895), p. 209.

[69] On Jew as outsider and pollutant, see Shmuel Trigano, "From Individual to Collectivity: The Rebirth of the 'Jewish Nation' in France," in Malino and Wasserstrom, op. cit., pp. 245-281, and Caron, op. cit., p. 18.

[70] Hyppolite Prague, "Kippour et l'ésprit du sacrifice," *Archives israëlites* 77b (5 October 1916), p. 157.

[71] Hyppolite Prague, "Purim", *Archives israëlites* 77 (16 March 1916): 41.

[72] *Archives israëlites* 15 July 1915, p. 114, and 28 October 1915, p. 173.

[73] Quoted in S. Halff, "The Participation of the Jews of France in the Great War," in *American Jewish Yearbook* 21 (1919-20), pp. 85f.

[74] André Spire, *Les juifs et la guerre* (Paris, 1917), pp. 18f.

IVAN STRENSKI

FRANCE, PRACTICE OF JUDAISM IN, FROM DE GAULLE TO THE PRESENT: To understand recent developments in French Jewry, we must keep in mind four important events: the French Revolution, the Décret Crémieux that gave French nationality to Algerian

Jews, the Holocaust, and the independence of Algeria or, in general, the post-colonization era. The modern period for French Jewry begins in the last decade of the eighteenth century, when, *de jure*, the Jews of the kingdom of France received equality of rights. But this new status was, indeed, a matter of law alone, not of practice, as the Jews' integration into the French bourgeoisie was postponed or delayed because of several waves of rabid antisemitism, culminating in the Dreyfus affair of 1894. During the nineteenth century, amid serious attacks on religion, which were even harsher when they had Judaism as a target, the actual process of emancipation went hand in hand with assimilation. Many conversions to Christianity seriously weakened Jewish religious practice, even as, in the academic world, learned non-Jews like Ernest Renan (1823-1892) criticized Judaism on many levels.

Between the two world wars, French Jewry had a brilliant religious leadership, very active not only in the synagogue but also in the academic world. Despite this vibrant leadership, in the decades following the end of World War II, as French Jewry bemoaned huge losses, many survivors who returned from the concentration camps turned their backs to religion and religious practice. This led the late chief rabbi of France, Jacob Kaplan (d. 1995), to speak of the need to restore souls rather than simply to rebuild stones, that is, to reconstruct the synagogues. Similarly, a former president of the Consistoire Central, the main religious organization of French Jewry, the well-respected Baron Alain de Rothschild, spoke of the French Jewish community as a desert.

A revival took place only after 1962, when almost the whole of Algerian Jewry determined to emigrate to metropolitan France, completely changing the face of Judaism in that country. The legacy of the North African emigration was felt as a refreshing and vivifying potion that gave new energy to the "dried bones" of the existing Ashkenazic Jews. At the same time, of course, this complete change of physiognomy had significant and far-reaching consequences on Jewish-

religious practice in the country. Suddenly the Consistoire de Paris, the biggest and most important of all other Consistoires in the Consistoire Central de France, was confronted with new demands: synagogues needed to be built very rapidly, not only in Paris but even more importantly in the suburbs now housing huge Jewish communities: Créteil, Sarcelles, Garges, Saint Brice, and so on. The Séminaire Israélite de France, heir to the Ecole Centrale Rabbinique of Metz, where rabbis are educated and ordained, needed to furnish these newly-born communities with appropriately trained clergy. And the Consistoire needed as well to meet the demands for schools to educate children, for certification of kosher restaurants, butcher-shops, and slaughterer-houses, and for synagogue administrators and staff.

Meeting these tremendous needs created significant difficulties that remain obvious to this day. These difficulties are exacerbated, moreover, by the range of religious cultures and social backgrounds now present within French Jewry. The religion of the immigrants remains intermingled with superstition and local rites that appear, in France, to be completely obsolete. Even so, Sephardic religious practices, alongside those of the oriental communities in general (including, now, Jews from Turkey, Egypt, Libya, and elsewhere), gradually have permeated the entire French Jewish community. The result is that today in Paris, where almost half a million Jews live, it is difficult to find more than one Ashkenazic synagogue. Nor is there any longer even a single kosher restaurant in which Ashkenazic religious customers can taste chopped liver, an Eastern European dish! This is despite the fact that about forty kosher butcher-shops stand in Paris,with more than thirty additional ones in the suburbs,[1] alongside more than a hundred kosher restaurants that operate in Paris under Bet Din supervision and fifty-one Jewish caterers that can supply weddings and Bar Mitzvah celebrations with kosher food.

The continued attention to religious practice evident in these numbers should not hide a worrying consequences of the presence of the Sephardic element, especially in religious life. While the heirs of the first emigration wave have become dentists, surgeons, university professors, judges, lawyers, barristers, members of parliament, and so on, their social evolution has not involved the area of religious practice, in which they stick to the religious manners of their fathers, considering an enlightened religion a betrayal of the religion of their ancestors. But this has not provided an appropriate context for Jewish practice of less traditionally oriented French Jews. Thus, except at the great Synagogue La Victoire, where there is a choir and opera singers, worship remains quite simple and reminds one of the old good habits of North Africa. Sephardic Jews continue to sing the prayers together with the cantor, even as Ashkenazic Jews are content to sit and listen. Formerly the Rabbinic elite was almost thoroughly form Alsace-Lorraine; now the only chief rabbi who is also a Rabbinic judge and the head of the Seminaire Rabbinique is Michel Gugenheim, whose own father, Ernest Gugenheim, had the same function.

At least, overall, it is not difficult to practice Judaism in France, where most big cities have synagogues, Jewish schools, ritual baths (miqvaot), and butcher-shops. But shortcomings must also be delineated, shortcomings that go to the heart of the question of the extent to which modern French Jews will remain integrated, as Jews, within European-French society. Thus we find today great competition between the moderate Jewish practice of the Consistoire and Bet Din, on the one side, and Lubavitch Hasidism (Chabad), on the other. This competition is conspicuous particularly in the areas of education and Rabbinic ideology. Some of the about fifty Jewish schools in Paris that cover the nursery ages through grammar school belong to the Lubavitch movement, which would like to rebuild the entire system of Jewish education according to its ideology. Another fact is equally or even more worrying: some directors of schools that belong to the Consistoire de Paris reject the use of meat slaughtered under the supervision of

the Bet Din. The result is both a potentially serious split in the Jewish community and the rejection by the Jews of tomorrow of the previously accepted ideology of religious learning with secular knowledge (Torah im derekh erets), which has allowed several generations of French Jews to live as Jews even as they have participated fully in French culture and society. This inner conflict within the Jewish community seems likely to prove very harmful and dangerous if a way is not found to unify the several contemporary tendencies.

Still, most of the Jewish schools today present a well-balanced program of Jewish religious and secular academic disciplines: the Ecole Maïmonide (Boulogne sur Seine), the Ecole Yavné (Paris), and the Ecole Lucien de Hirsch (Paris) are among the schools that have the best results at the Baccalauréat (the last step before university) and that stick to the ideals of Samson Raphael Hirsch, formalized in the modern orthodox movement. The situation is different when we look at religious practice within the general population, for, as a matter of fact, the so-called traditionalist communities, even those belonging to the Consistoire de Paris, tend to be much less traditional than they pretend to be. The traditionalists, of course, worship in orthodox synagogues on Friday evenings and Saturday mornings and on the most important Jewish festivals. But driving to synagogue, forbidden under Sabbath and festival law, is common, and these Jews, unlike their strictly orthodox rabbis, do not necessarily observe the dietary regulations or drink only kosher wine.

As in other western countries, this discrepancy between the life-style chosen by Jews and the demands of the orthodox rabbinate has led to the development of a quite strong liberal and reform community. There are today three liberal synagogues in Paris, offering family seating (rather than the traditional separation of the sexes), the recitation of segments of the worship in French, the chanting of a shortened weekly Torah portion, and the reading of the prophetic Haftorah in French as well as Hebrew. The introduction of egalitarian practices, allowing women full

participation in the service, and the centrality of the rabbi's sermon also mark liberal
worship, as does the availability to Jews who
marry non-Jewish partners of some rabbis
who will perform the wedding according to
Jewish tradition. This is in marked contrast
to the strict policy of the Consistoire de Paris,
which, besides refusing to sanction such
marriages, will not even allow a non-Jew's
conversion to Judaism explicitly for purposes
of marriage to a Jew.

At the same time, liberal Judaism has
influenced the orthodox in some positive directions. Between the two world wars, it was
common practice even in traditional synagogues to mark a girl's reaching of the age
of religious majority through the bat mitzvah
ceremony. For a time after the war, perhaps
in response to orthodoxy's attempt to maintain its boundaries, this practice was discon-
tinued. Now, as the reform movement has
become stronger, this custom has prevailed
anew, and orthodox rabbis have been compelled to accept it. The readings done by the
young girls take place at the end of the worship, after the conclusion of public prayer
proper. But, nevertheless, they are heard by
the entire congregation.

The demographics of French Jewry:
While we surmise that the Jewish population
in France today is between 700,000 and
750,000, for several reasons the exact number cannot be ascertained. The main difficulty
is that large numbers of Jews do not wish to
be considered members of the community.
This is for two related reasons, first, the desire to escape antisemitism, which has led,
second, to total assimilation into the culture
of Christian France, including acceptance of
French socio-culture—celebration of Christ-
mas and Easter, and so on. Another difficulty
in ascertaining the exact Jewish population
is structural. While Anglo-Saxon and formerly German Jews traditionally were members of synagogues, in which they paid Bar
Mitzvah and weddings fees and the like, this
is no longer uniformly the case. A similar
problem pertains to North-African Jews, who
have always had a much looser community
system. Once, simply counting all French

synagogue members would have provided at
least a foundation for establishing a reliable
figure of the number of Jews in France. But
this clearly is no longer the case (fig. 48).

But one feature of the Jewish population
is quite certain: about 80% of Jews live in
Paris or in the vicinity, that is, on the Ile de
France. The other big Jewish centers are
Strasbourg, Lyon, Marseilles. These big
cities are strong enough to have their own
Consistoire Regional, their own slaughtering system, and their own rabbinical courts.
Even for these cities, however, the Paris community remains an institutional center, for instance, providing the rabbinical supervisors
to organize sales of kosher wines. This is, of
course, paradoxical, since Strasbourg, Lyon,
and Marseilles have many vineyards, while
Paris has none.

As just noted, social evolution has loos-
ened French Jews' ties to their religious community, leading to the significant problem
of intermarriage. While there are no hard
statistics, it is likely that the rate of Jews' marrying non-Jews is now fifty percent. While
French traditional rabbis refuse to sanction
or participate in such wedding celebrations,
one rabbi, Marcel Stourdze, a survivor of
Auschwitz and the son of the late Haim
Stourdze, an orthodox but also enlightened
rabbi in Paris, has done so. The situation,
as already noted, is different within the liberal rabbinate.

Community organization: The Consistoire de Paris controls about a hundred
synagogues, primarily in Paris' XVI arron-
dissement, which includes the Mishkenot
Israel Synagogue, alongside the Synagogue
La Victoire, one of only two Ashkenazic
synagogues in Paris controlled by the Consistoire. Several others do not belong to the
Consistoire de Paris, that of Rue Cadet and
that of Rue Montevideo, in the XVI arron-
dissement, the so-called west side of Paris,
where the wealthiest Jews generally live. The
principal synagogues of Paris are the great
Synagogue La Victoire, Buffault (Portuguese rite), Salnt-Lazare (Algerian rite), Les
Tournelles, Don Isaac Abrabanel (a somewhat Turkish rite), and Chassloup-Laubat

(Sephardic). There are also some smaller synagogues, referred to as "oratoires," located in community centers, such as Edmond Fleg (Latin Quarter or Centre Communautaire; Rue Rochechouart) and the Centre Rachi, which is the largest Jewish community center in Europe. This community center houses the Jewish community's most important radio station, the monthly journal *L'Arche*, and large conference facilities.

Centre Rachi also houses many Jewish organizations, such as the Conseil Representatif des Institutions Juives de France (CRIJF), WIZO, the Cooperation Feminine, associations of Jewish schools, and the smaller organizations of war refugees and Holocaust survivors (fig. 49).

Liberal synagogues include that on the Rue Gaston de Caillavet (XV Arrdss.) and the one on Rue Copernic, which is the best known. While the Talmud Torah—the grammar school system—of the liberal community has enjoyed a very good reputation, significant problems divide the liberal and orthodox Jewish communities, especially regarding matters of personal status involving the impact of intermarriage and conversions not performed according to orthodox standards. The Bet Din of Paris, the central Jewish legal body, is orthodox, and from the perspective of this body, the liberal community's laxity in allowing weddings or conversions that do not meet the strictest guidelines of traditional law is very problematic.

Division is also caused by the Consistoire's and large traditional community's failure to play a leading part in introducing the participation of women in communal life. This is despite the fact that, gradually, a number of meritorious women have been integrated into the Consistoire's commissions for synagogue administration. Even so, in 1997, for the first time, four women are now elected to sit on the Consistoire proper. If they are elected, a serious cultural revolution will have been consummated within French Jewry, very much against the desires of some high-ranking religious leaders.

Fund raising within French Jewry is under the almost exclusive control of the Fonds Social Juif Unifie (FSJU), which created the Appel Unifie Juif de France (AUJF), and which, in Paris and other cities, raises money mainly for Israel.

It bears noting that only eight or nine percent of French Jews—50,000 to 60,000—are involved in any formal way within the "organized community." Even so, the existence today of the new medium of the Jewish radio station has completely changed the daily consciousness of the Jews in France. These stations reach thousands and thousands of Jews, whom they can call to public demonstrations or other meetings immediately. The stations thus may increase the activity and Jewish self-consciousness even of Jews who do not formally belong to the organized community. The radio-stations serve a different purpose as well. Despite the opposition of the rabbinate, they broadcast the liturgical rites of all the Jewish festivals, so that even Jews who are uninvolved in religious practice often know that to it is a holiday and have some sense of participation in religious worship.

Contemporary French Jewish leadership: Owing to the Napoleonic tradition, France has thirteen chief rabbis and eighty ancillary rabbis; among them, some visit the sick in the hospitals and others, the prisoners in jail, whom they supply with kosher food, especially for Jewish festivals. A main personality within this leadership is the chief rabbi, Joseph Sitruk, a rather young, charismatic man, who speaks monthly to more than two thousand persons in the great Synagogue La Victoire. He also takes part in some television ceremonies, for instance, the Journee des Deportes, directly broadcast all over France, and he lectures in freemason lodges and testifies on behalf of the Jewish community before French courts of justice, for instance, in cases involving antisemitism, such as, recently, the profanation of the cemetery in Carpentras.

The chief rabbi is the highest spiritual leader of French Jewry and the *ex officio* highest authority of the French Jewish court (Bet Din). Thus he is also the final arbiter of all Rabbinic placements, which are determined initially by the Consistoire de Paris. Below the Chief Rabbi of France are chief rabbis of large cities. The current chief rabbi of Paris, David Messas, is a Moroccan Jew who previously was chief rabbi of Geneva. His father, Shalom Messas, is chief rabbi of Jerusalem.

The court system is under the leadership of the Av Bet Din, currently Nessim Rebibo, also a Moroccan Jew, who studied in the U.S.A. and holds U.S. citizenship. He supervises the system of kashrut certification and presides in cases of personal status, which concern whether or not, under the law, a particular individual is to be deemed a Jew.

The lay leadership includes Jean Kahn, a wealthy businessman of Luxembourg with residence in Strasbourg, who presides over the Consistoire Central. The French government has appointed him president of the National Commission on Human Rights. He is also president of the Consistoire Israelite du Bas Rhin in Strasbourg. Moise Cohen is president of the Consistoire de Paris and has mightily contributed to its modernization, including the determination finally to include women in the Consistoire's Assembly. This author, Maurice-Ruben Hayoun, university professor in Paris and Heidelberg, is Secretaire Rapporteur of the Consistoire de Paris and presents the *rappon moral* each year in front of the assembly. He is also president of the Commission Culture et Reflexion sur l'Avenir du Judaïsme. Rabbi Gilles Bernheim, Shmuel Trigano, Armand Abecassis, and also Rabbi Josy Eisenberg are important thinkers and philosophers with a great interest in the French Jewish community.

The community's institutions and the involvement in them of a new generation of highly educated and charismatic advocates for Judaism reflect French Jewry's continued vibrancy in the face of demographic circumstances that in France, as in the rest of the western Jewish world, have given Jews reason for great concern. This suggests that, despite the community's general strength today, the continued vitality of French Jewry will depend on the development of higher standards of learning, especially with greater opportunities for Torah study. In conjunction with the increased dialog with European culture that is certain to emerge, the main features of the French Jew of the second millennium will be shaped.

Notes

[1] *Calendrier [luah] de l'ACIP*, 1997-1998.

MAURICE-RUBEN HAYOUN

FREE WILL, FATE, PROVIDENCE, IN CLASSICAL JUDAISM: The opposing concepts of free will and determinism (that is, fate) represent contrasting ways of understanding the world in which we live and of comprehending the ability of people to shape that world and to control their place in it. Ileana Marcoulesco defines the doctrines of free will and fate as follows:[1]

> [B]elief in free will amounts to the conviction that, as individuals, human beings are endowed with the capacity for choice of action, for decision among alternatives, and specifically that, given an innate moral sense, man can freely discern good and evil and choose the good, though he often does not. Determinism is the philosophical view that, given certain initial conditions, everything that ensues is bound to happen as it does and in no other possible way; thus nothing in nature is contingent, nor is there any room for human freedom.

The doctrine of fate thus holds that "events are unalterably predetermined from eternity" (*OED*), unfolding within an interrelated chain of causality. In light of these fixed interrelationships, individual choice cannot exist. Since everything stands in a predetermined relationship to everything else, no independent decisions are possible. The most extreme forms of determinism hold that even what appears to be a choice or to represent an individual's exercise of free will in fact is necessitated by the structure of history, determined by God at the time of creation. This is to say that even though, in daily life, people seem to face an array of possible alternatives, if fact, they can only "choose" the option that already is preordained and required within the structure of causality that comprises the world. The doctrine of determinism thus understands no provision to exist for the exercise of free will. For, according to this way of looking at the world, any free choice, unanticipated within the fixed cosmic order, would nullify that entire order, invalidating all other preordained interrelationships.

The doctrine of determinism stands in opposition to the concept of free will, referred to also as chance. Rejecting the idea of fate, those who conceive of the existence of free will hold that events unfold only in direct response to the decisions people make in their exercise of free choice.[2] This doctrine rejects the notion that there is a preset order or plan for the unfolding of history. Rather, the doctrine of free will holds that the decisions and choices of individual human actors shape the world and determine its future. In this view, people innately know how to identify and choose that which is good, even though they do not necessarily do so. But however they choose, their choices are free, and humans pay the consequences, living in a world created by decisions made by individuals as well as by the collective decisions of all people who comprise family, community, nation, and humankind.

While theories of free will or chance insist that people are free to choose good and evil and so to shape the world in which they live, these theories do not necessarily deny the existence of a deity directly connected with and interested in the human sphere. Doctrines of free will, this is to say, may be conjoined with a concept of providence, the idea of the benevolent care for the world of a God who is intimately concerned with and responds to the actions of human beings. Biblical Judaism, for instance, understands God to have made a promise to Abraham, later renewed with each patriarch and, finally, formalized with the people of Israel as a whole in the covenant at Sinai. According to this covenant, the people of Israel will become a great and mighty nation and possess a land flowing with milk and honey. Even though it claims that the future is preordained, in the Israelite perspective, this divine plan does not negate the existence of free will. Rather, within the Israelite comprehension of the divine plan, human responsibility, and, hence, free will, have a central importance. For the ancient Israelites perceived

each individual to have the obligation and the freedom to make choices commensurate with achieving the goal God set for them. Scripture thus presents a theory of divine providence that holds that, when the people act in accordance with the terms of the covenant, they will be protected by God, who providentially cares for those who are true to his law. But those who sin, or the sinful nation as a whole, are subject to punishment. In the biblical view, then, the eventual fulfillment of God's promise is certain, even though the path to its realization is dependent upon the behavior of the people of Israel, who have free will and whose actions God rewards or punishes as appropriate.

At the same time, we should be clear that the biblical concept of free choice masks the extent to which Scripture joins its view of divine providence with a deterministic notion of history. Deut. 30:16-20, first, highlights the idea of free choice. The Israelites here are depicted as having the power to choose God's blessing or curse, to act in accordance with the terms of the covenant or to reject God's law:

> If you obey the commandments of the Lord your God which I command you this day, by loving the Lord your God, by walking in his ways, and by keeping his commandments and his statutes and his ordinances, then you shall live and multiply, and the Lord your God will bless you in the land which you are entering to take possession of it. But if your heart turns away, and you will not hear, but are drawn away to worship other gods and serve them, I declare to you this day, that you shall perish; you shall not live long in the land which you are going over the Jordan to enter and possess. I call heaven and earth to witness against you this day, that I have set before you life and death, blessing and curse; therefore choose life, that you and your descendants may live, loving the Lord your God, obeying his voice, and cleaving to him; for that means life to you and length of days, that you may dwell in the land which the Lord swore to your fathers, to Abraham, to Isaac, and to Jacob, to give them.

Despite the picture of free will presented by this passage in Deuteronomy and many like it, throughout Scripture's story of the people of Israel, it also is clear that God already knows everything that will happen, including the choices people will make. This is evident in Gen. 15:12-16's depiction of God's original promise to Abraham:

> As the sun was going down, a deep sleep fell on Abram; and lo, a dread and great darkness fell upon him. Then the Lord said to Abram, "Know of a surety that your descendants will be sojourners in a land that is not theirs, and will be slaves there, and they will be oppressed for four hundred years; but I will bring judgment on the nation which they serve, and afterward they shall come out with great possessions. As for yourself, you shall go to your fathers in peace; you shall be buried in a good old age. And they shall come back here in the fourth generation; for the iniquity of the Amorites is not yet complete."

In the continuation of the narrative, God details for Abraham the rules that he must follow as obligations under the covenant with God. In this, Scripture clearly comprehends the existence of free will, to be exercised by Abraham and his descendants in their decision to abide by or reject God's law. At the same time, Gen. 15:12-16 proposes that God already knows exactly what will occur over the next approximately seven hundred years of Israelite history and, presumably, beyond. The promise that Abraham's progeny will be a great and mighty nation living where Abraham now dwells will be kept. But this will occur only after Abraham's death, when "the iniquity of the Amorites" is complete. This comment about the Amorites itself illustrates precisely how Scripture mixes ideas of determinism and free will. On the one hand, the Amorites surely are understood here to exercise free will. If they do not have the ability to choose to be righteous, it is hardly possible to speak of their iniquity. And yet, on the other hand, God already knows the outcome: the Amorites will "choose" to continue to transgress, and, as a result, God will turn their land over to the Israelite people. The Amorites, like the Israelites, seem to have free will. But, since the choices they will make already are known to God, they may also be understood to have no real choices at all.

To explain this dichotomy, the Bible's perspective may be described as a "soft" determinism. This perspective holds that even though our destiny is preordained, so that our actions are caused, this causality does not *entirely* compel our will. People thus still exercise some level of free choice.[3] This system alternatively may be described as a doctrine of providential free will. In this understanding, God's providence does not take the form of a preset and unchanging plan for the world. Providence is evidenced, rather, in the deity's continuing interaction with the human sphere. People are free to make their choices, and God responds appropriately, punishing or rewarding human beings as appropriate, but always guiding them—whether as individuals or communities—towards a preordained future. Small, individual choices thus are free, even though the larger trajectory of history is pre-ordained.

Concepts of free will and fate in post-biblical Judaism: The Hebrew Bible thus merges the conceptions of free will, fate, and providence. (1) It describes a God who is intimately connected with the workings of the world and with individuals in that world; (2) it perceives God already to know the future, such that a divine plan for the world determines everything that will happen; (3) yet Scripture understands God to have granted humans free will, the ability freely to choose whether to live righteously in accordance with God's will (which will bring divine reward) or to violate God's commandments (which will lead to divine retribution).

Scripture's unsystematic conjoining of these at least partially contradictory ideas leads, in the formative period of classical Judaism, to a range of different approaches to the question of free will and fate, each of which, as we shall see, focuses upon one element of the biblical perspective. Indeed, the contrasting approaches encompassed by Scripture are understood by Josephus to have yielded the chief philosophical differences among the main Judaic sects of his day. At *Antiquities* 13:171, he writes:

> Now at this time there were three schools of thought among the Jews, which held different opinions concerning human affairs; the first being that of the Pharisees, the second

that of the Sadducees, and the third that of the Essenes. As for the Pharisees, they say that certain events are the work of Fate, but not all; as to other events, it depends upon ourselves whether they take place or not. The sect of Essenes, however, declares that Fate is mistress of all things, and that nothing befalls men unless it be in accordance with her decree. But the Sadducees do away with Fate, holding that there is no such thing and that human actions are not achieved in accordance with her decree, but that all things lie within our own power, so that we ourselves are responsible for our well-being, while we suffer misfortune through our own thoughtlessness.[4]

Josephus thus describes the central Jewish sects of his day as philosophical schools, differentiated by their attitudes towards free will. The Pharisees, he here says, combine notions of fate and free will. At *Antiquities* 18:12, he offers a more detailed explanation of this contrast:

> Though they [that is, the Pharisees] postulate that everything is brought about by fate, they still do not deprive the human will of the pursuit of what is in man's power, since it was God's good pleasure that there should be a fusion and that the will of man with his virtue and vice should be admitted to the council-chamber of fate.[5]

God, the Pharisees believe, guides individual lives and human history, responding as appropriate to the choices people make in their exercise of free will. Thus the Pharisees account for both free will and divine providence, very much like the soft determinism that, as we saw above, is central in Scripture itself. The Sadducees, by contrast, take the idea of free will to its logical outcome. If people indeed are free to choose to live as they desire, then everything that happens must be a matter of chance, that is, of the confluence of decisions made by individuals in the exercise of their free will. Such an approach leaves no place for fate, which denies or at least severely restricts people's ability freely to choose. Unlike both of these views, finally, the Essenes view the world according to a doctrine of strict determinism. According to this view, everything is predestined and unfolds according to a preordained divine plan. There is no free will at all.

The distinct approaches to the problem of free will represented by the Pharisees, Sadducees, and Essenes awaken us to the unsystematic nature of the Bible's approach to this issue. As we see here, classical Jewish thinkers had difficulty maintaining Scripture's conception of an all-knowing, providential God while also allowing for free will. Within the Rabbinic literature, to which we now turn, yet another resolution—again an unsystematic one—is suggested for this dichotomy.

The Rabbinic linking of determinism and free will: The particular historical setting of early Rabbinic Judaism shaped the Rabbinic concepts of fate and free will. For in the first centuries C.E., the rabbis worked to make sense of events that had belied the Israelites' ability, whether through adherence to the law or through use of military might, to control their own destiny. The destruction of the Second Temple in 70 C.E., the failed Bar Kokhba revolt of 133-135 C.E., and the firm establishment of Christianity as the official religion of the Roman world in the fourth-sixth centuries had a dramatic impact on both the political and theological contexts in which Judaism existed. In light of these historical developments, all contemporary theologies of Judaism had to respond to the question that had been phrased succinctly and emotionally shortly after the destruction of the Second Temple when the author of 4 Ezra asked (3:32-34, 6:59):

> Have the deeds of Babylon been better than those of Zion? Has any other nation known You besides Zion? . . . If the world has indeed been created for our sakes, why do we not enter into possession of our world? How long shall this endure?

The Rabbinic response to questions such as these was two fold. The emergence of a firm determinism claimed that all is in the hands of God and that, despite the nation's current circumstances, God has established an overall plan by which, ultimately, the Israelites will regain their land and former glory. This theory of fate proposed that, in the meantime, the people's lowered social station and lack of political power neither reflected their actual standing in the eyes of God nor anticipated God's eventual goal for them.

At the same time, Rabbinic authorities could not and did not entirely give up the biblical notion that people in all events have the power of free will, that they are empowered to choose whether or not to abide by God's commandments, and that, by electing to follow the covenantal law, they assure God's providential protection. While the reward for obedience might not be immediately felt, the rabbis, like Scripture, are clear that God protects those who follow the divine will and that when the nation as a whole conforms to God's expectations, the suffering will end. Even as the character and direction of one's life were seen as largely predetermined, people thus were understood to have free will, and God, in his providential concern for humanity, was believed to respond positively to those who followed his dictates.

This combination of fate, free will, and providence allowed the rabbis to explain the current circumstance of the Jewish people—despised yet destined for glory; politically and militarily powerless yet, through their determination to abide by the covenantal law, empowered and assured of future salvation. The joining of these essentially contradictory ideas is nowhere clearer than in the paradoxical concept, expressed by Aqiba, that "everything is foreseen, yet free choice is given" (M. Ab. 3:15). This statement both responds to the dichotomous circumstance of the Jews, and, additionally, recognizes the paradoxical nature of human thinking about fate in the first place: from the point of view of the ordinary individual, it makes no difference whether all is determined by fate or up to chance, whether people's actions are predetermined or the result of their exercise of free will.[6] This is because, even if, as the rabbis themselves largely hold, everything is predestined, people have no foreknowledge of the path they are ordained to follow. As a result, they must perforce approach each choice as though they in fact exercise free will. While the outcome of their deliberation may indeed already be known to God, from the human standpoint, the decision appears freely to be made.

While thus avowing the existence of free will, the rabbis generally focus on the idea that, from the beginning, God knew how things would turn out, such that all is predestined. This idea emerges from the comprehension that the world was created as a cogent whole, with its purpose preexisting the actual creation. The rabbis thus understand all that was needed to accomplish God's ultimate purpose has having been provided from the beginning of time (Gen. Rab. I.IV):[7]

1.A. ["In the beginning God created" (Gen. 1:1)] Six things came before the creation of the world, some created, some at least considered as candidates for creation.

B. The Torah and the throne of glory were created [before the creation of the world].

C. The Torah, as it is written, "The Lord made me as the beginning of his way, prior to his works of old" (Prov. 8:22).

D. The throne of glory, as it is written, "Your throne is established of old" (Ps. 93:2).

E. The patriarchs were considered as candidates for creation, as it is written, "I saw your fathers as the first-ripe fruit in the fig tree at her first season" (Hos. 9:10).

F. Israel was considered [as a candidate for creation], as it is written, "Remember your congregation, which you got aforetime" (Ps. 74:2).

G. The Temple was considered as a candidate for creation, as it is written, "You, throne of glory, on high from the beginning, the place of our sanctuary" (Jer. 17:12).

H. The name of the messiah was kept in mind, as it is written, "His name exists before the sun" (Ps. 72:17).

I. R. Ahbah bar Zeira said, "Also [the power of] repentance.

J. "That is in line with the following verse of Scripture: 'Before the mountains were brought forth' (Ps. 90:2). From that hour: 'You turn man to contrition and say, Repent, you children of men' (Ps. 90:3)."

K. Nonetheless, I do not know which of these came first, that is, whether the Torah was prior to the throne of glory, or the throne of glory to the Torah.

L. Said R. Abba bar Kahana, "The Torah came first, prior to the throne of glory.

M. "For it is said, 'The Lord made me as the beginning of his way, before his works of old' (Prov. 8:22)."

N. "It came prior to that concerning which

it is written, 'For your throne is established of old' (Ps. 93:2)."

2.A. R. Huna, R. Jeremiah in the name of R. Samuel b. R. Isaac: "Intention concerning the creation of Israel came before all else.

B. "The matter may be compared to the case of a king who married a noble lady but had no son with her. One time the king turned up in the market place, saying, 'Buy this ink, inkwell, and pen on account of my son.'

C. "People said, 'He has no son. Why does he need ink, inkwell, and pen?'

D. "But then people went and said, 'The king is an astrologer, so he sees into the future and he therefore is expecting to produce a son!'

E. "Along these same lines, if the holy one, blessed be he, had not foreseen that, after twenty-six generations, the Israelites would be destined to accept the Torah, he would never have written in it, 'Command the children of Israel.'" [This proves that God foresaw Israel and created the world on that account.]

3.A. Said R. Benaiah, "The world and everything in it were created only on account of the merit of the Torah.

B. "'The Lord for the sake of wisdom [that is, Torah] founded the earth' (Prov. 3:19)."

C. R. Berekiah said, "It was for the merit of Moses.

D. "'And he saw the beginning for himself, for there a portion of a ruler [that is, Moses] was reserved' (Deut. 33:21)."

4.A. R. Huna in the name of Rab repeated [the following]: "For the merit of three things was the world created, for the merit of dough-offerings, tithes, and first fruits.

B. "For it is said, 'On account of [the merit of] what is first, God created . . .' (Gen. 1:1).

C. "And the word 'first' refers only to dough-offering, for it is written, 'Of the first of your dough' (Num. 15:20).

D. "The same word refers to tithes, as it is written, 'The first fruits of your grain' (Deut. 18:4).

E. "And the word 'first' refers to first fruits, for it is written, 'The choicest of your land's first fruit' (Exod. 23:19)."

This extended exposition sees a link between the natural world of creation and the historical world of Israel, its life and salvation. The world was created because of Israel.

The details of creation thus were specific to the world as it would later exist. The Torah, in particular, is a blueprint that describes exactly what will happen throughout time. Underlying this perspective is the comprehension that a correspondence and relationship exist between all aspects of the world as humans encounter them. The world was created on account of the Torah, including all that was necessary to assure fulfillment of what is stated in the Torah. This is an extreme statement of determinism, holding that everything is preordained by God and so controlled by fate.

Alongside the plan for what would occur throughout history, the rabbis hold that, at the time of creation, God made the specific objects through which that history would evolve. This means that Israel and the other nations, for their part, act out prepared roles in the preordained plan (M. Ab. 5:6):[8]

A. Ten things were created on the eve of the [first] Sabbath at twilight, and these are they:

B. (1) the mouth of the earth [Num. 16:32]; (2) the mouth of the well [Num. 21:16-18]; (3) the mouth of the ass [Num. 22:28]; (4) the rainbow [Gen. 9:13]; (5) the manna [Exod. 16:15]; (6) the rod [Exod. 4:17]; (7) the Shamir;[9] (8) letters; (9) writing, (10) and the tables of stone [of the ten commandments, Exod. 32:15].

C. And some say, "Also the destroyers, the grave of Moses, and the tamarisk of Abraham, our father."

D. And some say, "Also: the tongs made with tongs [with which the first tongs of the cult were made]."

Since, from the time of creation, God knew what would happen and prepared for it, there appears to be no room in the world for the chance outcomes that result from people's exercise of free choice. For instance, rather than God's surprise at human sinfulness, described at Gen. 6:5-6, which leads God to bring a flood (Gen. 6:6), the rabbis understand the rainbow to have been created before the first Sabbath. This means that God already knew that people would sin, that there would be a flood, and that, afterwards, God would promise never again to destroy the earth and would offer the rainbow as a sign of that commitment. In the Rabbinic view, there are no surprises for God. All is in place and ready for the preordained time to arrive.

In keeping with this attitude, the rabbis even reject the notion, explicit in Scripture, that God can determine at will to respond through miracles to the condition of the world or situation of the Israelite people. The rabbis rather understood even the miracles described in the Bible to have been preordained, arranged and prepared for at the time of creation. As the just cited passage explains, both the manna consumed by the Israelites after the Exodus from Egypt and the mouth of Balaam's talking ass were created by God in the beginning. These eventualities were part of the order of the cosmos, not a violation of that order. Only to people do they appear as extraordinary. Similarly, the rabbis explain that even the splitting of the Red Sea had been preordained (Exod. Rab. 21:6):

A. "Lift up your rod, [and stretch out your hand over the sea and divide it, that the people of Israel may go on dry ground through the sea;" Exod. 14:16]:
B. Said Moses in the presence of the holy one, blessed be he, "You are telling me that I should split the sea and make the sea into dry land!
C. "But [suggesting that this is impossible] thus it is written [Jer. 5:22]: 'I placed the sand as the bound for the sea, [a perpetual barrier which it cannot pass; though the waves toss, they cannot prevail, though they roar, they cannot pass over it].'
D. "So, lo, you have promised that you would never split [the sea, and, accordingly, I cannot do so now]!"
E. Said R. Eleazar Haqappar, "Said to him Moses, 'Is it not so that you said that the sea would not be made dry land, as it is said [Jer. 5:22]: "I placed the sand as the bound for the sea'"?
F. "'And it is [further] written [Job 38:8], "Or who shut in the sea with doors, when it burst forth from the womb?"'
G. "Said to him the holy one, blessed be he, '[You have erred in your exposition, since] you have not read from the beginning of the Torah!
H. "'What is written [there]? "And God said," 'Let the waters under the heavens be gathered together [into one place, and let the dry land appear;"' Gen. 1:9].

I. "'I am the one who made the stipulation with [the sea regarding its condition].
J. "'Thus I stipulated from the beginning that I would split it, as it says [Exod. 14:27]: "And the sea returned to its wonted [or 'stipulated;' the root appears to be the same] flow when the morning appeared."
K. "'[This means that it returned] in light of the stipulation that I stipulated for it from the beginning.'"

History unfolds as the logical and necessary consequence of plans that were made at the time of creation. Everything was prepared from the beginning, so that history represents a series of events linked in causal relationships. All derive ultimately from God's original, encompassing plan and so are independent of any decisions that people might believe they make in the exercise of their free will. This perspective is well illustrated by the notion that, in order later to be able to carry out the Exodus from Egypt, God needed already at the time of creation to stipulate that, during the Exodus, the sea would split and allow the Israelites to cross. Were it not for this precondition, even God could not later issue a command that would divide the sea. Once the preordained progression of history was set in motion at the time of creation, even God no longer had the power of free choice so as to change what already had been planned. God, it seems, is as subject to fate as are people.

To a striking extent, the rabbis understand the same rules of predetermination that apply to the people of Israel as a whole to extend even to individuals within the people. This means that, just as the course of Israelite and human history is predetermined and unchangeable, so individuals do not have the ability, through exercise of free choice, to change their own personal circumstances. This is clear at B. Ta. 25a, where the Talmud reports an incident involving the impoverished sage Eleazar b. Pedat:

A. R. Eleazar b. Pedat was in great need.
B. He was bled [to relieve an illness], but had nothing to eat [afterwards].
C. He took the skin of a garlic bulb and threw it into his mouth [whereupon he] became faint and fell asleep.

D. Rabbis went to ask about him and saw him crying and laughing [at the same time], while a ray of light shone from his forehead.

E. When he awoke they said to him, "Why did you cry and laugh?"

F. He said to them, "For the holy one, blessed be he, sat with me, and I said to him, 'For how long must I suffer in this world?'"

G. "And he said to me, 'Eleazar, my son, would you be satisfied that [to improve your situation], I return the entire world to its beginning?'

H. "'[If I did so] *perhaps* you would be born at a time of sustenance [that is, a more propitious time]!'

I. "I said to him, 'All of this [would be necessary to change my fortune], and [still] it is only a possibility [that I would wind up better off]?!'"

This passage, like the ones cited before it, goes well beyond the simple notion of divine providence and expresses instead a hard determinism. There is nothing that Eleazar can do—nothing, in fact, that God can do—to change Eleazar's earthly circumstance. That circumstance has been ordained in the structure of the world, not just from the time of his birth but from creation itself. To change it accordingly would require restructuring that world, going back to the very time of creation. But even were God to do this, there could be no guarantee that Eleazar would wind up better off. This is the case for only one possible reason: God's providential concern for humanity does not extend to, or allow God to respond to, the particular needs of any individual.

The denial of God's providential power to intercede stands, on the one hand, in contrast to what often is suggested in the Rabbinic literature, that a watchful God is intimately involved with the affairs of individual human beings. This idea of personal providence is expressed, for instance, when Hanina reports that "a person does not hurt his finger on earth unless it has been decreed from above" (B. Hul. 7b) or when Ec. Rab. 10:11 states that all occurrences in people's lives, ranging from snake bites to the actions of governments, are incited by God.[10] But, on the other hand, in denying God's power

to change the circumstance of an individual, B. Ta. 25a reflects the encompassing perspective of materials such as we have been reviewing, which hold that everything is dependent upon fate and which insist that the foreordained order of things cannot be altered, even by God. In this Rabbinic perspective, the fate of each individual is inextricably tied to the system created by God at the beginning. God has the power, perhaps, to change the entire world and so to change the system. But even God cannot alter a single part of the system or guarantee that revising the system as a whole will benefit a specific individual.

The way in which this approach responds to the world in which the rabbis themselves lived, referred to above, should be clear. Eleazar b. Pedat is righteous and learned, and yet he suffers. God recognizes his piety and yet is unable to change that which has been preordained. Speaking within the Talmudic period, such thinking surely offered at least the beginning of an explanation for the suffering the people of Israel experienced in exile and under foreign dominion. Eleazar's story suggests that God is all-powerful and remains with the people. God further has a plan by which his original promises under the covenant will eventually be fulfilled. In the meantime, the people must accept their condition, an aspect of the suffering that God inflicts upon those whom God loves (B. Ber. 5a; see below). Contrary to what might otherwise be thought, the current diminution of Israel's status does not demonstrate the end of God's power over the world or the cessation of God's providential concern for the Israelite nation. It is simply beyond human reason or comprehension, part of the divine plan that will end with Israelite glory.

The existence of free will: The stance detailed so far, which holds that God determined everything at the time of creation, leaves little room for people, through their exercise of free will, to make choices that will change their relationship to the world around them and allow them to transcend their current circumstance. This perspective suggests, rather, that everything is fated. In keeping with this approach, the rabbis even held that such individual matters as the determination of whom one will marry is predetermined by God (B. Sot. 2a).

But even as the rabbis' determinism flows from the biblical conception of an all-powerful and all-knowing God, the denial of free will that this determinism carries in its wake belies the central biblical tenet that individuals have the capacity and obligation to choose whether or not they will accept and follow the terms of the covenant. Scripture, this is to say, is clear that people are free to choose how they will live their lives and that their choices—by determining how God treats them—affect the order of the world. This idea of free choice stands, of course, at the heart of the covenantal agreement between God and the people of Israel, as it is described at Deut. 30:16-20, cited above. In the Deuteronomic perspective, people have the free option of choosing life or death, the blessing or the curse. In response to this choice, God determines the quality and length of the individual's life, on the one side, and how the nation as a whole will fair in relationship to the other nations of the world, on the other. So contrary to the strict determinism that we have reviewed so far, Scripture is clear that people have free will, the ability to choose their actions and so to affect their individual and national destiny.

In response to this biblical thinking, even while maintaining a deterministic notion of fate, Rabbinic Judaism finds a way also to allow for free will. The rabbis accomplish this through the ironic notion that, despite the existence of a preordained plan and program for the world and each individual in it, people still have the ability freely to choose whether or not to accede to God's will. This idea is expressed in the concept that "All is in the hands of heaven except for the fear of heaven" (B. Ber. 33b). The rabbis thus distinguish between material existence, in which, as we have seen, they understand everything to be predetermined, and spiritual life, in which they understand people to have the choice of abiding by or rejecting God's will.

In line with this thinking, God can be depicted as all-knowing and all-powerful even though, at the same time, people are seen to be empowered to choose righteousness and, through this exercise of their free will, to assure their ultimate salvation. B. Ber. 33b explains the matter as follows:[11]

A. And R. Hanina said, "Everything is in the hands of heaven except fear of heaven.
B. "For it is said, 'And now, Israel, what does the Lord, your God, require of you but to fear' (Deut. 10:12)."
C. Is fear of heaven such a small thing?
D. And has not R. Hanina said in the name of R. Simeon b. Yohai, "What the Holy One, blessed be he, has in his treasury is only a treasure of fear of heaven.
E. "For it is said, 'The fear of the Lord is his treasure' (Is. 33:6)."
F. Indeed, so far as Moses was concerned, it was a small thing!
G. For R. Hanina said, "The matter is to be compared to a man from whom people sought a big utensil. If he has it, to him it seems a small thing. If they ask for a small utensil and he does not have it, to him it seems a big thing."

Fate determines everything except whether or not people will choose to fear heaven, the one thing God has left up to people. But, the passage points out, this is the most central decision people can possibly make. It is the only choice that really matters, since, even though choosing to fear heaven does not assure earthly rewards, it does determine whether or not the individual will acquire spiritual treasures.

This approach to the problem of free will appears to respond profoundly to the real world in which people live and especially to the world of the Jews of the Talmudic age. For this approach recognizes that people in fact do not generally have the power to change their physical condition and that, however we wish to believe in God's providence, the righteous and the wicked seem to suffer the same fate (as Eccl. 3:17-19, for instance, had pointed out long before Talmudic times). At B. Ber. 33b the rabbis responded by arguing that such earthly rewards are not in any event important. Proper conduct under the law, rather, provides a spiritual reward, the most valuable thing a person can possess. This means that, despite the political and social condition of the Israelite nation, its people retain the power, through the exercise of their will, to follow the covenant, and so to reap the most important rewards God can offer, the spiritual awards offered to those who follow the covenant.

Still, as we see, contrary to the view of Scripture, the Rabbinic notion of free choice does not carry with it a conception of direct and immediate divine reward or punishment. The rabbis, unlike Scripture, that is, do not focus upon or insist that there is a direct connection between one's choices and one's earthly fate. In keeping with its overall determinism, even while acknowledging that an individual's sins may account for suffering and that the free choice to repent can bringing suffering to an end, the Rabbinic literature still asserts that, in the final analysis, one's fate is determined by God and so is not in his or her own hands. This means that the correlation between behavior and fate is not certain; even a righteous person may suffer. The point is made at B. Ber. 5a:[12]

A. Said Raba, and some say, R. Hisda, "If a person sees that sufferings afflict him, let him examine his deeds.

B. "For it is said, 'Let us search and try our ways and return to the Lord' (Lam. 3:40).

C. "If he examined his ways and found no cause [for his suffering], let him blame the matter on his wasting [time better spent in studying] the Torah.

D. "For it is said, 'Happy is the man whom you chastise, O Lord, and teach out of your Torah' (Ps. 94:12).

E. "If he blamed it on something and found [after correcting the fault] that that had not, in fact, been the cause at all, he may be sure that he suffers the afflictions that come from God's love.

F. "For it is said, 'For the one whom the Lord loves he corrects' (Prov. 3:12).

G. Said Raba said R. Sehorah said R. Huna, "Whomever the holy one, blessed be he, prefers he crushes with suffering.

H. "For it is said, 'The Lord was pleased with him, hence he crushed him with disease' (Is. 53:10).

I. "Is it possible that even if the victim did not accept the suffering with love, the same is so?

J. "Scripture states, 'To see if his soul would offer itself in restitution' (Is. 53:10).

K. "Just as the offering must be offered with the knowledge and consent [of the sacrifier], so sufferings must be accepted with knowledge and consent.

L. "If one accepted them in that way, what is his reward?

M. "'He will see his seed, prolong his days' (Is. 53:10).

N. "Not only so, but his learning will remain with him, as it is said, 'The purpose of the Lord will prosper in his hand' (Is. 53:10)."

A person may be able to bring an end to suffering by atoning and changing his ways. But this is not necessarily the case, since God also chooses to afflict those who are righteous. Such afflictions flow from God's love, and, in the view of the passage before us, one who accepts them ultimately will prosper.

But contrary to this view, not all Rabbinic sources even accept the notion that suffering can be understood as an aspect of God's love, let alone that it invariably will be rewarded. For the rabbis elsewhere assert that God's preordained plan and program for the universe are entirely beyond human comprehension. Things are the way they are because that is how God has made them; there is no comprehending or questioning God's logic. This attitude is expressed clearly in the often cited passage at B. Men. 29b:

A. Said R. Judah said Rab, "At the time that Moses went up on high, he found the holy one in session, affixing crowns to the letters [of the Torah]. He said to him, 'Lord of the universe, who is stopping you [from regarding the Torah as perfect without these crowns]?'

B. "He said to him, 'There is a man who will arrive at the end of many generations, and Aqiba b. Joseph is his name, who will interpret on the basis of each point of the crowns heaps and heaps of laws.'

C. "He said to him, 'Lord of the universe, show him to me.'

D. "He said to him, 'Turn around.'

E. "[Moses] went and took a seat at the end of eight rows, but he could not grasp what the people were saying. He felt faint. But when the discourse reached a certain matter, and the disciples said [to Aqiba], 'My lord, how do you know this?' and he answered, 'It is a law given to Moses from Sinai,' [Moses] regained his composure.'

F. "[Moses] went and came before the holy one. He said before him, 'Lord of the universe, How come you have someone like that and yet you give the Torah through me?'

G. "He said to him, 'Silence! That is how I have determined it.'

H. "[Moses] said to him, 'Lord of the Universe, you have shown me his Torah, now show me his reward.'

I. "He said to him, 'Turn around.'

J. "[Moses] turned around and saw [Aqiba's] flesh being weighed out at the butcher-stalls in the market.

K. "He said to him, 'Lord of the universe, such is Torah, such is the reward?'

L. "He said to him, 'Silence! That is how I have determined it.'"

When God established the Torah he knew that, generations later, a particular human would interpret it. This suggests that already at the time of creation, God had in mind that people's intellect, through their involvement with Torah and their decisions regarding the law, would determine the meaning and content of that law. This ability to interpret Torah suggests both free will and people's ability to make decisions that are not preordained by or known to God. And yet, in describing Aqiba's fate, the passage suggests that, in all events, what will happen to people *is* preordained and known to God, and, moreover, has no clear, logical relationship to what the person deserves. The greatest scholar of Torah will die a martyr's death simply because that is how God has determined things. This means that, so far as humanity is concerned, there can be no understanding of God's decisions. Aqiba's fate—the fate of all the people of Israel—has been preordained, and no humanly comprehensible motivation or meaning explains it. Fate unfolds simply in the way that God has decided it should.

This attitude is familiar from the book of Ecclesiastes, which notes that the limited perspective of mortal humans makes it impossible for them to perceive the point and meaning of God's overall plan (see, e.g.,

Eccl. 3:1-15). What is left for people, exactly as the statement of Hanina at B. Ber. 33b puts it, is to fear heaven. That is the extent of the free will God has granted humankind. All else is preordained, so that even following the mandate to fear God cannot assure an immediate reward. Even so, the rabbis depict people's love of God—and God's love of Israel that comes in return—as the greatest treasure one can possess. People freely choose to serve God, and with that choice comes the assurance that some day, at the end of time, God's plan for the people of Israel, described in the covenant at Sinai, will be fulfilled. The rabbis thus unite the disparate conceptions of fate and free will under a larger, encompassing doctrine of divine providence.[13]

Notes

[1] *Encyclopedia of Religion* (New York, 1987), vol. 5, p. 419.

[2] See John M. Dillon, "Fate, Greek Conception of," in *Anchor Bible Dictionary*, vol. 2, p. 776.

[3] See Marcoulesco, who distinguishes such an approach from "hard" determinism, which holds that "none of our actions is free, but only appear to be so; consequently, moral responsibility is an illusion as well."

[4] Translation: R. Marcus, *Antiquities VII.* (Cambridge, 1957), pp. 311-312.

[5] Translation: L. Feldman, *Antiquities IX.* (Cambridge, 1969), pp. 11-12.

[6] On the emergence of this idea in Greek though, see Dillon, op. cit., pp. 776-778.

[7] For further reflections on this theme, see Lev. Rab. 36.

[8] See also B. Pes. 54a and Sif. Deut. 355.

[9] An insect that cut stones with its glance (see M. Sot. 9:12), understood in Rabbinic sources to have been used by Moses to cut the jewels used in the ephod worn by the high priest.

[10] See in this vein B. B.B. 11a, which records that when Benjamin the righteous fell ill and was dying, the ministering angels reminded God of Benjamin's piety in giving charity, and God, in response, healed him and added twenty-two years to his life. So in certain settings, the Rabbinic literature also portrays quite graphically God's providential concern as being evidenced in direct interventions into the lives of individuals.

[11] Translation, Tzvee Zahavy.

[12] Translation, Tzvee Zahavy.

[13] On the concepts of fate and free will in medieval Jewish philosophy, see JUDAISM, PHILOSOPHY AND THEOLOGY OF, IN MEDIEVAL TIMES.

ALAN J. AVERY-PECK

G

GOD IN JUDAISM, THE CLASSICAL STATE-MENT: The religion, Judaism is made up of three components: [1] the Torah, oral and written, [2] Israel the holy people, and [3] God. God is creator of the world, giver of the Torah, and redeemer of Israel. Israel the holy people meets God in the Torah at Sinai, when God—not Moses—proclaims, "The Lord, the Lord! a God compassionate and gracious, slow to anger, abounding in kindness and faithfulness, extending kindness to the thousandth generation, forgiving iniquity, transgression, and sin" (Exod. 34:6). Only in the revelation of the Torah does Israel attain that certain knowledge about God that holy Israel offers humanity.

To state matters in more general terms: the religion that the world calls "Judaism" calls itself "the Torah." Judaism knows God through the Torah. The Torah tells the story of God's self-revelation to humanity through Israel, beginning with Abraham. It is because God wants to be known and makes himself known that Israel claims to know God, and the Torah—the teaching of God from Sinai, written and oral—contains that knowledge that God wishes to impart to humanity. For those who practice Judaism, the encounter with God takes place in the Torah, hence, in the study of the Torah. The place and time for meeting God is not only at prayer, then, but in the holy circle of sage and disciples, and it is in books that portray God's self-revelation to Moses at the burning bush (Exod. 3) or in the still small voice Elijah heard (1 Kgs. 19:12-13), that through all time Israel finds God. In more secular language, Judaism knows God through God's self-manifestation in the Torah—and otherwise, so Judaism maintains, there should be no specific, reliable knowledge of God, Creator of heaven and earth, who reveals the Torah and who redeems humanity at the end of days.

God of vengeance: Does that mean that God is the angry and vengeful God that many see described in the Old Testament?

The picture of God whom we meet in the Old Testament when read without sages' interpretation and the God whom the Judaic faithful worship in synagogue prayer under the tutelage of the sages of the oral Torah are not quite the same, for the Hebrew Scriptures that Christianity knows as the Old Testament do not exhaust the Judaic doctrine of God. The Torah of Judaism encompasses not only Scripture—the written part of revelation—but also an oral tradition. Only in the whole Torah, written and oral, do we find the complete doctrine of God that Judaism sets forth. In that one whole Torah that is God's self-manifestation to the supernatural community that God has called into being, called "Israel," God appears as infinitely merciful and loving, passionate as a teen-age lover, whom the Judaic community knows above all by the name, "the All-Merciful." God is made manifest to Israel in many ways, but is always one and the same.

Characterization of God: Certainly one of the most memorable characterizations presents God as a warrior, but the following passage shows that that presentation is only partial (Mekhilta Attributed to R. Ishmael Shirata Chapter One = XXIX:2):

A. "The Lord is a man of war, the Lord is his name" (Exod. 15:3):

B. Why is this stated?

C. Since when he appeared at the sea, it was in the form of a mighty soldier making war, as it is said, "The Lord is a man of war,"

D. and when he appeared to them at Sinai, it was as an elder, full of mercy, as it is said, "And they saw the God of Israel" (Exod. 24:10),

E. and when they were redeemed, what does Scripture say? "And the like of the very heaven for clearness" (Exod. 24:10); "I beheld until thrones were placed and one that was ancient of days sat" (Dan. 7:9); "A fiery stream issued" (Dan. 7:10)—.

F. [so God took on many forms.] It was, therefore, not to provide the nations of the world with an occasion to claim that there are two dominions in heaven [but that the same God acts in different ways and appears in different forms].

G. that Scripture says, "The Lord is a man of war, the Lord is his name."

H. [This then bears the message:] The one in Egypt is the one at the sea, the one in the past is the one in the age to come, the one in this age is the one in the world to come: "See now that I, even I, am he" (Deut. 32:39); "Who has wrought and done it? He who called the generations from the beginning. I the Lord, the first, and with the last I am the same" (Is. 41:4).

The main point is clear: however we know God, in whatever form or aspect, it is always one and the same God.

The supernatural community that calls itself "Israel"—that is, the Judaic equivalent of "the Church"—knows and loves God as the heart and soul of its life. Three times a day the faithful pray, morning, dusk, and after dark, and throughout the day, responding to blessings that cascade over them, faithful Israelites (that is, Jews who practice the religion, Judaism) respond with blessings of thanks, for matters as humble as a glass of water, or as remarkable as surviving a car crash. So faithful Israel knows God as intimate friend and companion and never wanders far from God's sight or God's love.

But what about philosophy, particularly philosophy of religion? People in general suppose that philosophers can prove the existence of God, that nature's plan or history's course points toward a Creator and Savior. But the specific truths about God that Judaism learns—the ones that the Torah teaches—come only from God's own self-revelation in the Torah itself. Philosophy sets forth knowledge of God in general, that is, the knowledge to be gained by sifting our experience in this world and drawing conclusions from it. Arguments for the existence of God that move from creation to Creator exemplify how philosophy affords such knowledge. The written Torah presents its argument in behalf of divine dominion from the facts of nature: "Where were you when I laid the earth's foundations? Speak if you have understanding. Do you know who decided its dimensions or who measured it with a knife?

Onto what were its bases sunk? Who set its cornerstone when the morning stars sang together and all the divine beings shouted for joy?" (Job 38:4-7).

Since Israel knows God through the Torah, which reports to Israel exactly what God has told and what sages have handed on from the revelation at Sinai, an account of the instruction concerning God in the several documents of the oral part of the Torah provides a precis of what it is that Israel knows about God. In the first of the documents that make up the oral part of the Torah, which is the Mishnah, we may accurately speak of what Israel knows about God. But in later compilations, Israel no longer knows only about God. God then is set forth as more than a principle and a premise of being (such as philosophers know about God), and more, even, than as a presence, as pious people know about God through prayer. Rather, Israel knows God as a person and, at the end of the formation of the oral Torah, even as a fully-embodied personality. Sages know God in four aspects:

[1] principle or premise, that is, the one who created the world and gave the Torah;

[2] presence, e.g., supernatural being resident in the Temple and present where two or more persons engaged in discourse concerning the Torah;

[3] person, e.g., the one to whom prayer is addressed; and

[4] personality, a God we can know and make our model.

When God emerges as a personality, God is represented [1] as corporeal; [2] exhibits traits of emotions like those of human beings; [3] does deeds that women and men do, in the way in which they do them.

In the Mishnah read along with its related writings, God makes an appearance as principle or premise and also as presence; the God of Judaism is never merely the God that followers must invoke to explain how things got going and work as they do. In the next stage in the unfolding of the oral Torah, represented by the Talmud of the Land of Israel and related writings, God is portrayed not only as principle and presence, but as a person. In the third and final stage, God emerges as a fully-exposed personality, whom we can know and love. It goes without saying that, since God is known through the Torah, sages recognize no need to prove the existence of God. The Torah proves the existence of God, and the glories of the natural world demonstrate the workings of God in the world. What humanity must do is explore what it means to be "in our image, after our likeness" (Gen. 1:26), that is, to be "like God." That fact explains why through its account of God, Rabbinic Judaism sets forth its ethics, the account of the proper way of life. The sages bear the task of setting forth, through the oral Torah that they transmit, precisely the answer to that question: how ought humanity to form itself so as to be "in God's image," "after God's likeness," and what does that mean.

In the oral part of the Torah, as much as in the written part of the Torah, God, who created the world and gave the Torah to Moses, encounters Israel in a vivid and personal way. But while some of the documents of the oral Torah portray God only as a premise, presence, and person, but not as a personality with whom human beings may identify, others represent God as a personality, specifically like a human being whom people may know and love and emulate. The categories of premise, presence, and person hardly require much explanation. As premise, God forms (in philosophical terms) the ground of being. That is how God plays a principal part in the Mishnah. Otherwise uncharacterized, God may form a presence and be present in all things. As a person, again without further amplification, God is a "you," for example, to whom people address prayers. When portrayed as a personality, God is represented in an incarnate way, not merely by appeal to anthropomorphic metaphors, but by resort to allusions to God's corporeal form, traits of attitude and emotion like those of human beings, capacity to do the sorts of things mortals do in the ways in which they do them, again, corporeally. In all of these ways, the incarnation of God is accomplished by treating God as a personality.

In writings redacted in the earlier stages in the formation of the Judaism of the dual Torah, beginning with the Mishnah, therefore, God does not make an appearance as a vital personality, with whom other personalities—human ones—transact affairs. Other documents, in particular in the later stages in the unfolding of that same canonical system, by contrast, represent God in quite personal terms. These, as already suggested, are three: outer traits, inner characteristics, and capacity for concrete action done as human beings carry out their wishes. That is to say, in some of these later documents God appears in corporeal form. God exhibits traits of emotion and exemplifies virtuous attitudes. God carries out actions as human beings do—and does them in the same way. That is the portrait of God appearing as a personality, not as a mere premise of being, abstract presence, or even disembodied person.

What we shall see, therefore, is that the Babylonian Talmud represents God in the flesh on the analogy of the human person. Prior to the Bavli, the faithful encountered God as abstract premise, as unseen presence, as a "you" without richly defined traits of soul, body, spirit, mind, or feeling. The Bavli's authorship for the first time in the formation of Judaism presented God as a fully-formed personality, like a human being in corporeal traits, attitudes, emotions, and other virtues, in actions and the means of carrying out actions. God then looked the way human beings look, felt and responded the way they do, and did the actions that they do in the ways in which they do them. And yet in that portrayal of the character of divinity, God always remained God. The insistent comparison of God with humanity "in our image and likeness" comes to its conclusion in one sentence that draws humanity upward and does not bring God downward. For, despite its treatment of the sage as a holy man, the Bavli's characterization of God never confused God with a sage or a sage with God. Quite to the contrary, the point and purpose of that characterization reach their climax in a story that in powerful language demands that in the encounter with the sage of all sages God be left to be God.

God as Premise, Presence, Person, and Personality: The oral Torah portrays God in four ways: as premise, presence, person, and personality.

[1] God as premise, occurs in passages in which an authorship reaches a particular decision because that authorship believes God created the world and has revealed the Torah to Israel. We therefore know that God forms the premise of a passage because the particular proposition of that passage appeals to God as premise of all being, e.g., author and authority of the Torah. Things are decided one way, rather than some other, on that basis. That conviction of the givenness of God who created the world and gave the Torah self-evidently, defines the premise of all Judaisms before our own times. There is nothing surprising in it. But a particular indicator, in so general a fact, derives from the cases in which for concrete and specific reasons, in quite particular cases, sages invoke God as foundation and premise of the world. When do they decide a case or reach a decision because they appeal to God as premise, and when do they not do so? But this conception is much more subtle, since the entire foundation of the Mishnah, the initial statement of the oral Torah, rests upon the conception of the unity of God. The purpose of the Mishnah is to show how, in the here and now of the social and natural world, we see what it means that God is one.

[2] God as presence stands for yet another consideration. It involves an authorship's referring to God as part of a situation in the here and now. When an authorship—e.g., of the Mishnah—speaks of an ox goring another ox, it does not appeal to God to reach a decision for them and does not suggest that God in particular has witnessed the event and plans to intervene. But when an authorship—also in the Mishnah—speaks of a wife's being accused of unfaithfulness to her husband, by contrast, that authorship expects that God will intervene in a particular case, in the required ordeal and so declare the decision for the case at hand. In the former instance, God is assuredly a premise of discourse, having revealed in the Torah the rule governing a goring ox. In the latter, God is not only premise but very present in discourse and in making a decision. God furthermore constitutes a person in certain settings, not in others.

[3] One may readily envisage God as premise without invoking a notion of the particular traits or personality of God. So too, in the case of God as presence, no aspect of the case at hand demands that we specify particular attitudes or traits of character to be imputed to God. But there is a setting in which God is held always to know and pay attention to specific cases, and that involves God as a "you," that is, as a presence. For example, all discourse concerning liturgy in the Mishnah (obviously not alone in that document) understands that God also hears prayer, hence is not only a presence but a person, a you, responding to what is said, requiring certain attitudes and rejecting others. In a later document, by contrast, God is not only present but a participant, if only implicitly, when the Torah is studied among disciples of sages. Here too we find an interesting indicator of how God is portrayed in one situation as a premise, in a second as a presence, and in a third as a person.

In cases in which God is portrayed as a person, however, there are regulations to which God adheres. These permit us to imagine that God is present, without wondering what particular response God may make to a quite specific situation, e.g., within the liturgy. We do not have to wonder, because the rules tell us. Accordingly, while God is a liturgical "you," God as person still is not represented in full particularity, reaching a decision on a specific case in accord with traits of mind or heart or soul that yield out of a unique personality, different (by nature) from all other personalities, a concrete decision or feeling or action. God as person but not as personality remains within the framework established at the outset when we considered the matters of God as premise and as presence.

[4] God emerges as a vivid and highly distinctive personality, actor, conversation-partner, hero. In references to God as a personality, God is given corporeal traits. God looks like God in particular, just as each

person exhibits distinctive physical traits. Not only so, but in matters of heart and mind and spirit, well-limned individual traits of personality and action alike endow God with that particularity that identifies every individual human being. When God is given attitudes but no active role in discourse, referred to but not invoked as part of a statement, God serves as person. When God participates as a hero and protagonist in a narrative, God gains traits of personality and emerges as God like humanity: God incarnate.

The Hebrew Scriptures had long ago portrayed God in richly personal terms: God wants, cares, demands, regrets, says and does—just like human beings. In the written Torah God is not merely a collection of abstract theological attributes and thus rules for governance of reality, nor a mere person to be revered and feared. God is not a mere composite of regularities, but a very specific, highly particular personality, whom people can know, envision, engage, persuade, impress. Sages painted this portrait of a personality by making up narratives, telling stories in which God figures like other (incarnate) heroes. When therefore the authorships of documents of the canon of the Judaism of the oral half of the dual Torah began to represent God as personality, not merely premise, presence, or person, they reentered that realm of discourse about God that Scripture had originally laid out.

True, that legacy of Scripture's God as actor and personality constituted for the sages who in the first six centuries C.E. created the Judaism of the dual Torah an available treasury of established facts about God—hence, God incarnate. But within the books and verses of Scripture sages picked and chose, and they did so for God as well. In some points in the unfolding corpus, without regard to the entire range of available facts of Scripture, God was represented only as implicit premise, in others, as presence and source of action, in still others as person. So the repertoire of Scripture tells us solely what might have been. It is only at the end, in the Bavli, that we reach to what did come about, which is the portrayal, much as in Scripture and on the strength of Scripture's facts, of God as personality, with that same passionate love for Israel that, as Scripture's authorships had portrayed matters, had defined God in the received, written Torah.

A definitive statement of the proposition that God appears to humanity in diverse forms is at Pesiqta deRab Kahana XII:XXV, which represents the state of opinion of the fully-exposed religious system of Judaism, at the time of the Talmud of the Land of Israel:

> 1.A. Another interpretation of *I am the Lord your God [who brought you out of the land of Egypt]* (Exod. 20:2):
> B. Said R. Hinena bar Papa, "The Holy One, blessed be he, had made his appearance to them with a stern face, with a neutral face, with a friendly face, with a happy face."
> C. "with a stern face: in Scripture. When a man teaches his son Torah, he has to teach him in a spirit of awe."
> D. "with a neutral face: in Mishnah."
> E. "with a friendly face: in Talmud."
> F. "with a happy face: in lore."
> G. "Said to them the Holy One, blessed be he, 'Even though you may see all of these diverse faces of mine, nonetheless: *I am the Lord your God who brought you out of the land of Egypt* (Exod. 20:2)."

So far we deal with attitudes. As to the iconic representation of God, the continuation of the passage is explicit:

> 2.A. Said R. Levi, "The Holy One, blessed be he, had appeared to them like an icon that has faces in all directions, so that if a thousand people look at it, it appears to look at them as well."
> B. "So too when the Holy One, blessed be he, when he was speaking, each Israelite would say, 'With me in particular the Word speaks.'"
> C. "What is written here is not, I am the Lord, your [plural] God, but rather, *I am the Lord your [singular] God who brought you out of the land of Egypt* (Exod. 20:2)."

That God may show diverse faces to various people is now established. The reason for God's variety is made explicit. People differ, and God, in the image of whom all mortals are made, must therefore sustain diverse images—all of them formed in the model of human beings:

3.A. Said R. Yose bar Hanina, "And it was in accord with the capacity of each one of them to listen and understand what the Word spoke with him.

B. "And do not be surprised at this matter, for when the manna came down to Israel, all would find its taste appropriate to their circumstance, infants in accord with their capacity, young people in accord with their capacity, old people in accord with their capacity."

C. "infants in accord with their capacity: just as an infant sucks from the teat of his mother, so was its flavor, as it is said, *Its taste was like the taste of rich cream* (Num. 11:8)."

D. "young people in accord with their capacity: as it is said, *My bread also which I gave you, bread and oil and honey* (Ez. 16:19)."

E. "old people in accord with their capacity: as it is said *the taste of it was like wafers made with honey* (Exod. 16:31)."

F. "Now if in the case of manna, each one would find its taste appropriate to his capacity, so in the matter of the Word, each one understood in accord with capacity."

G. "Said David, *The voice of the Lord is in [accord with one's] strength* (Ps. 29:4)."

H. "What is written is not, *in accord with his strength in particular*, but rather, *in accord with one's strength*, meaning, in accord with the capacity of each one."

I. "Said to them the Holy One, blessed be He, 'It is not in accord with the fact that you hear a great many voices, but you should know that it is I who [speaks to all of you individually]: *I am the Lord your God who brought you out of the land of Egypt* (Exod. 20:2).'"

The individuality and particularity of God rest upon the diversity of humanity. But, it must follow, the model of humanity—"in our image"—dictates how we are to envisage the face of God. And that is the starting point of our inquiry. The Torah defines what we know about God—but the Torah also tells us that we find God in the face of the other: in our image, after our likeness, means, everyone is in God's image, so if we want to know God, we had best look closely into the face

of all humanity, one by one, one by one. But let us start at the beginning.

God as Premise: Philosophers work by rational steps, from premises to propositions, then, sifting evidence, conducting argument, reaching upward to conclusions. For the philosophers of the Mishnah, God is both the unitary premise of all being and also the unitary goal of all being. In the Mishnah—as in all other writings of Judaism—God is present not merely in details, when actually mentioned, but at the foundations. To characterize the encounter with God, whether intellectual or concrete and everyday, we must therefore pay attention not alone to passages that speak of God in some explicit way, but, even more so, to the fundamental givens on which all particular doctrines or stories of a document depend. In the case of the Mishnah this is simple. That great philosophical law code demonstrates over and over again that all things are one, complex things yield uniform and similar components, and, rightly understood, there is a hierarchy of being, to be discovered through the proper classification of all things.

The most important thing the philosophers who wrote the Mishnah wished to demonstrate about God is that God is one. And this they proposed to prove by showing, in a vast array of everyday circumstances, the fundamental order and unity of all things and the unity of all things in a hierarchy that ascends upward to God. So all things through their unity and order flow to one thing; all being derives from One God.

In the Mishnah many things are placed into sequence and order—"hierarchized"—and the order of all things is shown to have a purpose, so that the order, or hierarchization, is purposive, or "teleological." The Mishnah time and again demonstrates these two contrary propositions: many things join together by their nature into one thing, and one thing yields many things. These propositions complement each other, because, in forming matched opposites, the two set forth an ontological judgment. All things are not only orderly, but, in their deepest traits of being, are so ordered that many things fall into one classification, and one thing may hold together many things of a single classification. For this philosophy, then, rationality consists in the hierarchy of the order of things, a rationality tested and proved, time and again, by the possibility always of effecting the hierarchical classification of all things. The proposition that is the Mishnah's is a theory of the right ordering of each thing in its classification (or taxon), all the categories (or taxa) in correct sequence, from least to greatest. And showing that all things can be ordered, and that all orders can be set into relationship with one another, we transform the ontological message into its components of proposition, argument, and demonstration.

God serves as premise and principle (and whether or not it is one God or many gods, a unique being or a being that finds a place in a class of similar beings hardly is germane!), and philosophy serves not to demonstrate principles or to explore premises, but to analyze the unknown, to answer important questions. In such an enterprise the premise, God, turns out to be merely instrumental. But for philosophers, intellectuals, God can live not in the details, but in the unknowns, in the as-yet unsolved problem and the unresolved dilemma. So in the Mishnah God lives in the excluded middle, is revealed in the interstitial case, is made known through the phenomena that form a single phenomenon, is perceived in the one that is many, is encountered in the many that are one. For that is the dimension of being—that immanental and sacramental dimension of being—that defines for this philosophy its statement of ultimate concern, its recurrent point of tension, its generative problematic.

That then is the urgent question, and the ineluctable and self-evidently truthful answer finds God in the form, God in the order, God in the structure, God in the heights, God at the head of the great chain of well-ordered being, in its proper hierarchy. True, God is premise, scarcely mentioned. But it is because God's name does not have to be mentioned when the whole of the order of being says that name, and only that name, and always that name, the Name unspoken because it is always in the echo, the silent, thin voice, the numinous in all phenomena of relationship: the interstitial God of the Mishnah.

God in person: Had Judaism emerged from the Mishnah, philosophers over the ages would have found themselves with an easy task in setting forth in a systematic and abstract way the doctrine of God and our relationship with God: the first principle, much like the unmoved mover of Greek philosophy, the premise, the presence, above all, the one who made the rules and keeps them in place. But that philosophical God will have puzzled the faithful over time, who found in the written Torah the commandment to "love the Lord your God with all your heart, with all your soul, and with all your might," a commandment not readily carried out in behalf of the unmoved mover, the principle and premise of being. Such a God as the philosophers set forth is to be affirmed and acknowledged, but by knowledge few are changed, and all one's love is not all that easily lavished on an abstract presence. When we come to the Talmud of the Land of Israel we meet God in familiar but also fresh representation.

The context in which the Yerushalmi took shape—the legitimation, then state-sponsorship, of Christianity—requires mention. The symbolic system of Christianity, with Christ triumphant, with the cross as the now-regnant symbol, with the canon of Christianity now defined and recognized as authoritative, called forth from the sages of the Land of Israel a symbolic system strikingly responsive to the crisis. The representation of God in man, God incarnate, in Jesus Christ, as the Christians saw him, found a powerful reply in sages' re-presentation of God as person, individual and active. God is no longer only, or mainly, the premise of all being, nor is God only or mainly the one who makes the rules and enforces them. God is now presented in the additional form of the one who makes decisions in the here and now of everyday life, responding to the individual and his or her actions. Not only so, but the actions of an individual are treated one by one, in the specific context of the person, and not all together, in the general context of the social world overall. And, as we saw in the

Mishnah, that is not the primary activity of God at all.

At Y. San. 10:1.IX, God serves as the origin of all great teachings, but as we have seen, that fact bears no consequences for the description of God as a person or personality:

> E. "Given by one shepherd" (Exod. 12:11)—
> F. Said the Holy One, blessed be he, "If you hear a teaching from an Israelite minor, and the teaching gave pleasure to you, let it not be in your sight as if you have heard it from a minor, but as if you have heard it from an adult,"
> G. "and let it not be as if you have heard it from an adult, but as if one has heard it from a sage,"
> H. "and let it not be as if you have heard it from a sage, but as if one has heard it from a prophet,"
> I. "and let it not be as if you have heard it from a prophet, but as if one has heard it from the shepherd,"
> J. "and there is as a shepherd only Moses, in line with the following passage: 'Then he remembered the days of old, of Moses his servant. Where is he who brought out of the sea the shepherds of his flock? Where is he who put in the midst of them his holy Spirit?'" (Is. 63:11).
> K. "It is not as if one has heard it from the shepherd but as if one has heard it from the Almighty."
> L. "Given by one Shepherd"—and there is only One who is the Holy One, blessed be he, in line with that which you read in Scripture: "Hear, O Israel: the Lord our God is one Lord" (Deut. 6:4).

In studying the Torah, sages and disciples clearly met the living God and recorded a direct encounter with and experience of God through the revealed word of God. But in a statement such as this, alluding to, but not clearly describing, what it means to hear the word of the Almighty, God simply forms the premise of revelation. There is no further effort at characterization. The exposition of the work of Creation (Y. Hag. 2:1.IIff.) refers to God's deeds, mainly by citing verses of Scripture, e.g., "Then he made the snow: 'He casts forth his ice like morsels' (Ps. 147:17)," and so on. So too God has wants and desires, e.g., God wants Israel to repent, at which time God will save Israel (Y. Ta.

1:1X.U), but there is no effort to characterize God.

God is understood to establish a presence in the world. This is accomplished both through intermediaries such as a retinue of angels and also through the hypostatization of divine attributes, e.g., the Holy Spirit, the Presence of Shekhinah, and the like. The Holy Spirit makes its appearance, e.g., "They were delighted that their opinion proved to be the same as that of the Holy Spirit" (Y. Hor. 3:5.III.PP, Y. A.Z. 3:1.II.AA, etc.). God is understood to enjoy a retinue, a court (Y. San. 1:1IV.Q); God's seal is truth. These and similar statements restate the notion that God forms a living presence in the world. Heaven reaches decisions and conveys them to humankind through the working of chance, e.g., a lottery (Y. San. 1:4.V.FF-GG):

> To whomever turned up in his hand a slip marked "Elder," he said, "They have indeed chosen you in Heaven." To whomever turned up in his hand a blank slip, he would say, "What can I do for you? It is from Heaven."

The notion that the lottery conveys God's will and therefore represents God's presence in the decision-making process will not have surprised the authorship of the book of Esther. It is one way in which God's presence is given concrete form. Another, also supplied by Scripture, posited that God in the very Presence intervened in Israel's history, e.g., at the Sea of Reeds (Y. San. 2:1.III.O):

> When the All-Merciful came forth to redeem Israel from Egypt, he did not send a messenger or an angel, but the Holy One, blessed be he, himself came forth, as it is said, "For I will pass through the Land of Egypt that night" (Exod. 12:12)—and not only so, but it was he and his entire retinue.

The familiar idea that God's presence went into Exile with Israel recurs (Y. Ta. 1:1. X.Eff.). But not a single passage in the entire Yerushalmi alleges that God's personal presence at a historical event in the time of sages changed the course of events. The notion that God's presence remained in Exile leaves God without personality or even ample description.

Where God does take up a presence, it is not uncommonly a literary device, with no important narrative implications. For example, God is assumed to speak through any given verse of Scripture. Therefore the first person will be introduced in connection with citing such a verse, as at Y. San. 5:1.IV.E, "[God answers,] 'It was an act of love that I did . . . [citing a verse,]' 'for I said,' 'The world will be built upon merciful love'" (Ps. 89:2). Here since the cited verse has an "I," God is given a presence in the colloquy. But it is a mere formality. So too we may say that God has made such and such a statement, which serves not to characterize God but only to supply an attribution for an opinion (Y. Ned. 6:9.III.CCCC):

> A. It is written, "These are the words of the letter that Jeremiah . . . sent from Jerusalem to the rest of the elders of the exiles" (Jer. 29:1).
> B. Said the Holy One, blessed be he, "The elders of the exile are valuable to me. Yet more beloved to me is the smallest circle that is located in the Land of Israel than a great Sanhedrin located outside of the Land."

All we have here is a paraphrase and restatement of the cited verse.

Where actions are attributed to God, we have to recognize God's presence in context, e.g., "The Holy One, blessed be he, kept to himself [and did not announce] the reward that is coming to those who carry out their religious duties, so that they should do them in true faith [without expecting a reward]" (Y. Qid. 1:7.IX.B). But such a statement hardly constitutes evidence that God is present and active in a given circumstance. It rather forms into a personal statement the principle that one should do religious duties for the right motive, not expecting a reward—a view we found commonplace in tractate Abot. So too statements of God's action carry slight characterization, e.g., "Even if 999 aspects of the argument of an angel incline against someone, but a single aspect of the case of that angel argues in favor, the Holy One . . . still inclines the scales in favor of the accused" (Y. Qid. 1:9.II.S).

It remains to observe that when we find in the Yerushalmi a sizable narrative of intensely-important events, such as the destruction of Betar in the time of Bar Kokhba (Y. Ta. 4:5.Xff.), God scarcely appears except, again, as premise and source of all that happens. There is no characterization, nor even the claim that God intervened in some direct and immediate way, though we can hardly imagine anyone thought otherwise. That simple affirmation reaches expression, for instance, in the observation, in connection with the destruction of the Temple, "It appears that the Holy One, blessed be he, wants to exact from our hand vengeance for his blood" (Y. Ta. 4:5.XIV.Q). That sort of intrusion hardly suggests a vivid presence of God as part of the narrative scheme, let alone a characterization of God as person.

God does occur as a "you" throughout the Yerushalmi, most commonly in a liturgical setting. As in the earlier documents of the oral part of the Torah, so in the Yerushalmi, we have a broad range of prayers to God as "you," illustrated by the following (Y. Ber. 1:4.VIII.D, trans. Tzvee Zahavy):

> R. Ba bar Zabeda in the name of Rab: "[The congregation says this prayer in an undertone:] 'We give thanks to you, for we must praise your name.' 'My lips will shout for joy when I sing praises to you, my soul also, which you have rescued' (Ps. 71:23). Blessed are you, Lord, God of praises."

Since the formula of the blessing invokes "you," we find nothing surprising in the liturgical person imagined by the framers of various prayers. God's ad hoc intervention, as an active and participating personality, in specific situations is treated as more or less a formality, in that the rules are given and will come into play without ordinarily requiring God to join in a given transaction:

God was encountered as a very real presence, actively listening to prayers, as in the following (Y. Ber. 9:1.VII.E):

> See how high the Holy One, blessed be he, is above his world. Yet a person can enter a synagogue, stand behind a pillar, and pray in an undertone, and the Holy One, blessed be he, hears his prayers, as it says, "Hannah was speaking in her heart; only her lips

moved, and her voice was not heard" (1 Sam. 1:13). Yet the Holy One, blessed be he, heard her prayer.

When, however, we distinguish God as person, "you," from God as a well-portrayed active personality, liturgical formulas give a fine instance of the one side of the distinction. In the Yerushalmi's sizable corpus of such prayers, individual and community alike, we never find testimony to a material change in God's decision in a case based on setting aside known rules in favor of an episodic act of intervention, and, it follows, thought on God as person remains continuous with what has gone before. Sages, like everyone else in Israel, believed that God hears and answers prayer. But that belief did not require them to preserve stories about specific instances in which the rules of hearing and answering prayer attested to a particular trait of personality or character to be imputed to God. A specific episode or incident never served to highlight the characterization of divinity in one way, rather than in some other, in a manner parallel to the use of stories by the authors of Scripture to portray God as a sharply-etched personality.

God's personality: For sages, God and humanity are indistinguishable in their physical traits. They are distinguished in other, important ways. The issue of the Talmud of Babylonia is the re-presentation of God in the form of humanity, but as God. Let us begin with the conception that God and the human being are mirror images of one another. Here we find the simple claim that the angels could not discern any physical difference whatever between man—Adam—and God (Gen. Rab. VIII:X):

A. Said R. Hoshaiah, "When the Holy One, blessed be he, came to create the first man, the ministering angels mistook him [for God, since man was in God's image,] and wanted to say before the latter, 'Holy, [holy, holy is the Lord of hosts].'"

B. "To what may the matter be compared? To the case of a king and a governor who were set in a chariot, and the provincials wanted to greet the king, 'Sovereign!' But they did not know which one of them

was which. What did the king do? He turned the governor out and put him away from the chariot, so that people would know who was king."

C. "So too when the Holy One, blessed be he, created the first man, the angels mistook him [for God]. What did the Holy One, blessed be he, do? He put him to sleep, so everyone knew that he was a mere man."

D. "That is in line with the following verse of Scripture: 'Cease you from man, in whose nostrils is a breath, for how little is he to be accounted' (Is. 2:22)."

In the Talmud of Babylonia in particular God is represented as a fully-exposed personality, like man. There we see in a variety of dimensions the single characterization of God as a personality that humanity can know and love.

Telling stories provides the particular means by which theological traits that many generations had affirmed now are portrayed as qualities of the personality of God, who is like a human being. It is one thing to hypostatize a theological abstraction, e.g., "The quality of mercy said before the Holy One, blessed be he. . . ." It is quite another to construct a conversation between God and, e.g., David, with a complete argument and a rich interchange, in which God's merciful character is spelled out as the trait of a specific personality. And that is what we find in the Bavli, and not in any prior document. Specifically, it is in the Bavli that the specification of an attribute of God, such as being long-suffering, is restated by means of narrative. God then emerges not as an abstract entity with theological traits but as a fully-exposed personality. God is portrayed as engaged in conversation with human beings because God and humanity can understand one another within the same rules of discourse. When we speak of the personality of God, we shall see, traits of a corporeal, emotional, and social character form the repertoire of appropriate characteristics.

The following story shows us the movement from the abstract and theological to the concrete and narrative mode of discourse about God (B. San. 111a-b, VI):

A. "And Moses made haste and bowed his head toward the earth and worshipped: (Exod. 34:8)":

B. What did Moses see?

C. Hanina b. Gamula said, "He saw [God's attribute of] being long-suffering [Exod. 34:7]."

D. Rabbis say, "He saw [the attribute of] truth [Exod. 34:7]." "It has been taught on Tannaite authority in accord with him who has said," "He saw God's attribute of being long-suffering."

E. For it has been taught on Tannaite authority:

F. When Moses went up on high, he found the Holy One, blessed be he, sitting and writing, "Long-suffering."

G. He said before him, "Lord of the world, 'Long-suffering for the righteous?'"

H. He said to him, "Also for the wicked."

I. [Moses] said to him, "Let the wicked perish."

J. He said to him, "Now you will see what you want."

K. When the Israelites sinned, he said to him, "Did I not say to you, 'Long-suffering for the righteous'?"

L. [Moses] said to him, "Lord of the world, did I not say to you, 'Also for the wicked'?"

M. That is in line with what is written, "And now I beseech you, let the power of my Lord be great, according as you have spoken, saying" (Num. 14:17). [Freedman, *The Babylonian Talmud. Sanhedrin*, p. 764, n. 7: What called forth Moses' worship of God when Israel sinned through the Golden Calf was his vision of the Almighty as long-suffering.]

The statement at the outset is repeated in narrative form at F. Once we are told that God is long-suffering, then it is in particular, narrative form that that trait is given definition. God then emerges as a personality, specifically because Moses engages in argument with God. He reproaches God, questions God's actions and judgments, holds God to a standard of consistency—and receives appropriate responses. God in heaven does not argue with humanity on earth. God in heaven issues decrees, forms the premise of the earthly rules, constitutes a presence, may even take the form of a "you" for hearing and answering prayers.

When God argues, discusses, defends and explains actions, emerges as a personality

etched in words, then God attains that personality that imparts to God the status of a being consubstantial with humanity. It is in particular through narrative that that transformation of God from person to personality takes place. Since personality involves physical traits, attitudes of mind, emotion, and intellect consubstantial with those of human beings, and the doing of the deeds people do in the way in which they do them, we shall now see that all three modes of personality come to full expression in the Bavli. This we do in sequence, ending with a clear demonstration that God incarnate takes the particular form of a sage. And that will yield the problem, referred to below, of the difference between God and all (other) sages.

Scripture knows that God has a face, upon which human beings are not permitted to gaze. But was that face understood in a physical way, and did God enjoy other physical characteristics? An affirmative answer emerges in the following, which settles the question (B. Ber. 7a, LVI):

A. "And he said, 'You cannot see my face'" (Exod. 33:20).

B. It was taught on Tannaite authority in the name of R. Joshua b. Qorha, "This is what the Holy One, blessed be he, said to Moses:"

C. "'When I wanted [you to see my face], you did not want to; now that you want to see my face, I do not want you to.'"

D. This differs from what R. Samuel bar Nahmani said R. Jonathan said.

E. For R. Samuel bar Nahmani said R. Jonathan said, "As a reward for three things he received the merit of three things.

F. "As a reward for: 'And Moses hid his face,' (Exod. 3:6), he had the merit of having a glistening face."

G. "As a reward for: 'Because he was afraid to' (Exod. 3:6), he had the merit that "They were afraid to come near him" (Exod. 34:30)."

H. "As a reward for: 'To look upon God' (Exod. 3:6), he had the merit: 'The similitude of the Lord does he behold' (Num. 12:8)."

I. "And I shall remove my hand and you shall see my back" (Exod. 33:23).

J. Said R. Hana bar Bizna said R. Simeon

the Pious, "This teaches that the Holy One, blessed be he, showed Moses [how to tie] the knot of the phylacteries."

That God is able to tie the knot indicates that God has fingers and other physical gifts. God furthermore is portrayed as wearing phylacteries as well. It follows that God has an arm and a forehead. There is no element of a figurative reading of the indicated traits. That is why, when God is further represented as having eyes and teeth, we have no reason to assign that picture to the status of (mere) poetry:

A. "His eyes shall be red with wine, and his teeth white with milk" (Gen. 49:12):
B. R. Dimi, when he came, interpreted the verse in this way: "The congregation of Israel said to the Holy One, blessed be he, 'Lord of the Universe, wink to me with your eyes, which gesture will be sweeter than wine, and show me your teeth, which gesture will be sweeter than milk.'"

In the Bavli's stories God not only looks like a human being but also does the acts that human beings do. For example, God spends the day much as does a mortal ruler of Israel, at least as sages imagine such a figure. That is, he studies the Torah, makes practical decisions, and sustains the world (meaning, administers public funds for public needs)—just as (in sages' picture of themselves) sages do. What gives us a deeply human God is that for the final part of the day, God plays with his pet, leviathan, who was like Hydra, the great sea serpent with multiple heads. Some correct that view and hold that God spends the rest of the day teaching youngsters. In passages such as these we therefore see the concrete expression of a process of the personality of God (B. A.Z. 3b):

A. Said R. Judah said Rab, "The day is twelve hours long. During the first three, the Holy One, blessed be he, is engaged in the study of the Torah."
B. "During the next three God sits in judgment on the world and when he sees the world sufficiently guilty to deserve destruction, he moves from the seat of justice to the seat of mercy."
C. "During the third he feeds the whole world, from the horned buffalo to vermin.
D. "During the fourth he plays with the leviathan, as it is said, 'There is leviathan, whom you have made to play with' (Ps. 104:26)."
E. [Another authority denies this final point and says,] "What then does God do in the fourth quarter of the day?"
F. "He sits and teaches schoolchildren, as it is said, 'Whom shall one teach knowledge, and whom shall one make to understand the message? Those who are weaned from milk' (Is. 28:9)."
G. And what does God do by night?
H. If you like, I shall propose that he does what he does in daytime.
I. Or if you prefer: he rides a translucent cherub and floats in eighteen thousand worlds. . . .
J. Or if you prefer: he sits and listens to the song of the heavenly creatures, as it is said, "By the day the Lord will command his loving kindness and in the night his song shall be with me" (Ps. 42:9).

The personality of God encompassed not only physical but also emotional or attitudinal traits. In the final stage of the Judaism of the dual Torah God emerged as a fully-exposed personality. The character of divinity, therefore, encompassed God's virtue, the specific traits of character and personality that God exhibited above and here below. Above all, humility, the virtue sages most often asked of themselves, characterized the divinity. God wanted people to be humble, and God therefore showed humility.

A. Said R. Joshua b. Levi, "When Moses came down from before the Holy One, blessed be he, Satan came and asked [God], 'Lord of the world, Where is the Torah? [What have you done with it? Do you really intend to give it to mortals?]'"
B. "He said to him, 'I have given it to the earth . . .' [Satan ultimately was told by God to look for the Torah by finding the son of Amram.]"
C. "He went to Moses and asked him, 'Where is the Torah that the Holy One, blessed be he, gave you?'"
D. "He said to him, 'Who am I that the Holy One, blessed be he, should give me the Torah?'"
E. "Said the Holy One, blessed be he, to Moses, 'Moses, you are a liar!'"

F. "He said to him, 'Lord of the world, you have a treasure in store which you have enjoyed everyday. Shall I keep it to myself?'"

G. "He said to him, 'Moses, since you have acted with humility, it will bear your name: 'Remember the Torah of Moses, my servant' (Mal. 3:22).'"

At B. Shab. 89a, God is represented as favoring humility and rewarding the humble with honor. What is important is that God does not here cite Scripture or merely paraphrase it; the conversation is an exchange between two vivid personalities. True enough, Moses, not God, is the hero. But the personality of God emerges in vivid ways.

God in Person; Corporeality of God: Just as Israel glorifies God, so God responds and celebrates Israel. In the passages at hand the complete personality of God, in physical, emotional, and social traits, comes to expression. God wears phylacteries, an indication of a corporeal sort. God further forms the correct attitude toward Israel, which is one of love, an indication of an attitude on the part of divinity corresponding to right attitudes on the part of human beings. Finally, to close the circle, just as there is a "you" to whom humanity prays, so God too says prayers—to God, and the point of these prayers is that God should elicit from himself forgiveness for Israel (B. Ber. 6a-7a):

A. Said R. Nahman bar Isaac to R. Hiyya bar Abin, "As to the phylacteries of the Lord of the world, what is written in them?"

B. He said to him, "'And who is like your people Israel, a singular nation on earth' (1 Chr. 17:21)."

C. "And does the Holy One, blessed be he, sing praises for Israel?"

D. "Yes, for it is written, 'You have avouched the Lord this day . . . and the Lord has avouched you this day' (Deut. 26:17, 18)."

E. "Said the Holy One, blessed be he, to Israel, 'You have made me a singular entity in the world, and I shall make you a singular entity in the world.'"

F. "'You have made me a singular entity in the world,' as it is said, 'Hear O Israel, the Lord, our God, the Lord is one' (Deut. 6:4)."

G. "'And I shall make you a singular entity

in the world,' as it is said, 'And who is like your people, Israel, a singular nation in the earth' (1 Chr. 17:21)."

H. Said R. Aha, son of Raba to R. Ashi, "That takes care of one of the four subdivisions of the phylactery. What is written in the others?"

I. He said to him, "'For what great nation is there. . . . And what great nation is there . . .' (Deut. 4:7, 8), 'Happy are you, O Israel . . .' (Deut. 33:29), 'Or has God tried . . .,' (Deut. 4:34). And 'To make you high above all nations' (Deut. 26:19)."

J. "If so, there are too many boxes!"

K. "But the verses, 'For what great nation is there' and 'And what great nation is there,' which are equivalent, are in one box, and 'Happy are you, O Israel' and 'Who is like your people Israel' are in one box, and 'Or has God tried . . .,' in one box, and 'To make you high' in one box."

L. "And all of them are written in the phylactery that is on the arm."

B. Ber. 6a-b XXXIX

A. Said R. Yohanan in the name of R. Yose, "How do we know that the Holy One, blessed be he, says prayers?"

B. "Since it is said, 'Even them will I bring to my holy mountain and make them joyful in my house of prayer' (Is. 56:7)."

C. "'Their house of prayer' is not stated, but rather, 'my house of prayer.'"

D. "On the basis of that usage we see that the Holy One, blessed be he, says prayers."

E. What prayers does he say?

F. Said R. Zutra bar Tobiah said Rab, "'May it be my will that my mercy overcome my anger, and that my mercy prevail over my attributes, so that I may treat my children in accord with the trait of mercy and in their regard go beyond the strict measure of the law.'"

B. Ber. 7A. XLIX

A. It has been taught on Tannaite authority:

B. Said R. Ishmael b. Elisha [who is supposed to been a priest in Temple times], "One time I went in to offer up incense on the innermost altar, and I saw the crown of the Lord, enthroned on the highest throne, and he said to me, 'Ishmael, my son, bless me.'

C. "I said to him, 'May it be your will that your mercy overcome your anger, and that your mercy prevail over your attributes, so that you treat your children in accord with the trait of mercy and in their regard go beyond the strict measure of the law.'"

D. "And he nodded his head to me."

E. And from that story we learn that the blessing of a common person should not be negligible in your view.

B. Ber. 7a

The corporeal side to the personality of God is clear at the outset, God's wearing phylacteries. The consubstantial traits of attitude and feeling—just as humanity feels joy, so does God, just as humanity celebrates God, so does God celebrate Israel—are made explicit. The social transactions of personality are specified as well. Just as Israel declares God to be unique, so God declares Israel to be unique. And just as Israel prays to God, so God says prayers. What God asks of God is that God transcend God—which is what, in prayer, humanity asks for as well. In the end, therefore, to be "in our image, after our likeness," the power of the powerless, the riches of the disinherited, the valuation and valorization of the will of those who have no right to will is to be not the mirror image of God but very much to be like God. That is how, once more, the dimension of *zekhut*—unearned merit—enters in. And with *zekhut*, we come to the category that defines the proper relationship of a human being to God: one in which what a person does does not coerce God but invokes in God an attitude of concern and love for the person. We now turn to the single most characteristic and important theological idea in Rabbinic Judaism—and one that is most difficult to grasp and most profound in its theological implications.

The humanity of God: As in the written Torah, so in the oral Torah, the covenant prevails, and God enters into transactions with human beings and accords with the rules that govern those relationships. So God exhibits precisely the social attributes that human beings do. A number of stories, rather protracted and detailed, tell the story of God as a social being, living among and doing business with mortals. These stories provide extended portraits of God's relationships, in particular arguments, with important figures, such as angelic figures, as well as Moses,

David, and Hosea. In them God negotiates, persuades, teaches, argues, exchanges reasons. The personality of God therefore comes to expression in a variety of portraits of how God will engage in arguments with men and angels, and so enters into the existence of ordinary people. These disputes, negotiations, transactions yield a portrait of God who is reasonable and capable of give and take, as in the following (B. Ar. 15a-b):

A. Rabbah bar Mari said, "What is the meaning of this verse: 'But they were rebellious at the sea, even at the Red Sea; nonetheless he saved them for his name's sake' (Ps. 106:7)?

B. "This teaches that the Israelites were rebellious at that time, saying, 'Just as we will go up on this side, so the Egyptians will go up on the other side.' Said the Holy One, blessed be he, to the angelic prince who reigns over the sea, 'Cast them [the Israelites] out on dry land.'"

C. "He said before him, 'Lord of the world, is there any case of a slave [namely, myself] to whom his master [you] gives a gift [the Israelites], and then the master goes and takes [the gift] away again? [You gave me the Israelites, now you want to take them away and place them on dry land!]'"

D. "He said to him, 'I'll give you one-and-a-half times their number.'"

E. "He said before him, 'Lord of the world, is there a possibility that a slave can claim anything against his master? [How do I know that you will really do it?]'"

F. "He said to him, 'The Kishon brook will be my pledge [that I shall carry out my word. Nine hundred chariots at the brook were sunk (Judg. 3:23), while Pharaoh at the sea had only six hundred. Thus the pledge is one-and-a-half times greater than the sum at issue].'"

G. "Forthwith [the angelic prince of the sea] spit them out onto dry land, for it is written, 'And the Israelites saw the Egyptians dead on the seashore' (Exod. 14:30)."

God is willing to give a pledge to guarantee his word. He furthermore sees the right claim of the counterpart actor in the story. Hence we see how God obeys precisely the same social laws of exchange and reason that govern other incarnate beings.

Still more interesting is the picture of God's argument with Abraham. God is represented as accepting accountability, by the standards of humanity, for what God does (B. Men. 53b):

> A. Said R. Isaac, "When the Temple was destroyed, the Holy One, blessed be he, found Abraham standing in the Temple. He said to him, 'What is my beloved doing in my house?'"
> B. "He said to him, 'I have come because of what is going on with my children.'"
> C. "He said to him, 'Your children sinned and have been sent into exile.'"
> D. "He said to him, 'But wasn't it by mistake that they sinned?'"
> E. "He said to him, 'She has wrought lewdness' (Jer. 11:15)."
> F. "He said to him, 'But wasn't it just a minority of them that did it?'"
> G. "He said to him, 'It was a majority' (Jer. 11:15)."
> H. "He said to him, 'You should at least have taken account of the covenant of circumcision [which should have secured forgiveness despite their sin]!'"
> I. "He said to him, 'The holy flesh is passed from you' (Jer. 11:15)."
> J. "And if you had waited for them, they might have repented!'"
> K. "He said to him, 'When you do evil, then you are happy' (Jer. 11:15)."
> L. "He said to him, 'He put his hands on his head, crying out and weeping, saying to them, 'God forbid! Perhaps they have no remedy at all!'
> M. "A heavenly voice came forth and said, 'The Lord called you' a leafy olive tree, fair with excellent fruit'" (Jer. 11:16).
> N. "'Just as in the case of an olive tree, its future comes only at the end [that is, it is only after a long while that it produces its best fruit], so in the case of Israel, their future comes at the end of their time.'"

God relates to Abraham as to an equal. That is shown by God's implicit agreement that he is answerable to Abraham for what has taken place with the destruction of the Temple. God does not impose silence on Abraham, saying that that is a decree not to be contested but only accepted. God as a social being accepts that he must provide sound reasons for his actions, as must any other reasonable person in a world governed by rules applicable to everyone. Abraham is a fine choice for the protagonist, since he engaged in the argument concerning Sodom (Gen. 18:20-33). His complaint is expressed at B: God is called to explain himself. At each following point Abraham offers arguments in behalf of sinning Israel, and God responds, item by item. The climax has God promising Israel a future worth having. God emerges as both just and merciful, reasonable but sympathetic. The transaction attests to God's conformity to rules of reasoned transactions in a coherent society.

The divinity of God; God as wholly other: Though God has the image of the sage, he towers over other sages, disposes of their lives, and determines their destinies. Portraying God as sage allowed the storytellers to state in vivid way convictions on the disparity between sages' great intellectual achievements and their this-worldly standing and fate. But God remains within the model of other sages, takes up the rulings, follows the arguments, participates in the sessions that distinguish sages and mark them off from all other people (B. Men. 29b):

> A. Said R. Judah said Rab, "When Moses went up to the height, he found the Holy One, blessed be he, sitting and tying crowns to the letters [of the Torah]."
> B. "He said to him, 'Lord of the universe, why is this necessary?'"
> C. "He said to him, 'There is a certain man who is going to come into being at the end of some generations, by the name of Aqiba b. Joseph. He is going to find expositions to attach mounds and mounds of laws to each point [of a crown].'"
> D. "He said to him, 'Lord of the universe, show him to me.'"
> E. "He said to him, 'Turn around.'"
> F. "[Moses] went and took his seat at the end of eight rows, but he could not understand what the people were saying. He felt weak. When discourse came to a certain matter, one of [Aqiba's] disciples said to him, 'My lord, how do you know this?'"
> G. "He said to him, 'It is a law revealed by God to Moses at Mount Sinai.'"
> H. "Moses' spirits were restored."
> I. "He turned back and returned to the Holy One, blessed be he. He said to him, 'Lord of the universe, now if you have such a man available, how can you give the Torah through me?'"
> J. "He said to him, 'Be silent. That is how I have decided matters.'"
> K. "He said to him, 'Lord of the universe, you have now shown me his mastery of the Torah. Now show me his reward.'"

L. "He said to him, 'Turn around.'"

M. "He turned around and saw people weighing out his flesh in the butcher-shop.'"

N. "He said to him, 'Lord of the universe, such is his mastery of Torah, and such is his reward?'"

O. "He said to him, 'Be silent. That is how I have decided matters.'"

This is the single most important narrative about the personality of God, indicating the point at which humanity cannot imitate God but must relate to God in an attitude of profound humility and obedience. For God's role in the story finds definition as hero and principal actor. He is no longer the mere interlocutor, nor does he simply answer questions by citing Scripture.

Quite to the contrary, God is always God. God makes all the decisions and guides the unfolding of the story. Moses appears as the straight man. He asks the questions that permit God to make the stunning replies. Moses, who is called "our rabbi" and forms the prototype and ideal of the sage, does not understand. God tells him to shut up and accept his decree. God does what he likes, with whom he likes. Perhaps the story-teller had in mind a polemic against rebellious brilliance, as against dumb subservience. But that does not seem to be the urgent message, which rather requires acceptance of God's decrees, whatever they are, when the undeserving receive glory, when the accomplished come to nothing. That God emerges as a fully-formed personality—the model for the sage—hardly requires restatement.

Just as Israel glorifies God, so God responds and celebrates Israel. Just as there is a "you" to whom humanity prays, so God too says prayers—to God, and the point of these prayers is that God should elicit from himself forgiveness for Israel (B. Ber. 7a):

A. Said R. Yohanan in the name of R. Yose, "How do we know that the Holy One, blessed be he, says prayers?"

B. "Since it is said, 'Even them will I bring to my holy mountain and make them joyful in my house of prayer' (Is. 56:7).

C. "'Their house of prayer' is not stated, but rather, 'my house of prayer.'"

D. "On the basis of that usage we see

that the Holy One, blessed be he, says prayers."

E. What prayers does he say?

F. Said R. Zutra bar Tobiah said Rab, "'May it be my will that my mercy overcome my anger, and that my mercy prevail over my attributes, so that I may treat my children in accord with the trait of mercy and in their regard go beyond the strict measure of the law.'"

Sages' vision of God encompassed God's yearning for Israel, God's eagerness to forgive Israel its sins. God's power to overcome anger in favor of mercy and love (B. Ber. 7a):

A. It has been taught on Tannaite authority:

B. Said R. Ishmael b. Elisha [who is supposed to been a priest in Temple times], "One time I went in to offer up incense on the innermost altar, and I saw the crown of the Lord, enthroned on the highest throne, and he said to me, 'Ishmael, my son, bless me.'

C. "I said to him, 'May it be your will that your mercy overcome your anger, and that your mercy prevail over your attributes, so that you treat your children in accord with the trait of mercy and in their regard go beyond the strict measure of the law.'"

D. "And he nodded his head to me."

E. And from that story we learn that the blessing of a common person should not be negligible in your view.

Just as Israel prays to God, so God says prayers. What God asks of God is that God transcend God—which is what, in prayer, humanity asks for as well. In the end, therefore, to be "in our image, after our likeness," the power of the powerless, the riches of the disinherited, the valuation and valorization of the will of those who have no right to will is to be not the mirror image of God but very much to be like God.

What, exactly, are we expected to be and to do because we wish to be "like God"? The answer is given at Lev. 19:1, "You shall be holy, for I the Lord your God am holy." Sages spell out the meaning of holiness, and that means, to be merciful and compassionate (B. Shab. 133b):

A. "This is my God and I will adorn him" (Exod. 15:2)—adorn yourself before him by truly elegant fulfillment of the religious duties, for example: A beautiful tabernacle, a beautiful palm branch, a beautiful ram's horn, beautiful show fringes, a beautiful scroll of the Torah, written in fine ink, with a fine reed, by a skilled penman, wrapped with beautiful silks.

B. Abba Saul says, "'I will adorn him'—be like him: Just as he is gracious and compassionate, so you be gracious and compassionate."

Abba Saul's statement says in a few words the entire knowledge of God that the Torah—meaning Judaism—provides. The real imitation of God comes about in our capacity to love one another.

What we know about God and ourselves we know because God's grace has permitted us to know—that alone. So the proposition is, the facts provided by the Torah themselves comprise an act of grace. This is demonstrated syllogistically, on the basis of three fundamental truths that govern throughout: humanity is made in the image of God; Israel are children of God; Israel possesses the most precious of gifts. These are givens. Wherein lies the gift? The act of grace is that we are told that they are God's gifts to us. We are not only in God's image—something we cannot have known on our own—but God has told us so. Israel are not only God's children—it would have been arrogance to have supposed so on their own—but God has so stated in so many words. Israel possesses the

greatest gift of all. They know it: God has said so. So the syllogism draws on three facts to make one point that is not stated but that lies at the goal of the argument.

A. Aqiba says, "Precious is the human being, who was created in the image [of God]."

B. "It was an act of still greater love that it was made known to him that he was created in the image [of God], as it is said, 'For in the image of God he made man' (Gen. 9:6)."

C. "Precious are Israelites, who are called children to the Omnipresent."

D. "It was an act of still greater love that they were called children to the Omnipresent, as it is said, 'You are the children of the Lord your God' (Dt. 14:1)."

E. "Precious are Israelites, to whom was given the precious thing."

F. "It was an act of still greater love that it was made known to them that to them was given that precious thing with which the world was made, as it is said, 'For I give you a good doctrine. Do not forsake my Torah' (Prov. 4:2)."

These six statements at M. Ab. 3:13-14 form the paradigm of Judaic theology: not truth alone, but truth enhanced because of the Torah's verification and validation. That is what it means to say, Israel knows God through the Torah. God is known because God makes himself known.

JACOB NEUSNER

H

HALAKHAH, LAW IN JUDAISM: Jewish law—*Halakhah*—denotes the entire subject matter of the Jewish legal system, including public, private, and ritual law. Within the Jewish tradition, law's purview encompasses not only those activities a judicial system normally is understood as able to compel or prohibit (as US Supreme Court Justice Oliver Wendell Holmes, Jr., 1841-1935, defined the scope of American law, in his famous "bad man's rule"), but also includes the ethical and moral component of conduct in both the pub-

lic and private realms. Reflective of this comprehensive understanding of law, the Hebrew word "Halakhah" means simply "the path," that is, the direction for properly living every aspect of life.

The pre-Talmudic period: The Pentateuch, referred to by Jews as the Torah, is the touchstone of Jewish law and, according to religious tradition and its derived legal theory, is the manifestation of the divine word, having been revealed to Moses at Mt. Sinai. According to traditional belief, alongside God's revelation of the written Torah, represented in the text of the Pentateuch, was a collection of material originally handed on orally—hence referred to as the Oral Torah—which consists of a variety of additional laws, rules, and interpretive tools. The divine and therefore binding nature of both of these Torahs is the predicate belief of normative Jewish law.

The biblical books contained in the Prophets and Writings, which together with the Torah constitute the Hebrew Bible, were written during the 700 years following composition of the Pentateuch. The Jewish biblical canon as a whole appears to have been completed no later than the year 150 C.E. While the Prophets and Writings are traditionally understood to have been written with divine inspiration and certainly had considerable impact on both the discourse and the homiletical material that appear in the primary documents of Jewish law, they are of far less significance than the Torah for establishing either the legal or ethical norms of Judaism. Indeed, very little historical information is available to us about the nature of normative Jewish law through the end of the prophetic period. Religious authority during this period was shared by a triumvirate of the monarchy, prophets, and high priests (*Kohen Gadol*). Interestingly, Jewish legal theory identifies Moses—who received the Torah directly from God—as the only Jewish leader who held all three titles, this being one of the indicia of his unique status.

The interval from the close of the canon until approximately 250 C.E. is known as the era of the Tannaim, the first redactors of Jewish law, whose period closed with the editing of the Mishnah, traditionally ascribed to Judah the Patriarch. This document, a redaction of nearly all areas of Jewish law then extant, became the basis of subsequent Jewish legal literature and is composed of material thematically structured in six "orders," dealing with agricultural law, family law, civil and criminal law, law pertaining to the holidays, Temple law, and the law relating to ritual purity.

The Tannaitic period witnessed the trans-formation of the very nature of Jewish law in three crucial ways. First, religious leadership was permanently transferred from the triumvirate of king/priest/prophet to the rabbis, who assumed the mantle of expositors of Jewish oral and written law, thereby becoming the architects of authoritative Rabbinic decrees and customs. Second, during this period, the oral law gradually came to be set in writing, a process that culminated in Judah the Patriarch's pivotal decision to permit creation of an authoritative writing down of the oral law, fixed in the text of the Mishnah. Finally, by the end of this period, Jewish law, indeed Judaism itself, was firmly rooted in the diaspora and no longer geographically confined to the land of Israel. These three transitions caused profound changes in Jewish law.

The next five or six centuries saw the writing of the Babylonian and Jerusalem Talmuds, two running commentaries on most sections of the Mishnah, containing elaboration and explanation of the rules and cases found therein. These documents were written and edited by scholars called Amoraim ("those who recount [Jewish law]") and, to a lesser extent, Savoraim ("those who ponder [Jewish law]"). On the whole, the Babylonian Talmud is a far more complete and refined work than the Jerusalem Talmud. As a result—and for a variety of additional reasons—its authority ultimately eclipsed that of the Jerusalem Talmud, giving it far greater significance through most of Jewish legal history. The material of the Talmud is diffuse and loosely edited and frequently presents multiple explanations of a given difficulty without resolving the problems presented. A variety of hermeneutic methodologies are used repeatedly throughout the Talmuds, representing approaches to Jewish law, tradition, and ethics. In addition, the dissemination of the Talmud resulted in the codification of many customs, practices, and decrees as normative in the Rabbinic tradition (although, in accordance with its largely dialogic character, the Talmud also records many subordinate traditions that did not become normative).

The fundamental significance of the Talmuds to Jewish law cannot be overstated. As Asher ben Yehiel of thirteenth century Spain notes (in Sanhedrin 3:4), Jewish authorities accept that Talmudic law provides the touchstone base for all discussions of Jewish law. Its authority is beyond dispute, so that denial of the authority of the Talmud excludes one from the community of adherents. While the Talmud might in certain circumstances be unclear, might itself accept more than one view as normative, or may cite many different views without resolving the matter under discussion, it nonetheless sets the framework of analysis for all that is Jewish within Jewish law.

The post-Talmudic period: The post-Talmudic era is divided into three periods: the *geonic* era, named for the geonim, or scholars who lived in Babylonia until its destruction in the middle of the eleventh century; the era of the *Rishonim* (the early authorities), who lived in North Africa, Spain, Franco-Germany, and Egypt until the end of the fourteenth century; and the period of the *Aharonim* (the latter authorities), which encompasses all scholars of Jewish law from the appearance of the Shulhan Arukh until the present.

The geonim: The history of the geonic era remains shrouded in uncertainty. Both modern scholarship and traditional Jewish law are hard-pressed to define an exact dividing line between the Savoraim, who ended the Talmudic era, and the geonim. Indeed, in a number of cases, it appears that geonic authorities engaged in argument with Talmudic statements, as though they were contemporaneous with the Talmudic authorities themselves. Although these instances appear to be confined to cases of custom rather than law, this apparent ongoing dialogue may nonetheless indicate that the geonim perceived themselves as a continuation of the Talmudic period and tradition, not as a distinctive group of authorities. Two primary figures of this period were Hai Gaon (939-1038) and Sherira ben Hanina (tenth century), both of the Pumbedita academy in Babylonia. Based on manuscripts now available, it appears that the geonic era was an active period of recodification within Jewish law. However, at the current time, only tentative inferences are possible, as sufficient data is not available for this early period.

The Rishonim: In the era of the Rishonim, the division of Jewish law into geographic schools of thought first developed. The Franco-German school, led by Solomon Yitzhaki (known by the acronym "Rashi," 1040-1105) in Northern France and his students and descendants, such as his grandson, Jacob ben Meir Tam ("Rabbenu Tam," 1100-1171), created the system of practice and interpretation that shaped Ashkenazic Jewry. The North African, Egyptian, and remaining Persian communities, under the leadership of Isaac Alfasi (1013-1103) and Moses ben Maimon, or Maimonides (known by the acronym "Rambam," 1135-1204), eventually became recognizable as a distinctive Sephardic Jewry. In this period, a sizable Jewish community also existed in Provence, with its own unique customs and significant scholars, including Menahem Meiri (1249-c. 1316) and Abraham ben David of Posquieres (c. 1120-1198). The same was true in Spain, where Moses ben Nahman, or Nahmanides (known by the acronym "Ramban," 1194-1270), Solomon ben Abraham Adret (c. 1235-1310), and Yom Tov ben Abraham Ishbilli (thirteenth-fourteenth centuries) were among the most significant scholars. These last two communities, Provence and Spain, eventually merged into Ashkenazic and Sephardic Jewry respectively. Asher ben Yehiel served as a transitional figure between the Franco-German school and the Muslim Spanish communities, making him another very significant figure of the period, as was his son, Jacob ben Asher (c. 1270-1340), author of the important law code the Arba'ah Turim (see below).

The literary methodologies of the Rishonim varied considerably, although adherence to a particular genre or literary style does not seem to correlate with geographical location. Three primary literary methodologies were employed during this period: codification, responsa, and Talmudic commentary. Codification involved the redaction of normative Jewish law into concise rules, typified by

Maimonides' *Mishneh Torah*, which remains to date the only comprehensive rendering of all of Jewish law. The responsa literature (in Hebrew, *she'alot u'teshuvot*, lit., "questions and answers"), typified by the 2,500 letters written by Rabbi Adret to Spanish Jewry, was generated by the exchange of written questions and answers between individual rabbis and congregants or communities. The issues tend to be fact-specific rather than general restatements of law. The responsa form is one of the unique literary contributions of Jewish law to the general body of legal literature, as the genre is not found in other legal systems. Talmudic commentary, the most common form of Rabbinic literature of the era, was the process by which scholars interpreted uncertainties within the Talmud or criticized and elaborated on the commentaries of others. It frequently directly involved discussions of normative Jewish law. Note that many rabbis wrote in more than one literary format. For example, in addition to his thousands of responsa, Rabbi Adret wrote commentaries on all areas of the Talmud, commonly published under the title *Hidushei HaRashba*, as well as a codification of the dietary laws, *Torat Habayit LeRashba*.

The Shulhan Arukh: From the mid-fourteenth century until the early seventeenth century, Jewish law underwent a period of codification, which led to the eventual acceptance of the Shulhan Arukh, the law code of Joseph Karo (1488-1575), as the basis for modern Jewish law. The Shulhan Arukh (and the Arba'ah Turim of Jacob ben Asher, which preceded it) divided Jewish law into four separate areas: the portion of the text referred to as *Orah Hayyim* is devoted to daily, Sabbath, and holiday laws; *Even Ha-Ezer* addresses family law, including financial aspects; *Hoshen Mishpat* codifies financial law; and *Yoreh Deah* contains dietary laws as well as miscellaneous legal matters.

While the Arba'ah Turim was not the first law code—Maimonides' Mishneh Torah was completed approximately a century earlier—it was unique in that it did not attempt to present a final and authoritative version of Halakhah. Rather, it collected and presented the range of opinions found among the Rishonim. Combined with Karo's Talmudic commentaries, known as the *Beit Yosef*, and Yoel ben Samuel Sirkes' (1561-1640) *Beit Hadash*, it remains the classic restatement of the principles of Jewish law. It is important to emphasize the much overlooked difference in methodology between the Arba'ah Turim of Rabbi Asher and the Shulhan Arukh of Rabbi Karo: The Tur, as it is called, may not strictly be considered a codification of Jewish law in that Asher did not judge among conflicting opinions within the received halakhic traditions. Rather, he sought only to redact Halakhah topically in organized chapters, faithfully collecting *all* opinions that he thought plausible, while only rarely voicing an opinion as to what should be the normative approach on a given question. Conversely, the Shulhan Arukh was intended as a code, rarely citing more than one opinion and attempting to provide definitive answers to questions of Halakhah.

Many significant scholars—themselves as important as Karo in status and authority—wrote annotations to the Shulhan Arukh that made the work and its surrounding comments the modern touchstone of Jewish law. But despite Karo's clear intention that the Shulhan Arukh should serve as a final and authoritative code of Jewish law, the text did not in fact attain this status. Instead, repeated commentaries have used the Shulhan Arukh as a reference point in collecting areas of disagreement with Karo and others decisors. The most significant of these commentators is Moses Isserles (c. 1525-1572), a Polish scholar whose glosses on the Shulhan Arukh present normative Ashkenazic practice. Among the other significant commentaries are: *Turei Zahav*, on all four sections, by David ben Samuel Halevi of Poland (1586-1667); *Magen Avraham*, on *Orah Hayyim*, by Abraham Abele ben Hayyim Halevi Gombiner (Poland, 1637-1683); *Sefer Meirat Einayim*, on *Hoshen Mishpat*, by Joshua ben Alexander Hacohen Falk (Poland, c. 1555-1614); and *Siftei Kohen*, on *Hoshen Mishpat* and *Yoreh Deah*, by Shabbetai ben Meir Hakohen of Lithuania (1621-1662). The most recent annotated edition of the *Shulhan Arukh* (Vilna, 1896) contains no less than 113 separate commentaries on Karo's text. In addition, hundreds of other volumes of commentary have been published as self-standing works, a process that continues to this very day. Significant works among this body of literature include Israel Meir Hakohen's (1838-1933) *Mishnah Berurah* on *Orah Hayyim* and the *Arukh Ha-Shulkhan* of Yehiel Mikhal Epstein (Belorussia, 1829-1908), the most recent comprehensive restatement of normative Jewish law.

The Aharonim: Since the time of the Shulhan Arukh, conventional Jewish law has viewed itself as being in the ultimate stages of development. Accordingly, this era is referred to as that of the Aharonim, or latter authorities. The normative view is that these later authorities may not—except in rare circumstances—engage in dispute with the views of earlier masters. Their task, rather, is only to determine which earlier view should prevail in a matter under dispute and to establish how inherited positions are to be applied in factual settings not addressed in the prior literature.

The greatest concentration of scholarly activity during the time of the later Aharonim (1750 and onward) occurred in Eastern Europe, the location of the vast majority of the world's Jewish population. Ashkenazic Jewry developed a highly intellectual and analytical approach to the study of Jewish law, focusing less on the establishment of normative Jewish law (as in the era of the codifiers) and more on the law's conceptual basis and, equally significantly, on the concept of the study of Torah as a form of divine worship. Typical of this approach was the work of three Lithuanian scholars, Hayyim ben Isaac Volozhiner (1749-1821), Naftali Tsevi Judah Berlin (1816-1893), and Hayyim Soloveitchik (1853-1918), each of whom emphasized the abstract study of Jewish law. The division between Ashkenazic and Sephardic authorities also sharpened considerably during this time; the terms themselves came to denote schools of thought and tradition, rather than merely geographi-

cal locations: while the Ashkenazic Jewish community lived in eastern Europe and the Sephardic predominately in Iran/Iraq, neither stayed geographically constant.

The literary style of the Aharonim appears similar to that of the Rishonim, although there is considerably more emphasis on responsa and codes than on commentaries. Some scholars, pointing to the significant differences in the nature of the problems confronted after a major historical shift, maintain that the era of the Aharonim should be divided into two periods: pre-emancipation and post-emancipation. Still others have argued that the proper division is pre- and post-Holocaust.

Halakhah today: Two principal Jewish communities exist in the world today, and thus two major areas of Jewish legal activity, each with its own distinct character: Israel and the United States. In addition, there are significant Jewish communities in England and France, and smaller ones in North Africa and Iran. The vast majority of Jewish legal scholarship is centered in Israel, with its many yeshivot (classical Talmudic academies) and academic institutions. A smaller—but still considerable—number exists in America. These two significant communities differ profoundly in institutional structure, in that Israel has a government-supported rabbinate directed jointly by a Sephardic and Ashkenazic chief rabbi. The rabbinate in Israel performs both governmental and pseudo-governmental functions, including the supervision of marriage and divorce, as well as involvement in many other official areas of Jewish public life. In general, Judaism, as the state religion of Israel, is publicly funded. This financial support extends to the students of Jewish law and to the institutions for halakhic study, including *hesder* (which combines military service with yeshiva studies), religious Zionist yeshivot (which defer military service until completion of yeshiva studies), and eastern European style yeshivot (which discourage military service).

The development of Jewish law in America has taken a different path, for Judaism in

America functions with essentially no governmental support: rabbis are paid by the congregations they serve, and yeshivot are supported by donations and tuition and provide scholarships based on need and ability. Even within Orthodoxy, this structural discrepancy has created vast cultural differences between American institutions and their Israeli counterparts. Moreover, beyond Orthodoxy, the United States has provided the primary context for the development of contemporary approaches to Jewish law, represented within the Reform and, in particular, the Conservative movements. The latter is a most interesting case, since, at one time, it appeared that Conservative Judaism might develop a coherent system of Jewish law that would remain grounded in the traditional sources and yet function independently of the Orthodox model. Such development, however, has not been consistent, for, from the mid-1960s until the present, the Law Committee of the movement's Rabbinical Assembly has provided little direction in developing a systematic approach to Jewish law, predicated on principles other than those found in either Orthodox or Reform Judaism. Instead, in the last twenty years, Conservative legal decisions have embodied decreasing fidelity to classical Jewish sources and legal processes.

Issues of content: A proper understanding of Jewish law may not be gained by reference only to historical data or trends. Jewish law has always had ethical, religious, and communal functions that continue to provide direction to the adherents thereof. This ethical component, while not ahistorical, is best summarized by a review of principles and ideals rather than via a historical review.

Many significant principles inform and direct Jewish law in the ethical arena. Primary among these is the mandate to imitate the divine (*imitatio dei*), which provides that adherents of Jewish law seek to function in an ethical and just manner, aspiring to do as the divine would. Furthermore, adherents must seek to promote correct conduct and values in the hope that all humanity—created in the image of God (Gen. 1:26)—may come to act accordingly. This principle provides a religious imperative as to what the results of the Jewish tradition should look towards. Second, Jewish tradition recognizes the related mandate of *tikkun olam*, "fixing the world," which imposes a duty on members of society to seek to improve the daily life of God's creatures through a variety of socially constructive projects. *Tikkun olam* mandates an outward looking, ethically positive view of one's obligations to ensure that the general community adheres to proper values and that Jews, through Jewish law, participate in that process. In addition, there is the philosophical mandate that arises from Is. 42:6, to be a "light unto the nations." David Kimchi (c. 1160-1235) presents one interpretation of this concept: "because of the influence of the Jews, the gentiles will observe the seven [Noahide] commandments and follow the right path." But more typically in Rabbinic contexts, the phrase "light unto the nations" is understood to mean that Jews should behave in an exemplary manner that non-Jews will wish to imitate, not as a mandate to proselytize observance. This is exemplified by Isaiah's prophesy: "Nations shall walk by your light, kings by your shining radiance" (Is. 60:3).

Two interrelated concepts, "the ways of peace" (*darchei shalom*) and "lest there be hatred" (*meshum e'va*), have sometimes been used to sanction actions that would not normally be permitted under Jewish law. The recognition that Jews are part of the larger society and need to participate in societal activities is used by Maimonides as the basis for the obligation to participate in public charities and to support poor people of all faiths. The notion that a Jew's conduct has the potential to incite antisemitism and thus to endanger the welfare of other Jews leads to the concept of "lest there be hatred." This principle has resulted in mandates such as the duty to desecrate the Sabbath to save the life of a non-Jew, not technically permitted by Jewish law. The force of these two concepts within the Jewish tradition is not to be understated.

Notably, Jewish tradition points clearly to

natural law as a force in the development of Halakhah. B. Erub. 100b recounts in the name of Yohanan that "if Torah had not given us certain rules, we would have learned modesty from the cat, the prohibition against stealing from the weasel, the prohibition of adultery from the dove," and so on. The exact parameters of natural law and its status vis à vis revealed law are matters of great controversy, especially for circumstances in which the two might be in conflict. Nonetheless, it is clear that natural law plays a role in the Jewish legal tradition, creating an inherent ethical basis for activity.

Natural law thinkers fall into two categories, those whose conception is *a priori* and those whose conception is *a posteriori*. The former depend on pure reason and intuition, the latter, on the experience of most nations. Judaism—which rebelled against what prevailed among the nations with which it came into contact—would not consider the *a posteriori* of any consequence. However *a priori* natural law is found not only in the Code of Maimonides but also very clearly in the Talmud. Without calling them natural rights, the rabbis recognized and enforced rights that were precisely that. For example, when the schools of Shammai and Hillel debated the status of a person who is half slave and half free—owned by one partner and emancipated by the other—the Shammaites convinced the Hillelites with an argument from natural law. The latter had thought it would be possible for such a person to work for himself one day and for his half-owner the next. The rejoinder of the school of Shammai is classic: "You have taken good care of the master but have you taken care of the slave himself? He cannot marry a female slave, because he is half free, and he cannot marry a free woman, because he is half slave. How will he fulfill God's will to populate the earth?" Needless to say, if his status does not allow him—because of God's law—to populate the earth, then he is under no obligation to do it: *God's* law stops him. But the school of Shammai was concerned with the slave's *natural* right, though that term is not used. The slave is not to be denied his humanity.

This controversy clearly indicates that the rabbis are concerned with the existence of natural rights, in this instance, the right to have and raise a family equal in status to that enjoyed by others in that society. It is not simply because God gave the command to be fruitful and multiply to all humans, and this person—half-slave and half-free—is entitled to fulfill that command given to him by God. Rather, his right is broader. Even in his half-slave and half-free condition, he could procreate. There are women with whom he may cohabit, at the very least women in the same status as he. But what he cannot do is to procreate and have completely free offspring. It is this very right that rabbis safeguarded for him, a natural right, to be equal to all in his society with regard to having and raising a family.

Indeed, in the halakhic context, ethical obligations were not merely ideals without means of enforcement; Jewish law recognized the need to provide practical incentives for ethical conduct. The Talmudic sages, and—continuing in this tradition—Jewish courts to this day, ensure that improper behavior, even when technically permitted according to Halakhah, results in sanction. For example, sages decreed that one who enters into a commercial transaction that is not technically binding, but is viewed as such by many, and then seeks to back out when the terms are no longer advantageous should be publicly cursed. Such public denouncements were designed to deter unethical behavior by making it difficult to engage in such conduct and remain a participant in the public market. The rabbis similarly aver that the spirit of the sages does not reside with a person who engages in particular types of conduct that ought to be discouraged. Many halakhic authorities even rule that one who ignores an ethical mandate of the law is to be considered an "evil-doer" (Heb., *rasha*) and must be treated as one with no legal credibility in court. This serious penalty carries significant consequences, for it deprives such a person of the trustworthiness in commercial matters that merchants otherwise legally possess.

Just as unethical conduct that is technically permitted by Jewish law will be condemned, so righteous conduct not directly mandated by Jewish law is encouraged. Hence the Talmudic category of conduct that is "beyond the letter of the law." Consider the case addressed by Isserles in his commentary to the Shulhan Arukh, of a lost object whose owner has relinquished hope of return prior to the moment that the finder discovers it. Since the owner has given up all thought of possession, in such circumstances, Jewish law does not require return of the object; the finder may keep it. Even so, returning such an object is recognized as ethically proper and therefore is encouraged. One who goes beyond the letter of the law to fulfill such an ethical responsibility is considered to have fulfilled the "mandate of heaven." Similarly, while a licensed medical practitioner is under no legal obligation to pay compensation for damage he caused that was truly accidental, the practitioner, who did in fact cause the damage, is encouraged to fulfill the mandate of heaven by making such compensation. Thus, just as unethical, but permitted, behavior can be subject to legal sanction, so Jewish courts sometimes can require the performance of pious or ethical conduct not strictly required by Jewish law. In this we see the difference in scope between Halakhah and legal systems guided by the idea that the job of the courts is only to determine what is legal, not what is ethical or proper.

Rabbinical decrees to promote justice are not only of the ethical-religious variety. A number of decrees in the financial area also are designed to allow for ethical-religious conduct. Consider, for example, the Talmudic taqqanat hashavim, "decree for those who wish to repent." Jewish law rules that a person who steals must return what he stole; if he has sold it, he becomes indebted to the victim in the amount of its value. Talmudic scholars considered the predicament of the thief who wished to repent, but was burdened with so many debts—obligations to repay the value of goods he had stolen and sold—that he would never contemplate repentance for fear of being hounded by his creditors. Thus, the rabbis ruled that in certain circumstances, so as to allow for and encourage repentance, a thief is exempt from the duty to repay those

from whom he stole, so long as the stolen item is no longer in the thief's possession.

Yet other decrees seem to have both economic and ethical foundations. Consider, for example, the "decree of the marketplace" (taqqanat hashuk). According to biblical law, when a thief sells a stolen item, he conveys no title at all to the purchaser, even if the purchaser is completely unaware that the goods were stolen. The original owner therefore may reclaim possession from the purchaser, who absorbs the loss. Talmudic rabbis decreed that in order that the marketplace should continue to function properly, goods sold in open market (in common law, "market overt") convey valid title, even though the one who sold them—the thief—did not possess valid title. This decree was grounded in economic concerns—to allow for the free sale of goods—as well as ethical ones—to rectify the injustice done to the buyer.

Wider implications: Halakhah not only regulates the conduct of Jews but also insists on the existence of a universal legal code, referred to as the Noahide law, understood to be binding on all descendants of Noah, that is, everyone. The Talmud enumerates seven Noahide prohibitions: idol worship, taking God's name in vain, murder, prohibited sexual activity, theft, eating flesh from a living animal, and the obligation to enforce laws. Each of these items represents a broad legal category, which itself comprises many distinct injunctions. Thus, for example, the prohibition against sexual promiscuity includes both adultery and all forms of incest. The Noahide laws thus encompass nearly sixty of the total 613 biblical commandments understood to be incumbent upon Jews and nearly a quarter of those commandments generally thought still to apply in post-Temple times. However, because of non-Jews' and early Jewish authorities' historical inattention to Noahide laws—only recently has interest increased in the ramifications of Jewish ethical law for a secular society—many of them remain unclear.

The halakhic understanding of divorce for those outside of the Jewish community exemplifies this unclarity. The Jerusalem Talmud states that, within Noahide law, there is no formal divorce. Later commentators understand this in three radically different ways. Some claim the statement means that divorce is not available to gentiles, so that they have no legal means of ending marriages. Others maintain that the passage suggests only that there is no *formal* process of divorce for non-Jews, so that either spouse can end the marriage simply by leaving the union. Yet other authorities insist that, according to Noahide law, while a man may never divorce his wife, she may divorce him at will. Since Jewish law cannot be expected generally to control the behavior of non-Jews in our society, this particular issue does not have obvious practical ramifications. But similar ones are important, for instance, concerning the interaction of Jewish and Noahide law in the area of commerce, a topic that also remains clouded in uncertainty. Thus we see the extent to which the Noahide law might be part of normative Jewish law but has not been adequately developed. Such development would be significant since, as a jurisdictional mandate, Jewish law does have a component that seeks to regulate the conduct of general society.

Halakhic foundations of Jewish self-governance: At the beginning of this century, Professor Nathan Isaacs wrote an essay on "Study as a Form of Worship," which described the unique fact that, in Judaism, study, in addition to prayer, is a most honorable way of expressing and fulfilling one's love of God. He referred, needless to say, to the study of Bible, Talmud, and other sacred writings. As a matter of fact, samples of all the different works are incorporated into the prayer book and were prescribed for different occasions.

For many Jews, even in modern times, this is the ideal, to spend one's life studying Torah, and the less relevant the study to the art of living or the advancement of human knowledge, the more it fulfills the religious goal of learning Torah exclusively for Torah's sake. Today the study of Jewish law by most Jews who engage in it is for that reason. One example of the irrelevancy of the study is impressive. Few Talmudic texts and

themes are as popular as Jewish criminal law. Yet, even though texts and themes accommodated more to the realistic requirements of the social order have become obsolete, the fact is that ancient and medieval Jewish society required a stronger hand for the authorities charged with the maintenance of public order and safety. For example the biblical rules of evidence too often made possible avoidance of prosecution and punishment. Consequently there was resort to a virtually parallel system of law. Professor Arnold N. Enker described this in a brilliant essay in whose summary he wrote:

> Jewish criminal law for Jews functions on two tracks. One which for want of a better term might be call the purely religious track concerns man's relation with God. The religious courts have exclusive jurisdiction in this area. Special procedures and unusual rules of evidence and of substantive law apply in these cases and serve to limit punishment of offenders to the most serious and brazen acts of open defiance of God's will. The second track involves the day-to-day concerns of law enforcement and the protection of the social order. On this track, which is administered apparently primarily by the king's courts, although the religious courts also have such jurisdiction, the courts are mostly free to apply whatever rules of practice and evidence they see fit, to evaluate the evidence free of restraint by formal rules and to punish the defendant as seems to them appropriate to accomplish the protection and preservation of the social order.

The parallel system of law, called "The King's Law," was based on Josh. 1:18, which states that the people invested Joshua with the power to give orders and to impose the death penalty on anyone who defied him. This blanket grant of power later became the basis for many a medieval monarch's claim that his right to rule derived from the people. In the same period, Jewish communities in Europe hesitated to arrogate unto themselves such power. They preferred another biblical source upon which to predicate their power to exercise control over the economy, and in this way, they managed to maintain law and order.

The Talmud understood that, at Ezra 10:8, the people had granted Ezra the power to issue orders disobedience of which would result in forfeiture of all an offender's property. This grant of power became the justification for the rule that a duly constituted rabbinical court can declare anyone's property ownerless and also transfer it to another. It was because of this power, one view in the Talmud holds, that Hillel was able to avoid the cancellation of debts in the Sabbatical year. He had created the Prozbul and so provided a way for creditors to collect from debtors, which in effect was an expropriation of debtors in favor of creditors. Circumstances warranted his innovation. It was not a capricious ruling, and it was for the benefit of the debtors—to make credit available in the years preceding the sabbatical. But, nonetheless, it was revolutionary legislation. In the middle ages, this power enabled the Jewish communities—and their councils and judiciary—to govern, to impose taxes and collect them, as well as to punish offenders against all laws of the community. The combination of the two powers—that of the "King's Law" and that of declaring property ownerless—made it possible for communities to legislate in many areas pertaining to the economy, such as rent control, prohibiting resort by litigants to non-Jewish courts, punishment of informers, etc. In a general way, biblical law pertaining to virtually every area of commerce and industry could be updated to cope with general or local needs.

Issues of contemporary Halakhah: More than any generation in the last hundred years, the current one has witnessed the revival of the study of Halakhah. The classical Talmud-based yeshivot promote intense study of Jewish law through the classical methodologies of analysis, analogy, and precedent, with a particular focus on the codification of normative Jewish law. Indeed, a new legal genre, the Jewish law hornbook, has emerged to become a significant form of literature within the field of modern Jewish law. Classical commentaries on Jewish law were principally devoted to the Shulhan Arukh, which in many respects had become the authoritative standard of Halakhah; consequently they were organized according to its chapter and content divisions. In contrast, these recent works present the Halakhah on a single topic in a systematic, rule-based manner, with references and variant opinions in the notes. Such hornbooks have been published on both significant and less significant topics.

In addition, the re-establishment of the state of Israel has created a rabbinical court system with adjudicative legal authority of the type not seen since the Golden Age of Spanish Jewry. This has given rise to additional types of literature in Jewish law. While there were always responsa, there now emerges a body of formal case law, reporting the rulings of rabbinical courts. Particularly in light of the decrees of Abraham Isaac Hacohen Kook (1865-1935; the first Chief Ashkenazic Rabbi of Palestine) and Isaac Halevi Herzog (1888-1959; Chief Ashkenazic Rabbi of Israel, 1937-1959) and the creation of an appellate rabbinical court system, there is now a significant source of normative Jewish law for areas in which the rabbinical courts have jurisdiction, such as family law.

The study of Jewish law in the state of Israel has taken yet another direction as well. There are those who argue that Jewish commercial law should form the basis for modern Israeli law, and that Jewish financial law exists as a self standing commercial legal code, awaiting implementation in Israeli society. Recently advocated by Justice Menahem Elon (1923-), the *mishpat ivri* ("the Law of the Hebrews") school argues that Jewish law can be divided into sections and that secular society may accept as binding only its commercial or family portions. Individuals who accept this approach focus almost exclusively on those areas of Jewish law applicable to a secular society. Still, while a number of modern Israeli statutes originate in Jewish law, one would be hard pressed to claim that the *mishpat ivri* school has yet succeeded in its goals. *Mishpat ivri* has, however, been a significant source of scholarship in the Israeli academic study of Jewish law.

In modern biomedical ethics, Jewish law and ethics have been significant. Unlike most other areas of normative Halakhah, which have had little impact on secular ethics and values, the Halakhah relating to bioethics has become an accepted partner in general discourse, even in the American diaspora. In all areas of current bioethical debate and scholarship, including abortion, neo-natal testing, and cloning, the Jewish legal tradition has played an active role and has had a significant impact on the development of the general ethical discourse.

Other areas of Jewish law, however, are developing more slowly. For example, the Jewish court, or *beit din* system, has never been fully functional in the diaspora and retains a weak and uncertain status. Thus, although Eastern European Jewry could claim a well established *beit din* system as late as 1920, America cannot, and even in Israel it appears limited to those areas in which there is a clear governmental mandate.

Conclusion: In all, however, it is an exercise in futility to ponder, as many have and still do, whether Jewish law at the end of the millennium has a future. First and foremost, so long as there will be Jews practicing Orthodox Judaism, Jewish law will be studied for its guidance in all matters of religious observance. One most never forget that the literature of Jewish law is integrated: civil law, criminal law, public law, the law of prayer and holidays, family law all interface with each other, and new religious problems may be resolved from all the precedents available. Moreover, as already indicated, for practicing Jews, the study of Jewish law is a form of worship no matter how irrelevant the texts and the arguments are for modern life. Many still study the law of animal sacrifices in anticipation of the coming of the messiah and the rebuilding of the Jerusalem Temple.

Moreover, Jewish law remains the best source for the study of Jewish history, especially the history of the half-century before the common era and the millennium and a half thereafter. The legal literature provides a vast amount of information about the Jews' political, social, and economic institutions and their dealings with the ruling authorities of the countries in which they lived.

For the study of American Jewish history, the legal literature is perhaps least important,

but even that will not be true in the future. While American Jews up until the beginning of this millennium contributed little to the legal literature, they contributed enormously to knowledge of the history of the Jews in earlier years. Now one finds many significant contributions from which one can glean how Jewish law is being studied and enriched in the light of word-literature and modern jurisprudence. This will deepen one's appreciation of the ancients as well as broaden the horizons of modern Jewish scholars in discovering insights heretofore not appreciated and views that may make a difference in Jewish life as Jewish law applies to that life. Overall, then, that Jewish law will remain a central and evolving aspect of Jewish civilization seems a certainty. This is guaranteed by the centrality of Jewish law in scholars' study of the history of Judaism, assured by its central place of in the ongoing life of Orthodox Jewry, and promoted by its role in the legal system of the modern Jewish state.

EMMANUEL RACKMAN, MICHAEL BROYDE,
AND AMY LYNNE FISHKIN

HALAKHAH, RELIGIOUS MEANING OF: The normative law, or *Halakhah*, of the Oral Torah defines the principal medium by which the sages set forth their message. Norms of conduct, more than norms of conviction, convey the sages' statement. And from the closure of the Talmud of Babylonia to our own day, those who mastered the documents of the Oral Torah themselves insisted upon the priority of the Halakhah, which is clearly signaled as normative, over the Aggadah, which commonly is not treated as normative in the same way as the Halakhah.

The aggadic statement addresses the exteriorities, the halakhic one, the interiorities, of Israel's life with God. When we consider the program of the Halakhah, the topics that define its native categories, we find a quite distinct and autonomous construction, one that hardly intersects, *categorically*, with the Aggadah. How so? If the native categories of the Aggadah find definition in the story of humankind, derive their dynamism and energy in the conflict of God's word and human will, compose their system in the working of repentance and (ultimate) restoration of humanity to Eden, none of these categories is matched by a counterpart in the Halakhah's category-formation—not repentance, not redemption, not Eden and the fall and the restoration. If the Aggadah organizes large components of its entire system within such categories as Eden/land of Israel or Adam/Israel or fall/exile, the Halakhah responds with large categories that deal with Kilayim—mixed seeds—Shebiit—the Sabbatical year—and Orlah—produce of a tree in the first three years after its planting. The Halakhah embodies the extension of God's design for world order into the inner-facing relationships of 1) God and Israel, 2) Israel's inner order in its own terms, and 3) the Israelite's household viewed on its own in time and space and social circumstance. If we wish to explore the interiority of Israel in relationship with God, as a shared order, and of Israel's autonomous building block, the household, we are required to take up the norms of everyday conduct that define Israel and signify its sanctification.

[1] BETWEEN GOD AND ISRAEL: the interior dimensions of Israel's relationships with God, laid out in the Mishnaic Division of Agriculture and Division of Holy Things. The Division of Agriculture defines what the people Israel in the land of Israel owes God as his share of the produce of the Holy Land, encompassing also Israel's conformity to God's regulation on how that produce is to be garnered; the anomalous tractate, Berakhot, on blessings, concerns exactly the same set of relationships. The Division of Holy Things corresponds by specifying the way in which the gifts of the Land—meat, grain, oil, wine—are to be offered to Heaven, inclusive of the priesthood, as well as the manner in which the Temple and its staff are supported and the offerings paid for. Two tractates, moreover, describe the Temple and its rite, and one of them sets forth special problems in connection with the same. The sole anomalous tractate, Hullin, which takes up the correct slaughter of animals for secular

purposes, belongs, because its rules pertain, also, to the conduct of the cult.

[2] WITHIN ISRAEL'S SOCIAL ORDER: the social order that is realized by Israelites' relationships with one another, discussed in the Division of Damages. This division spells out the civil law that maintains justice and equity in the social order, the institutions of government and the sanctions they legitimately impose.

[3] INSIDE THE ISRAELITE HOUSEHOLD: INTERIOR TIME AND SPACE AND CIRCUMSTANCE; SUSTAINING LIFE: the inner life of the household, encompassing the individual Israelite, with God, covered in the Divisions of Women, Appointed Times, and the Division of Purities, as well as in some singleton-tractates, such as Hullin. The Division of Women deals with the way in which relationships of man and woman are governed by the rules of sanctification enforced by Heaven, which takes an interest in how family relationships are formed, maintained, and dissolved, and the affects, upon the family, of invoking Heaven's name in vows. The Division of Appointed Times addresses the affect upon the conduct of ordinary life of the advent of holy time, with special reference to the Sabbath and the pilgrim festivals (Passover, Tabernacles), the pilgrimage, and the intermediate days of festivals, the New Year and Day of Atonement, Fast Days, and Purim. While parts of some of these tractates, and nearly the whole of a few of them, concern conduct in the Temple, the main point of the tractates is to explore the impact upon the household and village of the appointed times. The same interstitial position—between household and village, on the one side, and Temple and cult, on the other—serves the Division of Purity. The laws of these tractates concern mainly the household, since the cleanness-rules spelled out here concern purity at home. But, it goes without saying, the same uncleanness that prevents eating at home food that is to be preserved in conditions of cultic cleanness also prevents the Israelite from entering the restricted space of the Temple. But in the balance, the division concerns cleanness in that private

domain that is occupied by the Israelite household. We now address exemplary cases of Halakhah falling into each of the specified rubrics.

Between Israel and God—Orlah: God as the ultimate owner of the Land sets the terms of Israel's utilization of the Land, and the rules that he imposes form the condition of Israel's tenure on the Land, as Lev. 19:23-25 states explicitly:

> When you come into the land and plant all kinds of trees for food, then you shall count their fruit as forbidden; three years it shall be forbidden to you, it must not be eaten. And in the fourth year all their fruit shall be holy, an offering of praise to the Lord. But in the fifth year you may eat of their fruit, that they may yield more richly for you: I am the Lord your God.

The yield of the Land responds to Israel's obedience to God's rules for cultivating the Land, and that having been said, why this particular rule carries with it the stated consequence hardly matters. The religious premise of the treatment of the topic of Orlah is the same as the one that sustains tractate Shebiit, concerning the Sabbatical Year: God relates to Israel through the Land and the arrangements that he imposes upon the Land. What happens to Israel in the Land takes the measure of that relationship.

But apart from these traits that characterize all Halakhah of enlandisement, the Halakhah of Orlah makes particular points that are accessible, indeed, possible, only within the framework of that topic. The specificities of the law turn out to define with some precision a message on the relationship of Israel to the land of Israel and to God. If we turn to Sifra CCII:I.1, our attention is drawn to a number of quite specific traits of the law of Orlah, and these make explicit matters of religious conviction that we might otherwise miss. The first is that the prohibition of orlah-fruit applies solely within the land of Israel and not in the neighboring territories occupied by Israelites. The union of Israel with the Land of Israel invokes the prohibition:

A. "When you come [into the land and plant all kinds of trees for food, then you shall

count their fruit as forbidden; three years it shall be forbidden to you, it must not be eaten. And in the fourth year all their fruit shall be holy, an offering of praise to the Lord. But in the fifth year you may eat of their fruit, that they may yield more richly for you: I am the Lord your God" (Lev. 19:23-25).]

B. Might one suppose that the law applied once they came to Transjordan?

C. Scripture says, ". . . into the land,"

D. the particular Land [of Israel].

What that means is that some trait deemed to inhere in the land of Israel and no other territory must define the law, and a particular message ought to inhere in this law. This same point registers once more: only trees that Israelites plant in the Land are subject to the prohibition, not those that gentiles planted before the Israelites inherited the Land (Sifra CCII:I.2):

A. "When you come into the Land and plant":

B. excluding those that gentiles have planted prior to the Israelites' coming into the Land.

C. Or should I then exclude those that gentiles planted even after the Israelites came into the Land?

D. Scripture says, "all kinds of trees."

A further point of special interest requires that the Israelite plant the tree as an act of deliberation; if the tree merely grows up on its own, it is not subject to the prohibition. So Israelite action joined to Israelite intention is required (Sifra CCII:I.4):

A. ". . . and plant . . .":

B. excluding one that grows up on its own.

C. ". . . and plant . . .":

D. excluding one that grows out of a grafting or sinking a root.

The several points on which Sifra's reading of the Halakhah and the verses of Scripture that declare the Halakhah alert us to a very specific religious principle embedded in the Halakhah of Orlah.

First, the law takes effect only from the point at which Israel enters the Land. That is to say, the point of Israel's entry into the Land marks the beginning of the Land's consequential fecundity. In simpler language, the fact that trees produce fruit matters only from Israel's entry onward. To see what is at stake, we recall that the entry of Israel into the Land marks the restoration of Eden (and will again, within Judaism's restorationist theology), so there is no missing the point. The Land bears fruit of which God takes cognizance only when the counterpart-moment of creation has struck. The Halakhah has no better way of saying that the entry of Israel into the Land compares with the moment at which the creation of Eden took place—and in no other way does the Halakhah make that point. In this way, moreover, the law of Shebiit finds its counterpart. Shebiit concerns telling time, marking off seven years to the Sabbath of creation, the one that affords rest to the Land. The Halakhah of Orlah also means telling time. Specifically, Orlah-law marks the time of the creation of produce from the moment of Israel's entry into the Land. Israel's entry into the Land marks a new beginning, comparable to the very creation of the world, just as the Land at the end matches Eden at the outset.

Second, Israelite intentionality is required to subject a tree to the Orlah-rule. If an Israelite does not plant the tree with the plan of producing fruit, the tree is not subject to the rule. If the tree grows up on its own, not by the act and precipitating intentionality of the Israelite, the Orlah-rule does not apply. And given the character of creation, which marks the norm, the tree must be planted in the ordinary way; if grafted or sunk as a root, the law does not apply. In a moment, this heavy emphasis upon Israelite intentionality will produce a critical result. But first let us ask some more fundamental questions.

What is the counterpart to Israelite observance of the restraint of three years? And why should Israelite intentionality play so critical a role, since, Sifra itself notes, the Orlah-rule applies to trees planted even by gentiles? The answer becomes obvious when we ask another question: Can we think of any other commandments concerning fruit-trees in the Land that—sages say time and again—is Eden? Of course we can: "Of every tree of the garden you are free to eat; but as for the tree of knowledge of good and evil, you must not eat of it" (Gen. 2:16). But the Halakhah of Orlah imposes upon Israel a more demanding commandment. Of *no* tree in the new Eden may Israel eat for three years. That demands considerable restraint.

Not only so, but it is Israel's own intentionality—not God's—that imposes upon every fruit-bearing tree—and not only the one of Eden—the prohibition of three years. So once Israel wants the fruit, it must show that it can restrain its desire and wait for three years. By Israel's act of will, Israel has imposed upon itself the requirement of restraint. Taking the entry-point as our guide, we may say that, from the entry into the Land and for the next three years, trees that Israelites value for their fruit and plant with the produce in mind must be left untouched. And, for all time thereafter, when Israelites plant fruit-trees, they must recapitulate that same exercise of self-restraint, that is, act as though, for the case at hand, they have just come into the Land.

To find the context in which these rules make their statement, we consider details, then the main point. First, why three years in particular? Fruit trees were created on the third day of creation. Then, when Israel by intention and action designates a tree—any tree—as fruit-bearing, Israel must wait for three years, as creation waited for three years.

Then the planting of every tree imposes upon Israel the occasion to meet once more the temptation the first Adam could not overcome. Israel now recapitulates the temptation of Adam then, but Israel, the new Adam, possesses, and is possessed by, the Torah. By its own action and intention in planting fruit trees, Israel finds itself in a veritable orchard of trees like the tree of knowledge of good and evil. The difference between Adam and Israel—permitted to eat all fruit but one, Adam ate the forbidden fruit, while Israel refrains for a specified span of time from fruit from all trees—marks what has taken place, which is the regeneration of humanity. The enlandisement of the Halakhah bears that very special message, and how better make that statement through law than in the explicit concern sages register for the fruit-trees of the land of Israel. No wonder, then, that Orlah-law finds its position, in the Priestly Code, in the rules of sanctification.

So when Israel enters the Land, in exactly the right detail Israel recapitulates the drama of Adam in Eden, but with this formidable difference. The outcome is not the same. By its own act of will Israel addresses the temptation of Adam and overcomes the same temptation, not once but every day through time beyond measure. Adam could not wait out the week, but Israel waits for three years—as long as God waited in creating fruit trees. Adam picked and ate. But here too there is a detail not to be missed. Even after three years, Israel may not eat the fruit wherever it chooses. Rather, in the fourth year from planting, Israel will still show restraint, bringing the fruit only "for jubilation before the Lord" in Jerusalem. The once-forbidden fruit is now eaten in public, not in secret, before the Lord, as a moment of celebration. That detail too recalls the Fall and makes its comment upon the horror of the Fall. That is, when Adam ate the fruit, he shamefully hid from God for having eaten the fruit. But when Israel eats the fruit, it does so proudly, joyfully, before the Lord. The contrast is not to be missed, so too the message. Faithful Israel refrains when it is supposed to, and so it has every reason to cease to refrain and to eat "before the Lord." It has nothing to hide and everything to show.

And there is more. In the fifth year Israel may eat on its own, the time of any restraint from enjoying the gifts of the Land having ended. That sequence provides fruit for the second Sabbath of creation, and so through time. How so? Placing Adam's sin on the first day after the first Sabbath, thus Sunday, then calculating the three forbidden years as Monday, Tuesday, and Wednesday of the second week of creation, reckoning on the jubilation of Thursday, we come to the Friday, eve of the second Sabbath of creation. So now, a year representing a day of the Sabbatical week, just as Leviticus says so many times in connection with the Sabbatical year, the three prohibited years allow Israel to show its true character, fully regenerate, wholly and humbly accepting God's commandment, the one Adam broke.

Here, then, is the message of the Orlah-Halakhah, the statement that only through the details of the laws of Orlah as laid out in both parts of the Torah, written and oral, the Halakhah could hope to make. By its own act of restraint, the new Adam, Israel, in detailed action displays its repentance in respect to the very sin that the old Adam committed, the sin of disobedience and rebellion. Facing the same opportunity to sin, Israel again and again over time refrains from the very sin that cost Adam Eden. So by its manner of cultivation of the Land and its orchards, Israel manifests what in the very condition of humanity has changed by the giving of the Torah: the advent of humanity's second chance, through Israel. Only in the Land that succeeds Eden can Israel, succeeding Adam, carry out the acts of regeneration that the Torah makes possible.

Within Israel's social order—Abodah Zarah: Those who worship idols are called idolaters, and those who worship the one true God, who has made himself known in the Torah, are called Israel[ites]. In the Oral Torah, that is the difference, the only consequential distinction between Israel and the gentiles. But the Halakhah takes as its religious problem the concretization of that distinction, the demonstration of where and how the distinction in theory makes a huge difference in the practice, the conduct, of everyday affairs. What is at stake is that Israel stands for life, and gentiles, like their idols, for death. Thus an asherah-tree, like a corpse, conveys uncleanness to those who pass underneath it (M. A.Z. 3:8). Why does idolatry define the boundary between Israel and everybody else? The reason is that idolatry—rebellious arrogance against God—encompasses the entire Torah. The religious duty to avoid idolatry is primary; if one violates the religious duties, he breaks the yoke of commandments, and if he violates that single religious duty, he violates the entire Torah. Violating the prohibition against idolatry is equivalent to transgressing all Ten Commandments.

The Halakhah treats gentiles as undifferentiated, but as individuals. The Aggadah treats gentiles as "the nations" and takes no interest in individuals or in transactions between private persons. In the theology of the

Oral Torah, the category "the gentiles" or "the nations," without elaborate differentiation, encompasses all who are not Israelites, that is, who do not belong to the people Israel and therefore do not know and serve God. That category takes on meaning only as complement and opposite to its generative counterpart, having no self-defining characteristics on its own. That is, since Israel encompasses the sector of humanity that knows and serves God by reason of God's self-manifestation in the Torah, the gentiles are comprised by everybody else: those placed by their own intention and active decision beyond the limits of God's revelation. Guided by the Torah, Israel worships God; without its illumination, gentiles worship idols. At the outset, therefore, the main point registers: by "gentiles" sages understand God's enemies; and by "Israel" they understand those who know God as God has made himself known, which is, through the Torah. In no way do we deal with secular categories, but with theological ones.

The Halakhah then serves as the means for the translation of theological conviction into social policy. Gentiles are assumed to be ready to murder any Israelite they can get their hands on, rape any Israelite women, commit bestiality with any Israelite cow. The Oral Torah cites few cases to indicate that that conviction responds to ordinary, everyday events; the hostility to gentiles flows from a theory of idolatry, not the facts of everyday social intercourse, which, as we have seen, sages recognize is full of neighborly cordiality. Then why take for granted gentiles routinely commit the mortal sins of not merely idolatry but bestiality, fornication, and murder? That is because the Halakhah takes as its task the realization of the theological principle that those who hate Israel hate God, those who hate God hate Israel, and God will ultimately vanquish Israel's enemies as his own—just as God too was redeemed from Egypt. So the theory of idolatry, involving alienation from God, accounts for the wicked conduct imputed to idolaters, without regard to whether, in fact, that is how idolaters conduct themselves.

When we come to the Halakhah's treatment of the idolatry and idolaters, our first question must be, Why do sages define a principal category of the Halakhah in this wise? It is because sages must devote a considerable account to the challenge to that justice represented by gentile power and prosperity, Israel's subordination and penury. For if the story of the moral order tells about justice that encompasses all creation, the chapter of gentile rule vastly disrupts the account. Gentile rule forms the point of tension, the source of conflict, attracting attention and demanding explanation. For the critical problematic inherent in the category, Israel, is that its anti-category, the gentiles, dominates. So the urgent question to which the system must respond asks by what rationality a world ordered through justice can be ruled by gentiles. And that explains why the systemic problematic focuses upon the question, How can justice be thought to order the world if the gentiles rule? That formulation furthermore forms the public counterpart to the private perplexity: How is it that the wicked prosper and the righteous suffer? The two challenges to the conviction of the rule of moral rationality—gentile hegemony, matched by the prosperity of wicked persons—match.

Yet here the Halakhah turns out to make its own point, one that we ought not to miss. The Halakhah presupposes not gentile hegemony but only gentile power; and it further takes for granted that Israelites may make choices, may specifically refrain from trading in what gentiles value in the service of their gods, and may hold back from gentiles what gentiles require for that service. In this regard the Halakhah parts company from the Aggadah, the picture gained by looking inward not corresponding to the outward-facing perspective. Focused upon interiorities that prove real and tangible, not matters of theological theory at all, the Halakhah of Abodah Zarah legislates for a world in which Israelites, while subordinate in some ways, control their own conduct and govern their own destiny.

Israelites may live in a world governed by gentiles, but they form intentions and carry them out. They decide what to sell and what not to sell, whom to hire for what particular act of labor and to whom not to sell their own labor, and, above all, Israelite traders may determine to give up opportunities offered them by the circumstance of gentile idolatry. The Halakhah therefore makes a formidable statement of Israel's freedom to make choices, its opportunity within the context of everyday life to preserve a territory free of idolatrous contamination, just as Israel in entering the Land was to create a territory free of the worship and presence of idols. In the setting of world order, Israel may find itself subject to the will of others, but in the house of Israel, Israelites can and should establish a realm for God's rule and presence, free of idolatry. And if to establish a domain for God, Israelites must practice self-abnegation, refrain from actions of considerable weight and consequence, well, much of the Torah concerns itself with what people are not supposed to do, and God's rule comes to realization in acts of restraint.

Accordingly, the religious problem of the Halakhah focuses on the inner world of Israel in command of itself. The religious problem of the Aggadah, by contrast, explains, rationalizes as best it can, gentile hegemony such as the Halakhah takes for granted gentiles simply do not exercise. The Halakhah sees that world within Israel's dominion for which Israel bears responsibility; there sages legislate. The Aggadah forms a perspective upon the world subject to gentile rule, that is, the world beyond the limits of Israel's own power. The Halakhah speaks of Israel at the heart of matters, the Aggadah, of Israel within humanity.

To see the contrast between the Halakhah and the Aggadah on gentiles, let me briefly reprise the aggadic account of the matter. Who, speaking categorically not historically, indeed are these "non-Israelites," called gentiles ("the nations," "the peoples," and the like)? The answer is dictated by the form of the question: who exactly is a "non-Israelite"? Then the answer concerning the signified is always relative to its signifier, Israel. Within humanity-other-than-Israel, differentiation articulates itself along gross, political lines, always in relationship to Is-

rael. If humanity is differentiated politically, then, it is a differentiation imposed by what has happened between a differentiated portion of humanity and Israel. It is, then, that segment of humanity that under given circumstances has interacted with Israel: 1) Israel arising at the end and climax of the class of world empires, Babylonia, Media, Greece, Rome; or 2) Israel against Egypt; or 3) Israel against Canaan. That is the point at which Babylonia, Media, Greece, Rome, Egypt, or Canaan take a place in the narrative, become actors for the moment, but never givens, never enduring native categories. Then, when politics does not impose its structure of power-relationships, then humanity is divided between Israel and everyone else.

What then is the difference between the gentile and the Israelite, individually and collectively (there being no distinction between the private person and the public, social and political entity)? A picture in cartographic form of the theological anthropology of the Oral Torah would portray a many-colored Israel at the center of the circle, with the perimeter comprised by all-white gentiles; since, in the Halakhah, gentiles like their idols, as we have seen, are a source of uncleanness of the same virulence as corpse-uncleanness, the perimeter would be an undifferentiated white, the color of death. The law of uncleanness bears its theological counterpart in the lore of death and resurrection, a single theology animating both. Gentile-idolaters and Israelite worshippers of the one and only God part company at death. For the moment Israelites die but rise from the grave, gentiles die and remain there. The roads intersect at the grave, each component of humanity taking its own path beyond. Israelites—meaning, those possessed of right conviction—will rise from the grave, stand in judgment, but then enter upon eternal life, to which no one else will enjoy access. So, in substance, humanity viewed whole is divided between those who get a share in the world to come, Israel, who will stand when subject to divine judgment and those who will not.

Clearly, the moral ordering of the world

encompasses all humanity. But God does not neglect the gentiles or fail to exercise dominion over them. For even now, gentiles are subject to a number of commandments or religious obligations. God cares for gentiles as for Israel, God wants gentiles as much as Israel to enter the kingdom of Heaven and assigns to gentiles opportunities to evince their acceptance of his rule. One of these commandments is not to curse God's name, so B. San. 7:5 I.2/56a:

> "Any man who curses his God shall bear his sin" (Lev. 24:15): It would have been clear had the text simply said, "A man." Why does it specify, "Any"? It serves to encompass idolaters, who are admonished not to curse the Name, just as Israelites are so admonished.

Not cursing God, even while worshipping idols, seems a minimal expectation.

Gentiles, by reason of their condition outside of the Torah, are characterized by certain traits natural to their situation, and these are worldly. Not only so, but the sages' theology of gentiles shapes the normative law in how to relate to them. If an Israelite is by nature forbearing and forgiving, the gentile by nature is ferocious. That explains why in the Halakhah as much as in the Aggadah gentiles are always suspect of the cardinal sins, bestiality, fornication, and bloodshed, as well as constant idolatry. That view of matters is embodied in normative law, as we have seen. The law of the Mishnah corresponds to the lore of scriptural exegesis; the theory of the gentiles governs in both. Beyond the Torah there not only is no salvation from death, there is not even the possibility of a common decency. The Torah makes all the difference. The upshot may be stated very simply. Israel and the gentiles form the two divisions of humanity. The one will die but rise from the grave to eternal life with God. When the other dies, it perishes; that is the end. Moses said it very well: "Choose life" (Deut. 30:19). The gentiles sustain comparison and contrast with Israel, the point of ultimate division being death for the one, eternal life for the other.

While Israel and the gentiles are deemed comparable, the gentiles do not acknowledge or know God. Therefore, while they are like Israelites in sharing a common humanity by reason of mythic genealogy—deriving from Noah—the gentiles do not receive in a meritorious manner the blessings that God bestows upon them. So much for the points of stress of the Aggadah. When it comes to the Halakhah, the religious problematic focuses not upon the gentiles but upon Israel: what, given the world as it is, can Israel do in the dominion subject to Israel's own will and intention? That is the question that the Halakhah fully answers. For the Halakhah constructs, indeed defines, the interiority of an Israel sustaining God's service in a world of idolatry: life against death in the two concrete and tangible dimensions by which life is sustained: trade and the production of food, the foci of the Halakhah. No wonder Israel must refrain from engaging with idolatry on days of the festivals for idols that the great fairs embody—then especially. The presentation of the Halakhah commences with the single most important, comprehensive point—as usual.

Inside the walls of the Israelite household—Pesahim: For the Halakhah as for the Aggadah, Passover marks the advent of Israel's freedom, which is to say, the beginning of Israel. The liturgy for the occasion makes that matter explicit, calling Passover "the season of our freedom," and that represents a halakhic statement of a norm. But that only focuses the question of the Halakhah: what is that freedom that Israel gained at Passover, freedom from what? And to what, in the halakhic framework, had Israel been enslaved?

Alas, on the surface, the Halakhah in its classical formulation is not only remarkably reticent on that question but lays its emphasis elsewhere altogether. What makes Israel Israel, and what defines its trait as Israel, so far as the Halakhah is concerned, is two matters: 1) the preparation of the home for the festival through the removal of leaven, which may not be consumed or seen at that time; and 2) the preparation and presentation of the Passover offering and the consumption of its meat in the household. These define the topics of halakhic interest—and no others pertinent to the festival register. So the celebration of Israel's freedom turns into the transformation of Israel into a kingdom of priests and a holy people, celebrating its birth by recapitulating the blood-rite that marked the separation of Israel from Egypt and the redemption of Israel for life out of death, Israel's firstborn being saved from the judgment visited upon Egypt's. That defines the focus of the Halakhah: the act of sanctification unto life that marks, and re-marks every year, the advent of Israel out of the nations. The freedom that is celebrated is freedom from death.

Its message for the occasion of Israel's beginning as a free people focuses upon Israel's sanctification, and that message comes to the fore in the stress in the Halakhah upon the analogy of the Israelite household and the Temple in Jerusalem, an analogy that takes effect on Passover in particular. The upshot is, Passover marks the celebration of Israel's redemption, meaning, its separation from Egypt—the separation being marked off by blood rites on both sides—and its entry into the condition of cleanness so that a Temple offering may be eaten in the very household of the Israelite. True enough, the Temple offering is one of the very few—the offering of the red cow for the preparation of ashes for the purification water (Num. 19:1-20) is another—that may be conducted in a state of uncleanness. The second Passover explicitly provides for that circumstance. But the point of the Halakhah should not be lost: conforming with God's explicit instructions in the written Torah, on Passover Israel differentiates itself from the nations (Egypt) and chooses as the signification of its identity the attainment of the condition of cleanness in the household, such that Temple meat may be eaten there.

Like the Halakhah of Yoma, concerning the Day of Atonement, most of which is devoted to the Temple rite on that occasion, the Halakhah of Pesahim therefore stresses the cultic aspect of the occasion: the disposition of the Passover offering. In volume, nearly half of the Halakhah is devoted to that one theme—M. Pes. 5:1-9:11—and in complexity, by far the best articulated and most searching halakhic problems derive from that same theme. But the Halakhah of Pesahim belongs to the realm of the Israelite household and yields a statement on the character of that household that the Halakhah of Yoma does not even contemplate. The household is made ready to serve as part of the cult by the removal of leaven and all marks of fermentation; now people eat only that same unleavened bread that, offered in the Temple alongside the sacrifices, is God's portion through the year. The household is further made the locus of a rite of consuming other specified foods (bitter herbs, for example). But the main point is, the offering sacrificed in the Temple yields meat to be eaten in the household, at home, not only in the Temple courtyard.

That rule pertains only to Lesser Holy Things, the peace-offerings and the festal offering, for example—and to the Passover, so M. Zeb. 9:14: Most Holy Things were eaten within the veils [of the Temple], Lesser Holy Things and second tithe within the wall [of Jerusalem]. Among offerings eaten in Jerusalem in the household but outside of the Temple walls, the Passover offering is the only one precipitated by the advent of a particular occasion (as distinct from peace- and festal-offerings). The festivals of Tabernacles and Pentecost, by contrast, do not entail a home-offering of a similar character, nor does the celebration of the New Month. For its part, the Halakhah of Yoma describes an occasion that is celebrated at the Temple or in relationship to the Temple. In this context, then, the Halakhah of Pesahim alone sets forth an occasion in the life of all Israel that commences in the Temple but concludes at home. Its message, then, is that for Passover in particular—"season of our freedom"—the home and the Temple form a single continuum. That is why the Halakhah is seen to characterize the advent of Israel's freedom from Egypt as an occasion of sanctification: the differentiation through a blood rite in particular of Israel from the nations, represented by Egypt.

On what basis, then, does the Halakhah

before us pertain to the world within the walls of the Israelite household in a way in which the Halakhah of Yoma, the counterpart, does not? Why have sages treated in a single tractate so distinct a set of venues as the home and the Temple, rather than leaving the exposition of the Passover offering to take its place in tractate Zebahim, on the general rules of the cult, where the Passover offering makes its appearance in context? Once the question is framed in that way, the obvious answer emerges. Sages through their emphases transformed the festival of freedom into the celebration of Israel's sanctification, embodied here and now in the act of eating the Passover offering at home, in a family, natural or fabricated, that stands for the Israelite household. So as God abides in the Temple, so on this occasion God's abode extends to the household. That is why the Passover offering takes place in two locations, the Temple for the blood-rite, the home for the consumption of the meat assigned to the sacrifiers, those who benefit from the offering.

The law is explicit that people bring the animals to the Temple, where the beasts are sacrificed, the blood collected, and the sacrificial portions placed on the altar-fires. Then the people take the remaining meat home and roast it. So Passover is represented as a pilgrim festival alone; the home ritual hardly rates a single penetrating halakhic inquiry, being presented as a set of inert facts. It follows that, on the occasion at hand, the household (at least in Jerusalem) forms a continuum with the Temple. That means, also, that the Passover sacrifice then stands in an intermediate situation, not an offering that takes place in a state of uncleanness, like the offering of the red cow, which takes place outside of the Temple (Num. 19:1-20), nor an offering that is presented and eaten in the Temple in a state of cleanness, with the meat eaten by the priests in the Temple itself, like the sin-offering and other Most Holy Things. As to where the sacrifier eats his share of the Passover offering (and its comparable ones), the Halakhah takes for granted it is in a state of cleanness. So far as the Passover is concerned, it is not eaten in the Temple but at home or in a banquet hall, which by definition must be in Jerusalem. That consideration gains weight when we take account of the unleavened character of the bread with which the meat is eaten, in the model of nearly all meal-offerings: "All meal offerings are brought unleavened (Lev. 2:4-5, 6:7-9), except for the leaven[ed cakes] in the thank offerings and the two loaves of bread [of Pentecost], which are brought leavened [Lev. 7:13, 23:17]" (M. Men. 5:1).

By treating the sacrifice in that intermediate realm—the sacrifice in the Temple, the meat eaten at home—the Halakhah takes account of the requirement of the Written Torah, which, read as a harmonious statement, dictates that the Passover take place in two locations, the home and the Temple. Deut. 16:1-8 places the rite in the Temple in Jerusalem. It is explicit that only in the Temple is the Passover offering to be sacrificed, no where else. It is to be boiled and eaten in the same place, not at home, and in the morning the people are to go home. With that statement in hand, we should treat the Passover offering as a Temple rite, just as the sacrifice for the Day of Atonement is a Temple rite.

Then where is the altar in the home? Exod. 12:1-28 treats the offering as a rite for the home, with the blood tossed on the lintel of the house as a mark of an Israelite dwelling. The lintel then serves as the counterpart to the altar. That is where the blood rite takes place, where the blood of the sacrifice is tossed. Here we find as clear a statement as is possible that the Israelite home compares to the Temple, the lintel to the altar, the abode of Israel to the abode of God. Why the lintel? It is the gateway, marking the household apart from the world beyond. Inside the walls of the Israelite household conditions of genealogical and cultic cleanness pertain, in a way comparable to the space inside the contained space of the Temple courtyard.

What contribution the Oral Torah makes to the Halakhah of Passover emerges when we ask, To what offering may we then compare the Passover? The answer is, to the sin-offering. This is stated explicitly. But first, to advance the argument, we ask for the foci of the analogy. It is temporal and occasional, not permanent and spatial. True, the Oral Torah associates the lintel of the Israelite home with the altar, treats the contained space of the Israelite household as comparable to the Temple courtyard, has the household serve as the venue for an offering comparable to the sin-offering. But that analogy takes effect only at a very specific moment, just as the household compares to Eden only at the specific moment of the Sabbath day, the invisible wall descending to mark of the temporal Eden in the particular space consecrated by the Israelite abode. The advent of the first new moon after the vernal equinox then compares with the advent of sunset on the sixth day, the beginning of the Sabbath comparing to the beginning of the lunar calendar marked by the first new moon of spring. The Sabbath places Israel in Eden. Passover, the fifteenth of Nisan, places the Israelite household into a continuum with the Temple, the lintel with the altar (in the Written Torah's reading). With Passover, the Israelite, in the halakhic theory of the Oral Torah, carries his offering to the Temple and brings home the sacrificial parts to be consumed by himself and his family (or the surrogate family formed by an association organized for that particular purpose), so treating the household as an extension of the Temple for the purpose at hand. That same conception extends to other Lesser Holy Things, eaten in Jerusalem but not in the Temple; but Passover among festivals is unique in having its own offering, celebrating its own specific event in the natural year and in the rhythm of Israel's paradigmatic existence as well.

The Passover, moreover, may be subject to the rules of Lesser Holy Things but bears its own very particular signification. Some of the Lesser Holy Things are interchangeable: if an animal is designated for one purpose but offered for another, it may serve, e.g., as a freewill offering. But in the case of the Passover, we deal with a Lesser Holy Thing that is not interchangeable. The Oral Torah stresses that the rite is analogous to the sin-offering, in that the animal that is designated

for the rite must be offered for that purpose— and for that particular sacrifier. If it is designated for the benefit of one party but offered for some other sacrifier and it is not possible to clarify the situation, the animal is simply disposed of, so M. Pes. 9:9 for example:

A. An association, the Passover-offering of which was lost, and which said to someone, "Go and find and slaughter another one for us," and that one went and found and slaughtered [another], but they, too, went and bought and slaughtered [one for themselves]—
B. if his was slaughtered first, he eats his, and they eat with him of his.
C. But if theirs was slaughtered first, they eat of theirs, and he eats of his.
D. And if it is not known which of them was slaughtered first, or if both of them were slaughtered simultaneously, then he eats of his, and they do not eat with him, and theirs goes forth to the place of burning,
E. but they are exempt from having to observe the second Passover.

The stress on the specificity of identification of the beast and sacrifier aligns the Passover offering with the sin-offering, not with peace- or free-will offerings. That analogy is stated explicitly at M. Zeb. 1:1:

A. All animal offerings that were slaughtered not for their own name are valid [so that the blood is tossed, the entrails burned],
B. but they do not go to the owner's credit in fulfillment of an obligation, except for the Passover and the sin offering—
C. the Passover at its appointed time [the afternoon of the fourteenth of Nisan], and the sin offering of any time.

The theory is explained in the subsequent argument of Eliezer that the guilt-offering should be subject to the same rule: "The sin offering comes on account of sin, and the guilt offering comes on account of sin. Just as the sin offering is unfit [if it is offered] not for its own name, so the guilt offering is unfit [if offered] not for its own name]." Eliezer's statement takes for granted that the sin-offering is brought in expiation of (inadvertent) sin, and, it must follow, the Halakhah in general must concur that the same category encompasses also the Passover-offering. That matches the story of the blood on the lintel, an offering that expiates Israel and atones for those sins for which, at the same moment, Egypt will atone through the offering of the firstborn among men and cattle alike. Within that theory, how shall we find in the account of the offering the basis for treating it as comparable to the sin-offering, which is offered to expiate inadvertent sin? Since the Passover offering signals that Israel is to be spared the judgment the Lord executed against the first-born of Egypt, it is reasonable to suppose that the blood of the Passover lamb, placed on the lintel, not only marks the household as Israelite but also expiates inadvertent sin carried out in that household.

True, the Written Torah itself imposed the requirement of celebrating Passover in two different places: according to Deuteronomy, it is in the Temple, with the meat consumed in Jerusalem; according to Exodus, it is at home, with the meat consumed there. But in joining the two conceptions, with its rules for the household wherever it is located, the Halakhah has made a statement of its own out of the disharmonious facts received from Scripture. That statement is in two parts. First, the Israelite abode is treated as comparable to the Temple not merely in the aspect of cultic cleanness, but in the aspect of cultic activity: the place where the sacrificial meat was consumed, within the unfolding of the rite of expiation of inadvertent sin itself. That analogy, between the Passover on the fourteenth of Nisan and the sin-offering at any time, forms the critical nexus between the Israelite abode and the Temple altar. So the question arises, why that particular analogy, and to what effect? Or to state matters differently, what statement do we make when we say, the Passover offering is comparable to the sin-offering?

The answer derives from the occasion itself, Israel on the eve of the Exodus from Egypt, at the threshold of its formation into a kingdom of priests and a holy people. When God executed judgment of Egypt, exacting the first-born of man and beast as the sanction, he saw the blood, that—the

Oral Torah now tells us—compared with the blood of the sin-offering. Israel then had expiated its inadvertent sin and attained a state of atonement, so entering a right relationship with God. On the eve of Israel's formation, the Passover offered at home, with the blood on the lintel, marked Israel as having expiated its sin. The sinless people was kept alive at the time of judgment—just as, at the end of days, nearly all Israel will stand in judgment and pass on to life eternal.

Sin and atonement, death and life—these form the foci of Passover. If sages had wished to make the theological statement that Israel differs from the Egyptians as does life from death and that what makes the difference is that Israel is sanctified even—or especially—within its household walls, not only within the Temple veils, how better to say so than through the Halakhah of Passover? Eat unleavened bread as God does in the meal-offerings, consume the meat left over from the blood rite of the Passover offering, analogous to the sin-offering in its very particular identification with a given family-unit, and the actions speak for themselves. These are the two facts out of the repertoire of the data of Passover that the halakhic statement from the Mishnah through the Babylonian Talmud chooses to explore and articulate. The Written Torah sets forth the facts; Oral Torah explores their implications for the norms of conduct, while, in doing so, imparting its sense for the proportion, therefore the meaning and significance, of the whole.

Why these two topics in particular? The sages will assuredly have maintained they said no more than the Written Torah implied, and, as we have seen, that claim enjoys powerful support in the content of the Halakhah. But sages are the ones who framed the law, chose its points of proportion and emphasis. In doing so, they shaped the law into a statement congruent with the stresses of their system as a whole. Theirs was a theology of restoration, Israel to the Land standing for humankind to Eden. To such a statement, the fact that fully half of the halakhic formulations were monumentally irrelevant to the practical affairs of life made no difference. Sages knew full well that all Israel was resident outside of Jerusalem; in the time that the halakhic statement was being formulated, Israel could not enter Jerusalem, let alone sacrifice on the ruined, plowed-over Temple mount. But to the realities of the moment, sages chose to make no statement at all; these meant nothing of enduring consequence to them. For the situation of Israel in the here and now did not define the focus of the Halakhah, only its venue.

For sages, at stake in the Halakhah is the transformation of Israel by time and circumstance, the reconciliation of Israel and God by rites of atonement for sin, and the location of Israel and God into a single abode: the household now, Eden then. What is at stake in the Halakhah of innermost Israel, the Israel embodied in the abode of the household? It is what takes place in the Holy of Holies on the Day of Atonement: the encounter of Israel, its sins atoned for, its reconciliation in the aftermath of the fall from Eden complete—the encounter of Israel with God, the occasion of eternity, the moment at which, for now, death is transcended. Scripture said no less, sages no more (Exod. 12:11-13):

> It is the Lord's passover. For I will pass through the land of Egypt that night, and I will smite all the first-born in the land of Egypt, both man and beast; and on all the gods of Egypt I will execute judgments; I am the Lord. The blood shall be a sign for you, upon the houses where you are; and when I see the blood I will pass over you, and no plague shall fall upon you to destroy you, when I smite the land of Egypt.

The Halakhah makes the statement that the freedom Passover celebrates is Israel's freedom from death. Where Israel lives, there life is lived that transcends the grave. When, as is the custom, some people at the Passover Seder wear their burial garment, the gesture says no less than that.

Inside the walls of the Israelite household—Sukkah: The temporary abode of the Israelite, suspended between heaven and earth, the sukkah-booth built for the festival of Tabernacles in its transience matches Israel's condition in the wilderness, wandering between Egypt and the Land, death and eternal life. Just as Passover marks the differentiation of Israel, expiating sin through the Passover offering and so attaining life, from Egypt, expiating sin through the death of the first-born, so the festival of Tabernacles addresses the condition of Israel. We deal, we must remind ourselves, with the generation of the wilderness, that is, the generation that must die out before Israel can enter the Land. So entering the sukkah reminds Israel not only of the fragility of its condition but also—in the aftermath of the penitential season—of its actuality: yet sinful, yet awaiting death, so that a new generation will be ready for the Land. So the Festival recapitulates that interstitial circumstance, between death in Egypt and eternal life in the Land. Sages maintain that had Israel not sinned, the Torah would have contained only the Pentateuch and the book of Joshua, a neat way of stating in a few words the conviction that permeates the aggadic reading of the Land as counterpart to Eden, Israel as counterpart to Adam. It is on that basis that the wilderness marks the interval between death in Egypt and eternal life in the Land. The booth of Tabernacles, the now-abode of Israel-in-between, is the house that is not a house, protected by a roof that is open to the elements but serves somewhat: Israel en route to death (for those here now) and then eternal life (for everyone then).

It is at the sukkah itself that we find the center of the halakhic repertoire concerning the festival of Tabernacles. Israel in the wilderness, replicated annually from the first New Moon after the autumnal equinox, lived in houses open to the rain and affording protection only from the harsh sunlight, shade if not continuous shadow such as a roof provides. Their abode was constructed of what was otherwise useless, bits and pieces of this and that, and, hence, insusceptible to uncleanness. This is the abode in which Israel is directed to take up residence. The odd timing should not be missed. It is not with the coming of the spring and the dry season, when the booth serves a useful purpose against the sun, but at the advent of the autumn and the rainy one, when it does not protect against the rain.

It is an abode that cannot serve in the season that is coming, announced by the New Moon that occasions the festival. Israel is to take shelter, in reverting to the wilderness, in any random, ramshackle hut, covered with what nature has provided but in form and purpose what people otherwise do not value. Israel's dwelling in the wilderness is fragile, random, and transient—like Israel in the wilderness. Out of Egypt, Israel atoned and lived, now, after the season of repentance, Israel has atoned and lived—but only in the condition of the wilderness, like the generation that, after all, had to die out before Israel could enter the Land and its intended-eternal life.

Annually putting the Israelites into booths to remind them that Israel now lives like the generation of the wilderness then, sinful and meant to die, the Halakhah underscores not only transience. It emphasizes the contemporaneity of the wilderness-condition: the sukkah is constructed fresh, every year. Israel annually is directed to replicate the wilderness generation—Scripture says no less. The dual message is not to be missed: Israel is en route to the Land that stands for Eden; but Israel, even beyond the penitential season, bears its sin and must, on the near term, die, but in death enjoys the certainty of resurrection, judgment, and eternal life to come. What we are dealing with here is a re-definition of the meaning of Israel's abode and its definition. All seven days a person treats his sukkah as his regular dwelling and his house as his sometime dwelling. On the occasion of Tabernacles, Israel regains the wilderness and its message of death but also transcendence over death in the entry into the Land. Only in the context of the New Year and the Day of Atonement, only as the final act in the penitential season and its intense drama, does Sukkot make sense. It is the Halakhah that draws out that sense, in the provisions that define the valid sukkah upon which such heavy emphasis is to be laid.

True, the Written Torah tells more about the observance of than the historical reason or occasion for the festival of Sukkot. But what it does say—"that your generations may know that I made the people of Israel dwell in booths when I brought them out of the land of Egypt" (Lev. 23:43)—suffices. The reversion to the wilderness, the recapitulation of the wandering, the return to Israel's condition outside of the Land and before access to the Land, the remembrance of the character of that generation, its feet scarcely dry after passing through the mud of the Reed Sea when it has already built the Golden Calf—that is the other half of the cycle that commences at Passover and concludes at Sukkot. Who can have missed the point of the Tabernacles, with Scripture's words in hand, "that I made the people of Israel dwell in booths"? The rabbis of the Halakhah certainly did not.

Let us return to the eternal present established by the Halakhah and compare the provisions for the principal halakhic moments, Pesahim and Sukkah. Viewing the festival of Tabernacles in the model of the festival of Passover, we find that three elements require attention, in two divisions: what happens in the home, what happens in the Temple, and what happens in the home that connects the home to the Temple. Passover has the home cleansed of leaven, with the result that the bread of the holiday corresponds to the bread served to God in (most of) the meal offerings. What happens in the Temple is the sacrifice of the Passover offering. What happens in the home that connects the home to the Temple is the eating of the portions of the Passover offering that the ordinary Israelite on Passover eats, just as the priest in the Temple eats portions of the sin-offering (among other Most Holy Things). So, as we have seen, Passover marks the moment at which the home and the Temple are made to correspond, the whole taking place within the walls of Jerusalem.

That perspective turns out to clarify the divisions of the Halakhah of Sukkah as well: what happens in the Temple is a celebratory rite involving the utilization of certain objects (lulab, etrog) and the recitation of the Hallel-Psalms. What happens in the home? The home is abandoned altogether, a new house being constructed for the occasion. During Tabernacles, the Israelite moves out of his home altogether, eating meals and (where possible) sleeping in the sukkah, making the sukkah into the regular home, and the home into the random shelter. Just as, in the wilderness, God's abode shifted along with Israel from place to place, the tabernacle being taken down and reconstructed time and again, so, in recapitulating the life of the wilderness, Israel's abode shifts, losing that permanence that it ordinarily possesses. What happens in the home that connects the home to the Temple? At first glance, nothing, there being no counterpart to the Passover Seder. But a second look shows something more striking. To see the connection we must recall that during Tabernacles a huge volume of offerings is presented day by day. Then God consumed the festal offering (*hagigah*) and other sacrificial meat, e.g., from the freewill offering. Israel removes to the housing of the wilderness to eat the Festival meat, doing in the sukkah what God previously had done in the Tabernacle in that wilderness.

To find the religious meaning of the Halakhah of Sukkot, therefore, we must ask, What does the abode in the wilderness represent? To answer that question within the framework of the Halakhah, we introduce two well-established facts. First, one cannot over-stress that, as the Halakhah knows, Tabernacles continues the penitential season commencing with the advent of Elul, which reaches its climax in the season of judgment and atonement of the Days of Awe, from the first through the tenth of the month of Tishre, Rosh Hashanah, the New Year, and Yom Hakkippurim, the Day of Atonement. Tabernacles finds its place in the context of a season of sin and atonement. And since, as the rites themselves indicate, it celebrates the advent of the rainy season with prayers and activities meant to encourage the now-conciliated God to give ample rain to sustain the life of the Land and its people, the message cannot be missed. Israel has rebelled and sinned, but Israel has also atoned and repented: this is the meaning of the first days of the season of repentance.

At the new moon following, having atoned and been forgiven, Israel takes up residence as if it were in the wilderness. Why so? Because in the wilderness, en route to the Land, still-sinful Israel depended wholly and completely on God's mercy and good will and infinite capacity to forgive in response to repentance and atonement. Israel depends for all things on God, eating food he sends down from heaven, drinking water he divines in rocks, and living in fragile booths. Even Israel's very household in the mundane sense, its shelter, now is made to depend upon divine grace: the wind can blow it down, the rain prevent its very use. Returning to these booths, built specifically for this occasion (not last year's), manipulating the sacred objects owned in particular by the Israelite who utilizes them, as the rainy season impends, Israelites here and now recapitulate their total dependence upon God's mercy.

Accordingly, requiring that everything be renewed for the present occasion and the particular person, the Halakhah transforms commemoration of the wandering into recapitulation of the condition of the wilderness. The sukkah makes the statement that Israel of the here and now, sinful like the Israel that dwelt in the wilderness, depends wholly upon, looks only to, God. Israelites turn their eyes to that God whose just-now forgiveness of last year's sins and acts of rebellion and whose acceptance of Israel's immediate act of repentance will recapitulate God's ongoing nurture that kept Israel alive in the wilderness. The Halakhah's provisions for the sukkah underscore not so much the transience of Israel's present life in general as Israel's particular condition. The Halakhah renders Israel in the sukkah as the people that is en route to the Land, which is Eden. Yes, Israel is en route, but it is not there. A generation comes, a generation goes, but Israel will get there, all together at the end.

So in defining the sukkah as it does, the

Halakhah also underscores the given of God's providence and remarkable forbearance. In a negative way, the Halakhah says exactly that at M. Suk. 2:9:

A. [If] it began to rain, at what point is it permitted to empty out [the sukkah]?
B. From the point at which the porridge will spoil.
C. They made a parable: To what is the matter comparable? To a slave who came to mix a cup of wine for his master, and his master threw the flagon into his face.

No wonder, then, that, in the Aggadah, Sukkot is supposed to mark the opportunity for the messiah to present himself and raise the dead.

Conclusion: The Aggadah's structure and system and those of the Halakhah address a single topic, but from different angles of vision of Israel's existence, the one, outward-looking and the other, inner-facing. But both engaged by relationships, the one transitive ones and the other intransitive. It is the Aggadah, fully set forth, that affords perspective on the Halakhah—and vice versa. The Halakhah in its way makes exactly the same statement about the same matters that the Aggadah does in its categories and terms. But the Aggadah speaks in large and general terms to the world at large, while the Halakhah uses small and particular rules to speak to the everyday concerns of ordinary Israelites; the Aggadah addresses exteriorities, the Halakhah, interiorities, of Israel in relationship with God.

Categorically, the Aggadah faces outward toward humanity in general and shows the relationship of that humanity and Israel in particular. The theological system of a just world order answerable to one God that animates the Aggadah, specifically, sets forth the parallel stories of humanity and Israel, each beginning with Eden, marked by sin and punishment (Adam's and Israel's respective acts of rebellion against God, the one through disobedience, the other through violating the Torah), and exile for the purpose of bringing about repentance and atonement (Adam from Eden, Israel from the Land). The system therefore takes as its critical problem the

comparison of Israel with the Torah and the nations with idolatry. It comes to a climax in showing how the comparable stories intersect and diverge at the grave. For from there Israel is destined to the resurrection, judgment, and eternity (the world to come), the nations (that is, the idolaters to the end) to death. When we examine the category-formation of the Halakhah, by contrast, we see an account of Israel not in its external relationship to the nations but viewed wholly on its own. The lines of structure impart order from within. Each formation responds to the rules of construction of the same social order—God's justice—but the aggadic one concerns Israel's social order in the context of God's transaction with humanity, the other, Israel's social order articulated within its own interior architectonics, thus the one, transitive, the other, intransitive.

The theology of the Oral Torah that the aggadic documents, and aggadic segments of halakhic ones portray focuses our attention upon one perspective and neglects the other. The outward-facing theology that coheres in the aggadic documents investigates the logic of creation, the fall, the regeneration made possible by the Torah, the separation of Israel and the Torah from the nations and idolatry, the one for life through repentance and resurrection, the other for death, and the ultimate restoration of creation's perfection attempted with Adam at Eden, but now through Israel in the land of Israel. Encompassing the whole of humanity that knows God in the Torah and rejects idolatry, Israel encompasses nearly the whole of humankind, along with nearly the whole of the Israel of the epoch of the Torah and of the messiah that has preceded. Thus the Aggadah tells about Israel in the context of humanity and hence speaks of exteriorities. Its perspectives are taken up at the border between outside and inside, the position of standing at the border inside and looking outward—hence 1) God and the world, 2) the Torah, and 3) Israel and the nations.

That other perspective, the one gained by standing at the border, inside and turning, looking still deeper within, responds to the same logic, seeking the coherence and rationality of all things. That perspective focuses upon relationships too. But now they are not those between God and humankind or Israel and the nations, but the ones involving 1) God and Israel, 2) Israel in its own terms, and 3) Israelites in their own situation, that is, within the household in particular—terms that are amply defined only in the halakhic context.

JACOB NEUSNER

HERESY, APOSTASY IN JUDAISM: Heresy refers to holding unauthorized beliefs and performing unaccepted practices within one's religion; apostasy means abandoning that religion for another. The terms are significant in western culture because of their importance in Christianity. When, in the fourth century, Christianity became the West's primary political as well as religious doctrine, heresy and apostasy became definitive markers of cultural difference. One's place in society, indeed, one's social legitimacy was determined by the character of one's practice and the content of one's faith. Because Christianity both shaped the social order and was viewed as the only path to salvation, alienation from the Church meant separation from life in this world and in the hereafter.

As in the example of Christianity, religions must establish limits of tolerance in thought and behavior, for only in this way can they define what it means to be a member of a particular community. Therefore, categories for dissent, separation, and alienation are necessary components in the morphology of religion. Just as the opposition of Israel and "the Nations" is essential to Judaism's claim of distinctiveness, so too categories for heresy and apostasy are important to the religion's self-definition. Even so, in Judaism, heresy and apostasy do not occupy quite the same place they do in Christianity. In the foundational Rabbinic texts, heresy and apostasy are just two among several types of significant religious dissent; in later medieval and modern Judaism, the categories exist but are defined and applied in varied ways, depending on a range of factors—primarily social and political. Thus, in Judaism, heresy

and apostasy do not simply, or only, distinguish an "authentic" Jew from a renegade. Rather, they are part of a larger problem: how Judaism understands itself by defining and demarcating what is different or "other."

A notion of the "other" is essential to any religion's self-definition. Without an "other," there can be no "us." But "otherness" is not necessarily a natural or neutral trait. Not all differences are sufficiently problematic or challenging to make someone else into "not-us" or "anti-us." This means that "otherness" is a matter of imagination as well as confrontation. A religion "constructs" rather than merely encounters its "others." It fabricates definitive difference by focusing on a characteristic trait of dissenters or outsiders—behavior, belief, dress, food, etc.—and making it symbolize their difference. A religion decides which trait of the outsider pushes them beyond the pale. To evoke the significant disparity that constitutes "otherness," the symbol of difference must correspond powerfully to the naming religion's sense of its own distinctiveness. It must correlate to something the religion's adherents believe authentically represents their religion itself. Religions thus perceive their "others" in terms of traits, values, or practices that matter to themselves.

In so constructing "otherness," religions do not see the outsiders whole. Rather, a religion mistakes some part of the outsider for the outsider and a piece of itself for itself, and it construes each in terms of the other. Each negation of the "other" is simultaneously an affirmation of self, in terms of some particular trait. This mean that "otherness" is as much about the naming religion as it is about outsiders named. It is an important way in which adherents of a religion think about themselves and the limits and the potential weaknesses of their community. "Otherness," therefore, is at least as much a reflection of the religious community's self-understanding as it is a response to actual conflicts with a real other.

Two other features of the construction of "otherness" deserve mention. First, difference correlates with proximity. When multiple groups inhabit the same or adjoining space, or when they practice similar rites or read the same text—in general, when they are too much alike—the specification of difference is an urgent necessity. The religion's survival may depend on its ability to establish a clear distinction between itself and others. Second, the same trait or symbol need not evoke difference in all times and places. Although the form of difference is constant, its substance is not.

The components of difference in Judaism: Three basic factors ground the attitudes towards dissent and difference that shape the development of apostasy and heresy in Judaism: biblical monotheism, the Israelite covenant with God, and the Judaism's status as a colonial religion.

Biblical monotheism denies divine self-contradiction and expects of Israel exclusive loyalty to God. This theological framework emphasizes God's selectivity, singularity of purpose, and consistency of will. It consequently precludes doctrinal disparity among those who understand themselves to be Israel. From the perspective of monotheism, the one and only God cannot say conflicting things to the people chosen to act out God's desires. Within Israel, the claim to be right about God is necessarily a claim to be exclusively right. The "logic" of monotheism, therefore, makes dissent difficult to absorb and tends to deal with difference through separation.

The biblical covenant with God, however, complicates the understanding of Israelite identity and therefore the implications of dissent. Scripture contains two covenantal definitions of membership in Israel, God's people. The covenant at Sinai supposes that membership in Israel is conditional and that failure to fulfill the commandments can end one's membership. The covenant with Abraham, however, conceives God's bond with Abraham's descendants as "eternal" or "everlasting" (*brit 'olam*): "And I will establish my covenant between me and you and your descendants after you throughout their generations for an everlasting covenant, to be God to you and to your descendants after you" (Gen. 17:7). This form of covenant understanding makes membership in Israel indelible and makes exclusion from the community or the people difficult to justify or carry out.

These two formulations for membership in Israel—one conditional the other indelible—establish the polar limits within which the criteria for, and consequences of, apostasy and heresy developed in Judaism. The issues of apostasy and heresy set one covenant against the other. The basic questions are: Do heresy and apostasy constitute the kinds of dissent, of violation of commandments, that can nullify one's membership in Israel? Are heresy and apostasy procedural and juridical, matters of community discipline, or are they ontological, matters of one's ultimate relationship with God? Because of Judaism's political situation, the history of Judaism offers—and can offer—no single answer to that question.

From its inception, Judaism was—and outside of the State of Israel today remains—a religion of political dependents and dependence. Judaism's classic and foundational texts, which shaped and defined its approaches to dissent and exclusion, all were developed and composed in the context of political, cultural, and social domination by non-Jewish powers. The Hebrew Scriptures and the Babylonian Talmud are products of the diaspora. The Mishnah, the midrashic collections, and the Palestinian Talmud were composed and redacted under Roman control.

Moreover, Judaism's classic sources, the literature of the ancient rabbinate, emerged from—and to some extent within—the factionalism that characterized Jewish religious life in the land of Israel during the Persian, Hellenistic, and early Roman periods. Even when sectarianism diminished after the destruction of the Temple in 70 and the Bar Kokhba rebellion in 135, Rabbinic Judaism was not the only form of Judaism practiced by Jews. Thus, Rabbinic Judaism had to contend with internal diversity from the very outset.

For most of its history, Judaism has existed without a native center. Consequently, religious leaders in Judaism never had the political power to develop a centralized body to establish a single definition and uniform consequences of heresy and apostasy.

There are no Rabbinic equivalents to the Church councils or the papacy. Because Judaism remained a minority and politically dependent religion, it lacked a congruent political structure to endorse its world-view. Moreover, some key concepts in Rabbinic literature appear to advocate decentralized religious authority in Judaism. The Talmudic notion of *mara' d'atra'* ("master of the place"), for example, actively discourages rabbis from making legal rulings for one another's communities. Thus, although various nations and regions, particularly in modern times, supported and support leaders called "chief rabbi," the authority of such leaders extends only to a particular minority of Jews that voluntarily gives its assent. An overarching religious authority in Judaism that can set and enforce consistent standards and sanctions for heresy and apostasy appears neither politically possible nor religiously desirable.

This background of political dependence and internal religious diversity means that for the foundational texts of Judaism, heresy and apostasy are more likely to be issues of principle and theory than of practice. Thus, the questions of dissent and separation from Judaism are not central preoccupations of Rabbinic texts, and the varied terms for heresy and apostasy exhibit a range of meanings across and even within documents.

The Talmudic literature contains at least six terms for Jews who in the rabbis' judgment occupy a continuum from dissent within to abandonment of Judaism. The terms are: *min* ("sectarian," "heretic"), *mumar* ("apostate," "heretic"), *meshummad* ("apostate," "one who forces abandonment of religion"), *kofer* [*b'ikkar*] ("denier [of a principle of religion]"), *apikoros* ("Epicurean," "heretic"), and *poshe'a yisra'el* ("rebellious Jew"). The accepted translations indicate that there is some overlap among these terms. Their definitions are neither always uniform nor practical. *Min*, for instance, can refer to both a Jew and a gentile.[1]

An *apikoros* can be a Sadducee (B. Qid. 66a) or one who shames neighbors before a sage (B. San. 99b).[2] The term *mumar* can apply to one who consistently transgresses a single commandment or one who is judged alien with respect to the "entire Torah" (B Hul. 4b). Likewise, B. Hor. 11b defines a *meshummad* as follows:

> Our rabbis taught: If one ate forbidden fat, he is a *meshummad*. And who is a *meshummad*? One who ate animals not ritually slaughtered or afflicted with fatal diseases, forbidden animals or reptiles, or who drank the wine of libation. R. Yose, son of R. Judah, says, "Even one who wears a garment of wool and linen."

Alternatively, Sifra to Lev. 12 describes a *meshummad* as one who does "not accept the covenant" or who declares the covenant "void."

The relative fluidity of the terms suggests that Rabbinic texts are working on theoretical questions rather than practical ones. Indeed, in general, early Rabbinic documents focus on religious questions, such as the individual Jew's relationship to God and participation in resurrection and inclusion in rabbinism's eschatological realm, "the World to Come." Medieval and modern writings are more likely to conceive heresy and apostasy in social terms, such as ostracism from a community.

All of this means that in the history of Judaism heresy and apostasy are necessarily local phenomena. Their meaning and implications depend on the community in which, and the authority by whom, they are applied. The sanctions imposed on those judged in a given setting to be heretics or apostates also vary by community and context. A *herem* or "ban" applied to a person in one community has no force in another.

Moreover, although there is often legal consensus on some aspects of apostasy and heresy, there is almost never uniformity. In the halakhic literature of the middle ages and later, nearly every significant ruling on the treatment of heretics or apostates has a meaningful and considered dissent. Thus, for instance, in harmony with the covenant with Abraham, many Rabbinic and medieval legal sources understand membership in Israel—the community of Judaism—to be indelible. On this view, following B. San. 44a, apostates are sinning Jews and do not need to undergo a ritual of conversion in order to re-join the community of Judaism. Indeed, there is no rite in Judaism that revokes the status of being Israel, that transforms a Jew into a gentile. There also is no generally required ceremony of return or reentry for those who have abandoned Judaism for another religion. Repentance is sufficient. Other authorities, however, conform to the idea of the covenant at Sinai and hold the opposite position. They require immersion in a *mikveh* ("ritual bath") before a repentant apostate is allowed back into the community of Judaism. This view apparently first appears in the thirteenth century.[3]

The patterns of the two covenants can be seen in what Gerald Blidstein calls the "medieval consensus" on the religious status of an apostate Jew in Judaism. Most medieval authorities concurred that for "marital status and related issues, Jewish status was irreversible and inalienable."[4] The general legal principle is that a halakhic marriage between two apostates or an apostate and a Jew is valid. For one of them to marry someone else, therefore, requires a divorce, and they remain married until a halakhic divorce is performed. On matters of personal status, an apostate remained a Jew in perpetuity. For instance, the child of an apostate mother is regarded as a Jew. However, on other matters—including reliability as a witness—the apostate was treated as a gentile.

> In other areas—Levirate, inheritance, usury—the apostate was considered an alien by a respectable and large school. The depth of this alienation varied. . . . In the contexts of the Levirate and usury the "brotherhood" of the apostate, understood as a continuum of shared ideological commitment, was denied; for the purposes of inheritance his less definable but clearly vital "Jewish holiness," an aspect of Jewish status, was diminished. . . . The components of Jewish belonging are thus divisible.[5]

In the view of medieval halakhists, the two covenants balanced one another. With respect to personal status, membership in Israel was forever. With respect to property, inheritance, and related matters, membership was conditional.

The categories of heresy and apostasy play two important roles in Judaism, one in the realm of theory, the other in the arena of practice. In the theoretical realm, the categories of heresy and apostasy allow Judaism's intellectual and community leaders, from well inside the religion, to determine experimentally what can and cannot be compromised when the religion's boundaries are challenged. The categories provide a means to think along Judaism's edges, to imagine scenarios of rupture. But on a practical level, the adherents of a lived and living Judaism must be able to know that it is possible to go too far and what to do when that happens. Discrete communities must be able to understand which principles of difference to apply and when and why to apply them. But it must be stressed again that heresy and apostasy are local decisions. Perhaps because political authority is diffuse in Judaism, legal actions against heretics do not occupy a significant place in its history, and the actions themselves do not appear to have had significant consequences. Some groups now regarded as mainstream—such as Hasidism and Reform Judaism—were once declared heretical by other Judaic groups. They survived and thrived nonetheless.

> For the reasons explained above, we focus here more on the theoretical aspect of heresy and apostasy than on the practical. We review the biblical and historical foundations of apostasy and heresy in Judaism, examine in detail the case of classical Judaism's best known apostate, and briefly describe a case of alleged heresy in contemporary Judaism.

Biblical and historical foundations: The Hebrew Bible appears to have no specialized vocabulary for heresy and apostasy, but its approach to dissent and disloyalty appears to follow the conditional covenant associated with Sinai. Biblical law sets unalterable limits to Israelites who transgress core community values. Those who commit idolatry, blasphemy, sorcery, or Sabbath-violation are liable to death, either though execution (usually stoning) or divine extirpation (*karet*). Ezra 10:7-8 establishes the foundation for excluding from the community those who fail to follow its practices: "Then a proclamation was issued in Judah and Jerusalem that all who had returned from exile should assemble in Jerusalem, and that anyone who did not come in three days would, by decision of the officers and elders, have his property confiscated and himself excluded from the congregation of the returning exiles."

It is no accident that the idea of exclusion from the community as the consequence of dissent emerges so strongly in the Book of Ezra. The Persian period marks the transformation of Israelite religion into Judaism, and its colonial context is central to understanding the basic biblical attitudes towards difference that ground the approaches to apostasy and heresy in Judaism.

The Babylonian Exile, which began with the destruction of the Jerusalem Temple in 587 B.C.E. and forced the upper echelons of Israelite society to migrate from the land of Israel to Babylon, was a period of decisive transition in which the exiles' social organization, type of leadership, and religious practice underwent significant change. Daniel L. Smith suggests that the exile was a traumatic experience—exilic literature is preoccupied with the theme of suffering—and that the Israelites had to resist or face cultural death. They had three options for resistance: military, political, and cultural. Counseled by their prophets, particularly Jeremiah, the exiles chose to resist culturally but forge useful political relations with the ruling powers. They built strong cultural boundaries between themselves and their non-Israelite neighbors and transformed elements of their pre-exilic heritage into symbols of their identity. In this period, the Sabbath, intermarriage, and purity rules loom large. Smith explains this dynamic lucidly with reference to laws of ritual purity:

> It was not the *formulation* of laws of purity that represented the most creative response to Exile by the priestly writer, for . . . many of these laws . . . rest on older traditions. It was rather the *elaboration* of these laws to emphasize the *transfer* of pollution and the association of holiness with *separation*. While the post-exilic community reflected the results of these concerns, the most logical Sitz im Leben for their primary function was the Exile itself. The presence of these ritual

elaborations of the meaning of separation lends . . . weight to our thesis that the Exile represented a threat to the Jewish minority. In sum what we see in the development of purity law is a creative, Priestly mechanism of social survival and maintenance. To dismiss this creativity as "legalism" is to forget, or ignore, the sociopolitical circumstances in which it was formulated. Majority cultures rarely understand, much less appreciate, the actions of minorities to preserve and maintain identity.[6]

The exiles' survival strategy makes resistance to oppression internal rather than external and tries to make the ruling powers work to the advantage of the internal culture. It responds to a circumstance of nearly total political powerlessness. The identification of separation with holiness has self-evident and far-reaching consequences for the conception of difference in ancient Judaism.

In the next chapter in Israel's history, the context shifts. In 538 B.C.E., nearly three-quarters of a century after the exile began, the Persian emperor Cyrus, who had conquered Babylon the year before, issued an edict allowing the Jews to return to their native land to rebuild their destroyed Temple. Under a sequence of leaders—Zerubbabel, Nehemiah, and Ezra—and as clients of the Persian emperor, the Jews returned "home," to a land in which most of them had never lived. They imported the religion of separation and holiness they so brilliantly crafted for an exile of powerlessness.

At "home," however, the ideology of protection and cultural maintenance that was developed to protect them from real aliens was turned on their cousins, so to speak, the descendants of Israelites left behind—people claiming to be Israel but with no experience of exile and deprivation. The returnees have more political power than they did in exile, but, like those left behind ("the people of the Land"), they are still colonized. In effect, there are now two Israels, each claiming to be the real Israel, and each dependent on Persian colonial power to legitimate its status. This establishes the setting for the internal application of a model of otherness developed in exile to defend against absorption by an alien culture. Ezra 4:1-3, whatever the historicity of its specifics, illustrates these dynamics:

> When the enemies of Judah and Benjamin heard that the returned exiles (*bene ha-golah*) were building a temple to the Lord the God of Israel, they approached Zerubbabel and Jeshua and the heads of the families (*roshe ha-avot*) and said to them, "Let us join you in the building, for like you we seek your God, and we have been sacrificing to him ever since the days of Esarhaddon king of Assyria, who brought us here. But Zerubbabel and Jeshua the rest of the heads of families in Israel said to them," The house which we are building for our God is no concern of yours. We alone will build it, as his majesty Cyrus king of Persia commanded us.

The passage demonstrates how the colonial context shapes biblical attitudes towards dissent and difference. The returnees legitimate their claim that they alone will build God's temple not with an appeal to the God of Israel but rather with the imprimatur of the pagan king. Indeed, the passage suggests a direct connection between legitimacy in the Lord's house and the emperor's support. The competition for legitimacy, which can be resolved only by the imperial power, pits sectors of the conquered people against one another. To reiterate: "the enemies of Judah and Benjamin" defined in this passage as those different and excluded are not aliens but people who also claim to be Israel.

In exile, the religion of holiness and separation protected the Jews from becoming culturally similar to those who were different. At home, in the land of Israel, the same religion allowed them to declare themselves different from those who were culturally similar. This model shaped intragroup relations within Jewish society under colonial rule. In the early centuries of Judaism (and Christianity), within a context of political weakness—or perceived weakness—when Jews disagreed with one another religiously, the result tended to be mutual exclusion rather than negotiation. This is the context within which all Judaisms of antiquity developed, and it constitutes the background to the development of heresy and apostasy in Judaism.

This model calls into question the con-

ventional notion that ancient Jewry, including its various subdivisions, constituted a single cultural entity whose members held a reasonably uniform, mutually applied self-understanding that decisively separated them from the definitive others, the non-Jews. This argument holds that ancient Jews shared a common national or religio-ethnic self-definition and that ancient Judaism therefore manifested considerable tolerance of internal dissent. On this view, in ancient Judaism, one was either in or out, and otherness meant—and can only have meant—being outside "the Jewish community," or bereft of "Jewish identity," or excluded from "the Jewish people."[7]

The evidence, however, suggests otherwise. The colonial context, in which political legitimacy—and perhaps cultural legitimacy as well—was in the hands of foreign rather than native powers, generated competition rather than cooperation among Jewish groups. The various divisions, sometimes known as "sects," that flourished beginning with the late Persian period were far more interested in differentiating themselves from one another than in marking their differences from non-Jews. The response of the Dead Sea Scrolls to the "defiled" priests of the Jerusalem Temple and the utterly gratuitous scorn the Gospel of Matthew heaps on its hated "scribes and Pharisees" are but two of the most obvious examples.

The concern to mark dissenting Jews as "other" is also strongly present in early Rabbinic literature, which became the foundation for later Judaism. The earliest writings of Rabbinic Judaism, the Mishnah and its companion commentary, the Tosefta, manifest little tolerance for Judaic alternatives. Even a cursory survey of those documents reveals not a term or two, but a virtual lexicon of titles employed or devised by rabbis to designate those besides themselves, those, that is, whom they could not trust or whose presence they could not abide. A comprehensive register of such terms would include all those named in Mishnah Sanhedrin Chapters 7-9 and 11 who qualify for execution, whether by stoning, burning, beheading, or strangling—a list of at least thirty items. Most of these terms—including murderer, blasphemer, idolater, Sabbath-violator, beguiler, sorcerer, and so forth—derive from Scripture, the Mishnah's foundation. Whether such figures were historically present or not, they constitute a part of the Mishnah's semantic universe and are objects of both reflection and legislation.

A more conservative and pertinent listing includes those with whom rabbis claim to have had social interaction or those whom they exclude from "the World to Come," the one realm rabbis were certain they controlled. The former would include the *am haaretz* and the Samaritan (often designated as *kuti*, to emphasize foreign origin). The latter, first from M. San. 10:1, are the following: the denier of resurrection of the dead, the denier that the Torah is from heaven, the Epicurean, the reader of outside books, the reciter of charms over wounds, and the pronouncer of God's name with the proper letters. A comparable list in T. San. 13:5 is more elaborate. It includes *minim, meshummadim*, informers, Epicureans, deniers of Torah, separators from the community, deniers of resurrection from the dead, and sinners who cause the public to sin.

Scholars have attempted to account for several of these titles by seeking evidence of historical—that is, real flesh-and-blood— groups to which these names should be attached. Any serious advance on that research is unlikely. But the work in structuralism and semiotics has taught us that words are not necessarily representative of things or persons. We thus can understand early rabbinism's lexicon of otherness as both a reaction to external political pressures and as a consequence of internal cultural preoccupations.

If conceiving the other entails a double metonymy, seeing a part of "them" in terms of an essential piece of "ourselves," and if proximity, spatial and cultural, makes differentiation urgent, then perhaps it is legitimate to conceive this list of excluded "others" in terms of a single trait. Since "Torah" was Rabbinic Judaism's dominant cultural symbol, and since it was visualized and acted out as knowledge associated with a text, perhaps

this list can be explained in terms of what we might call "textual proximity," as follows: The *am haaretz* has no text and cannot be trusted. The Samaritan has the wrong text and must be watched. The outsiders write their own texts and have no part in "us." The Epicurean discards the text. The deniers of resurrection and Torah deny the text. Those who utter charms over wounds and those who pronounce the name use the text improperly. The informers expose the text to inappropriate others. The apostates violate the text (T. Hor. 1:5), and some sinners cause other Jews to do so. Finally, the *minim*, who wear phylacteries (M. Meg. 4:8), offer sacrifices (T. Hul. 1:1), and write and read Torah (T. Shab. 13:5, T. San. 8:7), appropriate our text and pretend to be "us." The *minim* appear to be too close for comfort, and it is hardly accidental that for them early rabbinism reserved the following uncharacteristic and bitter fury:

> The sacrifice of a *min* is idolatry. Their bread is the bread of a Samaritan, and their wine is deemed the wine of idolatry, and their produce is deemed wholly untithed, and their books are deemed magical books, and their children are *mamzerim*. People do not sell anything to them or buy anything from them. And they do not take wives from them or give children in marriage to them. And they do not teach their sons a craft. And they do not seek assistance from them, either financial or medical (T. Shehitat Hullin 2:20-22).

In all, it seems that the presence of the *minim* was especially intolerable, both in this world and the next.

A final point about this list of excluded others merits attention. All who are denied a place in the World to Come are Jews. Nothing in the text denies that. However, their status as Jews does not moderate the judgment of their ultimate fate. This raises serious doubt about the pervasiveness and power of "Jewish identity" and "Jewish peoplehood," at least in early Rabbinic writing. The materials considered above, in fact, demonstrate that early rabbis were preoccupied with fixing the boundaries of their own group and that they devoted extensive linguistic energy to a remarkably detailed elaboration of their own periphery. The precision of that elaboration is especially telling when contrasted with the documents' failure to differentiate among gentiles of diverse nationalities. Early rabbinism can tell one Jewish dissenter from another, but gentiles appear more or less indistinguishable. In the semantic universe they created for themselves, early rabbis do not appear as leaders or devotees of "the Jewish people," religiously or ethnically construed, but rather as a wary and watchful group of Jewish textualists, surrounded from within. This is the legacy of otherness inherited by the framers of later Rabbinic writings.

Otherness within—A Rabbinic heretic: We have considered a theory of difference and an analytical model of rabbinism and have explored both against a sample of early Rabbinic literary data. To complete this exercise, it will be helpful to do the same for a specimen of later Rabbinic writing. A useful example is the Talmudic picture of Elisha ben Abuyah, an alleged second century Palestinian rabbi who is characterized in the scholarly literature as the sole Rabbinic heretic. Elisha's pertinence to this inquiry, however, derives not from scholarly interpretation but from native Rabbinic classification. In most Rabbinic texts he is called by the sobriquet *Aher*, "Other." A rabbi labeled by other rabbis as different is particularly appropriate to any study of the problem of otherness in Rabbinic Judaism. The two principal accounts of Elisha occur in the Palestinian Talmud (Y. Hag. 2:1, beginning at 77b) and in the Babylonian Talmud (B. Hag., beginning at 14b). This paper considers only the first of these. It reads as follows:

    A. Four entered a garden.
    B. One looked and died; one looked and was smitten; one looked and cut the shoots; one entered safely and went out safely.
    C. Ben Azzai looked and was smitten.
    D. Concerning him Scripture says, *If you have found honey, eat only your fill [lest you become filled with it, and vomit]* (Prov. 26:16).
    E. Ben Zoma looked and died.
    F. Concerning him Scripture says, *Precious in the eyes of the Lord is death to his saints* (Ps. 116:15).
    G. Aher looked and cut the shoots.
    H. Who is Aher?

    I. Elisha ben Abuyah, who would kill the masters of Torah.
    J. They say, "Every disciple whom he would see praised in Torah, he would kill him.
    K. "And not only that, but he would enter the house of meeting, and he would see young men before the teacher. He would say, 'What are those sitting and doing here? This one's profession [will be] a builder; this one's profession a carpenter; this one's profession a fowler; this one's profession a tailor.'
    L. "And when they would hear [him speak] so, they would depart from him [their teacher] and go to them [the professions]."
    M. Concerning him Scripture says, *Do not let your mouth bring flesh into sin [and do not say before the angel that it is an error; why should God become angry at your voice and ruin your handiwork.]* (Eccl. 5:5).
    N. —for he ruined the handiwork of that very same man [= his own].
    O. Even in the hour of persecution, they [the Romans] would make them [the Jews] carry burdens [on the Sabbath].
    P. And they [the Jews] intended [that] two would carry one burden, on account of [the principle that] two who perform a single labor [on the Sabbath are exempt from a sin-offering].
    Q. He said, "Make them carry them singly."
    R. They [the Romans] went and made them carry them singly.
    S. They [the Jews] intended to deliver them [their burdens] in a *karmalit*, so as not to [violate the Sabbath law and] bring [something] out from the private domain to the public domain.
    T. He said, "Let them carry them straight through [from the private to the public domain]."
    U. They [the Romans] went and made them carry them straight through.
    V. R. Aqiba entered safely and went out safely.
    W. Concerning him Scripture says, *Draw me, let us run after you; [the king has brought me into his chambers.]* (Song 1:4).
    1. R. Meir was sitting expounding in the house of study of Tiberias.
    2. Elisha, his master, passed, riding on a horse on the Sabbath day.
    3. They came and said to him, "Behold, your master is outside."
    4. He stopped his exposition and went out to him.
    5. He said to him, "What were you expounding today?"

6. He said to him, "*And the Lord blessed the end of Job's life more than the beginning* (Job 42:12)."

7. He said to him, "And how did you begin it?"

8. He said to him, "*And the Lord doubled all Job's possessions* (Job 42:10)—for he doubled all his property."

9. He said, "Alas for what is lost and not found.

10. "Aqiba your master would not have expounded so, rather,

11. "*And the Lord blessed . . .* (Job. 42:12)—By the merit of the commandments that were in his hand from his beginning [= that he performed from the beginning of his life]."

12. He said to him, "And what more have you been expounding?"

13. He said to him, "*The end of a thing is better than its beginning* (Eccl. 7:8)."

14. He said to him, "And how did you begin it?"

15. He said to him, "To a man who begat children in his youth, and they died, and in his old age they were replaced [for him], lo, *The end of a thing is better than its beginning* (Eccl. 7:8).

16. "To a man who produced goods in his youth, and lost [them], and in his old age profited, lo, *The end of a thing is better than its beginning* (Eccl. 7:8).

17. "To a man who studied Torah in his youth and forgot it, and in his old age recovered it, lo, *The end of a thing is better than its beginning* (Eccl. 7:8)."

18. He said, "Alas for what is lost and not found.

19. "Aqiba your master would not have expounded so, rather,

20. "*The end of a thing is better than its beginning* (Eccl. 7:8)—when it is good from its beginning.

21. "And to me the [following] incident [occurred]:

22. "Abuyah, my father, was among the notables of Jerusalem.

23. "On the day that came to circumcise me, he invited all the notables of Jerusalem and seated them in one house.

24. "And R. Eliezer and R. Joshua in one house.

25. "And when they had eaten and drunk, they began to clap hands and dance.

26. "Said R. Liezer to R. Joshua, 'Since they are occupied with theirs, let us be occupied with ours.'

27. "And they sat and occupied themselves with the words of Torah,

28. "from the Torah to the Prophets, and

from the Prophets to the Writings.

29. "And fire descended from heaven and surrounded them.

30. "Abuyah said to them, 'My masters, have you come to burn [down] my house upon me?'

31. "They said to him, 'Heaven forfend! Rather, we were sitting and reciting the words of Torah,

32. "from the Torah to the Prophets, and from the Prophets to the Writings,

33. "and the words were as bright as at their delivery from Sinai.'

34. "And the fire lapped them as it lapped them from Sinai."

35. "And the origin of their delivery from Sinai [is that] they were delivered only in fire,

36. "*And the mountain burned with fire to the heart of heaven* (Deut. 4:11).

37. "Abuyah, my father, said to them, 'If such is the power of Torah, if this son survives for me, I [will] dedicate him to Torah.'

38. "Because his intention was not for the sake of heaven, therefore they [the words of Torah] were not established in that man [= me, Elisha]."

39. He said to him, "And what else did you expound?"

40. He said to him, "*Gold and glass cannot be compared to it, nor can it be exchanged for work of fine gold* (Job. 28:17)."

41. He said to him, "And how did you begin it?"

42. He said to him, "The words of Torah are as difficult to acquire as vessels of gold and as easy to lose as vessels of glass.

43. "And just as vessels of gold and vessels of glass, if they are broken, he [their owner] can return and make them vessels as [they were] at the outset, so a disciple who forgot his learning, he can return and study it as at the beginning."

44. He said to him, "Enough, Meir, until here is the Sabbath limit."

45. He said to him, "How do you know?"

46. He said to him, "From the hoofs of my horse, for I have been counting, and he has gone two thousand cubits."

47. He said to him, "And you have all this wisdom, and you do not return?"

48. He said to him, "I cannot."

49. He said to him, "Why?"

50. He said to him, "For once I was passing before the House of the Holy of Holes, riding on my horse, on the Day of atonement that fell on the Sabbath, and I heard a *bat qol* go out from the House

of the Holy of Holies, and it says, 'Return, O children!—except for Elisha ben Abuyah,

51. "'who knew my power and rebelled against me.'"

52. And whence did all this come to him [= How did all this happen to him?]

53. Rather, once he was sitting and studying in Bikat Ginisar, and he saw one man go up to the top of the palm tree and take a dam [from] upon the fledglings, and he [the man] descended from there in peace.

54. The next day he saw another man who went up to the top of the palm tree and take the fledglings and send the mother away, and he came down from there, and a serpent bit him and he died.

55. He said, "It is written, *You shall surely send the dam away and take the fledglings for yourself, so that it may be good for you and lengthen your days* (Deut. 22:7).

56. "Where is the good of this?

57. "Where is the length of days of this?"

58. And he did not know that R. Jacob had expounded before him,

59. . . . . *so that it may be good for you* (Deut. 22:7)—[This refers] to the World to Come, which is wholly good.

60. *. . . and lengthen your days* (Deut. 22:7)—[This refers] to the future [world], which is wholly long.

61. And there are those who say [that it was] because

62. he saw the tongue of R. Judah ha-Nahtom, dripping blood, in the mouth of a dog.

63. He said, "This is Torah, and this is its reward?

64. "This is the tongue that would give forth words of Torah flawlessly.

65. "This is the tongue that was concerned with Torah all its days.

66. "This is Torah, and this is its reward?

67. "It seems that there is no reward and no resurrection of the dead."

68. And there are those who say [that]

69. his mother, when she was pregnant with him, was passing by temples of idolatry and smelled [the smell of their] kind [of incense], and the odor penetrated her body like the venom of a snake."

70. After several days, Elisha became ill.

71. They came and said to R. Meir, "Behold, your master is ill."

72. He went, wanting to visit him, and found him ill.

73. He said to him, "Do you not repent?"

74. He said to him, "And if they repent, are they received?"

75. He said to him, "Is it not written, *You*

return man to dust (Ps. 90:3)?—Until the soul is crushed, they accept [repentance]."

76. In that very hour Elisha wept, and departed [from the world], and died.

77. And R. Meir was happy in his heart.

78. And he said, "It seems that in the midst of repentance my master died."

79. After they buried him, fire descended from heaven and burned his grave.

80. They came and said to R. Meir, "Behold, the grave of your master is on fire."

81. He went out, wanting to visit it, and found it on fire.

82. What did he do?

83. He took up his prayer cloak and spread it upon it.

84. He said, "*Sleep through the night, and in the morning, if he redeems you, well, let him redeem you; and if he does not want to redeem you, I swear by the Lord, I will redeem you* (Ruth 3:13)—

85. "*Sleep* (Ruth 3:13)—in this world, for it resembles night.

86. "*in the morning* (Ruth 3:13)—This is the World to Come, which is wholly morning.

87. "*If he redeems you, well, let him redeem you* (Ruth 3:13)—This is the Holy One, Blessed be He, for he is good,

88. "for it is written of him, *The Lord is good to all, and his mercies are over all his works* (Ps. 145:9).

89. "And *if he does not want to redeem you, I swear by the Lord, I will redeem you* (Ruth 3:13)."

90. And it [the fire] was extinguished.

91. They said to R. Meir, "If they say to you in that world, whom do you want to bring near, your father or your master, [what will you do]?

92. He said to them, "I [will] bring my master first and my father afterwards."

93. They said to him, "And will they listen to you?"

94. He said to them, "And have we not learned thus:

95. "They save the book chest with the book, the phylactery bag with the phylacteries?

96. "They save Elisha, Aher, by the merit of his Torah."

97. After [several] days, his [Elisha's] daughters went to collect charity from Rabbi [Judah the Patriarch].

98. Rabbi decreed [no], and he said, "*Let there be no one to extend him kindness, and let no one be generous to his orphaned offspring* (Ps. 109:12)?"

99. They said to him, Rabbi, do not look at his deeds, look at his Torah."

100. At that very hour Rabbi wept and de-
     creed that they be supported.
101. He said, "If this is what one who la-
     bors at Torah not for its own sake pro-
     duces—one who labors at Torah for its
     own sake—how much the moreso!"

The text is long, interesting, and quite rich,
and a comprehensive textual, literary, and
historical analysis is impossible here. The
following remarks concentrate on those elements that address the question of theories
of the other in Rabbinic Judaism. For that
purpose, we need to explore the text with four
questions in mind: What, from the point of
view of the text, made Elisha into an outsider,
an "other," an *aher*? How does the text account for him? What are the consequences
of his "otherness"? Finally and most important, why is the story told at all?

At the outset, one brief literary observation is apposite. The passage easily can be
divided into two large segments, differentiated by letters and numbers. There is good
reason to suppose that the segment I-U,
which is interpolated into the well known
passage of T. Hag. 2:3-4, was composed
independently of the lengthy narrative of
1-101. Although perhaps not a pristine unity,
that narrative clearly has received considerable editorial attention. But since the long
narrative of 1-101 assumes that Elisha is
known to the reader, since I-U constitutes an
explicit introduction of him, and since the
two segments are presented in direct sequence, it is plausible to suppose that some
redactor expected them to be read together,
as a piece. Let us now turn to the text.

At I-J, Elisha is baldly cast as a murderer,
a killer of masters and disciples of Torah.
At K-L, he dissuades young men from the
study of Torah and urges them into practical
professions. M appears to take this as an act
of leading others into sin, and N assures the
reader that Elisha was the principal victim
of his own behavior. Since the Palestinian
Talmud understands the rabbi as "Torah incarnate," in I-N, Elisha is also the destroyer
of the text, the wrecker of Torah's present
and its future. Then at O-U, Elisha is depicted
as an informer, who exposes the details of
Torah to the Romans and thus forces the
Jews into serious acts of Sabbath violation.

The long narrative that attempts to account for Elisha's treachery and to describe
his fate is introduced at lines 1-4 with the
curious image of Meir's interrupting his Sabbath sermon to accompany his teacher Elisha
and engage in exegetical discussion. Elisha
passes the house of study riding a horse, an
act that, if not strictly prohibited in all Palestinian Rabbinic circles, surely is starkly unconventional for anyone trained in Torah.
The exchanges between them at lines 5-21
accomplish two purposes. First, they set the
stage for Elisha's autobiographical account
of his circumcision (lines 21-38) by having
Elisha insist that a good end depends on a
good beginning. Of equal significance, they
begin to establish Elisha's own expertise
in Torah, for at lines 10 and 19 he chides
Meir for forgetting or not knowing what
his teacher, Aqiba, taught. Since in Rabbinic
imagination Aqiba is a much admired figure,
the association of him with Elisha is hardly
trivial.

At lines 21-38, Elisha recounts the story
of the day of his circumcision and his father's
disingenuous dedication of him to Torah.
Interestingly, Eliezer and Joshua, the two
rabbis, are seated separately from the other
notables, and at line 26 they engage one
another and their text while the rest of the
company rejoices at the circumcision. The
distinction between the Rabbinic "us" and
the laymen's "them" is explicit at line 26, and
is underscored by Abuyah's incomprehension
of the heavenly sign of delight in the rabbis'
Torah, at line 30. For our purposes, however,
the important point comes at line 38, which
blames Abuyah's impure motives for the failure of Torah to take root in his son.

Lines 39-43 contain another exegetical exchange, but now the focus has shifted from
the question about the beginning of life to a
concern about its end, and at line 43 Meir
raises the theme of return to, and recovery
of, Torah.

The brief exchange at lines 44-46 exhibits a stunning reversal. While urging his
teacher to return to and reacquire Torah, Meir
forgets it himself and must be prevented by
Elisha from violating the Sabbath limit.

Meir's question at line 45, "How do you know?," is thus at least as defensive as it is curious. Elisha's answer betrays irony because his horse, the very instrument of his unRabbinic behavior, is the means he uses to defend the sanctity of the Sabbath day.

Meir's question at line 47 could not be more fitting: "And you have all this wisdom, and you do not return?" Elisha's answer is straightforward. Because he knew God's power and rebelled against him—in Rabbinic terms, because he knew Torah and deliberately violated it—even the possibility of his repentance is definitively foreclosed by Heaven.

Line 52 introduces the Talmud's attempt to understand Elisha's alienation from Heaven, and lines 53-69 offer three explanations. At lines 53-60, Elisha witnesses an unmistakable and concrete disconfirmation of a scriptural promise. Lines 61-67 present a comparable circumstance, and Elisha implicitly denies the power of Torah and explicitly denies the resurrection of the dead. Both segments offer cases in which experience contradicts Torah and leads Elisha to think his way out of the text and to renounce its efficacy. By contrast, lines 68-69 depict his alienation from Torah as the result of his mother's accidental encounter with idolatry.

At lines 70-89, we turn to the consequences of Elisha's behavior. He becomes ill, and Meir arrives to urge his repentance and to affirm its attainability (lines 73-75). Whether or not Elisha actually repents at line 76 is unclear, but Meir takes his tears as evidence of a decisive change of heart (lines 77-78). It makes no difference in any case, because Heaven's negative judgment, which we saw at line 51, is confirmed when fire descends to consume Elisha's grave (line 79). The scene at lines 79-90 must constitute one of the most poignant passages in Rabbinic literature. In a gesture of unremitting loyalty to his teacher and a clear demonstration of ancient rabbis' conception of their own power, Meir contravenes Heaven's verdict. Through an exegesis of Ruth 3:13, which he allows to speak for him without elaboration at line 89, he vows that if God refuses to do so he himself will redeem Elisha in the World to Come. At line 90, the heavenly sentence is lifted.

Lines 91-101 explain both the reason for Meir's action and for Heaven's decision. In answer to a question about whom he would save first in the World to Come, Meir replies, in standard Rabbinic fashion, that his teacher would precede his natural father. His questioners are incredulous, and he answers them with a citation of M. Shab. 16:1. Elisha is likened to a container of Torah books or of phylacteries. Since on the Sabbath they are saved from fire because of their contents, so Elisha is brought into the World to Come on account of his. The same rationale is repeated in the exchange between Judah the Patriarch and Elisha's daughters, lines 97-101. Despite his willful misdeeds, Elisha is saved, not on account of repentance, but because of the Torah that is in him.

We saw earlier that the framers of the Palestinian Talmud inherited from the Mishnah and Tosefta an elaborate set of categories for marking otherness. In this narrative, Elisha falls into at least three, and probably four, of them. He is an informer, a sinner who causes others to sin, a denier of resurrection from the dead, and probably a denier of Torah. Any one of these should prohibit him from a place in World to Come; any one would represent a definitive sign of otherness. But, while Elisha richly earns the label "other," the framers of the text refuse to apply it to him. He is an "other," but the Talmud will not let him occupy that status. The problem now is to understand how and why the text accomplishes this remarkable result.

First, it offers no consistent picture of Elisha. He is both a committer of heinous crimes and a master of Torah. He interrupts a Sabbath sermon, yet teaches Torah to his student. He violates Torah, yet ends in the World to Come. In all, he hangs in the interstices of rabbinism, sometimes in and sometimes out. In some cultural settings such liminality might make Elisha a witch or a trickster. But in the context of the Rabbinic community, this figuration serves to reveal more than one side of him and to enhance his subjectivity.

This fuller vision is especially evident in

the text's incapacity to provide a uniform explanation of Elisha's deviance. Two of the accounts place the responsibility squarely on Elisha. His experience belies the Torah, and he reasons his way to a rejection of the text. But the two other accounts present him as a victim. His mother, quite by accident, affects him in the womb. His father, through improper designs, guarantees before the fact that Elisha will follow another path. So Elisha is both accountable and not, deserving of rejection and not.

Second, the text highlights Elisha's subjectivity by presenting his circumstance not only from the textual point of view, but also from his own. The unusual autobiographical story of the day of his circumcision and his telling of the *bat qol* that denies him the possibility of repentance both depict him as he sees himself. These accounts, along with his repeated exchanges with Meir, make him an interesting, somewhat complex, and even sympathetic character.

But, in the nature of things, the Rabbinic community would prefer not to manipulate its categories or undercut its texts. So the reasons for doing so in this case must be pressing indeed. However closely bound rabbis were to one another and to their Torah, Rabbinic Judaism was not a tribe. Ethnicity could not serve to define it or defend it. Ancient rabbis conceived Torah to be a material object and a body of teaching that stands at the center of Judaism and delimits its periphery. To remain authoritative, Torah must be a source of continual study, reflection and intellectual engagement. If one can enter the community through Torah, however, one can depart from it in the same way. The walls of the Rabbinic community are, in principle, scalable and vulnerable. But if one can depart from Torah, and Torah, once acquired, can depart from him, then Torah's ultimacy, primacy, and constitutive character are corrupted and diminished. It is one thing to declare as "other" someone who is outside the Torah to begin with. It is quite something else to declare that one who had the Torah from the beginning can be on the outside. To do so makes Torah a victim of subjectivity, reduces its stature, and destroys it as the com-

munity's center. This can explain why Talmudic narrators are prepared to relativize Elisha, to humanize him, but ultimately revert to the model of Torah as objectified knowledge. In Meir's response to his questioners, he likens Elisha to a chest of books or a bag of phylacteries, hardly a personal image. Likewise, Elisha's daughters urge Rabbi to forget their father's deeds, to ignore the behaviors that made him distinctive, and to remember instead his Torah, knowledge that is hardly peculiar to him.

Thus, Elisha ben Abuyah, whose deeds make him an outsider, is preserved by Talmudic narrators as an insider because the consequences of letting him out are too severe. And because they keep him inside, they can use him as a vehicle to test the boundaries of their textual community and to sort out the internal ambiguities of their own culture. Whatever the historical reality of this figure, this Talmudic account of Elisha ben Abuyah answers the question, "What would happen if. . . .?" It is an experiment of intellect and emotion that explores a most dangerous, destructive circumstance and renders it nugatory. A necessary cultural exercise, it allows the Rabbinic community, from inside the safety of Torah, to experience the most threatening kind of "otherness," the "otherness" represented by heresy and apostasy, the "otherness" within.

A contemporary case: The theory and dynamics of heresy and apostasy in Judaism are evident in a contemporary case involving Lubavitch Hasidism. After the death of the Lubavitcher Rebbe, some of his followers began to assert that he is the messiah. In the fall of 1996, the Israeli weekly *Sihat HaGeullah* revised the standard messianist slogan to read: "May our Master, Teacher, and Creator (instead of "Rabbi"), the King Messiah live forever." A number of other Lubavitch publications suggested that the Rebbe should be the focus of prayers.

To these developments, David Berger, professor of history at Brooklyn College, an ordained rabbi and president of the Association of Jewish Studies in the United States, responded with the charge of heresy. His remarks are worth citing at some length:

... despite the dominant efforts of a handful of brave Hassidim, the dominant institutions of the Lubavitch movement are either overtly Messianist or unwilling to declare unequivocally that the Rebbe is not the Messiah. A formal legal ruling (*psak din*) has just been issued by the head of the Crown Heights Rabbbinical Court, the Rabbi of Kfar Chabad [the Lubavitch center in Israel], the Lubavitch Vice-Chair of Agudat Ha-Rabbanim, and other major leaders of the movement, asserting that Jewish law requires belief in the Messiahship of the Rebbe.... In my view, this declaration alone is sufficient to exclude its promulgators from Orthodox Judaism....

It is evident ... that this belief, that the Rebbe is literally God and that he should be the object of prayer, has entered mainstream Lubavitch. In the terminology of Jewish law, this is idolatry. One who teaches this theology and urges that it be ritually expressed is an inciter to idolatry.... One who supports an institution in which this is taught violates a prohibition so severe that there is a requirement to die rather than to transgress. If a believer in this theology slaughtered an animal ritually, it has the status of a non-kosher carcass, which can undermine the kashrut of a restaurant or a home. A divorce document signed by such a believer or a Torah scroll written by him are invalid. A Jew who converts to this sort of Judaism remains, nonetheless, a non-Jew.[8]

In reply, Rabbi Gedalyahu Axelrod, who heads a rabbinical court in Haifa, wrote, in part, as follows:

There is no halakhic dispensation that will enable anyone to evade accepting the yoke of the Rebbe's Messiahship, because of Maimonides' ruling that obligates all Jews to do so.

Maimonides, in his Hilchot Yesodai HaTorah [Laws of the Foundation of the Torah], Chapter 10, determines the criteria for a great and wise prophet: that he has "broad knowledge," "is in full control of himself," "predicts the future," and, most important, that he declares that the Lord sent him to be a prophet. The Lubavitcher Rebbe, in session with thousands of his followers, dropped a spiritual and historic bombshell by declaring himself the prophet of the generation....

I would like to address the claim of idolatry—Heaven forbid!—raised in this article. I can only marvel at the way people are willing to destroy a movement known all over the world for its staunch devotion to the observance of commandments and to bringing Jews closer to Judaism.... I believe that David Berger must beg the forgiveness of the tens of thousands of followers of Lubavitch who proudly carry high the torch of Judaism and are not deterred by those who would destroy it from the day of its foundation.[9]

This exchange illustrates the double distortion that is basic to the construction of difference. Each side in the dispute sees the other in terms of a single trait—which, of course, fully represents neither. For Berger, the core issue is idolatry. He charges that those Lubavitch hassidim who regard the late Rebbe as "our Creator" and pray to him have crossed out of the realm of Judaic belief into "not-Judaism." They have violated a fundamental principal of Judaism, and for ritual purposes at least, they are gentiles. His insistent and severe tone evokes that of the Tosefta's comments on the *minim*, cited above. For Axelrod, the core issue is halakhic practice. He defends Lubavitch Hasidism against the charge of idolatry with an appeal to Lubavitch's well-known piety and evangelism for Judaism. And he casts Berger as an enemy of piety. On each side, the tendency in the exchange is to delegitimate and exclude.

Conclusion: The two examples reviewed above illustrate the theoretical and practical aspects, as well as the local nature, of heresy and apostasy in Judaism. They also show how difficult it is to identify a single ritual act or theological position that can mark an individual or group as heretical, let alone to have lost its status as part of the people Israel.

The case of Lubavitch Hasidism is current and practical. David Berger draws a firm theological line to place out of Judaism's bounds those who view the late Lubavitcher Rebbe as the messiah. He also points to the practical implications of his view. Heresy has consequences, even on the status of one's kitchen. But Berger's position—however carefully reasoned and supported by traditional sources—remains his. Indeed, outside of Professor Berger's declaration, the Lubavitchers' messianic claim, while widely reported and discussed in the Jewish community, did not generate Jewish public discourse about "correct" or "authentic" Jewish beliefs.

Moreover, neither Professor Berger nor his Lubavitcher opposition has the capacity to transform its opinion into Jewish community policy. Those whose kitchen tables Professor Berger regards as religiously unfit will still judge themselves supremely kosher.

In this instance, even a central theological disagreement on the coming of the messiah or the proper object of prayer did not—as a matter of practice—demarcate authentic from inauthentic Judaism.

The case of Elisha ben Abuyah appears far more theoretical than practical. In it, heresy and apostasy clearly are categories to think with, means by which Rabbinic authorities explore areas of risk and potential rupture in-ternal to their own tradition. Whatever the historical reality of Elisha ben Abuyah, the Talmudic account about him answers the question, "What would happen if. . . .?" Elisha's story is an experiment of intellect and emotion that explores a most dangerous, destructive circumstance and renders it nugatory. It is a necessary cultural exercise for it allows the Rabbinic community, from inside the safety of Torah, to experience the most threatening kind of "otherness," the "otherness" represented by heresy and apostasy, the "otherness" within.

Because of Judaism's perpetual political dependence, major theological differences about religious belief and practice coexisted historically and coexist today without generating a permanent rupture within the Jewish community. In the end, heresy and apostasy are floating targets in Judaism. The categories are less about true and authentic faith in objective terms than about finding and affirming oneself by identifying and marking the other.

Notes

1 Daniel Sperber, "Min," in *Encyclopedia Judaica* (Jerusalem, 1971), vol. 6, cols. 2-3.
2 Daniel Jeremy Silver, "Heresy," in ibid., vol. 8, cols. 358-362.
3 Jacob Katz, *Exclusiveness and Tolerance* (New York, 1962), p. 73. David ben Solomon Ibn Avi, *Teshuvot ha-Radbaz*, vol. 3, chapter 476.
4 Gerald Blidstein, "Who Is Not a Jew?—The Medieval Discussion," in *Israel Law Review* 11 (1976), pp. 377.
5 Ibid., p. 389.
6 Daniel L. Smith, *The Religion of the Landless* (Bloomington, 1989), p. 149.
7 E.E. Urbach, "Self-Isolation or Self-Affirmation in Judaism in the First Three Centuries: Theory and Practice," in E.P. Sanders, ed., *Jewish and Christian Self-Definition, Volume Two: Aspects of Judaism in the Greco-Roman Period* (Philadelphia, 1981), p. 292. L.H. Schiffman, "At the Crossroads: Tannaitic Perspectives on the Jewish-Christian Schism," in ibid., pp. 115-116.
8 "On False Messianism, Idolatry, and Lubavitch," in *Ha'aretz*, English Edition, January 11, 1998.
9 "The Prophet of God," in *Ha'aretz*, English Edition, January 15, 1998.

WILLIAM S. GREEN

HISTORY, THE CONCEPTION OF IN CLASSICAL JUDAISM: Rabbinic Judaism reached its full statement in the first six centuries of the Common Era, an age in which the people, Israel, confronted enormous historical crises. The first took place in 70 C.E., when the Temple was destroyed by the Romans, and the political foundations of Israel's life changed. The second was marked by the defeat of Bar Kokhba, who led a war aimed at regaining Jerusalem and rebuilding the Temple, in 132-135 C.E. As a result the established paradigm, destruction, repentance, restoration, that Scripture set forth, lost purchase. The third crisis confronted Israel in the fourth century, when Christianity, reading the same Scriptures and speaking in many of the same categories, became the official religion of the Roman Empire and claimed that its political triumph validated its reading of Scripture and invalidated that of Judaism. These cataclysmic events required sages to explain history and define the future for which Israel could and should wait in patience and hope.

By "history" is meant how happenings identified as consequential, that is to say, as events, are so organized and narrated as to teach lessons, reveal patterns, tell what people must do and why, predict what will happen tomorrow. The Pentateuchal and Prophetic writings of Scripture lay heavy stress on history in the sense just now given. By contrast, the framers of the Mishnah present a kind of historical thinking quite different from the one they, along with all Israel, had inherited in Scripture. The legacy of prophecy, apocalypse, and mythic-history handed on by the writers of the books of the Old Testament exhibits a single and quite familiar conception of history seen whole. Events bear meaning, God's message and judgment. What happens is singular, therefore, an event to be noted, and points toward lessons to be drawn for where things are heading and why.

If things do not happen at random, they also do not form indifferent patterns of merely secular, social facts. What happens is important because of the meaning contained therein. That meaning is to be discovered and revealed through the narrative of what has happened. So for all forms of Judaism until the Mishnah, the writing of history serves as a form of prophecy. Just as prophecy takes up the interpretation of historical events, so historians retell these events in the frame of prophetic theses. And out of the two—historiography as a mode of mythic reflection, prophecy as a means of mythic construction—emerges a picture of future history, that is, what is going to happen. That picture, framed in terms of visions and supernatural symbols, in the end focuses, as much as do prophecy and history-writing, upon the here and now.

History in the Mishnah: The Mishnah, by its own word, finds nothing to say about time and change, history and the teleology of history defined by eschatology, with its implication of movement from here to there; for the Mishnah, all things were to be formed into a hierarchical classification, for, in the fantasy of the Mishnah's framers, nothing much happened; the issue of intellect was ordering the chaotic, not confronting the permanence of change such as the concept of history entailed.

The Mishnah contains no sustained narrative whatsoever, a very few tales, and no large-scale conception of history. It organizes its system in non-historical and socially unspecific terms, lacking all precedent in prior systems of Judaism or in prior kinds of Judaic literature. Instead of narrative, it gives description of how things are done, that is, descriptive laws. Instead of reflection on the meaning and end of history, it constructs a world in which history plays little part. Instead of narratives full of didactic meaning, it provides lists of events so as to expose the traits that they share and thus the rules to which they conform. The definitive components of a historical-eschatological system of Judaism—description of events as one time happenings, analysis of the meaning and end of events, and interpretation of the end and future of singular events—none of these commonplace constituents of all other systems of Judaism (including nascent Christianity) of ancient times finds a place in the Mishnah's system of Judaism.

Disorderly historical events entered the system of the Mishnah and found their place within the larger framework of the Mishnah's orderly world. So to claim that the Mishnah's framers merely ignored what was happening would be incorrect. They worked out their own way of dealing with historical events, the disruptive power of which they not only conceded but freely recognized. Further, the Mishnah's authors to begin with did not intend to compose a history book or a work of prophecy or apocalypse. Even if they had wanted to narrate the course of events, they could hardly have done so through the medium of the Mishnah. Yet the Mishnah presents its philosophy in full awareness of the issues of historical calamity confronting the Jewish nation. So far as the philosophy of the document confronts the totality of Israel's existence, the Mishnah by definition also presents a philosophy of history.

But the Mishnah finds no precedent in prior Israelite writings for its mode of dealing with things that happen. The Mishnah's way of identifying happenings as consequential and describing them, its way of analyzing those events it chooses as bearing meaning, its interpretation of the future to which significant events point—all those in context were unique. Yet to say that the Mishnah's system is ahistorical could not be more wrong. The Mishnah presents a different kind of history. More to the point, it revises the inherited conception of history and reshapes that conception to fit into its own system. When we consider the power of the biblical myth, the force of its eschatological and messianic interpretation of history, the effect of apocalypse, we must find astonishing the capacity of the Mishnah's framers to think in a different way about the same things. As teleology constructed outside the eschatological mode of thought in the setting of the biblical world of ancient Israel, the Mishnah's formulation proves amazing, since Scripture framed teleology in historical terms, therefore invoked the conception of eschatology as the medium for thought about the goal and purpose of matters. By contrast the sages in the Mishnah set forth a teleology entirely outside of the framework of historical-eschatological thinking.

The framers of the Mishnah explicitly refer to very few events, treating those they do mention within a focus quite separate from what happened—the unfolding of the events themselves. They rarely create or use narratives. More probative still, historical events do not supply organizing categories or taxonomic classifications. We find no tractate devoted to the destruction of the Temple, no complete chapter detailing the events of Bar Kokhba, nor even a sustained celebration of the events of the sages' own historical life. When things that have happened are mentioned, it is neither in order to narrate nor to interpret and draw lessons from the event. It is either to illustrate a point of law or to pose a problem of the law—always *en passant*, never in a pointed way.

So when sages refer to what has happened, this is casual and tangential to the main thrust of discourse. Famous events of enduring meaning, such as the return to Zion from Babylonia in the sixth century and onward to the time of Ezra and Nehemiah, gain entry into the Mishnah's discourse only because of the genealogical divisions of Israelite society into castes among the immigrants (M. Qid. 4:1). Where the Mishnah provides little tales or narratives, moreover, they more often treat how things in the cult are done in general than what, in particular, happened on some one day. It is sufficient to refer casually to well-known incidents. Narrative, in the Mishnah's limited rhetorical repertoire, is reserved for the narrow framework of what priests and others do on recurrent occasions

and around the Temple. In all, that staple of history, stories about dramatic events and important deeds, in the minds of the Mishnah's jurisprudents, provide little nourishment. Events, if they appear at all, are treated as trivial. They may be well-known but are consequential in some way other than would be revealed in a detailed account of what actually happened.

Sages' treatment of events determines what in the Mishnah is important about what happens. Since the greatest event in the century-and-a-half, from ca. 50 C.E. to ca. 200, in which the Mishnah's materials came into being, was the destruction of the Temple in 70 C.E., we must expect the Mishnah's treatment of that incident to illustrate the document's larger theory of history: what is important and unimportant about what happens. The treatment of the destruction occurs in two ways. First, the destruction of the Temple constitutes a noteworthy fact in the history of the law. Why? Because various laws about rite and cult had to undergo revision on account of the destruction. The following provides a stunningly apt example of how the Mishnah's philosophers regard what actually happened as being simply changes in the law (M. R.H. 4:1-4):

4:1.A. On the festival day of the New Year that coincided with the Sabbath—
B. in the Temple they would sound the *shofar*.
C. But not in the provinces.
D. When the Temple was destroyed, Rabban Yohanan ben Zakkai made the rule that they should sound the *shofar* in every locale in which there was a court.
E. Said R. Eleazar, "Rabban Yohanan b. Zakkai made that rule in the case of Yavneh alone."
F. They said to him, "All the same are Yavneh and every locale in which there is a court."
4:2.A. And in this regard also was Jerusalem ahead of Yavneh:
B. in every town that is within sight and sound [of Jerusalem], and nearby and able to come to Jerusalem, they sound the *shofar*.
C. But as to Yavneh, they sound the *shofar* only in the court alone.
4:3.A. In olden times the *lulab* was taken up

in the Temple for seven days, and in the provinces for one day.

B. When the Temple was destroyed, Rabban Yohanan ben Zakkai made the rule that in the provinces the *lulab* should be taken up for seven days, as a memorial to the Temple;

C. and that the day [the sixteenth of Nisan] on which the *omer* [sheaf of first barley, the waving of which permits the utilization of crops of the new growing season, from the fifteenth of Nisan] is waved should be wholly prohibited [in regard to the eating of new produce] (M. Suk. 3:12).

4:4.A. At first [in order to determine whether the month of Tishre had begun, such that it was the festival day of the New Year] they would receive testimony about the new moon all day long.

B. One time the witnesses came late, and the Levites consequently were mixed up as to [what] song [they should sing, whether the one appropriate to the New Year festival or for a regular weekday].

C. They made the rule that they should receive testimony [about the new moon] only up to the afternoon offering.

D. Then, if witnesses came after the afternoon-offering, they would treat that entire day as holy, and the next day as holy too.

E. When the Temple was destroyed [so that the Levites no longer sang in any event], Rabban Yohanan b. Zakkai made the rule that they should [once more] receive testimony about the new moon all day long.

F. Said R. Joshua b. Qorha, "This rule too did Rabban Yohanan B. Zakkai make:

G. "Even if the head of the court is located somewhere else, the witnesses should come only to the location of the council [to give testimony, and not to the location of the head of the court]."

The passages before us leave no doubt about what sages selected as important about the destruction: it produced changes in festival rites.

Second, although the sages surely mourned for the destruction and the loss of Israel's principal mode of worship, and certainly recorded the event of the ninth of Ab in the year 70 C.E., they did so in their characteristic way: they listed the event as an item in a catalogue of things that are like one another and so demand the same response. But then the destruction no longer appears as a unique event. It is absorbed into a pattern of like disasters, all exhibiting similar taxonomic traits, events to which the people, now well-schooled in tragedy, knows full well the appropriate response. So in demonstrating regularity sages reveal their way of coping. Then the uniqueness of the event fades away, its mundane character is emphasized. The power of classification in imposing order upon chaos once more does its healing work. The consequence was reassurance that historical events obeyed discoverable laws. Israel's ongoing life would override disruptive, onetime happenings. So catalogues of events, as much as lists of species of melons, served as brilliant apologetic by providing reassurance that nothing lies beyond the range and power of an ordering system and stabilizing pattern. This is clear at M. Ta. 4:6-7:

4:6.A. Five events took place for our fathers on the seventeenth of Tammuz, and five on the ninth of Ab.

B. On the seventeenth of Tammuz (1) the tablets [of the Torah] were broken, (2) the daily whole offering was canceled, (3) the city wall [of Jerusalem] was breached, (4) Apostemos burned the Torah, and (5) he set up an idol in the Temple.

C. On the ninth of Ab (1) the decree was made against our forefathers that they should not enter the land, (2) the first Temple and (3) the second [Temple] were destroyed, (4) Betar was taken, and (5) the city was plowed up [after the war of Hadrian].

D. When Ab comes, rejoicing diminishes.

4:7.A. In the week in which the ninth of Ab occurs it is prohibited to get a haircut and to wash one's clothes.

B. But on Thursday of that week these are permitted,

C. because of the honor due the Sabbath [which follows, beginning on Friday evening].

D. On the eve of the ninth of Ab a person should not eat two prepared dishes, nor should one eat meat or drink wine.

E. Rabban Simeon b. Gamaliel says, "He should make some change from ordinary procedures."

F. R. Judah declares people obligated to turn over beds.
G. But sages did not concur with him.

M. Ta. 4:7 shows the context in which the list of M. Ta. 4:6 stands. The stunning calamities catalogued at M. Ta. 4:6 form groups, reveal common traits, so are subject to classification. Then the laws of M. Ta. 4:7 provide regular rules for responding to, coping with, these untimely catastrophes, all in a single classification. So the raw materials of history are absorbed into the ahistorical, supernatural system of the Mishnah. The process of absorption and regularization of the unique and onetime moment is illustrated in the passage at hand.

The Mishnah absorbs into its encompassing system all events, small and large. With what happens the sages accomplish what they do with everything else: a vast labor of classification, an immense construction of the order and rules governing the classification of everything on earth and in Heaven. The disruptive character of history—onetime events of ineluctable significance—scarcely impresses the philosophers. They find no difficulty in showing that what appears unique and beyond classification has in fact happened before and so falls within the range of trustworthy rules and known procedures. Once history's components, onetime events, lose their distinctiveness, then history as a didactic intellectual construct, as a source of lessons and rules, also loses all pertinence. So lessons and rules come from sorting things out and classifying them, that is, from the procedures and modes of thought of the philosopher seeking regularity. To this labor of classification, the historian's way of selecting data and arranging them into patterns of meaning to teach lessons, proves inconsequential. Onetime events are not what matters. The world is composed of nature and supernature. The repetitious laws that count are those to be discovered in Heaven and, in Heaven's creation and counterpart, on earth. Keep those laws and things will work out. Break them, and the result is predictable: calamity of whatever sort will supervene in accordance with the rules. But just because it is predictable, a catastrophic happening testifies to what has always been and must always be, in accordance with reliable rules and within categories already discovered and well explained.

The framers of the Mishnah recognized the past-ness of the past and hence, by definition, laid out a conception of the past that constitutes a historical doctrine. But it is a different conception from the familiar one. For modern history-writing, what is important is to describe what is unique and individual, not what is ongoing and unremarkable. History is the story of change, development, movement, not of what does not change, develop, or move. For the thinkers of the Mishnah, historical patterning emerges as today scientific knowledge does, through classification, the classification of the unique and individual, the organization of change and movement within unchanging categories. That is why the dichotomy between history and eternity, change and permanence, signals an unnuanced exegesis of what was, in fact, a subtle and reflective doctrine of history. That doctrine proves entirely consistent with the large perspectives of scribes, from the ones who made omen-series in ancient Babylonia to the ones who made the Mishnah. That is why the category of salvation does not serve, but the one of sanctification fits admirably.

History as an account of a meaningful pattern of events, making sense of the past and giving guidance about the future, begins with the necessary conviction that events matter, one after another. The Mishnah's framers, however, present us with no elaborate theory of events, a fact fully consonant with their systematic points of insistence and encompassing concern. Events do not matter, one by one. The philosopher-lawyers exhibited no theory of history either. Their conception of Israel's destiny in no way called upon historical categories of either narrative or didactic explanation to describe and account for the future. The small importance attributed to the figure of the Messiah as an historical-eschatological figure, therefore, fully accords with the larger traits of the system as a whole. If what is important in Israel's existence is sanctification, an ongoing process, and not salvation, understood as a onetime event at the end, then no one will find reason to narrate history.

But even on the foundation of the Mishnah, Judaism was to emerge from late antiquity richly eschatological, obsessed with the Messiah and his coming, engaged by the history of Israel and the nations. Judaism at the end did indeed provide an ample account and explanation of Israel's history and destiny. The explanation emerged as the generative problematic of Judaism; the theory of "Israel" set forth here framed the social reality confronted by Jews wherever they lived. So, to seek the map that shows the road from the Mishnah, at the beginning, to the fully articulated Judaism of the end of the formative age in late antiquity, we have to look beyond the Mishnah, first to the Talmud of the Land of Israel.

The conception of history in the Talmud of the Land of Israel: The Mishnah's subordination of historical events contradicts the emphasis of a thousand years of Israelite thought. The biblical histories, the ancient prophets, the apocalyptic visionaries—all had testified that what happened mattered. Events carried the message of the living God. That is, events constituted history, pointed toward, and so explained, Israel's destiny. An essentially ahistorical system of timeless sanctification, worked out through construction of an eternal rhythm centered on the movement of the moon and stars and seasons, represented a choice taken by few outside of the priesthood. Furthermore, the pretense that what happens matters less than what is testified against palpable and remembered reality. For Israel had suffered enormous loss of life. The Talmud of the Land of Israel takes these events seriously and treats them as unique and remarkable. The memories proved real. The hopes evoked by the Mishnah's promise of sanctification of the world in static perfection did not. We should not be surprised to observe that the Talmud of the Land of Israel contains evidence pointing toward substantial steps taken in rabbinical circles away from the position of the Mishnah. We find materials that fall entirely outside the framework of historical doctrine established within the Mishnah. These are,

first, an interest in the periodization of history, and second, a willingness to include events of far greater diversity than those in the Mishnah. So the Yerushalmi contains an expanded view of the range of human life encompassed to begin with by the conception of history.

Let us take the second point first. So far as things happen that demand attention and so constitute "events," within the Mishnah these fall into two classifications: (1) biblical history, and (2) events involving the Temple. In the Talmud at hand, by contrast, in addition to Temple-events, we find also two other sorts of *Geschichten*: Torah-events, that is, important stories about the legal and supernatural doings of rabbis, and also political events. These events, moreover, involved people not considered in the Mishnah: gentiles as much as Jews, Rome as much as Israel. The Mishnah's history, such as it is, knows only Israel. The Talmud greatly expands the range of historical interest when it develops a theory of Rome's relationship to Israel and, of necessity also, Israel's relationship to Rome. Only by taking account of the world at large can the Talmud's theory of history yield a philosophy of history worthy of the name, that is, an account of who Israel is, the meaning of what happens to Israel, and the destiny of Israel in this world and at the end of time. Israel by itself—as the priests had claimed—lived in eternity, beyond time. Israel and Rome together struggled in historical time: an age with a beginning, a middle, and an end. That is the importance of the expanded range of historical topics found in the present Talmud. When, in the other Talmud, created in Babylonia, we find a still broader interest, in Iran (Persia in the biblical and Rabbinic writings) as much as Rome, in the sequence of world empires past and present, we see how rich and encompassing a theory of historical events begins with a simple step toward a universal perspective. It was a step that the scribes and priests represented by the Mishnah were incapable of taking.

As to the second, the concept of periodization—the raw material of historical thought—hardly presents surprises, since apocalyptic writers began their work by differentiating one age from another. When the Mishnah includes a statement of the "periods" into which time is divided, however, it speaks only of stages of the cult: Shiloh, Nob, Jerusalem. One age is differentiated from the next not by reference to world-historical changes but only by the location of sacrifice and the eating of the victim. The rules governing each locale impose tax upon otherwise undifferentiated time. So periodization constitutes a function of the larger system of sanctification through sacrifice. The contrast between "this world" and "the world to come," which is not a narrowly historical conception in the Mishnah, now finds a counterpart in the Talmud's contrast between "this age" and the age in which the Temple stood. And that distinction is very much an act of this-worldly historical differentiation. It not only yields apocalyptic speculation. It also generates sober and worldly reflection on the movement of events and the meaning of history in the prophetic-apocalyptic tradition. Accordingly, the Talmud of the Land of Israel presents both the expected amplification of the established concepts familiar from the Mishnah, and also a separate set of ideas, perhaps rooted in prior times but still autonomous of what the Mishnah in particular had encompassed.

From the viewpoint of the Mishnah the single most unlikely development is interest in the history of a nation other than Israel. For the Mishnah views the world beyond the sacred Land as unclean, tainted in particular with corpse-uncleanness. Outside the holy lies the realm of death. The faces of that world are painted in the monotonous white of the grave. Only within the range of the sacred do things happen. There, events may be classified and arranged, all in relationship to the Temple and its cult. But, standing majestically unchanged by the vicissitudes of time, the cult rises above history. Now the ancient Israelite interest in the history of the great empires of the world—perceived, to be sure, in relationship to the history of Israel— reemerges within the framework of the documents that succeeded the Mishnah. Naturally, in the Land of Israel only one empire

mattered. This is Rome, which, in the Yerushalmi, is viewed solely as the counterpart to Israel. The world then consists of two nations: Israel, the weaker, Rome, the stronger. Jews enjoy a sense of vastly enhanced importance when they contemplate such a world, containing as it does only two peoples that matter, of whom one is Israel. But from our perspective, the utility for the morale of the defeated people holds no interest. What strikes us is the evidence of the formation of a second and separate system of historical interpretation, beyond that of the Mishnah.

History and doctrine merge, with history made to yield doctrine. What is stunning is the perception of Rome as an autonomous actor, that is, as an entity with a point of origin, just as Israel has a point of origin, and a tradition of wisdom, just as Israel has such a tradition. These are the two points at which the large-scale conception of historical Israel finds a counterpart in the present literary composition. This sense of poised opposites, Israel and Rome, comes to expression in two ways. The first is that it is Israel's own history that calls into being its counterpoint, the anti-history of Rome. Without Israel, there would be no Rome—a wonderful consolation to the defeated nation. For if Israel's sin created Rome's power, then Israel's repentance will bring Rome's downfall. Here is the way in which the Talmud presents the match (Y. A.Z. 1:2):

> IV.E. Saturnalia means "hidden hatred" [sina'ah temunah]: The Lord hates, takes vengeance, and punishes
>
> F. This is in accord with the following verse: "Now Esau hated Jacob" (Gen. 27:41).
>
> G. Said R. Isaac b. R. Eleazar, "In Rome they call it Esau's Saturnalia."
>
> H. Kratesis: It is the day on which the Romans seized power.
>
> K. Said R. Levi, "It is the day on which Solomon intermarried with the family of Pharaoh Neco, King of Egypt. On that day Michael came down and thrust a reed into the sea, and pulled up muddy alluvium, and this was turned into a huge pot, and this was the great city of Rome. On the day on which Jeroboam set up the two golden calves, Remus and Romulus came and built two huts in the city

of Rome. On the day on which Elijah disappeared, a king was appointed in Rome: 'There was no king in Edom, a deputy was king' (1 Kgs. 22:47)."

The important point is that Solomon's sin provoked Heaven's founding of Rome, thus history, lived by Israel, and anti-history, lived by Rome. Quite naturally, the conception of history and anti-history will assign to the actors in the anti-history—the Romans—motives explicable in terms of history, that is, the history of Israel. The entire world and what happens in it enter into the framework of meaning established by Israel's Torah. So what the Romans do, their historical actions, can be explained in terms of Israel's conception of the world.

The most important change is the shift in historical thinking adumbrated in the pages of the Yerushalmi, a shift from focus upon the Temple and its supernatural history to close attention to the people, Israel, and its natural, this-worldly history. Once Israel, holy Israel, had come to form the counterpart to the Temple and its supernatural life, that other history—Israel's—would stand at the center of things. Accordingly, a new sort of memorable event came to the fore in the Talmud of the Land of Israel. It was the story of the suffering of Israel, the remembrance of that suffering, on the one side, and the effort to explain events of that tragic kind, on the other. So a composite "history" constructed out of the Yerushalmi's units of discourse pertinent to consequential events would contain long chapters on what happened to Israel, the Jewish people, and not only, or mainly, what had earlier occurred in the Temple.

This expansion in the range of historical interest and theme forms the counterpart to the emphasis, throughout the law, upon the enduring sanctity of Israel, the people, which paralleled the sanctity of the Temple in its time. What is striking in the Yerushalmi's materials on Israel's suffering is the sages' interest in finding a motive for what the Romans had done. That motive derived specifically from the repertoire of explanations already available in Israelite thought. In adducing scriptural reasons for the Roman

policy, sages extended to the world at large that same principle of intelligibility, in terms of Israel's own Scripture and logic that, in the law itself, made everything sensible and reliable. So the labor of history-writing (or at least, telling stories about historical events) went together with the work of lawmaking. The whole formed a single exercise in explanation of things that had happened—that is, historical explanation. True, one enterprise involved historical events, the other legal constructions. But the outcome was one and the same.

Clearly, for the authorship of the Talmud of the Land of Israel, as much as for the ancient prophets, history taught lessons, and in their view, Israel had best learn the lesson of its history. When it did so, it also would take command of its own destiny. So the stakes were very high. What lesson, precisely, did the sages represented by the document at hand propose Israel should learn? Stated first negatively, then positively, the framers of the Talmud of the Land of Israel were not telling the Jews to please God by doing commandments in order that they should thereby gain control of their own destiny. On the contrary, the paradox of the Yerushalmi's system lies in the fact that Israel frees itself from control by other nations only by humbly agreeing to accept God's rule instead.

The heavy weight of prophecy, apocalyptic, and biblical historiography, with their emphasis upon history as the indicator of Israel's salvation, stood against the Mishnah's quite separate thesis of what truly mattered. What, from their viewpoint, demanded description and analysis and required interpretation? It was the category of sanctification, for eternity. The true issue framed by history and apocalypse was how to move toward the foreordained end of salvation, how to act in time so as to reach salvation at the end of time. The Mishnah's teleology beyond time, its capacity to posit an eschatology lacking all place for a historical Messiah—these take a position beyond the imagination of the entire antecedent sacred literature of Israel. Only one strand or stream, the priestly one, had ever taken so extreme a position on the centrality of sanctification, the peripherality of salvation. Wisdom had stood in between, with its own concerns, drawing attention both to what happened and to what endured. But to wisdom what finally mattered was not nature or supernature, but rather abiding relationships in historical time.

This reversion by the authors of the Talmud to Scripture's paramount motifs, with Israel's history and destiny foremost among them, forms a complement to the Yerushalmi's principal judgment upon the Mishnah itself. For an important exegetical initiative of the Yerushalmi was to provide, for statements of the Mishnah, proof texts deriving from Scripture. Whereas the framers of the Mishnah did not think their statements required support, the authors of the Talmud's units of Mishnah-exegesis took proof texts drawn from Scripture to be the prime necessity. Accordingly, at hand is yet another testimony to the effort, among third-and-fourth-century heirs of the Mishnah, to draw that document back within the orbit of Scripture, to "biblicize" what the Mishnah's authors had sent forth as a freestanding and "non-biblical" Torah.

The centerpiece of the rehistoricization of Judaism accomplished by the framers of the Talmud of the Land of Israel and related writings is the reversion to Scripture. The Scriptures that, after all, also lay to hand offered testimony to the centrality of history as a sequence of meaningful events. To the message and uses of history as a source of teleology for an Israelite system, biblical writings amply testified. Prophecy and apocalyptic had long coped quite well with defeat and dislocation. Yet, in the Mishnah, Israel's deeds found no counterpart in Roman history, while, in the Talmud of the Land of Israel, they did. In the Mishnah, time is differentiated entirely in other than national-historical categories. For, as in Abot, "this world" is when one is alive, "the world to come" is when a person dies. True, we find also "this world" and "the time of the Messiah."

But detailed differentiation among the ages of "this world" or "this age" hardly generates problems in Mishnaic thought. Indeed, no such differentiation appears. Accordingly, the developments briefly outlined here constitute

a significant shift in the course of intellectual events, to which the sources at hand—the Mishnah and Talmud of the Land of Israel—amply testify. In ca. 200 C.E. events posed a problem of classification and generalization. In ca. 400 C.E., events were singular and demanded interpretation because, in all their particularity, they bore messages just as, in prophetic thought, they had. In the reconsideration of the singularity of events and the systematic effort at interpreting them and the lessons to be drawn from them, the sages of the Talmud of the Land of Israel regained for their theological thought the powerful resources of history, the single most powerful arena for, and principal medium of, Judaic theology then as now. The ethos of Rabbinic Judaism comes to full expression not in the mere concession that history matters, but in specific lessons that are spelled out. Scripture forms a handbook for making sense of this morning's headlines. Genesis Rabbah explains that handbook.

Genesis Rabbah and Israel's history: In looking to the past to explain the present, the Judaic sages turned to the story of the beginnings of creation, humanity, and Israel, that is, to the book of Genesis. This was on the supposition that if we can discern beginnings, we can understand the end. The Israelite sages took up the beginnings that marked the original pattern for ongoing history. Sages could not imagine, after all, that what had happened in their own day marked the goal and climax of historical time. Rome formed an episode, not the end. But then, sages had to state what they thought constituted the real history of the world and of Israel.

Accordingly, sages read Genesis as the history of the world with emphasis on Israel. So the lives portrayed, the domestic quarrels and petty conflicts with the neighbors, all serve to yield insight into what was to be. Why so? Because the deeds of the patriarchs taught lessons on how the children were to act, and, it further followed, the lives of the patriarchs signaled the history of Israel. Israel constituted one extended family, and the metaphor of the family, serving the nation as it did, imparted to the stories of Genesis the character of a family record. History become genealogy conveyed the message of salvation. These propositions really laid down the same judgment, one for the individual and the family, the other for the community and the nation, since there was no differentiating. Every detail of the narrative therefore served to prefigure what was to be, and Israel found itself, time and again, in the revealed facts of the history of the creation of the world, the decline of humanity down to the time of Noah, and, finally, its ascent to Abraham, Isaac, and Israel.

What are the laws of history, and, more important, how do they apply to the crisis at hand? The principal message of the story of the beginnings, as sages read Genesis, is that the world depends upon the *zekhut*—merit—of Abraham, Isaac, and Jacob; Israel, for its part, enjoys access to that *zekhut*, being today the family of the patriarchs and matriarchs. That conception of matters constitutes the sages' doctrine of history: the family forms the basic and irreducible historical unit. Israel is not so much a nation as a family, and the heritage of the patriarchs and matriarchs sustains that family from the beginning even to the end. So the sages' doctrine of history transforms history into genealogy. The consequence, for sages, will take the form of the symbolization through family relationships of the conflict between (Christian) Rome and eternal Israel. The rivalry of brothers, Esau and Jacob, then contains the history of the fourth century—from sages' viewpoint a perfectly logical mode of historical reflection. That, in detail, expresses the main point of the system of historical thought yielded by Genesis Rabbah.

Genesis now is read as both a literal statement and also as an effort to prefigure the history of Israel's suffering and redemption. Ishmael, standing now for Christian Rome, claims God's blessing, but Isaac gets it, as Jacob will take it from Esau. Details, as much as the main point, yielded laws of history. In the following passage, the sages take up the detail of Rebecca's provision of a little water, showing what that act had to do with the history of Israel later on. The passage at hand is somewhat protracted, but it contains in a whole and cogent way the mode of

thought and the results: salvation is going to derive from the *zekhut* of the matriarchs and patriarchs.

2.A. "Let a little water be brought" (Gen. 18:4):

B. Said to him the Holy One, blessed be he, "You have said, 'Let a little water be brought' (Gen. 18:4). By your life, I shall pay your descendants back for this: 'Then sang Israel this song," spring up O well, sing you to it'" (Num. 21:7)."

C. That recompense took place in the wilderness. Where do we find that it took place in the Land of Israel as well?

D. "A land of brooks of water" (Deut. 8:7).

E. And where do we find that it will take place in the age to come?

F. "And it shall come to pass in that day that living waters shall go out of Jerusalem" (Zech. 14:8).

G. ["And wash your feet" (Gen. 18:4)]: [Said to him the Holy One, blessed be he,] "You have said, 'And wash your feet.' By your life, I shall pay your descendants back for this: 'Then I washed you in water' (Ez. 16:9)."

H. That recompense took place in the wilderness. Where do we find that it took place in the Land of Israel as well?

I. "Wash you, make you clean" (Is. 1:16).

J. And where do we find that it will take place in the age to come?

K. "When the Lord will have washed away the filth of the daughters of Zion" (Is. 4:4).

L. [Said to him the Holy One, blessed be he,] "You have said, 'And rest yourselves under the tree' (Gen. 18:4). By your life, I shall pay your descendants back for this: 'He spread a cloud for a screen' (Ps. 105:39)."

M. That recompense took place in the wilderness. Where do we find that it took place in the Land of Israel as well?

N. "You shall dwell in booths for seven days" (Lev. 23:42).

O. And where do we find that it will take place in the age to come?

P. "And there shall be a pavilion for a shadow in the daytime from the heat" (Is. 4:6).

Q. [Said to him the Holy One, blessed be he,] "You have said, 'While I fetch a morsel of bread that you may refresh yourself' (Gen. 18:5). By your life, I shall pay your descendants back for this: 'Behold I will cause to rain bread from heaven for you' (Ex. 16:45)"

R. That recompense took place in the wilderness. Where do we find that it took place in the Land of Israel as well?

S. "A land of wheat and barley" (Deut. 8:8).

T. And where do we find that it will take place in the age to come?

U. "He will be as a rich grain field in the land" (Ps. 82:6).

V. [Said to him the Holy One, blessed be he,] "You ran after the herd ['And Abraham ran to the herd' (Gen. 18:7)]. By your life, I shall pay your descendants back for this: 'And there went forth a wind from the Lord and brought across quails from the sea' (Num. 11:27)."

W. That recompense took place in the wilderness. Where do we find that it took place in the Land of Israel as well?

X. "Now the children of Reuben and the children of Gad had a very great multitude of cattle" (Num. 32:1).

Y. And where do we find that it will take place in the age to come?

Z. "And it will come to pass in that day that a man shall rear a young cow and two sheep" (Is. 7:21).

AA. [Said to him the Holy One, blessed be he,] "You stood by them: 'And he stood by them under the tree while they ate' (Gen. 18:8). By your life, I shall pay your descendants back for this: 'And the Lord went before them' (Ex. 13:21)."

BB. That recompense took place in the wilderness. Where do we find that it took place in the Land of Israel as well?

CC. "God stands in the congregation of God" (Ps. 82:1).

DD. And where do we find that it will take place in the age to come?

EE. "The breaker is gone up before them . . . and the Lord at the head of them" (Mic. 2:13).

Gen. Rab. XLVIII:X.

This sizable and beautifully disciplined construction makes one point again and again. Everything that the matriarchs and patriarchs did brought a reward to their descendants. The enormous emphasis on the way in which Abraham's deeds prefigured the history of Israel, both in the wilderness, and in the Land, and, finally, in the age to come, provokes us to wonder who held that there were children of Abraham beside Israel. The answer then is clear. We note that there are five statements of the same proposition, each drawing upon a clause in the base verse. The extended statement moreover serves as a sustained introduction to the treatment of the individual clauses that now follow, item by item. When we recall how Christian exegetes imparted to the Old Testament the lessons of the New, we realize that sages constructed an equally epochal and encompassing reading of Scripture. They now understood the meaning of what happened then, and, therefore, they also grasped from what had happened then the sense and direction of events of their own day. So history yielded patterns, and patterns proved points, and the points at hand indicated the direction of Israel. The substance of historical doctrine remains social in its focus. Sages present their theory of the meaning of history within a larger theory of the identification of Israel. Specifically, they see Israel as an extended family, children of one original ancestral couple, Abraham and Sarah. Whatever happens, then, constitutes family history, which is why the inheritance of *zekhut* from the ancestors protects their children even now, in the fourth century. In this typological reading Israel's history takes place under the aspect of eternity. Events do not take place one time only. Events, to make a difference and so to matter, constitute paradigms and generate patterns. Salvation is all the same; its particularization is all that history records. The lessons of history therefore do not derive from sequences of unique moments but from patterns that generate recurring and reliable rules. Accordingly, sages read the present in light of the past, rather than following the way of reading the past in light of the present. Given their present, they had little choice.

Sages found a place for Rome in Israel's history only by assigning to Rome a place in the family. Their larger theory of the social identity of Israel left them no choice. But it also permitted them to assign to Rome an appropriately significant place in world history, while preserving for Israel the climactic role. Whatever future history finds adumbration in the life of Jacob derives from the struggle with Esau. Israel and Rome—these two contend for the world. Still, Isaac plays his part in the matter. Rome does have a legitimate claim, and that claim demands recognition, an amazing, if grudging, concession on the part of sages that Christian Rome at least is Esau.

> 1.A. "When Esau heard the words of his father, he cried out with an exceedingly great and bitter cry [and said to his father, 'Bless me, even me also, O my father!']" (Gen. 27:34):
> B. Said R. Hanina, "Whoever says that the Holy One, blessed be he, is lax, may his intestines become lax. While he is patient, he does collect what is coming to him.
> C. "Jacob made Esau cry out one cry, and where was he penalized? It was in the castle of Shushan: 'And he cried with a loud and bitter cry' (Est. 4:1)."
> 2.A. "But he said, 'Your brother came with guile and he has taken away your blessing'" (Gen. 33:35):
> B. R. Yohanan said, "[He came] with the wisdom of his knowledge of the Torah."
> Gen. Rab. LXVII:IV

So Rome really is Israel's brother. No pagan empire ever enjoyed an equivalent place; no pagan era ever found identification with an event in Israel's family history. The passage presents a stunning concession and an astounding claim. The history of the two brothers forms a set of counterpoints, the rise of one standing for the decline of the other. There can be no more powerful claim for Israel: the ultimate end, Israel's final glory, will permanently mark the subjugation of Esau. Israel then will follow, the fifth and final monarchy. The point of No. 1 is to link the present passage to the history of Israel's redemption later on. In this case, however, the matter concerns Israel's paying recompense for causing anguish to Esau. No. 2 introduces Jacob's knowledge of Torah in place of Esau's view of Jacob as full of guile.

From Scripture's historical thinking to Judaism's paradigmatic structure: All scholarship on the Hebrew Scriptures concurs that ancient Israel set forth its theology through the media of historical narrative and thought. The Hebrew Scriptures set forth Israel's life as history, with a beginning, middle, and end; a purpose and a coherence; a teleological system. All accounts agree that Scriptures distinguished past from present, present from future and composed a sustained narrative, made up of one-time, irreversible events. In Scripture's historical portrait, Israel's present condition appealed for explanation to Israel's past, perceived as a coherent sequence of weighty events, each unique, all formed into a great chain of meaning. But that is not how for most of the history of Western civilization the Hebrew Scriptures have been read by Judaism and Christianity. The idea of history, with its rigid distinction between past and present and its careful sifting of connections from the one to the other, came quite late onto the scene of intellectual life. Both Judaism and Christianity for most of their histories have read the Hebrew Scriptures in an other-than-historical framework. They found in Scripture's words paradigms of an enduring present, by which all things must take their measure; they possessed no conception whatsoever of the pastness of the past.

Rabbinic Judaism formulated out of Scripture not only rules validated by appeal to arguments resting on facts recorded therein, such as Leviticus Rabbah yields. Rabbinic Judaism, like nascent Christianity, also invented an entirely new way to think about times past and to keep all time, past, present, and future, within a single framework. For that purpose, a model was constructed, consisting of selected events held to form a pattern that imposes order and meaning on the chaos of what happens, whether past or present or future. Time measured in the paradigmatic manner is time formulated by a free-standing, (incidentally) atemporal model, not appealing to the course of sun and moon, not concerned with the metaphor of human life and its cyclicality either. Not only so, but the paradigm obliterates distinctions between past, present, and future, between here and now and then and there. The past participates in the present, the present recapitulates the past, and the future finds itself determined, predetermined really, within the same free-standing structure comprised by God's way of telling time.

Theological paradigms of time are set forth by neither nature (by definition) nor natural history (what happens on its own here on earth); by neither the cosmos (sun and moon) nor the natural history of humanity (the life cycle and analogies drawn therefrom). In the setting of Judaism and Christianity, paradigms are set forth in revelation; they explain the Creator's sense of order and regularity, which is neither imposed upon, nor derived from, nature's time, not to be discovered through history's time. And that is why to paradigmatic time, history is wildly incongruous, and considerations of linearity, temporality, and historical order beyond all comprehension. God has set forth the paradigms that measure time by indicators of an other-than-natural character: supernatural time, which of course is beyond all conception of time.

Accordingly, a paradigm forms a way of keeping time that invokes its own differentiating indicators, its own counterparts to the indicators of nature's time. Nature defines time as that span that is marked off by one spell of night and day; or by one sequence of positions and phases of the moon; or by one cycle of the sun around the earth (in the pre-Copernican paradigm). History further defines nature's time by marking off a solar year by reference to an important human event, e.g., a reign, a battle, a building. So history's time intersects with, and is superimposed upon, nature's time. Cyclical time forms a modification of history's time, appealing for its divisions of the aggregates of time to the analogy, in human life, to nature's time: the natural sequence of events in a human life viewed as counterpart to the natural sequence of events in solar and lunar time.

So much for a theological formulation of matters. What, in this-worldly language, is to be said about the same conception? Paradigmatic thinking constitutes a mode of argument about the meaning of events, about the formation of the social order. Appealing to the pattern, parties to a debate, for instance about the meaning of an event or the interpretation of a social fact, frame their arguments within the limits of the pattern: that event corresponds to this component of the paradigm shared among all parties to debate. Paradigms derive from human invention and human imagination, imposed on nature and on history alike. Nature is absorbed, history recast, through time paradigmatic; that is, time invented, not time discovered; time defined for a purpose determined by humanity (the social order, the faithful, for instance), time that is not natural or formed in correspondence to nature, or imposed upon nature at specified intersections; but time that is defined completely in terms of the prior pattern or the determined paradigm or fabricated model itself: time wholly invented for the purposes of the social order that invents and recognizes time.

Let me make these abstractions concrete, since time paradigmatic refers to perfectly familiar ways of thinking about the passage of time, besides the natural and historical ways of thinking. Once we define time paradigmatic as time invented by humanity for humanity's own purposes, time framed by a system set forth to make sense of a social order, for example, the examples multiply. The common use of B.C. and A.D. forms one obvious paradigm: all time is divided into two parts by reference to the advent of Jesus Christ. Another paradigm is marked by the history of humanity set forth in Scripture: Eden, then after Eden; or Adam vs. Israel, Eden vs. the Land; Adam's fall vs. Israel's loss of the Land. The sages will impose a further, critical variable on the pattern of Eden vs. Land of Israel, Adam vs. Israel, and that is, Sinai. A pattern then will recognize the divisions of time between before Sinai and afterward.

These general definitions should be made still more concrete in the setting of Rabbinic Judaism. Let me give a single example of time paradigmatic, in contrast to the conceptions of time that govern in the Hebrew Scriptures. The character of paradigmatic time is captured in the following, which encompasses the entirety of Israel's being (its "history" in conventional language) within the conversation that is portrayed between Boaz and Ruth; I abbreviate the passage to highlight only the critical components (Ruth Rab., Parashah 5):

XL:i.1.A. "And at mealtime Boaz said to her, 'Come here and eat some bread, and dip your morsel in the wine.' So she sat beside the reapers, and he passed to her parched grain; and she ate until she was satisfied, and she had some left over" (Ruth 2:14):

B. R. Yohanan interpreted the phrase "come here" in six ways:

C. "The first speaks of David.

D. "'Come here': means, to the throne: 'That you have brought me here' (2 Sam. 7:18).

E. "'. . . and eat some bread': the bread of the throne.

F. "'. . . and dip your morsel in vinegar': this speaks of his sufferings: 'O Lord, do not rebuke me in your anger' (Ps. 6:2).

G. "'So she sat beside the reapers': for the throne was taken from him for a time."

I. [Resuming from G:] "'and he passed to her parched grain': he was restored to the throne: 'Now I know that the Lord saves his anointed' (Ps. 20:7).

J. "'. . . and she ate and was satisfied and left some over': this indicates that he would eat in this world, in the days of the messiah, and in the age to come.

2.A. "The second interpretation refers to Solomon: 'Come here': means, to the throne.

B. "'. . . and eat some bread': this is the bread of the throne: "And Solomon's provision for one day was thirty measures of fine flour and three score measures of meal' (1 Kgs. 5:2).

C. "'. . . and dip your morsel in vinegar': this refers to [his] dirty deeds.

D. "'So she sat beside the reapers': for the throne was taken from him for a time."

G. [Reverting to D:] "'and he passed to her parched grain': for he was restored to the throne.

H. "'. . . and she ate and was satisfied and left some over': this indicates that he would eat in this world, in the days of the messiah, and in the age to come.

3.A. "The third interpretation speaks of Hezekiah: 'Come here': means, to the throne.

B. "'. . . and eat some bread': this is the bread of the throne.

C. "'. . . and dip your morsel in vinegar': this refers to sufferings [Is. 5:1]: 'And Isaiah said, Let them take a cake of figs' (Is. 38:21).

D. "'So she sat beside the reapers': for the throne was taken from him for a time: 'Thus says Hezekiah, This day is a day of trouble and rebuke' (Is. 37:3).

E. "'. . . and he passed to her parched grain': for he was restored to the throne: 'So that he was exalted in the sight of all nations from then on' (2 Chr. 32:23).

F. "'. . . and she ate and was satisfied and left some over': this indicates that he would eat in this world, in the days of the messiah, and in the age to come.

4.A. "The fourth interpretation refers to Manasseh: 'Come here': means, to the throne.

B. "'. . . and eat some bread': this is the bread of the throne.

C. "'. . . and dip your morsel in vinegar': for his dirty deeds were like vinegar, on account of wicked actions.

D. "'So she sat beside the reapers': for the throne was taken from him for a time: 'And the Lord spoke to Manasseh and to his people, but they did not listen. So the Lord brought them the captains of the host of the king of Assyria, who took Manasseh with hooks' (2 Chr. 33:10-11)." . . .

K. [Reverting to D:] "'and he passed to her parched grain': for he was restored to the throne: 'And brought him back to Jerusalem to his kingdom' (2 Chr. 33:13).

N. "'. . . and she ate and was satisfied and left some over': this indicates that he would eat in this world, in the days of the messiah, and in the age to come.

5.A. "The fifth interpretation refers to the Messiah: 'Come here': means, to the throne.

B. "'. . . and eat some bread': this is the bread of the throne.

C. "'. . . and dip your morsel in vinegar': this refers to suffering: 'But he was wounded because of our transgressions' (Is. 53:5).

D. "'So she sat beside the reapers': for the throne is destined to be taken from him for a time: For I will gather all nations against Jerusalem to battle and the city shall be taken' (Zech. 14:2).

E. "'. . . and he passed to her parched grain': for he will be restored to the throne: 'And he shall smite the land with the rod of his mouth' (Is. 11:4)."

I. [Reverting to G:] "so the last redeemer will be revealed to them and then hidden from them."

The paradigm here emerges in these units: David's monarchy; Solomon's reign; Hezekiah's reign; Manasseh's reign; the Messiah's reign. So paradigmatic time compresses events to the dimensions of its model. All things happen on a single plane of time. Past, present, future are undifferentiated, and that is why a single action contains within itself an entire account of Israel's social order under the aspect of eternity.

The foundations of the paradigm, of course, rest on the fact that David, Solomon, Hezekiah, Manasseh, and therefore also, the Messiah, all descend from Ruth's and Boaz's union. Then, within the framework of the paradigm, what is described at Ruth 2:14 forms not an event but a pattern. The pattern transcends time; or more accurately, aggregates of time, the passage of time, the course of events—these are all simply irrelevant to what is in play in Scripture. Rather we have a tableau, joining persons who lived at widely separated moments, linking them all as presences at this simple exchange between Boaz and Ruth; imputing to them all, whenever they came into existence, the shape and structure of that simple moment: the presence of the past, for David, Solomon, Hezekiah, and so on, but the pastness of the present in which David or Solomon—or the Messiah for that matter—lived or would live (it hardly matters, verb tenses prove hopelessly irrelevant to paradigmatic thinking).

Taking account of both the simple example of B.C. and A.D. and the complex one involving the Israelite monarchy and the Messiah, we ask ourselves how time has been framed within the paradigmatic mode of thought. The negative is now clear. Paradigmatic time has no relationship whatsoever to nature's time. It is time invented, not discovered; time predetermined in accord with a model or pattern, not time negotiated in the interplay between time as defined by nature and time as differentiated by human cognizance and recognition.

Here the points of differentiation scarcely intersect with either nature's or history's time; time is not sequential, whether in natural or historical terms; it is not made up of unique events, whether in nature or in the social order; it is not differentiated by indicators of a commonplace character. Divisions between past, present, and future lie beyond all comprehension. Natural time is simply ignored here; years do not count, months do not register; the passage of time marked by the sun, correlated with, or ignored by, the course of human events, plays no role at all. All flows from that model—in the present instance, the model of time divided into chapters of Davidic dynastic rulers, time before the Messiah but tightly bound to the person of the Messiah; the division of time here then can take the form of before Boaz's gesture of offering food to Ruth and afterward; before David and after the Messiah; and the like. A variety of interpretations of the passage may yield a range of paradigms; but the model of paradigmatic time will remain one and the same. Not much imagination is required for the invention of symbols to correspond to B.C. and A.D. as a medium for expressing paradigmatic time.

The case now permits us further to generalize. The paradigm takes its measures quite atemporally, in terms of not historical movements or recurrent cycles but rather a temporal units of experience, those same aggregates of time, such as nature makes available through the movement of the sun and moon and the passing of the seasons, on the one hand, and through the life of the human being, on the other. A model or pattern or paradigm will set forth an account of the life of the social entity (village, kingdom, people, territory) in terms of differentiated events—wars, reigns, for one example, building a given building and destroying it, for another—yet entirely out of phase with sequences of time.

A paradigm imposed upon time does not call upon the day or month or year to accomplish its task. It will simply set aside nature's time altogether, regarding years and months as bearing a significance other than the temporal one (sequence, span of time, aggregates of time) that history, inclusive of cyclical time's history, posits. Time paradigmatic then views humanity's time as formed into aggregates out of all phase with nature's time, measured in aggregates not coherent with those of the solar year and the lunar month. The aggregates of humanity's time are dictated by humanity's life, as much as the aggregates of nature's time are defined by the course of nature. Nature's time serves not to correlate with humanity's patterns (no longer, humanity's time), but rather to mark off units of time to be correlated with the paradigm's aggregates.

It remains to reconsider those systematic comparisons between history's time and other modes of keeping time that have already served us well. Since the comparison of historical and cyclical time is now in hand, let us turn directly to ask how we shall read the paradigmatic, as distinct from the cyclical mode of formulating a human counterpart to nature's time? Here are the point by point correspondences:

[1] in time paradigmatic, human events do not form givens, any more than natural events form givens, in the measurement of time; while both of those definitions of the eventful correspond in character to the course of nature, paradigmatic events find their definition in the paradigm, within the logic of the system, in accord with the predetermined pattern, and not in response to the givens of the natural world, whether in the heavens or in the life cycle; paradigmatic time also follows a fixed and predictable pattern, but its identification of what is eventful out of what happens in the world at large derives from its own logic and its own perception; nothing is dictated by nature, not nature's time, not history's time, not the linear progress of historical events, not the cyclical progress of historical patterns;

[2] the matter is scarcely adumbrated in the case before us—nature's time plays no independent rule in paradigmatic time; cut down to human size by cyclical time in nature's way, nature's time in paradigmatic thinking is simply absorbed into the system and treated as neutral—nature's time is marked, celebrated, sanctified, but removed from the entire range of history, which is wholly taken over and defined by the paradigm.

[3] consequently, nature's time plays no role in paradigmatic time; time is neither cyclical nor linear, it is not marked off by unique events, it is simply neutral and inert. Time is inconsequential; the issue is not whether or not time is reversible in direction from past to future, or whether or not time is to be differentiated (for the same reason) into past, present, and future.

Nature's time, with its sense of forward movement (within the natural analogy supplied by the human life, from birth to death) is simply beyond the paradigmatic limits, for the paradigm admits of neither past nor present nor future, differentiated but also linked; nor cycle and recurrence. These conceptions contradict its very character. A paradigm predetermines, selects happenings in accord with a pattern possessed of its own logic and meaning, unresponsive to the illogic of happenings, whether chaotic, whether orderly, from the human perspective. A model is just that: there to dictate, there to organize, there to take over, make selections, recognize connections, draw conclusions. To characterize paradigmatic time as atemporal therefore proves accurate but tangential, since atemporality is not a definitive taxic trait, merely a byproduct of that trait. Indeed, the very phrase, "paradigmatic time," standing by itself presents an oxymoron. Paradigms admit to time—the spell that intervenes between this and that, the this and the that beyond defined within the paradigm. In that sense, time pertains, as much as the spell between sunset and sunset or new moon and new moon pertains in nature's time.

But in situating the events in the scale of human time, as history would have matters, to the model of Ruth and Boaz, David, Solomon, and the Messiah, captured in the little gesture described at Ruth 2:14, the matter of time simply does not pertain. For the action was not one-time (even for all-time) nor cyclical, but altogether out of history's and nature's time. Time is contingent, within the model. The paradigm serves to select events; model to endow events with order and meaning, structure and familiarity. Rich in time-sequences, the scene is a tableau, full of action but lacking temporality.

Paradigmatic time organizes events in patterns, invokes a model that everywhere pertains; the atemporality then is a byproduct of the very character of thinking about time and change that governs. Time and change mark chaos; order is not discovered within time and change.

Clearly, in paradigmatic existence, time is not differentiated by merely noteworthy events, whether natural or social. Time is differentiated in another way altogether, and that way so recasts what happens on earth as to formulate a view of existence to which any notion of events strung together into sequential history or of time as distinguished by one event rather than some other is not so much irrelevant as beyond all comprehension. To characterize Rabbinic Judaism as atemporal or ahistorical is both accurate and irrelevant. That Judaism sets forth a different conception of existence, besides the historical one that depends upon nature's and humanity's conventions on the definition and division of time.

Existence takes on sense and meaning not by reason of sequence and order, as history maintains in its response to nature's time. Rather, existence takes shape and acquires structure in accord with a paradigm that is independent of nature and the givens of the social order: God's structure, God's paradigm, our sages of blessed memory would call it; but in secular terms, a model or a pattern that in no way responds to the givens of nature or the social order. It is a conception of time that is undifferentiated by events, because time is comprised of components that themselves dictate the character of events: what is noteworthy, chosen out of the variety of things that merely happen. And what is remarkable conforms to the conventions of the paradigm.

Paradigmatic thinking presents a mode of making connections and drawing conclusions and is captured in its essence by two statements of Augustine (*Confessions* 10:13):

> We live only in the present, but this present has several dimensions: the present of past things, the present of present things, and the present of future things. . . .
> Your years are like a single day . . . and

this today does not give way to a tomorrow, any more than it follows a yesterday. Your today is Eternity. . . .

For our sages of blessed memory, the Torah, the written part of the Torah in particular, defined a set of paradigms that served without regard to circumstance, context, or, for that matter, dimension and scale of happening. A very small number of models emerged from Scripture, captured in the sets [1] Eden and Adam, [2] Sinai and the Torah, [3] the Land and people of Israel, and [4] the Temple and its building, destruction, rebuilding.

These paradigms served severally and jointly, e.g., Eden and Adam on its own but also superimposed upon the Land and Israel; Sinai and the Torah on its own but also superimposed upon the Land and Israel, and, of course, the Temple, embodying natural creation and its intersection with national and social history, could stand entirely on its own or be superimposed upon any and all of the other paradigms. In many ways, then, we have the symbolic equivalent of a set of two- and three- or even four-dimensional grids. A given pattern forms a grid on its own, one set of lines being set forth in terms of, e.g., Eden, timeless perfection, in contrast against the other set of lines, Adam, temporal disobedience; but upon that grid, a comparable grid can be superimposed, the Land and people of Israel being an obvious one; and upon the two, yet a third and fourth, Sinai and Torah, Temple and the confluence of nature and history.

By reference to these grids, severally or jointly, the critical issues of existence, whether historical, whether contemporary, played themselves out in the system and structure of Rabbinic Judaism. In particular, we may identify four models by which, out of happenings of various sorts, consequential or meaningful events would be selected. By reference to these models, selected events would be shown connected ("meaningful") and explicable in terms of that available logic of paradigm that governed both the making of connections and the drawing of conclusions.

The paradigm of Israel's past, present, and future (= "History" in the counterpart structure of historical thinking): How shall

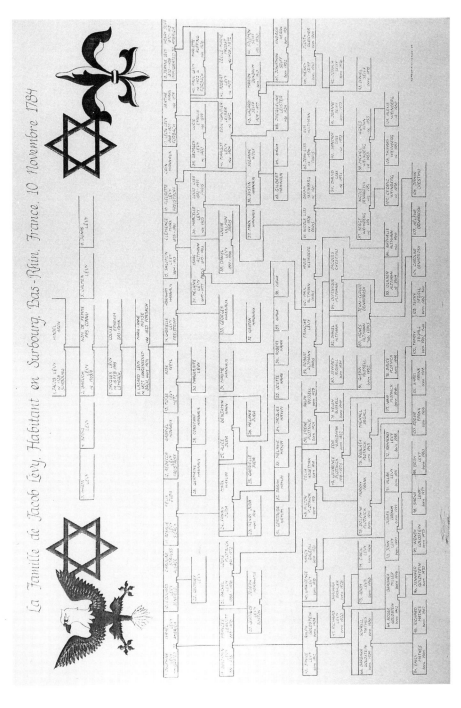

Figure 48. Vernan Nickerson made this family tree. Cousins Janice Goldstein and Marcelle Liss traced their lineage back to 1784 to connect their family's French and American branches.

Figure 49. Three Bar Mitzvah boys in a children's home of the Eclaireurs Israélites de France, the French Jewish Scouts, which took in children of Jews interned in camps. Members of the EIF also were active in the resistance. Moissac, France, c. 1940.

Figure 50. Mismatched phylacteries *(tefillin)*, one of which was obtained by Shmuel Stern in exchange for a sweater, Buchenwald, Germany, January 1945. In the camp, a sweater was precious. To Stern, the tefillin were even more so.

Figure 51. Drawing of Hanukkah lamp by a young child, Ludwig Biermann, Terezin ghetto, Czechoslovakia, 1943.

Figure 52. Mezuzah hidden by Miklos Weisz in Buchenwald concentration camp and the Terezin ghetto, 1944 to 1945. The devout Weisz felt this religious object helped keep him alive.

Figure 53. Spice box carved by Salamon Katz for the ceremony ending the Sabbath *(havdalah)*, Bamberg Displaced Persons camp, Germany, c. 1945-1946. In labor camps and at Auschwitz, he survived through his carpentry skills and made the spice box to celebrate his survival.

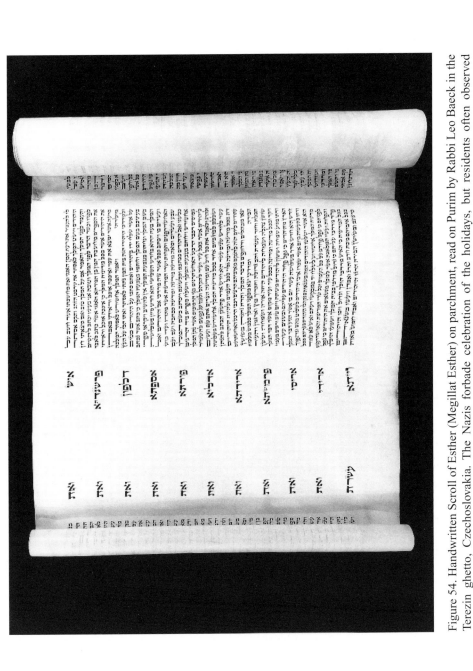

Figure 54. Handwritten Scroll of Esther (Megillat Esther) on parchment, read on Purim by Rabbi Leo Baeck in the Terezin ghetto, Czechoslovakia. The Nazis forbade celebration of the holidays, but residents often observed them in secret.

Figure 55. Sewing box and card made as a Jewish New Year gift for her parents by fourteen-year old Sigrid Ansbacher, Terezin ghetto, Czechoslovakia, c. 1943.

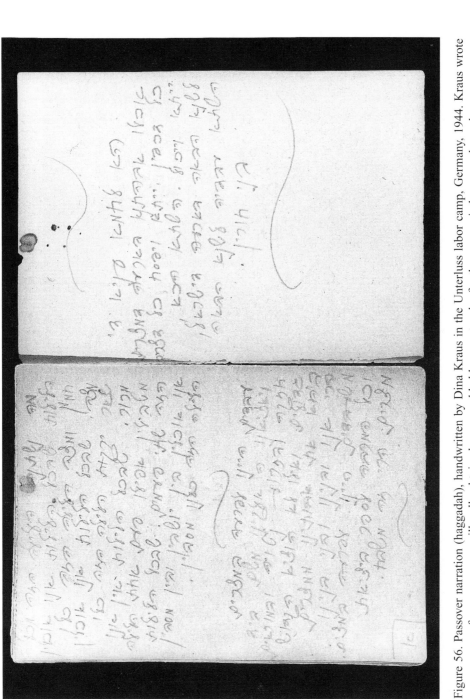

Figure 56. Passover narration (haggadah), handwritten by Dina Kraus in the Unterluss labor camp, Germany, 1944. Kraus wrote from memory on illegally obtained paper and held a secret seder for the women in her camp barrack.

Figure 57. "Hanukkah in the Attic," drawing in ink by fourteen-year old Helga Weissová, Terezín ghetto, Czechoslovakia, 1943. Helga chronicled a Hanukkah celebration in a ghetto children's home.

Figure 58. Talmud Torah and Yeshiva Netzach Yisrael, Polaniec, Poland, 1939.

Figure 59. Wedding of Dr. Tibor Paszternak and Magdalena Reichova, standing in front of the wedding canopy (*huppah*) surrounded by family and friends. Kosice, Czechoslovakia, June 18, 1942.

Figure 60. The Oxman family seder in a Displaced Persons camp in Germany, 1946.

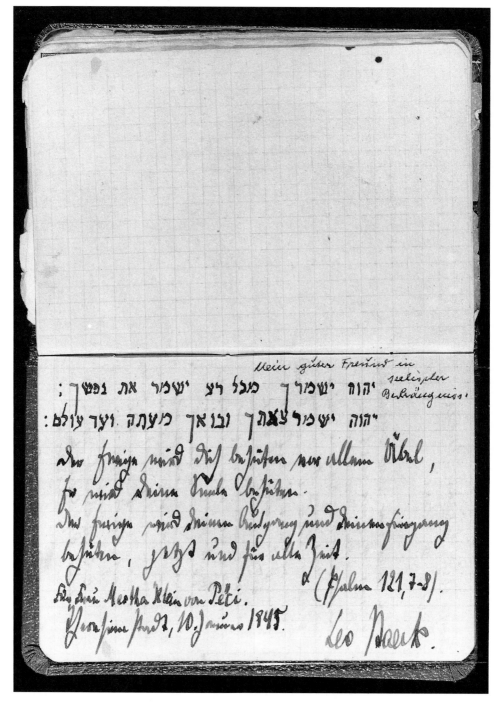

Figure 61. Book of Remembrances kept by Martha Klein von Peci while in Terezin ghetto, Czechoslovakia, 1942-1945. Klein worked in barrack L126 where prominent Jews such as Rabbi Leo Baeck expressed gratitude for her friendship with drawings, inscriptions, and poems.

Figure 62. Services for soldiers and liberated inmates conducted by Chaplain Herschel Schacter from Brooklyn, New York, at the Buchenwald concentration camp, May 18, 1945.

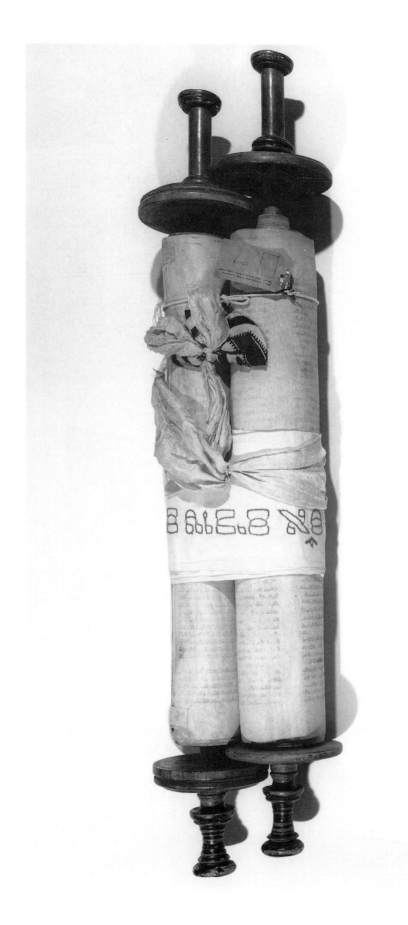

Figure 63. Bound with a cloth wimple and pieces of torn prayer shawl (*tallit*), this Torah was part of a vast collection of Jewish property looted by the Nazis for display in Prague, in a museum of the "extinct Jewish Race."

we organize happenings into events? On the largest scale the question concerns the division into periods of not sequences but mere sets of happenings. Periodization involves explanation, of course, since even in a paradigmatic structure, once matters are set forth as periods, then an element of sequence is admitted into the processes of description and therefore analysis and explanation.

Israel and the Nations: Moving from large aggregates, bordering on abstraction, we turn to the very concrete question of how Israel relates to the rest of the world. This involves explaining not what happened this morning in particular, but what always happens, that is, defining the structure of Israel's life in the politics of this world, explaining the order of things in both the social, political structure of the world and also the sequence of actions that may occur and recur over time (the difference, paradigmatically, hardly matters).

Explaining the pattern of events—Making connections, drawing conclusions: Paradigmatic thinking, no less than historical, explains matters; but the explanation derives from the character of the pattern, rather than the order of events, which governs historical explanation. Connections that are drawn between one thing and something else define a paradigm rather than convey a temporal explanation based on sequences, first this, then that, therefore this explains why that happened. The paradigm bears a different explanation altogether, one that derives from its principle of selection, and therefore the kinds of explanations paradigmatic thinking sets forth, expressed through its principles of selection in making connections and drawing conclusions, will demand rich instantiation.

The future history of Israel: Just as studying the past is supposed to explain the present and point to the future—surely the rationale for historical thinking and writing—so paradigmatic thinking bears the same responsibility. That concerns not so much explaining the present as permitting informed speculation about what will happen in the future. And that speculation will appeal to those principles of order, structure, and explanation that the paradigm to begin with sets

forth. So future history in historical thinking projects out of past and present a trajectory over time to come, and future history in paradigmatic thinking projects along other lines altogether.

The paradigm does its work on all data, without regard to scale or context or circumstance. What this means is that any paradigmatic case—personality, event, idea—imposes structure and order on all data; and the structure will be the same for the small and the large, the now and the then. By that criterion of paradigmatic structuring of "history," we should be able to tell the story of Israel's past, present, and future, by appeal to any identified model, and what we need not predict is which model will yield what pattern, for the patterns are always the same, whatever the choice of the model. In the following, for a striking example, we are able to define the paradigm of Israel's history out of the lives of the founders of the Israelite tribes. That is not a matter of mere generalities. The tribal progenitors moreover correspond to the kingdoms that will rule over Israel, so there is a correspondence of opposites. In the following, as the single best formulation of paradigmatic thinking in the Rabbinic canon, Israel's history is taken over into the structure of Israel's life of sanctification, and all that happens to Israel forms part of the structure of holiness built around cult, Torah, synagogue, sages, Zion, and the like; I give only a small part (Gen. Rab. LXX:VIII):

> 2.A. "As he looked, he saw a well in the field, [and lo, three flocks of sheep lying beside it; for out of that well the flocks were watered;" Gen. 29:2):
> B. R. Hama bar Hanina interpreted the verse in six ways [dividing the verse into six clauses and reading each in light of the others and in line with an overriding theme]:
> C. "'As he looked, he saw a well in the field:' this refers to the well [of water in the wilderness, Num. 21:17].
> D. "'... and lo, three flocks of sheep lying beside it:' specifically, Moses, Aaron, and Miriam.
> E. "'... for out of that well the flocks were watered:' from there each one drew water for his standard, tribe, and family."

F. "And the stone upon the well's mouth was great:"

G. Said R. Hanina, "It was only the size of a little sieve."

H. [Reverting to Hama's statement:] "'. . . and put the stone back in its place upon the mouth of the well:' for the coming journeys. [Thus the first interpretation applies the passage at hand to the life of Israel in the wilderness.]

3.A. "'As he looked, he saw a well in the field:' refers to Zion.

B. "'. . . and lo, three flocks of sheep lying beside it:' refers to the three festivals.

C. "'. . . . for out of that well the flocks were watered:' from there they drank of the holy spirit.

D. "'. . . The stone on the well's mouth was large:' this refers to the rejoicing of the house of the water-drawing."

E. Said R. Hoshaiah, "Why is it called 'the house of the water drawing'? Because from there they drink of the Holy Spirit."

F. [Resuming Hama b. Hanina's discourse:] "'. . . and when all the flocks were gathered there:' coming from 'the entrance of Hamath to the brook of Egypt' (1 Kgs. 8:66).

G. "'. . . the shepherds would roll the stone from the mouth of the well and water the sheep:' for from there they would drink of the Holy Spirit.

H. "'. . . and put the stone back in its place upon the mouth of the well:' leaving it in place until the coming festival. [Thus the second interpretation reads the verse in light of the Temple celebration of the Festival of Tabernacles.]

5.A. "'As he looked, he saw a well in the field:' this refers to Zion.

B. "'. . . and lo, three flocks of sheep lying beside it:' this refers to the first three kingdoms [Babylonia, Media, Greece].

C. "'. . . for out of that well the flocks were watered:' for they enriched the treasures that were laid up in the chambers of the Temple.

D. "'. . . The stone on the well's mouth was large:' this refers to the merit attained by the patriarchs.

E. "'. . . and when all the flocks were gathered there:' this refers to the wicked kingdom, which collects troops through levies over all the nations of the world.

F. "'. . . the shepherds would roll the stone from the mouth of the well and water the sheep:' for they enriched the treasures that were laid up in the chambers of the Temple.

G. "'. . . and put the stone back in its place upon the mouth of the well:' in the age to come the merit attained by the patriarchs will stand [in defense of Israel].' [So the fourth interpretation interweaves the themes of the Temple cult and the domination of the four monarchies.]

7.A. "'As he looked, he saw a well in the field:' this refers to the synagogue.

B. "'. . . and lo, three flocks of sheep lying beside it:' this refers to the three who are called to the reading of the Torah on weekdays.

C. "'. . . for out of that well the flocks were watered:' for from there they hear the reading of the Torah.

D. "'. . . The stone on the well's mouth was large:' this refers to the impulse to do evil.

E. "'. . . and when all the flocks were gathered there:' this refers to the congregation.

F. "'. . . the shepherds would roll the stone from the mouth of the well and water the sheep:' for from there they hear the reading of the Torah.

G. "'. . . and put the stone back in its place upon the mouth of the well:' for once they go forth [from the hearing of the reading of the Torah] the impulse to do evil reverts to its place." [The sixth and last interpretation turns to the twin themes of the reading of the Torah in the synagogue and the evil impulse, temporarily driven off through the hearing of the Torah.]

So much for the correlation of the structures of the social and cosmic order with the condition of Israel. In the passage just reviewed, paradigms take over the organization of events. Time is no longer sequential and linear. What endures are the structures of cosmos and society: Zion, holy seasons, synagogue, and on and on. Clearly, the one thing that plays no role whatsoever in this tableau and frieze is Israel's linear history; past and future take place in an eternal present.

That formulation, however, cannot complete the picture, since Israel's experience encompasses the nations, on the one side, Rome, on the other. Any claim to classify spells of time has to take account of the worldly political experience of Israel; that, after all, establishes the agenda of thought to begin with. The periodization of history can be worked out in terms of Rome's rule now, Israel's dominance in the age to come. The comparability of the two is expressed in various ways, e.g. (Gen. Rab. LXIII:VII):

2.A. "Two nations are in your womb, [and two peoples, born of you, shall be divided; the one shall be stronger than the other, and the elder shall serve the younger]" (Gen. 25:23):
  B. There are two proud nations in your womb, this one takes pride in his world, and that one takes pride in his world.
  C. This one takes pride in his monarchy, and that one takes pride in his monarchy.
  D. There are two proud nations in your womb.
  E. Hadrian represents the nations, Solomon, Israel.
  F. There are two who are hated by the nations in your womb. All the nations hate Esau, and all the nations hate Israel.
  G. The one whom your creator hates is in your womb: "And Esau I hated" (Mal. 1:3).

Thus far, paradigmatic thinking has come to expression in the transformation of actions or traits of the patriarchs into markers of time, modes of the characterization of what history treats as historical. But any conception that thinking about social experience by appeal to patterns or models, rather than sequences in teleological order, requires attention to data of a narrowly historical character, e.g., persons or events paradigmatized, misconstrues the character of the mode of thinking that is before us. We may indeed make sense of Israel's social world by appeal to the deeds or traits of the patriarchs or tribal progenitors. But other statements of the Torah serve equally well as sources for paradigmatic interpretation: models of how things are to be organized and made sensible, against which how things actually are is to be measured.

The purpose of paradigmatic thinking, as much as historical, points toward the future. History is important to explain the present, also to help peer into the future; and paradigms serve precisely the same purpose. The

choice between the one model and the other, then, rests upon which appeals to the more authentic data. In that competition, Scripture, treated as paradigm, met no competition in linear history, and it was paradigmatic, not historical, thinking that proved compelling for a thousand years or more. The future history of Israel is written in Scripture, and what happened in the beginning is what is going to happen at the end of time. That sense of order and balance prevailed. It comes to expression in a variety of passages, of which a severely truncated selection will have to suffice (Gen. Rab. XLII:II):

2.A. Said R. Abin, "Just as [Israel's history] began with the encounter with four kingdoms, so [Israel's history] will conclude with the encounter with the four kingdoms.
  B. "'Chedorlaomer, king of Elam, Tidal, king of Goiim, Amraphel, king of Shinar, and Arioch, king of Ellasar, four kings against five' (Gen. 14:9).
  C. "So [Israel's history] will conclude with the encounter with the four kingdoms: the kingdom of Babylonia, the kingdom of Medea, the kingdom of Greece, and the kingdom of Edom."

A single formulation of matters suffices to show how the entire history of Israel was foreseen at the outset (Pesiqta deRab Kahana XXI:V):

1.A. R. Hiyya taught on Tannaite authority, "At the beginning of the creation of the world the Holy One, blessed be He, foresaw that the Temple would be built, destroyed, and rebuilt.
  B. "'In the beginning God created the heaven and the earth' (Gen. 1:1) [refers to the Temple] when it was built, in line with the following verse: 'That I may plant the heavens and lay the foundations of the earth and say to Zion, You are my people' (Is. 51:16).
  C. "'And the earth was unformed'—lo, this refers to the destruction, in line with this verse: 'I saw the earth, and lo, it was unformed' (Jer. 4:23).
  D. "'And God said, Let there be light'—lo, it was built and well constructed in the age to come."

A single specific example of the foregoing proposition suffices. It is drawn from that same mode of paradigmatic thinking that imposes the model of the beginning upon the end. In the present case the yield is consequential: we know what God is going to do to Rome. What God did to the Egyptians foreshadows what God will do to the Romans at the end of time. What we have here is the opposite of cyclical history; here history conforms to a pattern, end-time recapitulates creation's events and complements them; here we see a good example of how paradigmatic thinking addresses the possibility of cyclicality and insists instead upon closure (Pesiqta deRab Kahana VII:XI.3):

A. R. Levi in the name of R. Hama bar Hanina: "He who exacted vengeance from the former [oppressor] will exact vengeance from the latter.
B. "Just as, in Egypt, it was with blood, so with Edom it will be the same: 'I will show wonders in the heavens and in the earth, blood, and fire, and pillars of smoke' (Job 3:3).
C. "Just as, in Egypt, it was with frogs, so with Edom it will be the same: 'The sound of an uproar from the city, an uproar because of the palace, an uproar of the Lord who renders recompense to his enemies' (Is. 66:6).
D. "Just as, in Egypt, it was with lice, so with Edom it will be the same: 'The streams of Bosrah will be turned into pitch, and the dust thereof into brimstone, and the land thereof shall become burning pitch' (Is. 34:9). 'Smite the dust of the earth that it may become lice' (Ex. 8:12).
E. "Just as, in Egypt, it was with swarms of wild beasts, so with Edom it will be the same: 'The pelican and the bittern shall possess it' (Is. 34:11).
F. "Just as, in Egypt, it was with pestilence, so with Edom it will be the same: 'I will plead against Gog with pestilence and with blood' (Ez. 38:22).
G. "Just as, in Egypt, it was with boils, so with Edom it will be the same: 'This shall be the plague wherewith the Lord will smite all the peoples that have warred against Jerusalem: their flesh shall consume away while they stand upon their feet' (Zech. 14:12).
H. "Just as, in Egypt, it was with great stones, so with Edom it will be the same: 'I will cause to rain upon Gog . . . an overflowing shower and great hailstones' (Ez. 38:22).
I. "Just as, in Egypt, it was with locusts, so with Edom it will be the same: 'And you,

son of man, thus says the Lord God: Speak to birds of every sort . . . the flesh of the mighty shall you eat . . . blood shall you drink . . . you shall eat fat until you are full and drink blood until you are drunk' (Ez. 39:17-19).
J. "Just as, in Egypt, it was with darkness, so with Edom it will be the same: 'He shall stretch over Edom the line of chaos and the plummet of emptiness' (Is. 34:11).
K. "Just as, in Egypt, he took out their greatest figure and killed him, so with Edom it will be the same: 'A great slaughter in the land of Edom, among them to come down shall be the wild oxen' (Is. 34:6-7).

The exposition of matters through the small sample given here leaves no doubt on precisely how paradigmatic thinking recast Israel's recorded experience ("history") into a set of models that pertained everywhere and all the time.

This survey of the way in which paradigmatic thinking comes to expression now permits a more general statement of matters. As a medium of organizing and accounting for experience, history—the linear narrative of singular events intended to explain how things got to their present state and therefore why—does not enjoy the status of a given. Nor does historical thinking concerning the social order self-evidently lay claim on plausibility. It is one possibility among many. Historical thinking—sequential narrative of one-time events—presupposes order, linearity, distinction between time past and time present, and teleology, among data that do not self-evidently sustain such presuppositions. Questions of chaos intervene; the very possibility of historical narrative meets a challenge in the diversity of story-lines, the complexity of events, the bias of the principle of selection of what is eventful, of historical interest, among a broad choice of happenings: why this, not that. Narrative history first posits a gap between past and present, but then bridges the gap; why not entertain the possibility that to begin with there is none? These and similar considerations invite a different way of thinking about how things have been and now are, a different tense structure altogether.

A way of thinking about the experience of humanity, whether past or contemporary, that makes other distinctions than the historical ones between past and present and that eschews linear narrative and so takes account of the chaos that ultimately prevails, now competes with historical thinking. Paradigmatic thinking, a different medium for organizing and explaining things that happen, deals with the same data that occupy historical thinking, and that is why when we refer to paradigmatic thinking, the word "history" gains its quotation marks: it is not a datum of thought, merely a choice; contradicting to its core the character of paradigmatic thinking, the category then joins its opposite, paradigm, only by forming the oxymoron before us: paradigmatic thinking about "history."

The category, "history," as conventionally defined and as further realized in the Authorized History of Scripture, Genesis through Kings, therefore forms merely one way of addressing the past in order to find sense and meaning therein. Clearly, with its emphasis on linear, irreversible events and the division between past and present, history is not the way taken by Rabbinic Judaism in organizing Israel's experience: selecting what matters and explaining that. We know that is the fact because none of the indicators of historical writing and thinking come to the surface in the documents under study. The very opposite traits predominate. Rabbinic literature contains no sustained historical or biographical narrative, only anecdotes, makes no distinction between past and present but melds them. But that writing, resting as it does on the Hebrew Scriptures, presents a paradox. A set of writings of a one-sidedly historical character, the Hebrew Scripture deriving from ancient Israel, finds itself expounded in an utterly ahistorical way by its heirs, both Judaic and Christian.

For, it is clear, the records represented as recording events of the past—the written Torah, the Old Testament—form a massive presence in Judaism and Christianity respectively. So history in the conventional sense formed a principal mode of thinking in the documents that educated the framers of the dual Torah of Judaism and the Bible of

Christianity. It must follow, both of those religions defined as an important component of God's revelation to humanity documents that by all accounts constituted systematic statements of the past: history-books above all else. But, we shall now see, these accounts of the past, received into the entire Torah, oral and written, of Judaism, and into the Bible, Old and New Testaments, of Christianity, received a reading that we define as one of a paradigmatic character. Given the fundamentally historical character of the Hebrew Scriptures transformed into written Torah and Old Testament, respectively, we must identify the basis for the rereading imposed thereon by the heirs.

That is to say, what Scripture ("written Torah," "Old Testament") yields for Rabbinic Judaism is not one-time events, arranged in sequence to dictate meaning, but models or patterns of conduct and consequence. These models are defined by the written Torah or the Old Testament (read in light of the perspective of the Oral Torah, by Jews, or the New Testament, by Christians). No component of the paradigm emerges from other than the selected experience set forth by Scripture. But the paradigms are at the same time pertinent without regard to considerations of scale and formulated without interest in matters of singular context. Forthrightly selective—this matters, that is ignored—the principle of selection is not framed in terms of sequence; order of a different sort is found.

The models or paradigms that are so discerned then pertain not to one time alone—past time—but to all times equally—past, present and future. Then "time" no longer forms an organizing category of understanding and interpretation. The spells marked out by moon and sun and fixed stars bear meaning, to be sure. But that meaning has no bearing upon the designation of one year as past, another as present. The meaning imputed to the lunar and solar marking of time derives from the cult, on the one side, and the calendar of holy time, on the other: seven solar days, a Sabbath; a lunar cycle, a new month to be celebrated, the first new moon after the vernal equinox, the Passover, and after the autumnal, Tabernacles.

Rabbinic Judaism tells time the way nature does and only in that way; events in Rabbinic Judaism deemed worth recording in time take place the way events in nature do. What accounts for the difference between history's time and paradigmatic time as set forth here is a conception of time quite different from the definition of historical time that operates in Scripture: the confluence of the nature's time and history's way of telling time: two distinct chronographies brought together, the human one then imposed upon the natural one.

In Rabbinic Judaism the natural way of telling time precipitated celebration of nature. True, those same events were associated with moments of Israel's experience as well: the exodus above all. The language of prayer, e.g., the Sabbath's classification as a memorial to creation and also a remembrance of the exodus from Egypt, leaves no doubt on the dual character of the annotation of time. But the exodus, memorialized hither and yon through the solar seasons and the Sabbath alike, constituted no more a specific, never-to-be-repeated, one-time historical event, part of a sustained narrative of such events, than any other moment in Israel's time, inclusive of the building and the destruction of the Temple. Quite to the contrary, linking creation and exodus classified both in a single category; the character of that category—historical or paradigmatic—is not difficult to define; the exodus is treated as consubstantial with creation, a paradigm, not a one-time event.

It follows that this Judaism's Israel kept time in two ways, and the one particular to Israel (in the way in which the natural calendar was not particular to Israel) through its formulation as a model instead of a singular event was made to accord with the natural calendar, not vice versa. That is to say, just as the natural calendar recorded time that was the opposite of historical, because it was not linear and singular and teleological but reversible and repetitive, so Israel kept time with reference to events, whether past or present, that also were not singular, linear, or teleological. These were, rather, reconstitutive in the forever of here and now—not

a return to a perfect time but a recapitulation of a model forever present. Israel could treat as comparable the creation of the world and the exodus from Egypt (as the liturgy commonly does, e.g., in connection with the Sabbath) because Israel's paradigm (not "history") and nature's time corresponded in character, were consubstantial and not mutually contradictory.

And that consubstantiality explains why paradigm and natural time work so well together. Now, "time" bears a different signification. It is here one not limited to the definition assigned by nature—yet also not imposed upon natural time but treated as congruent and complementary with nature's time. How so? Events—things that happen that are deemed consequential—are eventful, meaningful, by a criterion of selection congruent in character with nature's own. To understand why that is so, we must recall the character of the Torah's paradigms:

[1] Scripture set forth certain patterns which, applied to the chaos of the moment, selected out of a broad range of candidates some things and omitted reference to others.

[2] The selected things then are given their structure and order by appeal to the paradigm, indifference to scale forming the systemic counterpart to the paradigm's indifference to context, time, circumstance.

[3] That explains how some events narrated by Scripture emerged as patterns, imposing their lines of order and structure upon happenings of other times.

And this yields the basis for the claim of consubstantiality:

[4] Scripture's paradigms—Eden, the Land—appealed to nature in another form.

The upshot, then, we state with heavy emphasis: *the rhythms of the sun and moon are celebrated in the very forum in which the Land, Israel's Eden, yields its celebration to the Creator.* The rhythmic quality of the paradigm then compares with the rhythmic quality of natural time: not cyclical, but also not linear. Nature's way of telling time and the Torah's way meet in the Temple: its events are nature's, its story a tale of nature too. Past and present flow together and join in future time too because, as in nature, what is past is what is now and what will be. The paradigms, specified in a moment, form counterparts to the significations of nature's time.

These events of Israel's life (we cannot now refer to Israel's "history")—or, rather, the models or patterns that they yielded—served as the criteria for selection, among happenings of any time, past, present, or future, of the things that mattered out of the things that did not matter: a way of keeping track, a mode of marking time. The model or paradigm that set forth the measure of meaning then applied whether to events of vast consequence or to the trivialities of everyday concern alone. Sense was where sense was found by the measure of the paradigm; everything else lost consequence. Connections were then to be made between this and that, and the other thing did not count. Conclusions then were to be drawn between the connection of this and that, and no consequences were to be imputed into the thing that did not count.

That is not an ideal way of discovering or positing order amid chaos; much was left, if not unaccounted for, then not counted to begin with. We cannot take for granted that the range of events chosen for paradigms struck everyone concerned as urgent or even deserving of high priority, and we also must assume that other Israelites, besides those responsible for writing and preserving the books surveyed here, will have identified other paradigms altogether. But—for those who accorded to these books authority and self-evidence—the paradigm encompassing the things that did conform to the pattern and did replicate its structure excluded what it did not explain. So it left the sense that while chaos characterized the realm beyond consciousness, the things of which people took cognizance also made sense—a self-fulfilling system of enormously compelling logic. For the system could explain what it regarded as important, and also dismiss what it regarded as inconsequential or meaningless, therefore defining the data that fit and dismissing those that did not.

At stake in the paradigm is discerning order and regularity not everywhere—in the setting of these books, "everywhere" defied imagining—but in some few sets of happenings. The scale revised both upward and downward the range of concern: these are not all happenings, but they are the ones that matter—and they matter very much. Realizing or replicating the paradigm, they uniquely constitute events, and, that is why by definition these are the only events that matter. Paradigmatic thinking about past, present, and future ignores issues of linear order and temporal sequence because it recognizes another logic all together, besides the one of priority and posteriority and causation formulated in historical terms.

That mode of thinking, as its name states, appeals to the logic of models or patterns that serve without regard to time and circumstance, on the one side, or scale, on the other. The sense for order unfolds, first of all, through that logic of selection that dictates what matters and what does not. And, out of the things that matter, that same logic defines the connections of things, so forming a system of description, analysis, and explanation that consists in the making of connections between this and that, but not the other thing, and the drawing of conclusions from those ineluctable, self-evident connections. At stake now is the definition of self-evidence: how did our sages know the difference between a paradigmatic event and a mere happening?

When we speak of the presence of the past, we raise not generalities or possibilities but the concrete experience that generations actively mourning the Temple endured. When we speak of the pastness of the present, we describe the consciousness of people who could open Scripture and find themselves right there, in its record—but not only Lamentations, but also prophecy, and, especially, in the books of the Torah. Here we deal with not the spiritualization of Scripture, but with the acutely contemporary and immediate realization of Scripture: once again, as then; Scripture in the present day, the present day in Scripture. That is why it was possible for sages to formulate out of Scripture a paradigm that imposed structure and order upon the world that they themselves encountered.

Since sages did not see themselves as removed in time and space from the generative events to which they referred the experience of the here and now, they also had no need to make the past contemporary. If the Exodus was a irreversible, once for all time event, then, as we see, our sages saw matters in a different way altogether. They neither relived nor transformed one-time historical events, for they found another way to overcome the barrier of chronological separation. Specifically, if history began when the gap between present and past shaped consciousness, then we naturally ask ourselves whether the point at which historical modes of thought concluded and a different mode of thought took over produced an opposite consciousness from the historical one: not cycle but paradigm. For, it seems to me clear, the premise that time and space separated our sages of the Rabbinic writings from the great events of the past simply did not win attention. The opposite premise defined matters: barriers of space and time in no way separated sages from great events, the great events of the past enduring for all time. How then are we to account for this remarkably different way of encounter, experience, and, consequently, explanation? The answer has already been adumbrated.

Sages in the documents of Rabbinic Judaism, from the Mishnah forward, all recognized the destruction of the Second Temple and took for granted that that event was to be understood by reference to the model of the destruction of the first. A variety of sources maintain precisely that position and express it in so many words, e.g., the colloquy between Aqiba and sages about the comfort to be derived from the ephemeral glory of Rome and the temporary ruin of Jerusalem. It follows that for our sages of blessed memory, the destruction of the Temple in 70 did not mark a break with the past, such as it had for their predecessors some five hundred years earlier, but rather a recapitulation of the past. Paradigmatic thinking then began in that very event that precipitated thought about history to begin with, the end of the old order. But paradigm replaced his-

tory because what had taken place the first time as unique and unprecedented took place the second time in precisely the same pattern and therefore formed of an episode a series. Paradigmatic thinking replaced historical when history as an account of one-time, irreversible, unique events, arranged in linear sequence and pointing toward a teleological conclusion, lost all plausibility. If the first time around, history—with the past marked off from the present, with events arranged in linear sequence, with narrative of a sustained character serving as the medium of thought— provided the medium for making sense of matters, then the second time around, history lost all currency.

The real choice facing our sages was not linear history as against paradigmatic thinking, but rather, paradigm as against cycle. For the conclusion to be drawn from the destruction of the Second Temple, once history, its premises disallowed, yielded no explanation, can have taken the form of a theory of the cyclicality of events. As nature yielded its spring, summer, fall, and winter, so the events of humanity or of Israel in particular can have been asked to conform to a cyclical pattern, in line, for example, with Ecclesiastes' view that what has been is what will be. But our sages obviously did not take that position at all.

They rejected cyclicality in favor of a different ordering of events altogether. They did not believe the Temple would be rebuilt and destroyed again, rebuilt and destroyed, and so on into endless time. They stated the very opposite: the Temple would be rebuilt but never again destroyed. And that represented a view of the second destruction that rejected cyclicality altogether. Sages instead opted for patterns of history and against cycles because they retained that notion for the specific and concrete meaning of events that characterized Scripture's history, even while rejecting the historicism of Scripture. They maintained, as we have seen, that a pattern governed, and the pattern was not a cyclical one. Here, Scripture itself imposed its structures, its order, its system—its paradigm. And the Official History left no room for the conception of cyclicality. If matters do not repeat themselves but do conform to a pattern, then the pattern itself must be identified.

Paradigmatic thinking formed the alternative to cyclical thinking because Scripture, its history subverted, nonetheless defined how matters were to be understood. Viewed whole, the Official History indeed defined the paradigm of Israel's existence, formed out of the components of Eden and the Land, Adam and Israel, Sinai, then given movement through Israel's responsibility to the covenant and Israel's adherence to, or violation, of God's will, fully exposed in the Torah that marked the covenant of Sinai. Scripture laid matters out, and from that lay-out our sages drew conclusions that conformed to their experience. So the second destruction precipitated thinking about paradigms of Israel's life such as came to full exposure in the thinking behind the Midrash-compilations we have surveyed. The episode made into a series, sages' paradigmatic thinking asked of Scripture different questions from the historical ones of the time of the first destruction because our sages brought to Scripture different premises; drew from Scripture different conclusions. But in point of fact, not a single paradigm set forth by sages can be distinguished in any important component from the counterpart in Scripture, not Eden and Adam in comparison to the Land and people of Israel, and not the tale of Israel's experience in the spinning out of the tension between the word of God and the will of Israel.

The contrast between history's time and nature's time shows that history recognizes natural time and imposes its points of differentiation upon it. History knows days, months, years, but proposes to differentiate among them, treating this day as different from that because on this day, such and such happened, but on that day, it did not. History's time takes over nature's time and imposes upon it a second set of indicators or points of differentiation. History therefore defines and measures time through two intersecting indicators, the meeting of the natural and the human. As is clear in the foregoing remarks, the context in which "time" is now defined is the passage of days,

weeks, months, and years, as marked by the movement of the sun and the stars in the heavens and the recognition of noteworthy events that have taken place in specific occasions during the passage of those days and months and years. By contrast, paradigmatic time in the context of Judaism tells time through the events of nature, to which are correlated the events of Israel's life: its social structure, its reckoning of time, its disposition of its natural resources, and its history too. That is, through the point at which nature is celebrated, the Temple, there Israel tells time.

Predictably, therefore, the only history our sages would deem worth narrating—and not in sustained narrative even then—is the story of the Temple cult through days and months and years, and the history of the Temple and its priesthood and administration through time and into eternity. We now fully understand that fact. It is because, to begin with, the very conception of paradigmatic thinking as against the historical kind took shape in deep reflection on the meaning of events: what happened before has happened again— to the Temple. Ways of telling time before give way, history's premises having lost plausibility here as much as elsewhere. Now Israel will tell time in nature's way, shaping history solely in response to what happens in the cult and to the Temple. There is no other history, because, to begin with, there is no history.

Nature's time is the sole way of marking time, and Israel's paradigm conforms to nature's time and proves enduringly congruent with it. Israel's conforming to nature yields not cyclical history but a reality formed by appeal to the paradigm of cult and Temple, just as God had defined that pattern and paradigm to Moses in the Torah. Genesis begins with nature's time and systematically explains how the resources of nature came to Israel's service to God. History's time yielded an Israel against and despite history, nature's time, as the Torah tells it, an Israel fully harmonious with nature. At stake in the paradigm then is creation: how come? So long as the Judaism set forth by the sages in the Mishnah, Tosefta, Talmuds, and Midrash-compilations governed, Israel formed itself in response to the eternities of nature's time, bringing into conformity the ephemera of the here and now. That answers the questions, why here? why now? so what? And with the powerful answers set forth in paradigmatic as against historical thinking, Rabbinic Judaism would settle all points of conflict through compelling, irrefutable arguments.

JACOB NEUSNER

HOLOCAUST, JUDAIC THEOLOGY AND THE: The intentional murder of six million Jews during World War II—called the Holocaust or Shoah—raises a host of fundamental theological questions. Some of the most pressing methodologically and philosophically are:

(1) What is the status of "history," of historical events, in Jewish thought? This is to ask: is Judaism a historical religion? If yes, can historical events disconfirm Judaism's basic theological affirmations?

(2) How does one weigh and evaluate good and evil as historical phenomena *vis a vis* theological judgments?

(3) How does one divide up and evaluate the meaning of Jewish history?

(4) Is Jewish history in any way singular?

(5) Is the Shoah unique? And if it is, does this uniqueness matter philosophically and theologically?

(6) What is the status of empirical disconfirmation as a criterion and procedure in Jewish thought?

(7) What does it mean to speak of providence and of God's intervention into human affairs?

(8) What is "revelation"? What is "covenant"? The essential need for precision in the use of such technical terms is widely ignored by contemporary thinkers, even though the meaning of such terms is decisive in relation to claims made for the putative "revelatory" character of the Shoah and the reborn state of Israel.

(9) Recognizing the existence of a long tradition of "theological and philosophical" reflection on this matter, what limits, if any, are we bound by in interpreting God's attributes?

(10) What traditional biblical, Rabbinic, and contemporary sources, if any, have an authoritative status in this discussion?

(11) Last but not least, theological conversation about the Shoah raises a host of conceptual questions relating to the philosophical and theological meaning of the land of Israel, Zionism, and the state of Israel. For example, is the reborn state God's compensation for the death camps? Is it the fulfillment of biblical prophecy? Is it even "the beginning of the dawn of Jewish redemption"?

While we cannot here analyze all of these complex issues directly and fully, we begin with them in order to alert readers to the concerns to which they need to be sensitive when reflecting on the elemental conceptual matters dealt with in this essay.

It should also be noted at the outset that, while the Holocaust raises the host of questions already cited and directly challenges almost all of the basic traditional Jewish theological categories, it does not *necessarily* falsify or discredit them such that they require alteration, reformulation, or negation. Any argument in this direction that asks either for specific modifications or reformulations or, more radically, proposes total rejection of the Jewish theological tradition, requires coherent and compelling reasons. And, to anticipate parts of our further analysis, to produce such reasons, such an argument, is no easy matter.

Theological approaches to the Shoah: In responding theologically to the Holocaust, Jewish thinkers have explored many possible conceptual avenues, some old, some new. Jewish history is no stranger to national tragedy and, as a consequence, there are an abundance of traditional explanatory "models" that can be, and have been, adapted and reapplied to the Holocaust. Of these, six have regularly been looked to by modern thinkers as providing some map for dealing with the theological complexities of our own time.

1. *The Akedah* (The "Binding of Isaac"): The biblical narrative recounted in Gen. 22:2ff. is often appealed to as a possible paradigm for treating the Holocaust. Such a move is rooted in Jewish tradition, especially that of the medieval martyrologies of the crusader and post-crusader period, during which the biblical event became the prism through which the horrific medieval experience became refracted and "intelligible." In this perspective, like Isaac of old, the Jewish children

of Europe, and, more generally, all of slaughtered Israel, are martyrs to God and willingly sacrifice themselves and their loved ones in order to prove beyond all doubt their faithfulness to the almighty.[1] The appeal of this decipherment lies in its heroic imputation to the dead, in the defense of their sanctity and obedience to the God of Israel. Their death is not due to sin, to any imperfection on their part, or to any violation of the covenant. It is the climactic evidence of their unwavering devotion to the faith of their fathers rather than its abandonment. This view thus rejects the traditional as well as more contemporary approaches that explain that what befalls Israel is "because of our sins." Not sin but piety is the key factor in accounting for the genocidal event. God makes unique demands upon those who love him and whom he loves, and, as with Abraham, so too the Jewish people in our time respond with a fidelity of unmatched purity and selflessness. As such, the dreadful events are made a test, the occasion for the maximal religious service, the absolute existential moment of the religious life, whose benefits are enjoyed both by the martyrs in the world-to-come and by the world as a whole, which benefits from such dedication.

In evaluating this reading of the Holocaust, one appreciates the positive elements it stresses: its avoidance of the imputation of sin to the victims, its denial of sin as the cause of the horrific events that unfolded, its praise of Israel's heroism and faithfulness. Yet the analogy between biblical and contemporary events breaks down in the face of other elemental features of the *Akedah* paradigm. (A) In Genesis, God commands the test; are we likewise to deem Auschwitz a command of God? Or is such a direct claim so terrible as to shatter all belief in the compassionate God of Israel? (B) In the original, it is Abraham, God's especially faithful servant, who is tested—and tested because of his special religious status. Can we transfer, as is required by the analogy, Hitler and his SS into the pivotal role of Abraham? Abraham who sacrifices his "beloved," as compared to the *Einsatzgruppen* who murdered Jews as lice, as sub-humans, as the principle

of all that was negative, parasitical, polluting in creation. (C) Above all, in the biblical circumstance, the angel of the Lord brings the matter to a conclusion with no blood being shed: "Lay not thy hand upon the lad, neither do thou anything to him" (Gen. 12:12).

2. *Job*: The book of Job, the best known treatment of theodicy in the Hebrew Bible, naturally enough presents itself as a possible model for decoding the Holocaust. According to such a rendering, and parallel in certain ways to the modality suggested by the *Akedah*, Job provides an inviting paradigm because again Job's suffering is caused not by his sinfulness but by his righteousness— perceived by Satan as a cause for jealousy. Moreover, the tale ends on a "happy" note: God's double blessing rewards Job's faithfulness. On a deeper level, of course, the issues are far more problematic and their meaning ambiguous, i.e., the resolution of Job's doubts is never really clear, God's reply through the whirlwind is, in important ways, no answer to Job's questions and, perhaps most telling, Job's first wife and family are still dead through no fault of their own.

Beyond the inherent difficulties in ascertaining the correct reading of Job, the story presents details that lead away from rather than towards an analogy with the Holocaust. (A) The reader of Job knows, via the prologue, that the pact between God and Satan over the conditions of Job's trial explicitly include that Job not be killed. This, above all, renders the situations of Job and Auschwitz altogether different. (B) Outside of the writings of the few who survived, all other theological ruminations about the Shoah are by those who were not in the hell of the death-camps; hence our situation is not that of Job but, as Eliezer Berkovits has said, of Job's brother. So, our cry is a different cry, our faith a different faith. (C) Third, the haunting matter of those who died in order to make the test possible finds no "resolution" in Job. God's capriciousness appears all too manifest. (D) Finally, the climax of Job occurs with God's self-revelation. God may not provide answers to the specific complaints Job raises, but at least Job sees that there is a God. This means that, even if he does not understand God's ways, at a minimum, he has reason to "trust in the Lord." Through this manifestation of God's presence, Job receives some sort of "answer," as Martin Buber among others emphasized: "I had heard of thee by the hearing of the ear, but now mine eyes see thee; wherefore I abhor my words and repent" (Job 42:5-6).

Knowing there is a God makes a fundamental difference, even if one does not know how God balances the equation of good and evil, righteousness and reward. By contrast, and inescapable, those who went to their death in the death-camps, or those murdered by SS men in mass graves, or those children thrown alive into open fires, received no such comforting revelation of the divine. This unbroken silence makes the totality of the Holocaust irreconcilable with a Joban mode.

3. *The Suffering Servant*: One of the richest theological doctrines of biblical theodicy is that of the "Suffering Servant." Given its classic presentation in the book of Isaiah (especially chapter 53), the "Suffering Servant" doctrine is that of vicarious suffering and atonement in which the righteous suffer for the wicked and hence allay, in some mysterious way, God's wrath and judgment, thus making the continuation of history possible. According to Jewish tradition, the "Suffering Servant" is Israel, the people of the covenant, who suffer with and for God in the midst of the evil of creation. As God is long-suffering with his creation, so Israel, God's people, must be long suffering. In this they mirror the divine in their own reality and through this religiously rooted courage they, by suffering for others, make it possible for creation to endure. In this act of faithfulness, the guiltless establish a unique bond with the almighty. As they suffer for and with God, God suffers their suffering, shares their agony, and comes to love them in a special way for loving God with fortitude and without limit.

This theme has been enunciated in Jewish theological writings emanating from the Holocaust era itself and continuing down to our own day. One finds it in the writings of Hasidic rebbes, of conservative thinkers, such as Abraham Joshua Heschel (*Man's Quest for God* and *God in Search of Man*), and Or-

thodox thinkers such as Eliezer Berkovits (*Faith After the Holocaust*, pp. 124-127). In these many sources, it receives a classical exposition: "God's servant," Berkovits writes, for example, "carries upon his shoulders God's dilemma with man through history. God's people share in all the fortunes of God's dilemma as man is bungling his way through toward Messianic realization" (p. 127).

One contemporary Jewish theologian has gone beyond the traditional framework and used it to construct a more elaborate, systematic, theological deconstruction of the Holocaust. For Ignaz Maybaum, a German Reform rabbi who survived the war in London, the pattern of the "Suffering Servant" is the paradigm of Israel's way in history. First in the "Servant of God" in Isaiah, then in the Jew Jesus, and now at Treblinka and Auschwitz, God uses the Jewish people to address the world and to save it: "They died though innocent so that others might live." According to this reading of the Holocaust, the perennial dialectic of history is God's desire that the gentile nations come close to him, while they resist this call. To foster and facilitate this relationship is the special task, the "mission," of Israel. It is they who must make God's message accessible in terms the gentile nations will understand and respond to. But what language, what symbols, will speak to the nations? Not that of the *Akedah* in which Isaac is spared and no blood is shed but, rather, and only, that of the crucifixion, i.e., a sacrifice in which the innocent die for the guilty, where some die vicariously so that others might live.

In this view, the modern people Israel repeats collectively the single crucifixion of one Jew two millennia ago, and by so doing the Jews again reveal to humankind its weaknesses as well as the need for turning to heaven. In a daring parallelism, Maybaum writes: "The Golgotha of modern mankind is Auschwitz. The cross, the Roman gallows, was replaced by the gas chamber. The gentiles, it seems, must first be terrified by the blood of the sacrificed scapegoat to have the mercy of God revealed to them and become converted, become baptized gentiles, become Christians" (*The Face of God After*

Auschwitz, p. 36). For Maybaum, through the Holocaust, the world moves again forward and upward, from the final vestiges of medieval obscurantism and intolerance, of which the Shoah is a product, to a new era of spiritual maturity, human morality and divine-human encounter.

The difficulties inherent in the Suffering Servant theology are twofold. As to the thesis in its generality, it "solves" the problem of the Shoah by appeal to a doctrine that is equally in need of explanation, the notion of vicarious suffering, especially suffering on so monumental a scale and involving such systematic indignity, incalculable pain, and vast death. Indeed, as a "rationalization" of the Shoah, the doctrine of the Servant seems worse than the problem it hopes to explain: a God who acts in such a way, who demands such sacrifices, who regulates creation by such means, is a God whose nature requires more than a little explanation within the covenantal framework of biblical faith. Surely the omnipotent, omniscient creator could have found a more satisfactory principle for directing and sustaining creation. If, at this juncture, one defends the doctrine of vicarious suffering, one can only do so by recourse to mystery: "God's ways are not our ways." But this is not an explanation but a capitulation before the immensity of the Shoah, a cry of faith.

In the more specific, elaborate, form given to the doctrine by Maybaum, the problem is sharper. First, it empties Jewish life of all meaning other than that intelligible to and directed towards gentile nations. Only the Christocentric pattern now applied to the people of Israel gives meaning to this people's history and spirituality. Second, and urgent, is the realization that this view is predicated on a fundamentally false analogy between the Holocaust and Good Friday. Christians are able to declare that "Christ died for the sins of mankind," for (at least) two cardinal reasons. The first and most weighty is that Christ is believed to be God incarnate, the Second Person of the Trinity: the crucifixion is God's taking the sins of mankind on himself. He is the vicarious atonement for humankind. There is thus no terrible cruelty or unspeakable "crime" but only divine love, the presence of unlimited divine grace. Secondly, the human yet divine Christ, the hypostatic union of man and God, mounts the cross voluntarily. He willingly "dies so that others might live." How very different was the Shoah. How very dissimilar its victims (not martyrs) and their fate. The murdered, including the million Jewish children, were not divine—they were all too human creatures crushed in the most unspeakable brutality. If God was the cause of their suffering, how at odds from the traditional Christian picture, for here God purchases life for some by sacrificing others, not himself. Here grace, if present, is so only in a most paradoxical way, and certainly not in the reality of the victims. Here there is only Golgotha, crucifixion, death; there is no Easter for the crucified. Furthermore, the Jews were singled out "unwillingly;" they were not martyrs in the classical sense, though we may wish to so transform their fate for our needs.

The disanalogy of the Holocaust and Good Friday reveals yet something more. According to Maybaum, the symbol of the crucifixion is that of vicarious atonement. But given the circumstances of this vicarious sacrifice, of Auschwitz and Treblinka, of *Einsatzgruppen* and gas chambers, is it not the case that the nature of the atonement is far more criminal and infinitely more depraved than the sins for which it atones? What sort of reconciliation can the work of Hitler and the SS have been? What sort of *kohanim* (priests) were these and what sort of sacrifice can they bring? Can one truly envision God, the God of Israel, making such vicarious expiation?

4. *Hester Panim—God hides his face*: The Bible, in wrestling with human suffering, appeals, especially in the Psalms, to the notion of *Hester Panim*: "The hiding of the face of God." This concept has two meanings. The first, as in Deut. 31:17-18 and later in Mic. 3:4, is casual, linking God's absence to human sin: God turns away from the sinner. The second sense, found particularly in a number of Psalms (e.g., Pss. 44, 69, 88 and variants in, e.g., Pss. 9, 10, 13; see also Job 13:24), suggests protest, despair, confusion

over the absence of God for no clear reason and certainly not, e.g., in the mind of the Psalmist, as a consequence of sin. Here humankind stands "abandoned" for reasons that appear unknown and unfathomable. The divine presence has been removed and chaos unloosed upon the world. Thus the repetitive theme of lament sounded in the Psalms, "Why" or "How long" God will you be absent? Is it possible for God to be continually indifferent to human affairs, to be passive in the struggle of good and evil, to be unmoved by suffering and its overcoming?

In applying this difficult doctrine to the Holocaust, modern theologians are attempting three things: (a) to vindicate Israel; (b) to remove God as the direct cause of the evil, i.e., it is something people do to other people; and (c) to affirm the reality and even saving nature of the divine despite the empirical evidence to the contrary. The first two points need no further explanation, the third and most significant does. Framed in this way *Hester Panim* is not merely or only the absence of God but rather entails a more complex exegesis of divine providence stemming from an analysis of the ontological nature of the divine. God's absence is a necessary, active, condition of his saving mercy, i.e., God's "hiddenness" is the obverse of his "long-suffering" patience with sinners, since being patient with sinners means allowing sin. "One may call it the divine dilemma that God's *Erek Apayim*, his patiently waiting countenance to some, is, of necessity, identical with his *Hester Panim*, his hiding of the countenance, to others" (Berkovits, *Faith*, p. 107). Placed in the still larger mosaic of human purpose *Hester Panim* also is dialectically related to the fundamental character of human freedom without which humans would not be human. (We return in detail to this doctrine below in point 6.) It needs also to be recognized that this notion is an affirmation of faith. The lament addressed to God is a sign that God is and that his manifest presence is still possible. Even more, it declaims that God in his absence is still, paradoxically, present. It is a sign that one believes that ultimately evil will not triumph, for God will not always hide his face. For

some contemporary Jewish theologians, like Emil Fackenheim, Eliezer Berkovits, Yitzchak Greenberg, and Martin Buber, the state of Israel is proof of this.

Martin Buber, in his contemporary idiom, modernized the biblical phrase and spoke of our time during and after the Holocaust as one of "The Eclipse of God" (his 1952 book by that title). Like the believers of old, he too wished, through this felicitous description, to continue to affirm the existence of God despite the counter evidence of Auschwitz. Yet such affirmations stand under two critical judgments. First, it is again an appeal to faith and mystery despite strong evidence to the contrary. Second and related, this gambit still has to answer the pressing question: Where was God in the death camps? Given the moral attributes, the qualities of love and concern that are integral to God's nature, how can we rest in the assertion of his self-willed absence, God's passivity in the face of the murder of a million Jewish children. Thus, this solution only produces a larger metaphysical and moral conundrum.

5. *Mipnei Chataeynu—"Because of our sins we are punished:"* In biblical and later Jewish sources, the principal, though as we have already seen not unique, "explanation" for human suffering was sin. A balance in the universal order was inescapable: good brought forth blessing, sin retribution. Both on the individual and collective level, the law of cause and effect, sin and grief, operated. In our time, it is not surprising that some, particularly traditional, theologians and certain Rabbinic sages have responded to the tragedy of European Jewry with this classical "answer." Harsh as it is, the argument advanced is that Israel sinned "grievously," and God, after much patience and hope of "return," finally "cut off" the generation of the wicked. Though the majority of those who have wrestled with the theological implications of the Shoah have rejected this line of analysis, an important, if small, segment of the religious community has consistently advanced it.

Two questions immediately arise in pursuing the application of this millennial old doctrine to the contemporary tragedy of the

Holocaust. The first is: "What kind of God would exact such retribution?" In all the writings of those who advance this "explanation," no real effort has been made to truly grapple with this shattering concern. Christian thinkers who "explain" Auschwitz as another in the age-old punishments on a rebellious Israel for the crime of deicide, and Jewish thinkers who pronounce on Israel's sinfulness, are obligated to reflect, to be self-conscious, about the implications of such dogmatics for their God-idea. Could a God of love, the God of Israel, use a Hitler, use the SS, to consume the Jewish people in medical experiments without purpose, unbridled sadism, *Einsatzgruppen* "actions," and gas chambers?

Second, of what sin could Israel be guilty to warrant such retribution? Here the explanations vary depending on one's perspective. For some, such as the late Satmar rebbe, Joel Teitelbaum, and his small circle of Hasidic and extreme right wing, anti-Zionist followers, the sin which precipitated the Holocaust was Zionism. In Zionism, the Jewish people broke their covenant with God, which demanded that they not try to end their exile and thereby hasten the coming of messiah through their own means. In return, "we have witnessed the immense manifestation of God's anger (the Holocaust)" (*Sefer VaYoel Moshe*, Brooklyn, 1961, p. 5 [in Hebrew]). For others on the right of the religious spectrum, the primary crime was not Zionism but Reform Judaism. In this view, the centrality of Germany as the land that gave birth both to Reform Judaism and, according to the principle of "measure for measure," to Nazism is undeniable proof of a causal connection.[2]

In a similar, if broader view, others of this theological predisposition identified Jewish assimilation as the root issue. Again, the key role played by Germany is "proof" of the mechanism of cause and effect. Alternatively and interestingly, in these same very traditional orthodox circles, Isaachar Teichtal saw the negative catalyst not in the Jewish people's Zionist activity but just the reverse, in their passionate commitment to life in exile and their failure to willingly, freely, support the sanctified activity of the Zionist upbuilding that would end the exile. In his *Eim Habanim S'mechah*, written in Hungary in 1943, Teichtal, writing under the belief that the twin events of the Holocaust and the growth of the Zionist movement marked the beginning of the messianic era, declaimed: "And these (anti-Zionist leaders) have caused even more lamentation; [and because of their opposition] we have arrived at the situation we are in today . . . this abomination in the house of Israel—endless trouble and sorrow upon sorrow—all because we despised our precious land."[3]

All these "justifications" and "explanations" are both *ad hoc* and of extremely limited plausibility. To accept any one of them, one has first to accept the world view of their authors, idiosyncrasies and all, as in the case of the Satmar rebbe, and even then all appear to be *post hoc* rationalizations of little independent, philosophically coercive force. It is not an accident, nor is it regrettable, that this entire line of blaming the Jewish people for their own destruction has had so few champions.

6. *The burden of human freedom—"The Free Will Defense:"* Among philosophical reflections concerning theodicy, none has an older or more distinguished lineage than that known as the "Free-Will Defense." According to this argument, human evil is the necessary and ever-present possibility entailed by the reality of human freedom. If human beings are to have the potential for majesty, they must, conversely, have an equal potential for corruption; if they are to be capable of acts of authentic morality, they must be capable of acts of authentic immorality. Freedom is a two-edged sword, hence its challenge and its cost. Applying this consideration to the events of the Nazi epoch, the Shoah becomes a case of people's inhumanity to people, the extreme misuse of human freedom. Such a position in no way forces a reconsideration of the cosmological structure in which the anthropological drama unfolds; nor does it call into question God's goodness and solicitude, for it is people, not God, who perpetrate genocide. God observes these events with the unique divine pathos, but, in order

to allow human morality to be substantively real, God refrains from intercession. At the same time, while God is long-suffering with an evil humanity, his patience results in the suffering of others.

If God must absent himself for people to be, God must also be present in order that meaninglessness does not gain final victory. Thus, God's presence in history must be sensed as hiddenness, and God's anonymity must be understood as the sign of his presence. God reveals his power in history by curbing his might so that humans too might be powerful. In this scenario, the only enduring witness to God's ultimate control over the course of things is the Jewish people. In Israel's experience, as Berkovits declares in making this case, one sees both attributes of God. The continued existence of Israel despite its long record of suffering is the strongest single proof that God does exist despite his concealment. Israel is the witness to his accompaniment of happenings in space and time. Nazism, in its luciferian power, understood this fact, and its slaughter of the Jews was an attempt to slaughter the God of history. The Nazis were aware, even as Israel sometimes fails to be, that God's manifest reality in the world is necessarily linked to the fate of the Jewish people.

Given its history and intellectual power, this defense, not surprisingly, has been widely advocated by post-Holocaust thinkers of all shades of theological opinion. The two most notable presentations of the theme in the general theological literature are in Eliezer Berkovits, *Faith After the Holocaust* and Arthur A. Cohen, *The Tremendum*. Berkovits employs it to defend a traditional Jewish theological position, while Cohen utilized it to develop a Jewish "Process-Theology," discussed in detail below.

In trying to estimate the power of the "Free-Will" argument in the face of Auschwitz, two counter-arguments are salient. First, could not God, possessed of omniscience, omnipotence, and absolute goodness, have created a world in which there was human freedom but less, or even no, evil? The sheer gratuitous evil manifest during the Holocaust goes beyond anything that appears logically or metaphysically necessary for the existence of freedom and beyond the bounds of "toleration" for a just, all powerful God. One has to recognize, moreover, that for those committed to a belief in the biblical God, one miracle, even a "small" one, could have reduced the tragedy of the Shoah without canceling the moral autonomy of the murderers. Second, it might be argued that it would be preferable, morally preferable, to have a world in which "evil" did not exist, at least not in the magnitude witnessed during the Shoah, even if this meant doing without certain heroic moral attributes or accomplishments. That is to say, for example, though feeding and caring for the sick or hungry is a great virtue, it would be far better if there were no sickness or hunger and hence no need for such care. The price is just too high. This is true even for the much exalted value of freedom itself. Better to introduce limits, even limits on that freedom of the will requisite to moral choice, than to allow Auschwitz.

Here it is salient to recognize that free will is not, despite a widespread tendency to so understand it, all of one piece. One can limit free will in certain aspects, that is, with respect, for example, to specific types of circumstances, just as one constrains action in particular ways. Consider, too, that God could have created a humankind that, while possessing free will, nonetheless also had a proportionately stronger inclination for good and a correspondingly weaker inclination to evil. God could also have endowed us with a greater capacity for moral education. Neither of these alterations in the scheme of thing would have obviated the reality of free will, though they would have appreciatively improved humankind's moral record, perhaps even to the point of significantly reducing the moral evil done to the innocent by a Hitler. In sum, then, the "Free-Will Defense," while full of theological interest and intellectual attraction, fails to satisfy the theological demands raised by the Holocaust.

Contemporary post-Holocaust thought: The six positions analyzed above are all predicated upon, and extensions of, classical Jewish responses to national tragedy. In the last two decades, by contrast, post-Holocaust thinkers have proposed a number of innovative, more radical responses. Five, in particular, merit serious attention.

1. *Auschwitz—A New Revelation*: The first of these emerges from the work of Emil Fackenheim, who contends that the Holocaust represents a new revelation. Rejecting any account that analyzes Auschwitz as the result of Jews' sin as well as repudiating the literal notion of "explanation" as regards the Holocaust, Fackenheim employs a Buberian-type model of dialogical revelation, of revelation as the personal encounter of an I with the Eternal Thou (God). Thus Fackenheim urges Israel to continue to believe despite the moral outrage of the Shoah. God, on this view, is always present in Jewish history, even at Auschwitz. We do not, and cannot, understand what he was doing at Auschwitz, or why he allowed it, but we must insist that he was there. Still more, from the death camps, as from Sinai, God commands Israel. The nature of this commanding voice, what Fackenheim has called the "614th commandment" (there are 613 commandments in traditional Judaism) is that "Jews are forbidden to hand Hitler posthumous victories;" Jews are, that is, under a sacred obligation to survive. After the death camps, Jewish existence itself is a holy act; Jews are under a sacred obligation to remember their martyrs; Jews are, as Jews, forbidden to despair of redemption, or to become cynical about the world and humanity, for to submit to cynicism is to abdicate responsibility for the world and to deliver the world into the hands of the luciferian forces of Nazism. And, above all, Jews are "forbidden to despair of the God of Israel, lest Judaism perish." The voice that speaks from Auschwitz demands above all that Hitler win no posthumous victories, that no Jew do what Hitler could not do. The Jewish will for survival is natural enough, but Fackenheim invests it with transcendental significance. Precisely because others would eradicate Jews from the earth, Jews are commanded to resist annihilation. Paradoxically, Hitler makes Judaism after Auschwitz a necessity. To say "no" to Hitler is to say "yes" to the God of Sinai; to say "no" to the God of Sinai is to say "yes" to Hitler.

This interesting, highly influential response to the Shoah requires detailed analysis of a sort that is beyond our present possibilities. However, it needs to be stressed that the main line of critical inquiry into Fackenheim's position must center on the dialogical notion of revelation and the related idea of commandment, as that traditional notion is here employed. That is to ask: (a) how do historical events become "revelatory? and (b) what exactly does Fackenheim mean by the term "commandment?" In the older, traditional theological vocabulary of Judaism, it meant something God actually "spoke" to the people of Israel. Fackenheim, however, would reject this literal meaning in line with his dialogical premises. But then what does "commanded" here mean? It would seem that the word has only analogical or metaphorical sense in this case, but, if so, what urgency and compelling power does it retain? Second, is it appropriate that Hitler gains such prominence in Jewish theology, that Judaism survives primarily to spite his dark memory? In raising these issues, we only begin to do justice to the richness and ingenuity of Fackenheim's position.

2. *The covenant broken—A new age*: A second contemporary thinker who has urged continued belief in the God of Israel, though on new terms, is Yitzchak (Irving) Greenberg. For Greenberg, all the old truths and certainties, all the old commitments and obligations, have been destroyed by the Holocaust. Moreover, any simple faith is now impossible. The Holocaust ends the old era of Jewish covenantal existence and ushers in a new and different one. Greenberg explicates this radical notion in this way. There are three major periods in the covenantal history of Israel. The first is the biblical era. What characterizes this first covenantal stage is the a-symmetry of the relationship between God and Israel. The biblical encounter may be a covenant but it is clearly a covenant in which "God is the initiator, the senior partner, who punishes, rewards and enforces the punishment if the Jews slacken."[4] This type of relationship culminated in the crisis engendered

by the destruction of the First Temple in 586 B.C.E. To this tragedy, Israel, through the prophets, in keeping with the "logic" of this position, responded primarily through the doctrine of self-chastisement: the destruction was divine punishment rather than rejection or proof of God's nonexistence.

The second, rabbinical phase in the transformation of the covenant idea is marked by the destruction of the Second Temple. The "meaning" adduced from this event, the reaction of the rabbis, was to argue that now Jews must take a more equal role in the covenant, becoming true-partners with the almighty. The manifest divine presence and activity was being reduced but the covenant was actually being renewed. The destruction of 70 C.E. signaled the initiation of an age in which God would be less manifest though still present.

This brings us to what is decisive and radical in Greenberg's ruminations, what he has termed the "Third Great Cycle in Jewish History," which has come about as a consequence of the Holocaust. The Shoah marks a new era in which the Sinaitic covenantal relationship was shattered; now, if there is to be any covenantal relationship at all, an unprecedented form of it must come into being. "In retrospect, it is now clear that the divine assignment to the Jews was untenable. After the Holocaust, it is obvious that this role opened the Jews to a total murderous fury from which there was no escape.... Morally speaking, then, God can have no claims on the Jews by dint of the Covenant." What this means, Greenberg argues, is that the Covenant, "can no longer be commanded and subject to a serious external enforcement. It cannot be commanded because morally speaking—covenantally speaking—one cannot order another to step forward to die. One can give an order like this to an enemy, but in a moral relationship, I cannot demand giving up one's life. I can ask for it or plead for it— but I cannot order it" (p. 23).

Out of this complex of considerations, Greenberg pronounces the fateful judgment: *The Jewish covenant with God is now voluntary!* Jews have, quite miraculously, chosen to continue to live Jewish lives and collec-

tively to build a Jewish state the ultimate symbol of Jewish continuity, but these acts are, after Auschwitz, the result of the free choice of the Jewish people. "I submit," writes Greenberg, "that the covenant was broken. God was in no position to command anymore but the Jewish people was so in love with the dream of redemption that it volunteered to carry on with its mission" (p. 25). The consequence of this voluntary action transforms the existing convenantal order. First Israel was a junior partner, then an equal partner. Finally, after Auschwitz, it becomes "the senior partner in action."

Israel's voluntary acceptance of the covenant and continued will to survive suggest three corollaries. First, it points, if obliquely, to the continued existence of the God of Israel. By creating the state of Israel, by having Jewish children, Israel shows that "covenantal hope is not in vain." Second, and very important, in an age of voluntarism rather than coercion, living Jewishly under the covenant can no longer be interpreted monolithically, i.e., only in strict halakhic (traditional Rabbinic) fashion. Third, any aspect of religious behavior that demeans the image of the divine or of people, for example, prejudice, sexism, and oppression of all sorts, must be purged.

Greenberg's reconstruction of Jewish theology after the Holocaust presents a fascinating, creative reaction to the unprecedented evil manifest in the death camps. The question of the maintenance of his view, however, turns on the issues of: (a) the correctness of his theological reading of Jewish history, an open and difficult question; and (b) the theological meaning and status of key categories such as "covenant," "revelation," "commandment," and the like. That is to ask, on the one hand, whether Greenberg has done justice to their classical employment, and, second, whether his revised rendering is justifiable and functional; and (c) whether we should allow Hitler and the Holocaust such decisive power in determining the inner, authentic nature of Jewish theology. A careful reading of Greenberg's essays suggests that unresolved problems and internal contradictions remain within this novel deconstruction. These mean that a final judgment regarding Greenberg's proposals awaits future elaboration and reflection.

3. *A redefinition of God*: An important school in modern theological circles known as "Process Theology," inspired by the work of Alfred North Whitehead and Charles Hartshorne, has argued that the classical understanding of God has to be dramatically revised, not least in terms of our conception of God's power and direct, causal, involvement in human affairs. According to those who advance this thesis, God certainly exists, but the old-new difficulties of theodicy and related metaphysical problems emanating from classical theism arise precisely because of an inadequate "description" of the divine, which misascribes to him attributes of omnipotence and omniscience that God does not possess.

Arthur A. Cohen, in his *The Tremendum: A Theological Interpretation of the Holocaust* (New York, 1981), made a related proposal that drew on Schelling, Rosenzweig, and Jewish mysticism, though there is no doubt that he was familiar with the work of the process theologians. After arguing for the enormity of the Holocaust, its uniqueness, and its transcendence of any "meaning," Cohen suggests that the way out of the dilemma posed by classical thought is to rethink whether "national catastrophes are compatible with our traditional notions of a beneficent and providential God" (p. 50). For Cohen, the answer is "no," at least to the degree that the activity and nature of the providential God have to be re-conceptualized. Against the traditional view that asks, given its understanding of God's action in history, "How could it be that God witnessed the Holocaust and remained silent?," Cohen would pose the contrary "dipolar" thesis that, "what is taken as God's speech is really always man's hearing, that God is not the strategist of our particularities or of our historical condition, but rather the mystery of our futurity, always our *posse*, never our acts." That is, "if we begin to see God less as an interferer whose insertion is welcome (when it accords with our needs) and more as the immensity whose reality is our prefiguration . . . we shall have

won a sense of God whom we may love and honor, but whom we no longer fear and from whom we no longer demand" (p. 97). This redescription of God, coupled with a form of the "Free Will Defense," made all the more plausible because God is now not a direct causal agent in human affairs, resolves much of the tension created by the *tremendum*.

The difficulty, however, lies in the price paid for this success. This deconstruction of classical theism and its substitution by theological di-polarity fails to deal adequately with the problem of God's attributes. Is "God" still God if he is no longer the providential agency in history? Is "God" still God if he lacks the power to enter history vertically to perform the miraculous? Is such a "dipolar" God still the God to whom one prays, the God of salvation? Put the other way round, it certainly does not appear to be the God of the covenant, nor again the God of Exodus-Sinai, nor yet again the God of the prophets and the destructions of the First and Second Temples. Now, none of these objections count logically against Cohen's theism *qua* an independent non-Jewish theism, for he is free to speculate as he will. But, alternatively, these counter evidences suggest that Cohen's God is not the God of the Bible and Jewish tradition. Hence it is legitimate to ask whether, if Cohen is right, indeed, particularly if Cohen is right, there is any meaning left to Judaism, to the God-idea of Jewish tradition, and any covenantal role or meaning left to the Jewish people? Cohen's revisionism in this particular area is so radical that it sweeps away the biblical ground of Jewish faith and tradition and allows the biblical evidence to count not at all against his own speculative metaphysical hypotheses.

Secondly, is the dipolar, non-interfering God "whom we no longer fear and from whom we no longer demand" yet worthy of our "love and honor?" This God seems closer, say, to Plato's *Demiurgos* or perhaps better still to the innocuous and irrelevant God of the Deists. Such a God hardly seems to count in how we act or in how history devolves or transpires. What difference in our lives between this God and no God at all? What sense is there, given his non-interference, in calling him a God of love and salvation.

4. *God is dead*: It is natural that many should have responded to the horror of the Holocaust with unbelief. How, they asked quite legitimately, could one continue to believe in God when such a God did nothing to halt the demonic fury of Hitler and his minions. Such skepticism usually takes a non-systematic, almost intuitive, form: "I can no longer believe." However, one contemporary Jewish theologian, Richard Rubenstein, has provided a formally structured "Death of God" theology as a response to the Shoah.

In Rubenstein's view the only honest response to the death camps is the rejection of God, "God is dead," and the open recognition of the meaninglessness of existence. Our life is neither planned nor purposeful, there is no divine will nor does the world reflect divine concern. The world is indifferent to human beings. Humankind must now reject its illusions and recognize the existential truth that life is not intrinsically valuable, that the human condition reflects no transcendental purpose; history reveals no providence. All theological "rationalizations" of Auschwitz pale before its enormity and, for Rubenstein, the only reaction that is worthy is the rejection of the entire Jewish theological framework: there is no God and no covenant with Israel.

Humankind must turn away from transcendental myths and face its actual existential situation. Drawing heavily upon the atheistic existentialists, Rubenstein interprets this to mean that in the face of the world's nihilism, individuals must assert value; in response to history's meaninglessness, human beings must create and project meaning.

Had Rubenstein merely asserted the "death of God," his would not be a Jewish theology. What makes it "Jewish" are the implications he draws from his radical negation with respect to the people of Israel. It might be expected that the denial of God's covenantal relation with Israel would entail the end of Judaism and so the end of the Jewish people. From the perspective of traditional Jewish theology, this would certainly be the case. Rubenstein, however, again inverts our ordinary perception and argues that with the "death of God," the existence of "peoplehood," of the community of Israel, is all the more important. Now that there is nowhere else to turn for meaning, Jews need each other all the more to create meaning: "it is precisely because human existence is tragic, ultimately hopeless, and without meaning that we treasure our religious community" (*After Auschwitz*, Indianapolis, 1966, p. 68). Though Judaism has to be "demythologized"—has to renounce all normative claims to a unique "chosen" status—in the process, it paradoxically gains heightened importance.

Coupled, in Rubenstein's ontology, to this psychoanalytic revisionism is a mystical paganism in which the Jew is urged to forgo history and return to the cosmic rhythms of natural existence, to recognize the priorities of nature. So, for example, Jews must come to understand that the real meaning of messianism is "the proclamation of the end of history and return to nature and nature's cyclical repetitiveness" (*After Auschwitz*, p. 135). The future and final redemption is not to be the conquest of nature by history, as traditionally conceived in the Jewish tradition, but rather the conquest of history by nature and the return of all things to their primal origins. Humanity must rediscover the sanctity of bodily life and reject forever the delusions of overcoming it; people must submit to and enjoy their physicality—not try to transform or transcend it. Rubenstein sees the renewal of Zion and the rebuilding of the land, with its return to the soil, as a harbinger of this return to nature on the part of the Jew who, for almost two thousand years, has been removed from the earth (symbolic of nature) by theology and necessity. The return to the land points toward the final escape of the Jew from the negativity of history to the vitality and promise of self-liberation through nature.

Rubenstein's challenging position raises many pressing, fundamental issues, but two especially take us to the heart of the matter. The first has to do with how one evaluates Jewish history as "evidence" for and against the existence of God. It may well be that the radical theologian sees Jewish history too narrowly, as focused solely in and through the Holocaust. He takes *the* decisive event of Jewish history to be the death camps. But this is a distorted image at least to the degree that there was a pre-Holocaust and is a post-Holocaust Jewish history that includes, among other things, the reborn state of Israel. Logic and conceptual adequacy require that if we give (negative) theological weight to Auschwitz, we give (positive) theological weight to the recreation of the Jewish state, an event of equal or greater valence in Jewish history. Second, again an issue raised by the question of "evidence," is the adoption by Rubenstein of the philosophically unsatisfactory "empiricist theory of meaning" as the measure by which to judge the status of God's existence. This basic premise of his argument will not, however, satisfy, for ultimately not only is the theory itself logically deficient, but history, in its totality, provides evidence both for and against the non-existence of God on empirical-verifications grounds, since there is both good and bad in history. In sum, Rubenstein's criteria are less than convincing. His work, while highly provocative in the best sense, is not yet theologically definitive.

5. *Silence*: In the face of the abyss, the devouring of Israel by the dark forces of evil incarnate, recourse to human silence is not an unworthy option. However, there are two kinds of silence. The first is closer to the attitude of the agnostic: "I cannot know," and hence all profound existential and intellectual wrestling with the enormous problems raised by the Shoah, and with God after the Shoah, are avoided. The second is the silence and mystery that Job and many of the prophets reveal, to which the Bible points in its recognition of God's elemental otherness. This is the silence that comes after struggling with God, after reproaching God, after feeling God's closeness or painful absence. This silence, this mystery, is the silence and mystery of seriousness, of that authenticity that will not diminish the tragedy by a too-quick, too-gauche, answer, yet which, having forced reason to its limits, recognizes the limits of reason. Had Abraham accepted God's judgment at Sodom too quickly or Job his suffering in a too easy silence, they would have betrayed the majesty and morality of the God in whom they trusted. In the literary responses to Auschwitz by survivors, one finds this attitude more commonly expressed than in more formal works of overt theology. For example, it is pre-eminent in the novels of Elie Wiesel, Andre Schwarzbart, and Primo Levi and in the poetry of Nellie Sachs. Assuredly, there is great difficulty in ascertaining when thought has reached its limit and silence becomes proper, but, at the same time, there is the need to know when to speak in silence.

Yet silence, too, can be problematic for, ultimately, if employed incorrectly as a theological move, it removes the Holocaust from history and all post-Holocaust human experience and thus may produce the unintended consequence of making the Holocaust irrelevant. If the generations that come after Auschwitz cannot speak of it, and thus cannot raises deep questions as a consequence of it, then it becomes literally meaningless to them.

The appeal to mystery: There are two additional elemental matters that need to be addressed, however briefly. The first is what might fairly be called the "appeal to mystery" in thinking about, and responding to, the Shoah. This appeal takes several forms, all of which are intellectually unconvincing and problematic.

First, there is linguistic mystification according to which the Shoah is said to transcend all language. If any event X is described as being mysterious or a mystery in this absolute sense, that is, in the strict form that "for X no predicates apply," then X effectively drops out of our language and with its departure any coherent discussion of, or reference to, X becomes logically impossible. Entailed in such a self-sacrificing logical scenario is the elimination of the notion of mystery itself, for what is incomprehensible—that X to which no predicates apply—cannot be said to be mysterious or a mystery. The incomprehensible, the unintelligible, is not a mystery, it is merely incomprehensible and unintelligible.

Second, the metaphysical mystification of the Shoah must be rejected. For this reason, one must oppose, for example, the language (and approach) employed by the Eckardts, who draw an analogy between the Shoah and religious experience as such experience is described by Rudolf Otto. They write:

> The response that finds in the Holocaust a transcendent, crushing mystery incarnates the dimension of the numinous, as described by Rudolf Otto in *Das heilige*. The mental state called the numinous by Otto presents itself as *ganz andere*, wholly other, a condition absolutely *sui generis* and incomparable whereby the human being finds himself utterly abashed. There is a feeling of terror before an awe-inspiring mystery, but a mystery that also fascinates infinitely.[5]

But this is to confuse the issue, not clarify it. It must be shown, not merely asserted, that the Shoah is, in the mystical sense, *ganz andere*, and this, despite their well-intentioned efforts, the Eckardts have not been able to do. And they have not been able to do it because the assumed analogy between the Shoah and God, the *ganz andere*, is wholly misconceived. Whatever else the Holocaust is or is not, it is not beyond space-time, nor does it stand in the same oblique relation to the categories of human understanding and meaning as does the *Eyn Sof* ("The Ineffable One") of the mystics.

The Shoah is not an ontological reality that is necessarily (i.e., logically or metaphysically) incomprehensible, except when it is so defined, as it often is. But creating incomprehensibility by stipulation does not make for a convincing philosophical argument. This is not to claim that anyone who was not there can "know" the Shoah like those who were, but this salient epistemological disparity obtains with regard to all historical experiences—indeed, it is inherent in the difference between first- and third-person experience as such. The epistemic dilemma is, of course, made far more complex in its actuality when we are dealing with a multi-dimensional, many-person event like the Shoah. But the philosophical problem of how can we know that past of which we were not a part is in no way unique to the experience of the Shoah.

Third, one should reject the psychological mystification of the Shoah, according to which the Holocaust is said to be irrational *per se* and therefore beyond discussion and analysis—except by psychoanalysts or psychohistories—and beyond morality "by virtue of insanity."

Whatever the real contribution of the irrational, the pathological, and the insane to the murder of European Jewry, these psychological elements have to be placed within the larger, encompassing, metaphysical, historical, and sociopolitical context of the event itself, lest the Holocaust be understood as little more than a Rorschach test. In so contextualizing the psychological, one comes to recognize that Nazism had a logic of its own, its own way of organizing the world, so that, once its premises were accepted—most especially its racial theory—its program became "reasonable," however evil on alternative moral and ontological criteria. This is to acknowledge that racial theory, *per se*, is not inherently irrational, even if it is false and even though its fallacious imperatives led to genocidal enactment. Similarly, Nazism's romantic embrace of *volkisch* "feeling" is not deranged but rather a rational, if unacceptable, theory of what is fundamental, decisive, in individual and group behavior. One may disagree with or despair at this conclusion, but it does not violate any canon of reason as such.

Fourth, one must reject the historiographical mystification of the Shoah according to which the confused and erroneous claim is made that because we cannot know everything about this event and because we cannot know it like those who lived it knew it, we can know nothing at all about it. Post-Holocaust scholars can, despite their indirect relationship to the horrors, know about the Shoah even while acknowledging the real epistemological and existential limits and difficulties involved in their ability to know. Conversely, given their distance from the event, such observers may actually be at an advantage, at least as regards certain non-existential types of historical and philosophical knowledge.

A similar, acute epistemic sensitivity helps illuminate the analysis of the search for causes in regard to the Shoah. Insofar as there were undoubtedly multiple causes at work in creating the Shoah, their complete specification is difficult, in practice even impossible. However, this fact does not justify the argument that because we can supply only a partial and incomplete causal explanation, we should resist offering any causal explanation whatsoever. The often-made presumption underpinning this false contention that causal explanations must be complete explanations is merely a prejudice. If we can offer partial and incremental explanations that cumulatively build a progressively clearer account of the Holocaust, we should not on the grounds of some dubious *a priori* principle reject these explanations or this approach to explanations.

The "uniqueness" of the Shoah: The last item to be briefly explored is the "uniqueness" of the Holocaust. This issue, as already indicated, has played a considerable role in the theological debate concerning the implications of the destruction of European Jewry. Here two different matters arise. First is the historical-philosophical question: Is the Holocaust unique? Second is the related, but separate, question: If the Holocaust is unique, what theological implications does this have. To answer the first question—"Is the Holocaust unique?"—we have, of necessity, to specify in what particular sense we are using the notions "unique" and "uniqueness." That is, we have to delineate the conditions of "unique" and "uniqueness"—H is unique in respect of conditions A, B, C, . . . X.

I would argue that the individuating criteria conditions A, B, C, . . . X should not include moral or transcendental criteria. Instead, I propose that the criteria be phenomenological. And on such criteria I would argue that: "The Holocaust is phenomenologically unique by virtue of the fact that never before has a state set out, as a matter of intentional principle and actualized policy, to annihilate physically every man, woman, and child belonging to a specific people." This entails that the Holocaust would not be the Holocaust if the property of "intentionally pursuing the physical annihilation of a people without remainder" were not present. Other occasions of mass death that lack this nec-

essary intentionality are not comparable to the Holocaust, at least as regards this property. Certainly a *full* description of the Holocaust would include consideration of such elements as technology, bureaucracy, dehumanization, and the like. But the presence of these complementary phenomena without the property of genocidal intentionality would not, in my view, be sufficient to establish either the character of the Shoah as such or, in particular, its uniqueness.

Now, proceeding on the basis of the claim that the Holocaust is phenomenologically unique, we turn to our second inter-related query: does this matter theologically. As I understand the many issues involved in answering this question, and as I have defined the concept of "uniqueness," it is not at all clear to me that there is a direct, and preferred, theological meaning to be drawn from the exceptionality of this event. In dealing with—or not dealing with—the multiple epistemological and metaphysical issues that are here relevant, both the theological radicals and the theological conservatives have all run ahead of the available evidence and the extant philosophical-theological argumentation to posit conclusions that are neither epistemologically nor intellectually persuasive. Neither Rubenstein's endorsement of the "death of God" nor the Lubavitcher Rebbe's conservative kabbalistic pronouncements on the Shoah as a *tikkun* flow necessarily from the event itself. Both these and other denominational expositions are premature and inconclusive. They represent, in essence, *a priori* impositions: explanations extrinsic to the death camps grounded in deeply held prior theological positions.

Any theological position, at present, is compatible with the singularity of the Shoah. Religious conservatives who intuitively reject the uniqueness of the Holocaust on the usually implicit grounds that such an unequivocal conclusion would *necessarily* entail ominous alterations in the inherited normative *Weltanschauung* are simply mistaken. That is, one can without self-contradiction adopt an unexceptional conservative theological posture (either Jewish or Christian) while accepting the discrete contention that the destruction of European Jewry was a historical *novum*, given the disciplined understanding of the concept of a historical *novum* that has been proposed above. Conversely, the theological radicals who hold that the singularity of the Shoah necessarily entails religious transformations, and within Jewish parameters halakhic changes, have not shown this to be the case. They have merely assumed it to be so, positing the "required changes" they take to be obligatory without providing either halakhic or philosophical justification for such innovations. It may be that one or the other of these alternative positions is true, but so far none has made a convincing case for itself.

As is evident, then, the death camps and *Einsatzgruppen* do challenge traditional Jewish theological claims. However, just what this challenge entails and what it ultimately may mean—despite all the serious work done in this area—remains yet to be seen.

Bibliography

Katz, Steven T., *Post-Holocaust Dialogues: Critical Studies in Modern Jewish Thought* (New York, 1983).

Katz, Steven T., *Historicism, the Holocaust and Zionism* (New York, 1992).

Katz, Steven T., *The Holocaust in Historical Context* (vol. 1: New York, 1994).

Notes

[1] See Shalom Spiegel, *The Last Trial* (New York, 1967) and the medieval religious poems collected in A.M. Habermann, *Sefer Gezerot Ashkenaz VeTzarfat* (Jerusalem, 1945).

[2] For the presentation of this position, see Elhanan Wasserman, *In the Footsteps of the Messiah* (Tel Aviv, 1942), p. 6 [in Hebrew]; Haim Ozer Grodzinsky, *Ahiezer* (Vilna, 1939) [in Hebrew]; and Jacob Israel Kanyevsky, *Hayyai Olam* (Rishon Le Zion, 1972) [in Hebrew].

[3] *Eim Habanim S'mechah* (Budapest, 1942), p. 17 [in Hebrew].

[4] Irving Greenberg, *Third Great Cycle of Jewish History* (New York, 1981), p. 6.

[5] A. and R. Eckardt, "The Holocaust and the Enigma of Uniqueness," *Annals of the American Academy of Political and Social Science* 45 [July 1980], p. 169.

STEVEN T. KATZ

HOLOCAUST, THE PRACTICE OF JUDAISM DURING: Since the end of WWII, the Holocaust's unprecedented levels of murder and destruction have challenged, and, for some, destroyed, traditional belief in a caring and providential God. But what of those Jews who lived, and died, in the period of the Nazi atrocities? In what ways and to what ends did they continue to maintain Jewish belief and to lead Jewish lives? The following analysis of the practice of Judaism in the ghettos and camps shows that, even as the faith of many of the Nazis' victims was challenged, large numbers continued through their religious practice and belief to order and make sense of their lives. Retention of the ideals of Judaism and maintenance at whatever level was possible of the structure of Jewish life—an educational system, worship services, study of Torah—helped Jews keep their human dignity and benefit from as much of a sense of normalcy as was possible. In the most difficult of circumstance, Jews who had practiced Judaism continued to do so, holding firm to the idea of their special place in God's eyes and to the certainty that a better future would come. Their practice and faith provided comfort, some sense of normalcy, and the assurance that, somehow, their suffering would be requited.

The Nazi period represents the most horrific era in the nearly four thousand year history of the Jewish people. It started on January 30, 1933, when President Paul von Hindenberg appointed Adolph Hitler Reich Chancellor of Germany's NSDAP (National Sozialistische Deutsche Arbeiterpartei). On March 23, 1933, the first concentration camp, Dachau, was established, and in subsequent months racial anti-Jewish legislation was passed and the Gestapo (Secret State Police) was formed. By December 11, 1933, Hitler declared the legal unity of the German state and the NSDAP. This ushered in more aggressive propaganda, legislative acts, and street assaults against the Jews, highlighted on November 9-10, 1938, by the infamous *Reichspogromnacht* (generally known as *Kristallnacht*, "Night of the Broken Glass"), an organized pogrom against the Jews in Germany and Austria.

Six years to the day from when he was appointed *Reichskanzler*, Hitler declared in the *Reichstag* that the millennial age of a new world order would lead to a Europe cleansed of Jews (*Judenrein*). Mass killing of Jews began on June 22, 1941, following the German invasion of the Soviet Union, and Hitler's obscene goal was made manifest by Heinrich Himmler when, in November, 1941, he ordered the liquidation of the Riga Ghetto in Latvia, stating, "It is my order and also the Führer's wish." On January 20, 1942, the Wannsee Conference was convened by Reinhard Heidrich and prepared by Adolph Eichmann, head of the Jewish section of the Gestapo and in charge of transporting the Jews of Europe to their final destruction. At this meeting methodical and systematic plans were drawn for implementing "der Führers Wunch." An estimated six million Jewish men, women, and children from more than ten thousand communities were brutally murdered in the "Final Solution," two thirds of the Jews of Europe, whose sole crime was to be Jews.

In the second half of the twentieth century, in successive waves of analysis, advances in understanding the causes and effects of the Shoah have been dramatic and widely chronicled. The first wave of analysis recounted the horror of the Nazi treatment of Europe's Jews in the historical context of deeply rooted prejudices and antisemitism. Also documented, primarily from German sources and war crime trials (e.g., the International Military Tribunal at Nuremberg), was the technologically of mass death administered in twelve years of Nazi *Aktionen* against the Jews and other minorities and the effect on the victims. Then came the indictment of the German and Austrian nations, the Church leadership, the French, English, and Soviet governments, and the entire free world for their lack of intent and will to combat the Nazi death machine.

Additionally, scholars have asked how much Eastern European Jewry, the main victim of Nazism, contributed to its own demise. Conclusions reached by Bruno Bettelheim (*The Informed Heart*, 1960), Raul Hilberg (*The Destruction of the European Jews*, 1961), and Hannah Arendt (*Eichmann in Jerusalem*, 1963) are critical of the Jewish leadership and the masses who did not revolt against the Nazi evil. Others refute this stern judgment, referring to the increasing number of Jewish documents that describe exemplary Jewish resistance under the most dire circumstances. These newly available sources compensate for the limited documentation available to Bettelheim, the predominantly German sources used by Hilberg, and the largely theoretical reconstruction promoted by Arendt.

The next phase in the study of the Holocaust has augmented the previous questions of history, political science, and sociology by raising questions of psychology, philosophy, and literature. Particularly imaginative have been the recent theological questions: What about God? Where was the God of promises when millions of the innocent went up in smoke? What is human and divine responsibility after Auschwitz? Recent trends in research, methodology, and interpretation thus have added new issues and challenged all past statements on the Shoah.

Leaving aside the questions of the roots of the Holocaust and its implications for life today, the present discussion focuses upon the experience of the Nazis' victims during the Holocaust itself. How did Jews in the ghettos and camps maintain and, in some cases, create anew Jewish rituals and elements of Jewish theological belief? We ask, that is, how Jews—religious and secular, assimilated and traditional, rich and poor—actually practiced their religion during the Holocaust, questioning the ways in which Judaism offered them spiritual sustenance in a period of ubiquitous physical starvation, torture, and death. Before turning to these issues, however, let us briefly discuss what it is in fact possible to know and how we are to discover it.

Holocaust historiography: A central issue for all Holocaust research concerns the reliability of the historical evidence. What is *Historie*, controlled objective facts, and what is *Geschichte*, beyond the historical but connected to it by emotive factors?

This issue is clearly illustrated by the example of the role played by Rabbi Arye Leib Langfus, a judge in the Jewish religious court of Makow-Mazowieck and author of a diary buried near the crematoria in Auschwitz and published after the war. As a matter of history, Langfus was killed by the Germans on October 10, 1944, a few days after the ill-fated Sonderkommando uprising in Auschwitz II (Birkenau). The *Geschichte*, however, relates another viewpoint, that, with explosives attached to his body, Rabbi Langfus went into the crematoria III-IV area and blew up the building, killing himself in the explosion. Did this really happen or is it only a heroic myth, a possibility given weight by doubts that an Orthodox rabbi knowingly and willingly would have committed suicide on the Sabbath (October 7, 1944).

Even if one separates successfully what Lucy S. Dawidowicz calls "the documentary wheat from the epistaphic chaff" (*The War Against the Jews*, 1975), the basic value of the latter remains. Dawidowicz maintains that the most widespread example of historical falsification in Holocaust history is the story of the ninety-three Beit Ya'akob maidens who chose mass suicide over the degradation of a German brothel. Their alleged last will and testament is a letter in their name written by their teacher, Chaya Feldman, one of the suicides, which states a religious affirmation, "It is good to live for God, but it is also good to die for Him," and ends with a request, "Say Kaddish for us, your ninety-three children."

The question of the authenticity and accuracy of Chaya Feldman's epistle, as of the story of Rabbi Langfus, is not the only issue; what is significant is the contribution made by such simple and sublime thoughts to the "faith knowledge" of the sanctification of God's name. In evaluating the practice of Judaism during the Holocaust, that is, we must examine not only what happened but what people perceived to have happened or believed to have been possible and appropriate.

To do this, we must be cognizant of the many primary documents—particularly, responsa literature and protocols from *Judenrat* meetings—and varied secondary sources—diaries, letters, journalistic accounts, and eye-witness documentation—that depict religious conditions and ideology. Exemplifying this literature are Emanuel Ringelblum, *Notes from the Warsaw Ghetto* (1958), Chaim A. Kaplan, *A Scroll of Agony* (1964, reprinted as *The Warsaw Diary of Chaim A. Kaplan* [1973]), and Simon Huberband, *Kiddush ha-Shem: Kitavim mi-yome ha-Shoah* (1969). In these books we learn that the hideous plot of the Nazi regime to obliterate all remnant and meaning of European Jewry was met by a resounding Jewish urge to affirm life, maintain Jewish pride, and preserve the Jewish people. Consider two diary entries of Warsaw Hebrew teacher and educator, Chaim A. Kaplan:

> The enemy of the Jews attested long ago that if war broke out, Jews would be eliminated from Europe. Now half of the Jewish people are under his domain. Why has God embittered our lives so cruelly? Have we indeed sinned more than any other nation? We are more disgraced that any other people (September 10, 1939).
>
> The Nazis have condemned the entire Polish Jewish community to death by one means or another, but I am certain that "the eternity of Israel" will not be destroyed (November 11, 1941).

A plethora of raw material on the theme of survival—in some views to be achieved at any cost; in others, only with dignity—appears in the prolific *Yizkor* ("remembrance") literature in Yiddish and Hebrew, in documents and minutes from prewar *Kehillot* ("communities") and war time *Judenraete*, and in the multiple references, casual remarks, subjective appraisals, and partisan arguments devoted to and stemming from individual communities of that era. Though Holocaust historians attempt to separate fact from memoristic "fiction," the effort, I emphasize, is neither totally successful nor desirable. Why so? The mass of material and memories from each corner of Hitler's inferno, unleashing an unlimited stream of fears and feelings, appears so detailed, parochial, and incomprehensible that no scientific, comprehensive research on this topic has been or perhaps can be attempted.

Terminology: Along with questions about the historical accuracy of the sources, examination of the practice of Judaism during the Third Reich is stymied by the range of possible meanings of the terminology that applies to this event. As the following examples illustrate, caution is in order regarding the meaning of all words, phrases, and terms.

Today the term *Judenrat* is routinely used to refer to all forms of Jewish councils set in place by the Nazi occupying forces to deceive Jews with a false sense of internal autonomy and to prepare the way for the Final Solution. But this single, post-World War II term does not accurately capture the different organizational forms and agendas of Jewish "self-government" in the Nazi regime. For example, the *Reichsvertretung* of the Jews of Germany, inspired by the *Schnellbrief* of Reinhold Heydrich (September 29, 1939), was not a representative council but an appointed body with a leadership, and its internal function differed from the OGIF (France), the Center of Jewish Communities (upper Silesia), the Jewish Central Body (Romanian), and other *Altestenrat*.

Similarly, for the unknowing, the word *Yiddishkeit* is synonymous with an observant lifestyle of worldliness and other-worldliness among East European Jews. But *Yiddishkeit* properly refers to the cultural aura of Yiddish language and literature (*mama-loshen*) that understands well the significance of dispersion and therefore yearns for a rejuvenation of Jewish life to make it better. *Yiddishkeit* was the ethos and pathos in Central and especially Eastern Europe. In the words of Irving Howe, "Theirs was a community and a society: internally a community, a spiritual kingdom; and externally a society in peril, a society on the margin." Shielded by the way of Torah and the world of the *shtetl*, Eastern European Jewish communities withstood the inroads of westernization and the internal signs of stagnation, only to be destroyed beginning in 1939 by the forces of evil from without.

Another problem is what to call the Nazi genocide. The terms normally used, "Holocaust," "Hurban," and "Shoah," are neither etymologically, historically, nor culturally the same. "Holocaust" primarily means "something wholly burnt up," but its contemporary use to signify "total destruction" is largely misleading. From the Greek *'olokaustos* via the Latin *Holocaustum*, pre-Nazi period dictionaries use the word "holocaust" simply to translate the Hebrew term *olah*, that is, a whole-burnt offering (e.g., 1 Sam 7:9). The use of this specifically religious term for the annihilation of European Jews is objectionable insofar as it seemingly designates the Nazi murderers as priestly officiants engaged in acts of divine propitiation.

Most Yiddish speaking victims and survivors refer to the Nazi period as the *Hurban*, a Rabbinic term describing the destruction of the First Temple in 586 B.C.E. and the Second in 70 C.E., or simply as *die milhomeh yohrn* ("the war years"). But neither do these terms seem particularly appropriate to the Nazi genocide. The former is associated with other national calamities, thus failing to reflect the category-shattering character of the German Judeocide. The latter is simply a Yiddish reference to the second World War, hardly a fitting designation for the murder of six million at all.

Unlike the theologically associated terms *Holocaust* and *Hurban* and the non-emotional designation *die milhomeh yohrn*, the biblical Hebrew word *Shoah* refers to devastation and catastrophe that effect man, nature, and land in categories more of history than religion. First used in the booklet *Shoat Yehudei Polin* ("Devastation of Polish Jewry," Jerusalem, 1940), the word today is widely used in academic and ecclesiastical circles and is becoming more recognized in popular usage.

A final term that must be understood is *Kiddush ha-Shem*, "sanctification of God's name," referring to the noblest possible expression of service to the people Israel, represented in the martyr's death. In the Psalms, "The keeper of Israel that neither slumbers nor sleeps" (Ps 121:4) is implored to save Israel, and, by so doing, to "give glory unto thy name" (Ps 115:1). This view focuses on the idea that God is inseparably linked with the destiny of Israel and that, in the face of unremitting tragedy, when many nameless sanctify God's name, God is besieged with prayers to manifest the divine name—holiness, righteousness, mercy—by demonstrating the power to save the chosen people before all the nations.

With the shift from pre-modern to modern Jewish thinking, the function and underpinnings of "the sanctification of God's name" were dramatically altered. For the traditional Jew, martyrdom may be a consequence of the inherited religious values of passivism, pietism, and quietism, which open the door wide for Jewish powerlessness and helplessness in the face of destruction. For the modern ethnic, political, and secular Jew, by contrast, martyrdom is valued not primarily as the result of submission to the "yoke of heaven" but as the consequence of a human fist held firm against heavenly and earthly decrees. Thus the inherited ideal of *kiddush ha-shem* reverberates in, even as it is transformed by, the proclamation of the Zionist and Bundist youth of the ghettos of Poland, Galicia, Lithuania, Belorussia, and elsewhere: "Avenge the death of the saintly martyrs and be not sheep for the slaughter (Ps 44:23) but fighters of honor."

Theology and practice: The pre-war Jewish communities of Central, Northern, and Eastern Europe observed the Sabbath and festivals in accordance with ritual law and local custom. This was to change despairingly at the start of World War II, when German occupation authorities decreed Jews to be a race, replaced the cultural and religious concept of the community (*kehillah*) with a national, racial, and political idea (*Judenraete*), and compelled Jews to work on the Sabbath and holidays. Thus, in September, 1940, in Cracow and Lublin, under the threat of severe penalties from the authorities, the *Judenraete* issued calls for all Jews to work on New Year (Rosh ha-Shanah) and the Day of Atonement (Yom Kippur) and warned against arbitrarily leaving work on either of these High Holiday. Similarly, in 1939, the Lodz authorities had compelled the opening of all Jewish stores and offices on the Day of Atonement, but during the High Holidays in 1940 and 1941 announced instead that these days and the Sabbath were again to be deemed days of rest. Later, on January 29, 1943, Sunday was declared the official day of rest in the ghetto, a proclamation that was not too strictly observed by the large population of religious Jewry.

In general, the Nazis exploited Jewish festival and religious practices to increase the Jews' feelings of demoralization. For instance, on Tabernacles (Sukkot), September 29, 1939, German forces triumphantly entered Warsaw, home to 375,000 Jews (29.1 percent of the total population). Two weeks before, on New Year, Chaim A. Kaplan had written in his diary: "Yesterday was a day of horror and destruction. Between five o'clock and seven o'clock on the eve of Rosh ha-Shanah there was an air raid on the North Quarter, which is predominantly Jewish." On the eve of the Day of Atonement, September 22, 1939, Adam Czerniakow, who, on December 4, 1939, would be appointed chairman of the Warsaw Judenrat, recorded in his journal: "Today is the Day of Atonement, truly the day of judgment. All night long the guns were shelling the city."

In January, 1940, under the pretext that they housed large numbers of refugees and were a breeding grounds for diseases, the authorities shut down all the synagogues and public places of religious gathering, including ritual baths. When, in mid-November, 1940, the Jewish ghetto of Warsaw was formally sealed off from the rest of the city by a high wall, the *Judenrat* petitioned the authorities to declare the Sabbath as a day of rest, since all contacts with the Aryan-Christian part of the city had been severed. The general government agreed, and, on March 4, 1941, Jews were granted permission to recognize as days of rest and public and private prayer the Sabbath, Passover, Pentecost, New Year, and the Day of Atonement.

Based on this decision, three synagogues, including the "Great Synagogue" on Tlomackie Street, were able to open for Pentecost services, June 1, 1941. Nonetheless many Jews avoided public gatherings for fear of visits from sadistic S.S. personnel, who delighted in mocking the appearance and behavior of religious Jews, or from concerns about being snatched to compulsory labor details. The preferred place of worship for the approximately one third of Poland's Jews who maintained an overtly religious lifestyle was the *shtibl* (private conventicle, usually Hasidic) or private home.

The following tales of three cities are different, but the outcomes are the same. Illustrative of what happened in occupied areas outside of Poland, on the holiest day of the year, the Day of Atonement, September 4, 1942, the *Äetestenrat* of Siauliai, a city in northern Lithuania, summoned Jewish laborers to work. Once a burgeoning Jewish community that supported institutions of talmudic study, Hebrew schools, synagogues, and libraries, Siauliai was at the start of World War II in dismay: a few hundred fled to Russia and several thousands were murdered by the Germans and Lithuanians; about 5000 were restricted to the ghetto, and, by January, 1944, those who managed to survive these *Aktionen* were sent to the concentration camps Stuttgard and Dachau to die.

Riga, in Latvia, fell under German occupation on July 1, 1941. At the end of 1941/beginning of 1942, Jewish deportees from Germany, Austria, and Czechoslovakia were interned in a designated area of the Riga ghetto. Under the supervision of their own *Judenraete*, they were permitted public synagogue services on the Sabbath and holidays. This was denied to the local Jews, who worshipped in private conventicles. *Aktionen* by the Einsatzgruppen, aided by Latvian fascists, murdered in three years' activity about eighty percent of the local Jewish population. By the summer of 1944, the Riga ghetto was no longer.

Finally, in the district of Galicia, German government authority prohibited public worship. Services were driven underground, normally at the price of one's life if discovered. When a *shtibl* in Lvov, captured by the Germans in July, 1941, at the outbreak of the German-Soviet war, was disclosed by an informant, all worshippers were taken to prison, never to return. By September, 1943, major *Aktionen* (November, 1942, January and June, 1943) obliterated what had been at the beginning of World War II the 150,000 person Jewish population of Lvov and the environs.

Education: Despite slight differences from one area to another, during the nineteenth and early twentieth centuries, the stages of education within the religious life of Ashkenazic Jewry were essentially the same across the *shtetl* world of Eastern Europe. In the province of Lublin (East Poland), for example, the child's life became bound up with the school house (*heyder*) from the day of his birth. *Shir ha-ma'alot* ("Song of Ascent") amulets were posted in the room of the child's birth, and school children after class came to the home of the newborn and sang the *Shema*. At three years of age, a boy was wrapped in a prayer shawl, serving as a symbol of the Lord's curving of Mt. Sinai over the children of Israel when they received of Torah, and brought to *heyder*. The first Hebrew expression taught to him was *shadai 'emet*—"The Lord is truth" (fig. 53).

In Suisloch, in Grodono, Belorussian S.S.R., a child of five years old was sent to *heyder*, usually in the teacher's home, where he was taught the Hebrew-Yiddish alphabet and reading. A communal Talmud Torah was available for students whose households could not pay full tuition. At six years the child studied Torah and, after the initial introduction, was taught every week the first section of the weekly Torah portion in a word-by-word translation. In addition, the children were taught prayers, holidays of the year, customs, folkways, traditions, and blessing for various occasions.

The last stage of Torah study in elementary school was the study of Rashi's commentary on the Pentateuch, and, before Bar Mitzvah age, the beginning of Talmud study. Additionally, between twelve and fourteen, a number of diligent students left home for the yeshivas—the talmudic academies—to continue with advanced study in the sacred literature. The education of girls began later than boys, at about seven or eight years old, and centered on the mechanics of reading and writing. Afterwards, they would study the *tsene urene* with a women teacher.[1] At adolescence, many entered apprenticeships to seamstresses, and some worked in their parents' shops. After World War I and until 1939, a network of Yiddish and Hebrew schools largely replaced the old-fashioned *heyders*.

German forces invaded Poland on the day of the beginning of the academic year, 1939-

1940, and the schools did not open. In Warsaw the occupying army reduced public education to the training of workers, artisans, and farmers for the benefit of Germany. Secondary and higher education were forbidden, and all Jewish schools at every level were explicitly shut down. Within CENTOS (Federation of Associations for the Care of Orphans in Poland), unemployed teachers managed an unofficial program of daily education for thousands of youngsters.

In 1940-1941, the *Judenrat* petitioned local authorities to open elementary schools, but permission was initially denied on grounds of "the danger of typhus epidemic." In April, 1941, permission was granted, and the *Judenrat* set up a school system comprised of religious (Beit Ya'akob, Horev, Yavne) and secular (Tsysho, Tarbut, Shulkolt) schools, which instructed about 10,000 children of primary schools age. Prohibited secondary education was conducted in small contingents of six to twenty students meeting clandestinely in private homes of students or teachers. Instruction in Yiddish, Hebrew, or Polish followed the former state education code and was altered to fit the ideological philosophy of different Jewish groups, including, alongside the traditionalists, the religious Zionists (Mizrahi) and the socialist Zionists (ha-Shomer ha-Tsair). In time, authorities granted permission to teach specialized subjects (pharmaceuticals, nursing, medicine) and practical skills (gardening, farming, trades) to provide the labor of necessity and normalcy in the ghetto. In reality, of course, this provided a service to the Hitler's armies, since carpenters, locksmiths, and seamstresses, for instance, were part of the ghetto industry that furnished the compulsory Jewish labor force.

In October and November, 1941, the *Judenrat* in Bialystock in Northeastern Poland opened two schools: a secularist school for some 1600 students, divided into three shifts of thirty-nine classrooms of students in grades one and two, and a religious school for 500 pupils, with separate classes for boys and girls. By the second school year, in November 1942, the Gestapo and S.S. were in control, and all school activity came to a halt. The final liquidation occurred in August, 1943. A similar fate characterized other ghetto schools: Zamoss, Lvov, Zydowska, Rzeszow, Cracow, Gorlice, Miedzyrzee, Jaslo, etc.

The *Judenraete* that sponsored the educational committees that supervised the schools all faced more or less identical problems: delays by the authorities, whose permission was required to open classes; difficulty in finding qualified teachers and procuring suitable accommodations; reaching agreement on a common language of instruction; lack of textbooks; problems with weather and health; and the need to approve a Jewish religious studies curriculum. Still, in imposing a Jewish agenda, the *Judenraete* in the large ghettos of Lodz in central Poland and Vilna in Lithuania met less than usual interference from the authorities. As a result, in Lodz, there were forty-five elementary schools, two gymnasiums, a vocational school, and lyceum classes. All these contributed to a rich program of Jewish studies, with Yiddish as the language of instruction. In the Vilna ghetto, gymnasium classes conducted in Yiddish were offered in the sciences, geography, history, arithmetic, languages (Greek, Latin, German, Hebrew), and Jewish history and religion. Also, a rich program in extra-curricular activities existed: arts and crafts, drama, folklore, history, literature, and philosophy. In addition, several religious elementary schools and yeshivas were housed in the Orthodox prayer and study hall. The network of Jewish education in Vilna functioned up to the last days of the ghetto, in September, 1943.

Jews had settled in Austria in the tenth century, and the history of Jews in this central European country from the late Middle Ages on centered in Vienna and its surrounding areas. At the time of the Nazi annexation of Austria, 176,000 Jews lived in the capital, ninety-two percent of the Austrian Jewish population. The political, cultural, educational, and religious life of Viennese Jewry was coordinated by the *Israelitische Kultusgemeinde Wein*, which for decades spoke against antisemitism, dire economic prospects caused by the depression, emigration policy, etc. At one time or another, all major

Jewish parties were represented on the *Kultusgemeinde*: Agudah, Mizrahi, Progressive Religious Judaism, National Zionists, socialists. Under pressure from the religious traditionalists, major departures from Jewish tradition and custom had been rejected; however, minor innovations, e.g., the installation of a loud speaker system in the Leopoldstadt Temple, were sanctioned.

Between the two world wars, a theological seminary, a girls trade school, and three day schools (communal Volksschule, Orthodox Talmud Torah, and the *Chajes Realgymnasium*) existed in Vienna. All factions of the organized Viennese Jewish community supported strong commitment to traditional Jewish education and values: the nationalist *Chajes Realgymnasium*, established in 1919 by Galician Jews, taught Bible, Talmud, Hebrew literature, and land of Israel studies; the Liberal synagogues sponsored weekly Sabbath youth services; and the community provided Bar Mitzvah instruction, prayer shawls, phylacteries, and prayer books for boys in need and conformation classes for girls. Nearly 28,000 youngsters received public education in 1917-1918; due to emigration and low birth rate, this number fell to nine thousand by 1935-1936.

On more than one occasion, broad policy issues—for example, how was the *Kultusgemeinde* to define the essence of Judaism—threatened the unity of the community. Thus, the communal elections of 1932 enabled the Zionists to control the *Kultusgemeinde*. In 1934, in response, the ultra-orthodox Adas Yisrael threatened succession. Meanwhile, Josef Ticho, a prominent liberal leader embarrassed the leadership by charging in a public article that the Board has strayed from its mandate "to stay on confessional matters;" and Mizrahi leader Rabbi Solomon Friedman criticized the Agudah for appealing to non-Jewish authorities to resolve internal Jewish problems.

This atmosphere of debate over communal self-definition came to an end when, soon after the annexation on March 13, 1938, Austrian Jews lost all basic civil and religious rights: no more emigration, property rights, synagogue and group activities, education,

professions; and in their place, forced labor and death camps. In 1942, the *Altestenrat der Juden im Wein* replaced the *Kultusgemeinde* to represent the dwindling community before the authorities. It is estimated that 50,000 Jews were deported from Austria or died there during the Shoah.

Between 1933-1939, Nazi Germany passed more than four hundred laws and edicts, including twenty concerning the education of Jewish youth. The anti-education laws promulgated against Jewish students—ranging from quotas at high schools, colleges, and universities (April 25, 1933) to the total prohibition of Jewish children from attending German schools (November 15, 1938) and Jewish adults from attending universities (December 8, 1938)—altered radically the composition and goals of the Jewish school movement. Thousands of youngsters whose families, often marginal to the Jewish community, believed that public education was a direct entrance to the university and to the professions now entered the Jewish schools. Socially and culturally assimilated upper and middle class youngsters who had been weaned away from the religious tradition were now integrated with more traditional lower middle class students.

The educational objective of the *Reichsvertretung* during these turbulent years was to fortify the Jewish child ethnically, morally, and spiritually. Viewing the Jews as a *Schecksalsgemeinschaft* ("community of fate"), the *Reichsvertretung* intensified *Volkskunde* (study of the people) by increasing hours of instruction in Bible and Hebrew and by emphasizing knowledge of Jewish texts. Further, it encouraged participation in festival celebrations and other Jewish religious and cultural activities, including the development of a sense of connection to the land of Israel.

In the summer of 1939, the *Reichsvertretung* was replaced by the government imposed *Reichsvereinigung der Juden in Deutschland*, to which all Jews were compelled to belong (State Citizen Law, July 4, 1939). For three years the *Reichsvereinigung* supervised Jewish schools, until, on June 20, 1942, the Reich Minister of Interior ordered them closed permanently. Even so, Jewish schools in the Third Reich succeeded in seeding Jewish pride, encouraging self-respect, and imparting a cultural and religious inheritance that defied the Nazi agenda. In a sense, the Jews who stayed in Germany and those who emigrated benefited from adherence to the charge proclaimed by Martin Buber in the year Hitler rose to power:

> You can translate Jewish values into Jewish living. You can study our language, rich lore, Hebrew, and our own heroic history: Nay, study is not enough; it must become part of our daily living; it must enter our bloodstream. We must live, yes live as Jews, as a people, as a community! Teach your children Jewish values! Make your lives Jewish! Begin with yourselves—and your children will follow.[2]

Hasidic Judaism in the Holocaust: In the period of the Shoah, classical Hasidic thought permeated the life and contemplation of the Hasidim of Beltz, Bratslav, Ger, Lubavitch, and other dynasties. The Hasids' mystical belief system regarding the symbolic interaction of God and humankind, in which actions in the lower world have an impact on the upper world, informed both activist and quietistic schools of Hasidism during the traumatic Nazi years. Pesah Schindler[3] makes a compelling case regarding the single-mindedness of most Hasidim, who defiantly opposed the Nazis' evil mandates but, in the end, accepted joyfully what they viewed as a divine decree.

Schindler shows that, for the Hasidim, the sense of God's presence in history was not diminished by the Shoah, even though God's justice, compassion, goodness, and kindness appeared hidden to finite human knowledge. The Hasidim survived suffering and personal sacrifice (*meserat nefesh*) on the strength of their faith in the covenantal interrelationship between God and Israel and in light of their trust in God's ultimate defeat of evil. For the Hasidim, the phenomenon of redemption thus was architectonic: rebuke, destruction, and exile would be followed by salvation. This meant that, for the Hasid, the Nazi evil could be thwarted not by obliterating its reality, but by viewing it in a cosmic or mythic

perspective, subordinate to God's overall plans for redemption.

The Hasidic response to the Shoah reveals the nature of empathy, how faith, a Jewish life-style, and the observing of Jewish law prepared a grief-stricken community for a life of woe and calamity. Hasidim maintain classical Orthodox belief, rooted in spontaneous religious experience. By placing the Shoah in a kabbalistic frame, they responded to the Final Solution in accordance with meaningful, clearly defined Hasidic tenets. In the course of the terrible trauma, the Hasidic Rebbe thus played an altruistic role as a source of encouragement, and Hasidic victims themselves engaged in multiple acts of sanctifying God's name, not only by martyrdom but through obligatory and voluntary acts of holiness in the service of God and humankind.

Take, for example, the relationship of the Hasidic groups' Rabbinic leaders, the *Zaddikim*, to their followers. In a time of gathering insanity, the cadre of pious Hasidic rabbis—*rebbeim*—collectively acted as a kind of sponge for misery, absorbing pain and cruelty before it spilled out and overcame everything. By insisting that sanity could be restored in the world only when the natural order was restored through some established ceremony or rite—fraternal meal, Hasidic worship, strict adherence to the rules of holy time and space—the *Zaddik* played a major role in diminishing despair, which in turn helped the Hasidim to cope in extreme circumstances. In an existentialist way, *Zaddik* and Hasid believed that their actions transcended ordinary events laced with danger (e.g., survival at the expense of abuse of one's fellow) and helped to rediscover dignity and self-respect, necessary ingredients for the total salvation of Israel and the world.

The city of Lublin, once the seat of the central institution of Jewish self-government in Poland and a major center of Torah instruction represented by the Yeshiva of Lublin, was the site of the first detention camp (*Reservat*) the Nazis erected on Polish soil. Here, it is said, in the face of murderous and sadistic acts by the Nazis, a Hasidic ditty regarding penance evolved into a cry-

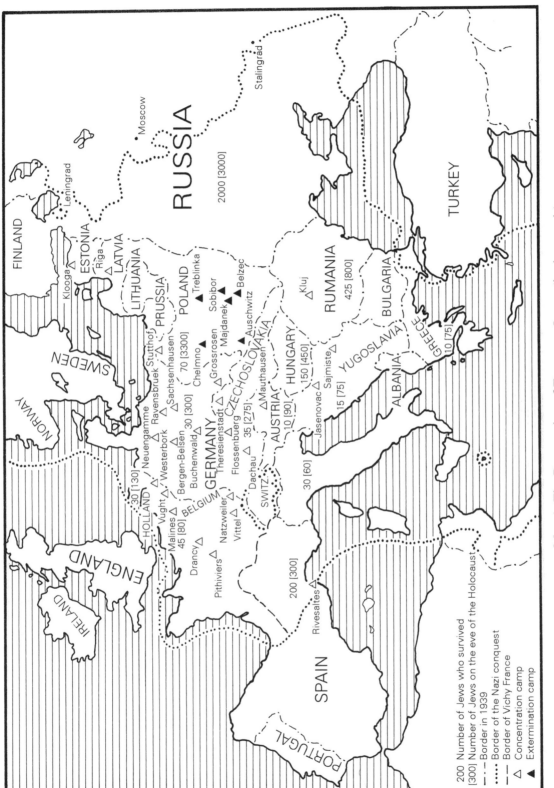

Map 1. The Destruction of European Jewry (in thousands).

Legend:
200 Number of Jews who survived
[300] Number of Jews on the eve of the Holocaust
–·– Border in 1939
········· Border of the Nazi conquest
—·— Border of Vichy France
△ Concentration camp
▲ Extermination camp

RUSSIA 2000 [3000]
POLAND
GERMANY
Buchenwald 30 [300]
Chelmno 70 [3300]
HOLLAND 30 [130]
BELGIUM 45 [80]
SWITZ. 200 [300]
AUSTRIA 10 [90]
CZECHOSLOVAKIA 35 [275]
HUNGARY 150 [450]
RUMANIA 425 [800]
BULGARIA 15 [75]
YUGOSLAVIA
GREECE 10 [75]

Camps:
Klooga △
Stutthof △
Sachsenhausen △
Ravensbruek △
Neuengamme △
Westerbork △
Vught △
Malines △
Drancy △
Pithiviers △
Natzweiler △
Vittel △
Rivesaltes △
Bergen-Belsen △
Flossenbuerg △
Dachau △
Mauthausen △
Theresienstadt △
Grossrosen △
Kluj △
Sajmiste △
Jasenovac △

Extermination camps:
Treblinka ▲
Sobibor ▲
Majdanek ▲
Belzec ▲
Auschwitz ▲
Chelmno ▲

ing chant that gave succor to the sad fate of Lublin's Jews:

> Lomir zich iberbeiten, avinu shebashamayim
> Lomir zich iberbeiten, iberbeiten, iberbeiten
> Let us be reconciled, our Heavenly Father
> Let us be reconciled, let us make up
> Mir velen zey iberleben, iberleben, avinu
> Mir velen zey iberleben, iberleben, iberleben
> We shall outlive them, our heavenly Father
> We shall outlive them, outlive them, outlive them.

This is truly a statement of immense courage and love of the Jewish people in the face of almost certain destruction.

Religious life in the camps: Theologians argue about human and divine responsibility after Auschwitz by focusing on a continuum of questions asked by the incarcerated: Why your people, O Lord, why us? Is this the reward for loyalty to the Torah? "Lord, how long shall the wicked, how long shall the wicked exult?" (Ps. 94:3).

But in truth, most people in the camps could not and did not bother with philosophical and logical problems or with the concept of death and the world-to-come. Rather they concerned themselves with staying alive and clinging to the hope that their own loved ones might survive. For some, to seize life was equated with remaining alive as a Jew, irrespective of religious observance. As one witness said: "The Nazis persecuted the Jews as *Jews* and not as religious Jews. So the issue wasn't to remain religious or to remain a believing Jew, but simply to remain a Jew!"[4] Such testimony argues that every single Jew who remained alive meant the entire nation's survival, even though this would be under the most trying and ethically difficult circumstances.

Hunger, for example, was the greatest privation suffered in the camps. Survivors typically comment that they needed to do "anything not to starve" and "in order to be able to endure, you have to eat whatever you can lay your hands on." This might have required taking bread from a dead person's hand, but rarely meant snatching bread from a living stranger, let alone from a friend, and never led to engaging in cannibalism.

Young people in the camps relate that their elders instructed them to violate the Jewish dietary laws (kashrut) in order to survive. This was deemed permissible under the authority of the Rabbinic doctrine that human life must be saved at almost all costs:

> After my father and I arrived at (concentration camp) *Golleschau* (forty kilometers from Auschwitz) we walked and ate together. When there were little specks of meat in his water soup, my father always picked them out and put them in my soup. Never would we eat *trefah* in its pure form even in Auschwitz. Maybe it was the additional specks of meat that helped me survive and their removal that helped cause his demise.[5]

Alongside such physical assistance, many spiritual factors contributed to people's inner strength to survive the camps. Among the most sacred was parents' will that children know from where they came (*shtetl*, life style), that they carry on the Jewish heritage, and that they survive to give living testimony to the Nazi destruction.

Hundreds of testimonies bear witness to children's observing of the religious commandment of honoring parents: they said prayers in secret, either from memory or by imitating another's recitation, repeating the words or simply listening and responding "amen;" they followed the Jewish calendar as best as was possible, fasting on Yom Kippur, telling the story of Purim even in the absence of noisemakers, children, and hamentaschen, the traditional Purim pastry; they ate matzah and boiled potatoes on Passover; they remembered even if they could not necessarily observe the Sabbath (see Exod. 20:8 and Deut. 12:15); and they performed acts of mutual assistance. Thus we read of how sibling helped sibling, giving each other the strength to hold out, and of how many were saved by total strangers who risked their own lives to do so.

How does one say Kaddish at Auschwitz? Does one say the deathbed confession on the Sabbath? Indeed, does the Sabbath of creation, a day of peace and tranquillity, exist on planet Auschwitz at all? How does one traverse the paths of Judaism (halakhah) when all roads pass before a king who appears not to hear words spoken to him from either near or far?[6]

In light of such practical problems and

theological dilemmas, the unofficial prayer of many religious victims of the Holocaust may well have been, "God, be there when I need you; do not leave me when I contest your hiding of your face from your people in need." Yet despite such theological problems and the confrontational attitude they created in some, for the believing Jew in the ghettos and death camps, prayer remained the key that unlocked the silence of heart, mind, and universe. The desire to say one's prayers in hell was both self-searching and soul-reaching, creating a dialogue and releasing frustration with the Lord of the Universe.

At great personal peril, phylacteries were smuggled into the camps, and witnesses testify to their use as people prayed in community (fig. 50). In the slave labor camps of Gross-Rosen and Plaszow and the death camps of Auschwitz, Buchenwald, and Maidanek, pages of the Talmud were ransomed from garbage heaps. Attested in Plaszow were pages from prayer books, torn prayer shawls, and a small Talmud volume (*gemorhle*). Groups of religious Jews who, whenever and wherever possible, met in secret for prayer and study gave new life to these sacred remains. And if no "written" Torah was found, then "oral" Torah—passages of the Mishnah from memory, for example—was passed on from teacher to student, from detention site to place of work and back (see figs. 51-57).

In this setting, verses from Psalms became personal credos, especially statements such as, "I shall not die but live and proclaim the works of the Lord. The Lord punished me severely but did not hand me over to death" (Ps. 118:17-18); "May God answer you on your day of trouble, the name of Jacob's God keep you safe" (Ps. 20:1); and "God of retribution, Lord, God of retribution, appear!" (Ps. 94:1). Similarly, the weekly liturgy as well as that of New Year, the Day of Atonement, and the other holy days infused with meaning moments of deepest grief and despair. It is not difficult to comprehend the power for believing Jews of words such as those of the Amidah, the central prayer of all worship services: "Lord our God, put your awe upon all whom you have made, your dread upon all whom you have created," fol-lowed, several passages later, by "the righteous will see and rejoice . . . iniquity shall shut its mouth, wickedness shall vanish like smoke, when you will abolish the rule of tyranny on earth." Affirmed by numerous attestations and declarations, it is clear that prayer directed to heaven brought in return solace on earth.

Rabbinic responsa: The Nazis' near-complete destruction of European Jewry represented the worst threat ever to the existence of Jews and Judaism. Life and the ever present likelihood of death raised again and again the question of how the people were to respond to the commandment "Choose life, that you may live, you and your seed" (Deut. 30:19). The issue may be approached from two angles, the rules for preserving and taking life and the theory of the sanctification of life through death.

The ethics of preserving life: Preserving life is a core teaching of Judaism. While Scripture contains no specific injunction against suicide, based on Gen. 9:5 ("For your lifeblood I will surely require a reckoning"), the sages taught that suicide is wrong and punishable by divine decree. In the community, it meant burial outside the sacred precincts of the cemetery and suspension of mourning laws and customs.

This strong edict intended to discourage Jews who contemplated suicide, but caused great grief and embarrassment for the family of those who anyway committed suicide. To mitigate this problem, the sages ruled that, to be treated as suicide under the law, a death must be both voluntary and premeditated. The rabbinical presumption was that people who kill themselves—axiomatic in cases of child suicide—do so without the premeditation. So their death is not considered a suicide at all. This idea is founded on the suicide of King Saul, who is described as having been in great mental distress "lest these uncircumcised (Philistines) come and thrust me through, and make a mock of me" (1 Sam. 3:14). His death by his own sword is used by many rabbis as a precedent for not stigmatizing a person who, in a situation of anguish, stress, and despair, takes his or her own life.[7]

Thus, while in normal times acts of suicide may be blameworthy, in stressful times—Masada, the Bar Kokhba rebellion, the crusades, Inquisition, pogroms—letting oneself be killed or even killing oneself for "the sanctification of God's name" is deemed by many to be praiseworthy. Maimonides, who codified Jewish attitudes toward martyrdom, taught that a Jew made to transgress the commandments in public or in a time of great religious persecution is expected to suffer death instead (Mishneh Torah, Yesode ha-Torah V.3). On the other hand, Maimonides made clear that a person who unnecessarily suffers death—e.g., in circumstances under which Jewish law should be set aside in the interest of saving a life—is an ordinary suicide. But medieval French and German commentators opposed this decision. They felt that all people who sacrificed themselves—even when not strictly required to do so—are worthy of admiration and respect.

This disagreement concerning the appropriateness of suicide is reflected in Holocaust responsa concerning matters of life and death during such humiliating times of personal anguish, degradation, and torture. Rabbi H.J. Zimmels'[8] opinion is illustrative:

> A different outlook on suicide in general can be found in the era of the Nazi Holocaust. Humiliation, fear of torture and starvation produced two dramatically opposed feelings among the Jews living under the Nazi heel. These feelings had great consequences in their attitude to life.
>
> One was pessimism, resignation, despair and abandonment of any hope for the future, leading to suicide. The other was optimism, a strong will to survive and to bear patiently all sufferings and hope for a change for the better. The former view was shared mainly by the Jews of Germany and Austria, while the latter attitude can be found among Jews of Poland and other Eastern territories.

It would appear that most responsa from the ashes agree: one may not commit suicide to avoid Nazi imprisonment and suffering, mental or physical. This attitude was inspired by the ancient sage Hananiah ben Teradyon (B. A.Z. 18a), who did not hasten his death even while he was being burned at the stake: "It is best that he who has given life should also take it away; no one may hasten his own death" (B. A.Z. 18a and the martyrology of the Day of Atonement). Following this pattern, Rabbi Ephraim Oshry of Kovno denied a Jew's request for a legal ruling permitting suicide even on a day on which some 10,000 men, women, and children were taken away to be slaughtered. He opined that any action to suicide "is a profanation of God's Name, because it shows that the Jews do not trust in God to save them."[9] Oshry goes on to say with admiration that in the "ghetto of Kovno there were no cases of suicide save in three instances. All the other inmates of the ghetto believed with perfect faith that God would not forsake His people."

At the same time (1941), in another place, the diarist Chaim A. Kaplan concurs that suicide was not an option for the broken Jews of Poland: "We are left naked, but as long as this secret power is still within us we do not give up hope. And the strength of this power lies in the indigenous nature of Polish Jewry, which is rooted in our eternal tradition that commands us to live."

Idealism and pragmatism are the engines that moved Rabbinic decisors, who understood that since "the day the Temple was destroyed, the Holy one, blessed be He, is only to be found in the four cubits of the law—halakhah" (B. Ber. 8a). Thus, from the perspective of the Jewish legal tradition they addressed the deepest questions of the meaning and responsibility of human life. Is it permitted to endanger one's own life in order to save that of another? Yes, in theory, but only if the danger to the rescuer's life is not certain, since, even to save someone else, one may not go to a certain death.[10] Despite this attitude, to risk one's life to save another was viewed as commendable, and, indeed, in situations in which all life was in danger, all things within reason and halakhah, including the despicable, were deemed allowable, including, for example, the stifling of an infant whose crying would expose a group in hiding, causing all to be killed. The crying child was seen as a pursuer, one who jeopardizes innocent life. While we may not set aside one life for another, pragmatically speaking, a possessor of life can stave off the threat presented by an antagonist, even an unwitting one, such as a baby.

The Talmud permits a community to save itself by surrendering to the authorities an individual whom the government has asked for by name. This is permitted if the individual is a legally condemned criminal, like the fugitive Sheba ben Bikri (2 Sam. 20) and has been called for specifically, by name. But if these conditions are not met, it is prohibited under Jewish law to hand over a Jewish soul, even if this means that an entire community will be killed (Y. Ter. 8:12).

Under this approach, Jewish communities could not surrender any Jew to the Nazis, since the charge of Jewish criminality flowed not from an ethical legal system but from a decree of genocide based on political and racial antisemitism, mixed with an abhorrent, callous, and divisive redefinition of Jewish identity. Alas, within the ghettos, the halakhah on this matter could not be followed. The German authorities commanded the *Judenraete* to prepare lists of candidates for "deportation" and ultimately death. Based on Y. Ter. 8:12 and Rabbah's famous injunction, "Be killed and kill not (the innocent); who has told you that your blood is redder than his?" (B. A.Z. 27b; B. Pes. 25b; B. San. 74a; B. Yom. 82a), the Jewish councils of Vilna, Heidemuehle, Sosnowiec, and elsewhere were advised by their local rabbinates not to comply. But other councils of elders resigned themselves to sacrificing segments of their communities in the hope and anticipation that others could be saved. Rabbi Abraham Dubner Cahane of Kovno justified this by reasoning that if all were in immediate and actual danger of death, the possibility of ransoming a few by preparing the deportation lists offered a possible gain at no real cost, since all were lost anyway. "Who should live and who should die?" Whoever has the power of life, let that individual live.[11]

The place of martyrdom: Persecution and destruction of Jews and Jewish communities over the centuries has contributed to the importance in the Jewish tradition of the concept of *Kiddush ha-Shem*, sanctification of God's name through martyrdom. The talmudic dictum "be killed and do not transgress" has been the spine of a martyred Jewish people whose limbs were torn in nearly every time and place. In the medieval period, the Sephardim responded to acts of isolation, vilification, and expulsion by a policy of outward adaptation to the host culture and belief, coupled with an inward turning to a messianic Jewish ideology. To combat relentless terror and forced apostasy, Ashkenazim, on the other hand, demonstrated a very strong belief in resurrection of the dead.[12] Whole communities of Ashkenazim thus embraced martyrdom, and accounts of righteous martyrs of the past became part of the everyday teaching and veneration of Central and Eastern European Jews. Indeed, a central focus on the commandment of martyrdom—to be preceded by its own benediction: "Blessed are you, Lord our God, King of the universe, who has commanded us to sanctify his name publicly"—is found in the famous work *Shenei lukot ha-berit*, known by the acronym, "Shelah," written by the Prague-born and Polish educated legal decisor and mystic Isaiah ben Abraham ha-Levi Horowitz (1565?-1630), published in Amsterdam in 1649.

Nevertheless, the pietistic, quietistic, and pacifistic way to heaven represented by the traditional approach to martyrdom was challenged by individual religious Zionist rabbis and Hasidic *rebbes* alike, who responded to the unparalleled horrors of the Shoah by advocating spontaneous, as well as planned, acts of sanctifying life (*kiddush ha-hayyim*) *even to death*. The pattern of spiritual resistance falls into three categories, each responding to a different stimulus but united by the intention to combat the enemy's determined goal of total annihilation of the Jewish people:

1. Remember that in past religious persecutions, the enemy demanded the soul of the Jew, who responded by offering a martyred body. The Nazis demand the body of the Jew, and it is the Jew's obligation to fight and resist in order to preserve life (Rabbis Isaac Nissenbaum and Menahem Zemba, Warsaw Ghetto).

2. Observe Jewish belief, faith, rites of passage, and the sacred calendar, however minimally and symbolically, for they con-

tribute to reconstruction (*tiqqun*) in the midst of destruction (Shoah) (Rabbi Kaloni Kalmush Shapiro, Piaseczno).

3. Return to Zion and by rebuilding the Land of Promise, the souls in burnt bodies can be restored to life by a people reborn (Rabbi Issachar Schlomo Teechthal, Budapest).

Conclusion: The religious imagination does not merely deal with the Shoah as controlled, objective facts of historiography. Rather, it sees the Shoah as historiosophy, a paradigm above the historical, attached to history but by no means limited by it. What are some of the last words out of the whirlwind? For Schlomo Zlicovsky, a religious Jew, in the ghetto of the city of Lodz, *Shema Yisrael* ("Hear O Israel"). For Roza Robota, a Zionist Jew, and her three companions (Ala Gertner, Regina Safirsztan, Estera Wajcblum) at the last public hanging on the gallows at Auschwitz (January 6, 1945), *Nekama* ("vengance"). For many of the Jews on the crooked road to the crematoria, *'ani ma'amin*: I believe in the Jewish faith at any cost and, though it may tarry, in the final triumph of the Jewish spirit and way:

> Do not become embittered by wailing and tears. Speak of these matters with calmness and serenity, as did our holy Sages in the midrash, "Lamentations Rabbati." And do as our holy Sages had done—pour forth your words and cast them into letters. This will be the greatest retribution which you can wreck upon these wicked men. Despite the ranging of our foes the holy soul of your brothers and sisters will then remain alive. These evil ones schemed to blot out their names from the face of the earth, but a man cannot destroy letters. For words have wings; they mount up to heavenly heights and they endure for eternity.[13]

For the generation of the Shoah, who must ponder the imponderable, the war years are understood in terms of the Aqedah narrative, describing Abraham's binding and near sacrifice of Isaac.[14] Aqedah is the image that binds a Jew to death and to new beginnings. Aqedah encourages the Jewish people through trial, tribulation, and catastrophe, and offers, hopefully, the blue print to rebuild. Faith and affirmation in the eye of the storm

signify sensing the always abrupt end of life and the challenge to make every minute qualitatively meaningful. Thus, the generation of the Shoah—victims and survivors—has a deeper sensitivity to the mysteries of death and the values of life than those generations that have not experienced isolation, vilification, expulsion, slave labor, and extermination. The collective experience of victims and survivors bears testimony to survival and a life of Torah: fear of God and human responsibility (figs. 60-62).

For the generation after, Aqedah is a communication of vicarious sacrifice, applying not only to the ritual concept but to the social context as well. By virtue of the sacrifice offered (real or otherwise), the victimized (and, by extension, members of the entire victimized group) feel entitled to special treatment.[15] Thus surviving the Shoah leads to *zekhut*—merit in God's eyes. The generation after, for its part, acquires *zekut* by remembering the exemplary acts of religious heroism and martyrdom of the Shoah's victims. This memory of *kedushat 'am Yisrael*—sanctification of the people Israel—represents the dominant motivating force for *tiqqun 'am Yisrael*—the revitalization of the people Israel—in our day. The result is that, in the aftermath of the Holocaust as in it, even as Judaism and the people of Israel have suffered grievous losses, they have survived. In the period of Nazi atrocities, Jews who had practiced Judaism continued to do so, creating, in that way, lives of dignity and meaning. And so, at least in part in the memory of their heroism, Jews continue through the practice of Judaism to the revitalize themselves and to work towards the creation of a better world. And so, as they believed it would be, the suffering of the victims is at least in some small measure requited.

Bibliography

Dawidowicz, Lucy S., *The War against the Jews, 1933-1945* (New York, 1975).

Garber, Zev, *Shoah: The Paradigmatic Genocide* (Lanham, 1994).

Oshry, Ephraim, *Responsa from the Holocaust* (New York, 1983).

Schindler, Pesach, *Hasidic Responses to the Holocaust in Light of Hasidic Thought* (Hoboken, 1990).

Notes

[1] *Tsene Urene* is an exegetical and homiletical rendering of the Sabbath Torah and Haftarot readings and festival scrolls reading in order "to understand the word of God in simple language." The language is old Yiddish with a mixture of German words. Composed in the sixteenth century and intended for a general audience, the work over the centuries became a book for women.

[2] Martin Buber, "The Children," in *Judische Rundschau*, no. 43-44 (May 30, 1933), p. 227. Cited by Solomon Colodner in his thesis, "Jewish Education In Nazi Germany," presented to the School of Education of Dropsie College (Philadelphia, 1951).

[3] *Hasidic Responses to the Holocaust in Light of Hasidic Thought* (Hoboken, 1990).

[4] Moshe Davis and Meir Hovav, eds., *The Living Testify* (Jerusalem, 1994), p. 113. Originally published in Hebrew in 1990 as *Eda'i Hayim*, the publication commemorates the fiftieth anniversary of the Hungarian Shoah, in which 565,000 of the approximately 825,000 Hungarian Jews perished.

[5] Michael Klein, "Faith and Affirmation in Auschwitz," in *Midstream*, August/September, 1994, p. 34.

[6] The converse of the parable on reason and revelation found near the end of Maimonides' *A Guide to the Perplexed*, III:51.

[7] A brief summary of martyrdom and suicide for the "sanctification of the Name" is found in H.J. Zimmels, *The Echo of the Nazi Holocaust in Rabbinic Literature* (Republic of Ireland, 1975), pp. 82-86, and in Irving J. Rosenbaum, *The Holocaust and Halakhah* (New York, 1976), pp. 35-40.

[8] Zimmels, op. cit., p. 83.

[9] Ephraim Oshry, *Sheilos u-teshuvos mi-ma'amakim* (New York, 1949), vol. 1, no. 6, cited in an abridged English version, *Responsa from the Holocaust* (New York, 1983), pp. 32-33.

[10] B. San. 73a instructs, "Whence do we know that if a man sees his companion drowning, being mauled by a wild beast, or attacked by bandits, that he is obliged to save him? The Torah says, 'Do not stand idly by the blood of your neighbor' (Lev. 19:16)."

[11] The responsa is adjusted to B. B.M. 62a, which states that a traveler should not share a flask of water with a companion if *both* will then die in the desert heat. But are the fiendishly-given "meal tickets" argued about in the "Maimonides debate"—life and death issues debated in certain ghettos and related to Maimonides' ruling on capital cases—comparable to the water canteen mentioned in the Talmud?

[12] This may explain why the medieval liturgical poem *U-netaneh tokep* ("Let us tell how utterly holy this day is . . ."), associated with Rabbi Amnon's hesitancy at the point of personal martyrdom, and the *'Eleh 'ezkerah* martyrology are of central importance in the Ashkenazic Yom Kippur service. Though the latter may well originate with the memory of the ten rabbis killed by Hadrian, the prayer's psychological appeal was shaped by Jewish martyrdom in the medieval lands of Ashkenaz. Among Sephardic Jews, by contrast, the Kol Nidre prayer acquired intense significance, since its cancellation of personal vows was interpreted to include the renunciation of vows to forswear Judaism and adopt Christianity in the period of persecution in Spain, Portugal, and elsewhere.

[13] Rabbi Nahum Yanchiker, the last Rosh Metivta of the Slabodka Musar-Yeshiva in the outskirts of Kovno. See Joseph Gutfersteen, "The Indestructible Dignity of Man," in *Judaism* 19.3, summer 1970, pp. 262-263.

[14] Gen. 22, recalled in the daily, Sabbath, and festival morning service; it is also the Torah reading for the second day of New Year.

[15] Note the role of animal sacrifice in classical Judaism and animal/human offerings in faiths. The use and psychology of sacrificial-laden labels like "the Holocaust" is discussed in Zev Garber, *Shoah: The Paradigmatic Genocide* (Lanham, 1994), pp. 51-66.

ZEV GARBER

I

IDOLATRY IN JUDAISM: The worship of a physical representation of a deity was a central aspect of Mesopotamian and Egyptian religions in the period of the emergence of the religion of Israel, detailed in the Hebrew Scriptures.[1] In light of the prevailing practices of the peoples around them, practices that we refer to as idolatry, the official religion of the Israelites was striking. In contrast to those religions, the Israelite doctrine took as its fundamental precept the prohibition against creating and worshiping any representation of the Israelites' own God, let alone of the gods of other peoples. Exod. 20:4-5 makes this point clear:[2]

> You shall not make for yourself a graven image, or any likeness of anything that is in heaven above, or that is in the earth beneath,

or that is in the water under the earth; you shall not bow down to them or serve them; for I the Lord your God am a jealous God, visiting the iniquity of the fathers upon the children to the third and the fourth generation of those who hate me.

The heart of the covenant between God and the people of Israel was the exclusive relationship between these two parties. God took Israel alone as his people and, in recognition of this exclusive bond, the Israelites were obligated to worship God alone. In the setting of the covenant, the prohibition against worship of other gods meant more than that the Israelites could not create images consciously conceived to be deities. Rather, insofar as any icon might be thought to represent a god, the people of Israel were prohibited from making images or likenesses of anything.

The Israelites' comprehension of God as invisible derives from the fact that God almost always appears to the people without physical form. The implication of this, as Deut. 4:12-18 makes clear, is that God cannot accurately be depicted by an icon:

Then the Lord spoke to you out of the midst of the fire; you heard the sound of words, but saw no form; there was only a voice. And he declared to you his covenant, which he commanded you to perform, that is, the ten commandments; and he wrote them upon two tables of stone. And the Lord commanded me at that time to teach you statutes and ordinances, that you might do them in the land which you are going over to possess. Therefore take good heed to yourselves. Since you saw no form on the day that the Lord spoke to you at Horeb out of the midst of the fire, beware lest you act corruptly by making a graven image for yourselves, in the form of any figure, the likeness of male or female, the likeness of any beast that is on the earth, the likeness of any winged bird that flies in the air, the likeness of anything that creeps on the ground, the likeness of any fish that is in the water under the earth.

The point is not that God may not, on occasion, be manifest in a visible image. To the contrary, Scripture itself on occasion describes God as taking a physical form. At Exod. 33:20-23, for instance, when Moses demands to be allowed to see God, he is shown God's back. God has a face, but Moses may not see it, since "man shall not see me and live." Accordingly God instructs Moses:

Behold, there is a place by me where you shall stand upon the rock; and while my glory passes by I will put you in a cleft of the rock, and I will cover you with my hand until I have passed by; then I will take away my hand, and you shall see my back; but my face shall not be seen.

Similarly, at Exod. 24:10-11 the elders of Israel have the opportunity to look upon God:

[A]nd they saw the God of Israel; and there was under his feet as it were a pavement of sapphire stone, like the very heaven for clearness. And he did not lay his hand on the chief men of the people of Israel; they beheld God, and ate and drank.

Scripture's point in prohibiting icons accordingly is not that God does not have or might never take a corporeal form. Rather, the prohibition against the creation and worship of images is based upon the fact that God has chosen to make himself manifest to the people of Israel only through verbal revelation. For this reason, the people are to conceive of and worship their deity without the use of any image. But in stating this requirement, even the Bible itself recognizes the contrast between the people's experience and that of Moses. Moses sees and speaks to God directly. All others, including other prophets, do not have this opportunity. The point is explicit at Num. 12:6-8, where God questions how anyone among the people of Israel can challenge Moses' authority:

Hear my words: If there is a prophet among you, I the Lord make myself known to him in a vision, I speak with him in a dream. Not so with my servant Moses; he is entrusted with all my house. With him I speak mouth to mouth, clearly, and not in dark speech; and he beholds the form of the Lord. Why then were you not afraid to speak against my servant Moses?

The point again is not that God has no physical image or does not, at least on occasion, assume a corporeal form. Rather, it is that Moses alone has been allowed to see this image and so is different from all other Israelite prophets, let alone from all other Israelites. To all people other than Moses, God makes himself known in a vision or dream but not in a material image.

The people's experience at Sinai of a God who speaks but is not seen is paradigmatic of the way in which God was always to be known to the people: through a revelation in words rather than in a corporeal form or image. The logical development of this conception that God does not appear in a physical image appears at Is. 40:18-25. Here we are told not simply that God *should not* be depicted with an image but, more than this, that God is so great and incomparable that he *cannot* be depicted, insofar as no image can satisfactorily portray him:

> To whom then will you liken God, or what likeness compare with him? The idol! a workman casts it, and a goldsmith overlays it with gold, and casts for it silver chains. He who is impoverished chooses for an offering wood that will not rot; he seeks out a skillful craftsman to set up an image that will not move. Have you not known? Have you not heard? Has it not been told you from the beginning? Have you not understood from the foundations of the earth? It is he who sits above the circle of the earth, and its inhabitants are like grasshoppers; who stretches out the heavens like a curtain, and spreads them like a tent to dwell in; who brings princes to nought, and makes the rulers of the earth as nothing. Scarcely are they planted, scarcely sown, scarcely has their stem taken root in the earth, when he blows upon them, and they wither, and the tempest carries them off like stubble. To whom then will you compare me, that I should be like him? says the Holy One.

From the ideology of Exodus, which holds that God may not be depicted graphically because God has chosen to appear to the Israelites without corporeal form, we move to the more developed prophetic ideology, which holds that God is incomparable and therefore cannot adequately be depicted. The result is that Israelites are forbidden not only from engaging in idolatry, that is, in the worship of foreign gods. They are, rather, also prohibited from iconolatry, that is, the use of images even in the worship of their own God.[3]

One result of its view that God cannot be accurately depicted and so is to be experienced only through verbal revelation is that Israelite religion comes to express contempt for all idols and their worship. Among many such passages, this perspective is explicit at Jer. 10:2-5:

> Thus says the Lord: "Learn not the way of the nations, nor be dismayed at the signs of the heavens because the nations are dismayed at them, for the customs of the peoples are false. A tree from the forest is cut down, and worked with an ax by the hands of a craftsman. Men deck it with silver and gold; they fasten it with hammer and nails so that it cannot move. Their idols are like scarecrows in a cucumber field, and they cannot speak; they have to be carried, for they cannot walk. Be not afraid of them, for they cannot do evil, neither is it in them to do good."

In passages such as this, the Israelite attitude towards images of gods reaches its logical conclusion. The point is not simply that Israelites are forbidden from worshipping idols, though, of course, they are. More important, they are to recognize that such images are not deities at all but only the products of human hands. Unlike the Israelite God, they have no power either to hurt or to help those who worship them. This means that idol worship is not simply a violation of the covenant with God. Rather, since idols are powerless, worshipping them is folly.[4]

The vocabulary used by Scripture to refer to idols matches this contemptuous attitude. Alongside terms that describe the method by which the idol is created,[5] a number of terms found especially in the prophetic literature reflect the prophets' attitude towards idols. Normally translated as simply "idols," the word *gilulim* is associated with a root meaning "dung."[6] *Elilim*, though it sounds like *el*, the term commonly used for God, is more likely associated with the adjective *elil*, meaning "worthless" or "weak," yielding the meaning "worthless gods."[7] Elsewhere, idols are described with equally derisive adjectives: they are "works of delusion" (Jer. 10:15), "false" (Jer. 51:17), and "empty" (Ps. 31:7). Ezek. 20:7-8 refers to idols as "detestable things;" Is. 44:19, Jer. 16:18, and Ezek. 5:11 call them "abominations." The latter two sources state that idols defile the sanctuary and pollute the land.

The perspective expressed in Scripture's prohibitions against the worship of idols and the attitude towards idolatry revealed in the Bible's specific terminology were part of the continuing battle of the leaders of the Israelite cult against the actual practices of the people. For despite the clear and fundamental stance of the official Israelite religion against idolatry, many passages in Scripture make clear that the people of Israel continually participated in, and were excoriated for, syncretistic religious practices in which they created and worshipped idols. Examples range from the incident of the Golden Calf (Exod. 32-34) to the affair involving Micah, who, at Judg. 17-18, sets up a shrine for an idol made by his mother out of silver he had stolen from her and then returned. One of many prophetic exhortations against the Israelites for their constant idolatry is at Jer. 11:10-13:

> They have turned back to the iniquities of their forefathers, who refused to hear my words; they have gone after other gods to serve them; the house of Israel and the house of Judah have broken my covenant which I made with their fathers. Therefore, thus says the Lord, Behold, I am bringing evil upon them which they cannot escape; though they cry to me, I will not listen to them. Then the cities of Judah and the inhabitants of Jerusalem will go and cry to the gods to whom they burn incense, but they cannot save them in the time of their trouble. For your gods have become as many as your cities, O Judah; and as many as the streets of Jerusalem are the altars you have set up to shame, altars to burn incense to Baal.

Scripture thus attests to continuing, powerful syncretistic tendencies, described in detail throughout the hagiographa and prophets.[8] Solomon, 1 Kgs. 11:3-8, condoned and participated in the idol worship of his foreign wives. His great-grandson Asa destroyed idols made by his father and "removed" his own mother because of her idolatry (1 Kgs. 15:11-13). But even Asa, who "did what was right in the eyes of the Lord," did not destroy the high places at which foreign gods were worshipped. Jeroboam introduced golden calves into Israelite worship, proclaiming, as in the incident of the Golden Calf after the Exodus from Egypt, "Behold your gods, O Israel, who brought you up out of the land of Egypt" (see 1 Kgs. 12:28-33). The marriage of the Israelite king Ahab to Jezebel, daughter of the Sidonian king, led him to introduce and promote the cult of Baal (1 Kgs. 16:31). Jezebel's entourage included 450 priests of Baal and 400 priests of Asherah (1 Kgs. 19:18). This meant that, subsequent to Ahab's actions, Elijah and Elishah continually confronted devotees of Baal and their followers among the people of Israel (see, e.g., 1 Kgs. 18:20-39).

These images of the syncretistic practices of Israelite kings and common people point to the long period of time that passed before the Deuteronomic ideal of the Israelite nation's worshipping only Yahweh and only at the single chosen cult-site—Jerusalem—became a reality. Still, the literature's frequent references to idol worship and to royal campaigns against idolatry[9] should not lead us to assume that during the monarchy idolatry was always rampant, let alone normative. Rather, we should be clear that this literature's often negative focus upon the Israelite leadership served to legitimate the official religion and its cultic leaders, whose "correct" practice was contrasted with what others supposedly did and believed. The presence of this underlying polemic makes it difficult to ascertain the extent to which the common people in fact produced or worshipped images of deities or of the Israelite God. Many people appear to have engaged in idolatry, while many others did not. Edward Curtis surveys the problem as follows:[10]

> The texts describing the participation of the people in idolatry give a conflicting impression of its extent. The accounts of Baal worship during the time of Ahab suggest that the worship had a fairly extensive popular following. 1 Kgs 18:19 reports that there were 850 prophets of Baal and Asherah on Mt. Carmel with Elijah. In the midst of Elijah's discouragement, God declares that there were 7,000 who had not bowed down to Baal. If the number is not a figurative one, it would represent a fairly small portion of the population that had remained loyal to Yahweh. At the same time that Jehu killed all the worshippers of Baal—some 10 years after the death of Ahab—he gathered them together in one temple and had 80 soldiers kill

the entire group (2 Kgs. 10:18-28). The perspective of the prophets is that the people of both Israel and Judah were, at many points in their history, not deeply committed to strict obedience to the covenant; instead, they were involved, at least at a popular and superstitious level, in syncretistic religious practices, often influenced by their Canaanite neighbors. . . .

While many Israelites were true to the covenant ideal, a significant portion of the people also appears to have been attracted to the Canaanite religion from which their own faith had grown and with which it still shared important characteristics.[11] This dualistic picture, drawn on the basis of the biblical literature, is confirmed by archaeological evidence. For, on the one hand, this evidence suggests that, by the eighth century B.C.E, the majority of the people in fact worshipped the God of Israel. And yet, on the other hand, the number of Israelite cult-shrines uncovered from this period shows that Israelite religious practice remained diverse and had not yet achieved the Deuteronomic ideal that emerged in this period and that demanded the worship of an invisible God in the one place that God would choose.[12]

Idolatry in the Talmudic literature: Following the clear perspective of the Hebrew Scriptures, the rabbis describe an Israelite's worship of any deity other than the God of Israel to be one of the worst sins possible. Idolatry accordingly ranks as one of only three sins (alongside murder and sexual licentiousness) that one must not commit even at the cost of his life (B. San. 74a). Indeed, the rabbis see acceptance of the prohibition against idolatry as so definitive of what it means to be a member of the Israelite people that, in their view, a gentile who denies idols may actually be called a Jew or, in different terms, can be held to have accepted the entire Torah (B. Meg. 13a). By contrast, recognition by a Jew of idols is tantamount to denying the entirety of law, as Sif. Deut. 54.LIV:III makes clear:

A. "[. . . and the curse, if you do not obey the commandments of the Lord your God but turn away from the path] that I enjoin upon you this day and follow other gods, whom you have not experienced" (Deut. 11:28):

B. On the basis of this statement sages have ruled: Whoever confesses to idolatry denies the entire Torah, and whoever denies idolatry confesses to the entire Torah.

Idolatry brings God's curse upon the people of Israel, as Deut. 11:28 indicates. Accordingly, the rabbis recognized in idolatry the denial of the essence of the Torah, adherence to which, by contrast, brings blessing upon the people of Israel. But the opposite also is true: to reject idolatry is to accept the principle that stands behind the multitude of laws understood together to portray the single, essential truth of Judaism, that there is but one God.

Scripture lists in only general terms the actions prohibited as idolatry. One may not engage in pagan rituals (Deut. 12:30), bow down to idols (Exod. 20:5, 34:14), or offer sacrifices to them (Exod. 22:20). Expanding upon these brief references, M. San. 7:6 contrasts aspects of actual idol worship, for which one is culpable to death, with actions that involve an idol, so as to be forbidden, but that are not in the category of idolatry:

A. He who performs an act of worship for an idol:

B. all the same are the one who performs an act of service, who actually sacrifices, who offers up incense, who pours out a libation offering, who bows down,

C. and the one who accepts [the idol] upon himself as a god, saying to it, "You are my god."

D. But the one who hugs it, kisses it, polishes it, sweeps it, and washes it,

E. anoints it, puts clothing on it, and puts shoes on it, [merely] transgresses a negative commandment [Exod. 20:5].

F. He who takes a vow in its name, and he who carries out a vow made in its name transgress a negative commandment [Exod. 23:13].

G. He who uncovers himself to Baal Peor—[he is stoned, for] this is how one performs an act of service to it.

H. He who tosses a pebble at Merkolis [that is, Hermes] [is stoned, for] this is how one performs an act of service to it.

In elaborating the content of idol worship, the rabbis thus distinguish actual acts of worship from acts that, although they show respect for the idol, do not comprise worship. While all such behaviors are forbidden, only the former, involving actual acts of idol worship, render one subject to the death penalty.

The rabbis devote an entire Talmudic tractate, Avodah Zarah, to idolatry. Despite this fact, they do not appear to have believed that, in their own time, idolatry was a serious threat. Song of Songs Rabbah to Song of Songs 7:7 makes this explicit:

A. "You are stately as a palm tree" [Song 7:7]:
B. R. Hunia in the name of R. Dosa b. R. Tebet: "Two inclinations to do evil did the holy one, blessed be he, create in his world, the impulse to worship idols, and the impulse to fornicate. The impulse to worship idols has already been eliminated, but the impulse to fornicate still endures.
C. "Said the holy one, blessed be he, 'Whoever can withstand the impulse to fornicate do I credit as though he had withstood them both.'"
D. Said R. Judah, "The matter may be compared to the case of a snake-charmer who had [two] snakes. He charmed the larger and left the smaller, saying, 'Whoever can withstand this one is certainly credited as though he had withstood them both.'
E. "So the holy one, blessed be he, eliminated the impulse to worship idols but left the impulse to fornicate. He said, 'Whoever can withstand the impulse to fornicate do I credit as though he had withstood them both.'"

Of the two main inclinations towards evil, only the inclination to fornicate remains in effect. Striking is the explanation for this, C and D-E, which, contrary to what Scripture portrays, holds that the desire to worship idols never had a very strong influence over the people of Israel in the first place. The continuation of the passage contains a debate concerning when God eliminated the impulse to worship idols, whether in the time of Esther and Mordechai or the period of Nebuchadnezzer and the Babylonian exile. In either view, the rabbis understand idolatry long to have ceased to be a problem for the people of Israel.

The rabbis depicted idolatry's threat to Israelite monotheism by claiming that so many idols are worshipped in the world that sufficient parchment does not exist to contain all their names (Sifre Deuteronomy 43). But despite this pronouncement, they seem to have had little concrete worry that the Jews of their period would actually engage in the worship of these idols. Indeed, the fact of the matter is that in the rabbis' own day, as in the Second Temple period, Jews quickly revolted when other nations' introduced into Israelite territory the slightest aspects of idol worship. This meant that, rather than focusing upon stemming Jewish acceptance of pagan gods, which was in all events unnecessary, the Rabbinic treatment of idolatry could concern the broader question of how to assure that, in their contact with non-Jews, Jews did not *inadvertently* participate in or contribute to idol worship. This goal of preventing unintentional Israelite idolatry was accomplished through the placing of strict controls upon all contact between Jew and gentile. For instance, within three days of gentile festivals, Jews were forbidden from having contact with gentiles or from selling them objects that might be used in idol worship (M. A.Z. 1:1-2):

A. Before the festivals of gentiles for three days it is forbidden to do business with them,
B. to lend anything to them or to borrow anything from them,
C. to lend money to them or to borrow money from them,
D. to repay them or to be repaid by them.
E. R. Judah says, "They accept repayment from them, because it is distressing to him [that is, to the gentile, to remain in debt to the Israelite]."
F. They said to him, "Even though it is distressing to him now, he will be happy about it later [that is, after the festival, when he repays the loan]."
G. R. Ishmael says, "Three days before them and three days after them [doing business with gentiles] is prohibited."
H. And sages say, "Before their festivals it is prohibited, but after their festivals it is permitted."

Before, and, according to some authorities, after a pagan festival, economic exchange with an idol-worshipper is forbidden, since such interaction appears to be an acknowledgment by the Israelite of the pagan's religious practices. Especially repaying money owed to the gentile is forbidden, since the money might then immediately be used to support idol worship, and the Israelite then could be understood to have promoted idolatry. But while the concern for Israelite acknowledgment or promotion of idol worship appears real, we see at the same time a striking desire to assure friendly and appropriate relationships between Jews and non-Jews. In Judah's view, E, this goal even takes precedence over the concern that the Israelite acknowledge idolatry. Judah relaxes restrictions that in all events do not entail concrete Israelite monetary support of pagan rights, allowing, for instance, an Israelite to accept a gentile's loan repayment immediately prior to a pagan festival.

In dealing with the problem of an Israelite's travel around and business in cities that contain idols, the rabbis make a similar point. Business, they say, may not be done in an area containing an idol, and one is prohibited from using a road that leads to that city alone. But if there is no appearance that the Israelite intends to support or be involved in idol worship, these restrictions are relaxed (M. A.Z. 1:4):

> A. A city in which there is an idol—
> B. [in the area] outside of it one is permitted [to do business].
> C. [If] an idol was outside of it, [in the area] inside it is permitted.
> D. What is the rule as to going to that place?
> E. When the road is set aside for going to that place only, it is prohibited.
> F. But if one is able to take that same road to some other place, it is permitted.
> G. A town in which there is an idol,
> H. and there were in it shops that were adorned and shops which were not adorned—
> I. this was a case in Beth Shean, and sages ruled, "Those which are adorned are prohibited, but those which are not adorned are permitted."

There is here no evidence of a concern that the Israelite might *actually* engage in idol worship. At issue, rather, is the appearance his actions project. Israelites may not travel on a road that only goes to a place where there is an idol, since others who see this might assume that the person is going there to engage in idol worship and might, in this way, be encouraged themselves to stray from worship of the one God. But Israelites may use a road that also leads to other places, even if their destination in fact is the place with the idol. As before, the concern with preventing a Jew from inadvertently supporting idol worship or from creating the impression of being involved in idolatry is ameliorated by the desire to allow Jews to engage as openly as possible in economic relations with those who worship idols.

Even the use by Jews of bath houses and other public areas in which idols stood could be countenanced. This was the case so long as there was no suggestion of the Israelite's participation in a cultic activity and no reason to believe that the individual's presence in that place somehow showed respect to the idol (M. A.Z. 3:4):

> A. Peroqlos b. Philosephos[13] asked Rabban Gamaliel in Akko, when he was washing in Aphrodite's bath house, saying to him, "It is written in your Torah, 'And there shall cleave nothing of a devoted thing to your hand' [Deut. 13:18]. How is it that you are taking a bath in Aphrodite's bath house?"
> B. He said to him, "They do not give answers in a bathhouse."
> C. When he went out, he said to him, "I never came into her domain. She came into mine, [for] they don't say, 'Let's make a bathhouse as an ornament for Aphrodite;' but they say, 'Let's make Aphrodite as an ornament for the bathhouse.'
> D. "Another matter: Even if someone gave you a lot of money, you would never walk into your temple of idolatry naked or suffering a flux, nor would you urinate in its presence.
> E. "Yet this thing is standing there at the head of the gutter and everybody urinates right in front of her.
> F. "It is said only, '[You shall hew down the graven images of] their gods' (Deut. 12:3)—[this means] that which one treats as a god is prohibited, but that which one treats not as a god is permitted."

As B makes explicit, Gamaliel is scrupulous about the rules of the Torah that control Israelite behavior. Within a bath house, he will not even so much as answer a question regarding covenantal law, an action that would show disrespect to God. But, since he does not understand the figure of Aphrodite to be an object of actual worship, he sees no problem with using the bath house in which it stands. Rather, the placement of the statue and the way gentiles treat it suggest that it is mere ornamentation and so not subject to any prohibition. Within this line of reasoning, Israelites might be permitted to make open use of many of the public spaces and facilities within the Greco-Roman world in which they lived. It need not have been assumed that contact with the statues of Greek or other gods that stood in these places was a threat to Israelite religion.

That the threat of idolatry in this period was viewed as more theoretical than actual further is suggested by the rabbis' frequent reference to idolatry as a metaphor for the worst sin people can commit rather than as an actual sin that people in fact do commit. Rabbis, this is to say, often refer to other types of immorality as being tantamount to idolatry. Thus "a drunk who says a prayer is like one who worships an idol" (B. Ber. 31b), and failing to give charity is tantamount to idolatry (B. Ket. 68a). T. B.Q. 9:31 even associates excessive anger with idol worship:

A. R. Simeon b. Eleazar says in the name of R. Hilpai b. Agra which he said in the name of R. Yohanan b. Nuri, "If a person pulled out his own hair, tore his clothing, broke his utensils, scattered his coins, in a fit of anger, he should be regarded by you as though he performed an act of service for an idol.

B. "For if his temper should say to him, 'Go do an act of service for an idol,' he would go and do it.

C. "And that is the sort of thing that the evil impulse can do: Today it says to him, 'Do this,' tomorrow 'Do that,' until he tells him, 'Go serve idols,' and he goes and does just that."

As understood in this and similar passages, idol worship is no longer defined as the concrete religious practice forbidden by Scripture. It is not, this is to say, the result of the Israelite's belief in the existence of deities other than God or the outcome of the person's reasoned hope that by following pagan rituals he or she can harness for personal benefit powers in the world besides those of the Israelite deity. The term idolatry, rather, has taken on a general significance, so as to symbolize any sin in which an Israelite loses control of him or herself and so ceases to follow any of the precepts of the Torah. Idolatry thus is no longer about the actual making and worshipping of idols. It is, rather, a metaphor for what happens whenever a Jew loses his or her focus upon the tenets and ideals of the covenant with God. Through this development, the concept of idolatry remained a useful symbol of what Israelite's must not do even in a period in which actual Israelite worship of idols had long been a thing of the past.

The Rabbinic literature contains numerous references to specific deities, idolatrous rites, and products used in idol worship. Some actual practices and many familiar deities are mentioned, e.g., Peor, Aphrodite, Mercurius, and Asherah. Much of what is mentioned however seems idiosyncratic to the Rabbinic understanding of pagan rites, especially insofar as the rabbis more frequently mention biblical deities, no longer worshipped in their day, than they do the actual gods of the Greco-Roman world in which they lived. Included in the category of cult items mentioned by the rabbis but unknown from other sources are long lists of foods and animal products that, according to the rabbis, may not be sold to or bought from a gentile, lest they are to be used in idolatry. One such list appears at M. A.Z. 1:5:

A. These are things [which it is] forbidden to sell to gentiles:

B. fir cones, white figs, and their stalks, frankincense, and a white cock.

C. R. Judah says, "It is permitted to sell him a white cock among other cocks.

D. "And when it is all by itself, one cuts off its spur and sells it to him,

E. "for they do not offer to an idol one which is lacking [a spur]."

F. And as to everything else, [if] they are left without specification [as to their proposed use], it is permitted, but [if] they are specified [for use for idolatry], it is prohibited.

G. R. Meir says, "Also fine dates, Hasab, and Nicolaus dates it is prohibited to sell to gentiles."

The association between these specific items and actual practices of idol worship is unknown, as is the source or currency of certain rites the rabbis associated with idol-worship, e.g., cutting a round incision through an animal's hide at the heart (M. A.Z. 2:3).

Unlike Scripture, the Talmud makes no specific mention of Israelites' obligation to destroy objects of idol worship or actively to prevent gentiles from engaging in their worship. Indeed, although idolatry is included among the seven Noahide commandments that apply to all people, as the economic statutes listed above suggest, the rabbis overall take a mostly neutral stance towards other people's practice of idol worship. Thus Tarfon held that idolaters are less dangerous than Israelite sectarians (Y. Shab. 16:9, 15c):

> A. Said R. Tarfon, "I swear by the life of my children [lit.: May I bury my children!], that if [sectarians] came to my house, I would burn them and all memory of them!
> B. "For if a pursuer were pursuing me, I would escape into the house of an idolater, but I would not escape into the house of a sectarian.
> C. "For idol-worshippers do not know him [that is, the true God], and [as a result unintentionally] deny him.
> D. "But sectarians recognize him and [even so] they deny him.
> E. "And regarding them, David said [Ps. 129:31], 'Do I not hate them that hate thee, O Lord?'"

The rabbis were able to excuse idol worshippers, whom they understood to act out of ignorance. This was not the case for Jews who disregarded or denied the "true" practice of the religion of the covenant, as it was defined and described, of course, by the rabbis themselves. We see again in this attitude the extent to which the Talmudic rabbis defined idol worship as something other than a problem for Jews and Judaism. Idolatry, rather, was what other, misinformed people did. Unlike in the view of the Hebrew Scriptures, it was not acknowledged as a very real threat to the integrity of Israelite beliefs. These were threatened only by sectarian movements emerging from within Judaism itself, movements that, interestingly enough,

were accused not of worshipping idols but only of incorrectly worshipping or thinking about the Israelite God.

A similar resignation to other people's idolatry and a sense that the worship of idols was not dangerous to Israelite practices may stand behind the understanding that, outside of the land of Israel, Israelites are not even required to destroy idols. Commenting on Deut. 12:1-3, which states, "Tear down their altars, smash their pillars, put their sacred posts to the fire, and cut down the images of their gods, obliterating their name from that site," Sif. Deut. 61 explains:

> A. Is it possible that one is required to pursue them abroad?
> B. Scripture says, ". . . obliterating their name from *that* site."
> C. In the land of Israel one is required to pursue them, and one is not required to pursue them abroad.

Despite this general acceptance of idol worship practiced by other people, the rabbis were confident of the exclusive truth of their religious beliefs, stating that idols should not be referred to by favorable names (Sif. Deut. 61) and permitting Israelites to mock idolaters (B. Meg. 25b):

> A. Said R. Nahman, "All mocking is forbidden, except for ridiculing idols,
> B. "as it says [Is. 46:1]: 'Bel bows down, Nebo stoops.' And it [further] says [Is. 46:2]: 'They stoop, they bow down together, they cannot save the burden, [but themselves go into captivity].'"

The Mishnah moreover provides a benediction to be recited when one sees a place in the land of Israel in which idols previously were worshipped: "Blessed is he who uprooted idolatry from our land" (M. Ber. 9:1).

Idolatry in the post-Talmudic times: In the post Talmudic period, in particular by the fourteenth century, Rabbinic authorities largely rejected the notion that idol worship continued to exist within the religions with which Jews had regular contact. While adherents of religions other than Judaism continued regularly to be referred to as "worshippers of stars and constellations," rabbis of the medieval period and on denied that these people engaged in, or even knew, the rudiments of the actual practice of idolatry.[14] Like the earlier Talmudic discussions of idolatry, this determination by Rabbinic authorities had concrete implications for business and social relationships between Jews and non-Jews. It established, for instance, that wine produced by gentiles should not be forbidden to Jews simply on the assumption that a gentile would pour out some of each vat as a libation offering to a false god. While other considerations, such as the desire to prevent inter-religious socializing that might lead to Jewish assimilation, continued to be taken seriously, no longer would the fear of intentional or unwitting Jewish participation in idolatry have a role in the determination of Jewish law.

Notes

[1] On the following, see Edward M. Curtis, "Idol, Idolatry," in *ABD*, vol. 3, pp. 376-381.

[2] See also Exod. 20:23, 34:17, Lev. 19:4, 267:1, Deut. 4:15-19, 4:25, and 5:8.

[3] Note, however, that some iconolatry at least appears to have been accepted as appropriate in the time of the patriarchs and in some other settings: Abraham (Gen. 21:33) planted a tree in Beer Sheba, where he called upon God; at Beth El, Jacob (Gen. 18:18, 18:22, 35:14) set up a pillar used in the worship of God (this practice was later prohibited by Deut. 16:22); the curtains of the tabernacle were embroidered with figures of cherubim (Exod. 26:1, 36:8), and there were also there and in the later Temple two golden cherubim (Exod. 25:18-22, 1 Kgs. 6:23-28), understood to be the resting place of God. These images also were carved on the doors and walls of the Temple (1 Kgs. 6:29, etc.). But other forms of iconolatry clearly were proscribed as idolatry, e.g., the making of the Golden Calf (Exod. 32:1-8), which Aaron declared actually to be the god that brought the Israelites out of Egypt.

[4] This point is made dramatically at 1 Kgs. 18:21-35, where the prophets of Baal are unsuccessful in bringing down fire from Baal to ignite sacrifices laid out on an altar. Yahweh, by contrast, responds to Elijah, leading the Israelites to recognize that "The Lord, he is God."

[5] E.g., *Pesel*, from the root meaning "to hew;" *'Asab*, from a root meaning "to form;" *Tabnit*, from the root meaning "pattern." See Curtis, op. cit., p. 378.

[6] See, e.g., Jer. 50:2, Ezek. 22:3-4, and 1 Kgs. 15:12. See Curtis, ibid., and Francis Brown, et al., *A Hebrew and English Lexicon of the Old Testament* (Oxford, reprint, 1974), p. 165.

[7] See, e.g., Jer. 14:14, Lev. 19:4, Ezek. 30:13. See Curtis, ibid., and Brown, ibid., p. 47.

[8] See on this Curtis, pp. 379-400.

[9] See, e.g., the actions of Jehu, 2 Kgs. 9:33 and 10:18-28; the uprising led by the priest Jehoiada, 2 Kgs. 11:17; and, most important, the purge of idolatry in Judah under Hezekiah, 2 Kgs. 18:3-5 and 2 Chr. 29-31. But then Hezekiah's own son, Manasseh, reinstituted idolatry in perhaps the most consequential manner possible. Along with rebuilding the high places torn down by his father, he built altars for foreign deities within the central Israelite Temple in Jerusalem (2 Kgs. 18), something that even Queen Jezebel, who built new sanctuaries for pagan gods, had not done.

[10] Curtis, ibid., p. 380.

[11] See R.A. Oden, Jr., "The Persistence of Canaanite Religion," in *Biblical Archaeologist*, 1976, vol. 39, pp. 31-36.

[12] See W. Dever, "Material Remains and the Cult in Ancient Israel. An Essay in Archaeological Systematics," in C. Meyers and M. O'Connor, eds., *The Word of the Lord Shall Go Forth: Essays in Honor of David Noel Freedman* (Winona Lake, 1983), pp. 571-587, and J. Tigay, *You Shall Have No Other Gods Before Me: Israelite Religion in the Light of Hebrew Inscriptions* (Atlanta, 1986). Both are cited by Curtis.

[13] A "philosopher" clearly is intended. Perhaps the text should read: Peroqlos the philosopher.

[14] See, e.g., Tosafot to B. A.Z. 57b, s.v., *leafuqei miderav*. On this issue, see OTHER RELIGIONS, JUDAIC DOCTRINES OF.

ALAN J. AVERY-PECK

INTENTIONALITY IN JUDAISM: In the classical sources of Judaism, people match God in possessing freedom of will. The sole player in the cosmic drama with the power to upset God's plans is the human, who alone is like God, "in our image, after our likeness" (Gen. 1:26). Humanity bears a single trait that most accords with the likeness of God, the possession of will and the power of free exercise thereof. In justice and good will, God makes the rules; humanity willfully breaks them. The theology of the Oral Torah thus identifies free will as the principal point of correspondence between God and humans, the point at which God's image makes its deepest mark upon humankind's visage. Just as God freely chooses, so do people. In humankind, God has not met but made his match.

Humans have the power to violate the rules of order, but the rationality of justice then dictates the result. For when humanity rebels against God, rejecting God's dominion instead of loving God, that sin disrupts the world order. Punishment, "the proper fruit of his deeds" (Prov. 14:14), follows. That is why classical Judaism takes as its critical theological problem the tension between the word of God and the will of humans, in full recognition that God judges what humankind does by reason of the exercise of free will. Set forth in many ways, the simplest statement is that of Aqiba: "Everything is foreseen, and free choice is given; in goodness the world is judged; and all is in accord with the abundance of deeds" (M. Abot 3:15).

Free will, moreover, reaches concrete expression in the deeds a person does by reason of the plans or intentions he or she independently shapes. The high value accorded by God to a human's voluntary act of accepting God's dominion, the enthusiastic response made by God to a person's supererogatory deeds of uncoerced love and uncompelled generosity, the heavy emphasis upon the virtues of self-abnegation and self-restraint—these emblematic traits of a coherent theology attest to the uncertainty of humankind's response that, from the beginning, God has built into creation. For the one power that lies beyond the rules of reason, that defies predicting, is humankind's power to make up its own mind.

To show the importance of intentionality in classical Judaism, we note first that Scripture provides a very precise answer to the question of how to differentiate among sins or crimes and why to do so. Not only so, but the point of differentiation must rest with one's attitude or intentionality. Two stories tell how the power of God—the power to command—conflicts with the power of humanity—the power to obey or to rebel. The first such story of power differentiated by the will of the human being in communion or conflict with the word of the commanding God comes to us from the Garden of Eden. We cannot too often reread the following astonishing words (Gen. 2:15-3:24):

> The Lord God took the man and placed him in the garden of Eden . . . and the Lord God commanded the man, saying, "Of every tree of the garden you are free to eat; but as for the tree of knowledge of good and bad, you must not eat of it; for as soon as you eat of it, you shall die."
>
> . . . When the woman saw that the tree was

good for eating and a delight to the eyes, and that the tree was desirable as a source of wisdom, she took of its fruit and ate; she also gave some to her husband, and he ate. . . .

> The Lord God called out to the man and said to him, "Where are you?"
>
> He replied, "I heard the sound of you in the garden, and I was afraid, because I was naked, so I hid."
>
> Then he asked, "Who told you that you were naked? Did you eat of the tree from which I had forbidden you to eat?"
>
> . . . And the Lord God said to the woman, "What is this you have done!"
>
> The woman replied, "The serpent deceived me, and I ate."
>
> Then the Lord said to the serpent, "Because you did this, more cursed shall you be than all cattle. . . ."
>
> So the Lord God banished him from the garden of Eden. . . .

Now a reprise of the exchange between God, Adam, and Eve tells us that at stake was responsibility: not simply who violated the law, but who bears responsibility for *deliberately* violating the law. Each blames the next, and God sorts things out, responding to each in accord with the facts of the case: whose intentionality matches the actual deed?

> "The woman you put at my side—she gave me of the tree, and I ate."
> "The serpent duped me, and I ate."
> Then the Lord God said to the serpent, *"Because you did this. . . ."*

The ultimate responsibility lies with the one who acted deliberately, not under constraint or on account of deception or misinformation, as did Adam because of Eve, and Eve because of the serpent. True enough, all are punished, the serpent, but also woman—"I will make most severe your pangs in childbearing"—and Adam—"Because you did as your wife advised and ate of the tree about which I commanded you, 'you shall not eat of it,' cursed be the ground because of you." All are punished, but the punishment is differentiated; those who were duped are distinguished from the one who acted wholly on his own: the serpent is cursed; the woman is subjected to pain in childbearing, which ought to have been pain-free; because of man, the earth is cursed. This is a diminishing scale of penalties, each in accord with the level of intentionality or free, uncoerced will involved in the infraction. The sanction applies most severely to the one who, by intention and an act of will, violated God's intention and will.

We turn to a second story of disobedience and its consequences, the tale of Moses' hitting the rock (Num. 20:1-13):

> The community was without water, and they joined against Moses and Aaron. . . . Moses and Aaron came away from the congregation to the entrance of the Tent of Meeting and fell on their faces. The presence of the Lord appeared to them, and the Lord spoke to Moses, saying, "You and your brother Aaron take the rod and assemble the community, and before their very eyes order the rock to yield its water. Thus you shall produce water for them from the rock and provide drink for the congregation and their beasts."

> Moses took the rod from before the Lord as he had commanded him. Moses and Aaron assembled the congregation in front of the rock; and he said to them, "Listen, you rebels, shall we get water for you out of this rock?" And Moses raised his hand and struck the rock twice with his rod. Out came copious water, and the community and their beasts drank.

> But the Lord said to Moses and Aaron, "Because you did not trust me enough to affirm my sanctity in the sight of the Israelite people, therefore you shall not lead this congregation into the land that I have given them."

> Those are the waters of Meribah, meaning that the Israelites quarreled with the Lord—through which he affirmed his sanctity.

Clearly intentional disobedience here leads to the penalty of extirpation. Thus, both stories direct attention to the generative conception that at stake is the will of God over against the will of the human being, and, in particular, the Israelite human being. So Scripture records the story of God's commandment, humanity's disobedience, and God's sanction for the sin or crime (and, again and again, humanity's atonement and reconciliation). There is clearly drawn the distinction between what is deliberate and what is mitigated by an attitude that is not culpable, a distinction set forth in the trag-

edy of Adam and Eve, in the failure of Moses and Aaron, elsewhere, in the distinction between murder and manslaughter that the Written Torah works out, and in countless other passages in the Pentateuch, Prophetic Books, and Writings.

Let us turn to some of the many passages of the Oral Torah that illustrate that same principle. By "intentionality," sages mean the attitude that motivates a given action, the intention of the person who performs the action: what that person hopes to accomplish, to effect or prevent. That intentionality, or expression of an attitude, governs the action's classification, its effect or lack of effect, its acceptability or lack of acceptability, its culpability or lack of culpability. Even when the term for intention, *kavvanah*, is absent, the category of intentionality is shown by context to pertain. Thus intentionality classifies actions, so that with one intention an action is cursed, but with the opposite, it is blessed (T. Bik. 2:15):

> A. He who sells a Torah scroll never sees a sign of blessing.
> B. Scribes who copy Torah scrolls, phylactery-parchments, and mezuzah-parchments—they and their dealers who buy these items from scribes, and their dealers' dealers who buy them from other merchants, and all those who deal in sacred objects for the sake of making a profit will never see a sign of blessing.
> C. But if they were dealing with these objects for the sake of heaven, lo, they shall be blessed.

Dealing in holy objects for profit is not acceptable, for the sake of heaven is. So the same action can mean two different things, depending upon the intention of the individual who carries it out. One's intention thus affects the assessment of one's deed, whether for good or ill. Another example is Miriam, who criticized Moses and was punished. But her intention was honorable; had it been dishonorable, the punishment would have been greater (Sifre Num. XCIX:II.1-2):

> 1.A. "Miriam and Aaron spoke against Moses [because of the Cushite woman whom he had married; Num. 12:1]."

B. [It is taken for granted that they criticized Moses for ceasing to have sexual relations with his wife, Zipporah.] Now how did Miriam know Moses had ceased to have sexual relations with his wife? She realized that Zipporah was not making herself up with women's ornaments. She said to her, "How come you're not making up like other women?"

C. She said to her, "Your brother does not pay any attention to such things." Thus Miriam realized and told her brother, and both of them spoke against him.

D. R. Nathan says, "Miriam was standing alongside Zipporah when it was said, 'And the youth ran' [Num. 11:27]. When Zipporah heard the message, she said, 'Woe for the wives of these men [who have become prophets, since they now will lose their husbands' attention].'"

E. "On that basis Miriam realized the situation and told her brother and both of them spoke against him."

2.A. Now it is an argument *a fortiori*: if Miriam, who intended to speak against her brother not to his detriment but to his credit, and not to lessen procreation but to increase it, and who spoke only in private, yet she was punished, if someone intends to speak ill of his fellow and not in praise, to diminish and not to increase procreation, and speaks not in private but among others—how much the more so [will such a one be punished]!

B. Now it is an argument *a fortiori*: if Uzziah the king, who had no intention of arrogating greatness to himself for his own honor but for the honor of his creator, was punished as he was [2 Chr. 26:19], one who arrogates greatness to himself for his own honor and not for the honor of his creator—how much the more so [will such a one be punished]!

The premise once more is the power of intentionality to differentiate among actions, even of the same classification, and to designate the one as weightier, the other as less consequential.

Concrete actions take on consequence only by reference to the intention with which they are carried out. For example, what matters in sacrifices is intentionality; the size of the offering makes no difference, only the intent

of the person who presents it (B. Men. 13:11 I.2/110a):

A. It is said of the burnt offering of a beast, 'An offering by fire, a smell of sweet savor' (Lev. 1:9), and of the bird offering, 'An offering by fire, a smell of sweet savor' (Lev. 1:17), and even of the meal offering, 'An offering by fire, a smell of sweet savor' (Lev. 2:9)—to teach that all the same are the one who offers much and the one who offers little, on condition that a man will direct his intention to heaven.

B. Now lest you might say, 'Then it is because God needs the food,' Scripture states, 'If I were hungry, I would not tell you, for the world is mine and the fullness thereof' (Ps. 50:12); 'For every beast of the forest is mine and the cattle upon a thousand hills; I know all the fowl of the mountains and wild beasts of the field are mine; do I eat the meat of bulls or drink the blood of goats' (Ps. 50:10, 11, 13). I did not order you to make sacrifices so you might say, 'I will do what he wants so he will do what I wants.' You do not make sacrifices for my sake but for your sake: 'you shall sacrifice at your own volition' (Lev. 19:5)."

The correct intentionality involves submission to God's will, and that is what governs under all conditions. The same point is made at M. R.H. 3:8:

A. "Now it happened that when Moses held up his hand, Israel prevailed, and when he let his hand fall, Amalek prevailed" (Ex. 17:11).

B. Now do Moses's hands make war or stop it? But the purpose is to say this to you: So long as the Israelites would set their eyes upward and submit their hearts to their father in heaven, they would grow stronger. And if not, they fell.

More than this, the sources hold that God plays a direct role by responding to a person's intentionality as is appropriate (T. Pe. 1:4): "As regards a good intention—the Omnipresent, blessed be he, refines it so that it produces a corresponding deed. As for an evil intention—the Omnipresent does not refine it, so that it does not produce a corresponding deed."

Intentionality thus is critical in fulfilling one's religious duties. For even when it comes to doing religious deeds, intentionality dictates the value of what is done; while one may well carry out one's obligation to heaven through correct action, lack of matching intentionality negates the action. Purity of heart, desire to serve God and not to aggrandize oneself—these govern the effect of the act. Regarding such correct intentionality, the sources are clear. One must carry out the requirements of the Torah for their own sake, not for the sake of a reward. This is expressed, first of all, in terms of Torah-study itself, and, further, in the setting of carrying out the commandment (B. Ned. 8:3-4 II.8/ 62A):

A. It has been taught on Tannaite authority:
B. "That you may love the Lord your God and that you may obey his voice and that you may cleave to him" (Deut. 30:20):
C. This means that someone shouldn't say, "I shall study Scripture, so as to be called a sage, I shall repeat Mishnah teachings, so as to be called 'my lord.' I shall reason critically, so that I may be an elder and take a seat at the session."
D. Rather: Learn out of love, and honor will come on its own: "Bind them on your fingers, write them on the table of your heart" (Prov. 7:3); "Her ways are ways of pleasantness" (Prov. 3:17); "She is a tree of life to those that hold onto her, and happy is everyone who keeps her" (Prov. 3:18).

Sincerity means doing the deed for its own sake, in all contexts as an act of willing, uncoerced obedience to the kingdom of heaven. In this theory, sages can go so far as to say, "A transgression committed for its own sake, in a sincere spirit, is greater in value than a religious duty carried out not for its own sake, but in a spirit of insincerity." Fulfillment of the teachings of Torah must be motivated by the correct attitude of faith, not improper aspirations (Sifre Deut. CCCVI:XXII.1):

A. Another teaching concerning the phrase, "May my discourse come down as the rain, [my speech distill as the dew, like showers on young growths, like droplets on the grass. For the name of the Lord I proclaim]:"
B. R. Benaiah would say, "If you carry out the teachings of the Torah for their own sake, the teachings of the Torah will live for you.

C. "For it is said, 'For they are life to those that find them' (Prov. 4:22).
D. "But if you do not carry out teachings of the Torah for their own sake, they will kill you.
E. "For it is said, "My doctrine shall drop as the rain.'
F. "And the word for 'drop' yields the sense of 'killing,' in line with its usage in the following verse: 'And he shall break the heifer's neck there in the valley' (Deut. 21:4).
G. "'For she has cast down many wounded, yes, a mighty host are all those she has slain' (Prov. 7:26)."

The right attitude involves sincerity, a total commitment to the action for its own sake, which means, for the sake of heaven.

This idea carries us to the matter of faith, where intentionality shades over into attitude. It is a subtle matter, but sages treat as a cluster the virtues of proper intentionality, good faith, and faith as an act and attitude of trust. That is why faith forms another chapter in the story of intentionality. It represents an act of confidence in the true and benevolent intentionality of God. In sages' view, acting in good faith, in complete sincerity, makes a person worthy of encountering the Holy Spirit, because one thereby imputes to the Holy Spirit or to God that same attitude of correct and honest intention that God values (Mekhilta XXV:I.26):

A. R. Nehemiah says, "How do you know that whoever takes upon himself the obligation to carry out a single religious duty in faith is worthy that the Holy Spirit should rest upon him?
B. "For so we find in the case of our ancestors that as a reward for the act of faith that they made, they achieved merit, so that the Holy Spirit rested on them, as it is said [Ex. 14:21-15:1], 'and they believed in the Lord and in his servant Moses. Then Moses and the people of Israel sang this song [to the Lord, saying, "I will sing to the Lord, for he has triumphed gloriously; the horse and his rider he has thrown into the sea].'"

Here "in faith" means, "in good faith," that is, with sincerity—proper intentionality. But the passage forthwith shifts from "in faith" to "faith," and that speaks of confidence in the correct intentionality of the other, in this case, God.

What governs the relationship between intentionality and action? Here the critical importance of classification in the mode of thought of sages—natural historians of transcendence, we might call them—accounts for much. Intentionality governs, we already anticipate, because it has the power to classify actions, one sort of action being valid, another, invalid. The intentionality of the actor, then, defines the effect of an action; the same action, performed in the same way, may produce diverse results, based on the will that one brings to bear upon the action. In religious duties, the effect of intentionality proves especially critical, for the intention to carry out one's obligation must accompany the act that effects that obligation; otherwise, the act bears no effect, as M. Ber. 2:1A-C makes explicit:

A. One who was reading the verses of the Shema in the Torah and the time for the [required, liturgical] recitation of the Shema arrived:
B. If he directed his heart towards fulfilling the obligation to recite the Shema, he fulfilled his obligation to recite.
C. And if he did not direct his heart, he did not fulfill his obligation.

Similarly, whether or not the recitation of the Eighteen Benedictions, the central prayer of supplication, requires intentionality is subject to discussion, e.g., at M. Ber. 4:4 A, where Eliezer states, "One who makes his prayers a fixed task—his prayers are not valid supplications of God."

Intentionality may even take precedence over actual activity, as M. Ber. 4:5A-C indicates: "If he was riding on an ass, he should dismount to recite the Prayer [of Eighteen Benedictions]. But if he cannot dismount, he should turn his face toward the east. And if he cannot turn his face, he should direct his heart toward the Chamber of the Holy of Holies." In like manner, those who pray are to direct their hearts to God (M. Ber. 5:1 A-E):

A. One may stand to pray only in a solemn frame of mind.
B. The early pious ones used to tarry one hour before they would pray, so that they could direct their hearts to the Omnipresent.

C. While one is praying even if the king greets him, he may not respond.
D. And even if a serpent is entwined around his heel, he may not interrupt his prayer.

Intentionality indeed governs the effect of all rites (M. R.H. 3:7D-J):

A. He who was going along behind a synagogue, or whose house was near a synagogue, and who heard the sound of the shofar or the sound of the reading of the Scroll of Esther, if he paid attention [thereby intending to carry out his obligation], he has fulfilled his obligation.
B. But if not, he has not fulfilled his obligation.
C. That is the rule even if this one heard and that one heard, for this one paid attention, and that one did not pay attention to what he heard.

This approach to law and ritual suggests that intention always validates the consequent action. Strikingly, the converse is also true: violations of the law, if unintentional, may well be exempt from culpability. Done without the intention to violate God's law, the deed is not deemed an act of rebellion against the Torah (M. Ter. 2:3 [translation, A. Avery-Peck]):

A. One who immerses unclean utensils on the Sabbath [in violation of the restrictions of that day]—if he does so unintentionally, he may use them; but if he does so intentionally, he may not use them.
B. One who tithes his produce or who cooks on the Sabbath—if he does so unintentionally, he may eat the food he has prepared; but if he does so intentionally, he may not eat the food.
C. One who plants a tree on the Sabbath—if he does so unintentionally, he may leave it to grow; but if he does so intentionally, he must uproot it.
D. But in the Seventh Year of the Sabbatical cycle [the laws of which are violated by the continued growth of the tree], whether he has planted the tree unintentionally or intentionally, he must uproot it.

T. Shab. 2:17-18 makes the same point, distinguishing inadvertence from deliberation in action, with appropriately diverse penalties:

A. He who slaughters an animal on the Sabbath—if he did so inadvertently, it may be eaten at the end of the Sabbath. If he did so deliberately, it may not be eaten.
B. Produce one gathered on the Sabbath—

if he did so inadvertently, it may be eaten at the end of the Sabbath. If he did so deliberately, it may not be eaten.

The approach applied in the preceding two passages to interpreting the significance of physical actions (tithing, cooking, slaughtering, etc.) applies as well within the psychological realm. Intentionality thus forms, for instance, the principal criterion for effecting atonement through repentance, meaning that if one manifests the inappropriate intentionality, the rite of repentance is null (M. Yoma 8:9 A): "He who says, 'I shall sin and repent, sin and repent'—they give him no chance to do repentance. 'I will sin and the Day of Atonement will atone'—the Day of Atonement does not atone."

The individual did not really intend to repent, and, therefore, despite his statement to the contrary, repentance has not occurred. Similarly, mere *accidents* of speech are not binding; one must say exactly what is intended for the act of speech to be effective, whether in regard to oaths or offerings (M. Ter. 3:8 [translation, A. Avery-Peck]):

A. One who [in designating agricultural gifts] intends to say, "heave offering," but says, "tithe," "tithe," but says, "heave offering;"
B. [or who, in designating a sacrifice, intends to say,] "burnt offering," but says, "peace offering," "peace offering," but says, "burnt offering;"
C. [or who, in making a vow, intends to say], "that I will not enter this house," but says, "that house," "that I will not derive benefit from this one," but says, "from that one"—
D. has not said anything,
E. until his mouth and heart agree.

The status of produce that has been designated for God thus is dictated by the match of intentionality and deed; the person must say what he means; if he does, his intentionality takes over and transforms the produce, sanctifying it. An act of sanctification effects the will and intention of the actor—or is null.

One's intentionality further governs the effect of one's deeds when it comes to dealing with consecrated money or produce. For example, M. M.S. 1:5 rules:

A. One who buys pieces of fruit outside Jerusalem with money in the status of second tithe[which is to be eaten only in Jerusalem]—
B. if he did so unintentionally [not realizing the coins were consecrated], let their payment be returned to its former place [that is: the purchaser, who used these coins by mistake, gets them back in return; the produce he bought has not become second tithe];
C. if he did so on purpose [the produce takes on the status of second tithe; therefore, as is required in the case of this agricultural tithe], let the pieces of fruit be brought up and eaten in the holy place [Jerusalem]. And if the Temple does not exist, let the pieces of fruit rot.

Human intention similarly is central in determining when produce is subject to tithing in the first place. For it is exactly the intentionality of the farmer towards the use of produce that arouses God's response, a commensurate claim upon the share of the produce that, as tithes, must be put to the uses required by God. Thus, when the farmer decides to benefit from the crop, e.g., to take it to market for sale, then God's rights of ownership also are activated, and then the crop must be tithed, for the farmer's intention to take the crop as his own signifies the point at which God, as co-owner, also wants his share. Until this point, random nibbling, which does not suggest a claim upon the crop as a whole, is permitted without tithing. The action—plucking the produce—superficially is the same as harvesting. But the intention—to take it all or to take only a bit—controls the action's meaning.

But how do we know what farmers intend to do and whether their actions should be seen as rendering the produce subject to tithing? Their particular actions convey their attitude and intention vis à vis the crop (M. Ma. 1:5 [translation, Martin Jaffee]):

A. At what point after the harvest must tithes be removed from produce?
B. (1) Cucumbers and gourds—after he removes the fuzz [from them].
C. But if he does not remove the fuzz, [tithes need not be removed] until he stacks them up.
D. (2) Chatemelons—after he scalds [them in order to remove the fuzz].

E. But if he does not scald [them, tithes need not be removed] until he makes a store [of melons].

F. (3) Green vegetables that are [normally] tied in bunches—after he ties [them].

G. But if he does not tie them, [tithes need not be removed] until the vessel [into which he places the picked greens] is filled.

H. But if he does not fill the vessel, [tithes need not be removed] until he collects all he needs.

I. (4) [The contents of] a basket [need not be tithed] until he covers [the basket].

J. But if he does not cover [it, tithes need not be removed] until he fills the vessel.

K. But if he does not fill the vessel, [tithes need not be removed] until he collects all he needs [in that basket].

L. Under what circumstances [do these criteria apply]? If he is bringing the produce to market.

M. But if he is bringing it home, [it is not liable to the removal of tithes, and] he eats some of it as a random snack until he reaches home.

What people do indicates their attitude and intention, to use the produce in a formal way, which is subject to tithing, or simply to take a bit for a snack, which is not. So intentionality again classifies a set of similar actions into diverse categories, each governed by its own rule.

In light of what we have seen, it is hardly surprising to find that, to incur guilt, one must intend the action one carries out. But those who act in a manner different from what was intended are not culpable as they would be had they accomplished their purpose (M. San. 9:4):

A. [If] he intended to kill a beast but killed a man,

B. a gentile but killed an Israelite,

C. an untimely birth but killed an offspring that was viable,

D. he is exempt.

E. [If] he intended to hit him on his loins with a blow that was not sufficient to kill him when it struck his loins, but it hit his heart, and there was sufficient force in that blow to kill him when it struck his heart, and he died, he is exempt.

F. [If] he intended to hit him on his heart, and there was in that blow sufficient force to kill when it struck his heart, and it hit him on his loins, and there was not sufficient force in that blow to kill him

when it struck his loins, but he died,

G. he is exempt.

H. [If I he intended to hit a large person, and there was not sufficient force in that blow to kill a large person, but it hit a small person, and there was sufficient force in that blow to kill a small person, and he died,

I. he is exempt.

J. [If] he intended to hit a small person, and there was in that blow sufficient force to kill a small person, and it struck the large person, and there was not sufficient force in that blow to kill the large person, but he died,

K. he is exempt.

L. But: [if] he intended to hit him on his loins, and there was sufficient force in the blow to kill him when it struck his loins, and it hit him on his heart and he died,

M. he is liable.

N. [If] he intended to hit a large person, and there was in that blow sufficient force to kill the large person, and it hit a small person and he died,

O. he is liable.

P. R. Simeon says, "Even if he intended to kill this party, and he actually killed some other party, he is exempt."

The system of criminal justice thus vastly expands on the distinction between manslaughter and murder. Once, like Scripture, we take account of intentionality in the matter of killing a person, we amplify and elaborate the issue to accommodate the exact correspondence between what one proposed to do and what he has actually done.

Still more: the entire system of animal sacrifices in atonement of sin rests on the distinction between intentional and unintentional actions. Indeed, that fact looms large in matter of repentance, which matches the correct intention now against the improper intention then and so rights the balance between God's and the human's will by bringing the person's will back into synchroneity with God's. Take the sin-offering, which is efficacious only as atonement for a sin committed through an inadvertent act. A deliberate action is not covered, so M. Shab. 11:6J-K:

A. This is the general principle: All those who may be liable to sin offerings in fact are not liable unless at the beginning and the end, their sin is done inadvertently.

B. But if the beginning of their sin is inadvertent and the end is deliberate, or the beginning deliberate and the end inadvertent, they are exempt—

C. unless at the beginning and at the end their sin is inadvertent.

The matter of intentionality also governs the penalty to be paid by means of an animal sacrifice or some other form of sanction, e.g., extirpation (premature death), death at the hands of heaven, or death at the hands of an earthly court, (M. Ker. 1:2):

A. For those transgressions are people liable, for deliberately doing them, to the punishment of extirpation, and for accidentally doing them, to the bringing of a sin offering, and for not being certain of whether or not one has done them, to a suspensive guilt offering (Lev. 5:17)—

B. "except for the one who imparts uncleanness to the sanctuary and its Holy Things, because he is subject to bringing a sliding scale offering (Lev. 5:6-7, 11)," the words of R. Meir.

C. And sages say, "Also: except for the one who blasphemes, as it is said, 'You shall have one law for him that does anything unwittingly' (Num. 15:29)—excluding the blasphemer, who does no concrete deed."

Intentionality governs the acceptability of some classes of animal offerings but not others. Specifically, if an animal is designated for use as a Passover offering or as a sin offering, but then the officiating priest offers the animal up under some other designation, that is, in a classification other than that specified by the donor's intent, the offering is null (M. Zeb. 1:1 = M. Men. 1:1 for meal offerings):

A. All animal offerings slaughtered not for their own name are valid, so that the blood is tossed, the entrails burned, etc., but they do not go to the owner's credit in fulfillment of an obligation, except for the Passover and the sin offering—the Passover at its appointed time the afternoon of the fourteenth of Nisan.

So too M. Zeb. 2:3:

A. This is the general rule: Whoever slaughters, or receives the blood, or conveys the blood, or sprinkles the blood intending to eat something that is usually eaten flesh, to burn something which is usually burned entrails, outside of its proper place the court for Most Holy Things, Jerusalem

for Lesser Holy Things—it is invalid and the flesh may not be eaten. And extirpation does not apply to it.

B. Whoever slaughters, or receives the blood, or conveys the blood, or sprinkles [the blood], intending to eat something that is usually eaten, to burn something that is usually burned outside of its proper time—it is refuse. And they are liable on its account to extirpation even if they eat the flesh within the time limit.

The intentionality of the animal offering covers six matters, and for each of these matters, the animal must be offered up under the donor's correct intentionality (M. Zeb. 4:6):

A. For the sake of six things is the animal offering sacrificed: (1) for the sake of the animal offering, (2) for the sake of the one who sacrifices it, (3) for the sake of the Lord, (4) for the sake of the altar fires, (5) for the sake of the odor, (6) for the sake of the pleasing smell.

B. And as to the sin offering and the guilt offering, for the sake of the sin expiated thereby.

C. Said R. Yose, "Even: One who was not mindful in his heart for the sake of one of all of these but slaughtered without specifying these things—it is valid, for it is a condition imposed by the court, that intention follows only the mind of the one who carries out the act, not the owner; and the officiant does not specify the six things at all."

We not only assess intentionality, we take account of the probability that someone will have acted in accord with the proper intentionality even in avoiding the cultic contamination of objects, so b. Hag. 2:7 II.3-2/18b:

A. Said R. Jonathan b. Eleazar, "If someone's head-band fell from him, and he said to his fellow, 'Give it to me,' and he gave it to him, the headband is unclean, for we cannot assume that he took it upon himself to guard it from uncleanness while he handled it, since the owner did not ask whether he was clean or not, nor can we say that the owner guarded it against defilement while it was not in his possession.

B. Said R. Jonathan b. Amram, "If one's garments for the Sabbath were mixed up with his garments for everyday, and he put them on, they are made unclean."

If someone protects something assuming it is one thing and finds it to be another, it is unclean. Here, once more, intentionality serves to classify an action and its consequence.

Intentionality extends to other matters besides concrete issues of the law and its practice. Intentionality shades over into attitude, the abstract becoming concrete through feelings or emotions. The right attitude is one of accommodation of one's own will to the will of others, self-abnegation, restraint, prudence. The most prized virtue is humility, on account of which Judah merited that the monarchy be assigned to his tribe, so too Saul (T. Ber. 4:18). A person should conform to the prevailing practice of the community and not stand out, so Hillel the Elder says at T. Ber. 2:21:

> Do not appear naked where others go clothed, and do not appear clothed where others go naked, and do not appear standing where others sit, and do not appear sitting where others stand, and do not appear laughing where others weep, and do not appear weeping where others laugh, because Scripture states, 'a time to weep, a time to laugh, a time to embrace, a time to refrain from embracing' (Ec. 3:4, 5).

And altruism is the right attitude, e.g., M. Abot 5:16:

> A. In any loving relationship that depends upon something, when that thing is gone, the love is gone. But any that does not depend upon something will never come to an end.
> B. What is a loving relationship that depends upon something? That is the love of Amnon and Tamar (2 Sam. 13:15). And one that does not depend upon something? That is the love of David and Jonathan.

So too the right intention is what validates contention (M. Abot 5:17):

> A. Any dispute that is for the sake of heaven will in the end yield results, and any that is not for the sake of heaven will in the end not yield results.
> B. What is a dispute for the sake of heaven? This is the sort of dispute between Hillel and Shammai.
> C. And what is one that is not for the sake of heaven? It is the dispute of Korah and all his party. One from whom people do not take pleasure, the Omnipresent does not take pleasure."

In line with what we have seen, the ability to form a valid intention in respect to religious obligations determines the point at which a minor may first carry out those obligations (T. Hag. 1:2):

> A. If he knows how to shake an object, he is liable to observe the commandment of the lulab. If he knows how to cloak himself, he is liable for the commandment of fringes. If he knows how to speak, his father teaches him the Shema, Torah, and the Holy Language Hebrew.
> B. And if not, it would have been better had he not come into the world.
> C. If he knows how to take care of his phylacteries, his father purchases phylacteries for him. If he knows how to take care of his person, they eat food preserved in a state of cultic cleanness depending upon the cleanness of his person. If he knows how to take care of his hands, they eat food preserved in a state of cultic cleanness depending upon the cleanness of his hands.
> D. If he has sufficient intelligence to answer a question, then a doubt involving him in private domain is resolved as unclean, and one involving him in public domain is resolved as clean.
> E. If he knows how to effect proper slaughter of an animal, then an act of slaughter on his part is valid.

The intention to do evil, even if the action is not done, is culpable and to be repented (B. Qid. 4:13/II.13/81b):

> A. R. Hiyyam bar Ashi was accustomed, whenever he prostrated himself to his face, to say, "May the All-Merciful save us from the Evil Impulse." Once his wife heard this. She said, "Now how many years he has kept away from me, so how come he says this?"
> B. One day he was studying in his garden, and she dressed up in disguise and walked back and forth before him. He said to him, "How are you?" She said to him, "I'm Haruta the famous whore, and I've come back today." He lusted after her. She said to him, "Bring me that pomegranate from the top bough." He climbed up and got it for her.
> C. When he went back inside his house, his wife was heating the oven, so he climbed up and sat down in it. She said to him, "So what's going on?" He told her what had happened. She said to him, "So it was really me." But he wouldn't believe her

until she gave him the pomegranate. He said to her, "Well, anyhow, my intention was to do what is prohibited."

D. For the rest of the life of that righteous man he fasted in penitence until he died on that account.

E. So too in the following: When R. Aqiba would come to this verse, he wept, saying, "If someone intended to eat ham and really had in hand veal, yet the Torah has said that he requires atonement and forgiveness, one who intends to eat ham and really had in hand ham—all the more so!"

F. Along these same lines: "Though he knew it not, yet he is guilty and shall bear his iniquity" (Lev. 5:17)—when R. Aqiba would come to this verse of Scripture, he would weep: "If someone intended to eat permitted fat and really had in hand forbidden fat, yet the Torah has said, 'Though he knew it not, yet he is guilty and shall bear his iniquity,' one who really did intend to eat forbidden fat and had in hand forbidden fat—all the more so is he guilty!"

G. Issi b. Judah says, "'Though he knew it not, yet he is guilty and shall bear his iniquity' (Lev. 5:17)—for such a thing as this that we are sinful even not by intent let all those who are mournful mourn."

It would be difficult to assemble a more uniform set of diverse formulations of a single principle. Intentionality forms the systemic dynamics of the entire structure of sanctification and morality that the Oral Torah constructs. It is the principal variable, because it is the one thing that God has created that is possessed of its own autonomy. That is why, also, it is intentionality that explains sin, and it is sin that, as we know, accounts for the imperfect condition of the world and of Israel therein.

JACOB NEUSNER

ISLAMIC DOCTRINES OF JUDAISM: "Islam," no less than "Judaism," is a construct, and its contents vary according to what Muslims, or Jews, or indeed anyone else, chooses to include in it. But in the case of Muslims and Jews, at least there are foundational texts that establish the general outlines of the construct and to some extent point the direction of its future development. What Muslims hold "Islam" to be is dictated in its broadest terms by the Quran, the text whose affirmation as the Word of God precisely marks the Muslim as Muslim. And if the Quran tells the Muslim and (somewhat less successfully) others what Islam is and ought to be, the same Holy Book also lays out for the Muslim what is Judaism and Christianity, Islam's covenantal siblings.

None of these constructs remained fixed with Muhammad's death in 632 C.E. and the consequent closure of the Quran. They were outlines to be continuously expanded and modified by subsequent generations of Muslims, substantially and obviously by Islam's religious elite of lawyers and theologians but not less remarkably by ordinary believers who century after century brought their own plentiful nuances to both "Islam" and "Judaism." Nor did thinking alone make it so. Muslims have not only thought about Judaism; they have also acted and reacted with the countless Jews who have lived under Muslim sovereignty from 629 C.E. to the present. The Muslim construct "Judaism" is indeed deep and rich.

To take the measure, then, of either "Islam" or "Judaism" in a Muslim context is to attempt to step into a rapidly flowing stream, and when that stream is as long and wide and as clogged with clerics and paper as the Islamic experience, the task becomes impractical as well as unproductive. We must settle here for the more modest but more certain blueprint of Judaism sketched in the Quran and the foundation stones laid down by the Prophet Muhammad's own rather complex experience with Jews. Whatever their subsequent interpretation, both are normative for Muslims everywhere, and so we shall confine out attention chiefly to them.

Every Muslim who opens the Quran hears only the voice of God there, but every Jew and Christian who looks into the Sacred Scripture of Islam is immediately impressed by the familiarity of its contents, its objectives, and even its style. Before the Quran ends, it has touched upon Adam, Cain and Abel, Noah and the flood, Abraham and his sons Ishmael and Isaac. Lot, Jacob, Joseph and his brethren—Joseph has an entire chapter, or *sûra* (Sura 12), devoted to his story—

Moses and Aaron, the Pharaoh, the escape of the Israelites from Egypt, Saul, David, Solomon, Jonah, and Job. This is a fairly extensive repertoire, but the absences are equally interesting. Though Muhammad was obviously interested in the prophetic office, and many of the early biblical figures from Adam to Solomon are treated as prophets, the classic prophets of the biblical canon like Jeremiah and Isaiah, two of the prophets, incidentally, most favored by Christians, are not mentioned at all. The Babylonian Exile and the Return are likewise ignored, as is all subsequent Jewish history. Muhammad was interested in history in a very narrow sense. He was not so much explaining the past as *using* it, and the biblical stories in the Quran are generally told for a reason: sometimes as *âyât*, "signs," or, more commonly, as *mathâni*, "punishment stories" about the consequences of ignoring prophets, particularly when they refer to the people of Abraham, of Lot, of Noah, or Moses.

In addition to these reflections on the biblical past, which appear in the earliest part of the Quran, the book contains numerous references to contemporary Jews with whom Muhammad came in contact, and, more particularly, to the Jews of Medina, the oasis where, twelve years after he began his prophetic mission, he had his first religious and political exchange with a Jewish community. Those Jews of Medina, though they are sometimes characterized, are never named or described, in the manner of all his revelations. But for all their opacity, they provide important clues to Muhammad's attitude not merely to the religion of the Jews but to his reactions to actual members of that faith community.

There is, then, every indication that the prophet of the Quran knew about and meditated upon the subject of Jews and Judaism. We shall look somewhat more closely into the sources of that knowledge and the consequences of his meditation.

The Jews of Arabia: We know too little to speak of "Arabian Judaism" on the eve of Islam. We know only that there was in the sixth century a considerable Jewish presence in the once prosperous land of the Yemen

and that there were other tribes, often the paramount tribes, that were identifiably Jewish to their Arab contemporaries and who dwelled in the oases strung like a necklace from Medina, 275 miles north-northeast of Mecca all the way north to the present border between Jordan and Saudi Arabia. The Yemen was a settled land with a literate people—South Arabian, with its linear script, is well-preserved and related to the Ethiopic of the peoples across the narrow straits of the Red Sea—and so we are somewhat better informed about them than we are of the northern oasis-dwellers.

Two pieces of information are pertinent here. In the sixth century, Jewish monotheism is on prominent display in the preserved South Arabian inscriptions, and in the same era a Jewish royal house, probably indigenous, came to rule in the Yemen. This Jewish rise to prominence brought Jews into direct conflict with a growing Christian presence that had originated with missionaries from Christian Abyssinia and was supplemented and augmented in the sixth century by an actual Abyssinian colonial force in the Yemen. By the early sixth century, Jews and Christians there were locked into a cycle of mutual persecution that came to a head in a slaughter of Christians at various towns in the Yemen, followed by an Abyssinian intervention and the death of the notorious Dhû Nuwâs, the last Jewish king of South Arabia. Most of the Abyssinians eventually went home, but they left behind one of their generals, Abraha, who soon declared his independence and ruled the Yemen, a Christian dominated Yemen, in his own name. The Jews there had lost their political power, but they were neither annihilated nor expelled, and not too long afterward Islam was drawing some of its most illustrious converts, and the source of much later information on the biblical background of the Quran, from among the Yemeni Jews, like the semi-legendary Ka'b "the Rabbi" (*al-Ahbâr*), who was reportedly converted in 638 C.E. and who seems to stand behind so many of the "Israelite tales" that filled in the later Muslims' knowledge of the Bible.

Little of this rich background, which was

known to the later (eighth-ninth centuries) biographers of Muhammad, appears in the Quran, which does make what appears to be a single, oblique reference to an attack by Abraha (?) against Mecca (Sura 105). Where the Quran does, however, betray some Yemeni, possibly Jewish, influence is in its early references to the god *Rahman*, "The Merciful One," who shows up often in the South Arabian inscriptions. Though at first *Rahman* does not always seem to be identical with Allah, soon the two are harmonized (cf., Sura 17:110), and the term *rahmân* eventually takes its place as a simple title or attribute of the High God of Islam.

Turning northward from Mecca, we encounter the other already noted Jewish communities in the oases of northwestern Arabia. Epigraphical evidence, the Quran and the Talmud, as well as the later Arab historical tradition all attest to their existence, though not very certainly to their beliefs and practices. We cannot say how they got there—though likely it was by emigration from the north—or precisely when. But if they were ethnic outsiders, the Jews of the Hijaz oases were fairly thoroughly acculturated, though by no means assimilated, to the Arab ways of their neighbors. Muhammad encountered Jews in the oasis of Medina when he arrived there in 622 C.E., but there is no evidence of a fixed or identifiable Jewish community at Mecca, which was not, like the other Jewish settlement sites, an oasis but a shrine center with closely linked trade and commercial ambitions. It is not unlikely, however, that before and during Muhammad's lifetime there were Jews in his native town as transient merchants perhaps, and, as will be shown, the Meccans' obvious familiarity with the Quran's frequent biblical allusions promotes to a strong probability the likelihood of some kind of pre-Islamic Jewish presence at Mecca.

The Bible and the Quran: An investigation into the origin and scope of the connection between Islam and the Jews must perforce begin with that first community's founding document, the Quran, the collection into 114 *sûras* or chapters of the revelations given to Muhammad between 610 and his death in 632 C.E. Taken together, they constitute his God-given message, which is nothing more or less than *islâm*, submission to the will of the one true God. Two characteristics of these revelations concern us here. First, they are ongoing, that is, they were dispensed—to Muhammad privately, and then proclaimed by him publicly and verbatim to whoever would attend—over a period of twenty-two years, in two different places, Mecca and Medina, and in changing social, political, and economic circumstances. Thus, for all its supernatural origins, the Quran is a historically conditioned document. Muslim jurisprudence is in fact based upon that assumption. Quranic commentators displayed great energy and ingenuity in laying out the "occasions," that is, the historical setting and circumstances of each of the revelations in the Quran, and the jurisprudents then attempted to sort out how a later revelation might have modified or even abrogated an earlier one.

History has a second claim upon the Quran, and so upon Islam. As the Quran itself makes clear, the message given to Muhammad stands in close historical, moral, and providential relationship to earlier such revelations, chief among them, that given to the *Banû Isrâ'îl*, as the Quran calls the Jews. This is a primary theme of Muhammad's revelation, never disowned or rescinded despite the Prophet's increasing political difficulties with the latter-day bearers of that revelation. Indeed, the Quran itself invites the comparison with the earlier Scriptures (Sura 41:43; 43:45-65), and even the most cursory glance shows that the "warner," as Muhammad is styled, and those Meccans to whom the "guidance" and "good news" was directed were both of them familiar with the chief personages of the Bible and to some degree with the covenantal progress from Abraham through the prophets, the latter including Jesus ('Îsâ). But Muhammad was a pagan, albeit a rather off-handed one, and his native Mecca was far from the Jewish Holy Land. Still the Quran is filled with what are apparently Jewish stories, and Muhammad himself is reported to have once prayed facing Jerusalem, and he likely fasted on Yom Kippur as well.

In the present context, we can afford to disregard these latter behavioral questions, principally on the basis of a systematic doubt that has grown up around the material in the biographies of Muhammad, and to concentrate on the Quran, whose authenticity is more firmly established and which in any event antedates the extant versions of the biographies by a century or more.

The Quran, Judaism, and Jews: Though the Quran makes no explicit mention of "Judaism," it shows a fairly elaborate knowledge of, and theory about, Jews, Jewish history (almost exclusively pre-exilic), and Jewish practices and beliefs. This information falls into two, overlapping categories that concern the biblical Israelites and another, less distinctly articulated but more deeply felt, corpus on the Jews of contemporary Arabia.

The Quran speaks often of the Children of Israel (*Banû Isrâ'îl*)—it prefers this biblical term to the more common contemporary appellation, "Israel"—who constitute both a community (*umma*) and a religion (*dîn*). Unlike the legislation of the Christian Roman Empire, which reserved the designation *religio* uniquely for Christianity and characterized Judaism as *superstitio*, the Quran exceptionally recognizes a multiplicity of religions in the world, of which Islam is one, along with that of the Children of Israel, the Christians, and the pagans, "those who associate (others) with God." Of these latter groups, Muhammad is made to say in the Quran, "To them their religion and to me, mine." The community of the Children of Israel is tribal—it takes Muhammad some time, and probably some Jewish assistance, to sort out the correct progenetic sequence of Abraham, Isaac, Jacob/Israel—but their religion is scriptural. Like Christianity and Islam after it, the *dîn* of the Children of Israel is founded on the contents of a divinely revealed book. Jews and Christians are in fact often characterized in the Quran simply as "People of the Book" without further description or distinction.

Although there were other divine books, that given to Abraham for example, the primacy of honor in the Israelite revelation belongs to the Torah (*Tawrât*) sent down to Moses. Moses is central to Muhammad's closure with Judaism, and this is true from the very earliest of the Quranic revelations. The Torah revelation, its prehistory, form, and modalities, is the prototype of the Quranic one. And it is the example of Moses, particularly in his dealings with the Pharaoh, that provides the moral paradigm—persecution, then vindication—of Muhammad's own mission.

For Muhammad, the contents of the Mosaic revelation constitute the substance of Judaism. What that content is emerges indirectly but fairly distinctly from the Quran's frequent but allusive references. The Torah is a moral code "commanding the good and prohibiting the reprehensible," to use the language of the Muslims' own moral imperative, as well as a series of specific behavioral prescriptions, like the observance of the Sabbath. The most pervasive of these prescriptions, or at least those that receive the greatest attention in the Quran, are the dietary laws. The reason may be that it was here that Muhammad was most aware that he was departing from Jewish norms. Only a few foods are forbidden to Muslims (Sura 16:116-124)—later jurists considerably extended the list—and this difference elicits an explanation of the Torah's even more varied prohibitions: the Israelites were "recompensed for their willful disobedience" (Sura 6:147; 4:158; 16:119). And the debate obviously continued into later days. The Jewish dietary laws continued to be discussed in the *hadîth* (the body of traditions ascribed to the Prophet but generally regarded by non-Muslim scholars as the creation of a later generation of believers), though by then the debate was more about Jewish-Muslim legal differences and appears to have turned away from the subject of food to that of sexual practices.

The Quran betrays a deep ambivalence toward the Jews of history. The Children of Israel were indeed the people whom God chose "in his knowledge" in preference to all the world (Sura 44:32; 45:16) and were destined to dwell in the land God gave them (Sura 17:104; 7:137; 10:93). But the Israelites were not content with their destiny. They did "mischief on the earth" and as a result were twice punished by an awful destruction of their Temple (Sura 17:4-8; which destructions are meant is not clear from the text). But more consequential to the Quran is the Israelites' persistent habit of contention and disputation. The Children of Israel fell out among themselves as soon as "the knowledge" was given them (Sura 10:93; 45:16-17). Indeed, Muhammad's view of contemporary Judaism, even before he went to Medina and had first-hand experience of a Jewish community—and of Jewish rejection—was that it was and remained a religion wracked with schism and sectarianism. God will judge among their factions at the resurrection, but, in the meantime, Muhammad has been sent to the Jews as an arbiter of religious matters: only the Quran can explain the things on which they continue to disagree (Sura 27:76-78; 45:16-18).

The Quran insists, Muslims believe, and historians affirm that Muhammad and his followers worship the same God as the Jews (Sura 29:46). Conceptually, at least, this is true, though the portrait of Yahweh that unfolds in the Bible is both more complex and psychologically nuanced and more directly engaged in history, if not in secondary causality, than the majestic but rather abstract and remote Allah of the Quran. Muhammad also understands that his Book is a confirmation of what has been sent beforehand to the Jews (Sura 2:41). Indeed, early in his career the Prophet had been instructed to turn to the Jews if he had any doubts about the revelation that had been sent down to him, and the Meccans are offered as a proof of the truth of Muhammad's message the fact that "the scholars of the *Banû Isrâ'îl* know it" (Sura 26:196-197).

We know little of what to make of either Muhammad's information about the Bible and the Jews or of his attitude toward them. Mecca, as has been said, had no fixed Jewish or Christian population, though there may have been members of both groups passing through it from Abyssinia across the Red Sea or from the Yemen on the south. There was, then, probably no lack of informants for both Muhammad and the Meccans, since his audience seems to have shared to some

degree—how else would his preaching have made sense?—his biblical knowledge. It is the quality of that knowledge that defies exact definition. The shape and tone of the Quran's biblical stories suggest that we are dealing with orally transmitted midrash rather than direct textual acquaintance. As far as the Bible is concerned, Muhammad may indeed have been retelling "old stories," as his Meccan opponents claimed (Sura 6:25; 8:31; 16:24; 23:83), but they owe far more to the midrashic Genesis Rabbah than to Genesis. Nor is there any evidence that the Prophet was reading the Bible (or anything else, for that matter; he obviously was, as the Muslim tradition insists, Sura 7:157-158, an *ummi*, a "scriptural illiterate"); what he got, he heard at Mecca, though we do not know precisely from whom.

Was it Jewish or Christian, that midrashic background buzz that provided the Quran's richly textured *Heilsgeschichte*? Both groups shared the same biblical accounts, of course, and given the syncretizing tendencies of religious communities on the margins of culture, as the Jews and Christians of the Hijaz were, there is little to choose between them as sources for the biblical perspectives on view in the Meccan suras of the Quran. But there are clues. The notion that the Jews were highly factionalized, the repeated insistence that Jesus was of the Children of Israel (Sura 43:57-59), and Muhammad's own exalted, though hardly mainstream Christian, view that Jesus was both mortal and the prophetic messiah (Sura 3:59; 4:171-172), all suggest that we are dealing in the Meccan environment, and perhaps at Medina as well, with some version of a Judeo-Christian remnant surviving in Arabia in the early seventh century, the Hijazi equivalent of the Mandeans of Iraq, a similar group that Muhammad apparently knew as the "Sabians."

"Israelite tales:" As already noted, the Quran's earliest references to biblical events and personages are allusive in the extreme, and there was an effort in the Medina suras to supply further—and more accurate—details on such matters as well as to sharpen their exegetical thrust. If the Quran's brief but pointed biblical references were enough to ground the faith of the first believers, they did not entirely satisfy the pious curiosity of succeeding generations of Muslims, some of whom, at least, had been Jews or Christians and so, presumably, had a fuller knowledge of the Bible, and, we may suspect, of the *midrashim*. Jewish converts in particular served as informants for the body of biblical amplification later known simply as *Isrâ'îliyyât*. The word means not "Judaica" or "stories from Jews," whom the Muslims called *Yahûd*, but, rather, from their content, "biblical stories." If Abraham and Ishmael built the Meccan Ka'ba, for example, as the Quran asserts (Sura 2:127), how did Ishmael, much less Abraham, find himself in that remote Arabian town? The quite elaborate and, on the face of it, quite plausible answer is provided in the *Isrâ'îliyyât*. Driven from the Negev, Hagar took the young—actually, infant in this version—Ishmael into Arabia and finally settled at Mecca, where Abraham later sought out and discovered his former concubine and firstborn son. Many more details were to follow in the tale, though the Quran itself shows no awareness of them. Ishmael grows to manhood at Mecca, marries a local Arab princess, and raises a family. The career of his descendants was not brilliant: they were forced to yield control of Mecca to outsiders and, more, they ignominiously lapsed from the monotheistic faith of their illustrious grandfather into a litholatrous paganism.

This segment of biblical midrash mainly concerns the Quran's brief Abraham-Ishmael allusions and provided rich material for Muhammad's biographers, who used the information to flesh out the earliest history of Mecca and to explain its obvious paganism at the time of Muhammad's call to prophecy. But the *Isrâ'îliyyât* ranged backward and forward among all the prophets—Solomon was a particular favorite, as he was in parallel Jewish tales—and eventually led to the creation of an entire literary genre known as "Tales of the Prophets." These were, quite professedly, entertainments rather than history. Jewish converts to Islam may indeed have been the source of the material, and much of it, like the stories of Abraham and

Ishmael in Mecca, may in fact antedate Islam. But stories improve with the telling, and the early Muslim entertainers responsible for creating, or performing, the "Tales of the Prophets" doubtless added their own creative touches to the narratives.

If the *Isrâ'îliyyât* began innocuously enough as bible amplifications, once attention began to be directed more to their origins than to their content, the fact that they had been supplied by Jews, albeit converts, bothered some Muslims, and the *Isrâ'îliyyât* began to be excluded from serious consideration as history—"It is reported by the Jews; it is prohibited (to be used) . . ."—even though they were never really intended as such. But well before this reaction, the *Isrâ'îliyyât* had worked themselves deep into the Muslim view of the prophets who had received and spread God's message in earlier times. Indeed, much of Louis Ginzberg's *Legends of the Jews* can be echoed, if not duplicated, directly out of the Muslims' "Tales of the Prophets."

Muhammad at Medina: In 622 C.E., after twelve generally unsuccessful years as a prophetic preacher in Mecca, Muhammad's fortunes were radically changed and, with them, his knowledge and understanding of the "Children of Israel." In that year, Muhammad managed to extricate himself and his followers from an increasingly dangerous Mecca and settle into Medina, whither he had been invited in the hope that this Arabian holy man might arbitrate the social and economic problems that were troubling the settlement. The two chief Arab tribes of Medina, the Aws and Khazraj, had slid into chronic confrontation within its narrow and heavily fortified confines, and they had each carried with them into the fray their Jewish tribal allies within the oasis. Arab history later recalled that the Jews had once been the masters of the oasis of Medina, as they still were of some of the other oases, but by this time of troubles they were merely clients. The Jews of Medina, chief among them the tribes of Qaynuqa', Nadir, and Qurayyza, had no part in inviting Muhammad to Medina, but they were certainly parties to the agreement drawn up between Muhammad and the

Medinese in the earliest days of his stay there. Like all the others, Muslims and pagans, they pledged themselves in the so-called "Constitution of Medina" to cease their quarrels and henceforward refer all disputes to "God and Muhammad." Few of the signatories could have imagined what followed.

In the sequel, there was little to refer to the new arbiter, since events moved rapidly in what must have been for most an unexpected direction. In 624 C.E., at a place called Badr Wells, Muhammad and his Muslim followers fell upon a Meccan caravan returning to that latter city; booty was taken, and the success of the bold venture created new attention and respect for Muhammad in Medina. The Meccans attempted, unsuccessfully, to riposte, and, from that moment on, the dynamic of history swung strongly behind the Prophet of Islam. This new political turn must have caused consternation among the Jews of Medina, who had already encountered Muhammad on religious ground and had become aware that this was no mere Arabian poet or seer, much less a mere arbitrator.

Tracing that first confrontation is a delicate work of reading between the lines of the Quran, but the revelations of what we calculate to be the early Medina period show Muhammad's rather abrupt departure from his own apparently Jewish practices in cultic matters. Where earlier he had prayed facing Jerusalem, for example, he announced, to the apparent confusion of his followers (Sura 2:142-145), that henceforward Muslims would pray facing the Ka'ba in Mecca. And where earlier Muhammad and the Muslims appear to have fasted, like the Jews, on the tenth of Tishre, Yom Kippur, he changed the practice early on at Medina and moved the fast to the month of Ramadan, associated now not with the giving of the Torah to Moses but with the "sending down" of the Quran to himself on the "night of destiny" (cf., Sura 97:1-5; 44:1-6). It was at Medina as well that Gabriel as the agent for the revelation of the Quran appears and, more important, that what was being preached in the Quran was neither Judaism nor Christianity but a return to the pristine "religion of Abraham."

"Abraham," the Quran explains, "was neither a Jew nor a Christian; rather, he was a monotheist (*hanîf*), a submitter (*muslim*), and not an idolater. Among men the nearest to Abraham are those who follow him, as are this prophet and those who believe . . ." (Sura 3:76-68).

Where once the Jews were called upon to verify Muhammad's message, at Medina they are accused of changing, distorting, and even inventing Scripture deliberately to deceive the Prophet (Sura 2:75-79, 89, 101). There is likely some historical echo here of Muhammad's debates about Scripture with what passed at Medina as Jewish scholars. But whatever the case, the conclusion is firm: the Torah presently in the hands of the Jews was worthless and will remain so forever more. Unlike the Christians, who must read the Old Testament to discover the messiah of the New, Muslims need not, and, given the Jewish tampering, in fact should not read the Bible. Not many did, in any event, after Muhammad: it was a number of centuries before the Bible was available in Arabic—it certainly was not in the Prophet's lifetime—and even Muslim polemicists long contented themselves with drawing upon biblical florilegia for the matter of their disputes with Jews of Islamic lands.

At Medina too emerges Muhammad's most distinctive theory about the relationship between Judaism and Islam. Jewish religion (*dîn*) is the direct consequence of the revelation of the Torah law, but there was a religious community that antedated Moses and was neither Jewish nor Christian. This was the religion (*millah*) of Abraham (Sura 2:135-136, 140), the pristine faith that is the prototype of all the subsequent monotheistic communities and to which Islam is the preeminent heir. Like Paul, Muhammad went behind Moses to find in Abraham a figure and a religious event, Abraham's conversion from paganism (which the Quran describes in greater detail than the Bible), which effectively trumps the Jewish claim to primacy. But where Paul stressed the quality of Abraham's faith, the Quran insists rather upon its object, the unique creator God, over against the false gods of paganism.

This is a watershed proclamation, the Prophet's declaration of emancipation from Judaism. It is of a piece with the ritual changes that preceded and accompanied it and with the increasing insistence that the Quran, which had from the first been characterized as a "recitation" (*qur'ân*), was indeed also a "Scripture" (*kitâb*), like the "*Tawrât*" and the "*Injîl*". These new attitudes and practices are doubtless the result of that first encounter with the Jews of Medina in the first year or two after the "migration" (*hijra*) of 622 C.E. Muhammad—who at Mecca thought he was announcing no more than what the earlier biblical prophets had said—likely expected the Jews of Medina to recognize this and to acknowledge his own firmly held conviction of his prophetic calling. When they did not, not only does the Quran's tone regarding the Jews generally (*Yahûd*, as it now prefers to call the *Banû Isrâ'îl*) grow more harsh and critical, but there follow violent political consequences for the Jewish tribes of Medina.

In the afterglow of Muhammad's first success against Mecca, his followers attacked the Qaynuqa' and expelled them from the oasis (Sura 59:2-4). The alleged motives are somewhat unconvincing in the sources, but we may discern in the act a fear of Jewish treason—the Medina Jews did in fact turn to Mecca for support against this now fearsome man—and the desire to possess Jewish wealth and property for the benefit of the still-impoverished Muslim migrants in Medina. Soon it was the turn of the Nadir: they too were expelled from the oasis and their property divided among the Muslims. Finally, the Qurayza were attacked in their fortified Medina redoubts, and upon their surrender they were taken to the market of Medina and slaughtered, 600 or 700 of them in all (Sura 33:26-27). Muslim jurists later judged that the Qurayza had broken their treaty with the Prophet by assisting the Meccans and pointed in justification to Sura 8:55-58: "The worst of beasts in the sight of God are those who reject Him . . . They are those with whom you made a pact, then they break their compact every time. . . . If you fear treachery from any group, dissolve it (that is,

your covenant) with them equally, for God does not love the treacherous."

Dhimma and Dhimmis: There was, however, one last political act to be played out between Muhammad and the Jews. In the year 628 C.E., temporarily freed from the threat of reprisal by his still hostile countrymen at Mecca, Muhammad conducted a raid against Medina's neighbor oasis of Khaybar. This was an entirely Jewish settlement, now swollen by Jewish refugees—and, in Muhammad's eyes, traitors—from Medina. The Muslim raiders attacked the settlement and, after a brief resistance, the oasis-dwellers capitulated. This was the first Muslim territorial conquest in which a settlement outside of Medina surrendered its sovereignty and liberty to Muhammad, without, at the same time, expressing a willingness to profess Islam. Of the courses of action open to him, Muhammad chose to offer the Jews of Khaybar a type of treaty (*dhimma*). Muhammad dictated the terms, and by them the defeated retained possession (though not ownership) of their homes and lands but had, in return, to surrender half the oasis' annual produce to Muhammad and the Muslims.

The Jews of Khaybar surrendered their sovereignty, though not their assent, to Islam and thus became in effect the first Sephardim, that is, Jews living as Jews under Muslim rule. And at a stroke, the Islamic Muslim community (*umma*), which to this point was constituted of the religious city-state of Medina (now entirely Muslim), was converted into a territorial domain under the governorship of Muhammad. And it now embraced within its expanding political boundaries non-Muslims as well as Muslims. At Khaybar, the imperial "Abode of Islam" (*dâr al-islâm*) came into existence and with it a major precedent for the Muslims' subsequent political and religious treatment of all the Jews and Christians swept by conquest under Islamic sovereignty.

The Quran sometimes distinguishes between Jews and Christians—in the latest revelations it shows a marked preference for the latter (Sura 5:82)—and sometimes combines them under the general rubric "People of the Book." But as the sequel to the Khaybar *dhimma* was to show, from the juridical point of view, the distinction now ceased to exist. As more conquered peoples were extended the *dhimma*, and as the *ad hoc* terms granted to the Jews of Khaybar grew increasingly detailed and increasingly standardized over the decades of conquest, it becomes clear that, in the eyes of Islamic law, Jews and Christians (and whoever else might qualify as "People of the Book") had an identical juridical status. They were "protected communities" (*dhimmis*). The People of the Book, who for centuries constituted the overwhelming majority of the population of the explosively expanding Dar al-Islam, were constrained to pay an annual poll-tax—Muslims paid none—and, though permitted to retain their beliefs and cult, had imposed upon them a number of political, social, and economic restrictions that reached into their public religious life as well. Like all the *dhimmis*, the Jews of the Dar al-Islam could not proselytize among the Muslims, build new places of worship—every construction had to be justified as "repair"—or conduct public cult observances. And like all previsions of Islamic canon law, the submissive *dhimma*, with both its guarantees and restrictions, is still in effect in Muslim lands.

Muslim-Jewish polemic: Muslim polemic against Jews and Judaism begins with the Quran and continues into modern times. In the present era "Zionism" has chiefly subsumed both those other categories, but for most of the encounter between the two communities, Islam's literary and theological attention—what Muslim governors and judges did in given historical circumstances is another matter—was directed more toward Judaism than toward Jews, and, to be more specific, to the question of the Bible. The Muslims engaged the Christians on their theology, and the Christians the Muslims on their ethics, but the Bible was the primary and almost exclusive battleground between Muslims and Jews into the modern era.

Both the divine origin and the imperfection of the present copy of the Jewish Scriptures is certified in the Quran. The case might thus be considered closed from the Muslim side, save that the Quran went somewhat further. Sura 7:156 claims that the Prophet was already known to both the Torah and the Gospel, and Sura 61:6 asserts that those earlier Scriptures referred to him as "Ahmad" or, if that is not a proper name, as "the praised one." The Quran as the Word of God could simply make those assertions apodictically. But there are no such manifest statements in the Scriptures of either the Jews or Christians, and so later Muslims had either to charge tampering with the original or locate the appropriately prophetic meaning beneath the literal sense of the present texts. Muslim apologists and commentators tried both approaches, and so the Jews had to defend both the integrity of their version of the Bible—against the allegation, for example, that the Mosaic text had been lost or disintegrated and that, after the Exile, Ezra had unsuccessfully tried to reconstitute it—and the validity of their interpretation of passages like Deut. 18:15-18, 33:2-3, and Is. 21:6-9, which Muslims claimed predicted Muhammad's coming and mission.

Where the Muslims got their information about the Bible and how they learned to deploy it is a difficult question, since there is very little evidence that they had any direct knowledge of the Masoretic text or the Septuagint. It could have come from Jewish converts to Islam like Samaw'al al-Maghribi, whose *Silencing of the Jews* was written in Baghdad in 1163. But far more likely is contact—oral rather than written—with a whole range of earlier biblical polemicists of various Jewish, Samaritan, Christian, and Manichean stripes, whose views survived into Islamic times in a bewildering variety of hardy Near Eastern sectarian communities. Warfare over biblical texts had a long history and Islam fell heir to many of its weapons and strategies.

The Jewish response, in notable contrast to aggressive Christian polemic against Islam, is quite restrained. There are preserved no formal anti-Islamic polemics written in Arabic by Jews living under Islam, and where there is counter-exegesis of the Muslim prooftexts, they invariably appear in general commentaries on Scripture written in Hebrew and intended for the comfort and conviction of a Jewish readership, not a Muslim one. Jewish authors might occasionally characterize Muhammad as *meshugga' chez eux*, but they were not themselves so addled as to make public remark of it. Two contradictory, but equally plausible, reasons have been suggested for this reticence. One is that the Jews were so threatened that to indulge in polemic would be to court enormous danger; the other is that the Jews were so secure that it was unnecessary. More likely the reason lies elsewhere. Christians were the Muslims' chief antagonists throughout the long Middle Ages, and the great mass of Muslim polemic was directed against these political, economic, and military rivals both inside and outside Islam. The Christians replied in kind. The Jewish presence inside Islam was considerably more subdued and its political presence on the frontiers of the Abode of Islam nonexistent. The Muslims were apparently content to make their exegetical points about the Bible and let it go at that. And so were the Jews.

Bibliography

Cohen, Mark R., *Under Crescent and Cross. The Jews in the Middle Ages* (Princeton, 1994).

Firestone, Reuben, *Journeys in Holy Lands. The Evolution of Abraham-Ishmael Legend in Islamic Exegesis* (Albany, 1990).

Lazarus-Yafeh, Hava, *Intertwined Worlds. Medieval Islam and Bible Criticism* (Princeton, 1992).

Lewis, Bernard, *The Jews of Islam* (Princeton, 1984).

Peters, F.E., *Muhammad and the Origins of Islam* (Albany, 1994).

F.E. PETERS

ISRAEL, LAND OF, IN CLASSICAL JUDAISM: The land of Israel in the classical sources of Judaism, both the Oral Torah and the liturgy of the synagogue and the home, is the counterpart of Eden, just as, in these same sources, the people of Israel is presented as the counterpart of Adam. The parallel is appropriate, because gaining the land, at the end of the forty years in the wilderness, marked the completion of Israel's history. Or, it would have marked that end, had Israel not sinned and ultimately lost the land, the metaphorical counterpart to the Fall from Eden. In the mythology of classical Judaism, separation of the people Israel from the land of Israel through exile is the divine penalty for the people's violating the covenant. Concomitantly, return to the land will mark the fulfillment of history, bringing with it the last judgment, the resurrection of the dead, and the advent of the age to come.

The idea that the people of Israel's return to the land of Israel will mark the completion of the divine plan for the world derives from the notion that, in the plan of creation, humans were meant to live in Eden and Israel in the land of Israel in time without end. The restoration will bring about that long and tragically-postponed perfection of the world order, further demonstrating the justice of God's plan for creation. Risen from the dead, humankind will be judged in accord with its deeds. The people of Israel for its part, when it repents and conforms its will to God's, recovers its Eden, returning to the land of Israel. So the consequences of rebellion and sin having been overcome, the struggle of the human will and God's word having been resolved, God's original plan for the people Israel in the land of Israel will be realized at the last.

In line with the centrality of the land of Israel in God's messianic scheme, in classical Judaism, the only territories differentiated in world geography are the land of Israel and, therein, the metropolis of Jerusalem. These are heavily differentiated, e.g., as to levels of sanctification, while no other territory or city is differentiated in any way at all. But these are holy, and no other territory or city is holy. The land of Israel is that territory that God promised to Abraham and gave to the children of Israel on condition that they keep the covenant, so Scripture made clear. Still more indicative of its enchanted standing, the question of the borders of the land at various points in the history of Judaism is moot; for Judaism, the religion, what matters is the holiness of the land, which is enhanced when the land is occupied by the holy people. The union of land and people marked Israel's attainment of Eden when Joshua led Israel into the land. That union would have stood for ever, had Israel not sinned. Sinning, Israel lost the land. The restoration for good will take place, classical Judaism teaches, when the people of Israel has repented its sin, atoned, attained reconciliation with God, and been forgiven. Then the messiah will gather in the exiles of Israel and restore the people to the land of Israel, the new Eden of the world to come. At that time, humanity at large will acknowledge the unity of God and enter into the condition of Israel too. So the land in concrete and in theological terms defines a principal component of classical Judaism.

The election of Israel is matched by the election of the land: God examined all the nations and chose Israel among them, considered all generations and chose the generation of the wilderness to receive the Torah, inspected all lands and chose *the* land, so Lev. R. XIII:II.1:

> A. R. Simeon b. Yohai opened [discourse by citing the following verse:] "'He stood and measured the earth; he looked and shook [YTR = released] the nations; [then the eternal mountains were scattered as the everlasting hills sank low. His ways were as of old]' [Hab. 3:6].
> B. "The Holy One, blessed be he, took the measure of all the nations and found no nation but Israel that was truly worthy to receive the Torah.
> C. "The Holy One, blessed be he, further took the measure of all generations and found no generation but the generation of the wilderness that was truly worthy to receive the Torah.

Here we come to the matter of geography. Moriah, where the Temple was built, is compared to all other mountains and found worthy of God's presence:

> D. "The Holy One, blessed be he, further took the measure of all mountains and found no mountain but Mount Moriah that was truly worthy for the presence of God to come to rest upon it.

Jerusalem similarly is compared with all other cities and is the one place worthy of having the sanctuary built in its limits:

> E. "The Holy One, blessed be he, further took the measure of all cities and found no city but Jerusalem that was truly worthy to have the house of the sanctuary built in it.

> F. "The Holy One, blessed be he, further took the measure of all mountains and found no mountain but Sinai that was truly worthy for the Torah to be given upon it.

Now comes the land of Israel, the only place truly worthy of the holy people, Israel:

> G. "The Holy One, blessed be he, further took the measure of all lands and found no land but the land of Israel that was truly worthy for the people Israel.
> H. "That is in line with the following verse of Scripture: 'He stood and took the measure of the earth.'"

The question that is answered is, why did God choose Israel, the generation that received the Torah, Moriah, Sinai, the land of Israel, and so on? The answer is, there was no better, more worthy choice, because of Israel's willingness to receive the Torah, just that generation, just that location being added.

Israel's claim to the land of Israel derives from observing the commandments. This is worked out in an argument involving Abraham and his inheritance of the land, in line with the statement of Simeon b. Yohai at T. Sot. 6:9: "Now if Abraham, who had received only a few commandments, inherits the land, we, who have been commanded concerning all of the commandments, surely should inherit the land." That is to say, because Israel inherits many commandments (the conventional number is 613), Israel inherits the land just as Abraham did. The land of Israel also is so distinguished because the dead who are buried there will be the first to come to life in the messianic era, being the land that gives breath to the people upon it (Y. Kil. 9:3 VI). Dying in the land of Israel is preferable to dying anywhere else (Y. Kil. 9:3 VI).

What gives God the right to give the land of Israel to the people of Israel? It is because God created the world and recorded that act in the Torah, establishing the right to dispose of the land as God wished. Indeed, the point of the story of creation is to explain why Israel possesses the land of Israel, so Gen. R. I:II.1:

> A. Joshua of Sikhnin in the name of R. Levi commenced discourse by citing the fol-

lowing verse: "'He has declared to his people the power of his works, in giving them the heritage of the nations' (Ps. 111:6).

B. "What is the reason that the Holy One, blessed be he, revealed to Israel what was created on the first day and what on the second? It was on account of the nations of the world. It was so that they should not ridicule the Israelites, saying to them, 'Are you not a nation of robbers having stolen the land from the Canaanites?'

C. "It allows the Israelites to answer them, 'And as to you, is there no spoil in your hands? For surely: "The Caphtorim, who came forth out of Caphtor, destroyed them and dwelled in their place"' (Deut. 2:23)!

D. "'The world and everything in it belongs to the Holy One, blessed be he. When he wanted, he gave it to you, and when he wanted, he took it from you and gave it to us.'

E. "That is in line with what is written, '. . . .in giving them the heritage of the nations, he has declared to his people the power of his works' (Ps. 111:6).

F. "So as to give them the land, he established his right to do so by informing them that he had created it. He told them about the beginning: 'In the beginning God created . . .'" (Gen. 1:1).

The sages thus read the story of the creation of the world in Genesis as an account of how God acquired the Holy Land and gained the right to give ownership of it to the people Israel.

That is why the union of the people of Israel and the Holy Land is so important. Indeed, merely living in the land is a form of atonement for sin, so Sifre Deut. CCC-XXXIII:VI.1:

A. R. Meir would say, "For whoever lives in the land of Israel, the land of Israel atones. For it is said, 'The people who live there will be forgiven their iniquity' (Is. 33:24).

B. "Still, the matter is not entirely settled, for we do not know whether they bear their sins upon it or whether their sins are forgiven upon it.

C. "When Scripture says, 'and cleanse the land of his people,' one must conclude that they bear their sins upon it, and their sins are not forgiven upon it."

D. And so did R. Meir say, "Whoever lives in the land of Israel, recites the *Shema* morning and evening, and speaks the

holy language, lo, such a one is destined for the world to come."

Meir's holds that when an Israelite takes up residence in the land of Israel and lives there, that very act forms an atonement for sin, and living in the land, reciting the Shema ("Hear O Israel, the Lord our God, the Lord is One"), and speaking the holy language of Hebrew suffice to win for a person a place in the world to come.

Israel's story in the land of Israel is the counterpart to Adam's in Eden, so the land of Israel is the counterpart, after the flood, to Eden before, as we see when we compare the people of Israel in its land with Adam in Eden. By reason of disobedience, Adam sinned and was justly punished by exile from Eden; that represented an act of mercy; he was not wiped out, as God had said he would be. Because of disobedience, Israel sinned and was justly punished by exile from the land of Israel, counterpart to Eden. Accordingly, Gen. Rabbah XIX:IX.2 systematically compares Adam and Israel, the first man and the last, in Eden and in the land of Israel, and shows how the story of Adam matches the story of Israel—but with a difference:

A. R. Abbahu in the name of R. Yose bar Haninah: "It is written, 'But they are like a man [Adam], they have transgressed the covenant' (Hos. 6:7).

B. "'They are like a man,' specifically, like the first man.

Now the composer identifies an action in regard to Adam with a counterpart action in regard to Israel, in each case matching verse for verse, beginning with Eden and Adam:

C. "'In the case of the first man, I brought him into the garden of Eden, I commanded him, he violated my commandment, I judged him to be sent away and driven out, but I mourned for him, saying, "How . . ."' [which begins the book of Lamentations, hence standing for a lament].

D. "'I brought him into the garden of Eden,' as it is written, 'And the Lord God took the man and put him into the garden of Eden' (Gen. 2:15).

E. "'I commanded him,' as it is written, 'And the Lord God commanded . . .' (Gen. 2:16).

F. "'And he violated my commandment,' as it is written, 'Did you eat from the tree concerning which I commanded you' (Gen. 3:11).

G. "'I judged him to be sent away,' as it is written, 'And the Lord God sent him from the garden of Eden' (Gen. 3:23).

H. "'And I judged him to be driven out.' 'And he drove out the man' (Gen. 3:24).

I. "'But I mourned for him, saying, "How . . .".' 'And he said to him, "Where are you"' (Gen. 3:9), since the word for 'where are you' is written [the same as], 'How. . . .'

Now comes the systematic comparison of Adam and Eden with the people and land of Israel:

J. "'So too in the case of his descendants, [God continues to speak,] I brought them into the land of Israel, I commanded them, they violated my commandment, I judged them to be sent out and driven away, but I mourned for them, saying, "How. . . ."'"

K. "'I brought them into the land of Israel.' 'And I brought you into the land of Carmel' (Jer. 2:7).

L. "'I commanded them.' 'And you, command the children of Israel' (Ex. 27:20). 'Command the children of Israel' (Lev. 24:2).

M. "'They violated my commandment.' 'And all Israel have violated your Torah' (Dan. 9:11).

N. "'I judged them to be sent out.' 'Send them away, out of my sight and let them go forth' (Jer. 15:1).

O. "'. . . .and driven away.' 'From my house I shall drive them' (Hos. 9:15).

P. "'But I mourned for them, saying, "How. . . ."' 'How has the city sat solitary, that was full of people' (Lam. 1:1)."

Here we end where we began, Israel in exile from the land, like Adam in exile from Eden. But the Torah is clear that there is a difference: Israel can repent.

God not only took up residence in the land, at the Temple, but, when God sent Israel into exile, he himself left the Temple and the land in stages. In Lam. Rabbah XXV:i.3, the relationship of God to the land is shown in its unraveling, as God responded to Israel's sin stage by stage:

A. In ten upward stages the presence of God departed: from the cherub to the cherub, from the cherub to the threshold of the Temple-building; from the threshold of the Temple to the two cherubim; from the two cherubim to the eastern gate of the sanctuary; from the eastern gate of the sanctuary to the [wall of the] Temple court; from the [wall of the] Temple court to the altar; from the altar to the roof; from the roof to the city wall, from the city wall to the city, from the city to the Mount of Olives.

B. . . . from the ark cover to the cherub: "And he rode upon a cherub and flew" (2 Sam. 22:11).

C. . . . from the cherub to the cherub: "And the glory of the Lord mounted up from the cherub to the threshold of the house" (Ezek. 10:45).

D. . . . from the cherub to the threshold of the house: "And the glory of the God of Israel was gone up from the cherub, whereupon it was to the threshold of the house" (Ezek. 9:3).

E. . . . from the threshold of the Temple to the two cherubim: "And the glory of the Lord went forth from off the threshold of the house and stood over the cherubim" (Ezek. 10:18). . . .

H. . . . from the two cherubim to the eastern gate of the sanctuary: "The cherubs raised their wings and flew above the earth before my eyes" (Ezek. 10:9).

I. . . . from the eastern gate of the sanctuary to the [wall of the] Temple court: "And the courtyard was filled with the splendor of the glory of the Lord" (Ezek. 10:4).

J. . . . from the [wall of the] Temple court to the altar: "I saw the Lord standing beside the altar" (Amos 9:1).

K. . . . from the altar to the roof: "It is better to dwell on the corner of the roof" (Prov. 21:9).

L. . . . from the roof to the altar: "I saw the Lord standing beside the altar" (Amos 9:1).

M. . . . from the altar to the wall: "and behold, the Lord was standing on the wall made by a plumb line" (Amos 7:7).

S. Said R. Judah bar Simon, "It was from the wall to the city, as it is said, 'Listen, the Lord cries to the city' (Micah 6:9)."

T. . . . from the city to the Mount of Olives: "And the glory of the Lord went up from the midst of the city and stood on the mountain" (Ezek. 11:23).

So, as Israel lost Jerusalem and the land of Israel, God took leave as well. God's intimate relationship with Israel and with the land is expressed in the view that God mourned over

Jerusalem like a mortal king. Thus, when God left the land, that marked exile for him as much as for Israel, for God goes into exile where Israelites are exiled (Y. Ta. 1:1 II:5):

> A. It has been taught by R. Simeon b. Yohai, "To every place to which the Israelites went into exile, the presence of God went with them into exile.

The account now specifies the several places to which Israel went into exile and indicates proof in Scripture that God went with them. First comes Egypt:

> B. "They were sent into exile to Egypt, and the presence of God went into exile with them. What is the scriptural basis for this claim? '[And there came a man of God to Eli, and said to him, "Thus the Lord has said], 'I revealed myself to the house of your father when they were in Egypt subject to the house of Pharaoh'"' (1 Sam. 2:27).

Second is Babylon:

> C. "They were sent into exile to Babylonia, and the presence of God went into exile with them. What is the scriptural basis for this claim? '[Thus says the Lord, your Redeemer, the Holy One of Israel]: For your sake I will send to Babylon [and break down all the bars, and the shouting of the Chaldeans will be turned to lamentations]' (Is. 43:14).

Third, in the conventional list, is Media:

> D. "They were sent into exile into Media, and the presence of God went into exile with them. What is the scriptural basis for this claim? 'And I will set my throne in Elam [and destroy their king and princes, says the Lord]' (Jer. 49:38). And Elam means only Media, as it is said, '[And I saw in the vision; and when I saw], I was in Susa the capital, which is in the province of Elam; [and I saw in the vision, and I was at the river Ulai]' (Dan. 8:2).

Fourth is Greece:

> E. "They went into exile to Greece, and the presence of God went into exile with them. What is the scriptural basis for this claim? '[For I have bent Judah as my bow; I have made Ephraim its arrow]. I will brandish your sons, O Zion, over your sons, O Greece, [and wield you like a warrior's sword]' (Zech. 9:13).

Finally comes Rome, the last pagan kingdom, at the fall of which, the classical sources maintain, Israel will be restored to the land of Israel:

> F. "They went into exile to Rome, and the presence of God went into exile with them. What is the scriptural basis for this claim? '[The oracle concerning Dumah]. One is calling to me from Seir, "Watchman, what of the night? Watchman, what of the night?" Is. 21:11).'"

Thus God remains with Israel wherever Israel is exiled, and that is even in a condition of uncleanness, a point made at Sifre to Numbers CLXI:III.2. The exposition takes for granted that all places outside the land of Israel suffer the uncleanness that corpses impart (as at Numbers 19), and so when God goes into exile beyond the limits of the holy land, God accepts the condition of uncleanness of the overseas exiles:

> A. "in the midst of which I dwell:"
> B. So precious is Israel that even though the people suffer uncleanness, the presence of God is among them, as it is said, "Thus he shall make atonement for the holy place, because of the uncleanness of the people of Israel . . . and so he shall do for the tent of meeting, which abides with them in the midst of their uncleannesses" (Lev. 16:16).
> C. And Scripture says, "Through their imparting uncleanness to my tabernacle, which is in their midst" (Lev. 15:31).
> D. And Scripture says, "That they not make their camp unclean" (Num. 5:3).
> E. And Scripture says, "'You shall not defile the land in which you live.'
> F. R. Nathan says, "So precious is Israel that, wherever they have been carried away into exile, the presence of God is with them.
> G. "They were carried into exile to Egypt, the presence of God was with them, as it is said, 'Thus the Lord has said, I exiled myself with the house of your father when they were in Egypt subject to the house of Pharaoh' (1 Sam. 2:27).
> H. "When they went into exile to Babylonia, the presence of God was with them, as it is said, 'On your account I was sent to Babylonia' (Is. 43:14).
> I. "When they went into exile to Elam, the presence of God was with them, as it is said, 'And I will set my throne in Elam and destroy their king and princes' (Jer. 49:38).

For sages, "Edom" stands for Rome:

> J. "When they went into exile to Edom, the presence of God was with them, as it is said, 'Who is this that comes from Edom, in crimsoned garments from Bozrah, he that is glorious in his apparel, marching in the greatness of his strength' (Is. 63:1).

Now comes the return to the Holy Land:

> K. "And when they return, the presence of God will return with them, as it is said, 'Then the Lord your God will restore your fortunes and have compassion upon you, and he will gather you again from all the peoples where the Lord your God has scattered you. If your outcasts are in the uttermost parts of heaven, from there the Lord your God will gather you, and from there he will fetch you; and the Lord your God will bring you into the land which your fathers possessed, that you may possess it' (Deut. 30:4-5). The word that is used is not, 'restore,' but 'the Lord your God will return.'
> L. "And Scripture says, 'Come with me from Lebanon, my bride; come with me from Lebanon; depart from the peak of Amana, from the peak of Senir and Hermon, from the dens of lions, from the mountains of leopards' (Song 4:7-8)."
> M. Rabbi says, "There is a parable: to what is the matter to be compared? To the case of a king who said to his servant, 'If you seek me, lo, I shall be with my son. Whenever you seek me, lo, I shall be with my son.'
> N. "And so Scripture says, 'Who dwells with them in the midst of their uncleanness' (Lev. 17:16).
> O. "And it says, 'Through their imparting uncleanness to my tabernacle, which is in their midst' (Lev. 15:31).
> P. "And it says, 'That they not make their camp unlearn, where I dwell in their midst' (Num. 5:3).
> Q. "And it says, 'You shall not defile the land in which you live, in the midst of which I dwell; for I the Lord dwell in the midst of the people of Israel.'"

The unity of God, the land of Israel, Israel the people, clearly forms a primary conviction of classical Judaism. Despite Israel's sin and God's estrangement from Israel, the land, and the people, God remains with Israel, the divine presence never leaving them. Scripture proves that point. God and Israel are united in love beyond all dissolution. That explains why God is both estranged from and perpetually present in and with Israel.

The critical place of the land of Israel in the system of classical Judaism is reflected in the Oral Torah's understanding, developing the ideas of the written Scriptures, that the union of the Israelites and promised land marks that land and its produce as holy, with God claiming a share as a partner in the production of crops. The disposition of the crops is governed by the wishes of both partners, that is, God and the farmer. In the Written Torah, God specified a variety of ways in which his share of the land was to be distributed. First fruits, for example, are to be designated and set aside and brought to Jerusalem, to the Temple, but only by an Israelite who actually owns the land on which the produce is grown (M. Bik. 1:2). Only the seven species by which the land is distinguished are subject to the requirement: wheat, barley, grapes, figs, pomegranates, olives used for oil, and dates for honey. A declaration of faith is made when the first fruits are presented, in line with Deut. 26:3, reflecting the historical connection of the people and the land. Similarly, dough-offering is to be separated from loaves of bread made from five types of grain grown in the land of Israel: (1) wheat, (2) barley, (3) spelt, (4) oats, and (5) rye (M. Hal. 1:1).

The manner in which the land of Israel is to be farmed by Israelites further is specified in Scripture and carefully elaborated in the Oral Torah. Diverse genera are not to be mixed together in the same field, though diverse species of the same genus may be (M. Kil.). The laws of the sabbatical year, requiring that the land be left fallow, are augmented, so that farm work carried out before the advent of the seventh year that benefits the crop in the seventh year may not be performed (M. Sheb. 1:1). Additionally, in the seventh year, produce must be removed from one's possession when similar produce is no longer available in the fields, and the money received when produce is sold similarly is subject to removal. The rule of leaving a corner of the field for the gleaning of the poor is to be observed (M. Peah) as is the prohibition against using the produce of a fruit tree for the first three years of its growth (M. Orlah).

Commensurate with this complex system of rules that reflect God's ownership of the land, the land enjoys supernatural grace, reflected in its remarkable productivity (B. Ket. 111b-113a):

A. R. Hiyya bar Adda was an elementary teacher for the children of R. Simeon b. Laqish. He took a three-day absence and did not come.

B. When he came, [Simeon b. Laqish] said to him, "Why were you absent?"

C. He said to him, "Because my father left me one espalier, and, on the first day I was absent, I cut three hundred grape clusters from it, each yielding a keg; on the second, three hundred, each two of which yielded a keg. On the third day, three hundred, three each of which yielded a keg. And I renounced my ownership of more than half of the yield."

D. He said to him, "Well, if you hadn't been absent, it would have yielded even more."

E. R. Ammi bar Ezekiel visited Bene Beraq. He saw goats grazing under fig trees, with honey flowing from the figs, and milk running from the goats, and the honey and milk mingled. He said, "That is in line with 'a land flowing with milk and honey' (Exod. 3:8, Num. 13:27)."

F. Said R. Jacob b. Dosetai, "From Lud to Ono is three Roman miles. Once I got up early at down and I walked up to my ankles in fig honey."

G. Said R. Simeon b. Laqish, "I personally saw the flood of milk and honey of Sepphoris, and it extended over sixteen square miles."

H. Said Rabbah bar bar Hannah, "I personally saw the flood of milk and honey of the entirety of the land of Israel, and it extended from Be Mikse to the Fort of Tulbanqi, twenty-two parasangs long, six parasangs wide."

I. Helbo, R. Avira, and R. Yose bar Hanina came to a certain place. They brought before them a peach as large as a pot of Kefar Hino—and how big is that? Five *seahs*. A third of the peach they ate, a third they declared ownerless, and a third they placed before their animals.

J. The next year, R. Eleazar came there. They brought one to him. He took it into his one hand and said, "'A fruitful land into a salt waste, for the wickedness of them that dwell therein (Ps. 107:34).'"

K. R. Joshua b. Levi came to Gabela. He

saw vines heavy with grape clusters, standing up like calves. He said, "Calves among the vines?"

L. They said to him, "All they are are clusters of ripe grapes."

M. He exclaimed, "Land, land, hold back your produce? To whom do you yield it? To those Arabs who stood against us on account of our sins?"

N. A year later, R. Hiyya came there. He saw them standing like goats. He said, "Goats among the vines?"

O. They said to him, "All they are are clusters of ripe grapes. Get out of here, don't do to us what your friend did."

P. What is the extent of the blessings that are bestowed on the land of Israel? A *bet seah* produces fifty thousand *kor*.

Q. Said R. Yose, "A *seah's* land in Judah would yield five *seahs*: a *seah* of flour, a *seah* of fine flour, a *seah* of bran, a *seah* of coarse bran, and a *seah* of cibarium."

R. A certain Sadducee said to R. Hanina, "It is quite right that you should sing the praises of your land. My father left me one *bet seah* in it, and from that ground I get oil, wine, grain, pulse, and my cattle feed on it."

S. Said an Amorite to someone who lives in the land of Israel, "How much do you collect from that date tree on the bank of the Jordan?"

T. He said to him, "Sixty *kor*."

U. He said to him, "You haven't improved it, you've ruined it, because we used to collect from it a hundred and twenty *kor*."

V. "Well, I was talking to you about the yield of only one side."

W. Said R. Hisda, "What is the meaning of the verse of Scripture: 'I give you a pleasant land, the heritage of the deer' (Jer. 3:19)?

X. "How come the land of Israel is compared to a deer? To tell you, just as a deer's hide cannot, when flayed, contain its flesh, so the land of Israel cannot contain its produce there being insufficient facilities to store that much.

Y. "Another explanation: Just as the deer is swiftest of all wild beasts, so the land of Israel is the swiftest among all the lands in ripening its fruit.

Z. "Might you say, just as the deer is swift but its meat is not fat, so the land of Israel ripens swiftly, but its produce is not fat, Scripture says, 'flowing with milk and honey,' which are richer than milk, sweeter than honey."

AA. When R. Eleazar went up to the land

of Israel, he said, "I have escaped one thing." When he was ordained, he said, "Now I have escaped two." When they seated him on the council for intercalating the year, he said, "Now I have escaped three: 'And my hand shall be against the prophets that see vanity . . . they shall not be in the council of my people' (Ezek. 13:9)—this refers to the council for intercalating the year. '. . . neither shall they be written in the register of the house of Israel' (Ezek. 13:9)—this refers to ordination. '. . . neither shall they enter into the land of Israel' (Ezek. 13:9)—this means what it says."

BB. When R. Zira went up to the land of Israel, he did not find a ferry to cross the river, so he took hold of a rope bridge and crossed.

CC. A Sadducee said to him, "Hasty people, you put your mouths before your ears: 'we shall do and we shall listen;' you still as always hold on to your rashness."

DD. He said to him, "A place that Moses and Aaron did not have the heavenly favor of seeing—as for me, who is going to tell me that I am going to have the grace of entering it; this accounts for my haste!"

EE. Abba would kiss the cliffs of Akko. Hanina would go out and repair the roads. Ammi and R. Assi would get up and move from sun to shade and from shade to sun. Hiyya bar Gameda would roll himself in the dust of the land: "For your servants take pleasure in her stones and love her very dust."

FF. Said R. Zira said R. Jeremiah bar Abba, "'The generation to which the son of David will come will be marked by persecution of disciples of sages.' Now, when I said this before Samuel, he said, 'Test after test: "And if there be yet a tenth of it, it shall again be eaten up" (Is. 6:11).'"

GG. Joseph repeated as a Tannaite statement, "Plunderers and plunderers of the plunderers."

HH. Said R. Hiyya bar Ashi said Rab, "All of the barren trees that are located in the land of Israel are destined to bear fruit: 'For the tree bears its fruit, the fig tree and vine yield their strength' (Joel 2:22)."

Except for the sin of the people of Israel, the land of Israel would produce quantities of produce commensurate with its chosen and holy status. Yet, even in the period of exile,

the land's special status and messianic destiny remain, as indicated in the final, poignant statement: "All of the barren trees that are located in the land of Israel are destined to bear fruit."

The holiness of the land is expressed in its election and its place in the hierarchy of sanctification and uncleanness. Hierarchization organizes the data of both sanctification and uncleanness in a single structure, even though there is no correspondence of the details of the one to those of the other. The points of differentiation, both as to sanctification and as to uncleanness, are the same, arrayed in sets of opposites at M. Kel. 1:5 and 1:6-8. We consider only the section on the hierarchy of holiness involving the land of Israel:

1:6A. There are ten [degrees of] holiness(es):
B. (1) The land of Israel is holier than all lands.
C. And what is its holiness? For they bring from it the *omer*, the first fruits, and the two Loaves, which they do not bring from all lands.

The land of Israel is marked as holy because from its produce are brought the offerings given to God at the Temple altar in Jerusalem. But there are gradations of holiness even within the land:

1:7A. (2) The cities surrounded by a wall are more holy than it [the land].
B. For they send from them the lepers, and they carry around in their midst a corpse so long as they like. [But once] it has gone forth, they do not bring it back.
1:8A. (3) Within the wall [of Jerusalem] is more holy than these [other places].
B. For they eat there lesser sanctities and second tithe.
C. (4) The Temple mount is more holy than it.
D. For men and women who have suffered an emission, menstruating women, and those that have given birth do not enter there.
E. (5) The rampart is more holy than it.
F. For gentiles and he who is made unclean by a corpse do not enter there.
G. (6) The court of women is more holy than it.
H. For one who immersed on that day and awaits sunset to be deemed clean

does not enter there, but they are not liable on its account for a sin offering.

I. (7) The court of Israel is more holy than it.

J. For one who [yet] lacks atonement [offerings made in the completion of the purification rite] does not enter there, and they are liable on its account for a sin-offering.

K. (8) The court of the priests is more holy than it.

L. For Israelite(s) do not enter there except in the time of their [cultic] requirements: for laying on of hands, for slaughtering, and for waving.

1:9A. (9) [The area] between the porch and the altar is more holy than it.

B. For those [priests] who are blemished or whose hair is unloosed do not enter there.

C. (10) The sanctuary is more holy than it.

D. For [a priest] whose hands and feet are not washed does not enter there.

E. (11) The Holy of Holies is more holy than they.

F. For only the high priest on the Day of Atonement at the time of the service enters there.

The pattern for sanctification is clear: a set of available facts is organized and laid out in a pattern of ascension to ever higher levels; but the facts are available, not established through any program of investigation. The single standard pertains: relationship to the same locus of sanctification. The centrality of the land of Israel in the hierarchical sanctification of Israel, the people, is self-evident. It is not surprising, therefore, that the classical sources of Judaism hold that the people of Israel truly worships God only when situated in the land of Israel (T. A.Z. 4:5):

A. And it says, "I am the Lord your God, who brought you forth out of the land of Egypt to give you the land of Canaan, and to be your God" (Lev. 25:38). So long as you are in the land of Canaan, lo, I am your God. If you are not in the land of Canaan, it is as if I am not God for you.

B. And so it says, "About forty thousand ready armed for war passed over before the Lord for battle to the plains of Jericho" (Josh. 4:13).

C. And would it ever enter your mind that the Israelites would conquer the land before the omnipresent? But the

meaning is this: so long as they are located upon it, it is as if it is conquered. Lo, if they are not located upon it, it is as if it is not conquered.

D. And so Scripture says, "For they have driven me out this day, that I should have no share in the heritage of the Lord, saying, 'Go, serve other gods'" (I Sam. 26:19). Now would it ever enter your mind that David would go and worship idols? But David made the following exegesis: Whoever leaves the land in a time of peace and goes abroad is as if he worships idolatry, as it is said, "I will plant them in this land in faithfulness, with all my heart and all my soul" (Jer. 33:31).

E. So long as they are located upon it, it is as if they are planted before me in faithfulness with all my heart and all my soul. Lo, if they are not located upon it, they are not placed before me in faithfulness with all my heart and all my soul.

Not only is the true worship of God possible only in the Holy Land, but Israelites living outside of the land worship idols and do not even know it (Abot d'Rabbi Natan XXVI: VI.1):

A. R. Simeon b. Eliezer says, "Israelites who live outside of the land worship idols in all innocence.

B. "How so? A gentile who makes a banquet for his son sends and invites all the Jews in his town. Even though they bring and eat their own food and drink their own wine and take along their own servant who stands over them and pours for them, Scripture regards them as though they had eaten from sacrifices of corpses, as it is said, 'And they will invite you and you will eat of their sacrifice' (Exod. 34:15)."

By contrast to the inherent unholiness of life outside of the land, many sources suggest that life in the land naturally conveys spiritual and other benefits. Since, for instance, in classical Judaism, a principal act of sanctification requires studying the Torah, the link between the holiness of the land and Torah-study is established: dwelling in the land of Israel secures Torah-learning of the highest quality (Abot d'Rabbi Natan XXVIII:I.1-II.1):

A. R. Nathan says, "You have no love like the love for the Torah, wisdom like the wisdom of the land of Israel, beauty like the beauty of Jerusalem, wealth like the wealth of Rome, power like the power of Persia, lewdness like the lewdness of the Arabs, arrogance like the arrogance of Elam, hypocrisy like the hypocrisy of Babylonia or witchcraft like the witchcraft of Egypt."

B. R. Simeon b. Eleazar says, "A sage who has dwelled in the land of Israel and then left for overseas becomes flawed. One who remains in the land is more praiseworthy than he. And even though the former is flawed, he is nonetheless more praiseworthy than all those who live in other lands never having lived in the land.

C. "The matter yields a parable. To what may it be likened? To Indian iron that comes from overseas. Even though it is less than it was, it is still better than the best iron made in all other lands."

As is appropriate to the land's place within the God's messianic scheme, dwelling there also secures benefits at the end of time. For when the messiah comes and raises the dead, he will carry out his mission in the land of Israel. That is why it is best to be buried there (Abot d'Rabbi Natan XXVI:III.1):

A. He would say, "Whoever is buried in other lands is as though he were buried in Babylonia. Whoever is buried in Babylonia is as if he were buried in the land of Israel. Whoever is buried in the land of Israel is as if he were buried under the altar. For the whole of the land of Israel is suitable as a location for the altar. And whoever is buried under the altar is as if he were buried under the throne of glory. As it is said, 'You throne of glory, on high from the beginning, you place of our sanctuary' (Jer. 17:12)."

Living in the land of Israel similarly guarantees entry into the world to come (Y. Shab. 1:3 V.3):

A. It has been taught in the name of R. Meir, "Whoever lives permanently in the land of Israel, eats his unconsecrated produce in a state of cultic cleanness, speaks in the Holy Language of Hebrew, and recites the *Shema* morning and night may be certain that he belongs among those who will live in the world to come."

The sacred character of the holy land thus comes to expression throughout the classical sources of Judaism. That is because of the equation of the land of Israel with Eden, the people of Israel with Adam, the exile with the fall from grace, and the end of days with the return to Zion and the restoration of Israel to the land. These are key-convictions of Rabbinic Judaism.

In line with its centrality, the land of Israel takes its place within a number of formative themes, clusters that hold together in single statements. Creation, revelation, redemption form one such paramount cluster; land, liberation, covenant, Torah, another; Israel, land of Israel, Jerusalem, restoration, a third. In the Grace after Meals, recited whenever pious Jews eat bread, one such cluster is expressed, and we see in it the centrality of the land of Israel within the key-concepts of Rabbinic Judaism. To understand the setting, we must recall that, in classical Judaism, the table at which meals were eaten was regarded as the equivalent of the sacred altar in the Temple. Judaism taught that each Jew before eating had to attain the same state of ritual purity as a priest in the sacred act of making a sacrifice. So in the classical tradition, the Grace after Meals is recited in a sacerdotal circumstance. In this setting, the entire theology of the Oral Torah, expressing the centrality of the land of Israel, comes to realization in a single, simple liturgy:

[1] Blessed art thou, Lord our God, King of the Universe, who nourishes all the world by his goodness, in grace, in mercy, and in compassion: He gives bread to all flesh, for his mercy is everlasting. And because of his great goodness we have never lacked, and so may we never lack, sustenance—for the sake of his great Name. For he nourishes and feeds everyone, is good to all, and provides food for each one of the creatures he created.
Blessed art thou, O Lord, who feeds everyone.

[2] We thank thee, Lord our God, for having given our fathers as a heritage a pleasant, a good and spacious land; for having taken us out of the land of Egypt, for having redeemed us from the house of bondage; for thy covenant, which thou hast set as a seal in our flesh, for thy Torah which thou has taught us, for thy statutes which thou hast made known to us, for the life of grace and mercy thou

hast graciously bestowed upon us, and for the nourishment with which thou dost nourish us and feed us always, every day, in every season, and every hour.

For all these things, Lord our God, we thank and praise thee; may thy praises continually be in the mouth of every living thing, as it is written, And thou shalt eat and be satisfied, and bless the Lord thy God for the good land which he hath given thee.

Blessed art thou, O Lord, for the land and its food.

[3] O Lord our God, have pity on thy people Israel, on thy city Jerusalem, on Zion the place of thy glory, on the royal house of David thy messiah, and on the great and holy house which is called by thy name. Our God, our father, feed us and speed us, nourish us and make us flourish, unstintingly, O Lord our God, speedily free us from all distress. And let us not, O Lord our God, find ourselves in need of gifts from flesh and blood, or of a loan from anyone save from thy full, generous, abundant, wide-open hand; so we may never be humiliated, or put to shame.

O rebuild Jerusalem, the holy city, speedily in our day. Blessed art thou, Lord, who in mercy will rebuild Jerusalem. Amen.

The context of grace is enjoyment of creation, the arena for creation is the land. The land lay at the end of redemption from Egyptian bondage. Holding it, enjoying it is a sign that the covenant is intact and in force and that Israel is loyal to its part of the contract and God to his. The land, the Exodus, the covenant—these all depend upon the Torah, statutes, and a life of grace and mercy, here embodied in and evoked by the nourishment of the meal. The restorationist dynamic— returning Israel to the land of Israel—frames the end in terms of the beginning, the restoration of Israel to the land of Israel, that the liturgy bespeaks. The restorationist theme recurs throughout, redemption and hope for return, and then future prosperity in the land: "May God pity the people, the city, Zion, the royal house of the messiah, the holy Temple." The nourishment of this meal is but a foretaste of the nourishment of the messianic time, just as the joy of a wedding, as expressed in its liturgy, is a foretaste of the messianic rejoicing. Creation and re-creation,

exile and return to the land—these are the particular clusters that point to the substrate of the sages' theology and underscore the centrality of the land of Israel within that theology.

JACOB NEUSNER

ISRAEL, LAND OF, IN MEDIEVAL AND RENAISSANCE JUDAISM: Treatments of the land of Israel in medieval Jewish thought address a number of central issues: (1) the scientific status (in the medieval sense of the term) of the country, mainly in terms of climatology and astrology; (2) the conceptual and metaphysical status of the country; (3) the relationship of the country to the religious commandments; and (4) the messianic significance of the country. Some thinkers, like Judah Halevi and Abraham ibn Ezra, discussed all these issues; others considered only some, such as Maimonides, who was not interested in the unique metaphysical status or all the messianic implications of the land of Israel; and still others concerned themselves with a single issue, such as the Halakhists, who considered the legal dimension of the country exclusively, and some mystics, who were interested only in its conceptual-metaphysical aspect.

Within this range of issues, three main approaches arose: (1) The rational. Some thinkers believed that the status of the country could be completely reduced to rational terms. This reduction might be positive or negative, that is, the character of the country might amount to certain "objective," scientific virtues; or the country might have no scientific standing whatever, other than its being "national" soil in a religious sense of the term. Rationalist philosophers like Maimonides and some of his thirteenth- and fourteenth-century spiritual followers held some such view. (2) The irrational. For some thinkers, no reduction of the status of the land of Israel to rational terms was possible. The country's virtues, they argued, stemmed from its unique, chosen quality, of which only people possessing special "knowledge" (*gnosis*), or specific groups (a specific nation, a group of adepts) could be aware or derive benefit. Kabbalistic conceptions, in which the soil itself was a manifestation of divine power, represent extreme irrational approaches to the land of Israel. (3) The integrative. Some agreed that the land has special spiritual qualities but nevertheless adduced scientific and rational reasons for its superiority and uniqueness. Such an approach was taken by Judah Halevi and by rationalists who did not take their rationalism to its ultimate conclusion.

Crystallization of approaches up to the end of the twelfth century: Prior to the twelfth century, Rabbinic thought did not address the status of the land of Israel as a topic of independent philosophical discussion at all. One possible reason is polemics. The Karaite movement known as *Avelei Zion* ("Mourners of Zion") focused on the ruined land, calling for voluntary immigration to the land of Israel to lament over its ruins and hasten redemption. In reaction, Rabbanite Jews opposed such action or avoided the subject entirely. For example, Saadiah Gaon, considered the first systematic Jewish thinker, dismissed the whole issue in trivial terms, and his avoidance of any systematic discussion of the country's philosophical status was probably motivated by a desire to push the issue aside. Another reason was the process of centralization, by which many of the philosophical works written before the beginning of the twelfth century came to focus on a single subject rather than to propose a broad, comprehensive interpretation of Judaism as a whole. Hence they refrained from dealing with the status of the country. A few examples of such works were Bahya ibn Paquda's *Duties of the Heart*, the anonymous *Book of Matters of the Soul*, and Solomon ibn Gabirol's *Source of Life* and *Improvement of the Moral Qualities*.

Thus the discussion of the status of the land of Israel moved from the periphery to the center only in the works of a group of thinkers in twelfth-century Spain. Aside from the theological necessity of the discussion, it also had a polemical thrust, directed at the Islamic concept of the Arabian Peninsula as the best of all possible countries (one of the principles of the *arabiyya*). Four philosophers in particular formulated approaches to the question of the land of Israel: Abraham bar Hiyya the Patriarch, Judah Halevi, Abraham ibn Ezra, and Maimonides. Despite a generally multifaceted attitude to the land, each of these four was particularly inclined towards one of the four issues mentioned above. Abraham bar Hiyya took a messianic approach; Judah Halevi's attitude was contemplative and metaphysical; Abraham ibn Ezra displayed a scientific approach (or, more correctly; one built on scientific premises); and Maimonides adopted a Halakhic perspective, indifferent to other aspects of the land of Israel. These four approaches became the four central philosophical paths informing perceptions of the land of Israel in Jewish thought during the Middle Ages, the Renaissance, and later.

Abraham bar Hiyya: Abraham bar Hiyya embraced an apocalyptic version of the messianic idea. Following the thought of Saadiah Gaon, he placed apocalyptic messianism in a historical-conceptual framework, establishing its legitimacy in the world of ideas. Apocalyptic messianism relied on the plain meaning of the messianic legends of the midrash, which assigned the land of Israel a major role. Abraham insisted that "all the countries of the world will be called the land of Israel, or the land of Israel will expand considerably, until it fills the entire world" (*Megillat ha-Megalleh*, end of Portal 4). Legend becomes reality, and the land of Israel—at least, as an alternative—will encompass the whole world; this will be one of the miracles to take place in the messianic age. The expansion of the land does not imply any derogation of its worth; on the contrary, it will become a model for the whole universe. Abraham bar Hiyya, for the first time, made the land of Israel an immanent component of apocalyptic messianic thought.

Judah Halevi: Undoubtedly the first thinker to propose a systematic, comprehensive philosophy of the land of Israel, in his *Sefer ha-Kuzari* (II:9-24), Judah Halevi deals with the unique status of the land on three levels:

Philosophical level. Halevi posits two parallel hierarchies: a hierarchy of levels of reality (inanimate, vegetable, animal, man, prophet) and a hierarchy of soils (the theory of climates, fully developed in the Hellenistic period, according to which the country was divided into seven climatic regions, each with characteristic geophysical and astrological conditions). The two summits of the hierarchies are interrelated and influence one another. A Jew may become a prophet only when he or she is in (or refers to) the land of Israel, which is the choicest region of the fourth climate, itself the best of all possible climates. Residence on the soil of the land of Israel becomes a necessary condition for the perfection of any Jew, and prophecy may exist only in (or for) it. This principle is explained through the parable of a vineyard, which can thrive only in mountainous soil. A vineyard uprooted from its native soil will wither and die. The vineyard symbolizes the people of Israel; the soil, the land of Israel. But the uniqueness of the land of Israel is not just a question of climatology. Jews, who need the land in order to grow and develop, are essentially and qualitatively different from gentiles; hence the land of Israel, too, has a special quality that is conducive to the appearance of a new level of reality, the prophets.

Interpretive level. Halevi laid the foundations for an exegesis of the Bible and Midrash in which various issues are based on the importance of the land of Israel. Sometimes he unhesitatingly departs from explicit midrashic traditions in order to highlight the sterling qualities of the land. For example, he insists that Adam was created in the land of Israel, contrary to midrashic traditions that declare that his creation was universal ("his dust was accumulated from the four corners of the Earth;" B. San. 38a). For Halevi, Cain and Abel fought over who would rule the land of Israel, while midrash speaks only of two alternative motives, control of the whole world or of the site of the Temple (Gen. Rabbah 22).

Halakhic level. Halevi bases on the importance of the land of Israel Halakhic rulings that are sometimes contrary to standard legal positions. Thus he argues that the International Date Line must pass through China. Since the earth is round, it has no *natural*

mid-point, a view contrary to the biblical and Rabbinic perception of the land of Israel as the world's center. Halevi, by contrast, places the land of Israel in the middle of the *inhabited* world (covering the area from China to England, since, of course, the people of Spain in his day were unaware of the New World). Halevi reinforces this perspective by situating the date line in China, thus proposing that world time is determined in accordance with the principle that the land of Israel is at the center of the earth. He also argues that days begin in the land of Israel: when the sun sets there on Saturday evening, the coming day is first referred to as "Sunday;" only eighteen hours later will it be Sunday in China as well. Thus the whole question of world time is dependent on the land of Israel.

Judah Halevi accordingly formulated a comprehensive doctrine of the importance of the land of Israel. But his greatest intellectual achievement was to define the land as a necessary condition for the perfection of any Jew. As this perfection depends on a series of factors that are indifferent to reason (the genetic constraint, according to which only a Jew can become a prophet; the religious constraint, according to which only fulfillment of *all* the commandments by all parts of the Jewish people makes prophecy possible), the land of Israel itself assumes a non-rational dimension (we should not say "irrational," since Halevi was speaking of indifference to, but not rejection of, reason). Halevi drew much from the Shi'ite Muslim notion of ṣafwa, that is, uniqueness or inherent religious superiority; but he laid the foundations for the idea of the very soil of the Holy Land as a necessary component in the personal and collective perfection of the Jew. This doctrine would reach its full, extreme implications only in the near future, as developed by Kabbalah. As to the possible link between Halevi's conception of the land of Israel, his intended immigration to the land, and his messianic activism, in the sense of the call to actual immigration, opinions are still divided.

ibn Ezra: Abraham ibn Ezra's point of departure is the scientific theory of climates, following the principles of which he holds that any geographical place has unique geophysical and astrological qualities. In rather brief and enigmatic language, he writes: "There is a place that receives power, and the Lord's might is seen there" (first commentary on Gen. 4:14), and "There are places that have received supernal power more than any other place" (second commentary on Gen. 4:13). In Ibn Ezra's terminology, "supernal power" denotes the forces emanating from the stars; hence it is clear that some places are more favorably situated, in astrological terms, than others. The land of Israel enjoys superiority on account of its astrological position, or, in Ibn Ezra's terminology, it is the abode of the "Glory" (Heb., *kavod*; commentary to Ps. 85:11). Then, again, within the land of Israel itself are astrologically superior places: Jerusalem and the Temple (long commentary to Exod. 15:17). Just what astrological position, in precise, "scientific" terms, renders the land of Israel superior is unclear, but Ibn Ezra undoubtedly believes that such a position existed.

ibn Ezra's awareness of the magical and antinomistic implications of the scientific principle shows clearly through his obscure language. Since every climate and geographical place have their own astral positions, it follows that, by using suitable techniques, one can mobilize the astral forces for useful and religious purposes. The theological implication is that many commandments in the Torah were meant as special techniques, suited only for the land of Israel, as they are correlated with its particular astral position. "Most of the commandments depend on the land" (second commentary to Gen. 47:30). That is to say, the religious commandments are seen as techniques for utilizing the astral forces specific to a certain place, namely, the land of Israel. Ibn Ezra in fact alludes to the antinomistic implications of this approach: "The essence of worship is to maintain the receptive power appropriate to the place, therefore . . . Jacob said: 'Rid yourselves of the alien gods . . .' [Gen. 35:2]" (commentary to Deut. 31:16). Elsewhere, the astral forces are brought down onto idols, but in the land of Israel the same function is performed by the commandments. Jacob, therefore, about to enter the Holy Land, told his company to discard their idols. Jacob married two sisters when abroad, as this particular union was forbidden only in the land of Israel (commentary to Lev. 18:26). This explains Rachel's death upon entering the Holy Land, which cannot "tolerate" such incestuous relations from the standpoint of astral worship. Ibn Ezra also explains the exile of Israel as an outcome of failure to observe the commandments, so that the astral worship unique to the land of Israel is not maintained. Thus Ibn Ezra's scientific approach had far-reaching theological implications.

Moses Maimonides: The major innovation in Maimonides' treatment of the conceptual significance of the Holy Land lies in his disregard for the issue. In his greatest philosophical work, *Guide of the Perplexed*, Maimonides conducts a profound discussion of numerous areas in Judaism, but nowhere in that framework does he deliberately discuss the land of Israel. In fact, he demonstrates that one can engage in a philosophical discussion of Judaism without even touching on the Holy Land. Accordingly, Maimonides' view of the land of Israel may only be determined from sources of two categories, direct and indirect: one includes various conceptual and national considerations that depend for their definitions and realization on the land of Israel; the other includes the Halakhic material pertaining to the land of Israel, as expressed in his legal writings.

We begin with the first category. Maimonides presents a series of objectives that can be achieved only on national soil. Clearly, here, the land of Israel is understood in a purely instrumental sense: it permits the realization of certain ends. These objectives are as follows.

The historiosophical approach of autonomy and exile. According to Maimonides, adversity and persecution prevent the perfect person from devoting himself to the acquisition of knowledge. Insofar as prophecy depends on intellectual virtues, stressful situations such as exile do not further its realization. Thus the intellectual perfection of any individual is dependent on leading an autonomous, peaceful existence in the land of Israel.

Importance of the political dimension in religious and intellectual life. Scholars do not agree on the significance of political aims in Maimonides' thought. Some consider the ultimate Maimonidean political end to be creation of a just government, while others see political perfection as merely a step on the way to individual perfection. In either case, the political dimension is essential to Maimonidean thought, as it is a major station on the road to perfection. Government and leadership are also considered part of the personal ideal of *imitatio Dei*. The land of Israel makes it possible to establish a proper government and is therefore of paramount significance for realization of the political ideal.

The place of the realization of messianism. In view of the previous two considerations, messianism serves personal perfection, releasing people from the deprivations of exile and restoring the political ideal. The land of Israel is also an indispensable precondition for the realization of messianism.

It is clear from these three considerations that the land of Israel does not stand on its own. Maimonides never discusses it in and for itself; its whole existence is instrumental. In this respect, Maimonides has retreated from the positions taken by his three predecessors: like Abraham bar Hiyya, he refers to the land of Israel in a messianic context, but unlike him he treats it as an instrumental factor; like Judah Halevi and Abraham ibn Ezra, he accepts climatology in general, but unlike them he never speaks of the special climate of the land of Israel, certainly not giving it the prominent metaphysical role it receives in Halevi's thought.

Turning now to the second category of sources, one finds Maimonides referring with great frequency to the Halakhic status of the land of Israel. As the whole legal system is, for him, an instrument in the achievement of political or intellectual perfection (*Guide of the Perplexed* III:27, etc.), that is, a means toward other ends, it is only natural that the land of Israel should find a distinctive place in that system. This category of Maimonidean sources also begins with a negative point: Maimonides does not count the settle-ment of the Holy Land as one of the 613 commandments listed in his *Book of Commandments*. That is to say, the conquest of the land is a commandment, given in the Torah, but residence in the land of Israel is not considered a biblical precept. This remains Maimonides' view in his discussion of messianic times (end of *Hilkhot Melakhim* in his Mishneh Torah), that is to say, the settlement of the land of Israel will not be a religious duty even in the future.

On the other hand, in a series of rulings, Maimonides establishes the legal status of the land of Israel, an act significant beyond the Halakhic achievements of the geonim and of other diaspora scholars. Thanks to the unique qualities of the Mishneh Torah as a comprehensive, systematic legal code, it was here that the legal status of the land of Israel was clearly stated and founded on definite Halakhic criteria; here lies Maimonides' contribution to the subject. Despite the fact that he is essentially reworking and rewriting things said by earlier Rabbinic authorities and diaspora scholars, such as Judah Halevi, his choice of laws and rulings and their inclusion in the monumental framework of the Mishneh Torah clearly defined the unique legal status of the land of Israel. This status, according to Maimonides, is based on the following principles:

(1) Jewish presence in the land of Israel is crucial for the authority of the Great Court (*Bet ha-Din ha-Gadol*). Once the dominant position of the Jews in their land had become impaired, the supreme legal authority of that body was also undermined. In *Hilkhot Qiddush ha-Hodesh* 5:3, Maimonides states that the original sanctification of the New Moon by witnesses was replaced by sanctification by calculation "at the time the land of Israel was destroyed." Before then, "everyone relied on the determination of the land of Israel." Thus, a Jewish presence in the land of Israel is a criterion of institutional Halakhic authority. This also follows from other issues, such as the interrupted ordination of judges owing to the exile from the land (*Hilkhot Sanhedrin* 4:11).

(2) The importance of the land of Israel is a Halakhic consideration. The scroll of Esther

is read on Purim on the fifteenth of Adar in cities that have been walled since the time of Joshua, although the actual site of the miracle—Susa—was not walled at that time. The distinction was made solely "to express respect for the land of Israel, which was in ruins at that time" (*Hilkhot Megillah* 1:5). Thus, even commandments originating in the diaspora are linked with the status of the Holy Land.

(3) Various elements in personal law are dependent on the sanctity of the land of Israel. Maimonides systematically restated the laws that derive from the rule: "Everyone may be brought up to the land of Israel, but not everyone may be brought out" (*Hilkhot Ishut* 13:20). These laws perpetuate the superiority of the land of Israel in such matters as a dispute between husband and wife, one wishing to immigrate to the Holy Land and the other refusing.

One could extend this list of examples, of course, with the many legal situations that arise only in the land of Israel, such as the commandments dependent on the Holy Land, the laws of the Temple, and the laws of Nazirites. In the last-named category, for example, Maimonides disagrees with other authorities, ruling that a person who takes a Nazirite's vow in the diaspora must immigrate to the land of Israel to keep that vow (*Hilkhot Nezirut* 2:21). In general, Maimonides relates to the sanctity of the land of Israel on a purely Halakhic level (*Hilkhot Beit ha-Behirah* 7:12). His approach, therefore, may be defined as rejecting any objective, "scientific" merit—or, *a fortiori*, uniqueness—of the land. The unique feature of the Holy Land is that it is national ground, on which the nation can maintain its autonomous legal and political life.

The process of symbolization—rationalism and Kabbalah: During the thirteenth to fifteenth centuries, thinkers faced three alternative understandings of the status of the land of Israel: inherent superiority irreducible to rational terms, scientifically based superiority, and indifference to any inherent, philosophical or scientific superiority of the land, with or without focus on the Halakhic substrate. Most of the rationalists, up until the

late fourteenth century, chose the second alternative. Judah Halevi's doctrine, with its inherent religious superiority, was embraced by the Kabbalists from the very beginnings of Spanish Kabbalah but was assimilated by rationalists only towards the end of the fourteenth century and during the fifteenth century. Maimonidean indifference on the specific issue of the status of the Holy Land was discarded by most of the rationalists, except for a few Yemenite scholars of the Middle Ages, such as Nathaniel al-Fayyumi, Nathaniel b. Isaiah, and Zechariah b. Solomon the Physician, who followed in Maimonides' footsteps, among other things, in not considering the status of the land of Israel on a systematic, philosophical level. Maimonides' crucial influence on the philosophers who succeeded him did not extend to the question of the chosen land.

One phenomenon in the world of ideas that profoundly affected the status of the land of Israel was an expansion of the horizons of biblical interpretation, resulting in the massive production of two methods of exegesis, particularly around the end of the twelfth century and the beginning of the thirteenth. The rationalist-philosophical world developed far-reaching allegorical techniques, while the Kabbalistic world evolved a rich variety of symbolic ones. This hermeneutic development directly shaped the understanding of the status of the Holy Land in the writings of both rationalists and Kabbalists.

We begin with the rationalists, whose problem was this: any perception of the land of Israel as something unique, a tract of land whose soil differed from any other, was at odds with the universal ideal of rationalism. Indeed, it was quite consistent of Maimonides to reject any "objective scientific" uniqueness of the land and, accordingly, to pay scant attention to biblical and midrashic sources that postulated such a particularistic view. The post-Maimonidean rationalists, however, could not accept such a dichotomy. Their object was to adapt the sources that refer to the uniqueness of the Holy Land to conform to their philosophy. To that end they expanded the techniques and scope of allegorical exegesis. Rationalist allegory presumes that the sacred text contains a profound inner meaning. This inner meaning consists (a) of fundamental scientific truths, whether they stem from the life sciences and physics, or from astronomical, astrological, and metaphysical disciplines; (b) of instruction and guidance that help the rationalist achieve perfection, that is, acquire knowledge and sciences leading to the desired conjunction with the Active Intellect, which is a cosmic intellectual entity. The well-versed rationalist knows how to use interpretive codes to expose that inner meaning.

The rationalist dilemma thus gradually led to the development of an allegorical school of exegesis that left practically no theological issue, biblical-historical narrative, or commandment without inner meanings. Public, historical events became symbols of a personal, intimate process, an intellectual development through which the individual strove to achieve personal conjunction while acquiring sciences and truths. In the dispute over philosophy that broke out in the 1220s and continued, with ups and downs, to the beginning of the fourteenth century, philosophical allegory was a favorite target of attack by fundamentalists, who believed that such massive exegesis would cause the plain, historical meaning to be forgotten and moreover nullify the validity of religious observance and who challenged the authority of Aristotelian science. These motives should be added to the historical and political reasons for the controversy.

The land of Israel was thus subjected to allegorical interpretation in two stages. At first, the land was seen as an ideal place for the study of sciences and intellection, since its climate was moderate, its astrological aspect was the best possible and, as national soil, it offered its inhabitants security. Menahem ha-Meiri, a Provençal thinker of the late thirteenth and early fourteenth centuries, expressed the idea as follows: "The land of Israel in itself is blessed with wisdom and fear of sin, to the extent that from them people apprehend the Glory of their Creator and are deemed worthy of enjoying the radiance of the Divine Presence" (*Beit ha-Behirah*, B. Ket. 111a). The very air of the land was seen as a cause "for removing the stupidity of improper views and for apprehending proper ones" (Solomon al-Constantini, a mid-fourteenth century Spanish philosopher, quoted from *Megalleh Amuqqot* on Deut., MS. Vat. 59).

In the second stage, the land became a symbol of the ideal of wisdom and learning. The land of Israel in general, and Jerusalem in particular, became expressions reflecting the goal of allegorical rationalism. Of the many examples, three suffice here. The Bible says that the land is "the fairest of all lands" (Ezek. 20:6, 15). The thirteenth-century Italian thinker Jacob Anatoli, playing on the Hebrew text of Ezekiel, which uses the word *zevi*, literally meaning "gazelle," writes: "Because wisdom is a crown of beauty [Heb., *ateret zevi*] and a diadem of glory and a graceful wreath [Heb., *livyat hen*] for its possessor, therefore was it called a graceful mountain goat [Heb., *yaalat hen*], for it arouses grace in the Lord's eyes" (*Malmad ha-Talmidim* 172a). Anatoli had just previously remarked that Jerusalem was a symbol of wisdom and apprehension, going on to intimate that the whole land of Israel reflected the acquisition of knowledge. Settlement on the land thus symbolizes the acquisition of wisdom.

Somewhat later, the fourteenth-century Provençal and Spanish scholar Moses of Narbonne explained the entire book of Lamentations from a rationalistic viewpoint, ending with the remark that the author of the book had also been referring to "Heavenly Jerusalem." In other words, the profound meaning of the destruction and the struggle to make amends are concerned with ignorance and lack of understanding, on the one hand, and the quest for personal, intellectual conjunction, on the other. One finds a similar allegorization of the land of Israel in the fifteenth century as well, in Isaac Arama's interpretation of Moses' survey of the Promised Land from a mountain-top before his death. According to Arama, God showed Moses the cosmological structure of the three worlds: the world of separate intellects (angels), the world of celestial bodies, and the terrestrial world. Thus, the land of Israel symbolizes the entire universe (*Aqedat Yizhaq*, Portal 105). The real, physical land was slowly supplanted in the rationalists' mind by the personal process of acquiring knowledge.

The Kabbalah: The Kabbalistic literature, which reached its proper formulation at the beginning of the thirteenth century, exhibits three approaches to the land of Israel: 1) the theosophical, beginning with the works of the Provençal Isaac the Blind and the Kabbalists of Gerona, Ezra and Azriel, which reflect, in the main, the symbolic development of the image of the land of Israel; 2) the theurgic, as expressed in the writings of Nahmanides; and 3) the personal, as in the ecstatic Kabbalah of Abraham Abulafia.

We begin with the theosophical approach. In the earliest stages of Kabbalah, the land of Israel in general and Jerusalem in particular were assumed to represent the uppermost *sefirot*, particularly, Wisdom, Foundation, and Kingship. As the *sefirot* represent hidden divine powers, the land of Israel itself becomes a manifestation of supernal, divine aspects. The Kabbalists thus set the terrestrial land aside in favor of the celestial land of Israel, focusing attention on its inner, divine dimensions. At Leviticus, 84a, the Zohar, edited at the end of the thirteenth century, illustrates this approach. The text comments on a talmudic legend according to which the entire land of Israel was "rolled up" beneath Jacob as he slept on his flight from Beersheba to Haran (B. Hul. 91b):

> How is it possible that the land of Israel, which measures four hundred by four hundred miles, was uprooted from its place to come beneath him? Nay, the Holy One, blessed be he, has another, supernal, Holy Land, also called the land of Israel, and it is beneath the level of Jacob on which he stands.

This "other land" of the mystic is the *sefirah* of Kingship, which stands beneath the *sefirah* of Glory, symbolized both by the term "the Holy One, blessed be he" and by the name "Jacob."

This fundamental symbolism of the land has further implications and ramifications. First, the land of Israel reflects the ineffable name of God, which is surrounded by other divine names (Ezra of Gerona). Second, the land of Israel and its cities also represent a sexual aspect. The first sin caused a split between the masculine principle of the divine powers (symbolized by the *sefirah* of Glory or Foundation) and the feminine principle (symbolized by Kingship). The coupling of the two principles is already symbolized in early Kabbalah by the unification of "Zion" (Glory or Foundation) and "Jerusalem" (Kingship). Since the righteous person similarly is symbolized by the *sefirah* of Foundation, the sexual aspect is also reflected in the fact that only perfectly righteous people can possess the land. Third, there were mixed implications for messianic activism. Some authorities considered the Kabbalistic activity symbolized by the land of Israel as a substitute for active immigration to that country, while others, on the contrary, considered it a catalyst for immigration.

The Zohar presents a broad variety of concepts of the land of Israel besides the theosophical dimension and its sexual implications; all these combined with the philosophies already formulated by Judah Halevi and Abraham ibn Ezra in a final consolidation of the theosophical conception. The Zohar uses climatological considerations to explain the position of the land of Israel at the center of the universe, the fact that the land is suited exclusively for the Jewish nation and that, contrary to other countries, it is not affected by the normal astrological system. The various theosophical traditions were summed up and merged with other conceptions of the status of the land of Israel in the many works of Moses Cordovero (Safed, sixteenth cent.), particularly in his commentary *Or Yaqar* to the Zohar. A more concise account may be found in *Hesed le-Avraham* by Abraham Azulai (Morocco and Palestine, sixteenth century).

The second approach to the land of Israel among thirteenth-century Kabbalists is well represented by the thought of Moses b. Nahman of Gerona, better known as Nahmanides or by the acronym Ramban. This approach is more concerned with the theurgic action of the commandments in the Holy Land than with its symbolism, though it too relies directly and indirectly on Judah Halevi and Abraham ibn Ezra. An important point here is Nahmanides' sharp criticism of Maimonides' failure to count settlement of the land of Israel as one of the 613 commandments. Among the commandments that Nahmanides added in his *hassagot* ("criticisms") of Maimonides' *Sefer ha-Mizvot* was the injunction "to inherit the land that God, blessed and praised be he, gave our ancestors, Abraham, Isaac, and Jacob, and it has never been abandoned to the hands of any other nation or to desolation." In Ramban's view, this injunction is "a positive commandment for all generations, binding upon every individual even in the time of exile, as stated frequently in the Talmud."

In addition, Nahmanides insisted that observance of the commandments was intended solely for the land of Israel, with their observance in the diaspora merely a preparation for the nation's future return to its land. Nahmanides took his own conclusions seriously and immigrated to the land of Israel. It is noteworthy that, by contrast, several Ashkenazic scholars ruled out immigration to the Holy Land, not only because of the dangers attendant on the journey but also because not all the commandments can be fulfilled in the present. This is the approach taken in a responsum of Hayyim b. Hananel Hakohen (Paris, second half of twelfth cent.), cited in *Tosafot* to B. Ket. 110a. But Nahmanides thought otherwise, and his conception of the commandments was in full accord with his Kabbalistic ideas, for, arguing that we have no tradition concerning the secrets of the *Merkavah* (the "Divine Chariot" or Throne of God), he confined his Kabbalistic deliberations to the reasons for the commandments.

Accordingly, Nahmanides' view of the Kabbalistic significance of the land focused on the theurgic effect of religious observance there. As he enveloped his teachings in enigmatic language, this theurgic action may be explained in two ways: harmony in the world of the *sefirot* is achieved by proper observance of the commandments, which possess authentic meaning in the Holy Land alone, or the commandments are also understood as

instruments through which the divine emanation (*shefa*), which exists in its most supreme manifestations in the Holy Land, is brought down to earth. Thus, Nahmanides evolved a special magical-astral theory, according to which divine emanation in itself is uniform but of dual significance: in its supreme aspect it is the theosophical emanation, emitted and brought down from the world of the *sefirot*; in its lowly aspect it is an astral emanation, which can be captured by magical-astral means, such as sacrifices or expiation (as in the case of the "scapegoat").

In this connection, it should be noted that Nahmanides had considerable esteem for magic, viewed as "an ancient and true science" the Jews had possessed but lost in exile. In his view, astral magic was the basis for all other forms of magic. A similar magical-astral conception had evolved in North African Kabbalah as well, as represented by Judah b. Nissim ibn Malkah. Thus the land of Israel was of supreme significance for Nahmanides, whether from a theosophical standpoint or an astrological one. It was there that the attraction of emanation is the most efficient and massive. This view of the centrality of the Holy Land in theosophical and theurgic lore pervaded the writings of Nahmanides' circle in the late thirteenth and early fourteenth centuries, as represented by such thinkers as Solomon b. Adret and Bahya b. Asher.

A third approach is represented by the circle of Abraham Abulafia, the creator of ecstatic Kabbalah, active in the mid-thirteenth and fourteenth centuries. Members of this circle were active in the land of Israel, such as the author of the book *Shaarei Zedeq* (*Gates of Righteousness*) and Isaac of Acre. Abulafia and Isaac considered the land of Israel and its cities symbols of the individual's soul or of the inner processes taking place in the soul, which lead to communion and conjunction with the deity. Isaac of Acre writes (*Ozar Hayyim*, MS. Moscow 775, fol. 94a):

> The secret of foreign lands and the land of Israel . . . is not a land of earthly soil, but it is the souls that reside in a lump of earth. . . .

And even though it [the soul] is in a foreign land, the Divine Presence (Heb., *Shekhina*) rests upon it, and that is surely the land of Israel.

In this sense, Abulafia's group took a view close to that of the philosophical allegory considered above, which transplanted the real existence of the land of Israel to an intimate personal level. The implications of this approach in counteracting the thrust of messianism are obvious, in direct opposition to the school of Nahmanides.

Late Middle Ages and Renaissance: Philosophy of the fourteenth and early fifteenth centuries is typified by the emergence of rationalist circles, each comprising a series of thinkers who shared certain characteristics and interests. These circles shaped for themselves definite constructions of the land of Israel that developed ibn Ezra's approach and rationalism in general, taking both to extremes. Their attitudes to the status of the land of Israel were marked by two main motifs, the astrological and at times also magical-astral qualities of the land, on the one side, and the land of Israel as the seat of wisdom and knowledge, on the other. These motifs first appeared in the early years of the fourteenth century in the biblical exegesis of Gersonides (Levi b. Gershom known as Ralbag), who postulated a connection between the earth and the power of the stars facing it (commentary to Gen. 4:13-14) and described the land of Israel as a receptacle for divine emanation. Nevertheless, in his major philosophical work, *Milhamot Adonai*, Gersonides did not devote special attention to the land of Israel, and the relevant remarks in his biblical commentaries are sporadic. Clearly, the subject was not of overriding importance for him, or, perhaps, he kept his authentic philosophical views strictly apart from his biblical exegesis—meant for the public at large—as he did, for example, his view on messianism. By contrast, the philosophical circles mentioned above discussed consciously and at length both intellectual and astrological aspects of the land of Israel.

One of these circles, active throughout the second half of the fourteenth century in Castile and Valencia in Spain, emphasized both aspects. Among the members of this circle were Solomon Al-Constantini, Solomon Franco, Ezra Gatigno, Samuel ibn Zarza, Shem Tov ibn Shaprut, and, to some extent, Joseph Bonfils (Tov Elem), most of whom wrote supercommentaries to Ibn Ezra's commentary on the Pentateuch. They tried to merge Ibn Ezra's teachings with Maimonidean thought, bringing out Neoplatonic elements in addition to the overt Aristotelian background. For them, the land of Israel was the home of prophecy according to the rational conception, that is, only there were both intellection and knowledge possible. In particular, they considered astral emanation to be most beneficial to the Jews in the land, and Joseph Bonfils in fact wrote that "the emanation reaches it before it reaches other countries" (*Zafenat Paaneah*, ed. Herzog, I, p. 127). This circle of commentators on Ibn Ezra accepted the antinomistic implications of the magical-astral outlook, according to which the commandments are unique to the land of Israel because of its astrological constellation. Thus Ezra Gatigno, for example, wrote (*Sod Adonai li-Yre'av*, MS. Munich 15, fol. 258a):

> There are places whose aspect permits one to make images in accordance with the power of the star that rules there in that place and to bring down supreme [= astral] power, to foretell the future, to procure success from them for the perfection of the people who live there and for the terrestrial world in part thereof. . . . And there are places in which the making of images to receive supreme power is contrary to their aspect. The land of Israel was one of those places whose aspect forbids one to make therein any image, and for that reason it was forbidden to make images there in the land of Israel.

According to Gatigno, idolatry is permitted everywhere but in the land of Israel, where it is strictly forbidden, because there emanation is not received by idols and images but only by the commandments. This idea recurs in different variations in the writings of Solomon Franco, Ibn Zarza, and Ibn Shaprut.

While active in the same region, Hasdai Crescas opposed the circle of commentators on Ibn Ezra and was vehemently critical of

Aristotelian science. Still, he embraced a model of the land of Israel similar to that of the circle, recognizing its astrological uniqueness and its ability to attract astral influx through the observance of the commandments, in the magical-astral style. Crescas, however, avoided the antinomistic implications of that conception. He emphasized the special position of the land of Israel in relation to divine providence, and, in the style of Judah Halevi, its being the only country in which prophecy could occur (*Or Adonai* II, 2, 6). However, Abraham ibn Ezra's perception of the land of Israel was the major influence on Crescas as much as on the commentators on Ibn Ezra's works.

Another circle, active in Provence at the end of the fourteenth and beginning of the fifteenth centuries, was mainly concerned with the land as the seat of wisdom. This circle consisted of one authoritative master, Solomon b. Menahem (Prat Maimon), and three disciples, Nethanel Kaspi, Jacob Farissol, and Solomon b. Judah, each of whom wrote a commentary on Judah Halevi's *Sefer ha-Kuzari*. Guided by purely rational considerations, they presented a unique interpretation of Halevi's work, completely overturning its original objective. In their view, the *Kuzari* was a rational work, as if Judah Halevi had been acquainted with, and composed his book in light of, the teachings of Maimonides and his disciples. The three commentators omitted the non-rational meaning of uniqueness in Halevi's theory, basing the superiority of the Holy Land on its capacity to further the apprehension of intelligibles and sciences and to lead the perfect man to conjunction with the Active Intellect. In a comment on the discussion of the land of Israel in the *Kuzari*, Nethanel Kaspi, for example, wrote, "the land is chosen and unique for you [= the Jews] to achieve true intellection and conjunction with spiritual existents, as is no other land" (MS. Paris 677, fol. 24a). Hence the Holy Land served the rationalist interest of the ideal of wisdom.

These two circles, the commentators on Ibn Ezra and those on the *Kuzari*, represent the spread of rationalism in different variations among the intelligentsia of the late Middle Ages. They espoused a well-defined, lucid perception of the land of Israel, in accord with their rational principles. Grappling with the dilemma described above, they ruled that the uniqueness of the land of Israel stemmed from its contribution to apprehension of the ideal of wisdom or from its scientific qualities. Neither circle assigned much weight to Judah Halevi's authentic notion of the uniqueness of the Holy Land.

Not so the third circle of moderate rationalists, active in fourteenth-century Spain, whose members were disciples of Asher b. Jehiel and Solomon b. Adret. They evolved a conception that fused the scientific and intellectual merits of the land with Judah Halevi's non-rational uniqueness. Among these moderate rationalists were such thinkers as Pinhas Halevi, Nissim Gerondi, Menahem b. Zerah, and Meir Aldabi. Nissim Gerondi and his pupil Joseph of Saragossa expressed the affinity between the land of Israel and its unique position *vis-à-vis* Providence as follows (*Derashot ha-Ran*, fifth homily; commentary of R. Nissim's disciple to Genesis, beginning of portion *Va-Yeze*):

> The superiority of the land of Israel over the other lands is that it is the ladder on which the righteous, those known as the angels of God, ascend to the Heavens, for these [= the angels] were designed to show him [= Jacob] that everything that is done in the land is through angels.

Menahem of Zerah added that the divine emanation that vitalizes and nourishes the countries of the world is emanated through the land of Israel (*Zedah la-Derekh* I, 1, 36). As mentioned, this uniqueness was merged with the Holy Land's quality of having air that was "moderate and good and the best of all [climates]" (Meir Aldabi, *Shevilei Emunah* II, 2). Thus, moderate rationalism was able to make the best of both a scientific approach and the notion of uniqueness.

This model was current in rationalist thought throughout the fifteenth century. For example, Shem Tov b. Joseph ibn Shem Tov argued that God's revelation to Abraham in Ur of the Chaldeans was not to be understood as prophecy but as merely intuition ("the divine spirit or inferior to the levels of prophecy"); this was because only in the land of Israel was authentic prophecy possible (*Derashot ha-Torah*, portion *Lekh-Lekha*). Another author, Abraham Shalom, also believed that the main part of prophetic emanation reached the land of Israel (*Neveh Shalom* VII, ii, 6). Moreover, he insisted, the land was by its very essence exclusive to the people of Israel: "The Chosen Land is exclusive to the Chosen People—though aliens may reside upon it, they will not possess it forever" (*ibid.*, IX, 9). The point was taken farther by Abraham Bibago, whose views of the ontological uniqueness of the Jews were also very similar to those of Judah Halevi, while his evaluation of the land of Israel followed the Kabbalists (*Derekh Emunah*, Portal III).

The comprehensive exegetical and philosophical thought of Isaac Abravanel offers a good summary of this view of the land of Israel. Abravanel bitterly disputed the rationalist definitions of prophecy proposed by Maimonides and Gersonides; in his view, contrary to that of the philosophical universalists, prophecy was a purely miraculous phenomenon, possible only in the Holy Land. Finally, this brief survey of fifteenth-century philosophy would not be complete without mention of the unique, ethically motivated approach of Isaac Arama. He singled out the small dimensions of the land, which supply its inhabitants with their basic needs, "enough for their livelihood, but measured and limited, not in great plenty" (*Aqedat Yizhaq*, Portal 77). The land was granted barely adequate crops, sufficient to avert starvation; thus the inhabitants would not be tempted to engage in commerce and trading but would learn to be thrifty and frugal, being more intent on perfecting their souls.

After the expulsion of the Jews from Spain, the Jewish centers of Italy, Palestine, Byzantium, and North Africa gained in importance, evolving their own theories of the land of Israel. In Salonika, the various medieval motifs of the uniqueness of the land of Israel (climatological and astrological merits, seat of wisdom and knowledge) received elaborate homiletical treatment, as in Moses Almosnino's sermons. Some thinkers

took up the theme of the land of Israel as a focus of astral magic as well. In Italy, humanists like Leone Modena described the Chosen Land as the ideal substrate for the creation of a perfect state. Thinkers in Safed wrote ethical and homiletical works that pondered the ethical and behavioral implications of the virtues of the Holy Land. In an extreme manifestation of this trend, Joseph Caro yearned to be burned there at the stake as a martyr.

Perhaps the most intense conceptual vigor of the period was revealed by Lurianic Kabbalah, which took shape in the second half of the sixteenth century. The land of Israel is assigned a special place in one of the mythical schemes presented in a book named *Shaar Maamrei Rashbi* ("Portal of Sayings of R. Simeon bar Yohai;" for the Torah portion *Qedoshim*). This scheme is concerned with Adam's sin and its results. The usual scheme in Lurianic writings is a dramatic fall of the worlds from the heavens, down into the depths of the forces of evil (*kelippot*). These worlds may be raised up again by retrieving the sparks or spiritual lights (*nizozot*) that fell into the impure regions as a result of the "breaking of the vessels" (*shevirat ha-kelim*). In *Shaar Maamrei Rashbi*, however, the descent of the worlds is described as gradual, each level of cosmic reality dropping by one step. The ascent is also to take place one step at a time. The reference point by which the descent and ascent are detected is the land of Israel, which stands on a supreme level, and the gradual descent of the worlds is measured against it.

This scheme presents the land of Israel with powerful imagery, as an ontological entity upon which the whole of creation depends. In actual fact, however, Lurianic Kabbalah held the potential of legitimizing life in the diaspora. For in Kabbalistic theory, the sparks of spiritual light, scattered by the shattering of the vessels, had to be retrieved all over the world. In other words, exile became a mission: to release the sparks from their fetters, the Jews were scattered to the four corners of the earth. The Lurianic circle (Menahem Azariah of Fano, Naphtali Bacharach) that stressed this exilic mission put forward the idea that, in the future, the whole world would become the land of Israel. Lurianic Kabbalah thus brought the land of Israel to its highest mythical dimensions, higher than ever in the past. These dimensions were commensurate with the ethical atmosphere of Safed Kabbalah, as is evident from Joseph Caro's and Solomon Alkabez's aspirations to achieve prophecy thanks to its specific association with the land of Israel. Thus Lurianic Kabbalah presented the most essential affinity between the land of Israel and the messianic idea.

Bibliography
Cohen, R.I., ed., *Vision and Conflict in the Holy Land* (Jerusalem and New York, 1985).
Hoffman, Lawrence, ed., *The Land of Israel: Jewish Perspectives* (Indiana, 1986)

DOV SCHWARTZ

ISRAEL THE PEOPLE IN JUDAISM, THE CLASSICAL STATEMENT: In the religion, Judaism, "Israel" stands for the holy people, whom God has called into being through Abraham and Sarah and their descendants, to whom the prophetic promises were made, and with whom the covenants were entered. In every Judaism "Israel" is a theological category, not solely a fact of sociology or ethnic culture or secular politics. The "Israel" of Judaism—of every Judaism—forms a supernatural social entity, "chosen," "holy," subject to God's special love and concern. That "Israel" is not to be confused with the Jewish people, an ethnic group, the people of Israel in a this-worldly framework, let alone the State of Israel, a modern nation-state. "Israel" in Judaism compares to "the Torah," in that, just as the latter is not just another book, so the former is not just another social entity. Just as the story of the Torah speaks of transcendent matters, so the tale of Israel, in Judaism, tells of God's relationship with humanity through the instrument God has chosen for self-manifestation: "You alone have I singled out of all the families of the earth—that is why I will call you to account for all your iniquities," as the prophet Amos put it (Amos 3:2, trans. NJPS).

Every Judaism uses the word "Israel" to refer to the social entity that it proposes to establish or define, and each Judaism deems its "Israel" to form a continuity of the Israel of whom the Hebrew Scriptures ("Old Testament") speak. Some deem the connection to be genealogical and fundamentally ethnic, putting forth a secular definition of their "Israel." But Rabbinic Judaism defines its Israel in supernatural terms, deeming the social entity to form a transcendental community, by faith. To Rabbinic Judaism "Israel" does not speak of a merely-ethnic, this-worldly people, but of a social entity defined by matters of supernatural genealogy, on the one side, and religious conversion, on the other. That is shown by the simple fact that a gentile of any origin or status, slave or free, Greek or barbarian, may enter its "Israel" on equal terms with those born into the community, becoming one of the children of Abraham and Sarah. The children of converts become Israelite without qualification. No distinction is made between the child of a convert and the child of a native-born Israelite. Since that fact bears concrete and material consequences, e.g., in the right to marry any other Israelite without distinction by reason of familial origin, it follows that the "Israel" of Rabbinic Judaism must be understood in a wholly theological framework. This Judaism knows no distinction between children of the flesh and children of the promise and therefore cannot address a merely ethnic "Israel," because for Rabbinic Judaism, "Israel" is always and only defined by the Torah received and represented by "our sages of blessed memory" as the word of God, never by the happenstance of secular history.

That does not mean that Rabbinic Judaism's Israel ignored this-worldly facts of the life of everyday Israel after the flesh. The fundamental social unit in Israelite society was the household, encompassing the large-scale economic unit of the farmer, his wife and children, slaves, dependent craftsmen and artisans, reaching outward to other such households to form a neatly-composed social unit, the village—and like villages. But Rabbinic Judaism's systemic social entity transformed the extended family into a representation, in the here-and-now, of mythic "Israel." In that way, the social unit adopted for itself and adapted for its purposes the social entity of Scripture and identified itself with the whole life and destiny of that entity. Clearly, therefore, Rabbinic Judaism set forth a theory of the ethnic entity that invoked a metaphor in order to explain the group and identify it. That fundamental act of metaphorization, from which all else follows, was the comparison of persons—Jews—of the here-and-now to the "Israel" of which the Hebrew Scriptures—"the Torah"—speak, and the identification of those Jews with that "Israel." Treating the social group—two or more persons—as other than they actually are in the present, as more than a (mere) given, means that the group is something else than what it appears to be.

To explain what is at stake in the category, "Israel," we have to recognize that the raw materials of definition are not the facts of the social order—how things are in practical terms—but the imagination of the system-builders. An "Israel"—that is, a theory of what Israel is and who is counted as part of Israel—in any Judaic system finds its shape and structure within that system. That "Israel" takes shape out of materials selected by the systemic framers from a miscellaneous, received or invented repertoire of possibilities. It goes without saying that, in the context of the description of the structure of a Judaism, its "Israel" is the sole Israel (whether social group, whether caste, whether family, whether class or "population," and whether any of the many social entities admirably identified by sociology) defined by that "Judaism." The best systemic indicator is a system's definition of its Israel, and Judaisms, or Judaic systems, from the priests' Pentateuchal system onward, made their statement principally through their response to the question framed in contemporary Judaic and Jewish-ethnic discourse as "who is a Jew?"

But the systemic component, Israel, finds its definition within the systemic imagination, not out of the raw materials of the social world beyond the system. For a system never accommodates the givens of politics and a sheltering society. The notion that society gives birth to religion is systemically beside the point. Systems do not recapitulate a given social order, they define one, and their framers, if they can, then go about realizing their fantasy. An "Israel" within a given Judaic system forms the invention of the system's builders and presents traits that they deem self-evidently true. That is quite without regard to realities beyond the range of systemic control. All that the context presents is a repertoire of possibilities. The framers of the contents then make their choices among those possibilities, and, outside of the framework of the system, there is no predicting the shape and structure of those choices. The system unfolds within its own inner logic, making things up as it goes along—because it knows precisely how to do so.

"Israel" in the Mishnah: While in first century Christianity, Christians claimed to form "the Israel after the spirit," while Jews who did not adopt Christianity were merely "Israel after the flesh," and while Christianity would deny to the Jewish people the status of the "Israel" of whom Scriptures spoke and to whom the prophets prophesied, these views did not play a role in the thinking of the earlier Rabbinic writings about "Israel." The Mishnah took shape at a time at which Christianity formed a minor irritant, perhaps in some places a competing Judaism, but not a formative component of the social order, and certainly not the political power that it was to become. Hence the Mishnah's framers' thinking about "Israel" in no way took account of the competing claim to form the true Israel put forth by Christianity; "Israel" remained intransitive, bearing no relationships to any other distinct social entity. The opposite of "Israel" in the Mishnah is "the nations," on the one side, or "Levite, priest," on the other: always taxonomical, never defined out of relationship to others within the same theoretical structure. As we shall see, the opposite of "Israel" in the Yerushalmi—which came to closure after Christianity had become the state religion of the Roman Empire—became "Rome," and Israel found itself defined as a family, with good and bad seed. Now the nations were differentiated, and a different world-order conceived; Israel entered into relationships of comparison and contrast, not merely hierarchy, because Christianity, sharing the same Scriptures, now called into question the very claim of the Jews to constitute "Israel."

As the Mishnah defines "Israel," the category bears two identical meanings: the "Israel" of (all) the Jews now and here, but also the "Israel" of which Scripture—the Torah—spoke. And that encompassed both the individual and the group, without linguistic differentiation of any kind. Thus in the Mishnah "Israel" may refer to an individual Jew (always male) or to "all Jews," that is, the collectivity of Jews. The individual woman is nearly always called *bat yisrael*, daughter of (an) Israel(ite). The sages in the Mishnah did not merely assemble facts and define the social entity as a matter of mere description of the given. Rather, they portrayed it as they wished to. They imputed to the social group, Jews, the status of a systemic entity, "Israel." To others within Jewry it was not at all self-evident that "all Jews" constituted one "Israel," and that that one "Israel" formed the direct and immediate continuation, in the here-and-now, of the "Israel" of holy writ and revelation. As we shall see, the Essene community at Qumran did not come to that conclusion, and the sense and meaning of "Israel" proposed by the authorships of the Mishnah and related writings did not strike Philo, for instance, as the main point at all. Paul, for his part, reflected on "Israel" within categories not at all symmetrical with those of the Mishnah.

The Mishnaic identification of Jewry in the here-and-now with the "Israel" of Scripture therefore constituted an act of metaphor, comparison, contrast, identification and analogy. It is that Judaism's most daring social metaphor. Implicitly, moreover, the metaphor excluded a broad range of candidates from the status of (an) "Israel," the Samaritans for one example, the scheduled castes of Mishnah-tractate Qiddushin Chapter Four, for another. Calling (some) Jews "Israel" established the comprehensive and generative metaphor that gives the Mishnaic system its energy. From that metaphor all else derived momentum.

The Mishnah defines "Israel" in antonymic relationships of two sorts, first, "Israel" as against "not-Israel," gentile, and second, "Israel" as against "priest," or "Levite." "Israel" serves as a taxonomic indicator, specifically part of a more encompassing system of hierarchization; "Israel" defined the frontiers, on the outer side of society, and the social boundaries within, on the other. To understand the meaning of "Israel" as the Mishnah and its associated documents of the second and third centuries sort matters out, we consider the sense of "gentile." The authorship of the Mishnah does not differentiate among gentiles, who represent an undifferentiated mass. To the system of the Mishnah, whether or not a gentile is a Roman or an Aramaean or a Syrian or a Briton does not matter. That is to say, differentiation among gentiles rarely, if ever, makes a difference in systemic decision-making.

And, it is also the fact, to the system of the Mishnah, that in the relationship at hand, "Israel" is not differentiated either. The upshot is that just as "gentile" is an abstract category, so is "Israel." "Kohen," that is, descendent of the Aaronide priesthood, is a category, and so is "Israel." For the purposes for which Israel/priest are defined, no further differentiation is undertaken. That is where for the Mishnaic system matters end. But to the Judaic system represented by the Yerushalmi and its associated writings, "gentile" (in the collective) may be Rome or other-than-Rome, for instance, Babylonia, Media, or Greece. That act of further differentiation—we may call it "speciation"—makes a considerable difference in the identification of gentile. In the Israel of the Mishnah's authorship, therefore, we confront an abstraction in a system of philosophy.

If we measure the definition against the social facts in the world beyond, we see a curious contrast. The Mishnah's systemic categories within "Israel" did not encompass the social facts that required explanation. The Mishnah could explain village and "all Israel," just as its system used the word "Israel" for individual and entire social entity. But the region and its counterparts, the "we" composed of regions, the corporate society of the Jews of a given country, language-group, and the like, the real-life world of communities that transcended particular locations—these social facts of the middle distance did not constitute subdivisions of the "Israel" that knew all and each, but nothing in between. The omitted entity was the family itself, which played no important role in the Mishnah's system, except as one of the taxonomic indicators. By contrast, "Israel" as family imparted to the details an autonomy and a meaning of their own, so that each complex component formed a microcosm of the whole: family to village to "Israel" as one large family.

The village then comprised "Israel" as much as did the region, the neighborhood, the corporate society people could empirically identify, the theoretical social entity they could only imagine—all formed "all Israel," viewed under the aspect of Heaven, and, of still greater consequence, each household— that is, each building block of the village community—constituted in itself a model of, the model for, "Israel." The utter abstraction of the Mishnah had left "Israel" as individual or as "all Israel," thus without articulated linkage to the concrete middle range of the Jews' everyday social life. Dealing with exquisite detail and the intangible whole, the Mishnah's system had left that realm of the society of Jews in the workaday household and village outside the metaphorical frame of "Israel," and "Israel" viewed in the image, after the likeness of family made up that omitted middle range. In the Mishnah's "Israel" we confront an abstraction in a system of philosophy, one centered upon issues of sanctification.

"Israel" in the Talmud of the Land of Israel: Two metaphors, rarely present and scarcely explored in the writings of the first stage (ca. 70-300 C.E.) in the formation of the Judaism of the dual Torah, came to prominence in the second stage (ca. 400-600 C.E.). That stage is represented by the Talmud of the Land of Israel and Midrash-compilations put together at the same period. These were, first, the view of "Israel" as a family, the children and heirs of the man, Israel; second, the conception of Israel as sui generis. While "Israel" in the first phase of

the formation of Judaism perpetually finds definition in relationship to its opposite, "Israel" in the second phase constituted an intransitive entity, defined in its own terms and not solely or mainly in relationship to other comparable entities. The enormous investment in the conception of "Israel" as sui generis makes that point blatantly. But "Israel" as family bears that same trait of autonomy and self-evident definition.

The "Israel" in the second stratum of the canon of the Judaism of the dual Torah bears a socially vivid sense. Now "Israel" forms a family, and an encompassing theory of society built upon that conception of "Israel" permits us to describe the proportions and balances of the social entity at hand, showing how each component both is an "Israel" and contributes to the larger composite as well. "Israel" as sui generis carried in its wake a substantial doctrine of definition, a weighty collection of general laws of social history governing the particular traits and events of the social group. In comparing transitive to intransitive "Israel," we move from "Israel" as not-gentile and "Israel" as not-priest to powerful statements of what "Israel" is. Now to specify in concrete terms the reasons adduced to explain the rather striking shift before us. Two important changes account for the metaphorical revolution at hand, one out at the borders, the other within, the Jews' group.

By claiming that "Israel" constituted "Israel after the flesh," the actual, living, present family of Abraham and Sarah, Isaac and Rebekah, Jacob and Leah and Rachel, the sages met head-on the Christian claim that there was—or could ever be—some other "Israel," of a lineage not defined by the family connection at all, and that the existing Jews no longer constituted "Israel." By representing "Israel" as sui generis, the sages moreover focused upon the systemic teleology, with its definition of salvation, in response to the Christian claim that salvation is not of Israel but of the Church, now enthroned in this world as in heaven. The sage, model for Israel, in the model of Moses, our rabbi, represented on earth the Torah that had come from heaven. Like Christ, in earth as in heaven, like the Church, the body of Christ, ruler of earth (through the emperor) as of heaven, the sage embodied what Israel was and was to be. So Israel as family in the model of the sage, like Moses our rabbi, corresponded in its social definition to the Church of Jesus Christ, the New Israel, of salvation of humanity. The metaphors given prominence in the late fourth and fifth century writings of "our sages of blessed memory" then formed a remarkable counterpoint to the social metaphors important in the mind of significant Christian theologians, as both parties reflected on the political revolution that had taken place.

In response to the challenge of Christianity, the sages' thought about "Israel" centered on the issues of history and salvation, issues made not merely chronic but acute by the political triumph. That accounts for the unprecedented reading of the outsider as differentiated, a reading contained in the two propositions concerning Rome, first, as Esau or Edom or Ishmael, that is, as part of the family, second, of Rome as the pig. Differentiating Rome from other gentiles represented a striking concession indeed, without counterpart in the Mishnah. Rome is represented as only Christian Rome can have been represented: it looks kosher but it is unkosher. Pagan Rome cannot ever have looked kosher, but Christian Rome, with its appeal to ancient Israel, could and did and moreover claimed to. It bore some traits that validate, but lacked others that validate.

The metaphor of the family proved equally pointed. The sages framed their political ideas within the metaphor of genealogy, because to begin with they appealed to the fleshly connection, the family, as the rationale for Israel's social existence. A family beginning with Abraham, Isaac, and Jacob, Israel could best sort out its relationships by drawing into the family other social entities with which it found it had to relate. So Rome became the brother. That affinity came to light only when Rome had turned Christian, and that point marked the need for the extension of the genealogical net. But the conversion to Christianity also justified the sages' extending membership in the family

to Rome, for Christian Rome shared with Israel the common patrimony of Scripture—and said so. The character of the sages' thought on Israel therefore proved remarkably congruent to the conditions of public discourse that confronted them.

The metaphor of the family, "Israel's children:" When the sages wished to know what (an) "Israel" was, in the fourth century they reread the scriptural story of "Israel"'s origins for the answer. To begin with, as Scripture told them the story, "Israel" was a man, Jacob, and his children are "the children of Jacob." That man's name was also "Israel," and, it followed, "the children of Israel" comprised the extended family of that man. By extension, "Israel" formed the family of Abraham and Sarah, Isaac and Rebekah, Jacob and Leah and Rachel. "Israel" therefore invoked the metaphor of genealogy to explain the bonds that linked persons unseen into a single social entity; the shared traits were imputed, not empirical. That social metaphor of "Israel"—a simple one and easily grasped—bore consequences in two ways.

First, children in general are admonished to follow the good example of their parents. The deeds of the patriarchs and matriarchs therefore taught lessons on how the children were to act. Of greater interest in an account of "Israel" as a social metaphor, "Israel" lived twice, once in the patriarchs and matriarchs, a second time in the life of the heirs as the descendants relived those earlier lives. The stories of the family were carefully reread to provide a picture of the meaning of the latter day events of the descendants of that same family. Accordingly, the lives of the patriarchs signaled the history of Israel.

The polemical purpose of the claim that the abstraction, "Israel," was to be compared to the family of the mythic ancestor lies right at the surface. With another "Israel," the Christian Church, now claiming to constitute the true one, the sages found it possible to confront that claim and to turn it against the other side. "You claim to form 'Israel after the spirit.' Fine, and we are Israel after the flesh—and genealogy forms the link, that alone." (Converts did not present an anomaly since they were held to be children of Abraham and Sarah, who had "made souls," that is, converts, in Haran, a point repeated in the documents of the period.) That fleshly continuity formed of all of "us" a single family, rendering spurious the notion that "Israel" could be other than genealogically defined. But that polemic seems to me adventitious and not primary for the metaphor provided a quite separate component to the sages' larger system.

The metaphor of Israel as family supplied an encompassing theory of society. It not only explained who "Israel" as a whole was but also set forth the responsibilities of Israel's social entity, its society. The metaphor defined the character of that entity; it explained who owes what to whom and why, and it accounted for the inner structure and interplay of relationships within the community, here-and-now, constituted by Jews in their villages and neighborhoods of towns. Accordingly, "Israel" as family bridged the gap between an account of the entirety of the social group, "Israel," and a picture of the components of that social group as they lived out their lives in their households and villages. An encompassing theory of society, covering all components from least to greatest, holding the whole together in correct order and proportion, derived from "Israel" viewed as extended family.

The theory of "Israel" as a society made up of persons who, because they constituted a family, stood in a clear relationship of obligation and responsibility to one another corresponded to what people much later would call the social contract, a kind of compact that in palpable ways told families and households how in the aggregate they formed something larger and tangible. The web of interaction spun out of concrete interchange now was formed not of the gossamer thread of abstraction and theory but by the tough hemp of family ties. "Israel" formed a society because "Israel" was compared to an extended family. That, sum and substance, supplied to the Jews in their households (themselves a made-up category which, in the end, transformed the relationship of the nuclear family into an abstraction capable of holding together quite unrelated persons) an account of the tie from household to household, from village to village, encompassing ultimately "all Israel."

The power of the metaphor of "Israel" as family hardly requires specification. If "we" form a family, then we know full well what links us, the common ancestry, the obligations imposed by common ancestry upon the cousins who make up the family today. The link between the commonplace interactions and relationships that make "us" into a community, on the one side, and that encompassing entity, "Israel," "all Israel," now is drawn. The large comprehends the little, the abstraction of "us" overall gains concrete reality in the "us" of the here-and-now of home and village, all together, all forming a "family." In that fundamental way, the metaphor of "Israel" as family therefore provided the field theory of "Israel" linking the most abstract component, the entirety of the social group, to the most mundane, the specificity of the household. One theory, framed in that metaphor of such surpassing simplicity, now held the whole together. That is how the metaphor of family provided an encompassing theory of society, an account of the social contract encompassing all social entities, Jews' and gentiles' as well, that no other metaphor accomplished.

"Israel" as family comes to expression in, among other writings of the fifth century, the document that makes the most sustained and systematic statement of the matter, Genesis Rabbah. In this theory we should not miss the extraordinary polemic utility, of which, in passing, we have already taken note. "Israel" as family also understood itself to form a nation or people. That nation-people held a land, a rather peculiar, enchanted or holy, Land, one that, in its imputed traits, was as sui generis as (presently we shall see) in the metaphorical thought of the system, Israel also was. Competing for the same territory, Israel's claim to what it called the Land of Israel—thus, of Israel in particular—now rested on right of inheritance such as a family enjoyed, and this was made explicit. The following passage, Gen. Rab. LXI:VII, shows how high the stakes were in the claim to constitute the genealogical descendant of the ancestors.

    1.A. "But to the sons of his concubines, Abraham gave gifts, and while he was still living, he sent them away from his son Isaac, eastward to the east country" (Gen. 25:6):

    B. In the time of Alexander of Macedonia the sons of Ishmael came to dispute with Israel about the birthright, and with them came two wicked families, the Canaanites and the Egyptians.

    C. They said, "Who will go and engage in a disputation with them."

    D. Gebiah b. Qosem [the enchanter] said, "I shall go and engage in a disputation with them."

    E. They said to him, "Be careful not to let the Land of Israel fall into their possession."

    F. He said to them, "I shall go and engage in a disputation with them. If I win over them, well and good. And if not, you may say, 'Who is this hunchback to represent us?'"

    G. He went and engaged in a disputation with them. Said to them Alexander of Macedonia, "Who lays claim against whom?"

    H. The Ishmaelites said, "We lay claim, and we bring our evidence from their own Torah: 'But he shall acknowledge the first-born, the son of the hated' (Deut. 21:17). Now Ishmael was the first-born. [We therefore claim the land as heirs of the first-born of Abraham.]"

    I. Said to him Gebiah b. Qosem, "My royal lord, does a man not do whatever he likes with his sons?"

    J. He said to him, "Indeed so."

    K. "And lo, it is written, 'Abraham gave all that he had to Isaac' (Gen. 25:2)."

    L. [Alexander asked,] "Then where is the deed of gift to the other sons?"

    M. He said to him, "'But to the sons of his concubines, Abraham gave gifts, [and while he was still living, he sent them away from his son Isaac, eastward to the east country]' (Gen. 25:6)."

    N. [The Ishmaelites had no claim on the land.] They abandoned the field in shame.

The metaphor as refined, with the notion of Israel today as the family of Abraham, as against the Ishmaelites, also of the same family, gives way. But the theme of family records persists. The power of the metaphor of family is that it can explain not only the

social entity formed by Jews, but the social entities confronted by them. All fell into the same genus, making up diverse species. The theory of society before us thus accounts for all societies, and, as we shall see when we deal with Rome, does so with extraordinary force.

    O. The Canaanites said, "We lay claim, and we bring our evidence from their own Torah. Throughout their Torah it is written, 'the land of Canaan.' So let them give us back our land."

    P. Said to him Gebiah b. Qosem, "My royal lord, does a man not do whatever he likes with his slave?"

    Q. He said to him, "Indeed so."

    R. He said to him, "And lo, it is written, 'A slave of slaves shall Canaan be to his brothers' (Gen. 9:25). So they are really our slaves."

    S. [The Canaanites had no claim to the land and in fact should be serving Israel.] They abandoned the field in shame.

    T. The Egyptians said, "We lay claim, and we bring our evidence from their own Torah. Six hundred thousand of them left us, taking away our silver and gold utensils: 'They despoiled the Egyptians' (Ex. 12:36). Let them give them back to us."

    U. Gebiah b. Qosem said, "My royal lord, six hundred thousand men worked for them for two hundred and ten years, some as silversmiths and some as goldsmiths. Let them pay us our salary at the rate of a denar a day."

    V. The mathematicians went and added up what was owing, and they had not reached the sum covering a century before the Egyptians had to forfeit what they had claimed. They abandoned the field in shame.

    W. [Alexander] wanted to go up to Jerusalem. The Samaritans said to him, "Be careful. They will not permit you to enter their most holy sanctuary."

    X. When Gebiah b. Qosem found out about this, he went and made for himself two felt shoes, with two precious stones worth twenty-thousand pieces of silver set in them. When he got to the mountain of the house [of the Temple], he said to him, "My royal lord, take off your shoes and put on these two felt slippers, for the floor is slippery, and you should not slip and fall."

    Y. When they came to the most holy sanctuary, he said to him, "Up to this point, we have the right to enter. From this

point onward, we do not have the right
to enter."

Z. He said to him, "When we get out of
here, I'm going to even out your hump."

AA. He said to him, "You will be called a
great surgeon and get a big fee."

The same metaphor serves both "Israel" and
"Canaan." Each formed the latter-day heir of
the earliest family, and both lived out the
original paradigm. The mode of thought
imputes the same genus to both social entities, and then makes its possible to distinguish among the two species. We shall see
the same mode of thought—the family, but
which wing of the family—when we consider
the confrontation with Christianity and with
Rome, in each case conceived in the same
personal way. The metaphor applies to both
and yields its own meanings for each. The
final claim in the passage before us moves
away from the metaphor of family. But the
notion of a continuous, physical descent is
implicit here as well. "Israel" has inherited
the wealth of Egypt. This notion of inheritance forms a critical component of the metaphor of family found in the conception of the
supernatural patrimony of the "children of
Israel," represented in the sages' frequent
allusion to "merit of the ancestors."

**Israel as *sui generis*: The rules of nature,
the rules of history, and supernatural governance of Israel in Leviticus Rabbah:** The
definition of "Israel" comes to us not only in
what people expressly mean by the word, but
also in the implicit terms yielded by how they
discuss the social entity. In Leviticus Rabbah
the conception of "Israel" as *sui generis* is expressed in an implicit statement that Israel
is subject to its own laws, which are distinct
from the laws governing all other social entities. These laws may be discerned in the factual, scriptural record of "Israel"'s past, and
that past, by definition, belonged to "Israel"
alone. It followed, therefore, that by discerning the regularities in "Israel"'s history, implicitly understood as unique to "Israel," the
sages recorded the view that "Israel" like
God was not subject to analogy or comparison. Accordingly, while not labeled a genus
unto itself, Israel is treated in that way.

To understand how this view of "Israel"

comes to expression, we have to trace the
principal mode of thought characteristic of
the authorship of Leviticus Rabbah. It is an
exercise in proving hypotheses by tests of
concrete facts. The hypotheses derive from
the theology of Israel. The tests are worked
out by reference to those given facts of social
history that Scripture, for its part, contributes.
As with the whole range of ancient exegetes
of Scripture, Rabbinic authorships treated
Scripture as a set of facts. These facts concerned history, not nature, but they served,
much as did the facts of nature availed the
Greek natural philosophers, to prove or disprove hypotheses. The hypotheses concerned
the social rules to which Israel was subjected,
and the upshot was that Israel was subject
to its own rules, revealed by the historical
facts of Scripture.

The single most common way in which
the sages made the implicit statement that
"Israel" is *sui generis* derives from their
"as-if" mode of seeing "Israel"'s reality. The
sages read "Israel"'s history not as it seems—
that is, not as it would appear when treated
in accord with the same norms as the histories of other social entities—but as a series of mysteries. The facts are not what
appearances suggest. The deeper truth is not
revealed in those events that happen, in common, to "Israel" and to (other) nations over
the face of the earth. What is happening to
"Israel" is wholly other, different from what
seems to be happening and what is happening to ordinary groups. The fundamental
proposition pertinent to "Israel" in Leviticus
Rabbah is that things are not what they seem.
"Israel"'s reality does not correspond to the
perceived facts of this world.

Now if we ask ourselves the source of this
particular mode of thinking about "Israel,"
we find no difficulty in identifying the point
of origin. The beginning of seeing "Israel" as
if it were other than the here-and-now social
group people saw lay in the original metaphorization of the social group. When people
looked at themselves, their households and
villages, their regions and language-group,
and thought to themselves, "What more are
we? What else are we?" they began that process of abstraction that took the form of an

intellectual labor of comparison, contrast, analogy, and, as is clear, consequent metaphorization. The group is compared to something else (or to nothing else) and hence is treated as not fully represented by the here-and-now but as representative, itself, of something else beyond. And that very mode of seeing things, lying in the foundations of the thought of the Mishnah's authorship, implicit in the identification of the survivors as the present avatar of Scripture's "Israel," yielded an ongoing process of metaphorization.

The original use of the metaphor, "Israel," to serve as the explanation of who the surviving groups were made it natural, from that time forward, to see "Israel" under the aspect of the "as-if." How this mode of thought worked itself out in the documents is clear. The exegetes maintained that a given statement of Scripture, in the case of Leviticus, stood for and signified something other than that to which the verse openly referred. If, for instance—as was a given for these exegetes—water stands for Torah and the skin disease mentioned in Leviticus 13, in Hebrew called *sara'at* and translated as leprosy, stands for, is caused by, evil speech, then a reference to one thing may indeed mean some other thing entirely, and the mode of thought is simple.

And what is decisive for our inquiry is that that mode of thought pertained to "Israel" alone. Solely in the case of "Israel" did one thing symbolize another, speak not of itself but of some other thing entirely. When other social entities, e.g., Babylonia, Persia, or Rome, stood for something else, it was in relationship to "Israel," and in the context of the metaphorization of Israel. When treated in a neutral context, by contrast, we find no metaphors, e.g., Alexander of Macedonia is a person, and no symbol stands for that person. When Greece appears in the sequence of empires leading finally to the rule of "Israel," then Greece may be symbolized by the hare. And there is another side of the matter too. Other things—the bear, the eagle—could stand for the empires, but—in that metaphorical context—then "Israel" stands only for itself. Whichever way we have it, therefore, implicit in that view and mode of thought is the notion of "Israel" as sui generis, lacking all counterpart or parallel entity for purposes of comparison and contrast. The importance of the mode of reading Scripture "as if" it meant something else than what it said, in the case of the exegesis of Leviticus Rabbah, should not be missed. What lies beneath or beyond the surface—there is the true reality, the world of truth and meaning, discerned through metaphorical thinking.

Comparing "Israels" among various Judaisms: The shape and meaning imputed to the social component, "Israel," conform to the larger interests of the system and in detail express the system's main point. We see this fact when we contrast the "Israel" of Rabbinic Judaism with the "Israel" of Paul's thought. In his representation of his "Israel," Paul presents us with a metaphor for which, in the documents of the Judaism of the dual Torah, there is no counterpart in this context. "Israel" compared to an olive tree, standing for "Israel" encompassing gentiles who believe but also Jews by birth who do not believe, "Israel" standing for the elect and those saved by faith and therefore by grace—these complex and somewhat disjointed metaphors and definitions form a coherent and simple picture when we see them not in detail but as part of the larger whole of Paul's entire system. For the issue of "Israel" for Paul forms a detail of a system centered upon a case in favor of salvation through Christ and faith in him alone, even without keeping the rules of the Torah.

The Apostle Paul and "Israel:" The generative problematic that tells Paul what he wishes to know about "Israel" derives from the larger concerns of the Christian system Paul proposes to work out. That problematic was framed in the need, in general, to explain the difference, as to salvific condition, between those who believed, and those who did not believe, in Christ. But it focused, specifically, upon the matter of "Israel," and how those who believed in Christ but did not derive from "Israel" related to both those who believed and also derived from "Israel" and those who did not believe but derived from "Israel." Do the first-named have to keep the Torah? Are the non-believing Jews subject to justification? Since, had Paul been a "gentile" and not an "Israel," the issue cannot have proved critical in the working out of an individual system (but only in the address to the world at large), we may take for granted that Paul's own Jewish origin made the question important, if not critical. What transformed the matter from a chronic into an acute question—the matter of salvation through keeping the Torah—encompassed, also, the matter of who is "Israel."

For his part, Paul appeals for his taxic indicator of "Israel" to a consideration we have not found commonplace at all, namely, circumcision. It is certainly implicit in the Torah, but the Mishnah's laws accommodate as "Israel" persons who (for good and sufficient reasons) are not circumcised, and treat as "not-Israel" persons who are circumcised but otherwise do not qualify. So for the Mishnah's system circumcision forms a premise, not a presence, a datum, but not a decisive taxic indicator. But Paul, by contrast, can have called "Israel" all those who are circumcised, and "not-Israel" all those who are not circumcised—pure and simple. Jonathan Z. Smith states, "The strongest and most persistent use of circumcision as a taxic indicator is found in Paul and the deutero-Pauline literature. Paul's self-description is framed in terms of the two most fundamental halakhic definitions of the Jewish male: circumcision and birth from a Jewish mother. . . . 'Circumcised' is consistently used in the Pauline literature as a technical term for the Jew, 'uncircumcised,' for the gentile."[1] It must follow that for Paul, "Israel" is "the circumcised nation," and an "Israel" is a circumcised male.

The reason for the meaning attached to "Israel" is spelled out by Smith, "What is at issue . . . is the attempt to establish a new taxon: 'where there cannot be Greek and Jew, circumcised and uncircumcised, barbarian and Scythian' (Col. 3:11), 'for neither circumcision counts for anything nor uncircumcision but a new creation' (Gal. 6:15)." It follows that for Paul, the matter of "Israel" and its definition form part of a larger project of reclassifying Christians in terms not defined by the received categories, now a

third race, a new race, a new man, in a new story. Smith proceeds to make the matter entirely explicit to Paul's larger system: "Paul's theological arguments with respect to circumcision have their own internal logic and situation: that in the case of Abraham, it was posterior to faith (Rom. 4:9-12); that spiritual things are superior to physical things (Col. 3:11-14); that the Christian is the 'true circumcision' as opposed to the Jew (Phil. 3:3). . . . But these appear secondary to the fundamental taxonomic premise, the Christian is a member of a new taxon."

In this same context Paul's Letter to the Romans presents a consistent picture. In Chapters Nine through Eleven he presents his reflections on what and who is (an) "Israel." Having specified that the family of Abraham will inherit the world not through the law but through the righteousness of faith (Rom. 4:13), Paul confronts "Israel" as family and redefines the matter in a way coherent with his larger program. Then the children of Abraham will be those who "believe in him that raised from the dead Jesus our Lord, who was put to death for our trespasses and raised for our justification" (Rom. 4:24-5). For us the critical issue is whether or not Paul sees these children of Abraham as "Israel." The answer is in his address to "my kinsmen by race. They are Israelites, and to them belong the sonship, the glory, the covenants, the giving of the law, the worship, and the promises; to them belong the patriarchs, and of their race, according to the flesh, is the Christ. God who is over all be blessed for ever" (Rom. 9:3-4). "Israel" then is the holy people, the people of God. But Paul proceeds to invoke a fresh metaphor (commonplace in the Rabbinic writings later on, to be sure) of "Israel" as olive tree, and so to reframe the doctrine of "Israel" in a radical way:

> Not all who are descended from Israel belong to Israel, and not all are children of Abraham because they are his descendants . . . it is not the children of the flesh who are the children of God, but the children of the promise are reckoned as descendants (Rom. 9:6-7).

Here we have an explicit definition of "Israel," now not after the flesh but after the promise. "Israel" then is no longer a family in the concrete sense in which, in earlier materials, we have seen the notion. "Israel after the flesh" who pursued righteousness which is based on law did not succeed in fulfilling that law because they did not pursue it through faith (Rom. 9:31), "and gentiles who did not pursue righteousness have attained it, that is, righteousness through faith" (Rom. 9:30). Now there is an "Israel" after the flesh but also "a remnant chosen by grace . . . the elect obtained it . . ." (Rom. 11:5-6), with the consequence that the fleshly "Israel" remains, but gentiles ("a wild olive shoot") have been grafted "to share the richness of the olive tree" (Rom. 11:17). Do these constitute "Israel"? Yes and no. They share in the promise. They are "Israel" in the earlier definition of the children of Abraham. There remains an "Israel" after the flesh, which has its place as well. And that place remains with God: "As regards election they are beloved for the sake of their forefathers. For the gifts and the call of God are irrevocable" (Rom. 11:28-29).

The shape and meaning imputed to the social component, "Israel," here conform to the larger interests of the system constructed by Paul, both episodically, and, in Romans, quite systematically. "Israel" expresses, also, the system's main point. For Paul's Judaic system, encompassing believing (former) "gentiles" but also retaining a systemic status for non-believing Jews, "Israel" forms an important component within a larger structure. Not only so, but, more to the point, "Israel" finds definition on account of the logical requirements of that encompassing framework. Indeed, there is no making sense of the remarkably complex metaphor introduced by Paul—the metaphor of the olive tree—without understanding the problem of thought that confronted him, and that he solved through, among other details, his thinking on "Israel." The notion of entering "Israel" through belief but not behavior ("works") in one detail expresses the main point of Paul's system, which concerns not who is "Israel" but what faith in Christ means.

"Israel" in Rabbinic Judaism compared with "Israel" in the thought of Philo and of the Essene community at Qumran: By philosopher in the present context is meant an intellectual who attempts to state as a coherent whole, within a single system of thought and (implicit) explanation, diverse categories and classifications of data. By politician is meant a person of public parts, one who undertakes to shape a social polity, a person of standing in a social group, e.g., a community, who proposes to explain in some theoretical framework the meaning and character of the life of that group or nation or society or community. We classify the framers of the Mishnah as philosophers, those of the Yerushalmi and related writings (by their own word) as politicians. The related but distinct systems made by each group exhibit traits of philosophy and politics, respectively, for reasons now spelled out. The generalization is before us. Does it apply to more than our own case? For purposes of showing that the same phenomenon derives from other cases and therefore constitutes a law, not a mere generalization out of a case, we take up an individual, a philosopher, and an authorship, the formative intellects of the community at Qumran. Philo, the Jewish philosopher of Alexandria, serves as our example of the former, and the authorship of the more important writings of the Essene community of Qumran, the latter.

The Judaic philosopher, Philo: For Philo, "Israel" forms a paradigmatic metaphor, bearing three meanings. The first is ontological, which signifies the places of "Israel" in God's creation. The second is epistemological. This signifies the knowledge of God that "Israel" possesses. The third is political, referring to the polity that "Israel" possesses and projects in light of its ontological place and epistemological access to God. Our point of interest is achieved when we perceive even from a distance the basic contours of Philo's vision of "Israel." What we shall see is that, for Philo, "Israel" formed a category within a larger theory of how humanity knows divinity, an aspect of ontology and epistemology. What makes an "Israel" into "Israel" for Philo is a set of essentially philosophical considerations, concerning adherence to or perception of God. In the philosophical system of Philo, "Israel" constitutes a philosophical category, not a social entity in an everyday sense.

Philo does see Jews as a living social entity, a community. His Embassy to Gaius is perfectly clear that the Jews form a political group. But that fact makes no difference to Philo's philosophical "Israel." For when he constructs his philosophical statement, the importance of "Israel" derives from its singular capacity to gain knowledge of God which other categories of the system cannot have. When writing about the Jews in a political context, Philo does not appeal to their singular knowledge of God, and when writing about the Jews as "Israel" in the philosophical context, he does not appeal to their forming a this-worldly community. That again illustrates the claim that it is within the discipline of its own logic that the system invents its "Israel," without responding in any important way to social facts out there, in the larger world.

Seeing "Israel" as "the people that is dedicated to his [God's] service," Philo holds that "Israel" is the best of races and is capable of seeing God, and this capacity of seeing God is based upon the habit of his service to God.[2] The upshot of the innate capacity to receive a type of prophecy that comes directly from God is that one must be descended from "Israel" to receive that type of prophecy. An Egyptian, Hagar, cannot see the Supreme Cause. The notion of inherited "merit" (in this context an inappropriate metaphor) bears more than a single burden; here "merit" or inherited capacity involves a clearer perception of God than is attained by those without the same inheritance—a far cry indeed from the "merit of the ancestors" as the fourth-century sages would interpret it. Mere moral and intellectual qualifications, however, do not suffice. One has to enjoy divine grace, which Moses had, and which, on account of the merit of the patriarchs, the people have.

If Philo, serving as the counterpart to the authorship of the Mishnah, represents an intellectual's thinking about the entity, "Israel," we do well to identify a political reading, placing into perspective, for comparison and contrast, the deeply political definitions of "Israel" formed by the authorships of the

Yerushalmi, Genesis Rabbah, and Leviticus Rabbah. For they appeal to political metaphors—metaphors of the group as polis. They see "Israel" as a political entity, matched against "Rome," or treated as sui generis, or compared to a family—anything but a mere category. For that purpose we turn to the library that was selected by, and therefore presumably speaks for, the builders of an "Israel" that is the best documented, in its original site and condition, of any in antiquity: the Essene community of Qumran. Just as, for Philo, we appealed to the foremost authorities for guidance, so, for the Essene community at Qumran, we do the same.

"Israel" at Qumran: The Essenes of Qumran serve as a test case for the two hypotheses, first, that what matters to begin with is dictated by the traits of the one to whom the subject is important, not by the objective and indicative characteristics of the subject itself; second, that the importance of a topic derives from the character of the system that takes up that topic. We turn first to the systemic definition of "Israel:" what kind of "Israel" and for what purpose, then to the importance, within a system, of an "Israel." By "Israel" the authorships of the documents of the Essene library of Qumran mean "us"— and no one else. We start with that "us" and proceed from there to "Israel." In this way as with the authorship of the documents of the second phase of the dual Torah the movement of thought began with the particular and moved outward to the general. The group's principal documents comprised a Community Rule, which "legislates for a kind of monastic society," the Damascus Rule, "for an ordinary lay existence," and the War Rule and Messianic Rule, ". . . while associated with the other two, and no doubt reflecting to some extent a contemporary state of affairs, plan for a future age."[3] Among the four, the first two will tell us their authorships' understanding of the relationship between "us" and "Israel," and that is what is critical to the picture of the type of "us" which (as we shall see) is "Israel."

Stated simply, what our authorships meant by "us" was simply "Israel," or "the true Israel." The group did not recognize other Jews as "Israel." That is why the group organized itself as a replication of "all Israel," as they read about "Israel" in those passages of Scripture that impressed them. They structured their group—in Vermes' language, "so that it corresponded faithfully to that of Israel itself, dividing it into priests and laity, the priests being described as the 'sons of Zadok'—Zadok was High Priest in David's time—and the laity grouped after the biblical model into twelve tribes. This particular Israel then divided itself into units of thousands, hundreds, fifties, and tens. The Community Rule further knows divisions within the larger group, specifically, 'the men of holiness,' the men of perfect holiness," within a larger "Community." The corporate being of the community came to realization in common meals, prayers, and deliberations. Vermes says, "Perfectly obedient to each and every one of the laws of Moses and to all that was commanded by the prophets, they were to love one another and to share with one another their knowledge, powers, and possessions" (Vermes, p. 89). The description of the inner life of the group presents us with a division of a larger society. But—among many probative ones—one detail tells us that this group implicitly conceived of itself as "Israel."

The group lived apart from the Temple of Jerusalem and had its liturgical life worked out in utter isolation from that central cult. They had their own calendar, which differed from the one people take for granted was observed in general, for their calendar was reckoned not by the moon but by the sun. This yielded different dates for the holy days and effectively marked the group as utterly out of touch with other Jews (Vermes, p. 87). The solar calendar followed by the Essene community at Qumran meant that holy days for that group were working days for others and vice versa. The group furthermore had its own designation for various parts of the year. The year was divided into seven fifty-day periods, as Vermes says, each marked by an agricultural festival, e.g., the Feast of New Wine, Oil, and so on. On the Pentecost, treated as the Feast of the Renewal of the Covenant, the group would assemble in hi-

erarchical order: "the priests first, ranked in order of status, after them the Levites, and lastly 'all the people one after another in their Thousands, Hundreds, Fifties, and Tens, that every Israelite may know his place in the community of God according to the everlasting design" (Vermes, p. 178). There can be no doubt from this passage—and a vast array of counterparts can be assembled—that the documents address "Israel."

Defining Israel in diverse Judaisms: What an "Israel" is depends on who wants to know. Philo has given us a philosophical "Israel." The authorships of the documents preserved by the Essenes of Qumran define "Israel" not as a fictive entity possessing spiritual traits alone or mainly, but as a concrete social group, an entity in the here-and-now, that may be defined by traits of persons subject to the same sanctions and norms, sharing the same values and ideals. Builders of a community or a polis, and hence, politicians, the authorships of the Essenes of Qumran conceived and described in law a political "Israel." Their "Israel" and Philo's bear nothing in common. The one "Israel"—the Essenes'—constitutes a political entity and society.

The "Israel" of the Essenes is the "Israel" of history and eschatology of Scripture, as much as the "Israel" of the authorship of the Yerushalmi, Genesis Rabbah, and Leviticus Rabbah refers back to the "Israel" of Genesis and Leviticus. The other "Israel"—Philo's—comprises people of shared intellectual traits in a larger picture of how God is known, as much as the "Israel" of the authorship of the Mishnah and related writings exhibits taxonomic traits and serves a function of classification. Both sets of politicians present us with political "Israel"s, that is, each with an "Israel" that exhibits the traits of a polis, a community ("people," "nation"). Both sets of philosophers offer a philosophical "Israel," with traits of a taxonomic character—one set for one system, another set for the other—that carry out a larger systemic purpose of explanation and philosophical classification.

The place of "Israel" in a Judaic religious structure: Whether or not "Israel" takes an important place in a system is decided by the system and its logic, not the circumstance of the Jews in the here-and-now. Systemopoeia—a word I have invented to mean, the making of a system—is a symbolic transaction worked out in imagination, not a sifting and sorting of facts. But how do we know whether or not any systemic component plays a more, or a less, important role? A judgment on the importance of a given entity or category in one system by comparison to the importance of that same entity or category in another need not rely upon subjective criteria. A reasonably objective measure of the matter lends hope to test the stated hypothesis. That criterion is whether or not the system remains cogent without consideration of its "Israel." Philo's does, the Mishnah's does, Paul's does not, the Essenes' does not, and the second stage in Judaism's does not.

The criterion of importance therefore does not derive from merely counting up references to "Israel." What we must do is to assess the role and place of the social entity in a system by asking a simple question. Were the entity or trait "Israel" to be removed from a given system, would that system radically change in character or would it merely lose a detail? What is required is a mental experiment, but not a very difficult one. What we do is simply present a reprise of our systemic description. Three facts have emerged.

First, without an "Israel," Paul would have had no system. The generative question of his system required him to focus attention on the definition of the social entity, "Israel." Paul originated among Jews but addressed both Jews and gentiles, seeking to form the lot into a single social entity "in Christ Jesus." The social dimension of his system formed the generative question with which he proposed to contend.

Second, without an "Israel," Philo, by contrast, can have done very well indeed. For even our brief and schematic survey of Philo has shown us that, whatever mattered, "Israel" did not. It was a detail of a theory of knowledge of God, not the generative problematic even of the treatment of the knowl-edge of God, let alone of the system as a whole (which we scarcely approached and had no reason to approach!). We may therefore say that "Israel" formed an important category for Paul and not for Philo. Accordingly, the judgment of the matter rests on more than mere word-counts, on the one side, or exercises of impression and taste, on the other. It forms part of a larger interpretation of the system as a whole and what constitutes the system's generative problematic.

If, moreover, we ask whether "Israel" is critical to the Essenes of Qumran, a simple fact answers our question. Were we to remove "Israel" in general and in detail from the topical program, we should lose, if not the entirety of the library, then nearly the whole of some documents, and the larger part of many of them. The Essene library of Qumran constitutes a vast collection of writings about "Israel," its definition and conduct, history and destiny. We cannot make an equivalent statement about the entire corpus of Philo's writings, even though Philo obviously concerned himself with the life and welfare of the "Israel" of which, in Alexandria as well as world-over, he saw himself a part. The reason for the systemic importance among the Essenes of Qumran of "Israel," furthermore, derives from the meanings imputed to that category. The library stands for a social group that conceives of itself as "Israel," and that wishes, in these documents, to spell out what that "Israel" is and must do. The system as a whole forms an exercise in the definition of "Israel" as against that "non-Israel" composed not of gentiles but of erring (former) Israelites. The saving remnant is all that is left: "Israel."

If we wish to know whether "Israel" will constitute an important component in a Judaism, we ask about the categorical imperative and describe, as a matter of mere fact, the consequent categorical composition of that system, stated as a corpus of authoritative documents. A system in which "Israel"—the social entity to which the system's builders imagine they address themselves—plays an important role will treat "Israel" as part of its definitive structure. The reason is that the system's categorical imperative will find important consequences in the definition of its "Israel." A system whose builders work on entirely other questions than social ones, explore the logic of issues different from those addressing a social entity, also will not yield tractates on "Israel" and will not accord to the topic of "Israel" that categorical and systemic importance that we have identified in some Judaisms but not in others. Discourse on "Israel," in general (as in the second phase of the Judaism of the dual Torah) or in acute detail concerning internal structure (as in the Essene writings of Qumran) comes about because of the fundamental question addressed by the system viewed whole.

The systemically-generative circumstance finds its definition in the out-there of the world in which the system-builders—and their imagined audience—flourish. Extraordinary political crises, ongoing tensions of society, a religious crisis that challenges theological truth—these in time impose their definition upon thought, seizing the attention and focusing the concentration of the systemopoieic thinkers who propose to explain matters. Systems propose an orderly response to a disorderly situation, and that is their utility. Systems then come into existence at a point, and in a context, in which thoughtful people identify questions that cannot be avoided and must be solved. Such a circumstance emerges in the polis, that is, in the realm of politics and the context of persons in community, in the corporate society of shared discourse. The acute, systemopoieic question then derives from out-there; the system begins somewhere beyond the mind of the thoughtful intellects who build systems. Having ruled out the systemopoieic power of authors' or authorships' circumstance, therefore, we now invoke the systemopoieic power of the political setting of the social group of which the system-builders form a part (in their own minds, the exemplification and realization).

Matters in regard to the systems of Paul and the Essenes hardly require detailed specification. Paul's context told him that "Israel" constituted a categorical imperative, and it also told him what he had to discover about "Israel" in his thought on the encoun-

ter with Christ. The Essenes of Qumran by choice isolated themselves and in that context determined the generative issue of describing an "Israel" that, all by itself in the wilderness, would survive and form the saving remnant.

Paul—all scholarship concurs—faced a social entity ("church" or "Christian community") made up of Jews but also gentiles, and (some) Jews expected people to obey the law, e.g., to circumcise their sons. Given the natural course of lives, that was not a question to be long postponed, which imparts to it the acute, not merely chronic, character that it clearly displayed even in the earliest decade beyond Paul's vision. And that fact explains why, for Paul, circumcision formed a critical taxic indicator in a way in which, for Philo, for the Mishnah, and other Judaic systems, it did not.

The circumstance of the Essenes of Qumran is far better documented, since that community through its rereading of Scripture tells us that it originated in a break between its founder(s) and other officials. Consequently, characterizing the Essenes of Qumran hardly moves beyond the evidence in hand. They responded to their own social circumstance, isolated and alone as it was, and formed a community unto itself, hence seeing their "Israel," the social entity of their system, as what there was left of Scripture's "Israel," that is, the remnant of Israel.

The sages of the Rabbinic Judaism made their documentary statements in reply to two critical questions, the one concerning sanctification, presented by the final failure of efforts to regain Jerusalem and restore the Temple cult, the other concerning salvation, precipitated by the now-unavoidable fact of Christianity's political triumph.

Once each of the three Judaisms for which a precipitating, systemopoieic crisis can be identified passes before us, we readily see how the consequent program flowed from the particular politically-generative crisis. The case of the sages in both phases in the unfolding of the dual Torah is the obvious example of the interplay of context and contents. There we see with great clarify both the precipitating event and the logic of self-evidence out of which a system spun its categorical program. That program, correlated with the systemopoieic event, would then define all else. If sanctification is the issue imposed by events, then the Mishnah will ask a range of questions of detail, at each point providing an exegesis of the everyday in terms of the hermeneutics of the sacred: Israel as different and holy within the terms specified by Scripture. If salvation proves the paramount claim of a now-successful rival within "Israel," then the authorship of Genesis Rabbah will ask the matriarchs and patriarchs to spell out the rules of salvation, so far as they provide not merely precedents but paradigms of salvation. The authorship of Leviticus Rabbah will seek in the picture of sanctification supplied by the book of Leviticus the rules and laws that govern the salvation of "Israel." The history of an "Israel" that is a political entity—family, sui generis, either, both, it hardly matters—will dictate for the authorship for which the Yerushalmi speaks a paramount category.

The sages formed that group of Jews that identified the critical issue as that of sanctification, involving proper classification and ordering of all of the elements and components of Israel's reality. Not all Jews interpreted events within that framework, however, and it follows, circumstances by themselves did not govern. The symbol-change worked for those for whom it worked, which, ultimately, changed the face of the Jews' society. But in the second and fourth centuries were Jews who found persuasive a different interpretation of events—whether the defeat of Bar Kokhba or the conversion of Constantine—and became Christian.

Nor did all Christians concur with Paul that Jews and gentiles now formed a new social entity, another "Israel" than the familiar one; the same social circumstance that required Paul to design his system around "Israel" persuaded a later set of authorships to tell the story of Jesus' life and teachings, a story in which (as in the Mishnah's system) "Israel" formed a datum, a backdrop, but hardly the main focus of discourse or the precipitating consideration. It took a century for Paul's reading of matters to gain entry into the canon, and before Luther, Paul's system was absorbed and hardly paramount.

So too with the Essenes. Diverse groups in the age in which the Essenes of Qumran took shape and produced their library, hence the system expressed in their books, formed within the larger society of the Jews in the Land of Israel. And not all such smaller groups seized upon the option of regarding themselves as the whole of (surviving) "Israel." Many did not. One such group, the Pharisees, presents an important structural parallel, in its distinctive calculation of the holy calendar, in its provision of stages for entry into the group, in its interest in the rules of purity governing meals that realized, in a concrete communion, the social existence of the group, and in diverse other ways. The Pharisees did not regard themselves as coexistent with "all Israel," even while they remained part of the everyday corporate community. They proposed to exemplify their rules in the streets and marketplaces and to attain influence over the people at large. So merely forming what we now call a sect did not require a group to identify itself as "all Israel," as did the Essenes of Qumran.

The upshot is, what people mean by "Israel" depends upon how they see the world in general. Just as, in the world today, "Israel" stands for "the state of Israel," or "the Land of Israel," by reason of the prevailing theories of what it means to be a Jew, so in the setting of various Judaisms, "Israel" takes on its meaning from its context.

Notes

[1] "Fences and Neighbors," in W.S. Green ed., *Approaches to Ancient Judaism* (Missoula, 1978), pp. 1-25 and in Jonathan Z. Smith, *Imagining Religion. From Babylon to Jonestown* (Chicago, 1982), pp. 1-18.
[2] Harry A. Wolfson, *Philo: Foundations of Religious Philosophy in Judaism, Christianity and Islam* (Cambridge, rev. ed. 1962), vol. 1, pp. 51-2.
[3] Geza Vermes, *The Dead Sea Scrolls: Qumran in Perspective* (London, 1994), p. 87.

JACOB NEUSNER

ISRAEL THE PEOPLE IN JUDAISM, IN MEDIEVAL AND MODERN TIMES: Numerous recent studies by historians and social scientists have examined the nature of Jewish identity, attempting to discover how Jews create their identity, how they maintain their Jewishness, and what this means for our understanding of Jews in particular and other minority groups in general.[1] While these investigations have opened new avenues for comprehending Jewish identity and its construction, they largely have failed to investigate what major Jewish thinkers themselves have said on the subject throughout the medieval and modern periods. After quickly reviewing the theoretical literature, this essay fills this gap by focusing on the ways in which Jewish thinkers themselves have defined Jewish peoplehood and by identifying what they considered to be the essential aspects of Jewishness. Our goal is to determine the significance of the concept of the People of Israel from inside the Jewish tradition, thus supplementing studies that have investigated Jewish identity in light of current intellectual paradigms.

Like membership in any group with a long history, Jewish peoplehood is a complex phenomenon. As Asa Kasher observes, the variety within any collective makes it almost impossible to create a description that applies equally to all members of the group. A problem arises, he argues, because "a diversity condition" holds for a collective; that is, "for each common collective . . . the question Who is a . . .? has a variety of significantly different answers, held by members of different groups, even within the collective itself." This "diversity condition" results from the collective's "rich conceptual realm" and "its own rich history,"[2] that is, from the group members' diverse understandings even of shared concepts. One example of Judaism's "rich conceptual realm" concerns the concept "God." Surely a defining factor of membership in the People Israel is belief in God. But which God: the biblical creator, the Maimonidean Active Intellect, or the mystical *Eyn Sof*? The term "Torah" furnishes another example of Judaism's conceptual variety. While contemporary Reform, Orthodox, Conservative, and Reconstructionist Jews all speak of Torah, Orthodox Jews, for instance, can hardly agree with Reform Judaism's defini-

tion of Torah, found in its 1976 San Francisco Platform:[3]

> Torah results from the relationship between God and the Jewish people. . . . Lawgivers and prophets, historians and poets gave us a heritage whose study is a religious imperative and whose practice is our chief means to holiness. Rabbis and teachers, philosophers and mystics, gifted Jews in every age amplified the Torah tradition. For millennia, the creation of Torah has not ceased and Jewish creativity in our time is adding to the chain of Torah.

This contrasts with the Orthodox conception of Torah as a single, unchanging revelation that goes back to Sinai rather than as a product of the intellect of Jews in each age.

Kasher suggests that a group's historical circumstances inevitably create its vast conceptual variety:[4]

> The history of a collective is . . . an arena of modification; and the richer the history of this collective is, that is, the more internal and external problems its members encounter, tackle, and solve, the more significant are the modifications its conceptual realm sustains. In the history of any living collective, members of the collective, whether all of them at once, most of them, or just some of them first, are bound to view the conceptual realm of their collective as highly structured, some of its parts being conspicuously considered more central than others.

In exactly this way, the attempt to define the meaning of Jewish peoplehood faces the reality that various factions within Judaism have always debated exactly which are the core elements of Judaism.

A second problem arises when we seek to determine who within the Jewish community has the right to specify or serve as a model for answering the question, "What is a Jew?" In light of the group's "rich conceptual realm," Kasher would seek a definition by asking a variety of Jews. Others argue that one should turn to the *incontrovertible core* of Judaism, "that is, the set of those individuals who are unquestionably Collected"[5] under the title Jew, meaning those members of the collective who 1) consider themselves to be Jewish and 2) who are considered by non-Jews to be Jewish. Kasher asserts that only one who has a clear view of the nature of the Jewish People (throughout he speaks of the "collective") will make a self-declaration about membership in the Jewish People. Similarly, others who wish to identify a person as a member of the Jewish People must have a clear notion of the person and the meaning of Jewish peoplehood. If all of these persons agree that a given individual is a member of the Jewish People, the second condition is met. Furthermore, we must also be able to argue that even those who do not know the given individuals, would, if they knew them, assign them to the Jewish People (p. 60). For example, members of the Lubavitcher Hasidim would meet Kasher's criteria for being incontrovertible Jews. While some Jews may object to or dislike this form of Judaism, no Jew or non-Jew would deny the fact that the Lubavitchers are in fact Jews.

What if some people identify themselves as members of a collective, while members of the *incontrovertible core* are divided on the question, some considering them to part of the collective and others not? Kasher calls such individuals members of the *union* of the collective: "A person belongs to the union (of a collective) when he or she is considered to be a member of the collective according to the views held by some members of the incontrovertible core of this collective" (p. 63). By deriving our information about the collective from the members of the *union* instead of only from members of the *incontrovertible core*, we are able to draw upon a much wider range of individuals and opinions, thus reflecting more clearly the entire group's sense of identity. Following this method, we may seek an answer to our questions concerning the Jewish People from all types of Jews—Reform Jews, secular Jews, Reconstructionist Jews, Orthodox Jews, Zionists, non-Zionists, and so on. While some of the incontrovertible core of Judaism may not consider all of the above mentioned Jews to be Jews, those who ascribe to what we shall label below as the ethnic element of Jewish identity would accept them all, and, it is most likely that they would all be included in the Jewish People by non-Jews as well.

The Jewish People as an ethnic group or religious community: Virtually from their beginnings as a people, Jews have exhibited a complex identity that does not fit easily into any one category. Indeed, prior to the modern era, Jews rarely even referred to themselves as Jews. That term derives from the Latin *Judaeus*, the Greek *Ioudaios*, and the Hebrew *Yehudi*, all of which refer to inhabitants of the territory of Judea, the southern Israelite kingdom in the Land of Israel. Only occasionally in the ancient world did the Greek term *Ioudaïsmos* refer to the beliefs and customs of Jews. By contrast, the term "Jew" as we use it today originated with medieval Christians, who used it to differentiate themselves from the Old Testament people whom, they held, God had rejected.

For most of their history, the people we call "Jews" referred to themselves as *benai yisrael*, the children of Israel, that is, the descendants of the biblical patriarch Jacob. Thus, when speaking of themselves, "Jews" reflected on their common ancestry and their shared family line, not on their geographical origins. They named Jacob as their progenitor because he alone of the three Patriarchs had children all of whom worshipped YHWH. Abraham, after all, had fathered Ishmael, the ancestor of the Arabs, and Isaac had produced Esau, the forefather of Rome and the Christians.[6] All of Jacob's children, by contrast, worshipped their father's god, the God of Israel. Therefore, from the point of view of *benai yisrael*—the People Israel—a *ben* or *bat yisrael*—a man or woman of the People Israel—is someone who descends from Jacob.

By the first century C.E., people were counted among the People of Israel if their mother was a *bat yisrael*. This made sense, for, even when it is difficult to identify a child's father, the identify of the mother is certain, especially at the time of birth. In this same period, Jewish law prohibited Jews from marrying non-Jews. Such unions were not considered valid, and the children produced from a non-Jewish female were not considered to be members of the People Israel.[7] While, for the reason just given, the offspring of an illegal union between a Jewish female and a gentile male were classified as a member of the People Israel, they were *mamzerim*, bastards under Jewish law. The product of unacceptable unions, they suffered numerous religious and social disabilities.[8]

Seen from this point of view, membership in the People of Israel appears to be a matter of ethnicity, defined by a significant number of contemporary anthropologists and sociologists as connected to a perceived or actual common ancestry.[9] As Keyes puts it: "kin selection provides the underlying motivation that leads human beings to seek solidarity with those whom they recognize 'as being of the same people,' or as 'sharing descent.'"[10] In van den Berghe's definition, ethnicity is an extension of the idiom of kinship, an "attenuated form" of kinship selection.[11]

In this approach, the fact that the People of Israel constitutes an ethnic group is underscored by the prohibition of marriage with people outside of the group and the fact that group membership depends on the identity of one's mother. In this definition, someone without a Jewish mother cannot become a member of the group, and a person with a Jewish mother can never leave the collective. Membership in the Jewish People as a ethnic group depends solely on one's establishing legitimate maternity.

While witnessing the establishment of the prohibition against marriage outside the group, the first centuries C.E. saw an important change that, at least in practice, undermined this concept of Jewish ethnicity. The phenomenon of conversion clearly appears in Jewish sources at the same time that the tradition prohibits marriage between Jews and non-Jews and establishes that a Jewish mother alone produces a member of the People of Israel. While the Bible does not recognize the possibility of conversion, Jewish law codes beginning with the Mishnah treat conversion as a viable mode of becoming a member of the People of Israel. This means that, even as matrilineal descent became the norm, a method was devised by which a person without a Jewish mother could be classified by the People of Israel themselves as a member of the collective. Importantly, in the understanding of the legal system, the convert's assimilation into the group is for all practical purposes complete. Once con-

verted, the proselyte is comparable to any born Jew.

The possibility of conversion means that, contrary to initial appearances, the group comprises a religious community as much as an ethnic one.[12] And this should not surprise us, since the religious aspect of the community of Israel was always a central feature. Indeed, alongside its ethnic connotation, the very name *benai yisrael* points to a religious ideology, for it originates in Jacob's struggle with the divinity, when God changed his name from Jacob to Israel (Gen. 32:23-33). One even may argue that the *ethnicity* of Jews in fact results from the people's continuing encounter and relationship with YHWH. Indeed, most of biblical, Rabbinic, and post-Rabbinic Judaism emerges as a delineating of the interactions between the People Israel and YHWH.

On the one hand, then, the Jewish People are an ethnic group membership in which depends upon the identity of one's mother. On the other hand, the Jews comprise a religious community defined by the group's interactions with YHWH. Until the modern period, these two conflicting aspects of the Jewish People functioned jointly within the Jewish collective, with the emphasis shifting between the two poles, but never completely becoming disentangled. Only in modern times, as we shall see at the end, have these two aspects of Jewish identity been placed in opposition to each other, with the religious element in particular disappearing for many who self-identify with the Jewish People.

Medieval conceptions of Jewish peoplehood: Since Jewish communities in Europe, Asia, and Africa experienced modernity at different times, it is impossible to demarcate the medieval period in simple chronological terms. Instead, medieval and modern Judaisms are best conceptualized as frames of reference or states of mind held by Jews in particular social, economic, and political environments. From this perspective, the term medieval Judaism denotes a distinctive mythological structure, although the exact details of the myth or the ways in which Jewish communities translated that myth into concrete actions and rituals varied from location to location. Sometimes the variations were minor; at other times they were vast.

Just as the exact structure of medieval Judaism eludes description, so it is impossible to outline in broad strokes the social, political, and economic condition of the medieval Jew.[13] The situation was different in each locality, and it changed much from the tenth through the eighteenth centuries. However, in general terms we can characterize the European Jew, especially after the twelfth century, as completely outside of the main currents of European culture. While the feudal system placed the serfs at the bottom of the social ladder, it had absolutely no place for the Jews, who were totally outside of the complex rules of that society. Banned from owning real estate within much of Europe after the thirteenth century, Jews were excluded from participating in the agricultural economy that dominated until the sixteenth century. The Christian underpinnings of the guilds along with economic jealousies prevented the Jews from participating in petty manufacturing. The medieval legal system excluded or demeaned the Jews, especially through the practice of the *more judaico*, a special oath Jews were obliged to take in lawsuits, intended to humiliate and degrade them. Following the establishment of the first ghetto in Venice in 1516, throughout much of Europe, Jewish residential areas were formally separated from those of non-Jews. Finally, if the Jews viewed themselves as essentially different from the non-Jews, Christian mythology merely re-enforced that view. Popular Christian culture pictured Jews as sub-human creatures in league with the devil, bent on destroying western civilization and the Christians just as they had destroyed Christ on the cross.[14]

Even within this setting, medieval Judaism flourished and developed a rich culture. Jews believed that God exits, that God created the world according to a plan, that the Torah contains that plan for the world and humankind, and that, having entered into a covenant with the Jews, God revealed the Torah to them, obligating them to follow the Torah's law and empowering God to reward or to punish the people in accordance with their behavior. This system of beliefs held, finally, that God would eventually send a messiah who would usher in and/or rule over a perfected world in which the Jews, along with the rest of humankind, would live according to God's original intention.

Although the general outlines of this myth were commonly held, its details and implications varied over time and among different groups of Jews. Jewish philosophers differed over God's exact nature, how God created the universe, how humans might speak about God, and the like. The mystics spoke about the dynamic interrelationships of the ten *sefirot*—emanations of God—through which the power of the *Eyn Sof*—the infinite deity—flowed to humankind and into the created world, activating Jewish affairs even as they were influenced by them. The philosophical debates about creation *ex nihilo* were literally worlds apart from Lurianic mysticism's discussions of *tsimtsum*—God's contracting into himself in order to make space in which to create—and *shevirat ha-kelim*—the breaking of the vessels that led to the disordered stated of the created world. Similarly, an array of opinions concerned, among many disputed aspects of the myth, revelation, the Torah's nature and content, the signs of the Messiah, the character of the perfected world, the extent of God's knowledge of world events, and the details of God's working in the world.

All agreed that God had chosen the Jewish People to receive the revelation of God's will on Mt. Sinai and that the Jewish People had a unique relationship with God and a special role to play in the world. However, different opinions concerned exactly what constituted the Jews' uniqueness and what caused them to be different from other peoples. As Jacob Katz notes, the distinction between Jews and non-Jews can be, and was, formulated in two ways. One view describes "a mere divergence in articles of creed." The other connects the differences to "the dissimilar character of Jews and non-Jews respectively."[15] The former, theological approach stresses Judaism as a religion, while the latter, essentialist definition focuses on the ethnic side of Judaism.[16] Let us review the appearance of each of these definitions within the medieval Jewish thinkers themselves.

Judah Halevi argued that the Jews are *essentially* different from other peoples of the world. They are "the pick of humankind," defined, as it were, by a unique genetic feature that was passed down from generation to generation, beginning with Adam who:[17]

> was perfection itself, because no flaw could be found in the work of a wise and almighty creator . . ., and there was no contaminating influence from the sperm of the father and the blood of the mother, from nourishing and nursing in the years of childhood and growth, from air, water, and soil.

Halevi speaks of the "Divine power" that was passed through the Jewish People, the "heart" of humankind. Israel's uniqueness is that it has, in Guttmann's phrase, "a peculiar religious disposition,"[18] which is both the cause and the effect of Israel's special relationship and communion with God. This interaction and relationship between the People Israel and God is also Israel's mission and purpose.

In a similar fashion, the Jewish mystical traditions ascribed to the People Israel a unique quality deemed to be inherent in its very nature. The Zohar thus teaches that individual souls are pre-existent with the divine: "Since the day when it occurred to God to create the world and even before it was really created, all the souls of the righteous were hidden in the divine idea, even in its peculiar form."[19] This means that the souls of the People Israel were pre-ordained and pre-counted before the creation of the world. Carved from God's very being, they are different from those of non-Jews.

The Jews' essential distinctiveness is further represented by the complex of meanings of the term *knesset yisrael*, literally, "congregation of Israel," but used to refer to the earthly Israel, to the spiritual Israel, and to the *Shekhinah*, that is, the creative aspect of God that comprises the lowest of the ten *sefirot*. Because God interacts with humankind and the created world through the *Shekhinah*, depicted also as *knesset yisrael*, the community of Israel can see itself as a liminal entity, alone among the peoples of the

earth in straddling the boundary between the divine and mundane realms. The People Israel occupy this role because their nature is different from that of any other people on earth; Israel alone was formed from the essence of the God-head.[20]

Lurianic thought argues that each human soul and hence each people—Jew and non-Jew—has a role in the process of *tiqqun ha-olam*, in returning the world to its ideal form. Just as each nation participates in the cosmic drama, so each people is a unique entity carved out of the primordial soul, to which it will be rejoined when the process of *tiqqun* is finished. But even as it shares this task with other nations, Israel has an essentially distinctive role in the process, since the majority of divine sparks have been assigned to her. The People Israel in particular must now live in exile so that, by observing Torah, it can fulfill the mission of returning to the godhead the sparks of divine light that have been scattered throughout creation. Through their religious acts, that is, the Jewish People play the primary role in returning the world to the condition God meant it to have at the time of creation. When the Jews' work is complete, the exile will end and the messianic age will commence.

Judah Halevi and the mystical tradition's notions that the People Israel are inherently different from everyone else contrast with the approach of Maimonides, who argues that all humans are essentially the same. Maimonides' view emerges from his understanding that no one is born with a fully developed soul but that, instead, each person enters the world with only the potential to acquire a soul through intellectual activity. This means that any intellectually gifted and energetic person, whatever the circumstance of his or her birth, can reach fulfillment as an individual and that what differentiates Jews from non-Jews is not inborn but the result of what, during their lives, they choose to do with their intellect.[21]

Maimonides thus considers Jewish identity to be a matter of commitment, of religion, not descent. He defines a Jew as someone who subscribes to his thirteen articles of faith, thus insisting on a doctrinal orthodoxy as a condition for being called a Jew and inheriting life in the world to come. In line with this approach, he supports conversion and proselytizing, especially among Christians, arguing that Moses gave the Torah to the Jews as well as to all who wish to convert to Judaism. Anyone, that is, can follow the Torah's dictates and requirements, which include accepting Maimonides' thirteen principles of faith, and so become a Jew. In fact, Maimonides held that, at the end of time, all people would do this. He believed that, in the meantime, God treats all people equally, protecting the righteous in proportion to their righteousness, without differentiating between the righteous of Israel and the righteous of other nations.[22]

While arguing that Jews and non-Jews are potentially equal and that during the messianic era they will all be the same, Maimonides maintained that, because of their religion, in the present world, the Jews are completely superior to non-Jews. This superiority derives from God's promise to Abraham that his offspring would enjoy special benefits, but, more importantly, from Israel's possession of the Torah. Thus, while never belittling the importance of descent from Abraham, in his letter to the convert Obadiah, Maimonides stresses the importance of the Torah over ancestry: "Ours is the true and divine religion, revealed to us through Moses, chief of the former as well as the later prophets. . . . God has singled us out by His law and precepts, and our preeminence over the others was manifested in His rules and statutes." According to Maimonides, only those who fully adopt the Torah's doctrines can thoroughly realize their potential to be members of the Jewish people.[23]

Maimonides shifts emphasis from Halevi and the mystical traditions' ethnic definition of the Jewish People, offering, instead, primarily a religious interpretation. By stressing adherence to the Torah, its laws and the thirteen principles, Maimonides argues that acceptance and practice of the Torah is a necessary, but also sufficient, criteria for membership in the Jewish people. It is incorrect to argue that Maimonides' stress on doctrine is independent of his emphasis on the *mitzvot*,

which led to his codification of Jewish law. As Twersky[24] has demonstrated, Maimonides' *Mishneh Torah* reflects the same philosophical system as his *Moreh Nevukhim* (*The Guide for the Perplexed*). Both it and the monumental law code are inseparable parts of the Torah. Twersky writes (p. 78):

> It is clear that Maimonides intended from the outset not only to compile 'rules in respect of that which is forbidden and permitted, clean and unclean,' but also to elucidate 'Torah principles' and 'theological fundamentals,' to set forth 'true and exact opinion,' and to indicate how each person can understand 'the ultimate goal of the precepts, according to his capacity.'

Twersky writes that Maimonides' "ideal was a blending of that which in the *Moreh* is called 'the science of the law,' namely 'the legalistic study of the law . . . and the science of the law in its true sense', i.e., the philosophical foundations of the Talmud" (p. 360). Both the *Moreh* and the *Mishneh Torah* were designed to promote Jews' becoming fully realized members of the People Israel, and both accordingly stressed the religious aspect of Judaism and membership in the Jewish People.

Maimonides' emphasis on "right dogma," in the sense of both law and thought, was carried forward in subsequent generations and became a major touchstone of some definitions of the Jewish People. Building on the implications of Maimonides' thought, Simon ben Zemach Duran (1361-1444), for instance, claimed that any person who denies even the smallest detail of the Torah's doctrines, while knowing it to be one of the Torah's teachings, is an unbeliever. While Duran permitted disagreement concerning the specifics of the law, he would not accept a person's denying of what he saw as the Torah's essentials: the existence of God, revelation, and retribution.[25]

Joseph Albo, who also died in 1444, painted a broader picture of the essential Jewish beliefs. He maintained that one who rejects the details, or corollaries, derived from the three basic beliefs also denies the fundamental beliefs; therefore, Albo produced a list of eleven necessary dogmas. For example, from the basic concept of revelation he deduced God's knowledge, prophecy, and the authenticity of God's messenger. The result was the conception that Jewish law in all of its details had to be followed because biblical revelation was unique. God had publicly certified Moses' status, and only a prophet with the same certification and status could change or abrogate Mosaic law. Furthermore, Mosaic revelation was the only means by which humankind could establish the proper moral and political order in the world.[26] Still Albo held that one who failed to follow exactly the details of Jewish law was only a sinner, not a heretic, unless he or she claimed that the particular law did not derive from God at all. In that case, having in effect denied the concept of revelation, the person had excluded him or herself from the Jewish People. Thus in Albo, as in Maimonides, we find the conjunction of law and dogma as a means of defining membership in the Jewish People.

Modern conceptions of Jewish peoplehood: Modern Judaism inherited the medieval period's two distinct ways of defining Jewish peoplehood. The essentialist conception maintained, for instance, by the mystical tradition and Judah Halevi was passed on to the modern Jew through the many forms of Hasidism, which also stress the essential unity and distinctiveness of the Jews. On the other hand, the philosophical tradition's idea that a Jew is defined by beliefs and actions that conform to a particular paradigm and set of dogmas was developed in many modern definitions that hold that Judaism is a religion comparable to other religions. Both the essentialist and the religious definitions of Jewish peoplehood thus continue to flourish in the modern era.

If there was one event that signaled the onset of the process of modernization, it was the French Revolution, which ended the isolation of the Jews and set into motion the political and social forces that were to change the Jews and their views of themselves forever:[27]

> It was this cataclysmic event that shattered the heretofore insular religious-ethnic world in which Jews had lived for centuries. Isolated and surrounded by Gentile hostility, the Jews had developed a tendency toward exclusivity and separatism. They had transformed the ghetto into a religious-cultural and socioeconomic state-within-a state; as a result, the ghetto, confined geographically and functionally, acquired all the characteristics of a distinct civilization. The French Revolution abruptly and unexpectedly upset this exclusiveness and loosened the ethnocentric ties. The egalitarian forces unleashed by this social cataclysm breached not only the Bastille, but also the similarly impregnable walls of the Jewish ghettos inside and outside France's frontiers. As a result, the Jews were catapulted from their physical and spiritual isolation into the seething caldron of western Europe.

Goldscheider and Zuckerman[28] explain what happened to the Jews as follows:

> The modernization of Europe overwhelmed the traditional Jewish society and polity.... As economic opportunities developed and expanded, Jews took advantage of them. As mass education emerged, Jews went to the *gymnasia* and to the universities. As the walls of the Jewish quarters came down, Jews moved out. Modernization transformed the old order and the place of the Jews within it.... The absolute dependence of the traditional Jewish community on the non-Jewish authorities ensured that when the latter changed so would the place of the Jews.

The ultimate affect of these changes, modernization, is explained by Michael A. Meyer:[29]

> [M]odernization is best understood as the historical process whereby increased exposure to non-Jewish ideas and symbols progressively erodes the given generational continuities, first in one location, then another, first among certain classes of Jews, then among others. Its product is Jewish modernity: the ongoing situation where internal continuity stands in potential or actual conflict with forces exterior to Jewish tradition.

In modernity, the Jew moves from a position of complete outsider to that of a potential member of non-Jewish society and a prospective participant in non-Jewish culture. Eventually, especially in America, the Jew becomes a virtually complete member of the non-Jewish world, in all of its aspects and with all of its ramifications. Perhaps the most significant change that permits this transformation is the rejection by both Jews and non-Jews of the previous essentialist understanding of Judaism. While this is a complex process of change, at base it emerges from the reasoning that, if there are no "essential" differences among various groups of people, then all people must be treated equally and granted the same opportunities for social and economic success.

For the thinkers of the Enlightenment, reason and universalism were inseparable concepts, "because reason implies a universal community of rational persons, and universalism, in turn, requires a common, rational basis of discourse."[30] This meant that there could be no essential differences among the various groups of humankind. Distinctions that did occur were understood to be conditioned developments, the results of either natural phenomena, such as geography, climate, or ecology, or the consequences of societal phenomena, such as political, social, religious, or economic policy. For this reason, thinkers such as John Toland and Christian Wilhelm von Dohm could argue for the integration for Jews into the political, social, and economic spheres of European culture. In Dohm's words:[31]

> Let us concede that the Jews may be more morally corrupt than other nations; that they are guilty of a proportionately greater number of crimes than the Christians; that their character in general inclines more toward usury and fraud in commerce, that their religious prejudice is more antisocial and clannish; but I must add that this supposed greater moral corruption of the Jews is a necessary and natural consequence of the oppressed condition in which they have been living for so many centuries. . . . The hard and oppressive conditions under which the Jews live almost everywhere would explain, though not justify, an even worse corruption than they actually can be accused of.

Although it took a good deal of time to move from the margins into the mainstream of European society, ideas like those expressed by Dohm paved the way for the acceptance of Jews by many European nations and communities. If the Jews were not "essentially" different, then, should the situations in which they were forced to live and develop be altered, their ideas and culture would also be changed. Once liberated, they could and

would grow to participate as full members of society.

A second important factor that caused the Jews to reject an essentialist view of themselves was the emergence in this period of the concept of a universal natural religion. Since modern thinking increasingly held that theological claims were to be dismissed as irrational, the entire concept of religion needed to be rethought. This occurred as many Enlightenment theologians, such as Spalding, Reimarus, and Jerusalem, while not rejecting revelation, came to speak of the

> "human, cheerful, this-worldly, practical, simply understood and modern religion of healthy common sense." This religion set forth the principles of God, Providence, and immortality as the common foundation of all faiths, excluding only the atheist from its "religion of humanity."[32]

The test of a religion's validity thus was to be its rationality and the morality and ethical behavior of its adherents, not its claims to revelation. In this intellectual and political environment, it became easy and advantageous for Jews to classify themselves as members of a religion, and once some modern Jewish thinkers found a means of expunging the ritual law from the religion, they were able to claim that, unlike in Maimonides' system, the Jewish religion did not require one to follow the traditional commandments at all. Membership in the Jewish People no longer had to do with behaviors that distinguished one from other peoples.

For thinkers such as Moses Mendelssohn, 1729-1786, Jewishness became a matter of private conscience. He held that no person or institution had the right to interfere with any individual's religious thoughts or actions. Because Judaism was rational and universal, it was tolerant of other religious systems. "Judaism does not claim," Mendelssohn wrote, "to possess the exclusive revelation of eternal truths that are indispensable to salvation."[33] There was no conflict between Judaism and European culture, and there was no reason a Jew could not participate fully in the life of his or her country.

For our purposes, Mendelssohn's most important intellectual accomplishment was his dismantling of the medieval mythological structure. Mendelssohn divided the phenomenon of Judaism into three distinct constituent parts: 1) "Religious doctrines and tenets, or eternal truths about God, His rule, and Providence, without which man cannot be enlightened or happy;" 2) "Historical truths, or accounts of the events of former ages. . . . These historical accounts disclose the fundamental purposes of the people's national existence. As historical truths they must . . . be accepted on faith;" 3) Laws, precepts, commandments, rules of conduct peculiar to this people.[34] Although Mendelssohn lived his entire life as a fully observant Jew,[35] it soon was claimed that only his first category, the religious doctrines and tenets, which were rational and universal, were the essence of Judaism. In accepting these eternal and universal truths, the Jews as a people were essentially the same as everyone else. In this construction, Mendelssohn's second and third categories, the historical truths and the laws and precepts, were merely external matters that *formally* separated the Jews from other religious communities. Mendelssohn believed and lived his life as if there was no actual disjuncture between these two aspects of Judaism, its essential truths and the requirements of the traditional Jewish legal system. Those who followed, by contrast, saw the rational truths as qualitatively different from and superior to the laws and precepts. Under the guidance of these people, Judaism came to be viewed by many as a system of universal ethics in which historical truths, laws, and precepts distinctive to the Jews had no standing at all.

For many, the Jews thus became a religious group whose ideology was the same as that of all "true" religions. This way of thinking nullified the concept of a unique convenantal relationship with YHWH, the God of Sinai and the Jewish People. While their history, laws, and precepts were uniquely theirs, these things were no longer to be seen as grounded in a reality that transcended time and space. Nor were the distinctive features of Judaism to be connected to the ultimate actuality of the true divinity, seen now, rather, as a rationally demonstrable entity equally available to all humans. This line of reasoning produced the claim that the Jewish People and their religion were, in essence, no different from Christians and Christianity. Both religions at base promoted the same ethical system, even if they were created by particular accidents of history and expressed through distinctive ritual systems.

This new thinking also divorced salvation in Judaism from revelation and removed the theory of justice from the traditional concept of covenant, which held that God responded to the Jews' adherence to or violation of the commandments. In all, "By denying Judaism its unique prerogatives to metaphysical truth and salvation, Mendelssohn deprived Judaism of its very essence and its adherents of their source of spiritual affirmation."[36] His thought, that is, introduced the ideas that led subsequent generations to reject Judaism's traditional mythic structure altogether.

Mendelssohn carefully argued that Judaism was a religion and that the Jewish People were a religious community. On the one hand, Judaism shared with other valid enlightened religions, such as Islam and modern Christianity, the characteristics and tenets of "natural religion." One the other hand, Judaism had a unique history and set of laws and customs that it did not share with its sister religions and which, according to the logic of the Enlightenment, subsequent Jewish thinkers would deem outside the essence of Judaism.

Samson Raphael Hirsch, the founder of Modern Orthodoxy, flourished about sixty years after Mendelssohn's death. Hirsch appreciated much of the thinking of the Enlightenment, believed that secular learning was an asset to rabbis and to the Jewish laity, supported the social and political emancipation of the Jews, argued for the unconditional support by Jews of the German government, and undertook to modernize the worship service in his synagogue. In dress and demeanor, Hirsch looked like his Reform rabbinical colleagues. He even appeared in an engraving clean shaven and without any head covering.[37]

Because Hirsch retained traditional Jewish practices, understood to be demanded by God as distinctive indicators of Jewish peoplehood, he accepted in theory the ethnic as well as the religious definition of the People Israel. In response to those who sought to change Judaism, so that the people's Judaism would not interfere with their loyalty to the State, Hirsch argued that Judaism in its essence did not prevent Jews from being completely loyal to the secular government. True, Jews could not aspire to some government posts, and at times their religion might prevent them from taking advantage of all of the benefits enjoyed by the State's other citizens. But none of this prevented the Jews from completely supporting the State. Hirsch maintained that Jews might be pitied, but not scorned, for the disabilities they face, since they had not freely chosen their religion but had been born into it and therefore were helpless to alter their situation.[38]

In his early years as rabbi in Frankfurt am Main, Hirsch worked diligently to improve the status and increase the influence of his congregation. To the dismay of many traditional Jews, he distinguished between people's private lives and their actions as part of the organized Jewish community. In this way, he was able to include among the community's membership Jews who privately violated the dietary laws, desecrated the Sabbath, and in other ways did not observe Jewish law. People could be members of the community so long as they were circumcised and had married according to Jewish law. Although to increase the size and influence of the traditional community Hirsch thus emphasized the essentialist element in Jewish peoplehood, Rosenbloom argues that he did not reject observance of Torah as a defining element of Judaism; he merely examined this element from the perspective of the community rather than the individual Jew: "Not to individuals, but to the Jewish community as a whole has God entrusted His Torah as a heritage, for only the community lives on forever and only the community has means for everything."[39] Hirsch had taken a radical step that in some ways brought him close to the Reform position:

> Hirsch's act was tantamount to an endorsement of an incongruous but common concept in his day . . . ham-eating Orthodoxy. It is hardly conceivable that rabbis of a previous age, or even of that time in eastern Europe, would have concurred with Hirsch's elastic definition of Jewishness. While halakhically a nonobservant Jew does not cease being Jewish or part of Jewry, he was never accorded the status Hirsch now tacitly bestowed on him—the ability to violate Jewish law and simultaneously belong to or even hold office in the traditionalist . . . [community]. Hirsch did exactly what his opponents, the Reformers, had done—localize Judaism within the synagogue.

Because Hirsch was at the same time an Orthodox rabbi and a modern Jew, his thoughts on Jewish peoplehood clearly exhibit the intellectual conflicts of his day. On the one hand, he accepted the ethnic definition of Jewish peoplehood much more enthusiastically than did many of his Orthodox colleagues. On the other hand, he supported the Reformer's religious definition of Judaism. God had chosen the Jewish People for the mission of teaching the divinity's will to the rest of humankind. To be part of the people who were to carry out this mission, one had to belong to a community that faithfully observed the law. Observance of the Torah made the Jewish People distinct and allowed them to perform the mission for which God had selected them.

Responding to Mendelssohn's followers, Hirsch argued that the Torah and its commandments made the Jews unique and allowed them to play their assigned role in human history. The commandments' divine origin made them meaningful in every age. The misconception, he maintained, had started with Maimonides, who failed to see that, in Judaism, knowledge is only the means to an end, a foundation for the observance of Torah and following of all the commandments.[40] Hirsch similarly criticized Mendelssohn, who had failed to see that the Torah makes Judaism unique and differentiates Jews from all other people, just as consciousness, broadly construed, differentiates humans from other animals.

For Hirsch, Judaism has two aspects, an outward manifestation and an inner essence. In its outward form, it is an evolving civilization that participates in the events of history along with all other nations. Its inner being, however, is connected to God through the Torah and does not change through history. To discover this inner being, one must examine Judaism's original sources, the Bible, the Talmud, and the Midrash. The Bible contained the essential spirit of Judaism in its potential form, later actualized in the Rabbinic documents. If one carefully investigates the Torah in order to attain the full historical perspective, "the inner spirit that permeates Judaism will become evident." To fully understand the Jews, accordingly, one must place them within their historical contexts and in their relationship to God, revealed in the Torah.[41]

For Hirsch, the Absolute Mind, which is God, manifests its will in the Torah. Therefore, the Torah is a path to freedom. It is not limiting or restrictive, for by following the Torah one gives expression to "the legality of the heart, the law which is identified with the individual."[42] Through the Torah, Jews lose their subjectivity and become one with God's desires and the guiding principles of the whole of creation. It is only through the Torah that the Jews take their proper place as part of nature.

The Jewish People alone are subject to the Absolute Mind because they alone have the Torah. The other nations of the world, by contrast, come to know God a little at a time through the course of history. All peoples except for the Jews therefore are subject to Hegel's laws of historical process, in which nations are born, grow, and die. Because the Jews are directly related to God through the Torah, they defy this process, even though externally they are subordinate to the nations around them. Unlike other nations, which need a state to objectify their law and to overcome their subjectivity, for the Jewish People "the Torah, the fulfillment of the divine will, was to be its soil and country and aim; its national existence, therefore, was neither dependent upon, nor conditioned by, transitory things, but eternal as the spirit, the soul, and the word of the Eternal One."[43]

Mendelssohn and Hirsch were both men of the Enlightenment and, despite their differences, neither at base believed that the Jewish People is essentially different from the other peoples of the earth. This non-essentialist view of Jewish peoplehood reached its fullest expression in Reform Judaism, especially in America, which developed at the end of the nineteenth century, mainly among Jews of Western European origin. America of course was founded on the principles of the Enlightenment, and Reform Judaism's adherence to those principles led Jews to maintain and solidify their relatively secure position in American society.[44]

The leaders of American Reform Judaism have met several times over the last two centuries to delineate the tenets of Reform Judaism. As we should expect, the documents that those meetings have produced are fairly consistent in their description of the Jewish People as a religious community, not an ethnic group. The Pittsburgh Platform of 1885, the first such statement, described Judaism as "a progressive religion, ever striving to be in accord with the postulates of reason," and stated that Judaism "presents the highest conception of the God-idea as taught in our Holy Scripture . . . as the central religious truth for the human race." The Bible is "the most potent instrument of religious and moral instruction;" therefore, Jews should take from the biblical tradition "only the moral laws, and . . . only such ceremonies as elevate and sanctify [their] lives."[45] The document clearly defines Judaism as a religion, in fact, as the religion that contains "the highest conception of the God-idea," which it has made available to all of humankind. Judaism, like all natural religions, is available to everyone. The concept of Torah is limited to the Bible, and the Bible is reduced to its moral lessons, which, again, are available to all humankind. The only rituals that are still incumbent on Jews are those that "elevate and sanctify" their lives, and the only laws they must perform are "the moral laws." In brief, membership in the Jewish People is defined primarily by adherence to the moral precepts of the Bible.

The Columbus Platform of 1937 similarly claimed that Judaism's message "is universal, aiming at the union and perfection of mankind under the sovereignty of God." God is revealed "not only in the majesty, beauty and orderliness of nature, but also in the vision and moral striving of the human spirit." Of more interest for our purposes, the authors of that document "recognize in the group loyalty of Jews who have become estranged from our religious tradition, a bond which still unites them with us" even though they "maintain that it is by its religion and for its religion that the Jewish people has lived."[46] In this definition, Jews are part of humankind and can form a unity among themselves in both religious and non-religious terms. This document, composed under the ominous clouds of economic depression and the German Nazi terror, thus expresses the dual aspects of Jewish peoplehood: religion and ethnicity. Still, its authors repeatedly state that Judaism is a religion and that the Jewish People are united by their religion's moral and ethical teachings, teachings that are available to all humankind. Jews who have rejected the religious elements of Judaism still are recognized as being part of the Jewish People. But the ideal members of the community are those who recognize Judaism's religious nature and its essential moral quality.

In many ways, the San Francisco Platform of 1976 reflects the complex identities of American Reform Jews. It emphasizes the universal nature of Judaism's message even as it underscores Judaism's particularity: "A universal concern for humanity unaccompanied by a devotion to our particular people is self-destructive; a passion for our people without involvement in humankind contradicts what the prophets have meant to us. Judaism calls us simultaneously to universal and particular obligations." The document thus stresses the centrality of ethics to God's message, while at the same time encouraging Jews to observe the traditional Jewish holidays, to mark life-cycle events within the context of Judaism, and to participate in those "activities which promote the survival of the Jewish people and enhance its existence."[47]

Throughout the text, the survival of the Jewish People and the contemporary appropriation of the Jewish past are paramount. Yet at the same time, unlike the Columbus Platform, the San Francisco Platform does not expressly find a place for the non-religious Jew. Its message is simple: Jews must work for the survival of the Jewish People, and they will survive only if they continue to be a religious entity, drawing from and interpreting their past as a people of God. At its heart then, we see here the continuation of the shift away from an essentialist definition of the Jewish People, a shift that is perhaps most clearly represented in the recent Reform definition of a Jew as any person born of at least one Jewish parent—father or mother, convert or born Jew—who participates in the Jewish community and practices aspects of Judaism as a religion. The religious underpinnings of Judaism thus are made paramount even as the requirement of a Jewish lineage is placed far in the background.

American Reform Judaism is an excellent example of Judaism defined as an enlightened religion and held to contain a universal message that it shares with all humankind. On this foundation, Jews share a rightful place in society with members of all other religions. At the same time, this approach allows Jews to benefit from a distinctive identity, to see themselves as the product of a unique history, set of customs, traditions, and revelation that makes them what they are. Interestingly, within the Reform context, this sense of distinctive identity is achieved even as traditional commandments are rejected, so that Jews need not in any way feel excluded from the mainstream of American culture and society. Indeed, Reform has a difficult time specifying exactly what actions and activities are required of Jews.

The Conservative movement among American Jews traces it current history to the beginning of the twentieth century with the appointment of Solomon Schechter as the head of the Jewish Theological Seminary. The movement's membership is largely drawn from descendants of Eastern European Jewish immigrants who rejected Reform's abandonment of the traditional *mitzvot* but who wanted to participate fully in American life.[48] Unlike the Reform movement, the leaders of Conservative Judaism historically have found it difficult to express their collective view of Judaism. However, in 1988 the American Conservative movement published *Emet ve-Emunah: Statement of Principles of Conservative Judaism*,[49] the first set of principles sanctioned by Conservative Judaism.

Emet ve-Emunah is a complex and sometimes contradictory document, clearly reflecting its creation by a committee. While it says a good deal about the importance of traditional Jewish practices, the goal of flexibility and inclusiveness prevent the authors from mandating the traditional 613 commandments or from dictating an exacting set of dogma. Similarly, while it states that "Judaism is indeed a civilization in the fullest sense of the term" (p. 22), it also states that "the Jewish religion as reflected in the Jewish way of life constitutes the most significant factor that identifies, distinguishes, unties, and preserves the Jewish people" (p. 35). The Jewish People comprises a religious entity bound together through God's revelation and *halakhah*. The Jews "unlike other nations, emerged on the stage of history to be a people, dedicated to the service of God." Thus, while paying a good deal more heed to the tradition than do the statements of the leaders of Reform Judaism, the Conservative Jews also come down on the side of the religious definition of the Jewish People.

Within the modern period, however, we still find Jews who expressly accept an essentialist or ethnic definition of Judaism, or, as Krausz describes them, who think of themselves as "Jews by descent."[50] The Lubavitchers are the best known for the argument that Jews are essentially different from non-Jews. This is most clearly expressed in their belief that within every Jew is a *pintelle Yeed*: Jews, in this view, are different from non-Jews because their soul places them within the realm of Jewishness, as Shaffer[51] explains: "One has to remember that 'the soul itself was so much deeper than what appeared to the eye,' and hence surface appearances ought never to discourage one from attempting to tap a man's inner capacity for faith in and love for Judaism." Lubavitchers would argue that even converts possess a unique soul that eventually brought them openly to express their innate Jewishness.

This follows the Rabbinic tradition that claims that the souls of all born Jews as well as those who would convert to Judaism witnessed the revelation at Sinai.[52]

To this point we have seen that the major differences among most modern Jews concern the nature of the religious essence of Jewish People: Is it Torah or is it morals and ethics? Does membership in the Jewish People demand observance of the traditional commandments, their modern forms, or only the moral teachings of Judaism that are applicable to all humankind? Despite its pervasive interest within the religious movements, this debate, however, reflects the concerns and self-images of only a portion of contemporary Jews. There are a many people who identify themselves as Jews, and who usually are classified by others as Jews, who reject religiousness altogether. But, simply because they have Jewish mothers, even the "incontrovertible core" counts them as members of the Jewish People. Kenneth Stern writes:[53]

> As commonly conceived, a Jew is taken to be a person who (a) has certain religious beliefs, (b) belongs to a certain ethnic group by birth, and (c) has what Webster's calls a 'sense of community' with a particular cultural and historical tradition. . . . [I]t would be important to add that a person could properly be called a Jew even if he did not meet all three of these conditions, so long as he met one or two of them. Thus I should argue that a person (like me) might very well feel a sense of community with other Jews, but be an agnostic or an atheist and *still* be a Jew. For me, having a religious belief is not a *necessary* condition for being a Jew; it is not even a very important condition.

Stern provides us with an excellent definition of secular Jews; they are Jews who "feel a sense of community with other Jews," but who reject the religious nature and underpinnings of that community. In a similar manner Garry M. Brodsky writes:[54]

> I do not subscribe to any of the religious tenets of Judaism or practice the rituals of Judaism. . . . I am not a member of a synagogue. I have not studied Jewish history and culture. . . . [W]hile I am a Zionist, I have not lived in or visited Israel. . . . [W]ith one qualification the differences between me and my non-Jewish colleagues and friends

traceable to my Jewishness amount to little more than I pay more attention to American-Jewish culture and to the Holocaust than they do. The qualification . . . is that I feel a deep sense of Jewish identity and they, of course, do not. . . .

Brodsky's parents made no great demands of him except that:

> I marry a Jewish woman, that I be sympathetic to the plight of Jews and enthusiastic in my support of the State of Israel. Since what was wanted of me made eminently good sense on its own terms, it was not difficult for me to grow up as a kind of Jew and to live my adult life in this kind of way.

For secular Jews, the defining factor is their *feeling* of identification with the Jewish People. Although both Stern and Brodsky claim that secular Judaism is strongest among intellectuals and Jewish academics, it is impossible to determine its extend or the range of its adherents. Notably, however, in the 1980s fewer than 24% of American Jews "frequently" attended a synagogue (compared to 44% of Americans who attended church),[55] and the only widespread religious observances among American Jews are a Passover Seder, lighting Hanukkah candles, putting a *mezuzah* on the front doorpost, and fasting on Yom Kippur. This means that it is difficult to argue that the majority of American Jews are religious in any traditional, or even modern Reform, sense of the term. Wertheimer explains:[56]

> demographic data suggest diminishing involvement in Judaism among the masses of American Jews. Surveys conducted during the eighties show a decline in the percentage of Jews who identify with any religious denomination. . . . [There is] a large population of Jews moving toward religious minimalism. . . .

It would seem, therefore, that secular Judaism—an attachment to the Jewish People based on something other than religiosity—is quite widespread among contemporary American Jews.

Brodsky states that he differs from his non-Jewish friends in his attention to American-Jewish culture and the Holocaust. Stern writes that "I have been raised in a tradition that has deep emotional associations."[57] He appreciates Jewish jokes, Yiddish phrases, Jewish food. Taking Brodsky and Stern as representatives of secular Judaism, it is obvious that among many contemporary American Jews the essence of Jewish peoplehood has shifted radically away from religion. This modern identity offers a definition of a Jewish People not held together by religious beliefs or practices at all. Nor is this identity strictly speaking ethnic, for the increasing rate of marriage between Jews and non-Jews indicates that for most young Jews, the ethnic bond is no longer strong either. Rather, for secular Jews, Jewish peoplehood is defined simply by a "feeling" of "connectedness."

How does this identity emerge and function? Brodsky notes that one is born a Jew or a gentile and that this leaves an "imprint" on the individual. He writes:[58] "[W]e become conscious of ourselves and our surroundings through preconceptions, prejudices, and predispositions that can be traced to the life-worlds into which we are born . . . [and] are part of the raw materials out of which our lives and selves are fashioned." This implies that a Jew learns innately to feel an intimate connectedness to all other Jews and to all Jewish experiences. In similar terms, Stern writes of his feelings of attachment to the Jewish People: "I connect with my grandparents. . . . These feelings and this tradition are deeply related to them and their love as well as to my parents and other members of my family."[59] For both of these men, the feeling of Jewishness was transmitted from parent to child, shaping the child's personality and instilling a deep relatedness to all other Jews. Importantly, according to Brodsky, this innate sense of Jewishness becomes the lens through which the Jew interprets all of history and culture.

Given what both Brodsky and Stern write, the Jewishness secular Jews feel stands closer to the essential Jewishness described in the Zohar and Judah Halevi than to the religious Jewishness defined by Maimonides, Mendelssohn, Hirsch, and most modern Jewish religious movements. Secular Jews do not claim to be connected to the Jewish People by any rational means. They do not locate the essence of Jewishness in religious or moral concepts common to all humankind or found in the Torah and the specifically Jewish commandments. Rather, they have an almost mystical feeling, inherited from their families, of attachment to the Jewish People. Secular Jews thus feel an attachment to a Jewish history that they have not experienced and a connection to past, primarily religious, Jews with whom they have virtually nothing in common.

Conclusions: Individual identity is a complex phenomenon, group identity all the more so. Alongside the biological determinants inherited from one's progenitors, a person's sense of self clearly is connected to the familial, social, political, economic, cultural, and historical settings into which he or she is born and raised. In addition, one's sense of self emerges in relationship to others, so that one cannot construct an identity without at the same time constructing an "other."

In medieval and modern times, Jews accordingly have created their sense of identity in terms of descent and/or through external factors, religion primary among them. The very term by which Jews have traditionally named themselves points to these two components: the People Israel, denoting a familial heritage, on the one side, and a unique relationship to God, on the other. Although we found medieval writers who stressed one or the other of these two options, this seems to have been primarily a matter of emphasis. No medieval thinker chose one aspect at the exclusion of the other.

In the modern period this relative consensus concerning "what" is a Jew falls apart. New intellectual and theological paradigms, new political and social realities lead Jewish thinkers to construct a religious identity as a singular, independent phenomenon, without significant reference to the ethnic nature of Judaism. Mendelssohn and most Reform Jews defined the Jewish People in terms of its religious beliefs, not its ethnic nature. In fact, only in the Columbus Platform did we find a clear statement of inclusion for those Jews who had rejected the religious tenets of Judaism.

Most recently, secular Jews, who reject the religious definition of Jewish peoplehood,

characterize their identity as emerging from innate feelings. Have they merely replaced religion with another set of cultural creations, such as their historical past, or do they base their connection to other Jews on some "essential" aspect of the Jewish being? The answer to this question is not simple. Silberstein claims that Ahad HaAm created the possibility of the modern secular Jew,[60] but he consistently spoke of the "Jewish Spirit" that was to be reinvigorated in the Land of Israel.[61] Yet, modern secular Jews may in fact be more consistent with medieval conceptions than they or others have realized. The "feeling" for Jewish culture and identity that they speak of seems to reflect a non-religious ethnic form of Judaism, a form that believes that the Jewish People are innately, even essentially, connected. This idea is not unlike the claims of the Zohar and Judah Halevi.

The nature of the Jewish People in the twenty-first century cannot be determined. We see already now the difficulty of defining the Jewish People in ethnic and/or religious terms alone, and the high rate of intermarriage alongside the increasing assimilation and secularism of today's Jews are certain to have a radical impact. All that is clear is that, in the next century, as at the onset of modernity, Jews undoubtedly will rethink their current sense of the nature and meaning of membership in the People Israel.

Bibliography

Goldberg, David Theo and Michael Krausz, *Jewish Identity* (Philadelphia, 1993).

Meyer, Michael A., *Jewish Identity in the Modern World* (Seattle & London, 1990).

Porton, Gary G., *The Stranger Within Your Gates: Converts and Conversion in Rabbinic Literature* (Chicago, 1994).

Schiffman, Lawrence H., *Who Was a Jew? Rabbinic and Halakhic Perspectives on the Jewish-Christian Schism* (Hoboken, 1985).

Silberstein, Laurence J. and Robert L. Cohn, *The Other in Jewish Thought and History* (New York & London, 1994).

Notes

[1] See, e.g., David Theo Goldberg and Michael Krausz, *Jewish Identity* (Philadelphia, 1993); Laurence J. Silberstein and Robert L. Cohn, *The Other in Jewish Thought and History* (New York and London, 1994).

[2] Asa Kasher, "Jewish Collective Identity," in

Silberstein and Cohn, pp. 56-78. The quotes are from pp. 65-66.

[3] Michael A. Meyer, *Response to Modernity: A History of the Reform Movement in Judaism* (New York and Oxford, 1988), p. 392.

[4] Op. cit., pp. 68-69.

[5] Op. cit., p. 60.

[6] Jacob Neusner, *Judaism and Its Social Metaphor* (Cambridge), pp. 112-114.

[7] Shaye J.D. Cohen, "From the Bible to the Talmud: The Prohibition of Intermarriage," in Reuben Ahroni, ed., *Biblical and Other Studies in Honor of Robert Gordis, Hebrew Annual Review* 7 (1983), pp. 23-39.

[8] Lawrence H. Schiffman, *Who Was a Jew? Rabbinic and Halakhic Perspectives on the Jewish-Christian Schism* (Hoboken, 1985), pp. 10-11.

[9] Chester L. Hunt and Lewis Walker, *Ethnic Dynamics: Patters of Intergroup Relations in Various Societies* (Holmes Beach, 1974), p. 3; Gerald D. Berreman, "Race, Caste, and Other Invidious Distinctions in Social Stratification," in Norma R. Yetman, *Majority and Minority: The Dynamics of Race and Ethnicity in American Life* (Boston, Sydney, London, Toronto, 1985), p. 23.

[10] Charles F. Keyes, *Ethnic Change* (Seattle and London, 1981), p. 5.

[11] Pierre L. van den Berghe, "Race and Ethnicity: A Sociological Perspective," in Yetman, p. 56.

[12] Gary G. Porton, *The Stranger Within Your Gates: Converts and Conversion in Rabbinic Literature* (Chicago, 1994).

[13] For the following see Jacob Katz, *Exclusiveness and Tolerance: Studies in Jewish-Gentile Relations in Medieval and Modern Times* (Westport, 1980); Jacob Katz, *Tradition and Crisis: Jewish Society at the End of the Middle Ages* (New York, 1971); H.H. Ben Sasson, *A History of the Jewish People* (Cambridge, 1976), pp. 385-726.

[14] Joshua Trachtenberg, *The Devil and the Jews: The Medieval Conception of the Jews and Its Relation to Modern Antisemitism* (Philadelphia, 1983).

[15] *Tradition and Crisis*, pp. 26-27.

[16] Menachem Kellner, *Maimonides on the Jewish People* (Albany, 1991), p. 1.

[17] Isaak Heinemann, "Jehuda Halevi: Kuzari," in *Three Jewish Philosophers* (New York, 1965), p. 45.

[18] Julius Guttmann, *Philosophies of Judaism: A History of Jewish Philosophy from Biblical Times to Franz Rosenzweig* (New York, 1973), p. 143 and, on the following, p. 144.

[19] Gershom G. Scholem, *Major Trends in Jewish Mysticism* (New York, 1973), p. 242.

[20] Gershom G. Scholem, *On the Kabbalah and Its Symbolism*, translated by Ralph Manheim (New York, 1970), p. 105 and, on the following, p. 116. See also Moshe Idel, *Kabbalah: New Perspectives* (New Haven and London, 1988), p. 206.

[21] Kellner, op. cit., pp. 3, 11.

[22] Kellner, op. cit., pp. 23, 26, 35, 50, 53, 72.

[23] Kellner, op. cit., pp. 81, 83, 88, 98.

[24] Isadore Twersky, *Introduction to the Code of Maimonides (Mishneh Torah)* (New Haven and London, 1980).

[25] Guttmann, op. cit., pp. 278-279.

[26] Ibid., pp. 281-284.

[27] Noah H. Rosenbloom, *Tradition in an Age of Reform: The Religious Philosophy of Samson Raphael Hirsch* (Philadelphia, 1976), p. 4.

[28] Calvin Goldscheider and Alan S. Zuckerman, *The Transformation of the Jews* (Chicago and London, 1984), p. 31.

[29] Michael A. Meyer, *Jewish Identity in the Modern World* (Seattle and London, 1990), pp. 6-7.

[30] Ibid., p. 10.

[31] Cited in Paul Mendes-Flohr and Jehuda Reinharz, *The Jew In the Modern World: A Documentary History* (New York and Oxford, second edition, 1995), p. 31.

[32] Michael A. Meyer, *The Origins of the Modern Jew: Jewish Identity and European Culture in German, 1749-1824* (Detroit, 1967), p. 20.

[33] Alfred Jospe, *Moses Mendelssohn: Jerusalem and Other Writings* (New York, 1969), p. 68.

[34] Ibid., pp. 97-98.

[35] Alexander Altmann, *Moses Mendelssohn, A Biographical Study* (Philadelphia, 1973).

[36] Rosenbloom, op. cit.

[37] Ibid., p. 66.

[38] Ibid., pp. 81-82.

[39] Cited in ibid., p. 103. The following quote is on p. 102.

[40] Ibid., pp. 128-136.

[41] Ibid., pp. 153, 156.

[42] Ibid., p. 193.

[43] Ibid., pp. 166-167. The quote is on p. 169.

[44] Leon A. Jick, *The Americanization of the Synagogue, 1820-1870* (Hanover, 1976), pp. 79-96.

[45] Meyer, *Response to Modernity*, pp. 387-388.

[46] Ibid., pp. 388-390.

[47] The quotes are from ibid., p. 394 and 393 respectively.

[48] Gilbert S. Rosenthal, *Contemporary Judaism: Patterns of Survival*, Second Edition (New York, 1986), pp. 148-169.

[49] *Emet ve-Emunah: Statement of Principles of Conservative Judaism* (New York, 1988).

[50] Michael Krausz, "On Being Jewish," in Goldberg and Krausz, pp. 264-278.

[51] William Shaffir, "Boundaries and Self-Presentation among the Hasidim: A Study in Identity Maintenance" in Janet S. Belcove-Shalin, *New World Hasidim: Ethnographic Studies of Hasidic Jews in America* (Albany, 1995), pp. 31-68.

[52] Porton, op. cit., p. 311, note 250.

[53] Kenneth Stern, "Is Religion Necessary?" in Peter I. Rose, *The Ghetto and Beyond: Essays on Jewish Life in America* (New York, 1969), p. 190.

[54] Garry M. Brodsky, "A Way of Being a Jew; a Way of Being a Person," in Goldberg and Krausz, p. 247. The following quote is from p. 247.

[55] Jack Wertheimer, "Recent Trends in Ameri-

can Judaism," in *American Jewish Year Book, 1989* (Philadelphia, 1989), pp. 63-162.

[56] Ibid., p. 162.

[57] Stern, op. cit., p. 199.

[58] Brodsky, op. cit., p. 250. On the following see pp. 250-251.

[59] Ibid., p. 199.

[60] Laurence J. Silberstein, "Others Within and Others Without: Rethinking Jewish Identity and Culture," in Silberstein and Cohn, pp. 1-3.

[61] Steven J. Zipperstein, "Ahad Ha'am and the Politics of Assimilation," in Jonathan Frankel and Steven J. Zipperstein, *Assimilation and Community: The Jews in Nineteenth-Century Europe* (Cambridge, 1992), pp. 344-365; Arthur Hertzberg, *The Zionist Idea: A Historical Analysis and Reader* (New York, 1970), pp. 247-277.

GARY G. PORTON

ISRAELITE RELIGION: The way Israelite religion actually was practiced in biblical times frequently was different from what the biblical sources, written according to later ideologies, claim to have been the case. In the face of the tendentious character of the biblical sources, to determine what people actually did and believed, we must take into account the realities of Israelite history and the specific contexts in which the Hebrew Scriptures were composed. We recognize as well that religious practice changed over time and was different across the various areas of Israelite settlement. But the value of describing this religion as it in fact existed is great, allowing us better to understand the foundations of Scripture's writings and to comprehend the actual practices and beliefs that ultimately yielded the biblical legacy as a whole.

Of course, rendering an accurate description is not always easy or even possible, the result, first and foremost, of our limited and often ideologically slanted sources. Contrary to how we are accustomed to looking at matters, the Bible is not an informed source for the periods it claims to depict. It is, rather, a theologically determined work with a clear ideological bent, and, thus, an informed source only for the period in which it was finally composed, primarily after the Babylonian Exile. Certainly there are points at which Scripture reveals what really happened. Even so, much of it cannot be construed as historically accurate. The representations within what is called Primary History—Genesis

through 2 Kings—for instance, may correctly depict some practices. But these writings overall must be read as the products of a number of distinct sectarian groups, each with specific ideologies presented through apologistic renderings of history. More strikingly, rather than as the work of traditionalists they normally are seen to be, the writings of the prophets of the eighth and early to mid-seventh centuries must be viewed as the chronicles of individuals, even fanatics, seeking to overturn the social and religious systems of their day.

Indeed, although generally viewed as the most conservative and true defenders of traditional Israelite practice and belief, these prophets were anomalous within their society. They were religious and social revolutionaries who took up the cause of the disenfranchised and the poor. So far as we can tell, they had little following among their fellow Israelites and Judahites. Nor, as revolutionaries, did they necessarily champion mainstream traditions but, rather, observances hitherto not practiced by the people of Israel. Their prophetic predications were related to their attempts to alter the current religious practices with a new set of traditions, beliefs, and attitudes. Thus, their exclusively Yahwistic beliefs may be very different even from those of the biblical sources—D, Dtr, and P—that, as we shall see, are also exclusively Yahwistic. Since they have different foci, we cannot be sure of that. In any case, the theology of these canonical prophets does not correspond at all to what is found in the writings of J or E.

Despite the problems presented by the biblical literature, we have sufficient non-scriptural sources, some artifactual and some written, to begin to depict some aspects of the various types of Israelite worship. Moreover, even though the Hebrew Scriptures contain a largely idealistic representation, they can on occasion inform us of actual practice. Oddly, this is the case in particular when Scripture presents a practice as a type of apostasy, a criteria that is very important in the study of the eighth and early seventh century prophetic writings. Additionally, documentary and artifactual materials from the entirety of the ancient Near East and in particular from the land of Israel are useful in determining Israelite history from the thirteenth century onward. Notably, such material only sometimes supports the biblical text; for the most part it does not. For example, extra-biblical material shows that the patriarchal narratives have much in common with other ancient Near Eastern religious narratives, with which they share historical correlations. But, because there is no knowledge of the people Israel *per se* prior to the thirteenth century, and there was ample opportunity for the acquisition of this knowledge subsequent to that, we must conclude that the Hebrew Scriptures reflect interaction with the other ancient Near Eastern cultures that occurred much later than what the Bible claims.

Textual redaction and the nature of Israelite religion: The traditional religious belief maintaining that the Torah was given to Moses at Sinai has long been rejected by scholars, who accept the Hebrew Bible as a composite work. The so-called "Documentary Hypothesis" holds that Genesis through 2 Kings, that is, Primary History, was composed at different times and in different locales by various redactors. There is some debate about what a "redactor" actually did— write?, edit?—as well as about the number of such individuals involved. Most scholars think of redactors as not quite original authors but as more than editors. Some, however, imagine at least some of the redactors actually to have been original authors.

The earliest traditions in the Hebrew Bible may reflect a written or oral Canaanite epic, or perhaps epic traditions, from at least the thirteenth century B.C.E. The earliest redactor of Primary History is the Yahwist (J), who is traditionally dated to the tenth century court of Solomon, though new, controversial scholarship, reverts to nineteenth century ideas and places him much later, possibly after 538 B.C.E., the end of the Babylonian Exile. J's writings are found in various portions of the Tetrateuch (Genesis through Numbers), and they once existed in Joshua as well. Subsequent to J came the Elohist (E), traditionally dated in the eighth century kingdom of Israel, although some new scholarship places him too much later. His writings

are also found in the Tetrateuch, and they once were found in Joshua.

In the view of the now-standard early dating of J and E, a redactor in the eighth century B.C.E., referred to as R^{JE}, combined the Yahwistic and Elohistic narratives to create a single JE epic. This most likely occurred after the fall of the Israel, the Northern Kingdom, in 722 B.C.E. The Deuteronomistic source (D) then is dated to the time of Josiah's Reform (2 Kings 22-23; 622 B.C.E.). He is held responsible for the large central core of Deuteronomy. The Priestly Redactor (P) worked during the first half of the Babylonian Exile (586-561 B.C.E.), although new, debated scholarship places him later as well. P is responsible for the introduction to the Hebrew Scriptures (Gen. 1:1-2:4a), and his work is found throughout the Tetrateuch. Although other redactors are represented, P's work dominates the Sinai story (Exod. 19:2b-Num. 10:11).

In the early part of the twentieth century, Martin Noth suggested an additional redactor, whom he called the Deuteronomistic Historian (Dtr). Noth believed that the Deuteronomistic Historian created the Deuteronomistic History (DtrH) during the Babylonian Exile. This view is still accepted by some scholars today, although many have rejected it. Dtr may have been responsible for truncating Numbers, since there is no reason to suppose that this had been done by P. In any case, Dtr framed D's work and reworked what may have been an R^{JE} book of Joshua, making it clearly his own; and he composed the remainder of Primary History through 2 Kings.

In the middle twentieth century, Frank Moore Cross suggested that there had been two Deuteronomistic Historians (Dtr^1 and Dtr^2), with Dtr^1 living in Judah at the time of Josiah's Reform and redacting during the late seventh and early sixth centuries, and Dtr^2 working during the early part of the Babylonian Exile. Cross suggested that the first Deuteronomistic Historian is responsible for the greater part of the Deuteronomistic History, that is, Deuteronomy through 2 Kings. But he holds that a later redactor, the second Dtr, did light editorial work on

DtrH, bringing it up to date to his own time. Although the existence of a second Deuteronomistic Historian is still debated, we can say that one or more "Dtr" is responsible for the framework of Deuteronomy and all of Joshua through 2 Kings, as these books were published in what David Noel Freedman defines as the "earliest Bible" of 560 B.C.E.

Whatever the specifics, accepting that different redactions of the text were created, we recognize that some practices and beliefs Scripture associates with earlier ages may actually reflect at least some aspects of the historical reality and prejudices of the later times and locales in which the redactors lived. Accepting the traditional scholarly dating, the tenth century Yahwist, for instance, reflected the religious practices of *some* sectarian group(s) that existed in his time. But even though he may have written to glorify the Davidic line and flatter Solomon, we cannot in the end presume that his writings reflect all that was practiced in Solomon's court. In fact, we now understand that Solomon likely was more a petty prince than the monarch of a great nation, that the Temple built by him was based on a Phoenician model, and that Solomon himself may not have been exclusively Yahwistic. Consequently, there is little chance that the practices delineated by the Yahwist in fact were widespread, even if they represented traditional folk knowledge.

Likewise, the ninth century Elohist reflected contemporary religious practices of some segments of the northern kingdom (Israel), which at that time was more geopolitically important than the southern kingdom of Judah. However, based on the biblical text itself, we can say that the Elohistic narrative did not represent certain mainstream religious traditions, particularly not those of the courts of the various dynasties that had been ruling that kingdom. When, after the fall of the northern kingdom in 722 B.C.E., R[JE] combined J's and E's work, he unintentionally may even have colored the combined work in light of his own ideological desires or possibly sectarian practices. We thus see either his own sectarian practices or an ideological projection of hypothetical practices.

The Deuteronomistic School represented its own beliefs, practices, and perhaps fantasies. The same may be said for the work of the Priestly Redactor. But, Dtr and P seem to be theologically opposed to one another. P's work stresses covenant—particularly the Sinai covenant—and the binding nature of Yahweh's law-codes on the Israelites, who had voluntary accepted Yahweh's covenant. Dtr's work, while incorporating covenant, stresses the Israelite nation as sinners whom Yahweh nevertheless loves. Likewise, it stresses that Yahweh, who hears Israelites who call to him in its distress, repeatedly redeems the nation. Dtr's basic Leitmotif, whereby Israel sins, Yahweh sends an avenger, Israel repents and cries out to Yahweh, and Yahweh sends a redeemer, colors all of DtrH. At the same time that it highlights the hopelessness of the sinful nation, it maintains a hope of redemption, even as the people suffer exile.

The composition of Primary History can be viewed from yet another perspective. I. Engnell has suggested that only two distinct works comprise Primary History, that everything we have is from just the Deuteronomic and Priestly schools. If so, the written material is far later than many traditionalists acknowledge, although not necessarily as late as some suggest. Still, to maintain the material's antiquity and reliability, the Scandinavian school represented by Engnell and his followers posits a lengthy oral tradition that remained relatively intact. This, however, is not convincing, since oral traditions frequently undergo significant development and change over time. Lord Raglan believed that after even a hundred and fifty years oral traditions become so altered that they are totally different from what they were at their inception. Hence, although elements of truth may exist in a tradition when it first developed, traditions cannot be treated as accurate unless they are written down at a very early stage. And even if this occurs, some traditions continue to develop orally after being written down; well-developed oral versions of a tradition may cause the alteration of written traditions that had become conceptually outdated.

The emergence of Israelite religion: The Israelite religion presented in the Hebrew Scriptures has little substantial relationship to historical reality. For one thing, Israel as a people did not exist during the so-called patriarchal era. For another, the narrative in which Yahweh and/or Elohim rescued Israel from slavery in Egypt, brought the Israelites across the Sea of Reeds, and granted them a "Great Covenant" at the sacred mountain, called Sinai and Horeb but, for normative theological purposes, construed as one and the same, is actually an eschatological paradigm. Because these sacred mountains have different theological antecedents, stemming from different religious traditions, the Great Covenant of Sinai/Horeb must be viewed as representing two different traditions and, presumably, an interaction with at least two different gods.

Late Israelite theology is grounded in the belief that Yahweh is Elohim. He is the God of Israel, whom he has chosen to be his own people. Historically, however, the covenant-laws have significant ties to ancient Near Eastern laws as well as to some universal theological constructs regarding ritual purity. It is possible that the Israelites had adopted (and adapted) these laws early in their history, perhaps even during J's or E's era. It is the more likely, however, that this occurred rather late, perhaps during Josiah's Reform in 622 B.C.E. or in the early part of the Babylonian Exile. So, it is unlikely that the Israelites lived by the law codes appended to the covenant attributed to Yahweh, struck with the people of Israel at Sinai and/or Horeb by Moses, the mythical priest, "Covenant Mediator," and "Salvation Hero."

Significantly, historians are aware that there was no "Israel" before the thirteenth century B.C.E., the date most accept for the emergence of the historical Israelites. Although "Israel" seems to be mentioned in the late thirteenth century Merneptah Stele, there is great debate about this, including the possibility that the word in question merely sounds similar but is not identical to Israel. Moreover, many historians date the beginnings of Israel even later than the thirteenth century, some placing it well into the first millennium B.C.E. Therefore, the real question regarding the patriarchs, the covenants, the promise of "the Land," and the experiences at Sinai and/or Horeb is how to categorize them. Are they sacred stories knowingly or innocently developed to serve the Israelite need to establish an identity and justify a right to the land held by individual Canaanite cities? Or are they folk-tale traditions, legends, merely pious fiction, or some combination of all of these kinds of thinking and story-telling? In any case, their affect is clear: they establish a theo-political tradition in which the land of Canaan really belongs to those who call themselves Israel.

It is possible that a small group of invaders brought news of a liberating god, Yahweh, and, during the thirteenth century, inspired some type of Canaanite revolt, thereby bringing about the emergence of the Israelite people. But the fact that Yahweh was a weather god who, in the minds of those responsible for the Hebrew Scriptures, later became syncretized with the supreme deity El makes this scenario rather unlikely. The Israelites were, for the most part, Canaanites or those who had become adherents to or outcasts from Canaanite society. The canonical prophets' attacks on the practices of the aristocracy and kings of Israel and Judah, and Dtr's attacks on those of the kings of both nations, together make it clear that Israelite religions were Canaanite well into the seventh century B.C.E. Consequently, any claim of the existence of Israel before that time must take for granted a people whose religious practices were either non-Yahwistic or not exclusively Yahwistic.

The early Israelites were not monotheistic. Rather, they worshipped a pantheon of gods, among them Yahweh and Asherah. The data suggest that, no earlier than the mid-seventh century B.C.E., these deities had become very important in the Israelite component of Canaanite society and that, in some instances, Yahweh may even have been subordinated to Asherah. Granting this, that which, starting in the eighth century, the canonical prophets railed at as apostasy, and what the seventh/sixth century Deuteronomistic Historian deemed abandonment of the covenant, in fact represented established Israelite practice.

In the eighth century B.C.E., when the earliest of the canonical prophets arose, the lower classes in both Israel and Judah may have experienced hard times. Nevertheless, at least in the first half of the century, the two states were prospering economically, with the upper classes amassing great wealth and living in luxury. Rather than blaming the coming onslaught of a foreign enemy on geopolitics, the prophets used it to advance their own ideology. They blamed the plight of the poor, widows, and orphans on a national apostasy from an idealized Yahwism that had not hitherto been mainstream Israelite practice. In response to this apostasy, they argued, Yahweh had caused the geopolitical problems afflicting both Israel and Judah. Thus the causative role actually played by geopolitics was ignored and/or repressed, for it did not support or allow for expression of the prophets' peculiar *theo*-political ideology. It is not surprising that the prophets continued to blame Israelite apostasy for the fall of Israel to the Assyrians in 722 B.C.E. and for the troubles that befell Judah until it fell to the Babylonians in 597 B.C.E.

Insofar as we can tell, the religion of the canonical prophets is different from anything represented in the Primary History. Most likely, in fact, it is different from any form of Israelite religious belief that preceded it. Although there are indications in Primary History that the worship of gods other than Yahweh-Elohim will have dire consequences for the individual worshipper as well as for the entire nation, these are very late. Not representative of earlier worship and belief, these ideas post-date the eighth and early to mid-seventh century prophets, albeit not those of the late seventh and sixth centuries. The illusion is created that this theme of exclusive Yahwism, first developed by the canonical prophets, extends back throughout the periods depicted in Primary History as well. But, in fact, it does not. Rather, it postdates those redactors who first sounded the clarion for exclusive Yahwism. It is found only in the Deuteronomistic History (DtrH), written in the late sixth to the mid-fifth centuries B.C.E., extending, elaborating on, and including D's work from the period of Josiah's Reform, and in those of the Priestly Redactor (P), writing during the Babylonian Exile, and published in the First Bible of 560 B.C.E.

The illusion is effected precisely because P was the ultimate redactor of the entire work and Dtr the penultimate, or, more likely, *vice versa*, thereby enabling one or the other or both of them to influence the earlier material. P placed his material throughout the Tetrateuch. Dtr framed D's work when he composed DtrH, which forms the final portion of Primary History. And Dtr's hand possibly may be seen even in the Tetrateuch as well. So, Primary History begins with P, whose work threads its way through that of J and E. And the Primary History ends with DtrH. This framing stresses the two theologies of P and Dtr, no matter how much attention is paid to those of other redactors. Consequently, the appearance that the theologies of P, D, and Dtr are those of the entirety of Primary History is not accidental.

The laws, rules, and rituals of the Priestly Redactor (P), whose work emanates from the Babylonian Exile, represent an even more radical departure from earlier traditions than that of the canonical prophets or Deuteronomistic Historian. We mistakenly believe P's theological precepts to be early for two reasons: he delineated his law-code in the Sinai narrative (Exod. 19:2b–Num. 10:11), and he framed major portions of Genesis through Numbers (the Tetrateuch) with his own writings, whereby he expressed his own theology, even going so far as to place his own introduction (Gen. 1:12:4a) at the very beginning of the composite work scholars call Primary History.

The precepts of Israelite religion: As we have argued, Israelite religion varied throughout its history. At first, it could not be distinguished from other Canaanite religions precisely because it was a Canaanite religion, and, for the greater part of their history, the Israelites were Canaanites by extraction, affiliation, or some meaningful societal relationship. As they began to take on a self-identity, they seem to have represented themselves as those who worshipped Yahweh among other gods, then Yahweh before all other gods, and then Yahweh alone. Moreover, until Josiah's Reform and/ or the acceptance of the "Yahweh Alone" movement's precepts, the Israelites were not monotheists. As did other Canaanites, they worshipped various gods, whose names, in Scripture, have come to be treated as if they were alternative names for "the" God. But they also worshipped those very same Canaanite gods who are attacked occasionally in the Primary History and very frequently by the prophets.

While later normative religious practice(s) syncretized the names of the various gods, treating each name as a different designation for Yahweh, there is no reason to believe this is what the earliest Israelites had in mind. Rather, they associated a distinct deity with each of these names. The process of syncretism *may* have started as early as Hezekiah's reign. But save for the fanatical Yahweh Alone precepts of the canonical prophets, this is not likely. In any case, full syncretization was not realized as a norm until at least some time between Josiah's Reform (622 B.C.E.) and the Babylonian Exile (either 597 or in its more absolute form of 586 B.C.E.). Perhaps it did not become the norm until the period of the Exile itself (586-538/537 B.C.E.), when, in Second Isaiah, we find a clearly developed monotheism.

Although Dtr depicts a general acceptance of the Yahweh Alone movement as if it were a reformation rather than a new approach initiated by Josiah, little evidence suggests that the king's theological tendencies were uniformly embraced. Indeed, that Josiah's reform is somewhat late is meaningful. Since the Yahweh Alone movement had its roots in the rise of the canonical prophets during the eighth century, possibly gaining Hezekiah's attention, the delay in acceptance suggests that the theology was not widely embraced. Most likely, during the eighth or early seventh centuries, it had not attracted many politically powerful followers and possibly not even many adherents among the general populace. However, if Josiah's acceptance is based on realpolitik, then it is likely that the movement had gained sufficient strength by 622 B.C.E. that he would choose to transform his state's religion to conform to the alleged Mosaic law book. Possibly, those who wanted to advance the Yahweh Alone movement justified the fall of the Northern Kingdom a century earlier by charging that it was Yahweh's will to punish apostate Israelites who worshipped other (non-)gods. This view seems far more significant than it was at its inception, because the canonical prophets treated their theology as if it were the norm. They acted as if those who accepted their beliefs were the true Israelites, and everyone else was apostate. In fact, this was an illusion, and the canonical prophets had little influence in their own time.

In any case, we do not know that much about Yahweh other than that he was a late developing deity. We do not even know what Yahweh's name meant to his followers at various times in the history of his worship. The redactors of the Primary History suggest different meanings and note different times at which the name was revealed. According to J, it was revealed in the primeval period (Gen. 4:26), just after the expulsion from Eden. According to P, Moses was the first person to whom the name was revealed (Exod. 6:2-3). E seems to connect the name with the verb "to be" (Exod. 3:14), and various meanings have been attached to this.

Not only is Yahweh's name problematic, but so is the allegedly prehistoric formulation of his worship. We cannot assume that the "ancestors" to whom the worship of Yahweh is credited really existed. Rather, they represent a religious formulation by which the nation created its history as a socio-religious perception just as all non-universalistic religious formulations are created. We must not presume, however, that this was a deliberate invention, intending to deceive people into believing (although it might have been!). What we can say is that after Israel's "history" was invented and accepted as historical—not necessarily concomitantly with one another—the invented history colored Israelite worship and governance. Therefore, although normative Israelite religion is predicated on a belief in the existence of various ancestors and the covenants that they concluded with their God, that perception was fictive, whether or not it was believed by the Israelites themselves. In fact, even granting the analogues to second millennium ancient Near Eastern life, such ancestors as Abraham, Isaac, Jacob, Moses, and others who play roles in the traditions represented as early Israel never existed. Despite what is portrayed in the Primary History, they cannot be located in either time or place. Perhaps the ancestors had once been gods and became demythologized at some indeterminable point prior to the tenth century B.C.E., the date at which most scholars believe J wrote. But, if those scholars who believe J was written many centuries after that are correct, then Abraham, Isaac, Jacob, Moses, and the others may have been merely folk figures, accepted within some folks tradition as mythical ancestors.

The religion represented in the Hebrew Scriptures is predicated on the existence of these ancestors and on the belief that Yahweh, who governs the entire universe and watches out for the line descending from Seth, Adam and Eve's third son, made covenants with Abraham, Isaac, and Jacob to give them innumerable progeny and the land of Canaan. But these stories may be quite late, and, most important, the various covenants depicted in them as having been granted each of the patriarchs often seem like the same covenant. While presented as a multiplicity of covenants, each contains a variation or simple iteration of the same promise: the patriarch will have great progeny, and he and his descendants will inherit the land. Most important, although basic to the Israelite belief system, these covenants are of only secondary religious importance behind the great covenant depicted as having been concluded at Sinai/Horeb. It does not matter whether they predate the Sinai/Horeb formulation or not. For Israelite religion is first and foremost dependent on the eschatological paradigm that includes the model of the Great Covenant made by Yahweh and mediated by Moses on behalf of the *entire* people of Israel. The precept of this covenant—that, once

it was ratified, Yahweh would be their God and they would be his people—is basic to all Israelite religion.

The entirety of the paradigm is one in which God rescued Israel from slavery in Egypt, brought the people across the Sea of Reeds, and granted them a covenant—a type of suzerainty treaty—at the sacred mountain(s) Sinai and Horeb. Although these two sacred mountains, navels of the universe, are normatively construed as the same, descriptively they are not. The narratives in Scripture would have had historical antecedents in which they were different. So, at least two different "ancestor" stories, each with its own eschatological tradition, were syncretized. And, although we have no way of knowing when this occurred, it may have been when the Israelites began to think of themselves as one people, apart from their Canaanite "neighbors." However, despite the claims of the canonical prophets, this development may not have come about until Josiah's Reform in 622 B.C.E.

The alleged Great Covenant is legalistically formulated, and religio-social law is basic to it. It claims that since, in the Great Covenant, God took Israel as his people, and the people took Yahweh as its God, God rightfully gave the people its laws. This paradigm, however, does not accord with reality. Since so much of the legal material is incorporated in either the Priestly Redaction, which is generally dated in the period of the Babylonian Exile, or in the Deuteronomist's Redaction, which is generally dated to the time of Josiah's Reform, perhaps having a very few antecedents from Hezekiah's reign, we must assume that the law-codes were incorporated into Israelite traditions and beliefs at a very late date. This does not mean that the law-codes themselves were late. Some codes are clearly from earlier periods. But, their origin is not necessarily Israelite.

Worship and sacrifice: Worship, expressed as service to God, followed the ancient Near Eastern tradition that takes as its model the service given to a king. In the various eastern religions, the icon of a god, which the deity was understood to inhabit at will once the icon had been enlivened by a ritual ceremony, lived in his or her own house or temple. Priests took care of all of the icon's necessities, including food, washing, anointing, etc. Worshipers, acting as they would with human sovereigns, brought their offerings and performed their duties to their gods. Israelite worship was similar, and although the canonical prophets tried to alter this, it took several centuries for them to succeed. They wanted to incorporate ethical, moral, and legal standards different from the traditional ancient Near Eastern ritualistic practices. This alteration in the nature of Israelite worship was the only way in which their revolutionary attempt to separate Israelite religion from other religions could be accomplished. Unless the Israelite forms of worship were reshaped to distinguish them from other Near Eastern forms, the Yahweh Alone movement could not evolve into the distinctive Israelite religion its practitioners desired to establish.

The nature of sacrifice as expressed in Exodus, Leviticus, and Numbers is informed by P's presentation, thereby reflecting circumstances in the Babylonian Exile when and where he wrote. Despite P's retrojection of the instruction for sacrifice into the period of the Exodus, we must not construe it in its entirety as an ancient and long-standing form of Israelite practice. However, since some portions of the tradition may have been part of a long-standing priestly tradition, they may well have been practiced by some Israelites for some time; but this is not likely. Since some of the practices were based on Mesopotamian practices, they too may have been long-standing. But we do not know when Israelites first incorporated them into their own traditions, and they may well have been or even most likely were incorporated during the Exile.

The nature of sacrifice as depicted by J and E, expressive of practices in which there is no cult centralization, is clearly different from what is pictured by D, P, and Dtr, whose theology and practices reflect the cult centralization that was basic to their existence. J and E depict the Patriarchs as offering their own sacrifices. Burnt offerings were made on open-air altars or pillars set up for the occasion (Gen. 8:20; 12:7-8; 13:18; 22:13; 26:25; 28:18; 35:14). This is clearly unacceptable to the redactors from the time of Josiah's Reform onward. Sacrifice even more than worship is to be regulated closely. And, in a period in which sacrifice is not possible, the Israelite identity is tied to the nature of Israel's worship, based on an idyllic formulation of both worship and sacrifice, as elucidated in the Sinai pericope and the book of Deuteronomy.

Conclusions: The history and religion of Israel are not one and the same. Nor are they what is represented in the Hebrew Scriptures, particularly in the Primary History, a historically late, redacted composite that presents the diverse religious and historical perspectives of its several layers of editors. Indeed, while the final redaction wishes to establish itself as representing the totality of Israel, it reveals inconsistencies and variants that attest to attitudes and types of worship that predate the later "Yahweh Alone" theology of the redacted whole. Thus, despite what is called for in the early Canonical Prophets, until Josiah's reform or even the Babylonian Exile, there is no indication that Yahweh was the only god worshipped by the majority of those who defined themselves as Israelites.

Bibliography

Cross, Frank Moore, *Canaanite Myth and Hebrew Epic: Essays in the History of the Religion of Israel* (Cambridge, 1973).

Edelman, Diana Vikander, ed., *The Triumph of Elohim* (Grand Rapids, 1995).

Engnell, Ivan, *A Rigid Scrutiny: Critical Essays on the Old Testament* (Nashville, 1969).

Mandell, Sara R., "Religious and Sociopolitical Construction of Early Israel," in Jacob Neusner, ed., *Approaches to Ancient Judaism* X (Atlanta, 1997), 83-124.

SARA MANDELL